I0006139

Engraved by F. Halpin.

Respectfully Yours

Silas Wright

A

HISTORY

OF

ST. LAWRENCE AND FRANKLIN

COUNTIES, NEW YORK,

FROM THE

EARLIEST PERIOD TO THE PRESENT TIME.

BY

Benjamin

FRANKLIN B. HOUGH, A. M., M. D.,

CORRESPONDING MEMBER OF THE NEW YORK HISTORICAL SOCIETY.

ALBANY:

LITTLE & CO., 53 STATE STREET.

1853.

Entered according to Act of Congress, in the year 1853, by
FRANKLIN B. HOUGH,
In the Clerk's office of the District Court for the Northern District of New
York.

MUNSELL, PRINTER,
ALBANY.

PREFACE.

The interest which was manifested, in a lecture delivered in December, 1851, at Ogdensburgh, on the early history of the county, led to the belief that the subject was one that commended itself to the attention of the citizens generally, and induced the collection of the materials herewith offered to the public. To the numerous persons who have expressed an interest in the work, and in various ways aided in promoting it, our sincere thanks are tendered; but an attempt to enumerate those from whom facts and verbal statements were received, would be impossible. To the Hon. Henry S. Randall, secretary of state, and Mr. Archibald Campbell, his deputy, are we indebted, for access to the voluminous data which our state archives afford, and aid in procuring many facts not elsewhere existing. Dr. E. B. O'Callaghan has been of especial service, in directing our attention to various sources of information; and Dr. T. Romeyn Beck, in the loan of volumes relating to our subjects of investigation. To Messrs. James H. Titus and A. O. Brodie, of New York, and to Henry E. Pierrepont, Esq., of Brooklyn, are our acknowledgments due, for materials in aid of the work; as they are also to Dr. Amasa Trowbridge, of Watertown, and P. S. Stewart, Esq., of Carthage. The sketches from which most of the wood engravings were made, were, with the exceptions of the views of Gouverneur and Potsdam, drawn by Miss Levantia J. Woolworth, of Turin.

To Elijah B. Allen, president of the Ontario and St. Lawrence Steam Boat Company, and Mr. T. P. Chandler, president of the Northern Rail Road Company, are we especially indebted, for facilities in collecting materials, and to the following citizens, for direct aid, and written memoranda, used in these pages, viz: the Hon. Messrs. Henry Van Rensselaer, John Fine, David C. Judson, Preston King, Jas. G. Hopkins, Smith Stilwell and Bishop Perkins; the Rev. Messrs. L. M. Miller, J. P. Jennings and H. R. Peters; to Drs. S. N. Sherman and A. Tyler; and to Messrs. A. B. James, James C. Barter, Wm. E. Guest, A. C. Brown, L. Hasbrouck, B. H. Vary, H. F. Lawrence and R. G. Pettibone, of Ogdensburgh; D. W. Church and C. Ford, of Morristown; D. W. Baldwin and A. M. Church, of Rossie; H. D. Smith, Esq., C. Rich and Hon. E. Dodge, of Gouverneur; Dr. D. Clark, Rev. R. Pettibone and Messrs. M.

Thatcher, J. L. Russell, Geo. S. Winslow, F. Wood and L. R. Tupper, of Canton; E. A. Dayton, of Columbia village; I. Ogden, of Waddington; Hon. Wm. A. Dart, L. and W. L. Knowles, S. Raymond, Wm. H. Wallace, J. Blaisdell, B. G. Baldwin, Rev. I. Allen, E. W. Foster, W. M. Hitchcock, and Rev. —— Andrews, of Potsdam; L. C. Yale, of Norfolk; Rev. W. Whitfield, of Pierrepont; Rev. O. M. Moxley, of Parishville; Hon. H. Horton, Col. Charles L. Schlatter, F. Pellitier, S. C. F. Thorndike, A. B. Parmelee, G. Parker, Dr. E. Man, Dr. T. R. Powell, J. H. Jackson, U. D. Meeker, R. G. Foote, G. C. Cotton and Rev. A. Parmelee, of Malone; J. C. Spencer, of Fort Covington; A. Fulton, of Hogansburgh; and Rev. F. Marcoux, of St. Regis; and not least because last, to the several editors of the St. Lawrence Republican, Ogdensburgh Sentinel, The Laborer, Canton Independent, Potsdam Courier, St. Lawrence Journal, Franklin Gazette and Frontier Palladium, are our cordial thanks tendered, for the kind attention they have bestowed upon the enterprise.

The indulgence of the reader is solicited towards the typographical errors, that must unavoidably occur among so many names and dates; and the assurance may be received, that such statements only are given, as are believed to be facts. It is at all times a delicate task to write upon subjects of history relating to those living, or about which many of the readers must know more than the writer. How nearly truth has been attained, the reader must decide. It has been our aim to be strictly impartial; to injure the feelings or the interests of none: to do justice to the resources of the country, and to the memories of those whose acts make up our history. Many links in the chain of events are wanting, and the data from which history is derived, are daily becoming lost. It has been our aim to rescue from oblivion the incidents that attended the feeble beginnings and early struggles of a district of country which a combination of favoring causes is destined to place high in rank of wealth and importance; and if our efforts shall in any degree tend to this end, by making known our resources and our advantages, a prominent object which has been constantly before us, will have been attained.

FRANKLIN B. HOUGH.

Albany, February 7, 1853.

CONTENTS.

INTRODUCTION.

BEFORE entering upon the history of St. Lawrence and Franklin Counties, it may not be amiss to glance at the condition of the country at the time of its settlement, that the difficulties of forming the first beginning, and the embarrassments which delayed their growth, may be duly appreciated. The details of the minor events that make up the annals of rural districts, may want the *dignity* of history, but not the *interest*, especially to the citizens of these localities.

At the time when settlements began, here, the river front of Canada, for most of the distance above Montreal, had been settled about twenty years, principally by tories, refugees from the States, at the time of the revolution. These were known as U. E. Loyalists,* and many of them suffered extremely from the privations incident to their forlorn condition, as great numbers fled precipitately from their homes, leaving their property to be confiscated, and although the British government gave them lands, and in various ways assisted them in settling on the St. Lawrence, yet there remained many inconveniences which time alone could remedy. In the school of adversity they had learned the bitterness of want, and were more willing to extend aid to others, from having felt its need, and they appeared much gratified when they learned that the south shore was to be settled.

It is a well known fact, that permanent settlements were made at an early day along the St. Lawrence, at several places, and the features of that majestic river were familiar to these enterprising explorers, before New England had a white inhabitant. With an assiduity that does credit to their sagacity and forethought, they began at once the labor of conciliating the friendship, and securing the interests of the savages, that had previously roamed through the forest in quest of game, or in stealthy midnight marches in search of some unsuspecting victim of revenge. The few traces which we possess of aboriginal occupation, bespeak a

* U. E.—United English.

military pursuit, and these probably extend back to an ante Columbian period, and show that whatever evil practices the natives may have derived from Europeans, the art of war was at least indigenous on this continent, if it is not inherent in man's nature.

These wandering tribes, recognizing but few objects as property, knowing few wants but those of the appetite, and having few thoughts or desires above the groveling instincts of the brute creation, the French labored to locate in permanent villages, to teach them the art of cultivating the earth, and of surrounding themselves with some of the conveniences of life.

This was first attempted near the settlements at Montreal and Quebec, of which the present missions of St. Louis and Lorette are examples, but it was found that an atmosphere of moral desolation hung around the white settlements, peculiarly fatal to the natives, who were more easily corrupted than improved by associating with the whites. These facts led to a desire for some other plan, which should attach the natives to the French, while it alienated them from the English. The result of these efforts was the establishment of an Indian settlement at the present village of Ogdensburgh, of the rise, progress and result of which, a detailed account is given in the following pages. In the war between the French and English, which resulted in the ascendency of the latter, our district became the theatre of active operations, and from the Indian settlement *Swegatchi*, there continually issued small war parties, who fell upon the feeble settlements of the Mohawk valley, and slew, scalped, plundered, and burned, without restraint. These cruel and wanton outrages, by the terror which they excited, to a considerable degree depopulated the frontier settlements; nor was the cause of this annoyance removed, until the final evacuation of the posts on the St. Lawrence, either with or without resistance, on the expedition of General Amherst in 1760. During the American revolution, a similar series of incursions were instigated, under the direction of the British.

The French had for many years ceased to be masters of Canada, but a great part of the population of the lower province was of that nation, and they long continued the carrying trade, by the toilsome navigation of the St. Lawrence, dragging their bateaux up the rapids with incredible labor. These crafts usually proceeded in small brigades, and the fatigue of rowing was relieved by the rustic song of the steersman, in which the others joined in chorus, keeping time with the song in the measured dip of their oars. There was a poetry in these scenes, which impressed itself upon those who observed them, and some of the older inhabitants, recall with regret the memory of the cadence of the simple song of the voyageurs, as it died away in feeble echoes along the shore in the still evening. These have long since given place to the noisy steamer, that sends its swell to ripple along the banks, and the piercing note of the steam whistle, denotes the march of civilization, and gives promise of other and greater benefits, which the future has in store for us.

At an early day, the improvement of the navigation of the river had been begun, by cutting canals, with locks, across some of the more difficult points in the rapids. The proprietors and agents of Northern New York, were originally more favored with facilities for introducing settlers upon their lands, than those of the fertile plains and valleys of the great west, because, although both were equally destitute of roads, the former had the advantage of *distance,* and emigrants from the New England states, could enter these counties, with much less time and expense than was required to perform the journey to the Genesee country and Ohio.

The route to the latter was through miry swamps, and along streams and valleys, which when overspread with the decaying foliage of a luxuriant vegetation, were infested with deadly miasms, and offered to the adventurous emigrant but little inducement for the exercise of industry, when his little earnings were liable to be demanded by the expenses of sickness, and his frame on alternate days, chilled, parched, and drenched, with fever and ague. Accordingly we find, that during the years between 1802 and 1807, the tide of emigration from that prolific hive, *New England,* poured into the valleys of the Black and St. Lawrence rivers, which settled with a rapidity, especially in the former, which has been seldom equaled.

The proprietors seldom made their tracts their homes, but their agents were generally from the eastern states, and men of influence in their own localities, and we find that the first settlers in the several towns were often from the same neighborhoods.

Winter was usually selected for moving, as the streams and swamps were then bridged by ice, and routes became passable which at other times would be wholly impracticable. A few of the first settlers entered with their families by the tedious and expensive navigation of the Mohawk river, to Fort Stanwix, and thence by the canal at that place, through Wood creek, Oneida lake and river, Oswego river, lake Ontario and the St. Lawrence to their destination, and others by the equally toilsome and more dangerous water route from lake Champlain, and up the St. Lawrence. The rumors of war which darkened the political horizon, stopped the growth of the country, and at its occurrence the settlements diminished more rapidly than they had previously grown. The channel of trade down the St. Lawrence, which was fast becoming established was broken up, and the exigencies of the period, gave origin to the belief, that other avenues to market, independent of the casualties of war should be established, nor was this abandoned until by the most indefatigable exertions under repeated discouragements, the great want has been supplied, and there has not been in its history a period, when the future was opening more pleasantly, than the present, inviting the investment of capital and industry, with the promise of rich returns.

In tracing the birth and infancy of our settlements, through the weakness, and perhaps the waywardness of inexperienced youth, up to the maturity of manhood, it has been our uniform desire to render impartial justice to the merits of those to whom belongs the credit of having met and overcome the difficulties of a new country, and through a long course of years, with hope deferred, have waited and labored for the accomplishment of those objects which were calculated to secure a lasting benefit to the country. About 1818, the first attempt was made to establish the dairy interest, a branch of agriculture which will, to a considerable degree, supersede every other, as the broken nature of the surface, in towns underlaid by primary rock, renders pasturage the most profitable use to which much of the land can be applied. The direct access to the markets, at all times, which is now enjoyed, enables the farmer to avail himself of the calls of the market, and derive every advantage that has hitherto been felt only by those living in the vicinity of large cities. Although butter and cheese are required for consumption by millions, yet but a comparatively small part of our country is capable of producing them. The country that yields these articles is mainly limited to the northern border of the Union; the climate of the central and southern portions not being adapted to the purpose. This species of husbandry likewise possesses the elements of perpetuity within itself, from the very small amount of the produce of fields that are taken away. Of other sources of wealth our counties possess an enviable share, when these resources come to be known and appreciated, they can not but be improved.

The great and increasing amount of freight business done on the Northern railroad, and the corresponding addition to the commerce of the river and lakes to meet this road, bear evidence that the public are beginning to realize the advantages of the communication, and to reap the benefits to be derived from it.

The Canadian system of rail roads in progress, is destined to exert a favorable influence upon the prospects of this section of the state, by directing the tide of travel and business between the seaboard and the great west, through our midst, and the commercial interests of the country, with whom economy of time and money are leading questions, will not be long in finding this as one of the most direct and eligible avenues.

There at present exists a strong probability, that the desirable link between the Northern rail road and that from Rome to Cape Vincent, will be shortly built, which must tend greatly to promote the growth and wealth of the district through which it will pass, by placing it in communication with the markets. The enterprise which has originated and sustained these and other measures, tending to develop to the extent of their capacity, the resources of the country, may perhaps be traced to the restless progressive spirit characteristic of New England, from whence the mass of our population is derived.

Had any accidental circumstances thrown the fortunes of the war of 1758–1760, into the opposite scale, giving to the French the ascendency, this district might have continued as it begun, inhabited by a French population, and exhibiting that stationary and neglected aspect still seen in their settlements below Montreal; unless, perhaps, the commercial wants of the country might have called forth the expenditure of extraneous capital, in the opening of lines of communication. Thus the events of a remote historical period have modified the character of all that follow, and with those who take a pleasure in watching the relations of cause and effect, there can be nothing more instructive than observing how necessarily dependent upon the past are the events of the future.

The claims of history upon the attention of those who seek probabilities in precedents, is therefore direct; and of an importance proportionate to the proximity of time and place, rather than the magnitude of the events. The mighty changes in nations and empires, and the records of the virtues and vices of mankind which adorn or disgrace the pages of ancient history, are instructive as showing the lights and shades of human character, but they have to a great degree lost their practical bearing from their dissimilarity from existing conditions. Their consequences remain, but so interwoven in the fabric of our civilization, as to be inseparable. The nearer we approach the present, the more obvious are the effects of causes, and there are few prominent events of American history, which have not left their operation upon existing conditions, and between which may be traced the direct relation of cause and consequence.

In pursuing the history of any district, nothing is more obvious than the fact, that causes apparently the most trivial, often produce the most lasting effects; and hence the minor details of a settlement, may possess in reality more importance than was attached to them at the time of their occurrence. To borrow the figure of Macauley, " the sources of the noblest rivers, that spread fertility over continents and bear richly laden fleets to the sea, are to be sought in wild and barren mountain tracts, incorrectly laid down in maps, and rarely visited by travelers." To extend this figure we may add, that the slightest causes may give direction to the mountain rill, and thus influence the course of the river, and the consequent fertility of the country which it irrigates. The origin of our various institutions, literary, civil, religious, and social, are especially susceptible of receiving their future direction from causes operating at the time of origin; and hence arises the importance of knowing these data, to be able to appreciate in its various bearings existing relations and agencies.

If this had been done in times past, an explanation would have been afforded of many events which otherwise appear obscure. The unappreciated facts of the present, are too apt to pass unrecorded and unheeded, until at some future time, their value becomes known in their want. The probabilities of the future, both with individuals and communities, are derived from the past. By comparing existing facts or circumstances, with similar ones that preceded them, of which the results are known, we infer the probable effects that will ensue in the case before us. To enable us to do this successfully, the past must be known, and thus history becomes our index to the future. By it we are enabled to shun the errors of others by knowing the consequences which ensue from given causes, and to gain those ends in which others have failed, by profiting from their experience. The duties of the historian have been beautifully summed up by another, in the following language: " To gather from still living witnesses, and preserve for the future annalist, the important record of the teeming and romantic past; to seize while yet warm and glowing, and inscribe upon the page which shall be sought hereafter, the bright visions of song, and fair images of story, that gild the gloom and lighten the sorrows of the ever present; to search all history with a careful eye; sound all philosophy with a careful hand; question all experience with a fearless tongue, and thence draw lessons to fit us for, and light to guide us through, the shadowy but unknown future."

It has been our endeavor in the following pages, to act with strict impartiality in relation to local interests and natural advantages; to avoid any appearance that would lead to the suspicion that we wished to promote any sectional or local interest, or advance the personal sectarian or political measures of any person or class of persons.

Many subjects have been passed with a brief notice, that but from want of space, would have been more fully discussed, and numerous documents and data having a direct relation to the history of Northern New York, have been for the same reason entirely omitted. To this class belongs much relating to the events of the war, consisting of original letters, official despatches, and verbal statements; but perhaps enough will be found to satisfy the reader that with whatever merit or wisdom the measures of that period were planned, their execution was attempted in a manner that shows either an incapacity or disinclination on the part of the commanding officers for their successful accomplishment. The latter has been often suggested, but this question belongs not to our inquiries.

In coming down to a still more recent period, and giving the details of a movement which threatened to disturb the peace of the country, a difficulty was felt in relating the events of the affair from the different and often conflicting statements of the cotemporary press, and the verbal accounts of parties who acted with, or who discouraged the affairs. In our relation of these events, by being limited to an account of a few of the many acts that make up the history of the Patriot war, an opportunity was not afforded for exhibiting the movement in the light that would enable one to form a just estimate of its merits, and perhaps the time has not yet elapsed, when a candid opinion could be safely expressed, without encroaching upon the reputation of some of the agitators and promoters of the scheme still living. The blood of the betrayed and unfortunate youths who fell at the wind mill at Prescott, and who suffered the death penalty in consequence of that affair, is upon the hands of those who incited them to the enterprise, but from which they kept *themselves* aloof. The tragic issue of this melancholy affair, like other and more recent ones of a similar class on the southern border of the Union, should serve as a warning beacon to guard against any movement having for its object, the forcing of our institutions upon a people who manifest no wish to receive them, but who, as in the above instances, evinced a spirit of resistance, and a vindictiveness, which proved the sincerity of their feeling.

It would have been pleasant, to have been able to extend the last chapter of the work, and especially to relate with greater detail the metalic and mineral resources of these counties, which deservedly enjoy a high reputation for their extent and value, and which have only begun to be developed. An enumeration of localities where metalic ores have been found, or indications observed that lead to the belief of their existence, would show that they are widely scattered over the primitive region, and will without doubt hereafter form a branch of industry of great prominence. This remark is especially applicable to the ores of iron. Of the minerals interesting to the man of science, and of no practical use, few sections afford so great a variety, or those of more elegance, than the western part of St. Lawrence county, and particularly the towns of Rossie, Gouverneur, Fowler, Edwards, and Hermon. A brief enumeration of these, with the towns in which they occur, is only given. To have specified the particular locality of each, would have been tedious, except to the collector.

In the chapter of biographical notices, disappointment in not receiving materials where they were expected and had been promised, has deprived us of the ability of inserting several, that would have made a desirable acquisition in the history of Northern New York, from the prominent and active part they took in its settlement, and in the title and transfer of lands, before purchased by actual settlers. This branch of history is one of great importance, because the duty of the annalist is to a great degree but to record the acts of men, and the consequences growing out from them.

In collecting the details of the settlements of several towns, a considerable amount of materials were procured, which have not been used, consisting mostly of the names and short memoranda of the early settlers, and lists of those who first formed religious societies.

There will probably be found some errors in what is given, as from necessity the statements were often drawn from memory, and hence liable to uncertainty. Written memoranda, and records made at the time of occurrence, are in all cases to be preferred to the memory, however definite this latter may be, and this remark is equally applicable to every department of history.

In a few instances, we met with those who have habitually made a record of passing events, and thus were able to fix with much definiteness, the dates and circumstances of events which otherwise would have been obscure. This practice has in it that obvious utility and convenience, that commends itself to general adoption, and these memorials of the past lose none of their interest from age, but rather acquire new value in proportion as the event becomes distant.

The reliance to be placed upon oral evidence depends upon so many contingencies, that it possesses every degree of probability, from absolute certainty to indefinite fable. The greater part of the following work relates to a period within the memory of those living, or of the generation immediately preceding the present. Of the occurrences half a century ago, the surviving witnesses who then knew most of them, have become enfeebled by age, and those whose memories are most sound, were then young, so that between the extremes of youth and age, verbal accounts have begun to lose their reliability, and a few years longer would place them wholly beyond our reach.   Traditions extending back through more than two generations, may as a general rule, be rejected by the historian as idle tales, and more liable to mislead than instruct.

This work is submitted to the public with a consciousness of its imperfections, and a desire that the reader will regard with indulgence, the errors and the faults which the greatest vigilance could not wholly exclude.   If it shall but serve to awaken an interest in the community to which it applies, and lead to the preservation of the data which make up the materials for history; if it serves to impart an interest to localities, by their associations with the events of the olden time, and especially if it serve, though but in an humble degree, to attract notice to the resources and the advantages which they possess, our object will have been attained.   If it had been possible to have rendered it uniform and alike minute in the details, it should have been done; but from the omission of facts, of which no record remain, many links in the chain of events have been irrecoverably lost.   Had this labor been attempted twenty years ago, it would have been possible to have rendered the early details more perfect.   At an equal period in the future, much that is here related, would have passed beyond recovery.

HISTORY

OF

ST. LAWRENCE AND FRANKLIN COUNTIES.

CHAPTER I.

ABORIGINAL, FRENCH, AND ENGLISH HISTORY.

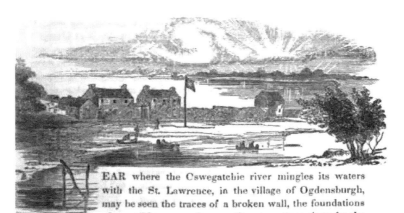

EAR where the Oswegatchie river mingles its waters with the St. Lawrence, in the village of Ogdensburgh, may be seen the traces of a broken wall, the foundations of an edifice erected more than a century since by the Sulpitians, for the purpose of attaching to the interests of the French, who were then the masters of Canada, such of the Iroquois confederacy or Six Nations of Indians, as might be induced to conform to their religion, and espouse their cause.*

* Several years since, the corner stone of the buildings represented at the head of this chapter was obtained in demolishing the walls. It is still preserved with much care by Mr. Louis Hasbrouck, of the village of Ogdensburgh, and bears the following inscription :

In nomine ✝ Dei omnipotentis

Huic habitationi initia dedit

Frans. Picquet 1849

Translated, this reads as follows " Francis Picquet laid the foundation of this habitation, in the name of the Almighty God, in 1749."

These buildings, or others erected on their site, were subsequently and for many years occupied by a British garrison, and within the memory of those yet living, as a court-house, jail, store, dwelling. and barracks for troops; and with them commences the earliest authentic history we possess of St. Lawrence county.

The Aboriginal inhabitants of the country, have left a few traces of their occupancy, in the remains of several ancient trench enclosures and paintings, of which we will give as full an account as can at present be obtained. In the adjoining county of Jefferson, not less than fifteen trench enclosures have been observed; how many more may have been levelled by the plow without exciting a suspicion of their true nature, can not be known. In St. Lawrence county, at least six are known to have existed, and perhaps more, besides localities which appear to have been a most favorite haunt of the red man, as evinced by the remains of his rude implements and ornaments scattered through the soil. It may be well to remark, that the observation made by De Witt Clinton,[*] that none of these remains occur below the level of the lake ridges, fails to be sustained in the instances which occur in St. Lawrence, and in several which occur in Jefferson counties. He attempted by this argument to prove the recent subsidence of the great lakes, and the modern origin of the *Lake Ridges*, which form so striking a feature connected with the geological structure of their borders.

Nothing is more common than to find along the lands that skirt the fertile meadow bottoms which form the shores of several of the tributaries of the St. Lawrence, the broken remains of rude pottery, seldom sufficiently entire to enable one to determine the original form, and usually sculptured or rather impressed while in a soft and yielding state with various fanciful figures, always differing from each other in fragments belonging to different utensils, but possessing a general resemblance, which is often much like that of the annexed figure. The cut here inserted represents an entire vessel of earthen ware dug up many years since in Jefferson county.

Not unfrequently a rude resemblance to the human face is noticed on these fragments. The material of this *terra cotta*, or baked earth, is usually clay and coarse sand, generally well tempered and baked.

Stone gouges for tapping maple trees; stone chisels for skinning deer;

* See the memoir of Mr. Clinton on this subject, read before the " Literary and Philosophical Society of New York," and published in a pamphlet form at Albany, in 1818.

arrowheads of flint, jasper, chalcedony, shale and other stone; amulets and beads of steatite, and other personal ornaments; implements of bone apparently used as needles, and as tools for marking impressions upon the pottery; and fragments of bones and broken shells, the remains of ancient feasts, indicate in broken and disconnected but intelligible language the pursuits of our predecessors upon our soil.

We will here mention those places where rude traces of embankments indicate the site of ancient strong-holds, illy adapted to the purposes of modern defense, but admirably fitted for resisting the modes of attack as then practised. As a general rule, those points were chosen which afforded naturally a protection upon one or more sides, as the bank of a stream, or the brow of a hill, leaving only defenses to be erected on the unprotected sides. The traces observed usually consisted, when first noticed, of a mound or bank of earth, surrounded by a ditch of proportionate extent, which evidently furnished the materials for the bank. There is reason to believe that the bank originally formed the foot of a palisade of timber, set upright in the ground, which, having entirely decayed, has left nothing but the earth remaining. In a few of the trench enclosures of western New York, the evidences of this are not wanting, for the holes which were left by the decaying of the pickets may still be traced. This is especially true of a work near Geneva, in Ontario county, which formed the last stronghold of the Senecas in the expedition of General Sullivan during the revolutionary war, and which owes its preservation entirely to the circumstance that the premises were expressly reserved at the time of the cession of their lands to the state, with the explicit understanding that it should never be brought under cultivation. "Here," said they, "sleep our fathers, and they can not rest well if they hear the plow of the white man above them."

In the town of Macomb, St. Lawrence county, are found the traces of three trench enclosures, and several places where beds of ashes mark the site of ancient hearths; the habitations and defences of a race, of whose period or history we have nothing to conjecture. One of these was on the farm of William Houghton, on the bank of Birch creek, and enclosed the premises now used as a mill-yard. It was somewhat in the form of a semicircle, the two ends resting on the creek, and might have enclosed half an acre. Every trace of the work has been long since erased by cultivation; but the line which formed the bank, and the space within and without, still occasionally afford fragments of pottery, ashes, shells, and stone implements. Great numbers of these have been picked up and carried off by the curious; and among other articles, numbers of stone and earthen-ware pipes, with a short clumsy stem two or three inches long, and a heavy massive bowl with a small cavity, have been found. On an adjoining hill, now partly occupied by an orchard, traces of an ancient work formerly existed, but this has also been obliterated. This locality is the one mentioned in most state gazetteers as occurring on the premises of Captain Washburn in Gouverneur (the former occupant of the farm when the adjacent country formed a part of that town); but the statement that "traces of rude sculpture exist within the enclosure," which has been often copied, is incorrect.

In the pond adjoining, there was found, many years since, a skeleton, said to have been of great size.

About half a mile northeast of this, is the trace of another enclosure, on the farms of William P. Houghton and Josiah Sweet; but the outlines are so indistinct, that they could not be traced with any degree of certainty. From what little remains, it appears to have consisted of a deep ditch, outside of a high bank; and it is said to have been irregularly semi-oval, with passages or gateways where the work was interrupted; and that its ends came up to a small stream, the present outlet of a tamarack swamp, but the former site of a beaver meadow. The evidences of the latter were found in digging a ditch for drainage some time since, when the sticks still bearing the marks of the teeth of beavers were found several feet below the surface.

This trench and bank could, at the author's visit, be traced about 160 paces, which appeared to be about half of its original circuit. Its longest direction was from N.N.E. to S.S.W. Numerous fire beds occurred within it, and in one instance a quantity of ashes and charcoal was found *five feet* below the surface.

In a field a few rods distant, in the direction of the work last described, the vestiges which abound in the soil seem to indicate that there was once an Indian village on the site.

On the premises of the St. Lawrence Lead Mining Company, and the farm of Robert Wilson, about three-fourths of a mile from the first described spot, is still another trace, which can still be easily made out, as the premises have never been plowed. In this instance the work was crescent-shaped, the open side being protected by a low ledge of limestone rock, and a branch which led down to a small stream, which may have served as a covered way to allow the inmates of the stockade to have access to the water. Not having been cultivated, the soil of this locality has not hitherto furnished any relics of interest, although it can scarcely fail to do so when plowed.

This is the only work of the three in the town of Macomb, which can still be seen entire.

On the farm of Henry E. Holbrook, in the northeastern part of Potsdam, on or near mile lot No. 10, was a remarkable trench enclosure in early times, but which is now entirely destroyed, except a very small portion in the public highway. It is on the road between Norfolk village and Raquetteville, west of the river, and half a mile from the railroad bridge at the latter place; and is situated on an elevated ridge of drift, in a commanding position, and at a point which affords a fine prospect of the surrounding country. The form of this work was said to have been semicircular, the open side resting on a swamp to the west, and several spaces or gateways are said to have occurred at irregular intervals. The ditch, which was exterior to the bank, appears to have furnished the earth for the bank, which was on the inside of the trench, and enclosed about two acres. Pine stumps still stand on the bank, four feet in diameter, which must have grown since the place was occupied, as beds of ashes have been found under their roots, mingled with broken earthen, flint arrows, and other relics of the builders. Within and without, scattered at irregular intervals, were found fireplaces, with charcoal, ashes, freshwater shells, bones, and broken pottery, which differed in no respect from that found in other trench enclosures in the state. On an island in the vicinity, Indian graves were found.

In the town of Massena, about half a mile west of Raquette river bridge, and on the western declivity of a slope near the summit of a dividing ridge which separates this river from Grass river, and in an open field which has long been cleared but never plowed, are plainly to be traced the outlines of a work which differs considerably from any above described, and which is by far the best preserved. Its form is irregular, being somewhat shaped like an ox-bow, with its open side towards Raquette river, and with numerous spaces or openings more especially on the southern side. The open side is in part protected by a ditch, which is not connected with the main work, being separated from it by a considerable interval on each side. The relics furnished by the soil in this vicinity do not differ essentially from those of other places, being mostly of earthen-ware and stone.

The summit of the ridge at this place commands an extensive and delightful prospect, and this vicinity must have formed a favorite haunt for the rude Indians who once made it their home. At no great distance on either side was a river abounding in fish, and affording a long navigation with an occasional carrying place, by which they could penetrate far into the interior; while a few miles below them, the mighty St. Lawrence, with its bays and islands, afforded equal facilities for hunting, and equal prospects for repaying the labors of the chase and the hazards of the fisheries.

If the intervening woods were cleared away, the locality in Potsdam, some eighteen or twenty miles distant, could be seen from this place; and perhaps the two may have been occupied by parties of the same tribe, who could exchange signals by night, as the fires gleaming upon one summit might be easily distinguished from the other.

The description of this enclosure, published in the third annual report of the Regents of the University on the condition of the State Cabinet is somewhat erroneous, as neither of the two works last mentioned are furnished with bastions and angles; and accordingly the inferences there drawn, that it must belong to a different historical period, are without foundation. The stumps of immense trees, standing on the bank and in the ditch, indicate at least an ante-Columbian age, and probably many centuries have elapsed since these stations have witnessed the events for which they were formed. Within this enclosure are one or two slight eminences, which may in their day have been sufficiently high to overlook the pickets by which they were probably surrounded.

In the town of Massena, not far from this work, there was found several years since, a pipe, formed of whitish steatite, or soapstone, having on its bowl and stem curiously wrought, the figure of a serpent, with its head rising a little above the level of the bowl. The figure of the serpent has been used by savages of all nations, apparently without the knowledge of each other, and this has given rise to the opinion that it originated in some religious notion, and that it is symbolical of some idea inherent in the human mind. The Egyptians represented the recurring cycle of the year, by a serpent with its tail in its mouth, and among the mounds of the south-west there is one which, when traced in its immense proportions along the ground, represents an enormous serpent. In the instance of the pipe found in Massena, there might, or might not, have been something more than the amusement of a leisure hour on its formation.

A semicircular trench, and bank, formerly existed in the town of Oswegatchie, near its western edge, and on the farm now owned by Benjamin Pope. A small portion of the present highway passes over it, at the only part which is now visible, cultivation having obliterated every trace of it elsewhere. It was somewhat semicircular, and no natural barrier can be noticed as forming, with the aid of the bank and ditch, a complete enclosure.

In this respect it differs from others, but we are not to infer from the non-existence of the bank that no defensive work existed. The outline of this bank may be traced in the spring by the unusual verdure of the grass along its line, and similar spots indicate the sites of fire places, both within and without. An unusual abundance of stone and earthenware fragments occurred here in former times.

INDIAN PAINTING *on the shore of the St. Lawrence opposite the village of* **Oak Point** *.*

On St. Regis Island, directly opposite the Indian village of that name, and at a point where the boundary of 1818 crossed the river, there still exists a barrow or sepulchral mound. " It was excavated by Colonel Hawkins of the United States boundary commission, in 1818, and found to contain near the surface human bones in considerable numbers, and in a good state of preservation, but at the base were found traces of fire, charcoal, burned bones, and fragments of pottery, together with stone implements and ornaments."[*]

Directly opposite to the church, on the east bank of St. Regis river, in the same neighborhood as the preceding, is another barrow or mound of somewhat similar character, which has at some period apparently been explored with the view of ascertaining the nature of its contents. There is no tradition in the village relating to either of them, and no probability that they were made by the existing race of Indians.

They doubtless date back to the era of the other earth-works above described, and belong to a remote period of our history, which has been lost. In making a canal around the rapids on the Canada shore of the St. Lawrence, many years since, a singular mound was dug through, which disclosed relics of copper and various ornaments, and among others a mask of the human face, in terra-cotta or earthen ware, which seemed to have belonged to some image.

Opposite the village of Oak Point, in Elizabeth township, C.W., is a painting on the rock,  representing a canoe with thirty-five men and a cross, evidently intended to commemo-rate some event, and done since the Catholic missionaries first came to Canada. From the direction of the boat, it appears that the party was passing down the river.

Opposite the village of Mor-

* Aboriginal Monuments of New York, by E. G. Squier. Smithsonian Contributions to Knowledge. Vol. 2, Art. 6, page 16.

2

ristown, and just below
the town of Brockville,
are two paintings, of
which engravings are
here inserted.

There is much pro-
bability that these paintings are of compara-
tively modern origin.
Indeed the Indians at
St. Regis village pos-
sess a vague tradition
concerning them, which
they related briefly as follows:

" A long time ago the Caughnawaga Indians were going west on a warlike expedition, and made these paintings on their way up. They were
all killed. The number of marks denote the number of the party."

The cross, the emblem of the Christian faith, and especially held in
reverence by the Catholics, indicates with sufficient clearness, the modern
origin of the sketches. Perhaps they may form a connecting link in the
chain of events that occurred under the French dynasty, or perhaps they
were traced from mere idle curiosity, or to pass away the tedium of a
leisure hour. In either event they are interesting as examples of the
symbolical records used by savages, to preserve the memory of events
or of the pastimes and tastes of a race which is fast passing away. The
sketch near Oak point was apparently done in vermillion, while the
others appear to have been made with ochre. All of these are less
brilliant than when first observed by the whites, and will in a few years
be entirely obliterated.

The shores of Black lake, in the town of Morristown, between the
village of Hammond, and The Narrows, contain traces of paintings
of an obscure character. A deer drawn very rudely, about eight inches
high; and seven figures in two groups, was at a short distance from the
former.

The deer was the emblem or mark in use among the Iroquois to designate one of their bands, and from the figures we give in our chapter on
titles, it will be seen that it was in use among the Oswegatchies. It is
therefore quite probable that this may be very modern, and its origin
may doubtless be ascribed to some incident connected with that clan.

The block on which the deer was drawn, is preserved in the collections of the state, at their historical and antiquarian museum at
Albany.

The following sketch represents the groups of human beings on the rocks at this place, drawn in the conventional form adopted among the savages.

Near the village of Edwardsville, or The Narrows, in the town of Morristown, on a hill a little east of that place, there was formerly found upon plowing, traces of an Indian village, as evinced by a row of hearths with burned stones, ashes, charcoal, shells, and fragments of bones. These were some little distance below the surface, and extended for a quarter of a mile.

The land here was excellent for the raising of corn, and the lake then, doubtless as now, abounded in fish, which would have made this an eligible residence for the rude Indian. Who? When? and in what numbers? are questions which echo only can answer.

With these exceptions we have no knowledge that any part of these counties had been inhabited, or the lands cultivated by any except the nomadic class, which still occasionally visits the hunting ground of his fathers.

There are no Indian fields, no traces of ancient occupancy by a foreign people, or evidence that the soil has ever been trod by the foot of man, except by a rude hunter in pursuit of his game. In some of the central and western parts of the state, in the fields of Iroquois, where that staple article of food had been cultivated from time immemorial, the hillocks on which it had been planted were distinctly to be traced at the time when possession was taken by the whites, but nothing of this has been observed in the northern part of the state.

The traces of ancient defensive works of which we have given an account, extend into Canada, and several of them occur in the townships of Augusta, Williamsburgh, Osnabruck, &c.

One of these is about seven and a half miles northwest of Prescott, C. W., on a farm occupied by Mr. Tarp. It is situated on a peninsula of elevated land, in the midst of a swamp, and accessible only by a narrow neck which bears the trace of an ancient defensive work. The land within this, is eighteen or twenty feet above the level of the surrounding swamp, and in two or three places are the traces of mounds of slight elevation, but which might have overlooked the surrounding country to a considerable distance. Within the breastwork at the isthmus, are lines of slight elevation, which mark the places of former dwelling (?); and in the soil has been found great quantities of the remains of rude pottery, which indicate the attainments which the tenants of this strong hold had acquired in this indispensible and primitive art.

The greatest quantity was found from fifteen to eighteen inches below the surface, and was accompanied by implements of bone, flint, green-stone, the bones of animals, that had doubtless been taken in the chase, and shells of fresh water molusca.

Among other relics was a flattened boulder of hornblende or gneiss, both sides of which had been rendered smooth and concave by the rub-bing of stone implements, and which might have served the purpose of a mortar for grinding corn. Boulders of immense size are often found in Jefferson county, and elsewhere, having shallow depressions upon their surface, apparently having been used as grindstones for sharpening and forming the rude stone implements of the rude people who once occupied the country.

The breastwork at the entrance of the enclosure above described, had at two places, openings about eighteen feet wide, which probably served as a passage way for the inmates, and the bank is evidently the foot of a pa-lisade of timber, set upright in the ground. The whole must have formed in its day a strong hold, easy of defense against any mode of attack then possessed.

Near Spencerville, is another trace of an ancient defensive work, and in the township of Augusta, in the second concession, still another.

At the latter is said to have been found an ornament of gold, but the account of this is so uncertain and obscure, that it is worthy of but little credit.

Several of the above works have been surveyed and examined, by William E. Guest, Esq., of Ogdensburgh, who has transmitted an account of them to the Smithsonian Institution at Washington, for publication.

At one of these works was found the broken portion of an immense tooth, supposed to have been that of a walrus. Both ends were broken, and it had been perforated as if to be worn as an amulet. This, with the copper implements found in this section, indicate that the commerce or travels of this people, whoever they were, must have extended from the seaboard to the copper regions of Lake Superior, which was doubt-less the source from which our aboriginal predecessors derived that metal.

To leave the period of the buried past, through which the stream of time has coursed its way, without leaving more to mark its path than the scattered relics and obscure traces, which tell of nothing, but that something was, and is not, we approach the period of authentic history; and here we find many links wanting in the chain of events, which might have enabled us to trace the progress of the discovery, and the settlement and the changes of dominion, which our country has undergone. Tradition relates, that the Adirondacks, and the Iroquois, or the nations of Canada, and those of New York, in ancient times. waged

long and bloody wars for the supremacy of the soil, and doubtless many
a stealthy march and midnight massacre, had they but had their historian,
would have made our district classic to those who dwell with interest
upon the recital of scenes of blood. It has been aptly said, that "that
country is the happiest which furnishes the fewest materials for history;"
yet, if rightly considered, the duty of the historian will be found not
limited to the narration of the dramatic events of war, but equally applicable to the arts of peace, and that the true heroes of mankind, are those
who have manfully encountered and overcome the difficulties which
might have hindered them from arriving at honorable ends by honest
means. Viewed in this light, the pioneer who has subdued the wildness
of nature, and surrounded his home with the luxuries of a well-directed
husbandry, is socially far above the victorious warrior, and his toils,
privations and successes are more worthy of record.

Before giving an account of the missions established on the St. Lawrence by the French missionaries, it may be interesting to glance at
the earlier discoveries of Canada, and note in a rapid manner, several of the primitive attempts to establish European colonies in this
quarter.

Two years after the discoveries of Columbus became known in
England, Henry VII engaged John Cabot, a Venetian merchant, to
sail in quest of discoveries in the west, and this navigator in 1497
reached the coast of Labrador, which he named *Prima-vista.* This
was doubtless the first visit of Europeans to this coast since the days of
the Scandinavians.

This voyage was succeeded by others under Sebastian Cabot, son of
the preceding, in 1498; and by Gaspar Cortereal in 1500, to whom the
discovery of the Gulf of St. Lawrence is said to be due.* This adven-
turer returned to Lisbon in the month of October of that year, laden
with timber and *slaves,* seized from among the natives of the coasts he
visited.

On a second voyage Cortereal perished at sea. In 1504, the French
first attempted a voyage to the New World; and in that year, some
Basque and Breton fishermen began to ply their calling on the bank
of Newfoundland and along its adjacent coasts. From these the island
of Cape Breton derived its name. The dreary picture of these bleak
and foggy coasts, and the mystery which hung upon the fate of the
second expedition of Verazzano, who had been sent out by Francis I.
from France, deterred for a time all efforts of the French to colonize

*This discovery has been also ascribed to Jacques Cartier, who entered the gulf on the 10th
of August, 1535. and gave it the name of the saint whose festival was celebrated on that day.—
Charlevoix.

this region. In 1525, Stefano Gomez sailed from Spain, and is supposed to have entered the Gulf of St. Lawrence, and to have traded upon its shores. A Castilian tradition relates, that finding neither gold nor silver upon the coasts, nor any thing which conveyed to these sordid adventurers an idea of mines or wealth of any kind, they frequently exclaimed "*Aca-nada*;" (signifying "here is nothing") and that the natives caught up the sound, which was repeated when other Europeans arrived, and thus gave origin to the designation of *Canada*. This origin of the word is also confirmed by Father Hennepin.

A. Geo. de Lorimier, an intelligent half breed, residing at the Saut St. Louis, and who is well acquainted with the native language, stated to the author that the word Canada was derived from the Indian word Ka-na-ta, which signifies, a village.

In 1534, Francis I, king of France, listening to the urgent advice of Philip Chabot, admiral of France, who portrayed to him in glowing colors the riches and growing power of Spain, derived from her transatlantic colonies, despatched Jacques Cartier, an able navigator of St. Malmo, who sailed on the 20th of April, 1534, with two ships of only sixty tons each, and a hundred and twenty men, and reached Newfoundland in May. After coasting along for some time, without knowing that it was an island, he at length passed the straits of Belleisle, and traversed the Gulf of St. Lawrence. Having spent a part of the summer on these coasts, he sailed on the 25th of July, highly pleased with the hospitable reception he had received from the natives, with whom he traded for furs and provisions.

His report induced the French king to attempt a colony in the newly discovered regions; and in May, 1535, Cartier again sailed with three small ships, with a numerous company of adventurers, which arrived on the coast of Newfoundland much scattered and weakened by a disastrous storm on the 26th of July.

Having taken in wood and water, they proceeded to explore the gulf but were overtaken on the 1st of August by a storm, which obliged them to seek a port, difficult of access, but with a safe anchorage, near the mouth of the Great river. They left this harbor on the 7th, and on the 10th came to a gulf filled with numerous and beautiful islands Cartier gave this gulf the name of *St. Lawrence*, having discovered it on that saint's festival day.* From this, the Great river and our county derive their name.

* "Cartier donna au golphe le nom de St. Laurent, ou plutot il le donna a une baye qui est entre l'isle d'Anticosti et la cote septentrionale, d'ou ce nom c'est etendu, a tout le golphe dont cette baye fait partie.—*Hist. de la Nouvelle France, Tome i, p. 15.*

According to Catholic accounts, Saint Lawrence, or Saint Lorenzo, was a deacon to Pope Xystus, or Sistus II, who suffered martyrdom for the faith of Christ, by being boiled on a

Proceeding on their voyage, they reached on the 15th, the isle since called Anticosti, and exploring both shores of the St. Lawrence, at length they discovered another island of great extent, fertility and beauty, covered with woods and laden with thick clustering vines, which they named the Isle de Bacchus, now called Orleans. Pleased with the friendly disposition of the natives and the comfortable prospects for a winter sojourn, Cartier moored his vessels where a little river flowed into a "goodly and pleasant sound," which stream he named the St. Croix, near the Indian village of Stadacona, the site of the modern city of Quebec. Cartier subsequently during the autumn ascended the river to the populous village of Hochelaga, and was every where received in the kindest manner by the natives. To a hill, three miles from the village, from whose summit the river and country for thirty leagues around was spread out in great beauty, he gave the name of Mont Royal, which has since been applied to the populous city on that island,—the modern Montreal, which lies at its foot.

The dreadful severity of the winter, with the scurvy, reduced the number of Cartier's companions considerably. In May, he sailed for France, with the Indian chief as a prisoner, who had treated him with uniform kindness. During each succeeding year, for some time after, expeditions were sent out to the newly discovered river, but misfortune attended them all, and no efficient attempt at colonizing the country was made till 1608, when De Monts, a Calvinist, who had obtained from the king the freedom of religious faith for himself and followers in America, but under the engagement that the Catholic worship should be established among the natives; after several perilous voyages, and much opposition, despatched Champlain and Pontgrave, two experienced adventurers, to establish the fur trade and begin a settlement. Champlain reached Tadousac on the 3d of June, and on the 3d of July he reached *Quebec*, where, nearly three quarters of a century before, Cartier had spent the winter. This magnificent site was at once chosen as the place for a future city; and centuries of experience have confirmed the wisdom of his choice.

During the first winter, the settlers endured the extremities of famine. On the 18th of April, 1609, Samuel Champlain, with two Frenchmen, ascended the Great river; and after a time, turning southward up a tributary, entered the beautiful lake which bears his name, and near its southern extremity, overcoming a rapid, they entered another lake, afterwards named *St. Sacrament*, now *Lake Horicon*, or *Lake George.*

In 1614, Champlain by his entreaties, procured four Recollects to

gridiron, A. D. 253. His festival is celebrated on the 10th of August, and his name occurs in the litany of the saints in the Catholic ritual.

undertake a mission to convert to the Catholic faith the Indians of the
country; these were the first missionaries who visited Acadia. To gain
a knowledge of the country and language of the natives, Champlain and
a father Joseph Le Cavon, united with them in an expedition against
the Iroquois, or confederates of New York, but the enterprise proved
unsuccessful, and Champlain was wounded.*

He was obliged to spend the winter with his savage allies, but improved the opportunity by informing himself of the resources and geo-
graphy of the country, to the greatest advantage.

In 1625, Henri de Levi, duke de Ventadour, who had purchased the
vice-royalty of New France, sent over the exemplary Father Lallemant,
and four other priests and laymen of the order of the Jesuits, who were
received by the Recollects with kindness, and admitted under their roof
on their first arrival. The next year, three other Jesuits arrived, with
artizans and settlers, when the settlement began to assume the appearance of a town. In 1629, the colony was seized by the English, but
restored by treaty in 1632; and in the year following, Champlain was
again installed as governor of New France. His death occurred in
December, 1635. From this time forward the Jesuit missionaries continued to explore the country, and labor with a zeal which has known
no parallel, to convert the roving savages to the Catholic faith. To
acquire their language and confidence, they adopted their dresses and
mode of life, assisted them in fishing and hunting, and joined in distant
and arduous marches for warlike purposes.

Every canton or tribe of the Iroquois of New York, and nearly every
nation throughout the range of the great lakes and the Mississippi valley
had its missionary, and many of them a depot for the purchase of furs
and sale of merchandise. To protect this trade, and especially to deprive
the English settlements of its benefits, military posts were early established at important points, and as Quebec was the principal port from
which exports were made, the St. Lawrence river became the highway
of the French to their distant stations.

The first military post of any note above Montreal was erected at
Cataraqui, now Kingston, of the founding of which a minute account is
preserved in the form of a journal of Count de Frontenac, a portion of
which describes the wild scenery of the St. Lawrence nearly two centuries ago, before the woodman's axe had echoed in the primeval forests,
which then shaded its waters. From it an idea may be formed of the

* The foregoing facts are mostly derived from the first volume of Warburton's Conquest
of Canada; where original authorities are cited. The expedition of Champlain is given in
full in the Documentary History of New York, Vol. III.

perils which these men encountered in the prosecution of their designs. The following extract from the journal of Count de Frontenac's voyage to Lake Ontario in 1673, was translated from the second volume of the collection of the Paris Documents in the office of the Secretary of State, by Dr. E. B. O'Callaghan, editor of the Documentary History of New York, who has kindly permitted this manuscript to be used for this work. It gives an interesting picture of the scenery and physical features of the St. Lawrence at that early period.

The object of this journey was to prevent the ratification of a treaty between Indian tribes, which he conceived would operate injuriously to the interests of the French. He proposed to effect this by the establishment of a military post on Lake Ontario, and this was the first beginning made at what is now the city of Kingston, C. W. He could thus prevent intercourse between the south and the north, and monopolize the fur trade of the Indians. He was still further induced to this, from the representations of the Jesuit missionaries, who had for some time labored among the Iroquois, and were over anxious that a station should be made in the country of the Indians, as well to promote their religion, as their commercial enterprises.

To impress the natives with a belief that cascades and rapids were no barrier against the French, Count de Frontenac resolved to take with him two flat bateaux, similar to that M. de Courcelles had two years previous carried to the head of the rapids, and even to mount them with small cannon, to inspire savages with awe. With these two boats, built after a particular model, holding sixteen men, and painted unlike any thing seen before, and with about one hundred and twenty bark canoes, he at length left Montreal on the 28th of June, having made all necessary arrangements for the government of the colony in his absence. On the 3d of July they had reached the islands at the head of Lake St. Francis, where they repaired their bateaux, which had been injured in the passing of rapids. We will quote the words of the journal:

"On the 4th, the route passed through the most delightful country in the world. The entire river was spangled with islands, on which were only oaks and hard wood; the soil is admirable, and the banks of the mainland on the north and south shores are equally handsome, the timber being very clean and lofty, forming a forest equal to the most beautiful in France. Both banks of the river are lined with prairies, full of excellent grass, interspersed with an infinity of beautiful flowers; so that it may be asserted, there would not be a more lovely country in the world than that from Lake St. Francis to the head of the rapids, were it cleared.

"Made three leagues up to noon, and halted at a spot more delightful than any we had yet seen. It was close to the little channel which stretches along the sault on the north side, and opposite the mouth of a

river by which people go to the Mohawk.* Sieur Le Moine was sent
to examine that which goes to the Mohawks, and reported that it formed
a large, circular, deep, and pleasant basin, behind the point where we
had halted, and that the Iroquois whom he had found there, had informed
him that there was five days' easy navigation in that river, and three when
the waters were lower. After having dined and rested awhile, the march
was resumed and it was resolved to take the south channel, with the
design to camp above the long saut, and cross over to that side at three
quarters of a league above it, but the rain which supervened obliged
Count de Frontenac to cause the entire fleet to come to anchor on the
north side, at the place where we intended to traverse, and he had time
only to get the bateaux to do this, and to encamp himself with the
Three Rivers' brigade, and his staff on the south shore opposite the
place where the other sections had anchored. We found in the western
forest, in the camp, a white flower, as beautiful as can be seen, with an
odor similar to that of the lily of the valley, but much finer. It was
sketched through curiosity.

" The 5th, the rain threatening, we contented ourselves in despatching
the bateaux at the break of day to get them past the rapids of the Long
Saut, and the order was sent to the fleet at the north side not to traverse,
until the weather was settled.

" Therefore it having cleared about ten o'clock, the fleet traversed and
advanced to the foot of the first rapid of the Long Saut, but one half
having passed, a storm sprang up, which obliged the count to go by land
as far as the rapid, to hasten on those who were in the middle, and to
prevent the last going further on; so that four only were able to pass,
and these camped half a league above. He sent the others into a cove,
after he had remained more than two hours under the rain, without a
cloak; very uneasy about the bateaux, which experienced much difficulty
in ascending the rapid, one of them had run adrift in the current, had
not the people behind, thrown themselves into the stream with incredible promptness and bravery.

It is impossible to conceive without witnessing, the fatigue of those
who dragged the bateaux. They were for the most part of the time in
the water up to the arm-pits, walking on rock so sharp that many had
their feet and legs covered with blood, yet their gaiety never failed, and
they made such a point of honor of taking these bateaux up, that as
soon as they arrived in the camp, some among them commenced jump-
ing, playing "prison bars," (*jouer aux barres*,) and other games of like
nature. The night of the 5th and 6th inst. was so wet, that the Count
could not sleep, so afraid was he of the biscuit getting wet, that he ordered Sieur de Chambly, not to allow the canoes to start until he saw
settled weather, and to push on the bateaux with experienced hands in
them as they did not carry any provisions capable of spoiling. He
waited till noon to set out, the weather having cleared up with appearances of no more rain; but a league had not been travelled, nor the bateaux overtaken, before a tempest burst so furiously, that all thought that
the provisions would be wet. With care however, very little harm happened, and after halting about three hours, we proceeded on with some
five or six canoes, to find out a place to camp; to give time to the people
in the canoes to follow them, with all the troops, and though there were
three or four very ugly rapids to be passed; they did not fail to surmount
all these difficulties, and to arrive before sundown at the head of the
Long Saut, where Count de Frontenac, had traced out the camp, oppo-

* Raquette River?

site a little Island, at the end of which the northern channel unites with that on the south.

The 7th, started the canoes, (bateaux?) very early, with orders to cross from the north side at the place where they should find the river narrower and less rapid, and he left with all the canoes two hours after, and proceeded until eleven o'clock, in better order than during the preceding days, because the navigation was easier. We stopped three or four hours about a quarter of a league from the rapid called the *Rapide Plat*.*

The weather appeared the finest in the world. This induced us to determine on passing the rapid, which is very difficult, on account of the trees on the water side tumbling into the river, which obliged the canoes to take outside, and so go into the strongest of the current. He detached six canoes in consequence, which he sent along to take axes to cut all the trees that might obstruct the passage of the batteaux, and took with him the Three Rivers' brigade and his staff, to lay out the camp, having left two brigades with the bateaux, and others for a rear guard. But on landing at 5 o'clock in the afternoon, there came a storm accompanied by thunder and lightning, more furious than all the others that preceded it, so that it was necessary to despatch orders in all haste to the bateaux, and to all the fleet to cast anchor, wherever they happened to be, which it was very difficult to effect, in consequence of some of the bateaux being in the midst of the rapid. The rain lasted nearly the whole night, during which the Count was extremely uneasy, lest precautions may not have been taken to prevent the provisions getting wet.

Next morning at break of day sent for intelligence, and news was brought, about 7 o'clock in the morning, that there was not much harm done, through the care every one took to preserve his provisions, and the bateaux arrived a quarter of an hour afterwards at the camp. As every one had suffered considerably from the fatigue of the night, it was resolved not to leave the camp before ten or eleven o'clock in order to collect all the people and give them time to rest.

The weather was so unsettled, that, through fear of rain, they waited until noon, and though a pretty strong south-west wind arose, and the river was very rough, we failed not to make considerable headway, and to camp at the foot of the last rapid.

The 9th, we had proceeded scarcely an hour, when the Montreal brigade, dispatched by Count Frontenac from our 3d encampment, by Sieur Lieut. de la Valtrie, under the direction of Sieur Morel, ensign, to make a second convoy, and carry provisions beyond the rapids, was found in a place which he had been ordered to occupy as a depot. As soon as our fleet was perceived, he crossed over from the south to the north, and came on board the admiral.

The Count wrote by him to M. Perrot, Governor of Montreal, to whom he sent orders to have new canoes furnished to Lieut. Lebert, to join this fleet, and endeavor to bring, in one voyage, what he had at first resolved to have brought in two. In two hours afterwards, we arrived at the place Sieur de la Valtrie had selected to build a storehouse. It was a

* This rapid is on the north side of Ogden's Island, at the present village of Waddington, in Madrid.

The Island was unknown to the early French voyageurs as the Isle au Rapide Plat, or island at the flat rapid.

The river here is underlaid by a limestone formation of very uniform surface, and has a descent of eleven feet in three miles.

3

point at the head of all the rapids, and at the entrance of the smooth navigation.*

The Count strongly approved Sieur de la Valtrio's selection, and resolved to sojourn there the whole day, to allow the troops to refresh, and to have leisure to send a second canoe to Montreal, with new orders and to hasten the return of the canoes, which were sent to bring provisions. At six o'clock in the evening, two Iroquois canoes arrived, bringing letters from Sieur de la Salle, who, having been sent into their country two months before, advised the Count, that, after some difficulty, founded on the apprehensions the savages entertained of his approach, they had, in fine resolved to come to assure him of their obedience, and that they awaited him at Kentè, to the number of more than two hundred of the most ancient and influential, though they had considerable objection to repair thither, in consequence of the jealousy they felt on seeing Onontio going to Kentè, as it implied a preference for that nation to the others. This obliged him to request the Abbès de Fènelon† and D'Urfè, to go in all haste to Kentè, which it had been resolved to visit, having judged by the map, after considerable consultation and different opinions, that it would be a very suitable place on which to erect the proposed establishment.

Though Count de Frontenac had appointed this interview with the savages, only with that view, he did not omit however taking advantage of the jealousy they entertained in their minds, and requested those gentlemen to assure them, that he expected them in that place only to let them know that he did not prefer the one to the other, and that he should be always their common father, so long as they remained in the obedience and respect they owed the king.

The 10th, left the camp about 5 o'clock in the morning, and though Count de Frontenac had determined on the preceding day, and before he received the news of the approach of the Iroquois, to leave the bateaux with the greater portion of the troops behind, and to take with him only two or three brigades, to reconnoitre as quickly as possible the outlet of the Great Lake, and the post he was about to fortify at the mouth of the Katarakoui, he changed his design and concluded he ought to proceed with more precaution, until he should be better informed of the intention of the Iroquois.

We therefore proceeded in a body, and in closer column than heretofore. The weather was so serene, and the navigation so smooth, that we made more than ten leagues, and went to camp at a cove about a league and a half from Otondiata, where the eel fishery begins. We had the pleasure on the march, to catch a small leon, a bird about as large as a European bustard (*Outarde*), of the most beautiful plumage, but so difficult to be caught alive, as it plunges constantly under water, that it is no small rarity to be able to take one. A cage was made for it, and orders were given to endeavor to raise it, in order to be able to send it to the king.

---

* Probably, Indian Point, in Lisbon, a short distance above Gallop Rapids.

† Fenelon, the Archbishop of Cambray, and author of the celebrated allegorical romance entitled, *Les Adventures de Télémaque*, was from 1667 till 1674 a missionary of the Sulpician order among the Iroquois, on the north shore of Lake Ontario. He was born, Aug. 6th, 1651; early engaged with zeal in ecclesiastical studies, became eminent as a missionary, author, and preceptor to the Duke of Burgundy, the heir apparent to the throne of France; was raised to the Archbishoprie of Cambray in 1697, and died in 1715

The 11th, the weather continuing fine, a good day's journey was made, having passed all that vast group of islands with which the river is spangled, and camped at a point above the river called by the Indians *Onnondakoui*,* up which many of them go hunting. It has a very considerable channel. Two more loons were caught alive, and a *scanoulou*, which is a kind of deer, but the head and branches of which are handsomer than that of the deer of France."

The narrative continues with an account of the stately and regal manner with which the Count de Frontenac entered the lake, and the interviews which he had with the natives. The pomp and ceremony with which he received the deputation of the savages, the glittering armor and polished steel which flashed and gleamed in the sun, the waving banners gayest colors that floated in the gentle breeze, and above all the roar of *cannon* and the destructive effect of shot, bewildered the minds of the simple-hearted natives, and impressed them with awe and astonishment. The Count then related to them in glowing colors the grandeur and importance of the King his master, whose humble servant he was, and thus conveyed a vague but overwhelming impression of the omnipotence of the French.

This speech is interesting, as an illustration of the motives which were held out to the natives by the French, and the manner in which they appealed to their passions and their interests in securing their adherence to their cause.

Count de Frontenac, having had a fire lighted near the place where they were seated, answered them in terms adapted to their manner of speaking, as follows :

"My Children : Onnontagués, Mohawks, Oneidas, Cayugas and Senecas. I am pleased to see you come hither, where I have had a fire lighted for you to smoke by, and for me to talk to you. It is well done, my children, to have followed the orders and commands of your Father. Take courage, then, my children: you will hear his word, which is full of tenderness and peace ; a word which will fill your cabins with joy and happiness, for think not that war is the object of my voyage. My spirit is full of peace, which accompanies me. Courage, then, my children, and rest yourselves."

The Count then presented them with six fathoms of tobacco, and added :

"My Children : You have taken great pains to come to see me, and I regret to have given you the trouble of so long a voyage, which I, however, tried to abridge, by not obliging you to go to Kenté, and by lighting the fire for you at Katarokoui.

Fear not : close your ears, nor distrust your minds. I am aware that there have been many evil disposed, who were desirous to persuade you that Onontio was coming into the cantons only to devour your villages; but, my children, that is not true. Those are busy bodies who would break the peace and union that exists between us; and you will never find

* Gannonoqui? from the Huron, *Ough-seanote*, a deer. Dr. O'CALLAGHAN.

in me any other than the feelings of a real father, so long as you will act like true children, and continue obedient.

Cheer up then your spirits, and be persuaded that I had no other design in this voyage, than to visit you; as it was very reasonable a father should be acquainted with his children, and the children with their father.

I can not, however, sufficiently testify to you the joy I feel to see that you not only fully obey my orders with promptness, and come in great numbers to meet me, but that you have also brought your wives and children with you, because this is a certain mark of the confidence you place in my words.

One regret only remains, that I can not speak your language, or that you do not understand mine, so that there might be no necessity for interpreter or spokesman.

But in order that you may be fully informed all I have said to you, I have selected Sieur Lemoine, to whom I shall communicate in writing what I have to state to you, so that you may not lose any of my remarks. Listen, then, attentively to him. There is something to open your ears, in order that you may be disposed in a day or two to hear the thoughts of Onontio."

The Count then handed the paper he held to Sieur Lemoine, and presented to each nation a gun, a quantity of prunes and raisins for the women, with some wine, brandy and biscuit.

The Indians appeared highly pleased with the speech which M. Lemoine explained to them in the commencement, and which appeared according to their fashion considerable, caused them to hope that magnificent ones would be made them at the close, when Onontio would communicate his intentions to them.

It was remarked that their countenances were much changed, and that Toronteshati, their orator, the ablest, most spiritual, and most influential man among them, from being sad and pensive before, assumed a gaiety not usual to him. He has been always an enemy to the French, and greatly in the interest of the Dutch. Count Frontenac was obliged in consequence, to pay him particular attention, and to keep him to dinner with him.

Sieur Rendieu was busy meanwhile, tracing out the fort at the place designated by the Count, and according to the plan which had been approved of by him, and as soon as they had dined, men were ordered to work at the trench, where pickets were to be set, until it was determined in what manner the troops should be employed, and until the tools were put in order. He then embarked in a canoe to visit the banks of the river, or harbor, and was delighted to find at the head of the bay, a prairie more than a league in length, as handsome and level as any in France, and to see the river winding through its centre, very wide, and capable of admitting barks and vessels for over three leagues continually.

He returned to the camp in great joy, on perceiving that he had found everything according to his wishes, and that God had seemingly blessed his enterprise, but what increased it still more, was to find that every body was so impatient for work, and so anxious to advance the undertaking, which he hoped to bring soon to an end. This ardor thus exhibited by them, caused him to alter his resolution, to divide the troops into four brigades, and to have them relieved every two hours, in order that the work should not intermit, and he accepted their proposal to divide the labor among them, each undertaking what may be allotted to him. This had so good an effect, that early in the evening, they began to make a clearing with such energy, that the officers found difficulty in drawing the people off to rest and sleep, so as to be able to work the next morning.

The 14th day had scarcely broken, when the entire brigade fell to work, according to the allotment that had been made, and all the officers and soldiers applied themselves to it with such heartiness and zeal, that the site of the fort was nearly cleared.

Sieur Lamoine had orders from the Count, to bring him at each meal two or three of the principal Iroquois, whom he entertained at his table. He fondled their children every time he met them, and had prunes, raisins. &c., distributed among them, which so gratified the Indians that they would not leave his tent, no more than the women, whom he treated, to induce them to dance in the evening.

The 15th, the work was continued with the same zeal; but the rain which fell throughout the morning of the 16th, prevented operations until noon, when every effort was made to recover lost time. The Indians were astonished to see the large clearance that had been made; some squaring timber in one place; others fetching pickets; others cutting trenches; and that different operations advanced at the same time. In the evening he caused notice to be given to the captain of the Five Nations, that he would give them an audience, on the next day, at eight o'clock in the morning.

On the 17th, everything being prepared to receive them, they came to the Count in the same manner as the first time, when he submitted to them in his speech all the conditions he desired of them, as may be seen from the copy annexed of his address, which was accompanied by magnificent presents in Indian fashion.

Count de Frontenac's speech to the Iroquois.

FIRST WORD.

" My children! Onnontagues, Mohawks, Oneidas, Cayugas, and Senecas I signified to you the other day, the joy I felt to see you arrive here with all your proofs of submission that children owe their father, and with such confidence that you have brought your wives and little ones.

You alleviate in truth thereby, all the trouble and fatigues I encountered on my voyage, and oblige me by the respect you have for my commands to give you every assurance that you can desire of my friendship, and the king, my majesty's protection, if you continue to observe faithfully his will, of which I am interpreter, and executor. I have even reason to persuade myself that you will not fail therein after the protestations you have given me, and the knowledge you have afforded me of the good understanding in which all the nations now live, inasmuch as you have informed me, that they were all of the same spirit, and had but one opinion. But as it is the duty of children to be obedient to their father, 'tis likewise the duty of a good father to communicate to his children, instructions and information, the most useful and necessary for them.

Children! Onontagues, Mohawks, Oneidas, Cayugas, and Senecas! I can not give you any advice more important or more profitable to you, than to exhort you to become Christians, and to adore the same God that I adore. He is the sovereign Lord of Heaven and Earth; the absolute master of your lives and properties; who hath created you; who preserves you; who furnishes you with food and drink; who can send death amongst you in a moment, inasmuch as he is Almighty, and acts as he willeth, not like men, who require time, but in an instant and at a word.

In fine, He it is who can render you happy or miserable, as he pleaseth. This God is called Jesus; and the Black Gowns here, who are his ministers and interpreters, will teach you to know Him, whenever you are so disposed. I leave them among you, and in your villages, only to teach you.

I therefore desire, that you respect them, and prevent any of your young braves daring or presuming to injure them in the smallest degree, as I shall consider the injuries done them as personal to myself, and such I will punish with like severity. Hearken well then to the advice I give you, and forget it not, as it is of great importance; and you ought to be aware that, in giving it, I labor more for you than for myself, and I study only your happiness The Hurons, here present in great numbers, must incline you thereto, since you see with your own eyes that they have learned to honor and serve the God of whom I speak to you.

Ancients! give herein the example to your children, as your judgment must be sounder than theirs; or at least, if you be not disposed to become Christians, at least do not prevent them becoming such, and learning the prayer of that great God whom the Black Gowns will willingly teach them, and his commandments. These consist of only two points, easy of observance. The first is, to love Him with your whole heart, and whole soul, and your whole strength. Ancients! is there any thing more easy than to love what is perfectly beautiful, what is sovereignly amiable, and what can constitute all our happiness?

The second thing he requires of us is, to love our brother as we love ourselves; that is to say, that we assist them in their necessities, and furnish them drink, and meat and clothing, when they are in need of them, as we would wish should be done to ourselves.

Again, Ancients—for to you I address myself. believing your minds to be sufficiently endowed to comprehend it—tell me frankly, if there is any thing more reasonable than this commandment? You ought to be more easily persuaded that I came not here save with a heart filled with gentleness and peace, to communicate these to my children, to assist them in all things, and to give them a proof of a true and sincere friendship.

Take courage, then, my children, Onontagues, Mohawks, Oneidas, Cayugas, and Senecas. Lend not an ear to the councils of certain busy bodies, who at my approach desire to excite distrust and suspicions, and who, assuming to be your friends, meditate only your ruin and destruction.

Listen to me, and trust my words. I am frank and sincere, and shall promise you nothing but what I shall exactly perform, desiring that you may on your side do likewise.

*   *   *   I content myself by telling you only to reflect on the past and on the present; consider well the greatness and power of Onontio; behold the number of persons accompanying and surrounding him; the ease and celerity with which he has surmounted all your *sauls* and rapids, and passed bateaux, mounted with cannon, over them, which you never thought could be steered through the smoothest and most tranquil of rivers, and that in a voyage made only through pleasure, and without necessity. Infer from this what he could effect if he desired to wage war and crush any of his enemies. If you reflect seriously on all of these things, you will acknowledge he is a good father, who is not cruel, and that he is absolute arbiter of War and Peace."

When we come to give an account of the founding of the mission on the St. Lawrence, nearly three quarters of a century after, it may be well to remember the nature of the motives which were brought to bear upon the minds of the savages, when we shall see that they were essentially the same as those offered by the Count de Frontenac.

From this time forward, the St. Lawrence was frequently traversed by French voyagers, and a post was established at *La Galette*, (meaning in the French language a *cake*, or *muffin*,) which is supposed to be near the site of Johnstown in Canada, a short distance below Prescott, or on Chimney Island.

In the celebrated expedition of De la Barre, the governor of Canada, against the Iroquois, in 1684,* La Galette is mentioned as one of his stopping places.

In laying a plan for the conquest of the Five Nations, de la Barre indicates the necessity of posting troops in Forts Frontenac and La Galette, to escort provisions, and keep the head of the country guarded and furnished.

This celebrated, and singularly unfortunate expedition, left Quebec on the ninth of July, 1684, and on the first of August arrived at Lake St. Francis, with about two hundred canoes, and fifteen bateaux, where he was joined by the Rev. Father Lamberville, junior, coming on behalf of his brother at Onondaga, and by the Rev. Father Millet, from the Oneidas.

On the second they reached the portage of the Long Saut, which was found very difficult, notwithstanding the care taken to send forward fifty men with axes to cut away the trees that projected from the bank, and prevented those passing who were dragging up the canoes and bateaux; because the trees being voluminous and the bank precipitous, the people were in the water the moment they abandoned the shore. During this delay, they were joined by the Christian Iroquois of the Saut St. Louis and of Montreal, who undertook for a few presents of brandy and

* See the Documentary History of New York, by E. B. O'Callaghan, Vol. I, p 93–142 where a full history of this event is given in the original documents. *La Famine*, which was in the work cited, located in Jefferson county, must doubtless have been Salmon river in Oswego county. In the Journal of Charlevoix, (12mo edition, vol. 5, p. 309–3) the following distances are given:

"From l'Isle aux Gallots, to l'Isle aux Cheves, (Goat Island) three leagues to a point, which is forty-three degrees thirty minutes; thence to *la pointe de la Traverse*, (Stoney Point,) a league and a half. The river *de Assomption* is a league from point de la Traverse; that *des Sables*, (Sandy Creek? three leagues further; that *de la Planche*, (Little Sandy Creek?) two leagues beyond; that *de la Grande Famine*, (Salmon river?) two other leagues; that *de la Petite Famine*, a league, that of *de la Grosse Ecorce*, (Thick Bark,) a league.

Colden in his history of the Five Nations mentions La Famine river, called by the Indians, Kaihahage, as falling into the south side of Cadaracui lake, about thirty miles from Onondago, (probably the mouth of Oswego river.) See vol. II. p. 64, of third London edition of Colden's History, 1755.

This correction is made with the knowledge and by the consent of Dr. O Callaghan.

tobacco, to pass the batteaux and largest canoes, a feat which was accomplished in two days, and without accident.

On the morning of the fifth, the governor had reached La Galette, where the provisions were taken from the canoes, which were sent back to La Chine for a new load.

The strong winds from the southwest which constantly prevailed, and which continued through the month, delayed the return of the canoes some time, and prevented the chance of his arriving at the fort at Cataraqui, until the ninth. After his arrival he despatched eight of his largest canoes to La Galette, for ten thousand weight of flour, provisions beginning to fail in the camp, which caused him much uneasiness, and which eventually contributed largely to his disasters.

This supply of flour was to be immediately baked into biscuit, and forwarded to the troops who had gone forward and encamped at La Famine, a post favorable for hunting and fishing, and which was four leagues from Onontague.

The canoes despatched to Galette returned with far less flour than was expected, and was immediately baked and sent to the troops.

The unfortunate result of this expedition is well known. Famine and sickness overtook the French army, and the governor was driven to the humiliating extremity of asking peace of those he had come to conquer.

The ever memorable speech of Garangula, the Onondaga orator, has often been quoted, and has ever been admired as a master-piece of eloquence.

Mortified and ashamed he returned to Montreal in September, having been to much pains to prove to the savages, that the French were not altogether invincible, but were, like themselves, liable to suffer from sickness and hunger, and doubtless did much towards weakening the confidence formerly reposed in their prowess.

In a letter from Father Lamberville to M. de la Barre, dated July 11, 1684, the establishment of a fort at La Galette, is alluded to as one of the best measures calculated to attain their ends with the natives. It was against the advice of this missionary, that the expedition was undertaken. In the same letter he wrote as follows:

"I do not believe you will derive any advantage this year from war, if you should wage it, for not only will the whole of the Iroquois prosecute the war in Canada, but you will not find the Senecas in their villages, in which they give out they will not shut themselves up, but conceal themselves in the grass and prepare ambuscaders for you everywhere. * * The warriors are to prowl everywhere, killing, without if possible being killed.

If their Indian corn be cut, it will cost much blood and men. You must also resolve to lose the harvest of the French grain, to which the Iroquois will set fire."

Causes of difficulty continued to exist between the Iroquois and the French, principally due to the jealousies which the English succeeded in disseminating among the former. This led to the expedition of the Marquis Denonville in the summer of 1687 against the Senecas, and that of the Count de Frontenac against the Onondagas in 1686. In neither of these did the French succeed in conquering their enemies, although in the former they succeeded in overrunning the country, and making a great many captures. Their prisoners were distributed among friendly tribes on the north shore of the lake.

Denonville founded the military post at Niagara, on the occasion of his expedition, and this formed one of the most important stations of the French, as it was at a portage between two navigable waters of great extent, and commanded the trade of an immense region of country.

The French were not always the aggressive party, for in 1688, the savages laid waste their country to the very gates of Montreal, and nothing but ignorance of the modes of attack practiced by civilized soldiers, prevented the entire destruction of their settlements.

The enemy disappeared as quickly as they came, and before they had recovered from the shock, and made preparations for defence, the assailants had vanished.

These vindictive wars were conducted along the valley of the St Lawrence for several years.*

In 1720 – 21, Father *Charlevoix*, a Jesuit, undertook, by command of the King of France, a journey to Canada. His observations, in an epistolary form, addressed to the Duchess de Lesdiguieres, were published at Paris in 1744; from the fifth volume of which we translate the following extracts from a letter dated " *Catarocoui*, 14th May, 1721:

"Above the Buisson, the river is a mile wide, and lands on both sides are very good and well wooded. They begin to clear those which are on the north side; and it would be very easy to make a road from the point which is over against the island of Montreal, to a bay which they call *la Galette*. They will shun by this forty leagues of navigation, which the falls render almost impracticable and very tedious. A fort would be much better situated and more necessary at la Galette than at Catarocoui, because a single canoe can not pass here without being seen, whereas at Catarocoui they may slip behind the islands without being observed.

* In January, 1851, a Mr. W. Merritt. a wheelwright at Malone, when dressing out wagon spokes, of oak timber, found a leaden bullet, which at some ancient period had been shot into the tree. It had been cut in Brasher, and the tree was eighteen inches in diameter, and the ball lay within an inch of the heart of the tree. It must from the appearance of the concentric lines of growth have laid in this situation about one hundred and seventy-five years, and may have been discharged by these early belligerents.

Moreover the lands about Galette are very good, and they might in consequence have always provisions in plenty, which would save many charges. Besides this, a bark might go in two days with a good wind to Niagara. One of the objects which they had in view in building the fort Catarocoui, was the trade with the Iroquois; but these savages would come as willingly to la Galette as to Catarocoui. They would have indeed something further to go, but they would avoid a passage of eight or nine leagues which they must make over the Lake Ontario. In short, a fort at la Galette would cover the whole country which is between the great river of the Outaouais and the river St. Lawrence; for they can not come into this country on the side of the river St. Lawrence, because of the falls, and nothing is more easy than to guard the banks of the river of the Outaouais. I have these remarks from a commissary of the Marine (M. de Clerambaut d'Aigremont), who was sent by the King to visit all the distant posts of Canada. * * * From Coteau du Lac to Lake St. François is but a good half league. This lake, which I passed on the fifth, is seven leagues long and three at the widest place. The land on both sides is low, but appears to be good. The course from Montreal to this is a little to the southwest, and the lake S. François runs west-southwest and east-northeast. I encamped just above it, and in the night was aroused by piercing cries as of persons in distress. I was at first alarmed, but soon recovered myself, when they told me they were *huars*, a kind of cormorants. They added that these cries prognosticated winds on the morrow, which proved true.

The sixth I passed the Chesnaux du Lac, thus called from some *channels* which form a great number of islands which almost cover the river in this place. I never saw a country more charming, and the lands appear good. The rest of the day was spent in passing the rapids, the principal one of which they call *le Moulinet* [the vortex] : it is frightful to behold, and we had much trouble in passing it. I went, however, that day seven leagues, and encamped at the foot of the *Long Saut*, which is a rapid half a league long, which canoes can not ascend with more than half a load. We passed it at seven in the morning, and sailed at three o'clock P. M.; but the rain obliged us to encamp, and detained us the following day. There fell on the eighth [May] a little snow, and at night it froze as it does in France in the month of January. We were nevertheless under the same parallels as Languedoc. On the ninth we passed the *Rapide Plat* [opposite the village of Waddington], distant from the Saut about seven leagues, and five from des Galots, which is the last of the rapids. La Galette is a league and a half further, and we arrived there on the tenth. I could not sufficiently admire the beauty of the country between this bay and les Galots. It is impossible to see finer forests, and I especially notice some oaks of extraordinary height.

Five or six leagues from la Galette is an island called *Tonihata*, where the soil appears fertile, and which is about half a league long. An Iroquois, whom they call *the Quaker*, I know not why, a very sensible man, and very affectionate to the French, obtained the dominion of it from the late Count de Frontenac, and shows his patent of concession to whoever wishes to see it. He has nevertheless sold the lordship for four pots of brandy, but has reserved to himself all other profits of the land, and has assembled here eighteen or twenty families of his nation. I arrived on the twelfth at his island, and paid him a visit. I found him laboring in his garden, which is not the custom of savages; but he affects all the customs of the French. He received me very kindly, and wished to regale me, but the beauty of the weather invited me to prosecute my journey. I took my leave of him, and went to pass the night two leagues from thence in a very fine place.

I had still thirteen leagues to Catarocoui: the weather was fine, and the night very clear, which induced me to embark at three o'clock in the morning. We passed through the midst of a kind of archipelago, which they call *Mille Isles* [Thousand Isles]. I believe there are about five hundred. When we had passed these, we had a league and a half to reach Catarocoui. The river is more open, and at least half a league wide: then we leave upon the right three great bays, very deep, and the fort is built in the third. This fort is square, with four bastions built with stone; and the ground it occupies is a quarter of a league in circuit, and its situation has really something very delightful. The banks of the river present in every way a varied scenery, and it is the same at the entrance of Lake Ontario, which is but a short league distant: it is studded with islands of different sizes, all well wooded, and nothing bounds the horizon on that side. This lake for some time bore the name of *Saint Louis*, afterwards that of *Frontenac*, as well as the fort of Catarocoui, of which the Count de Frontenac was the founder; but insensibly the lake has gained its ancient name, which is Huron or Iroquois, and the fort that of the place where it is built. The soil from this place to la Galette appears rather barren; but it is only on the edges, it being very good farther back. Opposite the fort is a very fine island, in the midst of the river. They placed some swine upon it, which have multiplied and given it the name of *Isle des Porcs* [Hog Island, now Grand Island]. There are two other islands somewhat smaller, which are lower, and half a league apart: one is named *l'Isle aux Cédres*, and the other *l'Isle aux Cerfs* [Cedar Island and Stag Island, neither of which names are now retained].

The bay of *Catarocoui* is double; that is to say, that almost in the midst of it is a point which runs out a great way, under which there is good anchorage for large barks. *M. de la Salle*, so famous for his discoveries and his misfortunes, who was lord of Catarocoui and governor of the fort, had two or three vessels here which were sunk in this place, and remain there still. Behind the fort is a marsh, where a great variety of wild game gives pleasant occupation for the garrison.

There was formerly a great trade here, especially with the Iroquois; and it was to entice them to us, as well as to hinder their carrying their skins to the English, and to keep these savages in awe, that the fort was built. But this trade did not last long, and the fort has not hindered the barbarians from doing us a great deal of mischief. They have still some families here, on the outskirts of the place; and also some *Missisaguex*, an Algonquin nation, which still have a village on the west side of Lake Ontario, another at Niagara, and a third at Detroit."

An English writer (Jeffrey) has written a book, entitled, "The French Dominion in America" (London, 1760, folio), in which he has freely quoted, without acknowledgment, from Charlevoix and other French writers, statements of facts and descriptions of places, of which he evidently had no knowledge beyond what he derived from these works.

The following is an extract from this writer (p. 15), which may be compared with the translation from Charlevoix which we have given.

"A fourth rift, two leagues and a half hence, is called the rift of St Francis, from whence to Lake St. Francis, you have only half a league. This lake is several leagues in length, and almost three in breadth where broadest. The land on both sides is low, but appears to be of an excellent soil. The route from Montreal hither lies a little towards the south-west, and the Lake St. Francis runs west-south-west and east-north-east.

From hence you come to the *chesneaux du lac*, for thus are called those channels formed by a cluster of islands, which take up almost the whole breadth of the river at this place. The soil seems here extraordinarily good, and never was prospect more charming than that of the country about it. The most remarkable falls here are, that of the *Moulinet*, which is even frightful to behold,* and exceeding difficult to get through, and that called the *Long Fall*, half a league in length, and passable only to canoes half loaded.

The next you come to, is called the Flat Rift [Rapide du Plat, opposite Ogden's Island and the village of Waddington], about seven leagues above the *Long Fall*, and five below that called *Les Galots*, which is the last of the falls. La Galette lies a league further, and no one can be weary of admiring the extraordinary beauty of the country, and of the noble forests, which overspread all the lands about this bay and *La Galette*, particularly the vast woods of oak of a prodigious height. A fort would perhaps be better situated, and much more necessary at *La Galette*, than at *Cadaraqui*, for this reason, that not so much as a single canoe could pass without being seen; whereas at *Cadaraqui* they may easily sail behind the isles without being perceived at all. The lands moreover about *La Galette* are excellent, whence there would always be plenty of provisions, which would be no small saving.

And, besides, a vessel could very well go from *La Galette* to *Niagara*, in two days, with a fair wind. One motive for building the fort at *Cadaraqui* was, the conveniency of trading with the *Iroquois*. But those Indians would as willingly go to *La Galette* as to the other place. Their way, indeed, would be much longer, but then it would save them a traverse of eight or nine leagues on Lake *Ontario*; not to mention that a fort at *la Galette* would secure all the country lying between the great river of the *Outawais* and the river *St. Lawrence*; for this country is inaccessible on the side of the river, on account of the rifts, and nothing is more practicable than to defend the banks of the great river; at least, these are the sentiments of those sent by the court of *France* to visit all the different posts of Canada.

One league and a half from *La Galette*, on the opposite shore, at the mouth of the *Oswegatchi* river, the *French* have lately built the fort *La Presentation*, which commands that river, and keeps open a communication, by land, between *Lake Champlain* and this place.

Four leagues above *La Presentation*, is the isle called *Tonihata*, about half a league in length, and of a very good soil. An *Iroquois*, called by the French writers, for what reason we are not told, the *Quaker*, a man of good natural sense, and much attached to the French nation, had, as they say, got the dominion of this island of a count of *Frontenac*, the patent of which, it seems, he was proud of showing to any body.

He sold his lordship for a gallon of brandy; reserving, however, the profits to himself, and taking care to settle eighteen or twenty families of his own nation upon this island.

It is ten leagues hence to *Cadaraqui*, and on your way to this place, you pass through a sort of Archipel, called the *Thousand Isles*, and there

---

* This is probably what is known at present as the Lost Channel, on the north side of Long Saut island. It has within a year or two been descended by steamers, and found safe, although the war of waters is frightful.

may possibly be about five hundred. From hence to *Cadaraqui*, they reckon four leagues.

The river here is freer and opener, and the breadth, half a league. On the right are three deep bays, in the third of which stands Fort *Cadaraqui* or *Frontenac.*"

From the earliest period of their settlement, the French appear to have been solicitous to withdraw the Iroquois from the interests of the English, and to establish them near their own borders, as well to secure their religious, as their political adherence to their interests. To effect their conversion, Father Ragueneau was sent to Onondaga, in 1657-8; Isaac Joques to the Mohawks (among whom he had been a captive, previously), in 1646; Frs. Jos. Lemercier to Onondaga, in 1656-8; Frs. Duperon to Onondaga, in 1657-8; Simon Le Moyne to Onondaga, in 1654, and subsequently to the Mohawks and Senecas; and many others, but none with more success than Jacques de Lamberville, who was among the Mohawks in 1675-8, subsequently at Onondaga, which place he left in 1686, and again in 1703 to 1709, he was engaged most zealousy in his work of proselyting to his faith the Indians of New York.

The result of the labors of these missionaries, was the emigration of a part of the Mohawk tribe, in 1675-6, to the saut St. Louis, in the vicinity of Montreal.

Some account of this emigration is given by Charlevoix which will here be given, as a specimen of the zealous devotion and religious strain in which the Catholic writers of that period were accustomed to speak and write, rather than for its importance as a historical document.

The success of their enterprise was proportioned to the zeal and energy with which it was prosecuted. The room in which Charlevoix dwelt while at this mission of the saut St. Louis is still pointed out to visitors, and the table on which he wrote forms a part of the furniture of the priest's house at that mission.

From vol. v of Charlevoix's Journal of Travels in North America, page 258, and subsequently. Letter to the Dutchess de Lesdiguieres:

Of the Iroquois Village of the Saut St. Louis, and of the different People who inhabit Canada.

"SAUT ST. LOUIS, *May* 1, 1721.

MADAME: I have come to this place to spend a part of Easter. It is a period of devotion, and every thing in this village is suggestive of pious emotions. All the religious exercises are performed in a very edifying manner, and leave an impression of fervor on the minds of the Habitants; for it is certain that it has long been the case in Canada, that we may witness the brightest examples of heroic virtue, with which God has been wont to adorn the growing church. The manner itself in which it has been formed is very marvelous.

The Missionaries, after having for a long time moistened the cantons of the Iroquois with their sweat, and some even with their blood, lost, at length, all hope of establishing there the Christian religión, upon a solid basis, but not of drawing a great number of savages under the yoke of the Faith. They felt that God had among these barbarians his elect, as in all nations, but they were convinced that to *assure their calling and their election*, it was necessary to separate them from their compatriots, and they formed the resolution of establishing in the colony, all those whom they found disposed to embrace Christianity. They opened their design to the Governor General and the Intendant, who carried their views still further, not only approving them, but conceiving that this establishment would be very serviceable to New France, as in fact it has been, as well as another, much like it, which had been established in the Isle of Montreal, under the name of *la Montagne*, of which the members of the Seminary of St. Sulpice have always had the direction.

To return to that which served as a model for the others, one of the Missionaries of the Iroquois opened his design to some of the Mohawks. They approved it, and especially that canton which had always most strongly opposed the ministers of the gospel, and where they had often been most cruelly treated. Thus, to the great wonder of French and Savages, were seen these inveterate enemies of God, and of our nation, touched with his victorious Grace, which thus deigned to triumph in the hardest and most rebellious hearts, abandoning all that they held most dear in the world to receive nothing, that they may serve the Lord with more freedom. A sacrifice more heroic still for savages than other people, because none are more attached than them to their families, and their natal land.

The number was much augmented in a short time; in part, from the zeal of the first proselytes who composed this chosen band."

This measure led to much persecution, and the converts were often tortured to compel them to renounce the faith. Others were confined in miserable dungeons in New York, from which they could be liberated only by abjuring their new religion, or at least by promising to leave the French.

M. de Saint Valier thus wrote in 1688: "The ordinary life of all the Christians at this mission, has nothing usual, and one would take the whole village to be a Monastery. As they only left the goods of their country to seek safety, they practice on all sides the most perfect disengagement, and preserve among each other, so perfect order for their sanctification, that it would be difficult to add any thing to it."

These savages of course carried with them their language and customs, but the latter gradually became adapted to those of the French, who labored to abolish those national ceremonies, and substitute in their place an observance of the ritual and requirements of the catholic religion. This measure succeeded so well, that, at the present day, the oldest Indians at the missions have lost all recollection of the existence of their ancient customs, and do not preserve the memory of national ceremonies of the olden time.

The emigration to Canada from among the Indians continued through many years, and at length, in 1749, led to the establishment of a missionary station and fort at the mouth of the river la Presentation [Oswegatchie], by Francis Picquet, a Sulpitian. An account of this is given in the Documentary History of New-York, which was taken from the Paris documents collected by an agent sent to Europe by this state for the purpose of obtaining historical materials.

"A large number of Iroquois savages having declared their willingness to embrace Christianity, it has been proposed to establish a mission in the neighborhood of Fort Frontenac. Abbé Picquet, a zealous missionary in whom the nations have evinced much confidence has taken charge of it, and of testing, as much as possible what reliance is to be placed on the dispositions of the Indians.*

Nevertheless, as Mr. de la Gallisonnière had remarked in the month of October, one thousand seven hundred and forty-eight, that too much dependence ought not to be placed on them, Mr. de la Jonquière was written to on the fourth of May one thousand seven hundred and forty-nine, that he should neglect nothing for the formation of this establishment, because if it at all succeeded it would not be difficult to give the Indians to understand that the only means they had to relieve themselves of the pretensions of the English to their lands, is the destruction of Choueguen which they founded solely with a view to bridle these Nations; but it was necessary to be prudent and circumspect to induce the savages to undertake it.

31st 8ber 1749. Mr. de la Jonquière sends a plan drawn by Siéur de Lery of the ground selected by the Abbé Picquet for his mission and a letter from that Abbé containing a relation of his voyage and the situation of the place.

He says he left the fourth of May of last year with twenty-five Frenchmen and four Iroquois Indians; he arrived the thirtieth at the River de la Presentation, called Soegatzy. The land there is the finest in Canada. There is oak timber in abundance, and trees of a prodigious size and height, but it will be necessary, for the defence of the settlement, to fell them without permission. Picquet reserved sufficient on the land he had cleared to build a bark.

He then set about building a store house to secure his effects; he next had erected a small fort of pickets and he will have a small house constructed which will serve as a bastion.

Sieur Picquet had a special interview with the Indians; they were satisfied with all he had done; and assured him they were willing to follow his advice and to immediately establish their village. To accomplish this, they are gone to regulate their affairs and have promised to return with their provisions.

The situation of this post is very advantageous; it is on the borders of the River de la Presentation, at the head of all the rapids, on the west side of a beautiful basin formed by that river, capable of easily holding forty or fifty barks.

* The following extract from Paris Doc. X., furnishes the date of the Abbe Picquet's departure to establish his colony on the Oswegatchie river:— "30 Sept. 1748. The Abbe Picquet's departs from Quebec for Fort Frontenac; he is to look in the neighborhood of that fort for a location best adapted for a village for the Iroquois of the Five Nations, who propose to embrace Christianity.

In all parts of it there has been found at least two fathoms and a half of water and often four fathoms. This basin is so located that no wind scarcely can prevent its being entered. The bank is very low, in a level country, the point of which runs far out. The passage across is hardly a quarter of a league, and all the canoes going up or down, can not pass elsewhere. A fort on this point would be impregnable; it would be impossible to approach, and nothing commands it. The east side is more elevated, and runs by a gradual inclination into an amphitheatre. A beautiful town could hereafter be built there.

This post is moreover so much the more advantageous, as the English and Iroquois can easily descend to Montreal by the river *de la Presentation*, which has its source in a lake bordering on the Mohawks and Corlar. If they take possession of this River they will block the passage to Fort Frontenac, and more easily assist Choueguen. Whereas by means of a fort at the point, it would be easy to have a force there in case of need to dispatch to Choueguen, and to intercept the English and Indians who may want to penetrate into the Colony, and the voyage to Missilimakinac could be made in safety.

Moreover, this establishment is only thirty-five leagues from Montreal; twenty-five from Fort Frontenac, and thirty-three from Choueguen;[*] a distance sufficient to remove the Indians from the disorders which the proximity of forts and towns ordinarily engenders among them. It is convenient for the reception of the Lake Ontario, and more distant Indians.

Abbé Picquet's views are to accustom these Indians to raise cows, hogs and poultry; there are beautiful prairies, acorns and wild oats.

On the other hand it can be so regulated that the bateaux carrying goods to the posts, may stop at *La Presentation*. The cost of freight would become smaller; men could be found to convey those bateaux at fifteen to twenty livres instead of forty-five and fifty livres which are given for the whole voyage. Other bateaux of *La Presentation* would convey them farther on, and the first would take in return plank, boards and other timber, abundant there. This timber would not come to more than twelve or fifteen livres, whilst they are purchased at sixty-eight livers at Montreal, and sometimes more. Eventually this post will be able to supply Fort Frontenac with provisions, which will save the king considerable expense.

The Abbé Picquet adds in his letter, that he examined in his voyage the nature of the rapids of the Fort Frontenac river, very important to secure to us the possession of Lake Ontario on which the English have an eye. The most dangerous of those rapids, in number fourteen, are the *Trou* (the Hole) and the *Buisson* (the Thicket). Abbé Picquet points out a mode of rendering this river navigable; and to meet the expense he proposes a tax of ten livres on each canoe sent up, and an *ecu* (fifty cents) on each of the crew, which according to him will produce three thousand livres, a sum sufficient for the workmen.

Messrs de la Jonquière and Bigot remark that they find this establishment necessary as well as the erection of a saw-mill, as it will diminish the expense in the purchase of timber; but as regards the rapids, they will verify them in order to ascertain if in fact the river can be rendered navigable, and they will send an estimate of the works.

---

[*] Ogdensburgh is 105 miles from Montreal; 60 from Kingston, Can., and about 60 from Oswego. The distances laid down in the text are very accurate, considering the time and the circumstances.

They have caused five cannon of two pound calibre to be sent to the Abbé Picquet for his little fort so as to give confidence to his Indians, and to persuade them that they will be in security there.

M. de la Jonquière in particular says, he will see if the proprietors of batteaux would contribute to the expense necessary to be incurred for the rapids; but he asks that convicts from the galleys or people out of work (*gens inutiles*) be sent every year to him to cultivate the ground. He is in want of men, and the few he has exact high wages.

1st 8ber, 1749. Mr. Bigot also sends a special memoir of the expense incurred by Abbé Picquet for improvements (*defrichemens*) amounting to three thousand four hundred and eighty-five livres ten sous.* Provisions were also furnished him for himself and workmen, and this settlement is only commenced. M. de la Jonquière can not dispense with sending an officer there and some soldiers. Sieur de la Morandiere, engineer, is to be sent there this winter to draw out a plan of quarters for these soldiers and a store for provisions. If there be not a garrison at that post, a considerable foreign trade will be carried on there.

7th 9ber 1749. Since all these letters M. de la Jonquière has written another in which he states that M. de Longueuil informed him that a band of savages believed to be Mohawks had attacked Sieur Picquet's mission on the twenty-sixth of October last—that Sieur de Vassau, commandant of Fort Frontenac, had sent a detachment thither which could not prevent the burning of two vessels loaded with hay and the palisades of the fort. Abbé Picquet's house alone was saved.

The loss by this fire is considerable. It would have been greater were it not for four Abenakis who furnished on this occasion a proof of there fidelity. The man named Perdreaux had half the hand carried away. His arm had to be cut off. One of the Abenakis received the discharge of a gun the ball of which remained in his blanket.

M. de Longueil has provided everything necessary. M. de la Jonquière gave him orders to have a detachment of ten soldiers sent there, and he will take measures, next spring, to secure that post. M. de la Jonquière adds that the savages were instignated to this attack by the English. The Iroquois who were on a complimentary visit at Montreal were surprized at it, and assured M. de Longueuil that it could only be Colonel Amson [Johnson?] who could have induced them. He omitted nothing to persuade those same Iroquois to undertake this expedition, and to prevent them going to compliment the governor, having offered them belts which they refused.

To induce the natives to settle here, the governor is said to have placed a large magazine of all kinds of clothing fitted for Indians, as also arms, provisions and ammunition, which were distributed very liberally among them.

Father Picquet having fortified his position in the year 1751, commenced the erection of a saw mill for the use of his settlement and the government.

In a document entitled " Titles and documents relating to the seignorial tenure," made to the Legislative Assembly of Canada in 1851, and published at Quebec in 1852, is a copy of the French grant to him. It is taken from pages 299 and 300, and runs as follows :

* Equal to $653·23.

4

"Le Marquis de Lajonquiere, &c.

Françoi Bigot, &c.

On the representation made to us by Monsieur l'Abbé Piquet, priest, missionary of the Indians of La Présentation, that in virtue of the permission which we gave him last year, he is building a saw-mill on the river called La Présentation or Souegatzy, with the view of contributing to the establishment of that new mission; but that for the usefulness of the said mill, it is necessary that there should be attached thereto a tract of land in the neighborhood, on which to receive the saw-logs, as well as the boards and other lumber : wherefore he prays that we would grant him a concession *en censive* of one arpent* and a half in front on the said river, that is to say, three-fourths of an arpent on each side of the said mill, by one arpent and a half in depth, having regard to the premises.

We, in virtue of the power jointly entrusted to us by His Majesty, have given, granted and conceded, and by these presents do give, grant and concede unto the Abbé Piquet the said extent of land of one arpent and a half in front, by the same depth, as herein above described : to have and to hold the said unto him and his assigns in full property for ever, on condition that the said tract of land, and the mill erected thereon, can not be sold or given to any person holding in mortmain (*gens de main morte*), in which case His Majesty shall reënter *pleno jure* into the possession of the said tract of land and mill; also on condition of the yearly payment of five *sols* of *rente* and six *deniers* of *cens*, payable to His Majesty's domain, on the festival day of St. Remy, the first of October each year, the first payment of which shall be due on the 1st October of next year, 1752; the said *cens* bearing profit of *lods et rentes, saisine et amende*, agreeably to the custom of Paris followed in this country; and that he shall have these presents confirmed within one year.

In testimony whereof, &c.

At Quebec, the 10th of October 1751.

Signed, LAJONQUIERE, and
BIGOT.

True Copy.
BIGOT.

It is rendered probable, from a comparison of dates, that Picquet on this occasion of his visit, took along with him a deputation of his neophites to present them to the governor, as is shown by the following documents, which explains the object of their journey (Paris Doc. X, *p.* 264,*et seq.*).

Speech of the Iroquois of the Five Nations, established at la Presentation, at Quebec, September 20, 1751.

SPEECH OF THE SAVAGES. 1.	REPLY OF MONSIEUR THE GENERAL. 1.
God has favored us with good weather yesterday, to enable us to arrive safely to see you; we are a people who come from the foot of the islands; we rejoice to find you in good health. These are chiefs and warriors, who have come to wish you much happiness.	I am pleased, my children, to see you. I thank you for the interest you express for my health.

* An *arpent* is a hundred perches of land, eighteen feet to the perch, or about three quarters of an acre. This is an old French land measure.

2.

We have not the talent of Frenchmen. We are savages; and we pray you to pardon us, if our expressions are not couched in appropriate language.

2.

I know that you are still young, and not yet able to be great orators. I am meanwhile very well satisfied with your harangue. It is very well spoken. You can not fail to acquire greater abilities by becoming identified with our interests, and in doing whatever M. l'Abbè Picquet shall direct you, for the service of the king, my master.

3.

We are like new-born children. We have heard speak of the attack which has been made upon the people! of the Saut, and we have made every effort that was possible to ascertain who were the authors of the attack.

3.

You can not but bewail the fate of your brethren at the Saut St. Louis, who have experienced a melancholy fate. I mourn for them equally with you.

4.

We have heard that it was the Chèraquis; and we ask if it is your will that we raise the hatchet to attack them: they have destroyed those of our own blood; our brothers, the people of the Saut, of the lake, and all who are under your wings, will unite with us.

4.

I can not disapprove of your raising the hatchet, to go and smite the Chèraques, who have stained their hands with the blood of your brethren; your brothers of the saut, of the lake, and all those who are under my wings, will afford me a pleasure by uniting with you.

5.

As you desire us to do, so we will act; we are, as it were, born but to day, and have embraced the faith. Our young warriors who have taken refuge amongst us, are at leisure, and desirous to strike, if you promote our Mission.

We must avenge the death of our brethren, after which, our Mission will increase more and more. Our father who instructs us, is as embarrassed as ourselves. He witnesses the arrival of young warriors who are anxious to set out on the war path the next morning.

By a Belt.

5.

I agree that you ought not to defer striking this blow, and I repeat, that I consent to it. And you ought not to omit any thing that will tend to increase your village, and afford me proofs of the zeal which you evince in favor of religion.

6.

We beg you to be assured, that we think like the French; we execute our projects; and we assure you by this belt, that we will set off at the breaking up of the ice, hatchet in hand, to strike the blow.

6.

I am very glad that you exhibit a constancy in your project, and that you will execute it. I receive your belt with pleasure, and I return you one, to assure you that at the breaking up of the ice, I will have the powder and lead furnished you which you require.

By a Belt.

I give you also this belt, by which I wish to bind myself to you; present it to the people of the saut, to the Iroquois of the Five Nations, and to all those who are under my wings. I bind them to you, that they may not separate themselves from it, until you shall have avenged the blood of your brethren.

7.

You now know the sentiments of your children, of La Presentation. You know we possess nothing. We throw ourselves into your arms. You know we are without weapons; yet we ask you for nothing. We leave you to infer what we require for the expedition which we are about to undertake.

.Our skin is tender; we see the snows which will not delay to fall upon the mountains; if we have not mittens, we shall freeze with the cold, and our nails will fall off.

7.

I open my arms to receive you. I repeat from the feeling of my heart, that I will provide for all your necessities. You see from others who are present, that I have done to them all you solicit for yourselves.

8.

I do not wish to weary you. I wish to depart in two days.

You know that the Five Nations are numerous. I wish to make an effort to assemble all those that it may be possible, to augment our village.

I cast my body into your hand. I wish to die for my dear Onontio Gwa.

8.

You do well to resolve to induce your brothers of the Five Nations to join you, and settle in your village.

• 9.

We have spoken to you, upon your word, and upon that of Monsieur the Bishop, to engage to increase our Mission. All those who have come to join our village, are under the hope that you will give us some utensils to assist us.

9.

There are quantities of these in the arsenals of the king at La Presentation. Monsieur the Abbé Picquet will take care of your brothers, when they arrive at your mission.

10.

If we were in a more comfortable situation, our village would sensibly increase. We want 37 brass kettles; our women make this request.

10.

I will not forget your women; there are the kettles which they ask.

The attempt of the French to establish a mission at Oswegatchie naturally excited the jealousies of the English, whose relations with their Canadian neighbors were every day tending to open hostilities. The industry of the French in founding establishments among the Indian tribes at this period, sufficiently evinces the anxiety they felt to secure the interest and influence of the savages, to the prejudice of the English colonies. The following communication from Lieut. Lindesay to Col. Johnson relates to the station at Swegage, or La Presentation, shortly before founded.

Oswego, 15th July, 1751.

"This day came here from Niagra the Bunt and the Black Prince's son, with their fighters. He first gave me an account how it had fared with them : told me he found two forts built by the French since he went out; one at Nigra, carrying place, and the other by John Cair on the river Ohieo. He said he heard a bird sing that a great many Indians from his castle, and others from the five nations, were gone to Swegage: all this, he said, grived him, and he saw things going very wrong; and if a stop was not put to it, the five nations wou'd be ruined soon. He said he was come home, for he lookt on this place as such: that ho was both hungry and poor; and hoped, as I represented the Governor and Coll. Johnson here, I would assist him in a little provisions and clothing to his fighters. I told him was sorry for the loss he had sustained, but was glad to find his thoughts and mine the same as to the French's building forts, and the Indians going to Swegage; and told him how wrong it was in our Indjans going to Cannada, and the consequences that would attend it, in the best light I could. He agreed with me in all I said, and promised to do everything in his power to have things better managed, and likewise promised in the strongest terms to all Coll. Johnson would desire of him. I gave him provisions and cloathing, &c. for his people, to the ualue of five pounds above what he gave me when he spoke, which was three bevers.

27th. This day came the Couse, and some other Sinaka sacham, in order to go to Cannada. He came to see me, and told me he was sent by the consent of the five nations to go to the Govn. of Cannada about the building the above said two forts, &c. I told him the consequence of Indjans going there; but as he is intirely French, all I said was to no purpose, though he seem'd to own the force of what I said, as all the other Indjans did, and I belive all but him might have been stopt; but as things are, I could do no more.

By all the Indjans that have been here, I find the French army landed at Nigra about the 26th July, in 20 large canoes, to the number of 250 or 300 French, with 200 Arondaks and Annogongers : they are to gather all the Indians as they pass, and allso French, and will at least amount to 1000 or 1200 French and Indjans. Their designs is to drive the English of that are at or near Ohieo, and oblidge the Meomies to come and live where they shall order them. All the Indjans who have been here, say they and all Indians are to join them. While the Bunt was here, I had him always with me, and did all lay in my powar to oblidge him. He showed the greatist sence of it, and said he would allways do what I asked, as he allways had done. He is much inclined to us; and am convinced that if Coll. Johnson sends for him, he will come and take our affairs in hand hertily; and I think he hath it more in his powar then any to bring things to rights, nor is it to be done without him. This is

my sentiments, and I hope you will pardon my liberty in giveing them. If you approve of what I have said, and desire me to bring him down with me, Ile do my indeavours, and he never yet hath refused what I asked of him.   There are some French here, who mett the army about hundred miles to the west of Nigra.   JOHN LINDESAY.
To the Honourable Coll. Wm. Johnson."*

On the 19th of June 1754, there assembled at Albany the celebrated Congress of Representatives from the several English colonies, to agree upon a *plan of union*, for the common defence against the encroachments of the French, and the hostilities of the Indians who were incited by them to make inroads upon the back settlements of the English.   Among the commissioners from the several colonies, appeared those who afterwards shone with distinguished reputation in the revolutionary war; and none more so than Benjamin Franklin.

The measure which was the great object of this congress ultimately, failed, from its strong republican tendency, which alarmed the minions of royalty then in power; but several points of interest were discussed, which have a direct relation with our subject.   In the representation of the affairs of the colonies which was agreed upon, were the following statements :

"That the Lake Champlain, formerly called Lake Iroquois, and the country southward of it as far as the Dutch or English settlements, the Lakes Ontario, Erie, and all the countries adjacent, have, by all ancient authors, French and English, been allowed to belong to the Five Cantons or Nations; and the whole of these countries, long before the treaty of Utrecht, were by said nations put under the protection of the Crown of Great Britain.   * * *

"That they [the French] are continually drawing off the Indians from the British interest, and have lately persuaded one half of the Onondaga tribe, with many from the other nations along with them, to remove to a place called Oswegatchie, on the River Caduraqui, where they have built them a church and fort; and many of the Senecas, the most numerous nation appear wavering, and rather inclined to the French; and it is a melancholy consideration that not more than 150 men of all the several nations have attended this treaty, although they had notice that all the governments would be here by their commissioners, and that a large present would be given."†

Hendrick the Mohawk chief, the warrior and orator, and ever the firm friend of the English, endeavored to dissuade the confederates of New York from joining the settlement at Oswegatchie; and at a conference of the Indian tribes with Sir William Johnson, held at Mount Johnson, September 24th, 1753, he thus addressed them in a speech replete with native eloquence and rhetorical ornament:

* See Doc. Hist. New York, Vol 2, p. 623.
† A full account of the proceedings of this congress will be found in the 2d vol. Doc. Hist. of New York, pp. 545 & 619.

" It grieves me sorely to find the road hither so grown up with weeds for want of being used, and your fire almost expiring at Onondaga, where it was agreed by the wisdom of our ancestors that it should never be extinguished. You know it was a saying among them, that when the fire was out here, you would be no longer a people.

I am now sent by your brother, the Governor, to clear the road, and make up the fire with such wood as will never burn out; and I earnestly desire you will take care to keep it up, so as to be found always the same when he shall send among you.—A belt.

I have now renewed the fire, swept and cleared all your rooms with a new white wing, and leave it hanging near the fireplace, that you may use it for cleaning all dust, dirt, &c. which may have been brought in by strangers, no friends to you or us.—A string of wampum.

I am sorry to find, on my arrival among you, that the fine shady tree which was planted by your forefathers for your ease and shelter, should be now leaning, being almost blown down by northerly winds. I shall now endeavor to set it upright, that it may flourish as formerly, while its roots spread abroad, so that when we sit or stand on them, you will feel them shake : should any storm blow, then should you be ready to secure it.—A belt.

Your fire now burns clearly at the old place. The tree of shelter and protection is set up and flourishes. I must now insist upon your quenching that fire made with brambles at Swegachey, and recall those to their proper home who have deserted thither. I can not leave dissuading you from going to Canada; the French are a delusive people, always endeavoring to divide you as much as they can, nor will they let slip any opportunity of making advantage of it. 'Tis formidable news we hear that the French are making a descent upon the Ohio: " Is it with your consent or leave that they proceed in this extraordinary manner, endeavoring by force of arms to dispossess your own native allies, as well as your bretheren, the English, and establishing themselves?" * * * A large belt.

At a general meeting of the Six Nations, held at Onondaga, they replied to the foregoing speech and that of the governor, through their speaker Red Head, as follows:

" We acknowledge with equal concern with you that the road between us has been obstructed, and almost grown up with weeds; that our fire is scattered and almost extinct. We return you our most hearty thanks for recruiting the fire with such wood as will burn clear, and not go out; and we promise that we shall, with the utmost care, dress and keep it up, as we are sensible from what has been said by our forefathers, that the neglect of it would be our ruin. A belt.

" We know very well the use of the white wing you recommended, and are determined to use it to sweep out whatever may hinder the fire from burning with a pure flame. A string.

" You may depend upon our care in defending the tree which you have replanted from the inclemency of the high winds from Canada. We are full of acknowledgments for your care and admonitions, and be assured we shall watch every threatening cloud from thence, that we may be ready to prop it up. A belt.

" We rejoice that we see the fire burn pure where it should do; the tree of shelter look strong and flourishing. And you may depend upon our quenching that false fire at Swegachey, and doing all we can to recall our brothers, too often seduced that way. Tho' we did not conceive we had done so much amiss in going thither, when we observe that you white people pray, and we had no nearer place to learn to pray, and have our children baptized than that. However, as you insist upon it, we will not go that way nor be any more divided. I must now say it is not with our consent that the French have committed any hostilities in Ohio. We know what you Christians, English and French together, intend. We are so hemmed in by both that we have hardly a hunting place left. In a little while, if we find a bear in a tree, there will immediately appear an owner of the land to challenge the property and hinder us from killing it, which is our livelihood. We are so perplexed between both that we hardly know what to say or think." A belt.

The sentiment expressed at the close of this last address, is so true and so melancholy, that it can not fail to excite our sympathy at the fate of the unfortunate race of which, and by which, it was spoken. The unlettered savages, in the simplicity of artless nature, and prompted by a sentiment of benevolence which has been but illy requited, admitted the European settlers to their lands, and proffered the hand of friendship. When once established, the whites finding themselves superior to their rude neighbors in the arts of trade, failed not in most instances, to avail themselves of this advantage, and overreach them in traffic, corrupt their morals, and impart to them the vices, without the benefits of civilization.

Under these influences, the presage of the orator just quoted has been soon and sadly realized, and the red man has retreated before the march of that civilization which he could not adopt, and those habits of industry which are at variance with his nature.

Like the wild flower that flourishes only in the shade, and withers in the sun as soon as its primitive thicket is gone, the race has vanished, leaving the homes and the graves of their ancestors for the wildness of the western forests, whence in a few years they must again retreat, until the last of the race has disappeared.

In an account of a military expedition consisting of a French regiment under de Béarre, which ascended the St. Lawrence in 1755, for the purpose of promoting the military operations which the French were carrying on at that time along the great lakes and western rivers, we find the following description of the works at la Presentation. [*See Paris Documents*, vol. X, p. 213.]

" On the 28th [of July, 1755,] ascended the two Galos rapids which are dangerous, doubled the point à Livrogne, and crossed from the north to the south, to encamp under Fort Presentation, which is six [?] leagues from the end of the rapids. This fort consists of four battlements, in the form of bastions, of which the curtains are palisades. It is sufficient to resist savages, but could be but poorly defended against troops who might attack it, and who could easily succeed. On the 29th, doubled two points, notwithstanding the wind blew with violence against us, and encamped upon point aux-Barils, at three leagues. On the 30th, passed the Thousand Islands, the River Toniata, and camped on an island very poorly adapted for the purpose, opposite a small strait a distance of seven leagues. On the 31st. crossed two large bays. Met in the former two canoes coming from Detroit, the conductors of whom said that the English had been defeated on the Ohio."

The Abbe Picquet joined this expedition with thirty-eight of his warriors, on the 12th of September, who desired to accompany the expedition to make prisoners at Chouagen. He left on the 16th, and rejoined at the Isle of Tonti.

On the 25th, his savages brought in two prisoners, having slain three who resisted them. These prisoners informed them that the fort at Oswego had been largely reinforced. Picquet left on the 26th to take his savages and his prisoners to Montreal to M. de Vaudreuil.

At the attack upon Fort George, which resulted in its capitulation, under Lt. Col. Munro, Aug. 9, 1757, a company of Iroquois warriors were present, under the command of De Longueil Sabervois. The Abbe Picquet, Sulpician missionary, is also enumerated as among the French force.

The savages were cunning politicians, and proved themselves oftentimes very willing to take sides with the strongest party, as is shown by the following address, which was returned to them by the governor-general of Canada, on an occasion in which they had sent him an address, by the hands of their friends the Oswegatchies; having, for some reason not related, chosen this indirect method of tendering their allegiance to the French, probably in consequence of the advantages which the latter had gained over the English, by the defeat of Bradock.

The address of the natives is not preserved, but that of the governor in reply to it, is given below, from which its nature and tenor may be ascertained.

We translate it from the eleventh volume of the Paris Documents, page 247, in the department of the Secretary of State, at Albany.

"*Reply of M. the Marquis de Vaudreuil, to the words which the Five Nations, sent him by their Deputies of the Mission of La Presentation, Oct. 22, 1755:*

My Children of the Five Nations,

I have listened attentively to the words you have addressed me by my children of la Presentation. You can not have better orators than those of this village, who knowing my sentiments to you, have had the goodness to bring me your belts, and to inform me of all which you have said.

I am now about to reply to your three words.

FIRST WORD.

You assure me, my children, by your first belt, not only of your neutrality, but even that you have embraced the good cause, and that no thing shall occur to separate you from it. You reply to me, concerning your young men, but you pray me not to ensanguine the land which you inhabit.

BY A BELT.

It appears, my children, that you know all the extent of my care for you, and that you are persuaded that it will be easy for you to influence me. You are right. If I should treat you as you deserve, I should reject your belt, and in place of being so complaisant as to answer you, I should prove to you the force of my resentment, which your treachery has deserved. But I see you are well convinced that my care exceeds all you had a right to expect.

If your sentiments towards me were as sincere as those of mine for you, you would blush at having a single thought of announcing your neutrality. Should children be neutral in what concerns their father? Surely you do not speak from the bottom of your hearts, and I ought to be persuaded that you really are beside yourselves: no matter — you wish to be neutral — be so.

I can not believe you have espoused the good cause. Ought you ever to have abandoned it? Have you not had, on the contrary, every reason to occupy yourselves on the part of the French? Have they ever induced you to commit the least thing against any one?

Have I not always assisted you in your wants, and by my councils in all your affairs?

In what have you profited thereby? You are ungrateful children, and it is with difficulty that I can restore you to your senses. You have been erring too far, and I can truly say, that you are no longer in the possession of your senses, for you have been robbed of these by the most cruel of your enemies.

You beg me not to ensanguine the land that you inhabit. What cause have you to make such a prayer? Have I any other business, than the preservation of it for you? Had it not been on account of kindness to you, I should have driven you away.

If you have not lost your senses, you should have thanked me for all I have done for you. In short, I retain your belt, not to recall to my mind the subject which induced you to send it, but because it comes from you, and you have still a place in my heart. I give you one that you may carry into all your villages, to make known to all my children, that I cease not to be their father, and expect that they will not delay to give me proof that they continue to be my children.

SECOND WORD.

You acknowledge, my children, that you have accepted the hatchet of the English, but that, having considered the alliance made with the French from time immemorial, you have rejected it, for no other reason, than to attach yourselves to the good cause. You pray me not to impute any thing to you of present affairs, and that nothing can induce you to conceal the belt which you have accepted.

BY A BELT.

Of all the proofs which you have received of my care, I desire, to-day, to give you one greater than you could have desired, in the acceptance of your belt, with the only view of recalling on all occasions, that you have been unnatural children, and that you have taken up the hatchet against your father, and that, from pity towards you, I have not visited you with the punishment which your black conduct deserved.

In vain you recall your alliance with the French, if I were not disposed towards you as a father full of goodness. You would have forfeited all the advantages which this alliance obtained for you on every occasion, from the moment that you renounced it by the most criminal treason; and scarcely had you taken the hatchet against me, than my children would have eaten and torn you with their teeth, even to the marrow of the bones, had I not restrained them; for it would have been of no use for you to tell them, that you had thrown away the hatchet, not wishing to be longer occupied in the good affairs. ·

How can you pray me to impute nothing to you of present affairs? Have you forgotten all that you have done, and do you think that I am ignorant of it?

No. Truly you are well persuaded that I have been a witness to your conduct, and that I have followed you in all your steps; that I have seen you; that I have heard you. Do you doubt that I have in my power the papers of general Braddock? I have the very words you have given; I have also your solemn council with colonel Johnson. My children of the upper country have always reported to me their words and their belts, which you, instead, have carried to your enemies and mine; but I forbear to repeat them.

You say that nothing could induce you to sully the belt which you have renewed. Ought I to believe it? How many times have you not deceived me? And how many times have you not obtained your pardon?

The belt which you have renewed is the ordinary means for recalling my goodness. You have too often tarnished it by your repeated treasons. I desire to establish it by that which I give you. Take good care of it, together. Make feasts from village to village, and from cabin to cabin, and proclaim daily, that you have had the misfortune to betray the best of fathers; that you deserved death, but found grace.

THIRD WORD.

You offer a condolence on the death of the officers who have been killed at the Ohio river, and at the portage of Lake St. Sacrament, particularly M. de Longueuil. In the mean time you say that you will be able to go down to avenge them yourselves.

BY A BELT.

How ought I to receive your belt? Will it not be with reason as an acknowledgment on your part, that it was yourselves, the five nations, who have killed these officers? Will I not be right to make pass from nation to nation, this belt, to arouse the vengeance of my children? Can you reasonably think that I have not seen the arms in hand against me? Have I not been a witness of all your actions; and that none of you would have been actually alive, if I had not exercised all my authority to arrest my children, who in their fury would have slaughtered you, your wives and children, and have ruined the land which you inhabit?

Ought you not to be overwhelmed at my great generosity! I receive your belt; but it is for you to exhibit upon all occasions that the French blood which you have shed unjustly, cries for vengeance upon you, and that at the first transgression you will be brought to submit to the lot which you have for so long a time deserved.

I give you this belt, in order that that which I have said may be indelible in your memories. Repeat it daily to your old men and your warriors, to your women and to your children, that they may never forget it; that they may one and all bewail their transgressions, and endeavor equally to repair them.

As regards M. the Baron de Longueuil, is this the time to do honor to his death? If your grief and regrets at his death had been sincere, would you have delayed till the present moment to come and give proofs of it? How often have you caused to be announced your departure to come and condole the death of this governor? Why do you differ?

If you wish to tell the truth, it is the evil spirit that prevents you. You have been too slow in coming to see me. You have been ashamed, and too negligent. You dared not to appear, because you knew yourselves to be guilty. Never mind : I receive you; and if you give me perfect proofs of your repentance of your crimes, and you avenge them upon those who have been at their root, and their true authors, your brothers and the domiciliated races, and the nations of the upper country, will continue to be your brothers and friends. * * *

Recall the memory of your ancestors, who possessed courage, and who gave on all occasions proofs of their good conduct. Learn from the old men of the age in which you live, concerning the times of my father, whom you loved as myself. Hear my word, as they heard his, and you will enjoy the most profound peace and tranquility.

Father Rigaud, Marquis de Vaudreuil, Commander of the Royal and Military Order of St. Louis, Governor and Lieutenant General for the King in all New France and the land and country of Louisiana.

We certify that the present copy is in conformity with the original remaining in our office : in testimony of which, we have signed these presents, and have sealed it with the seal of our arms, and countersigned by our secretary.

Done at Montreal, the 13th of February 1758.

Signed : VAUDREUIL."

An embassy of the Five Nations, held an interview with M. de Montcalm, on the 24th of April, 1757, to which measure they were inclined from the successes of the French in the last campaign, which resulted in the capture of Oswego. This council was addressed by orators from each of the Indian tribes, but a passage occurs in the original account of this council,* which is important as showing the standing of the Oswegatchies among their Indian neighbors at that period:

"There were also in attendance, the Iroquois of la Presentation, who were present at all the deliberations, but spoke not separately and in their own name. The reason was that they had been domiciled but a short time; they regarded themselves still as the "*fag ends*," [*natte*] of the Iroquois, who call the village of la Presentation the tail of the Five Nations." In a note to this in the original, this mission is mentioned as having been founded by the zeal of the Abbé Picquet, a Sulpician, and as equally important for religion as for the state.

* Paris Documents, vol. XIII, p. 194.

An interesting picture of the domestic life of the Oswegatchies, is given in the following extract from a narrative of a residence among them, which may be found entire in Drake's Indian Captivities.

Robert Eastburn, a tradesman, while in company with others, on their way to Oswego, in March, 1756, while stopping at Captain Williams's fort, at the carrying place, near the present village of Rome, was taken captive by the Oswegatchie Indians, and kept for sometime at their village near Fort Presentation, the site of Ogdensburgh.

The attacking party consisted of four hundred French, and three hundred Indians, commanded by one of the principal gentlemen of Quebec, and accompanied by a priest, probably Father Picquet.

The prisoners numbered eighteen or twenty, and their route led through Lewis and Jefferson counties, to Lake Ontario, and thence to the post at the mouth of the Oswegatchie.

They were seven days in reaching the lake, and suffered greatly from want of provisions. On the 4th of April, they were met by several French bateaux, with a supply of provisions, and having crossed the mouth of a river where it empties into the east end of Lake Ontario, a great part of the company set off on foot towards Oswegatchie, while the rest proceeded by bateaux down the St. Lawrence. The adventures with which the party met, are best given in the language of the original narrative:

" By reason of bad weather, wind, rain, and snow, whereby the waters of the lake were troubled, we were obliged to lay by, and haul our batteaux on shore. Here I lay on the cold shore two-days. Tuesday, set off and entered the head of St. Lawrence in the afternoon; came too, late at night, made fires, but did not lie down to sleep. Embarking long before day, and after some mile's progress down the river, saw many fires on our right hand, which were made by the men who left us, and went by land. With them we staid till day, and then embarked in our batteaux. The weather was very bad, (it snowed fast all day); near night we arrived at Oswegatchy. I was almost starved to death, but hoped to stay in this Indian town till warm weather; slept in an Indian wigwam, rose early in the morning, (being Thursday,) and soon to my grief discovered my disappointment.

Several of the prisoners had leave to tarry here, but I must go two hundred miles further down stream, to another Indian town. The morning being extremely cold, I applied to a French merchant or trader for some old rags of clothing, for I was almost naked, but to no purpose. About ten o'clock, I was ordered into a boat, to go down the river, with eight or nine Indians, one of whom was the man wounded in the skirmish above mentioned.*

At night we went on shore; the snow being much deeper than before, we cleared it away and made a large fire. Here, when the wounded Indian cast his eyes upon me, his old grudge revived, he took my blanket from me, and commanded me to dance around the fire barefoot,

* Referring to a portion of the narrative not quoted.

and sing the prisoner's song, which I utterly refused. This surprised one of my fellow prisoners, who told me they would put me to death, for he understood what they said. He therefore, tried to persuade me to comply, but I desired him to let me alone, and was through great mercy, enabled to reject his importunity with abhorrence.

This Indian also continued urging, saying, 'you shall dance and sing;' but apprehending my compliance sinful, I determined to persist in declining it at all adventures, and leave the issue to the divine disposal. The Indian perceiving his orders disobeyed, was fired with indignation, and endeavored to push me into the fire, which I leaped over, and he, being weak with his wounds, and not being assisted by any of his brethren, was obliged to desist. For this gracious interposure of Providence, in preserving me both from sin and danger, I desire to bless God while I live.

Friday morning, I was almost perished with cold. Saturday, we proceeded on our way, and soon came in sight of the upper part of the settlements of Canada."

The party continued their journey towards Canasadosega, and on the route the wounded Indian, assisted by a French inhabitant, endeavored again to compel Eastburn to dance and sing, but with no better success than before. On arriving at the town which was thirty miles northwest of Montreal, he was compelled to run the gauntlet, and was saved from destruction only through the interposition of the women. Being assigned to an Indian family at Oswegatchy, in which he was adopted, he set off on his return, and after a tedious and miserable voyage of several days, arrived within three miles of the town, on the opposite side of the river. The Oswegatchies inhabited the site of Johnstown until removed to Indian Point, in Lisbon, by Lord Dorchester, as stated elsewhere in the letters of Judge Ford.

The language of the narrative will be here resumed:

"Here I was to be adopted. My father and mother whom I had never seen before, were waiting, and ordered me into an Indian house, where we were directed to sit down silent for a considerable time. The Indians appeared very sad, and my mother began to cry, and continued to cry aloud for some time, and then dried up her tears, and received me for her son, and took me over the river to the Indian town. The next day I was ordered to go to mass with them, but I refused once and again; yet they continued their importunities several days. Seeing they could not prevail with me they seemed much displeased with their new son. I was then sent over the river to be employed in hard labor, as a punishment for not going to mass, and not allowed a sight of, or any conversation with, my fellow prisoners. The old Indian man with whom I was ordered to work, had a wife and children. He took me into the woods with him, and made signs for me to chop, and he soon saw that I could handle the axe. Here I tried to reconcile myself to this employ, that they might have no occasion against me, except concerning the law of my God. The old man began to appear kind, and his wife gave me milk and bread when we came home, and when she got fish, gave me the gills to eat, out of real kindness; but perceiving I did not like them, gave me my own choice, and behaved lovingly. When we had finished our fence, which had employed us about a week, I showed the old squaw my shirt, (having worn it from the time when I was first taken prisoner, which was about seven weeks,) all rags, dirt, and vermin. She brought me a new one, with ruffled sleeves, saying 'that is good,' which I thankfully accepted. The next day they carried me back to the Indian town, and permitted me to converse with my fellow prisoners. They told me we were all to be sent to Montreal, which accordingly came to pass."

At a grand council held at Montreal, Eastburn mentions a noted priest called Picquet. "who understood the Indian tongue well, and did more harm to the English than any other of his order in Canada. His dwelling was at Oswegatchy."

A plan of operations against Oswego was in progress; and great numbers of soldiers were in motion towards Lake Ontario, with bateaux laden with provisions and munitions of war. After a painful journey, Eastburn arrived again at Oswegatchie; having received from his adopted mother the choice of remaining at Montreal, or returning with her, and having chosen the latter alternative as affording the best chance of escape. While here, he daily saw many bateaux, with provisions and soldiers, passing up to Fort Frontenac; which greatly distressed him for the safety of Oswego, and led him to form a plan for notifying the English of the designs of their enemies.

"To this end, I told two of my fellow-prisoners that it was not a time to sleep, and asked them to go with me; to which they heartily agreed. But we had no provisions, and were closely eyed by the enemy, so that we could not lay up a stock out of our allowance.

However, at this time, Mr. Picket had concluded to dig a large trench round the town. I therefore went to a negro, the principal manager of this work (who could speak English, French, and Indian well), and asked him if he could get employment for two others and myself; which he soon did. For this service we were to have meat [board], and wages. Here we had a prospect of procuring provision for our flight. This, after some time, I obtained for myself, and then asked my brethren if they were ready. They said 'they were not yet, but that Ann Bowman (our fellow-prisoner) had brought one hundred and thirty dollars from Bull's fort [when it was destroyed as has been related], and would give them all they needed.' I told them it was not safe to disclose such a secret to her; but they blamed me for entertaining such fears, and applied to her for provisions, letting her know our intention. She immediately informed the priest of it! We were forthwith apprehended, the Indians informed of it, and a court called. Four of us were ordered by this court to be confined in a room, under a strong guard, within the fort, for several days. From hence, another and myself were sent to Cohnewago, under a strong guard of sixty Indians, to prevent my plotting any more against the French, and to banish all hope of my escape!" Here he met with unexpected kindness, and lodged at the house of the mother of a French smith, whose name was Mary Harris, and had been taken captive while a child at Deerfield in New England.

He soon after went to Montreal: and while there, saw the English captives and standards, the trophies of the French victory at Oswego of July 15th, 1756, brought into town. Among the prisoners, 1400 in number, he recognized his own son. He remained a prisoner about a year after, and was at length permitted to leave for England with other prisoners, and finally returned home.

The memoirs of Father Picquet have been written by M. de la Lande, of the Academie des Sciences, and are published in the fourteenth volume of a work entitled, " *Lettres Edifiantes et Curieuses* " (Lyons edition, 1819, *p.* 262, *et seq.*), from which an abridged translation is published in the Documentary History of New York, from which, and from the original essay, we derive the following.

"A missionary remarkable for his zeal, and the services which he has rendered to the church and the state, born in the same village as myself, and with whom I have enjoyed terms of particular intimacy, has given to me a relation of his labors, and I have thought that this notice deserved to find a place in the *Lettres Edifiantes*, having exactly the same object as the other articles in that collection, and I flatter myself that I shall be able to render an honorable testimony to the memory of a compatriot, and of a friend so amiable as M. l'abbé Picquet.

Francois Picquet, doctor of the Sorborne, King' Missionary and Prefect Apostolic to Canada, was born at Bourg, in Bresse, on the 6th Dec., 1708. The ceremonials of the church, from his infancy, were to him so engaging, that they seemed to announce his vocation.

The good instruction which he received from an estimable father, seconded by a happy disposition, enabled him to accomplish his earlier studies with the approbation of all his superiors, and of his professors, although in the dissipation and folly of youth, he was relieved by occupations altogether foreign to his studies. M. Picquet, in fact, loved to test his abilities in various ways, and in this he succeeded; but his first pastimes had announced his first preferences, and the church was his principal delight.

As early as the seventeenth year of his age, he successfully commenced the functions of a missionary in his country; and at twenty years, the Bishop of Sinope, Suffragan of the Diocese of Lyon, gave him, by a flattering exception, permission to preach in all the parishes of Bresse and Franche-Comté which depended on his diocese. The enthusiasm of his new state rendered him desirous to go to Rome, but the Archbishop of Lyons advised him to study theology at Paris. He followed this advice, and entered the congregation of St. Sulpice. The direction of the new converts was soon proposed to him; but the activity of his zeal induced him to seek a wider field, and led him beyond the seas in 1733, to the missions of North America, where he remained thirty years, and where his constitution, debilitated by labor, acquired a force and vigor, which secured for him a robust health to the end of his life.

After having for some time labored at Montreal, in common with other missionaries, he desired to undertake some new enterprise, by which France might profit by restoring peace to our vast colonies.

About 1740, he established himself at the *Lake of Two Mountains*,* to the North of Montreal, to draw the Algonquins, the Nipissings, and the savages of the lake Temiscaming to the head of the colony, and upon the route of all the nations of the north, which descend by the great river of Michilimakina, to Lake Huron.

There had been an ancient mission upon the Lake of Two Mountains, but it had been abandoned. M. Picquet took advantage of the peace which the country then enjoyed, in constructing a stone fort. This fort commanded the villages of the four nations, which composed the mission of the lake. He next caused a palisade to be built around each of the villages, of cedar posts, flanked by good redoubts. The King defrayed half of this expense; the missionaries incurred the rest by labor.

He there fixed the two nomadic nations of the Algonquins and the Nipissings, and caused them to build a fine village, and to sow and reap; a thing before regarded as next to impossible. These two nations, in the event, were first to give succor to the French. The pleasure which they experienced in this establishment attached them to France, and the king, in whose name M. Picquet procured them assistance in money, in provisions, and all that the wants of these two nations required.

He there erected a Calvary, which was the finest monument of religion in Canada, by the grandeur of the crosses which were planted upon the summit of one of the two mountains, by the different chapels and the different oratories, all alike built of stone, arched, ornamented with pictures, and distributed in stations for the space of three quarters of a league.

He here endeavored to gain an exact understanding with all the northern tribes, by means of the Algonquins and the Nipissings, and with those of the south and west, by means of the Iroquois and the Hurons. His negotiations resulted so well, that he annually, at the feast of the Passover and the Pentecost, baptized to the faith thirty to forty adults.

When the savage hunters had passed eight months in the woods, they remained a month in the village, which made it a kind of mission, receiving many each day with the two catechisms and with spiritual conferences. He taught them the prayers and the chants of the church, and he imposed penances upon those who created any disorder. A portion were settled and domiciled.

In short, he succeeded beyond all hope in persuading these nations to submit entirely to the King, and to render him the master of their national assemblies, with full liberty to make known his intentions and to nominate all their chiefs. From the commencement of the war of 1742, his savages showed their attachment to France and to the King, whose paternal character M. Picquet had announced to them, and who was regarded as the beloved and the idol of the nation.

The following is a letter which a savage warrior of the Lake of Two Mountains addressed to the King, in his enthusiasm, and which the three nations begged the governor to send to the King, at the beginning of the war. I will insert it to give an idea of their style, and of their oratorical figures. If it is not, word for word, the discourse of a savage, it is at

* About 36 miles N. W. of Montreal.—*Author*

5

least reported by those who knew the best, their style and their dispositions.

"MY FATHER:

Pay less attention to the fashion of my speech, than to the sentiments of my heart: no nation is capable of subduing me, or worthy of commanding me.

Thou art the only one in the world who is able to reign over me, and I prefer to all the advantages which the English can offer me to live with him, the glory of dieing in thy service.

Thou art great in thy name; I know it: *Onnontio* (the governor) who brings me thy word, and the Black Gown (the missionary) who announces to me that of the great spirit,* *Kichemaniton*, have told me that thou art the chief eldest son of the bride of Jesus, who is the great master of life; that thou commandest the world in wars, that thy nation is innumerable; that thou art the most absolute master of all the chiefs who command men, and govern the rest of the world.

Meanwhile, the noise of thy tread strikes my two ears; and I learn from thy enemies themselves, that thou hast only to appear, and forts fall to dust, and thy enemies are vanquished; that the quiet of night and the pleasures of the day yield to the glory which thou bringest; and the eye is wearied in following the courses and the labors of thy victories. I say that thou art great in thy name, and greater by thy heart that animates thee, and that thy warlike virtues surpass even mine. The nations know me: I was born in the midst of wars, and nourished with the blood of my enemies.

Ah my father, what joy for me, could I be able in thy service to assist thy arm, and behold myself the fire which war kindles in thy eye!

But if it should be that my blood should be shed for thy glory, under this sun, rely upon my fidelity, and the death of the English, and upon my bravery.

I have the war hatchet in my hand, and my eye fixed upon Onnontio, who governs me here in thy name.

I wait, upon one foot, only, and the hand raised, the signal which bids me strike thy enemy and mine.

Such, my father, is thy warrior of the Lake of Two Mountains."

The savages held their word, and the first blows that were struck upon the English in Canada, were by their hands.

M. Picquet was among the first to foresee the war which sprang up about 1742 between the English and the French. He prepared himself for it a long time beforehand. He began by drawing to his Mission (at the Lake of the Two Mountains) all the French scattered in the vicinity, to strengthen themselves and afford more liberty to the savages. These furnished all the necessary detachments; they were continually on the frontiers to spy the enemy's movements. M. Picquet learned, by one of these detachments, that the English were making preparations at Sarasto [Saratoga?], and were pushing their settlements up to Lake St. Sacrament.† He informed the general of the circumstance and proposed to him to send a body of troops there, at least to intimidate the enemy, if

---

* They call Matchimaniton, the bad spirit, or the devil. They call the king *Onnontio Goa.—Note in the original.*

† "I am building a fort at this lake, which the French call Lake St. Sacrament, but I have given it the name of Lake GEORGE, not only in honor to his Majesty, but to ascertain his undoubted dominion here."—*Sir Wm. Johnson to the Board of Trade, Sep. 3, 1775. Lond. Doc.* xxxii., 178.

we could do no more. The expedition was formed. M. Picquet accompanied M. Marin who commanded this detachment. They burnt the fort, the Lydius establishments,* several saw mills, the planks, boards and other building timber, the stock of supplies, provisions, the herds of cattle along nearly fifteen leagues of settlement, and made one hundred and forty-five prisoners, without having lost a single Frenchman or without having any even wounded.† This expedition alone prevented the English undertaking any thing at that side during the war.

Peace having been re-established in 1748, our missionary occupied himself with the means of remedying, for the future, the inconveniences which he had witnessed. The road he saw taken by the savages and other parties of the enemy sent by the English against us, caused him to select a post which could, hereafter, intercept the passage of the English. He proposed to M. de la Galissoniére to make a settlement of the mission of *La Presentation*, near Lake Ontario, an establishment which succeeded beyond his hopes, and has been the most useful of all those of Canada.

Mr. Rouillé, Minister of the Marine, wrote on the 4th May, 1749: " A large number of Iroquois having declared that they were desirous of embracing Christianity, it has been proposed to establish a mission towards Fort Frontenac, in order to attract the greatest number possible thither. It is Abbé Picquet, a zealous missionary and in whom these nations seem to have confidence, who has been entrusted with this negotiation. He was to have gone last year, to select a suitable site for the establishment of the mission, and verify, as precisely as was possible, what can be depended upon relative to the dispositions of these same nations. In a letter of the 5th October last, M. de la Galisonnière stated, that, though an entire confidence can not be placed in those they have manifested, it is notwithstanding of much importance, to succeed in dividing them, that nothing must be neglected that can contribute to it. It is for this reason that His Majesty desires you shall prosecute the design of the proposed settlement. If it could attain a certain success, it would not be difficult then to make the savages understand that the only means of extricating themselves from the pretensions of the English, to them and their lands, is to destroy Choueguen,‡ so as to deprive them thereby of a post which they established chiefly with a view to control their tribes. This destruction is of such great importance, both as regards our possessions and the attachment of the savages and their trade, that it is proper to use every means to engage the Iroquois to undertake it. This is actually the only means that can be employed, but you must feel that it requires much prudence and circumspection."'

Mr. Picquet eminently possessed the qualities requisite to effect the removal of the English from our neighborhood. Therefore the General, the Intendant, and the Bishop deferred absolutely to him in the selection of the settlement for this new mission; and despite the efforts of those who had opposite interests, he was entrusted with the undertaking.

---

* Now Fort Edward, Washington county.

† " I received an account on the 19th inst., by Express from Albany, that a party of French and their Indians had cut off a settlement in this province, called Saraghtoge, about fifty miles from Albany, and that about twenty houses with a fort (which the public would not repair) were burned to ashes, thirty persons killed and scalped, and about sixty taken prisoners. — *Gov. Clinton to the Board*, 30th Nov. 1745. *Lond. Doc.*xxvii., 187, 235.

‡ Oswego.

The fort of *La Presentation* is situated at 302 deg. 40 min. longitude, and at 44 deg. 50 min. latitude, on the Presentation river, which the Indians name *Soegasti*; thirty leagues above Mont-Real; fifteen leagues from Lake Ontario or Lake Frontenac, which with Lake Champlain gives rise to the River St. Lawrence: fifteen leagues west of the source of the River Hudson which falls into the sea at New York. Fort Frontenac had been built near there in 1671, to arrest the incursions of the English and the Iroquois; the bay served as a port for the mercantile and military marine which had been formed there on that sort of sea where the tempests are as frequent and as dangerous as on the ocean. But the post of *La Presentation* appeared still more important, because the harbor is very good, the river freezes there rarely, the barks can leave with northern, eastern and southern winds, the lands are excellent, and that quarter can be fortified most advantageously.

Besides, that mission was adapted by its situation to reconcile to us the Iroquois savages of the Five Nations who inhabit between Virginia and Lake Ontario. The Marquis of Beauharnois and afterwards M. de la Jonquière, Governor-General of New France, were very desirous that we should occupy it, especially at a time when English jealousy, irritated by a war of many years, sought to alienate from us the tribes of Canada.

This establishment was as if the key of the colony, because the English, French and Upper Canada savages could not pass elsewhere than under the cannon of Fort Presentation when coming down from the south, the Iroquois to the south, and the Micissagués to the north, were within its reach. Thus it eventually succeeded in collecting them together from over a distance of one hundred leagues. The officers, interpreters and traders, notwithstanding, then regarded that establishment as chimerical. Envy and opposition had effected its failure, had it not been for the firmness of the Abbé Picquet, supported by that of the administration. This establishment served to protect, aid and comfort the posts already erected on Lake Ontario. The barks and canoes, for the transportation of the king's effects, could be constructed there at a third less expense than elsewhere, because timber is in greater quantity and more accessible, especially when M. Picquet had had a saw mill erected there for preparing and manufacturing the timber. In fine, he could establish a very important settlement for the French colonists, and a point of reunion for Europeans and savages, where they would find themselves very convenient to the hunting and fishing in the upper part of Canada.

M. Picquet left with a detachment of soldiers, mechanics and some savages. He placed himself at first in as great security as possible against the insults of the enemy, which availed him ever since. On the 20th October, 1749, he had built a fort of palisades, a house, a barn, a stable, a redoubt, and an oven. He had lands cleared for the savages. His improvements were estimated at thirty to forty thousand *livres*, but he introduced as much judgment as economy. He animated the workmen, and they labored from three o'clock in the morning until nine at night. As for himself, his disinterestedness was extreme. He received at that time neither allowance nor presents; he supported himself by his industry and credit. From the king he had but one ration of two pounds of bread and one half pound of pork, which made the savages say, when they brought him a buck and some partridges: "We doubt not, father, but that there have been disagreeable expostulations in your stomach, because you have had nothing but pork to eat. Here's something to put your affairs in order." The hunters furnished him wherewithal to support the Frenchmen, and to treat the generals occasionally. The savages brought him trout weighing as many as eighty pounds.

FORT

Rapides

Moulin à Scie

bounden, and to treat the generals occasionally. The savages brought him trout weighing as many as eighty pounds.

When the court had granted him a pension, he employed it only for the benefit of his establishment. At first, he had six heads of families in 1749, eighty-seven the year following, and three hundred and ninety-six in 1751. All these were of the most antient and most influential families, so that this mission was, from that time, sufficiently powerful to attach the Five Nations to us, amounting to twenty-five thousand inhabitants, and he recokned as many as three thousand in his colony. By attaching the Iroquois cantons to France and establishing them fully in our interest, we were certain of having nothing to fear from the other savage tribes, and thus a limit could be put to the ambition of the English. Mr. Picquet took considerable advantage of the peace to increase that settlement, and he carried it in less than four years to the most desirable perfection, despite of the contradictions that he had to combat against; the obstacles he had to surmount; the jibes and unbecoming jokes which he was obliged to bear; but his happiness and glory suffered nothing therefrom. People saw with astonishment several villages start up almost at once; a convenient, habitable and pleasantly situated fort; vast clearances, covered almost at the same time with the finest maize. More than five hundred families, still all infidels, who congregated there, soon rendered this settlement the most beautiful, the most charming and the most abundant of the colony. Depending on it were La Presentation, La Galette, Suegatzi, L'isle au Galop, and L'isle Picquet in the River St. Lawrence. There were in the fort seven small stone guns and eleven four to six pounders.

The most distinguished of the Iroquois families were distributed at La Presentation in three villages: that which adjoined the French fort contained, in 1754, forty-nine bark cabins, some of which were from sixty to eighty feet long, and accommodated three to four families. The place pleased them on account of the abundance of hunting and fishing. This mission could no doubt be increased, but cleared land sufficient to allow all the families to plant and to aid them to subsist would be necessary, and each tribe should have a separate location.

M. Picquet had desired that in order to draw a large number, that they should clear during a certain time a hundred arpents of land each year, and build permanent cabins, and to surround their village with a palisade; that they should construct a church, and a house for seven or eight missionaries. The nations desired it, and it was an effectual means to establish them permanently. All this he could do with fifteen thousand livres a year, and he proposed to assign them a benefice, as tending to promote religion. Meanwhile our missionary applied himself to the instruction of the savages, and baptized great numbers.

The Bishop of Quebec, wishing to witness and assure himself personally of the wonders related to him of the establishment at *La Presentation*, went thither in 1749, accompanied by some officers, royal interpreters, priests from other missions and several other clergymen, and spent ten days examining and causing the catechumens to be examined. He himself baptized one hundred and thirty-two, and did not cease during his sojourn, blessing Heaven for the progress of religion among these infidels.

Scarcely were they baptized, when M. Picquet determined to give them a form of government. He established a council of twelve ancients; chose the most influential among the Five Nations; brought them to Mont-Real, where, at the hands of the Marquis du Quesne, they took the oath of allegiance to the King, to the great astonishment of the whole colony, where no person dared to hope for such an event.

Attentive as well to the good of the administration, as to the cause of religion, M. Picquet notified the chiefs of the colony of the abuses which he witnessed. He made for example, a remonstrance against the establishment of traders who had come to locate at the Long Saut, and at Carillon, to hold traffic and commerce, who cheated the savages, and sold them worthless things, at a dear price, and hindered them from coming to the mission, where they were undeceived, instructed in religion, and attached to France.

The garrisons which were established in the missions, embarrassed very much the projects of our missionary. "I have already seen," said he, in a memoir, "with gratification, the suppression of those of the Saut St. Louis, and at the lake of Two Mountains, and think that the government, informed by others as well as by myself, of the wrong they do to religion, as well as to the state, would withdraw that which is at la Presentation, where it is as useless, and even more pernicious than at the other missions.

No one knows better than myself, the disorders, which increase in proportion as the garrison becomes more numerous; the fervor of our first Christians is impaired by degrees by their bad example and bad councils; their docility towards the king is sensibly diminished; difficulties multiply almost continually between nations whose customs, and character, and interests, are so different; and in short, the commanders and guards of the magazines oppose habitually, a thousand obstacles to the fruits of the zeal of the missionaries.

During the twenty-eight years that I have had the charge and management of savages, I have always found with those who have studied their customs, and their character, that by free and frequent intercourse [*frequentation*] with the French, they become corrupt entirely, and that the bad examples, the bad councils, and the mercenary spirit and interests of the inhabitants of European nations who frequent their villages, are the principal causes why they make so little progress in religion.

Hence comes sometimes their indocility to the orders of governors, their infidelity to the king himself, and their apostacies. .

It is a thing of public notoriety, that at the Saut St. Louis, and at the Lake of Two Mountains, missions formerly so fervent, and which for almost a hundred years have rendered important services to the colony, they have there been the principal causes of these almost irreparable disorders; that they have not only introduced libertinism, and all kinds of debauchery, but even revolution and revolt."

M. Picquet feared above all, the introduction of crimes of the whites, happily unknown among savages.*

"The commandants were not then occupied in the missions which diminished the confidence of the savages in their missionaries. It seemed as if it were a victory gained, if they could detach some one, or even when they had adroitly prejudiced an officer against the missionaries, and wounded his feelings.

A devoutly religious missionary as indefatigable in the service of the king, as he was in that of his God, yielded himself at the foot of authority to the detriment of the mission of Saut St. Louis, under the force of accusations which the commandant of the fort fabricated against him. Then irreligion, libertinism, infidelity towards the king, and the insolence of the savages, immediately took the place of piety, of attachment, of submission, and of obedience, of which for a long period previous, they had given proofs under the guidance of the missionaries. At length, to

---

* A literal translation can not prudently be given.

remedy so many evils, they withdrew the garrisons which had placed two missionaries in the greatest danger; but the Jesuits were compelled to remove their mission from the Saut Saint Louis, below Lake St. Francis, to separate the savages from the frequent intercourse of the French.

Experience has always proved, that it was by religion, that we have succeeded best in attaching to us the savages, and that the missionaries formed and consolidated the union. In fact our missions have been always preserved in the same fidelity, when the missionaries have exercised liberally their ministry. But instead of which we see deserted the fine villages which were established at Fort Frontenac, at Niagara, below the portage, and nearly all the other posts of Upper Canada.

The commandants of these very posts, with their garrisons, have so dispersed and destroyed these establishments, that there remained no trace of them at the time of M. Picquet. These savages were without missionaries, without councils, and without sympathies, having all abandoned the French posts, to array themselves for the most part on the side of the English; and these kind of refugees are more dangerous to us than savages whom we have never known.

Before the missionaries had conciliated to us the people of Upper Canada, they conspired in all their posts against the French, and sought occasion to butcher them. Those who were on our side were of no assistance in time of war.

There were in all not more than forty in the expeditions of the first years of the war of 1755; and even except the domiciliated Christians, we saw almost none of the savages of the upper country, during more than three-quarters of a year, notwithstanding continual invitations and negociations; but the domesticated Christians, while they were quietly at home in their villages, with their missionaries, were always ready at the first signal to fly to the governor general.

We have seen them arrange themselves under their proper nations when the necessity came, and even not sparing their families; for in the affair of M. Diskau, they slew all the parents that they had made prisoners.

Instead of this, in the war of 1745, whilst they had garrisons in their villages, sometimes they refused to take up arms, and wished to remain neutral, and sometimes they betrayed us, and served our enemies, and could not be induced by the influence of entreaties, nor caresses, nor presents, and withstood until missionaries were sent to march with them.

But what is more strange, the governors general M. de Beauharnais, de la Galissonnière, de la Jonquière, and du Quesne, have themselves many times discovered that the savagos have been persuaded by the commandants of forts to go contrary to the orders of the generals, to the end, without doubt, that such faults would recoil upon the missionaries, and diminish the confidence which the generals reposed in them. When once got rid of, there was nothing to oppose the fire of age, the violence of the passions, and the inveterate habits of a great part of the soldiery.

The commanders of the magazine guards, were still more dangerous than the soldiers, the one by their authority, or their independence, as they had the disposal of the effects of the king; the other by the facilities which they equally had to make presents, and all the facilities which they enjoyed of corrupting the morals of the people. This has introduced confusion into the villages, to the contempt of the nation, and as a consequence the general alienation of these people from the French which has rendered it difficult for the missionaries to inspire them with courage, to engage on our side.

There might perhaps, meanwhile, be fear of withdrawing the garrison in time of war, but M. Picquet was persuaded that this would be still less hazardous than to allow them to remain; because, said he, the English think less of attacking a village in which there were only savages, than one in which is a garrison. They well know—

1st. That they have nothing to gain from the savages, whom it is difficult to surprise, and that one of their villages is like a nest of hornets, that take wing the moment they are disturbed, but who fall suddenly upon their aggressors from every quarter, and abandon them only on the last extremity.

2d. The English would have no longer to excuse themselves by the pretext of saying that they wished only to injure the French. He would set upon him all the nations, and irritate them in such a manner as to render them irreconcilable. It would be a happy blow for the French, but the English would be too much on his guard to undertake it.

In the month of June 1751, M. Picquet made a voyage around Lake Ontario, with a king's canoe and one of bark, in which he had five trusty savages, with the design of attracting some Indian families to the new settlement of La Presentation. There is a memoir among his papers on the subject, from which it is proposed to give an extract.

He visited Fort Frontenac or *Catarocoui*, situate twelve leagues west of La Presentation. He found no Indians there, though it was formerly the rendezvous of the Five Nations. The bread and milk, there, were bad: they had not even brandy there to staunch a wound. Arrived at a point of Lake Ontario called Kaoi, he found a negro fugitive from Virginia. He assured him on this occasion that there would be no difficulty to obtain a great part of the negroes of New England, who were received well in Canada, and supported the first year, and that lands were conceded to them as to habitants. The savages served them voluntarily as guides.

The negroes would be the most terrible enemies of the English, because they have no hope of pardon if the English become masters of Canada, and they contribute much to build up this colony by their labor. The same is the case with natives of Flanders, Lorraine and Switzerland, who have followed their example, because they were ill at ease with the English who loved them not.

At the Bay of Quinté, he visited the site of the ancient mission which M. Dollieres de Kleus and Abbé D'Urfé, priests of the Saint Sulpice Seminary, had established there. The quarter is beautiful, but the land is not good. He visited Fort Toronto, seventy leagues from Fort Frontenac, at the west end of Lake Ontario. He found good bread and good wine there, and every thing requisite for the trade, whilst they were in want of these at all the other posts. He found Mississagues there who flocked around him: they spoke first of the happiness their young people, the women and children, would feel, if the King would be as good to them as to the Iroquois for whom he procured missionaries. They complained that instead of building a church, they had constructed only a canton for them. M. Picquet did not allow them to finish, and answered them that they had been treated according to their fancy; that they had never evinced the least zeal for religion; that their conduct was much opposed to it; that the Iroquois, on the contrary, had manifested their love to christianity, but as he had no order to attract them to his mission, he avoided a more lengthy explanation.

He passed thence to Niagara. He examined the situation of that fort, not having any savages to whom he could speak. It is well located for defence, not being commanded from any point. The view extends to a great distance: they have the advantage of the landing of all the canoes and barks which land, and are in safety there; but the rain was washing the soil away by degrees, notwithstanding the vast expense which the King incurred to sustain it. M. Picquet was of opinion that the space between the land and the wharf might be filled in so as to support it, and make a glacis there. This place was important as a trading post, and as securing possession of the carrying place of Niagara and Lake Ontario.

From Niagara, Mr. Picquet went to the carrying place, which is six leagues from that post. He visited on the same day the famous Fall of Niagara, by which the four great Canada lakes discharge themselves into Lake Ontario. This cascade is as prodigious by its height and the quantity of water which falls there, as by the variety of its falls, which are to the number of six principal ones divided by a small island, leaving three to the north and three to the south. They produce of themselves a singular symmetry and wonderful effect. He measured the height of one of those falls from the south side, and he found it about one hundred and forty feet.* The establishment at this carrying place, the most important in a commercial point of view, was the worst stocked. The Indians, who came there in great numbers, were in the best disposition to trade; but not finding what they wanted, they went to Choueguen or Choëguenn [Oswego], at the mouth of the river of the same name. M. Picquet counted there as many as fifty canoes. There was notwithstanding at Niagara a trading house, where the commandant and trader lodged; but it was too small, and the King's property was not safe there.

M. Picquet negotiated with the Senecas, who promised to repair to his mission, and gave him twelve children as hostages; saying to him that their parents had nothing dearer to them, and followed him immediately, as well as the chief of the Little Rapid with all his family.

The young Indians who accompanied Picquet had spoken of this old man as a veritable apostle. M. Picquet withdrew with him to say his breviary; and the savagès and the Sonnotoans, without losing time, assembled themselves to hold council with M. de Touraine, who addressed them for some time at length, and said:

"You savages and the Sonnotoans know your firmness in your resolutions, and know that you have designed to pass by Choëguen [Oswego] in returning. Let me request you at once that you attempt to do nothing. They are informed of the bad disposition of the English, whom you regard as the formidable enemy of their colony, and as the one that has done them the most harm. They are disposed to destroy themselves, rather than that you should suffer the least harm; but all this amounts to nothing, and the savages will always lose by the approaches of this people who hate you. As for myself, added M. de Touraine, I entreat you earnestly not to pass that way. The Indians have told me nothing more."

M. Picquet immediately replied: *Ethonciaouin* (that is, as you desire, my children).

He set out with all those savages to return to Fort Niagara. M. Chabert de Joncaire would not abandon him. At each place where they encountered camps, cabins and entrepots, they were saluted with musquetry by the Indians, who never ceased testifying their consideration for the missionary. M. Picquet took the lead with the savages of the

* These are French feet. The falls on the American side are 164 feet high.—Burr's Atlas Intiod. p. 31.

hills; Messrs. Joncaire and Rigouille following with the recruits. He embarked with thirty-nine savages in his large canoe, and was received on arriving at the fort with the greatest ceremony, even with the discharge of cannon, which greatly pleased the Indians. On the morrow he assembled the Senecas, for the first time, in the chapel of the fort for religious services.

M. Picquet returned along the south coast of Lake Ontario. Alongside of Choëguen, a young Seneca met her uncle who was coming from his village with his wife and children. This young girl spoke so well to her uncle, though she had but little knowledge of religion, that he promised to repair to La Presentation early the following spring, and that he hoped to gain over also seven other cabins of Senecas of which he was chief. Twenty-five leagues from Niagara he visited the river Gascouchagou,* where he met a number of rattlesnakes. The young Indians jumped into the midst of them and killed forty-two without having been bitten by any.

He next visited the falls of this river. The first which appear in sight in ascending, resemble much the great cascade at Saint Cloud, except that they have not been ornamented and do not seem so high, but they possess natural beauties which render them very curious. The second, a quarter of a mile higher, are less considerable, yet are remarkable. The third, also a quarter of a league higher, has beauties truly admirable by its curtains and falls which form also, as at Niagara, a charming proportion and variety. They may be one hundred and some feet high.† In the intervals between the falls, there are a hundred little cascades, which present likewise a curious spectacle; and if the altitudes of each chute were joined together, and they made but one as at Niagara, the height would, perhaps, be four hundred feet; but there is four times less water than at the Niagara Fall, which will cause the latter to pass, for ever, as a wonder perhaps unique in the world.

The English, to throw disorder into this new levy, sent a good deal of brandy. Some savages did, in fact, get drunk, whom M. Picquet could not bring along. He therefore desired much that Choëguen were destroyed and the English prevented rebuilding it; and in order that we should be absolutely masters of the south side of Lake Ontario, he proposed erecting a fort near there at the bay of the Cayugas,‡ which would make a very good harbor and furnish very fine anchorage. No place is better adapted for a fort.

He examined attentively the fort of Choëguen, a post the most pernicious to France that the English could erect. It was commanded almost from all sides and could be very easily approached in time of war. It was a two story very low building; decked like a ship and surmounted on the top by a gallery; the whole was surrounded by a stone wall, flanked only with two bastions at the side towards the nearest hill. Two batteries, each of three twelve pounders, would have been more than sufficient to reduce that establishment to ashes. It was prejudicial to us by the facility it afforded the English of communicating with all the tribes of Canada, still more than by the trade carried on there as well by the French of the colony as by the savages: for Choëguen was supplied with merchandize adapted only to the French, at least as much

---

* The Genesee river. In Belin's map of *Partie Occidentale de la Nouvelle France*, 1755, (No. 902. W C. State Lib.) it is described as a " River unknown to Geographers, filled with Rapids and Waterfalls."

† The highest fall on the river is 105 feet.

‡ Sodus bay.

as with what suited to the savages,· a circumstance that indicated an
illicit trade. Had the minister's orders been executed, the Choëguen
trade, at least with the savages of Upper Canada, would be almost ruined.
But it was necessary to supply Niagara, especially the Portage, rather
than Toronto. The difference between the two first of these posts and
the last is, that three or four hundred canoes could come loaded with
furs to the Portage, and that no canoes could go to Toronto, except those
which can not pass before Niagara and to Fort Frontenac, such as the
Otaois of the head of the lake (*Fond du Lac*) and the Mississagues; so
that Toronto could not but diminish the trade of these two antient posts,
which would have been sufficient to stop all the savages had the stores
been furnished with goods to their liking. There was a wish to imitate
the English in the trifles they sold the savages, such as silver bracelets,
etc. The Indians compared and weighed them, as the storekeeper at
Niagara stated, and the Choëguen bracelets which were found as heavy,
of a purer silver, and more elegant, did not cost them two beavers, whilst
those at the king's posts wanted to sell them for ten beavers. Thus we
were discredited, and this silver ware remained a pure loss in the king's
stores. French brandy was preferred to the English, but that did not
prevent the Indians going to Choëguen. To destroy the trade the king's
posts ought to have been supplied with the same goods as Choëguen
and at the same price. The French ought also have been forbidden to
send the domiciliated Indians thither: but that would have been very
difficult.

Mr. Picquet next returned to Frontenac. Never was a reception more
imposing. The Nipissings and Algonquins who were going to war with
M. de Bellestre, drew up in a line, of their own accord, above Fort
Frontenac, where three standards were hoisted. They fired several
volleys of musketry and cheered incessantly. They were answered in
the same style from all the little craft of bark. M. de Verchere and M.
de la Valtrie caused the guns of the fort to be discharged at the same
time, and the Indians transported with joy at the honors paid them also
kept up a continual fire with shouts and acclamations which made every
one rejoice. The commandants and officers received our missionary at
the landing. No sooner had he debarked than all the Algonquins and
Nipissings of the lake came to embrace him, saying that they had been
told that the English had arrested him, and had that news been confirmed they would soon have themselves relieved him. Finally, when
he returned to La Presentation, he was received with that affection, that
tenderness which children would experience in recovering a father
whom they had lost.

In 1753, M. Picquet repaired to France to render an account of his
labors, and solicit assistance for the benefit of the colony. He took with
him three natives, the appearance of whom might create an interest in
the success of his establishments, and who, in the quality of hostages,
might serve to control the mission during his absence. The nations
there assembled consented to it, and even appeared to desire it, as well
as the chiefs of the colony. He conducted his savages to Paris, and to
the court, where they were received with so much kindness and attention that they said without ceasing, that could their nations know as well
as themselves, the character and the goodness of the French, they would
not fail to be otherwise than of the same heart and interests with that of
France.

While M. Picquet was in Paris, in 1754, M. Rouillé, then minister of
the marine, caused him to draw up sundry memoirs, especially a general
memoir upon Canada, in which he suggested infallible means for pre_

serving this colony to France. He also made observations upon the disturbances which certain inquiet spirits, rash and boisterous, had occasioned in Canada. The minister highly approved of them, and assured him that he would write to the general, to prevent in future the recurrence of like disorders, which could not fail to be pernicious in a colony still weak, and too distant from succors should they be necessary.

The minister wished to give him a pension of a thousand crowns, but M. de Laport, the first steward, conferred it upon the Abbé Maillard. The minister was displeased, while M. Picquet had only the pleasure of receiving a thousand crowns, of which in truth the ordinance was conceived in terms the most honorable. The king presented him some books, and when he took his leave, the minister said to him, "*Your majesty still gives you new marks of his pleasure.*"

The king always evinced the same sentiments towards him whenever he took occasion to mention him at Versailles or at Bellevue.

Meanwhile M. de Laporte was displeased with this journey of the Abbé Picquet, because it was leaving the other ecclesiastic jealous of the impression which this abbé was making with the court and the city. He restrained him from continually exhibiting his savages, and attempted to justify himself in what he had done.

At length he departed at the close of April, 1754, and returned to la Presentation with two missionaries.

The sojourn of the three natives in France produced a very good effect among the nations of Canada.

War was no sooner declared in 1754, than the new children of God, of the king, and of M. Picquet, thought only of giving fresh proofs of their fidelity and valor, as those of the Lake of the Two Mountains had done in the war preceding. The generals were indebted to M. Picquet for the destruction of all the forts as well on the river Corlac (Corlear) as on that of Choëguen. His Indians distinguished themselves especially at Fort George on Lake Ontario, where the warriors of La Presentation alone, with their bark canoes, destroyed the English fleet, commanded by Capt. Beccan, who was made prisoner with a number of others, and that in sight of the French army, commanded by M. de Villiers, who was at the Isle Galop. The war parties which departed and returned continually, filled the mission with so many prisoners that their numbers frequently surpassed that of the warriors, rendering it necessary to empty the villages and send them to Headquarters. In fine a number of other expeditions of which M. Picquet was the principal author, have procured the promotion of several officers, notwithstanding some have declared that there were neither honors, nor pensions, nor favors, nor promotions, nor marks of distinction, conferred by the king upon those who had served in Canada, who were prevented from receiving these by M. Picquet.

M. du Quesne, on the occasion of the army of General Braddock, recommended him to send as large a detachment of savages as was possible, and gave him on this occasion full powers. In fact, the exhortations which M. Picquet made them to give an example of zeal and courage for the king their father, and the instructions which he gave them produced, in short, the entire defeat of this general of the enemy, in the summer of 1755, near Fort Du Quesne, upon the Ohio.

This event, which conferred more honor upon the arms of the king than all the rest of the war, is due principally to the care which M. Picquet bestowed upon the execution of the commands of M. the Marquis du Quesne in this expedition, and by the choice which he made of warriors equally faithful and intrepid.

The assurance which he gave them, that they should conquer the enemy, so warmed their imaginations, that they thought in the combat that they saw the missionary at their head, cheering them on and promising them victory, although he was distant from them almost a hundred and fifty leagues; it was one of their superstitions, which he had taken pains to impart to them.

He frequently found himself in the vanguard when the king's troops were ordered to attack the enemy. He distinguished himself particularly in the expeditions of Sarasto (Saratoga), Lake Champlain, Pointe a la Chevelure (Crown Point), the Cascades, Carillon (Ticonderoga), Choëguen (Oswego), River Corlac (Mohawk), Isle au Galop, etc. The posts he established for the king protected the colony pending the entire war. M. du Quesne said that the Abbé Picquet was worth more than ten regiments.

He wrote to him on the 23d of September, 1754:

"I shall never forget as a good citizen, I shall remember as long as I live, the proofs which you have given me of your generosity, and for your unquenchable zeal for all that concerns the public good."

On the 9th of June, 1755, M. DuQuesne, upon the point of departing, sent word to him that the English thought of abandoning Niagara. He added, "the precautions to be taken must all emanate from your zeal, prudence and, foresight."

The English then endeavored, as well by menaces as by promises, to gain the savages, especially after the lesson which Du Quesne had given them at the Belle rivière (of the Ohio).

In the month of May, 1756, M. de Vaudreuil got M. Picquet to depute the chiefs of his mission to the Five Nations of Senecas, Cayugas, Onontaqués, Tuscaroras, and Oneidas to attach them more and more to the French. The English had surprised and killed their nephews in the three villages of the *Loups* (Mohegans?) M. de Vaudreuil requested him to form parties which could succeed each other in disquieting and harassing the English. He asked of him his projects in forming a camp; he prayed him to give a free expression to his ideas, and exhibited on his side the greatest confidence, and made him a part of all the operations which he proposed to undertake; and declared that the success of his measures was the work of M. Picquet.

The letters of M. de Vaudreuil from 1756 to 1759, which are among the papers of our missionary, are filled with these evidences of his confidence and satisfaction; but as those of M. Picquet are not to be found, it would be difficult to find wherewith to make a history of these events, of which alone M. Picquet has the greatest part.

In proportion as our circumstances became more embarrassing, the zeal of M. Picquet became more precious and more active.

In 1758, he destroyed the English forts on the banks of Corlac, but at length the battle of the 13th of September, 1759, in which the Marquis of Montcalm was killed, brought ruin on Quebec, and that of Canada followed. When he saw all thus lost, M. Picquet terminated his long and laborious career by his retreat on the 8th May, 1760, with the advice and consent of the General, the Bishop and Intendant, in order not to fall into the hands of the English.

The esteem which he had gained by his merit, the praises which in an especial manner he had received, might have induced him to remain there, but he had resolved never to swear allegiance to another power. Inducements were held out as motives by many French, by missionaries and by the savages themselves, who proposed to engage him, and labored to make him see the advantages that would result.

He still hoped to take with him in his retreat the grenadiers of each battalion, according to the advice of M. the Marquis de Lévis, to thus preserve the colors and the honor of their corps, but of this he was not the master.

He had the materials of subsistence abundantly, but was obliged to content himself with twenty-five Frenchmen who accompanied him as far as Louisiana, and he thus escaped with them from the English, although he had been the most exposed during the war, and although he did not receive the least help in so long a journey; but he had with him two little detachments of savages, one of which preceded him several leagues and the other accompanied him, who were successively relieved by similar detachments, as he passed through different tribes.

Those whom he left he sent each to his own nation, and advised them as a father. Every where they received him admirably, notwithstanding the deplorable circumstances in which he was in; every where he found the natives with the best dispositions, and he received their protestations of zeal and inviolable attachment to the king their father.

He passed to Michilimachina, between Lake Huron and Lake Michigan, but the savages, consisting of Iroquois or Algonquins, here left him, that M. Picquet might not be embarrassed from this cause;* proceeded thus by way of Upper Canada to the Illinois country and Louisiana, and sojourned twenty-two months at New Orleans.

Here he occupied himself in recovering his spirits, in quelling a sort of civil war which had sprung up between the governor and the inhabitants, and in preaching peace, both in public and in private.

He had the satisfaction of seeing this happily restored, during his sojourn.

General Amherst in taking possession of Canada, immediately informed himself of the place where M. Picquet had taken refuge, and upon the assurance which was given him that he had departed on his return to France by the west, he said haughtily; "I am mistaken in him, if this Abbé had not been less faithful to the King of England, had he taken the oath of allegiance to him, as had been to the King of France. We would then have given him all our confidence, and gained him to ourselves."

This General was mistaken. M. Picquet had an ardent love for his country, and he could not have adopted another.

Soon the English would have finished by proscribing him and offering a reward for his head, as a dangerous enemy.

Meanwhile the English themselves, have contributed to establish the glory and the services of this useful missionary; we read in one of their Gazettes: " *The Jesuit of the west has detached all the nations from us, and placed them in the interests of France.* " They called him a *Jesuit* because they had not then seen his girdle, nor the buttons of his cassock, as M. De Galissonniere wrote to him jocosely, in sending him the extract of their Gazette; or to speak seriously, the zeal of the Jesuits so well known in the new world, makes them believe that out of so great a number of missionaries, there can be none but Jesuits. They are represented as the authors of all the losses of the English, and the advantages which the French have gained over them. Some even insinuate that they possess supernatural powers. In short, our enemies believed themselves lost, when they were in the army, on account of the horde of savages that always attended them.

---

* I have much desired to find in his papers, his memoirs upon the customs of Canada; but I have heard M. Picquet say, that this subject was well treated of in the works of Father Lafitau, who had dwelt five years at the Sant St. Louis, near Montreal.—*Note in the Original.*

They spoke of nothing but of *Picquet, and of his good luck;* and this became even a proverb throughout the colony.

An English officer, having wished to make himself conspicuous, once offered a bounty for his head, whereupon the savages conspired to seize this English chief; he was led into their presence, and they danced around him with their tomahawks, awaiting the signal of the missionary, who made it not, in his courtesy to an enemy.

Thus did he endeavor, by every possible means, to act neutral, at least between the English and the French.

They had recourse to the mediation of the savages, and offered to allow him freely to preach the catholic faith to the nations, and even to domiciliated Europeans,—to pay him two thousand crowns pension, with all the assistance necessary for establishing himself;—to ratify the concession of Lake Ganenta and its environs; a charming place which the six cantons of the Iroquois had presented to M. Picquet, in a most illustrious council, which they had held at the Château of Quebec. The belts, which are the contracts of these nations, were deposited at his ancient mission, the Lake of Two Mountains; but he constantly declared that he preferred the stipend which the King gave him, and that all the overtures that could be made, and all the advantages that could be offered by a foreign power, were vain; that the idea of neutrality, under the circumstances, was idle, and an outrage upon his fidelity; in a word, that the thought itself was horrible. That he could make his fortunes without them, and that his character was very remote from this species of cupidity. The services, the fidelity, and the disinterestedness of father Picquet, merited for him a higher destiny.

Likewise the generals, commandants, and the troops, failed not by military honors, to evince their esteem and their respect for him, in a decisive manner, and worthy of the nature of his services. He received these honors as well from the army as at Quebec, Montreal, Three Rivers, and at all the forts which he passed, and even at the Cedars, notwithstanding the jealousy of certain menial subjects, such as M. De * * *, who had sought to tarnish the glory of the missionary; but he had been too vindictive in his assaults, to effect his object.

We have seen him at Bourg even, a long time after, receive tokens of veneration and regard from the officers of regiments who had seen him in Canada.

We see rendered in many letters of the ministers, similar testimonials rendered to his zeal and success. They give him the more credit, because they saw his anxieties of heart, under the obstacles he had to surmount, and upon the ancient hostility of these nations, who had been almost perpetually at war, but their experience with the English had led them to bestow their attachment upon the French, in proof of which the conduct of these people for a long time after the war was cited.

We see in the work of T. Raynal (vol. vii, p. 292), that the savages had a marked predilection for the French; that the missionaries were the principal cause of this; and that he says that this fact is especially applicable to the Abbé Picquet.

To give probability to what he says of his services, allow me to quote the testimony which he rendered in 1769, to the governor-general, after his return to France, and the loss of Canada.

" We, Marquis du Quesne, commander of the royal and military order of Saint Louis, chief of the squadron of the naval arm, ancient lieutenant-general, commandent of New France, and the governments of Louisburgh and Louisiana:

Certify, that upon the favorable testimony which we have received in

Canada, of the services of the Abbé Picquet, missionary of the king among savage nations; upon the confidence which our predecessors in this colony have bestowed upon him; and the great reputation which he has acquired by the fine establishments which he has formed for the king, the numerous and supernatural conversions of infidels, which he has attached not less to the state than to religion, by his zeal, his disinterestedness, his talents, and his activity, for the good of the service of His Majesty; that we have employed him on different objects of the same service, during the whole period of our administration as governor-general, and that he has always acted equal to our expectations, and ever beyond our hope.

He has equally served religion and the state, with incredible success, during nearly thirty years.

He had directly rendered the king absolute master of the national assembles of four nations who composed his first mission to the Lake of Two Mountains, with liberty to nominate all their chiefs at his will. He had caused all the chiefs of the nations which composed his last mission, at la Presentation, to swear allegiance and fidelity to His Majesty; and at these places he created most admirable establishments; in a word, he has rendered himself so much more worthy of our notice, that he would rather return to Canada, and continue his labors, than to live in his country, and recover the heritage of his parents, who have disowned him, as we have learned, for his not wishing to live in France, ten years since, when he was accompanied by three savages.

We would detail the important services which this abbé has rendered, if His Majesty or his ministers require it, and render justice to whom it is due, to obtain of the king those marks of approbation which are deserved; in the faith of which we have signed the present certificate, and sealed it with our arms.

Signed,   THE MARQUIS DU QUESNE.

M. de Vaudreuil, governor and lieutenant-general for the king in all of New France, certified the same in 1765, that M. Picquet had served nearly thirty years in this colony, with all the zeal and distinction possible, as well in relation to the direct interests of the state, as relatively to those of religion; that his talents for gaining the good will of the savages, his resources in critical moments, and his activity, have uniformly entitled him to the praises and the confidence of the governors and the bishops: that above all, he had proved useful by his services in the late war, by sundry negotiations with the Iroquois, and the domiciliated nations; by the establishments which he had formed, and which had been of great service, by the indefatigable and incessant care which he had taken to keep the savages fortified in their attachment to the French, and at the same time confirmed in their Christianity.

M. de Bougainville, celebrated by his maritime expeditions, and who participated in the first acts of the war in Canada, certified in 1760, that M. Picquet, king's missionary, known by the establishments which he had made alike serviceable to religion and the state, in all the campaigns in which he had been with him, had contributed by his zeal, his activity, and his talents, to the good of the service of the king, and to the glory of his arms; and his standing among savage tribes, and his personal services had been of the greatest service, as well in military as political affairs.

All those who had returned from Canada, labored to make appreciated the services so long and so constantly rendered to France during nearly thirty years, and to make known the merit of a citizen, who had expatriated himself to gratify the inclinations of his heart, who had sacrificed his youth, his heritage, and all the flattering hopes of France, who had exposed a thousand and a thousand times his life, preserving often the subjects of the king, and the glory of his arms, and who could himself say that he had nothing in his actions, but the glory of France, during his residence in Canada, in which he had spent much of his life.

His services had not the same result in the last war for the preservation of Canada, but the brilliant and almost incredible actions by which he contributed to it, have not the less preserved, with the savages, the notion and the high idea of French valor, and possible this feeling may here after result to our advantage.

I would wish to be able to report all of the letters of ministers, governors-general and private persons, of bishops, of intendants, and of other persons in authority, who witnessed with surprise the projects, the negotiations, and the operations of which this missionary had the charge, the congratulations which he received on his successes, as prompt as they were inspiring, upon his resources, upon the expedients which he suggested, his zeal and his experience in critical situations, and which his activity always put into execution.

I have often asked him to make a history of them, that should be alike curious and honorable for France.

We find a part of these letters among his papers; I have there seen among others, those of M. de Montcalm, who called him *" My dear and very worthy patriarch of the Five nations."*

M. the marquis de Lévis, desired especially to make known the labors and the successes of M. Picquet, of which he had been a witness, and which he had admired both for their disinterestedness, as well for regard to France as against the English, after the conquest of Canada; and I have witnessed the solicitations which M. de Lévis made to excite his ambition, or direct towards some important place, a zeal which was worthy of a bishopric.

The evidence of his ecclesiastical superiors, was not less favorable to the zeal of our missionary. The bishop of Quebec in 1760, departing for Europe, after having visited the new mission which M. Picquet had founded among the Iroquois, and where he had baptized more than a hundred adults, enjoined upon all the priests of his diocese, to aid him as much as they might be able; he conferred upon him all his powers, even those of approving the other priests, and of absolving from censures, reserved to the sovereign Pontiff.

M. Picquet after returning from France, passed several years in Paris, but a portion of his time was engaged in exercising the ministry of all the suburbs, where the archbishop of Paris deemed that he could be most useful. His alacrity for labor fixed him a long time at Mount Vallérien, where he erected a parish church.

He had been compelled to make a journey to sell books, which the king had presented him in 1754, which had survived the treatment he had experienced in Canada, and although he was reduced to a very small patrimony, he failed to employ his activity in obtaining the recompenses he had so well merited.

Meanwhile the general assembly of the clergy of 1765, offered him a gratuity of twelve hundred livres, and charged M. the archbishop of Rheims, and M. the archbishop of Arles, to solicit for him a recompense from the king.

The assembly next ensuing in 1770, gave him also a similar gratuity, but his departure from Paris interrupted the success of the hopes which his friends had entertained of the recompenses from the court.

6;

In 1772, he wished to retire to Bresse, where a numerous family desired it, and urged it with much earnestness.

He afterwards went to Verjon, where he caused to be built a house, with the view of making an establishment for the education of young people. He preached, he catechised, he confessed, and his zeal was never so much manifested.

The chapter of Bourg, decreed him the title of honorary canon. The ladies de la Visitation, asked him to become their director, and they thus attracted him to the capital of the province.

In 1777 he made a journey to Rome, where his reputation had preceded him, and where the Holy Father received him as a missionary worthy of being held dear by the church, and presented him with a gratuity of five thousand livres for his journey.

They there made the ineffectual endeavors to detain him; he returned to Bresse, and carried thither relics which he displayed for the veneration of the faithful, in the collegiate church at Bourg.

The reputation of the Abbey of Cluny, and the friendship which M. Picquet felt towards one of his nephews, established at Cluny, brought him to this habitation, so celebrated in Christianity. He purchased for himself, about 1779, a house and plat of land, which he wished to improve, but in 1781, he repaired with a sister to Verjon, for the settlement of affairs, where he was repeatedly attacked by an obstinate cold, and by a hemorrage, which reduced him considerably; and also by a kind of dropsy; lastly a hernior, which had existed a long time, became aggravated and caused his death, on the 15th of July; 1781.

M. Picquet had a very prepossessing and commanding figure, and a countenance open and engaging. He possessed a gay and cheerful humor. Notwithstanding the austerity of his manners, he exhibited nothing but gaiety, which he turned to account in his designs. He was a theologian, an orator, and a poet, be sung and composed songs in French, as well as in Iroquois, with which he interested and amused the savages. He was a child with one, and a hero with others. His mechanical ingenuity was often admired by the natives. In short, he resorted to every means to attract proselytes, and to attach them to him, and he accordingly had all the success which can reward industry, talents, and zeal.

It is thus I have thought best to make known a compatriot and a friend, worthy of being offered, as an example to incite those who are burning with zeal for religion and for their country.

Picquet was as much an object of abhorrence by the English, as he was of esteem by the French, a very natural result from the active partizan spirit which he evinced, and the zeal and success with which he prosecuted his plans for the aggrandizement of his faith, and his allegiance, which appear to have been equally the object of his ambition, and the aim and end of his life. Having given in the above biographical notice his memoirs drawn up in that florid style of paneygric, so common with the people and the age in which it was written, we will quote from an English historian of the French war. (Thos. Mante, in a work entitled The History of the Late War in America, London, 1772, quarto, page 231.) It is probably as much biased by prejudice, as the other by partiality.

" As to the Abbé Picquet, who distinguished himself so much by his brutal zeal, as he did not expose himself to any danger, he received no injury; and he yet lives, justly despised to such a degree by every one who knows any thing of his past conduct in America, that scarce any officer will admit him to his table.

However repugnant it must be to every idea of honor and humanity, not to give quarter to an enemy when subdued, it must be infinitely more so, not to spare women and children. Yet such had often been the objects of the Abbé Picquet's cruel advice, enforced by the most barbarous examples, especially in the English settlements on the back of Virginia and Pennsylvania."

To adopt either of these as a true account of the character of Picquet, would be equally unjust. Now that the times and circumstances in which he lived, have both passed away, and even the consequences resulting from his actions, have ceased to exist, we may perhaps from the data before us, in view of the times and the circumstances in which he acted, deduce the following conclusion:

That he was actuated by a controlling belief of the importance and the truth of the religion which he labored with such zeal to establish, and that this was the ruling passion of his life. That his energy and ability for the promotion of this object, at times led him to disregard the common claims of humanity, and to the performance of acts derogatory to our nature, and abhorred by civilized man.

That he evinced a capacity for the transaction of business and the promotion of the interests of his government, highly creditable to his character, and such as to entitle him to the esteem in which he was held by those in authority; and that especially in the selection of a location for a new settlement, which was the great act of his life, he proved himself the possessor of a sound mind, and a capacity for judiciously combining and comparing, the probable effects of causes, which must have made a prominent station of the post he selected.

The prophecy that a beautiful town might hereafter be built on the elevated plain opposite his fort, has been fully realized in the present village of Ogdensburgh, which the combination of favorable causes now existing, is destined soon to give a rank second to but few on our inland waters.

The portrait of Picquet is preserved at the Sulpician Mission of the Lake of Two Mountains, the scene of his early labors, and first success as a missionary. Picquet was succeeded in the mission of La Presentation, by Le Garde, a Sulpician, concerning whom the author has been unable to learn any particulars.

A French writer, whose initials only are given, (S— de C—) has left a memoir upon the war in Canada, and the affairs of that province from 1749 till 1760, which was published under the direction of the Literary and Historical Society of Quebec, in 1835, and which makes frequent mention of the post at Oswegatchie. From this work we will translate a few extracts.

The rancor with which he assails Picquet, almost leads us to believe that he was actuated by a personal enmity, although it appears not to have been limited to this missionary, but to have been directed towards the religious establishments of the country in general.

We shall endeavor to preserve the spirit of the original, in our translation. We are thus furnished with two versions of the conduct of Picquet; and prevented from being misled by an ex-parte narrative, like that which Lalande the astronomer, has given us.

"Thus M. de la Jonquière, persuaded that peace could not long continue, labored to inspire the savages with a hatred to the English; and especially endeavored to attach the five nations or Iroquois. These people had been always distinguished by their bravery; the French had waged with them long and cruel wars, and the inhabitants had been compelled to labor arms in hand, as we see in the history of Charlevoix, a jesuit, who has written an ecclesiastical history of this country.

This nation is divided into five branches, named the Onontagués, the Goyoguins, the Stonnontowans, [Senecas,] the Anniers, [Mohawks,] and the domiciliated tribes.

The Onondagas dwell upon a lake, at no great distance from the Mohawk river, in a fertile country, and the English pretend that it belongs to them. The Goyogowins, and the Stonnontowans, are a little beyond in the same direction, and approaching Niagara. The Anniers dwell upon the river Mohawk, not far from a dwelling belonging to Mr. Johnson, an English officer, who understands the Indian language, and has been very active during this war. The others reside at the Saut St. Louis, three leagues from Montreal; some at a place called la Presentation, and some at the lake of Two Mountains.

The general can well rely upon the fidelity of those who dwell near him, but it is not so of the others. Their cantons situated as we have seen, above, furnish in one way and another, difficulties not easy to surmount.

M. the Abbé Picquet, priest of the Seminary of St. Sulpice, was to this canton, what the Abbé de Laloutre, was to Acadia. He had as much ambition as he had, but he turned it to a different account.* He understood the Iroquois language, and this gave him a great advantage, and enabled him to put on foot the negotiations which he wished with the five nations, to draw them to our cause, and engage them to come and dwell with us. This Abbé, who could not endure the restraint of the seminary, was very willing to seize an occasion like that which offered, of freeing himself, and of forming a community over which he might rule and reign. He labored to decoy the five nations, and to form upon the River Cataraqui, or Frontenac, above the rapids, a village.

The place which he selected for his establishment, announced his little genius, and caused the fort which he had built to be called Picket's Folly; as for himself he called it la Presentation, of which we here insert a plan.

---

* Hocquart has given him the title of the *Apostle of the Iroquois*, and the English called him the *Jesuit of the West.*—[*Note in the original.*]

When the Abbé Picquet had assembled some families, he talked of building a fort, under the pretext of protecting them, and they sent him a Commandant, and a magazine guard, and enjoined it upon the commandant, to have much regard for the Abbé, and placed him, so to speak, under his tutelage, and gave full permission to this priest to conduct and administer the magazines; in short everything was under his orders.

This priest meanwhile did not prosper much, and it was felt that there was great difficulty in inducing the Iroquois to leave a fat and fertile country, to come and fix themselves upon an uncultivated tract, and to beg for their life of a priest. It was for this reason that de la Jonquière the elder, was sent to go and remain among them, and in the village which he might deem the most convenient for his negotiations, and they gave him a brevet of captain, without a company, to the end that he might not be disturbed in his residence, on account of his services.

There could not. have been chosen a more suitable person to remain with them. He understood their language perfectly, and for a long time had lived among them, as one of their number, and although he had been married in Canada, he had among the Iroquois many children; and in short, he had been as it were, adopted among them, and was regarded as one of their nation.

He had his cabin. His instructions were to second the Abbé Picquet, in his project, and above all to induce the Mohawks to leave entirely, the vicinity of the English, and to offer them such inducements, and advantages as they desired, to make them abandon their settlements, and come and live with us. If indeed he had been able to succeed in this, there can be no doubt that the remainder of the five nations would have followed their example. They alone were directly attached to the English, who had all along preserved in them a hostility to our nation. But Mr. Johnson, who was not ignorant of the designs of the French, laboured on the contrary, to maintain them in the alliance of his nation.

The Jesuits who had always sought their own aggrandizement, under the pious pretext of instructing the people, had not failed to seek to establish themselves in Canada.

Wishing to remain the sole masters they crossed, as much as possible, the Récollets in their projects of returning to the country, after the English had restored Canada, [in the treaty of St. Germain in 1632.] From the earliest times that these fathers, (the Jesuits,) were established in the country, they detached some of their number, to go and preach the gospel to the savages. They followed them in their marches, but wearied with their wandering life, which agreed not with their designs, which they had to accumulate large properties, they took great care to endeavor to establish their neophytes, without embarrassing themselves by those whom they abandoned.

They made great account of their zeal at the court, and showed large numbers of converts, and under the specious pretext of uniting them, to civilize them,* they demanded concessions of lands, and pensions. The court persuaded of the justice of their demands, accorded both the one and the other.

It was thus that they acquired the Seigniories of Charlesbourg; New and Old Lorette; Rastican, and the Prairie de la Magdeliene, and others, which are very well established, and of considerable repute. These concessions were given them under the titles of Seigneurie et ventes. (lods et ventes.) * * *

* The author in the MSS. neither renders justice to the motives, nor the conduct, of the Jesuits.—[Note in the original.]

The village of the Saut St. Louis, is situated upon the south bank of the river St. Lawrence, three leagues above Montreal. It is inhabited by Iroquois. The Jesuits have there a very fine and flourishing mission. Father Tournois governs this mission, and like a good Jesuit, puts the profit to his own interest, and that of his order. This seigniory has been directly assigned to the Iroquois; but the Jesuits had obtained subsequently to the Indians, a title of concession under the pretense of preventing the savages from going to Montreal to buy merchandize, where brandy was often given them, and to prevent them from drinking this liquor."

We find among the Bradstreet and Amherst MSS. (State Library,) a communication from the former, dated at Schenectady, Dec. 15, 1775, in which he complains of the danger there will be of depending upon the interest which Sir William Johnson was expected to secure, with the aid of £5000 sterling which had been given him in the spring of that year to be laid out among the six nations, exclusive of those who had settled at Swegache. He complains of this as very unwise because these Indians were in the frequent practice of visiting their relatives and urging them to espouse the cause of the French. The consequence was that great numbers who had early in the season been favorably inclined, became settled in their attachment to the enemies of the English.

The scalping parties fitted out at la Presentation, which proved so harrassing to the English settlements along the Mohawk river, and the frontier of New York during the year 1758-9, at length led to an attempt by Brigadier General Gage, in 1957, to put a stop to these outrages, by crushing the fortress from whence they issued.

This General had been instructed " in case Niagara should be reduced, to take post immediately at a place called by the French la Galette, near the entrance of the river St. Lawrence, and as soon as General Amherst was informed of the above event, he sent Major Christie to Brigadier Gage to enforce those orders, as by that means the English on the Mohawk river, would be as effectually free from the inroads of the enemy's scalping parties, and be enabled to live in as much security as the inhabitants of any part of the country, between Crown Point and New York, had already been. But however necessary it might be to take possession of this post, the difficulties which would attend the doing of it, appeared to Brigadier Gage so great, that he thought proper to make the General acquainted with them, and in the mean time defer the execution of his orders to a more favorable opportunity.

As the General deemed the post an object of the first consequence, he was greatly chagrined at the account from Brigadier Gage, especially as the season would be too far advanced before his orders, if he renewed them, could reach Brigadier Gage, for the Brigadier to execute them, he, therefore was obliged to postpone this necessary business to another campaign.[*]

The French fortress at Quebec, was reduced by the English army under the command of General Wolfe, in 1759.

The various French posts in the interior, still remained, and to complete the conquest three expeditions were fitted out early in the season of 1760. One of these ascended the St. Lawrence from Quebec, another proceeded towards Montreal by way of Lake Champlain, and the third, under Sir Jeffery Amherst, proceeded by way of Oswego, and down the St. Lawrence, encountering in its way the strong fortress on Isle Royal which he reduced. The details of this event, as related by Mante, the historian of that war, are here given. (P. 300.)

"The necessary preparations having been made to bring the whole power of the British forces in North America against Montreal, in order to finish by its reduction the war in this part of the world; and the season being sufficiently advanced to enable Sir Jeffery Amherst, the commander-in-chief, to commence his part of the operations, he embarked at New York on the 3d of May, and proceeded to Schenectady. From thence with a part of his army, he pursued his route to Oswego, where he encamped on the 9th of July. The remainder he ordered to follow with the greatest diligence, under the command of Brigadier Gage. On the 14th two vessels hove in sight on Lake Ontario, which proving to be those that had been fitted out at Niagara, under the command of Captain Loring, boats were immediately dispatched to him, with orders to look out for, and attack the French vessels cruising on the lake. On the 20th, two more vessels appeared, and proving to be the French vessels which had escaped Captain Loring's vigilance, a small boat was immediately dispatched to cruise for him, with an account of this discovery; and, at the same time, to prevent his being obliged to return to Oswego, for want of provisions, the General ordered Captain Willyamoz, with a detachment of one hundred and thirty men, in twelve boats, to take post on the Isle-Aux-Iroquois, and supply Captain Loring with everything he might want. On the 22d, Brigadier Gage arrived with the rear of the army; as did Sir William Johnson on the 23d, with a party of Indians.

On the 24th, the General received intelligence, that the French vessels had escaped into the river St. Lawrence, and that Captain Loring was returning with the Onondaga, and the Mohawk, of eighteen six pounders.

On the fifth of August, the General ordered the army to be in readiness to embark. It consisted of the following troops :

The first and second battalion of Royal Highlanders.
Forty-fourth regiment.
Forty-sixth.
Fifty-fifth,
Fourth battalion of the sixtieth.
Eight companies of the seventy-seventh.
Five of the eightieth.
Five hundred and ninety-seven grenadiers.
One hundred and forty-six rangers.

[*] History of the late war in North America, by Thomas Mante, p 217.

Three battalions of the New York regiment.

New Jersey regiment.

Four battalions of the Connecticut regiment, and one hundred and sixty-seven of the Royal Artillery, amounting in the whole, to ten thousand one hundred and forty-two effective men, officers included.

The Indians under Sir William Johnson, were seven hundred and six.

On the 7th Captain Loring sailed with his two vessels, and immediately after, the first battalion of Royal Highlanders, the grenadiers of the army, commanded by Lieutenant Colonel Massey, with Captain Campbell, of the forty second to assist him as Major; the light infantry, commanded by Lieutenant Colonel Amherst, with Captain Delancey as Major to assist him, with Ogden's and Whyte's companies of rangers, the whole under the command of Colonel Haldiman, embarked and sailed to take post at the entrance of the river St. Lawrence.

On the 10th, the general himself embarked, with the Royal Artillery, the regulars, Sir William Johnson and a part of his Indians, in boats and whale boats; but, the wind being very high, and the water of the lake very rough, they were forced to make for a small creek, at whose entrance there is a very dangerous bar, on which one of the artillery boats was lost. The next day, the weather being a little more moderate, the General at noon, proceeded for the river de la Motte, and on the 12th was joined by Brigadier Gage, with the provincials in a bay, where the enemy had lately encamped. On the 13th the whole embarked, and that very day encamped with Colonel Haldiman, at the post which he had taken at the head of the River St. Lawrence. Captain Loring, with his two vessels, having mistaken the channel from the lake to the River St. Lawrence, the army passed him, while he was endeavoring to extricate himself. On the 13th, the whole army gained Point de Baril, in the neighborhood of the post called La-Gallette, which Brigadier Gage was ordered to destroy the preceding year. Here the enemy had a very good dock, in which they built their vessels.

The grenadiers and light infantry, with the row-gallies, took post that day, without halting, at Oswegatchie, a few miles below Point au Baril.

All this while, one of the enemy's vessels kept hovering about the army; and as Captain Loring had not yet got into the right channel, it became necessary, for the safety of the army, either to compel this vessel to retire, or to take her.

The General was therefore obliged to order Colonel Williamson, with the row-gallies well manned, to do one or the other. On the 17th, the gallies advanced with the utmost intrepidity, under a heavy fire from the enemy; but it did not in the least dampen the ardor of the assailants; their fire was returned with such resolution and bravery, that after a severe contest of almost four hours, the French vessel struck her colors. She mounted ten twelve-pounders, and had on board one hundred men, twelve of whom were killed or wounded. The general immediately named the vessel the Williamson, in honor of the Colonel, and to perpetuate the memory of so gallant an action. The same day the army proceeded to Oswegatchie, from whence it was necessary to reconnoitre Isle-Royal, so that it was noon the next day before the army could proceed.

Fort Levi stood on this island, which was otherwise strongly fortified. Though the reduction of Fort Levi could be of little service, merely as a fort, yet it was certainly of too much consequence to be left in the rear of an army; besides, the number of pilots, perfectly acquainted with the navigation of the River St. Lawrence, which the making of the garrison prisoners would afford, was alone a sufficient motive for attacking it. It was therefore invested that very evening. Whilst the English were passing the point, the French kept up a very smart cannonade upon them, and destoyed one of the row-gallies, and a few boats, and killed two or three men; but notwithstanding this fire, and an uninterrupted continuance of it, the fort was so completely invested by the 20th, by the masterly disposition of the troops, as to make it impossible for the garrison to escape.

Captain Loring had arrived the day before, with his two vessels, and the Williamson brig, and the batteries being now ready, the general, on the 23d, determined to assault the fort, that as little time as possible might be wasted on it. He therefore ordered the vessels to fall down the stream, post themselves as close to the fort as possible, and man their tops well, in order to fall upon the enemy, and prevent their making use of their guns; whilst the grenadiers rowed in with their broadswords and tomahawks, facines and scaling ladders, under cover of three hundred of the light infantry, who were to fire into the embrasures.

The grenadiers received their orders with a cheerfulness that might be regarded as a sure omen of success; and with their usual alacrity, prepared for the attack, waiting in their shirts till the ships could take their proper stations.

This the Williamson brig, commanded by Lieutenant Sinclair, and the Mohawk, by Lieutenant Phipps, soon did; and both sustained and returned a very heavy fire. But the Onondaga, in which was Captain Loring, by some extraordinary blunder, ran a-ground. The enemy discovering his distress, plied her with such unceasing showers of great and small arms, that Captain Loring thought proper to strike his colors, and sent Thornton, his master, on shore, to the enemy, who endeavored to take possession of the vessel; but by Colonel Williamson's observing it, he turned upon them a battery, which obliged them to desist from the undertaking. The General then ordered Lieutenant Sinclair from the Williamson brig, and Lieutenant Pennington, with two detachments of grenadiers under their command, to take possession of the Onondaga, and they obeyed their orders with such undaunted resolution, that the English colors were again hoisted on board of her. But the vessel after all, could not be got off, and was therefore abandoned about midnight. The English batteries, however, put a stop to any further attempt of the enemy to board her. Captain Loring being wounded, was in the mean time sent ashore. This accident of the Onondaga's running aground, obliged the General to defer for the present his plan of assault, but this delay proved rather a fortunate event, as it saved a good deal of blood, for on the 25th, M. Pouchet, the commandant, beat a parley, demanding what terms he might expect; to which no answer was returned, but that the fort must be immediately given up, and the garrison surrendered prisoners of war, and but ten minutes were given for a reply. These terms where received within the ten minutes; and Lieutenant Colonel Massey, with the grenadiers, immediately took possession of the place.

The loss of the English before it, was twenty-one killed, and nineteen wounded. The first shot from the English battery killed the French officer of artillery. Eleven more were killed afterwards, and about forty wounded. The garrison, and all of the pilots, for the sake of whom chiefly the place had been attacked, were sent to New York; and the General named the fort, FORT WILLIAM AUGUSTUS.

On the surrender of Fort Levi, the Indians following the English army, prepared agreeably to their bloody custom, when at war, to enter the fort in order to tomahawk and massacre the garrison. But General Amherst, being apprised of their intentions, immediately sent orders to Sir William Johnson, to persuade them if possible, to desist, declaring at the same time, that, if they offered to enter the fort, he would compel them to retire. The stores he promised should be delivered to them, as his army was not in want of what few blankets might be found there; this message had its desired effect. The Indians though with great apparent reluctance, and ill humor, were prevailed on to return to their camp; however, their resentment increased to such a degree, that Sir William Johnson informed the General, he was apprehensive they would quit the army, and return to their respective villages and castles. The General replied: " That he believed his army fully sufficient for the service he was going upon, without their assistance; that, though he wished to preserve their friendship, he could not prevail on himself to purchase it at the expense of countenancing the horrid barbarities they wanted to perpetrate; and added, that, if they quitted the army, and on their return should commit any acts of cruelty, he should assuredly chastise them." Upon this most of these creatures, who amounted to about seven hundred, abandoned Sir William Johnson, and returned to their respective villages and castles, but without committing the least violence; the faithful few, in number about one hundred and seventy, who continued with the army, were afterwards distinguished by medals, which the General gave them, that they might be known at the English posts, and receive the civil treatment their humanity, and their affection for the English entitled them to.

If the French plan of policy had admitted of similar exertions of humanity towards their prisoners, there is no doubt but they might thereby have equally prevented the commission of acts, which, even had they conquered, would have been sufficient to sully the glory of their greatest achievements.

Till the 30th, the army was employed in leveling the batteries, and repairing boats and rafts for the artillery, which was now embarked with the necessary stores; and on the 31st, the General, with the first division of the army, consisting of the artillery, the grenadiers, and the light infantry, the 44th and 55th regiments, the 4th battalion of Royal Americans, and three regiments of provincials, embarked about noon, and in the evening reached the Isle-Aux-Chats, [opposite Louisville landing,] having passed the first rapids. On the 1st of September, they proceeded about ten miles further, and encamped. On the 2d, Brigadier Gage, with the other division, joined the General, having lost three Highlanders, in going over the Falls. The whole now proceeded together, entered Lake St. Francis, and that very evening reached Pointe-Aux-Boudets, where, the weather being extremely bad, the General halted. On the 3d, a prisoner was brought in, who gave intelligence that Colonel Haviland had taken possession of the Isle-Aux-Noix, the enemy having abandoned it on his approach.

The navigation of the River St. Lawrence, is, in this place, perhaps, the most intricate and dangerous of any actually used in North America, without the assistance of pilots accustomed to the force and direction of its various eddies. Though the French have been constantly going up and down the river ever since their possession of Canada, General Amherst's attempt to navigate it in the manner he did, was judged impracticable. No doubt, the route by Lake George and Lake Champlain, might have been the easiest to penetrate by into Canada; but this by the Mohawk River, Oswego, and the River St. Lawrence, opened a passage which had as yet, been unexplored by the English, and effectually deprived the French of the opportunity of carrying on the war another campaign, by retreating to their unconquered posts at Detroit, and elsewhere to the south. Those who declared the river impracticable to the English, grounded their opinion on the unsuccessfulness of the attempt made on La Galette, the preceding year, by General Gage; not considering the difference between a feeble irresolute effort, and a strong determined stroke.

The pilots taken at Fort Levi, contributed much to the safety of the army in this navigation; or, it would have been equally tedious.

The chief art of getting through these rapids with a number of boats, consists in the making them keep a proper distance. Without the greatest attention to this precaution, the lives of those who pass the Cedar Falls, especially, must be in the utmost danger.

It must be confessed, that the appearance of broken rocks, and inaccessible islands, interspersed in the current of a rapid river, and the foaming surges rebounding from them, without a direct channel to discharge itself by, presents a scene of horror unknown in Europe; yet the mind, by degrees, soon loses the sensation of terror, and becomes free enough to direct the actions of the body.

On the 4th of September, the General put the army in motion, and it soon cleared the Lake St. Francis, and entered a country lately well inhabited, but now a mere desert. About noon, the van of the army entered the Cedar Falls.

This, as we have already hinted, is by far the most dangerous part of the whole river, and had the boats crowded too close upon each other, most of them must have perished.

Accordingly, for the want of sufficient precaution, twenty-nine boats belonging to the regiments, seventeen whale boats, seventeen artillery boats, and one row galley, were dashed to pieces, with the loss of eighty-eight men; and this too before, on account of the night's approaching, the whole of the army could get through; what did, encamped on the Isle-Perrot. On the 5th, in the morning, the remainder, taking care to preserve a proper distance, passed the rapid with ease. During the stay, the General was obliged to make, to repair the damaged boats, the inhabitants came flocking in, and took the oath of allegiance to his Britannic Majesty.

Humanity and clemency ever attended on the victories of the Romans; the princes and the people who submitted to their arms, were sure of protection; and those who dared to oppose them, were made to feel the weight of their greatness and power.

True policy might alone be thought sufficient, especially after such an illustrious example, to make the generals of every nation adopt such conciliating measures. It would have been justly a matter of surprise, if, from the national feelings of his own heart, independent of any other motive, General Amherst had neglected to stretch forth the hand of commiseration, to the number of trembling, despairing wretches, who now appeared before him. The blood that had been shed in the wantonness of cruelty, had expunged from their breasts every hope of mercy; and they advanced like culprits approaching a judge, to receive the sentence due to their crimes.

Full as they were of conscious guilt, how great must have been their joy, to find themselves forgiven, restored to their possessions, and to their families; to be received as friends, and have every necessary provided for them as such, and to crown all, to know, for certain, that they might securely depend on a continuance, or rather an increase of these blessings."

From a map in Mante's History of the War in Canada, which represents the channel of the St. Lawrence, above and below Isle Royal, it appears that the English army were encamped on Indian Point, opposite the island where batteries were erected, and on the north shore. Batteries were opened on the islands under the Canada shore, and detached posts were established on the point opposite the Galloo Island, and upon that island, and the small one near its head.

The following account is preserved of the building of the fortress on Isle Royal, which was accomplished but the year before its reduction. It received its name from the French officer, who superintended its erection.—(See *Memoirs sur le Canada*, p. 168.)

"M. the chevalier de Lévis, had returned to the rapids, where he had ordered the construction of a fort, on an island called Oraconenton, about a league above the rapids. He gave orders that they should finish a bark, of which the building had been interrupted, in order to send the laborers to Quebec; the arrangement for the defense was, that the barks with the Jacobites, should form the first line; the Isle Oracouenton, and the others, the second, and the third at the Galops, which is at the commencement of the rapids; and thus they desired to defend themselves, from rapid to rapid.

This project would have been good, if they had had suitable bateaux to defend this river, which is extremely wide towards La Presentation, and defend the different passages of the rapids.

After these arrangements had been made, he descended to Montreal, where he learned that the Canadians had left their arms, to go to secure their harvest.

Against these he promulgated an ordinance, under pain of death; but it was represented to him, that it would be impossible to enforce this ordinance, as it did not emanate from M. de Vaudreuil, and this general did not have the power of the court, and that the Canadians could only be regarded as volunteers, who served without pay. * * *

M. de Lévis said, that if any one in the army wished to desert, he would cut off his head, but they boldly replied to him that if they knew that these were his sentiments, he would not find a single militia man, either at the Isle-Aux-Noix, nor at Oraconenton, and that they would take care that he should not find them. This threat intimidated him, and he said no more; he left to visit the Isle Aux Noix, and concerted with M. de Bourlamarque, for its defense, with whom a little time after, he ascended to Oraconenton, to the end that he might accelerate by his presence, the works there in progress, and defend in person the rapids, against the army of M. de Bostwick, who was still encamped at Chouaguen, and seemed preparing to descend. James Zouch, an English officer, had surprised La Presentation, having come through the woods from the army of Amherst, to La Presentation, to carry the letters of this general to Bostwick, and who had come out too low down. The five nations even sent belts to the savages of La Presentation, to invite them to withdraw.

These news which were received, one after the other, made him urge the works on the fort; and it was under these circumstances, that M. de Lévis received the tidings of the death of M. de Montcalm, and of the battle, with the order to descend as quickly as possible to Montreal, whence he continued his route to Jacques Cartier. * * *

M. de Lévis, having given orders to fortify Jacques Cartier, gave the command of this post to M. Dumas, and returned to Montreal. The fortification of the Isle Oraconenton, was given to M. Pouchot, who had been exchanged with many other prisoners, and they continued to labor at the Isle Aux Noix; they added to the middle of these entrenchments, a fort, *en étoile,* in which buildings were erected for the lodgement of the garrison and officers."

The St. Lawrence became a thoroughfare of prime importance, in the French and English war, that ended with the conquest of Canada, in 1760. From the paper from which we have previously quoted, (Memoire sur le Canada,) we will here translate, commencing near the close of the year 1758.

"In fine, M. de Vaudreuil, had decided to construct two barks in the place of those that were burned, and consequently to recall M. Duplessis from Frontenac, and to put there a commanding officer with a garrison. He had given orders to Duplessis, to retire entirely with his detachment; this was done on the 26th of October. He found at La Presentation, the orders which he had given to descend, and sent the Sieur Chevalier Benoit, the commander, to Fort Frontenac, with a detachment of troops and Canadians. He was sent as well to protect the baggage and the munitions of war, and the provisions, which were to pass by that way to the upper country, as to establish this post. Sieur Duplessis, also, had orders as well to send back those on the part of Montigni, to Niagara, who had come down, and who were to make this voyage with those sent in the canoes, in charge of the baggage and merchandise.
* * * Sieur the Chevalier Benoit, was of a Parisian family, and had absolutely nothing; he was one of those men, of nothing, who because they are such, charitably believe all others to be rogues. He was a man of chimeras, devout, with much wit, some little polish, and in addition to all, with some philosophy; and as for the rest, brave, and capable of doing honor to any service in which he was charged.
He departed therefore from La Presentation, with an inconsiderable detachment, and repaired to Frontenac, with a royal magazine guard. As the posts of the upper country were naturally wanting in articles of the greatest necessity, the instructions were issued, that as great a quantity should be forwarded as possible.
Officers were despatched to conduct these convoys, but theft and losses annihilated almost all of them.
The Canadians at this time, fatigued, and dying of hunger, did not wish to proceed further, and threatened to revolt; and to add to the misfortune, they demanded their payment; in short, they did us more harm than good at Niagara. Douville, commandant at Toronto, had evactuated that post, and retired to Niagara. Sieur de Cresse, assistant ship master of Canada, had been sent to Frontenac, with M. Laforce, captain of the builders, to construct two new gallies, as well to secure the supremacy of the lake, as to supply Niagara more easily, and to render the defense of this frontier the more respectable; but as he was unable to find the necessary timber at that point, here moved himself down towards La Presentation, to a strait known by the name of Point au Baril, where the construction was in every respect more easy.
He thence wrote to the General, in waiting M. Benoit, who had orders to fortify himself, either at the shipyard of Frontenac, or its environs. After having carefully examined, he decided to fortify himself near the fort,

and in consequence he cut down timber, to form four bastions, upon a prolongation fifty or sixty feet along the bank, and on the side of the fort. * * * But the General, who had received great complaints against Sieur de Lorimier, commanding officer at La Presensation, resolved to remove him, and to put in his place M. Benoit, and at the same time, in order to protect the works at Point au Baril, he gave the necessary orders to M. Benoit, who repaired there with all his garrison, and all that they had sent from Frontenac, and sent iron for the constructions at that place, and left not that which was at Frontenac.

Point au Baril is distant three leagues from La Presentation, in ascending towards Frontenac, upon the right bank of the river St. Lawrence.

Its location was less exposed to attack, than the coast at La Presentation, which of itself was a post too feeble and too badly situated, to sustain an attack. They therefore transported thither all that was destined for Frontenac, and built entrenchments around the spot, chosen for the building of the vessels, and sent thither a magazine guard, under a young man attached to M. de Montcalm."

From a map which accompanies the work from which we have been quoting, it appears that Point au Barril, [Barell Point,] was on the north shore of the river St. Lawrence, above La Presentation, and not far from the site of the present village of Maitland. We here insert the plan of the work as there given.

This point is mentioned very frequently on maps relating to the St. Lawrence river, of an old date.

* * * "It was from two prisoners sent by a detachment of Loups, by M. de Pouchot, that we learned that the army which descended by Chouaguen, and which was commanded by M. Amherst, at the head of 1500 men, was approaching.

It from this appeared beyond doubt, that the colony was about to be attacked at the same moment by three different ways, and that the slowness of the approach of Murrray, would avail nothing, when the three armies should assemble.

M. Amherst, having made his preparations, departed from Chouaguen, and appeared before Oraconenton.* The fort of La Presentation, had been dismantled, and the plan of defense of M de Lévis, could not be entertained, in consequence of the superiority of the army of the English General.

Accordingly, M. Amherst found no difficulty. Before commencing the siege of the Fort, he caused to be planted opposite to the fort, upon the main land, some batteries, which in a short time, razed the parapets, and ruined a part of the entrenchments. M. Pouchot conducted the defense in a manner, that failed not to elicit the admiration of the English General. At length, finding himself no longer able to retain it, he surrendered the place, and the garrison was made prisoners of war. * * *

The French Generals held frequent councils, but they amounted to nothing, because the junction of these armies, destroyed all plans of de-

* This fort appears to have been situated (See Smith's History, t. I. p 359,) upon Isle Royal, between La Presentation, (now Ogdensburgh,) and the beginning of the rapids. (Note in the original.)

fense which they had formed, and they were the more embarrassed because they had but a slender stock of provisions, and no hopes of drawing more from the country.

They did not know what lot M. Amherst would bring, nor how to treat with him in so unpleasant a place; and they could not hold out twenty-four hours. M. de Vaudreuil had, upon the departure of Amherst from Oraconenton, thought of submitting as soon as he should appear before the city.

M. Amherst, after having reduced Oraconenton, chose from among the Canadians whom he there found, those who were best qualified to conduct barges and canoes, and leaving the savages who had hitherto accompanied him, he descended to Soulauges, a small parish of the colony, and where are the last of the rapids, which were all passed hapily, at least without any considerable loss, and came and presented himself in good order, before the parish named Lachine, where his troops encamped without difficulty. The detachments which he had there, had orders to make preparations against the city."*

The following is an account given of this transaction in the Annual Register" for 1760, page 58.

" Having laid this general plan for completing the conquest of Canada, Lord Amherst, with an army of about 10,000 men, left Schenectady on the frontiers of New York, (June 21, 1760,) and passed up the Mohawks' river, and down that of the Oneidas', to Oswego. The army he had collected there, consisted of about 10,000 men, regulars and provincials, Sir William Johnson, brought about a thousand savages of the Iroquois, or Five Nations; the greatest number of that race of men which was ever seen in arms in the cause of England.

It was a matter of the greatest difficulty, to transport so numerous an army, the whole of its artillery, its ammunition, and all its provisions, over the expanse of that vast lake, in open boats, and galleys; it required the greatest caution, and the exactest order, least they should fall foul upon one another, least they should be driven out too far to gain the land, on the first threatening of a storm, or least they should come too near the shore. But all the dispositions were made with the most admirable method, and with that regularity of military arrangements which makes so considerable a part in the character of that able commander, so that the whole army embarked on the twentieth of August. A detachment had been sent some days before, to clear the passage of the river St. Lawrence of any obstructions, and to find the best passage for the vessels.

On the 27th, he had taken possession of Swegatchie, and made all dispositions for the attack of Isle Royal, a fort lower down the river, which commands the most important post, and as it were the key of Canada. The troops and boats were so disposed, that the Isle was completely invested, and the garrison was left no means of escape. The batteries were then raised, and opened, and after two days sharp firing, the fort surrendered.

This being a post of importance both to command Lake Ontario, and to cover our frontier, the general spent some days here in order to repair the fort, and at the same time to fit out his vessels, and to prepare all things for passing his troops down the river, the most dangerous part of which he was now to encounter, as all the rapids lie between this place and Montreal; but notwithstanding all precautions, nearly ninety men were drowned in passing these dangerous falls, and a great number of

* See note A. in the appendix of this work.

vessels broke to pieces. This loss from so large an embarkation, in such circumstances, is to be regarded as inconsiderable.

At length, after a tedious, fatiguing and dangerous voyage of two months and seventeen days, the English saw, to their great joy, the Isle of Montreal, the object of their ardent wishes, and the period of their labors."

There exists a tradition in the country, that the pilots who guided the vessels of Lord Amherst down the rapids, were bribed to pass them down the more dangerous routes, by the offer of large rewards by the enemy. It may well be questioned, whether men could be induced by any motive less than heroic patriotism, to conduct a craft down a channel in which a probability, amounting to little less than a certainty, existed, that it would be engulphed in the angry surges of the rapids.

Those who have passed down the river St. Lawrence, in steam boats, and witnessed the tumultuous war of waters, which this mighty Scylla and Charybdis, at once so wild, so grand, and so dreadful, presents; and reflects that a large army in a great number of boats, many of which were guided by inexperienced hands, constituted the flotilla, he will agree with the opinion of the author above quoted, that the number of lives lost is small compared with the whole number of the army, and the manifold dangers to which they were exposed.

There is still said to exist, in the St. Lawrence, opposite the town of Massena, the wreck of one or two vessels, which are supposed to have belonged to the French or the English fleet, and to have perished about this time.

General Israel Putnam, who afterwards shone most conspicuously in the revolutionary war, was in company with Lord Amherst in this expedition, and from what is well known of his energy and courage, there can be no doubt that he took an active part in the campaign, and was foremost in every enterprise that required the exercise of those traits of character, for which he was so eminent.

While the English account just quoted, (perhaps from a national prejudice, and a desire then manifested to keep in a subordinate station the provincials,) does not mention the name of Putnam, in connection with this event. The following extract from the miscellaneous works of David Humphrey, (New York, 1804, p. 280–1,) gives in an account of the reduction of Isle Royal, quite a different version of the affair, and is perhaps equally chargable with partiality, in giving all the credit of the enterprise to an American officer.

It appears probable that Humphrey's account is mostly fabulous.

"In 1760, Gen. Amherst, a sagacious, humane and experienced commander, planned the termination of the war in Canada, by a bloodless conquest. For this purpose, three armies were destined to co-operate by different routes against Montreal, the only remaining place of strength the enemy held in that country. The corps formerly commanded by Wolf, now by General Murray, was ordered to ascend the river St. Lawrence; another, under Col. Haviland, to penetrate by the Isle Aux Noix; and the third, consisting of about ten thousand men, commanded by the General himself, after passing up the Mohawk River, and taking its course by the Lake Ontario, was to form a junction by falling down the St. Lawrence.

In this progress, more than one occasion presented itself to manifest the intrepidity and soldiership of Lieut. Col. Putnam. Two armed vessels obstructed the passage and prevented the attack on Oswegatchie Putnam, with one thousand men, in fifty batteaux, undertook to board them. This dauntless officer, ever sparing of the blood of others, as prodigal of his own, to accomplish it with the less loss, put himself, (with a chosen crew, a beetle and wedges,) in the van, with a design to wedge the rudders, so that the vessels should not be able to turn their broadsides, or to perform any other maneuvre. All the men in his little fleet were ordered to strip to their waistcoats, and advance at the same time. He promised if he lived, to join and show them the way up the side. Animated by so daring an example, they moved swiftly, in profound stillness, as to certain victory or death. The people on board the ship, beholding the good countenance with which they approached, ran one of the vessels on shore, and struck the colors of the other.

Had it not been for the dastardly conduct of the ship's company in the latter, who compelled the captain to haul down his ensign, he would have given the assailants a bloody reception; for the vessels were well provided with spars, nettings, and every customary instrument of annoyance, as well as defence.

It now remained to attack the fortress, which stood on an island, and seemed to have been rendered inaccessible by a high abattis of black ash, that every where projected over the water. Lieutenant Colonel Putnam, proposed a mode of attack, and offered his services to carry it into effect. The General approved the proposal. Our partizan, accordingly, caused a sufficient number of boats to be fitted for the enterprise. The sides of each boat were surrounded with fascines, musket proof, which covered the men completely. A wide plank, twenty feet in length was then fitted to every boat, in such a manner by having an angular piece sawed from one extremity that when fastened by ropes on both sides of the bow, it might be raised or lowered at pleasure. The design was, that the plank should be held erect, while the oarsmen forced the bow with the utmost exertion against the abattis, and that afterwards being dropped on the pointed brush, it should serve as a kind of bridge to assist the men in passing over them. Lieutenant Colonel Putnam, having made his dispositions to attempt the escalade in many places at the same moment, advanced with his boats in admirable order. The garrison perceiving these extraordinary and unexpected machines, waited not the assault, but capitulated. Putnam was particularly honored by Gen. Amherst, for his ingenuity in this invention, and promptitude in its execution. The three armies arrived in Montreal within two days of each other, and the conquest of Canada became complete, without the loss of a single drop of blood."

It has been justly remarked, that there is an air of incredibility about this statement, which of itself sufficiently impairs its value as a historical fact. That a crew of an armed ship, should have been terror stricken at the approach of a handful of unarmed men, or possessing the means of annihilating at a single discharge the insignificant array brought against them, should have omitted to do so, implies a degree of cowardice or treachery which can scarcely be credited or believed.

With the fall of the fortress of Isle Royal, ceased the French dominion in St. Lawrence county.*

It was subsequently occupied by a small guard of British troops, and held till surrendered in accordance with the stipulations of Jay's treaty in the summer of 1796, to Judge Ford, who received it for the proprietors.

The remains of a cemetery still exist on the west side of the Oswegatchie, and several head stones mark the place where British soldiers were buried.

The history of this station, so far as our knowledge extends, from the time of the English conquest to the surrender under the treaty, is nearly or quite lost.

Such data as have fallen under our notice, will here be given:

In the summer of 1776, the following minute was forwarded from Oswego, by Lieut. Edward McMichael. (*See American Archives, fifth series, vol. i, page* 815.)

"Was informed at *Oswego,* that three regiments of Ministerial troops had arrived at *Oswegatchie,* at which place they were joined by a number of Tories and *Indians* under the command of Colonel *Johnson,* and were to embark immediately on board two armed vessels, bateaux and canoes, and proceed to *Oswego,* at which place they were to be joined by Colonel *Butler,* with all the *Indians* under his command, and likewise by Colonel *Caldwell,* with hat regulars could be spared from *Niagara.*

They intended repairing *Oswego Fort,* as soon as possible, in order that they might hold a treaty with the *Indians,* and be able to defend themselves against any attack."

In April, 1779, Lieutenants McClellan and Hardenburgh, of the Revolutionary army, were despatched from Fort Schuyler, on an expedition at the head of a body of Indians, against the British garrison at Oswegatchie, intending to steal upon it, and take it by surprise, but falling in with some straggling Indians, several shots were imprudently exchanged, which alarmed the garrison. They then attempted to draw the enemy

---

* *Antoine St. Martin,* a Frenchman, said to have inhabited the country since its occupation by the French, in 1760, died at an extreme age, (supposed to exceed by several years, a century) on the 4th of March 1849, at Ogdensburgh. In his latter years, he attracted some attention from his being made the personage of a romance, written and published at Poudam, by C. Boynton. His longevity appears to have been to him as much a solitude, as it was to others a wonder, and he would at times weep, and lament, that "God had forgotten him." With him perished the last survivors of the French period of our history, and it is much to be regretted that his narrative and recollections were not preserved.

from the fort by stratagem, and partly succeeded, but could not draw them at a sufficient distance to cut off their retreat, and on approaching the fort themselves, the assailants were so warmly received, that they were compelled to retreat without unnecessary delay. The only service performed, was to send a Caughnawaga Indian into Canada, with a letter in French by a French general, probably the Marquis de Lafayette, and addressed to the Canadians, and written the preceding autumn. The expedition was despatched from Fort Schuyler, on the day before Colone Van Schaick moved upon Onondaga; and from a letter addressed by Gen. Clinton, six weeks afterwards to General Sullivan, there is reason to believe, one object was to get clear of the Oneida Indians, then in the fort, until Colonel Van Schaick should have proceeded so far upon his expedition, that they or their people should not be able to give the Onondagas notice of his approach. All the Indians still remaining in Fort Schuyler on the 18th. were detained expressly for that purpose. Although professedly friendly, and reliable as scouts, they could not be trusted in expeditions against their fellows.*

The expedition of Lieutenants McClellan, and Hardenbergh returned to Fort Schuyler without having effected their purpose, on the 30th of April.

An incident happened in a military expedition from Fort Schuyler to Oswegatchie, during the Revolutionary war, and probably in the one just described, which shows in an amiable light, the finer feelings of the Indian character, and will serve as an offset for some of the darker phases of Indian warfare. The subject of the adventure afterwards for several years resided in St. Lawrence county, and often related the incident to the one from whose lips the account is written.

Belonging to a military party that was proceeding through the forest, was a little boy, about twelve years old, who served as a fifer to the company. Light hearted and innocent, he tripped along, sometimes running in advance to gather flowers, and at others lingering behind to listen to the music of the birds, which made the forest vocal with their songs. Seeing the unguarded deportment of the lad, his captain cautioned him against wandering from the company, for fear that some hostile Indian who might be lurking in the thicket, should take him off. The warning was heeded for some time, but ere long forgot, and he found himself many rods in advance of the party, culling the wild flowers which were scattered in his path, and inhaling the fragrance which the morning air with its exhilarating freshness inspired him, when he was suddenly startled by a rude grasp upon the shoulder, which upon looking around he saw was that of a sturdy Indian, who had been secreted behind a

* See Stone's Life of Brant. Vol. 1. p 91.

rock, and had darted from his concealment upon the unsuspecting victim, who had wandered from his protectors.

He attempted to scream, but fear paralyzed his tongue, and he saw the glittering tomahawk brandished over his head, which the next moment would terminate with a blow, his existence; but the savage, seeing the unarmed and terror stricken child, with no warlike implement but his fife, and doubtless touched with the innocence and terror of his trembling prisoner, relaxed his grasp, took the fife from under his arm, and having playfully blowed in its end he returned it to its owner, and bounded off into the forest. No further caution was needed, to keep him within the ranks, and they the next day reached their destination, which was Fort Oswegatchie.

In after years, when age had made him infirm, in relating this incident, he would weep with emotion at this perilous adventure, and always ended with the heartfelt acknowledgment, "that God had always protected him, and guarded him, from dangers seen and unseen, and from childhood to old age."

Isaac Weld, jr., published in London, in 1799, in two octavo volumes, a journal of travels in the States of North America, and the provinces of Upper and Lower Canada, in the years 1795-7, which describes among other interesting subjects, the condition and appearance of our frontier, and the fort at the mouth of the Oswegatchie, which we will quote. [Vol. ii, p. 38, et seq.] The voyage was undertaken in the month of August 1796.

"The Indians not only retain possession of the different islands, but likewise of the whole of the south-east shore of the St. Lawrence, situated within the bounds of the United States; they likewise have considerable strips of land on the opposite shore, within the British Dominions, bordering upon the river; these they have reserved to themselves, for hunting. The Iroquois Indians have a village upon the Isle of St. Regis, and another also upon the main land, on the south-east shore; as we passed, several of the inhabitants put off in canoes, and exchanged unripe heads of Indian corn with the men for bread; they also brought with them some very fine wild duck and fish, which they disposed of to us on very moderate terms.

On the fourth night of our voyage, we encamped as usual on the main land, opposite the Island of St. Regis, and the excellent viands which we had procured from the Indians having been cooked, we sat down to supper before a large fire, materials for which are never wanting in this woody country. The night was uncommonly serene, and we were induced to remain to a late hour in front of our tent talking of the various occurrences in the course of the day; but we had scarcely retired to rest when the sky became overcast, a dreadful storm arose, and by daybreak the next morning we found ourselves, and every thing belonging to us, drenched with rain.

Our situation now was by no means agreeable. Torrents still came pouring down; neither our tent nor the woods afforded us any shelter, and, the wind being very strong and as averse as it could blow, there was no prospect of our being enabled speedily to get into better quarters. In this state, we had remained for a considerable time, when one of the party, who had been rambling about in order 'to discover what sort of a neighborhood we were in, returned with the pleasing intelligence, that there was a house at no great distance, and that the owner had politely invited us to it. It was the house of an old provincial officer, who had received a grant of land in this part of the country for his past services. We gladly proceeded to it, and met with a most cordial welcome from the captain and his fair daughters, who had provided a plenteous breakfast, and spared no pains to make their habitation during our stay, as pleasing to us as possible.

We felt great satisfaction at the idea, that it would be in our power to spend the remainder of the day with these worthy and hospitable people, but alas! we had all formed an erroneous opinion of the weather, the wind veered suddenly about; the sun broke through the thick clouds, the conductor gave the parting order, and in a few minutes we found ourselves once more seated in our bateau. From hence upwards, for a distance of forty miles, the current of the river is exceedingly strong, and numberless rapids are to be encountered, which, though not so tremendous to appearance, as those at the Cascades, and Le Coteau du Lac, are, yet both more dangerous and more difficult to pass. The great danger consists however, in going down them; it arises from the shallowness of the water, and the great number of sharp rocks, in the midst of which the vessels are hurried along with such impetuosity, that if they unfortunately get into a wrong channel, nothing can save them from being dashed to pieces, but so intimately, are the people employed on this river, acquainted with the different channels, that an accident of the sort is scarcely ever heard of. " Le Long Saut," the Long Fall, or Rapid, situate about thirty miles above Lake St. Francis, is the most dangerous of any one on the river, and so difficult a matter is it to pass it, that it requires not less than six men on shore, to haul a single bateau against the current.

There is a third canal, with locks, at this place, in order to avoid a point, which it would be wholly impracticable to weather in the ordinary way. These different canals, and locks, have been made at the expense of government, and the profits arising from the tolls paid by each bateau that passes through them, are placed in the public treasury. At these rapids, and at several of the others, there are very extensive flour and saw mills.

On the fifth night, we arrived at a small farm house, at the top of the Long Saut, wet from head to foot, in consequence of having been obliged to walk past the rapids, through woods and bushes, still dripping after the heavy rain that had fallen in the morning. The woods in this neighborhood are far more majestic than on any other part of the St. Lawrence; the pines, in particular, are uncommonly tall, and seem to wave their tops in the very clouds. In Canada, pines grow on the richest soils, but in the United States, they grow mostly on poor ground; a tract of land covered with lofty pines, is there generally denominated "a pine barren," on account of its great poverty.

During a considerable part of the next day, we also proceeded on foot, in order to escape the tedious passage of the Rapide Plat, and some of the other dangerous rapids in this part of the river. As we passed along, we had an excellent diversion in shooting pigeons, several large flights of which we met with in the woods. The wild pigeons of Canada, are not unlike the common English wood pigeon, except that they are of a much smaller size; their flesh is very well flavored. During particular years these birds come down from the northern regions in flights that is marvelous to tell. A gentleman of the town of Niagara assured me, that once as he was embarking there on board a ship for Toronto, a flight of them was observed coming from that quarter, that as he sailed over Lake Ontario to Toronto, forty-five miles distant from Niagara, pigeons were seen flying over head the whole way, in a contrary direction to that from which the ship was proceeding; and that on arriving at the place of his destination, the birds were still observed coming down from the north, in as large bodies as had been noticed at any one time during the whole voyage; supposing therefore that the pigeons moved no faster than the vessel, the flight according to this gentleman's account, must at least have extended eighty miles.

Many persons may think this story surpassing belief; for my own part, however, I do not hesitate to give credit to it, knowing, as I do, the respectability of the gentleman who related it, and the accuracy of his observation. When these birds appear in such great numbers, they often light on the borders of rivers and lakes, and in the neighborhood of farm houses, at which time they are so unwary, that a man with a short stick might easily knock them down by hundreds.

It is not oftener than once in seven or eight years, perhaps, that such large flocks of these birds are seen in the country. The years in which they appear, are denominated " pigeon years."

There are also " bear years," and "squirrel years." This was both a bear and a squirrel year. The former, like the pigeons, come down from the northern regions, and were most numerous in the neighborhoods of lakes Erie and Ontario, and along the upper part of the river St. Lawrence. On arriving at the borders of these lakes, or of the river, if the opposite shore were in sight, they generally took to the water, and endeavored to reach it by swimming. Prodigious numbers of them are killed in crossing the St. Lawrence, by the Indians, who had hunting encampments at short distances from each other, the whole way along the bank of the river, from the island of St. Regis to lake Ontario. One bear of very large size, boldly entered the river, in the face of our bateau, and was killed by one of our men, while swimming from the main land to one of the islands. * * *

The squirrels this year, contrary to the bears, migrated from the south, from the territory of the United States. Like the bears, they took to the water, on arriving at it, but, as if conscious of their inability to cross a very wide piece of water, they bent their course towards Niagara river, above the falls, and at its narrowest and most tranquil part, crossed over into the British territory. It was calculated that upwards of fifty thousand of them crossed the river in the course of two or three days, and such great depredations did they commit, on arriving at the settlements on the opposite side, that in one part of the country, the farmers deemed themselves very fortunate where they got in as much as one-third of their crops of corn. These squirrels were all of the black kind, said to be peculiar to the continent of America.

* * * On the sixth evening of our voyage, we stopped nearly opposite to Point aux Iroquois, so named from a French family having been cruelly massacred there, by the Iroquois Indians, in the early ages of the colony. The ground being still extremely wet here, in consequence of the heavy rain of the preceding day, we did not much relish the thoughts of passing the night in our tent; yet there seemed to be no alternative, as the only house in sight was crowded with people, and not capable of affording us any accommodation. Luckily however, as we were searching about for the driest spot to pitch our tent upon, one

of the party espied a barn, at a little distance, belonging to the man of the adjoining house, of whom we procured the key; it was well stored with straw, and having mounted to the top of the mow, we laid ourselves down to rest, and slept soundly there, till awakened in the morning, by the crowing of some cocks, that were perched on the beams over our heads.

At an early hour we pursued our voyage, and before noon passed the last rapid, about three miles below the mouth of the Oswegatchie River, the most considerable of these within the limit of the United States, which fall into the St. Lawrence, it consists of three branches, that unite about fifteen miles above its mouth; the most western of which issues from a lake, twenty miles in length, and eight in breadth.

Another of the branches, issues from a small lake, or pond, only about four miles distant from the west branch of Hudson River, that flows past New York. Both the Hudson and the Oswegatchie, are said to be capable of being made navigable for light bateaux, as far as this spot, where they approach within so short a distance of each other, except only at a few places, so that the portages will be but very trifling. This however is a mere conjecture, for Oswegatchee River is but very imperfectly known, the country it passes through being quite uninhabited; but should it be found at a future period, that these rivers are indeed capable of being rendered navigable, so far up the country, it will probably be through this channel that the greatest of the trade that there may happen to be between New York and the country bordering upon Lake Ontario, will be carried on."

The small lake referred to by the author, was doubtless Raquette lake, in Hamilton county, which is even nearer the head waters of the Hudson, than above stated, but it lies at the source of the *Raquette* river, instead of the *Oswegatchie*.

"The trade is at present carried on between that city and the lake, by means of Hudson River, as far as Albany, and from thence by means of the Mohawks' River, Wood Creek, and Oswego River, which falls into Lake Ontario. The harbor at the mouth of Oswego river, is very bad, on account of the sand banks, none but flat bottomed vessels can approach with safety nearer to it than two miles, nor is there any good harbor on the south side of lake Ontario, in the neighborhood of any large rivers. Sharp built vessels, however, of a considerable size, can approach with safety to the mouth of Oswegatchee River. The Seneca, a British vessel of war, of twenty-six guns, used to ply constantly, formerly between Fort de la Galette, situated at the mouth of that river, and the fort at Niagara; and the British fur ships, on the lakes, used also at that time to discharge the cargoes there, brought down from the upper country.

As therefore the harbor at the mouth of Oswegatchee, is so much better than that at the mouth of the Oswego river, and as they are nearly an equal distance from New York, there is reason to suppose that if the river navigation should prove equally good, the trade between the lakes and New York, will be for the most part, if not wholly carried on by means of Oswegatchee River, rather than of Oswego River. With a fair wind the passage from Oswegatchee River to Niagara, is accomplished in two days, a voyage only one day longer than from Oswego to Niagara, with a fair wind.

Fort de la Galette was erected by the French, and though not built till long after fort Frontenac, now Kingston, yet they esteemed it by far the most important military post on the St. Lawrence, in the upper country, as it was impossible for any boat, or vessel, to pass up or down that river without being observed, whereas they might easily escape unseen behind the many islands, opposite to Kingston. Since the close of the American war, Fort de la Galette has been dismantled, as it was within the territories of the United States, nor would any advantage have arisen from its retention, for it was never of any importance to us but as a trading post, and as such, Kingston, which is in our own territory, is far more elligibly situated, in every point of view, it has a more safe and commodious harbor, the fur ships coming down from Niagara, by stopping there, are saved a voyage of sixty miles up and down the St. Lawrence, which was often found to be more tedious than the voyage from Niagara to Kingston. In the neighborhood of La Galette, on the Oswegatchee River, there is a village of the Oswegatchee Indians, whose numbers are estimated at one hundred warriors.

The current of the St. Lawrence, from Oswegatchee upwards, is much more gentle than in any other part between Montreal and Lake Ontario, except only where the river is considerably dilated, as at lakes St. Louis and St. François; however, notwithstanding its being so gentle, we did not advance more than twenty-five miles in the course of the day, owing to the numerous stops that we made, more from motives of pleasure than necessity. The evening was uncommonly fine, and towards sunset a brisk gale springing up, the conductor judged it advisable to take advantage of it, and to continue the voyage all night, in order to make up for the time we had lost during the day. We accordingly proceeded, but towards midnight the wind died away; this circumstance, however, did not alter the determination of the conductor. The men were ordered to the oars, and notwithstanding that they had labored hard during the preceding day, and had had no rest, yet they were kept closely at work until day break, except for one hour, during which they were allowed to stop to cook their provisions. Where there is a gentle current, as in this part of the river, the Canadians will work at the oar for many hours without intermission; they seemed to think it no hardship to be kept employed in this instance the whole night; on the contrary, they plied as vigorously as if they had but just set out, singing merrily the whole time. The French Canadians have in general a good ear for music, and sing duets with tolerable accuracy. They have one very favorite duet amongst them, called the " rowing duet," which, as they sing, they mark time to, with each stroke of the oar; indeed, when rowing in smooth water, they mark time the most of the airs they sing in the same manner.

About eight o'clock the next, and eighth morning of our voyage, we entered the last lake before you come to that of Ontario, called the Lake of a Thousand Islands, on account of the multiplicity of them which it contains. Many of these islands are scarcely larger than a bateau, and none of them, except such as are situated at the upper and lower extremities of the lake, appeared to me to contain more than fifteen English acres each. They are all covered with wood, even to the very smallest The trees on these last are stunted in their growth, but the larger islands produce as fine timber as is to be found on the main shores of the lake. Many of these islands are situated so closely together, that it would be easy to throw a pebble from one to the other, notwithstanding which circumstance, the passage between them is perfectly safe and commodious for bateaux, and between some of them that are even thus close to each other, is water sufficient for a frigate. The water is uncommonly clear, as it is in every part of the river, from Lake St. Francis upwards:

between that lake and the Utawas river downwards, it is discolored, as I have before observed, by passing over beds of marl. The shores of all these islands under our notice are rocky; most of them rise very boldly, and some exhibit perpendicular masses of rock towards the water, upwards of twenty feet high. The scenery presented to view in sailing between these islands is beautiful in the highest degree. Sometimes, after passing through a narrow strait, you find yourself in a basin, land locked on every side, that appears to have no communication with the lake, except by the passage through which you entered; you are looking about, perhaps, for an outlet to enable you to proceed, thinking at last to see some little channel which will just admit your bateau, when on a sudden an expanded sheet of water opens upon you, whose boundary is the horizon alone; again in a few minutes you find yourself land locked, and again a spacious passage as suddenly presents itself; at other times, when in the middle of one of these basins, between a cluster of islands, a dozen different channels, like so many noble rivers, meet the eye, perhaps equally unexpectedly, and on each side the islands appear regularly retiring till they sink from the sight in the distance. Every minute, during the passage of this lake, the prospect varies. The numerous Indian hunting encampments on the different islands, with the smoke of their fires rising up between the trees, added considerably to the beauty of the scenery as we passed it. The Lake of a Thousand Islands is twenty-five miles in length, and about six in breadth. From its upper end to Kingston, at which place we arrived early in the evening, the distance is fifteen miles.

The length of time required to ascend the River St. Lawrence, from Montreal to Kingston, is commonly found to be about seven days. If the wind should be strong and very favorable, the passage may be performed in a less time; but should it, on the contrary, be adverse, and blow very strong, the passage will be protracted somewhat longer; an adverse or favorable wind, however, seldom makes a difference of more than three days in the length of the passage upwards, as in each case it is necessary to work the bateaux along by means of poles for the greater part of the way. The passage downwards is performed in two or three days, according to the wind. The current is so strong, that a contrary wind seldom lengthens the passage in that direction more than a day."

The English are believed to have maintained the fort at Oswegatchie, as a protection to their fur trade; and this was made the cover of a pretension, to justify their retaining it after the peace which followed the revolution. The Oswegatchies, continued to reside in the vicinity after the English conquest, adopted the new allegiance, and as usual became corrupted in morals by their vicinity to the garrison. They are believed to have acted with the British in the war of the Revolution.

In the enumeration of Indian tribes made by Sir Wm. Johnson, in 1763,[*] the tribe is represented as numbering eighty warriors, at peace with the English. In the same enumeration, the Caughnawagas are reported at three hundred men, emigrants from the Mohawks, and with a colony at Aghquissasne, (St. Regis,) which was the seat of a mission. The latter had been founded but three years previously.

* Documentary History of New York, vol. i. page 27.

A portion of the Mohawk emigration had settled at the mission of the Lake of Two Mountains.

The English were careful not to molest them in their religious observances, which remain to this day, the same as when first established among them.

The Oswegatchies, at the time when the present class of settlers came on, were occupying a village of twenty-three houses, on Indian Point, in Lisbon, about three miles below Ogdensburgh. Spafford, in his Gazetteer, published in 1813, thus mentions them. "This village was built by the British government, after the Revolution, and when, of course, that government had no title to the land. The Indians remained here several years after the settlement of the country by the present proprietors, and were removed by order of the government of New York, on the complaint of the inhabitants. These Indians driven from New Johnstown, in Upper Canada, received this spot with improvements, in exchange from which driven by our government, they became destitute of a local habitation and a name, and the Oswegatchie tribe no longer exists, although a few individuals remain, scattered among the surrounding tribes."

This dispersion took place about 1806, or 7, and the remnants of the tribe, or their descendants, are found at St. Regis, Onondaga, and elsewhere.

While in Lisbon, they were under the direction of one Joseph Reoam, a Frenchman, who spoke their dialect of the Iroquois language, and is said to have been a chief, and to have married an Indian woman. They planted corn on Galloo island, and elsewhere in the vicinity.

Their village is described by one who saw it in 1802, as consisting of a street, running parallel with the river, with the houses ranged in a regular manner on each side of it, all uniformly built, with their ends to the street, sharp roofed, shingled with pointed shingles, and with glass windows. Every house was built for two families, had two doors in front, and a double fire place, and single chimney in the centre, with a partition equally dividing the interior. In 1802 there were about 24 families.

These Indians were accustomed to spend most of their summers on Black lake, in hunting and fishing, returning to their cabins for the winter. They used bark canoes, which they carried around rapids, and across portages, with perfect ease.

As many as forty Indians at a time were often seen in the settlement when new.

Directly opposite to the site of the Indian village of the Oswegatchies, is the island that was fortified by the French, and taken by the English under Lord Amherst in 1760. The ruins of the fortress upon it, are still to be seen, although mostly obliterated, and have given it the name of Chimney island. This island is low, and in shape irregular. It is on the American side of the channel, and has an area of six acres. There are said to be still seen on an island, opposite this, under the Canada shore, the traces of works erected by the English, to assist in its reduction.

A great number of iron and other metalic relics, have been found on this island, and the adjoining shores, as tomahawks, hoes, axes, picks, the hangings of gates and other relics of the French and Indian occupation of the place. These, like those found on the sites of the French establishments at Onondaga, and elsewhere, are rude and very coarse; scarcely appearing to be capable of being used for the purposes for which they were intended.

This island is three miles below the village of Ogdensburgh.

Like many other places having associations connected with the olden time, Chimney island has been the scene of *money digging*, on a somewhat extensive scale, by those who were weak enough to be led astray by the pretended indications of the divining rod, or the impositions of fortune tellers. As uniformly happens, there has been money lost instead of gained in these operations, and if stories are to be believed, certain of these adventurers have lost somewhat of credit and standing in community, by these speculations.[*]

[*] See Appendix, note B of this work.

CHAPTER II.

ST. REGIS.

N a beautiful and elevated point which juts into the St. Lawrence, where that river is crossed by the forty-fifth parallel of latitude, and between the mouths of the St. Regis and Racquette rivers, stands a dilapidated and antique looking village, whose massive and venerable church, with tin covered spire; whose narrow and filthy streets, and the general appearance of indolence and poverty of its inhabitants, and especially the accents of an unaccustomed language, almost convey to the casual visitor an impression that he is in a foreign land.

Such is the Indian village of St. Regis, whose origin and history we are about to relate. Its founders in selecting this site, evinced the possession of a taste at once judicious and correct, for it may well be questioned whether the shores of the St. Lawrence, abounding as they do in charming and lovely localities, affords anywhere a spot that will surpass this in beauty of scenery, or pleasantness of location. The village stands on a plain, moderately elevated above the river, which having for more than forty miles been broken by cascades and dangerous rapids, here becomes tranquil.

To the west, the ground swells into a gentle hill, which overlooks the village and river to a great distance; beyond which it again descends into a spacious plain, which for time immemorial has been the favorite ground for ball-playing, a pastime to which the natives are strongly attached, and in which they engage with much zeal.

The surrounding fields, are an open common, without separate enclosures, and are used as a public pasture by the inhabitants. Around the cabins of the villagers are usually small enclosures, devoted to the cultivation of corn, and culinary vegetables, which by the right of occupancy have come to be considered the private property of individuals, and as such are bought and sold among the natives, although the law recognizes no such private ownership, and holds them all as tenants in common, denying them the right of buying or selling land, except to the government.

Opposite to the village, lay several very fertile and beautiful islands, which are owned and cultivated by the villagers, and upon which is raised the grain upon which they subsist, and the grass which serves for their cattle during the winter months. The public points in the village, and the summits of the hill are crowned by the cross, which indicates the religious faith of the greater part of the inhabitants, and reminds us that the colony owes its origin to a religious movement. Such is St. Regis, as it appears to the stranger; a village which under Anglo-Saxon enterprise, would ere this have attained a preëminence equal to any place on the river, but which now exhibits nothing but an air of decay and litstlessness, peculiar of the Indian character, when it assumes the habits of civilization.

To one who traverses the streets, and observes the general aspect of its inhabitants, a leading trait will be noticed as their controlling principle, and he will recognize INDOLENCE in every feature, and in every action.

With this preliminary, we will proceed with our account of the origin of this village, which was formed by an emigration from the mission at Caughnawaga, or the Saut Saint Louis, about nine miles above Montreal. The latter at a remote period of American history, in its turn, was formed by a portion of the Mohawk tribe of Indians, who were induced by the French to emigrate to their vicinity and embrace the Catholic faith.

We will reserve for the appendix,* such notices as we may find, connected with this people, previous to the founding of St. Regis, and commence our account with a traditionary narrative upon which is based the causes that led to the measure.

About a hundred and thirty years ago, three children, (a girl about twelve or thirteen years of age, and two younger brothers,) were playing together in a barn, in the town of Groton, Massachusetts, and being absent from the house longer than was expected, their mother became solicitous about them, and went to find them. The girl was lying on the floor, with a limb broken, and the boys were missing.

She related that seeing some Indians coming, she fled to the upper part of the barn, and fell by accident from the beams above, and that they had seized the two boys, and carried them away. The stealthy manner of this seizure, and, the time that had elapsed, forbade pursuit, with any hope of success, and the distracted parents were left to mourn the loss without consolation or hope. The probable motive for the seizure of these children, was the expectation that a bounty would be

* See Appendix Note C of this work.

offered for their ransom; or perhaps they might be exchanged for French prisoners.

As afterwards appeared, these boys were taken by Caughnawaga Indians to their village near Montreal, where they were adopted as their own children, growing up in habits, manners, and language, as Indians, and in due time they married the daughters of chiefs of,that tribe. The names of these chiefs were Sa-kon-en-tsi-ask and Ata-wen-ta.

But they possessed the superiority of intellect, and enterprise, which belonged to their race, and this led to a series of petty quarrels, growing out of the jealousy of the young Indians of their age, which disquieted the village, and by the party spirit which it engendered, became a source of irritation and trouble in the settlement, and of anxiety on the part of their missionary, who labored in vain to reconcile the difficulties between them.

Failing in this, he advised the two young men, (one of whom they had named Ka-re-ko-wa) to remove with their families to a place by themselves, where they might enjoy tranquility, and be beyond the reach of annoyance from their comrades.

This advice they adopted; and taking with them their wives, and followed by their wives' parents, these four families departed in a bark canoe, with their effects, to seek in a new country, and in the secluded recesses of the forest, *a home*.

They coasted along up the St. Lawrence, and at length arrived at the delightful point on which the village of St. Regis now stands, where they landed and took possession.

The name of these youths, was TARBELL, and their descendants have always resided at St. Regis, and some of them have been distinguished as chiefs and head men of the tribe. One of these named Lesor Tarbell, and a son of his name, was a prominent chief, about fifty years since, and very much esteemed by the whites, for his prudence, candor, and great worth of character.

The name of Tarbell, is said to be very common in Groton, to this day.

Another traditional version of the account, differs in some particulars from that just related, and is as follows:

Three lads, and an elder sister, were playing together in a field, when they were surprised by a small party of Indians. One of the boys escaped, but the rest were seized, and marched that day about fourteen miles into the woods towards Canada, when it coming on dark, they came to a halt, and camped for the night. Thinking their prisoners secure, the Indians were less watchful than usual, and finally all fell asleep.

The girl, about twelve years old, kept awake, and seeing the rest asleep, her first thought was to awaken her brothers, and attempt to escape, but fearing to disturb the Indians, should she attempt this, and thus prevent any possibility of escape, she crept carefully out from among them, and struck off in the direction of her home, which she at length reached after undergoing great hardship.

One of the lads on growing up went off to the north west, the other married, and subsequently with his wife, and one or two other families, moved off, and made the first settlement at St. Regis.

From the abundance of partridges which the thicket afforded, they called it, AK-WIS-SAS-NE "where the partridge drums," and this name it still retains.*

These families were living very peaceably together, and had made small clearings for corn fields, when they were joined by Father Anthony Gordon, a Jesuit from Caughnawaga, with a colony of these Indians in 1760.

The year of this settlement is known by the fact that they were met near Coteau du Lac, by Lord Amherst, who was decending the St. Lawrence, to complete the conquest of Canada. Gordon named the place St. Regis.

With the belief that a biographical sketch of this saint, would be acceptable to our readers, in connection with this account, we will take the liberty of inserting it as it is given by a catholic author.

"Jean François Regis, of the society of Jesus, was born Jan. 31, 1597, at Foncouverte, a village in the diocese of Narbonne in Lauguedoc, France, and was a descendant of an ancient and noble family. At an early age he became strongly impressed with religious sentiments, and while a youth, was one of the first to enter the Jesuit School at Beziers, where he led a very exemplary life. At the completion of his earlier studies, he undertook the charge of instructing menial servants in Tournon. In 1631, his studies being finished, he visited Foncouverte to

---

* Another and equally consistent explanation of the adoption of this name, is given :

In the winter time, the ice from the rapids above, coming down under the firm ice at this place, often occasions a sort of tremor or earthquake in miniature, and is attended with a noise very much like the drumming of a partridge. A particular account of the singular phenomena of the ice in the rapids, will be given in our account of the town of Massena.

On the occasion of the author's visit to St. Regis in June 1852, the natives desired to give him a name, and proposed among others, that of their village. Objections being made, they decided upon, O-kwa-e-sen, a partridge, they regarding that bird somewhat as a national emblem, like the eagle to the United States. The idea was doubtless suggested by the particular inquiries made about the origin of their village. The custom of naming those who have business with them in common, and in former times when the drinking of rum was more prevalent, the ceremony of christening and adoption was conducted with excessive demonstration of joy. At present it consists in singing and shouting around the candidate, and the shaking of hands. At times a rude dance is performed, but this people have lost every recollection of the national feasts and dances, which are still maintained among the pagan party of the Iroquois at Onondaga and other Indian settlements, in the interior of the state.

They informed the author that they should consider him as belonging to the Ro-tis en-na-keh-te, or Little Turtle band, that being the smallest and feeblest one among them.

settle some family affairs, and there attracted much notice from the zeal
with which he preached to the people, and solicited alms for the poor.
He spent several years in missionary labors in France, always conspicuous for his zealous labors among the poor, over whom he acquired great
ascendency. This excited such persecution from the higher classes,
that he solicited an appointment as a missionary to the Hurons, and
Iroquois of Canada, but finally remained at home, much to his own
disappointment. He continued his labors among the lower classes till
his death, Dec. 31, 1640, at the age of 43 years, of which 26 were spent
as a Jesuit. This tomb at La Louvase, in Languedoc. is regarded by the
catholic population of France, as a shrine, and miracles are believed by
them to have been performed at it. He was cannonised by pope Clement
XII, in 1737, at the joint request of Kings Louis XV of France, and
Philip V, of Spain, and of the clergy of France, assembled at Paris, in
1735. His festival accurs on the 16th of June. [See *Butler's Lives of the
Saints*, 18mo edition, vol. vi, p. 261, 287.]

A painting of St. Regis, exists in the church at the mission of that
name. It was presented by Charles X, as hereafter stated.

It is not known how long the four families had been residing at this
place, when they were joined by the others, nor the numbers of the latter,
further than the vague tradition that "there were many canoe loads."
Probably they numbered several hundred souls.

The cause assigned for this emigration, was a desire to get the natives
away from the corrupting influences of rum, and the train of vices to
which they were particularly exposed from their proximity to Montreal.
It was hoped that by this means being withdrawn from the temptations
to which they were constantly liable, that a benefit would be derived.

In our account of Picquet's mission, we have seen that the missionaries
at the Indian establishments felt and deplored the contaminating influence
of the Europeans, and that the mission of St. Louis, was for this cause
obliged to be moved some distance up the river, to get the natives out of
the way of the moral miasm of Montreal, and the further emigration
to St. Regis, may without doubt be attributed to the same cause.

In these acts, these ecclesiastics evinced a commendable regard for
the moral welfare of their flocks, which challenges our admiration. In
order that the end desired might not be defeated, it was considered
essential that the new colony should be made up of a native population
entirely; that no military post should form a part of them, and that
traffic especially in spirituous liquors should be entirely interdicted.

Among the first duties of Gordon was the erection of a church, which
was built of logs and covered with barks.

This humble and primative temple of worship, was made to serve the
double purpose of a church and a dwelling, and one end of the hut was
partitioned off for the residence of their priest.

There being no bell, when the hour of worship arrived, an Indian went
through the village from hut to hut, and announced with a loud voice

the hour that they might assemble for prayer. This practice reminds one of the Mahomedan custom, of proclaiming the hour of prayer from the Minarets of mosques.

In about two years this church was burned, and with it the first two years of the parish records.

The first record extant, bears date Feb. 2, 1762, when Margarita Theretia an Abenika woman, married, and of unknown parentage, was baptized.

Since that date, the parish records are very perfect, they have been kept in the Latin and French languages.

Soon afterwards a small wooden church was erected on the ground now occupied by the priest's garden, which was furnished with a small cupola, and contained *a bell*.

It has been generally believed that this bell was the same as that taken in 1704, from Deerfield, in Massachusetts, but after careful inquiries, the author has arrived at the conclusion that that celebrated bell never was at St. Regis, but that it is none other than the smaller of the two that hangs in the steeple of the church of St. Louis, in Caughnawaga.

About fifteen years since, a bell belonging to the church of St. Regis, was broken up at Ogdensburgh, for recasting, and the Indians were very jealous lest some part should be abstracted, and are said to have appointed some of their number to watch the operation, and see that every part was remelted. This metal now forms a part of the larger bell in the church at St. Regis.

That the Deerfield bell could not have been taken directly to St. Regis, is evident, from the fact that fifty-six years elapsed between its capture and the founding of St. Regis.

The latter place was first begun by emigrants, in 1760, from Caughnawaga, the larger portion of the tribe remaining behind. It can scarcely be believed, that those that remained would allow themselves to be deprived of the only bell their church possessed, especially as the mission at the Saut St. Louis has been continued without interruption.

While on a visit to Caughnawaga, in October, 1852, the author found in the village a direct and consistent tradition of the bell, which is still used in their church, and among the records in the hands of the priest, a manuscript in the French language, of which we shall give a translation. The bell is a small one, and once possessed an inscription, which has been effaced.

The legend purports to have been found some fifteen years since, in an old English publication, and is regarded by the priest of the mission (Rev. Joseph Marcoux), who has for many years resided there, as in the main points reliable. If this view of the subject be correct, the legend loses none of its interest, except being transferred from the church of

8

St, Regis to the church of the Saut St. Louis. This village is on the south side of the St. Lawrence, opposite the village of Lachine, at the head of the Saut St. Louis, and nine miles above Montreal.

Legend of the Bell of Saut St. Louis (Caughnawaga), near Montreal.

" Father Nicolas having assembled a considerable number of Indians who had been converted to the catholic faith, had established them in the village which now bears the name of the Saut St. Louis, upon the River St. Lawrence.   The situation of this village is one of the most magnificent which the banks of that noble river presents, and is among the most picturesque which the country contains.

The church stands upon a point of land which juts into the river, and its bell sends its echoes over the waters with a clearness which forms a striking contrast with the iron bells which were formerly so common in Canada, while the tin covered spire of the church, glittering in the sunlight, with the dense and gloomy forests which surround it, give a character of romance to this little church, and the legend of its celebrated bell.*

Father Nicolas having, with the aid of the Indians, erected a church and a belfry; in one of his sermons explained to his humble auditors, that a bell was as necessary to a belfry, as a priest to a church, and exhorted them to lay aside a portion of the furs that they collected in hunting, until enough was accumulated to purchase a bell, which could only be procured · by sending to France.   The Indians exhibited an inconceivable ardor in performing this religious duty, and the packet of furs was promptly made out, and forwarded to Havre, where an ecclesiastical personage was delegated to make the purchase.   The bell was accordingly ordered, and in due time forwarded on board the *Grande Monarque,* which was on the point of sailing for Quebec.

It so happened that after her departure, one of the·wars which the French and the English then so often waged sprung up, and in consequence the Grande Monarque never attained her destined port, but was taken by a New England privateer, brought into the port of Salem, where she was condemned as a lawful prize, and sold for the benefit of her captors.

The bell was purchased by the village of Deerfield, upon the Connecticut river, for a church then about being erected by the congregation of the celebrated Rev. John Williams.

When Father Nicolas received news of the misfortune, he assembled

---

* The old church of Caughnawaga, was in 1845 replaced by the present large and substantial stone edifice, erected with funds given the Indians for that purpose in consideration of lands which the government had appropriated to itself, as having belonged to the Jesuits, but for which they awarded the value, on its being proved that this mission had never belonged to that order.   In 1830, a large bell was presented by the English government to the church, and hangs by the side of the time honored and venerable relic which forms the subject of the legend.   The latter originally bore an inscription in the Latin language, but this has been effaced by the chisel, probably by its New England owners, to prevent any identification by those for whom it was originally intended.   Adjoining the church, stands the priest's house, which still presents the same appearance as when Charlevoix the traveler abode in it.   The room is still pointed out in which he lived, and the desk on which he wrote a portion of that history which has made his name celebrated as a historian.

his Indians, related to them the miserable condition of the bell, retained in purgatory in the hands of heretics, and concluded by saying, that it would be a most praise worthy enterprise to go and recover it.

This appeal had in it as it were a kind of inspiration, and fell upon its hearers with all the force of the eloquence of Peter the Hermit, in preaching the crusades.

The Indians deplored together the misfortune of their bell, which had not hitherto received the rite of baptism: they had not the slightest idea of a bell, but it was enough for them, that Father Nicolas, who preached and said mass for them, in their church, said that it had some indispensable use in the services of the church.

Their eagerness for the chase was in a moment suspended, and they assembled together in groups, and seated on the banks of the river, conversed on the unhappy captivity of their bell, and each brought forward his plan which he deemed most likely to succeed in effecting its recovery.

Some of their number, who had heard a bell, said that it could be heard beyond the murmur of the rapid, and that its voice was more harmonious than that of the sweetest songster of the grove, heard in the quiet stillness of evening, when all nature was hushed in repose.

All were melancholy, and inspired with a holy enthusiasm; many fasted, and others performed severe penances to obtain the deliverance of the bell, or the palliation of its sufferings.

At length the day of its deliverance approached. The Marquis de Vaudreuil, Governor of Canada, resolved to send an expedition against the British colonies of Massachusetts and New Hampshire. The command of this expedition was given to Major Hertel de Rouville, and one of the priests of the Jesuit college, at Quebec, was sent to procure the services of Father Nicolas to accompany the expedition.

The Indians were immediately assembled in the church; the messenger was presented to the congregation, and Father Nicolas in a solemn discourse pointed to him as worthy of their veneration, from his being the bearer of glad tidings, who was about departing for his return to Quebec, to join the war. At the end of the discourse, the whole audience raised with one voice the cry of war, and demanded to be led to the place where their bell was detained by the heretics.

The savages immediately began to paint themselves in the most hideous colors, and were animated with a wild enthusiasm to join the expedition.

It was in the depth of winter when they departed to join the army of M. de Rouville, at Fort Chambly. Father Nicolas marched at their head, with a large banner, surmounted by a cross, and as they departed from their village, their wives and little ones, in imitation of women of the crusades, who animated the warriors of Godfrey of Bouillon, they sang a sacred hymn which their venerated priest had selected for the occasion.

They arrived at Chambly after a march of great hardship, at the moment that the French soldiers were preparing to start on their march up Lake Champlain.

The Indians followed in their rear, with that perseverance peculiar to their character. In this order the Indians remained, following in silence, until they reached Lake Champlain, where all the army had been ordered to rendezvous. This lake was then frozen and less covered by snow than the shores, and was taken as a more convenient route for the army. With their thoughts wrapped up in the single contemplation of the unhappy captivity of their bell, the Indians remained taciturn during this pensive march, exhibiting no symptoms of fatigue or of fear; no regret for their families or homes, and they regarded with equal indifference on the one hand the interminable line of forest, sometimes black from dense evergreens. and in others white from loads of snow; and on the other, the bleak lines of rocks and deserts of snow and ice, which bordered their path. The French soldiers, who suffered dreadfully from fatigue and cold regarded with admiration the agility and cheerfulness with which the Indians seemed to glide over the yielding surface of the snow on their snow shoes.

The quiet endurance of the proselytes of Father Nicolas formed a striking contrast with the irritability and impatience of the French soldiers.

When they arrived at the point where now stands the city of Burlington, the order was given for a general halt, to make more efficient arrangements for penetrating through the forests to Massachusetts. In leaving this point, de Rouville gave to Father Nicolas the command of his Indian warriors, and took the lead of his own himself, with compass in hand, to make the most direct course for Deerfield. Nothing which the troops had thus far suffered could compare with what they now endured on this march through a wild country, in the midst of deep snow, and with no supplies beyond what they could carry.

The French soldiers became impatient, and wasted their breath in curses and complaints at the hardships they suffered, but the Indians animated by a zeal which sustained them above the sense of hardships, remained steadfast in the midst of fatigue, which increased with the severity of their sufferings.

Their custom of travelling in the forest had qualified them for these hardships which elicited the curses and execrations of their not less brave, but more irritable companions.

Some time before the expedition arrived at its destination, the priest Nicolas, fell sick from over exertion. His feet were worn by the labor of traveling, and his face torn by the branches which he neglected to watch in his eagerness to follow the troops.

He felt that he was engaged in a holy expedition, and recalling to mind the martyrdom of the saints, and the persecutions which they endured, he looked forward to the glory reserved for his reward for the sufferings which he might encounter in recovering the bell.

On the evening of February 20th, 1704, the expedition arrived within two miles of Deerfield without being discovered.

De Rouville here ordered his men to rest, and refresh themselves a short time, and he here issued his orders for attacking the town.

The surface of the snow was frozen. and crushed under the feet, but De Rouville with a remarkable sagacity, adopted a stratagem to deceive the inhabitants and the garrison.

He gave orders that in advancing to the assault, his troops should make frequent pauses, and then rush forward with rapidity: thus imitating the noise made in the forest by the irregular blowing of the wind among branches laden with ice.

The alarm was at length given, and a severe combat ensued, which resulted in the capture of the town, and the slaughter or dispersion of the inhabitants, and the garrison.

This attack occurred in the night, and at daybreak the Indians who had been exhausted by the labors of the night, presented themselves before Father Nicolas in a body, and begged to be led to the bell, that they might by their homage prove their veneration for it. Their priest was greatly affected by this earnest request, and De Rouville and others of the French laughed immoderately at it, but the priest wished not to discourage them in their wishes, and he obtained of the French chief permission to send one of his soldiers to ring it in the hearing of the Indians.

The sound of the bell in the stillness of a cold morning, and in the midst of the calmness of the forest, echoed clear and far, and fell upon the ears of the simple Indians, like the voice of an oracle. They trembled, and were filled with fear and wonder.

The bell was taken from the belfry, and attached to a pole in such a manner that four men could carry it, and in this way it was borne off with their plunder in triumph, the Indians glorying in the deliverance of this miraculous wonder.

But they shortly perceived it was too heavy a burden for the rugged route they pursued, and the yielding nature of the snows over which they traveled. Accordingly upon arriving at the point on the lake, where they had left it, they buried their cherished treasure, with many benedictions of Father Nicolas, until the period should arrive when they could transport it with more convenience.

As soon as the ice had disappeared, and the bland air of spring had returned, giving foliage to the trees, and the fragrance and beauty of flowers to the forests, father Nicolas again assembled at the church, his Indian converts, to select a certain number of the tribe, who with the assistance of a yoke of oxen, should go and bring in the dearly prized bell.

During this interval, all the women and children of the Indian village, having been informed of the wonderful qualities of the bell, awaited its arrival with eagerness and impatience, and regarded its advent, as one of those events which but rarely mark the progress of ages. As the time approached, when the curious object should arrive, they were assembled on the bank of the river, and discoursing upon the subject, when far off in the stillness of the twilight, there was heard from the depths of the forest, a sound, which from being feeble and scarcely audible, became every moment louder. Every one listened, when presently the cry arose, *it is the bell! it is the bell !!* and in a moment after, the oxen were seen emerging from the wood, surrounded by a group of Indians, and bearing the precious burden on a pole between them. They had hung upon the beam and around the bell, clusters of wild flowers and leaves, and the oxen were adorned with garlands of flowers. Thus marching in triumph, Father Nicolas entered his village, more proud of his success, and received with more heartfelt joy, than a Roman general returning in triumph from the conquest of nations.

From this triumphal march in the midst of the quiet of the evening, which was broken only by the murmur of the rapid, softened by the distance arose the shouts of rejoicing, as the cortege entered the village, and the idol bell was deposited in the church. Every one gratified his eager curiosity by examining the strange and musical metal, and the crusade had been crowned with unqualified success.

In due time it was raised to its place in the belfry, and has ever since, at the accustomed hours, sent its clear tones over the broad bosom of the St. Lawrence, to announce the hour of prayer and lapse of time, and although its tones are shrill and feeble beside its modern companion, they possess a music, and call up an association, which will long give an interest to the church of the Saut St. Louis, at the Indian village of Caughnawaga."

Mrs. Sigourney, whose chaste and elegant poetry, is justly admired for the melody of its versification, as well as its delicacy of sentiment, has written a poetical account of this legend, which we will here take the liberty of quoting. It will be seen that it is in accordance with the erroneous belief of its being carried to the St. Regis, the inconsistency of which has been above stated.

THE BELL OF ST. REGIS.

" 'The red men came in their pride and wrath,
Deep vengeance fired their eye,
And the blood of the white was in their path,
And the flame from his roof rose high.

Then down from the burning church they tore
The bell of tuneful sound,
And on with their captive train they bore,
That wonderful thing toward their native shore,
The rude Canadian bound.

But now and then with a fearful tone,
It struck on their startled ear—
And sad it was 'mid the mountains lone,
Or the ruined tempest's muttered moan,
That terrible voice to hear.

It seemed like the question that stirs the soul,
Of its secret good or ill;
And they quaked as its stern and solemn toll,
Reechoed from rock to hill.

And they started up in their broken dream,
'Mid the lonely forest shade,
And thought that they heard the dying scream,
And saw the blood of slaughter stream
Afresh through the village glade.

Then they sat in council, those chieftains old,
And a mighty pit was made,
Where the lake with its silver waters rolled,
They buried the bell 'neath the verdant mould,
And crossed themselves and prayed.

And there till a stately powow came,
It slept in its tomb forgot,
With a mantle of fur, and a brow of flame,
He stood on that burial spot.

They wheeled the dance with its mystic round
At the stormy midnight hour,
And a dead man's hand on his breast he bound,
And invoked, ere he broke that awful ground,
The demons of pride and power.

Then he raised the bell with a nameless rite,
Which none but himself might tell,
In blanket and bear-skin he bound it tight,
And it journeyed in silence both day and night,
So strong was that magic spell.

It spake no more, till St. Regis's tower
In northern skies appeared,
And their legends extol that powow's power
Which lulled that knell like the poppy flower,
As conscience now slumbereth a little hour
In the cell of a heart that's seared."

The act of 1802, which will be hereafter given, empowered the trustees then created, to purchase a bell, and. it is very probable that this may have been the one that was broken up, and recast a few years since. The earliest settlers of the country agree in this statement that a bell was in the church at a very early period, and that the village presents now very nearly the same aspect that it did half a century since; with the difference that it now is more decayed and neglected than then.

The capture of Deerfield, divested of romance and tradition, occurred under the following circumstances.

"In the evening of the 29th of February, 1704, Major Hertel de Rouville, with 200 French, and 142 Indians, after a tedious march of between 2 and 300 miles through deep snows, arrived at an elevated pine forest about two miles north of the village, (now called Petty's plain,) bordering Deerfield meadow, where they lay concealed till after midnight. Finding all quiet, and the snow being covered with a crust sufficient to support the men, Rouville left his snow shoes and packs at the foot of the elevation, and, crossing Deerfield river, began his march through an open meadow before daylight, with the utmost caution, which however, was unnecessary, for the guard had retired to rest, a little before daylight. Arriving at the north west quarter of the fort, where the snow had drifted in many places nearly to the top of the palisades, the enemy entered the place, and found all in a profound sleep. Parties detached in various directions, broke into the houses, and dragged the astonished people from their beds, and whenever resistance was made they were generally killed. A party forced the door of the house of the Rev. Mr. John Williams, who awakened by the noise, seized a pistol from his bed tester and snapped it at one of the Indians who were entering the room. He was seized, bound, and kept standing in his shirt for nearly an hour. His house in the meantime was plundered, and two of his children, with a black female servant, were murdered before the door. They then permitted him and Mrs. Williams, with five other children to put on their clothes.
The house of Capt. John Sheldon was attacked, but as the door at which the Indians attempted to enter was firmly bolted, they found it difficult to penetrate. They then perforated it with their tomahawks, and thrusting through a musket, fired and killed the captain's wife, as she was rising from a bed in an adjoining room. The captain's son and wife, awakened by the assault, leaped from a chamber window at the

east end of the house, by which the latter strained her ancle, and was seized by the Indians, but the husband escaped to the woods and reached Hatfield. After gaining possession of the house, which was one of the largest in the place, the enemy reserved it as the depot for the prisoners, as they were collected from other parts of the village. The whole number made prisoners was 112, and the number of killed was 47. Having collected the prisoners, plundered and set fire to the buildings, Rouville left the place when the sun was about an hour high. Every building within the fort was reduced to ashes, except the meeting house, and that of Captain Sheldon, which was the last one fired, and saved by the English, who assembled immediately after the enemy left the place. The night following the attack, the enemy encamped in the meadow, in what is now Greenfield, about four miles from Deerfield village, where by clearing away the snow, and constructing slight cabins of brush, the prisoners were as comfortably lodged as circumstances would admit. The second day of the journey, Mrs. Williams, who had been confined but a few weeks previous, became exhausted through fatigue, and proving burdensome, her Indian master sank his tomahawk into her head, and left her dead at the foot of a hill near Green river. The march of the captives, on the Connecticut river continued several days without any incident of note, except now and then murdering an exhausted captive, and taking off his scalp.

At the mouth of White river, Rouville divided his force into several parties; that which Mr. Williams accompanied proceeded down Onion river to Lake Champlain, and from thence into Canada. After his arrival there he was treated with civility and even humanity. In 1706, a flag ship was sent to Quebec, and Mr. Williams and fifty seven other captives was redeemed and brought to Boston. All the surviving children of Mr. Williams were redeemed with the exception of his daughter Eunice, who was left behind, being about ten years old." *

She adopted the language, dress and religion of the Indians, and married one of the Caughnawagua tribe. She subsequently visited her New England relatives, but could not be induced to abandon her adopted people. Capt. Thomas Williams, at St. Regis, of whom we give a biographical notice, in this work, and whose name occurs on most of the treaties which the St. Regis Indians have held with the state, was a descendant of this daughter of the Rev. John Williams.

During the revolutionary war a considerable portion of the St. Regis and a part of the Caughnawaga Indians joined the British; others led by Colonel Louis Cook, of whom we shall give a particular account in the following pages, joined the American cause.

Concerning the history of the village during this period we have been unable to obtain any knowledge.

At the opening of the revolutionary war, the continental cause received much injury from the influence of the Johnson families, in Tryon county, and especially from Sir John Johnson, a baronet, and son of Sir

* See Historical Collections of Massachusetts, by John W. Barber, p. 250, 252 .Also a Biographical Memoir of the Rev. John Williams, by Stephen Williams, Deerfield 1837.

William, who secretly instigated the Indians to hostilities, and created much mischief on the frontier.

To prevent this calamity it was thought advisable by Gen. Schuyler, to arrest Sir John, and thus put it out of his power to do further mischief.

Accordingly in May, 1776, Col. Dayton, with a part of his regiment then on its way to Canada, was sent to prosecute this enterprise.[*]

Receiving timely notice of this, from his tory friends in Albany, he hastily assembled a large number of his tenants, and others, and prepared for retreat, which he successfully accomplished, taking to the woods and avoiding the route of lake Champlain, from fear of falling into the hands of the Continentals, supposed to be assembled in that direction, he struck deeper into the woods, by way of the head waters of the Hudson, and descended the Raquette to Canada. Their provisions were soon gone, their feet became sore from traveling, and numbers were left to be picked up by the Indians, sent back for their relief. After nineteen days of hardships, which have had few parallels in our history, they reached Montreal. So hasty was their flight, that the family papers were buried in the garden, and nothing was taken, but such articles as were of prime necessity. His extensive family estates were confiscated, and he thenceforth became a most active loyalist, and the scourge of the Mohawk settlement during the remainder of the war.

Some historians have supposed that an expedition of Mohawk Indians was despatched from Montreal to meet Sir John; and Brant long after, in rehearsing the exploits of his tribe, during the Revolution, says: " We then went in a body to a town, then in possession of the enemy, and rescued Sir John Johnson, bringing him fearlessly through the streets. "[†]

When on a visit of historical inquiry, at the Indian village of St Regis, in June 1852, the author obtained a tradition, that that people sent numbers of their warriors to meet the fugitives, carrying parched corn and sugar to preserve them from perishing, until they could reach the Canadian settlements.

We will return to the history of Gordon, and briefly trace the progress of the catholic mission, and then present the series of events which have marked the history of the village.

There is a tradition that a tract of land on the east side of the river, and extending up two miles, was granted to the priest as a support,

* Life of Brant, by William L. Stone, vol. i. p. 142, 144, and Sparke's Life and Writings of Washington, note in vol. iv. p. 409,410.

† Stone's Life of Brant, vol. i., p. 144, note.

but this claim has not been asserted, nor is it known that there is any written evidence of the fact.

Father Gordon's health failing, he went back to Caughnawaga, in 1775, where he died in 1777. The mission was then without a priest, five or six years. Father Denaut, Oct. 1784, from the Cedars, and Lebrun, a Jesuit from Caughnawaga, in January and September 1785, appear from the parish records, to have visited the place, to administer religious rites. - Denaut subsequently became Bishop of Quebec, and the mission at the Cedars was supplied by L'Archambault, who also occasionally visited St. Regis, in the absence of an established priest.

In December, 1785, Roderick McDonnell, a Scotch priest, succeeded, and remained till 1806, when he died. He is interred under the choir of the church. Being a part of the time sick, he was assisted by A. Van Felsen, of Quebec, who was here from May 5, 1800, till September 30, 1802.

During McDonnell's residence, the present church was erected in 1791 and 1792, at first without a belfry.

The frame church was then standing, but soon after demolished. The present church is a massive stone building, of ancient and venerable appearance, the walls nearly four feet thick, the windows high, and a door in the middle of the sash, for ventilation, after a custom prevalent in Canada. Across the end opposite the door is a railing, and beyond and elevated above the floor of the church, is an ample space for the altar, and the various fixtures of the catholic worship. The altar is unusually decorated with gilding and ornaments, and the interior of the church is adorned with paintings and prints of religious subjects. The history of two of these paintings will be given elsewhere.

A gallery extends across the end of the church over the door, for the accommodation of strangers and others, and in the body of the church near the wall, are a few seats for the singers. The greater part of the Indians, during worship, kneel or sit upon the floor, and the appearance presented to a stranger by the striking uniformity of dress and attitude, which he notices on first visiting the church during service, is very impressive.

Preaching is performed in the Mohawk dialect of the Iroquois language every sabbath, and all the ritual of the catholic church is observed with scrupulous care.

McDonnell was immediately succeeded by Father Rinfret, a Canadian, who remained a year, when he removed to Caughnawaga, where he died a few years after. He was followed by Jéan Baptiste Roupe, who arrived in the fall of 1807, and remained till the last of July, 1812. He was taken a prisoner in his house, at the affair which happened at St Regis, in the fall of 1812. He was succeeded by Joseph Marcoux, of Caughnawaga, who left in March, 1819, when Nicholas Dufresne, held the office of priest till 1825. He then removed to the Sulpician Seminary, at Montreal, and has been for ten or twelve years a missionary at Two Mountains, 36 miles northward from Montreal.

In 1825, Joseph Vallé arrived, and continued in the office till the fall of 1832, when he was succeeded by the Rev. Francis Marcoux, the present missionary. Father Vallé died in 1850, below Quebec.

The sovereignty of the soil of the northern part of the state, was anciently vested in the Mohawks, who, from the earliest period of authentic history, exercised jurisdiction over it. Upon the emigration of a part of this people to Canada, they claimed to carry with them the title from whence the villagers of St. Regis, asserted their claim to the northern part of the state, in common with the other Mohawk nations of Canada.

The Mohawks it is well known, espoused the royal cause in the revolution, through the influence of the Johnson family, and emigrated to Grand river in Upper Canada, where they still reside on lands given them by government. Whatever title to the land remained with them, was surrendered by the following treaty, held at Albany, March 29, 1795.

"At a treaty, held under the authority of the United States, with the Mohawk nation of Indians, residing in the province of Upper Canada, within the dominions of the King of Great Britain. Present, the Hon. Isaac Smith, Commissioner appointed by the United States, to hold this treaty, Abram Ten Broeck, Egbert Benson and Ezra L'Hommedieu, agents for the State of New York, Captain Joseph Brant and Capt. John Deserontyon, two of the said Indians, and deputies to represent the said nation at this treaty.

The said agents having in the presence, and with the approbation of the said commissioners, proposed to, and adjusted with the said deputies, the compensation as hereinafter mentioned, to be made to the said nation for their claim to be extinguished by this treaty, to all lands within the said state. It is thereupon finally agreed and done, between the said nations and the said deputies, as follows, that is to say: The said agents do agree to pay to the said deputies, the sum of one thousand dollars for the use of the said nation, to be by the said deputies paid over to, and distributed among the persons and families of the said nation, according to their usages, the sum of five hundred dollars, for the expenses of the said deputies, during the time they have attended this treaty, and the sum of one hundred dollars for their expenses in returning, and for carrying the said sum of one thousand dollars to where the said nation resides. And the said agents do accordingly for, and in the name of the *People of the State of New York*, pay the said three several sums to the deputies, in the presence of the said commissioners. And the said deputies do agree to cede and release, and these present witness that they accordingly do, for and in the name of the said nation, in consideration of the said compensation, cede and release to the people of the state of New York, forever, all the right or title of the said nation, to lands within the said state, and the claim of the said nation to lands within the said state, is hereby wholly and finally extinguished.

In testimony whereof, the said commissioner, the said agents, and the said deputies, have hereunto, and to two other acts of the same tenor and date, one to remain with the United States, one to remain with the said State, and one delivered to the said deputies, to remain with the said nation, set their hands and seals at the city of Albany, in the said State, the twenty-ninth day of March, in the year one thousand seven hundred and ninety-five."

Signed, sealed, and acknowledged.

(Copied from a MSS. volume entitled "Indian Deeds, and Treaties, 1712—1810," in the office of Secretary of State, at Albany. Page 187.)

Treaties with the Indians for their lands, were by a provision of the first constitution of the state, adopted April 20, 1777, reserved to the legislature. It was therein ordained,

"That no purchases or contracts for the sale of lands, made since the fourteenth day of October, 1775, or which may hereafter be made, with or of the said Indians, within the limits of this state, shall be binding on the said Indians, or deemed valid, unless made under the authority, and with the consent of the Legislature of the state." *(Laws of New York, vol. i, p. 16, 1813.)*

By an act passed April 4, 1801, it was provided:

"That if any person should without the authority and consent of the Legislature, in any manner or form, or on any terms whatsoever, purchase any lands within this state, of any Indian or Indians residing therein, or make any contract with any Indian or Indians, for the sale of any lands within this state, or shall in any manner, give, sell, demise, convey or otherwise dispose of any such lands or any interest therein, or offer to do so, or shall enter on, or take possession of, or to settle on any such lands by pretext or color of any right, or interest, in the same, in consequence of any such purchase, or contract, made since the 14th day of October, 1775, and not with the authority, and consent of the Legislature of this state, every such person shall in every such case, be deemed guilty of a public offence, and shall on conviction thereof, before any court having cognizance of the same, forfeit and pay to the people of this state, two hundred and fifty dollars, and be further punished by fine and imprisonment, at the discretion of the court."

The state being accordingly the only party whom the Indians could recognize, to them they applied for the settlement of their claims, to lands in the northern part of the state.

These claims were based upon ancient and primitive occupation, and especially upon the rights which they conceived they had, for compensation for services which some of them, particularly Colonel Louis Cook, their head chief, had rendered in the war. The nature and amount of these services we will give in our notice of that chief.

In 1789, he applied for a confirmation of a tract of land, in the present town of Massena, which he claimed was his own individual right, and this was subsequently confirmed to him by the Legislature.

In 1792, the Caughnawaga and St. Regis tribes, claiming to represent the Seven Nations of Canada, sent a deputation to the governor of the state of New York, to assert their claims, but this embassy produced no action in their favor.

As we shall have frequent occasion to allude to these *Seven Nations*, it would be well to understand who and what they were, but here our knowledge is less definite than might be desired, especially in relation to the origin of the term, and of the league or combination of tribes of which it consisted.

They appear to have been made up of several of the detached settlements of Iroquois emigrants from New York, and of Algonquins, &c., whom the catholic missionaries had domiciliated and settled in villages.

The St. Regis branch did not originally form, it is said, one of the seven, which consisted according to the Rev. F. Marcoux, of an Iroquois, an Algonquin, and a Nipessing nation at the Lake of Two Mountains, an Iroquo's tribe at Caughnawaga, the Oswegatchie tribe of Iroquois at La Presentation, a colony of Hurons at Lorett, nine miles north of Quebec, and a settlement of Abenekis at St. François, below Montreal, near the Sorel.

After the breaking up of the French at La Presentation, and the partial dispersion of the Oswegatchies, tradition relates, that a grand council was held, and it was therein resolved, that the St. Regis, who had formed a part of the Caughnawagas, at the formation of the league, should take the place of the scattered tribe, and they thenceforth represented them in the assemblies.

According to the gentlemen above mentioned, the tribes which represented the Seven Nations, have at present the following numbers, (June, 1852).

At the Lake of Two Mountains, of Iroquois,.................... 2ᴲ0

At the Lake of Two Mountains, Algonquins and Nipessing, together,   250

At Caughnawaga, of Iroquois,................................ 1300

At St. Regis, ... 1100

At Lorett, of Hurons, a very few.

At St. François of Abenakis, a few only. The numbers of the two
    latter were not known.

Failing in their first negotiation with the state, the St. Regis people prosecuted their claims, and in 1793 again appeared, by their deputies, at Albany, and laid their case before the governor, but without success. The following credentials are without date, but are believed to have been those furnished these Indians on this occasion:

" *The Chiefs at Cak-ne-wa-ge, head of the Seven Nations.*

To our brother, Commander and Governor, *Ni-haron-ta-go-wa,* George Clinton, at the State of New York. Brother, this is what we agreed upon, that we should have councils and conversations together, of peace and unity.

Now brother, we beg that you will pay attention that you can take the matter into good consideration betwixt you and us. We have sent the bearers, which will give you to understand our real minds and meaning, which is:

Thomas Aragrente,
Thomas Tharagwanegen,
Lumen Tiatoharopgiven,
William Gray,
Atthi naton.

All the chiefs' compliments to you, and beg you will not let the bearers want for victuals or drink, as much as may be for their good.

Te gan ni ta sen,	Ona sa te gen,
O na tri tsia wa ne,	On wa ni en te ni,
Sga na wa te,	Tha na ha,
Te ha sen,	Sga hen to wa ro ne,
Tha ia iak ge,	Si no he se,
Tha hen teh tha,	Sa ie gi sa ge ne,
Ga ron ia ra gon.	Ga ron ia tsi go wa."

(Signed by their marks.)

This negotiation also failed in its object, and the deputies returned home in disappointment.

In the winter of 1793-4, Colonel Louis, with three other warriors, again repaired to Albany, to get, if possible, some specific time designated, when the state would meet with them for their claim. They held an interview with the governor, but he declined at that time any negotiations with them on the subject, without referring their case to the legislature.

The journal of the assembly, for 1794 (page 106), contains the following record in relation to the St. Regis Indians:

"Mr. Havens, in behalf of Mr. Foote, from the committee appointed to take into consideration the communication made to this house by His Excellency the Governor, relative to the St. Regis Indians, reported that they have enquired into the several circumstances connected with the claim of the said Indians to certain lands within the jurisdiction of this state, and are of the opinion that it will be necessary to appoint commissioners to treat with the said Indians, and to authorize them, by law, to extinguish the said claim, or to take such measures relative to the said business, as shall be most beneficial to this state, and to the United States."

The following was the message of the governor, above alluded to. It was reported on the 21st of February of that year:

"GENTLEMEN,
You will receive with this message the conclusion of my conference with the Oneida Indians, and a copy of an additional speech of the Cayugas, and my answer thereto.

I also transmit to you a speech made to me by Colonel Lewis, of St. Regis, who, with three other warriors, arrived here some days ago, as a deputation from the chiefs of the seven nations, of Lower Canada. You will perceive by my answer to them, that I have, for the reasons therein mentioned, declined entering into conference with them on the subject of their deputation, other than that of receiving their communication, which is now submitted to the consideration of the Legislature.

GEO. CLINTON.

So far as we have been able to learn, the course advised by the committee was not adopted, and no encouragement was given the deputies further than the indefinite and unsatisfactory assurance that their claim should be examined at as early a day as might be consistent.

What the probable result would be, might perhaps be surmised, when we consider, that the state had already patented to Macomb and his associates the territory claimed by these Indians, reserving only a tract equal to six miles square, near the Indian village. It is very probable, that the Indians did not know of this sale, and still honestly believed themselves entitled to a large tract in the north part of the state.

In December, 1794, they again appeared at Albany to urge their claim. The governor appears to have been absent, and a communication intended for him was delivered to John Taylor, of Albany, who addressed the governor the following letter, inclosing that which he had received from the Indians:

ALBANY, 10th January, 1795.

" SIR:
The enclosed message was delivered me by one of the men who came down last winter, Col. Louis, and attended the Legislature at this place, on the subject of their lands. He says he was deputed by the Seven Nations for that purpose, and had directions to proceed to New York, if I could not do the business. As a journey to New York would have been attended by expense to the state, and trouble to you, I promised to transmit the message, and recommended him to return home.

I am your Excellency's
most obedient servant,

JOHN TAYLOR."

The letter referred to in the foregoing, was as follows:

" ALBANY, December, 1794.

NEWATAGHSA LEWEY:
Brother: The Seven Nations of Upper Canada are still of the same mind as they were when you spoke with them last winter; but they expected you would have met them this summer on the business that they came about to your great council last winter. They suppose that the business of the war, which was expected, prevented your meeting of them. They hope you will attend to the business, and meet them, as you promised, as early as possible next summer, as they are still of the same mind they were when they spoke to you, and expect you are so likewise."

The governor accordingly appointed Samuel Jones, Ezra L'Hommedieu, N. Lawrence, Richard Varick, Egbert Benson, John Lansing, Jr., and James Watson, commissioners, to hold an interview with the Indians, to settle some preliminaries with them, but without the power to treat definitely with them on the subject.

The following is the result of their negotiations, which was addressed to Governor Clinton:

"NEW YORK, 6 March, 1795.

SIR:

In consequence of your Excellency's appointment of us to that trust, we have this morning had an interview with the eleven Indians now in the city, from the nation or tribe, distinguished as the St. Regis Indians, or the Indians of the Seven Nations of Canada, and Colonel Lewis, one of their number, as their speaker, made a speech to us, purporting that during the last winter, they had come to Albany while the Legislature was sitting there, and made known their desire that a future meeting might be appointed, in order to treat, and finally conclude and settle with them respecting their right and claim to lands within the limits of this state; that they had returned home with what they received, as assurances that such future meeting would have been appointed; that they had waited in expectation of it during the whole of the last season; that they are not authorized to treat or conclude therefor; that the only object of their present journey is again to propose such meeting, when all the chiefs will attend, so that whatever may then be agreed upon, should be binding on all the tribes.

To this speech we have deferred giving an answer, supposing it most fit that we should previously be informed of the sense of the Legislature on the subject; it being most probably the interest of both houses, that the act of the 5th instant should be limited to an agreement or an arrangement to be made at this time, and with the Indians who are now present.

We have the honor to be, sir, with due respect, your most obedient, humble servants.

SAMUEL JONES,   RICHARD VARICK,
EZRA L'HOMMEDIEU,   EGBERT BENSON,
N. LAWRENCE,   JOHN LANSING, JUN.,
JAMES WATSON.

HIS EXCELLENCY, GOVERNOR CLINTON."

The following were the speeches exchanged on this occasion:

" Brothers :

Since that parchment was delivered us, which you will remember, as well as some of our chiefs now present, for it was during the Indian war when we were employed to make peace, and we made known to the other Indians the promises therein contained, and they made peace, we have claimed payment for those lands by means of that parchment, and he has promised to do us justice.

Brothers :

With respect to our affairs with you, we rest upon your word; you have promised to do us justice, and we depend upon it.

We have requested justice with the king, and he has promised to have a meeting, and to do us justice in the summer, and therefore we wish a settlement of our matter with you sooner. For if we should be engaged in settling that affair, and you should call upon us at the same time, we should have our hands full. Therefore, we wish a settlement with you first.

Brothers :

When we have made this settlement with you, we shall live with you like brothers, and not say that you have wronged us."

To the foregoing speech, the agents made the following reply:

" Brothers:
We have listened to what you have now told us.

Brothers:
The king and we are friends and neighbors, but he can not take a part in any business between you and us, nor can we take a part in any business between him and you.

Brothers:
You may rely on our promise, that the proposed meeting between you and us shall take place, but we can not now fix the time more precisely than we have done, for we do not know when we shall be ready, and if we should now fix a time, and should not then be ready, you would come to the place, and not finding us there, you would think we meant to deceive you.

Brothers:
We will certainly meet you as soon as we can, and we will give you seasonable notice.

NEW YORK, 11th March, 1795.

RICHARD VARICK,	EGBERT BENSON,
JAMES WATSON,	EZRA L'HOMMEDIEU.
SAMUEL JONES.	

The foregoing communication of the agents was transmitted to the Legislature on the 7th of March, 1795, by the governor, in the following message.

"Gentlemen:
With this message you will receive a communication from the agents appointed to confer with the representatives of the St. Regis Indians, which will necessarily require your immediate attention.

It must readily occur to you that no legislative direction exists with respect to the greater part of the expense incident to this occasion.

The concurrent resolution of the 3d instant, only refers to the accommodation of the Indians while in the city, and neither provides for the customary gratuities, nor the expenses arising from their journey here and their return.

I also transmit a letter from some of the chiefs of the Onondaga nation, respecting the agreement made with them in 1793, by the commissioners appointed for the purpose."

GEO. CLINTON.

Greenwich, 7 March, 1795.

In pursuance of this advice the following resolution was introduced in the senate and passed.

" Resolved. That his Excellency the Governor, be requested to direct that suitable accommodations be provided for twelve St. Regis Indians, who are expected in town this afternoon, on business relative to the claims on the State, and that the Legislature will make provision for defraying the expense."

On the 9th of March, 1795, the resolution of the senate was referred to the assembly, and the following record appears on their journal.

" Resolved. As the sense of both houses of the Legislature, that it is advisable a future meeting should be appointed by his Excellency the

9

Governor, to be held with the Indians, generally known and distinguished as the Indians of St. Regis, in order to treat, and finally to agree with the said Indians touching any right or claim which they may have, to any lands within the limits of this state; and further, that his Excellency the Governor, in addition to the request contained in the concurrent resolution of both houses, of the third instant, be also requested to cause the twelve Indians mentioned in said concurrent resolution, to be furnished with such sum of money as may be requisite to defray the expenses of their journey to this city, and on their return home, and also that his Excellency the Governor, be requested to cause such presents or gratuities as he shall deem proper to be given to the said Indians, in behalf of this state, and that the Legislature will make the requisite provision for carrying these resolutions into effect."

Ordered. That the consideration of the said resolutions be posponed until to-morrow.

The agents appointed by the Governor, held another interview with the Indians, and the speeches that were exchanged on the occasion are preserved, and were as follows:

Speech of the Agents for the State of New York to Colonel Louis, and other St. Regis Indians.

"*Brothers:*
When we met you, a few days ago, on your arrival in this city, we told you our chief the Governor, was sick, and that he had appointed us to meet you in his stead.

Brothers:
We then also bid you welcome, and which we now repeat to you.

Brothers:
You then told us that you had come to see us, and only to propose that there should be another meeting between us and you, when all your chiefs would attend, and treat and settle with us about land, which is within our state, and which you say belongs to you.

Brothers:
This was the substance of what you then told us, and we have told it to our chief the Governor, and our council the Legislature, and they have listened to it, and have directed us to tell you that they very willingly assent to what you have proposed, and that a message will be sent to you during the next summer, to inform you of the time and place, when, and where, we will meet you on the business, and we can now only promise, that the place will be as near where you live as conveniently may be, so as to save you the trouble of a long journey, and that the time will not be later in the next fall than when the travelling is good.

Brothers:
We wish you in the mean time to possess your minds in peace, for it is as much our wish as it is yours, that the business should be talked over and settled between you and us, in friendship and integrity, as between brothers, for as we do not desire any land which belongs to you, without paying you for it, so we hope you do not desire we should pay you for that which does not belong to you.

Brothers:
We now bid you farewell, for the present, and wish you a safe journey home, and that we may meet each other again in peace and in health, at the intended future meeting."

To this speech of the commissioners the St. Regis Indians through Colonel Louis, their speaker, replied as follows:

"*Brothers:*
It is usual when brothers meet, if it is even the next day, to thank Providence for preserving each of them, so as to meet again.

Brothers:
We are very thankful that you have taken so much pity on your brothers, who have come so great a distance to see you, that they were almost barefooted and uncovered, and you at our first arrival in the city, gave us a pair of shoes and hat each, for which we are thankful.

Brothers:
When we first arrived here, we told you the business we had come upon, and which we had come upon several seasons before, and particularly last winter. You then promised that you would meet us, but you have not done it.

We have business at home as well as you, brothers, and for that reason we request you to consider about the matter deliberately.

Brothers:
We think it is a long time hence that you have fixed upon. We told you when we came, that we had other business with the king, who also is on our lands. All the other nations to the westward are concerned in that business, and I expect I have that to see to, as they depend on my council. If that should take place at the same time as yours, it will be inconvenient, we therefore wish to have our business with you first settled, before we settle with the king.

Brothers:
We were at Albany when you received the speech of the king; I then told you the minds of our chiefs upon that subject, for I know it.

You told us then your minds were to do us justice, and that made our breasts cool. We returned home and told the king to perform the promise he had made to us.

[Here Colonel Louis produced a printed proclamation in parchment, by the late Sir William Johnson.]

For this reason we expect our matters with you first settled. For the king told us, that about midsummer he would come and settle with us for the lands of ours which he had possessed and improved.

Then, brothers, we shall be able to come and inform you how we have settled with him."

The Legislature by an act passed March 5, 1795, provided, " That it shall and may be lawful, for the person administering the government of this State, either by himself, or by such agent or agents as he shall thereunto appoint, to make such agreement and arrangements with the Indians of St. Regis, or with the representatives of the said Indians, respecting their claims to any lands within this State, or any part or parts thereof, as shall tend to ensure their good will and friendship to the people of the United States, and to extinguish any, and every such claim, and in such manner as he or such agents so to be appointed may think proper, but no such agreement or arrangement by such agents shall be valid, unless ratified and confirmed by the person administering the government of this State, any thing in the ' act relative to Indians resident within the State' passed the 27th of March, 1794, to the contrary hereof notwithstanding."

The act here referred to, was a law relative to the Indians resident within the state, which appointed the Governor, with William North, John Taylor, Abraham Van Vechten, Abraham Ten Broek, Peter Gansevoort, Jr., and Simeon Dewitt, trustees for the Indians within the state, and for each and every tribe of them, with full power to make such agreements and arrangements with the tribes of central New York, respecting their lands, as shall tend to produce an annual income to the said Indians, and to insure their good will and friendship to the people of the United States.

No grants were to be made by the Indians, except to the state.

They were further empowered to treat with any other Indians, for any other lands within the state, and the consideration paid for the extinguishment of these claims, was to be paid at the time of making the contract, or within one year thereafter.

Commissioners were again appointed, who met the deputies at Fort George, at the south end of Lake George, in September, 1795, where an interview was held, but without arriving at satisfactory results, or an agreement between the parties. We have not been able to procure the speeches that were made on this occasion, or what transpired between them, further than the intimations contained in the following pages.

The results were communicated by the agents of the state to Governor Jay, who in the month of January, transmitted the following message to the legislature.

GENTLEMEN:

" I have now the honor of laying before you the proceedings at a treaty with the Indians, denominated the Seven Nations of Canada, comprising those usually denominated the St. Regis Indians, held at the south end of Lake George, in this State, on the 26th day of September last, with a letter of the 2d instant, from the agents who were appointed to attend it on the part of the State.

It appears from the above mentioned letter, that the expenses incident to the said treaty have been paid, and the accounts duly audited and passed, except the allowance usually made by the United States to the commissioners whom they employ for holding treaties with Indians.

The compensation due to the said agents for their services, still remains to be ascertained and ordered by the Legislature.

NEW YORK, 23d January, 1796.

JOHN JAY."

On the 26th of March, 1796, the governor transmitted to the legislature a message, accompanying a letter from the department of war, dated the 19th inst., together with the report of the secretary of state, on the subject of claims made by the Indians called the Seven Nations of Canada, to lands within the state.

This message with the accompanying papers, was referred to the committee of the whole.

This was subsequently referred to a joint committee of the two houses, who reported on the 1st of April, as follows:

" That although the several matters stated by the agents of this State to the said Indians, at the late treaty held with them at Lake George, are to be relied on as true, and to be considered as sufficient to prevent the supposition that the said Indians have a right to lands claimed by them; and that although these matters both in respect to fact and inference, remain' unanswered by the said Indians, yet that it will be proper whenever a treaty shall be held for the purpose by the United States with the said Indians, that agents for this State should again attend, in order further to examine and discuss the said claim, and if they shall deem it eligible, then also further to propose and adjust with the said Indians, the compensation to be made by this State for the said claim."

This resolution met with the concurrence of the house.

In pursuance of this concurrent resolution of the senate and assembly, the governor appointed Egbert Benson, Richard Varick and Jas. Watson, agents on the part of the state, to meet the deputies of the St. Regis and Caughnawaga tribes, who then claimed, and have since been recognized by the state, to be the representatives of the Seven Nations of Canada, to negotiate in the presence of a commissioner appointed by the government of the United States, for the extinguishment of the Indian title to lands in the northern part of the state. The following is an account of the proceedings at this treaty, which we derive from the original manuscript in the office of the secretary of state, at Albany:

" At a treaty held at the city of New York, by the United States, with the nations of Indians denominating themselves the seven nations of Canada; Abraham Ogden, commissioner for the United States, appointed to hold the treaty, Ohnawito, alias Good Stream, a chief of the Caughnawagas, Oteatohatongwan, alias Colonel Louis Cook, a chief of the St. Regis Indians; Teholagwanegen, alias Thomas Williams, a chief of the Caughnawagas, and William Gray, deputies authorized to represent these nations or tribes at the treaty, and Mr. Gray also serving as interpreter.

Egbert Benson, Richard Varrick, and James Watson, agents for the state of New York.

MAY 23, 1796.

The deputy, Thomas Williams, being confined to his lodging in this city by sickness, was unable to be present; the other three deputies proposed, nevertheless, to proceed to the business of the treaty. The commissioner thereupon, informed them generally, that he was appointed to to hold the treaty; that the sole object of it was, to enable the state of New York, to extinguish by purchase, the claim or right of these nations or tribes of Indians, to lands within the limits of the state, and that agreeably to his instructions from the president, he would take care the negotiation for that purpose, between the agents for the state and the Indians, should be conducted with candor and fairness.

Mr. Gray, then read and delivered the following speech, as from the deputies, written in English.

A table from the seven nations of Indians residing in the state of New York, and Upper and Lower Canada, to the commissioner of the United States and state of New York, concerning a claim of lands in the state of New York.

Brothers:

We are sent from our nations to you, and fully empowered by them to treat with you respecting our lands, or on any other occasion that may be attended with a good meaning, or cause to brighten and stregthen the chain of friendship betwixt you and us. This power now given us, present, Colonel Louis Cook, Ohnawiio, Good Stream, Teholagwanegan, Thomas Williams, and William Gray, our interpreter at Caughnawaga, the place where our Great Council Fire is held, and where our nations were all assembled and in full council, and there to convince you, brothers, and in order that your business might be attended to with care, and speed, they gave us their full power, to act in behalf of our nations, and that whatsoever should be agreed upon betwixt you and us, the same should ever hereafter be indisputable, and stand for just, to us, or any of us. This power was given to us on paper, and signed by all our principal chiefs, and the same paper, lodged in the hands of our great brother, George Washington, the President, one who we had too much confidence in, to believe that he would have misplaced a paper, of that consequence, however it does not alter our power, as we have before mentioned. We are sent to you for the purpose of having a final settlement with you before we return to them, and brothers, our chief's last charge, when we parted with them at the great council at Caughnawaga, was to reason the case with our brothers, and to act with judgment; for that whatsoever was agreed on at this meeting, thro' us, should stand for just to the whole of our nations.

Brothers:

At our meeting last fall, at Fort George, you, after some conversations, desired us to point out the land we claimed in this state, and accordingly we did.

Brothers:

You then brought in several objections against our claim, but we could not find either of them to be reasonable, or in any way sufficiently weighty, if we had ever sold any of our lands, either to the king of France or Great Britain, or either of the United States, we should have of course signed our names to the agreement, which if that were the case, we are sensible that such papers would be brought forward against us, and that too with great justice, but so far from anything of the kind, that we bid defiance to the world, to produce any deed, or sale, or gift, or lease, of any of the lands in question, or any part of them, from us, to either the king of France, or Britian, or to either of the United States, or to any individual, excepting those we have adopted into our nation, and who reside with us.

Brothers:

You produced to us a copy of a deed from several Mohawks, for eight hundred thousand acres of land, which these Mohawks had as good a right to sell, as they have to come and dispose of the city of New York, notwithstanding this, you at the treaty of last fall, pointed those people out to us, to be too just a people, you thought to do a thing of the kind; but what makes them just in your eyes, we expect is because they stole from us, and sold to you. This is what makes them a just people.

Brothers:

Had we several years ago, done as those have, whom you call a just people, that is; had we sold off all our lands, then; underhandedly sold our brothers, and then fled our country; took up arms and come and killed men, women, and children, indiscriminately: burnt houses and committed every other act of devastation, and in short, done everything we could, against our once nearest friends, then according to what you say of these Mohawks, you would have esteemed us a just people, and therefore would not have disputed our claim.

Brothers:

From what we have seen, within a few years, we have reason to believe that a people as those, are most esteemed in your eyes; we need not mention to you the conduct of the western Indians, nor of their friends, you can judge who we mean, but it seems those who injure you the most, you are the readiest to serve.

Brothers:

It seems that before a nation can get justice of another, they must first go to war, and spill one another's blood, but brothers, we do not like this mode of settling differences; we wish justice to be done without, and it so far from the conduct of a Christian people, that we are fully determined we never will resort to such means, unless driven to it by necessity.

Brothers:

It is our earnest wish, to live in friendship and unity with you, and we have always endeavored to persuade our brother Indians to take pattern by us, and live peaceably with you, and to think that our brothers of the United States were a just people, and never would wrong them of any of their lands that justly belonged to them.

Brothers:

This we did on the strength of your former promises to us, which we think you remember too well to need them to be repeated. You who depend on ink and paper, which ought never to fade, must recollect better than we, who can not write, and who depend only on memory, yet your promises are fresh in our minds.

Brothers:

We ask for nothing but what is our just due, and that we ever shall expect to get, until such time as you deny your own words, not only by breaking your promises, but making false speakers of us in all that ever we said to our brother Indians, in your behalf, and encouraging those who always have been endeavoring to injure both you and us, all that ever lay in their power.

Brothers:

We entreat you only to look back, and consider the privileges your brother Indians formerly enjoyed, before we were interrupted by other nations of white people, who feign themselves to us as brothers, and let justice take place betwixt you and us, in place of arbitrary power, for that brothers, you very well know, is a thing that never gave contentment to any people, or nation whatsoever.

Brothers:

Formerly we enjoyed the privilege we expect is now called freedom; and liberty becomes an entire stranger to us, and in place of that, comes in flattery and deceit, to deprive poor ignorant people of their property, and bring them to poverty, and at last to become beggars and laughing-stocks to the world.

Brothers:

This is what we have already seen, but, however, we wish never to reflect on what is past, but trust in the Great Spirit who made us all, to so order it that justice may take place, and that better is to come.

Brothers:

We pray you to take this matter into good consideration, and do by us as you would wish to be done by brothers, that is what we wish for, that every brother might have their rights, throughout this continent, and all to be of one mind, and to live together in peace and love, as becometh brothers; and to have a chain of friendship made betwixt you and us, too strong ever to be broke, and polished and brightened so pure, as never to rust: This is our sincere wishes.

Brothers:

We wish likewise to enjoy our own laws and you yours, so far, that is, if any of our people, Indians, should commit a crime to any of their brothers, the white people of the United States, that he may be punished by his own nation, and his chiefs to make good all damages; and likewise on the other part, if any white person shall commit a crime to any Indian, that we the Indians, are not to take revenge on the person, but resign him up to justice, and there let him be punished according to the laws of his nation.

Brothers:

This we think will be one great step towards strengthening the chain of friendship, and to prevent all differences and disputes hereafter, and that is what we could wish that after this settlement with you brothers, that there never may hereafter arise differences or disputes betwixt you and us, but rather, if any nation, people or individual, should attempt to cause any difference or dispute betwixt you and us, or to intrude, or wish to injure either of us, that we may be all agreed as one, to drive such ill-minded people from off our continent, that does not wish to live amongst us in time of peace.

Brothers:

These are our sincere wishes, and we hope that you will consider this matter well, and let us make a good path for your children and ours to walk in after us; this brothers, is our greatest desire, and to live in peace and love with you.

Brothers:

As to our lands, we wish our children after us to share their part of the lands as well as us that are now living, and we are sensible, brothers, that if you do by us as you wish to be done, were it your case, as it is ours, and let justice speak, and make us an offer for our lands, yearly, exclusive of a small piece we wish to reserve for our own use, we are satisfied that as you know the value of lands so much better than we do, that your offer will prevent any further contention on the business.

Brothers:

We with patience wait your answer.

May 24, 1796.

Speech from the Agents of the State to the Deputies for the Indians.

Brothers:

We have considered your speech to us of yesterday, and we find the question respecting your claim, remains as it was at the conference betwixt you and us, at the treaty held at Lake George, last fall, were closed. Without some further evidence, it appears to be scarcely reasonable in you to expect we should admit your claim, and the only inducement with us to have it released or extinguished is, as we have before stated to you, because we desire to live in peace and good neighborhood with you, and to avoid all controversy in future, and consequently not any supposed merit or justice in the claim itself, but merely contentment and satisfaction to you, are the considerations in determining as to the amount of the compensation to be allowed you. We have therefore offered you three thousand dollars, which you declined accepting, without any offer or proposal in return from you; and although it was then intended as a definite offer from us, we are still willing to add to it or to vary it to an annuity, in order to which, however, you must now inform us what your wishes or expectations are. This will be necessary, otherwise the negotiations will not be conducted on terms duly fair and equal between us."

May 25, 1796.

Mr. Gray read and delivered to the agents the following speech, as from the deputies, written in English.

A speech from the Seven Nations of Canada and State of New York, to their Brothers of the State of New York.

" *Brothers:*

We have considered your answer of yesterday, to our speech to you on the day before, wherein you say, you find the question respecting our claim remaining as it was when we parted last fall from the treaty at Lake George. Very true, so it does; for if we remember right, you told us you would give us three thousand dollars for a release or quit claim for all the lands in our claim, exclusive of six miles square, to be reserved for the use of the village of St. Regis; and that was all you could offer, as you was sent there by them that was greater than you. We told you we was not able to comply with your offer, as we did not wish to bring our children to poverty by an action of that kind. Neither did you ask us what we did expect to have for our lands; if you had we should immediately have told you.

Brothers:

Now you say, without some further evidence, you can not see fit to admit our claim.

We want you brothers to tell us what further proof you wish us to shew than what we already have shown? We have told you, time past, and we tell you now, that our claim is just, and as to finding any other nation or people that say that our claim is not just, or that there is a better title can be procured than ours, as we told you before, we are sensible that can not be done, in justice; however, for your satisfaction, brothers, as we have mentioned several times before, that if you was not convinced that our claim was just, to be at the expense of calling the different nations whose boundaries join our claim, and let them be evidences for and against us. We likewise tell you, that if we ever had sold any part of the lands we now claim to bring forward the papers signed by our chiefs, and they will end the business betwixt you and us, and for further evidence, we think it, brothers, unnecessary.

Brothers:

We will now tell you what we expect to have, and do justice to you, and ourselves. That is, to reserve for our own use, in land, to begin at the village of St. Regis, and to run east ten miles on the line of the latitude of forty-five, then up the River St. Lawrence, from the village of St. Regis to a place called the Presque Isle, which we think is about thirty-five or forty miles from the village, and that distance to continue twenty miles in breadth. This piece we wish to reserve for our own use, which is but a very small piece. And the principal do we offer for your settlements, or any other use you may see fit to put it to. We should think it no ways out of reason or justice, to allow us the sum of three thousand pounds yearly, which will come to a trifle over one dollar for each person that is now living, and has a right in this claim, which is but a small sum towards clothing a person yearly, when before your clearing up our hunting grounds, we supported ourselves both in victuals and clothing, from what nature provided for us from off those lands.

Brothers:
Your compliances to these terms, will give contentment to the minds of your brethren, the Indians of the Seven Nations.

26th May, 1796.

Speech from the Agents to the Deputies.

Brothers:
We had intended to have avoided all further examination of the merits of your claim, and that the conferences between you and us should have been confined only to adjusting the compensation to be allowed to you for the extinguishment of it; but there are some parts of your speech of yesterday which we suppose ought not to remain wholly unnoticed by us.

Brothers:
You say there is no other people can be found, who can say your claim is not just, and if we are not convinced your claim is just, that we should be at the expense of calling the different nations whose boundaries join your claim, to be evidences for, and against your claim.

Brothers:
It would be sufficient for us merely to say, that considering the objections we have made to your claim, and the very unsatisfactory manner in which you have endeavored to answer them, that it is not reasonable in you to propose that we should be at the expense of procuring the attendance of the Indians, to whom you refer as witnesses. We will however, state a fact, to convince you that if they did attend, such is the probability that their testimony would be against your claim, as to render it unavailable even for you to call them.

Brothers:
The Six Nations of Indians, by a deed dated the 30th day of November, 1787, and in consideration of an annuity of two thousand dollars, sold to John Livingston, and his associates, for the term of nine hundred and ninety-nine years, lands described in the said deed as follows:
" All that certain tract or parcel of land, commonly called and known "by the name of the Lands of the Six Nations of Indians situate, "lying, and being, in the state of New York, and now in the actual pos- "session of the said chiefs, and sachems of the Six Nations. Beginning "at a place commonly known and called by the name of Canada Creek, "about seven miles west of Fort Stanwix, now Fort Schuyler, thence "north easterly, to the line of the province of Quebec, thence along the "said line to the Pennsylvania line, thence east on the said line, or Penn-

" sylvania line, to the line of Property, so called. by the state of New
" York, thence along said line of Property to ' Canada Creek' aforesaid."

These boundaries, you perceive, include nearly, if not all. the lands
you claim within this state, and the deed is signed by forty-five Indian
chiefs, and among the witnesses to it is Colonel Louis, the deputy here
present.

This deed was confirmed by another, bearing date the 9th day of July,
1788. Signed by sixty-six chiefs. and among the witnesses were Colonel
John Butler, and Captain Joseph Brant. These deeds having been
given up to the state, by the persons to whom they were made, have
been lodged in the Secretary's office, and they are now produced to you,
in order that you may see them. This purchase by Mr. Livingston, and
his associates, without the consent of the Legislature, was contrary to
the constitution of the state. and therefore void.

It is, notwithstanding, sufficient for the purpose for which we principally mention it, as it is not to be presumed, that these Indians would
ever declare that lands which they intended to sell, and be paid for, as
belonging to themselves, did belong to others. Not only so, but the
persons who have subscribed the deeds, as witnesses, and having a
knowledge of Indian affairs, and some of whom, even Colonel Louis
himself, if we are not much misinformed, assisted Mr. Livingston, and
his associates, in making the purchase, were called on as witnesses, between you and us, they must declare, that they never had heard or
believed, that any part of the lands described in these deeds, belonged
to any other nations than the Six Nations, otherwise they must declare
that they were witnesses to a transaction, which they knew to be intended fraudulent, and injurious to you; so that it must evidently be
fruitless in you to depend on the testimony of the neighboring nations,
to establish your claim.

Brothers :

When we first came together, at the treaty held last fall, and before
any formal speeches had passed between you and us, you mentioned,
that you claimed the lands also on the east side of the line between this
state, and the state of Vermont; but the intent of that treaty, being
only for the extinguishment of your claim to lands within this state, the
lands in Vermont were omitted out of the boundaries of your claim, as
you afterwards described it to us.

This you again affirmed to us verbally, yesterday, and you declared
the lands claimed by you, within the limits of Vermont, as running from
Ticonderoga to the Great Falls on Otter Creek, thence easterly to the
heights of land, dividing the waters which run eastwardly, from the
waters which run into Lake Champlain, thence along these heights, and
the heads of the waters running into Lake Champlain, to the forty-
fifth degree of latitude, and we take it for granted, you mean your claim
is the same as well with respect to the lands in Vermont as to the lands
in this state.

The king of Great Britain, however, when the territory was under the
jurisdiction of this state, as the colony of New York, made grants of
land, within the boundaries of your claim, as extending into Vermont,
without requiring a previous purchase from you, or any other nation, or
tribes of Indians, which is a further proof against the existence of any
title, in you, to the lands you claim.

Brothers :

In 1782 and 1788, we purchased from the Oneidas, Cayugas, and Onon-
dagoes, the whole of their lands, except some tracts which were reserved

for their own use, and the land which we purchased from each of these nations, and exclusive of the reservations, are certainly not less in value, than the lands you claim, as comprehended within this state.

Their title was not disputed—your title is not only disputed, but utterly denied by us. We are still willing however, but from motives of prudence and good will, only, to place you in respect to the amount of compensation, on an equal footing with them, and therefore will allow you, the average of what was then allowed them, which will be an immediate payment of one thousand pounds, six shillings and eight pence, an annuity of two hundred and thirteen pounds, six shillings and eight pence. The tract equal to six miles square, near the village of St. Regis, still to be applied to your use, as reserved in the sale to Alexander Macomb.

If this offer is accepted by you, it will then remain to be adjusted between you and us, as to the time, place and manner, in which the payments are to be made.

Brothers:

We shall now await for your answer.

28th May, 1796.

Speech from the Deputies to the Agents.

Brothers:

We have considered your offers to our last speech, and we think that we understand the greater part of them, and we are happy to think that after so long a time, you have thought fit to take some part of our speeches into good consideration.

Brothers:

We did say there was no people could with justice say your claim is not just, and we still repeat to you, brothers, that these deeds, you have shewn to us, are unjust, that is, we mean according to all information we can get from Colonel Louis, who was present when such purchase should have been made, and according to all the conversations we have had with the different nations, that should have sold this tract of land, belonging to us, and we never understood by these nations, that they had disposed of any lands within our boundaries.

We have strictly examined Colonel Louis that was present when these purchases were made, of those nations, and he solemnly declares that he did not know of their selling any part of our lands, or any other, only he lands that belonged to them, and we take him to be a man of better principles, than to be a witness to so great a piece of misconduct against his own tribe, and then not to inform us of it before this time; we therefore must needs tell you, that we think there is a great deception in those deeds, as there has been in many other former purchases from our brother Indians, and to convince you, brothers, that we do not make an unjust demand; was it not for our poverty, we should not have requested you to have been at the expense of calling the different nations for witnesses between you and us, as we wish to convince you that we are a people that always have acted on honest principles, and mean to continue in doing the same. However, it seems you are indifferent about having these nations to come forward, and for our parts, brothers, we think it a great honor to settle matters that concern you and us among ourselves, and not to trouble our neighbors with our business. We therefore are willing to comply with any thing in reason and justice, rather than it should be said by those ill-minded people that are always trying to invent mischief between us, that we could not agree. But there is one question we wish to ask you brothers;—have you not known us to be the right owners of these lands, why did you direct your good advice to us at the beginning of the trouble between you and the king of England?

We are sensible that a nation or people without lands, are like rogues without friends; of neither, is notice taken, or confidence put on them. But we received your council, heard your advice and your promises to us, and took them to be sincere, and we ever since have endeavored to live up to them with you as near us as possibly was in our power, and we believe we can with safety say, that since we have been neighbors, that we never have injured you or your properties, even to the value of a fowl. Neither have we made any demands from you while we could support ourselves by hunting, and always thought it to be a favor to our brothers in the new settlements, rather than to think or have the least mistrust that it would be a detriment to your justifying our claim when made. No brothers, we put too much confidence in your good and fair promises, to have the least mistrust of a thing of the kind.

Brothers:

Respecting our lands in Vermont, our claim in that state is as our claim in this state, which is just; and as to the king of Great Britain giving grants for settlements without requiring a purchase of us, that was not much for him to do at that time. If that had been the only mis-step he had taken towards the welfare of his children, we dare say you would not have rebelled against the government and laws of Great Britain, for the sake of obtaining liberty.

So we think that but a very small part of the reason why we should be deprived of our rights. And we have mentioned to you in a speech at the treaty last fall, at Fort George, that he did request us to sell those lands to him, and our answer was to him that we could not sell our lands, and that we had reserved them for the maintenance of our children, after us, and that has always been the advice of our forefathers, never to sell any part of our lands, but to lease them for an annuity, if it was ever so small, and we shall never forget their advice to us. And on these principles our lands were settled, and that was when we could not support ourselves by hunting, that those who resided on our lands must expect to give us some assistance for the use of our lands.

Brothers:

And in respect to your last offer to us for our lands in this State, we must beg you to have a little patience, and consider this matter once more, and we will now make an offer, which we are sure you will not think unreasonable, that is, brothers, we are not able to bring our reserve into as small a compass as possible, without interfering with our plantations, which will be resigning up to you about two thirds of the reserve, which we never did intend to dispose of on any consideration whatever. Still, as we have before mentioned, that we are willing to comply on any terms in reason, for the sake of good neighborhood and friendship with you, you will allow us to reserve to our own use, as follows:

Beginning at at the head of the second inland above Long Saut, on the river St. Lawrence, and run down the stream of the said river, ten miles below the village of St. Regis; then back into the woods twenty-one miles, then westwardly in rear the same distance as in front, and from thence to the river, opposite to said island, to the place of beginning. This reserve, brothers, we will not be able to make any less, brothers, without interfering with the plantations of our people, which is out of our power, so to do; and an annuity of four hundred and eighty pounds, with all expenses free, to the place where we may agree for the delivery of said payments; if so be you may see fit to agree to this offer, which we are sure you can not think unreasonable, for we are sensible it will not be more than half a cent per acre yearly; and the payment to be as you propose.

Brothers:

We hope you will not request us to vary from this offer, which we beg you rightly to consider, and let us live as well as yourselves. We will wait your answer.

28TH MAY, 1796.
Speeh from the Agents to the Deputies.

Brothers:

The offer which we made you the day before yesterday, was upon mature consideration, and appeared to us to be as liberal as you could possibly expect, and it is now to be considered, as definite between you and us, so that it only remains for you to give us your final answer, whether you are willing to accept it or not, in order that the negociations at the present treaty may be brought to a close. We would however, explain to you, that a reasonable allowance to you as deputies, for your services and expenses in attending this treaty, and such presents as are usual on these occasions, will be made to you, exclusive of the compensations which we have proposed, should be for the nations or tribes whom you represent.

30TH MAY, 1796.
Speech from the Agents to the Deputies.

Brothers:

After we had made our speech to you the day before yesterday, you verbally suggested to us, that the Indians of St. Regis had built a mill on a river, which you call Salmon river, and another on a river which you call Grass river, and that they had always supplied themselves with hay from the meadows on Grass river. You describe these rivers generally, only as emptying into the river St. Lawrence and being in the vicinity of St. Regis; and it is uncertain, whether they, and especially the places on them, where the mills are built, will be included in the tract equal to the six miles square, reserved in the sale to Mr. Macomb.

If you had seasonably informed the state of your claim, they might have reserved lands for your use, to any extent which might have been judged proper, but they have now sold all the lands on that quarter, to Mr. Macomb, and as reservations can not be made without the consent of the persons who have purchased from him, we have spoken to them on the subject, and they have consented, that we should further offer to you, that a convenient tract at each place where the mills are built, and the meadows on both sides of the Grass river, although thay may here-after be discovered to be not within the tract, equal to six miles square, shall be reserved to the use of the St. Regis Indians.

31ST MAY, 1796.

The deputies having declared their acceptance of the compensation, as proposed to them by the agents; three acts of the same tenor and date, one to remain with the United States, another to remain with the said Seven Nations, or tribes, and another to remain with the state, were thereupon this day executed, by the commissioners for the United States, the deputies for the Indians, the agents for the state, and Daniel McCormick, and William Constable, for themselves, and their associates, purchase under Alexander Macomb, containing a cession; release, and quit-claim from the Seven Nations or tribes of Indians, of

all lands within the state, and a covenant for the state, for the payment
of the said compensation, and also certain reservations of land, to be
applied to the use of the Indians of the village of St. Regis, as by the
said acts, reference being had to either of them, more fully may appear."
Signed,

ABRAM OGDEN.

The following is a copy of this treaty.

" *The People* of the State of New York, by the grace of God, free and
independent. To all to whom these presents shall come, greeting. Know
ye that we having inspected the records remaining in our Secretary's
office, do find there filed a certain instrument in the words following, to
wit:

" At a treaty held in the city of New York with the nation or title of
Indians, denominating themselves the Seven Nations of Canada, Abraham
Ogden, commissioner appointed under the authority of the United States
to hold the treaty, Ohnaweio, alias Good Stream, Teharagwanegen, alias
Thos, Williams, two chiefs of the Caughnawagas, Atiatobarongwan, alias
Colonel Louis Cook, a chief of the St. Regis Indians, and William Gray,
deputies authorized to represent these Seven Nations or tribes of Indians
at the treaty, and Mr. Gray serving also as interpreter, Egbert Benson,
Richard Varick and James Watson, agents for the state of New York.
Wm. Constable and Daniel McCormick, purchasers under Alex. Macomb.
The agents for the state, having in the presence and with the approbation
of the commissioners, proposed to the deputies for the Indians, the compensation hereinafter mentioned for the extinguishment of their claim to
all lands within the states, and the said deputies being willing to accept
the same, it is thereupon granted, agreed and concluded between the said
deputies and the said agents as follows: The said deputies do for, and
in the name of the said Seven Nations or tribes of Indians, cede, release
and quit claim to the people of the state of New York, forever, all the claim
right or title of them, the said Seven Nations or tribes of Indians, to lands
within the said state, provided nevertheless, that the tract equal to six
miles square reserved in the sale made by the commissioners of the land
office of the said state, to Alexander Macomb, to be applied to the use
of the Indians of the village of St. Regis, shall still remain so reserved.
The said agents do for and in the name of the people of the state of New
York, grant to the said Seven Nations or tribes of Indians, that the people of the state of New York shall pay to them at the mouth of the river
Chazy, on Lake Champlain, on the third Monday of August next, the sum
of one thousand two hundred and thirty pounds, six shillings and eight
pence, lawful money of the said state; and on the third Monday in August, yearly, forever thereafter, the like sum of two hundred and thirteen
pounds, six shillings and eight pence. Provided nevertheless, that the
people of the state of New York shall not be held to pay the said sums,
unless in respect to the two sums to be paid on the third Monday in August next, at least twenty, and in respect to the said yearly sum to be paid
thereafter, at least five of the principal men of the said Seven Nations or
tribes of Indians, shall attend as deputies to receive and to give receipts
for the same. The said deputies having suggested that the Indians of St.
Regis have built a mill on Salmon river and another on Grass river and that
the meadows on Grass river are necessary for hay, in order therefore to
secure to the Indians of the said village, the use of the said mills and
meadows, in case they should hereafter appear not to be included in the
above tract, so as to remain reserved.

It is therefore also agreed and concluded between the said deputies and the said agents and the said William Constable and Daniel McCormick, for themselves and their associates, purchasers under the said Alexander Macomb, of the adjacent lands, that there shall be reserved to be applied to the use of the Indians of the said village of St. Regis, in like manner as the said tract is to remain reserved, a tract of one mile square at each of the said mills, and the meadows on both sides of the said Grass river, from the said mills thereon, to its confluence with the river St. Lawrence.

In testimony whereof, the said commissioners, the said deputies, the said agents, and the said William Constable and Daniel McCormick, have hereunto, and to two other acts of the same tenor and date, one to remain with the United States, another to remain with the state of New York, and another to remain with the Seven Nations or tribes of Indians, set their hands and seals in the city of New York, the thirty-first day of May, in the twentieth year of the Independence of the United States, one thousand seven hundred and ninety-six. Abraham Ogden (L. S.), Ohnaweio, alias Good Stream (mark L. S.), Otiatoharongwan, alias Colonel Louis Cook (mark L. S.), Wm. Gray (L. S.), Teharagwan-gen, alias Thos. Williams (mark L. S.), Egbert Benson (L. S.), Richard Varick (L. S.), James Watson (L. S.), Wm. Constable (L. S.), Daniel McCormick (L. S.).

Signed, sealed and delivered in the presence of Samuel Jones, Recorder of the city of New York, John Taylor Recorder of the city of Albany, Jo's Ogden Hoffman, Attorney-General of the state of New York.

May 30th, 1797. Acknowledged before John Sloss Hobart, Justice of Supreme Court of Judicature.

Feb. 28, 1800. Exemplified signed and sealed by the Governor, John Jay."

The above treaty is engrossed upon a large size sheet of parchment, to which is affixed a large waxen seal, having on one side the state arms and inscription, " The great seal of the state," and on the other the device of waves beating against a rock, and the word " Frustra," " 1798." The back and margins are covered with receipts.

This and the other treaties which have been held between the St. Regis Indians and the state of New York, are carefully preserved by the clerk of the American party at St. Regis.

The agreements made in the treaty of May 31, 1796, were confirmed by an act which was passed April 4, 1801.

It had previously received the sanction of the general government, as appears from the following:

On the 20th of February, 1797, the governor sent to the senate the following message:

Gentlemen:
"I have the honor of laying before you a letter of the 18th ult., from the Secretary of the United States, for the department of war, enclosing a copy of the resolution of the Senate, advising and consenting to the ratification of the treaty concluded on behalf of the state with the Indians, calling themselves the Seven Nations of Canada.

JOHN JAY."

In the negociations between these Indians and the state, the name of Brant, the celebrated partisan Indian, was used in connection with pro-

ceedings, which the Mohawks had held with the state, in the cession of
their lands, in such a manner as to awaken a controversy between him
and the deputy superintendent, which ultimately became embittered by
mutual allegations of pecuniary delinquency. The six nations had
bargained with Colonel Livingston, in 1787, as we have previously
stated, for a large tract of land which the Caughnawaga and St. Regis
Indians insisted was fraudulent.

As Brant was a witness to the treaty, and was one of the most prominent of those by whom it was made, this denial of their right amounted
to little else than a charge that those who made it, had pocketed the
avails for their own benefit. This charge Brant indignantly repelled,
denying that the Caughnawagas had a right to a foot of the lands which
had been sold to Livingston, and demanding of them their authority, for
their charges against him, and the Grand River Indians. They replied
that their information was derived from the representations of the officers
of the state of New York, at Albany. To ascertain the ground there
might be for this, he addressed a letter to Governor Clinton, which
received the following reply.

GREENWICH, 1st DECEMBER, 1799.

Dear Sir:

"On my return from the country, about a month ago, I was favored
with your letter of the 4th of September. I am much gratified by the
determination you express, of furnishing Doctor Miller with the information he requested of you, and I hope as the work for which it is wanted
is progressing, you will find leisure to do it soon. I am confident he
will make a fair and honorable use of it; and, as far as he shall be enabled, correct the erroneous representations of former authors respecting
your nations.

I am surprised to find that you have not received my letter the 11th of
of January, last. It was enclosed and forwarded as requested, to Mr.
Peter W. Yates of Albany. Had it reached you; I presume you will find,
from the copy I now enclose, it would have been satisfactory; but as a
particular detail of what passed between the Caughnawagoes and me,
respecting their lands may be more agreable, I will now repeat it to you
as far as my recollection will enable me.

In the winter of 1792-1793, our Legislature being in session in Albany,
a committee from the Seven Nations or tribes of Lower Canada, attended
there, with whom I had several conferences. They complained that
some of our people had settled on their lands near Lake Champlain, and
on the River St. Lawrence, and requested that commissioners might be
appointed to enquire into the matter, and treat with them on the subject.
In my answer to their speeches, I answered that it was difficult to define
their rights and their boundaries; and that it was to be presumed that
the Indian rights to a considerable part of the lands on the borders of
the lake, had been extinguished by the French Government, before the
conquest of Canada, as those lands, or a greater part of them, had been
granted to individuals by that government before that period. In their
reply they described their southern boundary, as commencing at a creek
or run of water between Fort Edward and George, which empties into

South Bay, and from thence extending on a direct line to a large meadow or swamp where the Canada Creek, which empties into the Mohawk opposite Fort Hendrick, the Black and Oswegatchee Rivers have their sources. Upon which I observed to them that this line would interfere with lands patented by the British Government previous to the Revolution, and particularly mentioned Totten and Crossfield's purchase and Jessup's patent; but I mentioned at the same time that I was neither authorized or disposed to controvert their claims, that I would submit to the Legislature, who I could not doubt would pay due attention to them and adopt proper measures to effect a settlement with them upon fair and liberal terms. This I accordingly did, and some time after commissioners were appointed to treat with them in the presence of an agent of the United States, the result of which, I find you are informed of.

I believe you will readily agree that no inference could be drawn from any thing that passed on the above occasion to countenance the charge made against your nations. The mentioning and interference of their boundaries, as above stated, with tracts patented under the British Government, could certainly have no allusion to the cessions made by the Six Nations, or either of them to the state, especially as (if I recollect right) those cession are of the territory of the respective nations by whom they were made without defining them by any particular boundaries, and subject only to the reservations described in the deed.

I wish it was in my power to transmit to you copies of their speeches and my answer at full length; but it is not for the reasons mentioned in my former letter, should they, however, be deemed necessary to you, I will endeavor to procure and forward them; in the mean time you may rest assured that what I have related is the substance of them.

                    I am with great regard and esteem,
Col. Joseph Brant.   Your most obedient servant,
                                        GEO. CLINTON.

This correspondence, and that which ensued with Governor Jay, did not satisfy Brant, and he accordingly caused a deputation of his tribe to repair to Albany, at the head of which was his adopted nephew, John Norton, to meet a similar deputation of the Caughnawagas, face to face, and require his accusers connected with the government of the state of New York, either to substantiate their charges or acquit him in the presence of both delegations.

The result of this double mission is not known, save that the chiefs were not satisfied with it.

In July of the same year (1799,) Brant proceeded to the Caughnawaga country in person, accompanied by a body of chiefs of several of the tribes, for the purpose of a through investigation in general council. Such a council was convened; and the difficulties from the reports of speeches preserved in writing by Captain Brant, were fully discussed; and that too in a most amicable manner. From several intimations in these speeches, it appears that the whole of these difficulties had been caused by "chattering birds," and by the machinations against Captain

Brant, of the old Oneida sachem, Colonel Louis.* The council fire was kindled on the 8th of July, on the 9th Captain Brant was satisfied by the explanations given, and remarked, "that he had pulled up a pine, and planted down beneath it the small bird that tells stories."

On the 10th, the Caughnawaga chief replied:—" Brothers, we return you thanks; we also join with you to put the chattering bird under ground, from where the pine was taken up, there being a swift stream into which it will fall beneath, that will take it to the big sea, from whence it never can return." *(See Stone's Life of Brant, vol. ii, p.* 410, 414.)

The evident partiality of the writer of the life of Brant, has perhaps prevented him from giving to the Canada Indians their due in discussing their claims to the lands in the northern part of the state.

The St. Regis people having decided the question of the amount of land they were to receive, were desirous of having the boundaries known.

To settle definitely however their rights, they addressed the following letter to the governor.

To our Great Brother, John Jay, Governor of the State of New York.

Brother :
We the chiefs and chief warriors at St Regis, have sent the Bearers, Louis Cook, Sag Shaketlay, Loren Tarlelon, and William Gray, our interpreters, to enquire of you Brother, how we are to know the distance of our reserve, equal to six miles square, reserved to us by a treaty held at the city of New York, the 30th of May, 1796, with our deputies Louis Cook, Ohnaweio, Good Stream, Thomas Williams, and William Gray, and another reserve of one mile square on Salmon Creek, twelve miles below St. Regis, at a saw mill belonging to us chiefs.

Brother :
The reason of our sending the Bearers to you, is, that some time the latter part of last fall, some of your children, our brothers of this state, was marking and running lines within what we expect is our reserved lands, and we know no other way, but to come and inform you that we might know what to do, and we beg that you will inform the Bearers that they, as soon as is convenient to you may return home and inform us what to do.

We hope you will not let thy Bearers want for victuals and drink, what will be for their good, we wish you health and happiness with your family. From your Brothers the chiefs of St. Regis."

Chiefs.

For the Chiefs at
St. Regis, WILLIAM GRAY.

TIO-NA-TO-GEN-A,
THA-RON-IA-HE-NE,
TA-TE-GA-IEN-TON,
TO-TA-RO-WA-NE.

* We quote the language of Stone in his Life of Brant. This author was mistaken in supposing Colonel Louis an Oneida Indian.

This petition led to the passage on the 30th of March, 1799, of the following act:

" The surveyor general be, and he is hereby directed in his proper person. to lay out and survey, in such manner as the chiefs of the St. Regis Indians shall deem satisfactory, all the lands reserved to the said Indians, by the treaty held at the city of New York, and conformable thereto, the twenty-third day of May, in the year one thousand seven hundred and ninety six; and the treasurer is hereby required to pay to him, out of any money in the treasury, four hundred dollars to defray the expense thereof, which sum the surveyor general shall account for with the comptroller."

The surveyor general performed this duty and reported as follows:

" *Sir :*—Pursuant to the act of the legislature, directing the surveyor general to lay out and survey the lands reserved to the Indians residing at St. Regis. I have surveyed in a manner satisfactory to the chiefs of that tribe the tract equal to six miles square, reserved to them at their village; as also the two tracts of one mile square each, at the mills on Salmon river, and Grass river, maps descriptive of the boundaries of these I have the honor herewith to deliver.

When I was about to commence the survey of the meadows, reserved to the use of these Indians on Grass river, they informed me in council that they considered themselves entitled to a tract of half a mile on each side of the river, from its mouth up to the mill, and that they had caused it to be run out in that manner, for their meadow reservation, and intimated a desire that my survey should be made in a corresponding manner. I was obliged to inform them that I had no guide but their treaty, and consequently could regard no survey made without authority, and that nothing but the meadows barely, along that river, was pointed out as their property. They then pointedly desired me to make no marks on that ground, observing at the same time that as a deputation from their nation would have to repair to Albany on other business, during the sitting of the legislature, they wished by that opportunity to obtain an explanation of what they considered to be a misapprehension between the parties of the treaty.

Not being permitted to make a survey of the meadows, I availed myself of the opportunity of going up and down the river, of making an estimate of them, with a view to report the same as an article of information that might be serviceable in case a compromise respecting them should be contemplated.

These meadows consist of narrow strips along the margin of the river, where inundations have prevented the growth of timber. They lie in a number of patches, of from half a chain to three or four chains in width, making in the whole extent which is about six miles, not exceeding sixty acres altogether, as nearly as I could judge.

The grass on them with small exceptions, is all wild grass.

Their value, though of no very great consideration, as an appendage to the adjoining lands, is however esteemed as almost inestimable by Indians, who consider the clearing of land as a matter entirely beyond their power to accomplish. It will be impossible moreover, that the Indians should ever enclose the meadows with fences, so as to prevent their destruction by the cattle of the white inhabitants, who soon will settle thick in their neighborhood, and this will inevitably become the cause of disagreeable differences.

It is proper for me to observe that the ground on which these meadows are situated, as well as the mile square, at the mill on Grass river, has been patented in tracts distinct from Macomb's purchase; and therefore the sanction which the proprietors of that purchase gave to the treaty, will not exonerate the state from the duty of compensating the owners of the lands from which these parts of the reservation are taken."

[The remainder of the report relates to other subjects.]

Signed,
SIMEON DE WITT.

ALBANY JAN. 14, 1800.

The troubles from trespass anticipated in the above, were soon realized; for the particulars of these the reader is referred to our account of Massena.

On February 20, 1800, there was received in Assembly from the Senate, a resolution: "That the commissioners of the land office be directed to settle with the St. Regis Indians, for such tracts of land, included in the lands confirmed to them by the late treaty, and before located by individuals, and granted by this state, by making compensation for the lands so granted, or by satisfying the individuals owning such lands in such manner as they shall judge most advantageous to the state, and the legislature, will make provision for carrying into effect any agreement which may be made by the commissioners for extinguishing the claims of the said Indians, or of the individual proprietors aforesaid."

This resolution was postponed by the assembly, nor is it known what was the final action of the legislature upon it.

On the 9th of April, 1801, a law was passed making it lawful for the governor to cause a treaty to be holden with the St. Regis Indians, for the purpose of extinguishing their right to a tract of a mile square at the mill on Grass river, and for that purpose to appoint an agent on the part of the state, and procure the appointment of a commissioner, on the part of the United States, to attend the holding as such treaty. *Provided* that the consideration to be paid the said Indians for the said tract, shall not exceed a permanent annuity of two hundred dollars. A sum not exceeding $500 was appropriated to defray the expense of holding this treaty.

The surveyor general was directed to cause the meadows reserved to the use of the said Indians, upon Grass river, and which had been disposed of by the state, to be surveyed, and the quantity ascertained, and to report the same to the legislature at the next session.

It was further made lawful for the agent to extinguish the right of ferriage, belonging to the said Indians over the River St. Lawrence, adjoining their reservation, for such reasonable annuity as they may deem proper.

The future payments of the annuity stipulated with the said Indians, was directed to be made at the town of Plattsburgh, in the county of

Clinton. The act referred to makes a provision for the patenting by the
state to William Gray, of two hundred and fifty-seven acres of land, including the mill on Salmon river.

The president of the United States, by a message making sundry
nominations, and addressed to the senate, February 2, 1802, recommended the nomination of John Taylor of New York, to be a commissioner
to hold a treaty between the state of New York, and the St. Regis
Indians.

He was led to this, from having received a communication from the
governor of New York, purporting that the St. Regis Indians had proposed ceding one mile square, including the ferry, to the state of New
York, and requesting a commissioner to be appointed on the part of the
United States, to sanction the business, which it was proposed should be
accomplished during the ensuing winter at Albany.

(American State Papers, Indian Affairs, vol. i, p. 565.)

In 1802, agents were appointed to treat with the St. Regis Indians for
the sale of their mile square, and meadows. The following communication made to the Assembly by Governor Clinton, March, 15, 1802,
contains the results of their negociations. It was first reported to the
senate.

Gentlemen:
"I now submit to the Legislature, the report of the agents appointed
to treat with the St. Regis Indians, for the extinguishment of the mile
square, and the meadows on Grass river. I also present to you a petition
from those Indians, praying among other things, for legislative provisions,
to enable them to lease a part of their lands, to establish a ferry across
the St. Regis river, and to apply the income to the support of a school
for the instruction of their children. It may be proper to observe, that
as the petitioners have uniformly evinced a warm attachment, to the
state, and have made uncommon advances towards civilization, they have
a claim to the attention of the Legislature, arising as well from principles of policy, as benevolence. They discover an anxiety to return
home as soon as possible, but at the same time are unwilling to leave
this city, until the result of their application to the Legislature is known."
GEO. CLINTON.

The report of the agents referred to, in his excellency's said message,
and the petition of the St. Regis Indians, were also severally read, and
together with the message, referred to the committee of thee house. The
petition was as follows:

" *To our great and Honorable Brother, John Jay, Governor of the State
of New York:*
Brothers:
We, the chiefs and warriors of the village of St. Regis, have sent the
bearers, Colonel Louis Cook, Jacob Francis, Peter Tarbell, as deputies,
and William Gray as interpreter, to act and settle all business for us that

may concern this state, or us, the above mentioned village, or any individual belonging to this state.

Firstly, we beg you brother, to order means to have our meadows on Grass river, surveyed, and the number of acres contained there, to have as many acres cleared near our village, within the reservation made to us by this state, and then to have the use of the meadows on Grass river, till such time as those lands will be fit to mow grass on.

Secondly, brother, we wish to inform you, that at the west end of our meadows, on Grass river, we have one square mile of land, likewise reserved to us by the state, with a saw mill in the centre of the mile square, for which Amable Foshee is bound to pay us the sum of two hundred dollars per year, as long as he keeps it in his custody, and we are not satisfied with his usage to us.

Thirdly, brother; there is a route that leads from Plattsburgh on Lake Champlain, crosses the Chateaugay river, and comes straight to the village of St. Regis, where there ought to be a ferry kept up for the accommodation of the public, and the use of this ferry is like to create quarrels and disputes:

Now brothers in order to prevent all these disagreeable contentions, we wish to propose to you, for to take one hundred acres, and the privilege of the ferry, and where there may be a good potash works erected for those people who wish to give us two hundred and fifty dollars, as a yearly rent.

Fourthly, brother, we wish to inform you, that there are nine miles between houses, however the route runs through our reservation, and we mean to rent a part of our lands, in order to make it convenient for travelers, and as some benefit to ourselves and children, who may follow us, and we began to inform all our brothers who may see fit to rent the lands of us, that we expect they will pay their rents according to contract, as you have law and justice in your power, and we are not acquainted with our brother white people's laws.

Fifthly, brother, there is a request from your sisters of the village of St. Regis, the women of families, which is, that you pity them, and send them a school master, to learn their children to read and write.

Brother, your compliance to these requests will cause us ever to pray your welfare and happiness, who remain your brothers, chiefs, and their wives in the St. Regis."

TE-HA-TON-WEN-HEON-GATHA,
TI-E-HEN-NE.
TE-GA-RI-A-TA-RO-GEN,
ON-WA-RI-EN-TE.
ORI-WA-GE-TE,
TO-TA-TO-WA-NE,
AT-TI-AX-TO-TIE.

Witness, WILLIAM GRAY.

Accordingly two laws were enacted, relating to these people, at the ensuing session of the Legislature. The first was passed March 8, 1802. which provided, " that it shall and may be lawful for his Excellency the Governor, and the Surveyor general, to treat with the St. Regis Indians for the extinguishment of their claim to the mile square, and the meadows on Grass river, ceded to them in the year 1796, on such terms as they shall deem most condusive to the interests of the state, or to purchase the same from the individuals to whom it has been granted by the state before it was ceded to the said Indians, in case the latter purchase can be made on more favorable terms than the extinguishment of the Indian claim.

That in case the said lands can not be purchased of the said Indians, or of the said patentees at a reasonable price, his Excellency, the Governor, shall represent the same to the Legislature that further provisions may be made respecting those claims."

The meadows were subsequently purchased of the patentees for the Indians:

During the same session, an act was passed, relating to the St. Regis Indians, March 26, 1802, as follows.

"*Be it enacted by the people of the state of New York, in Senate and Assembly,* That William Gray, Louis Cook and Loren Tarbell, belonging to the tribe of the St. Regis Indians, be and they are hereby appointed trustees for the said tribe, for the purpose of leasing the ferry over St. Regis river, with one hundred acres of land adjoining, and also one mile square of land on Grass river, within their reservation within this state, for such term of time as they shall judge proper, not exceeding ten years, and it shall and may be lawful for the said trustees, to apply the rents and profits of the said ferry and lands for a support of a school for the instruction of the children of the said tribe, (of which the said trustees shall have the superintendence,) and for such other purposes as the said trustees shall judge most conducive to the interests of the said tribe, and the powers hereafter vested in the said trustees, may be exercised by them or any two of them.

And be it further enacted, That it shall and may be lawful for the said St. Regis Indians, on the first Tuesday of May next, and on the first Tuesday of May in every year thereafter, to hold a town meeting on their said reservation, within the state, and by a majority of male Indians above, twenty-one years of age, to choose a clerk, who shall keep order in such meeting, and enter in a book to be provided by him for that purpose, the proceedings of the said meetings.

And be it further enacted, That it shall and may be lawful for the said tribe, at any such meeting aforesaid, to make such rules, orders and regulations, respecting the improvement of any other of their lands in the said reservation, as they shall judge necessary, and to choose trustees for carrying the same into execution, if they shall judge such trustees to be necessary.

And be it further enacted, That it shall and may be lawful for the said William Gray, Louis Cook, and Loren Tarbell, to procure a bell for the church belonging to the said tribe, to be paid for out of their annuity.

And be it further enacted, That it shall and may be lawful for the person administering the government of this state, to cause to be sent to the said tribe at the place where their annuity is paid, two suits of silk colors, one with the arms of the United States, and the arms of this state as a gratuity, and to draw a warrant on the treasury for the expenses of the same."

On the approach of the war, the situation of St. Regis, on the national boundary, placed these people in a peculiar and delicate position. Up to this period, although residing in both governments, they had been as one, and in their internal affairs, were governed by twelve chiefs, who were elected by the tribe, and held their offices for life.

The annuities and presents of both governments were equally divided among them, and in the cultivation of their lands, and the division of the rents and profits arising from leases, they knew no distinction of party.

The war operated with peculiar severity against them, from the terror of Indian massacre, which the recollections and traditions of former wars, had generally inspired the inhabitants.

So great was the terror which these poor people excited, that they could not travel, even where acquainted, without procuring *a pass*, which they were accustomed to obtain from any of the principal inhabitants, whose names were publicly known. A paper, stating that the bearer was a quiet and peaceable Indian, with or without a signature, they were accustomed to solicit, and this they would hold up in sight, when still at a distance, that those who might meet them should not be alarmed. They were likewise accustomed to require persons traveling across their reservation, to have, if strangers, *a pass*, purporting the peaceable nature of their business. The chiefs, it is said, appointed certain persons to grant these passes, among whom was Captain Polley, of Massena Springs. As few of them could read, it became necessary to agree upon some emblem by which the signification could be known, and the following device was adopted: If a person were going through to French Mills, a bow was drawn on the paper, but if its bearer was designing to visit St. Regis village, an arrow was added thus.

Thus cut off from their usual means of subsistence, they were reduced to a wretched extremity, to obtain relief from which, Col. Louis repaired to Ogdensburgh, and sent the following letter to Gov. Tompkins:

"I address you these lines, for the purpose of expressing the situation of my nation, and of giving you assurances of our constantly cherishing good will and friendship towards the United States, and of our determination not to intermeddle with the war which has broken out between them and the English, and which has placed us in so critical a situation. Our young men being prevented from hunting, and obtaining a subsistence for their families, are in want of provisions, and I address myself in their behalf to the justice and liberality of the governor of this state, to obtain a supply of beef, pork and flour, to be delivered to us at St. Regis, during the time that we are compelled to give up our accustomed pursuits, which it seems, if continued, would give alarm to our white brethren. I have come myself to this place, to communicate the distressed situation of our nation to Col. Benedict, who has promised to submit the same to you, and in hopes of soon receiving a favorable answer to my request, I subscribe myself with much attachment, your affectionate brother and friend."

(Signed,)   LOUIS ✕ COOK,
                                                  his   mark.

One of the chiefs of the nation of the St. Regis Indians, and a Lt. Col. in the service of the United States of America.

In consequence of the foregoing letter, orders were issued that the St. Regis Indians should be supplied with rations during the war at French Mills. They accordingly received during the war, about 500 rations daily, at the hands of Wareham Hastings, the agent for the government.

The Indians, while drawing their rations, begged some for their priest, from the best of motives, which the latter received as a kindness from them; but this circumstance gave him more trouble than it conferred benefit, for it was with the greatest difficulty, that he was able to justify or explain this course, with the British and ecclesiastical authorities. He narrowly escaped imprisonment on suspicion of receiving bribes from the American government. It will be remembered that the priest's house is on the Canadian side of the boundary.

In 1812, it was agreed between a British and an American commissioner, that the natives should remain neutral in the approaching contest.

It is said that in the month of June, Isaac Le Clare, a Frenchman, then and still living at St. Regis, being down at Montreal with a raft of wood, was met by an uncle, who suggested an interview with the governor, which resulted in his receiving a lieutenant's commission, on the recommendation of Col. De Salaberry.

Before his return, the British company stationed at St. Regis, was captured as below stated, and Lieut. Le Clare succeeded to the pay, but not to the rank, of captain, in place of Montigney. He raised a company of about 80 Indian warriors, and crossed to Cornwall. These Indians participated in several engagements during the ensuing war. At the taking of Little York, they were posted at Kingston. At the attack upon Sackett's Harbor, twenty British St. Regis Indians were present under Lieut. St. Germain; and at Ogdensburgh, in Feb., 1813, about thirty of the same, under Capt. Le Clare, crossed to the town. At the battle of Chrysler's field, they were at Cornwall, and prevented by Col. McLean, of the British army, from engaging in the battle.

Chevalier Lorimier, an agent of the British government, in 1813, came up from Montreal with the customary presents to the Indians, and offered them, on condition of their crossing the river and taking up arms against the Americans. They would not do this, and he returned with his presents. This was after Capt. Le Clare had raised his company, or about the time.

During the fall of 1812, Capt. Montigney, with a small company of British troops, in violation to the previous agreement, arrived, and took post at St. Regis. Maj. Guilford Dudley Young, of the Troy militia, stationed at French Mills, receiving an account of this, resolved to surprise, and if possible capture this party; considering himself justified in entering upon neutral ground, as the enemy had first broken their agreement. He accordingly, about the 1st of October, 1812, proceeded quietly through the woods by an obscure path, guided by Wm. Gray, the Indian interpreter; but on arriving opposite the village of St. Regis, he found it impossible to cross, and was compelled to return.

Having allowed the alarm which his attempt had excited to subside, he resolved to make another descent, before the enemy should be reinforced, and for this purpose he marched a detachment at 11 o'clock at night, on the 21st of October, crossed the St. Regis river at Gray's Mills, (now Hogansburgh,) on a raft of boards, and arrived about 5 o'clock in the morning, within half a mile of the village, without attracting the notice of the enemy. Here the Major made such a judicious disposition of his men, that the enemy were entirely surrounded, and after a few discharges surrendered themselves prisoners, with the loss of five killed, among whom was Captain Rothalte. The fruits of this capture were forty prisoners, with their arms and equipments, and one stand of colors, two bateaux, &c. They returned to French Mills by 11 o'clock the next morning, without the loss of a man, and the prisoners were sent forward to Plattsburgh. Ex-Governor Wm. L. Marcy held a subordinate office in this affair.

This was the first stand of colors taken by the Americans during the war, and these were received at Albany with great ceremony. An account of the reception of the colors is taken from the *Albany Gazette* of Jan. 1813.

"On Thursday the 5th inst., at one o'clock, a detachment of the volunteer militia of Troy, entered this city, with the British colors, taken at St. Regis. The detachment, with two superb eagles in the centre, and the British colors in the rear, paraded to the music of Yankee Doodle and York Fusileers, through Market and State streets to the Capitol, the officers and colors in the centre. The remainder of the vestibule and the grand staircase leading to the hall of justice, and the galleries of the senate and assembly chambers were crowded with spectators. His excellency, the Governor, from illness being absent, his aids, Cols. Lamb and Lush, advanced from the council chamber to receive the standards. Upon which Major Young, in a truly military and gallant style, and with an appropriate address, presented it to the people of New York; to which Col. Lush, on the part of the state, replied in a highly complimentary speech, and the standard was deposited in the council room, amid the loud huzzas of the citizens and military salutes. Subsequently to this achievement Maj. Young was appointed a Colonel in the U. S. army."

This officer was a native of Lebanon, Ct.

"After the war, he entered the patriot service under Gen. Mina, and lost his life in the struggle for Mexican independence, in 1817. The patriots, 269 in number, had possession of a small fort which was invested by a royalist force of 3,500 men. The supplies of provisions and water being cut off, the sufferings of the garrison and women and children in the fort became intolerable; many of the soldiers deserted, so that not more than 150 effective men remained. Col. Young, however, knowing the perfidy of the enemy, determined to defend the fort to the last. After having bravely defeated the enemy in a number of endeavors to carry the fort by storm, Col. Young was killed by a cannon shot from the battery raised against the fort. On the enemy's last retreat, the Colonel, anxious to observe all their movements, fearlessly exposed his person by stepping on a large stone on the ramparts; and while conversing with Dr. Hennessay on the successes of the day and on the dastardly conduct of the enemy, the last shot that was fired from their battery, carried off his head. Col. Young was an officer whom next to Mina, the American part of the division had been accustomed to respect and admire. In every action he had been conspicuous for his daring courage and skill. Mina reposed unbounded confidence in him. In the hour of danger he was collected, gave his orders with precision, and sword in hand, was always in the hottest of the combat. Honor and firmness marked all his actions. He was generous in the extreme, and endured privations with a cheerfulness superior to that of any other officer of the division. He has been in the U. S. service as Lieut. Col. of the 29th regiment of infantry. His body was interred by the few Americans who could be spared from duty, with every possible mark of honor and respect, and the general gloom which pervaded the division on this occasion, was the sincerest tribute that could be offered by them to the memory of their brave chief."

(See Barber's Hist. Coll. and Antiquities of Ct.)

In the affair at St. Regis, the catholic priest was made prisoner, and this surprisal and attack soon after led to a retaliatory visit from the enemy, who captured the company of militia under Capt. Tilden, stationed at French Mills, a short time after. Those who were taken in this affair were mostly the identical troops who had been the aggressors at St. Regis, and for these they were subsequently exchanged.

During the war, considerable quantities of pork, flour and cattle, from the state of New York, it is said, were brought by night to St. Regis, and secretly conveyed across the river for the subsistence of the British army. These supplies were purchased by emmisaries under a variety of pretexts, and by offering the highest prices.

An Indian of the British party at St. Regis, was lately living, who was employed as a secret messenger to carry intelligence, and was very successful in avoiding suspicious and in accomplishing his errands.

It is a well known fact that there were American citizens who secretly countenanced these movements, and who openly denounced the war and its abettors; who hailed a British victory as a national blessing, and who mourned over the success of the American arms, with a pathos that proved their sincerity.

Impartial TRUTH would require their names to be held up to the execration of honest men, through all coming time, but CHARITY bids us pass them unnoticed, that they may perish with their memories.

By virtue of powers supposed to be vested in them by the law of 18 the trustees of these Indians had leased considerable tracts of the reservation in the vicinity of Salmon river, which had thus become settled and cleared up; but this measure was found to produce jars and discords, which led to the passage of a general enactment, passed June 19, 1812:

"That it shall be unlawful for any person or persons other than Indians, to settle or reside upon any lands belonging to any nation or tribe of Indians within this state; and if any person shall settle or reside upon any such lands, contrary to this act, he or she shall be deemed guilty of a misdemeanor, and shall on conviction, be punished by fine not less than twenty-five dollars, nor more than five hundred dollars, or be imprisoned not less than one month, nor more than six months, in the discretion of the court having cognizance thereof; and it shall be the duty of the courts of oyer and terminer, and general sessions of the peace in the several counties of this state, in which any part of said lands are or may be situated, to charge the grand juries of their respective counties, specially to indict all offenders against the provisions of this section."

Meanwhile many persons had in good faith expended considerable sums in improvements, which it was desirable should be secured to them by a more reliable tenure than Indian leases, which led in 1816, to the passage of a law:

"That in case the St. Regis Indians may be desirous of selling the mile square of land reserved by them. at or near the village of French Mills, in the town of Constable, in the county of Franklin, or any other lands lying within this state, to which the St. Regis Indians have any title or claim, the person administering the government of the state shall be and is hereby authorized to purchase the said lands from the said Indians, in behalf of this state, and that the treasurer be and is hereby authorized on the warrant of the comptroller, to pay to the order of the governor such sum of money to defray the expense of completing the said purchase as the governor may think reasonable to give for the said lands."

The following treaty was accordingly held March 15, 1816:

"A treaty made and executed between Daniel D. Tompkins, governor of the state of New York, in behalf of the people of the said state, of the one part, and Peter Tarbell, Jacob Francis and Thomas Williams, for and in behalf of the nation or tribe of Indians, known and called the St. Regis Indians, of the second part (at the city of Albany, this fifteenth day of March, in the year of our Lord, one thousand eight hundred and sixteen), witnesseth.

Article 1. The said tribe or nation of St. Regis Indians do hereby sell and convey to the people of the state of New York, for the consideration hereinafter mentioned, a certain piece or parcel of their reservation, called the one mile square, situated in the county of Franklin, on Salmon river, to have and to hold the same, to the said people of the state of New York, and their assigns for ever, and also a separate and additional tract of land, of their said reservation, situate in the county aforesaid, containing five thousand acres of the easterly part of their said reservation, adjoining their aforesaid mile square of land, within the territorial limits of the state of New York, to be measured from the east boundary line of said reservation, so as to make the said west boundary line of said five thousand acres to run due north and south; to have and to hold the said five thousand acres of land, to the said people of the state of New York, and their assigns for ever.

Article 2. The said Daniel D. Tompkins, governor, as aforesaid, for and in behalf of the people of the state of New York, covenants and agrees, with the St. Regis nation of Indians, that the said people, for the said several tracts of one mile square of land, and of five thousand acres of land hereinbefore granted and conveyed, shall pay to the said nation annually for ever hereafter, the sum of one thousand three hundred dollars, at French Mills, on said premises, the first payment of the said annuity to be paid on the first Tuesday of August next, and the whole annuity to be paid on the first Tuesday of August, in each year thereafter.

Article 3. The said St. Regis tribe or nation of Indians also covenant and agree to depute and authorize three of the chiefs or principal men of their tribe to attend at the times and places aforesaid, to receive the said annuity. And that the receipt of the said chiefs or principal men, so deputed, shall be considered a full and satisfactory discharge of the people of the state of New York, from the annuities which may be so received."

Signed, sealed, witnessed, acknowledged and recorded.

In consequence of the great distress among the St. Regis and other Indian tribes of the state, from the short crops in the cold summer of 1816, the legislature, at the recommendation of the governor, by an act passed February 12, 1817, authorized the payment of annuities to be anticipated for that year, for the purchase of the necessaries of life.

The concessions of the last treaty being found not to cover the territory that had been leased, another treaty was held on the 20th of February, 1818, as follows:

"At a treaty held at the city of Albany, the 20th day of February, in the year of our Lord one thousand eight hundred and eighteen, between his excellency Dewitt Clinton, governor of the state of New York, on behalf of the people of the said state, and Loran Tarbell, Peter Tarbell, Jacob Francis and Thomas Williams, on behalf of the nation or tribe of Indians, known and called the St. Regis Indians, it is covenanted, agreed and concluded as follows, to wit:

The said St. Regis Indians sell and convey to the people of the state of New York, two thousand acres out of the lands reserved by the said Indians, to be bounded as follows, to wit: On the north and south by the north and south bounds of said reservation; on the east by the lands ceded by said Indians to the people of the said state, by a treaty dated 16th March, 1816, and on the west by a line running parallel thereto, and at such a distance therefrom as to contain the said two thousand acres; also, four rods wide of land through the whole length of their reservation, for a public road, to the west bounds thereof, together with four rods wide of land, for the same purpose, commencing at the boundary line near the village of St. Regis, to run in a direction so as to intersect the aforementioned road a little westerly of the place where it shall cross the St. Regis river, which will be about one mile and three-quarters in length. On condition that both the said roads be laid out by Michael Hogan, with the assistance of Loran Tarbell, and such other person as his excellency, the governor of the said state, shall appoint; and further, that in case a turnpike gate, or gates, shall be established on said road, all the Indians of the said tribe shall be allowed to pass free of toll, and on the further condition that those on the lands they have now and heretofore sold, shall be compelled before the state gives them or any other person title thereto, to pay up the arrearages of rent due on the lands occupied by the said settlers.

In consideration of which cession or grant, it is hereby covenanted, on the part of the said people, to pay to the said Indians, annually, for ever hereafter, on the first Tuesday of August, at Plattsburgh, an annuity of two hundred dollars. And it is further covenanted by and between the said parties, that the annuities payable to the said Indians, in consequence of the former treaties between them and the said state, shall hereafter be paid them on the said first Tuesday of August, at Plattsburgh, instead of the places where they are made payable by such treaties. In testimony whereof, the said governor, on the part of the people of the said state, and the said Loran Tarbell, Peter Tarbell, Jacob Francis, and Thomas Williams have hereunto set their hands and seals, the day and year first above mentioned."

Signed, sealed, acknowledged and recorded.

The lands ceded by the treaty of 1818 were by an act of April 20th, of that year directed to be laid out into lots and farms and sold.

The report of the commissioners appointed by the governor to perform this duty, will be given in our account of Fort Covington.

The commissioners were to receive $4 per day for their services.

The following memorial explains itself, and indicates the necessity of the course which was subsequently to be pursued.

ALBANY 16, February, 1818.
"To his Excellency, Governor Clinton, of the state of New York:

The chiefs of the St. Regis Indians, by their petition, most respectfully approach your excellency, to shew, that in March 1802, a law was passed for the benefit of our tribe, appointing the trustees, namely: William Gray, Louis Cook, and Loren Tarbell, to manage and improve their affairs. From that period until the late war, they continued happy amongst themselves, but the war having produced a feeling of opposite interests in the tribe, they became divided almost equally in number, of young men, having your old chiefs, with their adherents steady in the cause and interests of the United States. In course of the war, their trustee, William Gray, was taken prisoner at St. Regis, and carried to Quebec, where he died a prisoner of war. Their other trustee, Colonel Louis Cook, after being actively engaged with General Brown, near Buffalo, died at that place. Since his death, your excellency's petitioner, Loren Tarbell, the surviving trustee, taking to his private council Peter Tarbell, and Jacob Francis, old chiefs, in whom the tribe have full faith, has continued to act as for the whole, and has the satisfaction of assuring your excellency, that the trust reposed in him, has been discharged conscientiously, and with full regard to justice.

Now your excellency's petitioner, growing old, and desirous to be relieved in part from the responsibility which he has felt in the discharge of his duties, humbly prays your excellency to get a law passed, appointing the above mentioned Peter Tarbell and Jacob Francis, to his aid, to fill the vacancies occasioned by the death of the former trustees, and confirming the acts of your petitioner done in conjunction with the latter, since the death of the former trustees.

And your petitioner will as in duty bound ever pray &c."

> LOREN TARBELL, (signed by his mark.)
> WILLIAM L. GRAY, Interpreter.

In consequence of the foregoing petition and memorial, an act was passed on the 3d of April, 1818, appointing Peter Tarbell and Jacob Francis, chiefs of the said tribe, to be trustees in place of Colonel Louis and William Gray, deceased, and to act with the surviving trustee Loren Tarbell.

Much difficulty arose between the Indians and their former tenants, in relation to their arrearges of rent, concerning which they memorialized the legislature, and on the 10th of March 1824, procured an act directing the Comptroller, to draw his warrant on the treasury, for the payment of any sum not exceeding $735.07 in favor of Asa Hascall, district attorney, for the county of Franklin, upon his certificate or certificates of the amount of rents due to the said St. Regis Indians, from settlers on certain lands ceded to them, by the people of this state, by treaty dated Feb 29, 1818, and it was made the duty of the said district attorney, on receiving the said money, to pay it over to the Indians as a full satisfaction and discharge of their claims.

On the 10th of April, 1824, the foregoing act was extended to include the lands ceded March 15, 1816.

The mill on Grass river, and one mile square reservation, continued to be the property of these people, until March 16, 1824, when at a treaty held at Albany between Joseph C. Yates, Governor, and Thomas Williams, Michael Cook, Lewis Doublehouse and Peter Tarbell, at which they sold and conveyed for the sum of $1,920, this property.

The following is a copy of the power of attorney, under which the deputies of the foregoing treaty acted:

"Know all men by these presents, that we, the undersigned, chief warriors of the tribe called St. Regis Indians, constitute and appoint Thomas Williams, Lewis Doublehouse, and Peter Tarbell, as our true and lawful attornies, to go to Albany, and sell such a quantity of our lands, to the people of this state, as they may think proper, and to transact all other business which shall be thought best for the welfare of our nation, and whatsoever our attornies shall lawfully act or do, we will ratify and confirm. Done at St. Regis in general council, this eighth day of March 1821."

Eleazer Skarestogowa,	Charles Sagahawita,
Peter Trewesti,	Ignace Garewess,
Loran Cook,	Joseph Bern,
Charles Williams,	Evrer Gagagen,
Thomas Turble,	Baptiste Satchweies,
Lewey Sabonrani.	

(signed mostly by their marks.)

The appointment made by the legislature in 1818 of trustees to fill the vacancy made by the death of Cook and Gray, appears to have been unsatisfactory to the tribe, as is seen from the following petition that was signed by the same parties as those who furnished the credentials of the deputies at the previous treaty.

" To the honorable the Legislature of the state of New York, in senate and assembly convened.

We the undersigned, chiefs and warriors of the St. Regis tribe of Indians, humbly represent to your honorable body, that our old chiefs that were appointed as trustees are all dead, except one, who is old and unable to transact public business. We therefore earnestly pray that your honorable body, will appoint Thomas Williams, Mitchel Cook, Lewis Doublehouse, and Peter Tarbell, as trustees to oversee and control the affairs of the St. Regis Indians.

Done in general council at St. Regis, this ninth day of March, 1824.

The following memorial was also prepared to be forwarded to the legislature:

" At a public council or town meeting, of the chiefs, head men, and warriors, of that part of the St. Regis nation, or tribe of Indians, which claim the protection and countenance of the state of New York, and which receive annuities from, and held lands under the authority of the said state; assembled on this 31st day of May, 1824, on their reservation lands, in the said state, it is unanimously resolved, that in order to put an end to all quarrels for power, we will not henceforth encourage any other individuals to be chiefs, or trustees, except Thomas Williams, Mitchel Cook, Lewis Doublehouse, Peter Tarbell, and Charles Cook; and we do hereby fully authorize, and empower them to transact for, and on behalf of our said tribe of American St. Regis Indians, all manner of business which they may deem for the general good.

We authorize them, especially, to receive all annuities, payable to us by virtue of any bargains or treaties, made, or to be made, by the state of New York, or of individuals under the sanction of law, and others, and to distribute all money or property, as received amongst the said tribe of American St. Regis Indians, according to our claims. We also authorize and require them, to execute to the governor of the said state, or other proper authority, all necessary grants, conveyances, releases, or receipts, which may be required, in consequence of any bargain or treaty heretofore made, or hereafter in their discretion to be made on our behalf, and for our benefit, with the governor of the said state.

We do further authorize and require them, to endeavor to make such a bargain with the governor, as that all the moneys which we are now, or shall be entitled unto, shall in future be paid on our reservation lands, to our said chiefs, and trustees, and not elsewhere. We also authorize them to make such arrangements with the governor, that some individual in whom the governor, as well as our said chiefs, can place confidence, may hereafter be considered the only proper channel of mutual communication between the governor and our said chiefs, on behalf of our said tribe, excepting all occasions in which our said chiefs may be at Albany. We fully approve all that was done by our deputies, and chiefs, Thomas Williams, Michael Cook, Louis Doublehouse, and Peter Tarbell, in the bargain or treaty made at Albany, on the 16th March last. We earnestly request that the governor will bear in mind, these resolutions

11

of the American St. Regis Indians, and that our minds may be known, we have each of us caused our several names and seals to be affixed to this paper, and another like it , and ordered one copy to be delivered to the governor, and one to be kept by our said chiefs."

[Signed by about sixty Indians.]

Copied from the duplicate at St. Regis.

As a further evidence of authenticity, the foregoing was accompanied by a declaration of allegiance, a copy of which is here given:

"Know all whom it may concern, that we, whose names are hereto annexed, do solemnly declare ourselves, to belong to the American Tribe of St. Regis Indians, that we owe no fealty to the British government, nor receive any annuities or benefits from the same; that we were friendly to the United States during the late war, and have continued to be so since, and that it is our fixed determination, to establish and continue our residence within the limits of the said United States, the protection and countenance, and especially of the state of New York, we hereby claim for said tribe. In witness of all which we have hereto caused our names and seals to be affixed this 31st day of May, in the year 1824, within our reservation lands, in the state of New York, done in duplicate one copy to be kept by our chiefs, and one copy to be delivered to the governor of the state of New York."

[Signed by about sixty Indians.]

The author has been unable to ascertain what action, if any, was taken on this subject by the legislature, further than in a treaty, held on the 29th of June, 1824, between Governor Yates, and Thomas Williams, Mitchel Cook, Louis Doublehouse, Peter Tarbell, and Charles Cook, the latter are recognized as trustees.

By this treaty, they ceded in consideration of $1,750 down, and an annuity of $60, payable on the 1st Tuesday in August, at the village of Plattsburgh, to the said chiefs and trustees, a tract of 1000 acres of land bounded as follows:

"On the northeast, by a line commencing on the easterly side of St. Regis river, at the termination of the roll way, so called, about four or five chains northerly from the mast road, and running thence southeast to the south bounds of the said reserved lands; on the south by the said south bounds; on the northwest by the said St. Regis river, and the land leased by the said Indians, to Michael Hogan, and on the southwest by a line to be run southeast, from the said St. Regis river, to the south bounds of said reserved lands."

On the 14th of December, 1824, the same Indians, who are styled, "Principal Chiefs and head men," confirmed to the people of the state of New York, for a payment of $1, and an annuity of $305, a certain tract of land which their predecessors had "in two certain indentures of lease, or instruments in writing, under seal, bearing date respectively, on the 20th and 23d days of October, in the year of our Lord 1817, and made and executed by and between their predecessors in office, and Michael Hogan, and subsequently confirmed by an act of the legislature."

On the 20th of April, 1825, the legislature confirmed this cession by an act, the preamble and body of which set forth the causes that led to the measure.

"Whereas the Indians of the St. Regis tribe did, by two certain inden tures of lease bearing date the 20th of October, and the 23d of October respectively, in the year 1817, (which leases were sanctioned and confirmed by the Legislature of this state,) convey certain premises therein described in consideration of a certain annuity or rent annually to be paid for a term of years, with the condition for the renewal of the said leases as often as the same might expire, and upon the same terms; And whereas, by the subdivision of said premises among a number of occupants, or by the removal of the said Indians from their present possessions, they may experience difficulty and loss in collecting and receiving the rents, reserved and annually due, by virtue of the conveyances aforesaid; Therefore,

Be it enacted by the People of the State of New York, That it shall and may be lawful for the grantee, in the said conveyances named, or his assigns, to convey the premises therein described to the people of this state; and whenever the said grantee or his assigns shall have paid or secured to be paid into the treasury of the state a sum equal to the principal of the annuity yearly payable to the said Indians by virtue of the conveyances aforesaid, at the rate of six per cent. per annum, it shall be the duty of the commissioners of the land office, to reconvey by letters patent to the said grantee or his assigns so paying or securing the payment of the sum above mentioned, and forever thereafter the annuity reserved in the conveyances aforesaid, shall annually be paid to the said Indians, in like manner as their other annuities from the state are now payable."

A treaty was held Sept. 23, 1825, between Governor De Witt Clinton and Thomas Williams, Mitchel Cook, Louis Doublehouse, Peter Tarbell, Charles Cook, Thomas Tarbell, Mitchel Tarbell, Louis Tarbell, Battice Tarbell, Jarvis Williams and William L. Gray, by which the latter as chiefs and trustees for the tribe, sold a tract of land,.of 840 acres, on the east side of the St. Regis river, which is now the site of a part of the village of Hogansburgh. For this they received $1100 down, in full of all demands.

This tract was bounded as follows:

"Beginning on the easterly side of the St. Regis river, at the most westerly corner of the lands ceded by said Indians to the people of said state, on the 12th day of June, in the year 1824, and running thence along the last mention lands, S. 45° E., to the south bounds of the said reserved lands; then along the same, westerly to the said St. Regis river, and then along the same to the place of beginning."

The foregoing are believed to be all the negotiations that have taken place between these people and the state in relation to their lands. There remains to be mentioned some notices on the personal history and present condition and habits of these Indians.

In 1826, a young Frenchman, by the name of Fovel, who had been for some time at Montreal, visited St. Regis, and induced one *Joseph Torakaron*, (sometimes known by his English name of Tarbell,) to consent to accompany him to Europe. Torakaron was to travel in the character of an Indian chief, (which office he then held at St. Regis,) and his companion in that of interpreter, solicitor, *treasurer* and agent. The motives held out to the chief were, that they should be able to obtain donations for the endowment of their church, and doubtless large sums as presents to themselves. Having made all necessary arrangements, and being furnished with letters from St. Regis, Montreal and Quebec, certifying the standing of Torakaron at home, the two proceeded by way of New York and Havre, to Paris. The conductor here obtained an interview with Charles X, and so favorable an impression was made upon the mind of the king, that he presented them with three fine paintings, and a large sum in money, and other valuable articles.

Thence they proceeded by way of Marseilles, to Rome, and obtained an interview with the pope.

During a conversation, the pope asked the Indian if he could converse in another language than his own, and finding him able to use the English and French to some degree, he invited him to a second interview alone. The result was, that a set of books and silver plate, for the service of the church, a rosary of jewels and gold, worth it is said $1400, and other articles of value, were given him. They thence returned to Marseilles, where they spent the winter, and in 1828 returned by way of Paris and Havre to New York. Here the treasurer, or interpreter, or whatever else he might be called, evinced his true character by absconding with every article of value, except the rosary and paintings, leaving Torakaron without means even to return home. He was enabled to do so through the charity of friends, and the paintings were soon after deposited in their destined place. Two are now at St. Regis, and the third at the church in Caughnawaga. Of the former, those who visit the church will recognise in a painting over the altar, the portrait of St. Regis, and in the one to the left, near the pulpit, that of St. François Xavier.

They are both evidently by the same hand, of the size of life, and very well executed. The third is the portrait of St. Louis, and is in the church dedicated to that saint in the Indian village near Montreal.

St. Regis is represented in the attitude of preaching; St. François as reclining on a bank, with a book before him and pointing to a cross, and St. Louis as a king, in royal robes, bowed in the attitude of the deepest humility, in prayer.

Fovel subsequently visited the Iroquois settlements of New York, as a priest, and occasioned much trouble, which rendered it necessary for Bishop Dubois to visit those places.

He afterwards went to Detroit, and appeared as a priest among the French at that city.

In the spring of 1829, the small pox appeared at the village of St. Regis, and swept off great numbers. All the tribe were then vaccinated, by direction of the British government.

In 1832, the Asiatic cholera broke out at this place, on the 20th of June, at first appearing in a mild form, for which the priest prescribed successfully for a short time, by administering large doses of laudanum and hot brandy. Of the first sixty cases thus dealt with, there are said to have been but two that were fatal.

Dr. McAuley, of Cornwall, was sent over by government, to attend the sick, and Dr. Bates, of Fort Covington, was also employed. The latter has remarked, that two in fifteen of those remaining in the village, died of this pestilence, and that when the east wind blowed, there were sure to be new cases. In one instance, a family of eleven were attacked, and but one survived. About 340 persons had the disease, some two or three times, making in all perhaps 500 cases. Friends became frightened, and fled away, leaving the sick, in some instances, to die unattended, and all mourning for the dead ceased.

This alarming pestilence was attended by the typhus fever, but it was observed that the two diseases did not attack the same persons, although they raged with equal severity. The cholera raged but eleven days, in which time 78 died, and the number of those who died in the year 1832, of this and other diseases, was 134.

As a natural consequence, this fearful visitation caused the greatest terror throughout the whole country, and exaggerated reports of its ravages at St. Regis spread rapidly to the neighboring villages, and led to the issuing of an order from the brigadier general of militia in the county, to the subordinate officers under his command, to take measures for preventing all intercourse with the infected village. Several persons volunteered to guard the road leading to Hogansburgh, and this vigilance was maintained about a week. It appeared to be unnecessary, because the epidemic limited itself to the vicinity of the river, and the village of Hogansburgh, two miles distant, was but very slightly affected.

In 1849, the cholera again appeared, taking off 29, and in the same year, the small pox broke out, with 500 cases, of which 30 were fatal. Bergen, of Cornwall, was employed by the British government on this occasion.

In 1850, the typhus raged the whole summer.

. A remark was made by the Rev. Mr. Marcoux, which is worthy of the attention of the medical profession, that the cholera and the typhus were associated in both cases, although they did not attack the same persons; and that they admitted and required alike a sustaining and stimulating course of treatment.

The filthy and negligent habits of these people appear to have rendered them fit subjects for any pestilence that might chance to make its appearance; and the observation so often made has been here confirmed, that rigid cleanliness and suitable regard for neatness, are the best preventives of contagion, and more efficient than cordons of troops, or quarantine regulations.

The annuities of the St. Regis Indians continued to be paid at Plattsburgh, until 1832, when, by a law passed April 24, the place of payment was transferred to the town of Fort Covington.

By this act the comptroller was directed to appoint an agent, who was to receive a sum not exceeding two percentum on all such disbursements.

He was directed to pay each of the heads of families under the direction of the trustees of the tribe, their equal shares of the annuities, taking the necessary receipts from the legal trustees of said tribes, for the annuities received.

As the village of St. Regis was then in the town of Fort Covington, these annuities have since been generally paid at that place.

The agents appointed by the comptroller, to pay these annuities, since this office was created, in 1832, have been, James B. Spencer, Amherst K. Williams, John S. Eldridge, Phineas Attwater, Wm. A. Wheeler, J. J. Seaver, and James C. Spencer.

During the summer of 1834, these Indins remonstrated against the payment of any part of the annuity of 1796, to the Caughnawagas, urging that previous to the war, a release was executed by the latter to them. During the war, the latter had not received their share. A few years after the war, through the agency and interference of Peter Sailly, of Plattsburgh, that moiety of the annuity was restored to them, with the express understanding, that $50 annually of that portion should be paid to Thomas Williams, who had left that tribe, with his family, during the war, at a great sacrifice, and joined the Americans. Williams was paid without objection, till 1833, when the Caughnawagas entered a protest, and he was not paid.

Before the war, the St. Regis Indians were allowed to hold, in common with their brethren in Canada, all the Indian lands, and also to receive the rents and profits of them. Since the war, the British government refused them the privilege of even occupying the lands on the St. Lawrence river, in common with their brethren in Canada.

For this reason, they conceived that they had an exclusive right to the state annuities. They accordingly applied to the legislature, in 1835, for the payment to them of the annuity which had been previously shared by the Caughnawagas.

They also asked that the payment of their annuities might be made at a more convenient season of the year, and to those who reside in the state of New York, or within the United States only.

They also applied for a change of the existing law for the election of trustees, and desired that the governor might be empowered to appoint not less than three nor more than six principal Indians, who should be called chiefs, and hold their office during pleasure, a majority of whom were to act for the tribe.

This memorial was referred to A. C. Flagg, the comptroller, who made a report to the legislature, in which he reviewed the history of the Indian title, and from which we will take the liberty of making a few extracts.

After briefly enumerating the several treaties made, by whom and for what consideration he gives the following summary of the compensation and annuities received for their lands.

				Sum paid at the treaty.	Amount of annuities.
Treaty of 1796 with the Seven Nations,				$3,179·96	$533·33
"	1816	"	St. Regis		1,300·00
"	1818	"	"		200·00
"	1824	"	"	1,920·00	
"	1824	"	"	1,750·00	60·00
"	1824 and act of 1825				305·00
"	1825 with the St. Regis,			2,100·00	
				$8,949·96	$2,398·33

In relation to the claims of these Indians, the comptroller said:

"It should be borne in mind, that the treaty was originally made with British as well as American Indians, which treaty is in the nature of a contract, on the part of the state, to pay annually a certain sum of money in consideration of the relinquishment, by the Seven Nations, of Canada, of certain lands belonging to them. When the treaty was made, the Caughnawagas were British Indians, as much as they are now; the state did not refuse to treat with them, and purchase their lands, because they resided in Canada; and having made the treaty with them, shall the state refuse to fulfill it?

If the annuity is to be confiscated because the Caughnawagas, or some of them, may have taken up arms against the United States during the late war, then the question would arise, whether the confiscation should be made for the benefit of the state treasury or the St. Regis tribe; and if the Caughnawagas are to be cut off, because some of their warriors aided the enemy, the same rule would deprive the St. Regis Indians of their annuities, since some of their warriors were understood to have joined the British army during the war. It should be recollected, however, that the Caughnawaga Indians did not promise allegiance, by the treaty of 1796, nor did they owe allegiance to the United States, or this state, when the war of 1812 was declared.

A request is made in the memorial, that the annuity of $533·33 may hereafter be paid only to such of the St. Regis tribe as reside in this state, or the United States. By the treaty of 1796, it was agreed, that if the Seven Nations of Canada, would relinquish their lands to the people of this state, they should receive forever an annuity of $533·33. After the Indians, in pursuance of this agreement, have relinquished their lands, and after the state has taken possession of and sold them, can the government of this state refuse to fulfil the stipulations of the treaty, because the Indians do not reside on the American side of the national line?

The St. Regis Indians represent that Thomas Williams left the Caughnawagas during the war, with his family, at a great sacrifice. It is true that he joined the American side during the war, and for doing this, his property may have been confiscated. But it will be seen by referring to the treaties, that Thomas Williams, who in 1796 was a Caughnawaga chief, in 1816, had become one of the chiefs and head men of the St. Regis tribe, and assisted in securing to the latter tribe an annuity of $1,300 for the sale of lands, reserved in the treaty with the Seven Nations of Canada. By joining the St. Regis Indians and aiding in the subsequent sale for the sole benefit of this tribe, of the lands reserved by the treaty of 1796, Williams would of course lose all favor with the tribe to which he had originally belonged.

The exclusion of the Caughnawagas from a participation in the annuity secured by the treaty of 1796, is only one of the disturbing questions with which the St. Regis Indians are agitated. There are two parties in the tribe, one denominated the American party, and the other the British party; and as they elect trustees under the authority of the laws of this state, the British Indians, it is alleged, join in and in some cases control these elections.

The strife in relation to the choice of trustees may have been increased and aggravated, from the circumstance that these trustees have been in the habit of issuing due bills, which are circulated and form a kind of paper currency. These due bills are made payable on the first Tuesday in August succeeding the date thereof, and are based of course on the money in the treasury and which is payable to the Indians on that day."

The comptroller advised against changing the time or mode of paying the annuities.

In 1834, there had been paid to one hundred and three families, comprising three hundred and thirty-six individuals, $2,131·66 to the St. Regis, and $266·67 to the Caughnawaga tribe.

It is stated that when the government, after the war, decided to restore one half of the annuity of 1796, to the latter, that Mr. Denniston, the agent, told their deputies, that Williams having been a party to the treaty, ought to have a share of the money, and accordingly $50 had been paid to him annually.

Those who wish to pursue this examination, will find by referring to the assembly documents of 1835, a further statement, with a copy of the paper purporting to confer upon the St. Regis Indians, authority to receive the annuities of 1796, which the comptroller decided to be spurious; and also a correspondence of James R. Spencer, at that time the agent, and documents showing that the St. Regis were deprived of certain rights previously enjoyed, in consequence of the course adopted in the war. Our space does not admit of further reference to this question.

The Caughnawagas being decided to be entitled to a portion of the annuity above mentioned, continued to receive it until 1841, (May 25,) when the commissioners of the land office were authorized,

"To direct the payment, in their discretion, to the Caughnawaga and St. Regis tribes, representing the Seven Nations of Canada, or any part or portion of them, of the principal of the annuities, or such portion thereof as they, the said commissioners, may from time to time deem proper, remaining under the control of this state, for the benefit of said Indians, or any portion of them. They were authorized also, to treat with any remaining tribes of Indians in the state for their lands, or the payment of moneys belonging to them, or in relation to roads running through their lands.

The acts of these commissioners were to be submitted to the governor for his approval, before they could have effect. Actions for trespass were to be prosecuted by the district attorney of the counties where they were committed, and the excess recovered, after paying the expense of prosecution, was to be distributed among the Indians. Three of the chiefs of the tribe might in like manner bring a suit for its benefit, with the written approbation of the supervisor of the town where the land was situated, or of any judge of the county courts, and security for costs in the latter case being given, approved by the supervisor or judge, at any time before or on the return of the first process in the suit."

The Caughnawagas have accordingly been paid the principal of their share of the annuity.

By an act passed April 27, 1841, the trustees of the St. Regis tribe duly elected, at a regular meeting, were authorized with the advice and consent of the agent for the payment of their annuities, to execute leases to white persons for any part of their unoccupied lands, for any term not exceeding twenty-one years, for such rents as may be agreed upon. The income of these leases was to be divided for the general benefit of the tribe. The district attorney of Franklin county, was to prepare the form of the lease, and none were to take effect unless with the written consent of the district attorney, or Indian agent, endorsed thereon. The fee for preparing the lease, attending to its execution, and endorsing it, was fixed at three dollars.

In pursuance with powers thus granted, considerable portions of the reservation have been leased, mostly to Canadian Frenchmen.

The question of the propriety of this measure, has ever been a subject of contention and party strife among them, at their annual election of trustees. For several years, the party opposed to leasing land, has been in the ascendancy, and the measure has been discontinued.

The grass meadows on Grass river, in the town of Massena, were purchased from the St. Regis Indians, by the commissioners of the land office, in pursuance of powers vested in them by the legislature, on the 21st of February, 1845.

The amount purchased was, according to Lay's Map of 1801, two hundred and ten acres, at three dollars per acre. It was stipulated that if the amount of land should be found to overrun, the excess should be paid for at the same rates.

The Indian meadows on Grass river were surveyed by John W. Tate, in 1845, and patented in small lots in the years 1846, '7, '8, '9, and 1851.

By an act making provision for the education of the different Indian tribes of the state, passed April 30, 1846, it was enacted: That the sum of two hundred and fifty dollars should be appropriated for the building and furnishing of a school house, on the lands of the St. Regis Indians; and the further sum of two hundred dollars a year, for the term of five years, for the payment of the wages of a teacher and other expenses of the said school.

These moneys were to be paid from time to time, by the agent, who was to give his usual official bond, and report annually to the superintendent of common schools.

This appropriation was very judiciously expended by Phineas Attwater, Esq., the agent, in the erection of a school house, on the reservation, and between the village and Hogansburgh.

In addition to the amount named in the previous act, a further sum of $75 was appropriated May 7, 1847, out of the United States deposite fund, to be expended by the agent paying annuities, in completing the school house on the St. Regis reservation, and in improving the school lot.

The act of 1846 was so amended as to give $300 per annum for the years 1847, 1848, for the payment of a teacher.

The novelty of the measure, with other causes, made it at first very popular, and the school was very fully attended. The parents evinced an interest in the measure that was surprising, and often visited the school, and took a deep interest in its success; but it became necessary to discharge the teacher, and those who have since been employed have failed to awaken the interest which was at first felt.

The British government have also maintained a school here for several years, but with no better success.

The natives have often expressed their sense of the degrading influences which the use of ardent spirits have exerted to their injury. The following memorial from the Oneidas, more than fifty years ago, addressed to the legislature as coming from the different Indian tribes, possesses a melancholy interest, and engages our sympathy as expressive of a refined sentiment of the heart, and a feeling that would do honor to man's nature, if expressed, not by the illiterate savage, but by one who had enjoyed all the advantages which civilization has conferred upon him.

" To the Legislature of the State of New York:

Brothers:
We, the sachems and chiefs of the different nations, desire your attention. You have often manifested a respect to our welfare, by way of good council. You have told us, that we should love one another, and to live in peace. You also exhorted us, to abandon our savage life, to adopt your mode of life in cultivating our land; to raise grain; to be sober and many other good things. We have made attempts to follow the good path you have pointed out for us, but find ourselves still deficient. And you seem to blame us for our backwardness, and we are to be blamed.

Brothers:
We have been often consulting upon our welfare. and to promote it— we made but slow progress. For we find our great obstacle which we look upon as our enemy, by whose means our nations are almost reduced to the ground. Our young men seem to be willing to become slaves to this tyrant, who goes in the name of SPIRITUOUS LIQUOR. To us he is a servant of evil spirit. When we found that our own endeavors and powers were too weak to prevent such an enraging tyrant, we united our voices, two years ago, to you for your assistance, that you might bind this tyrant. But you refused to give your assistance, which one brother had right to expect from another.

Brothers:
If such of your color, as sell us this article, were obliged to keep us in their houses while we are distracted with it, and suffer us in the desolation it makes, we then believe they would willingly call out as loud as we do for help, and existence. Therefore we can not but hope and firmly believe, that you will at this time, give all possible relief.

Brothers:
Remember, that we were willing to assist you to fight against your enemy. We were willing to let you have our lands when you needed. We were willing to maintain the chain of friendship with you, and we desire to live in peace, and to enjoy all your privileges. But how can we come to this, so long as you as it were willing to see us destroyed by this tyrant. In consequence of which, numberless audiences have taken place amongst us. And besides that you often told us, that the Great Spirit will send all drunkards to everlasting fire after death.

Brothers:
You are wise people, and you know the mind of the Great Spirit. But we are ignorant people, and you often call us savages. We know but little, and can do but little. And as you are our brothers, we would again look to you for help to lessen abundantly, that distracting article

by some law of yours that we may have fair trial to walk in that path which you so highly recommended to us.

And in compliance with this our request, we shall ever acknowledge your friendship, and we leave it to your wisdom and humanity."

By a general act passed April 10, 1813, it was enacted:

" That no pawn taken of any Indian within this state for any spirituous liquor, shall be retained by the person to whom such pawn shall be delivered, but the thing so pawned may be sued for, and recovered, with costs of suit, by the Indian who may have deposited the same, before any court having cognizance thereof."

It was made a penal offence to sell liquors to certain tribes by this act. By a law passed April 11, 1826, the provisions of a previous general act restricting the sale of ardent spirit, was extended to the Seneca and St. Regis tribe; and in this was prohibited the selling to any Indians of said tribes, or residing or visiting with them, any rum, brandy, gin, or other ardent spirits.

The traffic and use of ardent spirits with these people, was still further restricted by an act of April 20, 1835, which provides:

" That if any person shall knowingly sell or furnish to any Indians, belonging to or residing with the St. Regis tribe, any rum, brandy, gin, or other spirituous liquor, within the counties of Franklin or St. Lawrence, such person shall be deemed guilty of a misdemeanor, and on conviction thereof shall be fined at the discretion of the court, not exceeding twenty-five dollars for one offence, or may be imprisoned not exceeding thirty days, and shall also forfeit for every such offence the sum of five dollars, to be recovered with costs in an action of debt by any person who will sue for the same, one half of which forfeiture to be paid to the prosecutor and the residue to the commissioners of common schools in each town; and that on the recovery of such forfeiture, the offender shall not be liable for any other or further prosecution for the same offence."

The act of 1826 was by this repealed. A still more stringent law was passed April 16, 1849, which forbade the sale or gift of ardent spirits to the Indians, or receiving pawns from them, under a penalty of not less than twenty-five dollars for the former, and a forfeiture of ten times the value of the latter for each offence.

Notwithstanding the most stringent and explicit laws prohibiting the sale or gift of ardent spirits to the Indians, it has been found hitherto impossible to restrain many from habits of intemperence, although there is far less of this now, than formerly. The influence of the present priest appears to be decidedly in favor of temperance.

The state, in its negotiations with the Indian tribes within its borders, has regarded them as a foreign power, so far as the cession of their lands is concerned, and as wards or minors as relates to their internal affairs, and their intercourse with individuals.

A clause in an act passed April 11, 1808, directed that the district attorney in the county of Washington, should advise and direct the St. Regis Indians, in the controversy among themselves and with any other persons, and defend all actions brought against any of them by any white person, and commence and prosecute all such actions for them or any of them as he might find proper and necessary.

On the 11th of April, 1811, the substance of the foregoing act was repassed, with the following preamble and provision:

"And whereas, by the rules and customs of the said Indians, (many of whom are infants,) they are all tenants in common of their property, and all suits brought by them, or in their behalf, must be brought in the name of all of the individuals of the said tribe. Therefore;

Be it enacted, that it shall and may be lawful for the said district attorney, in all suits which he may find proper and necessary to commence and prosecute on behalf of the said Indians, to bring it in the name of the St. Regis Indians, without naming any of the individuals of the said tribe, any law, custom or usage to the contrary notwithstanding."

The district attorney of Washington county, continued to be charged with the trusts reposed in him by the foregoing acts, until April 21, 1818, when a law was passed directing the governor to appoint district attorneys in each of the counties of the state, and making it the especial duty of the one in Franklin county to perform all the duties previously required of the district attorney of the fifth judicial district relative to the St. Regis Indians.

It has since continued the duty of this officer to act in their behalf, but it is said that he is seldom called upon to settle the internal difficulties of the tribe, although upon several occasions individuals have become amenable to the laws and have been dealt with accordingly.

In their internal affairs, they have seldom troubled their neighbors, and have been at little or no expense to their town or county as paupers.

The St. Regis are at present nominally divided into five bands:

1st. OKAWAHO, *the wolf.* At present the most numerous.

2d. RATINIATEN, *the big turtle.* Second in numbers to the former.

3d. OKWARI, *the bear.*   Third   "   "

4th. ROTINESIIO, *the plover.*   Fourth   "   "

5th. ROTISENNAKEHTE, *the little turtle*, the least numerous.

This division is a traditionary one, the purport and meaning of which are entirely lost.

It anciently related to war parties, and rude pictures of these several objects were used as distinctive marks in designating or recording events. A satisfactory account of these and other bands, will be seen in the first volume of the Documentary History of New York.

These distinctions descend in a line by hereditary succession, from mother to son.

The female succession is common among all Indian tribes, and is accounted for by them in a characteristic manner, by saying that the *mother* of a person may be known with certainty, but not the father.

This classification is somewhat similar to that of the clans of Scotland, and probably had its origin under similar circumstances, namely, petty wars, led by small parties and extending not far from the locality where they originated.

The marks became distinctive symbols by which they were known, and constituted a kind of heraldic designation, when painted on their garments and weapons, or marked upon the bark of trees to indicate the class or band to which the wearer or maker of the device belonged.

The St. Regis Indians observe none of the festivals or ceremonies of their ancestors, and no public demonstrations are made, except those imposed by the canons of the catholic church. The principal rites of that sect are here observed, and none with more pomp and parade than *corpus christi*, which is depended upon easter, and falls generally in the first half of June. Preparations for this often occupy weeks; the streets are lined with green boughs and garlands of flowers, a military company from among their number, joins in the processions, and the ceremony usually attracts hundreds of curious spectators from the neighboring towns.

St. Regis day is not observed, but by a regulation of the bishops of Quebec, made several years since, the anniversary of patron saints of churches, is observed on the first Sunday of November. This day is observed with ceremonies in all the catholic churches in Canada.

The only national pastime which these Indians appear to possess, is that of *ball-playing*, in which they engage with much zeal, and for which they evince a strong passion.

The instrument which is used for this purpose, is formed of a rod about four feet in length, bent as in the following figure, and having drawn

across its curvature a net of deerskin thongs. The manner in which the game is conducted is as follows:

About a dozen Indians divided between two parties, and having no clothing but a girdle around the middle, and each with a bat like that above represented, repair to some spacious plain, in the middle of which is laid a ball. The game consists in seizing the ball on the net and tossing it from one to another till it arrives at the side of the field. Each party has its goal, to which it endeavors to tóss the ball, and the rivalry which it excites, leads them to the most active efforts. The ball is seldom allowed to touch the ground, and it rebounds from side to side, alternately favoring one and the other party. As a natural consequence, it often results in personal injuries, from blows aimed at the ball, but received by the ball players.

A company of these has lately held public exhibitions in our large towns and villages.

The exact number of the St. Regis tribe at the time of the athor's visit in June 1852, was 1120, of whom 632 souls belonged to the British, and 488 to the American party. Of this number there is said to be *not one individual of pure Indian blood*, being all more or less mixed with the French and other white races.

The war created a division which has since continued, and the British party still adhere to the election of their twelve chiefs, who hold their office for life.

Their affairs with government are transacted though an agent or clerk who resides in Cornwall, on the opposite shore of the St. Lawrence.

The American party elect three trustees annually, for the transaction of business, on the first Tuesday of May, in pursuance of statute.

The British party of the St. Regis tribe, at present, receive $1,000 as interest for a tract of land sold to that government. It will hereafter be somewhat greater. Besides, they receive rents for lands in Dundee, amounting to $1,000 annually, and blankets and clothing at certain rates, depending upon the age of the individual.

From five to nine, a child receives the value of $1·50. From nine to fourteen, about $2·50, and after that period, the worth of $4 or $5; besides, 1 pound of powder, and 4 pounds of shot and balls, for hunting. A woman receives the value of $4 in blankets and cloth.

Several of the British islands in the St. Lawrence, above and opposite St. Regis, belong to these Indians, and they cultivate or rent all that are valuable.

No section of the country possesses greater fertility or value for agricultural purposes, than most of these islands in the St. Lawrence.

The American party receive their annuity, amounting now to $2,131·67 equally divided between men, women and children, to the amount of $4 per head. Besides this, they receive rent for a tract of land near Hogansburgh, on the Indian reservation, amounting to about $700.

The money now paid by the state, is disbursed by an agent who is appointed by the comptroller, and holds his office at the will of the appointing power. He receives at present a salary of $70. The money is paid to heads of families in specie, in proportion to the number of members in each. It is equally divided among all.

A methodist mission has for some time existed at St. Regis, and they have a chapel in the village of Hogansburgh, on the line of the reservation, and as near the Indian village as a title for land on which to build a church could be procured. In the year 1847-8, the Rev. Ebenezer Arnold, of the Black River Conference, who was laboring in an adjoining charge, was led among them, and after preaching to them a few times succeeded in exciting that interest which resulted in the formation of a small and flourishing society, to which on the following conference the Rev. J. P. Jennings, was appointed missionary.

Through the indefatigable exertions of this gentleman, assisted by others who participated in his interest for the mission, and especially by Bishop Janes, who has the charge of the Indian mission for the time being, the present elegant chapel was erected at an expense of over $1,500, furnished with a fine toned bell, and having a convenient parsonage, pasture, and garden, the whole costing from $2,000, to $2,500. At the end of the second year of his labors, Mr. Jennings was succeeded by the Rev. R. E. King, the present incumbent.

The author is indebted to a work entitled Episcopal Methodism as it Was and Is, by the Rev. P. D. Gorrie, for most of the above data in relation to the methodist mission at St. Regis.

INDIAN NAMES OF PLACES.

It is scarcely two centuries since the territory now the United States, was an unbroken wild, traversed only by the rude natives, who pursued the bear, and the moose, and set his simple snares for such wild game as served to feed or clothe him. The advent of the European, was his misfortune; and step by step he has retreated before the march of civilization, leaving nothing, but here and there, his names of rivers and lakes, and even these, in too many instances, have been with a most singular injustice, and bad taste, exchanged for those of foreign origin, or of no signification of themselves.

The sonorous, and peculiarly appropriate names of the aborigines, have often been made the subject of commendation by foreigners, and should in most instances take the preference of those of modern origin.

In some cases this would be difficult, but in a new and growing country like ours, in which new sources of industry are daily being developed, and new places springing up, might we not with peculiar propriety adopt the euphonious and often elegant names of the Indians instead of the common place appellation of "———'s Mills," or "———'s Corners;" words which convey no association, but those of the most common and indifferent character, and which usually lose all their application after the first generation.

Let any one compare the splendid names of Saratoga, Niagara, and Ontario, with Sackett's Harbor, German Flats, or Lake George, and he will see the contrast between them, and can not fail to approve the taste that would restore the aboriginal names of places, where it may be found practicable.

In making his inquiries into the history of the mission at St. Regis, in June, 1852, the author took special pains to obtain, not only the Indian names of places in the northern part of the state, and immediately within the territory embraced in the work, but also of whatever other localities he might chance to be able, not doubting but that the subject would be regarded as one of general interest.

At the Indian village of Caughnawaga, near the Saut St. Louis, the author met an intelligent half breed, Mr. A. Geo. De Lorimier, alias Oronhiatekha, who is well acquainted with the Mohawk and other Indian languages, from whom he also derived some assistance, especially relating to distant and well known localities. The names derived from this source, will be designated by a † prefixed to the word.

Acknowledgements are especially due to the Rev. F. Marcoux, of St. Regis, for essential assistance in this and other inquiries. Those names received from this source will be thus marked, ‡.

RIVER AND STREAMS.

Black River.—(‡ Ni-ka-hi-on-ha-ko-wa) "big river." Mr. Squier, in a work entitled The Aboriginal Monuments of New York, has given the name of this river as Ka-mar-go. His authority is not cited.

In a map accompanying L. H. Morgan's work entitled The League of the Iroquois, the name given is Ka-hu-a-go, which is a Seneca word.

Chateaugay.—This by some is supposed to be an Indian name, but it is French, meaning, gay castle. The St. Regis call it †O-sar-he-hon, "a place so close or difficult that the more one tries to extricate himself the worse he is off." This probably relates to the narrow gorge in the river near the village.

Chippewa Creek.—In Hammond, (‡Tsi-o-he-ri-sen). This name also applies to Indian Hut Island.

Deer River—(‡Oie-ka-ront-ne) "trout river." The name also applies to the village of Helena, at its mouth.

French Creek.—(‡A-ten-ha-ra-kweh-ta-re) "the place where the fence or wall fell down." The same name applies to the adjoining island.

Gananoqui.—Not Iroquois, supposed to be Huron, and said to mean "wild potatoes," *Apios tuberosa,* (†Kah-non-no-kwen) "a meadow rising out of the water."

Grass River.—(‡Ni-kent-si-a-ke,) "full of large fishes," or, "where the fishes live." In former times this name was peculiarly applicable. Before

12

dams and saw mills were erected, salmon and other fish not now caught were taken in the greatest abundance, as far up as Russell. Its English name was suggested by the grass meadows near its mouth. On an old map in the clerk's office it is marked, Ey-en-saw-ye. The letter y, does not occur in the Iroquois language.

Indian River.—On Morgan's map, (O-je-quack). The St. Regis name it by the same appellation, as Black Lake, which see.

Oswegetchie, and the village of Ogdensburgh. (‡ Swe-kat-si), supposed to be a corrupted Huron word meaning " black water." This river in early times was sometimes called *Black river.*

Ohio.—(O-hi-on-hi-o,) " handsome river." The French designation of La Belle Riviere, was a translation of the original name.

Raquette River.—A French word meaning a " snow shoe." It is said to have been first so called, by a Frenchman named Parisein, long before settlements were begun in this quarter, and that the name was suggested by the shape of a marsh, near its mouth. The Iroquois name ‡ Ni-ha-na-wa-te, or " rapid river," is peculiarly applicable. It is said that Colonel Louis, the Indian chief, told Benjamin Raymond, when surveying, that its Indian name meant " noisy river," for which reason it has been usually written *Racket.*

As rapids are always noisy, this name would have an application, but we shall retain in the map the original orthography. The St. François name, as obtained by Prof. Emmons, was Mas-le-a-gui. On Morgan's map, above quoted, it is called Ta-na-wä-deh, supposed to be a Seneca word.

St. Lawrence River.—(‡ Cat-a-ro-qui,) said to be French or Huron. Signification unknown. On Morgan's map, Ga-na-wa-ge.

St. Regis River and Village.—(‡Ak-wis-sas-ne,) " where the partridge drums."

Salmon river.—(‡Kent-si-a-ko-wa-ne,) " big fish river."

Schoharie.—(‡Io-hsko-ha-re,) " a natural bridge," as that formed by timber floating down stream, and lodging firmly, so as to form a bridge.

†*Tioinata.*—A small river, tributary to the St. Lawrence, above Brockville. Signifies, " beyond the point."

LAKES.

Black Lake.—(‡ -tsi-kwa-ke,) " where the ash tree grows with large knobs for making clubs."

Champlain.—(†Ro-tsi-ich-ni,) " the coward spirit." The Iroquois are said to have originally possessed an obscure mythological notion, of three supreme beings, or spirits, the " good spirit," the " bad spirit," and the " coward spirit." The latter inhabited an island in lake Champlain, where it died, and from this it derived the name above given.

How far this fable prevailed, or what was its origin, could not be ascertained from the person of whom it was received.

Grass Lake.—Rossie, (‡O sa-ken-ta-ke,) " grass lake."

Ontario.—(†O-non-ta-ri-io,) " handsome lake."

Tupper's Lake.—(‡Tsit-kan i-a-ta-res-ko-wa,) " the biggest lake." A small lake below Tupper's lake is called ‡Tsi-kan-i-on-wa-res-ko-wa, " long pond." The name of Tupper's lake, in the dialect of the St. François Indians, as obtained by Professor Emmons, while making the geological survey of the second district, is Pas-kum-ga-meh, " a lake going out from the river," alluding to the peculiar feature, which it presents, of the lake, lying not in the course of, but by the side of, Raquette river, with which it communicates.

Yellow Lake.—In Rossie, (Kat-sen-e-kwa-r,) "a lake covered with yellow lilies."

ISLANDS.

Barnhart's Island.—(‡Ni-ion-en-hi-a-se-ko-wa-ne,) "big stone."
Baxter's Island.—Upper Long Saut Isle, (‡Tsi-io-wen-o-kwa-ka-ra-ts,) "high island."
Cornwall Island.—(‡Ka-wen-o-ko-wa-nen-ne,) "big island."
Isle au Gallop, and the rapid beside it, (‡Tsi-ia-ko-ten-nit-ser-ron-ti-e-tha.) "where the canoe must be pushed up stream with poles."
Isle au Rapid Plat.—Opposite Waddington, (‡Tie-hon-wi-ne-tha,) "where a canoe is towed with a rope."
Lower Long Saut Isle.—(‡Ka-ron-kwi.)
Sheik's Island.—(‡O-was-ne,) "feather island."
St. Regis island.—Same name with river and village.

NAMES OF PLACES.

Brasher Falls.—(‡Ti-o-hi-on-ho-ken,) "where the river divides."
Brasher Iron Works.—(‡Tsit-ka-res-ton-ni,) "where they make iron."
Canada.—(†Ka-na-ta,) "village."
Cayuga.—(†Koi-ok-wen,) "from the water to the shore," as the landing of prisoners.
†*Cataroqui.*—Ancient name of Kingston, "a bank of clay rising out of the waters."
Hochelaga.—Former name of Montreal, or its vicinity, (†O-ser-a-ke,) "Beaver dam."
Helena.—The same name as Deer river.
Hogansburgh.—(‡Te-kas-wen-ka-ro-rens,) "where they saw boards."
Kentucky.—(†Ken-ta-ke,) "among the meadows."
Malone.—(‡Te-kan-o-ta-ron-we,) "a village crossing a river."
Massena Village.—Same name as Grass river.
Massena Springs.—(‡Kan-a-swa-stak-e-ras,) "where the mud smells bad."
Moira.—(‡Sa-ko-ron-ta-keh-tas,) "where small trees are carried on the shoulder."
Montreal.—(‡Ti-o-ti-a-ke,) "deep water by the side of shallow."
New York.—(‡Ka-no-no,) signification not known.
Norfolk Village.—(‡Kan-a-tas-e-ke,) "new village."
Lower Falls in Norfolk on Raquette river, (Tsit-ri-os-ten-ron-we,) "natural dam."
The Oxbow, produced by the bend of the Oswegatchie river, (‡O-non-to-hen,) "a hill with the same river on each side."
Potsdam.—(‡Te-wa-ten-e-ta-ren-ies,) "a place where the gravel settles under the feet in dragging up a canoe."
Quebec.—(‡Te-kia-tan-ta-ri-kon,) "twin or double mountains."
Raymondville.—(‡Tsi-ia-ko-on-tie-ta,) "where they leave the canoe."
Saratoga.—(†Sa-ra-ta-ke,) "a place where the track of the heel may be seen," in allusion to a locality said to be in the neighborhood, where depressions like footsteps may be seen on the rock."
Schenectady.—(‡Ska-na-ta-ti,) "on the other side of the pines."
Ticonderoga.—(†Tia-on-ta-ro-ken,) "a fork or point between two lakes."
Toronto.—(†Tho-ron-to-hen,) "timber on the water."
Waddington.—(‡Ka-na-ta-ra-ken,) "wet village."

We will conclude our account of St. Regis, by a biographical notice of some of the more prominent of those who have flourished there.

TINENA, an Oswegatchie Indian, known as Peter the orator, was a man of great natural talent as a speaker. He was drowned about war time in crossing the St. Lawrence. He was an American Indian, and his descendants still live at St. Regis. On numerous occasions in council, he produced a great effect from his eloquence.

A half breed Indian, who usually was known as PETER THE BIG SPEAK, was a son of Lesor Tarbell, one of the lads who had been stolen away from Groton by the Indians, and who subsequently became one of the first settlers who preceded the founding of St. Regis.

He was a man of much address and ability as a speaker, and was selected as the mouth piece of the tribe on the more important occasions that presented themselves in their councils.

AT-I-ATON-HA-RON-KWEN,[*] better known as *Louis Cook* or *Col. Louis*, was unquestionably the greatest man that has ever flourished at St. Regis, among the native population. His influence with his tribe was very great, and they always relied upon his council, and entrusted him with the performance of their more important business, not only with the other tribes, but also with the two governments.

In all the treaties we have seen, and in all the reports of councils that are preserved, we uniformly find him mentioned, as one of the deputies of the tribe. He had the misfortune of being illiterate. Had he possessed the advantages of education, combined with his great native strength of mind, and soundest judgment, he would have shone with distinguished reputation in his day.

The following narrative of his life we have derived from his daughter, Mary Ka-wen-ni-ta-ke, at St. Regis, through the kindness of the Rev. F. Marcoux, as interpreter, and from a biographical notice written by the Rev. Eleazer Williams, which was obligingly loaned for the purpose. The author has also availed himself of whatever else came in his way, among the public archives at Albany.

Louis Cook was born about 1740, at Saratoga; his father being a colored man, in the service of one of the government officials at Montreal, and his mother, a St. François. In his features he strongly indicated his African parentage.

In an attack made upon Saratoga, towards the close of 1755, the parents of young Louis, were among the captives.

It is said that a French officer seized the boy, and would claim him as his property, but his mother incessantly cried out "ub-ni-ho-wa!," that is, " he is my child." No, no, said the officer, he is a negro, and he is mine. The afflicted mother made an appeal to the Iroquois chief warriors, for the

---

[*] This word signifies " one who pulls down the people."

restoration of her child, who immediately demanded of the officer, to have him delivered up to them as one of their own people, and he reluctantly gave up his prize. The mother out of gratitude to her Indian friends, would accompany them home on their return, and she repaired to Caughnawaga with them, where she spent the remainder of her life, and where she died. The Jesuit father of the mission persuaded young Louis to live with him as an attendant, and here he acquired the French language, which he spoke with ease.

His youth was not distinguished by any peculiarities differing from those of his age and condition, further, than that he indicated an enquiring mind, and took an interest in what was going on in the councils of the tribe, which was unusual for those of his age.

From these councils, he often said in his old age, he learned his first lessons of wisdom. His religious principles very naturally inclined with his early associations, and he became and continued through life a catholic, but there was nothing of intolerance or illiberality in his deportment towards others.

In the war between the French and English, which began in 1755, and ended by the complete success of the latter in 1760, Louis took up arms for the French, in common with his tribe, and was sent to watch the movements of the English on Lake George. Early in the spring of 1756, being in the vicinity of Ticonderoga, he was one of a scouting party sent out against the English, and encountered a party of the latter, under Major Rogers, and a skirmish ensued, in which he was wounded. The wound which he received, was long a source of annoyance, but his conduct had gained him a character for courage as a warrior, which he ever afterwards maintained. He was with the French troops at the defeat of Braddock, on the Ohio, and was also present at the taking of Oswego. At a later period, he was with the forces against Abercrombie at Ticonderoga, where he first received the command of a small party of Iroquois, for which service he was chosen, on account of his general reputation for consistency, and courage, and his command of the French as well as Indian languages.

In the attempt to retake Quebec which the French made, he was present, but after the conquest of Canada, his war spirit entirely ceased, and he returned to private life, and the gaining of a livelihood by the chase, respected by the Indians and the whites so far as he was known. His predilection, like those of the greater part of his race, were still with their former allies, the French, and although the opportunity for its exhibition did not recur, it prevented him from engaging zealously in the affairs of the English.

The troubles which preceded, and led to the American revolution, attracted his curiosity, as he heard the matters discussed among the whites, and he is said to have made once or twice a journey to Albany, to get information on the subject. From General Schuyler, and others, he derived an account of the difficulty, and news that he carried with him to Caughnawaga, is believed to have interested the chiefs of that tribe in behalf of the American cause.

When the storm which had so long darkened the political horizon at length broke, and the crisis had arrived when every one must choose a part, this independent minded Indian adopted a course, which, under the circumstances, must be considered remarkable, and resolved to identify his interests with those of the revolted colonies.

It is difficult to assign a probable reason for this course, as his residence was remote from the theatre of civil commotion, and his people could scarcely complain of the grievances which arose from the stamp act, or the trammels upon commerce and industry, of which the colonies loudly and justly complained.

It may perhaps be ascribed to a dislike for his old enemy the English, and a willingness to side with any party that would attempt their defeat. Whatever may have been the motive, the result was certain, that he enlisted with ardor in the cause of the revolution; served the interests of the colonies with zeal and ability in his sphere, and rendered essential service to his adopted cause, by the weight and influence which his abilities secured him among his race. He felt and declared that the cause was just, and would succeed; he had witnessed the military character of the provincials in the late war, and knew them to be brave, and he felt that the objects for which they contended were worthy of the trials and the sufferings which it would cost to achieve them.

After General Washington had assumed the command of the American army before Boston, Louis Cook resolved to pay him a visit.

In a letter to the president of congress, dated at the camp in Cambridge, August 4, 1775, General Washington says:

"On the first instant, a chief of the Caughnawaga tribe, who lives about six miles from Montreal, came in here, accompanied by a Colonel Bayley, of Coos. His accounts of the temper and disposition of the Indians, are very favorable. He says, they have been strongly solicited, by Governor Carlton, to engage against us, but his nation is totally averse: that threats as well as entreaties have been used, without effect; that the Canadians are well disposed to the English colonies, and if any expedition is meditated against Canada, the Indians in that quarter will give all their assistance. I have endeavored to cherish that favorable disposition, and have recommended him to cultivate them in return. What I have said, I have enforced with a present, which I understood would be agreeable to him; and he is represented as being a man of weight and consequence in his own tribe. I flatter myself, his visit will have a good effect. His account of General Carlton's force and situation of St. Johns, correspond with what we have had from that quarter.

(Washington's Life and Writings, by Sparks, vol iii, p. 53.)

The nature of the present which our Indian chief received at this time, is not known.

In after life, he was wont to exhibit to his friends a *silver pipe*, having neatly carved upon the bowl, the initials, G. W., as the dearly prized gift of a man he adored almost as his maker; and it admits of the conjecture, that this may have been the token which he received at the hands of Washington, on this occasion.

This visit of Louis afforded the general court of Massachusetts, then in session, an opportunity to learn something in relation to the existing condition of the Indians of Canada, and of the internal affairs of that province. There must have been an air of sincerity and intelligence in the Indian chief, to have secured this notice.

The minutes of the Massachusetts house of representatives for the 2d of August, 1775, contain the following memoranda:

" *Ordered*, That Mr. *Winthrop*, Mr. *Foster* and Mr. *White*, with such as the honorable House shall join, be a committee to confer with *Louis*, a chief of the *Caughnawaga* tribe of *Indians*, (who is now in town, being conducted here by Colonel *Bayley* of *Cohoss*,) in order to gain from him all the intelligence they can, respecting the temper and designs of the *Canadians* and Indians towards these colonies, or any other matter it may be of importance to us to know."

Read and concurred in, and Mr. *Howard*, Mr. *Batchelder*, Dr. *Church* and Colonel *Orne*, are joined to the committee of the honorable board.

On the following day, " Mr. *Chauncey* brought down the report of the committee of both Houses, who were appointed to confer with *Louis*, a chief of the *Caughnawaga* tribe of *Indians*, viz:

" *In Council, August* 3, 1775.

" The committee appointed to confer with *Louis*, a chief of the *Caughnawaga* tribe of *Indians*, (who is now in town, being conducted here by Colonel *Bayley* of *Cohoss*,) concerning the temper and designs of the *Canadians* and *Indians* towards these colonies, have attended to that service, and beg leave to lay before this honorable Court, the several questions proposed by the committee to the said *Louis*, and the answers made by him; which were as follows, viz:

Question. How many are there in the *Caughnawaga* tribe?

Answer. Five hundred men able to bear arms.

Q. How many in *St. François*?

A. I do not know. They are a different nation.

Q. How many in *Aronok*?

A. I do not know.

Q. Is there any other nation of *Indians* near your tribe?

A. Yes, *Cannastaug*. The number of them I can not tell.

Q. Has the Governor of *Canada* prevailed on the *St. François Indians* to take up arms against these colonies?

A. The Governor sent out Messrs. St. Lue and *Bahpassion*, to invite

the several tribes of *Indians* to take up arms against you.   At his desire
they held a Grand Council, and the *French officers* gave each man half a
pound of powder and a drink of brandy, and an ox among them, for a
feast.   They answered, nobody had taken arms against them, and they
would not take arms against any body to trouble them; and they chose
to rest in peace.   Upon this answer, the officers told them, 'if you do not
take up arms the *Yankees* will come and destroy you all.'   The Indians
answered again, when these men come here to destroy us, then we will
take up arms and defend ourselves; but we will not go to seek people to
quarrel with them.   The officers then told them, if you will not take up
arms, the regulars will come and destroy you, and take your lands.
They answered, they may come as soon as they have a mind to; and whoever comes to attack us, we will take up arms and defend ourselves.

The officers tried to engage their young men to take up arms, by putting two johannes apiece into their hands; but when the chiefs knew it
they took the money from them, and returned it to the officers, and told
the young men if they offered to engage, they would put them to death.

Q. Did you hear of any other nations of *Indians* that consented to take
arms?

A. There is another nation, called *Ottowas*, at a greater distance, which
the governor endeavored to engage, telling them that the other nations
had agreed to do it.   Upon which the *Ottowas* sent twenty of their tribe
to the General Council before mentioned, to inform them of the governor's message, and enquire whether they had agreed to take arms?
They answered they had not; and if they had any thought of it, they
would have given them notice.   The *French* officers had further told
them, that New York, and all the other governments to the southward,
were going to take arms against the *Yankees.*

Q. What do you know of the disposition of the French Canadians
towards us?

A. Their disposition is the same as that of the *Indians.*   The Governor
tried last winter to raise two thousand troops, but he could not engage
any.   They were disposed to remain upon their own land in peace.

Q. What number of regulars is there in Canada?

A. About five hundred in all.

Q. Where are they stationed?

A. A sergeant and five privates at *Quebeck*, twenty at *Montreal*, and
the rest are gone to *St. Johns.*

Q. What account did the French officers give of us?

A. When I went for my pass, the governor told me that you were not
capable of defending yourselves, and read me a letter purporting that
the king's troops had killed two thousand of your people, without reck-
oning the wounded, and burnt one of your towns.

All of which is humbly submitted.

By order of the committee."

J. WINTHROP.

(American Archives, fourth series, vol. iii, p. 301.)

Impressed with the warmest feelings of patriotism, and an earnest
desire to serve the cause of the colonies, he returned to his home, and
imparted to his fellows the things he had seen and heard.

In a letter from Sir Guy Carlton to General Gage, written in August,
1775, which was intercepted, the Canadian governor says:

" Many of the Indians have gone over to them (the Americans), and
large numbers of the Canadians are with them.

I had hopes of holding out for this year, though I seem abandoned by all the world, had the savages remained firm. I can not blame these poor people for securing themselves, as they see multitudes of the enemy at hand, and no succor from any part, though it is now four months since their operations against us first begun."

This occurred in the summer of 1775. The corn harvest having been secured, and some slight preparations for winter being made, he induced a dozen of the Caughnawaga warriors to visit with him the American camp, that they might learn, from actual observation, the condition of the cause which he was urging them to espouse. They first proceeded to the quarters of General Schuyler, and repaired thence to Cambridge. He had been probably advised to this course, by his friend General Schuyler, whom he had repeatedly visited, on his journeys to Albany, to gain intelligence of the approaching struggle. The latter had previously notified the commander-in-chief of the nature of the visit which he might soon expect to receive, but the journey was delayed a little longer than was expected. We find the occurrence mentioned in the correspondence of General Washington, who, in a letter to Major General Schuyler, dated at Cambridge, 16 January, 1776, says:

" Our Caughnawaga friends are not arrived yet. I will try to make suitable provisions for them during their stay, and use every means in my power to confirm their favorable disposition towards us. They will not, I am fearful, have such ideas of our strength, as I could wish. This, however, shall be strongly inculcated."

(Sparks's Washington, vol. iii, p. 245.)

Very soon after this letter was written, Louis with his comrades arrived in the American camp, to tender their allegiance to the cause of Liberty, and testify their respect to the character of the commander-in-chief.

In a letter to the president of congress, dated Cambridge, January 24, 1776, General Washington says:

" On Sunday evening, thirteen of the Caughnawaga Indians arrived here on a visit. I shall take care that they be so entertained during their stay, that they may return impressed with sentiments of friendship for us, and also of our great strength. One of them is Colonel Louis, who honored me with a visit once before."

(Sparks's Washington, vol. iii, p. 260.)

Louis had an ambition for military distinction, and it appears from what follows, that there was a hesitancy on the part of the American generals in granting this.

To entrust responsible posts in the hands of Indians, of whose character or history they knew little, would be unwise. To send them off without notice, would tend to make them dissatisfied, and for aught that could be known, might serve to render them disgusted with the cause.

The perplexity which the commander-in-chief experienced from this cause, is expressed in the following extract from his letter to General Schuyler, dated Cambridge, January 27, 1776:

" I am a little embarrassed to know in what manner to conduct myself with respect to the Caughnawaga Indians now here. They have, notwithstanding the treaty of neutrality which I find they entered into with you the other day, agreeably to what appears to be the sense of congress, signified to me a desire of taking up arms in behalf of the united colonies. The chief of them who, I understand, is now the first man of the nation, intends, as it is intimated, to apply to me for a commission, with the assurance of raising four or five hundred men, when he returns.

My embarrassment does not proceed so much from the impropriety of encouraging these people to depart from their neutrality, or rather accepting their own voluntary offer, as from the expense which probably may follow.

I am sensible that if they do not desire to be idle, they will be for or against us. I am sensible also, that no artifices will be left uneassayed to engage them against us. Their proffered services, therefore, ought not to be rejected; but how far, with the little knowledge I have of their real intentions, and your want of their aid, I ought to go, is the question that puzzles me. I will endeavor, however, to please them, by yielding, in appearance, to their demands; reserving, at the same time, the power to you to regulate the number and movements, of which you shall be more fully informed, when any thing is fixed."

In answer to this, General Schuyler wrote:

" It is extremely difficult to determine what should be done, in what you mention, respecting the offer made by the Caughnawaga Indians; but if we can get decently rid of their offer, I would prefer it to employing them. The expense we are at in the Indian department, is amazing: it will be more so, when they consider themselves in our service; nor would their intervention be of much consequence, unless we could procure that of the other nations. The hauteur of the Indians is much diminished since the taking of Montreal: they evidently see that they can not get any supplies, but through us."

(Sparks's Washington, vol. iii, p. 262.)

There is preserved a traditionary account of the interview between the Indian delegates, and the American general, at the audience or council which he gave them on this occasion. It was related by the Rev. Samuel Kirkland, the missionary of the Oneidas, who is said to have acted as interpreter to the one from whom we receive it.

One of the Caughnawaga chiefs arose and said:

" He perceived there was a war cloud rising in the east, which may make great trouble, and bring much distress upon the American people on account of which his very soul troubled him. War was a great evil to any nation or people. He knew this by sad experience, in the war between the English and the French, by which the latter were brought to ruin.

He rejoiced to see the Americans had such independent spirits, as to take up arms and defend their rights and liberties, and that they would succeed because he believed that God was on their side, but that this must be gained at the expense of much blood, and great distress, upon the people. That the king of England was a powerful king, or he could not have conquered the French in Canada, but the king of Heaven is stronger than any earthly king and will defend the oppressed; and with a strong voice he added, "brother Bostonians, be strong and courageous; your cause is good, you will assuredly be supported by the Great Spirit above, whose omnipotent arm will defend you, and in the end will give you a victory; a victory that will resound through all the earth, and this shall be a Sabbath day with you, and your children, and it shall be celebrated with joyful hearts, as long as the true American Spirit shall beat in their breasts. Your true Indian friends in the north, will do what they can in your favor. Indians are born free people; they love liberty, yes, they would wish to live as free as the deer in the forest, and the fowls in the air. Brother Bostonians, you are a great people, and able to meet the king of England, in the battle field. We are feeble compared to what we were once.

You will, I hope, always remember the feeble people who were once the lords of the soil, but who are now much reduced both in members and strength. But the war spirit is still in us, and we will do what we can to aid you, when the opportunity shall offer, even should it result in the destruction of our village by the British your enemies. Remember brother Bostonians, the words of your brothers of Caughnawaga.

Never forget that a portion of them are your friends at heart, and pray to the Great Spirit, that you become a free people, as the Indians your brothers."

Having been civilly treated at the camp the Indians returned to Albany, where they had an interview with General Schuyler, John Bleecker acting as interpreter; and here they again tendered their services to join the American cause.

After a considerable hesitation from the causes above indicated, it was resolved to grant the request, and Louis Cook, received a commission in the American army. From this time his residence at Caughnawaga became unsafe, and he returned thither no more during the war, unless stealthily.

A portion of the party remained with him, and others returned to Caughnawaga, warm in their friendship to the cause, and intending secretly to promote it as they might find themselves able.

These movements attracted the notice of Governor Carlton, of Canada, who endeavored to secure their adherence to the royal cause, but without effect.

In the winter of 1777-8, Colonel Louis repaired to Oneida, to raise a company of warriors among that tribe, and in this he succeeded. This is confirmed by a statement made in a petition of one Edward Johnson, to the legislature, for a grant of land for services rendered, in which he says:

" That winter I got acquainted with Louis Cook, a French Mohawk, who came to Oneida to get as many men to join him as he could in the American cause against Great Britain, for which he received a Lieutenant Colonel's commission from the first Congress, and said Louis asked me if I was willing to serve the country with him."

We also find a memorandum that the Oneidas entered Schenectady in July, 1780, under Col. Louis.

This tribe as is well known, was the only one that rendered efficient service to the American cause during the revolutionary war. The Mohawks were influenced by the Johnson families to take up the hatchet against the colonies, and it is well known that the western Indians of New York deserved the chastisement they received at the hands of General Sullivan.

In the summer of 1780, Count de Rochambeau, with a French fleet and army, arrived in the United States, as their allies, in their struggle for liberty.

"It was deemed advisable by General Schuyler, and others, that a deputation of friendly Indians should be encouarged to visit the French army and fleet at Newport. Many of the Iroquois had been strongly attached to the French in early times, particularly during the last war, and they still retained a lively remembrance the amicable intercourse that had then existed. When M. de Vaudreuil surrendered Canada to the British, he gave to the Indians as tokens of recognizance, a golden crucifix and a watch; and it was supposed that a renewal of the impressions which had in some degree been preserved among the tribes by these emblems of friendship, would have the effect to detach them from the British, and strengthen their union with the Americans and French. For this end their journey to Newport was planned.

General Schuyler who was at Albany, selected eighteen Indians for this deputation. Thirteen of these were Oneidas and Tuscaroras, and the other five Caghnawagas, from the Saut of St. Louis, near Montreal. They were accompanied by Mr. Deane, who was thoroughly acquainted with their language. They arrived at Newport on the 29th of August, 1780, and were received with a great deal of ceremony and attention by the French commanders. Entertainments and military shows were prepared for them, and they expressed much satisfaction at what they saw and heard. Suitable presents were distributed among them; and to the chiefs were given medals, representing the coronation of the French king. When they went away a written address was delivered to them, or rather a kind of proclamation, signed by Count de Rochambeau, copies of which were distributed among the friendly Indians. It was in the following words:

"The king of France, your father, has not forgotten his children. As a token of remembrance, I have presented gifts to your deputies in his name. He learned with concern that many nations deceived by the English who are his enemies, had attacked and lifted up the hatchet against his good and faithful allies, the United States. He has desired me to tell you, that he is a firm and faithful friend to all the friends of America, and a decided enemy to all its foes. He hopes that his children whom he loves sincerely, will take part with their father in this war against the English."

This paper was written both in the French and English languages, and sealed and signed in due form."

(Sparks's Washington, vol. vii, p. 183.)

General Washington in a letter to the Count de Rochambeau, of Sept. 3, 1780, says:

"The visit you have had from the Indians, gives me great pleasure. I felicitate you on that which you must have had in the company of such agreeable and respectable guests. I dare say the reception they met with, will have a good effect. It has been the policy of the English in regard to them, to discredit the accounts of an alliance between France and America; a conviction of which on the substantial evidence of your army and fleet, and not less of your presents and good cheer, will not fail to have a happy influence.". *(Ib., p. 183.)*

These Indians were principally useful as scouts, to carry intelligence and get information—a kind of service for which they are peculiarly adapted by nature, from the knowledge which they have of the forests, and the wary look-out they maintain against surprise or detection by their enemy.

On several of these occasions, Col. Louis was employed successfully. Once he was engaged to convey information to Canada, in connection with the expedition that was sent thither under General Montgomery, and at another time was sent to meet a messenger from Canada, at a designated place, near Lake Champlain. This duty he performed successfully, but when he reached the camp of the Americans, he was almost starved, having lost his provision bag, in crossing a river. He could not hunt on the way, as the British had Indian scouts in the woods.

On several of his expeditions as a bearer of despatches, he crossed Lake Champlain and the Green Mountains, to the upper settlements on the Connecticut.

In whatever enterprise he undertook, he uniformly acquitted himself with credit, and in every act of his life he confirmed the esteem which he had acquired among the officers of the army, who not only learned to trust his fidelity, but ask his opinion on subjects connected with Indian warfare, and varied affairs connected with the Indian tribes.

He continued in active service till the peace, and then not daring to return to his former associates at Caughnawaga, from the active partizan course which he had pursued, he repaired to Oneida, where he continued to reside until about the year 1789.

Many of the Caughnawagas had like him, lost their residence and their homes, by joining the Americans, and from some neglect no provision had been made for them, as for the Canada and Novia Scotia refugees, who for a like reason had become exiles; these patriotic Indians wandered here and there homeless, and a part of them finally settled at St. Regis to which as Caughnawagas they had a claim.

There can be little doubt that the claims of these Indians have been overlooked, as one may search in vain the public records for evidences that they have ever been remunerated by grants of land or otherwise, for their services, with the exception of Colonel Louis.

Some time after the revolution he visited Montreal, Caughnawaga, and St. François, and from his known influence with the Indian tribes, he was treated with respect by the agents of that government, who it is said, tendered him strong inducements to engage his friendship, but he rejected them all, that he might be free from this species of obligation, His wife, however, who accompanied him, accepted a gift of twenty dollars, with which she purchased a store that is said to be still owned by her descendents at St. Regis.

The western Indians towards the close of the last century, began to show symptoms of hostility to the United States, and endeavored to excite the same feeling among all the Indians in the country, to whom they sent messages, inviting them to meet in general council, to concert measures for promoting their measures, and of urging certain claims against the general government. The Canada Indians were also invited, and attended. The course which they pursued will be inferred from the following extracts.

"Colonel Louis of the Cougnawagas also came here to inform the government, that the Seven Castles, so called, in Canada, had been invited to the council, to be held at the Miami River, of Lake Erie. He also being convinced of the justice of the United States, promised to me his influence towards a peace. (*Letter of Gen. Knox, Feb.* 10, 1792. *American State Papers, Indian affairs. vol. i,* 12, 35.)

The deputies of these tribes accordingly attended the Indian council at the rapids of the Miami, on the 13th of August, 1793, and in the reports of the commissioners appointed on the part of the government, it is recorded, that they used their influence in settling the troubles then existing between the western tribes and the United States, which subsequently ripened into open hostilities.

They however with the others insisted that the Ohio river should be the boundary between the whites and the Indians.

His residence on the frontier of St. Regis was at first quite unpleasant as well as unsafe, from the hostility which his former course had created among the zealous loyalists who settled on the St. Lawrence, after the war.

During a portion of his life, before the war, he had resided at St. Regis, and occupied a tract of land afterwards known as the Mile Square, near the present village of Massena. This he endeavored to have secured to him by letters patent. The following is the petition in which he solicited this favor.

To the Honorable the Senate and Assembly of the State of New York, in Legislature convened;

"The petition of the subscriber respectfully showeth: That at the commencement of the late war, he resided near the village of St. Regis, within this state, and adjoining the north bounds thereof. That he occupied there a certain tract of land, lying on the Niconsiaga River, beginning on the first falls on the said river, and extending up the same on both sides thereof, about one mile, which land had descended to him by inheritance, and is his own distinct property.

That at the commencement of the late war, he left his said habitation, and joined the American army, and continued to serve his country in a military capacity, throughout the war, and that from the part he had taken in the American cause, he finds it inexpedient to return to his former residence, although the land so owned by him is still held and rented out by him. That your petitioner is desirous to have the said lands secured to him and his posterity, by a title to the same, under the authority of the state.

Your petitioner therefore most humbly prays, that the legislature will be pleased, in consideration of the premises, to direct letters patent to be issued to him, for the said tract of land.

And your petitioner will as in duty bound ever pray, &c.

Louis Cook.

Albany, 8th January, 1789.

The Journal of the senate of the state of New York for 1789, contains the following.

January 10, 1789.

"The petition of Louis Cook, alias Hadaguetogbrongwen, praying that his title to a certain piece of land, may be confirmed to him under the authority of the state, was read and committed to Mr. Clinton, Mr. Hawthorn, and Mr. Tredwell." (p. 30.)

February 19, 1789.

Mr. Clinton from the committee to whom was referred the petition of Louis Cook, alias Hadaguetoghrongwen, relative to his claim to a tract of land lying on the Niconsiaga River, near the village of St. Regis, within this state, reported that it was the opinion of the committee, that the prayer of the petitioner ought to be granted, and that a provision be made to direct the commissioners of the land office, to grant letters patent to the said Louis Cook, for such tract of land lying on the Niconsiaga river, beginning on the first falls on the said river, and extending up the same on both sides thereof as they shall find to be his distinct property; provided the same has not been otherwise appropriated; which report he read in his place, and delivered the same at the table where it was again read, and agreed to by the senate." (p. 68.)

This petition produced the passage of an act in his relief.

The 16th section of an act passed February 28, 1789, directed: "That it shall and may be lawful for the commissioners of the land office, to grant letters patent, to Louis Cook, alias Hadaquetoghrongwen, for such tract of land lying on the Niconsiaga River, beginning on the first falls on said river, and extending up the same on both sides thereof, as they shall find to be his distinct property; provided the same has not been otherwise appropriated."

It is not known to the author whether this tract was ever confirmed to him as his individual property, or what was the result of the action directed in the act for his relief.

It is probable, that Colonel Louis was induced to return to St. Regis, by those people, who were solicitous of securing his influence in settling the claim which they had against the state of New York, for lands, and in seeing that justice was done them in the matter of running the boundary between the two governments, which passed through their village.

He was not at first safe in his residence at St. Regis, being on several occasions in danger of his life, from the violence of the Mohawks. His friends, however, promptly informed him of the plots laid against him, in time for him to avoid them.

There is said to have been an especial feeling of ill will between Brant and Louis, arising from the active partizan course which they had pursued on opposite sides in the previous contest.

Colonel Louis took a leading part in the negotiations which finally resulted in the treaty of May 31, 1796, at the city of New York, by which the claims of the St. Regis Indians to the lands in the northern part of the state were extinguished, with the exception of the reservations then made. A history of the negotiations which preceded and attended this treaty, we have given in the foregoing pages. It will be seen that the terms offered by the agents of the state, bore no comparison with the demands of the deputies of the Indians, but here, as elsewhere, and ever, the latter found themselves at the mercy of those whose will was law, and were constrained to accept the terms offered, or none at all, having no tribunal of arbitration or appeal, by which to sustain their claims.

In sustaining his claims, Colonel Louis was seconded by Captain Thomas Williams, a chief of the tribe, and a descendant of the Rev. John Williams, of Deerfield, and by William Gray, a chief and interpreter, who, although a white by birth, had in every respect become an Indian in tastes and habits.

After the conclusion of the treaty, Colonel Louis had an opportunity of attending to his own private affairs, and he continued to be occupied with these, and with business connected with the internal management of matters connected with the tribes with whom the St. Regis people were associated, until the breaking out of the war in 1812.

By an act of the legislature, passed in 1802, he was, with Loren Tarbell and William Gray, made the trustee of his tribe, for the purpose of leasing a ferry, and a tract of land, and of establishing a school among the Indians.

Although without education himself, yet he was, for this reason, the more desirous that his people should acquire it; but the prejudices of the tribe were against it, and so far as we can learn, there was none established until a very recent period.

Louis was ever opposed to the leases and sales, by which the Indians, from time to time, alienated their lands in the vicinity of Salmon river, insisting most strenuously, that they belonged not to *them*, but to their *children*.

It is not our purpose to investigate the motives which were brought to operate in producing a contrary course, or the propriety of it.

On the declaration of war, Colonel Louis, although borne down by the weight of more than seventy years, and passed that time of life, when one would scarcely be expected to encounter the rugged toils of war; yet he felt rising within him the ancient martial spirit which had inspired him in former times, and he felt his age renewed, when he thought on the perils and the victories in which he had participated, and longed again to serve that cause which, in the prime of life, and vigor of youth, he had made his own.

The British early endeavored to secure the St. Regis people in their interests, and their agent, who had come up from Montreal, with the customary presents, which that government annually distributed in the payment of their annuities, returned without making the distribution, because they would not agree to take up arms for them.

The residence of Colonel Louis, in consequence of his engaging in the American cause, having become unpleasant, if not unsafe, at St. Regis, he repaired to Plattsburgh, where he spent a considerable portion of the summer. We notice the following in Niles's Weekly Register, of that period:

Oct. 17, 1812. "Gen. Louis, of the St. Regis Indians, a firm and undeviating friend of the United States, and his son, have been in this village (Plattsburgh), for several weeks. The St. Regis Indians are disposed to remain neutral, in the present contest; but what effect the British influence and British success may have upon them, we know not," &c.

We have noticed, in the foregoing pages, the miserable condition to which the St. Regis people were reduced by the war; as they could scarcely go out of sight of their village, without exciting alarm among the whites, and they had nothing to subsist upon at home.

Colonel Louis represented this condition of things to the governor, who directed, in consequence, that five hundred rations should be delivered daily to them, and they were thus enabled to avoid giving alarm to their white brethren.

During the summer of 1812, he visited General Brown, at Ogdensburgh, where he was received with attention: a new commission was presented him, and through the liberality of Mr. David Parisl, of that place, he was furnished with a new and elegant military dress and equipage, corresponding with the rank which his commissions conferred. On his return to his family, his appearance was so changed, that they did not

13

know him, and his children fled from the proffered caresses of their
father, as if he had been the spirit of evil.

His age and infirmities prevented him from active duty, but his *influence* with the Indian tribes, gave him an importance in the army, which
was of signal service to the American cause.

On the arrival of General Wilkinson, at French Mills, he joined that
army, and accompanied General Brown from thence to Sacketts Harbor,
in February, 1814.

In June following, he repaired to Buffalo, with his sons, and several
St. Regis warriors, and was present and actively engaged in the several
engagements that took place on the Niagara frontier.

In August, 1813, an affair had taken place near Fort George, in which
several Caughnawagas and British were taken prisoners; and colonel
Louis was induced, from motives of humanity, to undertake a mission
to Niagara for their release.

To excite a prejudice against him, some of his enemies wrote to an
officer in the American army, that he was on a visit to their camp, on a
secret mission, which reaching its destination before his arrival, led to
his arrest, and he was held a prisoner eight days, when some officers
from Plattsburgh arriving, he was recognized, and set at liberty. A further investigation was desired, and instituted, and he appeared before
the commission, and answered, with great modesty, the several questions
that were put to him, by the young officers: but the impertinence
of some of them aroused his spirit, and he replied : " You see
that I am old, and worn out, and you are young, and know little
of the service. You seem to doubt what I have been, and what I
am now. It is right that you should watch the interests of your
country in time of war. My history you can have." He then gave them
the names of several prominent officers of the northern frontier, as refer-
ences, and with a heavy hand, laid a large black pocket book upon the
table, and bid them examine its contents. It contained his commissions
as lieutenant colonel; general Washington's recommendatory letters, and
those of generals Schuyler, Gates, Knox, Mooers, and governor Tompkins, and a parchment certificate of membership, in a military masonic
lodge of the revolution.

These abundantly satisfied them, but he further insisted, that they
should write to Plattsburgh, which they did, more to gratify him, than
to satisfy themselves. The result was, of course, his complete exonera-
tion from any motives but those entirely consistent with honor and principle.

But time was having its work upon the frame of this worthy Indian
chief, and an injury which he sustained, by a fall from this horse, at the

head of a party of Tuscaroras, in one of the skirmishes of the campaign, was found to have seriously affected him, and he desired to be carried to the Indian settlements, to yield his last advice, and give up his parting breath among the people whose interests he had so long and so faithfully served.

Colonel Biddle, of the 11th regiment, the son of his former old friend, in Coos county, often sent to enquire after his welfare. Louis at length sent for the colonel, who hastened to his wigwam, and found him in a dying condition, but able to speak. He spoke at some length, on the interest he ever felt for the American cause, and the gratification he experienced in being able to die near their camp. He bid him remember him to his family at St. Regis, to colonel Williams, of that place, and to his friends, whom he named, at Plattsburgh.

To his son, he gave his two commissions which he had cherished as a treasure, and bid him carry them to his family at St. Regis, but this worthless fellow on returning pawned them at an inn for grog!

Colonel Louis died in October 1814, and was buried near Buffalo. His death was announced by the discharge of cannon, as was due to his rank in the army.

He was twice married, the first time at Caughnawaga, and the second at Onondaga, where he is said to have lived a short time after the revolution.

He had three sons, of whom one died at Caughnawaga, one at St. Regis, in 1832, and the third near Brasher Falls in 1833, while on a hunting excursion.

He had several daughters, one or two of whom still reside at St. Regis.

Colonel Louis was tall and athletic, broad shouldered and strongly built, with a very dark complexion, and somewhat curly hair, which in old age became gray.

He was very reserved in his speech, and by most people would be called taciturn. He seldom spoke without having something to say, and what he said, was received with deference, for it always had a meaning, and in all his deportment he strongly evinced possession of prudence, discretion and sense, and when once enlisted in any pursuit, he followed it with a constantcy and perseverance seldom equalled in the Indian character. He was prompt and generally correct in arriving at conclusions, and his judgment was relied upon, and his opinions sought by the officers of the army, with whom he was associated, with much confidence, and he possessed in a high degree the control of the affairs of his tribe, by whom he was beloved, respected, and obeyed.

He was illiterate, but spoke several languages with freedom. His portrait was taken while at Albany, but we have been unable to ascertian whether it be still reserved.

WILLIAM GRAY.—Probably no white person has had more influence with the Indian tribe of St. Regis, in their negociations than *William Gray*, and his name is constantly found as interpreter, or agent on the old treaties and other papers which were executed by these people. He was born at Cambridge, N. Y., joined the revolutionary army, at the age of seventeen. With a few others he was taken by surprise near White Hall, and carried to Quebec, where he remained till the peace. He then repaired to Caughnawaga, and resided for some time, from whence he removed to St. Regis, and married an Indian woman, and raised a family. He adopted the language, and customs of the tribe, and become their chief interpreter. While there, returned to Cambridge, and induced a large number of his father's family to remove to St. Regis, where they remained some time, but never inter married with the natives. His parents died on the Indian reservation.

He had acquired the rudiments of an education, which was subsequently of much advantage to him in his capacity of interpreter and chief.

Possessing considerable native enterprise, he acquired an ascendency with the Indians, and his advice was received with attention. At a very early period he erected a saw mill at what is now the village of Hogansburgh, and engaged in mercantile business at the Indian village.

He acted as interpreter at most of the treaties held previous to his death; and his conduct at that which occurred at New York in 1796, was such as secured him the following recommendation from the governor to the legislature.

Gentlemen :

"The agents who on the part of this state, concluded the agreement which has been laid before you, with the Indians called the Seven Nations of Canada, at the treaty held at New York in May last, have represented to me, that William Gray, one of the deputies from these Indians at that treaty, was during the late war captivated in this state by the Indians of St. Regis, that they adopted him into that tribe, and on the 21st of March, 1781, gave him the tract of land specified in the copy of the deed from them to him; with which a copy of the proceedings of that treaty, accompanies this message, and which he left with the said agents for your information.

That they have no reason to suppose otherwise, than that the said transaction was at the time intended, did take place between him, and the said Indians in good faith; that during the negotiations at the treaty, his conduct was fair and proper, and rather than that the treaty should be in the least impeded by his claims, he readily consented to waive the making of any stipulations in his favor, and to rely entirely on the state for such compensation or gratuity as the legislature should think reasonable."

JOHN JAY.

ALBANY, 28th February, 1797.

This however, failed to secure him the justice which he claimed, and he accordingly presented at a subsequent session, the following memorial, in which his claims are set forth.

" *To the Honorable, the Legislature of the State of New York.*

The petition of William Gray, respectfully sheweth:

That your petitioner was born in the county of Washington, in this state; that when a boy he was taken prisoner in the year eighty, in the late war, by the Indians of the Seven Nations of Canada, among whom he has ever since continued to reside; that by adoption and marriage, he has become entitled to all the rights and privileges of one of that people, and consequently is with them a proprietor of the lands secured to them by treaty with the state; that he now has a family of children whom he wishes to educate in the manner of their civilized ancestors, and leave some property to make them respectable and useful in society; that according to the customs of the tribe at St. Regis, the place where he resides, individuals have lands assigned to them for cultivation in severalty, yet the laws of the state can not take cognizance of it; that the nation of which he is a member, have set apart to him and wish to have confirmed to him a tract, as his exclusive proportion of the lands 257 acres, bounded on the north by the Salmon river mill tract, on the east by the east boundaries of the large reservation, on the west by a line parallel thereto, and on the south by the south bounds of said reservation, now held in common in their reservation, near the village of St. Regis. Your petitioner therefore, in consideration of all these circumstances, prays that it may be lawful for him to receive such a grant from the nation, and that it may receive the sanction of government, and your petitioner as in duty bound, shall ever pray."

WILLIAM GRAY.

ALBANY, the 19th February, 1800.

This petition secured him the advantages which he sought, in the passage of the following act, April 4, 1801, during the session next following:

" And whereas, William Gray of the village of St. Regis, having been early in life taken prisoner by the Indians calling themselves the Seven Nations of Canada, and since continued to reside among them, and being in consequence of adoption and marriage, considered as entitled to all rights and privileges as one of their nation, whereby he is equally and with others of them interested in the lands secured by the people of this state to the Indians residing at the village of St. Regis;

And whereas, it appears that the said Indians are disposed to give to the said William Gray, his proportion of their common property to be held in severalty by him and his heirs: therefore,

Be it further enacted, That it shall and may be lawful for the governor to direct the said agent to obtain from the said Indians, their grant to the people of this state, and to issue letters patent under the great seal of this state, to the said William Gray, his heirs and assigns, forever, for two hundred and fifty-seven acres, bounded on the north by the tract reserved and surveyed for the said Indians, and which includes the mill on Salmon river, on the south by the south bounds of the tract equal to six miles square, reserved to the said Indians, on the east by the east bounds of the said reservation, and on the west by a line parellal thereto, run from the eleventh mile mark, made by the surveyor general, in the south bounds of the said reservation, being in length north and south, one hundred and sixty-four chains and seventy links, and in width east and west, fifteen chains and sixty links."

A further history of the tract thus conveyed, will be given in our account of Fort Covington.

His residence during a few years previous to the war, was in what is now the village of Hogansburgh, west of the river; and this place at that period bore the name of Gray's Mills.

In the war of 1812, he took part with the Americans, and was employed by Colonel Young to conduct the party through the woods from French Mills, which surprised and captured a company of British at St. Regis, in the fall of 1812. Being considered a dangerous partizan, he was surprised and taken by a party of the enemy, on the east side of the St. Regis river, near the village, in December, 1813, and taken to Quebec, where he was confined in prison, and where he died in April or May following.

In his death the tribe lost a true friend and faithful servant. His descendants still reside at St. Regis.

TE-HO-RA-GWA-NE-GEN, alias *Thomas Williams*, whose name we have so often had occasion to mention in connection with the St. Regis tribe, was born about 1758 or 1759, at Caughnawaga, and was the third in descent from the Rev. John Williams of Deerfield. A daughter of this person by the name of Eunice, who was taken prisoner with him in 1704, became assimilated with the Indians, and afterwards married a young chief by the name of *De Roguers*, to whom she bore three children, viz: Catharine, Mary, and John. Mary was the mother of Thomas Williams, the subject of this notice. She died when her son was an infant, and he was reared by his aunt Catharine, whom he ever regarded as his mother. Having no cousin, he was the sole object of affection by his kind protector, and grew up an active and sprightly lad, in every respect of language and habits an Indian.

In 1772, the Rev. Levi Frisbee, was sent into Canada by the Rev. Dr. Wheelock, of Dartmouth College, who visited Caughnawaga, and took especial notice of Thomas, whose New England parentage was known to him and he obtained with some difficulty, the consent of his adopted parents to take him to Hanover, and place him in the Moore Charity School at that place, but sickness prevented him from attending. His adopted father often took him into the forest with him, on hunting excursions, and he became attached to his kind of life, often visiting in his rambles, Crown Point, Lake George, and vicinity of Fort Edward.

On the outbreak of the revolution, he is said to have participated in several of the expeditions against the colonies, but the lessons he had received from his grandmother Eunice, led him to exert his influence in favor of protecting defenceless women and children.

In 1777, he became a chief, and gradually acquired the esteem of the British officers. In the same year he was called upon with others of his tribe, to join General Burgoyne, but his feelings had begun to be enlisted in favor of the Americans, and he accompanied rather with the hope of being able to spare the effusion of blood, than of promoting the cause of his army, which he joined at Cumberland Head. On the retreat of the provincials from Ticonderoga, he was directed to pursue them, but under the pretense of falling upon their flanks, he is said to have purposely led his party by a too circuitous route to effect their object.

He was also sent with the detachment of the enemy against Bennington, but did little for the service in which he was engaged, and in the event almost came in collision with some of the British officers engaged on that expedition.

It is said that on the occasion of the death of Miss Jane McCrea, which formed so striking a tragedy in that campaign, that Thomas was solicited to undertake to bring her to the camp, but that he refused.

This service was according to the Rev. E. Williams, our informant afterwards accepted by some of the Indians of the Western tribes, who in two parties, each ignorant of the designs of the other, started on the expedition.

One of them had persuaded the girl to attend them to the British camp, and they were on their way thither, when they were met by the other; an altercation arose between them, and in the strife that ensued the girl was brutally tomahawked by one party, that the other might not be able draw the reward which had been offered by the young lady's lover, for bringing her in.

Our informant received this from a Winnebago chief, at Green Bay, who acknowledged having a hand in the murder, which some have attributed to St. Regis Indians.

This shocking barbarity, so abhorrent to human nature, led to a rebuke from Burgoyne, which is said to have weakened the attachment of the Indians for his course, and they afterwards left him.

Williams, among the rest of the Indians, abandoned the camp and returned home. In 1778, he joined an expedition to Oswego, with the view of invading some of the frontier settlements, but returned, and in the following year was one of the party who ravaged Royalton in Vermont, and afterwards participated in expeditions to Penobscot, Schoharie, &c.

In 1783 he visited for the first time his relatives in New England, and at Stockbridge met with the Rev. Samuel Kirkland, the Indian missionary, who served him as an interpreter. Among those whom he wished to visit, was the Rev. Dr. Stephen Williams, the brother of his grandmother Eunice, but he found him dead.

He subsequently visited repeatedly the friends of his grandmother, both in Massachusetts and Vermont, and always evinced a commendable regard for their welfare.

After the war, he resumed his hunting, and often visited Albany, and had a friendly intercourse with General Schuyler.

When the question of settlement of claims against the state came to be discussed, Thomas Williams was entrusted, in company with Gray and Cook, with the negotiation, the history of which we have given. In January, 1800, he visited his relatives in New England, and took with him his two boys, whom he left to be educated at Long Meadow, Mass. The names of these lads were John and Eleazer.

In 1801, with a party of Caughnawagas, in the service of the Northwest Company, he made a journey to the remote western prairies, and nearly to the Rocky mountains. In 1805, with his wife, he visited his sons, and the mother insisted on having John return, which he did, much to the regret of the benevolent gentlemen, who on account of their ancestry, felt a peculiar interest in the welfare of the youths.

The other remained some time longer at the school, and acquired a good English education, and subsequently became an episcopal clergyman, and was employed as a missionary for many years among the Oneidas and Onondagas, and also with the St. Regis Indians. For several years he was engaged in the settlements of the Green Bay emigrants, from the New York tribes, and is at present living near St. Regis, engaged in endeavoring to establish a school among the natives.

During the war of 1812, he is said to have held a colonel's commission, and to have been repeatedly engaged on responsible services for the Americans.

On the declaration of war, Williams resolved to take no part with the British, which led him to be reported with Colonel Louis, as refractory.

In August 1812, an agreement was entered into between Gen. Dearborn and Col. Baynes, that neither party should act offensively before the decision of certain measures then pending should be known.

A conference was subsequently held between agents of the two governments, at which it was agreed that the St. Regis tribe should remain neutral, but as afterwards appeared this was subsequently but little re-

ed. During the war Thomas Williams continued to exert an influ-
favorable to the Americans, and his two sons took active but oppo-
sides in the contest. In 1815 he visited Albany, and Washington, to
certain claims against government, but not being furnished with
necessary papers, he failed in his purpose.

consideration of the active part which he took in the treaty of 1796,
or several years after the war, till 1833, received $50 annually of the
nity which was paid by virtue of that treaty.

e died at his native village, August 16, 1849. In person he was
re the common size, with an intelligent countenance, and with that
is manner and deportment, which bespoke a superiority above his
ple in general.

he author is indebted to the Rev. Eleazer Williams, of St. Regis, for
t of the data from which the above account is written. Our space
not allowed the full use of the voluminous materials furnished.

CHAPTER III.

ORGANIZATION OF THE COUNTIES, PUBLIC BUILDINGS, &c.

HE causes which led to the organization of St. Lawrence county are set forth in the following interesting document, which is the original petition for its erection, and is preserved among the archives of the state, and possesses much value, from its being said to contain the signatures of nearly all the citizens then living in the county. The original is written in a remarkably neat and elegant hand, and the signatures are in every instance in the autograph of the signers.

" To the Honorable the Senate and Assembly of the State of New York.

The petition of the inhabitants, residing within the ten townships, upon the river St. Lawrence, beg leave humbly to represent the great inconvenience and hardships they labor under, by the ten townships being formed into one town, and annexing the same to the county of Clinton.* The principal inconvenience your petitioners labor under is the very remote distance they are placed from Plattsburgh, which is the county town of the county of Clinton. Not any of your petitioners are less than one hundred and twenty miles from Plattsburgh, and a great majority of them are from one hundred and thirty to forty miles.

Between the ten townships and Plattsburgh, much of the way there is no road, and the remainder of the way is a very bad one; this, together with the great inconvenience and expense which necessarily must arise to those whose private business, (as plaintiffs and defendants,) lead them into the county courts, is such, as to almost place your petitioners without the reach of that justice, which the laws of our country so happily provide for. This is a melancholy fact, which several of your petitioners have already experienced, and to which all are equally opposed, and when we add to this, the extreme difficulty, troubles, and expenses jurors and witnesses must be subjected to, in attending at such a distance, together with the attendance at Plattsburgh, for arranging and returning the town business, increases the burthen and expense beyond the ability of your petitioners to bear. Your petitioners forbear to mention many other inconveniences, tho' sensibly felt, your petitioners

---

* In the previous year, the town of Lisbon was erected, and attached to Clinton Co. See the original petition, &c., in our account of that town.

presume they will naturally occur to the minds of every individual member of your honorable body. Some of your petitioners, presented a petition to your honorable body, at their last session, praying for the formation of the town, and annexing it as it now is, but they did not then (neither could they,) anticipate the inconvenience and expense they find upon experiment attaches to their being so connected.

Your petitioners therefore beg leave humbly to state, that much less hardship and expense would arise to them. by having a county set off, upon the river St. Lawrence, and your petitioners humbly pray, that a county may be set off upon the aforesaid river, in such manner as your honorable body shall deem most proper; and your petitioners would beg leave further to shew, that one of the old stone buildings at the *Old Oswegatchie Fort*, (which the proprietors are willing to appropriate until the county is able to build a court house,) may at a small expense be repaired, and which when so repaired will make good accommodations, not only for the purpose of holding courts, but also for a gaol, and your petitioners pray, that place may be assigned for the above purpose.

Your petitioners would beg leave further to state, that Plattsburgh is totally out of their route to the city of Albany, which is the place to which they must resort, for their commercial business—Plattsburgh being as far distant from Albany, as the ten towns, consequently your petitioners are turned out of their way the whole distance, between the ten towns and Plattsburgh, which is not less than one hundred and thirty miles from the centre of the townships.

The peculiar inconvenience and hardships your petitioners labor under, is such, that your petitioners doubt not that relief will be cheerfully granted by your honorable body, and your petitioners as in duty bound will ever pray."

Nathan Ford,
John Tibbets,
Elisha Tibbetts,
Joseph Edsall,
Alex'r J. Turner,
John Tibbits, Jr.,
Alex'r Bough,
Jacob Redington,
Benjamin Stewart,
Joel Burns,
James G. Stewart,
Ashael Kent,*
Challis Fay,
Joseph Gilderslieve,
Elias Demmick,
Ephraim Smith Raymond,
Moses Patterson,
Henry Allen,
Edward Lawrence,
Jonathan Allen,*
James Pennock,
Asa Freeman,
Truman Wheeler,

Jacob Flemmen,
John Lyon,
Daniel Barker, Jun.
Jacob Morris,
Samuel Fairchild,
Alexander Leyers,
Daniel Sharp,*
Festus Tracy,
Septy Tracy,
John Armstrong,
Martin Easterly,
Alexander Brush,
James Harrison,
Stillman Foot,
Alex' Armstrong,
Jacob Cerner, Jun.,*
Christian Cerner,*
Jonathan Tuttle,
Benj'n Bacon, Sen.,
Benj'n Bacon, Jun.
Oliver Linsley,
Henry Erwin,
Nathan Shaw,
Caleb Pumroy,

James Sweeny,
George Foot,
Ashbel, Sikes,
John Farwell, Jr.
Joseph Erwin,
Moses McConnel,
Benjamin Campbell,
Godfrey Myers,
Seth Gates,
James Kilborn,
James Ferguson,
Solomon Linsley, Sen.
Isaac Bartholomew,
Solomon Linsley, Jun.,
Nathan Smith,
Jacob Cerner, Sen.,*
William Sweet,
William Morrison,
Dan'l Barker,
Sam'l Avens,
Elisha Johnes,
John Smith,
Benjamin Walker,
David Layton,

*Uncertain.

Coney Rice,
Andrew Rutherford,
Walter Rutherford,
Richard Rutherford,
Thomas Rutherford,
Isaac Parll,*
Jonathan Ingraham,
Joseph Thurber,
John Thurber,
Thomas J. Davies,
Reuben Hurd,
Aaron Welton,
George Davies,
Rial Dickonson,*
Major Watson,
Thomas Le Gard,*
Benj. Mellis, *
Elijah Carley,
Adam Williams,
David Carter,
William Sharp,
John King,
Thomas Kingsbury,
Peter Sharp,
James Salisbury,
Zina B. Hawley,*
John Lyttle,
Ezekiel Palmer,

Capt. Eben Arthur,
William Scott,
Jacob Pohlman,
David Rose,
John Stewert,
Samuel Thacher,
John Sharp,
John Armstrong,
David Linsley,
Jacobus Bouge, *
David Giffin,
William Peck,
Jeduthan Baker,
Kelsey Thurber,
John Cook,
James Harrington,
Joel Harrington,
Samuel Umberston,
Stephen Foot,
Jeremiah Comstock,
Daniel Mackneel,
Robert Sanford,
Justin Hitchcock,
Jeduthan Farrell,
Holden Farnsworth,*
Richard Harris,
James Higgins,
Samuel Steel,

John Pecor,
Peter Woodcock,
John Barnard,
Benj'n Nichols,
Seth Ranney,
Lazar Laryers,*
Titus Sikes, 3d,
William Lyttle,
William Lyttle, Jun.,
William Osborn,
Hira Pain,
Joseph Orcut,
Eliphalet Elsworth,
Robert Sample,
Isaac Cogswell,
Reuben Field,
Henry Reve,*
Asa Fenton,
Joshua Fenton,
Jason Fenton,
Joseph Freeman,
Josiah Page,
Peter Dudley,
Ahab Harrington,
Calvin Hubbard,
Amos Lay,
David ——,*
John Storring.

This petition was received in the Assembly on the 8th of February 1802, read and referred to a committee consisting of the following gentlemen:

MR. DIRCK TEN BROEK, of Albany County.

MR. SOLOMON MARTIN, of Otsego County.

MR. ARCHIBALD McINTYRE, of Montgomery County.

MR. WILLIAM BAILEY, of Clinton County.

MR. ABEL FRENCH, of Denmark, then Oneida County.

The bill passed the house of assembly on the 18th of that month, and subsequently resulted in the passage of the following:

"*An act to erect part of this State into a County, by the name of the County of St. Lawrence.*

Passed March 3, 1802.
I. *Be it enacted by the People of the State of New York, represented in Senate and Assembly,* That all that tract of land, beginning in the line of the River St. Lawrence, which divides the United States from the dominions of the king of Great Britain, where the same is intersected by a continuation of the division line of great lots, numbers three and four, of Macomb's purchase; thence running southeasterly, along the said line, until it comes opposite to the westerly corner of the township of Cambray; then in a straight line to the said corner of Cambray; then along the rear

*Uncertain.

lines of the said township of Cambray, and the townships of De Kalb, Canton, Potsdam and Stockholm, distinguished on a map of the said township, and filed in the secretary's office by the surveyor general; then by a line to be continued in a direct course from the line of the said township of Stockholm, until the same intersects the division line of the great lots numbers one and two in Macomb's purchase; thence northerly along the same to the lands reserved by the St. Regis Indians; then westerly along the bounds thereof, to the dominions of the king of Great Britain; thence along the same to the place of beginning, shall be, and is hereby erected into a separate county, and shall be called and known by the name of St. Lawrence.

II. *And be it further enacted*, That all that part of the said county lying westward of the boundary lines of the townships of Lisbon and Canton, as distinguished on the map aforesaid, shall be, and hereby is erected into a town by the name of Oswegatchie; and the first town meeting in the said town shall be held at the house of Nathan Ford; and the said townships of Lisbon and Canton shall continue and remain one town by the name of Lisbon. And that all that part of the said county, known and distinguished in the map aforesaid by the townships of Madrid and Potsdam, shall be, and hereby is, erected into a town by the name of Madrid; and the first town meeting in the said town shall be held at the house of Joseph Edsall. And that all the remaining part of the said county, shall be, and hereby is, erected into a town by the name of Massena; and that the first town meeting in the said town shall be held at the house of Amos Lay.

III. *And be it further enacted*, That the freeholders and inhabitants of the several towns erected or continued by this act, shall be, and are hereby empowered, to hold town meetings, and elect such town officers as the freeholders and inhabitants of any town in this state may do by law; and that the freeholders and inhabitants of the several towns, and the town officers to be by them elected respectively, shall have the like powers and privileges as the freeholders, inhabitants and town officers of any town in this state.

IV. *And be it further enacted*, That there shall be held, in and for the said county of St. Lawrence, a court of common pleas and general sessions of the peace, and that there shall be two terms of the same courts in every year, to commence and end as follows, that is to say: The first term of the said court shall begin on the first Tuesday in June, in every year, and may continue to be held until the Saturday following, inclusive; and the second term of the said court shall begin on the second Tuesday of November, in every year, and may continue to be held until the Saturday following, inclusive: And the said courts of common pleas, and general sessions of the peace, shall have the same jurisdiction, powers and authorities, in the same county, as the courts of common pleas and general sessions of the peace in the other counties of this state, have in their respective counties; *Provided, always*, That nothing in this act contained shall be construed to affect any suit or action already commenced, or that shall be commenced, before the first Tuesday in June next, so as to work a wrong or prejudice, to any of the parties therein, or to affect any criminal or other proceedings, on the part of the people of this state; but all such civil and criminal proceedings, shall and may be prosecuted to trial, judgment and execution, as if this act had never been passed.

V. *And be it further enacted*, That until legislative provision be made in the premises, the said court of common pleas and general sessions of the peace, shall be held in the old barracks, so called, in the said town of Oswegatchie, which shall be deemed in law, the court house and jail of the said county of St. Lawrence.

VI. *And be it further enacted*, That the freeholders and inhabitants of the said county, shall have and enjoy, within the same, all and every of the said rights, powers and privileges, as the freeholders and inhabitants of any county in this state, are by law entitled to have and enjoy.

VII. *And be it further enacted*, That it shall not be the duty of the supreme court to hold a circuit court in every year in the said county, unless, in their judgment, they shall deem it proper and necessary; any law to the contrary notwithstanding.

VIII. *And be it further enacted*, That the said county of St. Lawrence, shall be considered as part of the western district of this state.

IX. *And be it further enacted*, That all the residue of the tract of land lying between the division lines aforesaid, of great lots numbers three and four, and of great lots numbers one and two, in Macomb's purchase, and the north bounds of Totten and Crossfield's purchase, shall, until further legislative provision in the premises, be considered as part of the town of Massena, in the said county of St. Lawrence: And all that part of Macomb's purchase, included in great division number one, and the Indian reservation at the St. Regis village, shall be annexed to, and form part of, the town of Chateaugay, in the county of Clinton.

X. *And be it further enacted*, That the said county of St. Lawrence, shall be annexed to, and become part of the district now composed of the counties of Herkimer, Otsego, Oneida, and Chenango, as it respects all proceedings under the act entitled, 'An act relative to district attorneys.'

XI. *And be it further enacted*, That until other provision be made by law, the inspectors of election in the several towns in the said county of St. Lawrence, shall return the votes taken at any election for governor, lieutenant governor, senators, members of the assembly, and members of congress, to the clerk of the county of Oneida, to be by him estimated as a part of the aggregate number of votes given at such election, in the county of Oneida."

In accordance with this law, one of the stone buildings west of the Oswegatchie, was fitted up as a court house, and a bomb-proof magazine on the premises as a jail. Here the first courts were held, and first delinquents confined until the completion of the court house in 1803, under the provisions of a clause in an act passed April 2, 1803, which provided as follows:

"*And be it further enacted*, That it shall be lawful for the supervisors of the county of St. Lawrence, and they are hereby authorized, to receive the moneys subscribed by the inhabitants of the said county, for building a court house and gaol, on the east side of the mouth of the Oswegatchie river, opposite to the old barracks; and to apply such moneys for building the said court house and gaol, in such manner as they or the majority of them shall judge most for the interest of the said county; and shall account for the expenditures of the said money with the judges of the court of common pleas for the said county.

And be it further enacted, That as soon as the said supervisors, or a majority of them, shall, by writing under their hands, certify to the sheriff of the said county, that the gaol hereby authorized to be built, is fit for the reception of prisoners, it shall and may be lawful for the said sheriff, after filing the said certificate in the office of the clerk of the said county, to remove the prisoners into the said gaol; which gaol thereafter shall be the gaol of the said county; and that as soon as the said court house is finished sufficiently, so as to be comfortable for holding court, and a certificate thereof by the said supervisors, or a majority of them, delivered to the judges of the said court, and filed in the clerk's office, shall thereafter be the court house for the said county, to all intents and purposes.

And be it further enacted, That until further order of the legislature, it shall not be necessary for the sheriff of the said county, to give bonds to the people of this state, for a larger sum than four thousand dollars, and six sureties of five hundred dollars each."

An act of Feb. 12, 1813, required the board of supervisors to raise a tax of $900, for the purpose of erecting a fire-proof clerk's office. Previous to the completion of this, the records were kept in the office of Louis Hasbrouck, the clerk. The date of the first record in the office is May 29, 1802.

The house in which the clerk's office was kept for several of the first years is represented in the accompanying engraving, which possesses an additional interest from its having been one of the first dwellings erected in Ogdensburgh. It was completed in 1804. The lot on which it stood was sold to Mr. Hasbrouck for a guinea. Its central location has rendered it worth several thousand dollars.

This venerable dwelling was unfortunately consumed in a destructive fire that occurred in the autumn of 1852, together with the modern block of stores represented in the cut, and much valuable property on the opposite side of the street.

The engraving was taken from a daguerreotype by E. A. Olds.

The following resolutions in relation to the act authorizing the erection of a new clerk's office, were passed by the board of supervisors in Oct., 1821:

"Moved that the sum of $600 be raised and levied for the purpose of building a fire-proof clerk's office.

Action postponed for the present.

It was proposed to amend this, by inserting $500, and this amendment was passed.

Voted that the building should be erected in the village of Ogdensburgh. Louis Hasbrouck, David C. Judson, and Bishop Perkins, were appointed a committee to determine the size and plan, and to superintend its erection and finishing. It was further *Resolved*, that,

"Whereas, by an act of the legislature, passed February 12, 1813, authorizing the board of supervisors of the county of St. Lawrence, to raise money to build a fire-proof clerk's office, in said county; and whereas, it is considered probable that a division of the county may take place, and in such case, a location at Ogdensburgh would not benefit such new county; it was, therefore, resolved, that in case of such a division, such sum as may be assessed on the territory so set off into a new county, should be refunded to such new county."

In pursuance of the foregoing resolution, a stone building was erected on the corner of Ford and Green streets in the village of Ogdensburgh. It is now the land office of the Hon. Henry Van Rensselaer.

The proprietors and settlers of the central and southern sections of the county, were never entirely satisfied with the location of the public buildings at Ogdensburgh, and by referring to the letter from Judge Ford to S. Ogden, dated Jan. 11, 1805, it will be seen that secret jealousies were entertained on this subject. In 1818, the first direct effort was made to effect a removal, which was defeated through the efforts of persons residing in Ogdensburgh.

Among the arguments then adduced in favor of the measure, were the exposed situation of the frontier, and liability to hostile incursions in case of war, the inconvenience of the public buildings, and insecurity of the jail, and especially the distance from the centre of the county and the southern settlements.

The petition for the appointment of commissioners, to select a new site for public buildings, had 700 signatures, and the remonstrance 762. The inhabitants of Potsdam, also petitioned for the removal of the public buildings to their village.

Against the removal of the county seat, it was urged — that the condition of the buildings at Ogdensburgh did not call for a change; that a large amount of money was about to be expended upon roads, which would make that place easily accessible; that the county buildings, worth $2,000, would become forfeited, by reversion to the proprietor; that the taxable inhabitants then numbering 2,000, were then thinly scattered; and an uncertainty still existed, where the weight of population would ultimately preponderate.

A plan was at this time proposed for dividing the county, by a line

g between Lisbon and Canton on the west, and Madrid and Pots-
n the east, to extend in a direct line to the southern bounds of the
. The new county was to have been named *Fayette.*

estimate made at the time, is interesting, denoting the number of
ers in the several towns, and is as follows:

ern division. Oswegatchie, 193; Gouverneur, 89; De Kalb, 126;
, 119; Fowler, 28; Rossie, 62; Lisbon, 115; Canton, 202. Total,

ern division. Madrid, 260; Potsdam, 302; Parishville, 133; Stock-
99; Hopkinton, 81; Louisville, 106; Massena, 85. Total, 1,066.
subject of removal to a central location again came up for legis-
action in the session of 1827, but was permitted to lie over till the
ssion, for the purpose of obtaining a more distinct expression of
pular wish on the measure; and under these circumstances, it be-
test question in the election of members of assembly in that year.
considerations were dropped for the time, and it was expected,
e canvass would decide the preferences of the electors of the
upon the subject of removal. It resulted as follows:

For removal.	Against removal.
Moses Rowley, 2,364	Jason Fenton, 2,069
Jabez Willes, 2,178	Phineas Attwater, 1,688

members elected were nominated by a convention representing
tion desirous of a change of site, and with a distinct understand-
t they would labor to effect that object.

records of many of the towns, show that an expression of opinion
en on this subject, at their town meetings in 1828.

petition upon which the law, authorizing a change and appoint-
uninterested commissioners to designate a new site, was not nume-
signed, but embraced the names of those who possessed much
and influence in the county. It was dated December, 1827, and
d in the senate Jan. 18, 1828.

led, after the most active opposition from many of those interested
ensburgh, to the passage of the following law:

*Act, establishing the location of Court House and other Public Buildings
in St. Lawrence County.*

Passed Jan. 28, 1828.
seph Grant, George Brayton and John E. Hinman, of the county
da, be, and they are hereby appointed commissioners to examine,
ine and fix upon, the proper site for the erection of a new court
gaol and clerk's office, in and for the county of St. Lawrence, whose
shall be to go into the said county to examine the situation of the
with respect to its population, its territory, its roads, and the means
munication between the several towns and settlements in the said

14

county, together with the immediate prospect of settlements, and all other things which they shall think it necessary to examine and enquire into, the better to enable them to form a correct determination as to the site of a court house, gaol and clerk's office, for the said county, which shall best accommodate the population of the said county, in reference to its present territory.

II. The said commissioners, after having made such inquiries, and examinations as aforesaid, and as to them shall be satisfactory, shall on or after the fifteenth day of August next, fix upon and establish the site for the buildings aforesaid, and shall put their determination in writing, under their hands and seals, or the hands and seals of any two of them, and shall file the same in the office of the clerk of the said county, whose duty it shall be to receive and file the said paper, without any compensation for so doing; and the determination of the said commissioners, or any two of them, being so made and filed as aforesaid, shall be final and conclusive in the premises.

III. The said commissioners shall be entitled to receive three dollars per day each, for every day they shall be necessarily employed in discharging the duties of the said commission, and fifteen cents per mile each, for their travel, going and returning, to be computed from the residence of each commissioner, to the clerk's office of the said county; which shall be the compensation of the said commissioners, shall be raised levied and collected as the other contingent expenses of the said county are raised levied and collected.

IV. That Ansel Bailey, David C. Judson and Asa Sprague, Jr., be and they are hereby appointed commissioners to superintend the building of a court house, gaol and clerk's office, in and for the said county of St. Lawrence, upon the site to be fixed upon and established by the commissioners appointed in and by the first section of this act.

V. The commissioners appointed in and by the last preceding section of this act, or a majority of them, are hereby authorized and empowered to purchase materials, contract with workmen, and do all other things necessary to the building of the said court house, goal and clerk's office; to direct the size, shape and arrangement of the said buildings, and the materials of which the same shall be constructed; and that the said clerk's office shall be built of such materials, and be so constructed as to be fire proof.

VI. The comissioners last mentioned shall be, and they are hereby authorized to draw upon the treasurer of the said county of St. Lawrence, from time to time, for such sum or sums of money as shall come into the treasury of the said county, to be appropriated for the erection of the said buildings; and it shall be the duty of the said treasurer, to pay on the order of the said commissioners, or a majority of them, any sums of money in his hands, appropriated to the erection of the said buildings.

VII. The said commissioners appointed to superintend the erection of the said buildings, shall, before they enter upon the duties of their office, give bonds in the penal sum of $5,000, with approved sureties, to the supervisors of the said county, conditioned that they will faithfully discharge the duties of the said commission, and the moneys which shall come into their hands, as such commissioners, and that they will punctually and honestly account to the said supervisors, for all such moneys; and the said commissioners shall be entitled to receive each the sum of two dollars per day, for each day they be necessarily employed in the discharge of their duties, under this act, to be audited, levied and collected as the other contingent charges of the said county are audited, levied and collected."

nbstance of the remaining sections will only be given.

A tax of $2,500 to be levied on the county for the building.
he board of supervisors to sell the old court house, gaol and
ffice, and apply the proceeds towards the new building, &c.
pervisors to procure a deed in fee simple of the new site.
he site to be paid for out of the proceeds of the old buildings.
The supervisors to levy a sum in 1829, not to exceed $2,500, to
e new buildings.
Commissioners to give notice to the judges of the county court,
ompletion of the buildings.
The judges to meet and fix upon the gaol liberties.
The sheriff to remove prisoners to the new gaol, when directed by
es of the courts.
The sheriff alone, liable for escape of prisoners on removal.
. The clerk to remove records when directed by judges.
L. After the above, the new buildings shall be deemed the county
ouse, gaol and clerk's office, to all legal intents.
Vacancies among first commissioners, to be filled by governor.
Vacancies in building commissioners, to be filled by county

sum designated by the foregoing act being found inadequate to
e the buildings, an act was passed April 16, 1830, authorizing the
ors to raise $600 more for that purpose.

irst record made at the clerk's office after its removal, was on the
anuary, 1830, on which day it was opened.

ollowing extract from the report to the supervisors, of the com-
ers appointed to erect the county buildings, at Canton, describes
ginal construction:

h building is of stone. The court house is two stories in height,
by 40. The lower story is divided into four rooms, besides pas-
d stairways, viz, a grand jury room, a room for constables and
es attending the grand jury, and two rooms for petit jurors. The
tory is devoted entirely to a court room, 41 feet in length, by 37
th.
lerk's office is of the same height and size of the private clerk's
nd differing in its construction only, in making the front room
and the rear one larger. * * *
aol is 36 by 40, with the basement story rising about five feet
he ground, and a story and a half above. About 12 feet of the
end of all the stories is appropriated to prison rooms, except a
om in the lower story, for a sheriff's office, where the stove is
intended to give warmth to all the criminal rooms in the upper
well as the debtor's room immediately back on the same story.
lan of the criminal rooms has been entirely changed since the
ade at the last meeting of the board.
then contemplated to take the Jefferson county jail, as a model,
nstruction of ours, the strength of which consisted in the size,
n surface of the stone of which the walls are constructed. The
y of obtaining stone of sufficient size and evenness of surface to
dowaling, induced them to abandon that plan.
riminals' rooms are a block of cells, five in number, constructed

of wood and iron, placed in the second story, within and three feet distant from the outside walls.

The light is admitted into the cells through gratings in the upper part of the doors (which are to be wholly of iron), opening into the hall in the easterly end of the building into which the light is admitted, through four strong grated windows.

The cells are, with the exception of one, intended for the accommodation of single prisoners only.

The plan, though novel, as applied to county gaols, was suggested to the consideration of the committee, by an examination of the construction of the state prison, recently erected; and it appears to them to possess the same advantages for a county prison, which has given to those establishments a character for usefulness, in the prevention of crime, by the reformation of the criminal, in the measure of punishment that has revived the hope of the philanthropist, in the success of the penitentiary system; that from the world and from the contaminating influence of the society of his fellow prisoners, who may be more hardened in vice, and left to his own solitary reflections, if there is any chance for reformation, by punishment, it is under such circumstances. The safety of the arrangement strongly recommended itself to the consideration of the committee.

Confined singly, there can be no joint efforts.

Communication from the outside, except as to one cell, is believed to be impracticable and difficult, as to that; and should an escape from a cell be effected, the outside wall or grating would still remain to be forced."

The accommodation of the courthouse being deemed insufficient for the wants of the county, the subject of repairing and enlarging the building, was brought before the board of supervisors, at their session in 1850, and it was resolved,

" That a committee of five persons be appointed by the board, whose duty it shall be to examine the present building, and the cost and expense of an addition of 24 feet, of the same materials as the present building, and of the same height, including the expense of remodelling the inside in a convenient and suitable manner, and to receive proposals for the erection and completion of said addition."

This committee was authorized to contract for the erection of said addition to the court house, provided such addition shall be found practicable, for the sum of $1,600.

Two days afterwards, this vote was reconsidered, on a vote of 11 to 10, and three members of the board were appointed a committee to examine and determine what repairs and alterations in the court house were necessary. If, in the judgment of the committee, repairs and alterations should be made, and they might contract for the same, for a sum not exceeding $2,000, the committee were to file a certificate to this effect, with the clerk of the board, and they then might borrow, on the credit of the county, at par, such sums for seven per cent. annual interest, which they were authorized to expend in repairs and alterations of the court house.

The committee were to give their official bond for money so borrowed,

xceeding $2,000, in the aggregate, which was to be entered by the
of the board in his minutes, and certified by him, bearing 7 per
interest, payable annually. In case the committee should deter-
to make such repairs and alterations, they were to cause such
tions and repairs to be contracted for and made under their inspec-
nd direction.

urther amendment, which required that the committee in no case
d have authority to contract for the completion of the addition of
t on the east end of the court house, unless the same could be done
2,000, was adopted.

ssrs. Picket, Anthony, Cogswell, Foster, and Hazelton were appoint-
select a committee to carry the foregoing resolutions into effect,
bey reported the name of Messrs. Fisk, Thatcher and Cogswell,
were duly appointed.

additions contemplated, were effected during the year 1851, and St.
ence county can now justly boast of a court house which will com-
favorably in point of convenience, although perhaps not in splendor
hitectural display, with that of most of county buildings of the

is improvement had been suggested by the judges of the supreme

e records of the board of supervisors of St. Lawrence county pre-
to 1814 were lost in a fire at Ogdensburgh in the spring of 1839.
irst board is said to have been composed of the following:
han Ford, of *Ossegatche*; Alexander J. Turner, of *Lisbon*; Joseph
l, of *Madrid*; Matthew Perkins, of *Massena*.

early action of the supervisors in regard to public buildings, is
own. That in relation to subsequent buildings, has been given.
1825, the board resolved to avail itself of the provisions of the act
rizing certain counties to build county *poor houses*, by filing a cer-
to that effect, in the clerk's office of the county.
ried by a vote of 11 to 7.

sum of $2,400 was accordingly voted, for the purpose of purchas-
or more tracts of land, and to erect thereon suitable buildings
oor house. This sum was to be raised in three equal annual
nents.

th Stilwell, Jonah Sanford and Chauncey Pettibone were appoint-
missioners to locate the site, and make the purchase.

n adjourned meeting, held in January, 1826, several attempts were
to agree upon a site for the poor house, but without success: and
nmissioners previously appointed were discharged from that duty.

John C. Perkins, Samuel Northrup and Reuben Streeter were subsequently appointed for this purpose.

Asa Sprague, Jun., Daniel Walker, Smith Stilwell, Samuel Patridge, Silas Wright, Jun., Joseph Barnes and Ephraim S. Raymond were, at this session, appointed superintendents of the poor house.

A lot of eighty acres, one mile west of Canton village, was purchased, on which was a house and barn, for $1,250.

$500 was applied for repairing buildings, and stocking the farm. In 1827, the further sum of $500 was raised, for the purpose of erecting an additional building at the poor house.

-From the interruption in the series, we shall not attempt to give in connected order a synopsis of the proceedings of the board of supervisors in St. Lawrence county, but shall have frequent occasion to allude to them in this work.

Louis Hasbrouck was first appointed clerk of the board of supervisors, and held that office till the year 1810, when William W. Bowen was appointed, and held till 1819. During the session of that year, Chester Gurney officiated, and at that time, Bishop Perkins, of Ogdensburgh, was appointed to the office, which he held uninterruptedly, till the session of 1852, when having been elected to Congress, he resigned his office of clerk of the board, which he had held with the entire approbation of that body, for a third of a century, and Martin Thatcher was appointed his successor.

On his retiring from the office which he had held so long, Mr. Perkins received a unanimous vote of the board, expressive of their sense of the high esteem with which they regarded his services.

ORGANIZATION OF FRANKLIN COUNTY.

A Petition of John Porter, and others, inhabitants of the county of Clinton, was presented in the assembly, February 4th, 1808, praying for the erection of a new county therefrom, by the name of NORFOLK, and other provisions relating thereto, which was read, and with several similar petitions, was referred to a committee, consisting of Mr. Joshua Foreman of Onondaga, Mr. Elisha Arnold of Clinton, and Mr. Amos Hall of Alleghany, Genesee, and Ontario counties.

On the tenth of February, Mr. Foreman, from the above committee, reported as follows:

" That they had taken the facts set forth in said petition, into consideration, and do find, that the settlements in the western part of said

are so remote from the site of the courts in said county, as to
their attendance extremely difficult, and burthensome; that the
of said county is sufficiently large to admit of a division, and
each county a territory equal to the general size of counties in
e; that the application for such division, has been generally
n the county; the committee therefore presume that the princi-
ach division, as well as the line of division, are well understood
eed upon in said county; the committee also find that the town
me is very nearly central, in such proposed county, between the
west line, and from the quality of the soil in the north and
arts, the committee are of opinion, that said town will be at least
uth as the centre of population in said county; the committee
efore of opinion, that the prayer of the petitioners ought to be
, and that the place of holding courts in the new county, ought
tablished in the town of Malone; the committee have therefore
d a bill for that purpose, and directed their chairman to ask for
bring in the same."

being granted, the bill was introduced; read the first and
time, and referred to the committee of the whole. On the 15th
use as a committee, spent some time upon the bill, when the
resumed the chair, and Mr. Gold, from the said committee,
d, that the committee had gone through the said bill, made
ments, filled up the blanks, and agreed to the same, which he
ected to report to the house; and he read the report in his place
ivered the same to the table where it was again read, and agreed
ie house.

s then ordered that the bill be engrossed.
ie 16th, it was read the third time and passed; and on the same
ras sent to the senate, and read the first time.
ie 17th, it was read the second time, and referred to the commit-
ie whole.
ie same day Mr. Graham, from this committee, reported progress
ed leave to sit again, which was also done on the 26th. On the
larch, he reported that the committee had gone through the said
de amendments, and agreed to the same, which he was directed
t to the senate, and he read the report in his place, and delivered
ie at the table, where it was again read and agreed to by the

The amendments were ordered to be engrossed, and on the
iy it was passed and sent back to the assembly, where they
ncurred in.
ie 8th, it was by the assembly referred to the council of revision,
ubsequently received their sanction.

tlin county, was erected by an act, entitled:
act to divide the county of Clinton, and for other purposes."

Passed March 11, 1808.

"*Be it enacted, by the people of the state of New York, represented in senate and assembly*: That all that part of the county of Clinton, lying west of a line beginning in the line of the said county of Clinton, between number six and seven, of the old military townships, and running from thence southerly, along the east line of number seven, eight, nine, ten and eleven of the old military townships aforesaid, to the north line of the county of Essex, shall be, and is hereby erected into a separate county by the name of Franklin, and the residue of said county of Clinton, lying east of the aforesaid line, shall be, and remain a separate county by the name of Clinton.

And be it further enacted: That there shall be holden in, and for the said county of Franklin, a court of common pleas, and general session of the peace, and that there shall be two terms of said courts, in the said county, in every year, to commence as follows:—The first term of the said court of common pleas and general sessions of the peace, shall be holden on the third Tuesday of April, next, and may continue until the Saturday following, inclusive; and the second term of the said court, shall commence on the second Tuesday of October, next, and may continue to be holden until the Saturday following, inclusive; and the said courts of common pleas and general sessions of the peace, shall have the like jurisdiction, power and authority, in the said county, as the courts of common pleas and general sessions of the peace, in the other counties of this state, have in their respective counties.

Provided: That all suits now pending in the court of common pleas and general sessions in the county of Clinton, may be prosecuted to trial, judgment and execution, as if this act had not been passed.

And be it further enacted: That the said courts of common pleas and general sessions of the peace be holden at the academy, in the township of Malone, in and for the said county; and that the supervisors of the said county of Franklin be, and are hereby authorized to raise by tax, on the freeholders and inhabitants of said county, the sum of two hundred and fifty dollars, to be applied and appropriated by them to strengthen and secure one room in the said academy, as a gaol for said county, and the sheriff of the county of Franklin, and other officers, civil and criminal, are hereby authorized to confine their prisoners in such room of said academy, and in the gaol of the said county of Clinton, at their election.

And be it further enacted: That all those parts of the towns of Peru, and Plattsburgh, lying within the county of Franklin, west of the old military townships, be annexed to the town of Harrison, that all those parts of the said towns of Peru and Plattsburgh in the said county of Franklin, within the old military townships, be annexed to the town of Chateaugay; and that all that part of the town of Chateaugay, remaining in the county of Clinton, be annexed to the town of Mooers, in said county of Clinton; and the supervisors of the towns of Harrison and Chateaugay in the county of Franklin, and of Mooers, Peru and Plattsburgh in the county of Clinton, shall, as soon as may be, after the first Tuesday of April, next, on notice for that purpose being given, meet and divide the poor and money belonging to the said town of Peru, Plattsburgh, and Chateaugay, according to the distribution of the territory of said towns, and the last tax lists thereof.

And be it further enacted: That the said county of Franklin, shall be considered as part of the eastern district of this state, and until other provisions are made for that purpose, that the inspectors of elections in the several towns of said county of Franklin, return the votes taken therein at any election for governor, lieutenant governor, senators, mem-

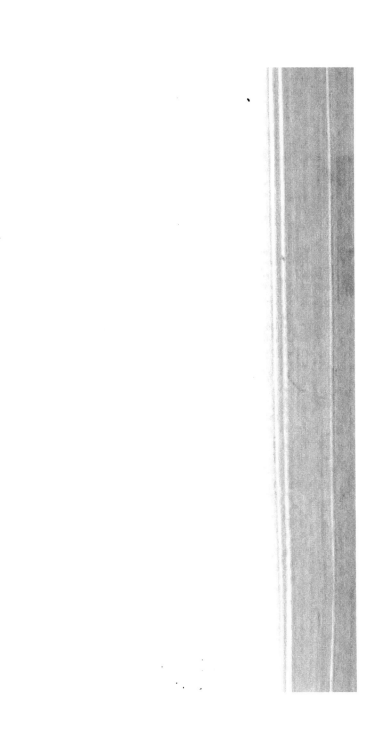

here of assembly, and representatives in congress, to the clerk of the county of Clinton, to be by him estimated as part of the aggregate number of votes given at such election in the county of Franklin, and that the said county of Franklin be considered as part of the said district to which the county of Franklin belongs, as it respects all proceedings under the act entitled, " *An act* relative to district attorneys."

The following remark, in relation to the origin of the name of this county, occurs in Spafford's Gazetteer of the State of New York, published in 1813:

" It can hardly be necessary to say, that this county received its name from the illustrious Franklin; and that nothing was meant by attaching it to the least valuable county of this state, though the doctor, who always saw a meaning in every thing, might be displeased with it, should he appear here in his butt of wine."

It was from insinuations like these, that northern New York has hitherto been looked upon by the law makers of the state, as unworthy of attention; and hence has led to a neglect of the just claims of its inhabitants to a participation in the benefits of our system of internal improvements. In 1813, there were four post offices in the county, Chateaugay, Constable, Dickinson and *Ezraville*, since changed to Malone.

By an act passed April 3, 1801, dividing the state into counties, the territory now embraced in St. Lawrence and Franklin counties was made a part of Clinton county, which included " all that part of the state bounded southerly by the county of Essex and Totten & Crossfield's purchase, easterly by the east bounds of the state, northerly by the north bounds of the state, and westerly by the west bounds of the state, and the division line between great lots No. 3 and 4, of Macomb's purchase, continued to the west bounds of this state.

By an act passed April 7, 1801, dividing the state into towns, the territory now embraced in Franklin county, was made to comprise the town of Chateaugay, when first erected, in 1799, this town included only that part of military townships in Nos. 5, 6, 7 and 8.

On the 22d of March, 1822, township No. 11, in the OLD MILITARY TRACT, was taken from Franklin and annexed to Essex county. The territory so transferred, was annexed to the town of Jay, and is embraced in the present town of St. Armand.

The building erected for an academy, and still standing on the premises of the Franklin Academy, continued to serve the purpose of a court house and jail until after the war. Measures were meanwhile taken as early as the beginning of 1809, to procure public buildings, and petitions were forwarded for the purpose.

From the journal of the assembly, February 20, 1809, it is learned:

" That it appears by the petition, that Noah Moody's dwelling house which stood on the rising ground a few rods west of the bridge, in the centre of the town of Malone, in the county of Franklin; has been selected by the inhabitants of the said county, for the site of their court house and gaol; that in consequence of such selection, the inhabitants of said town have bound themselves to contribute the sum of fifteen hundred dollars towards erecting the said court house and gaol within two years; that the act for the erection of said county does not designate the site, by reason whereof, it may be questionable whether the payment of the said bond can be enforced, wherefore the petitioners pray that the site be designated by law."

The committee reported favorably, and the act subsequently passed.

The location of the public buildings of this county was accordingly determined by an act passed March 24, 1809, which directed,

"That the court house and gaol in and for the county of Franklin, shall be erected at the place where Noah Moody's dwelling house stood, on the rising ground a few rods west of the bridge, in the center of the town of Ezraville, in said county."

By an act passed March 9, 1810, the supervisors of the county of Franklin were directed and empowered to raise the sum of $3,250, in three equal annual instalments, for the purpose of building a court house and jail, at the place previously established by law.

The sum of $250 was to be raised for the purpose of preparing a temporary room in the Academy, to answer the purpose of a jail, until one could be built.

The supervisors were directed to appoint a committee of three or five, to superintend the erection of the county buildings. When finished, the sheriff was to give notice of the fact by public proclamation.

By an act passed April 3, 1811, the supervisors of Franklin county were directed and empowered to raise the further sum of $500, in two equal annual instalments, to be levied and collected in the same manner as the other necessary and contingent charges are annually raised, together with five per cent. in addition for the commission of the collector, and one per cent. for treasurer's fees. This money was directed to be applied towards building a court house and jail.

By an act passed March 5, 1819, the supervisors were directed to raise a tax not to exceed $1,000, to build a fire proof clerk's office, in Franklin county.

The action of the board of supervisors in relation to the public buildings, will be given in the following synopsis of their proceedings.

The present court house was erected by Noah Moody, in 1811–1813, and contains within it the jail. During the summer of 1852, a separate and very appropriate building was erected for a jail.

Memoranda from the Records of the Board of Supervisors, of Franklin County, commencing October 4, 1808.

1808. The sessions, for several years, were held at the Academy. Present at the first session—Albon Man, of Constable; Nathaniel Blanchard, of Harrison; and Gates Hoit, of Chateaugay. John H. Russell appointed the clerk of the board.

Accounts audited for Constable, ... $391·30

" " Chateaugay, ... 470·05

" " Harrison, ... 704·94

Voted, that two mills and three-fourths be assessed to defray county charges, one and a half on Harrison, two and three-fourths on Constable, and two and a half on Chateaugay, to defray town charges.

A county bounty of $10 on wolves, and five on wolf whelps, voted.

The above bounties were to be paid on certificates issued by a justice of the peace, which were to have the following form:

"I hereby certify, that A B, personally appeared before me, and presented the pate and both ears of a full grown wolf (or wolf's whelp), and made solemn oath that he killed the same in the town of ———, in the county of Franklin, on the ——— day of ———, 1808.

The ears of which I have cut off and burned, and have given this certificate to ———, that he may be entitled to the county bounty, and a duplicate for the town bounty.

Franklin co. ———, 1808. Sworn before C D, justice of the peace."

$850 to be paid for roads and bridges, as follows : To Harrison, 310; Chateaugay, 200; Constable, 250.

Aggregate amount of county charges audited, $89·56.

Resolved, That out of the sum of $2,199·50, the sum of $250 be appropriated to strengthen a room for a gaol, in said county of Franklin, and the remainder to be appropriated as heretofore contemplated in the several resolves of this board, and for the purpose of defraying the contingent expenses of the county.

On the 7th of January, 1809, the supervisors of Franklin and Clinton counties, met to examine the accounts of the several towns, and the following resolution was passed:

Resolved, That no demands shall be made by either of the respective counties of Clinton and Franklin, against each other, in respect to the balance of town accounts unto this day. *Provided, nevertheless,* That the several items on the tax list, for arrears of taxes on nonresident property, which have been rejected by the comptroller, for defect in point of description or otherwise, and which deficiency has been charged to the several towns incurring the same in case assessed again by the respective counties, shall be paid, when recovered, to either of the counties entitled to the same; so far as the land on which these arrearages were assessed, remains, after the divisions of the county of Clinton, the territory of either of said counties.

The moneys coming hereafter for arrearages of taxes, were to be paid, three-fifths to Clinton, and two-fifths to Franklin counties.

1809. The board audited the several town accounts, which amounted to the following sums:

Chateaugay,	$463·50	Dickinson,	$686.73
Malone,	450·52	Constable,	407·00

Voted $2,276·05, it being three mills on a dollar, on the assessment for defraying contingent charges. $1,000 appropriated for bridges, as follows:

To Chateaugay, $230; Malone, $180; Dickinson, $265; Constable, $325.

1810. The sum of $1,069, applied for building court house and jail. The accounts of the several towns audited were as follows:

Chateaugay,	$486·25	Constable,	$351·65
Dickinson,	661·06	Malone,	461·99
	County charges, $1,329·65		

The sum of $2,499, it being three mills on a dollar, were voted as follows: $1,084 for building a court house and jail, and the remainder to defray the expenses of wolf bounties, and other incidental charges of the county.

The commissioners appointed to superintend the building of the court house, were authorized to draw on the treasury of the county the sum of $250, on the first of January, and the like sum on the first of June following, for the purpose of defraying the expense of building.

John Mazuzan, Cone Andrus, and James Ormsbey, were appointed a building committee. They were directed to take for their model, the court house in Clinton county, as near as might be, and not to exceed $5,000 in cost, including donations, which were expected to amount to at least $1,500. In addition to the sums above authorized to be drawn from the treasury, the further amount of $500, payable in the month of October next, was placed at the disposal of the building committee.

1811. The board proceeded to audit the several town accounts as follows:

Constable,	$379·58	Malone,	$516·50
Dickinson,	663·44	Chateaugay,	585·16
	County charges, $269·29		

The sum of $100 for Constable, $100 for Malone, $60 for Dickinson, was allowed for bridges.

The sum of $2,444·72, being two and a half mills on a dollar, was voted, out of which the treasurer was directed to pay to the commission-

harge of the erection of the court house, $1,353·33, towards de-
the expenses of that building.

The board audited the following accounts:

Constable,	$652·75	Malone,	$502·79
Dickinson,	516·01	Chateaugay,	211·01

County expenses, $643·86

ng the latter were $427·75, for bringing arms from Chateaugay.
mmittee appointed to draw a remonstrance to the legislature,
the division of the towns of Constable and Dickinson.
sum of $3,286·02, or four mills on a dollar, voted for county ex-
the ensuing year, of which $1,332·67 was to be applied for build-
court house, and the remainder for incidental expenses.

The board audited the following accounts:

Chateaugay,	$563·33	Dickinson,	$673·00
Bangor,	635·11	Malone,	613·57
Constable,	629·22		

Hoit directed to procure standard weights and measures for the
and to pay the necessary expense therefor. County charges
, $466·44. Three mills on a dollar, amounting to $1,699·97, voted
ensuing year.

The board audited the following accounts:

Chateaugay,	$539·08	Dickinson,	$583·59
Bangor,	522·60	Constable,	496·39
Malone,	569·72		

County charges, $1,281.56

e and a quarter mills, or $1,795·60, voted for the ensuing year.
ppropriated for a bridge at Chateaugay, $200 for the same in
ble, and $300 for the same in Malone, at the village, in place of a
formerly built at that place.

The board audited the following accounts:

Dickinson,	$519·05	Bangor,	$768·40
Chateaugay,	479·48	Constable,	1,208·16
Malone,	752·82		

County charges, $775·12

first school moneys received from the state, distributed as follows:
, $13·35; Chateaugay, $21·62; Dickinson, $9·88; Malone, $39·04;
ble, $52·52. Total, $136·43.

sum of $900, voted for roads and bridges, to be expended as
: Chateaugay, $200; Malone, $260, of which $200 was to be
ed on a stone bridge in the village; Constable, $200; Dickinson,
Bangor, $100.

mills on a dollar, and the state tax of two mills, voted to be
amounting to $7,284·25.

1816. The board audited the following accounts:

Dickinson,	$828·65	Bangor,	$640·65
Constable,	704·16	Malone,	743·16
Chateaugay,	722·10		

County expenses, $2,143·39

The sum of $3,300 levied to defray contingent charges. Of this, $400 applied for building a stone bridge in Malone village. The sum of $500 heretofore granted for this purpose, to be paid on the order of the board of supervisors.

1817. The board audited the following accounts:

Dickinson,	$745·18	Bangor,	$962·27¼
Malone,	776·82	Chateaugay,	620·20
Fort Covington,	684·83	Constable,	715·71

County charges, $2,345·19

" *Resolved*, That the board of supervisors has doubts respecting the legality of allowing bounties on squirrels, birds, &c., or any other noxious animals, except those particularly mentioned in the statute. Therefore, resolved, that this board think it improper to allow any bounties on the same hereafter, and that the supervisors' clerk be directed to notify each town in said county of this resolution."

$25 to be paid for each certificate of the killing of any full grown panther, and for a panther whelp, half this sum.

1818. The board audited the following accounts:

Bangor,	$712·15	Dickinson,	$512·52
Malone,	728·46	Fort Covington,	681·25
Chateaugay,	717·95	Constable,	725·96

County charges, $2,064·27

1819. The board audited the following accounts:

Fort Covington,	$548·67	Malone,	$1,068·64
Dickinson,	851·48	Constable,	689·23¼
Chateaugay,	752·90	Bangor,	671·87

Resolved, that the sum of $500 be raised for the purpose of building a fire-proof clerk's office. Benjamin Clark, Cone Andrus, and John L. Fuller, appointed a building committee.

1820. The board audited the following accounts:

Malone,	$656·72	Fort Covington,	$579·96
Constable,	770·00	Bangor,	902·21
Chateaugay,	1,801·62	Dickinson,	856·93

County accounts, $1,720·51

$218 voted to complete the fire-proof clerk's office.

1821. The board audited the following accounts:

Dickinson,	$1,073·90	Bangor,	$1,173·15
Malone,	3,226·99	Constable,	973·71
Fort Covington,	669·73	Chateaugay,	9,350·89

Total amount of county charges, including the enormous bounty allowed on wolves, $12,038·49.

On motion, resolved, that the treasurer be directed to pay to each of the persons or owners mentioned in the preceding schedule, the sums above allowed as charges against the county of Franklin, out of any moneys in the treasury not otherwise appropriated.

The sum of $28,794·04 voted to defray the expenses of the ensuing year, apportioned among the several towns as follows:

Dickinson,	$3,194·22	Constable,	$2,155·81
Fort Covington,	2,031·93	Bangor,	3,271·65
Chateaugay,	11,783·94	Malone,	6,356·49

On motion, resolved, that a bounty of twenty dollars be paid by the county of Franklin, on each full grown wolf in said county, and seven dollars and fifty cents on each wolf's whelp, the ensuing year.

Resolved, that a bounty of twenty-five dollars for each grown panther, and ten dollars for each panther kit, killed in the county of Franklin the ensuing year, be paid by the county out of any moneys not otherwise appropriated.

1822. The board proceeded to audit the following accounts:

Fort Covington,	$738·62	Chateaugay,	$3,687·98
Constable,	600·72	Dickinson,	738·95
Bangor,	5,811·42	Malone,	737·71

County charges amounted to $9,130·02

$100 voted for the agricultural society.

$500 voted for the military road.

1823. The board audited the following accounts:

Dickinson,	$662·70	Bangor,	$547·92
Fort Covington,	646·81	Chateaugay,	605·72
Constable,	523·23	Malone,	931·62

Amount of county charges, $1,887·65

$100 voted for the agricultural society.

$125 voted for a bell for the court house, to be purchased by the sheriff, on condition that $75 be first raised by voluntary subscription among the inhabitants for this purpose.

The sum of $4,000 voted to defray the state tax, county expenses the last year, and the necessary contingent expenses of the county.

1824. The board proceeded to audit the following accounts:

Constable,	$503·57	Dickinson,	$664·94
Bangor,	467·22	Malone,	678·63
Chateaugay,	583·51	Fort Covington,	665·75

County charges, $1,148·67

1825. The following accounts were audited:

Fort Covington,	$649·27	Malone,	$916·18
Bangor,	491·64	Constable,	529·32
Chateaugay,	561·88	Dickinson,	712·66

1826. The following accounts were audited.

Malone,	$915·96	Chateaugay,	$725·69
Bangór,	822·75	Fort Covington,	820·12
Dickinson,	736·92	Constable,	215·89

County charges, $1,996·68.

1827. The following accounts audited.

Constable,	$609·63	Malone,	$805·91
Dickinson	696·01	Chateaugay,	681·52
Fort Covington,	795 69	Bangor,	613·62

County charges, $1,777·12.

1828. The following accounts audited.

Chateaugay,	$573·87	Malone,	$700·17
Constable,	679·40	Bangor,	491·19
Fort Covington,	704·54	Dickinson,	589·43
Moira,	309·42	Brandon,	860·18
Duane,	296·75		

County charges audited, $2,256·47.

Voted that the treasurer be directed to pay only half of the poor moneys, and none of the wolf bounties, until he has returns from the comptroller.

1829. The board audited the following accounts:

Constable,	$353 66	Dickinson,	$521·96
Chateaugay,	652·12	Brandon.	438·20
Duane,	307·75	Malone	549·16
Westville	347·55	Bangor	463·26
Fort Covington,	1,125·93	Moira,	353·92

County charges, $2491·54.

A special session was held in February, 1830, at which it was resolved that five superintendents of the poor be elected, viz:

Jabez Parkhurst of Fort Covington,	Gideon Collins of Chateaugay,
Benjamin Clark, of Malone,	and
Freeman Bell, of Constable,	Orrin Lawrence of Moira.

These superintendents were directed to rent a tenement and lands not exceeding fifty acres, and cause the poor of the county to be maintained therein.

A special meeting held June 8th, 1830, for the purpose of taking into consideration the propriety of repairing the military road, and for appointing three commissioners for superintending the laying out of the same, agreable to an act of the legislature passed April 16, 1830.

It was resolved as the sense of the board, that a sufficient sum be raised, to make a road from the east line of Malone to the house of Plyna C. Daggett, in Chateaugay, and Joseph H. Jackson, Obediah T.

, and Jacob Smith, were appointed commissioners

The following accounts were audited:

Bangor,	$557·37	Duane,	$394·69
Brandon,	449·69	Fort Covington,	1194·68
Chateaugay,	1135·42	Malone,	1008·64
Constable,	449·07	Moira,	449·99
Dickinson,	565·84	Westville,	328·01

ved that the distinction between town and county poor in the of Franklin, be abolished.

County accounts audited, $2326·71.

To support poor house the ensuing year,	$1785·54
bridge money, " " "	1000·00
To defray the contingent expenses of towns, during the ensuing year,	2087·75

ved, that $7200 be raised to defray the contingent expenses of he ensuing year.

The following accounts were audited:

Bangor,	$557·21	Duane,	$364·48
Brandon,	469·68	Fort Covington,	1013·75
Chateaugay,	1249·85	Malone,	1133·95
Constable,	288·02	Westville,	342·51
Dickinson,	564·68	Moira,	354·40

nt of county charges, including $1500 for the support of the d $1000 for bridges, with the expense of courts &c., for the year, $5685·88.

voted on the towns of Chateaugay and Malone, for the purpose leting the road for which commissioners were appointed at a meeting.

that three superintendents of the poor be appointed. They horized to purchase some suitable place for the accommodation oor, and $2000 to be raised in five annual installments, for this $500 voted for the support of the poor.

The following accounts audited:

Bangor,	$538·78	Duane,	$374·68
Brandon,	430·33	Fort Covington,	856·00
Chateaugay,	1115·85	Malone,	810·76
Constable,	292·04	Moira,	417·35
Dickinson,	470·68	Westville,	353·41

Amount of county charges, $5496·62.

Accounts audited at this session.

Bangor,	$619·52	Duane,	$373·02
Brandon,	450·70	Fort Covington,	490·66
	471·79	Malone,	707·79

Chateaugay,	928·20	Moira,	379·00
Constable,	343·79	Westville,	485·62
Dickinson,	498·00		

County charges, $6,418·73.

The above, included $2500 for the support of the poor. $1,000 for bridges. $962·21 for courts, &c.

The sum of $2500 voted for the support of the poor the ensuing year.

1834. The following accounts audited:

Bangor,	$544·39	Duane,	$341·41
Bellmont,	755·93	Fort Covington,	528·09
Bombay,	441·95	Malone,	723·85
Brandon,	449·98	Moira,	392·33
Chateaugay,	799·39	Westville,	346·50
Constable,	311·80	County charges,	5690·76
Dickinson,	449·47		

A similar sum for the support of the poor, and for roads and bridges, as on the previous year.

1835. The following accounts audited:

Bangor,	$618·84	Dickinson,	$489·34
Bellmont,	765·76	Duane,	351·28
Bombay,	636·07	Fort Covington,	491·29
Brandon,	428·75	Malone,	701·31
Chateaugay,	758·22	Moira,	407·26
Constable,	316·16	Westville,	370·89

County charges, $6035·48.

The customary vote of $1000 for bridges, &c., passed.

1836. At a special meeting held August 25, 1836, it was resolved that an additional bounty of $10 be raised for the destruction of wolves, and $5 for that of wolf whelps.

1836. At the annual session the following accounts audited:

Bangor,	$591·29	Franklin,	$339·40
Bellmont,	654·63	Dickinson,	539·30
Bombay,	559·34	Duane,	339·30
Brandon,	469·58	Fort Covington,	580·39
Chateaugay,	991·64	Malone,	1,365·77
Constable,	320·87	Moira,	913·56
Westville,	434·84		

County charges, $6,213·62

$1,000 voted for bridges, $1,500 for the poor.

1837. The following accounts audited:

Bangor,	$559·95	Duane,	$319·66
Bellmont,	681·75	Fort Covington,	613·42
Bombay,	589·08	Franklin,	626·63
Brandon,	512·17	Malone,	1,358·89
Chateaugay,	724·29	Moira,	470·00

Constable,	298·74	Westville,	320·54
Dickinson,	468·58		

County charges, $7,013·75

1838. Accounts audited by the board:

Bangor,	$710·20	Duane,	$359·62
Bellmont,	498·25	Fort Covington,	637·03
Bombay,	536·00	Franklin,	642·77
Brandon,	553·55	Malone,	1,614·59
Chateaugay,	1,208·72	Moria,	368·42
Constable,	512·93	Westville,	· 494·06
Dickinson,	596·27		

County charges, $6,122·61

$2,500 voted for the support of the poor; $500 to repair the poor house.

The superintendents empowered to purchase, if thought advisable, a tract of land adjoining the poor house.

$300 of the sum above, voted for repairs of poor house to be applied for the support of the poor.

1839. The following accounts audited:

Bangor,	$697·85	Duane,	$359·48
Bellmont,	756·59	Fort Covington,	871·63
Bombay,	504·68	Franklin,	719·18
Brandon,	418·86	Malone,	1,392·21
Chateaugay,	748·49	Moria,	587·51
Constable,	554·88	Westville,	521·57
Dickinson,	635·45		

County charges, $8000·75

1840. The following accounts were audited:

Bangor,	$673·01	Duane,	$386·34
Bellmont,	1,035·27	Fort Covington,	623·01
Bombay,	734·30	Franklin,	446·96
Brandon,	583·29	Malone,	1,137·50
Chateaugay,	694·70	Moira,	615·62
Constable,	274·23	Westville,	457·58
Dickinson,	621·44		

County charges, $5,025·00

$2,500 voted for the support of the poor.

1841. The following accounts were audited:

Bangor,	$707·26	Fort Covington,	$569·74
Bellmont,	919·91	Harrietstown,	328·98
Bombay,	612·49	Malone,	1,173·19
Brandon,	577·97	Moira,	498·88
Chateaugay,	827·00	Westville,	449·93
Constable,	545·31	Franklin,	738·21
Dickinson,	598·83	Duane,	360·75

County charges, $6,179·85

$2,500 voted for the support of the poor.

$3,679 voted to defray the expense of courts, repairing court house, and other contingent expenses.

1842. The following accounts were audited:

Bangor,	$486·35	Fort Covington,	$732·45
Bellmont,	1,029·28	Franklin,	516·45
Bombay,	740·88	Harrietstown,	362·54
Brandon,	338·02	Malone,	964·15
Chateaugay,	1,133·62	Moira,	373·95
Constable,	512·20	Westville,	380·41
Dickinson,	652·09	Duane,	397·69
	County Charges, $6,410·00		

Resolved, That it is the opinion of this board, that all those who have demands against the county, ought not to demand any better currency than the current money of Lower Canada.

A petition of the board was forwarded praying the legislature to appropriate a part of the tolls of the military road, for the construction of a bridge in Chateaugay.

1843. The following accounts were audited:

Bangor,	$742·10	Constable,	$354·67
Bellmont,	567·73	Dickinson,	698·02
Bombay,	759·21	Duane,	335·08
Brandon,	492·87	Fort Covington,	724·85
Chateaugay,	1,078·55	Franklin,	484·96
Harrietstown,	613·96	Moira,	453·30
Malone,	1,167·35	Westville,	322·28
	County charges, $7,092·51		

The vote concerning Canada money again passed.

1844. The board proceeded to audit the following accounts.

Bangor,	$739·28	F Burke,	551·42
Bellmont,	782·49	Fort Covington,	$879·45
Bombay,	495·19	Franklin,	464·03
Brandon,	381·60	Harrietstown,	247·39
Chateaugay,	679·99	Malone,	1143·21
Constable,	357·78	Moira,	410·53
Dickinson,	705·69	Westville,	605·30
Duane,	458·58		
	County Charges, $8,056·11		

Resolution concerning Canada currency, renewed.

A special session was held, June 16, 1845, in consequence of the loss of the poor house building by fire.

The board proceeded to consider the expediency of abolishing the poor house system, and a committee of six was appointed to collect information on the subject.

Without any formal report from the above committee, it was resolved, that the superintendents of the poor be required to erect a good and substantial barn, on the poor house farm, and subsequently authorized the erection of a poor house of the same size, and on the same site of the former one.

The board resolved to petition the legislature at its next session to abolish the existing poor house system in the county.

1845. The board audited the following as town accounts.

Bangor,	$751,35	Duane,	360·34
Bellmont	517,89	Fort Covington,	915·96
Bombay,	747,85	Franklin,	429·17
Brandon,	309,95	Harrietstown,	373·27
Burke,	594,54	Malone,	1041·87
Chateaugay,	619,72	Moira,	467·70
Constable,	373,13	Westville,	621·36
Dickinson,	$40·426		

County accounts, $7 560·29.

In addition to the above, the board audited separate accounts against the several towns of sums varying from about $25 to $60.

Votes in relation to Canada currency again passed. The board voted to petition for the abolition of the distinction between the town and county poor.

1846. The following accounts were audited by the several town boards.

Bangor,	$665·99	Duane,	$337·24
Bellmont,	609·97	Fort Covington,	611·38
Bombay,	700·90	Franklin,	442·29
Brandon,	517·03	Harrietstown,	369·09
Burke,	594·06	Malone,	1112·04
Chateaugay,	528·32	Moira,	465·11
Constable,	560·33	Westville,	534 28
Dickinson,	435·39		

County charges, $5401·04

At an extra session held May 25, for the purpose of fixing the salary of the county judge, it was established at $600.

1847. The following accounts were audited by the several town boards.

Bangor,	$651·36	Duane,	$276·37
Bellmont,	531·52	Fort Covington,	838·52
Bombay,	678·91	Franklin,	494·50
Brandon,	414·03	Harrietstown,	352·04
Burke,	490·39	Malone,	1030·64
Chateaugay,	514·60	Moira,	459·43
Constable,	639·11	Westville,	602·99
Dickinson,	533·24		

County charges, $5,676·49.

Voted in favor of abolishing the office of superintendent of common schools.

1848. The following accounts were audited by the several town boards.

Bangor,	$702·87	Duane,	$396·76
Bellmont,	525·88	Fort Covington,	905·47

Bombay,	807·35	Franklin,	497·66
Brandon,	430·75	Harrietstown,	362·08
Burke,	393·00	Malone,	1379·29
Chateaugay,	592·93	Moira,	457·01
Constable,	592·66	Westville,	683·61
Dickinson,	554.60		

County charges $5465·74

1849. The following accounts were audited by the several town boards.

Bangor,	$691.93	Duane,	$178·66
Bellmont,	493·32	Fort Covington,	971·88
Bombay,	787·25	Franklin,	508·16
Burke,	568.66	Harrietstown,	353·25
Brandon,	445·03	Malone.	1363·93
Chateaugay,	530·90	Moira,	583·27
Constable,	458·27	Westville,	680·61
Dickinson,	608.61		

County charges $7988·77

$400 levied upon the town of Moira, for the purpose of erecting a town house. The sum to be divided between two years.

The board at this session passed the following laws :

" An act for the preservation of deer and fish." This law provides that a penalty of $5, should be required for the killing of any wild buck, doe, or fawn, at any time during the months of January, February, March, April, May, June or July.

The fact of exposing for sale any green deerskin or fresh venison, or having the same in his possession, during the above months, was to be deemed a violation of this law, unless the person having the same in his possesion, should be able to prove that the animals to which they belonged, were killed by some other person. Complaint is to be made to a justice of the peace, who may issue a warrant for search for fresh venison, or deerskins,

No person was allowed to kill any wild buck, doe or fawn, in the town of Duane, during three years from January 1, 1850.

No person allowed to·kill the above animals in Franklin, Dickinson, Brandon or Harrietstown, except in September, October and November.

Hunting any wild buck, doe or fawn, at any time with dogs or hounds, forbidden.

The taking of fish of any description, at any time with a seine or net in any lake or pond in the county of Franklin, in the south of townships Nos. 5 and 7, of Macomb's purchase, great lot number 1, and of township number 7, of the old military tract, or in any streams coming into or connecting said ponds or lakes, was forbidden under a penalty of $5. The same penalty for setting any trap, or spear for deer at any time.

The above penalties were to be prosecuted and recovered by the overseers of the poor of the town where the offence may be committed, and an action to be valid must be commenced within three months from the commission of the offence. This act took effect January 1, 1850.

The board passed an act, November 20, 1849, providing for a bounty of $15 to be paid for the destruction of wolves, and half that sum for wolf whelps, and $5 for every panther.

One half of all bounties for the destruction of noxious animals, is to be charged to the treasurer of the state. The usual precautions were to be observed by persons granting these certificates, that certificates be granted to none but those entitled to receive them, according to the true intent and meaning of the act.

1850. The following accounts were audited by the several town boards:

Bangor,	$471·65	Duane,	$364·99
Bellmont,	446·80	Fort Covington	741·13
Bombay,	637·91	Franklin	299 40
Brandon,	219·09	Harrietstown,	344·51
Burke,	631·64	Malone,	1,172·15
Chateaugay,	668·02	Moira,	580 89
Constable,	409·24	Westville,	476·13
Dickinson,	584·89		

County charges, $9,505·13

The member of assembly from this county, requested by the board to use his influence to procure the repeal of the act providing for the registration of births, deaths and marriages, and of the present militia system.

$500 appropriated for the erection of a new clerk's office, and William Andrus and Joseph R. Flanders, appointed a committee for superintending the building of the same.

1851. The following accounts were audited by the several town boards:

Bangor	$341·26	Duane,	$275·73
Bellmont,	416·52	Fort Covington,	447·16
Bombay,	455·63	Franklin,	589·63
Brandon,	329·06	Harrietstown,	428·55
Burke,	489·69	Malone,	613·22
Chateaugay,	450·31	Moira,	435·53
Constable,	448·37	Westville,	449·21
Dickinson,	475·32		

County charges, $7,713·55

Included in the above, was $1,949·23 for school fund, $1,500 for the poor, $1,700 for contingencies, $100 for the deaf, dumb and blind, and $600 for a clerk's office.

Resolved, That the board will not make any assessment under the military act, during this session.

$1,500 raised for the poor.

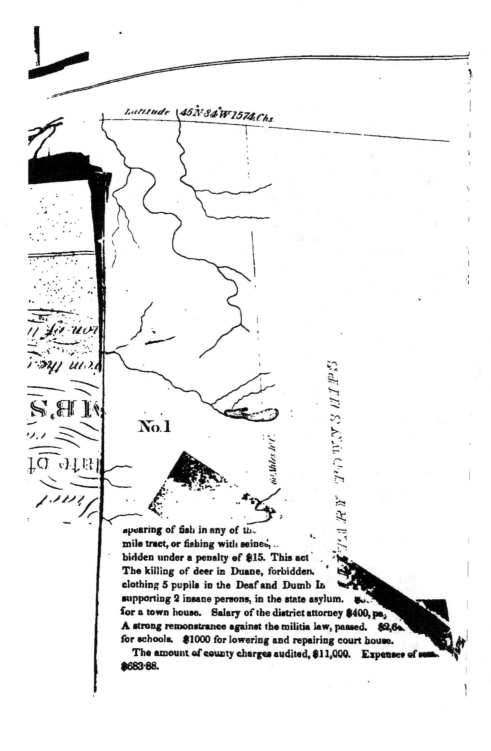

Latitude 45°N 84°W 1574 Chs.

No. 1

...pearing of fish in any of th...
mile tract, or fishing with seines, ...
bidden under a penalty of $15. This act
The killing of deer in Duane, forbidden.
clothing 5 pupils in the Deaf and Dumb In
supporting 2 insane persons, in the state asylum. ...
for a town house. Salary of the district attorney $400, pa...
A strong remonstrance against the militia law, passed. $2,6...
for schools. $1000 for lowering and repairing court house.

The amount of county charges audited, $11,000. Expenses of ...
$683·88.

Stephen Crossfield and others, from the Mohawk and Canajoharie tribes of Indians, at Johnson's Hall, in Tryon county, in the month of July, 1773. It was described as lying on the west side of Hudson river, and contained by estimation about 800,000 acres of land.[*]

This is believed to have been subsequently confirmed by a Royal grant.

The surveyors employed in running out the tract, found it a ragged and inhospitable wilderness, and the further north they went the worse they found it, from which it was inferred that the whole northern country was of the same character.[†]

In a map of Canada and the north part of Louisiana, in Jeffery's French Dominions in America, the country north of this tract, is described as the "*deer hunting grounds of the Iroquois*. Map No. 74, in Delisle's Atlas of 1785, (state library,) names it and the north of Vermont "*Irocoisia*," or the land of the Iroquois, and in an old map, republished in the 4th volume of the Documentary History of the state, it is called, *Coughsagrage*, or the beaver hunting country of the Six Nations. Across our two counties is written the following sentence :

"Through this tract of Land, runs a Chain of Mountains, which from Lake Champlain on one side, and the River St. Lawrence on the other side, shew their tops always white with snow, but altho this one unfavorable circumstance, has hitherto secured it from the claws of the Harpy Land Jobbers, yet no doubt it is as fertile as the Land on the East side of the Lake, and will in future furnish a comfortable retreat for many Industrious Families.

A desire to promote the settlement of the state, led the legislature to take early measures for bringing into market the unpatented lands.

An act was passed, May 5, 1786, entitled "an act for the speedy sale of the unappropriated lands of the state," creating land commissioners, and empowering them to dispose of such unsold lands as they might see proper, within the limits of the state. The outlines of the tracts were first to be run into townships of 64,000 acres, as nearly square as circumstances would permit. Each township was to be subdivided into mile square lots, to be numbered in arithmetical progression, from first to last, and on every fourth township was to be written, "*to be sold by single lots.*" The maps so numbered and lotted, were to be filed in the secretary's office, and the original thereof in the surveyor general's office ;

"And the said secretary and surveyor general respectively, shall cause maps so to be filed, to be put up in some conspicuous part of their respective offices, and shall permit any person whatever, freely to inspect such maps, between the hours of nine and twelve in the morning, and three and six in the afternoon in every day, Sundays only excepted, on

---

* See MSS., Council Minutes, vol. 31, p 31.

† On the authority of Henry E. Pierrepont, Esq., of Brooklyn.

paying for inspecting in morning six-pence, and the like in the afternoon.

Advertisement for the sale of these lands at public vendué, was to be duly given. The surveyor general was to put up as nearly as might be, one quarter part of the unappropriated and unreserved lands in every township, in lots contiguous to each other, and sell them to the highest bidder; reserving five acres out of every hundred for roads, but not selling any land for a less price than one shilling an acre.

The first, and every fourth township, was to be sold in single lots. One fourth of the purchase money was to be paid down, and the remainder was due within sixty days.

In every township the surveyor general was directed to mark one lot "*gospel and schools*," and another "*for promoting literature*," which lots were to be as nearly central as may be. The former was reserved for the support of the gospel and schools in the town, but the latter was reserved for promoting literature within the state.

The land commissioners were directed to designate each township which they might lay out, by such name as they might deem proper, and such name was to be respectively mentioned in the letters patent, for granting a township or part of a township.

It was made a condition that there should be an actual settlement made for every six hundred and forty acres, which may be granted to any person or persons, within seven years from the first day of January next, after the date of the patent by which such lands shall be granted; in failure of which the lands would revert to the people of the state.

Accordingly, in pursuance of powers vested in them, the board above created, on the 25th of May, 1787, passed the following resolution:

" *Resolved*, That the surveyor general be, and he is hereby required and directed, to lay down, on a map, two ranges of townships for sale, each township to contain as nearly as may be 64,000 acres, and as nearly in a square as local circumstances will permit, and to subdivide each township into lots, as nearly square as may be, and each lot to contain 640 acres, as nearly as may be.

That each range contain five townships adjoining each other, and one of the said ranges to be bounded on the River St. Lawrence, and the said ten townships to be laid out within the following limits and bounds, to wit:

Between a line to be run S. 28° E., from a point or place on the southern bank of the River St. Lawrence, bearing S. 28° E. from the N. W. end of the Isle áu Long Saut, and a line parallel with the said first line, and also to run from the south bank of the said river, and the said parallel lines to be distant fifty miles from each other, and that the said surveyor general advertise the said townships, and proceed to the sale thereof, agreeable to law, and that two of the said townships be sold in single lots."

(Land Office Minutes, vol. i, p. 256.)

The value of this tract was then but little known, and of the position and courses of lakes and streams, there was scarcely more knowledge than we now possess of Central Africa. The shores of the river were well known, and served as a guide in the laying out of the ten towns.

Accordingly, in pursuance of the statute, the following advertisement appeared in the papers. We copy from the *Albany Gazette* of June 7, 1787:

By virtue of an act of the Legislature entitled 'An act for the speedy sale of the unappropriated lands within this state, and for other purposes therein mentioned,' passed the 5th of May, 1786, and pursuant to a resolution of the Honorable the Commissioners of the Land Office:—

TEN TOWNSHIPS OF UNAPPROPRIATED LANDS,

On the southeast side of the RIVER ST. LAWRENCE, will be sold at Public Vendue, at the Coffee House in the City of NEW YORK. The sale to commence on TUESDAY, the 10th of JULY next, at XI o'clock, in the forenoon. Maps are filed for inspection in the offices of the Secretary of the State, and Surveyor General.

The fourth and eighth Townships, will be sold by single Lots, the rest by Quarters of Townships.

Such securities as are made receivable by law on the sales of forfeited lands, will be received in payment. The one Quarter of the Purchase Money on the day of sale, and the remainder within sixty days after.

SIMEON DEWITT,
June, 1787.   *Surveyor General.*

The names of the ten townships were established by a formal resolution of the commissioners of the land office, Sept. 10, 1787,* and with their corresponding numbers were as follows:

1. LOUISVILLE.	6. CANTON.
2. STOCKHOLM.	7. DEKALB.
3. POTSDAM.	8. OSWEGATCHIE.
4. MADRID.	9. HAGUE.
5. LISBON.	10. CAMBRAY.

They have been known by these names exclusively, and not by their numbers. All but the last two, are still retained. No. 9 was changed to Morristown, and No. 10 to Gouverneur. Three new towns have since been formed of these, viz: Macomb, from Gouverneur and Morristown; Depeyster, from Dekalb and Oswegatchie; and Norfolk, from Stockholm and Louisville.

A part of Hague has also been attached to Hammond, and of Dekalb to Hermon.

In accordance with the law, and previous advertisement, an auction sale took place at the Merchant's Coffee-house, in the city of New York, at the time advertised, at which the ten towns were offered for sale, in

---

* Land Office Minutes, vol, i, p. 296. Secretary's office.

quarters, except Oswegatchie and Madrid, which were sold in mile squares.

The obvious intention of the law in causing these lands to be offered in small parcels, was to afford an opportunity for those of limited means to compete at the sales; but this intention was defeated by a previous agreement, it is said, among the purchasers, in which they delegated one of their number to bid, and agreed to not compete in the sale.

The principal purchaser was Alexander Macomb, who subsequently acted a distinguished part in the northern land purchases.

Mr. Macomb had, for many years, resided in Detroit, and is said to have been a fur trader.

In the course of his business, he had often passed up and down the St. Lawrence, and thus became acquainted with the general aspect and probable value of the lands, and better qualified to engage in these purchases, than most of his associates.

To cover the private agreement, certain persons were employed to bid for Macomb, and the lots so sold were subsequently conveyed to him before patenting. In this manner, lots Nos. 11, 13, 14, 16, 17, 18, 20 and 21, in Madrid, were bid off by Michael Connoly; lots Nos. 47, 56 and 57, in the same town, by John Meyers; lots Nos. 48 and 49, in the same town, by Daniel McCormick; lots Nos. 18 and 19, in Oswegatchie, by John Meyers; and lot No. 23, in the same, by Thomas McFarren, and afterward made over to Macomb.[*]

The ten townships were sold as follows, to the original patentees, lots Nos. 55, 56 were not included in the first patents, but were sold long after.

Reference is made to the volume and page of patents, in the office of the secretary of state, where they are recorded. The quarters were numbered as follows: No. 1, the northeast; No. 2, the southeast; No. 3, the southwest; and No. 4, the northwest quarters. The gospel and school lot (No. 55), usually came out of No. 3, and the literature lot (No. 56), out of No. 2. As these towns were designated to be each ten miles square, the full quarters (1 and 4) would contain 16,000 acres, and the smaller quarters (2 and 3) 15,360 acres.

It may be proper here to notice, that the reserve for roads has seldom or never been regarded by subsequent purchasers, or made a condition in their deeds. The reserves of gold and silver mines, have, of course, proved superfluous.

1. *Louisville*, patented in quarters, to Alexander Macomb, on the 17th of December, 1787 (b. 20, p. 64).

[*] Land Office Minutes, vol. II, p. 4.

The literature lot was patented to Erastus Hall, January 20, 1806 (b. 32, p. 10).

A tier of lots numbered from 1 to 12, along the St. Lawrence, sold June 4, 1788, to John Taylor (b. 20, p. 311, 322).

These contained 500 acres each.

2. *Stockholm* was patented in quarters, to Alexander Macomb, Dec. 17, 1787 (b. 20, p. 68 to 70).

The literature lot was sold to Henry Foster, September 25, 1829 (b. 32, p. 265).

3. *Potsdam* was patented in quarters, to Alexander Macomb, Dec. 17, 1787 (b. 50, p. 72, 75).

4. *Madrid* was sold in lots of 640 acres, or one mile square each, as follows:

1 to 6, to Jeremiah Van Rensselaer, June 4, 1788 (b. 20, p. 322).

7 to 49, to Alexander Macomb, but on different dates, viz:

7 to 10.	Dec. 17, 1787 (b. 20, p. 96-99).
11.	April 19, 1788 { " 267).
12.	Dec. 17, 1787 { " 100).
13—14.	April 19, 1788 { " 268-9).
15.	Dec. 17, 1787 { " 101).
16.	April 19, 1788 { " 270).
17—18.	" " { " 271-2).
19.	Dec. 17, 1787 { " 101).
20—21.	April 19, 1788 { " 273-4).
22 to 30.	Dec. 17, 1797 { " 104-112).
31 to 46.	Dec. 20, 1787 { " 112-127).
47 to 49.	April 19, 1787 { " 275-277).

51. Literature lot sold to Thomas Peacock, March 24, 1827 (b. 32, p. 226).

52 to 95, to Alexander Macomb, but at different times, as follows:

52 to 55.	Dec. 20, 1787 (b. 20, p. 128-131).
56—57.	April 19, 1788 { " 278-9).
58 to 86.	Dec. 20, 1787 { " 132-160).
87 to 95.	Dec. 22, 1787 { " 161-169).

The river lots of 500 acres each, numbered from 12 to 17, sold to John Taylor, June 4, 1788 (b. 20, p. 322).

6. *Canton*, was patented in quarters to Alexander Macomb, Dec. 17, 1787, (b. 20, p. 80, 83). The literature lot was conveyed to the trustees of Lowville Academy, Nov. 20, 1818 (b. 26, p. 678).

7. *Dekalb*, was patented in quarters to Macomb, Dec. 17, 1787, (b. 20, p. 84, 87). The gospel and school lot was subdivided and sold in small lots to individuals between 1829 and 1836.

The literature lot, was subdivided and sold in small parcels to individuals, between 1829 and 1834.

8. *Oswegatchie*, was patented in mile squares, as follows:

. 1 to   9, to Alexander Macomb, Dec. 22, 1787, (b. 20, p. 170, 175).
—   10, to Henry Remsen, Jun. Oct. 15, 1787, (b. 20, p. 55).
11 to   12, (the latter of 1160 acres) to John Taylor, June 4, 1788 (b. 20, p. 328).
—   13, to Henry Remsen, Jun., Oct. 15, 1787 (b. 20, p. 56).
      500 acres at the mouth of Oswegatchie river, to John Taylor, April 22, 1789, (b. 21, p. 178).
- 14 to   15, (1700 acres) to John Taylor, June 4, 1788)b. 20, p. 329). .
16 to   17, to Henry Remsen, Jun., Oct. 15, 1787 (b. 20, p. 54, 58).
18 to   53, to Alexander Macomb, Dec. 22, 1787 (b. 20, p. 180, 201).
     54,   "   "   Dec. 24, 1787 (b. 20, p. 210).
57 to 100,   "   "   Dec. 24, 1787 (b. 20, p. 211, 244).
      500 acres to John Taylor, April 22, 1789 (b. 21, p. 178).

9. *Hague*, was patented in quarters to Macomb, Dec. 17, 1787, (b. 20, p. 88, 91).

The greater part of the gospel and school lots of this town came in Black Lake.

10. *Cambray*, was patented in quarters to Alexander Macomb, Dec. 17, 1787 (b. 20, p. 92).

On the 4th of July, 1788, Jeremiah Van Rensselaer, conveyed to Macomb, for £275, lots No. 1 to 6, in Madrid, and 10 and 11, in Lisbon. (Sec's office. Deeds, b. 2, 4, p. 305.)

On the same date Taylor sold his lands to Macomb, containing 10,830 acres, for £580. These were lots No. 1 to 11 in Louisville, containing 5,500 acres; No. 12, in Madrid and Louisville, of 500 acres; No. 13 to 17, in Madrid, containing 2,500 acres; and No. 11 to 15, in Oswegatchie, containing 2,330 acres. (b. 24, p. 307.)

On the 5th of April, 1788, Henry Remsen, conveyed to Macomb, for £120, the four lots he had bid off in Oswegatchie.

Macomb thus became the nominal owner of nearly the whole of the ten towns.

On the 16th of April, 1791, he appointed Gouverneur Morris, then in France, his attorney, to sell any portions of the ten towns which he might deem proper, excepting a tract in Lisbon previously sold.[*]

So far as our information extends, no sales were made by virtue of this power.

By an instrument executed May 3, 1792, Macomb conveyed to Samuel Ogden, in trust for himself, Gen. Henry Knox, Robert Morris, and Gouverneur Morris, four of his associates, for the consideration of £3,200,

* See Deeds, b. 22, p. 148. Secretary's office.

the four townships of Hague, Cambray, Oswegatchie, and Dekalb, with the stipulation that Ogden should convey to H. Knox, 44,114 acres; to R. Morris, 60,641 acres, and to Gouverneur Morris, 60,641 acres of this tract.*

In 1792, Macomb became involved by transaction with Wm. Duer, Isaac Whippo, and others of New York,† by which he was compelled to assign his interest in a tract of land of 1920,000 acres, for the benefit of his creditors, to William Edgar and Daniel McCormick.

On the same date with the foregoing, be sold to Wm. Constable, for £1,500, the towns of Madrid, Potsdam, and the west half of Stockholm, and Louisville, and to William Edgar, for £12,000, the towns of Lisbon, and Canton, excepting a tract in the former, previously sold to John Tibbets. The towns of Potsdam and Canton, appear to have been at first included in this conveyance, which Edgar in an instrument dated Oct. 24, 1793,‡ acknowledged to have been a deed of trust, and obligated himself to reconvey the same to Macomb when required.

The failure of Macomb, was in some way connected with a bank which it was attempted to get established, as a rival of the Bank of New York, in 1792. He was very much blamed for the course he took in the matter, and on his failure, was lodged in the debtor's prison. It is said that even in this retreat he was assailed by a rabble, and owed his preservation only to the strength of the building.

At the time this embarrassment occurred, Macomb was largely indebted to Alexander Ellice, and others of London. To satisfy this debt, he had conveyed on the 6th of June, 1792, the towns of Lisbon, Canton, Madrid and Potsdam, with the west half of Lousville and Stockholm, but Ellice disclaimed this transfer, and quit claimed his title to the conveyance.

The following is a brief summary of the transfers of the several towns of the first purchases, so far as we have been able to obtain it.

Louivsille.—We have shown how Constable became the owner of the west half of this town.

James Constable, John McVickar, and Hezekiah B. Pierrepont, executors of Wm. Constable, on the 15th of Dec. 1803, conveyed 2854 acres in a square at the S. W. corner to Gouverneur Morris, excepting parts previously sold.§

G. Morris, Jun., received the above by will from his father, and this is called the *Morris Tract*, at the village of Norfolk. At one period it was

* Deeds. b. 24, p. 309, Sec'. Office.
† Recital in a conveyance of Oct. 10, 1793. Deeds, b. 24, p. 437. Sec'. Office.
‡ ib. b. 26, p. 42.
§ Clark's Office, Deeds, b. 2, p. 142.

owned by Leray, and a part was afterwards purchased by Russell Attwater.

The remainder of the west half of the town was conveyed by Wm. C. to Eweretta Constable, Jan. 3, 1803, * James McVickar and Eweretta, his wife, conveyed the above to Wm. Stewart, Dec. 4, 1807, who reconveyed it to McVickar, Dec. 5, 1807.† The latter, Aug. 16, 1816, deeded lots, 58, 59, 60, 68, 69, 70, 78, 79, 80, 88, 89, 90, to Henry McVickar, ‡ who by will conveyed it to Edward McVickar.

The remainder of the west half of Louisville became the property of the McVickar families. The southern half of No. 16, 17, and the whole of 26, 27, 36, 37, became the property of John Jay, who married a daughter of Wm. Constable. This is called the *Jay Tract*.

The east half of Louisville and Stockholm, were conveyed June 2, 1792, by Macomb to Wm. Edgar, Wm. Laight and John Lamb, in trust, to be divided as follows: To Edgar, 30,618 acres; to Laight, 111,27 acres; to Lamb, 22,255 acres.§

Edgar sold his share April 3, 1795, to Nicholas Low, John Delafield and Josiah Ogden Hoffman, for $30,618. The latter, July 15, 1797, sold 5,103 acres to Elkanah Watson.

To divide their lands, the proprietors entered into a contract in August 1798, with Amos Lay, to survey it, and subdivide the lots by three qualities. Macomb also agreed with him, for a similar survey of the west half.

The survey having been made, and a deficiency being found, this was proportionally divided among the several proprietors, and they drew by lot for their tracts, Feb. 18, 1799.

Mr. Lay received for his survey and maps of Louisville, the sum of $500, and a further sum of $70, for cutting a road through the town.

In a communication of E. Watson, to the proprietors, accompanying the survey, was the remark that a road from Louisville to St. Regis, was expected to be completed in May or June, 1799.

Our space will not admit of a further account of the title of this township.

STOCKHOLM.—The west half of this town was sold by Wm. Constable, to John Constable, Jan. 3, 1803,‖ and the latter conveyed the same to Hezekiah B. Pierrepont, Sept. 28, 1809.¶

This was a deed in trust, for P. to settle and sell the lands, to raise $45,000, to pay C. The lands remaining unsold, to be divided equally

* Clerk's Office, b. 1, p. 86.   § Deeds, b. 24, p. 280, Secy's Office.
† Clerk's Office, b. 1, p. 322, 323.   ‖ Clerk's Office, deeds, b. 1, p. 85.
‡ Clerk's Office, b. 4, p. 306.   ¶ Clerk's Office, b. 2, p. 390.

16

between them. By an agreement dated April 10, 1813,[*] C. withdraws the 4th quarter of the town, which agreement P. signs, P. conveys to D. Mc Cormick, the 3d quarter of town, April 14, 1813.[†] McC. conveys back the same April 15, 1813.

By a subsequent deed, John Constable, as heir of Wm. Constable, deceased, releases with the other heirs of Wm. C., all their interest to H. B. Pierrepont, This half of the town has mostly been settled under agents of Hezekiah B. Pierrepont, and his heirs. Henry E. Pierrepont, Esq., of Brooklyn, has at present the management of this estate, and of other extensive tracts, in Franklin, St. Lawrence, Jefferson, Lewis and Oswego counties, which form a part of the Macomb purchases.

Of the eastern half of this town we have been unable to obtain the chain of title. Edward W. Laight, Samuel Reynolds, Wm. Onderdonk, Richard Gouverneur, Nicholas Low and others, were concerned in the early transfers.

POTSDAM.—Macomb, by way of Edgar to Constable, as above. The latter by deed, dated Nov. 18, 1802,[‡] conveyed to Garret Van Horne, David M. Clarkson, and their associates, " as joint tenants, and not as tenants in common," the town except 2 miles wide, on the N. W. side. G. Van Horne conveyed the above by deed of trust, on the 9th of April, 1821,[§] excepting parts previously sold to Matthew Clarkson, to be conveyed to the following proprietors, in separate parcels, and by separate deeds, viz: *Levinus Clarkson, Hermon Le Ray, Nicholas Fish, John C. Clarkson, Garret Van Horne, Wm. Bayard*, the executors of *Jas. McEvers*, deceased, *Thos. S. Clarkson, Levinus Clarkson* and *G. Van Horne.*

On April 10, 1821, M. Clarkson, as such trustee, executes conveyances of separate lots and parts of lots, in said town, to said persons.

All subsequent titles in this town (except the 2 mile strip) have been derived from the foregoing proprietors.

The strip by the side of Madrid, was divided into two tracts, of which the western is called the *Ogden Tract*, and the eastern the *Le Roux Tract.* The latter was sold to Charles Le Roux, by Constable, April 30, 1802. Le Roux died in 1810, and in his will directed that this should be sold by his executors, (John Doughty, Charles L. Ogden and Thos. L. Ogden,) as expeditiously as found convenient.

These executors deeded it June 26, 1811,[‖] to David A., and Gouverneur Ogden, as joint tenants in fee simple. The latter by deed, Oct. 2, 1823,[¶] conveyed to Joshua Waddington and Thomas L. Ogden, who, Nov. 1, 1824,[**] conveyed to Waddington.

---

[*] Ib. b. 3, p. 488.
[†] Ib. b. 3, p. 490, 902.
[‡] Ib. b. 1, p. 46.
[§] Ib. b. 7, p. 51, 76

[‖] Clerk's Office, b. 3, p. 293, 6.
[¶] Clerk's Office, b. 7, p. 442, &c.
[**] Ib. b. 8, p. 17, &c.

We have not the title of the western tract.

MADRID.—Macomb to Edgar, Oct. 24, 1793, as above. Edgar, by a conveyance, dated June 12, 1794, sold to Wm. Constable, the towns of Madrid and Potsdam, for five shillings, N. Y. currency.*

Constable sold to Abraham Ogden, Josiah Ogden Hoffman, David A. Ogden and Thomas L. Ogden, this town, June 6, 1796, for $60,000.† This was further confirmed by a deed from Thomas Cooper, master in chancery, June 30, 1801, to John McVickar,‡ who by deed, dated July 10, 1801,§ conveyed to David A. and Thomas L. Ogden, as tenants in common. These brothers, April, 1803,‖ deeded an undivided third of the town, to Joshua Waddington.

On the 29th of June, 1811, these parties executed partition deeds of lands, previously contracted and mortgaged.¶

CANTON and LISBON.—Macomb to Edgar, as above. Edgar to Alexander von Pfister, by deed June 12, 1794, for five shillings. This was doubtless in trust. In this was excepted a tract of 9,600 acres, sold by Macomb to John Tibbets, of Troy, Nov. 20, 1789, for £960.**

Von Pfister conveyed, March 3, 1795, to Stephen Van Rensselaer, Josiah Ogden Hoffman, and Richard Harrison, for £5,068, 16s.†† This is said to have been conveyed to them in payment for money loaned. On the 21st of January, 1805, Hoffman, by deed, released to Van Rensselaer his interest in the two towns.

By an agreement between the parties, Harrison retained one-third of the eastern part of the tract (about 39,460 acres), and Van Rensselaer the remainder (78,932 acres).‡‡ Stephen Van Rensselaer,§§ by deed dated Sept. 13, 1836, conveyed all his estate in these towns to his son Henry Van Rensselaer,‖‖ in whom the title of unsold portions is still vested.

DE KALB.—Macomb to Ogden as above. The subsequent transfers we have not obtained. Wm. Cooper, of Cooperstown, subsequently purchased the town and commenced its first settlement. After his death it was divided up into a number of tracts, among his heirs.

OSWEGATCHIE was patented by 98 patents as above stated. Macomb to S. Ogden, May 3, 1792, with three other towns. Col. Ogden purchased the share of Robert Morris, as appears in a deed recorded in the secretary's office January, 1793, and conveyed to the others their shares

---

* Secy's Office, deeds, b. 26, p. 41.
† Ib. deeds, b. 28, p. 391.
‡ Clerk's Office, b. 1, p. 17.
§ Clerk's Office, b. 1, p. 20.
‖ Ib. b. 1, p 78.
¶ Ib. b. 3, p. 191.

** Clerk's Office, deeds, b. 3, p. 100.
†† Secretary's Office.
‡‡ Clerk's Office. b. 1, p. 111.
§§ See note D, in this work.
‖‖ Clerk's Office, deeds, b. 25, p. 496, &c.

in the townships of Hague and Cambray. On the 29th of Feb., 1808. S. Ogden conveyed by quit claim, this town to his son David B. Ogden.[*] On the 21st of January, 1847, the latter quit claimed to David C. Judson, Esq., of Ogdensburgh,[†] with whom are the original patents.

Nathan Ford and others purchased large tracts in this town. By a deed of Aug. 17, 1798, Ogden conveyed to Ford[‡] an undivided half of three certain tracts, one of which contained 10,000 acres, and lay south of land at the outlet of Black lake.

The lot of 500 acres, on which stands the village of Ogdensburgh, was sold by John Taylor, the patentee, June 13, 1789, to Alexander Macomb, for £25.[§]

HAGUE and CAMBRAY.—To S. Ogden as above; May 3, 1792, endorsed in a release from Robert Morris for his proportion, and an acknowledgment signed by Gen. Knox of the receipt of his conveyance, dated May 23, and June 26, 1792.

The portion of the above which came to the share of General Knox, lay along the west side of Hague and Cambray, extending from the river to the rear line, and was two miles, forty-six chains and twenty-one links wide. This is known among early purchases as the *Knox Tract*, conveyed May 23, 24, 1792.

It was supposed to contain 32,994 acres, but was afterwards found to embrace only 32,748 acres. To make up the deficiency of his 44,114 acres, lands in Oswegatchie were conveyed to Gen. Knox.

Henry Knox conveyed the above to *Benjamin Walker*, June 8, 1792, by warranty deed.

Walker, March 3, 1794, executed an agreement for the sale and exchange of lands with Samuel Ogden, including the Knox tract, for the consideration of $16,497. Deeded as promised Dec. 2, 1794. A strip three chains, forty-one links, bounded on the north-east corner of the 60,641 acre tract, was conveyed by *S. Ogden* to *David Ford*, May 27, 1800. Ford exchanged lands Sept. 19, 1808, with Morris, by which the former receives a tract on the east border of the town.

S. Ogden, March 4, 1795, conveys 20,000 to John Delafield, for £6,000. This tract lay near the west border of the town. Feb. 12, 1796, D. sold to J. O. Hoffman for $10, one-sixth of this 20,000 acre strip. This strip was subsequently owned by Messrs. Nicholas Low, John Delafield,[‖] and

---

[*] Clerk's Office, deeds, b. 2, p. 132.

[†] Ib., B. A. 39, p 676, &c.

[‡] Oneida Clerk's Office, book B., No. 7, of deeds, p. 49.

[§] Secretary's Office, deeds, b. 24, p. 308.

[‖] Delafield was a great operator in financial matters, but was ultimately unfortunate in his speculations. Seixas was a Jew, and lived in New-York.

—— Seixas, and the tract was still further divided by lines running from the St. Lawrence to the rear. Of these the first on the west was subsequently conveyed to Philip Kearney. It was 64 chains, 71 links wide, and embraced 10,000 acres. A portion of this adjoining the town of Rossie, was sold to Mr. Parish. The next strip, 42 chains, 75 links wide, was purchased by Nicholas Low. It embraced 6666⸱66 acres. A tract, 18 chains, 71 links wide, next east of this, embracing half the above number of acres, became the property of Nicholas Gouverneur. A strip 52 chains, 80 links wide, embracing 8,000 acres, was sold to Hoffman and Ogden; and about 5,000 acres, or a strip 26 chains, 52 links wide, constituting the remainder of the Knox tract, was conveyed to Col. Samuel Ogden. Adjoining the Knox tract, and embracing 20,000 acres, was sold by *Samuel Ogden* to *Wm. Constable*, for £1,000, Feb. 24, 1794. (*Sec'y office, b. mortgages* 36, *p.* 341, *&c.*)

Wm. Constable to *Gouverneur Morris*. Deed of the same 20,000 acre strip, November 17, 1798. (*Clerk's office, b. No.* 1, *p.* 39.) Gouverneur Morris acquired of Samuel Ogden, by purchase, a second tract, adjoining the last, embracing 60,641 acres, May 13, 1799. (*Clerk's office, b. No.* 2, *p.* 401.)

About 9,500 acres remained in these two towns, which *Samuel Ogden and Wife* conveyed to *David B. Ogden*, Feb. 29, 1808. (*Clerk's office, b. No.* 2, *p.* 132-3.)

David B. Ogden conveyed to *Gouverneur Morris*, July 1, 1808, all that was conveyed to him by Samuel Ogden. (*Clerk's office, b. No.* 2, *p.* 151.)

Gouverneur Morris's title was subsequently sold to Edwin Dodge, David C. Judson, Augustus Chapman, Abraham Cooper, and others, but our space will not allow us to give the details.

THE GOSPEL AND SCHOOL LOTS were located near the centre of the town, and were usually numbers 55 and 56. The former have since been sold by the authority of the legislature, who, on the 21st of April, 1825, passed an act authorizing the freeholders and inhabitants of the several towns, at their annual town meeting, to vote directing the whole of the income of the gospel and school lots, to be appropriated to the schools in town.

The money received for the sale of these lands, has in most or all cases been invested, and the interest arising therefrom applied for the annual expenses of schools.

The literature lot in Canton, was given to the Lowville academy in Lewis county, and that of Potsdam, to the St. Lawrence academy, in that town.

The literature lots of Stockholm, Louisville, Lisbon, Oswegatchie,

Hague, and Cambray, were sold by the surveyor general, in pursuance of an act of the legislature, in 1832, and the avails placed in the general literature fund of the state for the common benefit of the academies and colleges under the direction of the regents of the university.

By an act passed March 23, 1823, the literature lot in Madrid, was appropriated to Middlebury academy, in the county of Genesee, and to settle the boundaries, a law was passed on the 17th of March, 1824, by which the E., N. and W. bounds, as surveyed in 1797, were declared the bounds of the mile square, and the southern line so ran as to make 640 acres. Upon receiving a fee simple conveyance of this from the proprietors, the state released to them their claim to the remainder of the township.

By an act of March 4, 1830, the inhabitants of any of the towns of St. Lawrence county having gospel and school lots therein, were authorized to apply the rents and profits to the gospel and schools, or either, as the people assembled in town meeting might direct. The part applied to schools was to be paid to the school commissioners, and that to the gospel was to be distributed to the different Christian orders in the ratio of resident members in full communion with any regularly organized church. It is believed that in no instance were the funds applied to the latter use.

OLD MILITARY TRACT, IN CLINTON AND FRANKLIN COUNTIES.—By the same act under which the "ten townships" were sold, (passed May 5, 1786). a provision was made for the laying out of a tract of land to pay for military services, rendered by persons in the revolutionary war. It was as follows:

"And whereas, by the act entitled, 'An act to prevent grants or locations of the lands therein mentioned, passed the 25th day of July, 1782, a certain tract of land was set apart for the use of such of the inhabitants of this state, as had served in the army of the United States. And whereas from sundry circumstances, which have intervened since the passage of the said act, the lands intended to be granted, would be of little use to the inhabitants having so served; Therefore, *Be it enacted, by the authority aforesaid*, that the said commissioners shall be and are hereby authorized to direct the surveyor general to lay out the following tract of land, to wit: Beginning at a certain point, in the north bounds of Jessup's purchase, thirty miles distant from the north east corner of two certain tracts of land, granted to Philip Skeene, by letters patent, bearing date the sixth day of July, one thousand seven hundred and seventy-one, and running thence north, to the north bounds of the state; thence easterly along the same twenty miles, thence south to the north bounds of Jessup's purchase, aforesaid, continued easterly to the place of beginning. All which tract of land, shall on a map thereof, to be made by the surveyor general, be laid out into townships of the ten miles square, and each township shall on the said map be numbered, and the commissioners shall therefrom, from time to time, devise such regulations, for laying out lots, of such dimensions as they shall think proper, for satisfying out of the said tract of lands such claims of all such persons who are or shall be entitled to grants of lands, by virtue of the tenth, eleventh and fourteenth, clauses of the act, entitled 'An act for granting certain lands promised to be given as bounty lands by the laws of this state, and for other purposes therein mentioned, or such of them as are still unsatisfied, as to the said commissioners shall appear best calculated to enable the persons holding such rights, to participate as equally as may be in the advantages derived from locating the said lands, to which they shall be respectively entitled. Provided, That all persons claiming such rights, and who have not already exhibted their claims, shall exhibit their respective claims to the said commissioners, on or before the first day of January next, or shall be precluded from the same."

Four of the ten townships so set apart constitute the present towns of Burke, Chateaugay, Bellmont and Franklin, in Franklin county. The causes which led to this were as follows:

" The frontiers of New York, in 1779, being much exposed to hostile incursions of the Indian tribes, who were incited to this by the British, it became necessary to provide some efficient mode of defence, and the necessity of the state of New York's relying upon her internal resources, became greater, from the failure of the several states to furnish their respective quotas of troops, for the general defence. The state legislature, therefore, proceeded to adopt the measures requisite to bring into the field a force sufficient for their purpose, and passed a law, on the 20th of March, 1781, providing for the enlistment of two regiments for the defence of the frontiers. The troops thus raised, were to be armed, subsisted, and paid by the United States, and to continue in service three years, unless sooner discharged.

The faith of the state was pledged to the officers and privates of these regiments, that at the end of their enlistment, they or their heirs, should receive lands in proportion to their rank. Noncommissioned officers and privates, were to receive five hundred acres, and officers as follows:

A major general, 5,500 acres; brigadier general, 4,250 acres; colonel, 2,500; lieut. col. 2,250 acres; major, 2,000 acres; captain and surgeon of regiment, 1,500 acres each; chaplain, 2,000 acres; each subaltern and surgeon's mate 1,000 acres. The lands were required to be settled within three years after the close of the war, or they would become forfeited and revert to the state.

In the following year Col. Lamb's regiment of artillery was raised, with the same privileges and bounties as the other regiments. Congress also granted lands to these soldiers, which were located in the state of Ohio. By a subsequent agreement between the state of New York and the United States, any soldier relinquishing his claim to his one hundred acres in Ohio, should draw a full right of 600 acres in New York, but failing to relinquish his right by neglect or otherwise, the 100 acres, over the 500, should revert to the state. This gave origin to the term *States Hundred*, once so much used on the military tract.

A very large tract of land, in the central part of the state, was surveyed out, to satisfy these claims, and the townships into which it was divided, were named after the most illustrious military characters of antiquity.

In May, 1784, commissioners were appointed to settle these claims, consisting of the governor, lieutenant governor, the speaker of assembly, secretary of state, treasurer and auditor.

The Indian title to this tract was not then extinguished, was at the time, some doubt and uncertainty when this could b

Some of the claimants becoming clamorous, an act was pas legislature, as above stated, authorizing the commissioners b office, to lay out several townships, where the Indian title has tinguished to satisfy these claimants, and accordingly these located in the northern part of the state.

These lands were numbered from south to north, and b number of twelve each, containing one hundred square miles. 1, 2, 11, and 12, are in Essex county; numbers 3, 4, 5, and 6, county, and numbers 7, 8, 9, and 10, in Franklin county. Th these lands compared with those of western New York, becom to the speculators, who had bought up many of the soldier's final settlement of claims was deferred until the Indian ti center of the state were extinguished." [a]

By a resolution of the land commissioners, of June 10, 178 veyor general was directed to lay out the tract, as indicated in

This was accordingly done, but no part of the tract was ever g military claimants, being sold like the other lands by the comm

Townships number 6 and 7, the former now in Clinton, an in Franklin counties, were patented by the state to James C Albany, on the 25th of Feb. 1785, with the usual conditions of

On the 6th of March, 1785, Caldwell sold to Col. McGregor York, for £500, currency, the above townships

On the 19th of December, 1795, Col. McGregor sold to Jr William Bell, George Bowne, Joseph Pearsall, Henry Hayd Edmund Prior, merchants of New York, as tenants in comm different proportions, of the lands in townships 6 and 7. The to be divided into lots, for which the purchasers agreed to ball ing to their respective interest therein. The following is the lots, that fell to the share of each, so far as relates to number present towns of Chateaugay, Burke, and a small part of

Col. McGregor drew numbers, 1, 2, 6, to 12, 14, to 21, 23, to 35, 37, 38, 39, 41, 42, 44, 50, 53, 54, 56, to 59, 61, to 65, 68, 69, 78, to 81, 84, to 87, and 90.

John Lamb drew, 76, 71, 3, 13, 22, 55, 62, 77.

William Bell, drew No.'s 43, 32, 66, 20, 75, 36, 52, 60, 313 68

George Bowne drew 4, 73, and 33.

Joseph Pearsall, drew No.'s 34 and 40,

Henry Haydock, drew No. 88.

Edmund Prior, drew No. 5.

Thomas H. Brantingham, who owned a part of each of th ships drew lots number 51, 28 and 67, which were convey McGregor.

* See Clarke's History of Onondago for further facts.   † Land office Minutes, e

These lots subsequently passed through various hands, and townships number seven at present forms almost the entire settled portion of the military tract in Franklin county.

No. 8 was patented to Col. McGregor Feb. 25, 1795, who sold to several parties, and the latter divided* it by ballot, as follows:

William Bell, Nos. 3, 4, 5, 7, 13, 14, 18, 34, 35, 37, 38, 39, 40, 42, 87, 88, 93, 94, 99, 43, 71, 72, 20, 26, 28; in all 25 lots.

B. Swartwout, Nos. 2, 12, 16, 30, 53, 57, 66, 69, 78, 80, 92; in all 11 lots.

R. L. Bowne, Nos. 1, 2, 9, 33, 70, 90, 91, 96; in all 7 lots.

Leonard Gansevoort, Nos. 17, 21, 22, 45, 55, 56, 59, 60, 73, 79, 84; in all 11 lots.

Sir W. Poultney, Nos. 9, 15, 27, 41, 44, 46, 52, 58, 64, 68, 81, 82, 97, 98, 100; in all 15 lots. His first agent was Col. R. Troop, present agent Joseph Fellows, of Geneva.

Edmund Prior, Nos. 62, 67, 74, 86; in all 4 lots.

Wm. Rhodes, Nos. 36, 51, 54, 76, 85; in all 5 lots.

Wm. Haydock, Nos. 32, 47; in all 2 lots.

Barent Staats, 20 lots, which he sold to the following individuals:

P. Van Rensselaer, Nos. 48, 49, 50, 61, 63, 65, 75, 77, 83, 82, 95; in all 11 lots. P. Van Loon and J. P. Douw, Nos. 6, 8, 11; in all 3 lots. A Van Schaak, No. 25. J. Plush, Nos. 10, 23, 31; in all 3 lots. M. Gregory, No. 19. J. Benson and D. B. Slingerland, No. 24. A considerable number of the above lots have been sold for taxes, and many of the present owners hold their titles in this way from the state.

Township No. 9 was patented by the state as follows:

Lots Nos. 1 to 48, to Gerrit Smith, August 10, 1849; h. 34, p. 505 Lot No. 51, to Guy Meigs and Sam'l C. Wead, June 20, 1849; b. 36, p. 291. Lots No. 61 to 87, to Gerrit Smith, Aug. 10, 1849; b. 34, p. 505. Lots 91 to 113, also 116 to 126, also 129 to 180, also 182 to 201, also 202, and 205 to 215, 217 to 228, 231 to 270, 272, 275 to 287, 290 to 292, 295 to 304, 321 to 323, 325 to 329, 331, 334 to 342, 355 to 360, to the same, at the same date as the other purchases. Portions of the remainder have been sold to individuals, and a part is still owned by the state.

Township No. 10 was surveyed by J. Richards, in 1813, and sold in part to individuals, between 1827 and the present time. A large part was sold to Gerrit Smith, August 10, 1849, and some lots are still owned by the state.

MASSENA.—This town was mostly granted in small and separate patents, to Jeremiah Van Rensselaer and others. The first of these grants was made Oct. 23, 1788, adjoining the present reservation, and at the mile square. These tracts were designated by letters, and extended to the letter N.

* Secretary's office, patents, b. 23, p. 393.

Colonel Louis, the Indian chief to whom a tract in this town was conditionally granted, in 1789, did not receive a patent. He however drew lots Nos. 72 and 98, of 600 acres each, and 55, 11 and 34, of 500 acres each, in Junius, N. Y., for his military services.

MACOMB'S GREAT PURCHASE.—The legislature of the state of New York, at their session in 1791, in order to promote the settlement of their lands, passed a law authorizing the commissioners of the land office to dispose of any of the waste and unappropriated lands of the state, in such quantities, and on such terms, and in such manner, as they should judge most conducive to the interest of the public.

The extraordinary powers granted by this law, have been rightly pronounced, in the language of a report made not long since to the legislature, on another subject, " too great to be entrusted to mortal hands."

Governor Clinton, in his annual message of 1792, communicated a report of the land commissioners, in which they said, that they had during the year, sold 5,542,170 acres, in less than forty parcels, for £412,173 16s. 8d., and that they had endeavored to serve the public interests therein.

In a list of applications that had been received for the tract, was one from Macomb, in April, for all the vacant lands between Lake Champlain and the St. Lawrence, for 8d. per acre, in 6 years without interest, which was rejected, on account of its extent, " and because it contained lands joining old patents, and fronts too great a proportion of water communication."

On the 2d of May, he applied as before, and it was accepted, the quantity being reduced.

Wm. Henderson had applied for all the military land at 9d. per acre, which was rejected. Macomb had no competitors in his purchase.

This report being in order, Mr. Talbott, of Montgomery, moved a series of resolutions, in which, after enumerating the several acts which had been passed relative to the waste lands, and declaring that the spirit and design of these had been to afford to those of small means, the ability to purchase, and to prevent the accumulation of large landed estates in the hands of a few; he directly intimated that the commissioners had violated the trust reposed in them. It appeared a mystery to him, that this immense tract had been sold for 8d., while adjoining tracts had been sold to the Roosevelts for 3s. 1d.; to Adgate, for 2s; to Caldwell, McGregor, and Henderson, at 1s. 8d. per acre.

The sale without interest, and privilege of discount by paying down, was severely censured.

These resolutions were warmly discussed but not passed. They were evidently designed as the foundation for an impeachment, but failed in their purpose. Colonel Burr not having attended the meetings of the board, was not included in the charges, as he appears to have been absent on official business. The discussion continued till a late hour, when the house adjourned without decision, until the next day. On the 10th of April, 1792, Mr. Melancton Smith moved the following resolution with a preamble, as a substitute for those formerly offered:

"*Resolved*, That this house do highly approve of the conduct of the commissioners of the land office, in the judicious sales by them, as aforesaid, which have been productive of the before mentioned beneficial effects "

This resolution was adopted by a vote of 35 to 20. The following is a copy of the application of Macomb, which was received by the commissioners:

"At a meeting of the commissioners of the land office, of the state of New York, held at the City Hall, in the city of New York, on Wednesday, the 22d day of June, 1791.

Present—His Excellency George Clinton, Esquire, Governor; Lewis A. Scott, Esquire, Secretary; Gerard Bancker, Esquire, Treasurer; Peter T. Curtenius, Esq., Auditor.

The application of Alexander Macomb, for the purchase of the following tract of land, was read, and is in the following words, to wit:

' To the commissioners of the land office of the state of New York, *Gentlemen:*

I take the liberty of requesting to withdraw my application to your honourable board, of April last, and to substitute the following p oposal, for the purchase of the waste and unappropriated lands comprised within the bounds herein after mentioned, and all the islands belonging to this state, in front of said lands, viz: Beginning at the northwest corner of the township called Hague, on the river St. Lawrence, and thence extending southerly along the westerly bounds of the said township, and the township called Cambray, to the most southerly corner of the latter, thence extending easterly, northerly and southerly, along the lines of the said township of Cambray, and of the townships of De Kalb, Canton and Potsdam, and Stockholm, to the eastermost corner of the latter, thence northwesterly along the line of the said township of Stockholm, and the township of Louis Ville, to the river St. Lawrence, thence along the shore thereof to the line, run for the north line of this state, in the 45th degree of north latitude, thence east along the same to the west bounds of the tract formerly set apart as bounty lands for the troops of this state, serving in the army of the United States, thence southerly along the same, to the north bounds of the tract known by the name of Totten and Crossfield's purchase, thence westerly along the north bounds of the tract last mentioned, to the westermost corner thereof, thence southerly along the westerly bounds thereof, to the most westerly corner of township number five, in the said tract, thence westerly on a direct line to the northwestermost corner of the tracts granted to Oothoudt, thence westerly on a direct line to the mouth of Salmon river, where it empties itself, into lake Ontario, thence northeasterly along the shore of the said lake, and the river St. Lawrence, to the place beginning, including all the islands belonging to this state, fronting the said tract in lake Ontario and the river St. Lawrence, five per cent. to be deducted for highways, and all lakes whose area exceeds one thousand acres, to be also deducted, for which, after the above deductions, I will give eight pence per acre, to be paid in the following manner, to wit : One-sixth part of the purchase money at the end of one year from the day on which this proposal shall be accepted, and the residue in five equal annual instalments on the same day, in the five next succeeding years. The 1st payment to be secured by bond, to the satisfaction of your honorable board, and if paid on the time limited and new bonds to the satisfaction of the board executed for another sixth of the purchase money, then I shall be entitled to a patent for one-sixth part of said tract, to be set off in a square, in one of the corners thereof, and the same rule to be observed as to the payments and securities and grants or patents, until the contract shall be fully completed. But if at any time I shall think fit to anticipate the payments, in whole or in part, in that case I am to have a deduction on the sum so paid, of an interest at the rate of six per cent. per annum, for the time I shall have paid any such sum before the time herein before stipulated.

I have the honor to be, gentlemen,

with great respect, your most obedient servant,

ALEXANDER MACOMB.

New York, May 2d, 1791.

I do hereby consent and agree, that the islands called Caleton's or Buck's islands, in the entrance of lake Ontario, and the isle Au Long Saut, in the river St. Lawrence, and a tract equal to six miles square, in the vicinity of the village of St. Regis, be excepted out of the above contract, and to remain the property of the state : Provided always, That if the said tract shall not be hereafter applied for the use of the Indians of the said village, that then the same shall be considered as included in this contract, and that I shall be entitled to a grant for the same, on my performance of the stipulations aforesaid.

ALEXANDER MACOMB."

The board, by a resolution, accepted this proposition, and directed the surveyor general to survey the said tract, at the expense of Macomb, and requiring him to secure the payment of the first-sixth part of the purchase money.

(Land Office Minutes, vol. ii, p. 192.)

On the 10th of January, 1792, the surveyor general having made a return of the survey above directed, and the security required having been deposited, for the payment of the southern half of the tract, containing 1,920,000 acres, the secretary was directed to issue letters patent accordingly,* which was done January 10, 1792.† This portion was tracts Nos. 4, 5 and 6, in Jefferson, Lewis and Oswego counties.

In the returns of the survey, made under the direction of the surveyor general, the lands were laid out into six tracts, of which number one lies entirely in Franklin county, and numbers two and three, in St. Lawrence county.

These were subsequently subdivided into townships, named and numbered as follows, with the origin of each so far as is known.‡

* Land Office Minutes, vol. ii, p 232.
† See Office Patents, b 23, p. 160; see recital in patent to McCormick, ib. b. 18, p. 193, &c.
‡ In obtaining the origin of these names, the author has been assisted by A. O Brodie, of N. Y., and Henry E Pierrepont, of Brooklyn.

NUMBER ONE embraced 27 townships.

1. *Macomb*, Alexander Macomb.
2. *Cormachus*,* Daniel McCormick.
3. *Constable*, Wm. Constable,
4. *Moira*, a place in Ireland.
5. *Bangor*, a town in Wales.
6. *Malone*, a name in the family of R. Harrison.
7. *Annastown*, a daughter of Constable.
8. *St. Patrick*, the Irish saint.
9. *Shelah*, a place in Ireland.
10. *Williamsville*, a son of Constable.
11. *Westerly*,
12. *Everettlaville*, a daughter of Constable.
13. *Dayton*, Jonathan Dayton.
14. *Ennis*.
15. *Fowler*, Thedosius Fowler.
16. *Johnsmanor*, A son of Constable.
17. *Gilchrist*, Jonathan Gilchrist.
18. *Brighton*, a town in England.
19. *Cheltenham*, "   "
20. *Margate*,   "   "
21. *Harrietstown*, a daughter of Constable.
22. *Lochneagh*, a lake in Ireland.
23. *Killarney*,   "   "
24. *Barrymore*, a place in Ireland.
25. *Mount Morris*.
26. *Cove Hill*.
27. *Tipperary*, a county in Ireland.

These were numbered from west to east, and from north to south. See map of Franklin county, where the original names and numbers are given.

NUMBER TWO embraced 18 townships, in the eastern part of St. Lawrence county, and south of the ten towns, viz:

1. *Sherwood*.
2. *Oakham*.
3. *Mortlake*.
4. *Harewood*.
5. *Janestown*, a daughter of Constable.
6. *Piercefield*.
7. *Granshuck*.
8. *Hollywood*.
9. *Kildare*.
10. *Matildavale*.
11. *Wick*.
12. *Riversdale*.
13. *Cookham*.
14. *Catharineville*.
15. *Islington*.
16. *Chesterfield*.
17. *Grange*.
18. *Crum ick*.

This tract was numbered from west to east, commencing at the south west corner, and ending at the north.

NUMBER THREE was divided into 15 townships, viz:

1. *Hammond*, Abijah Hammond.
2. *Somerville*,† a town in N. Jersey.
3. *Dewitt*, the surveyor general.
4. *Fitz William*.
5. *Ballybeen*, McCormick's native place.
6. *Clare*, a county in Ireland.
7. *Killarney*, "   "
8. *Edwards*, a brother of D. Mc Cormick.
9. *Sarahsburgh*.
10. *Clifton*, a town in England.
11. *Portaferry*, a town in Ireland.
12. *Scriba*, from George Scriba?
13. *Chaumont*, the name of T. D. Le Ray.
14. *Bloomfield*.
15. *Emilyville*, a daughter of Constable.

The numbering of this tract began at the north west, and ran irregularly from west to east. We have carefully retained these names and

* Or McCormick. This word is but a play upon the name.
‡ On some maps marked Caledonia. This was a favorite name of Mr. Parish.

numbers on our map of St. Lawrence county. Nos. 3, 4, 5, 6 and 21, in the first tract; and 1, 38, in the third tract, have been applied to towns. Most of the others have been discarded, or are used only in designating tracts of land.

Macomb, soon after his purchase, appointed Wm. Constable to go to Europe, and sell lands, which he did, but as they are not within our proposed limits, the details of these transactions will not be given. The report of this sale naturally spread through the state, and put a stop to further applications, which led the commissioners to direct the surveyor general (Oct. 11, 1791,) to advertise in all the papers in the state, that the Old Military tract, and large tracts east and south of this, were still for sale.

This was accordingly done.*

The failure of Macomb, interrupted the sale, and prevented him from receiving the patents.

On the 6th of June, 1792, he released to Wm. Constable, his interest in tracts 1, 2 and 3.†

As many of the transfers that ensued were confidential, it would be tedious to follow them, if our space allowed. William Constable and Daniel McCormick were the leading negotiators in this business, and after the death of the former, in May, 1803, James Constable, John McVickar and Hezekiah B. Pierrepont, as his executors, assumed the settlement of the estate and sale of lands. Macomb's interest in the three tracts was sold June 22, 1791, to Wm. S. Smith, Abijah Hammond and Richard Harrison, but the patents for these tracts were not issued till several years afterwards.

On the 3d of March, 1795, the commissioners of the land office directed the secretary of state to prepare letters patent to Daniel McCormick, for the third tract of 640,000 acres, the latter, who was an original proprietor with Macomb, having paid the sum required into the treasury. This was accordingly done.‡

On the 10th of July following, McCormick satisfied the claims of Smith, Hammond and Harrison, by deeding one-fifteenth part of the third tract, and two undivided tenths remaining after deducting the said one-fifteenth part, and also one-third part of the remainder§. The title of these gentlemen to the third tract would accordingly be represented by the following formula:

$$\frac{1}{15} + \frac{2(1-\frac{1}{15})}{10} + \frac{1-\frac{1}{15}}{3}.$$

Our limited mathematical attainments will not allow us to trace the

* Land Office records, p. 230.   † Sec.'s office, patents, b. 23, p. 160.
‡ Sec.'s office, patents, b. 23, p. 394.   § Sec.'s office, deeds, 29, p. 157.

complex and compound vulgar fractions that were employed in the subsequent sales.

On the 14th of May, 1798, McCormick applied for patents for the first and second tracts of Macomb's purchase, which were ordered, and on the day following, approved, and on the 17th of August, passed by the commissioners.[*] The first tract embraced 821,879 acres, and the second 553,020 acres.

The fees charged for issuing a patent for 1,374,839 acres granted to McCormick, amounted to $820, of which half was paid into the treasury, and the rest the land commissioners divided between them, by virtue of an act of February 25, 1789, establishing the fees which were a certain rate per township;[†] and of course proportioned to the magnitude of the sales.

On the 21st of June, 1797, the surveyor general was directed by the land commissioners to finish and return a survey of the lands contracted and sold to Macomb, and to employ none but competent and trusty surveyors on this duty. If difficulty arose in finding the starting point, he was to attend personally to the matter.[‡]

McCormick, by deed to Constable, September 20, 1793, conveyed an undivided third of great lot No. 2,[§] and December 19, 1800, a partition deed between Macomb and McCormick to Constable was executed.

Theodosius Fowler, Jonathan Dayton, and Robert Gilchrist, having become interested in the tract, a partition deed was executed January 19, 1802, in which Hammond, Harrison, Fowler, Gilchrist, and Dayton, released to McCormick, Constable and Macomb.

In July, 1804, James D. LeRay, by purchase from Constable, became interested in the townships of tracts Nos. 1, 2 and 3. He appointed Gouverneur Morris as his attorney.

We have prepared a detailed statement of the shares received by each, in these transfers, but our space will not admit of its insertion. The following tabular statement shows the names of those to whom the different townships were assigned. It is taken from a copy of an original map, kindly furnished to the author, by P. S. Stewart, Esq., of Carthage, the agent of Mr. LeRay.

To condense the statement, the following abbreviations will be used:

L. LE RAY DE CHAUMONT.	W. C. WM. CONSTABLE.
M. ALEX'R MACOMB.	F. THEODOSIUS FOWLER.
M. C. DANIEL McCORMICK.	G. F. GILCHRIST FOWLER.

[*] Land office records, iii, p 60. Patents, b. 19, p. 198, 294, sec.'s office.
[†] Ib., iii, p. 57.
[‡] Ib., iii, p. 18.
[§] Deeds, secretary's office, b. 22.

R. H. Richard Harrison. P. David Parish.
H. Abijah Hammond.

Great Tract No. 1, including 27 townships. 1, M.; 2, W. C.; 3, W. C.; 4, G. F.; 5, M. C.; 6, R. H.; 7, W. C.; 8, H.; 9. N. ⅓ W. C., middle ⅓ H., S. ⅓ M. C.; 10, W. C.; 11, R. H.; 12, W. C.; 13, N. W. ¼ R. H., E. ½ not marked; 14, not marked; 15, N. W. ¼ G. F., N. E. ¼ M. C., south part not marked; 16, W. C.; 17, N. ⅓ R. H., middle ⅓ M. C., S. ⅓ W. C.; 18, H.; 19, F.; 20, G. F.; 21, L.; 22, M. C.; 23, M. C.; 24, N. W. ¼ H., N. E. ¼ G. F., S. E. ¼ R. H., S. W. ¼ M. C.; 25, S. ½ G. F., the rest not marked: 26, M. C.; 27, N. W. ¼ M. C., the remainder L.

Great Tract No. 2, including 18 townships. 1, N. W. ¼ M. C., N. E. ¼ L., S. E. ¼ M. C., S. W. ¼ G. F.; 2, N. W. ¼ M., S. W. ¼ G. F., E. ½ L.; 3, W. C.; 4, N. W. ¼ L, N. E. ¼ H. S. E. ¼ M. C., S. W. ¼ C.; 5, M,; 6, S. ½ M. C., N. ½ M. C., R. H., H., G. F. and L.; 7, M. C.; 8, N. ½ R. M., S. ½ M. C.; 9, R. H.; 10. W. C.; 11, W. C.; 12, N. W. ¼ P., N. E. ¼ R. H., S. E. ¼ H., S. W. ¼ M; 13, P.; 14, P. and M.; 15, H.; 16, R. H.; 17, E. part M. C., middle part L., W. part G. F.; 18, not marked.

Great Tract No. 3, including 15 townships. 1, H.; 2, not marked; 3, not marked; 4, E. part H, middle part M. C., W. part S., (Madame de Stael?); 5, M. C.; 6, E. ½ L., W. ½ S.; 7, G. F.; 8, M. C.; 9, M.; 10, N. W. ¼ M., N. E. ¼ L.; S. E. ¼ R. H., S. W. ¼ H.; 11, M. C.; 12, M. C.; 13, L.; 14, not marked; 15, N. E. ¼ M. C., N. W. ¼ G. F., S. ½ L.; 15, N. E. ¼ L.; N. W. ¼ M. L., S. E. ¼ M. C., S. W. ¼ G. F.

The *islands* in the St. Lawrence were not patented with the lands opposite which they lay, nor were they included in the jurisdiction of any of the towns, although included in the contract of Macomb, with two exceptions. It was not deemed advisable to patent any of these until the national boundary was decided. By an act passed March 17, 1815, they were declared to be a part of the respective towns opposite which they lay, and this extended to the island in Lakes Erie and Ontario, and the Niagara river.

The islands were patented as follows:

All the islands which lie within this state, between a line drawn at right angles to the river, from the village of Morristown, situated on the shore of the river, and a meridian drawn through the western point of Grindstone island, in the county of Jefferson, containing fifteeen thousand, four hundred and. two acres, and nine-tenths of an acre, were granted to Elisha Camp, Feb. 15, 1823. In the above grant is included Grindstone island, containing 5,291 acres, Wells's island containing 8,068 acres, Indian Hut island containing 369 acres, and some small islands without names.

Lindy's island, 7·92 acres, to Elisha Camp, Dec. 9, 1823.

Nine small islands, 178·8 acres to Hezekiah B. Pierrepont, Oct. 21, 1824.

Isle du Gallop,	492·5	"	"	"
Tick island,	11·0	"	"	"
Tibbits island,	17·5	"	"	"
Chimney island,	6·2	"	"	"
Other small islands,	3·0	"	"	"

Rapid Plat, 9,763 acres, to Daniel McCormick, August, 1815; and to McCormick on the 15th of December, 1823, the following, with the number of acres in each. The title is recorded in book 25, p. 480, of patents, at Albany.

Smugglers' island and Johnson's island, 17·72.

An island near Johnson's island, between that and the United States shore, 2·46.

Snuy island, 55·20.	Upper Long Saut island, 868·80.
Chat island, 95·20.	C island, 3·1.
Chrystler's island, 52·80.	D Island, 2·5.
Hog island, 5·29.	Haynes' island, 134·56.
Goose Neck island, 405·87.	

The Isle au Long Saut, was reserved by the state in the original sale, from its supposed importance in a military point of view, and sold to individuals by the surveyor general, in pursuance of statute, between May 5, 1832, and the present time, at the land office in Albany.

Barnhart's island, 1692·95 acres; two-thirds to David A. Ogden and one-third to Gouverneur Ogden, Dec. 15, 1815.

This island, near St. Regis, lies very near the Canadian shore, and a considerable part of it north of the line of 45° N. latitude. It was accordingly regarded as British territory, and in 1795 it was leased of the St. Regis Indians, by George Barnhart, for a term of 999 years, at an annual rent of $30. The British government had made a practice of granting patents upon the issue of similar leases, and would doubtless have done so in this instance, had application been duly made.

In 1806, a saw mill was built, and arrangements made for the erection of a grist mill, when the Indians became dissatisfied and insisted upon a renewal of the lease, at an increased rent. Accordingly a lease was given for 999 years, at $60 annual rent. Deeds had been granted by Barnhart, who with all the other inhabitants of the island, were treated as British subjects, until upon running the line between the two nations, after the treaty of Ghent, the commissioners assigned the island to the United States, as an offset for the half of Grand island, at the outlet of Lake Ontario, which in justice would have been divided. In 1823, D. A. Ogden and G. Ogden purchased the islands in St. Lawrence county, and with them Barnhart's island. The settlers not complying with the offers made, were ejected by the state, and they in 1849 applied for redress at the state legislature. By an act passed April 10, 1850, Bishop Perkins, George Redington and John Fine, were appointed commissioners to examine these claims, and awarded to the petitioners the aggregate of $6,597, which was confirmed by an act passed at the following session of the legislature. The claimants received as follows: Wm.

17

Geo. Barnhart, $1,475; Jacob Barnhart, $3,284; Geo. Robertson, $1,127; Geo. Gallinger, $402, and Geo Snetzinger, $309.

The state, in disposing of its lands, conveys them by an instrument called a *patent*, in which there appears no consideration of payment, and which purports to be a gift, and to be executed by but one party. As reference is often made to the reservations of the patent, the form of one is here inserted:

"THE PEOPLE OF THE STATE OF NEW YORK, By the grace of GOD, free and independent. TO ALL to whom these Presents shall come greeting: KNOW YE, That WE HAVE Given, Granted and Confirmed, and by these Presents, DO Give, Grant and Confirm unto [here follows name, bounds of lands, &c.], TOGETHER with all and singular the Rights, Hereditaments and Appurtenances to the same belonging, or in any wise appertaining : EXCEPTING and RESERVING to ourselves all Gold and Silver Mines, and five Acres of every Hundred Acres of the said Tract of Land for Highways : TO HAVE AND TO HOLD the above described and granted Premises unto the said . . ., Heirs and Assigns, as a good and indefeasible Estate of Inheritance for ever.
ON CONDITION NEVERTHELESS, That within the Term of Seven Years to be computed from the . . . Date hereof, there shall be one Family actually settled on the said Tract of Land hereby Granted for every six hundred and forty acres thereof, otherwise these our Letters Patent and Estate hereby Granted shall cease, determine and become void : IN TESTIMONY WHEREOF, WE have caused these our Letters to be made Patent, and the great Seal of our said State to be hereunto affixed : WITNESS our trusty and well beloved [George Clinton] Esquire Governor of our State, General and Commander-in-Chief of all the Militia, and Admiral of the Navy of the same."

These instruments are made out by the secretary of state, on the order of the land commissioners, and bear the signature of the governor, and the great seal of the state, which, in former times, was a large waxen disc, with paper on each side, bearing the arms of the state on the face, and an impression on the back, which was styled "the reverse."

Tax Sales have caused large tracts of land in the rear townships of the great purchase to change hands, and many of the present owners hold their titles from this source.

In March, 1834, 116,873½ acres were sold in St. Lawrence and 28,323 acres in Franklin counties, amounting, in the latter, to $841·73 only. At this sale, Peter Smith bid off large amounts in these and other counties. In 1839, 43,164 acres in St. Lawrence and 65,881 acres in Franklin counties, were sold. In 1843, 93,690 acres in the former, and 45,457 acres in the latter.

These sales, which formerly took place at Albany, have, by a recent act of the legislature, been very judiciously transferred to the county seats. These lands have usually been sold at prices scarcely nominal.

The following are examples: 17,140 acres, $185·09; 20,568 acres $263·02; 21,165 acres, $671·03.

The state is said to own considerable tracts, which have been forfeited for taxes.

Landholders' Reserves have very frequently been made in the northern counties, and generally apply to mines and minerals. In some deeds, these reserves embrace certain specific ores or minerals, and in others the reservations are extended to mill seats and mill privileges. A clause is commonly inserted, by which it is stipulated, that all damages arising from entering upon the premises, in pursuance of the conditions of the reservation, shall be paid.

This has undoubtedly, in some cases, operated as a drawback upon the mining interests, as the occupant, having no claims upon ores that might exist upon his premises, would feel no solicitude about their discovery; and even would take pains to conceal their existence, preferring the undisturbed enjoyment of his farm, to the annoyance and disturbance that might arise from mineral explorations.

These reservations of ores are superfluous, in sections underlaid by Potsdam sandstone, or any of the sedimentary series of rock that overlay this formation; as none have hitherto been discovered or suspected to exist in any of these rocks.

It is only in primitive rock, or along the borders of this and sedimentary or stratified rocks, that useful ores have hitherto been discovered in this section of the state.

The Original Survey of Macomb's Purchase.

The following account of these surveys, was obtained from Mr. Gurdon Smith, a pioneer settler, and one of the surveyors who run out the great purchase.

The north line of Totten and Crossfield's purchase, was run during the revolutionary war, by Jacob Chambers, and forms the southern boundary of the great tract.

The ten towns had been supposed to be surveyed, previous to 1799, but some of the lines, if ever marked, could not then be found, and a part of them were run out, under the direction of Benjamin Wright, of Rome, in 1799.

The outlines of the great tract had been surveyed by Medad Mitchell, and —— Tupper; the former from New York, who laid out the great tracts numbers 1, 2 and 3, but did not subdivide it into townships. On finishing their work, they were at the extreme south east corner of Franklin county, from whence they proceeded through the woods towards Rome, but bearing too far to the north, they crossed Black river, below the High falls, and when they first recognized their situation, were in the town of Redfield, Oswego county, where one of them had previously surveyed.

When they reached Rome, they were nearly famished, having been several days on close allowance, and for a short time entirely destitute. From one of these surveyors, Tupper's lake, on the south border of. the county, derives its name. In the winter of 1798-9, Mr. Benjamin Wright, originally from Connecticut, but then a young man, residing in Rome, and by profession a surveyor, obtained from the proprietors in New York, a contract for surveying the three great tracts of Macomb's purchase, into townships. He had been engaged from 1795 till 1798, in company with his cousin, Moses Wright, in surveying large tracts, and among others, the Black river tract, in Jefferson, Lewis, and Oswego counties.

From his excellent reputation as a surveyor, he was employed as a suitable person to superintend the survey of the great northern purchase.

Early in June, Mr. Wright, with a party of about twenty men, started by way of Oneida lake, and the St. Lawrence rivers, with a six handed bateau, to commence their operations at St. Regis. They left arrangements for three of their number, G. Smith, Moses Wright, and Ebenezer Wright, with eight other men, to come through the woods, to meet them at Penet's bay, now the village French Creek. The latter party started on the 11th of June, 1799, having been prevented by the absence of one of their number from getting off, till several days after the main part of the company had left; and arrived after a march of about four days, at the point designated, but instead of finding their companions, they found a letter, stating that after waiting in vain several days, they had gone down the river. With the exception of a small supply left for their support, they were destitute of provisions, but making a virtue of the necessity, they divided their little stock equally between them, and pulling down the little log cabin which had served for their shelter, and which was then the only tenement in the country, they made of its timber, a raft, and following on, came to where some Canadian timber thieves were at work on the American shore, near the head of Chippewa bay.

Here they found provisions for supplying their most pressing hunger, and from hence they were taken in a boat to where Brockville now is, then a small settlement.

From this they proceeded to Oswegatchie where they overtook the others, and being assembled, they descended to St. Regis, to commence their operations at that place. At the head of the Long Saut, two of the number intimidated by the swiftness of the current, slipped out of the company, and attempted to gain St. Regis, by land, but on arriving at the mouth of Grass river, they were obliged to hire some Indians who were passing, to convey them to Cornwall, from whence they proceeded to St. Regis. A small party under the direction of G. Smith, was put on shore, to proceed by land from the Long Saut to St. Regis, to make a traverse of the river, who arrived two or three days later than those who proceeded by water.

The arrival of so many men upon their lands, at first greatly alarmed the Indians, who suspected evil designs upon their persons, or their property, and they assembled in arms, to repel them; but at length, being satisfied that their designs were altogether peaceable, they were received and treated with much kindness. The names of those assembled at this place for surveying, were as follows:

Benjamin Wright, (principal surveyor), Gurdon Smith, Moses Wright and Ebenezer Wright, (the latter cousins of B. Wright,) Clark Putnam, E. Hammond, Benjamin Raymond, surveyors at the head of parties, and each having his lines assigned him. Each had two axe men to mark the lines, and two chain men. B. Wright, superintended the operations of the others, and had the direction of supplying the several parties with provisions, at camps, that were established at different points. He had his head quarters at the mouth of Raquette river.

One of the first duties to be done, was to explore the Raquette river, and ascertain how far that stream was navigable, and at what points it was most eligible to establish camps. To Mr. G. Smith, was assigned this duty, and he with two men, followed the shore as far up as the present village of Potsdam, and in consequence of this, and other explorations, a camp was established at the present site of Norfolk village at the foot of the rapids on the west side; another near Coxe's Mills in Pierrepont; another at the Canton high falls; and another at Cooper's falls, in Dekalb, and at each of these a man was left to take charge of provisions.

In commencing operations, Mr. Wright found it a matter of the first importance, to ascertain the point where the line formerly run between the great lots of Macomb's purchase, intersected the south line on the southern border of the county.

To determine this, Mr. Hammond was despatched to find the point of intersection, but not only failed in this, but also was detained so long by various causes, that his absence became a serious source of uneasiness with those who were left. He at length came in nearly famished, having failed to accomplish his object.

Still in hopes of ascertaining these important data, Mr. Smith was next sent, with directions to make the most careful examinations, and not return until if possible, they were found.   After traveling nearly as far as was necessary to reach the point, the party camped near a river to spend a night, in hopes of being so fortunate as to find the object of their search the following day.   Next morning one of their party related a curious dream, which he had dreamed during the night, in which he related, that they seemed to be traveling along, and carefully examining every object for land marks, when they came to a bog meadow, with scarcely any vegetation but moss, and that on a solitary bush which grew apart from all others, might be found the mark.   This dream was treated with derision, but they had scarcely proceeded a quarter of a mile when they came to a marsh which the dreamer declared was like that which had appeared in his vision, and on careful examination, he detected the bush and the mark, much to the surprise of all.

The manner in which this anecdote was related, leaves no doubt of its truth, and it remains a subject for the speculation of the physiologist to offer a solution.   He might have heard it related casually, and years before, that such a mark had been made in such a place, and this, from its trifling nature, might have made no impression at the time, and was forgotten, but when it became an object of solicitude to ascertain it, the busy thoughts flitting through the mind in dreams, without the control of the will, and following each other in a succession of which we know no law or order, might have brought, unbidden, the welcome fact, long forgotten, and which no effort of memory in the waking state could have recalled.   In [no other rational manner can this singular instance of apparent revelation be satisfactorily explained.

These different surveying parties, spent the summer in running some of the principal lines of the great purchase, meeting at times with great hardships, from exposure to the elements, want of provisions, and misunderstanding of instructions, from the imperfect knowledge possessed of the different lakes, streams, and rivers in the country.

Towards fall, the several parties proceeded back to Rome, where they all resided, some by water, and two parties, (Smith's and Raymond's) through the forest.

An incident occured in Mr. Smith's party, worthy of record.   He had procured a supply of provisions, about 25 miles below Tupper's lake, of a party who had been sent by Mr. Wright, for this purpose, and thence in pursuance of instructions he had turned back to the south line, and had proceeded on this, to the extreme south western corner of St. Lawrence county, where they camped for the night.   In the morning, it being foggy and misty, two of his men had conceived that the course he proposed to take, in order to reach the High falls on Black river, (S. 25° W.) was not in the direction of their homes, notwithstanding the evidence of the compass, and peremptorily refused to accompany him. The course they proposed to take, was back on the south line towards Lake Champlain, and no argument or expostulation could convince them that they were in error.

Mr. Smith, endeavored to remonstrate, by showing that the line was obscure, and would soon be lost, and that they must then wander at random and perish in the forest, which had then no limits, but the St. Lawrence, Black, and Mohawk rivers. But finding entreaties vain, he divided his provisions equally between them, and they shouldered their knapsacks and started. At this trying moment, those that remained, tortured with fear that the missing men would be lost, and that their blood would be required at their hands, resolved to remain in the place they were a short time, in hopes that the deluded men would lose their course, and call for assistance before they had got beyond hailing distance; and so it providentially proved, for their receding forms had scarcely disappeared in the distance, than, from the very anxiety they felt to keep their line, they became confused, and perplexed, and a faint shout in the distance conveyed back to those who remained, the joyful news that the misguided men had discovered their folly, in time to be saved.

Mr. Smith, who had been listening intensely to learn whether such would not be the result, instantly sprang upon his feet, and bidding his men remain in the place they were, he darted off in the direction of the cry, and at length overtook them, much to the relief of all parties.

Being by this time convinced of their error, and willing to trust that most reliable guide *the compass*, they willingly consented to follow the others, thankful for having discovered their folly in season.

Had not the others remained where they were, the two parties would have been beyond hailing distance, and the consequences must have been fatal.

The company on the third day, arrived at the High falls, having struck the road, then newly cut from that place to Brown's tract, at a point seven miles from the falls.

In May, 1800, Mr. B. Wright, Mr. M. Wright, G. Smith, and B. Raymond, returned with men by way of Lake Ontario, and finished during that season, the survey of their contract, embracing the first three great lots of Macomb's purchase.

The head quarters during this summer was also at St. Regis, but nothing worthy of notice occurred. In the latter part of the summer, they returned home with their work finished.

CHAPTER V.

─────

ORGANIZATION AND SETTLEMENT OF THE SEVERAL TOWNS.

WITH most persons, the adventures of the pioneer settler, and the privations and inconveniences experienced in forming a new settlement, possess a great degree of interest; and if we consult the annals of any people, or of any age, we shall find that the *origin*, and the first feeble *beginnings*, of a new settlement or colony, are those which have been described with the greatest minuteness, and read with the greatest interest. The idea of an ERA, or STARTING POINT, from which future events shall be dated, of itself possesses an importance which engages the attention, and is afterwards recalled as an occurrence not easily forgotten; and the magnitude of the enterprise, enhances the importance of the initial steps. On this principle, the corner stone of the edifice, which is to be the pride of the architectural art, is laid with imposing ceremonies; and the first discovery and occupation of a new country, has been by voyagers and discoverers, celebrated with such acts as were well calculated to fix the event in the memory, and add to the importance of the *beginning* of a new series of events.

Thus it is in the formation of new settlements; the commencement of a labor which is to change the wilderness to the cultivated field, and the difficulties encountered in effecting a lodgment in a forest, remote from sympathy or assistance, and exposed to all the hardships which such a situation imposes, has in it a species of merit which deserves to be commemorated; and especially, if there be in this any self-sacrifice from principle, or for the good of others, or the exhibition of those traits of character which evince courage in the presence of danger, perseverance in defiance of obstacles, or the exercise of those ennobling traits of character which elevate and adorn the human mind, do they especially demand our favorable attention.

Entertaining such a view of the subject, the author has for several months, devoted his time exclusively to the laborious but pleasing task, of gleaning from the memories of the early inhabitants, and the scattered records of the various towns; from the periodical press, the records of societies, and from the public archives, the details which follow, in relation to the origin, progress and present condition of the towns of these two counties. The difficulties which attend this class of researches, can be realized only by one who has experienced them. To patiently listen to the broken and disconnected narrative of the aged, whose sluggish memories are scarcely able to recall the incidents which marked their prime; to submit to the verbose and disjointed accounts of the illiterate, and the loose statements of those who talk at random; to guard against the impositions of those who have an interest to be promoted, and the misstatements of those who are themselves in error, and from these to select those parts which have worth, and reject the worthless, and to connect and arrange the whole in such a manner as to form a consistent and impartial narrative, requires an amount of labor which is very great.

It is hoped that these statements will be remembered should the reader observe any deficiencies or errors in the following pages.

St. Lawrence county, is at present divided into twenty-eight towns, which were organized on the following dates, and from the following towns.

BRASHER, taken from *Massena*, April 21, 1825
CANTON, taken from *Lisbon*, March 28, 1808.
COLTON, taken from *Parishville*, April 12, 1843.
DEKALB, taken from *Oswegatchie*, February 21, 1806.
DEPEYSTER, taken from *Oswegatchie and Dekalb*, March 24, 1825.
EDWARDS, taken from *Fowler*, April 27, 1827.
FINE, taken from *Russell and Pierrepont*, March 27, 1849.
FOWLER, taken from *Rossie and Russell*, April 15, 1815.
GOUVERNEUR, taken from *Oswegatchie*, April 15, 1810.
HAMMOND, taken from *Rossie and Morristown*, March 30, 1827.
HERMON,* taken from *Edwards and Dekalb*, April 17, 1830.
HOPKINTON, taken from *Massena*, March 2, 1805.
LAWRENCE, taken from *Hopkinton and Brasher*, April 21, 1823.
LISBON, taken from (*the Ten towns,*) March 6, 1801.
LOUISVILLE, taken from *Massena*, April 5, 1810.
MACOMB, taken from *Gouverneur and Morristown*, April 30, 1841.
MADRID, taken from *Lisbon*, March 3, 1802.
MASSENA, taken from *Lisbon*, March 3, 1802.
MORRISTOWN, taken from *Oswegatchie*, March 27, 1821.
NORFOLK, taken from *Louisville and Stockholm*, April 9, 1823.
OSWEGATCHIE, taken from *Lisbon*, March 3, 1802.
PARISHVILLE, taken from *Hopkinton*, March 18, 1814.
PIERREPONT, taken from *Russell*, April 15, 1818.
PITCAIRN, taken from *Fowler*, March 24, 1836.
POTSDAM, taken from *Madrid*, February 21, 1806.
ROSSIE, taken from *Russell*, January 27, 1813.
RUSSELL, taken from *Hopkinton*, March 27, 1807.
STOCKHOLM, taken from *Massena*, February 21, 1806.

BRASHER.

Was erected from Massena, April 21, 1825, and the first town meeting

* Under the name of DEPEAU, changed to HERMON 28, Feb. 1834.

was directed to be held at the house of Benjamin Nevin. The poor moneys of the towns, were to be divided agreeably to the last tax list. It originally embraced the greater parts of townships No. 17 and 18. By an act of April 11, 1827, all that part of No. 16 or Chesterfield, north of the south line of Stockholm, extended to the county line, was added, without the knowledge or consent of its inhabitants. The latter part was taken off in 1828, in forming the town of Lawrence.

Town Officers.—The following is a list of the first town officers, elected June 6, 1825. Benjamin Nevin, *Supervisor;* David McMurphy, *Town Clerk;* Wm, Stowell, Jehiel Stevens, and Benjamin Watts, *Assessors;* John Burroughs, David Richardson, and Peter Corbin, *Commissioners of Highways;* Benjamin Watts, *Constable and Collector;* Francis Nevin, and David Richardson, *Overseers of the Poor;* Luman Kibble, Jehiel Stevens, and Francis Nevin, *Com'rs of Com. Schools;* David McMurphy, Benjamin Nevin, and Wm. Stowell. *Inspectors of Schools.*

Supervisors.—1825, Benj. Nevin; 1826, David McMurphy; 1827-8; Jehiel Stevens; 1829, B. Nevin; 1830; J. Stevens; 1831-3, B. Nevin, 1834. J. Stevens; 1835-6, David Richardson; 1837-8, Nicholas Watts; 1839-41, J. Stevens; 1842-3, John Phelps; 1844-7, Joseph A. Jacobr, 1848-9, John Phelps; 1850-1, James H. Morse; 1852, Hannibal Andrews.

The town of Brasher derives its name from Philip Brasher, of Brooklyn, who acquired by purchase at different times from the eight heirs of Thomas Marston, one of whom was his wife, a portion of the town. Mr. Marston had received his title, March 18, 1809, from G. V. Ludlow, Master in Chancery, and the tract thus conveyed, had been set off to Jonathan Dayton, in a division between Dayton, Gilchrist, and Fowler, in July, 1801. Mr. Brasher held for several years the office of 'alderman, and member of assembly, and had been in the legislature for several years, previous to the time the town was organized. It was the intention of the petitioners that this town should bear the name of *Helena*, and as such the bill passed the assembly, but was altered in the senate. This town has at present three villages and post offices, which were established as follows: *Helena,* Feb. 13, 1827; *Brasher Falls,* July 22, 1840; and *Brasher Iron Works,* July 14, 1849.

This town embraces most of the townships of *Grange* and *Crumack,* and was subdivided into strips running north and south. McCormick, one of the proprietors, conveyed to Joseph Pitcairn by deed dated July 6, 1818, the middle part, and under this proprietor the settlement first began. The eastern part, which is known as the Chandler tract, of 12,235 acres, was conveyed by McCormick to Samuel Ward, Dec. 15,1794, and formed a part of 192,000 acres to which the latter became entitled on a division of the great purchase. It passed thence to Samuel Havens, of Dedham, Mass., Dec. 6, 1806, and in 1834 the tract was surveyed into 33 lots, and sold Aug. 10, 1842, to T. P.

Chandler. The west third was confirmed by McCormick, Constable, and Macomb to Harrison and others, in a partition executed Jan 19, 1801, It ultimately became owned by Thomas Marston, and by inheritance and purchase by Brasher. The first improvement began in town was the erection of a saw mill on Deer river, and as was supposed on the Haven tract, by G. B. R. Gove in 1815. The first actual settlement was made March 17, 1817, near the village of Helena, by several families who came on and settled under the agency of Russell Attwater, of Norfolk, who in that year erected a saw mill, which afterwards contained a grist mill, with a single run of stones. Benjamin Nevin succeeded as agent in May, 1819. There were then living in town the following men, and their families: Wm. Johnson, Amos Eldridge, Jeremiah Shuff, Enoch Hall, ——— Brown and Francis Nevin, a young man. A grist mill erected by Mr. Nevin, was burned in April 1828, but immediately rebuilt, and is the one now at Helena. The first religious meetings were held by the Methodists, and the Rev. Squire Chase, preached the first sermon in town. The settlement at the mouth of Deer river, received the name of HELENA, from Helen, only daughter of Joseph Pitcairn. It was the intention of this proprietor to make the place his home, and he caused to be erected the large stone dwelling west of the village, for a residence, but domestic afflictions prevented him from carrying this intention into effect. This place is a small village, and a fall in Deer river, gives it a water power sufficient for common mechanical purposes.

Some importance was at an early day attached to the navigation of the St. Regis river in this town, and a boat capable of carrying ten barrels of potash, was run between Hogansburgh and the landing, seven miles below Brasher falls. The inhabitants of Stockholm and Hopkinton availed themselves of this communication, in reaching market. To promote this, an act of March 25, 1828, made it the "duty of the assessors of the town of Brasher, to designate in their next assessment all lands lying west of and within two miles of the St. Regis river, and above the place usually called the landing. The board of supervisors were authorized from this to levy a tax not exceeding twenty cents on an acre, in addition to the ordinary tax, to be expended by the road commissioners of the town in improving the roads through these lands." By an act passed April 18, 1831, the board of supervisors were authorized and required to tax the town of Brasher $1,000 to rebuild two bridges over the St. Regis river, where the main road from Potsdam and Stockholm to Hogansburgh passes through the town. This sum was not to be levied unless the same should have been previously fixed and determined upon by a vote of the freeholders and inhabitants, at a legal town meeting assembled.

On Deer river two and a half miles from Helena, is the small manufacturing village of *Brasher Iron Works*. The first beginning here, was about the 10th of September, 1835, by Stillman Fuller, formerly from Fullerville Iron Works. Mr. Pitcairn had known of the existence of bog ores in this town, and induced Mr. F. to come and examine the ores, and if practicable to erect a furnace. The first contract run ten years, and allowed Mr. Fuller the sole right of digging ores on his tract, by paying a tribute of twenty-five cents a ton. The furnace at Norfolk had previously been in part supplied from this town, but the new contract cut them off from all further supplies from this quarter. A furnace was erected on the left bank of Deer river, which was 31 feet square on the ground, of the same height. Inside diameter, 7 feet. Lining, sandstone from Potsdam, which was found to answer the purpose of a firestone admirably. It was made a quarter furnace, and at first fed by a cold blast. It was got in operation and the first casting of iron made on the 29th of October, 1836. The first blast continued till the last of January following, without delays or accidents, and about 250 tons were made on the first trial. At the end of the second blast, in the latter part of 1827, the premises were sold to Isaac W. Skinner, from Buffalo, and R. W. Bush, of Ogdensburgh, under the firm of Skinner & Bush, who continued about three years. At this time, Wm. H. Alexander, of Syracuse, took the place of Bush, under the firm of Alexander & Skinner, who have continued the business till the present time, with little interruption. It has been run exclusively on bog ore, mostly loam ore, which yields about twenty per cent, and makes a good quality of iron. The iron made has been partly exported in the pig, but since 1843, the greater part has been cast into stoves, and other castings, upon the premises. Two cupola furnaces have been erected, for remelting the iron for castings. About 1843, a machine shop was erected for finishing mill irons, and other articles, and a large amount of this business has been done here. A hot blast has been introduced, and is now used exclusively. The furnace has been three times burned. At the first of these burnings, the entire premises were consumed, but the latter only burned the casting house. Coal is obtained within from 1 to 3 miles, at a cost of about $4 per hundred bushels. Two brick coal kilns have been built, but their use here, as well as elsewhere, has been discontinued, the coal not being found to be of so good a quality as that burned in pits covered with earth in the usual way. Most of the inhabitants of this place are directly or indirectly dependent upon the iron works for employment. The surrounding country is much of it still a wilderness, the settlements being new and scattered, and presents an appearance of desolation from its having been overrun by a fire in the summer of 1849. This destructive fire spread through the woods, from Norfolk across the towns of Brasher, Bombay, Fort Covington, and Westville, taking in its course every thing combustible, and killing most of the standing timber, which still remains a dismal monument of its ravages. Many thousands of dollars worth of pine and other choice timber were destroyed; in some places every thing valuable of the soil was burned, fields of grain were overrun, miles of fence swept away, and many houses and barns burned. The work of destruction continued several weeks, but was most violent and uncontrollable about from the fifteenth to the twentieth of July. The efforts of the inhabitants succeeded in some instances in checking the conflagration, but in other cases human efforts were unavailing, and flaming surges swept onward without restraint. The scenery of the burning forests, especially at night, is said to have been awfully sublime and impressive.

An accident happened at the furnace, in September, 1843, which destroyed the building and fatally burned one of the laborers. This was caused by the blowing up of the furnace, an accident to which those supplied by loam ore, are more liable than others, and against which nothing but the greatest care of those having charge, can effectually guard. It is caused by the clogging up of the inside, by which the mass of ore and fuel does not settle down as the parts below waste away, before the blast, thus forming a cavern of intensely glowing heat. When the mass above becomes detached and falls, the water in the damp ore being instantly changed to steam, expands with terrific violence, always throwing out of the furnace whatever it contains, and usually setting fire to the wood work on the premises, and effectually putting a stop to the blast. On the occasion of the blowing up of this furnace in September, 1843, the liquid iron at the bottom was thrown out by the violence of the explosion, miserably burning one of the firemen, who died a few hours after in the greatest agony. Similar accidents have happened at Carthage, and other furnaces in Northern New York, that are supplied with bog ores.

The village of Brasher Falls, near the southwest corner of the town on St. Regis river, about a mile below the junction of the two branches, and the same distance from the Brasher and Stocholm depot on the Northern rail road, was first commenced by John Crapser, of New York, who, in the fall of 1826, built a dam and saw mill on the falls in the river at this place. The saw mill was got in operation for lumbering, and two or three dwellings erected the following spring; but no increase occurred in the place until the fall of 1839, when Calvin T. Hulburd, of Stockholm, purchased a tract of six hundred acres of land, on both sides of the river, including the site of the present village. In 1841 he commenced and finished a grist mill and dwelling; a small woolen factory was built soon after. A bridge had been built, partly at the expense of the town, several years previous to 1839. A fork and hoe factory was established by F. and T. R. Taylor in 1846, a manufactory of agricultural implements, by Davis & Co., from Maine, in 1851, and a foundery by the same company in 1852. The facilities of this place for manufacturing purposes, are worthy of especial notice; as the amount of water power is immense, and still but partly appropriated, and its vicinity to the railroad, gives it a direct access to market. The St. Regis river, the two branches of which unite near the rail road bridge, a mile above, here descends a declivity which, in a state of nature, must have presented a rapid of singular wildness and beauty. The volume of water is here amply sufficient for a large amount of power, and admits of being repeatedly used within a short distance. Among the manufactories at this place, those of forks and hoes, by Messrs. Taylor, and of agricultural implements, by Davis & Co., are quite extensive, and give employment to a great number of laborers. The former of these deserves mention' from its being the pioneer in the business of manufacturing cast steel polished forks in the country. Mr. F. Taylor commenced this business at Parishville in 1831. In 1840, he erected at Bicknellville machinery for facilitating the business, and here during five or six years, the number of forks and hoes made, ranged from fifteen to twenty thousand a year. In 1846 the manufactory was removed to Brasher Falls, where from twenty to thirty thousand forks, and from six to twelve thousand hoes, are made annually, and exported from hence to nearly every state of the union.

Religious Societies.—The First Presbyterian and Congregational church of Helena, was organized June 1, 1837; Benjamin Nevins, Linus Kibble and Grant Johnson, trustees. A church edifice was built in 1837-8, and the Rev. Messrs. Rufus R. Demming, of Massena, ——— Howe and Charles Jones have been employed as a partial supply, there having been no settled pastor. The First Presbyterian society of Brasher Falls, was incorporated under the general act, February 24, 1845. Ebenezer S. Hulburd, Martin Smith, Hiram Holcomb, Sidney Kelsey, Justin Bell, Jehiel Stevens and Elijah Wood, being the first trustees. The church was formed July 8, 1844, by about seventeen members, mostly from the church in East Stockholm, who employed the Rev. S. S. Howe, as their first clergyman. He has been succeeded by Rev. Charles Jones and Hiram Dyer, the present pastor. A church edifice was erected in 1847. The church at present numbers about 60. The First Society of the Methodist Episcopal church of Maple Ridge, was incorporated February 29, 1848; D. Wait, William F. Wait, Luther S. Carter, Benjamin Bell and V. G. Carter, trustees. The First Society of the M. E. church of Brasher Falls, incorporated April 10, 1848, had David Richards, Heman Holmes, Joseph Eester, Ethan Johnson and John S. Hall, as its first trustees. Each of these societies has a chapel, the one at the falls having been built in 1851. At Brasher Iron Works, a Baptist society has existed, but has been scattered. A Freewill Baptist church was formed in this town in July, 1848, by Eld. John Sweat. Its first number was 9, and present 13 members, Eld. A. P. Walcott is pastor. In 1851, a catholic church was built half a mile east of the village, by the Rev. Mr. Keveny, of Hogansburgh.

CANTON

Was erected from Lisbon, March 28, 1805, with its present limits, the first town meeting being held at the house of Stillman Foote. The poor moneys were to be divided by the last tax list. During this session, the settlers of Oswegatchie, Madrid and Massena had petitioned for a division of these towns, and Mr. B. Wright, in the assembly, from the committee to whom the matter had been referred, reported March 26th, that " they found their situation peculiarly inconvenient, as they had to travel from fifteen to thirty miles to town meeting."

Memoranda from the Town Records.—In 1806 and 1812, $5 bounties offered for wolves, and in 1810 and 1816, $10. In 1810, a fine of $12 imposed on all jugglers, mountebanks and wire dancers. $50 raised, for securing the rights and privileges of fish ; and S. Foote, D. Campbell and N. Walker, a committee for the purpose. This was afterwards a matter of solicitude with the town, and of legislative action. In 1815, C. Wilson, F. Tracy and Wm. Richardson were appointed a committee for making Grass river navigable for fish of all kinds to come up and down at pleasure, and $50 voted for the purpose. On the 12th of April, 1824, a law made Grass river a public highway, from its mouth to the high falls, in Canton, and dams were allowed to be erected, on condition that passages or sluices should be made for fish to pass. Neglecting this, or setting nets or weiers, was punishable by a fine of $25. As early as April 5, 1813, a law was passed, " that no person should draw any seine, set any net, or make any obstructions, in Oswego, Racket or St. Regis rivers, under a penalty of $25. The avowed object of this law was, to protect Salmon, which frequented these rivers in early times, and in 1806-7, were caught as far up Grass river as Russell. In 1825, the town appointed Minot Jenison and Thomas D. Olin to enquire into the condition of dams, and prosecute any violation of the law; promising to indemnify them for losses arising from law suits.

In 1811, resolved to preserve in the town records, the dates of births, deaths and marriages, which were to be reported to the clerk under a penalty of $1; and in 1812, it was made the duty of the assessors to collect these data. In 1823 and 1825, $500 voted for the support of the poor, and similar but smaller sums voted in other years. In 1835, the legislature was petitioned for a law, to tax the town $500, to be paid to the trustees of the public lands in trust for the academy, to be invested for its benefit, on condition that the trustees execute bonds for the conveyance of the lot and buildings for a school. In 1836, M. Jenison, J. H. Conkey, S. D. Olin, R. N. Harrison, D. Mack, J. Ames, 2d, C. Foote, S. Wright Jr., L. Moody, D. Clark, H. Barber and A. Smith appointed a committee to superintend the academy, and employ a teacher, and to attend to the interest of the town therein. In 1837, voted a tax of $500 for three years for the academy, on condition that a subscription of an equal sum be raised. In 1840, a crow bounty of one shilling, and in 1841-2, one of ten cents voted. In 1846, $1,000 voted for a town house, in three equal sums. Benjamin Squires and Cyrus Abernethy a committee to erect it. In 1849, at a special meeting, the legislature was petitioned for a law taxing the town $6,000, in six equal sums, for building a plank road, from the village to town line, towards Gouveneur, which was done. Luman Moody, Theodore Caldwell and Joseph J. Merriman were recommended as commissioners to build the road.

Supervisors.—1806, Stillman Foote; 1807-8, Daniel Walker; 1809-12, Daniel Campbell; 1813-22, Daniel Walker; 1823-4, Thomas D. Olin; 1825-6, Jeduthan Farwell; 1828-30, James Parkill; 1831-3, Silas Baldwin Jr.; 1834-5, John Heaton; 1836-40, Lemuel Buck; 1841-2, Henry Barber; 1843-4, Richard N. Harrison; 1845-6, Henry Barber; 1847-8, Cyrus Abernethy; 1849, William F. Cahoon; 1850-2, Hiram S. Johnson.

Canton was surveyed by Amos Lay, assisted by Reuben Sherwood and Joseph Edsall, in the summer of 1799. Their labors included both townships of Canton and Lisbon. Among the men who were employed to assist, were the following: Festus and Septimus Tracy, Nahum Allen, George Goss, Abner Hazelton, Alvin White, Jacob Redington, —— Thompson. The supplies of provisions for the summer's operations, were boated up in canoes, through Oswegatchie river and Indian creek (natural canal), and up the Grass river, to the site of the present village of Canton. While working near the St. Lawrence, their supplies were carried directly over at whatever point they might happen to need them. The survey of the two townships being completed, the hands returned to New England through Canada. While the survey was going on, the parties engaged on it were frequently back and forth from the front settlements in Canada, and the subject of the value of the lands was much discussed, and a high idea was entertained of their probable value for agricultural purposes. This led to the formation of an association, consisting of thirty or forty Canadians, who proposed to form a settlement on the tract, and who sent one of their number to Albany, to negotiate a bargain with the proprietors, for a purchase. This agent is said to have effected a conditional bargain for one-quarter of a township, wherever the company might wish to locate, in Lisbon or Canton. Upon receiving this intelligence, the whole party decided upon traversing the tract, to learn its actual value, by direct observation; and accordingly, taking several days' provisions on their backs, and guided by persons who had been employed in the survey, they separated in small parties, and pursued their course in various directions, through the woods. At night they would meet at an appointed place, kindle an immense fire of logs and dry materials which they collected, and camp around it for the night.

Every thing proceeded agreeably for a while, but unfortunately for their harmony, numbers of them came from different quarters upon a remarkably beautiful tract of land, in the southeastern part of Canton' where the hard timber was unusually clear and lofty, and a meandering stream wandered through the forest between banks that, in their native growth of timber and herbage, and the soil at the surface, betokened unusual richness and fertility. Here, without the knowledge of each other, several parties resolved to locate their interests, and in accordance with the prevalent custom, commenced slight improvements, which, in their opinions, would confer a preëmption right to the soil. These proceedings soon became known to the whole party, and the overlapping claims of rivals engendered a party strife, in which each loudly vociferated his claims, and insisted upon the priority of his arrival, and 'in an incredibly short space of time, the schemes of the whole party were dissipated. Of confidence in each other's honor, they had none; and the mutual distrust led to the dissolution of the company, who scattered immediately, and by different routes, sought the St. Lawrence, and crossed again to Canada. Some being ignorant of the course of the rivers, wandered from their way, and did not reach the great river, till they had arrived in Louisville; and when they gained the settlements, were well nigh exhausted with hunger and fatigue.

The first land that was taken up with the view of actual settlement in the town of Canton, was by Daniel Harrington, a native of Connecticut, but who had afterwards lived in Vermont, and in Canada. In 1800, he took up a tract of land on the east side of Grass river, where Canton village now is, having commenced a small improvement the fall before, which consisted of a slight clearing, near the present agricultural fair ground, and on the bank of the river, where he sowed less than an acre of land to wheat, in the fall of 1800; and having no team to assist him, he harrowed in the grain with a hand rake. , The crop was sold to Mr. Foote, and when harvested, yielded more than sixty bushels, notwithstanding the immense numbers of squirrels of that year. By a striking coincidence, the officers of the society in selecting their fair grounds located them almost exactly on the spot which had thus early betokened its capabilities for agricultural improvement. The cabin of this pioneer, stood on the spot where the flag staff of the fair ground is erected. In the fall of 1799, several men came into town, and made slight clearings, supposing that thereby they acqired a preemption right; but the first permanent settler, was Stillman Foote, Esq., from Middlebury, Vt., who came into town to look for lands, in 1800, and purchased the mile square, on which Canton village now stands. Harrington's title, including the wheat crop, he purchased for a horse, saddle and bridle. In March, 1801, Mr. Foote left his home in Vermont, for his location, with two teams laden with provisions and furniture; but upon the approach of warm weather, he was obliged to leave a great part of his load at Willsborough, on Lake

18

Champlain, to be taken, together with the irons for a mill, by the more circuitous route of Lake Champlain and St. Lawrence river to Lisbon, the nearest accessible point, about 18 miles from his destination. A very poor road conducted our emigrants as far as Chateaugay, where every trace of a road ended, and they were obliged to seek the St. Lawrence at St. Regis, where they crossed and proceeded along the Canada shore to opposite Lisbon. From this place they were guided to Canton by an obscure trace marked for a road. Mr. Daniel W. Church, who had been engaged as a millright, followed by water, having charge of the mill irons and remainder of the loading left at the lake. From his diary before us, the following memoranda are taken:-

"March 27th, took leave of my family and home. 29th, went to Bason Creek, and waited some days. April 1st, got a passage for old Mr. Foote, [Daniel F., the father of S. F.,] to Plattsburgh, in company with one Mr. Storer, who had a spare horse there, and sent my two men with him. Thought I had taken a prudent step to keep the old gentleman from catching the small pox, which he would be much exposed to, should he go with me through Canada. 4th. Got our loading on board, and set sail; got myself set on shore at Carlotte to get more loading. The vessel could not wait; I got aboard of another with Johnson, and set sail. Just at night the wind rises, and the evening is very dark. The passengers, of whom there were 50, begin to be very sick. The vessel is poorly manned, and I remain on deck to assist the captain in working it, as it is in some danger. Run in at Peru, and lay at anchor in the swell all night. Could hardly see land when within 20 yards; and suffered intolerably with cold, having no blanket, nor even great coat. 5th. The wind dies away, and we set our passengers on shore, and sail with a moderate breeze till the morning of the 6th, when we reached St. John. Met with Johnson and my other company, and walked to Laprairie. 8th. Go to the Indian village, 9 miles above Laprairie, and ferry across to Lachine. The Indian village is the handsomest town I have seen in my whole voyage, except Mt. Real. To see the Indians at their homes was quite new to me. 9th. Went back to Mt. Real, on foot, after a canal ticket. Set out just at evening, and it was dark before I left the place. Lost my way, and returning, was hindered some time, but arrived at my company in so short a time, as to surprise them. 10th. Agree with Mr. Tuttle concerning a boat, as follows: He is to have a boat and two hands, or one hand and work himself; and I am to find the rest of the help, and pay the canal ticket. Tuttle is clerk to one Crystler, and takes a passage in another boat, and agrees with Mr. Grant to hire two hands, but the latter can not, because it is seed-time with the Canadians. We set out without any help, but can not get along, the current is so strong. Happen to hear of two hands, who will go to Pt. Clair, 8 or 9 miles; hire them and arrive there. 11th. Go to Cedars with great difficulty. 12th. Arrive at the King's locks, where the hands being all beaten out, leave the boat, and we hire Canadians in their room. I go in the boat and come very near getting lost in the rapids. Meet with as much hardship as I know how to get along with, and after toiling as hard as possible, arrive at the head of Lake St. Francis, between 9 and 10, in the evening. 13th. Sail across the lake a little below Cornwall. 14th. Go above Cornwall. Tuttle hires 2 hands, one good, the other worse than none. We find it impossible to get any farther with our loading. 15th. Arranged business, and set out on foot,

hardly able to stir. Go to Crystlers, and have dfficulty in settling with
—— who refuses to allow some borrowed money. 16th. Arrive at Lisbon, at the house of James Turner. 17th. Reach Canton, with seventeen
blisters on my hand, occasioned by rowing and pulling the bateau along.
Find Thomas down with the fever and ague."

Mr. Church was accompanied by Libeus Johnson and sons; John
Flannegan, a journeyman, Thomas Marvin, an apprentice, and one or
two others. He found in the camp Mr. Foote and his father, who had
come through on horseback, and others to the number of twelve, who
all occupied the same shanty, and without the first convenience; as every
article not of prime necessity, had been left at Cornwall until a road
could so far be cleared as to allow of the passage to teams. An entire
week was consumed in getting the teams from Lisbon, and on Saturday
night they were still three miles from camp, where the cattle were left
to browse, and the men came on. The whole party then proceeded to
return to them, and the loads were got in. The first clearing was made
on the west side of the river near the water's edge just below the present
bridge. The party immediately set about preparing the frame of a sawmill, but had scarcely begun operations, when the camp was visited by
sickness, and one of the number stricken down by death. On the 2d of
May, Mr. Church, the mill-wright, was attacked by an intermittent fever,
contracted the summer previous, and about the same time, the elder Mr
Foote was taken with symptoms, at first not understood, but soon too
sadly recognized as the small pox. Five of the company had been inoculated, and this operation was forthwith performed upon the other
six. Although nearly four score years of age, the invalid bore his sickness well, and at one time it was hoped he would survive. But on the
accession of the secondary fever, he grew worse and died. His last
words were: " God's will be done." Mr. Church at this time, was not
able to sit up in his couch of hemlock boughs, and the symptoms were
beginning to appear upon those who had been inoculated. Stillman
Foote had fallen a few days previous, and broken a rib, which disabled
him from rendering assistance. They kept the corpse until the third
day, watching it by turns, and then committed it to the earth, wrapped
in the hammock on which he died, with a few hemlock boughs below
him, and the bark of an elm tree for a coffin. There was at this time,
no medical aid to be had, nearer than Johnstown, in Canada, and even
this was not to be reached, as the heavy rains had rendered all the
streams impassable, so that a young man who had been sent out, was
obliged to return. This is believed to be the first death of a white person in Canton, and occurred May 10th, 1801. We will here resume our
quotation from Mr. Church's diary, which describes the difficulties of

the settlers with vividness. It covers some of the events above described:

"May 2. Myself had the fever and ague. 4th. Had an intolerable fit of it. Gloomy times. 5th. Worked. Very rainy at night; camp leaks everywhere; no place to lay down in. Sleep none at all. Have free scope for my thoughts, not having anything to interrupt me, but the snoring of the rest of the company, soaking in water. With great difficulty I prevent the rain dropping on old Mr. Foote. Let any person imagine himself in the woods, fifteen miles from any house, sick of the fever and ague, one of the company rotten with the small pox, one with his ribs broke, one other ghostified with the fever and ague, three inoculated with the small pox, and only three well ones, and let him imagine himself exposed to all the rains, without physician, or nurse, or medicines; then let him awake and find it a dream, and see how glad he will be! 10th. More trouble; the old gentleman died, and I am growing worse every day. The three well ones bury the old man as well as they can in his hammock, and put some barks over him. Hard times for poor Stillman, who had to lay his own father in his winding sheet. 13th. Ride out to Lisbon with extreme difficulty. I can not sit on a horse. Ride bare-backed. Get wet with rain through and through. From Canton to Lisbon settlement is fifteen miles without the least opening; very little road, and very many swamps and mireholes. 14th. Go to Dr. Adams's and back on foot, fourteen miles. Half an hour before I set out while the fever was on, I could not walk across the house. 25th. So far recovered as to ride back to Canton."

Mr. Church was soon compelled to go back to his friends, and the rest of the party having partly finished the mill, returned back to spend the winter in Vt. In the spring of 1802, Mr. Foote returned with his family, consisting of a wife, two sons, and a daughter, and they took up their abode in a corner of the saw-mill. Mr. Church and three companions proceeded through the woods from Chateaugay, a distance of about 70 miles, without mark or guide, but a compass. Their goods were borne by a pack-horse, and they were five days on the pathless road, most of the time in the rain, and towards the last of their journey, so short of provisions, that they were obliged to subsist upon pork and partridges, of the latter of which they chanced to kill a few on the way. During this summer a single run of rock stones driven by a tub wheel, was got in operation in a part of the mill, and this was the first and only grist mill in town, until after the war.

During the summer of 1802, a thrilling incident happened, which well nigh proved fatal to one of the party. On a sabbath morning about 20 persons had assembled at the mill from the several clearings to spend a day in social intercourse, and discuss the news. Two men were crossing the river in the only boat in the place, and had gained an island, when the current unexpectedly caught the boat, and was taking it down stream. One jumped out, but in so doing, threw the bow of the boat further into the current, and the remaining one finding it impossible to gain the island, jumped overboard with his setting pole, and lodged on a rock where he could maintain himself but with great difficulty, while the boat was swept down, and broken among the rapids below. Mr. Church procured a rope and swam over to the island, where making one end fast to a tree, he let himself down stream till he could get the other end into the hands of the one in peril, who was thus rescued from what appeared to be certain destruction.

In 1802, the town began to settle rapidly, and among others, Peter R. Leonard, Moses Leonard, Thomas D. Olin, Chester Dewey, Lebeus Johnson, and five sons, James Parkil, Daniel Walker, Nathan Walker, —— Kingsbury, most of them with families, and from Vermont, immigrated. The first school was taught in 1804, by William Barker; and religious meetings began to be held the same year. The second death was that of one Osgood, who was killed in 1803, about three miles south of Foote's, by the fall of a tree. The first birth in town, was a daughter of L. Johnson, in 1803; and the first male born in town, is said to have been a son of P. R. Leonard, in 1803.

Before the war, a forge was built on the east side of the river by Mr. Foote, and run upon bog ores from the north part of the town. The extravagant price of iron at that period, justified an expense for its reduction, that would be now wholly inadmissible. A dam was built at the village soon after the mill, but the bridge not till after the war. The west side of the river long continued to be the principal seat of business. A Mr. Farwell is said to have been the first settler east of the river, where the most of the village of Canton is now located.

In 1831, (April 9,) the legislature voted a tax of $1,800 on the town, for a bridge at the village, naming Jno. Day, Isaac Heaton, and Thomas H. Conkey, commissioners for its erection, with power to anticipate by a loan, the fund to be raised. This bridge was destroyed by a freshet in June, 1843. It was soon rebuilt, and in 1852, again rebuilt.

The first inn in Canton, was opened by Mr. Foote, soon after he became established, and for several years the town settled very fast. In the south part of the town, in the vicinity of South Canton, Benjamin Rose, of Dorsett, Vt., began in 1806, and soon after, Ward Squires, Abner Wells, and John Rose. The village of Canton began to grow rapidly after the location of the court house, in 1828, and its central location, in the midst of a highly cultivated region and fine water power, give it much importance. A destructive fire occurred here on the 4th of October, 1843.

The village of Canton was incorporated May 14, 1845. Its bounds were made to include the jail limits, as they then existed, excepting thereout the bridge across Grass river. The officers of the village were

to be five trustees, two of whom shall be inhabitants of the two school
districts on the east side of the river, and the fifth to reside on the west
side of the river, with three assessors, one treasurer, one clerk, and one
collector, who were to be elected on the first Monday of May of each
year. The president of the board of trustees was to be chosen by themselves, out of their number, soon after each annual election. The powers
of the trustees extended to those subjects which relate to the internal governments of a village, including the organization and supervision of a
fire department, the care of roads and public squares, &c., coupled with
the power of enforcing their regulations by fines within certain limita-
tions fixed by statute. The following is a list of the trustees which have
been elected annually in the village of Canton, since its organization.
The persons elected as president are given in italics:

1846, Prosper Barrows, Benjamin Squire, Nathan Pratt, Barzillai Hodskin, and *Nathaniel Hodskin.*
1847, Ebenezer Miner, Daniel Mack, *Elias G. Page*, Harry Smith, Orville Page.
1848, Ebenezer Miner, B. Hodskin, Calvin Williams, Harry Smith,
Prosper Barrows.
1849, P. Barrows, S. J. Bingham, Harvey M. Childs, H. Smith, *Paul
Boynton.*
1850, E. Miner, Darius Clark, *A. R. Kipp*, O. Page, Nathaniel Hodskin.
1851, Wm. Blanchard, Theodore Caldwell, Vincent Coan, Martin
Thatcher, *P. Boynton.*
1852, Benjamin Squire, *Luman Moody*, Clapp Bailey, O. Page, L. B.
Storrs.

By an act passed April 21, 1846, the board of supervisors were directed to levy a tax of $333·33 annually, for three years, in Canton, for
the erection of a town house in that village, to be paid to Benjamin Squire
and Cyrus Abernethy, who were named in the act as commissioners to
expend the above sum for this purpose. The supervisor of the town is
ex-officio the trustee of the house, and has control of the same. The
town house was accordingly erected, and stands fronting a public square
before the county buildings, and near the academy.

On the 11th of April, 1832, the Canton Social Library was incorporated; Darius Clark, Moses Whitcomb, Wm. Perry, Jr., Lyman Langdon,
Wm. F. Cahoon, Elias C. Page, and Benjamin Walker, being first trustees.
Like most other library associations this is believed to have become
extinct since the formation of school district libraries.

On both sides of Grass river, but mostly on the west bank, and near
the north part of the town, is the village of *Morley*, which name it received in 1835 from the family name of the Harrison relatives. It was
formerly called *Long Rapids*, and first began to be settled in the spring
of 1810, by S. Foote, of Canton, who built a saw mill here. In 1811, a

second saw mill, and in 1815 a wooden grist mill, were built, the latter by Christopher Wilson. Mr. F. sold his interest in 1812. The sum of $150 was in 1817 voted for a bridge at this place. The present stone mill was built for Mr. Harrison, the proprietor. It is a place of considerable business, having two saw mills (one a gang mill of 32 saws), four shingle machines, a sash factory, tannery, two wagon shops, a tavern, three stores, and about fifty or sixty families. A plank road from Canton to the Northern Rail Road passes through the village.

Near the north-west corner of the town, on the Oswegatchie river, and 11 miles distant from Ogdensburgh, with which place it communicates by plank road, is the village of *Rensselaer Falls*, which began in 1839, by the erection of a forge, by Tate, Chafee & Co. It first had the name of *Tateville*, from Robert Tate, of the above firm, but it has been more generally known as *Canton Falls*, until the recent establishment of a post office. The forge was west of the river, and at first had three fires, and was worked on specular ore from Hermon, and bog ores from Lisbon. A saw mill was built in 1839 by Mr. Van Rensselaer, the proprietor, and in 1846 the present stone grist mill. This village has been surveyed into lots, and the Oswegatchie, which here has a fall of about six feet, gives it an abundant water power. A congregational church was formed here in 1842, and a society in 1847, who erected a church edifice in 1848. The Rev. —— Parsons, and Rev. Goreham Cross, have been employed here. A cemetery association at this place was incorporated April 15, 1852, with Jacob Shull, B. Morrison, Augustus Johnson, A. G. Pierce, G. W. Cooper, and Caleb S. Johnson, trustees.

Near this village the *Natural canal*, which forms so striking a feature of the country, joins the Oswegatchie. It was originally open both at this and Grass river, and navigable for small boats, and became the highway to mill by the pioneers. This channel is six miles long, and from 5 to 10 and even 25 rods wide, with a descent of three feet towards the Oswegatchie. It runs through an alluvial flat, of about 4500 acres, covered by a forest of black ash and soft maple, which has hitherto been too wet to cultivate, but is now in process of reclaiming. The outlet on the Oswegatchie has been closed, and a canal cut along the bank to below the dam, by which the water is expected to be lowered about four feet. It has cost about $6000. The outlet on Grass river has long since been closed. This channel is known on some maps, and among the inhabitants, as Indian creek.

In 1816, an act of 1807, relating to the gospel and school lots of central New York, was extended to this county, and authorized the supervisor, and two commissioners, chosen at a town meeting, to lease them for a term not over 21 years, and to apply the proceeds to the support of the gospel or schools, or both, as the town might vote. On the 21st of March, 1823, a law was passed allowing three trustees to be chosen, with powers similar to those of the town of Madrid previously created.

About a mile below the High falls on Grass river, near the south part of Canton, where that river issues from a romantic rocky ravine, its channel broken by rapids, and its banks discolored by reddish and yellow stains from the efflorescence of iron pyrites, which here form an important constituent of the rock, stand the remains of a manufactory of copperas and alum, which have for many years been going to ruin. This manufactory was commenced in the year 1832, by S. & H. Foote, of Canton, who on the following summer were joined by G. W. Shepard, and J. C. Bush, of Ogdensburgh, the premises having been leased for ten years for the purpose. During the first year, but little was done, but getting the works in order, and erecting suitable fixtures for the manufacture. In the summers of 1833-4-5, and a part of 1836, from sixty to eighty hands were employed, but the enterprise being found one that did not remunerate it was abandoned. The process of the manufacture depends upon chemical principles and was as follows. The rock abounding in iron pyrites, (sulphuret of iron) was first dug and broken by hand, a process easily effected, from the tender and porous texture of the mineral. A clay bed having been prepared on the ground, and a quanty of wood first laid, it was covered with the pulverized stone and ignited. When once fairly on fire, it would burn of itself, from the great percentage of sulphur in the mineral, and it needed no further care than to throw on new ore, with water, to reduce the pile to a smouldering heap, charged with the saline substances sought, which were lixiviated by the application of water; the ley collected and boiled in a large leaden tank, ten or twelve feet square, and two feet deep, and when sufficiently concentrated pumped into vats and allowed to crystalize on racks hung in them for the purpose. After the first crop of crystals of copperas was obtained, the residual liquor was again boiled with the addition of certain proportions of potash, and the second time set to crystalize, when alum was obtained. The proportions obtained were three parts of copperas to one of alum.

The fumes which arose from the burning and smouldering heaps were very disagreeable, and so noxious that a great number of trees in the vicinity were destroyed by those poisonous emanations. More than a thousand tons of copperas, and a third as much of alum, were made here while the works were in operation. Most of it found its way to the New York market. Unlimited quantities of iron pyrites, exist at this place which may hereafter offer inducements for the renewal of this manufacture, or the making of soda ash, should facilities for transportation to market be increased, or cheaper and more efficient methods of manufacture be discovered.

Religious Societies.—The earliest religious organization in town was by the Presbyterians, who united under the Rev. Amos Pettingill, in 1807. He was a missionary, sent by the New Hampshire Missionary Society, and was instrumental in forming several of the churches of this order in the county, for which reason a brief biographical notice may be appropriate. Mr. P. was born at Salem, N. H., Aug. 9, 1780, and in 1798, he entered Atkinson Academy, and afterwards Harvard College, as a charity student, where he graduated in 1805. In June, 1806, he was appointed a missionary to travel through the new settlements, between Lakes Champlain and Ontario, and spent sixteen weeks on this service, 'which by reason of the fewness of the inhabitants, the badness of the roads and the frequent want of comfortable lodgings, involved hardships little less than perilous.'* In December he was ordained as an evangelist, and employed by the Missionary Society, of Mass., and he the next year returned to his former labors, and in 1807, was installed over a church in Champlain, where he continued till after the war. He subsequently preached in several places, and died Aug. 19, 1830. In forming the Canton church, he was assisted by the Rev. Ebenezer Hibbard, of Vt. It consisted of the following persons: George Foote, John Richardson, Weltha Foote, Betsy Donegly, M. Conkey, Jane Ross, and P. Richardson. They were only occasionally supplied by the ministry until 1823, when the Rev. Hiram S. Johnson, became pastor, who remained until 1837, when he was dismissed from ill health, and in Feb. 1839, the Rev. Roswell Pettibone† was installed, who still remains the pastor. The First Presbyterian Society in the town of Canton, was incorporated, July 22, 1825, Elias C. Page, Silas Wright, Jr., Joseph Barnes, Henry Foot, Wm. Richardson, and Eden Ray, being the first trustees.

Presbyterian Church and Parsonage, Canton.

The church has received more than 300 members, but from deaths and removals, they number at present, but 183. In 1826 or 7, the public square in front of the church and parsonage, here represented, was presented to the town, by Silas Wright, and Joseph Barnes. The church in the census of 1850, is reported capable of seating 1200, and worth $6,500. It is built of Potsdam sandstone, and is quite ornamental to the village.

The First Congregational Society in the town of Canton, was incor-

* Memoir of Amos Pettingill, from which these facts are derived.
† We are indebted to Mr. P. for the above data.

porated Jan. 16, 1815. Geo. Foote, Hosea Catlin, and Hubbard Clark, trustees. The First Methodist Society in the town of Canton, was incorporated, Nov. 3, 1819; Jesse Barnes, Hugh Montgomery, Isaac Bull, Jeduthan Farwell, Wm. Perry, and Wm. Richardson, trustees. As a farther account of the denomination will be given by itself, further notices, except the dates of incorporation will be omitted. The Frst Baptist Evangelical Society, of Canton, was incorporated Dec. 10, 1823; R. Bacheller, T. D. Olin, and Jno' Paul, trustees. Members of this order had associated as early as 1814-15, under the Rev. Ruppe Batchelor, from Addison, Vt., and in June 1817, formed a church of 12 members. Mr. B. was ordained in 1818, and in 1819, Justin Olin and Joseph Olin, were appointed deacons. Meetings were first held in the north part of the town, and afterwards at the village. Eld. Richard Palmer succeeded as pastor, in 1825, Eld. Joel Peck, in 1831, and subsequently Henry Greene, O. Scott, Clement Havens, Silas Pratt, George Lile, and in Jan. 1842, L. D. Ford. After about two and a half years, Cha's Nickols, succeeded who remained two years. On the 8th of Dec. 1847, Eld. John Wilder, succeeded, from whom these dates are derived. For several years from 1831, a branch existed in the south part of the town, which has since been united with the main body. About 1830, this society united with the Universalists, in building the brick church, and in 1848 they built a separate church on an adjoining lot, at a cost of $1,200, which was dedicated by a sermon from Eld. Joseph Sawyer, Feb. 8, 1849. In a revival that soon followed, about forty members were added; the present number is 130. The First Calvanistic Congregational Society, of Canton, was incorporated Sept. 15, 1823, Jeduthan Farwell, Wm. Hatch, Luther Brown, and Samuel Clark, trustees.

The First Universalist Society, in the town of Canton, was incorporated March 10, 1836; Lemuel Buck, Joseph Ames, 2d, and Minot Jenison, trustees. This society has an elegant brick church, fronting the public square, which in the census of 1850, is reported capable of seating 1000 persons, and worth $5,000. This society has a church organization, and numbers about 300. The next society incorporated in town, was Grace Church, in the town of Canton, Aug. 22, 1836. Richard N. Harrison, Roswell Green, Wardens; John D. Burns, Darius Clark, Elam Russ, Harry Foote, Lyman Ellsworth, Thos. Viner, Chauncy Foote, and Henry Van Rensselaer, Vestrymen. A church was built in 1841-2, and consecrated Sept. 3, 1842, by the Bishop T .Onderdonk. At its organization it numbered 19, and at present it has fifty members. The clergymen employed here have been, Richard Bury (1836), Wm. Tutham, Johnson A. Brayton, Thos. P. Tyler, F. J. Hawley, Wm. G. French, Minot M. Wells, and Abel Ogden, now presiding. Richard F. Harrison, present clerk.

The First Methodist and Free-Will Baptist Union Society, of the village of Morley, was incorporated Feb. 1, 1842; Wm F. Hollenbeck, Henry Wells, Stephen D. Arnold, Thomas G. Meredith and Wesley Byington, trustees. The First Wesleyan Methodist Society, of the village of Morley, was incorporated, Sept. 23, 1843; D. Clemens, Joel Seger, Zelotus Whitney, John Allen, Wm. Allen, Thomas Buffam, trustees. This society has a church which in the census of 1850, is reported $1,000. The first Congregational Society of Canton Falls, was incorporated July 19, 1847, John Shull, Jun., Wm. Hanna, Theophilus T. Rathbone, trustees. This society has erected a church.

COLTON,

Was erected from Parishville, April 12, 1843, embracing townships

10, 7, 4, and 1. The first town meeting was directed to be held at the inn nearest the post office in Matildavale. This act took effect on the 1st of February, 1844. Pain Converse was appointed to preside at the first town meeting. By an act of the board of supervisors passed November 18, 1851, that part of the town of Parishville, known as Mile Squares, number one, six, and twelve, and all that part of Mile Square lot number two, west of Raquette river, was taken from that town and annexed to Colton. This act was to take effect on the 1st of February, following.

The town of Colton was erected in compliance with a petition from the town of Parishville, which at the town meeting of 1843, voted for the formation of a new town, by the name of Springfield. The present name is derived from the middle name of Jesse C. Higley, an inhabit-ant. A post office by the name of *Matildaville*, had been previously established, but this was soon changed to agree with that of the town.

Memoranda from records.—The first set of town officers elected, were, Pain Converse, *supervisor;* James H. Bridge, *clerk;* Zina Hepburn, Silas Hawley, Hiram Pierce, *justices;* Silas Hawley, Jessey C. Higley, *inspectors of elections;* J. C. Higley, James S. Ellis, Clark D. Norris, *assessors;* J. C. Higley, *sup. schools;* Israel C. Draper, Phineas Hepburn, Henry Gibbins, *com. of highways;* Zina Hepburn, Hiram Pierce, *over-seers of poor;* Hiram Leonard, *collector and constable;* Wait Perry, *sealer of weights and measures.*

In 1844, the poor moneys, from Parishville, voted for the support of schools. In 1848, voted against a division of the county.

Supervisors: 1844, Pain Converse; 1845-7, James S. Ellis; 1848-9, James H. Bridge; 1850-1, Silas Hawley; 1852, Lorenzo Chamberlain.

The first settlement in this town was made in March, 1824, by Abel Brown, and his son James Brown, and were very soon succeeded by Asahel Lyman and Wm. Bullard, who commenced their improvements a short distance south of the present village. In 1825, Horace Garfield, from Potsdam, erected a saw mill, and in 1828, Samuel Partridge built a forge of two fires on the right bank of the Raquette river, near the head of the falls. It was kept in operation until about 1840, and was run upon magnetic ores chiefly. Some bog ores were used, but the adventure was considered rather as an experiment, and proving unprofitable, was abandoned. A starch factory was built here in 1844, and continued a few years, making about thirty-five tons, annually, from potatoes. In 1828, a grist mill was built by Jonathan Culver. The recent impulse which has been given to the lumbering business, by the completion of the northern rail road, which has given new value to the immense forest which covers the southern part of the county, has created at the village of Colton, a lumbering interest of much importance, and more than

doubled the size of the place within two years. About 1850, A. M.
Adsit & Co., erected in the east bank of the river, a gang mill, of about
70 saws, which, working day and night, manufacture 35,000 feet of
boards, daily, and in 1852, Messrs. Pratt, Bacheller & Co., erected on
the opposite bank, a similar mill of 60 saws. In 1852, E. H. Southworth,
built a gang mill, on the west bank, two miles above.

The logs which supply these mills and several others below, come
down the Raquette, in the spring floods, from the remote recesses of the
forest, on the south border of the county, and from Franklin, Hamilton
and Essex counties. So long as this supply lasts, the village of Colton
will possess importance, and when it is gone, the superior water power,
and vicinity of iron ores, and fuel, may, if properly employed, make it a
manufacturing place of considerable consequence. The river at the
village plunges down a steep declivity, to the depth of about sixty feet,
and it is said to have a fall of three hundred feet, within two miles. The
wildness and grandeur of these rapids, when the river is swolen by the
melting of snow, can not be sufficiently admired.

The first school in town, was taught in the summer of 1826, by Miss
—— Young. The first death, was a child of James Brown, in 1829.
The first religious meetings were held by the Christian sect, at the house
of Mr. Lyman. There are at present, two religious organizations in town;
the Methodist and Universalist, each of which were in 1852, engaged in
erecting a church.

De Kalb.

This town, embracing the original township of ten miles square, was
erected from Oswegatchie, by the same act which formed Stockholm
from Massena, and Potsdam from Madrid, by an act which finally passed
the council of revision, February 21, 1806.

The first town meeting was, by the provisions of the statute, to be
held at the hotel, in said town. The limits of De Kalb have been twice
curtailed. In 1825, Depeyster was formed out of all that part of the town
lying north of Beaver creek, and in 1830, a strip one mile wide, and six
long, lying in the southeast corner, adjoining the township of Fitz William, was annexed to Depau, afterwards Hermon.

De Kalb derives its name from an illustrious personage of revolutionary memory.

" The Baron De Kalb, knight of the royal military order of merit, was
a native of Alsace (a German province ceded to France), and was educated in the art of war in the French army. He was connected with the
quarter-master general's department, and his experience in the duties of
that station rendered his services very valuable to the American army.
Toward the close of the Seven Years' War, he was dispatched to the
British colonies in America, as a secret agent of the French government.

He traveled in disguise; yet on one occasion, he was so strongly suspected, that he was arrested as a suspicious person. Nothing being found to confirm the suspicion, he was released, and soon afterward returned to Europe. De Kalb came to America again, in the spring of 1777, with La Fayettee and other foreign officers, and was one of the party who accompanied the marquis in his overland journey, from South Carolina to Philadelphia. Holding the office of brigadier in the French service, and coming highly recommended, Congress commissioned him a major general on the fifteenth of September, 1777. He immediately joined the main army under Washington, and was active in the events which preceded the encampment of the troops at Valley Forge. He was afterward in command at Elizabethtown and Amboy, in New Jersey; and while at Morristown in the spring of 1780, was placed at the head of the Maryland division. With these, and the Continental troops of Delaware, he marched southward in April, to reinforce General Lincoln, but was too late to afford him aid at Charleston. Gates succeeded Lincoln in the command of the Southern army, and reached De Kalb's camp, on the Deep river, on the 28th of July, 1780. In the battle near Camden, which soon followed, De Kalb, while trying to rally the scattered Americans, fell, pierced with eleven wounds. He died at Camden three days afterwards, and was buried there. An ornamental tree was placed at the head of his grave, and that was the only token of its place until a few years since, when the citizens of Camden erected over it an elegant marble monument. The corner stone was laid by La Fayette in 1825. It is upon the green, in front of the Presbyterian church, on De Kalb street. The large base, forming two steps, is of granite; the whole monument is about fifteen feet in height."

(Lossing's Field Book of the Revolution, ii, p. 667, note.)

Memoranda from the Town Records.—1808. Voted that the weed called tory weed (Cynoglossum officinale), shall not be allowed to grow on any man's improvements, or in the roads. Penalty $1 for every neglect to destroy it, after ten days' notice. This law passed annually until 1816. 1809. A penalty of $1 for allowing Canada thistles to go to seed. Renewed till 1816. 1810. $2 offered for every wolf scalp. 1813. A committee appointed to enforce the destruction of thistles and tory weed, or exact the penalty. 1818. The supervisor and town clerk a committee to petition for a road, to be laid out from Indian river to Hamilton (Antwerp to Waddington). 1820. $500 raised for the support of the poor. $10 bounty on wolves and panthers. Voted that all the public books in town be sent to the town library, and subject to its regulations, but not to be taken by persons out of town. 1823. Wolf bounty, $5. The avails of the gospel and school lots applied to common schools. 1828. Resolved, That it is inexpedient to pass any resolution in relation to the county buildings. 1849. A special town meeting called March 27, to consider the necessity and propriety of petitioning the legislature for a grant to pledge the credit of the town to raise money to build a plank road on the main stage road, through the villages of Richville and De Kalb. The petition was not sustained.

Supervisors.—1806, Isaac Stacy; 1807-15, Isaac Burnham; 1816-18, Gideon Townsley; 1819-20, Elisha Griffin; 1821-8, Asa Sprague, Jr.; 1829-30, Jonathan Round; 1831, Nathaniel Martin: upon his failing to qualify, Roswell White was appointed to fill vacancy. 1832-5, Asa Sprague; 1836-9, Seth Alexander; 1840-2, Harlow Godard; 1843-5, Asa

Sprague; 1846, Dwight Spencer; 1847-9, Orin M. Fisk; 1850, Edward H. Hopkins. In September, Orin M. Fisk appointed to fill vacancy; 1851-2, Orin M. Fisk.

The following is a list of the jurors in the town of De Kalb, in September, 1806:

Joseph Anderson, Elias Alexander, Seth Alexander, Ichabod Arnold, Isaac Burnham, Thomas B. Benedict, James Burnett, Amos Comly, James Farr, James Farr, Jr., Elisha Griffin, Potter Goff, Nathaniel Holt, Levi Holt, Jonathan Haskins, Horatio G. Johnson, Obediah Johnson, Israel Porter, Solomon Pratt, Solomon Rich, Isaac Stacy, Henry Smith, Nathaniel Smith, Timothy Utley, Abner Wright, Joseph Woodhouse, William Woodhouse, Joshua Sweet.

The following is a list of the electors in the town of De Kalb, on the 2d of December, 1807, made by Thomas B. Benedict and Joseph Woodhouse, who were appointed to take the census of the electors of that town. It embraces, with one exception (N. Holt), the heads of families:

Joseph Anderson, Ichabod Arnold, Elias Alexander, Seth Alexander, Daniel Barker, Ralph R. Bell, Mansfield Bristol, Truman Bristol, James Burnet, Isaac Burnham, Barton Carver, Abraham Cole, Elisha Cook, James Cooper, William Cleghorn, Abel Cook, David Day, James Farr, Elisha Farr, Joseph Fisk, Ephraim Fisk, Mathew Grover, Elisha Griffin, Potter Goff, Russell Goff, Nathaniel Holt, Levi Holt, Philo Hurlbut, John Jackson, David Judson, Philo Lord, Abial Lyon, Richard Merrill, James Merrill, Solomon Pratt, Jacob Preston, Samuel Phelps, Solomon Rich, Salmon Rich, Joseph Rounds, William Sloan, Nathaniel Smith, Joshua Sweet, John Seeley, Isaac Stacy, Elijah Stockwell, Marvil Thair, Josiah Thornton, Samuel Thatcher, Timothy Utley, William Van Booscirk, William Woodhouse, Abner Wright, Eseck Whipple.

It will be remembered that a part of the present town of Depeyster was a part of De Kalb, when the above census was taken.

De Kalb was purchased from Samuel Ogden, by judge William Cooper, the father of J. Fenimore Cooper, the illustrious author.

In May, 1803, judge Cooper, of Cooperstown, with a company of thirty-four persons, mostly from the towns of Cooperstown and Richfield, Otsego county, started to form a settlement on his purchase, in the town of De Kalb. A part of these, with two wagons, each drawn by a span of horses, and a cart drawn by two yoke of oxen, proceeded by way of the Black river country and the old state road, to the clearing of Abram Vrooman, near the present village of Ox Bow. Here, from the extreme badness of the road, it became necessary to build boats for a part of the loading, and two log canoes were made under the direction of Jehiel Dimick, which were lashed together, and loaded with a part of the freight. The party consisted of William Cooper, the proprietor, Salmon Rich, Isaac Stacy, Eseck Whipple, Richard Merrill, Elisha Cook, William Brown, Gardner Brown, William Stone, Asa Ransom, Timothy Utley, Elijah Utley, Abner Wright, Andrew McCollom, Asa Ransom, Jun.,

James Farr, Elijah Farr, wife and wife's sister, Joseph Woodhouse, William Woodhouse, Dr. Robert Campbell, Ralph R. Bell, wife, sister and daughter, Elijah Stockwell, Jehiel Dimick, John Hewlett and William Sloan. Of these, Dimick, Rich, Bell and Hewlett came down the Oswegatchie river with the load, and the remainder along the road towards Ogdensburgh. The first night was spent at a deserted shanty, five miles from the Ox Bow, and in the night the party were alarmed by the cries of one of their number, who discovered that a large dry birch tree, which they had fired to keep off the musquitoes, was about to fall upon them. They fled in the greatest haste, just in time to save themselves, for the tree fell with a heavy crash upon the hovel, crushing and consuming it. A part of their bedding was lost by this misfortune.

On the second night, they arrived at Bristol's, in the present town of Depeyster, where the women were left, and the men proceeded to open a road through to De Kalb. This was effected in eight days, and they proceeded to their location, just above Cooper's falls. Alexander McCollom, Potter Goff and Stephen Cook, who formed a part of the original party, came up the Mohawk, with goods, which Judge Cooper had bought in Albany, for the purpose of opening a small store, and with these, they reached the location in De Kalb, by way of Oneida lake, the St. Lawrence, and the Oswegatchie, arriving on the 12th of June, 1803, with the other parties, at the present village of Dekalb. On the first day, they put up the body of a house, and slept without a roof over their heads, the first night. On the second day, another house was built, and on the third day, a store, which like the others, was of logs, and covered by barks. Goff, Campbell and Andrew McCollom, were surveyors, and several farms were run out. Salmon Rich, took up 11,850 acres, in the south corner of the town, Mr. Farr, a larger tract, in the eastern corner, and Stacy, another large tract, near the north part of the town. Most of these afterwards reverted to Mr. Cooper's heirs. Clearings were begun in various places, and a party was set to work in preparing to erect a mill at the falls. A canal was blasted, and one or two houses built. Wm. Brown cleared and got in two acres of winter wheat. A saw mill was raised during 1803.

Three families, and most of the party remained the first winter. During the winter, and following spring, several families came in, among whom were Salmon Rich, Isaac Stacy, James Farr, Jonathan Haskins, James Merrill, Richard Merrill, Timothy Utley's family. Sackett Dodge, Dr. J. Seeley, Barton Carver, Seth, and Elias Alexander, Elijah Pooler, James Burnett, Nathaniel Holt, James Cooper, a brother of the proprietor, Elisha Griffin, and many others. In 1805, Philo Lord, Thomas B. Benedict Horatio Johnson, Obadiah Johnson, Jacob Preston, Wm. Cleghorn, Daniel Smith and sons, Harvey John, Nathaniel, Daniel, Phinness and

Richard. The latter were from Canada, Solomon Pratt and many others, came in. In the spring of 1804, Mr. Cooper commenced the erection of a grist mill, under the direction of three brothers by the name of Jackson, (Cyrus, Asahel and Asa,) and at the raising of the frame, Asa Jackson was severely |hurt by falling upon his head. Dr. John Seeley performed the operation of trephining, with no other instrument than a *steel thimble*, which was fashioned into an annular saw, and fitted on a handle. This was the first surgical operation performed in town, and was successful. Dr. Seeley died, May 24, 1829.

On the 13th of Sept. 1804, commenced a violent rain, which continued several days, and produced a freshet, which was very destructive, and raised the Oswegatchie as high as has since been known. Geo. Cowdry, one of the settlers, was drowned in going over the falls, at this time, and was the first white person known to have died in town. Early in May, 1804, the first birth occurred in the family of Jehiel Dimick. The second was a daughter in the family of Salmon Rich, May 16th, of the same year. The first marriage was May, 27, 1804, of Elisha Cook to Letta Willey, and the ceremony was performed by Stillman Foote, Esq., of Canton, then the nearest magistrate. The second was Alexander Mc Collom, and Olive Sprague, on the day following, and by the same magistrate. The first school in the town was taught by Bella Wills, a methodist minister, in the winter of 1807, at De Kalb village, then called Cooper's village. In 1805, Judge Cooper erected a large hotel, on a hill in the village, which was three stories high, sixty feet square, and a curb roof, and was the first public house in town. After a few years, it fell into decay, and has since been entirely destroyed. Isaac Stacy was the first tenant, and was soon succeeded by Wm. Cleghorn, who kept the house for some time.

The early settlers were often annoyed by their horses escaping into the woods, and wandering off in the direction of their former homes. Several were thus lost, and an incident occurred while in pursuit of some of these, which is worthy of notice. Late in December, it being very cold and the ground covered with snow, two men started in pursuit of some horses, which were tracked to a distance of many miles to the southwest, about into the present town of Fowler. The pursuit led them much further than anticipated, and they had not provided themselves with provisions sufficient for supporting the hardship of their journey, and in returning were oppressed with excessive hunger, cold and fatigue. Yielding to these, one of them wished to lie down and rest on the ground, a course which the other knew would be fatal, and against it he remonstrated in the strongest manner, but to no purpose, for the inclination to sleep was irresistible, and arguments were of no avail with one who lost in emergencies of the moment, all control of his reasoning powers, and all hope of safety, by continuing on. He accordingly threw himself upon the ground to sleep, but his companion acting upon the principle, that the end justifies the means, provided himeslf with a green beech twig of sufficient length and weight to give it effect, and with this he aroused the sleeper by several severe blows, and thus he continued to apply the rod, as occasion indicated, disregarding the present effect upon the temper of his friend, until they reached the settlements, both nearly exhausted and famished by the hardships they had encountered.

The St. Regis and St. François Indians sometimes visited the settlements on hunting expeditions. They were entirely peaceable, except when intoxicated. In 1806, Tom, a St. Regis Indian, and Joe, his father-in-law, got into a quarrel over a quart of whiskey, and Joe got badly wounded, but finally recovered. It was observed that although much addicted to drink, at least one would keep sober to take care of the guns, knives and tomahawks, which were concealed till the rest were sober.

The first settlement of Richville, originally called Rich's Settlement, was made in the spring of 1804. In March, Salmon Rich and Jonathan Haskins, having loaded a sleigh with provisions, cooking utensils and camp apparatus, at Cooper's village, with the assistance of three or four hired men, drew it by hand up the river on the ice, a distance of ten miles, opposite the present village of Richville, where they formed a camp and commenced clearing. On the approach of warm weather, their shanty got overflowed, and they were driven to another stand. In April, a small log house was built by Jonathan Haskins near the river, and in June following P. Rich began a clearing at the present village, and erected a log house covered with bark. A house afterwards built by Haskins, a little southeast of the present tannery, became the first school house a few years afterwards. Joseph Kneeland was the first teacher. He was shot at the taking of Ogdensburgh. About 1807, the first tavern was kept by Solomon Pratt. About 1810, Chas. Boreland erected a grist mill, the second one in town, on the stream which bears his name, a mile and a half above Richville. He had erected a saw mill the year previous.

In 1824, on the establishment of a post office, the place received the name of Richville, and John C. Rich was appointed post master. This office he held for about twenty-five years. The village at present contains two churches, three stores, a tavern, post office, tannery, grist mill, two saw mills, the usual variety of mechanic shops, and about thirty families.

19

In this, as in some other towns, a large amount of poor money had accumulated, by taxes levied ostensibly for the support of the poor, for which there was no use after the adoption of the poor house system. By an act of Feb. 22, 1830, the overseers of the poor in this town were directed to pay $1,000 to the trustees of the public lots, to be invested for the support of schools. From this source, and the sale of the school lot, this town has acquired a larger fund than any other in the county. The location of the two reserved lots was at first not known, and they were sold by Mr. Cooper. This afterwards became a subject of difference, to settle which, Simeon Dewitt, the surveyor general, was empowered by an act passed April 3, 1811, to settle with the legal representatives of Wm. Cooper, on such terms as he might deem just and reasonable, for any differences which might have arisen between the state and the said Cooper, in consequence of any mistakes committed in locating the public lots in De Kalb. In the general law relating to the gospel and school lots of these towns, De Kalb was excepted.

Religious Societies.—The first religious organization in town, was said to have been the Methodist, but they did not form a legal society, until Feb. 25, 1839, when the First Society of the Methodist Episcopal Church, in De Kalb, was incorporated, with Seth Alexander, Dwight Spencer, Obadiah R. Rundell, Orin C. Spencer, Elijah Pooler, Thomas Spafford and John D. Smith, trustees. The First Presbyterian Church and Society in the town of De Kalb, was incorporated Dec. 7, 1818, with Seth Pomeroy, Joshua Dewy, Isaac Burnham, Elisha Griffin, Isaac Stacy, Jun., and Jonathan Haskins, trustees. Elisha Griffin declining to serve, Gideon Townsley, was on the 18th of December, of the same year, chosen in his place. A church had been formed August 30, 1817, through efforts of missionaries, sent out by a missionary society of Massachusetts. The Rev. James Johnson, who was in the service of that society, in 1817, made an appointment to preach in the adjoining town of Russell, and at the urgent solicitation of Seth Pomeroy, of De Kalb, he consented to visit his town, which he did, and preached on a week day, and consulted with the inhabitants on the practicability of forming a church. He recommended that all who felt interested should meet and consult on the subject, on the next Lord's day, and notice to that effect was given. In relation to the prospects of forming a religious society at that time, we can not do better than copy from an original narrative drawn up by one of the first founders.

" The people were in general moral, but as to Christian or praying ones, I did not know any, except a Baptist elder, who preached one half of the time, and an old man with his wife, who were Methodists. You can not picture to yourself a more unlikely place to form a church; the prospect to me was all barren and dry, and I thought there was nothing to form a church with, unless it was dry trees. It was a time of anxiety and prayer to the Great Head of the church. The day arrived, and there came two elderly men who were many years ago, professors of religion, but who had wandered a great way from the fold of God. It was affecting to hear them give an account of themselves. Their wives were also professors, and one of them did indeed, pray earnestly that God would appear and build up his cause. Just as the meeting was opened, a kind Providence sent us a minister, the Rev. M. Bunt, from Massena, who was of great service to us, and before the meeting broke up, it was evident the Lord was there. The Rev. Mr. Johnson, came soon after, and the subject was pursued till we found in all, seven professors, and three who gave evidence of piety,—ten in all. These on the last Sabbath in August, 1817, were organized into a church, and the Lord's supper was for the first time, administered."

A revival soon after occurred, and about seventy professed to be converted, of whom forty or fifty joined the Methodist, and fifteen or twenty the Baptist churches.

The Rev. Mr. Johnson, was employed about eighteen months, when he left for Vermont, and the Rev. Thomas Kennan, was hired to preach three quarters of the time, for three years. The organization subsequently was at one time nearly lost, from death of members.

The first religious society formed in Richville, was the United Religious Society, June 15, 1827; Orson White, Orson Shead, Josiah Walker, Henry C. Miller, John C. Rich and Marshall Allen, trustees. This was succeeded by the United Baptist and Methodist Religious Society of Richville, March 16, 1836, of which Nathan Barker, Harlow Godard, John Chase, James Phelps, Danford Johnson and Russell Johnson, were trustees. By this society the church edifice by the cemetery in Richville, was built in 1837, mostly by the Baptists, and the other party not having assisted on the 2d of Oct., 1837, the First Baptist Society of Richville, was formed, having Eleazer Dewey, Jacob C. Temple, Jabez Bozworth, John C. Rich, H. Godard, and Simeon Millen, trustees.

The First Congregational Church and Society in DeKalb, was formed Dec. 1829, Stephen Thompson, Jun., Orson White and Marshall Allen, trustees. A church was formed in Richville, in 1827 or 8, as a branch from the First Presbyterian Church in DeKalb, which was in a year or two, changed into a Congregational one. On the 11th of Feb., 1840, the First Congregational Society of Richville, was formed, having Marshall Allen, Darius Wiser, Jonathan Barker, Josiah Walker, Orson White, and A. V. Chandler, the first trustees. The Presbyterians and Methodists, have each a church, on the Gouverneur and Canton plank road, and south of DeKalb village; the former reported in the census of 1850, worth $900, and the latter $800. The Baptist and Congregational societies have each a church in the village of Richville, the former worth $1000, and the latter $600. The years 1826 7, were marked by religious revivals at the latter place.

De Peyster,

Was erected from Oswegatchie and DeKalb, by an act which passed the legislature on the 24th of March, 1825, but did not take effect till the first of April following. The poor moneys belonging to the several towns, were to be equitably divided. It was first proposed to name the town *Stilwell*, from Mr. Smith Stilwell, who was at the time a prominent citizen in town, and many of the inhabitants were very anxious that it should receive this name, but Mr. Stilwell declined, on the ground that some one among the proprietors, might be willing to make the town a liberal present, for the privilege of giving it their name. A correspondence was opened with Mr. Frederick DePeyster, of NewYork, who owned a portion of the part that had been in DeKalb, and resulted in the selection of this name, for the new town. Its location rendered an organization necessary, for it was separated from the greater part of Oswegatchie by Black lake, and the Oswegatchie river, and from the settlements of DeKalb, by an intervening wilderness.

Frederick DePeyster, was an extensive shipping merchant for many years in the city of New York, and distinguished for his integrity, liberality and punctuality in business. At an early day he purchased of Judge Cooper, a part of the town of DeKalb. On the erection of a Union church in DeKalb he presented $300 to assist in it; and in 1840 his son made a present of a fine bell weighing about seven hundred pounds, which had belonged to a Spanish convent, and which was forwarded to its destination free of cost.

Memoranda from the Records. The first town meeting was held in pursuance of statute, at the house of Timothy Morris, May 3, 1825. Smith Stilwell, elected *supervisor;* Timothy Morris, *clerk;* John Wilson, Moses King, Horace Plympton, *assessors;* Jonathan Morris and Bela Bell, *overseers of the poor.*

Voted to raise a subscription for a town house and church, and a committee of three, consisting of Smith Stilwell, Nathan Dean, and Philo Hurlbert, were appointed for this purpose. A special town meeting was held on the last Monday of June, to decide on the subject of a town house, and it was resolved to erect one, at a cost not to exceed $1,500, The church in DePeyster village was erected accordingly.

The Bethel Union Society, which owns this church, was incorporated Oct. 23, 1827. Bela Bell, Luke Dean, Joseph Sweet, Zenas King, Jonathan Curtis, Horace Plympton, and Smith Stilwell, being named as the first trustees. 1828, voted in favor of the High falls on Grass river, as a county seat. 1841, voted to have those parts of Morristown and Gouverneur, annexed to this town, which were afterwards formed into the town of Macomb.

Supervisors—1825-9, Smith Stilwell; on the 7th of November, Luke Dean elected to fill vacancy, occasioned by the removal of Mr. Stilwell; 1830-4, Horace Plympton; 1835-9, Johnathan Curtis; 1840, Abner McMurphy; 1841-3, Sylvester Johnson; 1844, Jonathan Curtis; 1845, John Blaisdell; 1846-7. David Fuller; 1848, Thomas D. Witherell; 1849-51, Levi Fay; 1852, Thomas D. Witherell.

The first settlement in the present limits of De Peyster, was made by Samuel Bristol originally from Sandgate, Vt., but who had for a short time, lived on the St. Lawrence, four miles above Ogdensburgh, in the month of November, 1802. His location was on lot No. 12, on the extreme south border of the township of Oswegatchie, and two and a half miles from the line of Hague. This location had been selected the summer previous, and he had been sent thither by Judge Ford, to form a stopping place for the accommodation of travelers who about this time were beginning to come into the country from the central and southern parts of the state, in considerable numbers. He had a large family. During the first summer, he had cleared about thirty acres, and got three of them sowed with wheat, and a house erected for a tavern. No other settlers arrived until the next winter (1803–4), when Thomas Wilson, from Hebron, N. Y., Joseph Round, Samuel Barnard, —— Green, Ichabod Arnold, and Robert Hill, from Rhode Island, Frederick Plympton, from Sturbridge, Mass., and David Day, most or all, except the latter, having families, moved into town. The first school was opened at the house of Samuel Bristol, in the winter of 1805–6, by Bela Willes. He was also the first preacher who held regular meetings (Methodist), although traveling ministers had casually happened to stop and hold meetings. Silas Kellog, in 1806, came in and erected a tavern some distance west of the corner. The first store was opened by James Averell 2d, near Kellog's tavern. Mr. Averell was then a young man of about eighteen years of age, and was established in business by his father.

Capt. Rufus Washburn, who removed in 1806, to what is now Macomb, was among the first settlers of De Peyster. In 1809, Smith Stilwell, then from Albany, but a native of Saratoga county, came in, and purchased lands, but did not remove with his family until the year following.

This town suffered its full share from the cold and backward seasons which form a striking epoch, from which many of the oldest settlers are able to date events. In 1815, but little was raised in consequence of the cold, and most of that little, was claimed by the birds and squirrels, which in that year are said to have been extremely numerous.

In 1816, many families were obliged to live without bread, as flour was very expensive, and difficult to be bought at any price. During this year, the first barley in town (about two acres), was raised by Mr. Stilwell. While it was still growing, it was watched by the neighbors with great interest, and they would stand by the fence which enclosed it, and count the number of days that would elapse before it would be suitable to cut, with an anxiety which proved how much their hopes depended upon that little field for food. It was scarcely ripe, when with the owner's permission, it was reaped, dried, threshed, and ground in small quantities, by his neighbors. Oats and potatoes sold for $1 per bushel, and wheat at from $2 to $3 a bushel.

This settlement long bore the name of Bristol's settlement, from the first settler.

The story of Putnam and the wolf, has been often quoted as an instance of the display of courage, which has elicited the admiration and excited the interest of every class of readers, but an occurrence which happened in this town, about the year 1821, may be regarded as perhaps equally worthy of our attention, although its hero never wore epaulettes, or shone in public life as a prominent character.

A son of one of the pioneer settlers, who on sundry occasions had evinced that acuteness which led to his being called by his father, "his ingenious," was distinguished for nothing so much as for personal courage, and a disregard for consequences, in the attainment of his objects. This lad, being at the time of the incident about to be related, but seventeen years of age, was out with a dog and gun hunting, late in the fall of the year. A light snow being on the ground, he discovered the tracks of an unknown animal, which he traced some distance, to a place where they entered a cave. Determined not to be hindered from the attainment of his object, and finding the opening of convenient size for entering, he crept in some distance, with gun in hand, keeping his dog behind him, until having reached a part of the cave where it was quite dark, he discovered at no great distance from him, two globes, of fire like brilliancy, which gleamed in the dim obscurity full upon him. He here paused, and bringing his gun to bear upon a point directly between them, he deliberately fired. His dog upon this, rushed past him to attack whatever the enemy might be, while he retreated, and was soon followed by his dog. Hearing no noise, or signs of life within, he, after a short delay, again ventured into the den, and listened for some time, but heard no noise, and at length ventured up nearer, and groping in the dark, he laid his hand upon the paw of an animal, evidently dead, which he with much difficulty dragged out, and found to be *a panther*, of large size, which on being measured, was found *nine feet four inches in length.* The ball had entered a vital part of the brain, and proved instantly fatal.

The truth of the above narrative is vouched for by a very respectable authority, and it may be received as reliable.

Deer were at an early day, quite numerous here, and still occur in the forest which extends through portions of this town, and the adjoining sections of Macomb, Gouverneur and De Kalb. It is said that on one occasion, five were shot by a hunter within a brief interval, without removing from the place in which he stood.

Many of the inhabitants of De Peyster and vicinity, having been much annoyed by wolves, in the fall of 1836, a public meeting was called on the 17th of December, of that year, and a committee of about forty appointed to make arrangements for a general wolf hunt, on an appointed day, and advertised in the county papers, inviting citizens generally to attend and participate in the enterprise.

Religious societies.—Besides the one above mentioned, two others have been incorporated. The First Society of the Methodist Episcopal Church in De Peyster, Oct. 23, 1827, Bela Bell, Luke Dean and Joshua Sweet, trustees; and the First Congregational Society of De Peyster, July 29, 1850, John Humphrey, Joseph McCoy, and Chester Dyke, trustees.

EDWARDS

Was organized from Fowler, April 27, 1827, and at first comprised townships, Nos. 8 and 4, or Edwards and Fitz William, now Hermon. The first town meeting was held at the house of Wm. Martin. The township of Fitz William, was taken off in erecting Depeau, and by an act of the board of supervisors, passed November 17, 1852, all that part of the town of Hermon, situate at the north east corner, known as the south end of the east third of township number 4, of great tract number 3 of Macomb's purchase, being subdivision lots, numbered 32 to 37, according to Ashman's old survey, was annexed to the town of Edwards. This act took effect on the first of February, following, and gave the town of Edwards its present limits.

First Town Officers, 1827.—Orra Shead, *supervisor;* John C. Haile, *clerk;* J. C. Haile, Asa Brayton, Jr., Wm. Teall, *assessors;* Roswell Lillie, Arba Collisier, Peleg Haile, *commissioners of highways;* J. C. Haile, Asa Phelps, Wilkes Richardson, *commissioners of schools;* Warren Streeter, Guy Earl, *overseers of poor;* J. C. Haile, George Allen, Wm. Teall, *inspectors of schools.*

Supervisors.—1827-8, Orra Shead; 1829, Wm. Teall; 1830-3, Orra Shead; 1834-35, Hubbard Goodrich; 1836-40, John C. Haile; 1841-2, J. B. Pickit; 1843-5, Ingraham Winslow; 1846-7, James Noble; 1848, I. Winslow; 1849, Elijah Shaw; 1850, J. B. Pickit; 1851, Elijah Shaw; 1852, Horace Barnes.

This town derives its name from *Edward McCormick,* a brother of Daniel McCormick, the patentee of tracts 1 and 2. of the great purchase. He was a sea captain, in the East India trade, and was for many years, engaged in voyages between New York and various ports in the Indies.

Edwards was surveyed in the summer of 1806, by Reuben Ashman of Russell, and subsequently settled by agents of Joseph Pitcairn and A. O. Brodie. Mr. Pitcairn received his title from McCormick, and in his will dated May, 9, 1837, made Mr. Brodie his executor and heir. The town of Pitcairn has the same ownership and title.

In January, 1812, Asa Brayton and family, made the first location in this town, on the line of the St. Lawrence turnpike. This road had been commenced in 1810, and was built in this and the two following years, and from this improvement, the first settlement of several of the towns in the county date. The portion through Edwards, was built by Enos Chapin, contractor, Joseph M. Bonner, John Britton, Samuel and Elijah Jones, and several families by the name of Johnson, settled in 1812-13. In 1814, Orra Shead, from Russell, built a grist mill.

The first death in town, was that of —— Partridge, who was killed by an accident at a raising, in 1813. The first birth in town, was that of John B. Brayton, a son of Asa Brayton, in the fall of 1812. In 1817, the settlement was considerably increased by several Scotch emigrants, among whom were Robert Watson, Robert Brown, Alexander Noble, William Cleveland, Alexander Laidlaw, Alexander Kerr and James Grieve. In 1819, George Allen arrived as an agent for Mr. Pitcairn, having been preceded in this office by Phineas Attwater.

Near the south border of the town, is a settlement known as South Edwards. The earliest settlement here was made by Job Winslow, in the fall of 1824, who at that time, came in from Potsdam, and erected a saw mill. He had visited the place the year previous, and purchased a farm around the falls, where he afterwards built. In 1825, he erected a grist mill. In March 1825, Elijah Shaw settled in the vicinity, and became the first merchant. From him, the settlement is sometimes named *Shawville.* The village is situated on the west branch of the Oswegatchie, and at present contains a new and very fine grist mill, a saw mill, tannery, carding and cloth dressing works, store, and a few mechanic shops. It is on the mail route from Edwards to Lowville. On the Oswegatchie river, below Edwards village, in 1830, was erected a furnace, 24 feet square, 28 feet high, 6½ feet inside diameter, by A. Freeman. It was run about six blasts, and was burned in 1847. At first it used the cold blast, but from 1840 the hot blast was employed. A part of the iron was made into castings on the premises, and the ores used were bog ore from this town, and specular ore from the Kearney and Little York mines. In 1842 or 3, a forge was built, and run two or three years.

Religious Societies.—The Methodists first organized with but four members, and held the first religious meetings in town. In 1827, the Christian denomination effected an organization in South Edwards, under Elder Isaac Banister, and he remained its pastor till his death, January 15, 1852. This society has always been small, and the present number is about 25. The First Congregational Church and Society in Edwards, was formed May 10, 1828. Calvin Phelps, Robert Watson, John Whitehead, Levi W. Gleason, Arba Collister, Orra Shead and Robert Brown, being the trustees. A union church was built in the village, by the Presbyterians, Baptists and Methodists, at a cost of $1000, in 1850.

FINE

Was erected March 27, 1844, from Russell and Pierrepont, and made to embrace No. 14, or Bloomfield, No. 12, or Scriba, and the south half of No. 9, or Sarahsburgh, in the former town, and No. 15, or Emilyville, in the latter. The funds belonging to the respective towns, were to be equitably divided, and the first town meeting to be held at school house No. 20. It received its name from the Hon. John Fine, of Ogdensburgh, who is interested in an extensive tract in the town, and under whom the first settlement was begun. The supervisors have been, 1844-5, Amasa I. Brown; 1846-50, Daniel Truax; 1851, A. L. Brown; 1852, D. Truax.

This town is one of the newest and least settled in the county of St. Lawrence. The principal settlement is in the east half of Scriba, which is owned by the Hon. John Fine, and James Averell, of Ogdensburgh, Wm. H. Averell, of Otsego Co., and Frederick De Peyster, of New York city. The first settlement was commenced by Elias Teall, who on the 24th of October, 1823, made a contract with the proprietors of the east half of the township of Scriba, and undertook to establish settlers on the tract. He built a mill on a branch of the Oswegatchie, erected a log house, made some improvements, and got some inhabitants to come on, but did not succeed in his undertaking. On the 6th of September, 1828, James C. Haile, made a contract with the proprietors, and erected a saw mill on the Oswegatchie, and a small grist mill, of one run of rock stones, without bolt or other appendages; built a house and barn, and got in more settlers. In May, 1833, he also left the settlement, having been abandoned by his settlers.

· In February, 1834, Amasa I. Brown, made a contract with the owners, for the Haile improvements, with an additional tract of land, and on the 28th of March, of that year, he moved his family into the town, having no neighbors nearer than ten miles distant. In a few weeks he was followed by one G. Luther, who had previously attempted a settlement, and in the autumn of the same year, two more joined them, making four families who wintered in town the first season. About twenty persons took up land that fall, although but three or four ever came on to settle. At this time the owners of the west half of No. 12, and of No. 9 and 14, were intending to take measures to commence the settlements of their lands, but the rage of speculation then tended to the west, and their proposed measures were not carried into effect. This left the settlers in the eastern part of the town, exposed to much hardship, for the unsettled parts lay between them and their neighbors, in South Edwards and Pitcairn, and no roads existed through the forest but such as they made themselves. This inconvenience, joined with a series of unpropitious seasons, tended to keep back the settlement, and impoverish its inhabitants, so that numbers left, and there now remains of that first immigration, but two or three families. Others, however, came in to take the places of those that got discouraged and left, and in 1843, there were 43 or 44 voters, besides 5 or 6 aliens. In 1843 they petitioned for an incorporation as a town, but failed, but the next year they succeeded. The first town meeting was held June 18, 1844, at which the following town officers, were elected:

A. I Brown, *supervisor;* Joseph M. Beckwith, *town clerk;* J. M. Beckwith, James Marsh and Elijah C. Hill, *assessors;* John K. Ward, *collector;* John Marsh, George Young and William H. Perkins, *commissioners of highways;* A. I. Brown, I. M. Beckwith and Elijah C. Hill, *justices of the peace.*

From this time forward, the settlement has slowly but steadily improved, and they have a tolerably good road through to South Edwards, on each side of the Oswegatchie. They have a road now in contemplation, from the western part of the settlement, to run a southwesterly course, and communicate with the navigation on Black river. It has been laid to the county line, by the road commissioners, and some improvements made towards opening it.

On the 15th of April, 1814, a law was passed to construct a road from Turin to Emilyville, to intersect the Albany road, and commissioners appointed with power to tax adjacent lands; and in 1816, a further appropriation was made, but this route was never opened.

The legislature, at its session of 1852, passed an act providing for opening a road from the old St. Lawrence turnpike, in the town of Pierrepont, to intersect the Carthage and lake Champlain road. This route has already been laid from Pierrepont to the old Watson road, in Herkimer county, and would have been continued through, had the line between Herkimer and Lewis counties been known. This line passes on or near the east bounds of townships Nos. 9, 12 and 14, and through the eastern settlements in Fine. When these roads are opened, and the proposed state improvements, in progress of construction, are completed, the inhabitants in this secluded portion of the county will enjoy good advantages for markets. Many of the inhabitants, from narrow and short sighted views, are said to be opposed to both of these roads, but when completed, they can not fail to greatly promote the prosperity of the town. The soil of the town of Fine is generally a gravelly loam, with much of its surface broken; but most, susceptible of cultivation. The timber is much of it beech and maple, with birch, spruce and hemlock, interspersed with elm, ash and cherry. The country is well watered, and from its elevated situation, it is not subject to local causes of disease, and is remarkably healthy. The Oswegatchie here affords an abundance of water power, and iron ore is said to abound, so that this town possesses within itself resources that will eventually place it on an equality with most of adjoining and older settled districts. There is a saw mill five miles from South Edwards, and another in the east part of the settlement. A grist mill is contemplated another season, which will answer the purposes of the settlers.

The author is indebted to Mr. Amasa L Brown, for assistance in preparing the above notice. '

FOWLER

Was formed from Rossie and Russell, embracing Kilkenny (No. 7), and Portaferry (No. 11), April 15, 1816, the first town meeting to be

held at the house of Noah Holcomb. The poor moneys of the respective towns were to be equitably divided. At the time of its erection, No.
7 constituted school district No. 3, of Rossie. On the 10th of April,
1818, the townships of Edwards and Fitz William, previously in Russell,
were attached to Fowler. These have since been taken off in the erection of Edwards. In forming Pitcairn, in 1836, a triangular portion of
No. 11, lying west of a line commencing three miles S. E. of the W.
point of said township, and running at right angles to the S. W. line till
it intersected the line of No. 7 was retained by Fowler, and these limits
it has since maintained.

On the division of the Great tract, No. 7 fell to Gilchrist and Fowler.
On the 3d of August, 1810, the former conveyed his share to the latter
(*Clerk's office, b. iii, p.* 129), and Theodosius Fowler, on the 15th of May,
1821, conveyed to his son, T. O. Fowler (*Ib., b. vi, p.* 75), under whom
the most of the town has been settled.

The town received its name from Theodosius Fowler, of New York,
who was a captain in the continental army of the revolution. He received his commission as ensign in February or March, 1776, and was
promoted to a second lieutenant on the 10th of August, to be first lieutenant after November 21. In June, 1778, he was raised to the rank of
captain at first in the 1st N. Y. regiment, but in 1780, he was transferred
to the 2d regiment, in which he served till the close of the war; not
being absent in all fifty days, either in winter or summer. He was present and took a part in the battles of Long Island, Saratoga, Monmouth
and White Plains, and shared the hardships of the camp at Valley
Forge and Morristown, and the expeditions against the Indians of western New York, under Colonels Van Schaick and Willet, in 1779, and of
General Sullivan, in the summer of the same year. During the year
1780, the New York line of five regiments was reduced to two, commanded by Colonel Van Schaick and General Van Cortland, to the latter
of which Captain Fowler was assigned. In the fall of 1781, these were
ordered to Virginia, and aided in the capture of the British at Yorktown.

We have been under the necessity of condensing the above, from a
minute and extended account, written by Mr. Fowler himself, which we
had prepared for this work, and was loaned the author by the Hon. F.
Dodge, of Gouverneur.

First Set of Town Officers.—Theodosius O. Fowler, *supervisor;* Simeon Hazleton, *clerk;* Noah Holcomb, Elvan Cole, Benjamin Brown,
assessors; John Parker, Noah Holcomb, *com'rs of highways;* Noah
Holcomb, Benj. Brown, *overseers of the poor;* Simeon Hazleton, Samuel
B. Sprague, *overseers of highways;* Alvan Wright, *constable and col-*

lector; Alvan Wright, Simon Hazleton, Elam Cole, *com'rs com. schools;* Theodosius O. Fowler, Jedediah Kingsley, Richard Merrill, *inspectors of common schools.*

Supervisors.—1817. Theodosius O. Fowler; 1818, (Feb. 19,) Benjamin Brown to fill vacancy, 1815, 21, Eben Cole; 1825-9, Justus Pickit; 1830, Stillman Fuller, 1831-2, J. Picket; 1833-4, S. Fuller; 1835-6, William Hurlbut; 1837-8, J. Pickit; 1839-41, Henry H. Haile; 1842-3, Asa L. Hazleton; 1844-5, Alfred Burt; 1846-7. Heman Fuller, 1848-9; Addison Giles; 1850-1, Thomas T. Hazleton. 1852, E. W. Abbott.

In 1824, the town agreed to raise a bounty for wolves and wild cats agreeably to the late law. This is the only record of any votes having been taken by the town, for the destruction of noxious animals.

The first settlement in the town of Fowler, was made by Brigadier General James Haile, from Fairfield, Herkimer Co., who came into town to explore, and who purchased of Richard Townsend, agent for Gilchrist and Fowler, in the month of June, 1807, a tract one mile square, on the ground where the little village of Hailesboro now stands, under obligations to build mills within a year. In the fall of the same year, he came on with several men, to commence the erection of mills. One Capt. Ward, was millwright. and a Capt. Robinson, carpenter. A saw mill was built the same fall, and a small grist mill, with one run of stones attached to it, was also got into operation in 1808. The latter was swept away by a freshet in 1809, and rebuilt the following year. Timothy Campbell, was the millwright employed to build the second mill, which contained but one run of stones till 1819, when another was added. In 1844, the present mill was erected in a most superior manner, containing three run of stones, to which a fourth is about to be added. Mr. Elijah Sackett, from Hartford, N. Y., came into town in 1808, and was employed as a miller, until his death, in the spring of 1812. He was the first white person who is known to have died in town. Lemuel Arnold, John Ryan, —— Cleveland, Ebenezer Parker, and others, came on and settled soon after, and in 1811, Samuel B. Sprague, made the first stand in the neighborhood of Little York. Albin & Oliver Wright, were early settlers.

During the war several families left the country from fear of Indians, nor did the town begin to settle rapidly until 1820. Early in 1818, Gen. Haile moved into town with his family, having only come on himself, in the summer time previously. He resided here till his death, Dec. 17, 1821.

In 1825, a mill was erected at Hailesboro, by Jasper Clark, for sawing the white limestone, which abounds in the vicinity. The business was carried on by him, and continued by A. Giles, for several years. It was used for tomb stones, building stones, sills and caps for windows, and for jambs of fire places. The coarsely crystalized structure of this stone, has been found to render it unsuitable for lettering and the finer kind of ornamental work, but for the heavier uses of building, and especially for the manufacture of *lime*, it has no equal. The natural water privileges of Hailesboro, are superior. Within a distance of half a mile, the Oswegatchie river descends 84 feet, and within a mile above it has an equal descent, so that the same water could be used repeatedly, and such is the nature of the channel, at the island, in the village, that the supply can be regulated, and every liability to injury from floods avoided. In the lowest stages of the water, it is estimated that sufficient water flows in the river at this place, to drive eight run of mill stones. During a part of the year, the supply is much greater. A small mill with two saws, has recently been built about a mile above, and at the village a grist mill, saw mill, clothing works, wagon shop, &c., are erected. It has a tavern, store, the usual variety of mechanic shops, and about twenty families.

The first marriage in the town of Fowler, was Mr. John Parker, to Miss Elizabeth S. Sackett, in 1812. The first birth was in the family of —— Merrills. A small settlement began to be formed at the present village of Little York during the war, which received its name from the circumstance of the capture of Toronto (which then bore this name), at about the same time. The neighborhood is without the advantages which a water power confers, and is but a centre for the local business of a portion of the town. The village of Fullerville Iron Works, is situated on the Oswegatchie, three mills from Little York, and nine from Gouverneur.

The earliest settlement in this vicinity was made by John Parker, about three quarters of a mile below that place, where the St. Lawrence turnpike originally crossed the Oswegatchie in the year 1812. In 1813 he erected a saw mill at the falls in the present village of Fullerville, which being burned, was rebuilt in 1823-4. In 1826, a grist mill was erected by S. Fuller & Co, and sold in 1838, to Rockwell Bullard and company, who rebuilt the mills, which are the same that still remain.

In 1832, Sheldon Fuller, Stillman Fuller, Heman Fuller and Ashbell Fuller, brothers, originally from Ferrisburgh, Vt., but for eight years previous engaged at the Rossie iron works, came here, and commenced the erection of a blast furnace; and after them the place received its name. A furnace, erected by the firm of S. Fuller & Co., was about 30 feet square, on the ground, and 40 feet high, and was first got in operation in August, 1833. Their first operations were commenced on the ore from the vicinity of Little York, of which they used about 1,000 tons, and

this was the first ore raised from that mine. Subsequently several
thousand tons of bog ore, obtained from swamps in the Fine tract, from
two to three miles distant, in the town of Edwards, were used. During
the first years of their operations, a great number of experiments were
made, upon ores from numerous localities, the greater part of which
failed in producing useful results. The presence of sulphur and various
impurities, rendered many kinds of the ores tried entirely valueless for
the manufacture of iron. Besides the ores above mentioned, those from
the Kearney mine, in Gouveneur, the Keene or Thompson mine, in
Antwerp (both red specular ores), and the magnetic or primitive ores of
Pitcairn and Clifton, have been used at this furnace. The pig iron made
here, has principally been sold to cupola furnaces, in St. Lawrence and
Jefferson counties; and from its softness, is much prized for castings,
as it will admit of the mixture of old iron, and that which from repeated
melting has become hard.

The amount made at this furnace, as near as can be ascertained, is as
follows:

By S. Fuller & Co.,	about	600 tons,	at two blasts.
By Fullers & Maddock,	"	1,700 "	" "
By H. Fuller & Co.,	"	1,200 "	at four blasts.
By Fullers & Peck,	"	3,000 "	at five blasts.
Total number,		6,500 "	

The furnace was rebuilt by the latter company, in 1846, and a hot
blast subsequently used. Previous to this, the furnace was supplied by
the cold blast. About 133 bushels of coal have been required to make
a ton of iron, by the cold blast; and 125 by the hot blast. Iron made
by the latter process will not *chill;* but it is here thought to make more
iron from a given quantity of ore, and the process of separation is much
accelerated. At Fullerville are two forges for making malleable iron
from ore, scrap and pig iron. The first, adjoining the furnace, was
erected in 1835, by the Fullers, contains three fires, and is capable of
making 1,200 pounds per day. Previous to 1846, it was worked about
two-thirds of the time, and since, about three months in a year. In
1840, Edwin Rockwell, Luther Bullard, Chester H. Benton and Oliver
Benton, under the firm of Rockwell Bullard & Co., erected a forge on
the east bank of the river, which contained two fires, and was run very
steadily for two or three years, and since that time by different parties
more or less every year, till within one or two years. It is thought that
magnetic ore makes the best bar iron, although that from the specular or
red ores is soft, tough and suited to every purpose for which this useful

metal is applied. It has much local celebrity, and all the bar iron made at this place has been consumed within thirty miles of these forges.[*]

As no rolling mills have been erected, the iron is drawn out under a trip hammer. Coal for supplying the furnace and forges is obtained from within 1 to 5 miles, and the distances to several neighboring mines are as follows: to Kearney's and to Thompson's, 11 miles; to Tait's, in Hermon, 20 miles; to Pitcairn (Jayville), 15 miles; to Clifton mine, 21 miles; to Little York, 3 miles; to bog ore swamps, 2 to 3 miles.

The Fowler Library was incorporated April 12, 1831. Simeon Hazelton, Justus Pickit, George Draper, Charles C. Edgerton, Gaylord Graves, Theodosius O. Fowler, Reuben Wright, trustees.

Religious Societies.—The Baptist church of Fowler was organized February 9, 1822, and at the time of its formation, embraced 13 members, all of whom united by letter. This number was soon after increased, by baptism, until it amounted to forty, of whom twenty-one at present belong to the church. The first clergyman employed, was Elder Jonathan Paine. In December, 1822, Elder Noah Barrell was employed to preach a quarter of the time for one year. Elder William Gorrey commenced preaching in May, 1828, and remained until the close of May, 1831. The Rev. Mr. Gurnsey soon after was employed, end continued a year, when his place was supplied by Elder Wilkey (June, 1833). Elder Brand was afterwards invited to preach (May, 1836), and remained two years. Elder John Peck was invited to preach September 6, 1838, and left in November, 1840. Elder David Deuland was employed in March, 1843, and remained for one year. He was subsequently again invited to preach for one year. In September, 1851, Elder Nicols was employed to preach a part of the time. A church edifice was erected in the village of Fullerville, in 1835.

The foregoing data were furnished by Mr. Kentfield, the present clerk.

The Antwerp and Fowler Baptist society was incorporated December 31, 1825, James N. Graves, Peter Sigourney and Moses Burge, trustees. The church edifice of this society is in Jefferson county, near the line, and at Steele's corners. A Free Will Baptist church has existed for many years in the west part of the town. They have recently erected a church edifice.

A Presbyterian church and society was formed at Fullerville, about 1833, consisting of ten or fifteen members, and a church was erected. Most of the members having moved away, the organization has been lost for several years. The Rev Mr. Batchelor, from Hermon, officiated here as clergyman for a time.

The Little York Universalist society was formed March 22, 1841, Jabez Glazier, Leman Fuller, Simeon Hazelton, Albert A. Vedder and John P. Ryon being the first trustees. They own a church which, in the census of 1850, is reported worth $1,000.

---

[*] The experience of those who have dealt in this vicinity, might possibly establish the fact, that bar iron has, to some degree, served as a currency, or circulating medium, to facilitate trade. The advocates of hard money might here find arguments, both pro and con, in reference to this great national question.

GOUVERNEUR,

Was formed from Oswegatchie, April 5, 1810, and embraced the township of Cambray, until the recent division in erecting Macomb. It at this time contained 223 inhabitants, of which 30 were senatorial voters. An effort was made in 1841 to form a new town out of parts of this, De Kalb and Hermon, but failed. The first town meeting was held at the house of John Spencer, at which the following officers were elected:

Richard Townsend, *supervisor;* Amos Comly, *town clerk;* Rufus Washburn, Isaac Morgan, Pardon Babcock, *assesors;* Amos Comly, Benj. Smith, Ephriam Case, *commissioners highways;* Jonathan S. Colton, Israel Porter, *overseers of poor;* Barnabas Wood, *constable and collector;* Jonathan S. Colton, Isaac Morgan, *fence viewers;* Israel Porter, *pound master.*

Supervisors.—1811–4, Richard Townsend; 1815–9, John Brown; 1820–1, Israel Porter; 1822–6, Aaron Atwood; 1827–35, Harvey D. Smith; 1836, Almond Z. Madison; 1837, Harvey D. Smith; 1838, Almond Z. Madison; 1839–41, William E. Sterling; 1842, Peter Van Buren; 1843, Wm. E. Sterling; 1844–5, Peter Van Buren; 1846–9, Geo. S. Winslow; 1850–2, Charles Anthony.

Memoranda from the Records.—March 5, 1811, voted that Ephraim Case, Rufus Washburn, Pardon Babcock, Jonathan S. Colton and Benjamin Smith, be appointed a committee to superintend the destruction of noxious weeds, and any person who may discover any of these shall give notice to one of the above committee, on whose farm such weeds are growing; and it shall then be the duty of the committee man to go and give such person warning that such weeds are growing on his farm, and the place where they grow, and if such person do not cut such weeds in the month of June, so as to prevent their going to seed (provided such warning be given previous), shall forfeit and pay to said committee five dollars, the one half to go to the informant, and the other half to be paid into the hands of the overseers of the poor in this town for the support of the poor, and that this committee shall be allowed at and after the rate of $1 per day for their services in giving notice of the growth of such weeds.   1814. Voted that the block house be sold at vendue, and the avails applied to build a house of public worship. 1824, Nov. 25. Special town meeting to vote on receiving part of Rossie to this town. Resolved not to receive petition.   1828. "Since it is understood that certain persons in Potsdam, will give $3000 for public buildings, and since we are convinced that at no distant day the county will be divided; therefore.   *Resolved,* On condition of $3000 granted as above, that we recommend the location of the county building at that place.   1829. The sale of the gospel and school lots for school fund advised.   1835. Voted to remove the burying ground in the village. Rescinded in 1838.   1839. Trustees of academy requested to petition the legislature for an appropriation of $2000 to be refunded by a tax within 4 years, to rebuild the academic building destroyed by fire Jan. 1, 1839.   A very full town meeting voted for this, but five or six dissenting.   1839. Resolved that the county poor house system ought not to be abolished.   1841. Protest against any division of the town at present.   The only division practicable is Beaver Creek, and the creation of a new town between that creek and Black lake.   1841, Aug. 18. The fund derived from the sale of the gospel and school lot divided between Macomb and Gouverneur, as follows: to Macomb $281·38, to Gouverneur $2,082·37. 1842. Vote against the erection of a new town from parts of Gouverneur, De Kalb and Hermon. 1843. The town petitioned for the abolition of the office of deputy superintendent of schools. 1844. Resolves against the division of the town again passed, and in favor of the formation of a new county from Jefferson, Lewis and St. Lawrence. 1845. A committee of five to report on the expediency of erecting a town house. May 6, a special town meeting convened to hear the report of the committee which was in favor of the measure. [This plan failed from efforts made to secure its location west of the river.] 1846. A town map to be procured for the town and a copy to be deposited in the county clerk's office. In 1847 resolved to keep both copies. 1850. Resolved to sustain the resolution of the board of supervisors restoring the distinction between town and county poor. *Wolf bounties* were offered in 1819, 1820 and 1821, of $5, and in 1840 of $10, with half these sums for wolf's whelps. *Fox bounties* of 50 cents in 1820-1. In 1822, 25 cents penalty for every goose running in the highways.

Gouverneur and Morristown were named from Gouverneur Morris, an early and extensive proprietor in the lands of Northern New York. He was born at Morrisania, Westchester co., Jan. 31, 1752, and educated at Columbia college. At an early age he engaged in the political discussions of the day, and became a member of the provincial congress, and a delegate to the convention that framed the first constitution of the state. A few years after the war, he repaired to France on commercial business, and remained in Europe several years; during a portion of which time he held the office of minister from the United States to the French court. During his residence there he was a witness to the excesses of the French revolution, and incurred much personal danger in the discharge of the duties of his office. In 1798 he returned home with a justly acquired celebrity as a statesman, and with enlarged and liberal views acquired from extensive travel and careful observation upon European affairs, and was soon afterwards elected to fill a vacancy in the United States senate. On the death of Washington he delivered an oration in New York, at the request of the corporation, and it fell to his lot to perform the same duty to the memory of Hamilton and the elder Clinton. Mr. Morris died Nov. 6, 1816. An injury which he sustained by a fall from a carriage in 1780, deprived him of a leg, which was supplied by one of wood.

His life and writings by Jared Sparks form three octavo volumes. and to these the reader is referred for a minute account of this celebrated man.

In the summer of 1805, Dr. Richard Townsend, of Hartford, Washinton co., having procured of Gouverneur Morris of New York, an agency for the sale and settling of his lands in Cambray, started with several men, his neighbors, to visit the tract, and make arrangements for

20

beginning a settlement. The party consisted of Richard Townsend, Isaac Austin, Willard Smith, Pardon Babcock, Ambi Higby, John Alden and Morris Mead, the latter a surveyor. They proceeded to the head of Lake George, and thence with map and compass, and with three days provisions, they struck into the woods on a course which they supposed would bring them to their destination. Several incidents of interest happened to the pioneers on their journey. On one occasion having caught some fish in the morning, their dogs (two fine mastiffs), by their barking and manner, indicated that they were followed by some wild animal. On the approach of night, they built a row of fires, within which they camped, having placed their fish in the branches of a tree much elevated above the ground. In the morning, these were gone, and the tracks around the roots indicated that they had been followed by one or more large panthers.

They were seven days on the route, suffering towards the last from want of provisions, and first came into clearings in the Smith settlement in De Kalb. The sound of a bell attached to an ox, first indicated their approach to clearings, and by following this they were led into the settlement, where several men were chopping. One of the party hailed the owners of the cattle with a complaint that they had broken into and injured his cornfield, for which he demanded compensation.

The surprise of the settlers was unbounded, upon seeing a company of men emerge from the depths of the forest, and they could scarcely credit the story that they had traversed the wilderness from Lake George, with no guide but their compass, and an outfit of only three days provisions. The party thence proceeded on to Gouverneur, arriving just below the present village, and after a short stop most of them proceeded down, and crossing near the present Kearney bridge, returned by way of the Black river country to their homes, having been absent about three weeks. Townsend, Austin, Smith, and others, visited the town again late in the fall, proceeding on horseback by the Black river road as far as Boon's upper settlement, where they were obliged to leave their horses from the badness of the roads. Arriving by the route of the state road to Lee's tavern, three miles north of Antwerp, they proceeded thence to their destination on the Oswegatchie, where its placid course was broken by a small cascade, and its channel divided by two beautiful green islands, in the present village of Gouverneur. Here they constructed a float of logs, and crossed, arriving at their destination about the middle of October. A surveyor (Col. Edsall, of Madrid), was procured, and several farms surveyed, and slight beginnings made, when the party returned home by the route they came. In February 1806, Pardon Babcock, Wil-

lard Smith, Eleazer Nichols, and Isaac Austin, with their families, the
wife of the latter being borne an invalid, in a cradle, the whole journey,
arrived at Antwerp, on their way to Cambray, with the view of making
a permanent settlement. Here their families were left a few days, while
the men went forward to erect a shanty and provide accommodations.
One Jershom Matoon, was keeping an inn at Antwerp at this time, and
his was the only house in the place. It was a very humble log cabin,
with but one room, which served every purpose of bar room, bed room,
parlor, kitchen, and dining room, was without a chimney, and destitute
of every accommodation properly so called.

A slight shelter having been erected, these four families proceeded to
take possession, and crossing on the ice near the site of the Kearney
bridge, they arrived at their home, which was found to be an open shed
covered with boughs. This stood in the present road in front of Elwin
E. Austin's present dwelling house. On the next day, a flat roofed log
shanty, open on one side, and covered with wooden troughs, after the
manner still occasionally seen in sugar camps, was erected; and soon
after another, facing the first, but with a space between of a few feet,
which served the purpose of a door, as well as a chimney; and at each
side, a pile of logs was laid at night, and set on fire, for the triple purpose of light, warmth, and a defence against wild beasts.

This cabin furnished a common shelter for several weeks, until the
several families had provided for themselves separate huts. Isaac Morgan, from Orange co., Vt., arrived on the last of March, and the number
was soon after increased, and Dr. Townsend, during the summer, employed one John Simons, of Brownville, to survey into farms the lands
around the present village. In July 1806, the first religious meeting
was held in town, at the shanty of Esq. Austin, by Elders Nichols, and
Pettengill, two missionaries from Connecticut. A Mr. Heath, a methodist preacher, living in Rich's settlement in De Kalb, preached occasion
ally on sabbaths, the settlers always keeping up some form of divine
service on Sunday, at the hut of Mr. Austin, until a school house was
erected, when the meetings were held at that place.

A road was cut through to Richville, on the first summer, by voluntary
labor, and communications were soon opened with Antwerp. The first
birth in town, among the settlers, was a son (Allen Smith), in the family
of Willard Smith, May 8, 1806. The first death was Emily Porter, aged
two years, in Aug. 1808. The second a Mrs. Martin. The third death
was that of Stephen Patterson, who was crushed while stoning up a
well. The first marriage was Medad Cole to a daughter of Stephen
Patterson. Dr. John Spencer, from Windsor, Ct., was the first practising

physician, who moved into town, and for several years was the only one within many miles. On his arrival in April 1807, there were eleven families living in town, viz: Richard Townsend, Isaac and Daniel Austin, Pardon Babcock, Willard Smith, Eleazer Nichols, Stephen Patterson, Isaac Morgan, Benjamin Smith, Israel Porter, and Stephen Smith. Previous to his arrival Dr. Seeley, of De Kalb, was occasionally called. On the first occasion in which medical assistance was needed, the messenger got belated, and was compelled to lie out in a thunder storm, and returned in the morning by following in his dog. Gilchrist, Constable and others, of the great proprietors, traveled through the town in the summer of 1807, and made a short stay. The settlers feeling the want of a bridge, and hoping nothing from the town of Oswegatchie, of which they were then a part, raised in 1808, by voluntary subscription, the sum of $500, with which they hired Mr. Isaac Kendall, to build the first bridge in the village. It stood 12 years, and was then replaced by one costing $1000, built by Mr. James Parker. The chief contributors to the first, were the two Austins, Townsend, Babcock, Spencer, Porter and Morgan.

The shanty used by the workmen on the bridge, in the autumn of the same year, became the first school room, and was occupied by Miss Elizabeth S. Sackett, now Mrs. John Parker, of Fowler. It stood near where the Presbyterian church now is. The first man school, was taught by Sylvester McMasters, in a shop erected for mechanical purposes, by Capt. Babcock, but which was relinquished for this use. In 1811, the first school house was built of logs, on the ground now occupied by the Plank Road House, west of the bridge. In 1808, Mr. Porter opened the first public house, and soon after, John Brown commenced as a merchant. During this summer Gouverneur Morris, spent three weeks in town, at the house of Mr. Isaac Austin, from whence he proceeded by water to the Ox Bow, where his nephew Lewis R. Morris, was living. In 1809, a clearing of 80 acres was made for Morris by Joseph Bolton, near the natural dam, and a grist and saw mill were erected there at the proprietor's expense, by Mr. Austin, and the premises long afterwards bore the name of Morris's Mills. Lands first sold for $.50, but soon after were fixed at $3.00.

In the spring of 1809, the following families were living in town. Wm. Cleghorn, J. S. Colton, Wm. Colton, Henry Welch, Israel Porter, Elkanah Partridge, Dr. J. Spencer, Isaac Austin, Eleazar Nichols, Rockwell Barnes, Stephen Patterson, Joseph Bolton, Holenb Smith, Benjamin Smith, Caleb Drake, Benjamin Clark, James Barnes, Calvin Bullock, Ephraim Gates, Richard Townsend, Isaac Morgan, Timothy

Sheldon, Colburn Barrell, Reuben Nobles, Ephraim Case, Richard Kemble, John Hoyt, Pardon Babcock, Daniel Austin, Medad Cole. Besides these, Wm. Canning, Sela Coleman, Alfred Cole, Harvey Black, Charles McLane, James and John Parker, Josiah Waid, and a few others, the last mentioned being mostly single men, were living in town or came in very soon after. The settlers in 1812, participating in the general alarm, commenced the erection of a block house in the present village of Gouverneur, but it was never finished. The timbers were subsequently employed in the dam, and in buildings soon after erected. The dam in the village was erected in 1814, the first machinery being clothing works, put in operation by one Downs. A frame school house was built on the east side of the river, in 1815, which was replaced by the present brick edifice in 1827.

The war in this and many other towns, checked its growth, for many years, but it soon after began to increase in population quite rapidly, and in 1816-18, many families from Johnstown, located on the road leading to the Ox Bow, which still bears the name of Johnstown Street, from this cause. The first settler on that road was Jeremiah Merithue, in 1810. In 1825 Israel Porter built the first grist mill in the village, Mr. Daniel W. Church, being the mill wright. It was burned about 1825. A saw mill was built several years previously.

The following incident, which occurred in December, 1807, is worthy of record. It is derived from the person who was the subject of the adventure, and is reliable. Dr. Spencer had set out in the morning, on foot, to visit a patient beyond Antwerp, guided by a line of marked trees, and an obscure path through the woods, which extended but a part of the way. A light snow, followed by rain and frost, had fallen, which rendered the tread of men and animals audible to a great distance, and the air was chilly and uncomfortable. When he had proceeded about three miles, he was aroused by a rustling sound, and presently a deer pursued by a black wolf, past swiftly by him. He dropped behind a log to see the chase, without interrupting it, when he heard a louder sound behind him, and on looking back saw eleven other wolves, in a pack, which gave up the chase for the deer and stood gazing at the new game they had discovered. He jumped up, and with loud shouts and threatening gestures, endeavored to frighten them away, but without success, for they retreated but a few paces, and then turned to eye him narrowly. A short distance beyond, on the ground now covered by the house of Mr. G. Norton, stood the body of a log house, and his first thought was to run for that, in hopes that he could defend himself at the door, but upon second thought it was evident that but little hope of escape could be expected in flight. He next thought of climbing a tree, but then the wolves might watch him till he was exhausted with cold. At last finding that shouting and gestures, were of no avail, he laid down his pill bags, overcoat, and hat, and cutting a green beech stick, of sufficient size to be easily wielded, and of a weight that would give effect to a blow, he rushed at them swinging his weapon, and making all the uproar in his power, by beating the icy bushes until they were scattered, when losing that confidence which numbers had given them, they fled in different directions. His first thought was to return back, but dreading the jeers of his neighbors, who might say that he had been scared by a wolf, he kept on his course. Before out of hearing, he distinguished the cries of the pack, as they were again mustering, but he saw no more of them.

A separate account of the academy in this town will be given. The village of Gouverneur, was incorporated under a general act, Dec. 7, 1847. Its first officers were as follows:

Edwin Dodge, Peter Van Buren, S. B. Van Duzee, N. D. Arnod and I. P. Smith, *trustees.* H. Schermerhorn, Rich'd Parsons and O. G. Barnum, *assessors.* Zebina Smith, *collector.* Chauncey Dodge, *clerk.* H. D. Smith, *treasurer.* O. G. Barnum, *pound master.* Its present officers (1852,) are Peter Van Buren, M. Barney, J. Fosgate, R. Parsons and W. M. Goodrich, *trustees.* I. Smith, O. S. Barnum and S. Cone, *assessors.* H. L. Conklin, *clerk.* H. D. Smith *treasurer.* Z. Smith, *collecter and pound master.*

The inhabitants of Gouverneur and Morristown, were authorized, April 15, 1826, to elect three trustees, to have charge of the public lands, and apply the profits for the support of schools. On the 31st of March, 1828, the overseers of the poor were directed to pay to the trustees of the public lots, $1000 of the poor moneys in their hands, to be invested for the support of schools. From this fund and the proceeds from the sales of the school lot, a large fund has accrued. The trustees of the Baptist and Presbyterian societies, by an instrument on file, among the archives of the state, relinquished their claims in favor of schools.

The *Gouverneur Union Library* was incorporated Feb. 14, 1815. Richard Kimball, Benjamin Brown, Timothy Sheldon, Joseph Smith, Pardon Babcock, Aaron Atwood, Rockwell Barnes and Israel Porter, being the first trustees.

Religious Societies.—The first church formed in town, is said to have been by the Baptists, to which sect many of the first settlers belonged. They were organized in February, 1810, by Elder Jonathan Payne, and at first, numbered eleven members. Elder Payne has been succeeded by Elisha Morgan, Noah Barrell, Joseph Sawyer, Clement Haven, Newell Boughton, S. Pomeroy, N. O. Webb, J. Sawyer and Conant Sawyer. The First Baptist Society of Gouverneur was formed April 14, 1825. Wm.

W. Rhodes, Rufus Smith, Alanson Townsend, Benjamin Leavitt, Miles Turner and Moses Rowley, being the first trustees. It was reorganized July 2, 1835. In 1822, they erected a church; and in 1850 and 1851, their present very elegant church, at a cost of about $3000. It is the first one to the right of the Seminary, in our view of Gouverneur village.

The First Congregational or Presbyterian Church, was formed May 24, 1817, consisting of six persons, since which time up to Jan. 1, 1852, 538 have been admitted to membership. On the 20th of April, 1820, the First Congregational or Presbyterian Society in Gouverneur, was incorporated, with John Spencer, Richard Kimball, Wm. Cleghorn, William Colton, Rockwell Barnes and James Parker trustees. This church was not regularly supplied by a minister until the 1st of January, 1820, since which time the following clergyman have been employed.

Rev. James Murdock, 1820-25; Rev. Richard C. Hand, 1825-33; Rev. Jonathan Hovey, 1833-34; Rev. Robert F. Lawrence, 1835-38; Rev. Simeon Bicknell, 1838-42; Rev. B. B. Beckwith, 1843, till the present time. The first church edifice was erected in 1820, and completed in 1824. Cost $1,400.

The present meeting house was completed at a cost of $3,500, and dedicated in August, 1844. It is represented on the right in our engraving of Gouverneur village.

The author is indebted to Harvey D. Smith, Esq., the clerk of this society, for the foregoing facts.

A Congregational Church was formed in February, 1843, and on the 21st of March, a society was incorporated as the Second Congregational Church of Gouverneur. Rockwell Barnes, Nathan W. Smith and John Leach, being the trustees.

Being disappointed in not receiving materials which had been expected, we are unable to give that particular account of this and other societies, in this and other towns, which was desirable.

The first Universalist Society of Gouverneur and Hailesboro, was incorporated Jan. 7, 1849, with James Sherwin, Francis Farmer, Hall Tuttle, L. P. Smith, Addison Giles and Sanford Betts, as trustees.

HAMMOND

Was formed from Rossie and Morristown, March 30, 1827, to take effect on the 1st of May following. Its line on the side of Morristown, was changed May 2, 1837; a corner south of Black lake, was on the 11th of April, 1842, attached to Macomb; and the line bordering Rossie, which at first ran parallel with the original line of Somerville, one and a half miles southeast of it, was on the 7th of Feb., 1844, changed to its present course from the corner of the old township, to the head of Mile bay.

Supervisors.—1827-8, Sylvester Butrick; 1829-31, Roswell Ryon; 1832, Allen Cook; 1833, Orrin Brown; 1834-5, Loren Bailey; 1836-7, George C. Daniels; 1838, Orrin Brown; 1839-40, Enoch Taylor; 1841, Ebenezer N. Demick; 1842, Orville E. Wightman; 1843, E. N. Demick; 1844-7, Wm. H. Wright; 1848-9, Henry Zoller; 1850, Sidney S. Wait; 1851, Josiah Zoller; 1852, Abel P. Morse.

In 1831, the town voted to petition that the interest of the poor fund might be applied to the support of schools.

The town derives its name from Ahijah Hammond, of New York, who owned the township previous to the purchase of David Parish. He was a brother-in-law of David A. Ogden, and a merchant and speculator of New York, and at one time had in conjunction with others, a scheme of purchasing the vacant lands then existing above the settled parts of New York, but which now lie in the heart of the city. In the revolutionary war he held a commission as captain of artillery. He never visited his northern purchases, and took no further interest in them than as a subject for speculation. David Parish purchased of Hammond and wife, 28,871 acres Sept. 12, 1814. Slight beginnings had been made previously, but no titles of land passed to actual settlers until July, 1818, when Wm. Wiley took the first contract. Loren Bailey went into town as an agent, on the 31st of July, 1818, and it then began to settle rapidly. Mr. B. continued the agent till his death, when the office was removed to Rossie. The first actual resident in town is said to have been one Wm. McNeill, from Vermont, who had been in town several years previous to 1812. He attempted no clearing, lived a hermit's life, subsisted by hunting and fishing, and dwelt in a niche in the rocks, at Chippewa bay. The first clearing was commenced in the summer of 1812, by William Wiley, from Vermont, at the present village of Hammond Corners. In 1813, —— Barker, from Rossie, settled a mile south of the Corners, and opened a tavern. At this time the Ogdensburgh turnpike was laid through the town, and worked in this and the next year.

In the summer of 1814, an attempt was made by a party of fifty or sixty Canadians, under Duncan Fraser, to abduct one or two refugees who had taken up their abode in town, and had rendered themselves obnoxious to their former Canadian neighbors, by repeated depredations committed in revenge for real or supposed injuries. The party landed very early in the morning at Chippewa bay, and proceeded in quest of their object, but missed their path, which delayed their arrival till sunrise, at the inn of Mr. Barker, where the principal object of their search was sleeping. Alarmed by the family, this person fled half dressed to the woods, narrowly escaping the shower of balls aimed at him. The house was ransacked in vain for papers, and the party returned home disappointed in their pursuit.

The greater part of the town of Hammond, west of the village, and in the direction of Chippewa bay, was settled by Scotch emigrants, in 1818, 1819, and 1821. These families came over singly, and without any particular destination, and meeting the agents of Mr. Parish, were induced to locate on his tract, where they, or their immediate descendants, mostly continue to reside. The following persons located in 1818: John and

David Gregor, John Baird, Peter Allen, John Hill and James Hill, of whom all but the two latter, were married. A Mr. Cowan, one of their number, was killed in the following winter by the fall of a tree, and Mr. Parish, with characteristic liberality, paid the expenses of his widow's return to Scotland. In 1819, Thomas Caswell, Wm. Nickol, James Rogers, Robert Morris, Robert and Andrew Shields, John Mercer, Thomas Dodds, and Wm. Burke, an Englishman, came into the settlement; and in 1821, John Brown. Several of the latter were single men, and none of them past the middle of life, and the evidences of prosperity which meet the eye of the traveler, sufficiently prove that they have successfully encountered the hardships of a new settlement

A few years later, others were induced to emigrate through the representations of those already located. To those of the first and second year, who required it, Mr. Parish extended a similar credit with that of his settlers in Rossie.

The first school in the Scotch settlement, if not in town, was taught by Dr. James Scott, of Lisbon, in the winter of 1819–20. Mr. Bailey, the agent, settled at Chippewa bay, three and a half miles from the Corners. Abram Cooper soon after commenced improvements at this place, which at present although but a small settlement, forms an important port for the export of iron from Rossie, and lumber and produce from the surrounding country. A steam saw mill was erected here about 1844, by James E. Lyon.

Oak Point is a small village and landing, at the point where the original line of Hague and Hammond touched the river. George Elliot first commenced a settlement here, and was succeeded by —— Cowan, in 1824, who opened a small grocery store. Earl Atwood, Abram Schermerhorn, from Trenton, N. Y.; —— Matthews, and a few others, came soon after. In 1825, a wharf was built on a small island in the channel communicating with the shore by a bridge; and in 1838, this was rebuilt. A post office was established in 1840, and a custom house has existed for many years. The deputy collectors have been J. G. McCormick, Benjamin Franklin, and Amos Webster. The duties in 1850 were $2,461·31, and in 1851, $2,191·64, mostly on cattle, sheep and horses. This office had previously been located at the Corners, where Sylvester Butrick and Arnold Smith had held it. A light house was erected on Cross-Over island a short distance above, in 1847. The river steam boats formerly landed here regularly, but this practice has been for some time discontinued.

The south part of the town, on the military road, was first settled about 1819, by Samuel Webster and William Tappan, of Vermont. Jonathan

Ring, of Herkimer county, settled in the following year, and commenced keeping an inn. The military road from Sackett's Harbor to Hammond, had been cut through shortly before the war, but from disuse, had become impassable. It was reopened in 1823, by a company of about twenty-five soldiers from Sackett's Harbor, who volunteered for the service, and drew extra pay for their labor. They were under the direction of Capt. Wilkie, and afterwards of Capt. Ransom. The road was laid out as a highway, one or two years after, and has continued one of the principal thoroughfares from Watertown to Ogdensburgh. The South Hammond post office was established in 1833, Mr. King being postmaster. The office has continued in the care of him and his son, Henry King, until the present time. The hotel at South Hammond was erected in the summer of 1848. There is no village in this vicinity.

On the 19th of April, 1834, Loren Bailey, Azariah Walton and Elbridge G. Merrick were appointed commissioners to open a road from the line of Clayton and Lyme, to a road leading from Chippewa bay to Osdensburgh. This road was through the villages of French Creek and Alexandria Bay to Hammond. The lands adjacent were taxed to build it.

Opposite to the town of Hammond, in the channel of the St. Lawrence, lay the last of the Thousand Islands, a most beautiful and romantic group, which seldom fails to elicit the admiration of the traveler, as he threads his course among them. They commence near the outlet of Lake Ontario, and extend along the entire river front of Jefferson county, and consist principally of gneis rock, which rises from the green limpid waters of the great river, in an infinite variety of pleasing forms and groups; most of them still covered with the primitive forests, with here and there a clearing, and a curling spire of smoke rising among the trees, which indicates the site of the home of some secluded settler. The larger islands are mostly under a fine state of cultivation, and possess a fertile soil, and some of them have interesting mineral localities. The singularly romantic beauty of this group, struck in a most forcible manner the attention of the early French voyageurs, who dwelt upon the lovely spectacle which they presented, and described in language that would apply to the dream of a romance, the picturesque forms that every where rose above the water, and were reflected from its placid surface. Nor are they destitute of incident, which gives additional interest to the association, and the events of the early French and Indian wars of the revolution, of the war of 1812-15, and of the patriot war, so called, of a still recent period, give a charm to numerous localities, which few, who delight in the association of the incidents of former times, with present appearance, will fail to appreciate. Among the objects most likely to attract the notice of the traveler, as he passes the South channel, from Clayton to Cape Vincent, is a group of chimneys, which looms up from an elevated plain, at the head of Carlton island, and are the remains of a fortress that the French erected in early times, for the protection of their trade and travel, to more remote stations in the west. Indian Hut island, in Chippewa bay, is supposed to derive its name from the residence of the Quaker Indian, alluded to on page 44 of this work.

Religious Societies.—The first Presbyterian union society, in the town of Hammond, was incorporated December 14, 1827, with Luther Lanphear, James Hills and Walter Wilson, trustees. A church had been formed shortly before, by the Rev. Hiram S. Johnson, of 12 members, which was under the St. Lawrence Presbytery, and the pastoral care of Joseph Taylor. From sickness and other causes, this organization was lost. The present Presbyterian society, belonging to the Ogdensburgh Presbytery, is a separate church. They have a stone meeting house in Hammond Corners, and for several years have been under the pastoral care of the Rev. John McGregor. The first society of the M. E. church of Hammond, was incorporated September 29, 1832. Rev. Joel J. Emma, William S. Wait, Alonzo D. Carter, William Brown and Abel Franklin, trustees. A Free Will Baptist church was formed April 6, 1843, by Elder Samuel B. Padin, who preached two years. It was composed of 14 males and 13 females, most of whom reside in the south part of the town. They have formed no legal society, and have no house of worship. Trinity church, in the towns of Hammond and Rossie, was incorporated December 16, 1846. Henry W. Chapman and A. P. Morse, wardens; William B. Bostwick, Phirenda Butterfield, William Laidlaw, Sophereth Ophir, William Welch, Robert Morris, John Burrows, and James Hill, vestrymen. This society has never erected a church.

HERMON.

This town was formed from Edwards and De Kalb, under the name of DEPEAU, April 17, 1830. It received this name from Francis Depeau, of New York, who was also extensively concerned in the French purchase, in Jefferson county. He was interested in the middle third, which had passed from McCormick to George Lewis, July 12, 1804, who sold to John and Curtis Bolton, August 1, 1823. The latter sold to Depeau, June 6, 1828, and the latter May 3, 1830, conveyed to Sarah, wife of John Bolton. It originally embraced the township of Fitz William, or No. 4, and a strip, 1 mile by 6, from the southeast side of De Kalb. The board of supervisors have recently attached a part to Edwards, as stated in the preceeding pages, In a short time the inhabitants found it a source of annoyance, to have a name so near like Depeauville, in Jefferson county, to which their mails often went, and they procured a change of name on the 28th of February, 1834, to HERMON. A post office had been formed December 20, 1828, of this name, which was taken from the scriptures.

The first town meeting was held at the house of Nathaniel Kent, at which the following were elected:

William Teall, *supervisor;* Benjamin Healy, *clerk;* Wilkes Richardson, Isaac C. Pool, Silas Williams, *assessors;* Simeon Peterson, Jesse Worden, Shubael Parker, *commissioners of highways;* Wilkes Richardson, Robert Gotham, Henry Tanner, *commissioners of schools;* Benjamin Healy, Aaron Teall, C. D. Morehouse, *inspectors of schools;* Martin L. Cook, John Matoon, *overseers of poor;* Charles D. Redfield, *collector;* Ariel Wrisley, Charles C. Redfield, *constables.*

Supervisors.—1830-2. William Teall; 1833. Reuben L. Willson; 1834-6, Harry Tanner; 1837, Silas Williams; 1838 9, Henry P. Cook; 1840, Nathaniel Kent; 1841-2, H. P. Cooke; 1843-7, Silas Williams; 1848-51, Seymour Thatcher; 1852, David W. Weeks.

The first settlement in this town was begun by James Taylor, several years before the war, in the western part of the township of Fitz William, and near the line of Gouverneur. George Davis, James Farr, Philemon Stewart, Ariel Inman and Rufus Hopkins had settled in the town previous to 1812. Those who located on township No. 4, did so without previously making an arrangement with an agent, as none had been then appointed. David McCollom, from Rutland county, Vt., but then from Canada, came in 1812; Roger Story, in 1813; German Southerland, in 1816. The first saw mill was erected, in 1818, on Elm creek, in the present village of Hermon, by Milton Johnson, from Russell The first death in the town was that of Thomas Farr. In 1819, a grist mill and distillery were erected, in what is now the village of Hermon. by Milton Johnson. The latter was kept up till 1832 or 1833. The first religious meetings in town were held in 1811, by the Rev. Mr. Wright, a missionary from Massachusetts. The first schools were kept in the house of David McCollom, near the village of Hermon, in winters of 1817-18, by William D. Moore; and 1818-19, by Wesley McCollom. The first road opened through the town, was from De Kalb to Russell, during the war. The next was from the present village of Hermon, to De Kalb, in 1818. The settlers suffered rather more than the usual share of distress from the famine which ensued from the cold season of 1816. During the war, the settlement of the town was checked, and numbers left the country, from fear of Indian incursions. In 1822, 3, 4, 5, the town settled quite rapidly, and during the latter year, the numbers of settlers increased more rapidly than in any other. The second mill in town was built on Elm creek, one mile above the present village of Hermon, by Abram Fisk. In the following year, Amos Marsh bought the premises and erected a grist mill. From him the settlement in this vicinity was

named *Marshville.* William Teall opened a store in 1823, in the northern edge of the town, and soon after William Martin commenced the
first mercantile business in the village of Hermon. This place on Lay's
map of 1817, is named *Eastburnville,* which it never bore among the
inhabitants. The village of Hermon is a thriving and growing place,
and has a direct plank road communication with Ogdensburgh, Canton,
&c., and the Potsdam and Watertown rail road will pass between it and
De Kalb.

The county records show the incorporation of the cemetery associations in this town, viz:

The Marshville Cemetry Association.—March 11, 1850, Edmund Allen,
Sen., Martin McCollom, Clarke Maine, Ralph Fisher, Isaac C. Sherwin,
Thomas Campbell, *trustees.*

Hermon Hill Burying Ground Association.—January 18, 1851, Peter
Clintsman, Calvin Rhodes, P. D. Miller, Chester Winslow, J. B. Miller,
R. M. Hall, *trustees.*

Religious Societies.—The Methodist, Baptist, Christian and Presbyterian
sects, have or have had organization in town. In 1826, Elder James
Spooner, formed a small church of the Christian order, which once had
70 but now only 30 members. Elder J. Starkey, has the pastoral care at
present, and for the past twenty years, has filled the office.

The First Baptist Society of the town of Hermon, was incorporated
Dec. 3, 1845. Horatio Marsh, Daniel V. Babcock, Edward Maddock,
Wm. E. Tanner, Theodorus Frisby and Orle Gibbins, trustees.

The First Society of the Methodist Church, in the town of Hermon,
was incorporated November 1, 1847. Samuel I. Bingham, Seymour
Thatcher, Joseph H. Beard, Lorenzo H. Sheldon. Orin Nichols, Timothy
B. Hatch and Daniel McIntyre, trustees. These societies each erected
in Hermon village, in 1848, a church edifice, costing about $1400 each.
The Methodist church is furnished with a fine toned bell.

HOPKINTON

Was erected March 2, 1805, from Massena, and included Islington and
Catharineville, and so much of Chesterfield as was annexed to the town
of Massena. The first town meeting was to be held at the house of
Eliakim Seeley. All the remainder of Massena in the second tract,
without the bounds above mentioned, were annexed to Hopkinton, which
was declared to be a part of St. Lawrence county. By the erection of
Lawrence and Parishville, it has been reduced to its present limits, which
alone are sufficient for a small county, although the settled part is a strip
scarcely four miles wide across the north end. It embraces the most of
14, and the whole of 15, 12, 8, 9, 5, 6, 2, 3, of the second tract of the Great
purchase. The town was named in compliment to Judge Hopkins, the
first settler, and a man of much prominence in the early history of the
county. A biographical notice will be given in this work. The title to
No. 14, passed from McCormick to Macomb, June 24, 1801, by a deed

for 23,886 acres, and a part (7,675 acres,) from A. Macomb to A. M. Jr., January 1, 1808.

At the town meeting held March 4, 1806, Roswell Hopkins was elected *supervisor*; Henry McLaughlin, *clerk*; Amasa Blanchard, Joseph Armstrong, Reuben Post, *assessors*; A. Blanchard, Seth Abbot, *overseers of poor*; Abraham Sheldon, *constable and collector*; A. Sheldon, R. Post, H. McLaughlin, *commissioners of highways*; Eli Squier, Oliver Sheldon, A. Blanchard, *fence viewers*; Oliver Sheldon, *pound keeper*.

Supervisors.—1806, R. Hopkins; 1807, Benjamin W. Hopkins; 1808, Henry McLaughlin; 1809, R. Hopkins; 1810, B. W. Hopkins; 1811, J. R. Hopkins; 1820-2, Thadeus Laughlin; 1823-6, Jonah Sanford; 1827-9, Isaac R. Hopkins; 1830-2, Joseph Durfey; 1833, I. R. Hopkins; 1834-5, T. Laughlin; 1836, Phineas Durfey; 1837, Eliakim Seeley; 1838, T. Laughlin; 1839, I. R. Hopkins; 1840-1, Clark S. Chittenden; 1842-4, Elias Post; 1845, Gideon Sprague; 1846-7, Clark S. Chittenden; 1848-9, E. Post; 1850-1, C. S. Chitteuden; 1852, Joseph B. Durfey.

Memoranda from the Records.—1806. A committe appointed to decide upon a lawful fence, and report rules for the range of domestic animals. 1807, wolf bounty, $10. 1808, Henry Mc. Laughlin, Amasa Blanchard and Seth Abbott, appointed to prescribe rules for regulating the manner in which inoculation for the small pox shall be administered in town. $60 voted to buy a set of statute laws and blank books. At an adjourned meeting in March, $100 voted for destroying wolves, $5 bounty offered; $250 voted for the poor.

1809. $100 for the poor, and various sums often larger in following years. Wolf bounty $5.

1810. Bounty on wolves, $10, and $100 to destroy these animals. At a special meeting in June, $500 previously appropriated to bridges, given to the St. Lawrence Turnpike Co., on condition that the road be located in a certain route.

1811. At a special meeting the legislature petitioned to tax the town to aid the North West Bay road. Also, to petition for a lottery to raise the sum of $10,000 to repair this road; also, to pray for exemption from service on juries, during four years. $100 voted to encourage the destruction of wolves, and $5, "to be paid out of the above sum, for each wolf's scalp, capable of doing mischief." The same bounties in 1812-13-14-15. In 1816, $50 raised for wolf bounties, and a bounty of $10; with $5 "for every wolf's whelp scalped and destroyed in town."

1817. $10 wolf bounties; 75 cents for two bounties and $10 appropriated for this business. $50 to pay T. Meacham, for killing 2 panthers.

1818. $10 voted to pay for the destruction of every catamount in the town.

1819. Five hog constables elected; $20 panther bounty; $10 wolf bounty; $1 fox bounty.

1820. $10 wolf bounty; $15 panther bounty; $1 per hundred for the dedestruction of *mice*, $25 said to be paid for the latter.

1821. Bounties offered as follows; wolves $5; wolf whelps, $2-50; panthers, $15; their young, $7·50; foxes, $2; young foxes, $1.

1824. $10 wolf bounties, and $5 for wolf whelps.

1825. $5 for wolves, and half this sum for their young.

1835. Three hog constables elected.

In May, 1802, Roswell Hopkins, of Vergennes, Vt., having bought a part of Islington, of Hammond, came into town to make a settlement accompanied by Samuel Goodale, B. W. Hopkins, his son, Jared Dewey, Eliphalet Branch and Joel Goodale.

In June, having made arrangements for clearing land, Mr. H. started to return to Vermont, on horseback, by a line of marked trees, and in fording the St. Regis river, which was swollen by heavy rains, his house was partly thrown over by the violence of the current, and his portmanteau, containing in one end the provisions for his journey, and in the other, several hundred dollars in specie, were swept down stream, and lost. At the approach of winter, the party returned to Vermont. In March, 1803, Judge Hopkins, Abraham Sheldon, Eli and Ashbel Squire, moved their families into town. The first birth occurred in December, 1803, in the family of Mr. Sheldon. In this season, the first grist mill was erected by Mr. Hopkins, on Lyd brook, near the present village of Hopkinton. During the first year, and until the mill was built, the settlers were obliged to go to the Long Saut, on the Canadian shore, to mill. In addition to the foregoing, Thomas Remington, Gaius Sheldon, Reuben Post, Eliakim Seeley, Henry McLaughlin. Thadeus McLaughlin, Horace Train, Jasper Armstrong and Seth Abbott, came in 1804 and 1805, many of them with families, and from this time the settlement grew rapidly. The following interesting account was published in the *Northern Cabinet*, Sept. 3, 1845, and is understood to have been written by Elisha Risden, a pioneer settler and surveyor:

" The first settlers of Islington, now Hopkinton, came by the way of French Mills to St. Regis, and thence up the St. Regis river to Stockholm, and thus to their destination. Previous to 1805, the main road from the east into St. Lawrence county, passed through Chateaugay to Malone, Bangor, Moira, and Chesterfield (now Lawrence) to Stockholm, and thence to Potsdam, and on to a few new settlements beyond. A road had been opened on the western side of the St. Regis river, between Islington and Stockholm and another road from Islington, leading north east, crossed the St. Regis river, and intersected the road from Malone to Stockholm, half a mile west of Deer river. These roads were laid down with little regularity along the most favorable ground, were without bridges or causeways, and mostly impassable, except when bridged by the ice in the winter. In March 1805, there were no settlements between Islington and Deer river, nor between Deer river and Stockholm. Between Deer river and Malone a few scattered beginnings had been made. At the date above mentioned, several families moving into the county, had reached Deer river, where they were obliged to encamp, as the ice had broken up, and the river was impassable for teams. Hearing the condition of these families, Dr. Pettibone, of Stockholm, sent a message to Roswell Hopkins, Esq., of Islington, inviting the young men of that settlement, to meet those from Stockholm, at the river, and erect a bridge. The request was immediately circulated, and although at 10 o'clock at night, they mustered their forces and started on the expedition. The St. Regis river had first to be crossed, as the ice bridge had been broken up, and this was effected by wading on horseback at midnight, and with infinite peril, the rapid and swollen river. The night was dark and cloudy; there were but three horses to transport the party of nine men, which was at length effected at six times crossing, and the company met that from Stockholm at the appointed place, early in the morning, and at once proceeded to plan and execute a good and substantial log bridge—the first one across Deer river—at a point about one hundred rods below the present village of Lawienceville. The party from Islington, on their return home reached the St. Regis several hours sooner than the time appointed for the horses to be sent to meet them, and as the river had subsided somewhat, one or two of the company cut each of them a pole to support themselves against the current, and with their boots and axes slung to their backs, forded the river by wading. The horses were sent to transport the remainder, and the whole party returned without accident. From Deer river to Islington, was 8½ miles by the ford, and 15 by Stockholm. From Esq. Hopkins's to the ford 1¼ miles. Mr. Hopkins was remarkably attentive in assisting settlers to cross this ford, and kept a watch to give notice when teams arrived, and the young men could go down with two yoke of oxen and a strong sled, cross over to them, fasten their sleighs with withes and ropes to the top of the sled, and so recross. In crossing, the empty sled would float, and the ferrymen were obliged to wade by its side and work with all their might to keep it from floating down stream. The sleighs were lightened of their contents, hoisted with levers and skids on to the sled, bound fast, reloaded, and crossed over. Difficulty was often experienced in keeping the load upright, and the screams of the women and children as their craft veered and floundered along the angry stream, formed a picture strikingly characteristic of primitive times and known only to pioneers. In April of this year the sleighing ceased, but people continued to arrive on horseback and on foot, who were often disappointed at the difficulties in crossing, and in several instances travelers coming to Islington, after reaching the ford, retraced their steps and proceeded to their destination by the very circuitous route of Stockholm. To obviate these difficulties a foot bridge was built at the ferry, which although rude and temporary was very acceptable. The ford way road is now occupied by cultivated fields, and its route exists only in the recollections of the few remaining pioneer settlers.

In May 1807, the first death (that of an infant) occurred. Previous to this there had been 26 births. In 1809, Abram Sheldon built the first framed house. In 1807 the town contained 48 persons capable of voting for senators. In 1810 a social library was incorporated, 45 persons having subscribed $115 for the purpose. The first trustees were Roswell Hopkins, Amasa Blanchard, Henry McLaughlin, Rueben Post, Seth Abbott, Stephen Langworthy, Jasper Armstrong, Benjamin W. Hopkins. Dr. Stephen Langworthy was the first physician who settled in town, in a very early day. The second was Dr. Gideon Sprague, from New Haven, Addison Co., Vt., who settled in town in 1811, and is at present the second oldest practitioner in St. Lawrence county. Dr. E. Baker, of Canton, settled there in 1806. In 1824, Isaac R. Hopkins built a saw mill on the St. Regis river, north of the village, and at the raising it was christened Fort Jackson, which the little village at this place still bears. There are here two churches, saw mill, clothing works, starch factory,

&c., and in the vicinity a valuable quarry of Potsdam sandstone, which has been used for lining several furnaces. This beautiful building material should supersede every other in the vicinity, where it can be procured, and would be found more cheap, durable and elegant than any other that the country affords. Blocks of any convenient size and very uniform, can be readily procured here.

On the last of February 1814, after the British party had returned from their incursion to Malone, and had arrived at French Mills, they earned from a citizen spy, who acted as their guide that a large amount of flour belonging to the United States army, was stored in a barn in the village of Hopkinton, and that there was no guard at that place to protect it. Upon this they detached Major De Heirne, of the British regular service, with Lieut. Charlton, the second in command, and about thirty soldiers, who proceeded in sleighs, by way of Moira corners, to Hopkinton, twenty-seven miles from French Mills, and arrived at that place early in the morning, before the inhabitants were up. They first posted sentinels at the door of every house, and proceeded to search for arms in every place where they might be suspected to be found, and succeeded in obtaining about twenty stand, which had been distributed among the inhabitants. It is said that several muskets were saved, by being hastily laid in a bed, which had been occupied but a few moments previous, and thus eluded the search that was made for them. Their case has been described by the poet.

> " 'Tis odd, not one of all these seekers thought,
> And seems to me almost a sort of blunder,
> Of looking *in* the bed as well as *under*."

They found some three hundred barrels of flour stored in a barn owned by Judge Hopkins, and occupied by Dr. Sprague, but having no teams for conveying away more than half of that quantity, they began to destroy the remainder, but being dissuaded by the inhabitants, they desisted, and distributed the remainder among the citizens. During the brief sojourn of this party, they conducted themselves with strict propriety, and sacredly respected private property of every kind, using or receiving nothing for which they did not offer compensation. No parole was required of the inhabitants. Upon the passage of the detachment of the American army through Hopkinton, on their way from French Mills to Sackett's Harbor, but a very short time previously, the officers in command were importuned by Judge Hopkins and others, for the privilege of carrying the military supplies in their village further west, to a place of greater safety, dreading the very event which soon after happened. They offered to take their pay from the flour, at such prices as would be just and equitable, but no one appeared to feel themselves au-

21

thorized to order the removal, and it was not effectual. The surrounding country would have readily furnished volunteers sufficient for this duty, and gladly undertaken it, had they been allowed the privilege.

In 1816, snow and frost occrrued in every month in the year, and crops of all kinds, except grass and oats, were nearly destroyed. Flour was procured with the greatest difficulty, and sold at $22 per barrel.

Thomas Meacham, a noted Nimrod, who spent many years in hunting, in St. Lawrence and Franklin counties, died near this town, on the North west Bay road, May 7, 1849, aged 79. He kept an account of his successes, which resulted as follows: wolves 214; panthers, 77; bears, 210; deer, 2550. Mr. Meacham would relate many amusing anecdotes. His traps were always out, and one day in examining them he found two wolves and a bear, and shot another on the way, making, as bounties then were, a profit of $185. A further account of this pioneer was published by Wm. H. Wallace, in his paper, the St. Lawrence Mercury, Dec. 19, 1849.

Religious Societies.—July 6, 1808, five males and six females, were organized by the Rev. John W. Church, a missionary, into a Congregational church. A society was formed Sept. 30, 1814, with Amasa Blanchard, Reuben Post and Isaac R. Hopkins, trustees; Rev. Hiram S. Johnson, now of Canton, was ordained pastor, in December, 1815, and remained till 1822, when he was succeeded by the Rev. Roswell Pettibone, who was installed, July 21, 1824, and who remained till Aug., 1830. The Rev. Messrs. J. Butler, Cha's Bowles,—P. Montague, Bachelor, J. A. Northrop and E. Wood, have since been employed. The present number in the church is 84. A meeting house was built in 1827, at the cost of $2,800. Dr. Gideon, Sprague, Aaron Warner and Artemas Kent, being the building committee.

A Baptist church was formed by Eld. Rowley Sept. 11, 1808, of but 6 members. On the 12th of Sept. 1808, the sacrament of the supper was administered for the first time to the Congregational church, in the forenoon and to the Baptist church in the afternoon, in the same house. A Baptist society was formed, Feb. 17, 1818, with Abijah Chandler, Jonah Sanford, Sylvanus C. Kersey, and Samuel Eastman, trustees.

In 1815, these two societies erected a stone building for a place of worship and public business, which by a law of 1841, was repaired by a tax of $250, and now forms the village school house. On the 8th of July, 1830, the name of the Baptist church, was changed to the Hopkinton and Lawrence church, at which time they held their meetings alternately at Hopkinton and Nicholville. On the 5th of Aug., 1843, the word Hopkinton was dropped, and they have been since permanently located in Nicholville. A society of the M. E. church, was formed, Dec. 30, 1839, Josiah Smith, Martin Corey, Hiram B. Sheldon, Rufus Alden, Philip Mosher, Albert Sheldon, Bradley Adams, John Daniels, and John L. Ransom, trustees.

A Free-Will Baptist church was organized in 1844 by Elder John Sweat, and Elder Wm. Whitfield, of 16 members. This church erected a commodious house of worship in 1847, cost $1,000, dedicated Jan. 2, 1848, the sermon by Elder John W. Lewis. Elder John Sweat was chosen pastor at the organization of this church, and still retains this relation.

LAWRENCE.

This town was erected from Hopkinton and Brasher, April 21, 1828, to take effect on the 1st Monday of March, following. The first town meeting was to be held at the house of Carlton Mc Ewen. The poor moneys were to be equitably divided, and a part of the town having been formerly set off from Massena to Brasher without their knowledge or consent, and without any division of the poor fund, it was also made the duty of the supervisors of Lawrence and Massena to meet and divide this fund, in the same manner and subject to the same appeal as above stated.

The title is as follows: the proprietors to Harrison, Jan. 1, 1801, and from the latter to William Lawrence, Feb. 17, 1820. (*Clerk's office Deeds, b. 5, p. 596.*) Parts are now owned by D. Lynch Lawrence, a son of the above.

The town derives its name from William Lawrence, of New York, a gentleman who had spent the prime of his life as a merchant, and engaged in foreign commercial enterprises. Having retired from business, he purchased the unsold portions of Chesterfield, with the view of giving him some employment, and as he told one of his settlers to occupy his mind and prevent his time from dragging heavily, as he had been actively engaged in commerce in the four quarters of the globe, till, at the age of fifty, he found himself in circumstances which justified his retirement from active business. He died in New York, in 1824. It was his custom to spend his summers in town for two of three years before his death.

Memoranda from the Records.—Carlton McEwen, *supervisor;* Myron G. Peck, *town clerk;* James Trussell, Nathaniel Smith, Newel H. Lampson, *assessors;* Enos Burt, *collector;* James Trussell, Myron G. Peck, *overseers of poor;* Giles Hard, David S. Murray, John Ferris, *com's of highways;* Enos Burt, Warren Day, *constables;* George P. Farran, Samuel Bent, James Ferris, *com's of schools;* D. Wright, N. Higgins, David S. Murray, Levi H. Powers, *inspectors of schools.*

Supervisors.—1829-32, Carlton McEwen; 1833-4, George P. Farrar; 1835, C. McEwen; 1836, Myron G. Peck; 1837, Luther Whitney; 1838-9, Walter Smead; 1840, no choice, a tie between J. F. Saunders and C. McEwen, who received 140 votes each. The justice appointed the latter, who declined serving, and March 30, J. F. Saunders was elected at a special meeting; 1841, J. F. Saunders; 1842-3, Lucius Hubbard; 1844, J. F. Saunders; 1845, Jude Clark; 1846-8, C. McEwin; 1849-50, Milo L. Burnham; 1851, Peabody Newland; 1852, Noah D. Lawrence.

The first settlement, in the present town of Lawrence, was made by —— Brewer, who came in as a subagent for the proprietor, Mr.

Harrison, to show land to settlers; and located on the farm now owned by Carlton McEwen, where he erected a shanty in the summer of 1801 and remained till the summer following, when he sold out his interest and agency to Samuel Tyler. In the fall of 1806, Joseph and Samuel Tyler, from Piermont, N. H., Joseph St. Clair and Avery Sanders, from Middlesex, Vt., and Ephraim Martin from Bradford, Vt., and Abijah Chandler, from Lebanon, N. H., came in and selected farms, but did not move their families till the next spring. Having made a bargain with the agent, Judge Bailey of Chateaugay, for land, Abijah Chandler! and the others above named, moved in to reside, most of them having families. Mrs. Chandler was the first white woman who came into town.

These families first came to Hopkinton by sleighs, and proceeded thence to their destination after the snow had gone. Most of them settled in the central and northern parts of the present town, except Mr. Chandler, who settled a short distance from the present village of Nicholville. In May, 1807, these families were followed by Ira Allen, James and Jonathan Pierce, and Sidney Dunton. In June, Jonathan Stevens, Ambrose Lewis and families, and Jonathan Hartwell, without his family, located in town. The latter moved on in the following spring.

In July, 1807, Jonathan, Green, and James Saunders, and D. C. Bastain, and in the same year John Howard, Asa Griffin, and John Prouty, came in. In 1808-9, the settlement was largely increased from Vermont and New Hampshire, and continued till the war, when every family but five are said to have left, and most of them never returned. From this time the settlements languished, and the pioneers were exposed to unusual hardships from the difficulty of reclaiming their lands, and bringing them under cultivation. This arose from the very level surface, which when covered by forests, was wet and swampy, but which, now it is cleared up and cultivated, forms one of the finest and most valuable agricultural districts in the county. Deer were unusually plenty, and consequently wolves. An old lady, in relating these hardships, added, that "had it not been for the deer, they must all have starved, as venison was often the only food they had."

The first school was taught in 1810, by Miss S. Tyler, and meetings were held in 1808, by a Quaker from Peru, N. Y. The first framed house was built in 1808, by Daniel Harris.

It is only since the rail road has given value to the grazing districts of this section, that this town has begun to be most rapidly developed. Lands have advanced often one hundred per cent, and this increase is not a fictitious but a real addition to their value, especially for diarying; and this class of husbandry has in itself the elements of perpetuity, for the produce of the fields mostly returned to them to refertilize the soil, and when judiciously managed, to preserve it in its original fertility. These remarks apply not to this town alone, but to Northern New York generally.

There are in Lawrence three villages and post offices, viz: Nicholville, Lawrenceville, and North Lawrence.

Nicholville is situated on the east branch of St. Regis river, where crossed by the St. Lawrence turnpike, and mostly upon the north bank, and consequently in Lawrence. In the summer of 1817, Samuel Wilson erected a saw mill on the south bank, and in 1822 a grist mill was built on the same side, but was swept off in 1830 by a flood. John Pomeroy, Eli Bush, Chester Armstrong, Calvin Converse and Horace Higgens, purchased and settled here about 1820. In 1824 a distillery, and in 1826 a stone grist mill, were built. The village is named from E. S. Nichols, of N. Y., the executor of the estate of Wm. Lawrence, who afterwards absconded with a large amount of funds belonging to a company. For this reason an effort is being made to change the name of the village and post office. The river here runs in a deep and narrow valley, and the water power is occupied by two saw mills, a grist mill, a woolen factory, a machine shop, and the usual variety of mechanic shops; and the village has about a hundred families, three stores, a tavern, and a Baptist and a Union meeting house. The Port Kent road of 75 miles, through the central part of Franklin county, commences here on the north bank, and the old Northwest Bay road (recently reopened), a short distance west, on the road to Hopkinton.

Lawrenceville is on both sides of Deer river, where crossed by the main road from Potsdam to Malone. It forms the centre of business for a rapidly growing district, and has a water power sufficient for the ordinary wants of the place. A saw mill was built here in 1809, by Ephraim Martin, but the dam was soon swept away, and no further improvement was attempted until 1821, when another was built by Charles Kellogg, and in 1822 a grist mill. A store was opened in 1822, by Josiah F. Saunders, and about 1820 an inn, by John Shepard. In 1828, Dr. John Inman, the first physician, settled in town. In 1827-8, the place began to grow, and has at present three churches, several mills, stores, and shops, a starch factory, &c., and is progressing with the surrounding country in wealth and prosperity.

North Lawrence owes its existence entirely to the rail road, and is situated on the west bank of Deer river, where it is crossed by that road. A location had first been made here many years previous, by John W. Bean, who had erected a saw mill. Chauncey Bristol was the second settler in the vicinity. There is here a depot 50 by 100 feet, which receives the business of the county north and south, three saw mills, one of them having a gang of about 30 saws, and numerous new stores, dwellings, and other buildings, sufficiently indicate its thrift and prosperity.

Religious Societies.—A Free Will Baptist church was formed July, 1838, by Elder Benjamin Bundy and David Colby, of 5 members. Elders Samuel Newland, Samuel Hart and others; and at present the former have been pastors. Present number, 37. The first Baptist evangelical society in the town of Lawrence, was formed November 19, 1840; Peabody Newland, Walter Smead and Stephen Hammond, trustees. Reorganized, May 14, 1842. The church established by the Baptists in Hopkinton, and since moved to Nicholville, now numbers 82. The names of clergymen in the order of their succession, since 1808, are Solomon Johnson, Beriah N. Leach, Silas Pratt, Peter Robinson, James M. Beeman and Elias Goodspeed, who is at present employed. A small meeting house was built in 1832, and enlarged in 1836, and in 1852, a church 40 by 50 feet, which was designed to be opened early in January, 1853. These data were kindly furnished by Myron G. Peck, Esq., of that place.

The M. E. church, of Lawrenceville, was incorporated April 6, 1842; David Blish, John Shepard, Charles Kellogg, Samuel Meacham, Chase S. Wise, John F. Carpenter and Thomas Heale, trustees. They have a church reported in the census of 1850, worth $1,200.

The Congregational church and society of Lawrenceville, incorporated August 3, 1840; Heman Shepard, Avery Colling and John W. Bean, trustees. Their church is reported in the census worth $1,600. On the 17th of August, 1852, a church of this order was formed at N. Lawrence, of about 20 members, all but two of whom withdrew from the other for this purpose. They have been recently incorporated, and are about to erect a church.

LISBON

Owes its origin to the following petition, which is said to have been intended as a preliminary to the location of the county seat in this town:

"To the Honorable the Legislature of the State of New York; in Senate and Assembly convened.

The memorial of the subscribers, for themselves, and in behalf of the settlers on the ten townships of land, situate on the river St. Lawrence, heretofore sold by the people of the state, respectfully sheweth:

That many settlers are now established on the said townships, and have already made valuable improvements thereon; that great inconvenience ensues, by reason of their remoteness from the settled parts of the state, and they are daily exposed to loss and injury in their property, by the waste and spoil committed by persons from the opposite side of the river St. Lawrence, and having no magistrates or constables among themselves, such injuries can not be redressed; that the said ten towns are situate in the counties of Montgomery, Oneida and Herkimer; that it has become highly necessary for the encouragement and prosperity of the settlers on the said townships, that they should be incorporated into one town. They therefore humbly pray, that the said townships, as described in the map, filed in the secretary's office, and known by the names of Louisville, Stockholm, Madrid, Potsdam, Lisbon, Canton, Oswegatchie, De Kalb, Hague, and Cambray, may be erected into one town, and to be known by the town of Lisbon; and that the same may be annexed to the county of Clinton; and that the town meetings of the said town may be held in the township of Lisbon, being the center township, at the house of Alexander J. Turner, and as in duty bound they will ever pray.

Uri Barber, Calvin Hubbard, James Turner, Benj. Bartlett, Samuel Allen, Ahab Herington, Daniel Herington, Jacob Hoar, Alexander Turner, Jun., John De Lance, David Zoyten (?), Festus Tracy, Jacob Pohlman, John Tibbets, Alexander J. Turner, Stillman Foote, George Foote, Peter Sharp, R. F. Randolph, John Tibbets, Jun., Wesson Briggs, Benj. Pierce, Andrew O'Neil, Benjamin Stewart.

Received in Assembly, February 9, 1801. Read and referred to Mr. Shurtliff, Mr. Norton, Mr. Danforth.

Lisbon was accordingly erected March 6, 1801, and the first town officers were as follows:

Alexander J. Turner, *supervisor;* John Tibbets, *clerk;* John Tibbets, Jr., Benjamin Stewart, Joseph Edsall, Seth Raney, William Shaw, *assessors;* Calvin Hubbard, Jacob Redington, Benjamin Stewart, Wesson Briggs, Jacob Pohlman, *commissioners of highways;* Peter Sharp, Joseph Furman, John Thurber, *constables;* Peter Sharp, *collector;* Uri Barber, Benjamin Bartlett, John Lyon, *poormasters;* Samuel Allen, Benjamin Galloway, Wm. Shaw, Benjamin A. Stewart, Joseph Edsall, Reuben Fields, Adam Milyer, Joseph Thurber, *pathmasters;* Uri Barber, George Hilman, John Tibbets, Jr., Asa Furman, John Sharp, *fence viewers;* Benjamin Stewart, Reuben Fields, *pound keepers;* Alexander J. Turner, John Tibbets, Jr., Benjamin A. Stewart, *trustees for the glebe.*

Supervisors.—Most of the town election records previous to 1831, having been lost, the following imperfect list of supervisors is given as the best that could be obtained:

1801, and for several years after, Alexander J. Turner; 1814–15, George C. Conant; 1816–17, James Thompson; 1818, Bishop Perkins; 1819–20, Robert Livingston; 1821–8, Wesson Briggs; 1829, John Thompson; 1830–5, G. C. Conant; 1836, Joseph Chambers; 1837, G. C. Conant; 1838–9, David C. Gray; 1840–1, Charles Norway; 1842, Wm. H. Reynolds; 1843, D. C. Gray; 1844, G. C. Conant; 1845–9, Wm. Briggs; 1850–1, Aaron Rolf; 1852, David G. Lyttle.

The following return of electors was made in 1801, when this town embraced the present limits of the ten towns. The occurrence of the name of a *firm* on a poll list, is novel. Except the first two, who were reported worth a freehold of the value of £100 or upwards, the remainder were returned as renting real estate worth at least forty shillings per annum:

Ogden & Ford, Elijah Carley, Steven Foot, David Race, Thomas Lee, Benjamin Willson, Kelsey Thurber, Jonathan Comstock, Wm. G. Peck, John Lyon, Jacob Pohlman, Benjamin Nickler, Major Watson, Seth Rainey, Joseph Thurber, Jeduthan Barker, Adam Milyer, Thomas J. Davies, Jonathan Ingraham, Daniel McNeal, John Smith.

Tibbets's tract of 9,600 acres, lying on the river St. Lawrence, and near its western border, was purchased by John Tibbets, of Troy, from Alexander Macomb, Feb. 22, 1789, for the sum of £860 New York currency. In a mortgage bearing even date with the deed, it is stipulated concerning the interest:

"That should it so happen, that the said John Tibbets, his heirs or assigns, should not have the peaceable possession or enjoyment of the said premises, or should he be disturbed or kept out of the possession thereof by any Indians, or by reason of any claim which the Indians may have thereto, then in such case the interest on the above mentioned sums to cease during such time as the said John Tibbets shall be kept out of the peaceable possession of the said premises according to the true intent and meaning of this instrument."

The endorsements show that no interest was demanded on this mortgage from 1791 to 1796 inclusive, for this reason.

The author is indebted to Amos Bacon, Esq., of Ogdensburgh, with whom is the original mortgage, for a knowledge of the above fact.

The first white settler was Andrew O'Neal, from Canada, but originally from Ireland, who crossed the St. Lawrence in 1799, and settled about two miles below the present village of Gallooville. The town was then being surveyed for the proprietors, by Reuben Sherwood, a Canadian. Amos Lay, Isaac Beach, and William Preston, at different times surveyed the town into farms. Tibbets's tract was principally surveyed by Daniel W. Church. O'Neil employed men from Canada to build him a house. Early in February, 1800, Alexander J. Turner, of Salem, Washington county, came into town by way of Lake Champlain, as agent for the proprietors, and located on an eminence half a mile west of the present mills, having taken up the first three river lots, joining Tibbets's tract. He continued as agent till 1805, when he was succeeded by Louis Hasbrouck, of Ogdensburgh. He died March, 1806. At his death he was a judge of the court of common pleas, and formed one of the bench at its first organization. Peter Sharp and Peter Hinion, Germans, from Schoharie, came in 1800, took up farms and erected houses near the present mills. John Tibbets, of Troy, also came in and settled on his tract.* In 1801, Reuben Turner,† Wm. Shaw, Lemuel Hoskins, Wm. Lyttle, James Aikens, and Benjamin Steward, mostly from Vermont, moved into the town. Matthew Perkins, from Becket, Mass., Wesson Briggs and Hezekiah Pierce, also came into town, and settled in the same year. The three latter were connected by marriage with the family of Tibbets. The first birth was in the family of J. Tibbets, in September, 1800.

* Mr. Tibbets died in Detroit, September 23, 1826, at the age of 63.
† Mr. Turner was a soldier of the revolution, and died July, 1839, aged 92.

Many of the first settlers were from Washington county. In 1802, John,* Samuel, William, and James, sons of William Lyttle, Richard and John Flack, —— Crosset, Isaac and Elihu Gray, John McCrea and sons, John Jr., Samuel and Alexander, and others; and during the years 1803, '4, '5, and '6, a very large number arrived, among whom was Robert Livingston, who held the office of county judge from 1810 to 1829, and from whom most of the above facts are derived.

The first mill in Lisbon, was built for the proprietors in 1804, by D. W. Church, millwright. It had two run of rock stones and a saw mill, under the same roof, and from its being painted red, it long bore the name of *the Red Mills*, by which it is still often called by the old in-habitants, although the old mill has long since given place to the present substantial stone building on the Gallop rapid. The original mill was fifty by seventy feet, and three stories high. In 1803, Dr. Joseph W. Smith, the first regular physician in the county, settled and remained two years.

In 1813, great numbers died of the epidemic which pervaded the country at that time, and Lisbon is said to have suffered more severely than any other town in the county. In 1816–7, was much suffering from want of provisions, in consequence of short crops from cold summers. It is said that more corn was raised on the Gallop island, and in a field of eleven acres on Livingston's point, in 1816, than in all the rest of St. Lawrence county. Some local cause appears to have favored these localities, and the yield was bountiful. Common corn sold for $2·50 per bushel, and seed corn for $5. Potatoes were sold for $1 per bushel.

An incident happened during the war, which excited much attention at the time, and may be deemed worthy of record. A company of some sixty dragoons had been stationed for some time in the fall of 1813, at the house of Peter Wells, four or five miles back from the river on the road to Canton. About thirteen of these had come to "the mills," and were stopping at an inn kept by one Scott. A sufficient guard of sen-tries was stationed around the house, but during the night a party of two hundred men from Canada, having landed at Tibbets's point about mid-night, surprised the sentinels and surrounded the house, where the dra-goons were supposed to be, but not until several of them had escaped. One named Smith was shot, and another one, Mercer, was wounded. The latter was brutally stabbed several times after resistance ceased,

* *Captain John Lyttle* died in Lisbon, June 28, 1843, at the age of 64. He was a citizen of that town nearly forty years, and held several civil and military offices. During the war of 1812–15, he held the office of captain of a rifle corps, and was in several of the battles on the western frontier. For more than twenty years he held the office of justice of the peace in the town of Lisbon.

and he was left for dead, but subsequently recovered. Two dragoons, Scott and his son, and all of the horses that could be found, were taken to Canada. It is said that these dragoons made a very gallant resistance, and that it was found impossible to take Smith and Mercer alive. The house where this affair took place is still standing.

During the cholera panic of 1832, a board of health was formed; Dr. Wooster Carpenter appointed health officer, and the St. Lawrence, opposite the house of Obadiah Platt, not less than 300 yards from the shore, assigned as a quarantine ground for crafts from Canada; but it is believed that these regulations were never enforced.

The Northern rail road passes nearly through the centre of the town, and on it is a depot fifty by one hundred feet, at which, however, but little business is done. There is a post office here, at Gallopville, and on the Ogdensburgh and Canton road, eight miles from the former place, which bear the names of *Lisbon Centre*, *Lisbon*, and *Flackville*. The latter received its name from John P. Flack, the first postmaster.

An act was passed April 6, 1850, authorizing Henry Van Rensselaer, Esq., of Ogdensburgh, his heirs and assigns, to erect for hydraulic purposes, a dam from the south shore to Gallop island, a distance of about 1,200 feet. A fall of from 6 to 8 feet would thus be obtained, and an amount of power almost incalculable, afforded. The bottom of the river is rocky, and capable engineers have estimated the work practicable, at a cost of $50,000. This being the foot of navigation for sail vessels on the lakes, would doubtless, were a dam built, and a branch to the rail road laid, give an importance to this point, as a manufacturing place, which has scarcely a parallel in the country. This channel is used but little, if any, by boats; and the navigation north of the island, would be improved by diverting more water into that channel, as would necessarily result in the erection of a dam.

A circulating library was incorporated in this town March 11, 1828, with Wm. Marshall, Andrew O'Neil, Albert Tyler, John Glass, Joshua G. Pike, James Douglass, and James Moncrief, trustees.

Religious Societies.—This town was also the pioneer in the religious organizations, one having been formed by the Rev. Alexander Proudfoot, of Salem, who visited his old neighbors for the purpose. The Rev. Mr. Sherriff, a Scotchman, became their first pastor in 1804. The First Associate Reformed Congregation in Lisbon was incorporated Nov. 15, 1802, with A. J. Turner, J. Tibbets, Jun., John Farewell, Wm. Shaw, Benj. Stewart and Reuben Turner, trustees. This was reorganized Feb. 28, 1827, with Geo. C. Conant, John Thompson and Joseph Martin, trustees.

The first society of the Methodist Episcopal church of Lisbon, was incorporated April 25, 1822, with Daniel Aiken, Asa Baldwin, David Wells, Robert Briggs and Luke McCracken, trustees. It was reorganized

April 3, 1847, with George Fulton, Joseph Langtree, David Aiken, Stephen Mackley and Isaac Storking, trustees.

St. Luke's church, in the town of Lisbon, was formed Oct. 12, 1837, with Obadiah Platt and Samuel Patterson, *wardens;* Jesse Platt, Hugh Leach, Robert Leach, Henry Hunt, Simeon Dillingham, John Clarke, Wm. Spears and Dr. W. Carpenter, *vestrymen.*

The Reformed Presbyterian Church, in Lisbon, was formed June 28, 1842, with John Middleton, Wm. Glass, John Smith, John Cole, John Campbell and James Valentine, trustees.

The First Wesleyan Methodist Society, in the town of Lisbon, was formed Feb. 14, 1843, with Joseph Platt, David Aiken, Isaac Storms, Thomas Martin and John Martin, trustees.

The First Congregational Society in Lisbon, was formed March 3, 1843, with Wm. Briggs, John Dings, James Martin, Thomas McCarter, James Norway and Wm. H. Reynolds, trustees. A church had been formed Nov. 25, 1842, under Lewis Wickes, of Lewis county, and grew out of a revival arising during a protracted meeting held by him in that year. About 60 members united at first, and the present number is 80. The Rev. Wm. F. Buffett and Stephen Williams have been hired as ministers, but the Rev. Morgan L. Eastman, the pastor since Feb. 8, 1849, is the only one regularly installed. A church was built in 1845, costing $1000.

LOUISVILLE.

Erected from Massena, April 5, 1810, at first 10 miles square, but in 1823 divided in the formation of Norfolk, and in 1844 increased by strip taken without the knowledge of the inhabitants from that town. The first town meeting was directed to be held at the house of John Wilson; the poor moneys were to be equitably divided and the act to take effect Feb. 1, 1811.

Supervisors.—The early records could not be found. 1816-8, Elisha W. Barber; 1819, Christopher G. Stowe; 1820, Benjamin Raymond; 1821, Timothy W. Osborne; 1822-3, C. G. Stowe; 1824, Samuel B. Anderson; 1825-8, Wm. Bradford; 1829, Sept. 19—Gould to fill vacancy from B's death; 1829-33, Juba. E. Day; 1834, Allen McLeod, Jr.; 1835, J. E. Day; 1836, Allen McLeod; 1837-40, Samuel Bradford; 1841-2, John Doud; 1843, Thomas Bingham; 1844, S. Bradford; 1845, T. Bingham; 1846-7, Nathaniel D. Moore; 1848, John Gibson; 1848, March 25, Levi Miller, jr., to fill vacancy; 1849, Levi Miller, jr.; 1850-2, John Gibson.

In December, 1811, at a special town meeting the legislature was petitioned to take some action by which the public lots might be sold or leased.

In 1819 a wolf bounty of $10, and in 1821 a fox bounty of $1.

1823, two notices for the division of the town given; one of these was to have a town six miles square from Lisbon, Madrid, Stockholm, and Potsdam, having the present village of Norfolk as its centre; the other asking for the division of the town of Louisville, as was done by the legislature subsequently.

In 1828, Samuel Stacey, Otis G. Hosman and Samuel Bradford, appointed to wait upon the commissioners about to locate the court house, and represent the interests of the town.

In 1849, " resolved that the notice given for annexing a part of Louisville to Massena be laid under the table."

In April, 1800, Nahum Wilson, the first settler in Louisville, arrived with his family. He was originally from Peru, N. Y., but had resided a year in Canada, and was accompanied by Aaron Allen, and two sons, but did not move in his family until the following winter. These two pioneers took up each a farm, and commenced clearing immediately. A crop of corn was raised, and in the fall they sowed wheat. Great numbers were in town looking for land, but no one else formed a settlement during the first year. The next settler was John Wilson, who came from Vermont in the spring of 1801, and he was soon succeeded by Lyman Bostwick, Elisha W. Barber, Esq., and several brothers, Griffin Place, and others. The earliest settlement at Louisville Landing, was made about 1806, by Shirley, from New Hampshire. About this time the settlement began to increase quite rapidly, and continued until checked by the approach of war. The first birth in town was the son of Naham Wilson; the first death that of Philo Barber, in 1801 or '2 Elisha Barber taught the first school in 1808 or '9. In 1805, Asa Day erected a mill on Grass river, a mile below the present village of Millerville. On the approach of war many went off and never returned. Religious meetings were held at an early day by ministers from Canada Nahum Wilson kept the first public house.

The following incident was an important event in little settlement:

On the 6th of January, 1806, four persons (Dr. Barber and Mr. Chapman, from Madrid, Mr. Alexander and Mr. Powell, of Louisville), were accidentally drowned, while crossing the St. Lawrence, about opposite the centre of the town. They had been over to Canada, where they were detained by the roughness of the river, occasioned by a strong east wind, which always produces a swell, from its encountering the current. Towards night, the wind having abated, they attempted to cross in a log canoe, but their boat capsized, and two of them came supposed to have drowned immediately. The other two clung to their boat, and endeavored, by cries, to obtain assistance. These cries were heard on both shores of the river, and to a great distance below, as they floated down; but no one paid any particular attention to them, not realizing that they proceeded from persons in distress, and they all perished. Three of the bodies were found several miles below; but the fourth at a great distance below, among the islands. A large dog who was abroad had been bound to keep him quiet, and is supposed to have overturned them. This sad accident spread a gloom through the settlements, and was a cause of unavailing regret to those who had heard the cries, without hastening to their assistance. No blame was attached to any one, and the darkness of the night, and roughness of the river, were such, that aid could scarcely have been afforded, had the situation of the sufferers been appreciated. A touching incident that occurred on the morning of the day on which the accident happened, was rendered peculiarly affecting by the fatal event. As one of the number was about leaving home, a little daughter, who evinced great fondness for her father, came to him in a manner unusually affectionate, tenderly embraced and kissed him, and exacted of him a promise, that he would certainly return before night. She seemed to have an instinctive forboding of evil; and by the artless innocence of childlike entreaty, endeavored to prevent it.

The early settlers of Louisville, in an especial manner, were indebted to their Canadian neighbors for many kindnesses, which relieved them from those extremities that settlers of other towns, less favorably situated, endured. The St. Lawrence can here be crossed at most seasons in safety. Mills existed at various points along the north shore; and the inhabitants, mostly of German descent, who had been driven from the Schoharie and Mohawk settlements, for their adherence to the king's interest, in the revolutionary war, had already, in their own sufferings for want of that assistance which may be derived from neighbors, forgetting the bitterness of former times, in their anxiety for better. Previous to the declaration of war, the most friendly relations existed; families exchanged visits with as much freedom and frequency, as if the river was but a common street; and they were constantly in the habit of borrowing and lending those articles which their limited means did not allow each one to possess. The war, for a season, made each suspicious of the other, and entirely stopped all intercourse for a time; but necessity ere long led them to look back with regret on the customs of former times, and secretly long for their return. During the first summer of the war, many of the Canadian men were called off to perform military duty, and labor on the fortifications at Prescott, and their families were left to provide for themselves as they might best be able. Provisions became scarce, and want stared them in the face. Pressed with hunger, the children of one of their families, remembering the homely but wholesome fare which they had formerly observed on the south shore, one night entered a boat, and being skilful in its use, crossed over, and humbly begged at the door of a house, at which they were acquainted, for *food*. The family were overjoyed at the visit, and on their return, they sent back an invitation for their parents to come over on a certain night, and renew their old acquaintance. They did so, and never were people more delighted than these, when they met, exchanged salutations, and learned, by those expressions that come from the *heart*, that although the two governments had declared them *enemies*, they were still *friends*. The livelong night was spent in agreeable festivities; and with the approach of dawn, they returned.

News of this was confidentially spread, and these midnight visits became common; being at first strictly secret and confidential, but towards the close of the war, quite open, and performed by daylight. One loyalist, however, who felt the spirit of the olden time return, when called upon to sustain the interest of his king, although a very kind hearted man, and strongly attached by the ties of friendship, to his American neighbors, sternly refused all renewal of acquaintance, from a sense of duty, and discountenanced it among his neighbors. One evening an inhabitant of the south shore resolved to attempt to conquer this spirit by kindness, and boldly visited his house, as had been his former custom. Finding him absent, he followed him to a neighbor's, and warmly saluted him with a cordial grasp of the hand, and friendly chiding, for so long and so obstinately withstanding the claims of neighborship. This appeal to the heart, outweighed the decision of the head, and the salutation was, after a moment's hesitation, returned with a cordiality that showed him sensible of the truth, that man is by nature a social being, and intended to live by the side of neighbors. Peace was thus declared along this frontier, long before the fact was established by diplomatists, or published by the proclamation of the president.

Early in the summer of 1812, the inhabitants of Louisville, for their own protection, organized a volunteer company of about forty men, who constituted the male population of the town, capable of bearing arms. They elected Benjamin Daniels, one of their number, "high sergeant," whom they agreed to obey, in all matters touching the common interest. Soon after their organization, they received orders from General Brown, at Ogdensburgh, to bring to all crafts passing the river. In pursuance of these instructions, they, on one occasion, hailed and brought in a raft, and found in the cabin a large amount of valuable groceries, &c., the greater part of which was forwarded to the collector of the district. During the summer, a regular company of militia was formed, with Benjamin Willard, captain, which drew arms from the arsenal at Russell, and was kept in service from August till November. They were ordered to allow Indians to pass, but to stop all other crafts, and learn their business. At times, they had rumors of hostile visits from the north shore; but they were not executed.

The first death penalty inflicted in St. Lawrence county, under its present organization, was upon the person of Louis Gerteau, who was publicly executed in Ogdensburgh, on the 12th of July, in 1816, for the murder of three persons in Louisville, about a mile from Massena village 22d of February, 1816. The circumstances were briefly these: Michael' Scarborough, of this town, being engaged in lumbering, had gone away on business, leaving his wife and two children, one of them an infant, and a French lad about 14 or 15, named Macue, to look after his affairs in his absence. The latter was brother-in-law of the murderer, who was well acquainted with the family, and the premises, and at the time was living a neighbor. Mr. S. had incautiously displayed a large sum of money, which Gerteau supposed was in the house, and for obtaining this, he deliberately laid his plans.

On the night before the murder, he slept in the barn, and at dawn arose, and taking with him a sycthe, repaired to the house, which he entered, but finding an axe, he exchanged for this weapon, and cautiously entered the room, where his brother-in-law was sleeping in a bed upon the floor. He passed through this, to the bedroom where Mrs. Scarborough and her two children were asleep, and took up the money he was after, from its place in the corner of a drawer. With this he might have made his escape unobserved; but fearing detection, laid it down, raised his weapon, and with a blow nearly severed the neck of the woman. He then turned, and dispatched the lad with two blows, and the infant child, and wounded the other, seized the money, amounting in small change to about $22, which had incited him to the crime, fastened the door of the house and fled, having first feasted himself upon cakes and sweetmeats. By a circuitous route, he avoided the houses in Massena village, and gained the road towards St. Regis. About sunrise, some neighbors, having occasion to visit the house, were surprised to find it fastened, and a track in the new snow from it, and observing, through the window, the corpse of one of the victims, the door was forced open, and the alarm of the murder instantly spread. The ruffian was overtaken about two miles from St. Regis, and on being taken to the scene of his slaughter, he acknowledged the crime, and related the details of the shocking barbarity. It appeared that he had not traveled more than two miles an hour, after the murder, and had endeavored to rub out the stains of blood from his hat and coat.

He was tried at the circuit court, and court of oyer and terminer, at Ogdensburgh, in July, 1816. William Van Ness, Esq., one of the justice of the supreme court, presiding; Nathan Ford being first judge, Russell Attwater and Robert Livingston, judges; Caleb Hough and Jason Fenton, assistant justices. The grand jury presented three separate indictments, on the first day of their session, and upon being arraigned he pleaded, not guilty, to each. The names of the murdered persons as named in the indictments were, Maria Scarborough, Jean Baptiste Macue, and Adaline Scarborough. The records of the court contain the following entry of his sentence. (July 3, 1816.)

"Louis Couard, otherwise called Louis Gerteau, otherwise called Jean Baptiste Gerteau, for the murder of Maria Scarborough, whereof he was convicted, was called to the bar, and the court sentenced that he be taken to the place from whence he came, and from thence to the place of execution, and that on Friday, the twelfth instant, between the hours of one and three, to be hung by the neck until he is dead, and may God have mercy on his soul; and further, that his body be delivered to the medical society of this county, to be delivered to some person authorized to receive it."

The sentence was duly executed, in the presence of an immense crowd, who assembled to witness the punishment of a crime which has had but few parallels in our country.

The post office of Louisville is located at a small village on Grass river, near the centre of the town, which has acquired the name of *Millerville*, from the founder. A small clearing had been made at this place, by Oliver Ames, previous to 1823. In March, of that year, the Rev. Levi Miller, from Turin, Lewis county, a native of Wooster, and afterwards a resident of Chester, Mass., came on as an agent for James McVicker. A saw mill had been commenced in 1820, for the proprietor, but was not finished. A bridge had been built across Grass river at this place about the year 1820. In 1837, a grist mill was built by George Redington having two run of stones which has since been enlarged, and two other run added. Besides these mills, the place at present contains a tannery, clothing works; trip hammer &c., in which water power is used, a hotel, store and several mechanics. The Methodist Episcopal denomination had an organized church as early as 1820, but did not form a society until 1839, when the First Methodist Episcopal Society of the town of Louisville was formed, and the following trustees elected, June 3; Levi Miller, Levi Miller, Jun., Israel G. Stone, John Power and John Doud.

In June, 1841, the number of trustees of the society, was increased from five to nine, in accordance with the recommendation of the discipline of that denomination. A church edifice was built in 1849, the basement being for a town hall. A melancholy accident occurred at this place in the spring of 1823, in which two young men who were crossing the river in a canoe, were carried over the dam and drowned. The water being in its spring flood, their bodies were not found for several weeks. The post office of Louisville was first located on the St. Lawrence, but about 1827, it was removed to the Grass river, where it has since been kept. A post office has since been formed at Louisville landing. In 1832, a board of health was organized who appointed Dr. Ira Gibson, health officer, and designated the shore of the St. Lawrence, between Robert Crawford's and Allen McLeod's farms, as quarantine grounds. The difficulties at times attending the navigation of rafts, and the space they occupy rendered a somewhat extended location necessary. The quarantine regulations were not enforced, for the intercourse with Canada stopped of its own accord. The alarm passed off in a few weeks. About ten cases of cholera occurred in town of which one was fatal.

Opposite the lower part of Louisville is an island of some two thousand acres, known on Burr's map, as the Upper Long Saut island, but better known among the inhabitants, as Baxter's island, Stacy's island, and Croil's island, from the names of successive owners. The French named it, Isle au Chamailles; and the Indians, Tsi-io-wen-o-kwa-ka-ra-te, or High island. Like Barnhart's island, it was at its settlement considered a part of Canada, but in running the boundary in 1818, it was assigned to the state of New York. The deepest channel being north of the island, indicated the propriety of this according to the terms of the treaty.

MACOMB,

WAS organized from Morristown and Gouverneur, April 30, 1841, and made to include the district in the former, south of Black lake, and in the latter, north of Beaver creek, from the line of DeKalb to the Ogden tract which it followed to the Oswegatchie, and thence up that river to Rossie. A small tract south of the lake was still left in Hammond, which on the 11th of April, 1842, was attached to Macomb. The town derives its name from the proprietor, who was by birth an Irishman, and for many years a merchant in New York.

It has been said, that coming events cast their shadows before them, and this proverb was verified in the formation of this town. The inhabitants of those portions of Morristown, and Gouverneur, between Black lake and Beaver creek, having long felt the inconvenience of their seclusion from the places of holding town meetings; several years before they were organized into a town, began to importune for a separate town. In 1837, the inhabitants of Morristown, expressed their willingness for this, whenever those in the south of the lake should agree upon the measure. Similar resolutions were passed by Gouverneur. In the town meeting of Morristown in 1841, on the subject of setting off a new town on the southerly side of Black lake, it was *resolved*:

" That all those electors residing on the northerly side of Black lake, do now withdraw from the room, in order to obtain the voice of those on the southerly side; which being done, it was on motion, *resolved*, (with only one dissenting voice), that, that part of the town of Morristown which lies on the southerly side of Black lake, be set off by itself, a new town. The whole of the electors were then called in, and being all present, this resolution was again passed."

The first town meeting was held in pursuance of statute at the house of David Day, 2d.

Supervisors.—1841-2, David Day, 2d; 1843, John Parker; 1844-6 Enoch Taylor; 1847-50, Wm. Houghton; 1851-2, David Day, 2d.

The first settler in the limits of this town, was Samuel Bristol, who

22

located on the place now owned by Robert Wilson. He first made a stand at De Peyster, and was among the very first settlers of that place. Captain Rufus Washburn, formerly of Connecticut, but then from Exter, Otsego county, came into the town when almost entirely new. He lived the first summer at Ogdensburgh, and afterwards for five years at De Peyster. He was a blacksmith, and kept a public house for many years on the place now owned by Wm. Houghton. Samuel Wilson, E. Wilson and Samuel Peck, were early settlers. The improvements of this town were for many years limited to a small neighborhood on the State road, and schools were neglected till 1818. Capt. Washburn was drowned in the Oswegatchie while returning from a town meeting in Gouverneur village, on the 28th of April, 1817.

Pope's Mills is a small settlement on Fish creek, two miles from Black lake, to which it is navigable. It owes its origin and name to Timothy Pope, who moved from Oswegatchie to this place in 1816, and erected mills. He was originally from Otsego county, and settled in Oswegatchie in 1804. He was killed Nov. 7, 1835, with one —— Shaw, by the bursting of a defective millstone. A considerable portion of this town is still but thinly settled; but the greater part is susceptible of profitable cultivation, and it is without doubt destined to be a mining district of much importance. The Wesleyan and Episcopal Methodists have each an organization in town.

About 1836, a vein of lead, zinc-blende, and calcareous spar, was discovered near the shore of Black lake, at a place named Mineral Point, and somewhat extensive mining operations were commenced. A company styled the Morris Mining Company, was incorporated May 1, 1839, with James Averell, David C. Judson, Sylvester Gilbert, John W. Grant, Lewis Moss, Thomas L. Knapp and Edwin Dodge, trustees, for the purpose of mining in Morristown and Oswegatchie. To continue 25 years; capital $50,000, in shares of $100 each, and to be managed by seven directors.

About 1836, a vein containing galena was discovered on the land of Robert Wilson, near the Old State road; a company formed, and a shaft sunk to the depth of about 60 feet. A few years after, lead ore was discovered on the same range, near the road leading from the Washburn settlement to Gouverneur, and in 1850 small mining operations had been commenced, when in 1851 the right was purchased by parties in New York, and a company formed styled the St. Lawrence Mining Company, who became incorporated under the general mining law of Feb. 17, 1848. The articles of association were filed Sept. 16, 1851, in the clerk's office, and name Thomas Addis Emmet, Stephen Crocker and John L. Gratacat, trustees; capital $72,000 in shares of $2 each. Duration limited to

50 years. At a meeting of the stockholders in New York, May 17, 1852 the capital of the company was increased to $360,000. Extensive mining operations were commenced late in 1851, and are believed to be still continued. A furnace for reducing lead was erected, and a considerable amount of lead has been sent to market.

MADRID.

This was one of the four towns formed by the act incorporating the county, March 3, 1802, and at first embraced also the township of Potsdam. Since 1810, it has been of its present limits. In 1837 an effort was made to procure a new town from parts of Madrid, Lisbon, Canton and Potsdam, with Columbia village for its centre, but it was opposed by the other towns, and failed.

The first town officers in Madrid, were Joseph Edsall, *supervisor;* Jacob Redington, *clerk;* Cyrus Abernethy, Reuben Field, Alex. Brush, Henry Erwin, *assessors;* Henry Erwin, *constable and collector;* Jonathan Tuttle, Solomon Linsley, *overseers of the poor;* John Sharp, Isaac Bartholomew, Ephriam S. Raymond, *commissioners of highways;* Asa Freeman, Jonathan Allen, Cyrus Abernethy, *fence viewers;* Edward Lawrence, *pound keeper;* Jonathan Allen, Alexander Brush, Thomas Rutherford, Oliver Linsley Solomon Linsley, *overseers of highways.*

Supervisors.—1802-5, Joseph Edsall; 1806-7, Asa Freeman; 1808, Alex. Richards; 1809, Asa Freeman; 1810-12, Joseph Freeman; 1813, Wm. Meach; 1814-15, J. Freeman; 1816-22, Jason Fenton; 1823-28, J. Freeman; 1829-32, J. S. Chipman; 1833-6, Geo. Redington; 1838, R. Blood; 1839, Walter Wilson; 1840. G. Redington; 1841-2, Alfred Goss; 1843-4, A. T. Montgomery; 1845-6, T. Sears; 1847-8, A. T. Montgomery; 1849-50, Jesse Cogswell; 1851, Richard Edsall; 1852, Francis Fenton.

$5 bounty offered for wolves, in 1803, (excepting the township of Potsdam) and 1804. In 1806, $10 bounty for wolves.

This town began to settle along the St. Lawrence, about 1793, and the following names from the land books, give the dates of purchases, although not of location:

In May, 1798, John Sharp, Barton Edsall; in June, 1800, John Tuttle, Benjamin Bartlett, Godfrey Myers, Benjamin Campbell, Elias Dimick, Reuben Fields, Asa Freeman, Samuel Allen, Edward Lawrence, Asa and Jason Fenton, Alexander Brush, James Kilborn, Jacob Carnes, Allen Patterson, Jacob Redington, Robert Sample, Caleb and Cornelius Peck, Henry Allen, Wm. Osburne, Ira Paine, Oliver Linsley, Joseph Orcutt and Henry and Joseph Erwin.

In 1801, Isaac Bartholomew, Simon Linsley; in 1802, Allen Barber, Nathan Smith, Aaron Scott, Martin Rosenberg, John Allen, Geo. Rutherford, Thomas Andrews, Walter and Richard Rutherford, (brothers,) and many others, mostly from New England, who came through from Chateaugay, by way of Moria and Stockholm. In 1803, Samuel Chipman, from Vergennes, Vt., and others.

The first agent was Joseph Edsall, who was a native of Vernon, Sussex county, N. J., and died in Madrid, in 1844, aged 81. He received his agency June 8, 1796, and was instructed to sell river lots at $2.50, and rear lots at $2 per acre. A portion of the former were reserved that the owners might have the benefit of their rise in value. One fourth was to be paid down, and the rest in three equal payments.

The village of Waddington, is named from Joshua Waddington, of N. York, who was a joint proprietor with D. A. and T. L. Ogden, in the town of Madrid, at an early day. It was originally called *Hamilton*, from Alex. Hamilton, the celebrated lawyer and statesman, who had been associated in business with the Ogden brothers, and the post office originally bore this name. It was, by a vote of the town meeting of 1818 (March 3), changed to its present name, and the post office was soon after altered to correspond with it.

In official papers relating to the war, and in statute laws passed in early times, the name of Hamilton is often used. A grist and saw mill were erected here in 1803-4. The island opposite, the mills, water privilege, land in the bed of the river, and 1,135 acres, comprising the shore opposite the island, and extending one mile back, was in 1811, conveyed by T. L. Ogden and J. Waddington, to D. A. Ogden. This tract embraced the whole of the present village. The rapids on the north side of the island, is called the Rapide plat, and extends its whole length, a distance of three miles, and has a fall of eleven feet. On the south side, this fall was originally gained in a distance of fifty rods, constituting a wild and dangerous cascade, which the French voyageurs called La Petit Sauts. The principal fall was near the lower ledge of limestone, near the present dam, and had a height of about eight feet. The dam has destroyed the romantic scenery of the place, and made a basin of still water, the spot which was once a rapid. The primitive scenery of this romanic spot is described as having been one of unrivaled beauty and interest. The water, by flowing down the smooth declivity of rock, acquired an immense velocity on reaching the abrupt fall, where, striking the bottom, it rebounded with an immense surge, which threw back so large a volume of water as to make a strong upward current along the shore.

Fish abound in the waters, and the wild fowl and deer appeared to have chosen this spot as a resort. As a natural consequence, the rude Indian here found his favorite employment of hunting and fishing; there are those of the St. Regis tribe still living, who remember with regret, the peculiar advantages for their pursuits, which the locality afforded, and a few of the race annually visit the island, and camp in the woods near its head. The island was once covered by a pine forest, and large quantities of valuable timber having been cut in early times, under the direction of the St. Regis Indians. Mr. Joseph Edsall, agent for the town, forbid them to take it away. The Indians appeared to be anxious to settle the matter amicably, and accordingly in May, 1803, an instrument was drawn up between the agent and William Gray, Louis Cooke and Loren Tarbell, trustees of the Indians, by which Edsall was to be allowed to remove the timber *then down*, and to pay 60 cents for every tree, if the title to the island then in process of investigation, should be decided as belonging to the proprietors of Madrid.   In hopes of establishing a commercial and manufacturing interest at this point, the proprietors undertook the expensive task of building a stone dam across the southern branch of the St. Lawrence, which at the same time, should make it navigable, by having in it a lock, and create a water power of unlimited extent.   An act authorizing this, was passed in 1808, and allowed the taking of toll upon vessels passing, at the rate of twenty-five cents per ton for large boats, and double that rate for all boats under two tons.   The locks were to be fifty feet by ten, and allow of a draft of two feet.   These improvements were to be completed within three years.   A wooden lock was first attempted, but before done its foundation was undetermined, and it was abandoned.   In 1811 and 1815, the act was extended, and finally a stone lock was built in the line of the store dam, which proved of little or no use, as its dimensions only allowed the passage of Durham boats.   The era of steam boats followed, and the Canadian government assumed the task of locking and canaling around the principal rapids. An effort was made to secure the advantages of this trade, by digging a canal across to Grass river, but never carried out.   An account of this will be given in its proper place.

In 1832 the connection between the lock and island shore, gave way, being but imperfectly secured, and caused a considerable break in the dam.   To repair this and afford a work which in future should give control to the water in the south channel, the bridge above was filled in with stone, leaving openings through which boats could be admitted, and which when closed, should stop all water from passing.   By this means the water can at any time be drawn off below, and repairs made at but small expense.   A canal runs from the dam parallel with the river, in front of the village, which affords, in connection with the conveniences above mentioned, facilities of great importance.   Floods or drought are here unknown, and the supply of water for hydraulic purposes, has no limits which will ever be reached.   There are here a large stone flouring mill, built in 1832-33, and grist mill, woolen and carding shop, furnace and machine shop, trip hammer, saw mill, shingle, sash and stave machines, paper mill, and other machinery.   The manufacture of water lime, has been carried on to a limited extent, and rather as an experiment, at the village of Waddington.   The stone from which it was made, is said to have been derived from the drift formation which constitutes the island, and the supply must therefore be precarious and limited.

Waddington was incorporated April 26, 1839.

Mr. Spafford, in his Gazetteer of 1813, states that Hamilton then contained 135 houses, 2 saw mills, 1 grist mill, a fulling mill, trip hammer, &c.; and the *site of an academy* then building. The *site* is still probably there, but no building was ever erected or begun. At that period the want of an academy began to be felt; and this place, Ogdensburgh, and Potsdam, each wished to secure it; but while Mr. Ogden and others were waiting till the country should become stronger, Judge Raymond and his friends were exerting every effort, and succeeded in founding St· Lawrence Academy at Potsdam. The work above quoted, adds:

"Madrid was owned by J. Waddington, D. A. and T. L. Ogden, Esquires, of New York; men (say the inhabitants), of benevolent dispositions and well calculated to settle a new country, and who have used every possible means to promote the interest and prosperity of the settlers. The whole number of electors exceeded 200, and the probable population 6 or 700. There are 5 grist mills, 7 saw mills, several carding machines, fulling mills, tanneries, and one trip hammer, and a convenient number of mechanics. There are one Congregational and one Baptist society, but no settled ministers."

A furnace was built by the Ogdens at Waddington in 1834. It was what is termed by iron founders a quarter furnace, with one tewel and a cold blast. It was 26 feet square on the ground, 28 feet high, and run upon bog ore alone. The building, which was of brick, inclosed two stacks or separate furnaces, of which the latter was got in operation in 1836, and was used but in one blast. In 1840, the furnace was stopped, and has not since been worked. A portion of the iron made here was made into castings upon the premises, and the remainder sold as pig iron. The ore was got in swamps in the town, and made very good iron. Much of it was washed previous to using. It cost about $3 per ton delivered at the furnace. The inside diameter of the furnace was 6 feet 10 inches.

"The ore," according to Professor Beck, was "procured near Grass river, two and a half miles from Columbia village, and seven from Waddington. There were three varieties of the ore, viz: one large lumps, called *pan ore*, another in small masses more or less rounded, called *shot ore*, and lastly an ochery one called *loam ore*. All of these were of a reddish yellow color when reduced to powder, and by calcination lost from 18 to 20·5 per cent in weight, and became black and magnetic. An analysis yielded 71 per cent of the peroxyde of iron, 8·50 per cent of silica and alumina, and 20·50 per cent of water. The proportion of metalic iron was 49·23 per cent, although this variety of ore seldom yields in the large way more than 25 per cent."

(See Geological Report, 1837, p. 41.)

The first mills at Columbia village, were erected by Seth Roberts in the summer and fall of 1803, and from him it was often called Roberts's mills. It was also called Grass River falls, at an early day. Meetings were first held in the mill, and in 1803 the first school was taught in town by Dorothy Fields.

On the 4th of March, 1806, the dwelling of Uel Gray, which stood about three-fourths of a mile southwest from the present village of Madrid, was burned; and two children, of five and seven years of age, perished miserably in the flames.

On the 9th of April, 1818, six men were drowned in Columbia village by being carried over the dam in a boat, and although within sight of many, no relief could be extended. Their names were Asa Lord, Abraham and Joseph Loomis, Ezra Bigelow, Asa Dagett, and Leonard Reed.

The following statistics were collected by Mr. E. A. Dayton:

"Columbia village, on both banks of Grass river, but mostly on the west side, and one mile from the Canton and Madrid depot, had in the fall of 1852, 2 taverns, 6 stores, 1 drug store, 4 groceries, 1 book store, 2 shoe stores, 2 tin shops, 1 tannery and shoe shop, 1 grist mill, 1 saw and shingle mill, 1 furnace, 2 wagon and sleigh shops with water power, 1 chair factory and cabinet shop with water power, and 2 cabinet shops without, 1 woolen factory and carding mill, 1 jeweler, 3 blacksmith shops, 1 marble shop, and 2 harness shops. It has 3 lawyers and 4 physicians, a Congregational, Methodist, Baptist and Universalist church, each except the Methodist having a settled minister, except the second who have preaching on alternate sabbaths. It had 2 district schools and 1 select school. At the depot was 2 taverns, 1 blacksmith shop and 10 dwelling houses."

By a law of March 30, 1821, three trustees were to be annually chosen, to have charge of the public lands in town. They were not allowed to sell them on a shorter credit than ten years, or to receive more than a quarter of the purchase money at time of sale. Moneys thus arising were to be loaned on good securities upon lands to double the amount. Half the revenue was to be paid to the school commissioners for the several school districts, in the same proportion as the state moneys were distributed, and the other half was to be equally distributed among the several religious societies in town. These trustees of lands were to hold their offices until successors were elected.

Two *library associations* have formerly existed in town, both of which were incorporated; that at Columbia village, Jan. 10, 1821, with Charles Pitts, Abner Parmalee, David Holbrook, Anson Hall, and Justin Sparhawk; and that of Waddington, with Gouverneur and William Ogden, Nathaniel Tagert, Jas. L. Thayer, Robert W. Brigham, Thomas Rutherford, Jr., and John S. Chapman, trustees, May 10, 1831.

Religious Societies.—The Congregational church of Christ, was formed under the Rev. Amos Pettengill, 17th Feb. 1807, of 10 members. In March they were visited by Mr. Hubbard, of Vermont, a missionary, and letters of thanks were voted to the two societies, who had sent missionaries to them. In 1809, the Rev. Chauncey Cook, was hired. In 1811, Rev. John Winchester hired for three years on a salary of $91 in cash, and $273 in wheat, at the going price. In 1815, and in 1822, revivals. In 1817, Royal Phelps employed, and in 1821 Oliver Eastman. In 1824, members pledged the crops on certain pieces of land, be the same more or less, for the support of the gospel. These were half an acre of corn; ten rods of corn, &c., &c. One subscription was "a place for onions." In 1829, an attempt was made to pass a total abstinence vote, but without success; but ten members then signed a pledge, which was the first temperance movement in town. The Rev. Joseph Hurlbut, employed in 1829, and James Taylor in 1833. In 1840, S. M. Wood, was ordained pastor (Dec. 9), and in 1841, there were large accessions to the church, from meetings held by the Rev. J. Burchard, and in 1844, from the labors of A. Wicks. In 1849, the Rev. B. B. Parsons was employed, and in Jan. 15, 1850, was installed pastor. The society of this church was formed May 8, 1820, with Salmon Gray, A. Packard, Sen., Stephen Goodman, Charles McFarlan, Wm. Powell, and Abner Parmalee, trustees.

In 1825-6, the present stone church was built, thirty by forty feet, at a cost of $4000, under the direction of Wm. Powell, Thomas Wright, and Hiram Safford. The numbers received by this church up to the fall of 1852, 350. Present number 185. In 1850, a bell costing $300 was bought by general subscription and placed in the stone church.

The Second Congregational Society in town (at Waddington) was incorporated Dec. 29, 1828, with Samuel H. Dearborn, Benjamin W. Jackson, and Lorenzo Sheldon, trustees. On the 5th of Oct., 1841, it was reorganized, and in 1844 a church was began, and in 1848 finished.

The Baptist church of Madrid was formed Sept. 7, 1808, of ten members, under the Rev. Samuel Rowley, a missionary from the Vermont Baptist Association. In 1810-11, there was quite a revival. In 1818, Samuel Johnson was hired as a preacher one fourth of the time. In 1825, Elder Rhodes hired half of the time, and was succeeded by Elder Safford. In 1829, the hand of fellowship withheld from free masons. In the same year Elder Pratt was employed. Elder Dodge, Peck, Scott, Lyle, R. S. Palmer, O. W. Moxley, Daniel Sabin, —— Kyle, T. M. Beaman, and H. S. P. Warren, have since preached here. A society was formed July 11, 1836, with John S. Whitney, James Simons, Simon S, Clark, James Murphy, Arad Peck, Harvey Linsley, and Enos C. Eastman, trustees. A church was built in 1836. The number belonging to this church in Nov. 1822, was 126.

The First Universalist Society of Madrid, was formed in 1814, by a few early settlers. The first minister was John Foster, who in that year commenced his labors and remained two years. He was succeeded by the Rev. Jonathan Wallace, from Jericho, Vermont, was supported as their pastor for about half of the time for thirteen years. On the 31st of March, 1841, a society was incorporated, having Hiram Winslow, Wm. McEwen and Luther Abernethy, its first trustees. This society at first consisted of 107 members, and in 1842 a church edifice was built in Columbia village, at a cost of $3000. The Rev. Messrs. D. Mott, and J. Baker, of St. Albans, Vt., and in Jan. 1850, Rev. J. W. Bailey, from Wilmington, Vt., the present pastor, were employed. In 1852 a church organization, with 48 member was formed. The St. Lawrence Association in 1836, 1842, 1848 and 1852, held their sessions here.

The society owns a parsonage, and is said to be increasing in numbers.

REFERENCES

TO THE MAP OF

COLUMBIA VILLAGE.

1 Congregational Church, 2 sheds.
3 Universalist   "   4   "
5 Methodist   "
6 Baptist Church, 7 Sheds,
8 School House,
10 Bridge,
11 12 Dams,
13 Floom,
14 J. Horton's Grist Mill,
15   "   Saw and Shingle Mill,
16   "   Dwelling,
17 Merchants' Exchange; T. W. Crone,
   C. Powell, E. W. Dart & Co., Mer'h.
   and Odd Fellows' Hall.
18 J. Van Buren, Columbia Hotel.
19 G. F. Martin, dwelling.
20 W. L. Reed,   "
21 A. J Goss,   "
22 Doct. C. Pierce, "
23   "   Office,
24 Mrs. Enos Eastman, Dwelling,
25 N. Hosford,   "
26 W. B. Goodrich,   "
27 C. R. Brundriage, "
28 J. T. Rutherford, "
29 D. Sears,   "
30 Rev. B. B. Parson, dwelling, parsonage
   of Congregational Church,
31 Ezekiel Abernathy, dwelling,
32 C. R. McClelland,   "
33 H. K. Belding,   "
34 Rev. J. W. Raily, dwelling, Universalist Church Parsonage,
35 M. D. Hepburn, dwelling,
36 W. W. Hepburn,   "
37 H. B. Richardson   "
38 J. Cogswell,   "
39 McCall & Smith, Shoe Store,
40 G. F. Martin, Harness Shop,
41 J. Marshall, Grocery,
42 Fish & Stone, Tin and Stove Shop,
43 C. A. Loomis, Dwelling,
44 L. C. Lockwood   "
45 J. Whitney,   "
46 N Hosford, Blacksmith Shop,
47 J. T. Rutherford, Store,
47 Thos. Mea, Tailor,
48 A. J. Goss, Store,
49 J. A. Fuller   "
50 A. Ross, dwelling; G. E. Poor, Book
   Store, and O. Whitney, Stone Shop,
   and S. of T. Hall
51 J. A. Fuller, dwelling.
151 W. J. Manly,   "

52 P. S. Wescutt,   "   & Milliner shop,
53 G. E. Poor,   Dwelling
54 F. C. Powell,   "
55 A. M. Dixon,   "
56   "   Wagon Shop,
57 H. Dart,   Dwelling,
58 A. Reynolds,   "
59 J. A. Whighs,   "
60   "   Blacksmith Shop,
61 Mrs. Thomas Sears, Dwelling,
62 D. Whitney,   "
63 A. H. Joice,   "
64 W. Wheeler,   "
65 Mrs. Morrison,   "
66 C Powell,   "
67 D. E. Shurman.   "
68 J. Hughs,   "
69 I Fisk, Tin Shop,
70 H. B. Richardson, Cabinet Shop,
71 Thos. Furgison, Dwelling,
72 C. Averill, House,
73 A. Goss, Woolen Factory,
75 A. Goss, House,
76   "   Dwelling,
77 E. P. Hill   "
78 A. Pike,   "
79 D. P. Haskell   "
80 C. Goss,   "
81 A. Goss, house.
82 J. Curry,   Dwelling,
83 D. Monty   "
84 J. Bruce,   "
85 R. Blood,   "
86 L. Stebbings,   "
87 J. F. Jackson, "
88 L. Houghton,   "
89 W. S. Lockwood, "
90 W. Lockwood   "
91 M. W. Levings, "
92 J. R. Loucks,   "
93 Mrs. Beckwith, "
94 N. D. More, Brooklyn House,
95 Dayton's Shoe Store,
96 B. Dayton's Estate Property,
97 M W. Leving's Chair Factory,
98 W. L. Reed, Waggon Shop,
99 W. Lockwood,   "
100 N. & J. Meatt, Furnace,
101   "   Dwelling,
112 A. Goss, Store,
104   "   Farm Barns
Mrs. Dayton, dwelling, between 112 & 75
O. Whitney, Dwelling, adjoining 50.
T. W. Crone,   "   "   57.

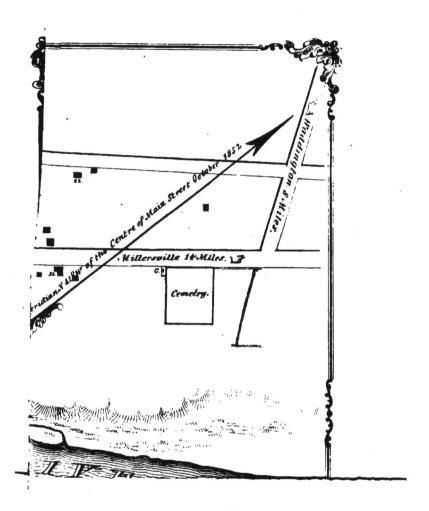

Meridian S 18 W of the Centre of Main Street October 1852

Huntington 8 Miles

Millersville 14 Miles.

Cemetry.

St. Paul's church, Waddington, was incorporated Oct. 19, 1818, with David A. Ogden, and Gouverneur Ogden, Wardens; Jason Fenton, Robert McDowall, Thomas Short, Thomas Archibald, John Dewey, John S. Chipman, Thomas Rutherford, and Elisha Meigs, Vestrymen. The church edifice had been finished the same year at the expense of Trinity church, New York, and David A. Ogden, and was consecrated by Bishop Henry Hobart, of the diocese of New York, on the 22d of August, 1818. The building was commenced in 1816, and built in that and the two following years. The first meeting of the vestry, was on the 17th of October, 1818, at which time Amos G. Baldwin was appointed Rector. William H. Vining, clerk and secretary; D. A. Ogden, treasurer. This church possesses a glebe of three hundred acres on Mile square number ten, about a mile from Waddington village. Jason Fenton, Gouverneur Ogden, Thomas Short, and Thomas Archibald, were the persons first mentioned, as charged with an examination of this property. It has since been managed by trustees appointed by the vestry. The following is a list of the rectors of this church since its organization: Rev. Amos G. Baldwin, Rev. Addison Searle, Rev. Seth W. Beardsley, Rev. Hiram Adams, Rev. Aaron Humphrey, Rev. John A. Childs, Rev. John H. Hanson. At the date of writing there is no rector to this church. The following quotation from the records of the church, under date of October 17, 1818, explains itself :

" It having been stated to the board that the Hon. John Ogilvie, his Britannic Majesty's commissioner, for ascertaining the line between the United States and his Majesty's province of Upper Canada, has presented a bell for the use of said church; therefore:—

Resolved, Unanimously, that the thanks of this board be presented to him, and further as a means of perpetuating our gratitude and his liberalty that the following inscription be engraved on the said bell, viz: "Presented by the Honorable John Ogilvie, of the city of Montreal, June 1818." In answer to this resolution, which was communicated to the honorable gentleman, he expressed a wish that the bell might " ring till the end of time," but this benevolent wish has not been fulfilled, because the bell has been accidentally broken and its place supplied by another.

The First Associate Reformed church in Madrid, was incorporated Sept 17, 1819, with Richard Rutherford, Mark Douglas, John Mofatt, John Rutherford, and Robert Ridu, trustees.

The First Catholic Congregation in Madrid, was incorporated May 28, 1859, with Wm. Fitz Geralds, John Hamlin, Patrick Welch, Thomas Fay, and Michael Hughs, trustees. The church was built by the Rev. James Mackey, now of Ogdensburgh.

The Waddington Methodist Episcopal church, was incorporated April 13, 1849, with Wm. Jordin, Miles M. Sheldon, Richard Tindale, John Tackereel, and John McDowal, trustees. That of Columbia village June 30, 1847 with Solomon S. Martin, Stephen F. Palmer, and Wm. L. Reed, trustees.

MASSENA.

Incorporated in the act that formed the county, March 3, 1803, the whole of Great tracts 2 and 3 being attached. By the erection of Hopkinton and Brasher, it has been reduced to its present limits, which were never a part of Macomb's purchase.

The earliest records extant are 1808, when John Wilson was elected *supervisor;* John E. Perkins, *clerk;* Elisha W. Barber, Thomas Stead-man, Enoch French, *assessors;* Aaron Wright, *collector;* Benj. Willard. Jarvis Kimball, Enoch French, *com'rs. highways;* Jno. Reeve, Aaron Wright, *constables;* Griffin Place, John Garvin, *fence viewers;* John Bullard, Griffin Place, *pound masters.* At this meeting, voted a petition for the erection of Louisville. In 1806, a wolf bounty of $3, and in 1810, of $5. In 1818, $500 voted for the poor. In 1820-1, a fox bounty of 50 cts. In 1825, voted to let the Deer river settlers have $200 out of the poor funds, in case they are set off, and no more. In 1826, voted in favor of allowing that part of No. 16, still belonging to Massena, to be attached to Brasher, and of allowing $10 of poor money to be allowed them. In 1828, J. B. Andrews, John E. Perkins and Lemuel Haskell appointed to wait upon the court house commissioners, and represent the interests of the town. The location at Columbia village advised. In 1849, voted to raise $100 to build a float, and furnish wires for a ferry on Grass river, near the centre of the town. In 1850, voted not to make a distinction between the town and county poor; and in 1851, against a tax for repairing the court house.

Supervisors.—1802, Amos Lay; 1806-9, John Wilson; 1810-11, Thomas Steadman; 1812, Calvin Hubbard; 1813-17, Willard Seaton; 1818-19, John E. Perkins; 1820-1, John Stone, Jr.; 1822-4, John B. Andrews; 1825-6, Chester Gurney; 1827-8, Lemuel Haskell; 1829-30, Ira Goodridge; 1831, John B. Andrews; 1832-3, L. Haskell; 1834-7, Ira Goodridge; 1838-9, John B. Judd; 1840-1, Benjamin Phillips; 1842-4, John B. Andrews; 1845, E. D. Ransom; 1846, Allen B. Phillips; 1847, E. D. Ransom; 1848-9, Allen B. Phillips; 1850, Willson Bridges; 1851-2, J. B. Andrews.

The first settlement in Massena began as early as 1792, by the erection of a saw mill on Grass river, a mile below the present village, on premises leased and owned by the St. Regis Indians. Amable Foucher, from Old Chateaugay, near Montreal, afterwards occupied them, and was in possession till 1808. The first dam built by F. was swept off *up stream,* by the back water from the St. Lawrence, thrown up by the obstruction of ice. The peculiarity of the great river, which caused this, deserves notice.

From the commencement of the rapids below the village of Ogdensburgh to the head of lake St. Francis, at St. Regis, the St. Lawrence seldom freezes sufficiently to allow of crossing on the ice, although at particular seasons, and for a short time there has been a bridge of ice sufficiently strong to support teams. The waters, however, being chilled by snows drifted into them, and obstructed by anchor ice, or masses formed at the bottom of the stream, as is common in running water in our climate, will commence forming a dam or slight obstruction usually near St. Regis, where its surface is covered with solid ice, and this being fixed by freezing, and increased by cakes of floating ice and snow, will accumulate at successive points above, raising the surface, and causing still water just above the obstruction, which allows the freezing process to take place. This has taken place during severe snow storms, and in intensely cold weather, so rapidly, *as to raise the waters of the St. Lawrence at certain points fifteen feet in as many minutes;* and the Long Saut rapids, where the waters usually shoot downward with the swiftness of an arrow, have been known to be as placid as the surface of a mill pond, from obstructions below. The descent of the water is, of course, the same, but the rapids are carried *further down stream*, and still water occurs at points where it is rapid at ordinary seasons. The extreme difference of level hitherto observed from these obstructions, is about *twenty-five feet*, in Robinson's bay; in Massena, about nine miles above St. Regis, and in Grass river, it has been known to raise to an equal height. No winter passes, without more or less of these ice dams and reflex currents, which usually happen towards the latter part of winter, after the waters have become chilled, and ice has formed below. Above the head of the Long Saut, they are seldom or never noticed. Similar occurrences happen at Montreal, at certain seasons, and have often caused serious accidents. The apparent solidity of the obstructions thus temporarily formed, is seldom trusted by those acquainted with the river; although there have been those, fool-hardy enough, to venture across the channel upon them. They will sometimes form and break away with astonishing rapidity; for such is the irresistible force of the mighty current, that no obstruction can long withstand its power. In 1833, a bridge at Massena Centre, supposed to be placed sufficiently high to be above the reach of all floods, was swept away from this cause, the waters having arisen nearly five feet higher than had been before observed; and it has been found quite impracticable to maintain bridges below Massena village across Grass river. The water has been seen to pour over the dam at Haskell's mill, *up stream*, for a short time, and the dam at Massena village has been preserved against the back water with extreme difficulty. The lower dam on Grass river is built to resist the current from both directions, and the level of this river, as well as the St. Lawrence, is from this cause higher through a portion of the winter than its normal level.

Settlements under the proprietors began in 1798, in the fall of which year Amos Lay began to survey.[*] In 1799, a road from Oswegatchie to St. Regis, was surveyed and partly opened, and portions of it are still traveled. The first land agent was said to be Henry Child, who was

---

[*] Mr. Lay was born Aug. 17, 1765, in Lyme, Ct.. and was early employed in the northern surveys, of Massena, in the fall of 1798; of Canton and Lisbon, in '99, and afterwards, of Stockholm and Louisville; and in 1820, No. 7, tract No. 2. In 1817, he published a map of New York, and afterwards one of the United States, which have gone through several editions. He was recently living in Lower Canada.

succeeded by Amos Lay, and the latter by Matthew Perkins. Mamri Victory, Calvin Plumley, Bliss Hoisington, Elijah Bailey, David Lytle, Seth Reed, Leonard Herrick, John Bullard, Nathaniel Keeser, Jacob and David Hutchins, Daniel Robinson and others had settled in 1802, mostly from Vermont, who came by way of Chateaugay and St. Regis. The town began about this time to settle rapidly, and in 1807, there were in the town, as it then was constituted, 96 voters, with property qualifications.   •

In the summer of 1803, Calvin Hubbard and Stephen Reed erected a saw mill on Grass river, at the village of Massena, which was the second one in town. In 1807 or 8, they built the first grist mill near the same place, which had a single run of rock stone. In 1810, they sold to James McDowell, of Montreal, who held the lower mill, and the Indian reservation on which it stood. He continued the owner of the upper mills until about 1828.

The first school is said to have been taught in the winter of 1803, by Gilbert Reed, at what is now Massena village.

The annoyances experienced from the Indians by the early proprietors and settlers, are set forth in the following memorials.

"To the Honorable the Legislature of the State of New York, in Senate and Assembly convened:
The petition of the subscriber, humbly sheweth: That he, together with a number of others, his associates, did, (at sundry times), locate on several tracts and pieces of land, and obtained grants for the same, on the southeast side of the river St. Lawrence, and easterly of and adjoining the township of *Louisville*. That your petitioner and associates, were induced to this distant object; *first*, to be clear of intefering with other claims, and *secondly*, by a stream of water passing through the middle of the said collected several tracts, then called and known by the name of *Little Black river*, and noted in a map of the state, published at the time of the Revolution, by the name of *Eyensauoye*, and now called by the St. Regis Indians, Grass river. That your petitioner and associates, attempted last season to commence settlements on the premises aforesaid, and were prevented from taking possession by the *St. Regis Indians*, who alleged that the said Black river and one half mile on each side thereof is reserved by treaty, and confirmed to them by the commissioners of the United States and the state of New York. That your petitioner, therefore, to investigate the claim, applied to the record of the state, and found the original treaty there desposited, dated the 31st May, 1796, whereby it appears, the premises so surrendered by the commissioners aforesaid, is about eight square miles, being the most valuable part of the property held by your petitioners, &c., under the solemn grants of the state, in the years 1788, and 1790. A copy of said treaty, and cession aforesaid, is hereunto annexed, together with a map of the several grants certified by the surveyor general. That your petitioner, previous to the discovery of the cession aforesaid, did subscribe, and is accountable to contribute a considerable proportion towards a road from Plattsburgh, jointly with the proprietors of Louisville, and is now without

the prospect of deriving the least benefit therefrom. In case thus circumstanced with the St. Regis Indians, who are not amenable to the laws, your petitioner and associates are induced to apply for legislative aid in the premises, and pray that they will be pleased to grant such relief as they in their wisdom will judge equitable and just.

JER'. V. RENSSELAER.

Albany, 17th January, 1799.   Himself and Associates."

In consequence of the above, the state purchased the grass meadows, paying, it is said, much more than they were worth, and more than afterwards sold for.

To His Excellency, John Jay, Esq., Governor of the State of New York, in council. The petition of the several persons, whose names are hereunto subscribed, settlers in the townships of Massena, and Louisville, on the banks of the river St. Lawrence, in the state of New York. *Humbly representeth;* that the Indian chiefs and warriors of St. Regis, are possessed of a tract of land, chiefly wild meadow, extending from the mouth of Grass river, in the township of Massena, up to the falls, which is about seven miles. That your petitioners having settled in the said townships of Massena and Louisville, are greatly annoyed by the said Indians, who threaten to kill and destroy their cattle unavoidably trespassing upon these meadows, they being exposed chiefly without fence, and several of their cattle are missing. Your petitioners therefore humbly pray your Excellency, in council, to take such measures of accommodation with the said Indians, as shall seem meet, in order to secure to your petitioners the peacable enjoyment of their lands and property, against the depredations of the said Indians. And your petitioners will ever pray, &c.

Signed, Amos Lay, Mamri Victory, Calvin Plumley, Kinner Newcomb, Samuel Newcomb, G. S. Descoteaux, Wm. Polley, Anthony Lamping, Aaron Allen and two illegible signatures. Dated June 24, 1800."

The first bridge over Grass river, was built in 1803, at the village, and has been rebuilt several times. In 1846 a tax of $873 was, by law, directed to be raised for the erection of a bridge, which was done in the same year. A bridge was built at the centre of the town, in 1832, but soon swept off. Raquette river is crossed by two bridges.

In early times, when from the insecurity of the laws and the tardiness of justice in overtaking and punishing offenders, there lived in the lower part of Massena, a class of people who sometimes executed the laws that pleased them best, and the "blue beech law" had perhaps, in some cases, the precedent of that formed upon the statute. Fighting was of frequent occurrence, and the only redress in certain cases, that could be appealed to, for the settlement of personal difficulties. When courts of justice came to be established, the decisions were at times very unsatisfactory, and sometimes absurd. It is said that on one occasion, a man having been convicted before a magistrate for fighting, was sent to Ogdensburgh jail, in the custody of a constable. To sustain the journey, hey took along a jug of rum, and both partook freely of its contents, until becoming nearly intoxicated, they fell to blows, and both being badly beaten and gory with blood, returned. The keeper of the prisoner then offered to again start, and the latter promised peaceably to go, on condition, that their jug should be replenished. The account does not relate whether this very reasonable offer was complied with, on the part of the worthy magistrate.

Early in the summer, 1812, an American Durham boat on its way up from Montreal, was stopped at Mille Roche, a corporal's guard was put on board, and it was ordered to Cornwall. The militia officer, (Mr. Grant,) being somewhat a stranger to the river and its channels, gave up to the captain and crew of the boat its management, and the latter in running it down, steered across the foot of Barnhart's island, and before the guard on board had time to realize their situation, they were moored to the shore, and taken prisoners by the inhabitants, who seeing the boat approaching, and comprehending the movement, had seized their arms and rushed to the water's edge, to await them. The boat's crew had moreover carelessly spattered water upon the guns of the guard, so as to render them entirelely useless. A militia training was then in progress at Massena village, and thither a messenger was despatched for help, but before they could arrive, the boat and the guard had been secured, and the latter were on their march to the village as prisoners. Their leader thenceforth bore the title of *Commodore Grant*, and the thing was looked upon as a good yankee trick. The boat was never recovered by the British, but the guard having been handsomely treated, were dismissed on parole.

During the same summer, the inhabitants of Massena village, by voluntary labor, undertook to enclose a portion of their premises with a stockade. This was built of timber set into the ground, with two sides hewed to make the joints somewhat perfect, and the tops cut off about twelve feet from the ground and sharpened. A difference of opinion having arisen, in relation to where the line of pickets should run, and what premises should be included, the work was abandoned, and of course never afforded any protection, if indeed any was in reality required. Quite an amount of labor was expended on this work. During the months of July and August of the same year, a barrack was erected near the centre of the town, north of Grass river, at the expense of the government, under the direction of Lieut. Emerson. It was a frame building, about one hundred feet in length, and occupied by militia of the county, under the command of Col. Fancher, of Madrid, for about three months. The numbers posted here were about 200 or 250. At the expiration of this period a part of these returned home and a part repaired to Ogdensburgh.

United States Hotel, Massena Springs, St. Lawrence Co., N. Y. Benjamin Phillips, Proprietor.

Harrowgate House—Rowing and Bathing House. Massena Springs, St. Lawrence Co., N. Y. B. Phillips, Proprietor.

In September, 1813, a company of some 300 provincial militia of the county of Stormont, in Canada, and under Major Joseph Anderson, crossed the St. Lawrence in the night, burned the barrack, and took several prisoners who were subsequently released. A building which had been used as a storehouse for provisions, &c., was spared, on the representation that it was private property. They also destroyed several Durham boats that had been sunk in the river, and which were partly exposed by the low water. This party crossed at the foot of Barnhart's island, and returned by way of Grass river, up which the boats that had brought them over had been sent to meet them.

Half a century since Massena was overspread with a forest that afforded superior lumber and timber for spars, which made the business of lumbering one of much prominence for many years. In 1810, $60,000 worth of timber was rafted to Quebec by one man. Spars from 80 to 110 feet long, were often obtained. This business ceased with the progress of the settlements about 1828, although wood, and certain qualities of timber are still annually rafted to Montreal.

Massena Springs are situated on the west bank of Raquette river, one mile from Massena village, which is on Grass river, and communicate with the depot of North Potsdam by a plank road. They have acquired a wide reputation for their medicinal qualities, and this celebrity is rapidly increasing. The early surveyors noticed them in 1799–1800, when a copious volume of clear cold water was thrown up, strongly charged with sulphur, and the earth around trod into a mire hole, by deer and moose, which frequented the spot on account of the saline qualities of the water. The Indians here found an abundance of this game at all seasons, and vague traditions exist, that they used the waters medicinally, but of this there is much doubt. The whites, however, began to use the waters at an early day, and Spafford, in 1813, mentioned them as occurring near Lay's falls, and as possessing a reputation for the cure of cutaneous complaints. In 1822, Capt. John Polley erected the first accommodations, and in 1828, the present Harrogate house was built by Ruel Taylor, for Parsons Taylor, of St. Regis, which was opened for the accommodation of invalids, by David Merrils. Other private houses were erected in the vicinity soon after, and the spring was curbed and the ground around improved by a platform. In 1848, Benjamin Phillips, Esq., erected the present spacious and convenient hotel represented in our accompanying engraving. It is of brick, 90 by 44 feet on the ground, three stories in height, with the wings and accommodations for about two hundred visitors. It is proposed to extend the building to the ground occupied by the barn, which would quite double its capacity. Both hotels are now owned by Mr. Phillips, who has provided every convenience as well for the sick, as for those who resort thither for purpose of recreation during the warm season. A neat building, supported by pillars, has been erected over the spring, and the grounds around planted with shade trees, and appliances for the external use of the water by warm and cold bath, have been prepared. The waters have been analyzed by Prof. Emmons, with the following results:

	Warm spring.	Cold spring
Chloride of Sodium,.........................	6,988	6,205
Magnesia,...................................	644	846
Calcium,...................................	1,026	466
Sulphate of Lime,...........................	2,794	1,960
Carbonate of Lime,..........................	1,630	1,100
Hydro Sulphuret of Sodium, Magnesia and Organic Matter,...............................		1,870
	13,082	12,447

The complaints for which these waters have been most used, are cutaneous diseases of nearly every description, dyspepsia, especially of the chronic variety, and chronic diarrhœa. For a disordered condition of the digestive organs in general, and for the debility arising from want of exercise, and close application to any sedentary employment, they have been found to exert a salutary influence. Active organic diseases of the liver and lungs have been oftener aggravated than relieved by the use of these waters. They are found serviceable also, in general debility, chronic ophthalmia, calculous affections, and the debilitating causes peculiar to the female constitution.

Religious Societies.—Meetings were held as early as 1803, by traveling preachers, and in 1806 two missionaries, one of whom was the Rev. Royal Phelps, visited the town, but no church was formed until February, 1819, when a Congregational one was formed under the Rev. Ambrose Porter, a native of Connecticut, and a graduate of Dartmouth College. The number at first, was 12. In five years he was succeeded by F. F. Packard, who stayed three years. In September, 1833, the 2d Congregational Church was formed at the village, the former being at the centre of the town. The same clergyman has usually preached at both. The Rev. Messrs. Philetus Montague, Justin Taylor, Joseph A. Northrup, Rufus R. Demming and Thomas N. Benedict, have been successively employed. The 1st Congregational Society, was incorporated August 6, 1825, with John E. Perkins, Benjamin Phillips, Charles Gurney, James G. Steadman and U. H. Orvis, trustees. This society, aided by other sects in 1836, erected near the centre of the town, west of Grass river, a brick meeting house, at a cost of $1,600. The 2d Congregational Society, was incorporated October 15, 1844, with Silas Joy, William S. Paddock, Samuel Tracey, Benjamin Phillips, Robert Dutton, John B. Judd and J. B. Andrews, trustees. A meeting house was built at the village in 1843-4, at a cost of $2000, including the site. The years 1825, 1842 and 1846, have been marked by religious revivals, in which other denominations shared.

AND FRANKLIN COUNTIES. 859
The Baptists and Methodists have each an organization in town. The church of the former is in the census of 1850, estimated worth $800. A Universalist Society was incorporated September 21, 1835, with Cornelius Barnes, Enos Beach and Joseph Tucker, trustees. They have no place of worship.

There is a Catholic church west of Grass river, about a mile below the village, which in the last census, is reported worth $900.

MORRISTOWN

Was formed from Oswegatchie, March 27, 1821, at first 10 miles square, but in the erection of Hammond and Macomb, reduced to its present limits.

The first town officers were David Ford, *supervisor;* David Hill, *clerk;* John Canfield, Paschal Miller, Horace Aldrich, *assessors;* Henry Hooker, *collector;* John Hooker, Daniel W. Church, John K. Thurber, *overseers of poor;* Wm. Swain, Alexander B. Miller, Wm. R. Ward, *commissioners of highways;* Powel Davis, James Burnham, *commissioners of schools;* Erastus Northum, John Grannis, Alexander R. Miller, *inspectors of schools.*

Supervisors.—1821, David Ford; 1822, Timothy Pope; 1823-4, Augustus Chapman; 1825-6, Paschal Miller; 1827, Augustus Chapman; 1828-9. Jacob J. Ford; 1830-2, Richard W. Colforx; 1833-4, John Parker; 1835-7, Jacob J. Ford; 1838-9, Isaac Ellwood; 1840-52, Moses Birdsall.

Notes from the Records.—1821, Canada thistles to be cut twice in the year, under a penalty of $5, to be sued by the poor masters. In 1833, voted against any part of the town being set on to Hammond. In 1836, efforts made to bridge Black lake at the Narrows. In 1844, voted against any division of the county. Resolved to build a town house, but this has not been done. In 1846, voted in favor of abolishing the office of deputy superintendent of schools. In 1848, resolved that an application be made to the legislature for an act granting the ferry money received at Morristown, to the support of common schools, and to give the care of the ferry to the town officers. The same resolution was passed in relation to a ferry across Black lake. The care of this ferry was asked to be given to the town officers of the two towns.

This town was settled principally under the agency of Col. David Ford, who in the summer of 1804, visited the town to make preliminary arrangements for improvements. The town was surveyed in 1799, by Jacob Brown, afterwards Gen. Brown, and a village plat laid out at the present village of Morristown, named *Morrisville,* and another at the Narrows, named *Marysburgh,* both of which names are discarded. Col. Ford first made an actual settlement about 1808. Mr. Arnold Smith and Thomas Hill, settled at about the same time, on the site of the present village.

The first house in the village was erected by Mr. Ford, and Arnold Smith kept the first public house. A wharf was built in 1817, by John Canfield, Sen., who also erected the first store house at this port. The first school in town was kept it is said, by George Couper.

23

To promote the settlement of the village, the agent, about the year 1817, offered to mechanics a village lot, and a park lot of some five acres, as a free gift, on condition that they should carry on their trade during five years, and within a limited time erect a house of specified dimensions. Several lots were thus taken up, but, except in one or two instances, the conditions were not complied with in such a manner as to acquire a title. It was the intention of the proprietor to have conveyed a glebe of two hundred acres for the benefit of the Episcopal church, but his death occurred before the legal conveyance was made, and his executors never carried his intention into effect. Mr. Morris, with the above exceptions, a part of which existed in intentions only, never gave any property for the use of the town of Morristown.

The first settler on Black lake was John K. Thurber. Henry Ellenwood located near this place in 1810, and Henry Harrison, Ephraim Story, Benjamin Tubbs and Benjamin Goodwin about the same time, in the vicinity of Black lake. The first tavern erected at the present village of Edwardsville, or the Narrows, was by Arnold Smith. A ferry was first established here by Mr. Ellenwood. A post office was erected March 22, 1837, Jonathan S. Edwards being the first post master; and the office, from him, was named *Edwardsville*, although the place has scarcely acquired that name among the inhabitants. A union church was erected here in 1847, and dedicated on the 3d of November of that year, by a sermon preached by clergymen of each of the two principal denominations, who erected the house, the Rev. Mr. Wait, a Presbyterian, and Rev. Mr. Carey, a Methodist.

A ferry across Black lake has existed for many years, at this place, but never under a regular license, until 1851. It was then leased in accordance with law, at the rate of $45 per annum, the income being equally divided between Macomb and Morristown, for the benefit of schools. This point is very favorably situated for the location of a bridge, as the lake is narrow, and near the middle divided by an island. The project has been brought forward several times, but more especially in 1836, about the time when high anticipations were entertained from the mineral wealth of the country south of the lake; but has not hitherto been carried into effect. The present ferry is admirably arranged, and affords a means for crossing adequate to the wants of the country.

This town scarcely began to be settled before 1817, during which year, and the two following, great numbers of settlers came in and took up lands. The sales continued until the year 1820, when they were suspended during the settlement of the estate of Gouverneur Morris, one of the principal proprietors of the town. In 1823, the lands were mostly again opened for sale, portions having been purchased by Augustus Chapman and others, and since that period the town has progressed steadily in wealth and improvement. Being underlaid by the Potsdam sandstone, it is generally fertile and productive, and but little if any land occurs in town which is not susceptible of profitable tillage. Along the shore of Black lake, in common with parts of Hammond, De Peyster and Macomb, considerable attention has, within a few years, been paid to the cultivation of hops. The town wants an adequate supply of water power, as the only stream which has any pretensions to hydraulic privileges, is Chippewa creek, which flows across the town, and affords at one or two places a limited supply of water during a part of the year. To remedy this inconvenience, a wind mill was erected in 1828, on a commanding elevation at the village, and for one or two years did good business; but the projector having been accidentally drowned, no one was found able or competent to undertake its continuance, and it was abandoned. This is believed to be the first and only wind mill for grinding grain, erected in the county; although at several points along the Canada shore, they have been erected and used. The ruins of the oldest of these, is on the bank of the St. Lawrence, between Prescott and Maitland, and was old and dismantled at the time when Ogdensburgh first began to be settled, in 1796. Steam has very generally superceded wind, as the motive power, and from its cheapness and efficiency, is justly preferred. There are, it is believed, two or three steam grist mills in town. The central and eastern part of Morristown was settled by English emigrants, in 1817-18, and a portion still bears the name of English settlement. They were Robert Long, George Bell, James McDugal, Robert Johnson, Edward Lovett, William Arnold, William Holliday (Irish), —— Carter, William Willson, George Couper, Wm. Osburne and Thomas Baldrum, in 1817, and John Pringle, Thomas Young, John Taylor, Joseph Taylor, John Willson, Joseph Couper, and a few others in the year following. These were principally from Roxburghshire, Northumberland, Yorkshire and Lincolnshire, and met casually without having previously been acquainted.

Religious Societies.—The Presbyterian church in this town, was formed by the Rev. Mr. Smart, of Brockville, assisted by the Rev. Isaac Clinton, of Lowville, in June, 1821, at first of eight members. A church was erected in 1837, at a cost of $1,950, and dedicated Feb. 14, 1838, by the Rev. J. Savage. The Rev. Messrs. James Rogers, James Taylor, John McGregor, Solomon Williams, Henry E. Eastman, Henry W. Wait, Samuel Youngs, and Robt. T. Conant have been successively employed.

The first religious Union society was formed Feb. 11, 1833, with Joel Carter, John Child, Abel Beardsley, Zenas Young and James Burnham, trustees.

The Presbyterian society was formed March 25, 1833, with Stephen

Canfield, David Palmer, Erastus Northam and Wm. N. Brown, trustees. The Baptist church was organized January 23, 1828, at the Narrows and first consisted of ten members. The first settled pastor was Elder Clement Havens, although several had been employed previously for a short time. Whole number since first formed, 155; present number, 51. Present pastor, Eld. Ayers.

Christ's church, of Morristown, was formed about 1830, and now numbers about 40 members. The society was incorporated July 6, 1846, with George Couper and Cuthbert Ramsey, wardens, and Augustus Chapman, Chilion Ford, Robert Ashton, Moses Birdsall, James W. Munsell, Thomas Boldram, John Brewer and Henry Hooker, vestrymes. The Rev. Messrs, Aaron Humphreys, David Griffith, J. A. Brayton, George A. Slack, E. J. W. Roberts and John Scovil have been employed in the ministry of this church. The church edifice was built in 1833, at a cost of between two and three thousand dollars.

The first Evangelical Lutheran congregation was formed March 18, 1847, with Joseph Weaver, John Dillenbeck and John Mitchell, trustees. A Methodist society was formed Nov. 16, 1847, with Wm. C. Griffin, Samuel N. Wright, J. C. Stodard, John Jewett, Lemuel Lewis, Cornelius Walrath and P. W. Hindmarsh, trustees. They erected a church that was dedicated Nov. 16, 1848, burned in Nov., 1850, and rebuilt in 1851, at a cost of $1,600.

A Congregational church was formed on Chippewa street, in May, 1852, of 25 members, under the ministry of the Rev. Samuel Young. A church edifice had been erected here in 1849, at a cost of $550.

NORFOLK.

An attempt was made, in 1817, to divide the towns, making one six miles square, with the present village the centre, and failed. On the 9th of April, 1823, Louisville was divided, embracing mile squares 36 to 95, and all of 34 and 35 south of Grass river. April 15, 1834, mile squares 6, 7, 8, 9, 10 and the north halves of 14 and 19 of Stockholm were added, and April 3, 1844, lots 36 to 44, and parts of 34, 35, 45 were annexed to Louisville. A swamp between Raquette and Grass rivers, rendered a division of Louisville necessary.

The first town meeting was held at the house of Elisha Adams. In 1828, a committee of five to wait upon the court house commissioners. In 1848, voted against dividing St. Lawrence into three counties. In 1851, voted strongly against enlarging court house. In 1852, $650 voted for a town house. This has been built of brick, 60 by 40, with a piazza 8 feet wide in front. It is decidedly the finest town hall in the county, and has cost about $1,000.

Supervisors.—1823, Christopher G. Stowe; 1824-9, Phineas Attwater; 1830-1, Wm. Blake; 1832-3, P. Attwater; 1834-6, Wm. Blake; 1837, Norman Sackrider; 1838, William Blake; 1839, N. Sackrider; 1840-1, Hiram Attwater; 1842-5, Ira Hale; 1846-7, Giles I. Hall; 1848-9, Calvin Elms; 1850-1, Nathaniel F. Beals; 1852, Christian Sackrider.

The first industrial operations in Norfolk, in common with many of the towns of St. Lawrence county, lying on the Great river or its tributaries, was commenced by timber thieves, previous to 1809. In that year Erastus Hall, from Tyrringham, Mass., came into town to explore, with a view of settlement. He arrived at Potsdam May 9, 1809, at the inn of Ruell Taylor, and meeting with Judge Raymond, was induced to go and look at lands, in which the latter had the agency, in what was then the town of Louisville. Ira Brewer, from the same place with Mr. Hall, accompanied him on his journey, and they proceeded through a bush road which had been cut as far as the present village of Raymondville, for the purpose of conveying potash to a point from whence it could be shipped in canoes for Canada. Arriving at their destination, but on the opposite side of the river from that which they wished to gain, they made a rude raft of logs, on which they placed their coats, guns, axes and fire works, and endeavored to paddle over, but soon found themselves at the mercy of the current, without the ability to guide their frail raft with the poles they had provided. Passing under a tree they threw on shore their freight, and with much difficulty rescued themselves by seizing and clinging to the branches. One lost his hat, but soon recovered it by swimming, and the two found shelter in a shanty erected by lumbermen in procuring timber. A great number of beautiful masts had been taken in the woods near Raquette river in this town. In returning they attempted to cross the river in an old bark canoe, but this instantly filled with water, and they were obliged to hasten back. On the first night they were unable to get to their destination, and slept under a log. Several days after, they returned, and had farms surveyed out by Sewall Raymond, of Potsdam. The first contract for land in town was given to Mr. Hall in June, 1809. The first framed building erected was a small ware house on the east side of the river at Raymondville.

By night the explorers built a ring of fires, as the only means of being free from the clouds of mosquitos and *black flies*, of which the latter in particular were very annoying. In fifteen minutes the faces of those exposed would be covered with blood, and on their return to the settlements their friends did not know them, they had become so disfigured During this summer the Raquette river was leveled and found boatable as far as the Morris tract, near the present village of Norfolk. Mr. Hall employed some persons at the Union in Potsdam, to erect him a house, and in the fall returned to New England for his family. Mr. Eben Judson, from Williston, Vt., and Martin Barney, came on the same year and made small beginnings. In March, 1810, Mr. Judson came on with his family, and his wife was the first white woman who settled in town. They started on the 7th of March, 1810, *on the first snow that had fallen that winter,* having been delayed several weeks waiting for snow, and arrived on the third day from Lake Champlain at the Union, in Potsdam, from which they proceeded to their destination. The company censisted of Mr. and Mrs. Judson and three children, a brother and a brother-in-law, and two brothers, Ashbell and John Hall, young men who remained several months and returned.   They had two horse teams, an ox team, and a cow.   The brother and brother-in-law of Mr. Judson immediately returned, leaving the family established in their house, which was a shanty 10 by 14 feet, built between two hemlock trees.   They also had a shed for their cattle, which was an open bower covered by boughs.*   Mr. Hall and wife arrived four days after.

In September, 1810, Timothy W. Osborne, from Georgia, Vt., came on with a company of eight or ten men, as an agent for Major Bohan Shepard, of St. Albans, Vt., and erected a saw mill on Trout brook.   The second mills were built by Jonathan Culver at a point then called Hutchen's falls, in 1812, and were at the lowest place on Raquette river ever occupied by mills.   It is about three miles below Raymondville. They were afterwards burned.   Judge Attwater erected the third mills in town, on the Morris tract, in the lower part of the present village of Norfolk, in the summer of 1816.   The first Durham boat ever run on the Raquette river, was in this year, and was laden with mill irons, goods, and provisions, from Schenectady, sent by Judge Attwater to begin the settlement at his mills.   It was drawn around Culver's dam, and afterwards for one or two seasons performed regular trips every week from Culver's to Norfolk, in connection with a line below the dam, which run to ports on the St. Lawrence.   The latter was required to be regularly furnished with clearance papers from the collector of customs.

Christopher G. Stowe, Martin Barney, Milo Brewer, and several others, came in and commenced improvements in 1810, but the families of Hall and Judson were the only ones that spent the winter in town.   In 1811 the settlement was increased by several families.   The first death was that of Mr. Judson, June 29, 1813.   Dr. Lemuel Winslow, from Williston, Vt., was the first physician; he located in 1811.   The first road towards Massena, was made in November, 1810, by Hall and Brewer. Great expectations were early based upon the supposed value of the navigation of the river, and Judge Raymond, with characteristic enthusiasm, supposed that his location would grow to great importance.   A village plat east of the river, was surveyed, and named *Racketon*, of which Spafford, in his Gazetter of 1813, says:

"The village of *Racketon* is a new and flourishing settlement, forming in the southeast part of the town, at the head of bateaux navigation on

---

* Judge Raymond happening to pass soon after, and being belated, accosted the family with the facetious remark " that they must be keeping tavern, since they had erected sheds," and accepted the humble accommodations of his settlers, with a good nature and familiarity which did credit to his character.

the Raquette river, 20 miles from its confluence with the St. Lawrence. At this place, immediately above the landing, is a fall of the waters of Raquette river of about 15 feet, and excellent accommodations for hydraulic works. Racketon is about 25 miles east of Ogdensburgh; and uniting its advantages for good navigation to the St. Lawrence with those of its central position, in a rich and fertile country, must become a rich and populous place."

About 1814 a bridge was built, and in 1816 Raymond moved his family to the place and remained several years. From him the inhabitants named the place Raymondville, and a post office of this name has been established. It is however still called the Lower village by many, to distinguish it from the Upper village, or Norfolk village proper. The place possesses a fine water power, and communicates with the rail road at North Potsdam, by a plank road.

The first settlement at Norfolk village was made in 1816, by Judge Russell Attwater, from Russell, who in June, the year previously, purchased one half of the Morris tract, and the west half of 88 of Louisville. This tract had been assigned to James D. Le Ray in a partition of lands, and sold by him to G. Morris. A clearing of ten acres had been made for Le Ray in the summer of 1811, in the lower part of what is now the village of Norfolk, on which in 1812 a crop of wheat was raised. A large stone grist mill, with two run of stones was built the first year, by Mr. Attwater, on the site of the stone mill of Mr. Sackrider. A chapel was fitted up with seats and a desk in the third story of a mill, and this was the first accommodation for public worship in town.

A company styling itself the Phœnix Iron Company, under the firm of E. Keyes & Co., was formed Oct. 7, 1825, and the year following, built in the village on the north bank, a furnace for making iron from bog ores, which existed abundantly in the swamps of this and neighboring towns. It passed through several hands and run about two hundred days in a year, till 1844, when it was burned by an incendiary. It produced about twelve tons daily, and was lined with sandstone, from Potsdam and Hopkinton. In 1846 a forge was built by Wm. Blake a little above the furnace, and run two or three years, until it was burned.

The village of Norfolk, possesses manufacturing facilities which are destined to render it a place of much importance. The Raquette river here has a descent of about 70 feet within a mile, passing over three dams already erected, and affording opportunity, for at least four more, at each of which the whole volume of the river could be used. Below the upper dam, the channel is divided by an island of about two acres in extent, which affords facilities for the erection of dams at its head and at its foot, and the water could be diverted to either side or used upon both sides of the island and the main shore. At the foot of the island the river turns to the left, and the bank on the inside of the bend is low and flat, and but little elevated above high water mark, while that on the outside of the bend is an elevated plain of easy ascent, and abruptly terminating upon the river. This elevated bank continues with a slight interruption to below the village. The left bank of the river is low, and on this the main part of the village is at present built. Throughout the whole extent, the bed of the river is formed of limestone, affording at the same time a secure foundation for building, and the materials for the erection of walls. Lime made from this stone is of good quality.

It is by plank road three miles distant from the Potsdam station, and the same distance to Knapp's station. At the time of writing, there exists a stone grist mill, with three run of stones, three saw mills, one planing machine eight shingle factories, a tannery, a woolen factory, a trip hammer, a furnace, and several other manufactories using water power. At none of the dams now erected is the entire water privilege occupied.

The town of Norfolk and especially the village of Raymondville, possesses great natural advantages for the manufacture of brick, which are of superior quality. Their durability and hardness is probably due to the clay of which they are made, and of which an account will be given in the chapter on the geology of the county.

Norfolk Union Library was incorporated May 25, 1834. Philander Kellogg, Wm. Grandy, Hiram G. Francis, Denis Kingsbury, Daniel Small, John W. Williams, and Nathaniel Brewer, trustees.

Religious Societies.—Meetings were held in the lower part of the town almost immediately after it was settled.

Neither Mr. Hall, nor Mr. Jordan were members of church, but believing that the observance of the sabbath conduced to morality, they soon after their arrival agreed to hold religious meetings alternately at the house of each, at which a sermon should be read, and that their families should not remain and visit after the meeting was dismissed. Occasionally others of the settlers would come in on the sabbath, and these weekly unions were kept up for some time, when one Montague, who came on with others, to build a mill on Trout Brook, having heard of these meetings, attended, and was the first worshiper who could sing and pray; and thenceforth they lacked none of the elements requisite in the protestant worship. In 1811, Seth Burt, a missionary from Massachusetts, came and left books. The Rev. James Johnson, from Potsdam, and the Rev. Mr. Winchester, from Madrid, occasionally visited the town, and held meetings in the vicinity of the present village of Raymondville. After Mr. Attwater's arrival in 1816, as soon as circumstances would admit, the upper story of his grist mill was fitted up for the purpose of divine worship, according to the rites and doctrines of the Episcopal church. Here he officiated for several years as a lay reader, and succeeded in making a few individuals acquainted with the doctrines of the church, among these was one who is now an able and honored bishop of the church, the Rt. Rev. L. Siliman Ives, D. D., of North Carolina. The parish of Grace church, in Norfolk was first organized in the year 1825, by the Rev. Seth M. Beardsley, then acting as missionary in the country, who also made an unsuccessful attempt to build a church. He was succeeded by the Rev. Hiram Adams, in 1828, and by the Rev. Henry Attwater in 1829. From July 1836, to March 1842, the public services of the church were discontinued, with the exception of occasional lay reading, and owing to the want of a clergyman, and the removal of several families, the organization of the parish was lost. A reorganization took place March 29, 1842, when the Rev John A. Childs, began to officiate as missionary. During the two years in which he ministered in this place, another effort was made to build a church but failed. In 1845, the Rev. John H. Hanson, the present missionary, was engaged by the parish. On July 30th, the corner stone of a church was laid by the Rt. Rev. Wm. H. Delancy, D. D., Bishop of Western New York, in a lot of ground purchased by the vestry, and situated in the centre of the village. The church thus begun, was fully enclosed in 1849, but is not yet completed within. It has cost about $2000 and will require about half as much more to complete it after the original design. It is after the Elizabethean style of church architecture, is 70 feet in length, including the porch, fifty feet across the transept and twenty-two across the nave. The ridge is thirty-four feet high. The walls are of stone and very massive, and the whole wants but the moss and the ivy to give it an appearance of venerable antiquity, consonant with the purposes for which it was erected. This is the only gothic edifice in St. Lawrence or Franklin counties.

The Presbyterian church so called, being Congregational in form, was organized July 1, 1817, by Rev. Royal Phelps, of the Cayuga Presbytery, then acting as a missionary, assisted Rev. John Ransom, of Hopkinton, at first of 17 members. The meetings were first held in the loft of a mill, and afterwards in the chamber of the tavern of J. Langworthy, and in the school house. The stated supplies have been numerous. The Rev. Adolphus Taylor, after preaching several years, died here. Loring Brewster was installed 1st pastor, April 28, 1828, and G. B. Rowley the present pastor, from whom these facts are received, Nov. 10, 1847. The society was incorporated Feb. 20, 1828, G. C. Stowe, Martin Beach, E. S. Tambling, Wm. Blake, Philemon Kellogg, and John C. Putnam, trustees. Reorganized Dec. 12, 1840. A meeting house was built in 1840, at a cost of $4000, and the church numbers now 153. The church of Raymondville, was a colony from this, and their brick meeting house was finished and dedicated in 1844, at a cost of $3000, and soon after, a bell of 300lbs, was placed in it. Rev. Moses Ordway was the first resident minister. The Methodists organized a society, April 19, 1831, with Royal Sheldon, Lucius Chandler, Justice Webber, Hiram Johnson, and Ebenezer Houghton, trustees. They reorganized, Feb. 10, 1840, and in that year built their present chapel in Norfolk village.

OSWEGATCHIE.

Incorporated with the county, March 3, 1802, from Lisbon. The town records were destroyed, April 17, 1839, in the great fire at Ogdensburgh, and the following list of supervisors is partly made up from other sources than the records.

Supervisors.—1802, and for several years, Nathan Ford; 1814-23, Louis Hasbrouck; 1825-8, Sylvester Gilbert; 1829, Washington Ford; 1830, Jacob Arnold; 1831, Baron S. Doty; 1832-4, Preston King; 1835, Joseph W. Smith; 1836, Royal Vilas; 1838, Baron S. Doty; 1839-44, Geo. W. Shepard; 1845-52, Geo. M. Foster.

Settlements were began here under Samuel Ogden, the proprietor, by Nathan Ford, his agent, in 1796, who on the 11th July, 1797, was made his attorney, to sell lands. It had been the intention to commence earlier, but possession of Fort Oswegatchie could not be got. Under the British administration, parties from Canada having obtained from the Oswegatchie Indians, leases of extensive tracts of land in this town, had commenced improvements, and were occupying them when first known to the purchasers. As the history of these spurious titles possesses much interest, we will here insert one or two of them.

" To all people to whom these presents shall come; Ogentago, Dowasundah, Sahundarish, and Canadaha, the four representatives of the Indian village of Oswegatchie, have this day, by and with the advice of the whole nation, being duly assembled in full council of the whole tribe or nation, as above mentioned, Men, Women and Children being all present, have this day bargained, agreed, and to farme let for ever, to Major Watson, of Oswegatchie, and to his heirs and assignes for ever, all that tract or parcel of Land, Situate, Lying, and Being, on the South Side of the River St. Lawrence, Beginning at the northwest corner of a tract of land granted to Daniel Smith, and running up along the stream of the river one League, or three English miles; thence East South-east from the Lake or River, into the woods three Leagues or Nine English Miles, thence Northeast one League or three English miles, thence North North west three Leagues or Nine English Miles, along the Line of said Daniel Smith to the place of Beginning, at the River Keeping the breadth of one League or three English miles, from the front of the River with Nine Miles in Depth; to him, his heirs and assigns, with the appurtenances thereunto Belonging, or anywise appertaining to him the Said Major Watson his heirs and assigns for ever, for the yearly Rents and Covenants herein Reserved to the above Ogentago, Dowasundah, Sahundarish and Canadaha, their heirs and successors or assigns, forever; to be yearly and Every year after the day of the date hearof, and to commence on the first day of December, one thousand Seven hundred and ninety three, the sum of Twenty Spanish Mill'd Dollars, thirteen and one third Bushels of wheat, and thirty three and one third pounds of pork, to be paid on the premices by the said Major Watson, his Heirs, Executors, administrators and assigns, to the above forementioned representatives, their heirs or assigns, if legally demanded on the premises, they giving sufficient discharges for the same, every year, hereafter, as the same rent becomes due. Now therefore this Indenture witnesseth, that the above Ogentago, Dowasunda, Sahundarish, and Canadaha, the four Representatives of the above mentioned village, and being the true and lawful owners of the above described Lands, and for, and in consideration of the yearly Rents and Covenants above mentioned, the receipt whereof they do here acknowledge, hath granted Bargained aliened released and confirmed, and by these presents doth, fully, freely, and Absolutely, do grant, Bargain, and sell; alien, Release, and Confirm, unto the said Major Watson, his heirs and assigns for ever all the Title, Interest, Property, Claim, and Demand, of and unto, the above mentioned Land, and premises, together with all the Trees, Timber, woods, ponds, pools, water, water courses, and streams of water, fishing, fowling, hawking, and hunting, Mines and Minerals, Standing, growing, Lying, and Being, or to be had, used, and enjoyed within the limits and Bounds aforesaid, and all other profits, Benefits, Liberties, priviledges, heriditiments, and appurtunanceys to the same Belonging, or in anywise appertaining, to have, and to hold, all the aforesaid Land, and premises, to the said Major Watson, his heirs, and assigns, to the proper use Benefit and Behoof of him, the said Major Watson, his Heirs and assigns for ever, So that neither of them the said Releasors nor their heirs or any other person or persons whatsoever for them or either of them, in their or either of their Names or write, Shall, or May, by any ways or means whatsoever, at any time hereafter, Claim, Challenge, or demand any Estate Right Title Interest, of, in, or to, the said above released premices, or any part thereof, But from all and every action and actions, Estate, Right, title, Claim, and Demand, of any kind, of, in, or to, the said premises, or any part thereof. they and Every of them, Shall be for ever Bound, by thease presents, and thay, and Every of them, tho above said premises, with the apportunances to the said Major Watson, his heirs and assigns, shall, and will, for Ever Warrant and Defend. In Witness whereof, they have hearunto Set their Hunds, and Seals, the Twenty Second day of August, in the year of our Lord one thousand seven hundred and ninety two.

Sealed and Delivered
in the Presents off,

Senhawe x his Mark.
Sahieh x his Mark.
Henry Galton.
Chrest. Swansichton.
Ogentago x his Mark.   L. s.
Dowasundah, x his Mark.   L. s.
Sawhundarish, x his Mark.   L. s.
Canadaha. x his Mark.   L. s.

T. B. A true Coppy.

Endorsement on Preceding.—Be it for Ever hereafter Remembered, that the chiefs of the Oswegatchie Nation, have received of Major Watson, Jared Seeley, and Daniel Smith, and John Livingston, an actual payment for the consideration contained in the Deeds executed by us and our fathers, comprehending ten miles on the river St. Lawrence, with nine miles back into the woods; we say received the rent in full, for the year of our Lord, one thousand seven hundred and ninety-seven, agreeable to the conditions of the within Lease or Deed, and the said parteys are hear by Regularly Discharged for the same, as witnesses our hands.

his

Witness present,
    Amos Ansley.

CANDAHA.

mark.

Lashalagenhas, ⋈ his mark.
Lewangelass, ⋈ his mark.

Onatchateyent, Totagoines, Onarios, Tiotaasera, Aonacta, Gatemontie, Ganonsenthe and Onente, Oswegatchie chiefs, at Grenville, U. C., June 1, 1795, in the presence of Joseph Anderson, John Stigman and Ephraim Jones, confirmed to Catharine and Frances, the wife and son of Capt. Verneuil Lorimier, a verbal lease, executed in 1785, of a tract on the south shore, half a mile on each side of the small river called Black river, and up to Black lake, for the yearly rent of one hundred silver dollars, or money equivalent thereto. This was a full warranty deed with covenant. Lorimier had been a French officer in command of Fort Presentation, and a tradition relates that he also possessed a French title, which with other papers, were scattered and lost in a gale of wind that unroofed his house.* It having been reported the St. Regis Indians discountenanced these proceedings. Watson and his associates wrote to them on the subject, and received the following answer, dated at St. Regis, April 10, 1795.

"Sir—We were favored with your letter of the 9 March, and we have to inform you that no Indian of St. Regis ever will molest or trouble you on your present possession. You pay our brothers of the Oswegatchie, a tolerable rent, and as long as you will make good payment of the same rent to our brothers, who are the same in all respects as ourselves, we shall and ever will be happy to keep you in full possession; do not ever believe any thing to the contrary from any person whatever. We are with esteem, your brothers and friends,

Tharonhiageton,   Ononsagenra,
Assorontonkota,   Tionategekha.
for ourselves and others of our village of St. Regis."

To still further substantiate their title, the lessees from the Indians procured of the commandent of the Fort at Oswegatchie, a permit to locate upon and occupy the tracts included in their leases. This document is given below, in the orthography and punctuation of the original.

"This is to cartifye that John Levingston Daniel Smith, Major Watson and Jered Seley have made a purchase of a tract of land from the Indians of the Oswegatchie within the Jurisdiction of the British post of Oswegatchie, I having examined said purchase and find it to be a fair one therefore the said John Levingston Daniel Smith Major Watson and Jered Seley are hereby ortherized to settle cultivate and improve the saim and I as cummanding officer of said post Do bereby Ratifie and Confirm said purchase and promis the Kings protection to them and Their associates Witness my hand And seal Don at oswegatchie this Tenth Day of June one thousand seven hundred ninty four

Richard Porter. L. S."

By virtue of these titles, and under protection of the British flag, a saw mill was erected west of the Oswegatchie, near its mouth, and the business of lumbering was commenced and prosecuted with spirit, under which the majestic forests so often alluded to in our first chapter, began rapidly to disappear; and these operations extended to the whole river front and the tributaries of the great river, capable of floating spars and rafts.

The following correspondence in relation to these claims and trespasses, passed several years before settlements were attempted:

---

* Stated on the authority of Wm. E. Guest, Esq., of Ogdensburgh.

NEW YORK, Nov. 1, 1793.

His Excellency George Clinton, Esquire:

Myself and associates, owners of ten townships of land lying on the east side of the river St. Lawrence, having had the honor of addressing you on the 2d of September, 1792, and stating to you as the head of the executive of this state, certain representations of trespasses daily committed on said townships, by subjects of the government of Great Britain, in hopes that through your aid some measures would be taken, either by the government of the state, or by the general government, to put a stop to the great evil of which we complained. But finding from good information that the trespass was not only continued, but very much increased, I conceived it for the interest of myself and the other gentlemen concerned, to take a journey to that country, as well to establish the facts contained in that letter, as to endeavor by making a representation thereof to the governor of Canada, to have an immediate stop put to the evil. How far my expectations have been realized, your excellency will judge from a perusal of the copies hereto annexed, of the letters which passed between Governor Simcoe, my Lord Dorchester, and myself.

You will allow me in behalf of myself and associates, to aver to you, that all the facts contained in our letter to you, as well as those contained in my letter to Governor Simcoe, and my Lord Dorchester, are true, and I trust you will readily see the necessity of some immediate and spirited measures to stop the trespass, or the greater of all our valuable timber will be destroyed, and carried out of the United States by a set of men whose only motive is to plunder and destroy. Our title under the state we know to be good, and we conceive we have every just claim for protection and indemnity from it. It is now upwards of eight years that we paid into the public treasury a large sum of money for this tract of country, under full expectation that we might make peaceable settlements thereon: But unfortunately for our interests, we are not only prevented by the British government from settling those lands, but the subjects thereof have already robbed us of the most valuable part of that property. It is the apprehension of consequences of a public nature, that restrains us from appealing to the law of the state for the protection of that property. There can be no doubt but that the justice of the legislature ought to give us an ample indemnity for our sufferings. How far then it may be proper for us through you, to make a representation of the hardships under which we labor to it, at the approaching session, is with much respect submitted to your wisdom, and we well knowing your anxiety for the dignity of the state, and the interests of its individuals, have no doubt that you will do every thing that may be proper in the premises.

I have the honor to be your most obedient humble servant,

SAM'L OGDEN.

YORK, UPPER CANADA, August 31, 1793.

" *His Excellency John G. Simcoe, Esq.:*

"SIR—Having obtained under the state of New York, a title to a large tract of land lying on the southeast side of the River St. Lawrence, at or about Oswegatchie, and being informed that many persons calling themselves subjects of your government, are daily committing great trespass on said tract of land, by cutting and transporting to Montreal large quantities of timber therefrom, I beg leave to represent the same to your excellency, in full confidence that your interposition will put an immediate stop to such proceedings as tend very much to my injury. It may not be improper to add, that previous to my leaving New York, I was advised, and well knew, that the executive of that state would, on my application, give his immediate aid for the protection of this property. But conceiving such an operation would involve a governmental question (which for very obvious reasons I conceive at this time ought to be avoided), at great expense and fatigue, I undertook a journey to this country, that I might make this representation to your excellency previous to any other measures being taken in the premises.

I have the honor to be, &c.,

SAM'L OGDEN."

YORK, August 31, 1793.

"*Samuel Ogden, Esquire:*

SIR—I am just favored with your letter of the 31st of August; I beg leave to observe to you, that last autumn on the representation of the Oswegatchie Indians, the magistrates of the town of Augusta, warned some of his majesty's subjects to quit those very lands. I apprehend you claim under a title from the state of New York. In regard to your intimation that the executive of the state of New York, would give its immediate aid for the protection of this property, I have to observe that you are perfectly just in your observation that such would be a governmental question, inasmuch as it is obvious to all *there is no treaty line,* nor can *be reasonably expected to be acknowledged by Great Britain,* until the prior articles of the treaty shall be fulfilled by the United States. But in the immediate point of view, as this question does not concern his majesty's subjects, who have already been forbidden at the request of the Indians claiming the land, to form settlements on that side of the river, I can only refer you to his excellency the commander-in-chief, for any further explanations you require, to whom your very liberal principles as expressed in your letters which I shall transmit to him, can not but be highly recommendatory, and impress those sentiments of respect, with which I am your obedient servant,

J. G. SIMCOE,
Lt. Gov'r Upper Canada."

QUEBEC, September 29, 1793.

"*His Excellency Guy Lord Carlton, Governor General, &c.:*

MY LORD—His excellency, Governor Simcoe, having in his letter to me of the 31st of August, referred me to your lordship on the subject about which I wrote him, I beg leave to address you thereon, and to inclose you for your information that correspondence, and a representation of some facts, which came to my knowledge since writing to Governor Simcoe. On examining the tract of country which I own, I found the most wanton and excessive waste of timber imaginable, so much so, that I conceive injury already committed to the amount of many thousand pounds. I found also, a large saw mill building, within two or three hundred yards of the fort of Oswegatchie, which if persisted in will destroy the most valuable tract of timber in all that country. This mill is building by Verne Francis Lorimier, a half pay captain, who lives opposite my tract on the western side of the river, with whom I had a conversation on the subject. After producing a copy of the records of New York, shewing my title to these lands, and representing the injury that would arise to me from the waste of timber which the mill would occasion, I offered in order to prevent any further difficulty, to pay him his disbursements in case he would desist. This he refused, and informed me that he was conductor of the Indians, on whose lands it was, and that so long as one of them were alive, he should possess the mill. This gentleman being in the employ of your government, for Indian affairs, or agency, and under that pretence is in the constant practice of selling large quantities of timber. It is not *my business*, my lord, to discuss any question of a public nature. I shall not, therefore, attempt to reason as to *the right* the Indians may have to those lands (which I am informed by the governor of New York have been long since purchased of them); on the propriety of the detention of the post at Oswegatchie, or on the *recent establishment* of an Indian village on my lands. Yet I can not help observing that no claim of title can in the *courts of New York*, justify those trespasses on my property, which the state stands bound to protect me in. I presume your goodness will excuse the earnest importunity of an individual who conceives himself a great sufferer, and feels a most anxious desire from various motives, that your interposition may prevent any further settlement or waste being committed on those lands, until the question of the posts, shall by the two governments be finally adjusted and settled.

I have the honor to be, your lordship's most obed't serv't,

SAM'L OGDEN.

In the summer of 1795, Mr. Ford was sent by Ogden to take further measures to obtain possession, and commence a settlement. His letter of instructions, dated Perth Amboy, July 12, 1795, will be read with interest.

" *Dear Nathan.*—By this opportunity I have written again to my brother * on the subject of his application to my Lord Dorchester, and have told him that you would stay a few days at Montreal, and requested him to communicate to you there (to the care of Mr. Forsyth) his lordship's determination. Now in case of his giving you permission to repair one or more of the houses, and placing inhabitants therein, you will then, while at Oswegatchie, make, with the advice of Major Drummond, the necessary arrangements, and procure some proper person to move therein as my tenant. The importance of this, you will see, and it *may become a question*, whether you had not better in this case, return from Toronto *via Oswegatchie, and spend some weeks, or perhaps months there, this summer and autumn*, so as to prepare and arrange things for your reception next spring. If you should succeed in the idea I gave you, respecting the *saw mill*, then *it* ought to be kept diligently at work in sawing pine boards and shingles proper for the buildings we mean to erect next year, which ought to be carefully set up when sawed, so as to be seasoned for use next summer. Can not you, by some means or other, possess yourself of a particular account of the distance and route from Oswegatchie up the river and lake, and so on to Fort Stanwix, or such route as the nearest direction may lead to? In doing this, attend to the following queries: 1. What falls of water between the Oswegatchie and the lake? 2. What distance from the fort to the lake? what streams put in and where? with a full description of lands, meadows, swamps, &c. *Be very particular as to this.* 3. A very particular description of the lake, as well as the outlet, and the land around its margin, with an estimate of its dimensions and course, so that we may

* The Hon. Isaac Ogden, of Montreal, who became a loyalist in the revolution, and afterwards filled a high judicial station in Canada.

form an estimate of its situation in the townships. Estimate its course with that of the great rivers. 4. What streams run up into the lake, and what water communication leads from towards Fort Stanwix, and what may be the supposed distance? 5. In your description of land, attend to timber, limestone, intervals, bog meadow, swamps, &c. Let your observations be made in writing, and do not spare paper. Perhaps a few dollars laid out in presents to the Oswegatchie Indians would be useful. You will procure from the commanding officer, at Montreal, a letter of introduction to the serjeant at Oswegatchie. This will become very necessary. Col. Gorden and Col. McDonald, if at Montreal, will aid you in this.

My health is mending. God bless you.

SAM'L OGDEN.

Major Ford.

In answer to the foregoing, the following letter was returned, dated Kingston, Aug. 28, 1795:

" *Dear Sir :*—I have this moment received your letter dated July 12th. Its contents shall be attended to. I wrote you the 2d and 7th inst., both of which I hope you have received. I left Montreal the 9th for Niagara; on my way I paid Oswegatchie a visit, and was much surprised to find the dam so completely out of repair. The north end of the dam is totally gone for fifteen or twenty feet, and all the gravel is off the dam,—indeed it does not appear there ever was any great quantity upon it. Such another built dam I never saw. It looks more like an old log house than it does like a dam. There is a kind of crib work built up, which supports logs, set nearly perpendicular, without having even the bark taken off, and chinked exactly like a log house. It appears there has been a little gravel thrown on but there is scarce a trace of it left.

Nothing has been done this summer, and I doubt much if they do repair. Honniwell has sold out to Lorimier, and he has rented to a number of people, and so confused a piece of business as it is, I never saw. There is no person about the place that can give me the whole history of the business. Honniwell is not at home, or I could have known all about it. I was happy to find that most of the people upon the other side are glad to find that a settlement is to be made, and many intend coming over. I did not go to see Lorimier, and for this reason. After conversing with Mr. Farrand fully upon this subject, we finally concluded it would be best for me to show the greatest indifference, merely call at the mill, look at the fort, and take care to impress the idea fully upon whoever I talked with, that by the treaty the fort was to be given up in June, that there would be a garrison sent there; that settlers would be brought on and business commenced extensively. This I have done in a way that I hope will have its desired effect. In my absence, Mr. Farrand will make business at Oswegatchie, and sound Lorimier on the subject, and if possible make him apply for terms. If he can be brought to this state, a negociation may be had upon better terms than if I should apply to him. Mr. Farrand concurred fully in this idea, and thinks it the most probable way to accomplish our wishes. Loromier's circumstances are in a very embarrassed state, the mill, together with the farm, are mortgaged to Honniwell, and many other demands are rising up against the estate. My intention is to return to Oswegatchie, if I keep my health (which thank God was never better). I intend leaving my baggage, and find my way through the woods to the Little falls. This idea I suggested to you in a former letter. Never was any body more unfortunate than I have been in passages. I had a long passage up the North river and a long passage to St. Johns, was detained longer at Montreal than was necessary, for want of a conveyance up the river; a a long passage up the river, and as the d——l must have it so, arrived here only two hours too late for a passage to Niagara, and this is the ninth day I have been here wind bound, and what is more than all, a packet which arrived two days ago from Niagara, brings word that the governor left that place six days ago for Long Point, at which place his stay is very uncertain. I shall go on to Niagara, and if I do not find his return certain in a short time, I shall go on to Fort Erie, and there hire an Indian to take me on in a birch canoe, until I find him. I think this will be saving time. The whole time I have been at this place, is completely lost, for I durst not be out of the way for fear the wind should come fair, in which case the vessel would leave me. Were not this the case, I should have visited the isle of Taunty, and the Grand isle.* All this must be left until I return. I believe there will be no doubt of a law suit respecting Grand isle. I have been to the mills upon the Thames, and find them very much out of repair. My time was so short that I could not get a very full account about them and the land. I shall see them again. The greatest object of all is the fixing of the Oswegatchie business, and no stone shall be unturned to bring this to a happy issue. Mr. Farrand tells me, that Lorimier relies upon a French title which he says he has. This Mr. Farrand will get a sight of, and should it be worth any thing, a negociation will be more necessary Mr. Farrand will be in full possession of all the business against my return, (which I shall make as speedy as possible,) and which I shall not leave until I see an end of. The boat which is going to Montreal is waiting for this, and hurries me so that I have not time to write you as fully as you wish.

N. FORD.

Col. Ogden, Newark.

NEWARK, IN UPPER CANADA, Sept. 10, 1795.
De r Sir:—I wrote you from Kingston, the 20th of August, which I hope you have received. In that I mentioned my ill luck in not arriving at Kingston a few hours sooner, which would have made me in time to have taken passage in the packet, by which misfortune I was detained at Kingston, from the 19th of August to the 1st September, and after another *gun-boat voyage* of six days arrived at this place, where I am now detained by the governor's not having returned from Long Point, from whence he is daily expected. I shall transact my business with him as soon after his return as possible, and return to Oswegatchie immediately, when I hope to settle that business. Should I not be so fortunate as to obtain leave of the governor to repair the houses, that will not prevent my negotiating with Lorimier. Mr. Farrand will have taken the necessary measures for bringing about a negotiation. I have this day written him, to meet me at Oswegatchie on my return. I take it for granted you have received all my former letters, which contain all the

---

* Mr. Ford was commissioned by Col. Ogden, and Nicholas Low, to make inquires into the titles and terms of these islands, and purchase them of Sir John Johnson, in the name of Alex'r Wallace an Englishman, (as they say in Canada), on speculation. He was authorized to offer £2000 sterling for the isle of Tante. Eleven families had been settled three years upon it. Grand isle had been purchased at Montreal from Mr. Curot, a Frenchman (who held it under a grant from the king of France) for £500 with a further sum of quarter dollar per acre, when the title was established These purchases were not made by Mr. Ford He examined them and made very full reports upon soil, timber &c., which are preserved with his papers." P. H. H.

information I have. I will write you thence by way of Montreal, and inform you of my success with his excellency. Unless something very unforseen takes place I shall undoubtedly leave my baggage at Oswegatchie, and go through the woods to the Mohawk river. I am of opinion that it will be best to strike the river as low down as the Little falls, which is said to be 120 miles from Oswegatchie. I am sorry to tell you, it is a very sickly season in this province; never was it more so, but I am very happy to add that it is less so about Oswegatchie. That part is looked upon to be the most healthy of any in Upper Canada. Should I pass through this country without a touch, I shall be peculiarly fortunate. It is said here that strangers are scarce ever exempt. I hope to reach the Fort in a state to be able to undertake the proposed march. I should recommend to you, not to sell before I return. I think there can be no doubt of those lands settling very fast. I hope to give you a very satisfactory account of them on my return. I have this moment heard that the governor is at Fort Erie, on his return. Believe me to be your very humble servant.

N. FORD.

Mr. Ford, in a letter dated Kingston, Sept. 23, 1795, mentioned that the governor had returned sick, and that his business could only be settled in council. He again states his intention of traversing the woods to the Mohawk, but it is not known whether this design was carried into effect. Jay's treaty, which was finally ratified in February, 1796, provided in its second articles, that his majesty's troops should be withdrawn from all posts within the states, on or before the 1st of June; the property of British subjects being secured to them by the pledge of the government, and they were to be free to remain or go as they saw fit.

The signature of the treaty having at length rendered it certain, that the surrender of Fort Oswegatchie would remove the last obstacle which had for several years hindered the settlement of Northern New York, Mr. Ford at length started with a company of men, a few goods, and articles of prime necessity, for a new settlement, with the design to repair or rebuild the dam and mills on the Oswegatchie, and survey and settle the country. As a guide for his operations, the proprietor drew up the following memorandum of instructions, which embody the designs and wishes of Col. Ogden, in relation to the new settlement:

" On your arrival at Oswegatchie, endeavor in as amicable a manner as possible, to gain immediate possession of the works, mills, and town. If difficulties do arise, you will of course exercise the best of your judgment and discretion, in order to remove them. This, perhaps, may be done best by soothing measures; perhaps by threats and perhaps by bribes, as to which, it must be entirely submitted to your judgment, as circumstances may turn up. It seems certain that you will have no difficulty in obtaining possession of the fort and works. These, therefore, I presume you will immediately possess. The mills seem the great difficulty, for which you will make every exertion after you have possession of the fort. After you have obtained possession of the mills, you will immediately commence the repairs thereof, so as to have the saw mill at work this autumn before you leave it. As to the manner of repairing the dam, it must be left to your own judgment. I must however recommend it to your particular attention, to have it solidly placed and well filled in with stone, and graveled, so as to render it permanent and secure. Perhaps it may be best for this fall's operation, to place the whole of the *saw* mill on the same site as it formerly stood, observing, however, that in our next summer's operations we shall place many other works *on the same dam*, and that those works must be carried so far down the river as to be placed on the navigable water, so that vessels may come to them to load and unload. If the old mill is destroyed, and you find that a new one must be constructed, I would recommend that you construct it so as to saw plank or timber of forty feet long. You will exercise your own judgment as to what repairs it may be proper for you to put on any of the buildings at the old fort. It strikes me that it will be best to repair the old stone houses, and as many of the frame as may be found sound and free from decay. Of this, however, you will be able to judge after a careful inspection thereof. Should you meet with any difficulty with the Indians who live below, send a letter to Mr. F * * * and enclosing one to —— Grey, (the interpreter), who lives at St. Regis; desire Grey to come up to you, and with him fall on such measures as may be proper for an accommodation.

If on experiment you find that a further supply of goods will be advantageous this autumn, write me so, and send me a memorandum thereof, so that I may forward them to you. If on experiment you find that any particular article of commerce will answer a good and speedy remittance, you will be very early in your communications to me thereof, and it is probable that you may point out the best and most expeditious manner of transporting the same.

It *may be*, that certain articles of remittance may offer, which it may be proper to send to Montreal for sale, in which case you will forward them to the care and direction of Thomas Forsyth, of that place, taking care to give him written instructions how to dispose thereof, and always remember in your *letter book* to keep regular copies of *all your letters*. Your sett of books must be regularly kept, so as to shew a very exact account of *all* expenditures and disbursements, so that every shilling may be explained and accounted for. Write me from Schenectady the result of your conversation with Tibbets, so that I may endeavor to fall on some measures for the completing that object. If on examination you find any tract of land without my purchase, and which you believe to be an object worth our attention, write me a *full account thereof*, and enable me to take it if it should be found an object. Mr. Grey gave me some rea son to believe he could find a mine of iron ore, within our ten townships. Pray extend your researches thereafter as early as possible, as it is very important that we should at as early a period as possible commence our iron work operation, and nothing can be done until the ore be found. The letters I forward you from hence, I shall forward to the care of D. Hale, Albany; any which you may write to me, (not by the post), you will also direct to his care.

July 12th, 1796.   S. Ogden."

Mr. Ford left New York in July, 1796, and on the 18th arrived at Albany, and crossed with teams to Schenectady, where he met Mr. Day and John Lyon,* men whom he had employed to come with him, together with Thomas Lee, carpenter, and Dick, a negro slave who was owned by Mr. Ford. These were considered sufficient to man one boat. To hire another would cost £85 to Oswegatchie, besides porterage and lock fees, which would amount to £5 more. Of the boatmen, Mr. Ford remarked: " So abandoned a set of rascals as the boatmen at this place are, never saw." Instead of complying with their demand he bought a four handed boat, and tried to hire men by the day, but here he was again met with a coalition, and was obliged to pay high wages to his hands.

* Mr. Lyon died in February, 1834, at the age of 81.

So impressed was he with the impositions and exactions that thus obstructed the gateway to the great west, that he predicted that at no distant day, if a change for the better did not soon occur, " the western country would seek a market in Montreal, rather than submit to the exactions of t'ese men." Could a prophetic vision but have carried him forward through but half a century, and placed him on that very spot, where he could have seen the throbs of those mighty arteries which transmit the wealth of millions along their channels, and on their iron tracks, in obedience to the electric message, and the beautiful Mohawk reduced to an insignificant stream, from the withdrawal of its waters, by the canals; the senses must have failed to impart to the understanding the vastness of the change, and the bewildered eye would have gazed without comprehension upon the scene, as belonging to a dream!

Is an equal change reserved for the coming half century?

Mr. Ford having purchased a boat for £16, prepared to leave the town, and the journal of his voyage will give the incidents which occurred, with much vividness, and will here be quoted:

" Left Schenectada on Friday, 22d July, 1796, at 2 o'clock, with two boats, for Oswegatchie; proceeded up the river as far as Maby's tavern, where he lodged, distance, 6 miles. 23d. Set out early in the morning, and got as far as Mill's tavern, where we lodged, distance 10 miles; had a very heavy shower this afternoon. 24th. Left Mill's tavern, and got to Connoly's, where we lodged, distance 17 miles. Our passage up the river is rendered very slow, owing to the lowness of the water, and our boats being full loaded. I have been under the necessity of loading them full for two reasons: 1st, because I could not make up three full loads; and 2d, because of the infamous price I was asked for taking a load. It will scarcely be believed, when I say that I was asked £85 for one boat load to be taken to Oswegatchie, besides locks and portage fees, which would make it amount, in the whole, to £90. This I thought so enormous, I could not think of submitting to it. I purchased a boat, and hired another with three batteauxmen, and with my own people, I set out, and thus far we have come on tolerably well. 25th. Left Connoly's this morning, and came on to what is called Caty's rift, distance 3 miles. At this unfortunate place commenced my ill fortune. I at first hired only two batteauxmen, but previous to my leaving Schenectada, I hired a third, hoping, by this, I had put it out of the power of any accident to happen. The boat being manned by three professed batteauxmen, and one good hand (though not a boatman), ascended this rift to within a boat's length of being over, when she took a shear and fell back, and soon acquired such velocity, that the resistance of the boatmen became quite inadequate to stopping her. The consequence was, she fell crosswise of the current, and when she had descended the rapids about half way, she brought up broadside upon a rock (which lays in the middle of the stream), and sunk almost instantly, about four or five inches under. In this situation she lay about two hours, before I could procure assistance to get her unloaded, the delay of getting to her, together with the difficulty of coming at her cargo, made us three hours before we could relieve the boat, during which time we expected to see her go to pieces which would undoubtedly have happened, had she not been a new boat and well built. It was particularly unfortunate, that it was on board this boat that I had almost all my dry goods, which got most thoroughly wet. Upon getting the boat off, I found she had two of her knees broke and one of her planks split, and leaky in several places. I immediatel had one-half the cargo reloaded, and set forward up the rapid, at th

head of which lives Mr. Spraker. Here I unloaded, and sent the boat
back for the residue. Upon their arrival, I set about opening the goods,
all of which w· re soaking wet. The casks I had the goods in, would
have turned water for a short time, but the length of time the boat was
under, gave an opportunity for all the casks to fill. The three boxes of
tea were all soaked through. The difficulty of getting this article dry,
was heightened by the very showery weather we had Tuesday and
Wednesday; but by paying the greatest attention, we were enabled to
get it all dry by Wednesday evening. The goods I had all dried and
repacked; the boat I had taken out of the water, and repaired; almost
every thing was now ready for setting out in the morning. Upon drying
the tea, I found it was too much damaged to take on; I concluded it
would be better to send it back to New York, and have it disposed of at
auction, for what it would bring, rather than have the reputation of
bringing forward damaged tea, and disposing of it for good; and that in
a country where my future success very much depends upon the reputation I establish. 28th. I finished packing up, and at 10 o'clock we got
on board, and proceeded upon our voyage again; got as far as Neller's
tavern, distance about 12 miles; rained very sharp this afternoon. 29th.
Got to the Little falls this afternoon, about three o'clock. The tea I left
boxed up, in the care of Mr. Spraker, to be forwarded to Mr. Murdock,
Schenectada. I have written him to forward it to Mr. McKie, you will
be so good as to give him directions about it. It was fortunate that two
chests of tea were left at Schenectada, as was also a barrel of snuff, &c.,
which I have ordered to be forwarded to Kingston. The two casks of
powder I have also sent back to Mr. McKie; that article was totally
spoiled (except to work over again). The best of the muslins was in
Richard's trunk, and did not get wet. I hope the dry goods are not so
damaged as to prevent a sale of them. The cutlery is very much injured,
notwithstanding the greatest attention. This is not only a heavy loss, but
is attended with vast fatigue and perplexity. I could not procure oil
cloths for the boats (the one you had was sold with the boat). I have
only tow cloths, which I fear will not be sufficient to protect the goods
against the very heavy rains we have had, and still have. It has been
raining about twelve hours very heavy, and should it continue, I apprehend the casks will not fully shed the water. No industry or perseverance shall be wanting on my part, to make the best of the voyage."

On the 1st of August, the voyagers arrived at Fort Stanwix (Rome),
on which date Mr. Ford wrote to Col. Ogden, that although the voyage
had thus far been disastrous and extremely unpleasant, yet he anticipated
arriving at Oswegatchie in a week, and hoped to go on pleasantly down
hill.

A copy of the letters of Judge Ford, from 1796 till 1807, is before us,
which describe the events of that period with minuteness, and are expressed in language remarkable for that force and originality so peculiar
to that singular man. They would of themselves form a volume of
considerable size, and we shall be under the necessity of gleaning from
them the succession of events, although we confess our utter inability to
approach that conciseness, and that striking peculiarity which indicate
the talents and genius of their writer.

He arrived August 11, 1796, and was accompanied by Richard Fitz
Randolph, a clerk, Thomas Lee, a carpenter, John Lyon and family, and

a few boatmen from Schenectady. His goods he set up in the sarjeant's room, which he used as a store; the family of Tuttle, whom he had sent on to stay in the fort and keep things in order, he placed in the barracks adjoining the store; Mr. Lyon, he placed in the mill house, and immediately crossed to Canada, and obtained three yoke of oxen, four milch cows, peas, wheat, &c., hired about forty men, and set about building a dam and saw mill. He found many persons the other side anxious to settle, but was not at the time authorized to sell lands, and could only defer their applications, by telling them that settlements could not be made, till the lands were surveyed. In a few days, Joseph Edsall arrived, and began to survey the town. He brought with him a small bag of orchard grass seed, half for Ford, and half for Mr. Farrand, on the north shore. On the 7th of September, he wrote to Mr. Ogden as follows:

" When I wrote you last, I mentioned Major Watson and several other persons, who had settled upon the lands up the river. These people have relinquished their pretentions, and find that they had better become purchasers. Watson, and several others of them, are at work for me. From what I had heard before, it was Watson I was expecting that would be the person who meant to give us trouble, but I am glad to find it is not like to be the case. But I am well informed that John Smith, or Joseph Smith (who goes by the name of Yankee Smith), is the man who says he will try the title with you. He lives upon the other side himself, and keeps a tavern. I believe he is a man of but little force to set about establishing title to such a tract. I have been told that he was on his way to warn me about my business, but was taken sick and returned. I have not seen him. It would be well to make an example of him, if we could get him over this side. Those fellows only want to be treated with promptness, to bring them to terms. I dare say, Smith's object is, to make a fuss, hoping that to get clear of him, you will give him a deed for a tract, which he is not able to purchase. This I would never indulge him in. It is through such fellows that so much trespass has been committed, and [by] this Smith particularly.

I have had all the chiefs of the St. Regis village to see and welcome me to this country, excepting Gray and two others, who are gone to the river Chazy, to receive the money from the state.

They gave me a hearty welcome, and pressed me very much to pay them a visit. I treated them with the utmost civility, and sent them all away drunk. As to the Oswegatchie Indians, I have never heard a word from them upon the possession of their lands,—many of them have been here to trade, &c. As to Lorimier's claim, I never heard any thing from them, until I had been here several days. I had been asked what I intended doing with the widow, &c., by people who were not interested, (and who, I suppose, informed her what I said upon the subject); my reply was that we had been very illy treated about the business heretofore, but I had understood that the widow was in indigent circumstances, and it was not your or my intention to distress the widow and fatherless: what was right we intended to do. Were Mr. Lorimier alive, we should hold a very differt language. This was my uniform reply to those who said anything to me upon the subject. Upon the 17th, Mr. Sherwood (a young lawyer), came over and presented me a letter from Mrs. Lorimier (a copy of which is annexed) which after I had read, he began to apologize for being under the necessity of formally forbidding me to proceed in my building upon the premises, and begged I would not be offended if he called in two witnesses, that he might do it'in form. He went on to say that he thought Mrs. Lorimier's right would hold good under the 2nd article of the treaty, &c. &c., to all which I made no other reply, but that I should not have any objection to his being as formal as he wished, and as to her coming within the 2nd article, I did not conceive it could be made to bear such a construction, and concluded by observing that if Mrs. Lorimier meant to set up title, it must be the hardest kind of one, and that all idea of charity must be at an end. He insinuated that the cause would be tried in their courts, it being a matter that the treaty was to decide. This idea I treated with levity, as did also Farrand, when I mentioned the thing to him. A few days after this transaction, I was over the river, where I saw Capt. Anderson, (who lives at Kingston,) to whom the estate is indebted. He told me he was going to administer on the estate, and wished to know if we intended to make the widow any compensation. I told him the widow had sent me a letter and a lawyer, to forbid my proceeding; that I supposed she meant to press her title if she had any, in which case charity would be entirely out of the question. That we had ever been disposed to do what was right, he, himself, very well knew. Who had advised her to the step she had taken, I did not know, neither did I care. If they thought the widow would do better by a law suit than relying upon our justice and generosity, she was at perfect liberty to try it; that I should give myself no further trouble about it. ·He told·me he thought it a very unwise step she had taken, and could not imagine who had advised her to it, that the thing was given up, and I should never hear any more of it. Notwithstanding all his protestations to the contrary, I did believe then, and ever shall, that he himself was the man—I took care not to insinuate such a belief. I then interrogated him as to her title, this he evaded, upon which I told him that he must be well enough acquainted with law to know that a widow could not dispose of real estate, and if they had any title to the land, I should not do any thing until the heir at law gave me a release and quit claim. That if I went into the business at all, I did not mean to do it by halves. This brought forward an elucidation of their title, as he has it from the widow, and as he says the lease which he has seen is:——. He states that in the year 1785, they built a saw mill and lived upon this side; that the dam and mill went away, and they removed over the river. That in the year 1793, the Indians gave Lorimier a *verbal lease* (for the land, as stated in her letter to me). That after Lorimier's death, the Indians came forward and confirmed to her in her own name (in writing), a lease for the same lands (the widow states) they gave Lorimier a verbal lease for. This last act was done this spring or last fall.

This he assures me on his honor, is all the title they have. After much conversation upon the subject, I told him that if their conduct towards me was such as it ought to be, I would take the business into consideration, and make an equitable valuation of the mill and house, and pay the widow therefor, provided they gave up all idea of title. This he assured me they would do, and rely upon our generosity. I am to write to him upon the subject, which when I do, he will come down, and we shall have an end to the business. I do not wish to be in too great a hurry, for fear that something may be behind, which I may find out. I shall be attentive to the business, and not lose too much time.

As to business in the mercantile way, it equals my expectation. I am confident much business may be done here in that way. I am sorry that

I have not a further supply of coarse goods here for the season. Provisions of every kind can be taken in here in abundance. It was impossible for me to know soon enough what would answer this country for you to forward them this autumn. I shall make the best and most of what I have,—it will go some way in making provision for our next summer's operations. I would suggest to you the propriety of sending to England this fall, to have the burr stones shipped to Montreal; they will come easier and much cheaper that way than coming up the Mohawk. It is astonishing what a mill may do here,—— Boulton's mill, which is at the Garlows, is now resorted to for fifty miles, and a worse mill I am sure, never was. I have not yet been able to get information relative to iron ore. If I can get the dam done soon enough, I intend to take a ramble back of the lake. If we get the saw mill under way this fall, which I hope will be the case, it will be absolutely necessary to have a bill of such timber as will be wanted for the grist mill, so that every preparation for that may be going on this winter. This you will be so good as not to fail sending me.

My carpenter will stay the winter. I can now give you an accurate account of the surveys and claims, made by the people who have leases from Indians.—Yankee Smith, begins 1 mile from the fort, runs 3 miles upon the river, and 9 miles back. Watson then begins, and has the same quantity. Sealy then begins and has a like quantity. Sealy lives upon the other side, he has been here, but I did not know at the time, of his pretentions. Watson tells me that Sealy's lease is in New England. I should not be surprised to find that he had sold it to the speculators there. The following is Mrs. Lorimier's letter to me.

EDWARDSBURGH, 16th August, 1796.

Sir.—I am informed you have arrived in Oswegatchie, with a number of people, and have taken possession of one of my houses there, and that you are about to make a dam across the Black river, first taking away what remained of mine. That you may not be deceived, I now inform you, that I have a good title to half a mile on each side of that river, from the mouth to the scource of it, which I can not think of relinquishing without a valuable consideration; and Christian charity obliges me to think, that you would not endeavor to wrong or in any manner distress the widow and fatherless, and as it appears you wish to form a settlement there, I hereby give you my first offer to purchase my title, and would be glad to have you answer upon the subject, as soon as possible, that I may know how to govern myself.

I am your most humble serv't,

To Major Ford.   CATHARINE LORIMIER.

I was not particular in stating to you that Lorimier's verbal lease, was obtained of the Indians, after you had warned him off the premises. I have drawn upon you through Mr. Foresyth, for five hundred dollars, payable ten days after sight. I hope he will honor the bill, I have requested him to forward me four hundred dollars in cash, and one hundred dollars in rum. Richard joins in best respects to Mrs. Ogden and family, and I am very anxious to hear from you, and when you write, pray let me know the news, and how the world is going. I believe you will begin to think it is time for me to stop, for you must be tired of reading, and I am sure I am of writing.—So God bless you, is the earnest prayer of your friend and humble servant.

Col. Samuel Ogden.   N. FORD."

On the approach of winter, Mr. Ford returned to New Jersey, and did not get back to Oswegatchie until the 9th of August, 1797. He found that the Canadian claimants had been over the spring before, held a town meeting, elected civil and military officers, and sent on Ensly their moderator to get their proceedings confirmed by the governor, and that they had opened a land office for selling and settling his tract. He wrote to his partner:

" I also found that some of those jockeys had come over and stripped a quantity of bark, I immediately sent Mr. Randolph, with a boat (properly manned), with orders to take on board as much bark as he could, and burn the residue. He accordingly set out, and did not, (unfortunately), arrive at the place before they got off with one boat load, but was fortunate enough to arrive just as they had got the second loaded, which he detained, and after making them assist in loading his boat, he ordered both to sail for the garrison, where they arrived in good order, and well conditioned. I immediately sent the bark to a tanner in Johnstown, where I send my hides, so that we shall have our hides tanned with our own bark. They have kept themselves very quiet upon the subject. I gave out that I wanted more bark, and only wait for trespassers to come over and get it for me. If it is possible for processes to be made out, leaving the names to be filled up, and a deputation made, I am clear for having some of the ringleaders in Herkimer jail,— this I am sure would settle the business. If this can be done, let friend Richard's name be mentioned for the deputation, and I will see that the business is properly executed, but you must write me particularly how it is to be done, and you must be particular that the opinion be given by a lawyer of New York, for depend upon it, there is a difference between New York and New Jersey laws upon these subjects."

In a letter written early in 1798, Ford stated his anxieties about the leases, and advised that influence should be used with the governor, and legislature, to prevent any mischief that might arise from the ex parte representations which he understood were being used, and added, that it would make a *fatal* hole in Oswegatchie township, should the claims happen to be by any means confirmed. The trouble about the lease was finally settled by purchase from Mrs. Lorimier and her son, Sept. 26, 1798, in which Mr. Ford paid £62 10s. Canada currency, for a quit claim, "during the rest residue and remainder of said term which is yet to come and unexpired, to wit: so long as wood shall grow and water run, peaceably and quietly to enter into, *have, hold, and occupy*, possess and enjoy." The original is extremely diffuse in its style, and abounds in repetitions. Watson was arrested on a charge of having violated the statute by dealing with the Indians for their lands;* taken to the county jail at Rome; indicted in June 1799, tried and convicted in June 1800, having laid in jail a year, and was released upon his signing a release and quit claim, and surrendering his papers.

* See page 128, of this work, for the law on this subject.

It appears that Watson and Ensly were the only ones of the lessees who had ventured to sell lands to settlers; the others only awaited the result to set up their claims. In his letter to his attorney, Tho's R. Gould of Whitestown, informing him of the condition of the affairs, and forwarded by Mr. Sherman the keeper of Watson, on his way to jail, he expressed his regret at the necessity which led him to the measure, and added that every milder means had been exhausted. His efforts to secure the others failed. In a letter of Sept. 14, 1798, he says:

" The sheriff then went in pursuit of Ansly, but by some means or other, he got suspicious that something more than common was preparing, and he made his escape over the river, by which means he eluded the officer Watson I have forwarded to jail, and as he is really the principal, I hope it will be sufficient to finish the business. I am sorry that Ansly was not taken, for he is a great villain. I am not sure but I shall lay a plan for taking him yet; nothing but the difficulty of sparing hands to send down with him will prevent; but should he recross the river, and be saucy, I will do it at all events. They have carried on with a tolerable high hand since my absence, in insulting our settlers. I have given it to the charge of all the people, if any person dare threaten them or abuse them, for settling under the title derived from the state, to make me instantly acquainted with the fact, and I will immediately issue a warrant for them, and send them to jail. This, by the state law, I have a right to do, and I certainly shall do it. The remote situation of this place has encouraged, and still does encourage, to do and act as they would not dare to act, were the jail a little handier, and there is no way to get the jail nigher to us but by cutting the road to the Mohawk. This is a thing you must take pains about, and with a little pains I am confident it may be effected, and if only a winter road can be got, the value of the lands will almost double. At present it is impossible for people to get here, the expense is so great. I shall draw upon you shortly for 6 or 800 dollars, and hope you will be prepared. Friend Richard joins in best respects to Mrs. Ogden and family. Believe me to be as ever your humble servant,

N. FORD."

In a letter of Sept. 16, 1798, to Samuel Ogden, he says:

" I wrote you the 11th inst., in which I mentioned having sent Watson to jail, &c. The minds of those in his and Ansly's interests, are much agitated at the circumstance. They are at present very quiet, and Ansly durst not be seen this side the river. It has been suggested that the Indians will be excited to do private mischief. I am not uneasy for my personal safety. We are so totally outside of the protection of government, that it may become absolutely necessary to go into some violence, should violence be threatened. Nothing but necessity will induce me to do a thing which will not be perfectly consistent with law, but when that necessity presents itself, I shall do that which is most effectual for self defence, and oppose violence with violence, and trust to common justice the event. I have been told the Indians have burnt a quantity of wild hay I had put up some distance from here; the truth of the fact I have not yet ascertained; I shall find out the persons who have done it. My line of conduct towards them I shall not pretend at present to say."

During the season of 1797, a grist mill was commenced, it being the same as that now owned by Wm. Furness, which was placed a considerable distance below the dam, in order that vessels might there load and unload. A large number of hands were employed, and to add to his cares Isaac Ogden had hired and sent up from Montreal, four French masons and five or six laborers, at high prices, and with the promise that they should be paid in money as soon as their work was done. There was no lack of ability or inclination on the part of Mr. S. Ogden to sustain these expenses, but the means of communication by letter, and especially the remittance of money, were very precarious and uncertain. This produced the greatest difficulties, and in this and the following years almost rendered the firm insolvent. It was in these extremities that the energy and perserverence of Mr. Ford were displayed in the most striking manner, and in such a way as to indicate his qualifications for founding a new colony, beyond the protection of the laws, and among those whose interests would have been promoted by his misfortunes. After complaining to his partner of the high prices promised ($30 for masons and $15 for laborers, while he could hire the latter for $11.25), he adds:

"There is a disadvantage over and above the very high price allowed the French laborers, because nothing but money will answer, for d——l the thing will they purchase. There is their expenses, which amounts to $30 or $40 exclusive of their pay. Your brother writes very anxiously, fearing he may be led into some scrape in the business. I will give you an extract of that part of his letter: 'You are to pay them at Oswegatchie, in *silver dollars;* be careful that you do not bring me into a law suit with them for non-compliance on your part, as you see I am bound; it would not be well for a judge to be sued.' He also mentions that he had wrote you upon the subject, &c., and you will see the positive necessity of putting it in my power to defray the heavy expenses which must unavoidably accrue in so extensive a building. The cash I am obliged to pay out for the supplies of last winter and this spring, will take every farthing of money I brought with me, and unless you take measures for my being immediately supplied, it will be impossible for me to go on. The store affords me a considerable assistance, but the sales fall vastly short of the supply wanted. I hope you will not let this escape your attention. The success of our operations very much depends upon this year's exertions. There are a number of people who wish to come over, who have not joined the *mob*, but they have no money to purchase, and are poor. How I shall do with them I know not. I must shape the thing by way of agreement. Another year I shall insist upon your sending an agent about your landed matters; it is positively more than I can attend to and take care of my business. I can not conclude without taking again the liberty of pressing upon your mind the necessity of forwarding me the ways and means; without it, I shall not be able to do much this year. You will have the goodness to present my best respects to Mrs. Ogden, and all the family, and believe me to be with every sentiment of esteem, your friend and humble servant,

N. FORD.

N. B. I took out my commission as a magistrate, but could not be sworn in by any other but a judge or clerk of the court of this county, and not any being handy, I could not spare the time to hunt them up. The invention of our friends over the river have been upon the stretch to invent lies to destroy our influence. Among the great number propagated I shall only mention was that you and I were both broke, and that Mr. Randolph had surest orders to quit the ground as soon as he possibly could plausibly do it, &c."

In a letter of Aug. 23, he urged the justice of the claims of the laborers, many of whom were poor, and whose families would be brought to want, and represented in strong language, the discredit that would be brought upon themselves in case of failure to pay them. The following bill of goods was probably the first ever ordered in town. They were directed to be sent to Fort Stanwix, to meet boats from Oswegatchie, and to be packed in tight barrels.

"Four doz. pieces of Hummums, that will come at 1s. 10d., or 2s. pr. yd.; 3 or 4 pieces of coarse blue, and mixed colored cloths; 200 yds. check flannel, yd wide; striped cotton, blue and white; 2 ps. of camblet, for cloaks (brown); 1 ps. swan's skin; 2 ps. coating; 1 ps. blue 2d cloth; 1 ps. yellow flannel; 1 ps. of red; 1 ps. of white; colored silk and twist; 10 or 20 ps calico, some of which to be large figured for Indians, the rest fashionable; 1 ps. Russian sheeting; 1 cwt bar lead; 500 oil flints; vermillion for Indians; 1 small case hats; 2 doz. of cotton handkerchiefs for men; 2 doz. do. for women; ¼ cwt indigo; 2 or 3 ps. of blue and black moreen; 2 or 3 ps. of caliminco; do. 2 ps. durant, do. If you should determine to send the above articles, you must do it immediately, and send me word. I do not know any body at Fort Stanwix, unless you shall write to Mr. Weston, and he will have them stored.

In a letter dated September 13, 1797, to S. Ogden, he wrote:

"I am still disappointed in not hearing from you; how to account for it I am totally at a loss. How, or in what manner, I am to turn myself to meet the present demands at present, I know not, and how I am to do when the season of work closes, I am still much more at a loss to know. I have not ten dollars at command, and have now forty-five hands (besides a number of women and children), to find in provisions. These must all be fed and paid, and unless you forward me the means, it will be out of my power to go on with the business. I have squeezed along; —— knows how until this time, but this will do no longer. The money must be paid for what has been had, as well as what is to be. Laying aside every other consideration, this way of carrying on business is extravagant, for supplies must be had, and at such prices as those who have them choose to ask, but if I had it in my power to send a man out and purchase with cash, I should be able to get things a little at my prices. The supply of provisions will amount to considerable, but when I come to pay off the hands, and then tell them I have no money, what must their opinion be of us! They have nothing but their labor to depend upon, and have been at work and still are at work, under the strongest impression, that the moment they want their money they can have it. The contract your brother made with the Frenchmen was such that they were to be paid monthly. They were so dissatisfied at the expiration of the first month, that it was with difficulty I prevented their going to Montreal, and demanding their pay from your brother. They said, 'he is the man they bargained with and he shall fulfil the contract.' Their second month will expire the 7th of next month, and then I suppose there will be more noise than all the work is worth, for I have not in my power to pay them, and I am sure they will then leave me, and your brother must stand in the gap. A noise at Montreal with the Frenchman, and a noise here with the people over the river, will be rather more than any one man can stand. Were I not quite confident that you had taken measures before now, I should be almost induced to run away."

In this letter he gave a minute account of the plan of the mill and fixtures, and his hopes and fears in relation the first raft which he was preparing to send to Montreal. As the business of the season was about being closed up, his embarrassment became extreme, and is fully set forth in the following letter, dated Oct. 7, 1797.

"I have this moment received your letter of the 13th of August, and my letter of the 13th September, (which I hope you have received) will be answering much of it. Some few days ago I received part of the money you had placed in your brother's hand, but the whole sum of $500, which I am authorized to draw upon him for, is so trifling, compared with our disbursements, (as you will see by my last letters, to which permit me to refer you), that I am almost discouraged. You know when I left you, you did not furnish me with any more cash than was necessary to get me here, and pay our debts. This you very well remember, I remonstrated against, but you assured me I should have a sufficiency forwarded to Montreal early enough to meet my exigencies, upon which promise I set out, and have struggled through the season thus far, at the close of which I receive $500, a sum that is only $5 more than will pay the four French masons, and six laborers from Montreal. Now what am I to do with all the rest? and how am I to pay for provisions, and lay in our winter stock? The mode you point out is to draw upon you at short sight. I have no doubt that the bills would be punctually paid, but let me ask to whom am I to sell the bills in this country? This cannot be done to any one short of Montreal, so that the very moment Mr. Randolph returns from that place, I must send him back to negotiate the bills: the very expense attending this will be considerable, and the loss of his service at this time will be much more than the expense; for it is more than I can possibly do to attend to keep upwards of forty hands at work, provide provisions, and tend the store, which I have been obliged to do ever since he has been gone to Montreal, which is upwards of three weeks. Added to all my own troubles I have been perplexed with Edsal's thirteen surveyors, whom he left unprovided for, and who have given me a great deal of trouble, and Tuesday next must be fitted out for home, and provided with cash, and before I can send to Montreal, and get returns, Odle and his party, and King and Vanriper, must be fitted out and they must have money to carry them home. Their wages will be paid in Jersey, but the five carpenters and thirty laborers, I have hired from over the river, must be paid here, and so must all our supplies. If you had received your money, the shortest way would have been to forward it by Mr. McDonald, and if you had not, you ought to have advised me to draw sooner. It is now the close of the season, when the hands want to be paid off, and now I have to do what might have been done long since. It is certainly placing me in a very cruel situation, in a strange country, and in a country where it is the interest of so many to be our enemies, and who lay hold of every opportunity to turn every slip to our disadvantage, and I am sorry to add, there are some among this number, who have professed friendship. God knows I have a heart that despises them, and a disposition to punish them for their scurrility, as soon as I can bring it home to any one who has the smallest pretentions to calling himself a gentleman. There has been much said of us, but I cannot trace it to those whom I suspect. If I am able to do so, I will call them to a settlement that shall make them tremble. In my former letter, I informed you that I had sent a raft of boards to Montreal, and the prospects of raising money from that source, &c. The raft contained 2800 boards—this number was as much as could go down the rapids at this season. My orders were for the boat to return as soon as the boards were landed, and friend Richard to remain and sell them to the best advantage. He has not yet returned. The boat has returned, and by it he has sent me four hundred dollars of the money in your brother's hands, the remainder he retained, and wrote he had done so because he feared the raft would not sell for enough to pay for the articles I had been under the necessity to purchase, such as rum, nails, tackles, to raise the mill, &c. Before the boat came away, he had sold one crib for $12½ per 100 boards, and did not expect a higher price for the remainder, so that when he comes to pay your brother about $40, which he advanced for the Frenchmen's outfit, and $40 which we owe to R. F. & Co., and for three barrels of rum, 15 bushels of salt, two casks of nails, window glass and tin, and add to this the cash he had to pay the hands at Montreal, I am sure he will have no raft money in hand, for at the most the raft will fetch no more than $380, supposing he is able to get $12½ per 100, which is very doubtful.

* * * My room door opens at this instant; enters my ten Frenchmen; what do you want? "Our month is out, and we want our moneys." Here I must stop and settle with them. * * * I have done it, thank God; and had I not received the money from Montreal, as I did, they would have left me, and gone to your brother. But by doing this, I am now stripped of cash again; and all the other people must do without. I have done this to save the noise which would otherwise be at Montreal. The noise here is bad enough, and I fear our fame will spread fast enough, without our assistance to propagate it. What I am to do now, I know not. Those from whom I have been in the constant habit of purchasing beef at 4d. York, now ask me 4½, and they keep the hide and tallow. This will bring our beef at 5½d., and this arises from no other cause, than a knowledge of my being without money, and the advantage is taken. They know I must have beef, and they know I must get it from those who can credit; and I can not help myself. Had I the cash, I could get it plenty, and I believe for less than 4d. This is also the case with my flour. If I had cash, I could purchase wheat for less than a dollar, but as I have not, I am under the necessity of purchasing of Mr. ———, who charges me four dollars per cwt. This is a loss of one dollar upon every hundred, which is no small matter, in the quantity I am obliged to use. This is doing business at a great loss, and if it can, ought to be, avoided. You certainly have no competent idea of the magnitude of our building, or you would never have sent me five hundred dollars, under the idea of its being sufficient for our summer's operations. The little map I sent you in my last, will furnish you with sufficient information to form a judgment of what we have to do, and from your knowledge in business, of the expense also. Every possible economy is made use of, and no object however trifling escapes my attention; and

could I be furnished with a capital equal to the object, I am bound to say, no work of equal magnitude would be set in motion for the same money this would be.

* * * If you would for a moment conceive yourself in my very, very unpleasant situation, I am confident your humanity would become excited to that degree, that no time would be lost in giving relief, but you are too far from the scene, and my pen too feeble to paint. I close the subject, not doubting you will take the earliest opportunity to furnish me with the means necessary for the occasion. In my last I told you we were almost through the stone work of the mill. That is finished, and a most complete wall it is. * * * Before I close this letter, I shall give you a description of the dam and race we expected to raise on the 12th. I should now have the pleasure to tell you it was, and partly covered, had not Odle met with the misfortune to stick the adze into his ancle, which has laid him up nearly a fortnight.

There is one question you will naturally ask me, about paying the Frenchmen, which is—why did I not draw a bill and send it to your brother at Montreal, to negotiate and pay them there? This I tried, and pressed it, in every way and shape I could devise; but their jealousy, or their ignorance, or the orders of their priests, to bring the money with them (so that they could have their share), or what it was, I know not; but nothing but the moneys would answer. I have kept the masons busy at the walls of the dam. I have found the race a more tedious job than any I ever undertook. I have drove it with the utmost industry, and have progressed in it as fast as could reasonably be expected, considering the disadvantage I labored under, in sending so many of my hands with the raft."

The mill was finally raised in October of that year. He proposed to have the mill stones brought to the place in sections, and put together there, to save the expense of taking them whole up the rapids in boats. His Frenchmen he finally sent to Mr. Ogden, of Montreal, for the balance due them; but was very soon enabled to remit the means of payment. His opinion of the settlers from Canada was subsequently modified:

"Those people upon the other side, who used to talk so much about purchasing and settling, say very little about the matter now. The intentions of some of them I have discovered, which was, to purchase upon the credit given, in hopes before the leases expired, the land would rise, so as to nett them a handsome profit; in this I prevented them by annexing to the terms, 'in case of actual settlement.' I think it much better the land should rise in your hands than theirs. There is another class which would come over but are so poor they durst not purchase. Knowing their own inability to pay, they are fearful that at the expiration of the time the land will be taken from them, and they lose their improvement; so that between the two classes, we are not like to get many from the other side. Indeed, the more I become acquainted with them, the less I fancy them as settlers. They are a strange medley, and I believe it is well the river is betwixt us. I am well convinced in my own mind, the country will settle, and by our own countrymen, one of whom is worth six of his majesty's beef-eaters. Let us get our buildings and our business well under way, and if possible get the legislature to assist in cutting a road from the Mohawk, and the country will soon settle itself. The road ought to be attended to this winter. You can, through the medium of your friends, get the thing pressed in the legislature. If this were done, the people on the other side assure me they would much rather take their produce to Albany in the winter, than go to Montreal. They have all a desire to trade with New York. Were this avenue once opened, it would be astonishing to see the number of people that would flock in. The navigation is too intricate and expensive for families to come in that way. The consequence is, hundreds are under the necessity of going to the army land, and the Genesee, and every other new country to which they can get with sleighs. The road finished, and our business under good way, will at once render Ogdensburgh the emporium of this part of the world. I hope Edsal has furnished you with a map and field book of his work. I charged them to do so as soon as they got home. I was happy to be informed that Mr. G. M. was so soon expected. I hope he has arrived safe. I am much at a loss to account for your writing me only once since I left Jersey. You promised me you would be very punctual."

Postscript of a letter dated Dec. 17, 1797, by N. Ford, to Samuel Ogden.

N. B. The Yankees I mentioned to you in a former letter, have been with me, and go out to-morrow to view the lands upon the east branch. There are four of them who will settle together, and as I conceive it an object to get a settlement going in that part of the tract, I have made it an object with them, by allowing them each to take 100 acres adjoining each other, for 10s. per acre, in four annual payments. There are four more who wish to join them, and make a like settlement, and I have promised Mr. Thurber (who is the leading character in the business), if they come forward, and go immediately on with him and his associates, they shall have a like quantity at 12s. per acre. Mr. Thurber tells me I may expect them. As soon as I can get this settlement under way, I shall venture to put the lands in that quarter at 16s. and 20s., and so on from time to time, as the settlement advances. I mentioned in a former letter the plan the people over the river had laid for speculation. They having been defeated in that, have laid another, which is, to purchase and strip off the timber, before the payment becomes due, and then give up the land. This scheme I have also discovered and by frustrating this plan, we shall not have many settlers from the other side, unless it should so turn out, upon finding they can get no advantage from their plans, some may become actual settlers. The Yankee immigration is commonly in the winter, and as the ice over Lake Champlain has not been good until lately, I expect there may be some along shortly. I shall have another opportunity to write you again in ten or twelve days, and when I return shall give you a full history of every thing. Don't forget the road to the Mohawk—every thing depends upon that. God bless you.   N. F.

On the 24th of October, 1798, Mr. Ford wrote to Ogden:

"I have sold eight or ten farms, but not one shilling of money; but I think it better to let settlers come on under contract. I consider most of them pioneers making way for another set, which will most assuredly succeed them. Many stand aloof yet, waiting the fate of Watson (who I suppose is now in jail), hoping or doubting as to the title.
* * * I mentioned to you the burning of our hay by the Indians, in consequence of Watson's arrest. The report was not true. I have had an opportunity of seeing the Indians who were suspected, and read

them a lecture upon the subject. I found them submissive; the white Indians are the worst; but I have so totally got the better of white and black Indians, that they are perfectly quiet, and I have not the least apprehension from either. I can not conclude without pressing your attention to the road. Be assured it is every thing to this country."

The great object of solicitude, *the mill*, was at length completed so as to get grinding done on the 1st of December, 1798. On the 22d he had ground about 1,500 bushels. During the summer of 1799, while the surveys of the towns were in progress, vague reports of iron mines, salt springs, &c., were circulated, and high expectations formed from the latter. During the season of 1799, a second saw mill was erected. During the first eleven months, the grist mill ground 3,954 bushels of wheat, 1,820 of corn, other grain 100 for customers, and 693 for the owners. In almost every letter which he wrote Mr. Ford brought in the subject of a road to the Mohawk, as an object of vast importance to the prosperity of the new settlement. He observed in a letter to the Hon. Stephen Van Rensselaer, as follows:

"The difficulty of getting to this country with families is beyond what is generally supposed. The present road through the Chateaugay country, accommodates the few who emigrate from the upper part of Vermont, but the immense flood of people who emigrate to the westward, go there because they have no choice. This road once opened as contemplated, the emigration would soon turn this way, not only because the distance would be less than to the Genesee, but also because the lands are better and more advantageously situated. If the legislature will not take up the business, I am fully of opinion the proprietors will find their account in cutting out the road at their own expense. I should suppose those who own in the big purchase, would unite partially in the thing. for that land can never settle until a road is cut The traveling and commerce which will go to Albany from Upper Canada, will far surpass the most sanguine idea. I am confident the farmer from this country will take his produce to Albany as easily as he can to Montreal, and he is sure of going to a better market. Over and above this (which is a sufficient reason for inducing them this way), is, that generally speaking, those who have settled upon the opposite side of the St. Lawrence, are from the North and Mohawk rivers, and their connexions are there. So they have a double advantage of seeing their friends, and doing business upon more advantageous principles. Vast numbers of the most leading farmers in that country, have assured me they would go to Albany in preference to Montreal, if it took them three days longer. I am confident that the commerce which would flow into Albany, through the medium of this road, would very soon reimburse the state for the expense. Those who live on our own side of the river, are compelled from necessity to trade at Montreal. This is the case with myself. My inclination is to trade to Albany, but it is impossible. It is highly political to prevent if possible, the commerce of this country from falling into a regular system through Montreal; for when people once form mercantile connections, it is vastly difficult to divert and turn the current into a new channel. I see no rational mode but having the road cut, to secure to Albany so desirable an object. I have taken the liberty of stating my
25

ideas upon this subject, which if they should meet yours, I trust and hope you will take such steps as will secure a benefit to the state, as well as promote the interest of the proprietors and settlers.

I can but be suspicious that you and Hoffman, have suffered an imposition in Mr. —— and Mr. ——'s survey. I shall mention the grounds of my suspicion, and you will be able to draw your own conclusions. Some short time before Mr. —— had finished his part of the survey, I had it hinted to me that ——'s work was all wrong. Not many days after, Mr. —— came to my place, when I mentioned the matter to him. He told me he had understood something of the matter, upon which I told him it was his business to ascertain the fact, and as an honest man, make you acquainted with the business early enough to prevent ——'s receiving his pay. This I told him was not a business that immediately concerned me, but I would not be in the knowledge of these things without communicating them, and he might take his choice of doing it himself, or I would do it for him. A day or two after he came to me, and affected to be very much distressed, and wanted my advice; that he was confident —— was a villain, and much feared he should be involved with him. I told him to get two surveyors, go into the woods, and take —— with them, examine the lines he, ——, had run, as well as the lines given him to lay out his work from, and if his work was false, convict him of it upon the spot; then let these surveyors certify the fact, and then write you a letter fully upon the subject, and inclose the certificate. This was done. The surveyors and —— told me they had never seen such infamous work done by any body who had the smallest pretensions of being a surveyor. They very particularly examined the line given him to lay off his work from, and found that right. —— wrote you a letter upon this subject, which I made him show me, also the certificate, both of which he promised to forward immediately. I have no doubt upon my mind he would have done it, for there never were two men who execrated each other more than they have, or appeared to be greater enemies, and I never was more surprised than to hear that they met by mutual agreement at the St. Regis village, and travelled on to Albany together, and found no difficulty in making up a very good survey, and getting their pay, and have now gone to N. Y. for another job of surveying. No alteration has taken place in the lines since they were examined and if they were wrong then, they certainly are wrong now. How Mr. —— reconciles this business, I cannot very well see. I should have been happier to have given this information earlier."

During the fall of 1800, Mr. Ford was visited by Gouverneur Morris, on a tour to see his northern lands, and wrote:—" I have done all I could to add to his accommodation, but that has been so trifling it scarce deserves a name; for there was no accommodation which he had not with him. He travels in the style of an eastern prince." In this season, a fulling mill was got in operation, and kettles for making potash were brought on at great expense. In the summer of 1801, Edsall was employed to survey a road through to the Black river, which was completed in September. It was intended to run to the High falls, but he found that after leaving the Ox Bow, "he came to a most intolerably swampy and ridgy ground, growing worse and worse as he progressed, and before he reached the falls became so perfectly confident of the impracticability of a road as well as the impossibility of settlement, that he abandoned the idea." This surveyor took a contract of continuing the road from Louisville to the east branch of Black lake, (Oswegatchie) and arrangements were made for extending it on to the Long falls, (now Carthage, Jefferson county,) to intersect the road through the Black river country, then about being laid out by Jacob Brown. At this time a project was on foot of opening a road through to Schroon lake, in the direction of Albany, but the roughness of the country, as found of Edsall's survey, deterred for a time, the prosecution of this plan. The road towards Black river, was so far cleared of underbrush during the fall, that it was resolved to attempt the journey through by sleigh as soon as the snows permitted. Mr. F. was strong in the faith that before the next summer he would have a road that should be drove with loaded wagons, and added: "I have no idea of putting up with such a thing as they have made through Chateaugay, which scarcely deserves the name of an apology for a road." Late in this season the arrival of a vessel from Oswego, with 120 bbls of salt, was recorded as a memorable event.

The erection of a new county was prosecuted with zeal, and in March, 1802, was successfully accomplished. Mr. Ford thus wrote to S. Ogden, concerning the first session of the county court:

"We had a respectable grand jury, and a numerous audience, and the business of the day was gone through with tolerable propriety. I was much disappointed in Edsall's not being here. I however brought forward my propositions respecting the court house, and should have gone through it tolerably well, but Turner and Tibbets, with the assistance of a Mr. Foote, who lives in Canton, rather seemed to think it had rather be put off. I did not think it good policy to urge the thing, and make party at that particular time. This is of too much importance to be omitted a moment. [Reflections upon the personal motives of certain parties omitted, in which the interests of other localities for securing the county seat, are surmised.] If we can preserve harmony in the county, it will be the better way, but if it is reduced to a certainty that we are to be opposed, I am determined to take the field, and we will try our strength. I would wish to try all other means first. *This letter* and our determination, ought to be kept a profound *secret*, and let us pursue the same *friendship* which they affect towards us; if we take them upon their own ground, we may have a chance to fight them with their own weapons, but to do this with effect, caution on our part is necessary. * * * You must let me hear as early as possible, for the board of supervisors must meet shortly, to fix about repairing the jail, and this can not be done for less than £100. It will be poor policy to tax the county that sum, in addition, for a thing that ultimately will be lost, and at this particular time, I do not think it practicable for the county to pay it; for wheat and flour have no market at Montreal, and the people have nothing that will bring money. The policy of the county ought to be the strictest economy, and make the taxes as light as possible; for nothing scares people like taxes, and particularly in a new country. A man will be hardly willing to emigrate to a new country where his little all is subject to be sold for taxes.

There is a curious circumstance about the law which perhaps it is not best to say any thing about at present, and which I am confident I am not mistaken in, and Turner stood by me when the law passed, and he is confident of the same thing. The bill as first reported, fixed the place of the court house here. That part was amended, and it was left with the judges and supervisors to fix the spot. But the bill now says, "to be left to the future order of the legislature." Another thing in the bill,— the time of opening the court was on the 2d Tuesday of June; the bill now says the 1st Tuesday, Turner and myself both stood by, and our attention was necessarily fixed on the bill, but we neither of us can remember any such amendments. How they have since found their way into the bill I do not understand. As we now must apply to the legislature to fix the place, it makes it necessary that we should be as unanimous as possible. If we are, and apply, there is no doubt but we can succeed. Edsall has been from home these four weeks; what has become of him, I do not know,—I fear some accident. I met with him at the Little falls, and mentioned my plan to him, which he approved. I have delayed doing any thing very pointed, because he was not here. The season thus far has been the wettest and most backward of any known in the country. Wheat has no market at Montreal, neither has any thing else."

In a letter to T. L. Ogden on the subject of taxes he said:

"It is of all consequence that taxes be kept out of view as much as possible, and a tax of £100 in addition to those which must be raised for other purposes, would when all put together be more to each, than any man within the county ever paid in his life, let him come from whatever part of the world he might, I need not tell you the influence this would have upon the mind as well as pockets of all the settlers, and also the influence it would have upon those who contemplated emigating to the county.

It is too obvious to need the smallest observation; for there can be none but will readily believe the emigration would very soon be from, instead of into, the country. You will most undoubtedly agree with me in opinion, that all measures ought to be pursued which will have a tendency to promote and encourage settlement. This I take to be a primary object with all those who possess lands within the county, from which they expect to draw resource. Whilst I am upon the subject of taxes, I can not omit mentioning one circumstance which applies forcibly to this country, and is one which requires address and management in the affairs of the county to obviate its effects, and this arises from our proximity to Canada, where the taxes are very small, and scarce deserve a name. People will be drawing a parrallel, and when they find the taxes upon this side of the river to be so much higher than upon the other, I fear it will be difficult to explain away the effects which may be produced. The taxes last year were three times as high on this side of the river, as they were upon the other. I however explained the thing away very much in my settlement. People however talked and affected not to see what could make the difference. Our taxes now of course must be something higher, but if things are judiciously managed, I hope taxation will be circumscribed so as not to be oppressive. Many difficulties have this long time presented themselves to my mind upon those subjects, but never so forcibly as they have since my return home; and upon mature deliberation I concluded to make the following propositions, and if the county thought proper to accept the offer, I would set about the court house and jail, and before this time next year, I would have a room for the court, and also one jail room fitted, and the whole should be finished as soon as possible, and not repair the barracks.

Proposition.—That every person should sign in wheat, as many bushels as they thought proper,—to be paid in *wheat*, delivered at our mill, in the following manner. ¼ in Feb., ¼ in the Feb. following, and ¼ the next Feb. The house to be set upon the east side of the Oswegatchie river. Ogden and Ford would subscribe $1000, take the wheat subscription upon themselves, and go on and finish the building at once. The county was very much disposed to take the offer, and very properly concluded that they could never get a house upon so good terms, but Tibbets Turner and Foote, threw cold water upon it, and I did not think proper to urge the thing. Their opposition did not extend beyond their own settlement, and many of *them* thought the offer too generous to be slighted."

In a confidential letter of August 8, 1802, the fear was expressed, that some project was on foot to extend the county back to the height of land, in which case the court house would undoubtedly fall in the great purchase, or of dividing it by a line from the rear to the river.

On the 18th of Sept., 1802, he wrote concerning *the* road.

"I have got all the worst places cross-wayed; and to convince you I have effected something like a road, a waggon from the Mohawk river came through to Ogdensburg with me. I do not mean to tell you it is at this minute a *good* waggon road, but before cold weather, I intend it shall be so. I have finished the bridge over the east branch, (now Heuvelton), and a most complete one it is; there are few so good in any of our old counties."

During this season, vigorous efforts were made to collect materials for the court house. On the 12th of Nov., 1802, he wrote concerning the settlement:

"Emigration this year has universally been less than it has been for several years past, and this I impute to the sudden fall of produce, in consequence of the peace From the high price of produce, land in our old settled country was proportionate, and lands not experiencing the same sudden fall are still kept up by those who meant to sell and emigrate; but the neighbor who meant to buy does not think he can (in consequence of the fall of produce), pay the price he expected he could, and the consequence is, the man does not sell, and as consequently does not emigrate. But this is a thing which will regulate itself, and emigration must soon go on with its usual rapidity; for I can not learn there are any less children got in New England now, than there were when wheat was three dollars per bushel, and it is equally necessary that yankees swarm as it is for the bees. We are getting on with our settlement, I have got three settlers out upon the new road, fifteen miles from this, and several intend going. I hope to have the road a good one, I mean to have it in my power to say it is by far the best new road I ever saw in a new country."

The lumber trade, although often a source of loss at times, continued to be prosecuted, and one or two rafts were sent annually to Montreal.

On the 10th of July, 1804, Mr. Ford wrote to Ogden concerning his raft, &c.:

"She sailed yesterday with flour, potash, pearl barley, boards and plank, all of which I fear will go to a dull market, but this is a fate attending doing business. We must hope for better times, and be the more industrious. I found our business at home in as good a train as I could expect. The difficulty of procuring labor in this country is unusually great. The high price of lumber last year, was such as to induce almost every body to drive at that business, which takes off all the surplus labor this year. In old times, 'all the world went up to Jerusalem to be taxed,' but in modern days all the world go to Montreal with rafts, which if I am not mistaken will prove a heavier tax to *them*, than the old times people experienced at Jerusalem. I have got our tanning business under way; we shall make about two hundred hides. I find the man I have employed in the business to be very industrious, and hope we shall find the business to answer. Since my arrival I have determined to set a still at work. I have employed a man who has the reputation of being clever at the distilling business. I have sent to Albany for a still of 150 gallons, and a rectifier of 50 gallons. The size of these I imagine is as profitable as any. At all events I do not wish to dip too deep before I make the experiment. I brought in three masons from Troy to work at the court house, and I hope to see the chimney above the roof to-morrow or next day at furtherest. My intention is to hold our November term in the house. After getting through this and the two foregoing objects, I intend laying aside all further considerations in the building way, until we find ore, except it be to build a house, which I intend shall be of stone. I can not consent to live in those old barracks much longer, and the groundwork of this fabric I intend shall be laid next summer. I found a number of settlers had got on before my return. I have sold several farms since, and a number more are intending to purchase, but money they have not. I can plainly perceive, there will not a great length of time elapse before a race of people will come along who will purchase improvements."

On the 17th of Nov., 1804, he wrote: "This season has passed away without hearing a word from you. Why you are thus silent I do not know. I told you in my last I was jogging away at the court house, and now I have the pleasure to tell you I have completed it, so as to be very comfortable and convenient. We have also finished one of the jails. The November term was held in the house, and the people of the county expressed much satisfaction in finding themselves in the possession of so much accommodation. It has been a pretty tough job to get along with it, for it has interfered very much with our business, but I hope the effect will be to put an end to any court house dispute in the county. I have had the certificates regularly filed in the proper office, and it now becomes the court house and jail of the county. I told you also in my former letter, I was about setting up a distillery, and upon examining I found it would be more trouble to convert one of the block houses into a distillery than it would be to build a new one. The court house delayed me so late in the fall that I only got at distilling a few days since. I hope we shall find it to answer. Our tannery we shall find to answer. The man whom I have employed I find to be very industrious, and a good workman. As to settlement, that progresses, but not with the same rapidity which some other part of the county does. I have made a number of sales this fall, and to some who are respectable people; and one sale I have made (which is not fully completed, and which if it takes place, which I do not doubt at present), of importance, for it is to a man who will pay half the money next spring, and the residue in one or two years. He has been over the land and likes it well, and also the country generally. He will purchase between 2 and 3,000 acres, and is to give $5 per acre. Should this sale take place, there are a number of men of handsome property in Ulster county (from whence this man comes), who will also purchase and remove here. Although our sales are not rapid, we shall ultimately do better than those who are pressing off their lands at the price they are, and upon so long a credit, for the rise of lands is much more advantageous to us than their interest will be to them. In either case no money is received. Nothing has been done or is doing about the road, and unless there is a different conduct among the proprietors there will not be by me."

The subject of the road to the Mohawk, was never lost sight of until accomplished, which was done by a law of April 9, 1804, in which a lottery was created, for the purpose of raising $22,000, with 10 per cent in addition for expenses, to construct a road from Troy to Greenwich, Washington county, and from or near the head of the Long falls on Black river, (Carthage), in the county of Oneida, to the mills of Nathan Ford, at Oswegatchie, in St. Lawrence county. The latter was to be six rods wide, and Nathan Ford, Alexander J. Turner, and Joseph Edsall, were appointed commissioners for making it. Owners of improved lands might require payment for damages. $12,000 of the above sum was appropriated for this road. If any person thought proper to advance money for either road, he might pay it into the treasury, to be repaid with interest out of the avails of the lottery. Vacancies in the office of commissioners were to be filled by the governor. They were to be paid $1·50 per day. The summer of 1805 was devoted to the location and opening of the road, and on the 26th of October, 1805, Judge Ford wrote:

"I have just returned from laying out the state road between Ogdensburgh and the Long falls upon Black river, and I am happy to tell you we have great alterations (from the old road), for the better, as well also as shortening distance. This business took me nine days, and most of the time it was stormy, disagreeable weather. The difficulty I find in forming a plan how our lottery money can be laid out to the best advantage, makes me wish for some abler head than mine, to consult, or those with whom I am associated in the commission. To contract by the mile is very difficult, and to contract by the job, comprehending the whole distance, is still worse. After consulting and turning the business in all the ways and shapes it is capable of, I proposed to my colleague the propriety of employing a man of reputation, who had weight of character equal to the procuring of thirty good hands to be paid by the month, and he to superintend the business. The superintendent to be handsomely paid, and he to carry on and conduct the business under the direction of the commissioners. This plan we have adopted, and I trust I have found a man who is fully adequate to the task, * and we shall make our engagements to begin on the 25th of May. I hope nothing will interfere which will obstruct our progressing. I am sorry to say I am not wholly without my fears, although I durst not whisper such an idea. You would be astonished to see how much pains are taken to counteract this object, by those who are settling lands to the east of us; and you would be equally astonished to see the exertion there is now making to get roads in every direction to lake Champlain. Their exertion is by no means fruitless, for they have worked through with several. This I however am happy to see; notwithstanding it produces to us a temporary evil, will eventually be a thing which can not fail to produce to us solid advantages; because through these avenues, we shall ultimately reap as great advantages as they will. All that can be said of the thing is, they are enjoying the first fruits. There is not now scarcely a town in the rear of us (in Macomb's great purchase), but what is open for sale, and have agents now on, that trumpet those lands to be the finest in the world; and these agents being yankees, who have connexions in the eastern states, have turned the most of emigration that way. Those lands are infinitely better, generally speaking, than we ever had an idea of, and the very low price they are held at, induce vast numbers to stop at them, notwithstanding their original intentions were otherwise. But it is a fact, that nine-tenths of the first emigrants enquire for cheap lands, and the reason for their so doing, is because they expect to sell their improvements, and jog further. Those agents cry down the front lands as a poor, sunken and fever and ague country, and that lands have got to their value, and a thousand other stories, equally false and ridiculous. These together (or some one of them), have the effect to divert the unware traveler. By the dexterity of those fellows in the east, and the Black river jockeys to the west (whose brains are equally inventive), they really have the effect to make our settlement interior. Were I to attempt to give you any adequate idea of the means made use of, to divert and keep back settlements upon the river towns, by these people, I should exhaust all my ingenuity, and then fall vastly short of the object. Suffice it to say, that no stone is left unturned; but however much it may avail them for the present, its duration must be short. The patroon having stopped the sales in Lisbon and Canton, has been of great injury to us, because it has enabled the people I have just described, to assert that the sales of the river lands are stopped, and this has prevented many from coming on to view lands in our town. Finding that every species of foul play is practised against us, I have thought it good policy to send a man (who is very well qualified), to that part of Vermont from whence the greatest emigration to this country comes, to make a true statement of the country, and lessen the force of misrepresentation, by exposing the fraud practised upon the credulity of those who seek a better country. I have also authorized him, after finding out proper influential characters, to privately assure them, if they come on and purchase, and use their influence to induce others to follow them, I will make it a consideration, which shall be *to them an object.* I have also employed another, who lives beyond the mountains, near the borders of New Hampshire, in the same business, and my determination is to show those fellows who have taken so much pains to prevent our town from settling, that it can be done. My time heretofore has been so much occupied with our business,

* David Seymour, of Springfield, Vt., the father of George N. Seymour, Esq., of Ogdensburgh.

and my winters so wholly taken up in carrying out measures with the legislature, that I have not had it in my power to traverse the eastern states, and meet those agents there, and have an opportunity to do away their misrepresentations. There are a number of people, who have been on their way to me (as has come to my knowledge), who have been turned aside by these fellows. Their wish was to settle upon the lands near the court-house. When they have mentioned this, they have been confidentially told there is no court house in the county established by authority, and that there is no likelihood of the thing being substantially fixed here; but that their lands are in the centre of the county, and that there is no doubt but it will be there. They have caught many by this stratagem. I should not be surprised if there should be an attempt to make a hub-bub about the court house; but I hope I have guarded that at all points, so as to baffle their designs. Envy and jealousy are very conspicuous concerning the court house, and you would be surprised to see how much pains have been taken to turn all the eastern roads from our town. This I have looked at, without its being known that I have observed it, and when they had got the whole fixed very much to their minds, and as they supposed, so as to keep the whole emigration interior. When the board of supervisors set, I proposed to them to appropriate a sum of money for the purpose of opening a road from the east branch bridge to the northeast line of Canton, for the purpose of accommodating that part of the county with a road which would fetch them to the court house six miles nearer than any other way; and as that interior country was rapidly settling, I thought it the duty of the board to facilitate their communication with the court house as much as possible. This idea the board fell in with, and we have appropriated between three and four hundred dollars to that object, and in drawing the resolution, I have taken care to word it in such a way as will run the road, not only so as to make the above accommodation, but also so as to strike their main road, at a point which will exactly embrace all their other roads, by which we shall open an avenue through that part of our purchase in Dewitt (now a part of Russell), and give a full chance for those who wish to settle at Ogdensburgh. This stroke has disturbed much of their plans, and I suppose the board will have to suffer a little slander for appropriating public money for the public accommodation against their local interest. We shall have the commissioners out this fall, and have the road laid and recorded, and if possible, have it opened. After we get it recorded, it will be out of their power (under present circumstances), to get it altered, and this is what they fear. Much pains were taken last year, to have a sufficient number of towns set off, for the purpose of overbalancing the board of supervisors. This they failed in. I foresee that much jarring interest and local consideration will compel us to meet that dissension which all new counties have experienced before us. It is a fatality incident to human nature, and we must not expect to be exempt from it.

I am happy to tell you, we have got the east branch bridge finished, and I think it is not such a one as will get away as soon as the other did.* In my former letter I told you I had been obliged to rebuild the lower side of our dam. The frost had so injured it that it would not do to risk it another winter. This has been a heavy job. This, together with the bridge, repairing the two houses in town, and our ordinary business, has found vent for all the money I have been able to muster. The want of capital obliges us to carry on business to a great disadvantage. If we

* The bridge at this place had been swept off in a freshet.

had capital sufficient to open business upon such a scale as the situation of this place is capable of, we could without doubt make the business support itself; but under the present circumstances it moves feebly in comparison to the dead capital. I' hope we shall not always stand at the same point. You doubtless recollect the letter you wrote me last fall upon the subject of a clergyman being sent here under the direction of the bishop. That letter I answered fully, in which I stated the feelings and wishes of the settlers. I also mentioned to them the measures pursuing by them to obtain a clergyman of their own persuasion. I also stated my opinion as to the policy of attempting to urge, or in any way to direct their wishes in this matter. To that letter I would beg leave to refer you. Finding them determined to get one of the Presbyterian order, and their minds being fully bent upon that object, I concluded it was proper for me not to oppose, but fall in with their views, and take such a lead in the business as to prevent their getting some poor character who would probably be a harm rather than advantage to the settlement. Under this impression I have united with them in giving a call to a Mr. Younglove, a gentleman of education and abilities, and who has been the first tutor of the college at Schenectada for three years.* His recommendations are highly honorable. He has spent six weeks with us, but has now returned to his friends in Washington county, and expects to be back in February. I have suggested to him the idea of taking the charge of an academy here. An institution I make no scruple will answer well, for there is no such thing in Canada short of Montreal. If I can succeed in effecting this object, which at present I make no doubt of, it will be the means of adding much reputation to this place, and particularly so, by having it under the guidance of a man who has already established a reputation as a teacher. Our court room will afford good accommodations for the present. Upon his return I shall form a plan for carrying this desirable object into effect, and advertise the thing in our papers, and also the eastern and Montreal papers. By this means full publicity will be given to the institution, and I think it can not fail to attach much reputation to the village of Ogdensburgh, and when we get a little more forward, and find the thing to succeed, we will build an academy. David and his family left this yesterday for their new habitation in Morristown, where I hope they will be comfortable the ensuing winter. He writes you by the present conveyance. I have written you a number of letters this summer, but I am sorry to tell you I have received none from you except the one by T. L. O. I can not conclude without telling you I fear the Indians will jockey about the lead mine, but if they should, we would have the gratification to know the speculation is a good one; the lands are settling rapidly. I am, however, not without hope we shall finally attain our object. Believe me with much affection, your friend,

    Col. Sam'l Ogden.   N. Ford.

To counteract the influence of traveling agents, Mr. Ford, in the winter of 1805, '6, also sent men to travel through the districts in which the emigrating epidemic prevailed, and published in two of the papers in Vermont, giving a little history of the county. Dr. J. W. Smith was one

---

* The Rev. John Younglove, A. M., S. T. D., graduated at Union College in 1801. In the following year he was appointed tutor, and was one of the two first who held that office in that college. He had held that place until 1805, when he received the call as above stated. It does not appear that he settled there, although he spent some time here.

of the persons employed to influence emigrants. Of the articles he said:

"I shall prepare another and forward in February. The doctor (to whom I shew them), says they're calculated to be useful in Vermont, and is surprised that something has not been done long since. I have ever been of opinion it was as easy to write the county into notice as it was the Genesee, and have frequently requested your sons David and Ludlow to do it, but it seems they did not, and I am conscious my pen is too feeble. But I presume I have done the thing in such a way as will do no harm if it does no good. All I can say is that a plain simple story sometimes takes effect, provided it be so told that no suspicion is attached to it, and I have tried to guard my expressions so as to prevent that. There has not been any opportunity for me to hear from Vermont yet. This I however expect daily. I very much suspect some attempt will be made at the legislature for dividing the avails of the lottery, for the purpose of expending a part of it upon the Champlain road. I have written to my friends in the legislature, guarding them against it. I mentioned to you that the board of supervisors have granted a sum of money for making a road from the east branch bridge to intersect that and other roads which had been laid out by those interior people, for the purpose of turning the emigration from the front towns, and that I expected it would make a noise. They kept themselves tolerably peaceable, hoping and expecting nothing would be done until after the next town meeting, when they would change the commissioners of Canton and Lisbon. In this they have been anticipated, for we have contracted for the making the road and building the bridge over the natural canal, and making the crossway through the swamp, and the hands are now at work at it. Before town meeting we hope to have the heaviest of it completed. They have no hope now to prevent the thing, but gratify themselves by railing against the supervisors for granting the money. This I disregard. Business as usual will take me to Albany in the latter part of February. How long I shall be detained there is very uncertain. I shall from thence pay you a visit."

Having quoted freely from the correspondence down to the time when it ceased to relate to the settlements, we will resume the history of Ogdensburgh. The village was surveyed the second or third year of the settlement, and the streets named at first as now, with trifling exceptions. The first house erected and finished was the present American hotel. The place was named from Samuel Ogden, who was a son of David Ogden, and had several brothers. On the occurrence of the revolutionary war, the father and all of the sons except Abram, (the father of David A. Ogden, an owner of Madrid,) and Samuel, adhered to the royal cause. These two were disinherited by their father for their political faith. Samuel Ogden was for many years engaged in the iron business in New Jersey. He bore the title of colonel, although he is believed to have held no office and took no part in the revolutionary war. He married a sister of Gouverneur Morris, and the acquaintance which resulted from this relation, led him to become concerned extensively in the land purchases of the western part of the state, and in the township of Oswegatchie and elsewhere. He lived for a time at Trenton, N. J., and owned an estate which afterwards was purchased by General Moreau. He subsequently resided in Newark, N. J., where he died about 1818. David B. Ogden, whom we have had occasion to mention as concerned in the titles was a son of S. Ogden.

In 1802, was held the first celebration of our national anniversary in Ogdensburgh, if not in the county. It was held at the old barracks, and Mr. John King, in the employment of Ogden & Ford, delivered the oration. In 1804, a pleasant celebration was held, at which a party of both sexes from Canada united with the villagers in the festivities of the occasion. A dinner was prepared by Judge Ford, as was his custom for several years, and in the evening fireworks were first displayed. They were prepared on the premises, and said to have been very fine. Many of the Canadians previous to the war, were accustomed to cross to our side, and join in celebrating our national anniversary, and even the war itself, although it temporarily checked the intercourse along the lines by inspiring mutual fear and suspicion, did not long separate those people who had many interests in common. In 1813, along the lower part of St. Lawrence county, old neighbors began to exchange visits by night, and continued to do so more or less privately till the peace.

There were living in the village of Ogdensburgh in 1804, but four families, viz: ———— Slosson, on the corner diagonally opposite the St. Lawrence hotel; Dr. Davis, on the ground now covered by E. B. Allen's residence; George Davis, who kept an inn at the American hotel; and a Mr. Chapin, in State street near the Ripley house. There was a store kept by Judge Ford at the old barracks, and occasionally the settlers had the opportunity of shopping on board of Durham boats from Utica, in which goods were displayed for sale.

In the summer of 1803, Mr. Washington Irving, then a young man, came into the county with some of the proprietors, and remained a short time. His name occurs on several old deeds as a witness. In 1804, Mr. Louis Hasbrouck, the first county clerk, who had been on for two years previously, removed with his family, and settled in the village.

In November, 1804, Francis Bromigem, David Griffin, Richard M. Lawrence, John M. Lawrence, John Lyons, Wm. B. Wright, Seth Warren, Archibald McClaren, and Stephen Slawson, were returned as grand jurors, and Daniel McNeill, Wm. Sharp, and John Stewart, as petit jurors in Oswegatchie.

In 1808, the unsold portions of the village plat was purchased by David Parish, who first visited the town in the fall of that year, and measures were immediately taken to create at this point a commercial interest that should contest with every other port on the river and lake for superiority. In this year a bridge was built by a Mr. Aldrich at a cost of $1,500, which was warranted to last five years, and which stood fifteen. In 1829 and in 1847 Legislative provision was made for rebuilding the bridge. In the fall of 1808, the firm of J Rosseel & Co., sustained by the capital of Mr. Parish, commenced mercantile operations and brought on $40,000 worth of goods, which were opened in a temporary store until a permanent building could be erected.

On November 10th, 1808, the building of two schooners was commenced by Mr. Jonathan Brown, of New York, who with Selick Howe was sent on from New York for that purpose by Mr. Parish. Two vessels, the *Collector* and the *Experiment* were built during that winter and the following summer. The first one launched was the schooner *Experiment*, which occurred on the 4th of July, 1809, and this formed a part of the exercises of the day. A very handsome celebration was got up for this occasion; an oration delivered by a Mr. Ogden, a lawyer from New Jersey, at the court house, and a dinner was prepared in a beautiful walnut grove, on the present site of the marble row. Great numbers of Canadians participated in the proceedings with spirit. The yard in which the Experiment was built, was on the site of Amos Bacon's store. She was subsequently commanded by Capt. Holmes, and had a burthen of 50 tons. The second vessel was the schooner *Collector*, launched in the latter part of the summer of 1809, and made several trips up the lake that season under Capt. Obed Mayo, and the next year she was run by Capt. Samuel Dixon. Her first arrival was Nov. 15, 1809, with salt and dry goods from Oswego. She was owned by Rosseel & Co. On the following summer (1810), the third schooner, the *Genesee Packet*, was launched and rigged. She was owned and commanded by Capt. Mayo. On the 5th of July, 1810, Mr. Rosseel wrote to his patron as follows: "We have renounced the project of building boats, since with them we could not enter into competition with the Kingstonians, in the line of transporting produce down the St. Lawrence, a rivalship which we are solicitous to maintain, though we work for glory; we therefore have resolved to combine building arks." Early in the season of 1809, Mr. Rosseel proceeded to Montreal, to procure from thence laborers, where he engaged about 40 Canadians to work by the month, and bought two bateaux to take them up to Ogdensburgh, with blankets, peas for soup, &c., each receiving a month's wages in advance for their families' support. These bateaux were afterwards used in bringing sand from Nettleton's point, above Prescott, for the mortar used in building, the cement of which is remarkably hard. The stone building at the wharf was commenced on the 7th of May, under the direction of D. W. Church, and in June Mr. David Parish's brick house. The commercial and mercantile enterprise of the company prospered for a season, and the vessels belonging to the port of Ogdensburgh became the carriers on the lake, and at the breaking out of the war it was growing more rapidly than any port on the lake.

The earliest record of a school in Ogdensburgh which we have been able to find, is the following memorandum furnished by Mr. Joseph Rosseel, dated Nov. 24, 1809: " Upon application of some of our villages, I have granted the house destined for Capt. Cherry's bivouac, as a place for the use of a school, for upwards of thirty children, whose parents have engaged Mr. Richard Hubbard for a teacher." Mr. H. was from Charleston, N. H., and his numbers increased from 6 up to 10 or 12. The accommodation having been found too small, a dwelling house was assigned, and soon after a school house was built.

In 1850, the spacious and elegant school house on Franklin street, in district No. 1, was erected. The accompanying engraving does not adequately represent the premises, which are arranged in a manner that might serve as a model for those school officers who contemplate the erection of a convenient and well arranged school house. It is located on a lot of about three-quarters of an acre in area, in what is at present near the border of the village, but which will shortly be the centre of a dense population. It is of brick, 48 by 60 feet on the ground, two stories high, and surmounted by a belfry containing a bell, and has cost with the fixtures and improvements nearly three thousand dollars. The first story is occupied by two school rooms for small scholars, with separate play grounds for the two sexes. These yards are with a high and close fence, and communicate with the street and school rooms, but not with each other. The second story is occupied by a single spacious room with arched ceiling, and conveniences for ensuring ventilation, and furnished with seventy seats. The whole building is capable of accommodating about four hundred and fifty scholars, under the supervision of three teachers, and lacks nothing in the way of maps and black boards for illustrating the rudiments of education, or of convenient yards, wood rooms and other fixtures to promote the comfort, health and happiness of children. It was built under the direction of Dr. S. N. Sherman, A. B. James, and Otis Glynn, trustees.

The approach of the war arrested the growth of the village, as well as that of the country in general, and the embargo entirely stopped its commerce. These evils began to be felt for several years previous, and judge Ford as early as August 18, 1807, in writing to S. Ogden, said:

" The sound of war has palsied the sales of land in this county. The

Gurdon Smith.—P. 262—641.

School House. District No. 1., Ogdensburgh.

prospect of immigration this fall to the county, was vastly flattering, and among the number were men of property and respectability. This unhappy affair will very materially affect our prospects in the money line. I yet hope I shall receive a payment, which if I do, I shall not fail to alleviate your present wants. I however, am apprehensive that the gentleman (who is now out) will fear to return, for much is said of the Indians, and much pains is taken by some people upon the other side of the river, to inspire a belief that the Indians will be employed by the British government, and their numbers are immensely magnified. This, as is natural, frightens the old women, and the anxiety and commotion among them is astonishing. Many are for flying immediately, whilst others are so frightened they do not know which way to run. This constant theme of fear, originating with the women, puts the d—l into some of the men, and some among them are becoming as old-womanish as the women themselves. These men I abuse for their cowardice, and the women's fears I soothe, but I fear all my exertions will be in vain, for it is incredible what frightful stories are going upon this subject. Should the war-whoop continue and curtail us in the receipt of that money so certainly expected, it will be totally out of my power to afford you that aid you wish. It would have been out of my power to have given you assistance when I was in Jersey, if Mr Lewis had not promised me he would answer my draft upon him in October. Upon the promise I purchased my goods upon 6 months credit, and gave you his note for what he could then pay, together with the ready money I had. These two, together with what money I had to pay upon our Dewitt purchase, made up a sum of almost two thousand dollars. By this means I was under the necessity of going in debt, and to people who are not in a situation to lay out of their money; with them we have not heretofore had dealings, and who count upon punctuality. * * * Out of all the money we have due in this country, I am confident I shall not be able to command five hundred dollars. I need not urge upon you the necessity of cherishing that credit and reputation which we have established in the course of our business, neither need I give you any new assurance how much pleasure it would afford me to have it in my power to help you to such sums as I may be able. I really viewed the time as having arrived when you might have calculated upon a certainty from your estate here, and nothing but the dreadful dilemma into which our country is now plunged, could have prevented it. I yet hope the whirlwind may pass by without material injury. * * What makes this war-whoop more particularly disadvantageous to us at this time, is the event which we have so long anticipated being upon the eve of taking place, of this becoming the place of a depot instead of Kingston. Two of the principal merchants residing at the head of the lake, called upon me when on their way down the river with their produce, to know if arrangements could not be made for receiving and forwarding their produce to market, provided they should be able to contract with the owners of vessels, so as to make it their interest to come to Ogdensburgh, instead of Kingston. I told them I was not prepared at that moment to answer them decisively, but if they would call upon me upon their way up, I would by that time make an estimate, and give them an answer what I could do the business for. Last week they called, and we found no difficulty in agreeing upon the price of forwarding, but they found this war business would interfere. They however, told .me they would make it a business to see the owners of vessels, and if this war sound should blow over, write me immediately, that I might make the necessary arrangements. To set this business properly in motion, will take considerable money. Therefore much caution is to be used, that a failure on our part should not take place. If we can but get the thing in motion, it will produce an effect that will be solid. Should the temper and times admit of going into this business, I shall be under the necessity of sending to the Susquehannah for those people who have been in the habit of making arks and managing them. I do not think the business of ark building is sufficiently understood by any person in this country, to hazard any thing to their management, and as the success of this business is very much to depend upon economy and accurate management, I think we had better go to the expense at once of procuring men who already understand the business, than hazard it to those who must learn from experience."

                                                                N. Ford.

On the 18th of December, 1807, he said:

" When I wrote you last, I told you the sound of war was like to palsy emigration, and I am sorry to add, a continuation of the war-whoop has completely produced that effect, and if one can judge from the acts of the administration, the chances are much in favor of war measures, though I presume Jefferson does not calculate to fight himself. I hope and trust there will good sense and moral honesty yet be found in the people of America, to avert the impending storm. The extreme wet season has prevented the post making the regular tours, by which I am much in the dark how prospects in the political hemisphere are likely to stand. ••• Should this unpleasant bustle blow over this winter, I presume we may calculate the ensuing summer will produce to the county many valuable settlers, who are laying back from no other cause than to see the fate of the present commotion. Very few sales have been made in the county this year, and most of those which have been made, were to that description of people who may be considered as the first run, and consequently are of the moneyless kind. The people in the county have very much got over their first fright about war, and I hope should it come, they will have spunk enough to stand their ground, and manfully defend their property. The d—l of it is, we have neither guns nor ammunition to do with. I suppose upon a proper representation to Jefferson, he might be induced to send us up one of his gun boats;—it might as well travel our new road, as plow through the sandy corn fields of Georgia. I think an application of this kind made through *Slone* of New Jersey, might be attended to at least by *Slone*, whose capacity is not equal to distinguishing but that such application and mode of conveyance would be perfectly proper and consistent. I hope you will write me often, and give me a sketch of the times. I should like to know a little before hand how the guillotine is like to work. That is a machine much more likely to travel than Jefferson gun boats, and my opinion is the Democrats will never rest until they erect a few of those kind of shaving mills."

The reader is referred to the chapter on the war, for the details of the incidents that occurred here during that period. For many years afterterwards business languished, and the country was a long time in recovering from the depression of business which it occasioned. A fort to be called *Fort Oswegatchie* was begun, and after the war some thoughts of finishing it were entertained, but the work was never prosecuted. During the summer of 1817, Mr. Monroe, the President, made a tour through the northern states, and visited Ogdensburgh. He reached Hamilton from Plattsburgh, July 31st, and on the following day he was met by a party of gentlemen from Ogdensburgh, and carried into town, preceded by a band of music; and became the guest of Mr. George Parish. He there received the respects of the citizens, and the trustees and inhabitants, through Louis Hasbrouck, Esq.; who delivered him the following address.

" *Sir*:—The trustees and inhabitants of this village welcome with peculiar satisfaction, your arrival in health among them, after your long and fatiguing journey, through many of our yet infant settlements. In common with the nation, we have viewed with much interest, your important tour along our seaboard and frontier, particularly confiding in your observation, wisdom, and experience, for the establishment of such points of national defence along our immediate border, as will best promote our individual prosperity, and strengthen the national security. Born and educated under a government whose laws we venerate, enjoying a soil rich in the bounties of Providence, and grateful for the invaluable blessings of liberty, bequeathed to us by the heroes of the revolution, no excitement shall be wanting on our part, to maintain, defend, and transmit to posterity, the benefits we so eminently possess. Experience however has taught us, that individual or sectional exertions, be they ever so ardent, unless aided by the protecting and strong arm of government, afford but a feeble defence against a powerful foe. Placed on a frontier contiguous to a warlike and powerful nation, enjoying the advantage of an extensive and increasing navigation, it is peculiarly important that our local situation should be well understood. At the commencement of the late war, the attention of government was in the first instance naturally drawn to the defence of that extensive line of sea coast, on which the immense maritime force of the enemy could be more effectually exerted, and consequently the more remote and interior defences did not perhaps, receive the protection which their importance warranted.

But commencing your administration in a time of profound peace, enjoying the confidence of the nation, and presiding over a government proud of its honor, tenacious of its rights, and possessing the requisite resources, we flatter ourselves, should any collision hereafter take place (which we pray heaven to avert), your penetration and judgment, aided by your local observations, will have pointed out and perfected such a line of defences, as will ensure our personal safety, and redound to the honor and prosperity of the nation. That you may establish these desirable objects, progress in your important tour in safety, and return happily to the bosom of your domestic circle, is, sir, the fervent prayer of your obedient servants."

His excellency made a verbal reply to the following effect:

" He thanked the citizens of Ogdensburgh for their attention, and very polite reception; he received them as marks of respect to the first magistrate of the nation, not by any means arrogating them to himself as an individual. It gave him great pleasure because it evinced an attachment of the people to that form of government, which they themselves had established. He was satisfied they held its value in just estimation, and were sincerely devoted to its preservation, and in administering it, he would support its principles, and, to his best ability, promote the interests of the country. As the address correctly stated, his journey was connected with objects of national defense, and was undertaken for the

26

purpose of acquiring such information, as would better enable him to discharge the duties of his office, that large sums of money had been appropriated by the government, the judicious application of which depended much on the executive. He perfectly agreed, that the time of peace was the best time to prepare for defense, but had much pleasure in stating, that the best understanding prevailed between our government and that of Great Britain, and was persuaded he had every reason to look for a permanent peace.. He said that the importance of the situation along the St. Lawrence had not escaped his observation, and during his progress in this country, he was much gratified to find it fertile and abundant, and inhabited by enterprising, industrious, and he believed a virtuous people."

In the evening the President was joined by Major General Brown, of the United States army, and his whole suite, accompanied by whom he repaired to Morristown, and lodged with the honorable Judge Ford.

On Saturday the 2nd, he viewed Mr. Parish's xtensive and very valuable iron works at Rossie, considered to be an establishment of great public importance, and usefulness to the surrounding country. From Rossie he proceeded to Antwerp, where he was met by Mr. Le Ray, and others, and conducted to Le Rayville, where he spent the night.

[*Narrative of a Tour of Observation, by James Monroe, p.* 187.]

The village of Ogdensburgh was incorporated April 5, 1817, and the charter then granted, has been amended, April 29, 1839, and June 20, 1851. By the latter act the bounds were extended eastward to the Tibbets tract in Lisbon, and westward to the lands of Henry Van Rensselaer, and it was divided into three wards, of which No. 1 includes all between the Oswegatchie and Franklin street. No. 2, all west of the Oswegatchie, and No. 3, the remainder. The officers consist of a president: a trustee, and an assessor, in each ward; a police justice, a collector, and one or more constables; a chief engineer and two assistants, for the fire department, and one or more street commissioners. The above down to constables, are elected annually on the 1st Tuesday of April. A fire department was organized in 1820, and a company formed in July 1827. The village at present owns three fire engines; a fourth is owned by individuals, and a fifth by the rail road company. Large reservoirs have very lately been built at central points for use in fires. On the 27th of May, 1824, the name of *Euphamia*, was changed to *Slate*, and of *Gertrude* to *Franklin* streets.

St. Lawrence county in general, and that portion bordering on the river in particular, partook of the general alarm that spread like an epidemic through the country, on the aproach of the Asiatic cholera in 1832. The village of Ogdensburgh suffered considerably from this pestilence, and strict sanitary regulations were adopted in this and other frontier towns, in pursuance of the recommendations of the legislature in an act passed at a special session convened for the occasion. Quarantine grounds were established, at first at the mouth of the Oswegatchie, and afterwards at Mile point, the site of the present depot, where crafts from Canada were to be detained fifteen days. The following facts are mostly derived from an address delivered before the St. Lawrence medical society, by their president, Dr. S N. Sherman, who had witnessed the progress of the pestilence at that place, and was a believer in its non-contagious character.

"In June, 1832, the disease appeared in America, the first case having occurred in Quebec, on the 8th of that month. On the 14th, it appeared at Montreal, and on the 17th, at Ogdensburgh, though not in its severest grade. On the 21st of June, the first fatal case occurred at that place. During the period from the 8th to the 21st of June, it was computed that from one hundred to one hundred and fifty citizens of Ogdensburgh and vicinity, were in the cities of Montreal and Quebec, or occupied on boats and rafts, in the passage to or from thence. Some, it is true, on their passage down, laid up their boats and returned, but of all that number engaged in navigating the St. Lawrence, not one, so far as was known, died of cholera, or was attacked by it. The case that occurred on the 21st of June, was that of a Frenchman, of dissipated habits, and broken down constitution. He assured those around him on his death bed, that he had not crossed the St. Lawrence in a fortnight, and could not therefore have caught the disease by ordinary contagion. The second fatal case, was that of a child four years of age, at least half a mile from the residence of the former. The third case was also that of a Frenchman, living in a quarter remote from the others, and who had not been out of the village for weeks. The fourth case occured near one of the wharves, and the subject of it had not left the village, but subsequently an aged couple with whom he boarded, sickened and died of the disease. The fifth case occurred a mile from the village, on the Heuvelton road, the subject of which had been in no other house, and not a stone's throw from her own, for the last fortnight.

Cases followed in quick succession; first here, tomorrow at a point half a mile distant, and next day in a quarter equally remote and under circumstances that strongly tended to prove the non-contagious character of the disease. Precise data of the mortality of the cholera at Ogdensburg are not preserved, as none of the physicians kept a journal of the cases, and the records of the board of health are lost. The number of cases reported was about 160, and of death, 49. In 1834, the numbers attacked were not more than ten, of whom seven died. It is but just, however, to remark, that the mortality in proportion to the number of cases in the above estimates, is too large, as no cases were counted in which the third stage or state of callapse, had not made more or less progress. In 1832, by common consent, the physicians reported no case as cholera, unless among other symptoms, the rice water discharges, vomiting, violent cramping of the muscles of the limbs or trunk, or both, the broken or cholera voice, and more or less blueness of the skin occurred. Had all the cases been reported, in which the disease was checked in the earlier stages, the number would have been increased to hundreds. This custom was adopted in Philadelphia, and other cities, and the less rate of mortality which they exhibit is thus explained. In the city of Paris, there were treated in a given time, 10,274 cases, of whom 1,453 died. In New York, of 5,814 cases, 2,935, or about 52 per cent were fatal. In Quebec, there had died of cholera, up to September 1, 1832, 2,218, and the city probably did not number over 28,000 inhabitants, which gives a mortality of eight per cent. of the whole population. In Philadelphia, there died 754, out of 2,500 cases. In Montreal, the mortality of the disease was greater than in any American city, except Quebec. No reports were made of it in 1834, from its having been deemed the wiser policy to excite as little as possible the attention of the public mind to the subject, and thus avoid the general state of the consternation and alarm which are well known to operate so powerfully in producing fatal results in numerous cases, and which is thought to have increased the mortality of the disease in 1832."

The state of alarm which pervaded the frontier on the approach of the cholera, and the stringent quarantine regulations which were imposed upon all persons coming from the provinces into the states, checked for a season, all business and communication on the St. Lawrence, and increased the alarm which was felt in relation to the disease. Intercourse was not established along the river for several weeks, and the public mind but slowly recovered from the panic which the pestilence had occasioned. We have given on page 167, an account of the ravages of the cholera at the Indian village of St. Regis, which in severity, has scarcely a parallel in the history of this fearful malady. The following memoranda from the records of the board of supervisors, show the expenses which were incurred in the several towns in the organization of boards of health, and the establishment of sanatary regulations.

"Brasher, $8.50; Canton, $120; Dekalb, $6.50; Edwards, $5; Fowler, $6; Gouverneur, $9; Hammond, $18.25; Depeau, $5; Hopkinton, $5; Lawrence, $5; Lisbon, $10; Louisville, $9.87; Madrid, $87.87; Massena, $13; Morristown,$164.37; Norfolk, $6; Oswegatchie, $24.63; (Ogdensburgh $780.33); Pierrepont, $4.25; Potsdam, $24.48; Stockholm, $7; Total, $1,351.46."

The completion of the Oswego canal was the first public work that conferred a benefit upon Ogdensburgh, or St. Lawrence county, as they thus first gained a direct avenue to market. The Erie canal hindered the growth of this portion of the state, more than it promoted it, by opening new, cheap and fertile land to the settler, the produce from which could be sent to market at less expense than that from this county, and thus great numbers were induced to emigrate. In the great era of speculation and high prices in 1836, in connection with the extraordinary mineral resources then being developed, a new impulse was given, and measures were adopted to improve the hydraulic power of the place, by the purchase of the water privilege and erection of mills.

This right had passed from Ford to Thomas Denny, and was bought by Smith Stilwell, in 1836, for $30,000, and has since been sold to individuals who are bound by certain regulations, to sustain the expenses which their maintenance may require. A canal is extended down to below the bridge, and with the exception of a few weeks in summer, affords an ample supply for the extensive mills and manufactories upon it. The dam built by Judge Ford, in .1796, has with some repairs, lasted till the present time, and is still good.

A most destructive fire occurred at Ogdensburgh on the night between the 16th and 17th of April, 1839, by which nearly half the business portion of the village was laid in ashes. The loss was estimated at but little less than $100,000. The irritation that then existed on the frontiers led to the suspicion that it was the work of an incendiary.

This fire consumed the premises on the southwest corner of State and Ford streets, including the post office, Republican printing office, and a large number of stores and shops. The loss has been estimated at nearly $100,000.

On the morning of the 1st of September, 1852, another fire consumed a large amount of property on Ford and Isabella streets, extending from the store of G. N. Seymour nearly to Washington street, and shortly after two other destructive fires burned a large amount of property on Ford street, including the office of the St. Lawrence Republican and the entire premises belonging to the Hasbrouck estate, and represented in our engraving on page 209.

Circumstances connected with these fires, excited suspicions with some that they were the work of an incendiary. A portion of the burnt district has been rebuilt, and ere long it is presumed the whole will be occupied by blocks of elegant buildings. As an emporium of commerce, and the natural limit of navigation by sail vessels, the port of Ogdensburgh enjoys advantages incomparably superior to those of any port on the river, and this feature of the location presented itself to the minds of the French in their selection of a site for a mission, the English in their retention of it as a fur station, and the early purchasers under the state as a point for the establishment of a commercial interest and the nucleus of a new settlement.

The completion of the Northern rail road has done infinitely more than all other causes combined to give an impulse to the prosperity of Ogdensburgh and of Northern New York generally, and in our history of improvements will be found an account of the origin, progress and completion of that work. This, in connection with the system of Canadian roads in progress and the great natural advantages of the place, can not fail to give it an eminence as [a commercial point which it so truly deserves. Its streets are adorned with many buildings that for elegance and durability would do credit to any of our largest cities. The traveler will find at its several hotels those conveniences and attentions which render the tourist's life agreeable, and the capitalist an opportunity for investment that can not fail to richly remunerate. We here present a view of one of the hotels.

St. Lawrence Hotel, Ogdensburgh, N. Y.

This hotel is on the corner of State and Ford streets; the main building on the corner was built in 1842, and the addition on the right, (the lower story of which is occupied by stores, and which is known as the Seymour block), in 1851. The whole has a front of 132 feet on State and 94 on Ford streets. Besides the public halls, parlors, &c., it has 86 sleeping apartments, and from the observatory on the top a splendid view of the village, the river, and the Canada shore for many miles, is afforded. It is owned by Geo. N. Seymour, Esq., and kept by Brown, Sperry & Co.

A cemetery association was incorporated under the general act July 26, 1847, with Geo. N. Seymour, Elijah B. Allen, John Fine, Collins A. Burnham, Edwin Clark, David C. Judson, Wm. Brown, Amos Bacon, and James G. Hopkins, trustees. It was dedicated on the 18th of Sept., 1847, by the clergy and citizens, at which an address was delivered by the Hon. John Fine, and suitable religious exercises and the singing of a hymn composed for the occasion by Mr. C. T. Pooler, closed the exercises of the day. The circumstances of such an occasion, were peculiarly calculated to make a serious and lasting impression; as a few revolving years would doubtless lay beneath the surface upon which they stood many who participated in the exercises of the day. The cemetery is situated on the bank of the Oswegatchie, about a mile from the village, and when the premises are completed after the contemplated plan, will be at once an appropriate and ornamental ground, and will compare favorably with the cemeteries of most towns of the size.

The *Ogdensburgh Library* was incorporated June 10, 1838, with George Guest, Bishop Perkins, James G. Hopkins, Charles Lawton, and Baron S. Doty, trustees. This is believed to have been dissolved several years. School district No. 1, in this village, has the largest public library in the county.

The *Ogdensburgh Atheneum* was the name of a society organized at that place in 1830, for the purpose of obtaining for the perusal of its members, the principal periodicals of Europe and America. It continued in operation about three years. This was the first effort for the establishment of an association for mutual benefit. Courses of lectures had occasionally been given by citizens and strangers, and in the winter of 1851-2, a very general interest was felt in a series of lectures which were got up under the name of a Lyceum, and at the expense of a fund raised for the purpose in the village. While these lectures were in progress, the project of a more permanent and useful organization was discussed, and on the last evening of the course, a consultation was held, which eventually resulted in the formation of a *Young Men's Association*, adopting for its constitution that of the Albany association.

This organization was effected May 8, 1852, there having been previously circulated a subscription for obtaining the means necessary for the purposes. The price of membership was fixed at $5, and the condition of the subscription was, that forty members should be procured before an association should be formed. In two months from the date of the adoption of the constitution and by-laws, the number was increased to fifty members. On the 9th of July the following officers were chosen:

Rev. L. Merrill Miller, *president*; S. Foote, A. B. James, Z. B. Bridges, *vice presidents*; R. Slade, *recording secretary*; E. M. Holbrook, *corresponding secretary*; George Morris, *treasurer*; J. G. Hopkins, H. G. Foote, W. C. Brown, P. R. Randall, R. W. Judson, R. G. Pettibone, R. Morris, S. S. Blodget, H. H. Humphrey, H. F. Lawrence, *managers*. The latter, with the other officers above named, constitute an executive committee. Sub committees on rooms and fixtures, on the supply of the reading room, the library, &c., and others to procure donations and subscriptions, and to make arrangements for lectures, were appointed. Commodious rooms in the second story of Judson's block, opposite the St. Lawrence hotel, were taken, a small but select library purchased, and a reading room supplied with all the standard magazines and numerous papers, was fitted up. These rooms are open daily and on evenings, to citizen members and strangers. The design of this association is to embrace, besides a library and reading room, a course of public lectures during the winter months. The interest which has thus far been very generally manifested in this measure, give assurance that the association will be one of a permanent character; well calculated to promote the intellectual welfare of the community in which it is located, and that its success will be proportioned to the excellent intentions which led to its institution. It is hoped that the model thus offered will find an imitation in other large villages in the county.

The earliest settlement in the vicinity of Black lake, in the town of Oswegatchie, was made in 1797, by Capt. Joseph Thurber, and his sons Kelsey J. and John K. Thurber, from the town of Augusta, in Canada, but originally from New Hampshire. Mr. Thurber had been a very early settler at Plattsburgh. David Rose, David Judson, Thomas J. Davies, and others, were very early settlers in this part of the town. Jacob Pohlman, a millwright, who had been employed in 1797 by Ford, on his mill at Ogdensburgh, was an early settler in this town in the vicinity of the lake. He emigrated from Germany when a young man, and first arrived in Philadelphia. At Albany he met with Mr. Ford, who persuaded him to remove to the new settlement, and he spent the remainder of his life in town.

The river road towards Morristown began to be settled at about the same time, Thomas Lee being the pioneer settler. Schools were first commenced in Oswegatchie in this settlement, and John K. Thurber was the first teacher. Capt. David Griffin, Adam Millis, and Elijah Carley, also located along this road. The first death in the town of Oswegatchie, after the arrival of Judge Ford and his party, was Mrs. Lyon. The first marriage among the settlers was that of James Chambers and Elizabeth Thurber, in 1796. As there was no magistrate or clergyman authorized to perform the marriage ceremony, the parties crossed to Canada to get yoked. In 1801, Mr. John King, from New Jersey, arrived as a clerk for Mr. Ford.

The village of *Heuvelton*, near the southern border of the town, was surveyed into a village plat by Judge Edsall, of Madrid, before it had an inhabitant, and received the name of *Fordsburgh*, from Nathan Ford. It was sometimes mentioned as the East Branch, meaning the place where the highway crossed the East Branch, or Oswegatchie. This river was sometimes so called, and Indian river bore the name of West Branch. Truman Bristol, and families by the name of Havens, Jones, and Osburne, began small improvements about 1805. In the fall of 1806, Jairus Remington, formerly a Presbyterian minister, a native of Massachusetts, but then from Putney, Vt., moved in by way of the Black river country, with his family, and commenced keeping a public house on the left bank of the river. He had been on several times before, and had made an arrangement with Judge Ford to establish an inn at this point, where it was very much needed for the accommodation of the numerous travelers and emigrants who were coming into the country by the State road then newly opened. Judge Ford wrote Jan. 6, 1806, as follows:

"I have also sold four lots in our village at the East Branch bridge, to a gentleman who is a man of education and influence in Massachusetts, and also in Vermont. His intention is to set up business, and from the representation he makes to me I am induced to believe he will be very serviceable, not only as an inhabitant, but as being a person who will bring with him a number of emigrants. I have made it his interest to be servicable to us this way, as I have also those who have gone to Vermont. This gentleman has also gone for his family. He has made arrangements for building, and as an evidence of his being in earnest, he has made considerable advances to carpenters here, for beginning early in the spring. From present appearances I have grounds to believe there will be a strong emigration to our settlement the ensuing season."

Judge Pinney and family settled here in 1808; Redfield and family soon after. David Burroughs, from Shaftsbury, Vt., arrived in 1811. There were few settlers besides these, till 1820, when Jacob A. Vanden Heuvel,* an enterprising gentleman from New York, having purchased the village and an extensive tract of land adjoining, commenced the erection of a grist mill, and numerous other improvements. His father was a Hollander, who emigrated to New York in 1792, having previously resided several years in the Dutch colony of Demarara, in Guiana, of which he was for some time the governor. In compliment to the new proprietor, the place received the name of *Heuvel*, which was in January, 1832, changed to Heuvelton, its present name. A saw mill and dam had been erected by Mr. Remington for many years. The place soon after began to increase in population quite rapidly. The bridge first erected, was above its present location, and was carried off. One or two others on the same place failed. The first school in the settlement was a very small one, taught by Mr. Dyer Badger in the winter of 1808, in a small shanty near the site of the present school house.

The first religious meetings were held by Methodists. Dr. S. N. Sherman was the first physician of the place, having located here in 1825. Mr. Van Heuvel with much liberality erected a church for the Episcopal worship, but it was never much used by this denomination, and has passed into the hands of the Universalists. The first death in this part of the town is said to have been that of Mr. David Seymour, who was drowned in 1806. He was at the time engaged in the erection of a bridge.

Religious Societies.—The annals of the Methodist Episcopal Church, show that a circuit denominated *Oswegatchie*, existed as early as 1793, and it is from this probable, that meetings were occasionally held by the Methodists at the garrison, while still a British post. The importance of some organization was early felt, and led to the formation of the First Church and Congregation of Christ, in the town of Oswegatchie, Oct. 10, 1805, with Nathan Ford, John Lyon, Aaron Welton, Louis Hasbrouck

* Mr. V. H. was authorized by an act of the legislature passed Feb. 8, 1832, to assume the name of Van Heuvel, by which he has since been known. His father, John Van Den Heuvel, died in New York, May 6, 1826.

and Thomas J. Davies, trustees. In a letter of November 29, 1804, Col'
Ogden wrote to Judge Ford, as follows:

"You have added hereto the state of my attempt to effect the establishment of a clergyman with you. From what has passed it seems pretty
certain that one will visit you with my *letter*, on the receipt of which I
pray you do every thing in your power to establish him with you, render
his visit as pleasing as possible, show him as extensive an annuity *as possible*. Will not Tibbets and and others from the other townships, as well
as from the other side of the river, contribute towards his establishment?
I am certain nothing will promote our object more than the settlement of
a proper clergyman and erection of a church. The following is a copy
of my letter to you which I have left with the bishop, dated New York,
23d November: "My desire that a church should early be established
at Ogdensburgh, has induced me to wait on bishop Moore, and some other
of the clergy of this place, desiring a clergyman might be induced to
make you a visit, under the belief that having explored the town, situation, &c., he will be desirous of becoming a resident with you."

The following are the proposals I have made: Samuel Ogden proposes to have *two town lots* laid out in the town, near the church and
court house lots, one to be held as a *parsonage*, and conveyed for its use,
the other to be conveyed in fee simple to the first clergyman who shall
reside in the town, and perform Episcopal duties therein, for the term of
ten years. One farm shall he also laid out in the vicinity of the town as
a parsonage, to be conveyed *for the use of the church*, also a convenient
lot in town whereon to build a church, and for a burying ground. The
bishop has presented you with two dozen prayer books. How shall I
send them?" This was rather an unwelcome duty to impose upon judge
Ford, who was a zealous Presbyterian, and the story is related as authentic, that he was so determined to establish one of this denomination, that
he declared *he would go to h—ll for one* rather than be disappointed. The
ingenious manner in which he answered the above letter is worthy of
perusal. It forms a part of a long letter dated Jan. 11, 1805.

"I confess I feel much embarrassment in answering that part of your
letter which relates to the establishing of a clergyman. Not because I
do not think your arrangements judicious and liberal, but because there
are local considerations which claim to be deliberately and cautiously
examined, for however much this measure may partake of yours and my
wish, I fear our interest will be materially affected by it at this time, because the whole emigration to this country is, and has been, with very
few exceptions, Presbyterian, and this summer pains have been taken to
settle a clergyman in Lisbon, of that denomination. A visible spring
has been given to emigration in that town in consequence of it. Our
neighbors are pursuing that kind of policy which comports with the feelings and wishes of the people in this respect, by which they expect to
profit, and they will. The moment a measure should be pursued, which
had the shadow of appearance to direct the religious opinions of the people, (no matter how pure our motives may be,) jealousies will be excited,
and uneasiness created. It is not necessary for me to tell you how quick
the sensibility of people are engaged when their religious notions and
prejudices are touched; reason loses its force, and passion and rancor are
the only visible features. Since Lisbon has settled their clergyman, our
people are anxious to have one also. The idea has been much pressed
and much urged by them, and they have determined to have one, but he
must be a Presbyterian. I have suggested our idea, but it will not take.
The question now is whether we shall find it our interest to resist their

wishes and the wishes of those who it is probable will come to our settlement, or whether it will not be better to let them follow their own prejudices, and please themselves in their religious pursuits. It unquestionably must be the means of casting a double emigration into Lisbon, and this I make no doubt, has operated as a reason for the haste with which Lisbon has settled their clergyman. We shall find it our interest to move in this thing with caution, and not hastily take a step by which our neighbors will gain in proportion as we lose, by a wrong move upon the chess board. We stand delicately situated at this time. There are those whose interest it is to take every advantage of any unguarded measure we may pursue, for however much there is of harmony and good understanding in the country at this time, there are jealousies and secret feelings in the breasts of *some people in this world*, on account of the court house. I have now and then heard them echoed in whispers. There was no belief the exertion which has been made would have been to have the court house built. It is certain that edifice was considered as a thing which might be visible seven years hence, but it is now fixed by law; consequently all hope of changing its situation has vanished. This circumstance gives us an evident advantage of the other towns, and they will naturally for a time, feel jealousies, for they are natural upon such occasions; and if by any means we should excite a religious clamor, we must expect advantage to be taken of it, in which case we shall lose more than we shall gain. I conceive this would be the case for the purpose of counteracting the advantage we now hold. As from any assistance from our neighbors on the opposite shore, it is out of the question, for they are universally Scotch Presbyterians or Methodists. As for ———, he never gave a farthing in his life for the support of any clergyman; he holds all alike in equal contempt. No assistance can reasonably be calculated upon from without, and want of accordance within our settlement must and will beget an expense which will not be favorable to our interests, for we can not calculate upon more than a mere trifle from the settlers, if any thing at all. It is only necessary for you to ask yourself what success it is probable you would meet with were you to set a subscription on foot to be subscribed by Presbyterians and Methodists, for the support of a Church of England clergyman? There are few who are better able to answer this question than yourself, for your knowledge of the exciting of prejudices which attach to different sects, is such as will enable you to make a prompt decision. I have tried to comprise my ideas upon this subject in as concise a manner as possible, and shall conclude them by observing that circumstanced as we are, whether it would be good policy to take any step upon this subject at present, but leave the people to act for themselves. * * *

Believe me to be with warmest affection, your friend,

N. FORD.

Samuel Ogden, Esq."

A Baptist church was formed July 29, 1809, under Elder Samuel Rowley, a missionary from Massachusetts, of 9 members. The present stone church in State street was erected in 1833. A society had been formed May 23, 1821, with Harry Eastman, Charles Hull and Erastus Vilas, as trustees.

The Presbyterian church was organized Dec. 8, 1819, of 9 males and 9 females. The whole number received into full communion up to Aug., 1852, was 646; present number, 255. The society was incorporated

Presbyterian Church and Parsonage, Ogdensburgh.

June 1, 1820, with N. Ford, T. Lyon, Duncan Turner, Joseph Rosseel, Wolcott Hubbell and Wm. I. Guest, trustees. Their clergymen have been Rev. Barnabas Bruen, 1819; James McAuley, 1821; James B. Ambler, 1827; E. G. Smith, 1829; J. A. Savage, 1832; L. Merrill Miller, 1851. The above dates are those in which they commenced their labors respectively. Mr. Savage, after a pastorate of nearly 20 years, was dismissed from his charge, in order to assume the presidency of Carroll College, Wisconsin. A temporary wooden building was erected for a church, in 1818, on the southwest corner of Ford and Caroline streets, and the present church was built in 1824, at a cost of $9,000, and in 1847, enlarged to its present size, at a cost of $3,000. The church has a clock, bell and a good organ, and adjoining, a parsonage lot, with dwelling and other fixtures, worth in the aggregate, including the church property, about $15,000. There is a flourishing sabbath school connected with the church, numbering over 200 scholars, and a library of about 500 volumes. The ladies' missionary society contribute $50 per year, and a Dorcas society $40, to charitable objects annually. Contribution to other benevolent associations, $250 per annum. Most of the above data were collected by the Rev. L. M. Miller, for this work.

St. John's Church. — The Rev. Daniel Nash, on a missionary tour, in 1816, visited this place, and in a report which he made says, that he was the first Episcopal clergyman who had visited that village and the county of St. Lawrence. The second one who

St. John's Church and Rectory, Ogdensburgh.

officiated, was the Rev. Amos G. Baldwin, a missionary who came early in June, 1818, and at times performed divine offices in the court house; and on the 23d of May, 1820, a society was incorporated, having Thomas

J. Davies and Isaac Plumb, wardens; George Parish, Louis Hasbrouck, David Ford, David C. Judson, Andrew McCollom, Junius Walton, Richard W. Colfax and Sylvester Gilbert, vestrymen. The first report to the bishop, was that of 15 members. In 1821, it was resolved to build a stone church edifice, and in the same year, Rev. L. Carter was invited to a temporary charge, which he immediately assumed, and on the 10th of August, 1821, he laid the corner stone on a lot of ground, given for that purpose, by David and George Parish. In October, 1823, the building was opened for worship. In 1824, the Rev. Addison Searle and Rev. Mr. Beardsley were called to take temporary charge of the congregation, and in 1825, the first measures were adopted by the vestry, for the erection of the present rectory. In the same year, the Rev. Mr. Todd accepted the charge of the parish. In 1830, the Rev. Nathaniel Huse was called to the parochial charge, and in 1833, the Rev. Richard Bury was chosen to a temporary charge. In 1838, the Rev. Francis Tremayne became the minister, and in 1836, the Rev. William Barton became the first rector, and continued until 1839, when he resigned, and the Rev. —— Brayton was temporarily employed. In 1840, the Rev. H. R. Peters was invited to the rectorship, and still remains. In 1843, the church was thoroughly repaired, enlarged and made to assume its present appearance. This work was undertaken by Hon. H. Van Rensselaer, one of the wardens, who very liberally proposed to make the addition, and carry up the tower to a proportionate height, in consideration of the additional pews. This increased the length 30 feet, making its present dimensions 90 by 42 feet, and the church is capable of seating from 500 to 600. In consequence of the growth of the congregation, further additions, or a new edifice will ere long be needed. The rectory adjoins the church in the same enclosure, is of stone, and was built on land given by George Parish. There is a large bell in the tower, and the church contains a fine organ. The author is indebted to the Rev. Mr. Peters for the foregoing data.

The first M. E. church in town was incorporated Feb. 22, 1825, with Ichabod Arnold Joseph Brooks, Joseph Cole, David Chapin and Joseph Arnold, trustees. It has been reorganized Nov. 13, 1827, and Feb. 17, 1828. A second M. E. society was incorporated June 1, 1840, with Benj. Nichols, Uriah Van Waters, Amasa Pace, Ransom Lovejoy, James Russell, Joseph D. Hutchinson and Hiram Young, trustees. It was reorganized Dec. 12, 1848. This denomination in 1850, erected the present large brick church on Franklin street. A society was formed at Heuvelton, Sept. 14, 1843, with Nathan F. Griffin, Isaac Gray and Amos H. Hewlett, trustees.

The second Presbyterian church and society in Oswegatchie, was formed April 4, 1832, with Alex. McCall, John J. Dorn, John Lamon, Ezra Day and David Griffin, trustees. · They have a church in the west part of the town.

The first congregational society of Heuvelton was formed Sept. 26, 1842, with G. T. Howard, Andrew M. Gray, Ebenezer Kate, John Pickens and A. H. McMurphy, trustees. It reorganized Nov. 3, 1850.

A Universalist society was formed April 16, 1842, with Allen Chaney, Wm. Gardner and O. S. Cummings, trustees, and reorganized Sept. 26, 1842, and April 15, 1843.

The Roman Catholic church of Ogdensburgh and its vicinity, incorporated November 29, 1848; James Kennaday, Daniel Burns, James Mc Nulty, John Feelyard and Mitchel Lequin, trustees. During the summer of 1852, a large stone church, 60 by 100 feet, has been built, by Rev. James Mackey.

PARISHVILLE

Was formed from Hopkinton, March 18, 1814, and at first embraced Sherwood, Harewood, Granshue, Matildavale, Wick, Cookham and the west third of Catharineville. The first town meeting was directed to be held at the house of Thomas C. Colbun. The poor masters of the two towns were directed to meet and divide any moneys in the hands of the poor masters of Hopkinton.

It at present embraces Cookham (29,541 acres), and 7,971 acres of the west part of Catharineville. Wick, or No. 11, tract 2, is annexed. The first town officers were as follows:

Daniel W. Church, *supervisor*; Abijah Abbott, *clerk*; Stephen Goodman, Ira Ransom and Daniel Rockwell, *assessors*; Ephraim Smith, *collector*; Jonathan M. Derbey and Stephen Paddock, *poor masters*; Abel Brown, Peter Mahew and Elisha Brooks, *com'rs of highways*; Ephraim Smith and Matthew Wallace, *constables*; Peter Mayhew, Abel Brown and Elisha Brooks, *fence viewers*; Russell Foot, *pound keeper*; Abel Brown, Peter Mayhew and Foster Brownell, *overseers of highways.*

Supervisors.—1814, Daniel W. Church; 1815, Abijah Abbott; 1816-20, Daniel Hoard; 1822, William Allen; 1823, Daniel Hoard; 1824-31, Wm. Allen; 1832-4, John Brownell; 1835-7, William Allen; 1838-9, John Hoit; 1840-1, John Brownell; 1842-44, Ethan H. Pease; 1845-7, Sylvanus B. Merrill; 1848-9, Erastus D. Brooks; 1850-1, Nathan Christy; 1852, William F. Gurley.

Notes from the Town Records.—1814-15-16—$5 dollars for wolves and panthers, with half this for the young of these animals. 1818, $10 offered for panthers. 1820, $15 offered for panthers, killed in town, to be proved by producing the head, with the skin and ears thereon, and by making oath to the same. $0.50 bounty for foxes and $0.25 for young foxes. 1821, $15 bounty offered for old panthers, and $7.50 for their young. $1 fox bounty, and half that sum for their young. 1826. Voted in favor of a division of county, and the formation of a new one. 1827, this action again taken, and William Allen, and Daniel Hamlin, were appointed a committee to represent the wishes of the town in a petition to the legislature. 1846. $600 voted to build or furnish a town house in the village of Parishville, to be raised in the years 1847-48, and appointed William Allen, D. S. Stevens, and E. D. Brooks, a committee to petition the legislature for the powers necessary for raising the tax. This measure was not carried into effect. 1850. The town voted against reviving the distinction between the town and county poor.

This town derives its name from David Parish, who, Dec. 2, 1808, bought the town of J. D. Le Ray de Chaumont.[*] The latter had purchased of the heirs of Wm. Constable, July 24, 1804.[†]

The first settlement was made under the direction of Daniel Hoard, as agent of Mr. David Parish. Mr. Hoard was a young man, a native of Springfield, Vermont, who with his brother Silvius Hoard, had been

---

[*] Clerk's office, b. 3. deeds, p 180.   [†] Ib. b. 2, p. 105.

brought to the notice of Mr. Parish, by Gen. Lewis R. Morris, of Springfield, who had been interested in the lands afterwards purchased in St. Lawrence and Jefferson counties. Both brothers were employed as agents; the first at Parishville, and the latter at Antwerp. Mr. Hoard in the fall of 1809, surveyed and cut a road from Potsdam line to the site of Parishville village, In April 1810, he returned with Luke Brown, Isaac Tower, and Hartwell Shattuck, from Springfield, Vermont, and Levi Sawyer, from Massachusetts. These were employed during the summer, in clearing lands, and during the season, they chopped about seventy acres, and cleared forty on the site of Parishville village. A Mr. Whitmore and wife came into town this summer, to board the men engaged in clearing lands, and this woman was the first who ever came into town to reside. A line of road through to the Black river had been marked previous to this year. The route led several miles further south than the St. Lawrence turnpike was afterwards made, and passed through the township of Matildavale, now Colton. During the summer and fall of 1810, a saw mill was built by two brothers from Oneida county, by the name of Barnes. It was got in operation the same season, and used during the winter. Towards spring, the family which had first moved in went away. Soon after (March 31, 1811) Luke Brown and family moved into town, and this was the first permanent family in Parishville. He settled about two and a half miles from the line of Potsdam, on a farm he had previously purchased, and commenced improvements upon. Ira Collins, Reuben Thomas, George A. Flower, Joel Hawkins, William Thomas, Richard Newton, Abijah Abbot, —— Champlin, and —— Dagget, several of these men with families, came in and settled soon after, During the year 1811, the turnpike from the Black river settlements was cut through the town; a grist mill was built by Daniel W. Church, for Mr. Parish, and a distillery was erected and inclosed by Mr. Hoard the same season. The latter was the property of the agent, and remained such as long as he resided in town. It has been worked, with a few interruptions, nearly every year since. It was not got in operation till the spring of 1812. During the summer of 1812, a large tavern stand was erected by Mr. Church, for the proprietor of the town, costing $12.000, and during this season the place received large accessions of inhabitants, many of whom fled from Ogdensburgh, and other places on the St. Lawrence, from the danger they apprehended from the war. This morbid growth gave business and life to the settlement, which has never since been equalled; and for a time the village and surrounding country increased in population and improvements, as if by magic. A forge was built and run at an early day at its place. In 1813, this prosperity continued, and extensive buildings and improvements were undertaken. During this season a building was erected at the expense of Mr. Parish for public purposes, and which has since been usually known as the *academy*, for which use it was originally designed. It has since been used as a town hall, school house, and place for public and religious meetings. It is a one story wooden building with single room. The first birth in the town of Parishville, was in the family of Luke Brown, in the spring of 1812. The first school was taught by Miss Harriet Bronson, in the summer of 1813, in the barn of Daniel Hoard. A school house was erected very soon after. Religious meetings were occasionally held in 1812-13, and subsequently by traveling preachers, but the first stated ministry was established by the Methodists in July 1818, at the house of Mr. L. Brown. Baptist meetings were first held by an Elder Johnson, from Jefferson county.

An affair occurred in this town, in the fall of 1812, which created much excitement at the time. A desperate character by the name of B——, living in the edge of Stockholm, had been charged with a crime which carried him to jail in Ogdensburgh, in the month of June of that year. While undergoing his trial, and afterwards, he threatened vengeance against the neighborhood where the crime was committed, and against a Mrs. Miller in particular, who had been the principal witness against him. Shortly after his imprisonment, he succeeded in breaking jail, and was not seen for some time, till early in the morning, on Monday, October 23d, he was seen to cross the bridge over Raquette river, near the line of Pierrepont. On Wednesday morning, following, Mrs. Miller was left by her husband in the act of rising from bed, while he went some distance from home to get fire at a neighbor's. On his return she was not in the house, and her shoes and parts of her clothing being left he supposed that she was not far distant. Nothing more was seen of her, and her absence during the day, became a subject of anxiety, which increased till the whole country, far and near was rallied, and a general search begun, which continued several days, and at length given up in despair of finding any trace of the absent one.
On Friday night several houses and barns in the vicinity, were burned, evidently by an incendiary, and on Saturday morning following, the jail bird was seen to recross the bridge, of Raquette river. Suspicion rested on B——, who was followed up and arrested at Carthage, having in his possession a stolen rifle. Nothing but suspicion resting upon him, in relation to the abduction and arson, he was tried for the theft, and sent to states prison, where he died. On the following spring, a woman's head, was found some distance from a headless body, in the woods about three miles above the village of Parishville, which, were identified as those of Mrs. Miller, who in all probability had been brutally murdered from a fiendish revenge, by the ruffian who, had afterwards set fire to his own house, and another which sheltered his wife and children.

Parishville was surveyed by Joseph Crary, in the fall of 1809. The village was surveyed into a plat, by Sewall Raymond, in 1812. It is located on St. Regis river, at a point where that river is crossed by the old St.

Lawrence turnpike. The river here affords a considerable amount of water power. The channel is pressed into a narrow gorge scarcely ten feet wide and the river descends about 125 feet in the distance of a mile. *Wick*, is owned by Dr. Samuel W. Moore, of New York whose wife is Emily, a daughter of Wm. Constable. There are in this township, three school houses, several mills and about 100 families.

Religious Societies.—A Congregational church was formed Aug. 7, 1823, by a council consisting of the Rev. Messrs. M. Parmelee of Stockholm, Rev. Oliver Eastman of Parishville, Mr. Custant Southworth, licentiate of Canton, R. Pettibone, do. of Hopkinton, Mr. Henry Winchester, delegate from Madrid, and Dea. Sam'l P. Reynolds of Potsdam. It began with 11 members. C. Eastman, Moses Ordway, Tertius Reynolds, *Wm. K. Talbot*, Bliss Burnap, Geo. P. Everest, *Milton Bradley*, Enos Wood, and Bliss Burnap have been employed; those in italics having been settled as pastors. Whole number admitted up to Sept. 20, 1852, 224; of whom 90 now belong to the church. The stone church in Parishville was built in 1834, at a cost of $3000. A society was incorporated April 23, 1827, with Noran Rockwell, James Hardy, and George A. Flower, trustees.

A Baptist church was formed in October, 1823, of about 13 members, present number, 172. A society was formed April 5, 1831, with Graton Brand, Seymour Flower, and David Burdit, trustees; they have a commodious church, costing about $1950. The pastors have been the Rev. Messrs. Solomon Johnson, —— Rhodes, B. N. Leach, J. H. Greene, G. Brand, L. T. Ford, and O. W. Moxley. The last named commenced his services with this church in May, 1840, and continued them until May, 1844, when he moved to Madrid, and labored with the Baptist church there until March, 1848, when he returned to Parishville, where he still continues; and has labored longer with this church than any other minister, since its organization. They have during the intervals been supplied by the Revs. Henry Greene and W. H. Rice.

A Methodist society was formed March 10, 1828, with Luke Brown, Francis Goodale, Nathan Christy, Levi Fuller and Isaac Russell, trustees. It was reorganized Aug. 23, 1833, and Oct. 26, 1846. A chapel was built in 1846-7, worth $1000. A Wesleyan Methodist society was incorporated Dec. 6, 1843, with Luke Brown, Walter W. Bloss and Leavitt Hatch, trustees.

PIERREPONT,

Was erected from Russell and Potsdam, April 15, 1818, including the townships of Emilyville, Chaumont, Clifton Clare, and so much of Dewitt as would lie east of a continuation of the west line of said townships to the rear line of Canton. The first town meeting was directed to be held at the house of Cyrus Grannis. The towns of Emilyville and Chaumont have been annexed to Fine, in the formation of that town. The poor moneys were to be equitably divided between the towns. The portion of Dewitt included in this town, was by an act of 1807, annexed to Potsdam. This portion comprises almost the entire settled part of the town. A small part on the west belongs to the Harrison estate, and the remainder to that of the late Hezekiah Beers

27

Pierrepont, by the agents of whom it has been principally settled, and from whom it derives its name.[*]

First Town Officers.—Cyrus Grannis, *supervisor;* Andrew A. Crampton, *clerk;* Wm. Yale, Elisha Woodruff, Gardner Cox, *assessors;* Peter R. Leonard, Joseph Dorothy, *poor masters;* Flavius J. Curtis, Ezra Crarey, Samuel Belding, *commissioners of roads;* Richard Weller, *constable and collector;* Seth Hale, *overseer of highways;* F. J. Curtis, Ebenezer Tupper, Gardner Cox, *commissioners of schools;* Cyrus Grannis, Wm. Yale, A. A. Crampton, *inspectors of schools;* Joseph Dorothy, Seth Hale, F. J. Curtis, Henry Axtell, *fence viewers;* E. Tupper, P. R. Leonard, *pound keepers.*

Supervisors.—1819, Cyrus Grannis; 1820-1, John Axtell; 1822 3, Ezra Crarey; 1824-9, Benjamin Squire; 1829, Aug. 22, Gardner Cox to fill vacancy; 1830-2, G. Cox; 1833-8, Samuel Northrup; 1839, Paine Converse; 1840, G. Cox; 1841-2, Andrew A. Crampton; 1843-4, Joshua Manley; 1845, Orin A. Howard; 1846-7, J. Manley, 1848-9, Truman Smith; 1850-1, Asa W. Briggs; 1852, Peter F. Ryerson.

Notes from the Town Records.—1819. At the first town meeting, $30 raised for the support of schools, and $100 for the poor. Similar appropriations were voted nearly every year for many years. The poor funds having accrued to a considerable amount, the town, at their town meeting in 1820, appointed a committee of three to draft a petition to the legislature, praying for the privilege of applying this to the support of schools. Benjamin Squire, Zuriel Waterman, and Samuel Northrup, were appointed on this committee. An act was accordingly passed April 29, 1829, making it the duty of the overseers of the poor, to pay over the funds in their hands to the commissioners of common schools, to be invested for the benefit of schools. The present amount of the school fund is $575·62, secured by bond and mortgage. In 1822, $1 bounty was offered for foxes and $5 for wolves and panthers. In 1825, 50 cents for foxes and $5 for wolves.

From the field notes of Benjamin Wright, made on the first survey of township number three, now Pierrepont, the following traditionary record is taken: " The Indians tell of a silver mine near the falls on Grass river, which was worked a little about 1776, but was stopped by an order of government soon after it was begun." In township No. 3 it is said : " The Indian line of navigation from Lake Champlain, or from St. Regis to Black river, or Lake Ontario, lies through this town by way of Fall river."

The first settler in the town of Pierrepont was Flavius J. Curtis, who located near the line of Canton about 1806-7. The town however did not begin to settle rapidly until the opening of the St. Lawrence turnpike through it in 1811-12. Davis Dunton, Peter R. Leonard, Joseph Mathers, Ebenezer Tupper, Clark Hutchins, Zuriel Waterman, Foster Shaw, Henry Axtell, Alanson Woodruff, and others, settled about 1812. Religious meetings were held by the Rev. A. Baldwin, an Episcopal clergyman, in 1816. Nathan Crarey taught the first school in 1815-16. Cyrus Grannis is said to have opened the first inn near the centre of the town, on the turnpike, and Mr. Tupper at the point where this road crosses Raquette river.

Near the northeast corner of the town of Pierrepont, on Raquette river, is the little village of *East Pierrepont* or *Cox's Mills.* The first settlement at this place was commenced by Gardner Cox, from Barnard, Vermont, who in 1817, purchased a small tract of land, including the water privilege, and in the fall of that year, in company with John P. Dimick, from the same place, who had purchased a piece of land adjoining, he commenced a clearing. These two persons shantied together several weeks, and cut over some twenty acres of land. They returned to Vermont in the winter. On the 9th of March, 1818, Benjamin Cox, who had become concerned with his brother in the purchase, moved in with his family, and this was the first family that settled in this part of the town. The three persons here mentioned remained during the summer, and in the fall of that year got out the frame of a saw mill. A dam and saw mill was built in the summer of 1819, John and Joseph Goulding, of Potsdam, being the millwrights. From 1818 to 1822, the surrounding country on both sides of the river, as far up as the turnpike, was settled mostly by people from Vermont, many of whom were induced to remove and locate through the recommendations of Mr. Cox. In 1822 Mr. Cox erected a grist mill with a single run of rock stones, to which a second was added two years after. This mill was of wood, and in 1836 was replaced by the present stone mill. A bridge was built across the river at this place in 1828. In 1845, a starch factory was erected by Mr. Gardner Cox, and has been in operation every year since, manufacturing about thirty tons annually. It is contemplated to erect fixtures for the manufacture of corn starch. During the present year (1852), a gang mill is in process of erection, by Ralph, Clark & Dornbery, who have for several years been concerned in the McIntyre iron works, in Essex county, and who own extensive tracts of timber in that county *which they propose to take to this place by the natural water communications of the interior.* Cold river, which flows through this tract, is a tributary of Raquette river, and forms a part of that wonderful system of waters in the interior of the southern wilderness, which renders access to market for the timber with which it is covered, easy. The mill at East Pierrepont is to have fifty saws, but is built of such dimensions as to receive double that number. Schools have existed at this settlement since 1822. No religious societies at present exist here, as from the vicinity to Potsdam (about four miles), the inhabitants have been associated with the several religious denominations of that place. In 1846, a large school house, built with reference to its being used as a place of worship, was erected, and is occasionally used by the several orders for that purpose. East Pierrepont affords the only valuable water privilege in town. The village is mostly on the east side of the river, and contains about forty families, a store, and the usual variety of mechanics.

In the summer of 1799, Judge Raymond, and others, engaged in surveying into townships the great northern purchase, had a provision camp near the village of East Pierrepont. An incident is related concerning this encampment, worthy of record. Some of his men, wearied with the labors of the survey, which was protracted till late in the season, became anxious to return home, and finally refusing to listen to reason or argument, became mutinous, and resolved to leave, with or without permission, and so declared their intention. The route they proposed to take, was through the southern forest, and their guide, the compass of Mr. Raymond. Hearing of this intention, the latter, having exhausted his patience in attempting to dissuade, resorted to another expedient, and privately stole out of the camp on the evening previous to the day appointed for their departure, and hid his compass. When the mutineers had made all their arrangements and were prepared to start, inquiry was made for the compass, but it could not be found. Mr. Raymond, having in this manner gained control over his men, succeeded at length in convincing them that it was their interest to continue the survey until it was completed, and then return home honorably; and having obtained from each a promise of obedience, the instrument was produced and the labors continued till completed.

From observations continued annually for more than thirty years, upon the height of the spring flood of the Raquette at Coxe's mills, in Pierrepont, by the owner, it has been noticed, that with but few exceptions, the highest water occurred on the last week in April. One of these exceptions was in July, 1830, when a memorable freshet prevailed throughout all the rivers of Northern New York and portions of the New England states. It was produced by heavy and protracted rains. The water at this place was then about three and a half feet above ordinary summer level on the dam, while the ordinary depth in spring floods does not exceed two and a half feet.

The citizens of Pierrepont at their annual town meeting in 1846, voted to choose a committee from different parts of the town, to draw a plan for a town house, and purchase a site for the same, and to erect the said house and have it finished at a cost of not to exceed $500, before the first of October, 1847, and also to petition the legislature for powers for this purpose. Joshua Manley, Nathan Crarey, Jun., Henry Gleason, Merritt Howard, Chileab Billings, Lucius Palmer, and Christopher W. Leonard, were appointed on this committee. An act was accordingly passed on the 27th of April, 1847, directing the board of supervisors of St. Lawrence county to levy the sum of $800 for the above purpose, and appointing the three first named on the committee to superintend its erection. The supervisor, town clerk, and superintendent of schools, are by virtue of office trustees of the town house. A town hall, of neat and ample proportions, was built the same year, near where the Canton and Colton road crosses the old turnpike. This edifice serves the purpose of a church, there being no meeting house erected expressly for the purpose in town.

A part of the township of Clare was formerly owned by Madam De Stael, the accomplished French authoress, and virulent enemy of Napoleon. She invested her money in these lands at the recommendation of Gouverneur Morris, with whom she was personally acquainted. On the 7th October, 1806, he wrote to her as follows:

"It has occurred to me that you would do well to purchase the remainder of the township of Clare. It lies next to that of Ballybeen [Russell], which is rapidly increasing in population. Thus in time a revenue will be drawn from it, inconsiderable indeed at first, but subsequently of great importance. Now such a provision for a son, is of more value than thrice the amount of money. The one directs to industry and economy, the other excites to dissipation unless indolence is allowed to exercise its ennervating power. It would perhaps be possible to purchase the remainder of Clare at the rate of one dollar an acre. It certainly would not be necessary to go higher than two dollars."

On the partition of lands between McCormick and others, 15,200 acres were conveyed to Herman Le Roy and Wm. Bayard, in trust for this lady. They were subsequently conveyed to Theodosius O. Fowler, and in 1846, purchased by S. Pratt and John L. Russell, upon directions to sell by Duc de Broglie and Ada Holstein de Stael, his wife, the only surviving child of Madame de Stael. In 1847, a question of alienage of Dutchess De Broglie, and of the operation of the New York statute of trusts, having arisen, the legislature, by separate acts, confirmed the title of Russell and Pratt to the Clare lands, and of Livingston to the Clifton lands, similarly circumstanced.

Religious Societies.—The Methodists have a society at East Pierrepont, which was incorporated Jan. 3, 1844, with Gardner Cox, Nathan Christy, Levi Fuller, John Hicks, and Harry Train, trustees. A Free Will Baptist church was organized by Elder S. W. Lewis, in September, 1850, of seventeen members. Present number twenty-five, who have employed Elder Wm. Whitfield, pastor.

PITCAIRN

Was erected from Fowler, March 29, 1836, and made to include township No. 11, or Portaferry, excepting a triangular tract on the west corner, which was retained by Fowler. The first town meeting was directed to be held at the house of David Brown.

At the first town meeting, the following officers were elected: John Sloper, *supervisor;* Stephen Seabury, *clerk;* Levi W. Gleason, Silvester Bacon, Aaron Geer, *justices;* Almond Howard, Samuel Gustin, Robert Leach, *assessors;* John Williams, George P. Burdick, Levi W. Gleason, *commissioners of highways;* Constant Wells, Jonathan Paine, Elijah Anderson, *commissioners of common schools;* Silvester Bacon, J. Paine, David Brown, *inspectors of schools;* Almond Howard, George P. Burdick, *overseers of the poor;* Matthew M. Geer, *collector;* M. M. Geer, Constant Wells, *constables.*

Supervisors.—1836-40, John Sloper; 1841-2, Silvester Bacon; 1843- 4, Horatio N. Dickinson; 1844, at a special meeting in October, Asaph Green; 1845-7, Asaph Green; 1848-50, Eli R. Paul; 1851-2, Asaph Green.

Joseph Pitcairn, from whom this town was named, was born in Fifeshire, Scotland, and was a son of a Scotch clergyman. In early life he came to the United States, and subsequently for several years he resided in the East Indies. At one time he held the office of consul for our government at Paris, from which office he was removed by Jefferson. Most of his life was spent in the capacity of a merchant, at Hamburgh, in Germany. In 1817, having acquired from Daniel McCormick, who took a great interest in his affairs, and to whom he is believed to have been somewhat related, the ownership of his unsold lands in St. Lawrence and Franklin counties, he came into the northern part of the state, appointed agents, and took measures for commencing settlements in Pitcairn, Edwards, Brasher, and other places. At one time he contemplated making the village of Helena, in Brasher, his summer residence, and the fine stone mansion of Mr. Nevins, of that village, was erected for him. He died in New York, in June, 1844.

The first settlement in Pitcairn was formed by emigrants from Potsdam. In the fall of 1824, Nathan Dickenson and sons, Nathan, Justin, Anson, Leonard, and Hubbard, with Levi W. Gleason and Nathan C. Scovil, came in to select land, and most of them erected the body of log houses. In December, Justin Dickenson and family moved into town, and for some time lived alone. In February he was joined by others. James Streeter, from Fowler, arrived in February, having made the first clearing in town the fall previous, on the site of the present cemetery near the log chapel. Nathaniel, Joseph and Elisha Lamphear, came in in 1824, but did not move till the next year. Joshua Sloper, George

Peabody, Aaron Geer and sons, Dayton Merrrill, Samuel Gustin, and others, came in 1824 and 1825. Elder Jonathan Paine in 1826, became the first Baptist preacher. In June, 1825, the first birth occurred in town, in the family of N. C. Scovil. The first school was taught by Miss Caroline Dickenson, in 1826. The first marriage was Aaron Bingham to Miss C. Dickenson. P. Jenny erected the first saw mill in 1828. There are two post-offices in town, both of which are on the route from Edwards to Lowville. Pitcairn post office was established 5th June, 1840, John Sloper, postmaster; and East Pitcairn post office, February 8, 1850, Charles Bowles, postmaster.

Near the southeast corner of the town, is a valuable depository of magnetic iron ore, which will doubtless hereafter give employment to the industry of great numbers. The supply is reported to be ample. About 100 tons have been taken, and the mine has acquired the name of the Jayville mine.

Mining explorations for lead were formerly carried on in town, and much money expended.

The following incident happened in Pitcairn near where Green's mill now stands, and some time before any settlers had located in town. James Streeter, then living in Fowler, was out hunting for deer, in the winter time, when there was about three feet of light snow on the ground. When on Portaferry creek, he noticed a great number of tracks, which as he traced across the ice, he discovered had been made by five panthers. Following these, he found a place where they had pawed away the snow to the ground, and had nested the night previous, and a few rods beyond this, he overtook a large male panther, which his dog treed, and which was killed by a single shot from his rifle. A few rods beyond, a young panther was treed and wounded. A second shot despatched this, and shortly after another young one was chased to a spruce tree and despatched by a single shot. The three were beheaded, and Streeter returned to the camp, and the next morning came back with a companion and despatched the remaining female panther. A large male remained, who was treed without difficulty but not killed till after many shots. This one evinced much venom, keeping his eyes fixed upon the hunters, disregarding the dog, gnashed his teeth, growling, spitting after the fashion of a cat, and would run up and down, as if about to attack them. Getting more composed, he would climb to the topmost branches, and seating himself, would purr like a cat. When wounded, he would again become enraged. He was killed by a shot through the head. The bounties on panthers were $25 each at this time, which made the day's work very profitable.

POTSDAM.

This town was erected from Madrid, by the same act which formed Stockholm from Massena, and De Kalb from Oswegatchie, Feb. 21, 1806. The first town meeting was directed to be held at the house of Benjamin Raymond. In 1807, a part of the present town of Pierrepont was annexed, which was taken off in the erection of that town. The officers elected at the first town meeting, were

Benjamin Raymond, *supervisor;* Gurdon Smith, *town clerk;* Bester Pierce, David French and Gurdon Smith, *com'rs of highways;* Giles Parmele, Horace Garfield and Benjamin Bailey, *assessors;* Benjamin Raymond, Benjamin Stewart, Levi Swift, Abner Ray, Jun., Archibald Rayer and Isaac Buck, *overseers of highways;* Ansel Baily, *constable and collector;* William Smith and Oliver Boyder, *pound masters;* Jabez Healy and David French, *overseers of poor;* Levi West, B. Pierce and Benj. Stewart, *fence viewers.*

At a special town meeting, convened at the academy, Sept. 1, 1813, in pursuance of an act entitled "an act for the establishment of common schools," passed June 19, 1812, the following named persons were elected school commissioners, viz: Benjamin Raymond, Gurdon Smith and Howard J. Pierce. Four school inspectors were chosen, viz: James Johnson, Liberty Knowles, Thomas Swift and Sylvester Bacon. These were the first persons who held that office in town.

Supervisors.—1806-7, Benjamin Raymond; 1808, Charles Cox; 1809, Benjamin Raymond; 1810-11, Charles Cox; 1812-17, Benjamin Raymond; 1818-21, Gurdon Smith; 1822. Samuel Partridge; 1823-4, Gurdon Smith; 1825, Samuel Partridge; 1826-7, Horace Allen; 1828-9, Samuel Partridge; 1830-4, Zenas Clark; 1835-7, Ansel Bailey; 1838, Amos W. Brown; 1839, Ansel Bailey; 1840-3, Aaron T. Hopkins; 1844-5, Thomas Swift; 1846-7, Isaac Parker; 1848-9, Charles Dart; 1850-1, Amos Blood; 1852, Isaac Parker.

Notes from the Records.—1810-11. A bounty of $5 offered for wolves. 1826-7. Voted that it was expedient to divide the county, and to erect a new one. 1837. Voted against any division of the town.

In June, 1799, Mr. Benjamin Wright, of Rome, having arrived at St. Regis with a surveying company of seven parties, despatched Mr. Gurdon Smith, one of his surveyors, up the Raquette river, to make observations, and ascertain how far the river was navigable, and what places were most suitable for provision camps. He proceeded with his boat as far as Norfolk, from whence he proceeded by land to the present village of Potsdam. Finding a commodious place for spending the night, on the rocks near where the mills now stand, and a snug shelter under a fallen pine, he spent the night.

Here, far removed from every settlement, in the untraversed wilderness, and in all probability on ground which the foot of the white man had never before trod, he discoved a tuft of *timothy grass,* evidently the product of a single seed, which had been wafted by winds, or carried by birds, to a spot congenial to its growth. Much pleased with this familiar object, he hailed it as the harbinger of civilization, and a herald sent forward to anticipate the future destiny of the county, as a great grazing region. The figure of the great and indispensible staple, so essential to our prosperity as a dairy district, might, with much propriety, be adopted by the citizens of Potsdam, as an emblem for their seal, with equal or more application than the thistle, the shamrock and the roses, of Scotland, Ireland and England, which have come to be considered as the national devices of these countries.

The first settlement of the town of Potsdam was begun by Benjamin Raymond, the agent for the proprietors, in 1803. In May of that year, he left Rome with a bateau laden with mill irons, provisions, and about half a dozen men, and proceeded by the difficult and tedious route of Oswego river, lake Ontario and the St. Lawrence, to Point Iroquois, above Waddington, where he left a part of his load, and proceeded to open his way through the forest, to his location in the present village of Potsdam. He first struck the river some distance below, and here he built a raft, and ascended about half a mile to the falls, where he arrived in June. He here erected a temporary hut on the rocks west of the river, and commenced building a saw mill, which was raised and got in operation the same year. During the summer, lines for roads were surveyed out in different directions, and some of them, among which was the route from Stockholm through Potsdam to Canton, was so far cleared of underbrush, as to allow the passage of teams. The frame of the saw mill was the first building erected in town. Mr. Raymond had, for two or three years, traversed the town as a surveyor, and was well acquainted with its location, and sensible, before commencing a settlement, of the natural superiority of the soil over that of some other parts of the country. Ebenezer Patterson is said to have been the first man who moved his family into town, and his wife was, during the year 1803, reported to have been the "handsomest woman in Potsdam." In 1804, Mr. Raymond returned with his family, coming by the way of the Long falls (Carthage).

William Smith, Gurdon Smith, Benjamin Stewart, John Delance, David French, Chester Dewey, Joseph Bailey, Bester Pierce, Roswell Parkhurst,* William Bullard, Abner Royce, Reuben Field, and others, came in, some only to select farms, on which they began small improvements, preparatory to removal, and others moving on directly.

* Roswell Parkhurst, who lived many years in Potsdam, and died there, was in his youth the subject of an incident which has formed a prominent place in the annals of Royalton, in Vermont. In 1776, a company of tories and Indians attacked that town, and took a number of prisoners, among whom were several men and children. The mother of one of the latter followed the Indians, and urged them to return her little son, whom they had taken, and plead her request with such earnestness, that she succeeded. Encouraged by this success, she urged the matter further; and had the address to prevail with the savages to give up twelve or fifteen of her neighbors' children, among whom was the subject of this note. In a fit of good humor, one of the savages then offered to carry her on his back over the river, which offer she accepted, and she was safely conveyed across on the shoulders of the gallant Indian.

(*Williams's History of Vermont*, 2d ed. vol. ii, p. 241.

During the summer, a frame grist mill was raised and partly finished, but not got in operation till the following year. Ebenezer Wright, a brother-in-law of Raymond, was the millwright. In 1805, Horace Garfield, Timothy Shepard, Jabez Healey, John Fobes, Oliver Boyden, Ansel Bailey and brothers, Giles Parmelee, David Corey, most of those who formed *The Union*, which will be described presently, and John and others by the name of Smith, from Tunbridge, Vermont, relatives of Joe Smith, the celebrated founder of the Mormon sect, came into town and settled. John Smith is at present the chief or high priest of the Morman settlement at Salt lake, in Utah territory. The first death in town among the settlers was that of James Chadwick, a young man from Tyrringham, Mass., which was caused by the falling of the limb of a tree, in July, 1805. The first birth in town, was a daughter, in the family of William Smith, in the year 1804. Levi Swift, Charles Cox, Asa and Ira Perrin, Abram Collins, and many others, came in and took up farms, and in that year the land around Potsdam village for quite a distance was contracted to actual settlers. The first frame dwelling in town was erected by Mr. Raymond, in 1804, on the west side of the river.

On the Raymond's again returning in the spring of 1805, he proceeded with a team and sleigh to the Ox Bow on the Oswegatchie river, in Jefferson county. Here the snow left them, and a company of some eighteen, who had come by different routes, and with different destinations, found themselves in the same dilemma; among these were Nathaniel Holt, James Burnett, Elijah Pooler, Isaac Burnham, Elisha Griffin, Dr. John Seeley, and perhaps one or two others, on their way to DeKalb. Mr. Raymond was accompanied by a brother in law, Mr. Ebenezer Wright, and his family. Finding no alternative, they constructed a raft of about thirty pine logs, which they bound together securely, and upon which they placed their three sleighs, their goods and families, and proceeded down the stream, at that time excessively swollen by rains and melting snows. At night they came to, about opposite the present village of Richville, and towards the close of the second day (April 1,) the emigrants arrived at Cooper's settlement in DeKalb. The horses were sent around by the state road, in charge of Sewall Raymond, a cousin of B. Raymond.

The land records of Potsdam show the following list of early settlers, in the order of their purchases, commencing June 9, 1803. During that year the following persons purchased.

Christopher Wilson, Jabez Healey, John Fobes, Moses Patterson, Elihu Knights, Ash Knapp, Elias Champion, Gurdon Smith, Joshua Coakley, Francis Whitney, John DeLance, Benjamin Stewart, Giles

Parmelee, Sylvanus Eaton, Archibald Royce, William Smith, Chester Dewey, Nathaniel Bailey, David French, Esau Rich, Reuben Ames, Barnabas Ames, Benjamin Bailey, Howard J. Pierce, Newel B. Smith, Ansel Bailey, Ebenezer Hubbard, Ebenezer Patterson. In 1804, Ebenezer Parkhurst, Jun., Wm. Ames, Barnabas Hogle, Thomas Bowker, David Covey, Jehiel Slafter, Joseph Wright, Lebeus Johnson, Bester Pierce, Roswell Parkhurst, Alvin Mills, Reuben Field, John Bowker, Spalding Waterman, William Bullard and associates, Ezra Crarey. In 1805, Ezekiel Wilson, Paul Raymond, Jehiel Slafter, Horace Garfield, Ebenezer Jackson, Dyer Bottum, Elijah Stevens, David French, Azariah Orton, David Hendee, Levi Wyman, Josiah Fuller, Wm. Pike, Charles Cox, Benjamin Pratt, Levi West, Jeremiah Gilmore, Abraham Collins, Samuel Harris, Levi Swift, Frederick Currier, Josiah Fuller, Ai Powers, Asa Goodnow, Abner Royce, Jun., Andrew Patterson, Timothy Parker, Luther Savin, William Isham, Timothy Shephard, Larned Rich, Moses Patterson.

On the 28th of Nov., 1804, Wm. Bullard and associates took up a tract of 2,427 acres, about two miles north of the present village, at a cost of $8656·04, with the view of establishing a colony, having a unity of interests, and on a plan which he had drawn up in New England. The records of the land office show, that his partners in the purchase were William, Thomas H. and Ammi Currier, J. Buttolph, J. Borroughs, J. and R. Field, N. Howe, J. McAllaster, E. and S. Shaw, M. Smith, D. and L. Wyman, and B. Wells. Some of these withdrew and others joined; and about the month of May, 1807, they formed an association styled *The Union*, a d consisting of the following members.

Wm. Bullard the projector, John Burroughs, Manassa Smith, Nathan Howe, Ammi Currier, Thomas Currier, Isaac Ellis, Wm. Currier, Alba Durkee, and John McAllaster. A constitution was formed, a clerk chosen, and all things relative to the Union was decided by a majority of votes, on strictly republican principles. The property of the company was held in common stock, each sharing equally in the proceeds, according to the amount of labor invested. An account was kept with each member, of the amount of stock invested, and day's works performed, and at the annual meeting of the stockholders, which occurred in January of each year, a settlement was made with each. The company were prospered to some degree. Bullard acted as agent, and Burroughs as clerk. They disclaimed all control over the political or religious views of the members. After dissolution, the land was divided, and most of the members continued to reside on the tract, and accumulated property. But two of the company are now living. Mr. Burroughs, in Potsdam, now in his 88th year, and Wm. Currier, in Ohio. Most of them afterwards adopted the religious tenets of the Christian sect. In March 1818, in this settlement, a great excitement was produced by finding in a hen's nest, an egg, on which was inscribed in white and raised characters, very legibly, the words, " *wo! wo! to those that deny the Trinity.*" Like the golden egg of the fable, this prodigy and the hen that laid it, attracted the greatest curiosity, and hundreds from the surrounding country flocked thither to wonder at the miraculous denunciation, and satisfy themselves by actual inspection of the prodigy. It is said that $500 were offered for the hen, and that this sum was refused!

Numbers were exceedingly alarmed, and others looked upon it as a direct communication from Heaven, while still another class, said that it was a *trick of some mischievous person, and that the characters were first traced with hot tallow, and then eroded by immersion in vinegar.* From the account book of the Union, before us, it is observed that a minute record was kept of every item of business, apparently with strict justice, and at its dissolution, the most friendly feeling existed between the members. In Spafford's Gazetteer, 1813, this society is erroneously stated to be composed of Moravians. The members were from New England and had formed the association before settling in Postdam. Mr. Bullard, the projector, had issued a pamphlet to set forth the advantage of the association, and labored zealously to establish it.

In 1809, a bridge was built on the present site, which lasted till 1830, when the supervisors of the county were directed by an act of the legislature, to levy a tax of $300 in town, for the purpose of rebuilding it. The bridge then erected, lasted till 1849, when the board of supervisors were, by an act passed March 28, 1849, authorized to levy another tax of $500, in addition to the tax of $250, ordinarily raised for improving roads and bridges, across Raquette river, in the village of Potsdam, to be expended under the direction of Benjamin G. Baldwin, and Williard M. Hitchcock. The additional sum of $250 was also directed to be raised in 1850, for the same purposes. With this appropriation the present elegant bridge across the Raquette river was built. In 1810, Judge Raymond erected a building near the centre of the village, for a public school, and place of worship, which subsequently was given to the St. Lawrence academy, and for many years was occupied by the trustees of that institution as an academic building. In 1820, the first church in the village, was erected by the Presbyterians, and in 1825 the north academic building was built. That on the south was built in 1835, after the organization of a teacher's department. A full account of the origin and history of this institution, will be found in the chapter devoted to this subject. For several years from the time that settlements began, they progressed quite rapidly, and in no town was more energy or industry displayed in promoting internal improvements, and thus offering inducements to settlement, than by Mr. Raymond.

The village early acquired a growth second only to Ogdensburgh, and the location of the St. Lawrence academy tended much to promote this prosperity. A fire company was incorporated by an act of April 9, 1823, by which Samuel Partridge, and all of those residing in the village, were constituted a body corporate, with the powers, privileges and immunities, usually granted to such associations, and with such exemptions from service, as militia, or jurymen, as is customary. On the incorporation of the village, in 1831, the fire department was placed under the jurisdiction of the village trustees, who reorganized it and formed a code of by-laws for its government. The village possesses at present, two good fire engines, but there is scarcely any organization of a fire department kept, further than suitable regulations for the care and preservation of the engines.

In 1825, the citizens of this town united in celebrating the national anniversary in a manner quite novel and utilitarian. The following extract from their programme, which was preceded by a series of patriotic resoluons, will be read with interest.

Resolved, therefore, that it be recommended to the inhabitants of said town, to assemble at the village, at an early hour on the 4th day of July next, with teams and suitable implements, for the purpose of embanking the meeting houses and gun house, and improving the public square in said town, as a principal part of the exercises of that day. *Resolved*, That Rev. Jonathan Wallace be requested to deliver an appropriate address on the square, at the close of said day. *Resolved*, That Messrs. Jabez Willes, John C. Smith, John Goulding and Anthony Y. Elderkin, be a committee of arrangements. *Resolved*, That the following persons be appointed as assistants of the said Committee, for the purpose of notifying the inhabitants of their respective neighborhoods, furnishing a due proportion of the several kinds of implements, and taking charge of the different portions of work, viz:

Warren Clark, Moses Cheeny, Ebenezer Brush, Solomon M Crary, Seth Benson, Ai Powers, David French, Ansel Bailey, Louis Plympton, William Smith, Sylvester Bacon, Giles Parmalee, Archibald Royce, James Murphey. Gurdon Smith, Stephen Buss, David Barnum, Thomas S. Hemenway, Perez Fobes, Joel Buckman, Ezra Lyman, Samuel Parker, 2nd, Samuel Stickney, Jacob Redington, Jonathan Hoit, Amini Currier, Frederick Currier, Daniel Pride, James Porter, John Chandler, Charles Edgerton, Thomas W. Durkee, Isaac Ellis, Jun., Isaac Austin, Stephen Maynard, John Smith, Almond Howard, Parley Perrin, Ira Perrin, Amos W. Brown, Aikins Foster, Bester Pierce, Horace Garfield, John Olmstead, John M. Call, Alanson Fisher, A. Lyman, John B. Judd, Eleazer Johnson.

L. KNOWLES, *Chairman.*

H. Allen, Secretary.

In pursuance of the above resolutions, the undersigned give notice for the (4th of July next) of the following

Order of the Day.—1. The day will be ushered in by the discharge of cannon.   2. At half past 7 o'clock, A. M., prayers will be attended on the common.   3. Labor will commence at 8 o'clock A. M , at the discharge of one gun.   4. At half past 12 o'clock, at noon, at the discharge of a gun and the sound of the bugle, the procession will form, and, aided by the band, will march to the table (on the common), to be furnished with the provisions which each man will bring with him; and it is presumed some appendages will be added by the people of the village.   Liquor will be furnished by the committee.   5. At half past one o'clock, P. M., labor will recommence, at the sound of the bugle.   6. At 5 o'clock, P. M., the sound of the bugle will announce the cessation of labor, when the procession will form and proceed to the place for receiving the address, from Rev. Mr. Wallace.   7. The day will close with music and the discharge of cannon.

J. WILLES,
A. Y. ELDERKIN,   } Committee
J. C. SMITH,   } of
JOHN GOULDING. } Arrangements.

Potsdam, June 23, 1825.

The trustees of public lands in the town of Potsdam, were by an act

of the legislature passed April 18, 1828, authorized to sell the gospel and
school lot, or any part thereof in that town, on such terms of credit less
than ten years, as they might deem most conducive to the interests of
the town. This was done.

The village of Potsdam, was incorporated March 3, 1831. The affairs
of the corporation were directed to be managed by five trustees, elected
annually on the first Monday of May, in each year, who were to elect one
of their number as president, and to appoint a clerk, treasurer, collector,
constable and pound master, who should hold their offices for one year
unless sooner removed by the trustees.

At a meeting of the trustees, held May 3, 1832, a seal was adopted
having for its device a tree, under the word *Potsdam.* July 3, 1832,
Zenas Clark, George Wilkinson and Justus Smith, were appointed a board
of health, and John Parmelee, health officer, in pursuance of the statute
law passed June 22, 1832. This board met soon after, and passed a series
of resolutions restraining persons from Canada from entering the village
without having first obtained a bill of health from some health officer
within the county, to be approved by the board. Regulations respecting
domestic nuisances, &c., were also passed, and vigilant measures taken
to remove all causes which might tend to generate disease.

The act of 1831, incorporating the village of Potsdam, was amended
April 10, 1849. The bounds of the village were by this act increased, and
additional powers were conferred upon the trustees in relation to the purchase and conveyance of real estate, the making and repairing of side-
walks, roads, &c., and the planting and protection of trees, and the construction of reservoirs, sewers and ditches.

About five miles from the village in the north west part of the town is
a small village commonly known as *Smith's Corners,* from Gurdon Smith,
the first settler. It is the centre of business for a rich agricultural district, and is the seat of the post office of West Potsdam of the U. States
Mutual Insurance Co. One mile south from this is a small settlement
which has acquired the name of *Yaleville.* The first beginning was made
here in 1806, by Moses Patterson. It contains two saw mills, grist mill,
tavern, two stores, several mechanic shops, and about eighteen families.
The post office of West Potsdam, was first established here in 1847.
Barnabas Yale and sons, Lloyd C. and John, settled here in 1836, and
from them the settlement derived its name.

Buck's Bridge is the name of a small village in the western corner
of the town, on Grass river, three miles from the rail road depot for Madrid
and Canton, and on the plank road between those places. The place
derives its name from Isaac Buck, from Shoreham, Vt., who settled here
about 1807. In 1809, a saw mill was built and in operation, and some
thirty or forty acres of land cleared. A store was opened by Mr. Buck,
about this time. A Methodist chapel has been erected here, and it is the
seat of a post office.

Raquetteville is the name of a village which has sprung up as if by
magic, near the point where the Northern rail road crosses Raquette river,
and at the depot for a rich and growing country, both north and south,
with which it communicates by plank road. Under the combined influences of these communications, a valuable water power, the characteristic energy of its spirited founder, and the very strong probability that
it will become the terminus of the rail road about to be built to Watertown,
it can not fail to attain that importance to which it is entitled. It has
sprung up since October, 1850, and is mostly upon a farm of 400 acres

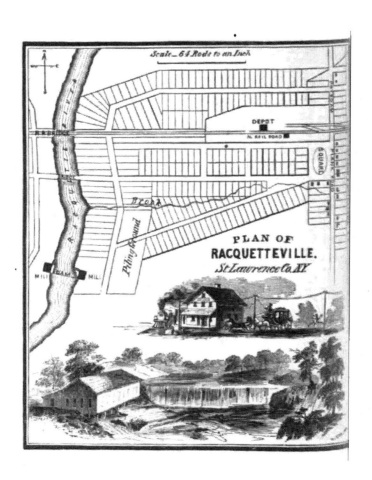

Scale...64 Rods to an Inch

DEPOT
R. ROAD

SQUARE

PLAN OF
RACQUETTEVILLE.
St.Lawrence Co. N.Y.

purchased by Benjamin G. Baldwin, 1836. This gentleman conveyed 15 acres to the company for a depot, besides road way; in 1850, he erected a tavern house, which burnt down the next March, and in 1851, two other taverns and several dwellings were built. In 1852, a substantial dam with eight feet fall, was erected on Raquette river, which affords a water power of great value; a highway bridge constructed a little below; the premises around laid out for a village, with ample reservations for public grounds and numerous dwellings, built. Among the latter was a large hotel built by Robert M. Gill, three stories in height. An extensive forwarding and mercantile interest has sprung up, and the returns of the rail road show an amount of business surpassed only by that of its two termini. It is anticipated that additions to the depot which is 50 by 100 feet, will soon be necessary for the accommodation of passengers. The water power is owned by a company, and there is in preparation for building a large gang saw mill on each bank, and other machinery on an extensive scale. The peculiar facilities for the transportation of timber which this river affords, will long give prominence to this department of industry,—the manufacture of wooden fabrics, and Raquetteville, in addition to the facilities of other points on the river, will possess the additional one of direct rail road communication with market. A post office named North Potsdam, is established here, and a telegraph station on the main line from Ogdensburgh to Burlington, uniting with most of the large cities.

By an act passed April 18, 1845, the board of supervisors were required to levy a tax of $600 in each of the years, 1846 and 1847, in the town of Potsdam, which moneys were to be paid over to the supervisors of the town, Henry L. Knowles, Samuel Partridge, Flavel Smith and William W. Goulding, for the purpose of being spent in the erection of a town house in the village. The committee hereby appointed were at liberty to anticipate this appropriation by loans, if they thought proper. The town was directed to choose by ballot some person who with the supervisor and town clerk, were to have charge of the town house, with liberty to grant its use for such purposes as might not be deemed inconsistent with the purposes for which it was erected, or the interests of the town. If it should be located upon the westerly side of the public square it should not be let for any such use on Sunday without the consent of the trustees of the societies occupying the two nearest churches.

A town hall was accordingly built the same year under a contract with Wm. J. Sweet. It is of wood, about 64 by 40 feet, and stands on the centre of the west side of the public square.

We are much indebted to William H. Wallace, Esq., for the following statistics of Potsdam village, as it was in the fall of 1852:

Population of village, 1,500 to 1,600; of town, 5,000 to 6,000. There were 175 dwellings; 5 churches; 2 large stone academic buildings; 12 dry goods stores, and six others in town; 1 furnace or hardware store; 1 book store; 3 shoe stores, and 1 shoe shop; 2 wholesale and retail grocery stores; 1 printing office (issuing a weekly paper, circulation 900); 6 groceries; 3 hotels; 2 jeweler shops and stores; 2 saddle and harness shops and stores; 2 tailor shops; 3 shoe and leather stores; 2 tanneries; 4 cabinet shops; 2 finishing machine shops; 1 foundry and furnace; 1 trip hammer shop; 5 blacksmith shops; 1 wholesale and retail tin store; 2 cooper shops; 1 carriage factory; 2 wheelwright shops; 1 chair shop and factory; 1 marble factory; 1 fanning mill factory; 1 large flouring and grist mill; 2 saw mills, one gang mill with 100 saws and 4 gates; 1 woolen factory; 1 cloth dressing and carding factory; 1 hoe factory; 2

asheries; 1 plaster mill; 1 drug store, excluding two-others who deal extensively in drugs; 1 bakery; 1 book bindery; 1 millinery furnishing store; 2 milliner shops; 4 physicians and surgeons; 5 practicing lawyers; 4 settled clergymen; 1 large gang saw mill, 2½ miles below Potsdam village, on Raquette river, 80 saws.

The second legal execution for murder in St. Lawrence, was that of John Donnovan, for the murder of James Rowley, at Potsdam, Jan. 23, 1852. Both were Irishmen. They had been drinking beer together, and afterwards a quarrel arose, hard words and blows were exchanged, but subsequently the matter was settled, and they parted, apparently as friends. Rowley had, however, proceeded but a short distance, when Donnovan followed, and with a jack knife inflicted several wounds, which proved fatal. The murderer was arrested, after somes how of resistance, and tried before judge Hand, in February, 1852, at Canton. The jury, after two hours' deliberation, brought in a verdict of guilty, which verdict the prisoner received with the same apparent indifference and stupidity he had evinced throughout the trial. On the 21st, he was arraigned and received his sentence, to be executed on the 16th of April, which sentence was carried into effect in the yard of the jail, in the presence of the limited number which were legally admitted, and several hundred, who gained a sight of the spectacle from the roofs of buildings and other places.

The Washington Benevolent Society Library was incorporated in Potsdam, June 14, 1814, under a general act, with Benjamin Raymond, Liberty Knowles, Azel Lyman, Robert McChesney, Pierce Shepard, Jacob Redington and Sewall Raymond, trustees.

The Union Library Association was incorporated Jan. 8, 1828, with Jabez Willes, Zenas Clark, Amos W. Brown, Myron G. Munson, Horace Allen, Solomon M. Crary, Solomon Parmeter, trustees.

Religious Societies.—A united religious society was formed in Potsdam, September 16, 1806, with Wm. Bullard, Jonathan Adams, Ammi Currier, Reuben Field, Manasseh Smith and Alba Durgee, trustees. This was the Union mentioned in our foregoing pages.

St. Paul's church society was formed August 14, 1811, with Liberty Knowles, Joseph P. Reynolds, and Azel Lyman, trustees. Exceptions having been taken at the name, it was, Dec. 16, 1820, changed to the first Presbyterian society in Potsdam, with A. Lyman, Sewall Raymond and Forest Morgan, trustees. A church organization was effected June 9, 1811, by about 20 members, who were united by the Rev. William Wright, and Rev James Johnson, the latter of whom became their first pastor, and was installed March 10, 1812. The council that performed this duty, were the Rev. Messrs. A. Pettengill, of Champlain; A. Parmelee, of Malone; E. Wright, of Russell; J. Winchester, of Madrid, and Amasa Blanchard and Salmon Gray, delegates; the former from Hopkinton, and the latter from Madrid. Ora P. Hoyt was ordained Jan. 18, 1826; F. E. Cannon, Sept. 7, 1831. He was succeeded by B. B. Hotchkin, and the latter by Elijah W. Plumb, the present pastor. Up to the close of 1826, 199 had joined the church. In 1846, 317 had united. The present edifice represented on our engraving, between the two academic buildings, was built in 1820, at a cost of $4,500, and dedicated Feb., 1822. In 1820, and in the fall and winter of 1826-7, were periods of unusual religious interest, and the number of members was largely increased.

The Christian sect, in the autumn of 1815, through the labors of Bela Palmer, for a church in the neighborhood of the Union. It numbered

J.J. Harrison, Sc. London.   Holy Trinity Church, Finsham, St Lancaster, &c.

from 30 to 40 members, most of whom had belonged to that community. Eld. Ira Allen commenced preaching here in 1819, and has since had the pastoral charge of the church with only two years interval. In all 177 have united, of whom 45 have died, which, with other causes, have reduced the numbers to 78.

A Baptist church was organized Jan. 9, 1824, of 6 males and 6 females, delegates being present from the churches in Hopkinton, Madrid, Stockholm, Canton and Parishville. The following have been employed as pastors: Rev. Messrs. —— Palmer, Silas Pratt, —— Bacheldor, Henry Green, Wm. H. Rice, I. Ide; some of them at several successive times. The present number of the church (Oct., 1852), is 58, and 150 have been received from the first. No society has been incorporated.

A Universalist society was incorporated October 2, 1825, with James Whitcomb, Asher Brown and Steward Banister, trustees. It had been formed on the 17th of Jan. previous, but this soon lost its organization, which was again effected Jan. 6, 1825. The early efforts failed to secure the means for building a church, until 1832, the meeting being previously held in the old academy. A committee was then appointed, who in 1835-6 erected the present church edifice. Rev. Jonathan Wallace, Rev. Wm. H. Waggoner and Rev. Jonathan Douglass, have been successively employed as clergymen. A church organization was effected January 17, 1852, of 24 members, and the present number (October, 1852), is 33.

A Methodist society was formed Feb. 4, 1833, with John Lockwood, Gersham Conger, Jonathan Paul, George Wright and John Byington, trustees. It was reorganized January 4, 1836. A Methodist society was formed in West Potsdam, June 1, 1846, with John Wellwood, Erastus Robbins and Wm. S. Horr, trustees.

Trinity church, Potsdam, was organized on the 23d, and incorporated on the 25th, of March, 1835, with John C. Clarkson and Augustus L. Clarkson, wardens; David L. Clarkson, Zenas Clark, Theodore Clark, Myron G. Munson, Noble S. Elderkin, Samuel Partridge, Frederick Miller, Jr. and Aaron T. Hopkins, vestrymen. Rev. Richard Bury, appears from the records of the vestry, to have been employed as a clergyman previously, and to have signed the records of the first meeting. He was employed on the 16th.of October, 1834. The elegant church edifice on the island in the village of Potsdam, represented on the opposite page, was erected in 1835, and consecrated on the 7th of August, 1836. In September, 1839, the Rev. Albin R. Putnam was employed as rector of the church. Having received a call to the rectorship of Immanuel church, of Bellows Falls, Vt., he resigned on the 20th of February, 1844, and was, on the 29th of April following, succeeded by the Rev. Nathan Watson Monroe, who resigned Aug. 10, 1846. The Rev. J. G. Hubbard was elected rector of the church, April 18, 1847, who held this office till February, 1851, when he resigned. The Rev. Kendrick Metcalf, D. D., was elected on the 29th of September, 1851. He had been previously employed as a professor of Greek and Latin, in Geneva College; and on the change of name and fuller endowment of that institution, in the early part of 1852, he resigned, and returned to that institution. He was immediately succeeded by the Rev. William Staunton, from Ridgefield, Ct., the present rector.

In the corner stone of the church edifice, was deposited the following inscription : " This church is erected to the worship and service of Almighty God, by the name of Trinity church, Potsdam, St. Lawrence county, state of New York, Anno Domini, 1835. Rt. Rev. Benjamin Onderdonk, bishop of the Diocese. Richard Bury, rector; John C. Clarkson, Augustus L. Clarkson, wardens; David L. Clarkson, Theodore

28

Clark, Zenas Clark, Aaron T. Hopkins, Samuel Partridge, Frederick Miller, Jun., Myron G. Munson, Noble S. Elderkin, vestrymen. Names of the building committee, John C. Clarkson, Augustus L. Clarkson, David C. Clarkson, Zenas Clark, Samuel Partridge, Theodore Clark. Master builders, Alanson Fisher, Jedidiah Reynolds."

There were also deposited in the box, one Bible, one Common Prayer Book, one copy of The Spiritual Character of the Liturgy, sundry tracts, religious periodicals, papers of the day, and coins. The ceremony of laying the corner stone, was performed on the 3d of June, 1835.

The Congregational church of West Potsdam was incorporated, July 8, 1842, with David Barnum, Bashin Heminway and Henry Dayton, trustees.

A Free-Will Baptist church was formed at West Potsdam, July 4, 1841, by Eld. D. F. Willis, of 30 members. Pastors; Elder Willis, in 1841-2, since then Elder William Whitfield has been, and still is their pastor. Present number 49. This church erected a house of worship in connection with the Methodist Episcopal society, in 1842, at the cost of about $600. It was dedicated, 2d Oct., 1842. Sermon by Eld. Moores Cole. The society was incorporated, June 29, 1843, with G. S. Hathaway, Horace Hathaway, and B. Lane, trustees.

There is a small congregation in Potsdam, calling itself the Catholic Apostolic church, which is one of a body of churches bearing that name now existing in England, Germany, and other parts of Europe, as well as in North America. It was gathered in the spring and summer of 1837, by the preaching of two Evangelists, who came from England to Canada, the year before, and were invited to Potsdam by some persons who had heard of their mission. As it is, with a single exception, the only one of the kind in the United States, the following account of the origin, government, faith, and worship of the body of which it forms a part, is given on the authority of one of its ministers.

"In the year 1830, remarkable spiritual manifestations began to appear in different parts of the church, at first in Scotland, and afterwards in England, under the form of prophesyings, speaking in tongues, healings &c. Many in those countries believed them to be true gifts of the Holy Ghost, as in the beginning, revived again to prepare the church for the coming of her Lord; and some ministers (amongst whom Mr. Irving of the Scotch Presbyterian church in London, stood foremost) gave liberty for their exercise in their congregations. This continued for a year or two, during which, the spiritual utterances were most abundant, throwing light upon the scriptures, and searching and cleansing the hearts of hearers, when a new form was given to the work by the naming of men to the office of Apostle, by the Holy Ghost, speaking, as was believed, through Prophets. The number was gradually increased until, after several years, the Apostolic college was completed, and stood twelvefold, as at the first. Under their rule, guided by the light of prophecy at a living ministry in the church, the work has gone forward, and been developing itself more and more to the present time. Churches have been set up in several of the countries of Europe, in Canada, and in the United States; and a well defined system of order and worship has been established, of which the following are the principal features. There is a fourfold ministry of Apostle, Prophet, Evangelist, and Pastor, by the conjoined working of all of whom in their several places the building up and perfecting of the church is to be accomplished. The Apostles, the peculiarity of whose office is, that they are sent immediately by the Lord, without the intervention of man, have the rule and guidance of all the churches; and are, under Christ, the heads of the whole body of the baptized. They have authority to ordain; they confer the gifts of the Holy Ghost by the laying on of their hands; and they serve as bands of unity, by the general oversight which they exercise over all the ministers and their flocks, in all matters of worship, doctrine, and discipline. Prophets are the channels through which the supernatural light of prophecy is given by the inspiration of the Holy Ghost; Evangelists have it for their special work to carry forth the gospel; and Pastors are entrusted with the care of souls in all the congregations that are gathered.

Each fully organized church is under the rule of an angel (a chief Pastor, or Bishop), assisted by Elders and Deacons; and there are also Under Deacons and Deaconesses, as the necessities of the people may require. All who are of the Priesthood, are called to their office by the voice of prophecy, and ordained by Apostles, (or those delegated by them for that purpose); but the Deacons are chosen by the people, to whom they act as counsellors in temporal matters, while they can also be used as Evangelists. In such churches, there is daily worship, at six in the morning and at five in the evening, with additional shorter services at nine and at three; and the Eucharist is celebrated every Sunday, and the Communion also administered every day at the close of the morning worship. Forms of prayer are used, embracing the most valuable parts of the existing rituals of the church, with such changes and additions as have been thought necessary to free them from error, to adopt the services to the present wants of Christendom, and to bring the worship of God into the highest form which the circumstances of the time allow. Vestments are worn by the ministers in fulfilling their public offices. As to their faith, it is that of the Church Catholic in all ages, as embodied in the three great creeds, commonly called the Apostles', the Nicene, and the Athanasian, all of which are used in their worship. The doctrine of the Holy Trinity, the apostacy of man, the Incarnation of the Son of God, the atonement for sin through His sufferings and death, the office of the Holy Ghost to regenerate and sanctify, and the eternal retributions of the judgment, are held by them as fundamental truths of Revelation. They expect the speedy coming of the Lord to establish his kingdom upon the earth, and to rule over it with his saints, risen and translated; at which time they also believe that God will fulfil His promises to the Jews, gather them to their own land, and make them a blessing to all nations. They look upon the church as embracing all the baptized, in all their divisions; and as being a divine institution, with ministries, sacraments, and ordinances appointed by the Lord himself. They recognize all Christian men as brethren, members with them of the one body of Christ, which however, they believe to be in a state of dismemberment and schism, and full of error and pollution, through the sins of many generations. They are distinguished from others only in being the first gathered under Apostles, whose work they believe to be to present the bride of Christ to Him at His coming, holy and undefiled. They look upon themselves, as standing in no other attitude to any part of the church, than that of brethren, to whom the returning grace of God has been first vouchsafed, and that only that they may be witnesses to all that His kingdom is at hand, and that He is visiting His people now at the end of the dispensation, to bring them back to His ways, and to adorn them with all the gifts of His spirit, they take no other name, therefore, than that which belongs to the whole church—Holy Catholic and Apostolic—as that which expresses its true standing before God, and which should never have been laid aside by any. In the congregation in Potsdam, which has never yet received the full organization of a church, and is only under the care of a Pastor and Deacons, there are regular services, sometimes daily, and sometimes only on Wednesdays and Fridays, of the week days; and the Lord's supper is administered every Sunday. There are between fifty and sixty communicants, amongst whom there have been some spiritual manifestations in the form of prophetic utterances."

Rossie

Was erected from Russell, Jan. 21, 1813. The following memorandum in relation to the organization of this town occurs on the records of the town of Russell:

"At a special meeting of the freeholders and other inhabitants of the town of Russell, assembled on Tuesday, the first day of January, 1811, at the dwelling house of Moses A. Bunnel, in said Russell, *voted*, To grant the request of Benjamin Pike, in behalf of the inhabitants living on that part of Russell called Somerville, that they be set off from Russell and annexed to the town of Gouverneur."

As originally formed, it embraced townships 1, 2 and 7, or Hammond, Somerville, and Kilkenny, of tract No. 3. Fowler and Hammond have since been taken off, and the line between Rossie and Hammond was altered Feb. 7, 1844. The town derives its name from Rossie castle in Scotland, which was owned by the husband of David Parish's sister. Her name was *Rossie*, but she usually bore the name of *Rosa*.

The first town meeting was directed to be held at the house of Reuben Streeter, but the day having passed the legislature appointed another, and the first town election was held in the block house, then the residence of Mr. S.

Supervisors.—1814, Reuben Streeter; 1815, Theodosius O. Fowler; 1816–18, Reuben Streeter; 1819, Ebenezer Marvin; 1820, Roswell Ryon; 1821, Reuben Streeter; 1822–4, Lewis Franklin; 1825, Ebenezer Marvin; 1826–7, James Howard; 1828, William Brown; 1829, Reuben Streeter; 1830–2, S. Pratt; 1833–4, William Skinner; 1835, S. Pratt; 1836–8, Robert Clark; 1839–40, Martin Thatcher; 1841, Sylvenus Barker; 1842, Martin Thatcher; 1843–4, Wm. B. Bostwick; 1845–6, S. Pratt; 1847–8, Henry V. R. Willmot; 1849, Zaccheus Gates; 1850, Adam Turnbull; 1851–2, Zaccheus Gates. Mr. Gates died in April, 1852, and S. Pratt was elected in his place.

The first school districts were organized March 30, 1815, when No. 1 embraced the present town of Fowler; No. 2, all Rossie southeast of Indian river; and No. 3, between Indian and St. Lawrence rivers. The town is very unpleasantly situated for the transaction of its business, in being so divided by the Oswegatchie and Yellow lake, that no communication can be had without going out of the town and county. In 1817–18–19–21, and 22, a wolf bounty of $5 offered. In 1828, the town voted in favor of Potsdam as a county seat. In 1844, voted unanimously in favor of a new county from parts of St. Lawrence, Jefferson and Lewis.

The earliest settlement in this town was commenced in 1807, by Joseph Teall, of Fairfield, and Reuben Streeter, of Salisbury, Herkimer county, who had contracted of Lewis R. Morris, the nephew of Gouverneur Morris, a tract lying between the Oswegatchie and the south line of Gouverneur extended to the county line. Mr. David Parish, Dec. 2, 1808, purchased the town (26,804 acres), the money going to G. Morris and J. D. Le Ray, with whom was the title previously. The land records at Ogdensburgh show the following purchases under date of October 1, 1806, at which time these men came into town and selected lands. They were mostly from Herkimer county. Ambrose Simons, Oliver Malterner, Amos Keeney, Jr., Samuel Bonfy, Silvius Waters, Joshua Stearns, Jerom Waldo, George W. Pike, Benjamin Pike, Jr., Ebenezer Bemis, David Shepard. The first improvement was made by Reuben Streeter, in 1807, on a farm about half a mile east of the present village of Wegatchie. In 1808, he commenced the erection of a mill on the Oswegatchie, and in the spring of 1811, the following families were living on the Teall and Streeter tract, besides those already named: David Freeman, James Streeter, Joseph Teall, Diamond Wheeler, Eli Winchell, Simeon Stevens, John and Wheaton Wilcox, and Daniel Wilcox, (single.) The first school in town was taught about a mile west of Somerville, by a Mr. Maynard. The following additional names of families appear on the first assessment roll, some of whom resided in the portions now Fowler and Hammond: Lemuel Arnold, Jeduthan Baker, James Barnes, Horatio G. Berthrong, (first innkeeper at Rossie,) Samuel B. Brown, Truman Bristol, Joseph Desbrow, James Haile, Samuel Hendrix, Jedediah Kingsley, Alexander Osburne, Ebenezer Parker, Richard Townsend, Joseph Teall, Jr., Elias Teall, Alvin Wright. Total number of acres wild land 90,575; tax payers 37, (some of them non-reidents); cleared 499¼ acres; total value, $183,754; value of buildings in the three townships, $2,990.

On receiving news of the war, the inhabitants of the southern part of Rossie, erected a block house on the road between Somerville and Wegatchie, about half a mile from the latter place, for mutual protection. Thither the inhabitants were accustomed to repair to spend their nights, on occasions of public alarm, which were very frequent, and as often entirely groundless. The sight of an Indian, however innocent his intentions, was sufficient to originate an alarm which lost nothing by passing from mouth to mouth, and stories are related which reflect little credit upon the courage of certain ones of the settlers. This block house was well built, of hewn timber, 24 by 30 feet, and stood till about 1840. It was used only in 1812. A similar one was built of round logs, near a small stream a few rods northeast of the present village of Somerville. It was only occupied a few nights.

In the summer of 1812, the mills built by Mr. Streeter were burned in the night time, as it was reported, by the Indians. This is believed to have been done by a man who lived in the edge of Gouverneur near the Kearney bridge, and who wanted a pretext for quitting the country. He fled to New York, and was not pursued or apprehended.

The mill was immediately rebuilt by Mr. Parish, and owned by him until sold to Mr. James Howard about the year 1817. It was his wish to have the settlement at his mills called *Caledonia*, and this it has in some measure retained, although it has been since known as *Howard's Mills*, *Church's Mills*, and *Wegatchie*. The latter name was given it upon the establishment of a post office in 1849. It was intended at one time that Caledonia should be the name of the town.

The first settlement at Rossie iron works was commenced by men sent by Mr. D. Parish, late in the summer of 1810, to erect mills, and make arrangements for settling lands.*

The stone store at Ogdensburgh being enclosed and nearly finished, Mr. D. W. Church, who had superintended its erection, with seven men, one of whom was accompanied by his wife to cook for the party, proceeded in a Canadian bateaux, with shanty furniture and tools, to the head of navigation on Indian river, and landed at sunset on a fine flat ock, on an island near where the foundry now is, and spreading their sail upon poles for a tent for the married pair, and their blankets on the rocks under the canopy of heaven, around a fire, for themselves, they spent the first night. The following evening saw a commodious hut with two rooms erected, near where the saw mill now is, and by winter a saw mill was erected and in operation. In December, the camp was broken up and abandoned till spring. During the winter, parties were engaged in getting out timber, which subsequently was employed in buildings then erecting at Ogdensburgh, and in the frame of the Genesee Packet, built soon after at that port.

During the summer of 1811, the lumber business was prosecuted with vigor, and in the following winter the bridge at the foot of the Big hill was built. The furnace was commenced in the summer of 1813, under the immediate direction of Mr. James Howard, and from this period the settlement exhibited much life and spirit under the enterprising direction of Mr. Parish, its proprietor. A road through to Ox Bow, had been run out in the fall of 1810, and was cut and cleared the following summer. It was subsequently made a turnpike under the name of the Ogdensburgh turnpike. The first male child said to have been born in town, was Wm. Rossie Williams, March 31, 1814.

Rossie furnace, was the first blast furnace erected in Northern New York, and is at this time by much the largest. It was built in the summer of 1813, and got in operation in 1815. The Caledonia iron mine, one mile and a half east of Somerville, began to be wrought at about the same time or the year before. The ore was first sent to Albany for trial. When first erected, the furnace consisted of two stacks, but only one of these was ever got in operation. They were about thirty-two feet square at the base, and of the same height.

The agent employed by Mr. Parish to build and run this furnace, was Wm. Bembo, an Englishman of great experience in this business, but unacquainted with the ores and fuel used in this country. The result was, that no iron could be made, and after spending large sums in experimenting, and in building a costly mansion for permanent residence, he abandoned the attempt in discouragement, and returned to England. At this juncture, Mr. Parish met with parties from New England, who *guessed* that the thing could be done, and he accordingly offered to Messrs. Keith, Marvin and Sykes, the free use of the furnace and coal, with the privilege of culling the best of the ore on the premises, and all they could make in three months, if they would make a trial. The result was that these men realized a large profit, and not the least difficulty was found in getting iron of a good quality and in the greatest abundance. From this time the furnace was run by S. Fullers & Co., for about three years, on a contract which was to have run five years, but Mr. George Parish having an opportunity of leasing it for a long term, bought the

* The early settlers found traces which indicate that the English or French had at some time contemplated the erection of some station at Rossie. It being at the head of a navigation of 27 miles towards Fort Stanwix, rendered it important. A Durham boat laden with stone, was found sunk in the river, with every appearance of having been a long time submerged, and an excavation apparently for a cellar existed where the stone store at Rossie now stands.

contract and leased to Robert R. Burr, of New Jersey, who run it two or three years, and left about 1827. It then lay idle about ten years. A forge was erected in 1816, which was subsequently burned. The first furnace was what is technically called a *quarter furnace*, with one tewel or pipe for air. During some considerable portion of the time, before 1826, bog ore was in part used. The principal supply has been derived from the Caledonia mine in Rossie, the Keene and Wicks mines in Antwerp, and a small opening adjoining the Kearney mine.

This furnace has been several times burnt and rebuilt. On the 12th of May, 1837, it was again got in operation by Mr. Parish, and has since been run by his agents with short intervals. A stack 32 feet square and 46 feet high was built in 1837, and stood till about 1844, when the present one was erected. It is 40 feet square, 46 feet high, 9 feet diameter within, and capable of making 11 tons a day with a hot blast. It is technically called a three quarter furnace, and has three tewels or air pipes. Since 1838 the hot blast has been used most of the time, the apparatus of which was put in by Mr. Alger, the patentee, in 1838.

From 110 to 120 bushels of charcoal are required to make a ton of iron with the hot blast, and 200 with the cold blast. Fire brick are used for lining. Formerly sandstone was employed for this purpose. The former is found to be much more durable. The following table derived from the books of Mr. D. W. Baldwin, the agent, will exhibit, to those acquainted with the iron trade an accurate idea of the operations of the furnace, and the average yield of the iron ores of Northern New York, from which a comparison can be drawn with the results of other furnaces and different ores. The table exhibits the number of tons and pounds of ore consumed, the tons and pounds of pig iron made, and the percentage of yield of each blast since 1837.

ORE.		IRON.			ORE.		IRON.		
tons.	lbs.	tons.	lbs.	per cent.	tons.	lbs.	tons.	lbs.	per cent.
1088	708	490	367	45·04	618	810	275	1125	44·56
666	825	382	556	57·36	3580	990	1698	1297	47·44
1328	992	746	136	56.16	1782	1725	908	1570	50·97
1251	1048	741	1222	59·25	1310	815	608	365	46.41
1580	1998	847	1747	53·62	3630	11	1687	485	46·48
1245	354	758	827	60·90	5297	231	2568	892	48·48
2078	717	1113	568	53·56	5398	1700	2724	1794	56·05
574	708	289	1560	50·45	1706	1950	851	1667	49·88
1281	162	616	769	50·06					

All of the above blasts, except the last, were made with heated air.

The iron mines in this town, situated a mile and a quarter east of the village of Somerville, began to be wrought in the fall of 1812, and have been continued with more or less interruption till the present time. The amount is inexhaustible, and the yield in the large way about 50 per cent. It is raised by laborers of little or no capital, at a stipulated price per ton, including the cost of draining and raising. The first ore that was taken to the Rossie furnace was not sorted, and a large amount of red stone was carried for smelting, which was one of the principal causes of the first failures in getting iron. Afterwards a large quantity of middling quality was thrown away, and none but the best was taken. From $1 to $3 has been paid per ton for drawing ore, 13 miles, to the furnace, and this business, done mostly in winter by sleighs, has enabled great numbers to pay for lands with their surplus labor. The Caledonia

mine belonging to the Parish estate, and the one that has been principally wrought, is estimated to have furnished 100,000 tons of ore.

The geological and mineralogical associations of this mine will be
found detailed in the chapter on these subjects.

The mills represented in the accompanying view of Rossie iron works,
were erected in 1845-6, and the large foundry on the opposite side of
the falls in 1848-9. This with the machine shop (not represented in the
engraving), are capable of producing every variety of castings, and machinery on the most extensive scale. The facilities of a plank road from
Watertown and Rome to the St. Lawrence river, has made this point accessible to market, and it can not fail to participate in the future prosperity of this section of the state. A large amount of rail road castings
have been made here, and the property of chilling which this iron possesses to a high degree when made with a blast of cold air, renders it
peculiarly well adapted for those purposes which require *hardness*, combined with *strength*. This property belongs in common to all the iron
made by the cold blast from the specular ores of Northern New York.
Rossie is nine miles from Chippewa bay, a port in Hammond, and most
of the distance over a plank road. It is from nine to thirteen miles from
the mines which supply it with ore, and from one to ten miles from forests which will for a long period furnish abundance of coal.

In Spafford's Gazetteer (1813), the following reference is made to this
place:

"Black lake seems a mere expansion of Indian river, which it receives
at the foot of a fine cascade, where is laid out the village plat named
Rosa, and some mills are here erected."

That portion of the town of Rossie, lying between the Oswegatchie
and the Indian rivers, is usually denominated the Scotch settlement,
from the fact that nearly every inhabitant within these limits is of Scotch
descent. The first of this settlement was begun in 1818, by ten families,
who emigrated from Scotland in that year, by way of Quebec and the St.
Lawrence river, viz:

Robert Ormiston, James Dickson, William Fachney, James Fairbairn,
Corlan McLaren, Donald McCarrie, Thomas Elliot, James Henderson,
James Douglas and Andrew Dodds. Their destination was uncertain; a
portion designed locating in Delaware county, but as they were proceeding up the river in a Durham boat, they stopped a short time at Prescot,
where they were visited by an agent of David Parish, and induced to
cross to Ogdensburgh, with their families. The latter were liberally provided for in the village, while the men went to view the lands then nearly
surveyed in Rossie. It is said that they passed up through the valleys and
across the richest portions, and that the existence of hills and ledges of
rock was not known until after they had located their farms, and commenced clearings. To assist the emigrants on first starting, Mr. Parish
caused 10 acres to be cleared for each, supplied each family with a cow,
seed, wheat and provisions for the first year, besides building a comfortable log house on each farm, and furnishing an ox team to every two of
his settlers. For these they were to pay, when they had got fairly settled
and were in a condition to earn something from their farms, but prices
were then very high, and the debt ran up faster than, with the means of
payment at the depreciated prices which followed, they could cancel.
The settlement was increased the following year by new emigrants from
Scotland, but to these the facilities extended to the first were not offered.
Meanwhile some of the former became disheartened by the burden of
debts which constantly increased, and some thought of giving up their

Rossie Iron Works. Rossie, St. Lawrence Co., N. Y.

location and beginning anew elsewhere. To avoid this and to place them in a condition more favorable and equal, Mr. Parish assembled these inhabitants at Rossie village, in the winter of 1823-4, and after ascertaining the indebtedness of each, reduced the whole to a common level, by canceling all above $500. This measure met with general approbation, and his tenants returned home with renewed courage. With but few exceptions the same families or their immediate descendants, still occupy the same farms that were then selected, and may be counted among the more thrifty, successful and industrious farmers in town. In 1819 the following families settled: Robert Clark, Andrew Culbertson, John Henderson, Andrew Flemming, John Dodds, James Hobkirk, John Tait, James Ormiston, David Storie, Wm. Laidlaw and James Lockey.

In 1820, John McRobbie, Thomas Turnbull and brothers, Michael, Adam, Andrew and William, and Scotch settlers continued to arrive occasionally until 1832. Roads had been made through the central part of the town before these Scotch emigrants arrived, and small beginnings made in one or two places.

Yellow lake derives its name from the circumstances of its being coverd with the blossoms of the nuphar or pond lily, when first noticed.

The village of *Somerville*, is situated upon the plank road between Antwerp and Gouverneur, six miles from the latter and seven from the former place. It derives its name from the township as given by surveyor General Dewitt, long before its settlement. Being without natural facilities it has remained but the centre of a fine agricultural district, and at present contains about a dozen dwellings and the usual variety of mechanic shops. The Universalist and Methodist societies have each a church which will compare favorably with those of any place in the county, in which the population and number of members are not greater. They were both erected in the summer of 1846. Perhaps no place in Northern New York, presents more inducements to the visit of the mineralogist than the country within fifteen miles of Somerville.

On the Oswegatchie river, two and a half miles from Somerville, is the little village of Wegatchie, containing a post office, a furnace, woolen factory, grist mill, saw mill, and about 20 dwellings. The furnace was begun in 1847, and got in operation in the spring of 1848, by Skinner and Blish. Up to the spring of 1852, it had made about 2000 tons of iron at two hot and one cold blasts. It is 30 feet square, 36 feet high, and has two tewels. It is capable of making four and five tons daily. No castings are made on the premises.

The celebrity which has been given to Rossie by its lead mines, will give interest to their history.

The Indians of St. Regis have a tradition that their ancestors knew of the existence of lead not far from the present mines, but the precise locality is not known. It was not where the workings at present exist, because it was said to be near a small stream. The natives were accustomed to smelt the lead in a small way by casting the ore upon a fire kindled upon a bark or piece of wood, and pouring the metal when melted into a groove in sand. The bar was then cut into small pieces and rolled into balls between flat stones. Many years before the mines were discovered, a quantity of pure galena was found on the bank of the Oswegatchie, in the village of Ogdensburgh, evidently a *caché* of some Indian, and the traditions of lead mines in the woods was common with the early proprietors. It is said that lead was first found at Rossie, among the ashes of a log heap, but its precise locality was not then known.

Arthur Bacon, of Rossie, is reported to have discovered masses of galena among the earth at the roots of an up turned tree, some time before particular attention was directed to the subject. This was at Coal hill, (so called from its being a *coal job* or place for making charcoal). The Victoria vein, so called, was subsequently discovered by a daughter of Joel Jepson. On the return of Mr. George Parish from Europe, in September, 1835, he learned that B. T. Nash proposed to search for ores, and on the 11th of December of that year, a contract was executed between him and Nash, with the following conditions:

A tribute of 50 cents per ton was to be paid for iron ore, and 75 cents per ton for lead ore, should mines of either be found. All the lead ore to be smelted into lead *in Rossie*, and no ore to be sent away for manufacture. The lease was to continue ten years from date.

Previous to the drawing of this contract, a company consisting of five persons, viz: B, T. Nash, Joseph Barber, Zadoc Day, Joseph Disbrow and ————, all of the town of Oswegatchie, had been formed for the purposes of mineral exploration, and Indian traditions had led them to the Rossie district, where indications of ore if not the mine itself, were discovered before the lease from Mr. Parish had been procured. The articles of agreement between the individuals of the company were drawn up in due form, signed and sealed. Mr. Nash soon after sold the right to J.C. Bush. The remainder applied for redress, and they or those to whom they sold their chances afterwards, compromised the matter, and two companies were incorporated by the legislature on the 12th of May, 1837, for the working of the lead mines.

The charters of these two companies were alike in date, limitation, powers and privileges. They were to continue till January 1, 1847; capital of each, $24,000, to be divided into 960 shares, of $25 each. The business of each company was to be managed by five directors, of whom the first were to be those named in the act, and these were to be chosen on the first Monday in Feb. annually. They were to choose a president annually. Stock was deemed personal property, and stockholders were made personally liable for the company's debts. The company holding the eastern division of the Coal hill vein, was styled *The Rossie Lead Mining Company*, and David C. Judson, James Averill, Erastus Vilas, Peter C. Oakley and Roylas Vilas were named its first directors.

The western 80 rods of the same vein was held by *The Rossie Galena Company*, of which John C. Bush, Bliss T. Narsh, Elias G. Drake, Sylvester Gilbert and David C. Judson, were named the first directors.

The vein upon which these two companies commenced their operations, was in a ridge of gneiss rock, about two miles southeast from Rossie iron works, and one from Indian river. The relative position of the several veins and the bearings of each are represented in the accompanying map. The appearance of the Rossie lead mines soon after they were first opened, is thus described by Prof. L. C. Beck, who visited the locality in the summer of 1836, as state mineralogist.[*]

" Following the road from the village of Rossie, at no great distance from the bank of Indian river, after passing through a dense forest, there appeared towards the west a precipitous ledge of rocks about fifty feet high. My attention being particularly directed to this hill, I observed a white deposite contrasting with the dark color of the rock, passing down perpendicularly or very nearly so, from the summit to the base. The part of the vein thus distinctly and beautifully exposed, was ascertained by measurement to be fifty feet, while its average width was two feet. Upon a more close inspection, the vein, before its sinking below the alluvium, was found to incline slightly towards the north, and the whitish

___

[*] See First Annual Report of New York Geological Survey, p. 64, 65.

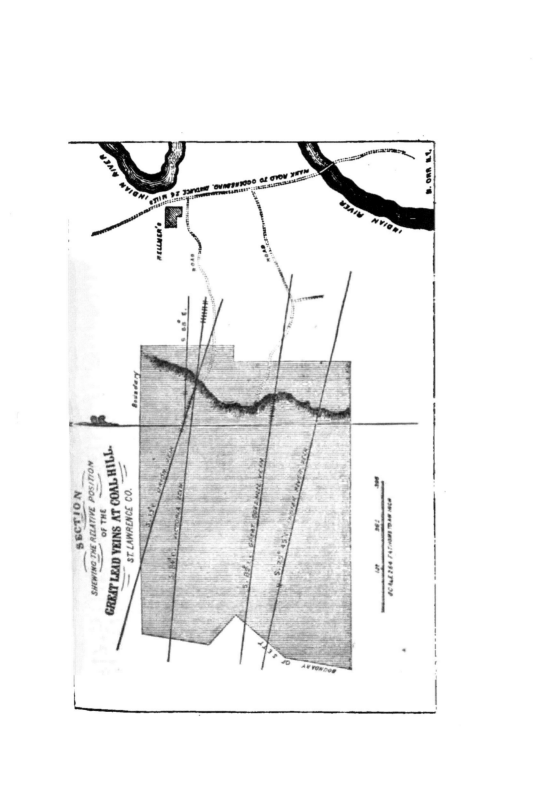

SECTION
SHEWING THE RELATIVE POSITION
OF THE
GREAT LEAD VEINS AT COAL HILL.
ST LAWRENCE CO.

INDIAN RIVER

INDIAN RIVER

MAIN ROAD TO OGDENSBURG. DISTANCE 26 MILES

B. ORR. ESQ.

MILLNER'S

ROAD

ROAD

Boundary

BOUNDARY OF B.ORR

COMPARATIVE VIEWS OF THE CLIFF COPPER MINE OF LAKE SUPERIOR AND THE COAL HILL LEAD MINE OF ROSSIE.

SECTION OF WORKINGS AT THE CLIFF MINE, LAKE SUPERIOR.

PRODUCT OF WHOLE EXCAVATION, $284,884·93
NUMBER OF FATHOMS EXCAVATED, 2,413
YIELD PER CUBIC FATHOM, - $118

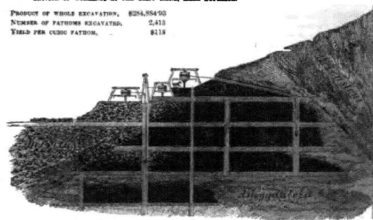

SCALE OF FEET.

SECTION OF WORKINGS AT COAL HILL, ST. LAWRENCE CO., N. Y.

PRODUCT OF WHOLE EXCAVATION, $241,000
NUMBER OF FATHOMS EXCAVATED, 1,396
YIELD PER CUBIC FATHOM, - $172

SCALE OF FEET.

appearance was found to be due to the salts of lead formed by the decomposition of the galena. On ascending the ledge of rocks, the course and extent of the vein could be easily determined by the excavations that had been made, and by the appearance of the surface at those parts where it had not been opened. It was exposed at that time to the extent of 450 feet, and every part of it seemed to be so distinctly characterized, as to excite surprise, that it had not long since been discovered."

From an examination made at the time, it was inferred that the ore contained no silver, or at least that the quantity was too small to denote its presence by the tests employed, and of no importance practically. The lead ashes were found by analysis to consist of the carbonate and sulphate of lead and the carbonate of lime, in variable proportions, formed by the action of the atmosphere.

Workings on the western section commenced in 1836, but systematic operations were not begun until Jan. 1, 1837, at which time the eastern company also commenced operations. An immense number of laborers were employed, and the business for a considerable time went on prosperously from the immense yield of lead, notwithstanding the entire inexperience of managers and miners, and the enormous expenditures for the erection of smelting houses and machinery, which were afterwards found to be inefficient. Wages to laborers, and prices for provisions were very high, and the whole operation was conducted without regard to economy; but with all these drawbacks, the companies divided large dividends, stock arose to extravagant prices, and people's heads seemed to be bewildered with the dazzling prospect of wealth which several persons suddenly realized. It has been estimated by one who was intimately acquainted with the operations, that $16,000 were paid for smelting works not used; $8,000 for experiments; $12,600 for an extra set of managers 3½ years, where one would have been better; $6,500 for drawing stone to the smelting house, which should have been separated at the mine; on contracts at excessive rates, $30,000, making $97,600, which might have been saved. The economical method of mining, is to sink vertical shafts at intervals of three or four hundred feet along the vein, and at every ten fathoms run levels as is represented in our section of the Cliff copper mine. The ore is then thrown *down* by blasting from above the levels, by a process called *stoping*, and the ore is then wheeled to the shafts and raised. Instead of this at the Rossie mines, the workings were mostly from above downwards. The amount of water at the worst season, was about 120 gallons per minute, but the machinery employed for raising this, from its being inefficient, was a constant source of expense for repairs, and the workings were, from this cause, often suspended. The ore was principally smelted by Messrs. Moss & Knapp, at a furnace on Indian river, 1¼ miles from the mines, at $25 per ton, with a clause in the contract giving them all over 68 per cent., which made it $28·16, besides drawing the mineral from the mines. A reverberatory furnace was erected at the mines, but this was found to waste more lead than it yielded. The Victoria and Union veins were wrought by Mr. Parish, and their yield is represented on the pages of the sections.

A working was commenced by him on the Robinson or Indian river vein, where ore was found on the surface, and about 300 pounds of lead were taken out directly over a cavity in the granite, which, on blasting to the solid vein proved to be 15 feet deep. A shaft 9 by 11, and 76 feet deep, was sunk here, which yielded 1,100 pounds of lead. No vein in the last 8 or 10 feet. Cost $1,600. In the branch of the Union vein, two shafts were sunk, the western, 55, the eastern, 50 feet deep. Both produced, and still show, some lead.

The following statement of yield, was drawn up by Mr. Charles L. Lum, who kept the books of Moss & Knapp, and had accurate means for knowing the product of their furnace. The numbers show the pounds of lead smelted in each month, for the two sections of the Coal hill mine.

Western Section.		Eastern Section.	
1837	1838	1837	1838
To J. 1, 110,434	(Slags,) 7,412	Jan.. 3, 60,690	Jan., 29,915
" 50,901	Jan., 110,292	Feb. 2 }	Feb., 38,222
F. &. M. 68,880	Feb., 48,613	Mar., } 80,872	Mar., 52.864
(Slags), 8,382	Mar., 68,954	Apr., } 121,888	(Slags) 5,285
Apr., 39,214	Apr., 34,609	May, }	Apr., 54,963
May, 25,836	May, 80,534	June, 60.714	May, 49,460
June, 90,298	June, 67.892	July, 45,071	June, 35,641
July, 76,113	July, 90,486	Aug., 60,802	July, 40,664
Aug., 73,749	Aug.. 111,349	Sept, 43.965	Aug., 51,921
Sept., 118,058	(Slags) 6,503	Oct., 83,753	Sept., 44,422
Oct., 188,788	Sept. 111,271	Nov. 16,927	Oct.
Nov., 54,842	Oct., 67,575	Dec., 20,996	Nov., &
Dec.. 101,211	Nov., 32,892		afterwards, 405,559
Total yield,	1,845,088	Total yield,	1,405,683

Making in all 3,250,690 lbs. or 1625 tons of metalic lead, the average yield of the ore, being 67 per cent, or 10½ tons per fathom.* The ore is associated with beautiful white calcareous spar, free from any mineral in intimate combination with it, which renders it very easy for dressing, and the smelting of it in the large way has been found not to exceed three dollars per ton of metalic lead. It is so favorable for smelting that it can be reduced for three dollars per ton of metal, which, when suitably dressed, yields seventy per cent of lead.

Both of these companies discontinued working about 1840, and numbers lost large sums from the depreciation of stock and loss from various causes, among which was the low price of lead in market.

An incident occurred during the earlier workings of the mines, that well nigh resulted in blood-shed. During the spring of 1837, nearly five hundred Irish laborers were employed in and about the mines, who may be supposed to have been actuated by the peculiar prejudices common to the lower classes of that people. On the evening preceding "St. Patrick's day in the morning," some mischievous persons had suspended by the neck, an effigy in Irish costume, before a house occupied by laborers as a boarding house, and affixed a label "St. Patrick," and a wish that this might be the fate of every Irishman. This had its natural effect, and the indignation towards the authors of this act knew no bounds. Those living near the place accused others from a neighboring locality of doing it, and mutual accusations led to threats of vengeance, and the whole crowd had armed themselves with such weapons as chanced to fall in their way, and were disuaded from acts of violence with the greatest difficulty, on the part of the overseers, who to appease them, offered large rewards for the offenders. Had the latter been discovered, nothing would have saved them from a violent death. This gave origin to a feud, which subsisted for a long time, and the laborers in the smelting house, in some way became obnoxious to the Irish, as

* Miners estimate by the *fathom* which is 6 feet in length and depth, without regard to thickness.

SECTION from GEOLOGICAL MAP of ST. LAWRENCE COUNTY.

Lyman Merriman, Alva Weeks, and Wm. Ayers, trustees. In 1846 they erected a church, which in the last census is reported worth $1,700.

The Methodist Episcopal church of Somerville, was incorporated Dec. 16, 1845, with Hiram Hall, Orin Freeman, John Johnson, Freedom Freeman, Augustus Preston, and A. C. Van Dycke, trustees. They erected in 1846, a chapel, reported in the census worth $1,500.

The Catholics several years since commenced a church at Rossie Iron Works, which was not enclosed.

RUSSELL,

Was formed by an act of March 27, 1807, embracing the whole of Great tract No. 3, except so much of township 3 as is now included in Pierrepont, which by this act was attached to Potsdam. The first town meeting was directed to be held at the house of Reuben Ashman.

By an act of April 10, 1818, the townships of Edwards and Fitz William (now Hermon and Edwards), were transferred from Russell to Fowler. The first town officers were: Russell Attwater, *supervisor;* Reuben Ashman, *clerk;* Ezra Moore, Jos. Hutchinson, Philip Viall, *assessors;* Calvin Hill, *constable and collector;* John Knox, Jos. Hutchinson, *overseers of the poor;* Sam'l Eaton, John Watson, John Knox, *commissioners highways;* John Watson, Thos. Gillmore, *fence viewers;* Azel Clark, Simeon Stiles, Elihu Morgan, Joel Clark, *overseers of highways.*

Supervisors.—1808-10, Russell Attwater; 1810, at special town meeting, R. Ashman; 1810-14, Reuben Ashman; 1815-18, Anthony C. Brown; 1819-21, Phinneas Attwater; 1822, R. Ashman; 1823-7, James Williams; 1828-33, Rollin Smith; 1834-8, Elihu Phelps; 1839-40, Holmes Nevin: 1841-2, R. Smith; 1843-6, Benjamin Smith; 1847, R. Smith; 1848, J. Williams; 1849-50, Nelson Doolittle; 1851-2, Rollin C. Jackson.

Notes.—1809, $250 raised for the poor, $250 for schools. 1810, $5 for wolf bounties, and $150 voted for this purpose; $250 raised for the poor, to be let on good security. 1811, same wolf tax and poor tax as 1810. Voted that the books sent to the town of Russell, by the Hampshire Missionary Society, be left in the care of Moses A. Bunnel, and to be returned to him within three months after taken away. Voted, that a sled shall be four feet wide. A fine of $2 for going on the public highway with a sled that is not four feet wide the present year. The same in 1812. $5 wolf bounty, $100 to pay these bounties; $250 for the poor; $1 penalty for allowing Canada thistles to grow and go to seed. 1813, $5 wolf bounty, payable out of the money previously raised for this purpose. 1814, $250 for the poor. 1815 to 1819, voted to raise three times the amount for schools that the town receives from the state. 1820, $5 bounty for wolves, payable from the money raised for this purpose in 1810, 1811 and 1812. In 1821, a committee of three appointed to examine and see if there is any money in town raised for the destruction of wolves in 1810, 1811 and 1812. *Resolved,* That such balance as may be found due, shall be collected and paid to the supervisor for the purpose of paying a bounty on noxious animals at the rate of $2-50 for each wolf, panther and bear, and $1 for each fox. In 1822 the money paid for bounties raised in 1810-12 to be paid in work on roads and bridges. 1823, voted to give up to Reuben Ashman $150, raised in 1810, for the destruction of wolves, on his securing the remainder. In 1832, voted that the territory called Scriba, and Bloomfield, be set off into a separate town, on condition that they will not call for any of the public funds of money now on hand, except road money. In 1838, remonstrated against the petition of the inhabitants of the town of Edwards, to have the townships Nos. 12 and 14, now belonging to this town, set off to the town of Edwards. In 1839, voted in favor of abolishing the poor house system, and agreed to unite in a petition to the legislature to that effect.

This town is named from Russell Attwater, and now embraces a part of Dewitt, the whole of Ballybeen, and the north half of Sarahsburgh. It was McCormick's wish that the town should bear the name of Ballybeen, after his native place in Ireland. Mr. Attwater had purchased of McCormick, in 1798, the north half of No. 5, a quarter of No. 6, a quarter of No. 14, of tract No. 2, and a quarter of No. 22 in Franklin county All but the half of No. 5, were subsequently reconveyed. This embraced about 13,600 acres, and was purchased at about forty cents per acre.

The town was first explored with the view of settlement by Mr. Russell Attwater, in the summer of 1804. In 1805, Timothy Blair, a surveyor from Blanford, (the former residence of Mr. A. and many of the first settlers), came on, and surveyed most of the town into farms. The party who came this year, arrived in the spring, and spent the whole summer in opening roads, surveying, and in clearing a field of about twelve acres, on a farm now owned by George L. Horsford. The company who spent the season of of 1805 in town, were mostly young men in the hire of Mr. Attwater, who boarded themselves in a shanty, and procured their provisions from Canada. The first family that settled in town was that of Nathaniel Higgens, who in the spring of 1805 commenced a clearing on a small lot near the village. Joel Clark and family, from Granby, Mass., came in the fall of 1805, and the first saw mill in the town of Russell was erected by him the same year, on Plum creek, half a mile from its mouth. These two families spent the winter of 1805-6 in town, with no neighbors within many miles.

The names of those who accompanied Mr. Attwater the first summer (1805), were Nathan Knox, Heman Morgan, Elias Hayden, Loren Knox, Reuben Ashman, Jesse Bunnell, Elihu Morgan, and David Knox. In April, 1806, Mr. Attwater returned with many others who proposed to form a settlement, and proceeded by way of the Black river country, and the State road, to Washburn's, in Macomb, and thence crossed to Foote's settlement, in Canton, and proceeded thence to their destination in the present village of Russell. A Mr. Alvin White, from Granville, Mass., lived near the south line of Canton, and was the only settler on the route. Dea. Joseph Hutchinson, of Shoreham, Vt., Michael Coffin, of Vt., Philip and Sampson Vial, John Potter, and John Cooper, from

Willsborough, N. Y., and a few others joined them. A field of corn planted among the logs in the month of June, yielded at a surprising rate, which greatly encouraged the emigrants, and led them to look forward with pleasing anticipations to the future. The reports of the fertility of the soil, carried back to New England, had an influence in inducing others to emigrate to the new settlement. Jacob Hutchins commenced the erection of a log grist mill, on Van Rensselaer creek, in Dewitt, about half a mile from the south line of Canton, in the summer of 1806, and this was the second mill erected in town.

The first child born in the town, was a son of Reuben Ashman, in October, 1806. The second was a daughter in the family of Nathaniel Higgens, in May, 1807. The first death was that of one Curtis, in the year 1807. The settlement was increased in 1807, by the addition of the following families: Simeon Stiles, Elihu Phelps, in the winter of that year; Samuel Clark, and several other families of the the same name; John Watson, Horace Dickenson, Enos Bunnell, Luther and David Phelps, and many others. Dr. Plinny Goddard, from Vermont, was the first physician who in 1807 located in town. In the winter of 1808-9, the first school was taught in town by Rollin Smith. The first religious meetings were conducted by the Rev. Royal Phelps, a Presbyterian missionary, in 1806, at the house of Mr. Attwater. The first Episcopal services were conducted by Bishop Hobart, about 1807. The earliest meetings of the Baptist church were held by a man named Sawyer. Calvin Hill and Harriet Knox, were the first persons married in the town of Russell. The ceremony was performed by the Rev. Mr. Phelps in the summer of 1806. The first saw mill at the village of Russell, was erected by Mr. Attwater in 1807, and a grist mill not long after.

An act was passed Feb. 24, 1809, which directed the governor to cause to be deposited, if he should deem necessary, an amount not exceeding 500 stands of arms, in such place in St. Lawrence county as he should select, with such quantities of ammunition and military stores as in his opinion would be necessary in case of invasion. The village, from its being interior and on the St. Lawrence turnpike, was selected, and a building erected. It stands on a commanding elevation, a little north of the village, on a lot given to the state by Mr. Attwater for the purpose of an arsenal, and is a massive stone building, three stories high, thirty by fifty feet on the ground, and originally surrounded by a high stone wall, bristling with iron spikes. The lower story was destined for artillery, the second for small arms, and the third for ammunition. During the war, a guard was posted around the premises for its protection, but since that period no further supervision has been maintained than the care of a keeper, who was a citizen residing in the vicinity. In the summer of 1850 the arsenal building was sold at auction, in pursuance of a general law, for the sum of $525. The arms, amounting to four hundred stand, and some twenty thousand cartridges, were sold in small lots at the same time. It is contemplated to convert the arsenal building into a high school, for which it is well adapted, and the surrounding country is abundantly able to sustain such an enterprise in a creditable manner.

During the first year of the war, the settlement at Russell village exhibited an activity and enterprise which has never been surpassed by any settlement in the county. The erection of the arsenal, and the opening of the roads towards Lake George and Albany, which concentrating in town were supposed to promise prospects of future greatness, and the St. Lawrence turnpike then in course of completion, by its enormous business during the first one or two years of its existence, gave encouragement that this prosperity would last; but the latter lost its importance on the close of the war, and the two southern roads soon fell into ruin from disuse, and their route can now be traced only with difficulty.

By an act passed April 26, 1831, the overseers of the poor were directed to pay over on the first day of January of each year, to the commissioners of common schools, the interest of all moneys arising from the poor fund, to be by them applied for the use of schools.

A forge was erected at the village on Grass river in 1846. It has two fires and is capable of making about 400 pounds of bar iron a day. It has been worked with bog and magnetic ores, and with scrap iron. The ores with which it is supplied are drawn from three to eleven miles from their localities, and can be obtained in unlimited quantities.

Religious Societies.—The Baptists organized July 15, 1809, under the Rev. Samuel Rowley, a missionary, and the early meetings were held at the house of Philip Viall. First number, seven; whole number, one hundred and eighty-five; present number, forty-two. A church was built in 1845, at a cost of $900, and dedicated October 15, 1845. The present pastor is the Rev. Myron R. Slater. A society was incorporated December 29, 1846, with Harry Van Aernam, Wm. G. Gibbons, and Gilbert Stewart, trustees. The Presbyterian and Episcopal denominations have formed societies in town. The latter under the name of Sion church, April 10, 1819, with Russell Attwater and Jesse Bunnell, *wardens;* Justis Ives, Levi Frost, John Boyd, Moses Bunnell, Reuben Ashman, Phineas Attwater, William Attwater, and Nathan Knox, *vestrymen.* The Wesleyan Methodists formed a church September 9, 1843. The following is a list of their clergymen: Hiram Wing (deceased), Joel Grennell, W. W. Sterricker, S. Soper, and Harvey Miles, the present pastor. A Methodist Episcopal society was incorporated Feb. 19, 1851, Hiram Derby, M. Van Brocklin and Charles Rundell, trustees.

29

STOCKHOLM,

Embracing the original township, was formed from Massena, Feb. 21, 1806, the first town meeting being directed to be held at the house of Luman Pettibone. By an act of April 15, 1834, mile squares 6, 7, 8, 9, 10, and the north half of 14 and 19, were annexed to Norfolk. A petition had been sent in 1805, to form the town, which was referred to the members from Oneida, who then represented this county, but nothing was done. The day of the first town meeting having passed without an election, Nathan Walker, of Canton, Gurdon Smith and Benjamin Raymond, of Potsdam, magistrates, proceeded to appoint under their hands and seals, town officers in pursuance of powers granted in an act of March 7, 1801, viz:

Ebenezer Hulburd, *supervisor*; Wm. Staples, *clerk*; Stephen A. Tambling, Benjamin Wright and Arba Woodward, *assessors*; Samuel Webster, *constable and collector*; S. A. Tambling, Luman Pettibone, *overseers of the poor*; S. A. Tambling, E. Hulburd and W. Webster, *com'rs of highways*; S. A. Tambling, B. Wright, *fence viewers*; E. Hulburd, *poundmaster*; L. Pettibone, *overseer of highways*. We regret that our space will not allow the publication of this instrument entire.

Supervisors.—1806, Ebenezer Hulburd; 1807, Simeon Nash; 1808–9, Zephaniah French; 1810–11, Stephen A. Tambling; 1812–13, Warren Webster; 1814–22, Nathaniel F. Winslow; 1823, at a special meeting, Chauncey Pettibone; 1823–9, Chauncey Pettibone; 1830–2, Shiverick Holmes; 1833, Joseph H. Sanford; 1834, Benjamin Holmes; 1835, Wm. T. Osborne; 1837–8, Joseph H. Sanford; 1839, Dorus Pettibone; 1840, Thomas Dunton; 1841–2, J. H. Sanford; 1843–5, Ziba L. Smith; 1846, Sidney Kelsey; 1847, B. Holmes; 1848–9, Allen Lyman; 1850–1, Daniel P. Rose; 1852, Hiram Hulburd.

Notes from the Records.—Wolf bounties of $5 offered in 1808, '9, '11, until the meeting of the supervisors, when it was to be increased or lessened to make it $20. $5 in 1814, '17; $10 in 1819, '20. On several years panther bounties. In 1817, voted against division, and in 1824, a strong remonstrance against annexing a part to Norfolk. In 1828, six ballot boxes to be provided for town elections, to be numbered, No. 1, supervisor and clerk; No. 2, assessors; No. 3, overseers of poor; No. 4, commissioners of highways; No. 5, constables and collector; No. 6, commissioners and inspectors of schools.

In 1830, clerk requested to endeavor to get Stockholm excepted from law requiring one ballot box for town elections. In 1833, supervisor and clerk to petition for a repeal of the law abolishing imprisonment for debt.

An adjourned town meeting was held March 19, 1822, to receive the report of a committee of five, consisting of Ebenezer Hulburd, Chauncey Pettibone, N. F. Winslow, John Simons and W. Webster, appointed to examine into the situation of the public lands in town. Ralph P. Stearns and Chauncey Pettibone were appointed the first commissioners of public lands. A committee was appointed to draw up a petition to the legislature to authorize these lands to be granted on durable leases.

An act passed Feb. 8, 1823, created the office of trustees of public lands in the town of Stockholm, who were to be elected by the inhabitants and to constitute a body politic for the care and preservation of gospel and school lot in the town of Stockholm. They were to have the powers of similar officers in Madrid.

Arrangements for settling this town began to be made in 1800 and 1801. In 1802, Ebenezer Hulburd and Dr. Luman Pettibone, agents, from Orwell, Vt., with Benj. Wright, Isaac Kelsey, Abram Sheldon, and others, came into town and commenced improvements. Mrs. Sheldon was the first woman in town. On the 7th of March, 1803, seven families, of which six were from Orwell, Vt., moved in. The heads of these were Isaac Kelsey, Wm. Staples, Abraham Sheldon, Luman Pettibone, John and Robert Bisbee, and Benj. Wright. They had the first year, raised some corn, oats and potatoes, which had been secured as well as circumstances allowed. They came by way of Chateaugay and St. Regis, and up that river on the ice. The houses and furniture constructed, were all of the rudest kind, and such as saws, axes and augers would make. With strips of elm bark, they made bedsteads and chairs, and all their furniture was of the rudest and simplest pattern.

In September, 1804, occurred the greatest flood ever known in the country, produced by heavy rains and swelling the St. Regis river far above its ordinary flood level. Four of the seven families living near the bank of the river, were compelled to flee from their homes. One family living near Trout brook, remained within doors until the under floor was raised from the sleepers, and the wood was floated from the fire-place, and with the greatest peril and difficulty they escaped with their lives.

The first saw mill in town was built in 1804, by Samuel Reynolds, a proprietor of several mile squares, about one and a half miles above the east village.

The first school was taught in the winter of 1807. Among the early settlers not above named were Stephen A. Tambling, Warren Webster, Alba Woodward, Samuel Webster, Simeon Nash, Luther Hulburd, Zephaniah French, Alpheus Johnson, John Graves, Josiah L. Hill, Ralph P. Stearns, Reuben Kelsey, and others.

The first agents for Stockholm (Pettibone and Hulburd), were in 1816, succeeded in the western part of the town, by Nathan Osburne, and shortly after by J. H. Sanford. The latter held the office for many years, and was the predecessor of Mr. E. M. Foster, the present agent for the proprietors.

The first sheep taken into Stockholm, and the first in the eastern part of St. Lawrence county, were driven from Vermont, in 1803. The flock consisted of about fifty. They arrived in October, 1803. Much trouble was encountered in getting them across some of the streams, particularly

the Salmon river, where the timbers of a bridge were laid only. A part
of the flock crossed on these, and the rest swam the river. From this
little flock the farmers of the neighboring towns derived their stock.
Much difficulty was experienced in keeping them from being destroyed
by wolves. 'Every night it was necessary to yard them in an enclosure,
well fenced against their troublesome enemies, and during the day, it
was found impossible to preserve them unless pastured in the immediate
vicinity of dwellings. Similar difficulties were felt in Hopkinton and
other towns, and led to the offer of bounties for the destruction of wolves,
which in these towns were doubtless necessary, and considered at the
time as no more than adequate to accomplish their object.

The first settler who located in the west half of Stockholm, was John
Thatcher, from Williston, Vt., who in March, 1805, started from the settlement in the east part of the town of Stockholm, taking his wife and
children, and the small sum of household articles which he was able to
carry in a vehicle drawn by a single horse, to locate in the western part
of the town. On arriving at the river, he found it swollen and rapid,
but providing himself with a pole to sustain himself against the current,
he forded it repeatedly, carrying on his back his children, and his household goods, and finally with much difficulty, assisted his wife in wading
the river. Here he constructed a rude shelter of hemlock boughs beside
a fallen tree, and kindling a cheerful fire on the site of the present little
village of Sanfordville, he spent the first night. The horse was comfortably provided for on the opposite bank of the river, and on the following
day he returned to the settlements to make further arrangements for his
residence. He is spoken of as a man capable of enduring fatigue to an
extraordinary degree, and was known to have carried the flour of three
bushels of wheat on his shoulders for miles, through the forest to his
family. The first log house in the west half of Stockholm was built near
the line of Potsdam, for a Mr. Dart, in the winter of 1805–6, by some
ten or a dozen of the settlers of East Stockholm, who went to the location a distance of eight miles, cut and rolled up the frame of a log house,
and returned in the evening of the same day. George Streight, John
Partridge, Stiles Nelson, and Eldad Taylor, were early settlers in the
west half of the town.

The first grist mill in Stockholm, was erected at the present village of
Bicknelville, and during the first one or two years, the citizens were
compelled to resort to Sheik's mill, in Canada, or to Canton, or to Roberts's mill, now Columbia village. In 1804, a mill was got in operation
in Hopkinton.

During the first summer, Mr. Pettibone had occasion to resort to the
mill at Columbia, through a densely wooded country, without roads wor-

thy of the name, and the trip was performed under circumstances of peculiar hardship. Dr. P. and a young man by the name of Abel Kelsey, started with an ox team and wagon, expecting to spend the night in a shanty which they supposed had been built, and was occupied by, a settler, who had commenced a small clearing on the west side of Raquette river, about a mile and a half below the present village of Potsdam. They accordingly neglected to take with them any apparatus for kindling a fire.

At the close of a day of toil and labor, they found themselves on the banks of the river, and succeeded in fording it, laying the grain bags on polls across the top of the wagon, to keep it dry; but to their great disappointment, the cheerful log hut and comfortable fire which they had anticipated as waiting them, was not there, and to add to their misery a cold, drenching rain set in, and continued through the night. They had been already half drowned in crossing the river, and were compelled to crawl under the best shelter they could find, and spend the night in as wretched a condition as possible. On the next morning, Mr. Pettibone found himself shaking with an ague, contracted in consequence of exposure, and with the greatest difficulty able to get through to his destination.

The journey to Foote's mill, in Canton, usually consumed five days, in going and returning, ten bushels being the amount that could be taken at a trip, which was performed with an ox team. Two or three men accompanied to guard against accidents, and clear away the underbrush for the cattle. On arriving at streams, the grain was taken over on their shoulders, or laid across the oxen, to keep it out of the water, and thus all the intervening rivers were forded, except Raquette river, which was crossed by a float, just below the falls, at Potsdam village. This was the only way of crossing at that place, till the erection of a bridge in the year 1809. The ox teams were driven into the water, sometimes much against their will, and forced to swim the river, their drivers with whips and loud shouts preventing their return to the banks. At night, if the pioneers found shelter and supper in the hut of some settler, it was well; and if not, it was as well; for they usually succeeded in striking a spark from steel, and setting fire to some dry standing or fallen tree, by the side of which they would spend the night, having care that the fire should not mount into the tree top, and detach the larger branches, or burrow among the roots, and overturn the flaming column upon them.

The journey to Canada was in part performed by canoes on the rivers, more or less difficulty being encountered in passing the rapids. Amid these rude and fatiguing labors, which would dishearten a majority of our present citizens, a certain amount of enjoyment existed. The hand of sympathy was extended to neighbors, and any luck that befel one, was regarded as a common benefit. If any needed a helping hand, his desire need but be announced, to be heeded, and a common interest and a *hope of better times*, stimulated to exertion, and dispelled gloom.

During the war, numbers of the inhabitants became alarmed, and left the county, from fear of the Indians, and those that remained proceeded to erect defences for their protection. One of these was a double line of pickets around the house of Dr. Pettibone, which enclosed a square area of about a quarter of an acre, and was finished with gate and fixtures complete. Here the inhabitants assembled on a few occasions of alarm, but no real danger ever presented itself. Another stockade was commenced around the house of Warren Webster, about a mile east of the centre of the town, which was finished on two or three sides only and a third was commenced around the dwelling of Jonathan Sager, in the west half. These pickets were timbers set upright in a trench, about three feet deep, in a double row, so that no openings existed between them. They were about sixteen feet high, sharpened at the top, and supported by earth banked against them on each side. On one occasion of a draft, the greatest fear was entertained from an attack of the St. Regis or some other Indian tribe, they knew not what, and a volunteer company was raised, and a guard mounted and maintained for several days on the road which led towards Canada. Arms were procured at the state arsenal at Russell, and distributed among the inhabitants. From the miry condition of the roads, these were procured with great difficulty, being borne by pack horses, which often required to be relieved in passing swamps and streams.

The miseries of war appear to be not limited to the actual amount of suffering which it directly entails, but include the privations and hardships sustained from apprehensions of danger, which often lead the timid to voluntarily encounter a needless amount of suffering.

The roads were at times thronged with groups of timid inhabitants, hastening away with such articles of furniture and provisions as they were able to snatch in their haste, and with such vehicles as they could command, and each augmented the fears of the others, by magnifying the rumors which they had received from those as timid as themselves. It is but just to say, that the class of fugitives did not form a majority of the existing population, and that there were many who ridiculed the fears of the timid, represented the absurdity of the alarms, and earnestly entreated them to behave like men, and stand ready to do their duty if real danger should arise, instead of stealing off in the cowardly manner of some. A portion of those who left the country never returned, and others came back to witness the waste and destruction which their own folly and neglect had brought upon them.

The village of *Bicknellville*, on the west branch of St. Regis, in the southwest quarter of Stockholm, and about half a mile south of the direct road from Potsdam to Malone, was first begun in 1811, by Amos Bicknell, originally from Barnard, Vt., but since 1806, a resident of Potsdam. In May, 1811, he removed to this place, with his family, consisting of his wife, six sons and three daughters, several of whom still reside in the vicinity, and commenced the erection of a grist and saw mill, which were built and got in operation the same season.

About 1815, the proprietor, Mr. Pierrepont, expended a large sum in opening a road from Parishville to Norfolk, which, from its importance as a communication by which potash from the new settlements could be taken to the navigable waters of Raquette river, was called the *Market road.* This route originally was laid about a mile east of this place, but eventually the principal travel from the back towns passed through by Bicknell's mills, and some portion of the original road has been discontinued.

In 1812 or 1813, a carding machine was got in operation at this place, and having a natural advantage in the possession of a good water power, it has gradually grown into a small village, with a grist and saw mill, small woolen factory, foundry and machine shop, and a number of mechanic shops. A fork and hoe factory was maintained there several years, but is at present discontinued. It has a Methodist chapel, a union store, a tavern, and about thirty families.

Southville is a small village having a post office of the same name, and situated near the south bounds of the town. The earliest settler in this place, is said to have been Shubel Gurley. Daniel Harrington and some others located soon after in the neighborhood.

Three miles from Potsdam Station, on the Northern Rail road, and on the direct line between Parishville and Norfolk, is the depot of Knapp's Station, which derives its name from Moses Knapp. The first settler in this vicinity was Eldad Taylor, on the farm of Mr. Knapp. The station at this place was first named *Stockholm*, while that near Brasher falls, also in this town, was named *Brasher*, and afterwards *Stockholm and Brasher*, but confusion arising from the similarity of names, the present one was adopted. The post office of *North Stockholm* is located at this place. This is a flag station, and passenger trains do not stop without a signal. The business at present limited, but is expected to increase with the opening of new routes, and the further settlement of the country. This is one of the points proposed for the terminus of the Potsdam and Watertown rail road, and should it be finally selected, it would become a place of much importance. It is often known by the inhabitants as Plum Brook.

A forge was erected on Trout brook, about a mile southwest of the centre of the town, by Benjamin Holmes and Harry Merrill, about 1825. It was run about ten years on bog ore, obtained from swamps in the vicinity. The enterprise was given up on account of the failure of the supply of ore.

Religious Societies,—In May, 1803, the settlers commenced holding religious meetings on Sundays. The first sermon preached in town was by a Baptist minister, Eld. Webster, from Orwell, Vt., (text, Acts xiv, 9.) and in 1806, the Rev. Amos Pettengill, and in 1807, the same with Rev. E. Hibbard, from Brandon, Vt., came and spent a few sabbaths with the people, which resulted in the formation of a Congregational church of 2 male and 5 female members, March 10, 1807. In summer the meetings were held in barns, and in winter, in private houses. In 1813, they employed the Rev. Hiram S. Johnson, who preached half of the time till 1819. In 1821, the Rev. Moses Parmelee was hired till 1824. For 20 years after this they had no pastor, but were most of the time supplied with preaching. In 1845, the Rev. Philo C. Pettibone, was installed over the congregation, and still remains their pastor. The society was incorporated June 6, 1837, with Sidney Kelsey, Ashbel Skinner, and Calvin T. Hulburd, trustees. A church of this denomination was formed at West Stockholm, about 1822-3, and consisted originally of 5 members.

The Rev. Roswell Pettibone, was employed as their first preacher. There has been no pastor regularly installed over this church. A church edifice was erected in 1831, at a cost of about $1,800, mainly through the influence of Mr. J. H. Sanford.

The Baptists organized at a very early day, but the data of their history has not been received. The society was incorporated May 25, 1822, with Ralph P. Sterns, Warren Webster and Luther Fuller, trustees. It was reorganized Jan. 7, 1839. They have a meeting house in town.

The Free-Will Baptists were organized into a church in June, 1839, by Eld. Samuel Hart, and is at present almost scattered. A Methodist Episcopal church was incorporated in West Stockholm, Nov. 19, 1840, with Loren Ashley, Ziba S. Smith, Ruel Lincoln, Roswell B. Webb, Horace Doud, Martin Strait, Henry B. Sumner, Norman Ashley, and Joseph Page, trustees.

The Wesleyan Methodist society of East Stockholm, was incorporated Oct. 11, 1852, with Ira Beach, Stillman Austin, Elias Jenkins, Hugh Allen and James Kelsey, trustees.

A church of the Christian order, was gathered by Eld. Palmer, many years since, which once numbered 40 members, but they have for some time been scattered and without a pastor.

FRANKLIN COUNTY,

Embraces 15 towns which are organized as follows:

BANGOR, taken from *Dickinson*, June, 15, 1812.
BELLMONT, taken from *Chateaugay*, March 25, 1833.
BOMBAY, taken from *Fort Covington*, March 30, 1833.
BRANDON, taken from *Bangor*, Jan. 28, 1828.
BURKE, taken from *Chateaugay*, April 26, 1844.
CHATEAUGAY, taken from *Champlain*, March 15, 1799.
CONSTABLE, taken from *Harrison*, March 13, 1807.
DICKINSON, taken from *Harrison*, April 11, 1808.
DUANE, taken from *Malone*, January 24, 1828.
FORT COVINGTON, taken from *Constable*, February 28, 1817.
FRANKLIN, taken from *Bellmont*, May 20, 1836.
HARRIETSTOWN, taken from *Duane*, March 19, 1841.
MALONE,* taken from *Chateaugay*, March 2, 1805.
MOIRA, taken from *Dickinson*, April 15, 1828.
WESTVILLE, taken from *Constable*, April 25, 1829.

BANGOR,

Was organized as above, the first town meeting being held at the house of Chester Tuller, and the poor moneys being equitably divided. The first town officers were

Joseph Plumb, *supervisor;* Eleazer Barnum, *clerk;* C. Fuller, John Marvin, Isaac Bigelow, *assessors;* C. Fuller, *collector;* Samuel Silsbee, Elijah Drury, *poor masters;* James Lawrence, Barnabas Barnum, Elijah Drury, *com. of highways;* Eleazer Barnum, David Sayle, *constables;* Jehiel Barnum, Gardner Dickinson, Jonathan Bower, John A. Buckland, Ebenezer R. Daggett, *fence viewers;* David Doty, *pound master;* Joseph

* As HARRISON, changed to EZRAVILLE, April 11, 1808, and to MALONE, June 10, 1812.

Plumb, Joel Griffin, Samuel Silsbe *com. of common schools;* Elisha Drury, Asa Worth, John Marvin, Chester Tuller, *inspectors of common schools.*

Supervisors.—1813-17, Joseph Plumb; 1818-20, Noah Moody; 1821-5, J. Plumb; 1826-7, George Adams; 1828, J. Plumb; 1829-32, G Adams; 1833, William Plumb; 1834, G. Adams; 1836-7, James Adams; 1838, G. Adams; 1839, Joshua Dickinson; 1840-2, G. Adams; 1843-4, Talmadge Barnum; 1845, J. Dickinson; 1846-8, Abel Wilcox; 1849-50 Allen Hinman, Jun.; 1851, George H. Stevens; 1852, Joseph Eldred.

Town bounties have been offered for "noxious animals" as follows:

For wolves, $10 in 1828-9; $15 in 1813-14-15-21; $20 in 1816-17-18-19-20; in 1816, half this sum for wolf whelps; for squirrels 12½ cents 1817; for panthers, $20 in 1817-18-19-20; $25 in 1821; for crows, 50 cts. 1817-19; for bears, $3 in 1817-18-19; $5 in 1820; $10 in 1821; for black birds, 12½ cents in 1817; for foxes, $2 in 1818-19-20; $3 in 1816; $5 in 1821; for wild cats, (lynx?) $2 in 1817-19; $3 in 1820; $5 in 1821.

At a special town meeting May 6, 1820, voted that the vote for raising a bounty on wolves, panthers and bears, taken at the last annual meeting, be amended to this effect: "that no person shall be entitled to any bounty from the town except actual residents of the town at this date."

A special town meeting November 21, convened for the purpose, passed a similar resolution. In 1826, voted in favor of building a county poor house, which was done, leaving a surplus poor fund with the several towns. To dispose of this a special town meeting was held December 29, 1830. Voted to apply the poor funds of the town for the purpose of building a town house, and a vote was taken locating said house. March 30, 1831, the vote locating the town house was reconsidered, and a committee of three from three different towns, was named for the purpose of selecting a site. Alric Mann, James Duane and Burnabas Heath, were named such committee. In case any one of these should be unable to attend, the one or two who did attend had power to appoint one or two as the case might be, to fill the vacancy. Such persons might not be residents of the town. The site was to be fixed by the first day of July next. Joseph Plumb, Joshua Dickinson and George Adams, were nominated as a town committee who were to receive from the poor masters, the funds in their hands, and erect a town house on the site designated by the commissioners. They were also empowered to collect materials, &c., on subscription for the above purpose. Silvester Langdon, was subsequently appointed in place of Mr. Duane. The committee thus constituted, reported,—"That in their opinion the interests of the said town would be best served by locating the town house on the high land between the north and south roads. They accordingly located it on lot No. 16. This decision not giving satisfaction, a meeting was held May 5, 1832, the former vote was reconsidered, and it was voted to divide the public money remaining in the hands of the overseers of the poor, equally between the north and south parts of the town. It was voted to appropriate the said money for the purpose of building two town houses to be located at the centre of the town from east to west, on the north and south roads, unless it should be thought best to vary somewhat from these points. Talmadge Barnum, Alanson Green, Jesse Smith and William Plumb, were appointed a committee for erecting the north house, and Jas. Lawrence, John L. Riggs, Joseph Conger and Samuel Brighton, for the other. A committee was to be appointed to see that the several religious societies in town have the the use of these houses in proportion to the amount that each should pay. The foregoing votes were finally reconsidered, and the meeting adjourned.

On the 7th of December, a meeting was again held, and all former votes annulled. The equal division of the public moneys was again voted, and the central location near the centre from east to west on the north and south roads, again adopted. James Adams, James Lawrence and Silvester Potter, were appointed a committee to erect the south house, and Jesse Plumb, David Doty and Ezra French, the other. The use of these houses was to be divided between the different religious societies in proportion to the amount subscribed by each towards the erection. Both were to be so far completed as to be valued at $1,200 each, within three years from date.

Two public buildings were accordingly erected. That on the north road in 1834, and the other in 1835. The former is of wood, and the latter of stone, and was only completed in 1851. At their town meeting in 1850, the town voted that their meetings should in future be held alternately at the village on the south road, and at North Bangor corners. The supervisor was instructed to oppose the plan of removing the site or rebuilding the county buildings. The town has uniformly voted for the support of schools as much money as the law allows.

Settlement in this town was commenced in the spring of 1806, by Benjamin Seeley, originally from Vermont, but who for several years lived in Moira. He located about 2½ miles east of the centre of the town. A winter road existed across the town previous to this, which was passable only by sleighs, and no wheeled vehicle had been taken into or through the town till afterwards. The next settler was Joseph Plumb,* in June, 1806, then from Moira, but originally from Middlebury, Vt., who took up a farm two miles east of the centre of the town. In the fall, Jehiel and James Barnum, originally from Vermont, commenced improvements, and moved on with their families the following winter. Chester Tuller, Robert Wilson, Joel Griffin, and many others, settled in 1807 along the central road, and several families had settled in the southern part of the town before the St. Lawrence turnpike was opened. Among these were Gardner Dickinson, H. Conger, Jonathan Bowen, Levi Sylvester and Andrew Potter, and others, all of whom were from Franklin co., Vt. At the time when the town began to settle, the north half belonged to McCormick. William Cooper owned the S. E. quarter, and Asahel Bacon, the S. W. quarter. Mr. Bacon lived in New Haven, Ct., and his first agent was Joseph Plumb. The Cooper tract was divided among the heirs of that gentleman, and it was surveyed in 1815. N. Baker surveyed the north half of the town in the fall of 1806, and the south half was surveyed by Potter Goff, of De Kalb, in the fall of 1815. The first school was taught in 1808, by Samuel Russell.

Religious Societies.—The first religious meetings are said to have been held by Rev. Alexander Proudfit, in 1808. A Congregational Church was formed in a barn of Mr. Southworth, near North Bangor, at an early day. It consisted at first of 9 members. This society was incorpoted

* Mr. Plumb died in Bangor, in 1838, at the age of 77.

February 9, 1833, with Joshua Dickinson, Jonathan H. Farr, D. Paine, F. Tilton and Henry Stevens, trustees.

The Christian sect were organized by Elder Uriah Smith and J. Spooner, in the fall of 1818, and was attended by a religious revival. Elder John Smith, was pastor of this church for many years. They have a church and hold meetings on alternate Sabbaths.

BELLMONT,

Was erected from Chateaugay, embracing townships 8, 9, and 10, of the Old Military tract, March 25, 1833, the first town meeting being held at the school house of dis. No. 8. On the 23d of March, 1838, the southern tier of mile square lots of No. 7, were annexed.

Supervisors:—1833-34, Roswell A. Weed; 1835 Henry B. Hatch; 1836, Jonathan H. Farr; 1837, Roswell A. Weed; 1838-39, John D. Mills, 1840-41, George Winkley; 1842, Pliny C Daggett; 1843, Marcus Heading; 1844-45, William Weed; 1846-47, Abraham Reynolds; 1848-49, William Weed; 1850, John D. Mills; 1851, Jonas G. Clark; 1852; William Weed.

The first survey of township No. 8, of the Old Military tract, was made in 1801, by Joseph Griffin. The town of Bellmont, derives its name from William Bell, one of the early proprietors of a portion of the town. Mr. Bell was engaged in mercantile business, and for several of the latter years of his life, was employed as a super cargo in the East India trade. While engaged in settling his lands, it was his custom to spend a portion of the summer months in Franklin county. Mr. James H. Titus, is the present owner of about one fifth part of Bellmont (No. 8), adjoining Malone. The attention of this gentleman, is now personally devoted to the settlement and improvement of this section of the county, which previous to the completion of the present avenue to market, scarcely found encouragement for the investment of labor. At present, the settlement of Bellmont is limited mostly to the north part of the town, and to a road running from east to west, parallel with the line of the town. Several romantic and beautiful lakes occur here, and none that surpasses that of Chateaugay lake, near the line of Clinton county.

There is a Presbyterian society of thirty to forty members in this town, which is a branch of the Malone church.

An alleged murder occurred in Bellmont, Nov. 3, 1851. Mr. Justin Bell, of Brasher, St. Lawrence county, had erected a shanty near Owlshead pond, about 8½ miles from Malone village, and one or two into the woods, for a residence while hunting and fishing. He had been there on this occasion several days, and on the morning of the day on which the fatal occurrence happened, Mr. B. H. Man, of Westville, a surveyor, who had been up beyond, to examine a piece of land, with others, left Bell and James Sherwin, at the shanty. The latter had arrived about 11 o'clock, partly intoxicated, and with a *jug of liquor*. He is said to have threatened to take possession of the shanty and the furs, and his swaggering manner made Bell uneasy at being left alone in his company, and he enquired of those who were leaving them, whether he would be safe in his company.   Early on Monday morning, Sherwin came into the settlement with the statement, that he had accidentally shot Bell, while attempting to discharge his gun.   Numbers immediately repaired to the premises, and a coroner's inquest was held. Discrepancies in the account given of the manner in which the alleged accident occurred, and the fact of some of the furs, the lamp, &c., being found at a considerable distance from the shanty, led to suspicion of crime, and Sherwin was arrested and committed for murder.   The Franklin county jail being thought unsafe, should any attempt be made to rescue the prisoner, he was confined for some time in the jail of St. Lawrence county, and at the July term of the court of oyer and terminer, held at Malone, in 1852, he was tried.

Augustus C. Hand, one of the justices of the supreme court presided, assisted by John Hutton, county judge, and Milton Heath, and Elisha Hollister, justices of sessions.   After a full and impartial trial, the jury, from the circumstances proved, after a deliberation of several hours, brought in a verdict of *guilty*. The prisoner received the verdict with apparent indifference. He was sentenced to be hung, Sept. 10, but this was commuted to imprisonment for life.

BOMBAY,

Was organized from Fort Covington, March 30, 1833, by an act which took effect on the first of May following. The first town meeting was directed to be held at the school house near Bombay Corners. This town embraces the present Indian reservation of the St. Regis tribe, and township No. 1, or *Macomb*, of Great tract number 1, of Macomb's purchase. The name of Bombay was derived from the commercial capital in the East Indies, and given by Michael Hogan, the founder of Hogansburgh, from its being the former home of his wife. Mr. Hogan died at Washington, D. C., on the 26th of March, 1833, at the age of 68. He had for several years held the office of consul general of the United States, at Valparaiso, in Chili, and was formerly a merchant in the city of New York. He was distinguished throughout various reverses of fortune, by his enterprise, intelligence and probity, as well as by his hospitable and liberal disposition, and the urbanity of his manners.

Supervisors:—1833-34, Wilson Randall; 1835-37, Amherst K. Williams; 1838-39, John S. Eldridge; 1840-1, Elias Bowker; 1842-43; Elvin K. Smith; 1844, Amasa Townsend; 1845, Elias Bowker; 1846-47; A. Townsend; 1848, Charles Russell; 1849-50, Jacob G. Reynolds; 1851, C. Russell; 1852; J. G. Reynolds.

The first improvements in the town, except at St. Regis village, were, it is said, begun by Gordon, the founder of St. Regis, who about 1762, caused mills to be erected at what is now Hogansburgh, but which then bore the name of St. Regis mills. From this place he is said to have sent rafts to Montreal. The tradition of this affair is obscure and un certain. A mill was burned about 1804, said to have been old. In December, 1808, there were no mills there. William Gray, the Indian interpreter, was living on the west bank during the early part of the war and for many years previous, and the place then bore the name of Gray's mills. From information derived from Joseph Lefonduze, a Frenchman, who has resided for many years at Hogansburgh, it is learned that Frenchmen, named Berön and Bouget, owned the first mills erected since 1808, who were succeeded by one Soufaçon and Jean Baptiste Parissien,* who left in 1816.

The first grist mill was erected for Michael Hogan, about 1818, on the east side of St. Regis river. He had previously purchased township number one, and mills were erected near the centre of the town, by Daniel W. Church, for him in 1811. The first settler in township number one is said to have been Joseph Hadley, a hunter, about 1803. Samuel Sanborn, with a large family, settled about the year 1805. The settlements in town were very few and feeble, previous to 1822, when immigration commenced, and proceeded so rapidly, that the greater part of the town, not reserved by the Indians, was taken up within two or three years. Much of the valuable timber had been stolen by parties from Canada, and by squatters, before it passed into the hands of actual settlers. The title of township number one, passed from Mr. Hogan to Robert Oliver, of Baltimore, and the estate has been subsequently divided among his heirs, by commissioners chosen for the purpose.

The village of Hogansburgh is accessible by steamers, and an American boat that plies between Cornwall and Montreal, has touched here during the past season, but notwithstanding this advantage, joined with a good water power, the place does not appear to thrive. Among other causes, the difficulty of obtaining titles on the reservation, and the impossibility, from this cause, of bringing under improvement lands which are susceptible of a high cultivation, are the principal. The first road across the Indian lands, was from French mills to St. Regis, and in the treaty of 1818, the right of way for one to the present village was ceded, and soon after a road was opened nearly east and west through the reservation. April 12, 1827, $1,000 was applied, and $1,000 subscribed, for improving this road, under the direction of James B. Spencer and Wm. Hogan. A law was passed May 26, 1841, appointing Gurdon S. Mills and James Hall Jr., to repair, straighten and improve this road, and the sum of $4,000 was applied for this purpose.

Religious Societies.—The Methodists organized a society in town March

* Owner at an early day of mills on Salmon river. Died at Isle au Perot, about 1823 aged 77.

26, 1832, with Joseph Elliot, James M. Roberts, Simon Alverson, John O'Riley and Wilson Randall, trustees. This society has a church at Bombay Corners.

The church of St. Patrick (in the Catholic Register named St. Mary's church), was incorporated Oct. 20, 1834, with the Rt. Rev. John Dubois, bishop, N. Y.; John Keesan and John Hammill, of Brasher, James Murphy, Davis O'Nail, of Bombay, Patrick Feely and Lanty Adams, of Hogansburgh, trustees. They have a stone church at Hogansburgh. Before its erection, there was no other Catholic church in the county, except at St. Regis.

An Episcopal church was commenced in 1837, a little east of the village, but was never finished.

BRANDON,

Was erected Jan. 28, 1828, and made to include all that part of Bangor south of No. 5, in Great tract No. 1 of Macomb's purchase. The first town meeting was directed to be held at the house of Elijah Prentiss. The poor moneys raised in Bangor in 1827, were to be divided according to the last assessment. At the first town meeting, the following officers were elected:

Henry Stephens, *supervisor;* Jonathan H. Farr, *clerk;* Shubert Hastings, Elijah Prentiss, *assessors;* Jonathan Hastings, *collector;* Josiah Hastings, Isaac Joy, *poor masters;* George Austin, Clark Adams, Rufus Whitney. *com'rs of highways;* Jonathan Hastings, Royal Whitman, *constable;* Andrew Stevens, Joseph Thomas, Thomas Wells, *com'rs of common schools;* James Wells, Ezekiel Hildreth, Calvin Farr, *fence viewers;* Peter H. Higgings, Ira Ewings, Thomas Wells, Joseph Thomas, Peter Willson, *overseers of highways.*

At the first meeting, $250 voted for the highways. At a special town meeting, held December 10, 1830, a vote was taken and carried, *that the poor money should be applied to pay the resident taxes in the year* 1830. A vote was also taken that the overseers of the poor should collect the poor money without delay, and pay it over to the collector of the said town of Brandon, and that the remainder of the poor money, after paying the resident taxes, is to apply towards paying the overseers of the poor for their services in the year 1830. This action was taken after the adoption of the poor house system, when the poor being otherwise provided for, the towns were allowed to specify the object for which the poor fund that had previously accumulated could be applied.

1850. Resolved unanimously, that the supervisor be instructed to oppose the removal of the court house from the present site. The board of supervisors was requested to cause the present buildings to be repaired. The town has usually voted for the support of schools all the money which the law allows, and $250 annually for public highways.

Supervisors.—1828-31, Henry Stevens, Jr.; 1832-3, Jonathan H. Farr; 1834, H. Stevens, Jr.;1835-6, J. H. Farr; 1837, Jason Baker; 1838, James H. Holland; 1839-40, H. Stevens, Jr.; 1841, J. H. Holland; 1842, Shubert Hastings; 1843-4, Henry Stevens; 1845-6, Alexander Sergeant; 1847-8, J. H. Holland; 1849-50, J. Baker; 1851-2, J. H. Farr.

This town derives its name from Brandon, Vt., from whence most of the first settlers emigrated. The settlement is at present mostly limited to the north third of No. 8. A few scattered settlers reside on the Port Kent road, in township No. 11. The town began to settle in 1820, and the following names, from the land book of Mr. Noah Moody, the agent, were those of first settlers: Josiah Hastings, Aaron Conger, Wilson Spooner, Luther Taylor and John Thomas.

In 1821, Andrew and Henry Stevens, Levi Conger, G. W. Taylor, Clark Adams, Daniel K. Davis, Jonathan H. Farr and Orrin Wellington; in 1832, ten, and in 1823, eight families, moved into town. The first saw mill was built by Ira Ewens, in 1825-6.

The following note is taken from the field notes of B. Wright, made on the survey of 1799:

" The Indian line of navigation from lake Champlain to Hudson's river, Rackett river, Black river and lake Ontario, lies through this town (No. 23, tract No. 1), by a path from Saranac lake to a small lake on a branch of the river Racket, and is much used by the various tribes of them."

It is marked on the original maps, as the Indian Pass.

BURKE

Was erected from Chateaugay, April 26, 1844, and comprises most of the western half of township No. 7 of the Old Military tract. It was proposed to name the town *Birney*, from the candidate of the liberty party for the presidency in that election; but this was changed in the legislature. The supervisors of this town have been, 1844-7, Loren Burk; 1848-9, Reuben Pike; 1850-51, Winthrop Newton; 1852, Elisha Marks. In 1850, the supervisor was instructed to use his influence against the removal of the county buildings, or the building of new ones.

In 1851, $500 was raised by authority of the legislature, for a town house, and one has been erected of wood, near the centre of the town, a mile northwest of the depot.

The town was settled at about the same time as Chateaugay, of which it formed a part. Jehiel Barnum, Noah Lee and others, enumerated in our account of Chateaugay, were among the earlier settlers. There is at present no village in town. A post office, town house, Presbyterian and Baptist churches (all built in 1852), exist near the centre of the town, near a neighborhood known as Burke Corners, which may form the neucleus of a village. Near the point where Trout river is crossed by the rail road, is a starch factory and several minor establishments, which the facilities of transportation which they enjoy, may be the means of making a place of business. A depot building has been lately erected here. It is only a flag station.

CHATEAUGAY,

Was formed from Champlain, embracing townships 5, 6, 7, 8, of the Old Military tract. On the erection of St. Lawrence county, Great tract No. 1, of Macomb's purchase, and the St. Regis reservation; and in forming Franklin county, Military townships 9 and 10 were annexed, and 5 and 6 taken off. Tract No. 1 was taken off in 1805, in forming Harrison, and by the two acts erecting and extending Bellmont, and in the erection of Burke, it has been reduced to its present limits.

At the first town meeting in 1799, Lewis Ransom was elected *supervisor and clerk;* Ralph Shepard, Jesse Ketchum, and Benj. Roberts, *assessors;* Amasa Farman, *collector;* Gilbert Raymond, L. Ransom, *poor masters;* Azeur Hawks, Geo. Platt, Nathan Beeman, *commissioners highways;* Thomas Smith, Amasa Farman, *constables;* Amasa Farman, Peleg Douglas, Ezekiel Hodges, Benj. Roberts, Jesse Ketchum, *path masters.* The town in 1800 gave 86 votes for senator.

Supervisors.—1799-1802, Lewis Ransom; 1803-5, William Bailey; 1806-8, Gates Hoit; 1809-10, William Bailey; 1811, James Ormesbee; 1812, Lebeus Fairman; 1813-21, G. Hoit; 1822-3, George W. Douglas; 1824-5, Gideon Collins; 1826, Ira Smith; 1827-8, G. Collins; 1829-31, Jacob Smith; 1832, John D. Miles; 1833-6, John Mitchel; 1837-8, Ezra Stiles; 1839, G. Collins; 1840-41, J. Mitchel; 1842, Henry R. Smith; 1843, Daniel N. Huntington; 1844, G. Collins; 1845-9, H. B. Smith; 1850, Jonathan Hoit; 1851, H. B. Smith; 1852, Thomas Bennet.

Bounties for noxious animals have been voted as follows: For panthers, $10 in 1815; $30 in 1818, '19, '20, '21. For wolves, $10 in 1807, '08,* '15; $15 in 1817, '18; $20 in 1819, '20, '26. For bears, $10 in 1818, '19, '20, '21. For foxes, $2 in 1817; $4 in 1818, '19; $5 in 1820, '21. For squirrels, $0·25 in 1817; $1 for every 12 in 1820, to residents of the town only. For wolvarines, $15 in 1819. For black birds, $0·25 in 1817. For crows, $0·50 in 1817, '18; $1 in 1820, '21.

Feb. 12, 1821, at a special meeting "held upon application of twelve freeholders, to see if the inhabitants will agree to drop these bounties," it was decided by ballot that no proceeding should be had in the matter. At a subsequent special meeting they were discontinued.

Notes from the Records.—1804, "If any man leave syrup so that it kill or injure cattle, he shall pay damage;" this vote again passed in 1806, '08. 1805, if any person having any thistle or tory weed growing in any of their improved lands, or in the highway passing these lands, and by them occupied, shall by the 1st of July cut or destroy the same to prevent their going to seed, on a penalty of $5 for each neglect. 1810, $80 for a pound; $150 of the poor money to purchase a merino ram to belong to the town. At an extra meeting 1809, resolved to raise $3,500 by tax in three years, for a court house and jail, after a law is passed authorizing it. 1820, $25 voted to purchase a compass and chain for the use of the town.

Townships 6 and 7 were surveyed in the summer of 1795 by Cochran & Ransom, assisted by Samuel and Nathan Beeman (father and son),

* Expressly stipulated that bounties should not be paid for the *unborn young.*

Benj. Roberts, and others, and the latter thus becoming acquainted with the quality of the land, resolved to purchase and settle here. The first improvement was begun by Benjamin Roberts, from Ferrisburgh, Vt., and Nathan Beeman,* from Plattsburgh, early in 1796. At this time the frontier settlement was in Beekmantown, six miles west of Plattsburgh.

Having decided upon emigrating far beyond the limits of civilized life, Mr. Roberts left his home in February, 1796, with his family and goods, and arrived safely at Plattsburgh, where he left his family, and attempted to proceed with a portion of his goods to his destination. With the assistance of some of the land proprietors, and others, who felt an interest in the proposed settlement, they proceeded with a number of teams as far as was practicable (about eighteen miles), where they were compelled from the depth of the snows to abandon the undertaking, and leaving their loading concealed in the woods with hemlock boughs, they returned to Plattsburgh. In March, Mr. Roberts, with Levi Trumbull, a young man whom he had hired, set out with an intention of making sugar, and there being a firm crust on the snow, they started with a hand sled for the place where their loading had been deposited, and taking a five-pail iron kettle, and an old fashioned Dutch iron pot, holding about ten gallons, some provisions, an axe, and tapping gouge, they proceeded with these, drawing them on the sled by hand to Chateaugay, a distance of about twenty-two miles, along a narrow path that had been partly cut through the fall before, in anticipation of a road. Mr. Roberts had also provided a hut the fall previous, which was not covered. They soon fitted up a quantity of bass wood troughs, and commenced making sugar. While occupying this camp, they were on one occasion visited by an Indian, who sold them a moose, the flesh of which they cut up and smoked over their fire, as they were making sugar. At the close of the sugar season they left their sugar, smoked meat, and kettles, in their camp, and returned to Plattsburgh.

In the early part of April, Mr. R. again started with his family, consisting of a wife and four children, and several hired men. These were Levi Trumbull, Joshua Chamberlin, Kinkade Chamberlin, Ethan A. Roberts, Jared Munson. Their outfit consisted of a yoke of oxen, and a pair of steers, for leaders, attached to a sled containing a few articles of indispensable use, but they had not proceeded more than a mile beyond the house of a Mr. Delong, the last settler in Beekmantown, when one of the oxen gave out from fatigue. He was here unyoked and left to provide for himself, as the spring was just opening and vegetation had advanced enough to afford a scanty supply of food; and Roberts proposed to his wife to return with her young children to the settlement, until another opportunity offered; but with heroic resolution she in-

* In his youth Mr. B. resided at Ticonderoga, and acted as the guide to Allen and Arnold, in the surprisal of that fortress, in March, 1775. Being but a lad, he like other children, was allowed the range of the premises, and was familiar with every nook and avenue. Under his guidance Ethan Allen was conducted to the chamber of the British commander, who was surprised and captured without resistance. In relating this occurrence, Mr. Beeman said, that Capt. Delaplace, after some conversation with Mr. Allen, happening to see him in company with the provincials, enquired: "What! are you here Nathan?" This question aroused a sense of conscious guilt and shame, for having betrayed the confidence reposed in him, in rewarding kindness with treachery. Mr. Beeman died in Chateaugay in 1850.

30

sisted upon sharing the hardships of the undertaking, and resolved to proceed. The husband, having placed in a rude bark saddle, such burden upon the odd ox as he was able conveniently to,carry, and suspended from the yoke of the steers a pack containing a few articles of first necessity, he took upon.his own back one of his boys, and led the way, driving his cattle before him, and followed by his wife, bearing an infant in her arms. His men and two older boys, then mere lads, bearing each such burdens as their strength permitted, brought up the rear. What could not be taken was left, covered up on the sled. A part of their loading was a barrel of rum, which was left, excepting a copper teakettle full, which they took along; and this being exhausted to within a quart, the remainder was preserved for Mrs. Roberts. Wherever night overtook them, they encamped in such a place as they might happen to be. They were from Monday till Saturday, in performing the journey of about forty miles, and reached their sugar camp about noon on Saturday, finding all safe. During this toilsome march, Mrs. Roberts was often compelled to pause and rest, and as they ascended the last hill, she enquired dispairingly how much further it was to the end of their journey.

The remainder of the first day and the next was spent in covering their hut with barks, and they completed this labor just in time to save themselves from a drenching rain. A set of table furniture was made of wood, upon which to eat, consisting of trenches and forks. To supply the family with provisions, the odd ox was sent once a week to Plattsburgh, with Chamberlain as driver, and with the regularity of the mails, this animal performed his weekly trips, bearing on his back a supply of flour and pork, upon which they relied for support during the first season. The party commenced a clearing on the south bank of Marble river, about half a mile north of the present village of Chateaugay, and during the summer of 1796, about forty acres were cut and partly cleared. A small patch of potatoes and turnips was got in, the seed of the former, being brought on the backs of Wm. Roberts and Nathan Beeman, from Cumberland Head. To economize weight, the seed ends and eyes of the potatoes, were only brought. Beeman from Plattsburgh, had been on several times during the summer, and having made arrangements for moving, brought on his family in the fall. Mrs. Roberts had been in the settlement three months, without seeing the face of any one of her sex, until the arival of Mrs. B. Within the first three years, John Allen, Samuel Haight, Lewis Ransom, Jacob Smith, Azur Hawks, Noah Lee, Gilbert Reynolds, Jesse Ketchum, Silas Pomeroy, David McMullen, Claudius Britton, Samuel Turner, Stephen Vaughan, Peleg Douglas, David Mallory, Thomas Smith, Gate Hoit, Ezekiel Hodges, Samuel Stoten, Israel Thayer, Avery Stiles, and Moses Corban, and perhaps a few others, mostly men of families, and from Vermont, came into the town, selected and purchased lands, commenced small improvements, and made arrangements for making a permanent settlement. David Mallory, during the second year of the settlement, commenced the erection of the first grist mill, on Marble river, about a mile and a half north west of the present village of Chateaugay. A mortar was rigged up during the first season, by excavating a hole in the top of a stump, the pestle being suspended from a bough, in such a manner, that the force of the grinder was required only in bringing down the pestle. The principal milling, however, was done in Plattsburgh, and the trip required generally a week. The first crop raised, was some seventy bushels of potatoes, and a quantity of turnips. The mill was built for

Nathaniel Platt, of Plattsburgh, who was somewhat interested in the titles of the town. The millwright was Elisha Howard, of Vermont. It was got in operation in the year it was begun. A saw mill was built by the same parties near the grist mill, and the same year. The first birth in town, is said to have been that of Alanson Roberts in 1796. The first school was taught about 1799. The settlement grew quite rapidly for several years, principally on the Fort Covington and the Malone roads, the former of which was opened as a winter road about the year 1798. These became the thoroughfares of emigrants from Vermont, on their way to St. Lawrence and at the time of the war a thriving settlement existed, numbers here as elsewhere, returned to New England, on the approach of war, and of this number, some never returned. The first road was worked by subscription and voluntary labor, so as to be passable in 1800. A turnpike company was incorporated April 8, 1805, to build a road from Plattsburgh to the Macomb purchase, and March 14, 1806, the limitation was extended 3 years; and should 10 miles be built, the company might for 7 years collect double tolls. This company, it is believed, did not organize. A law of April 9, 1811, directed the managers of the lottery for the purchase of the Botanic garden to raise $5,000 to improve the road to the county line. On the 8th of June, 1812, a law directed $5,000 to be paid out of the state treasury for the purpose. The preamble of this law, states that "the said county of Franklin forms a part of the northern frontier of this state, and the settlements therein are situated on the borders of a foreign territory, and at a great distance from the other settlement." The two counties were to tax themselves $150 annually, to repay the $5,000, until it should be repaid by the lottery. A sum not exceeding $750, annually, might be raised by tax, during two years, for the finishing of the road. During the military operations of the war, and especially in 1813, when General Wade Hampton was passing with his army through, to form a junction with Wilkinson on the St. Lawrence, necessity compelling him to improve it, in order to maintain a communication with the lake. In one of his letters, he states, that he had made it a perfect turnpike, In 1815-16, a party of United States troops, under Captain William F. Haile, built twenty miles of road towards Franklin Co., but it was continued no further by the general government. In 1830, a law directed a tax of $2,000 in Malone and Chateaugay, to be expended by commissioners, on the road from Plattsburgh to Malone. The Chateaugay Turnpike Company was incorporated April 21, 1828, to build a road from Malone Court House, by way of Chateaugay lake to Mooers, but was never organized.

A forge was erected by Wm. Bailey about 1803-4, about three miles above Chateaugay, on the river, but never made but a few tons of iron. Ore was derived from swamps in the vicinity of Chateaugay lake, but this proved to be in limited quantities. Some ore was afterwards drawn from Constable and from Clinton Co., but the manufacture under the circumstances was found to be a losing operation and was after a trial of two or three years abandoned. A large paper mill was begun by the same person in the vicinity of the forge, but never completed.

During the summer of 1812, the inhabitants for their own protection, and by voluntary labor and contributions, erected a block house on a commanding elevation on the bank of the Chateaugay river, three miles north west of the village. Upon the representation of Mr. Gate Hoit to Governor Tompkins, the sum of $100 was applied as a partial remuneration for the expense of erection. During the war it was occupied a part of the time by the troops stationed in town, and towards the close of the war or soon after, it was privately burned as was supposed, by

some one from Canada. In 1812, a detachment of regular troops under
Col's Wool and Snelling, were stationed a short time at Chateaugay. They
were encamped near the north part of the town. Gen. Wade Hampden,
with an army consisting mostly of new recruits from Vermont, and intended to coöperate in the unsuccessful enterprise of Gen. Wilkinson,
against Montreal, marched from Plattsburgh as far as this town in Aug.,
and camped in the vicinity of Chateaugay Corners. In November he returned to Plattsburgh. A quantity of flour with a small guard for its protection, was left. While he lay encamped near the Corners, small bodies
of troops occupied positions nearer the province line, and one of these
came near having an engagement with the enemy. One of the sentinels
was shot, and a small show of force was made which retreated, and it
was believed that an ambuscade had been laid in hopes of decoying the
party into it. On this occasion, they took one of the inhabitants (Salmon
Smith,) a prisoner into Canada, but he soon escaped and returned. I or
some years previous to the war, a settlement of New England people
had existed in Canada near Chateaugay river, but on the occurrence of
hostilities, they abandoned their improvements, and moved into the state.
Few if any of these ever returned or received any compensation for the
property left, which was subsequently sold by government to European
emigrants. Soon after the arrival of General Wilkinson at French Mills,
a regiment under Col. Bissell, which had formed a part of his force, proceeded to Chateaugay, and remained during the winter. On the evacuation of French Mills, the greater part of Wilkinson's army passed
through on their way to Plattsburgh, and were soon after followed by a
detachment of the enemy under Col. Scott, who pressed whatever teams
they could find, and succeeded in finding and in carrying away a considerable amount of provisions which had been left by the American army.
On returning, the British destroyed the bridges to hinder from pursuit.
At the time of their incursion they proceeded as far as where the
road crosses Marble river, towards Plattsburgh, and succeeded in inter-
cepting an express which had been dispatched to convey information to
the American forces at Plattsburgh. Upon finally receiving information,
a detachment started and had proceeded about a dozen miles, when they
were met by the intelligence that the invaders had retreated. The enemy
were joined at this place by a company of Indians under a white captain,
who came up the Chateaugay river from Canada. Much complaint was
made by the inhabitants about the seizure of private property by the enemy, who were said to have been not over particular in selecting public
from private stores.

After this occurrence, no military operations occurred in town during
the war. A portion of the citizens, in common with other parts of the
county, was called out on the eve of the battle of Plattsburgh, to assist in
the defense of that place, and proceeded under the command of General
Alric Man, by a southern route near Chateaugay lake, to avoid being intercepted by the enemy. This detachment did not arrive till after the
action. On approaching the village a firing of cannon was heard, and
they hastened on to afford any aid they might be able, but ascertained
that it was but the firing of minute guns at the burial of the dead.

By an act of March 20, 1843, the sum of $500 per annum for three
years, was applied towards the construction of a bridge over Chateaugay
river, near Douglass's mills, out of the tolls collected on the military road
from Plattsburgh. It was to be constructed under the joint direction of
the military road commissioners in Franklin county, and the road commissioners in Chateaugay.

Chataugay Tunnel and Embankment—Northern Railroad.

Among the most successful achievements in the line of rail road engineering in the state, may be reckoned the high embankment and tunnel a short distance west of the station at Chateaugay. The surface of the country in the northern part of Franklin county, is in the main level, and finely adapted to agricultural purposes, but the Chateaugay, Salmon and other rivers in their descent to the St. Lawrence, have worn for themselves deep and narrow valleys, which afford in numerous places, the most picturesque scenery, but which opposed an obstacle of great magnitude in the construction of the Northern rail road. To overcome that at Chateaugay, it was resolved to fill in the valley with earth, in order to bring it up level with the surface on each side. To ensure a channel for the river in such a manner that the embankment should not suffer from its encroachment, a tunnel 300 feet long, was first made through the solid rock, which bordered the valley, and permanent walls erected to direct the stream through its new channel, and to retain the earth of the embankment in its place. This great undertaking was completed after nearly two years labor, at a cost of about $130,000. The tunnel was begun in August, 1848, and made in five months. The embankment is over 800 feet long, and its top 160 feet above the level of the river. It contains 500,000 cubic yards of earth. The tunnel is 25 feet wide, 22 high. Retaining walls 50 feet high. This work was planned and executed under the direction of Col. Charles L. Schlatter, civil engineer.

About a mile south of the Chateaugay tunnel, there occurs on this river a beautiful cascade, which from the singular wildness and sublimity of the surrounding scenery, is well worthy of the visit of those who take pleasure in studying the wild and picturesque. This locality affords much more of interest than many other places which annually draw their thousands, and if known and suitably appreciated, would not fail to draw its share of wonder-loving visitors, who would return amply compensated for their labor. This fall occurs in a ravine which the stream has worn through the Potsdam sandstone, to the depth of nearly 200 feet, and the principal fall is at the outlet of a narrow gorge, and has a vertical height of about 50 feet.

About half a mile east of Chateaugay village, and but a few yards north of the rail road, occurs an intermittent spring, which is worthy of notice. This spring rises from two sources through the sand, and in such volume as, in ordinary seasons, to turn a water wheel for a mechanic shop. The water is remarkably clear and cold, is never known to freeze, and discharges bubbles of gas (said to be nitrogen), in considerable quantities while running. There is no certain period of its intermitting, nor does this appear to be affected by rains. Some times the period of its flowing will last for one or two years; but it is generally dry towards the close of summer. Once it failed in the month of February. It is said generally to stop quite abruptly, not occupying more than twenty-four hours from the time it begins to fail, till it is nearly or quite dry; but on again starting, it will but slowly increase, and not attain its full flow before one or two weeks. It has been said that the return of the water is preceded by a low subteranean murmur, but there is a difference of opinion on this point among the inhabitants of the vicinity sufficient to render the fact doubtful, as it is in itself improbable. There is a smaller but constant spring less than a mile northeast of this, which discharges gas, but the nature of these gaseous emanations has not been ascertained. Springs of ample volume are common along the northern border of Franklin county, and in the towns of Chateaugay, Westville, and perhaps other towns, there are several of sufficient volume to turn a mill, but with the exceptions above stated, there are none known that intermit or discharge gas. This curious spring in early time attracted the curiosity of the Indians, who called it Hu-nah-a-ta-ko-wah, " a big spring rushing out of the ground."

Religious Societies.—In 1800 or 1801, one Huntingdon, a Presbyterian, held the first meetings in town, at the house of Judge Bailey, and about 1802, Henry Ryan, a M. E. circuit preacher, visited the town. In 1805, a class of about 6, was formed with Benj. Emmons for leader. In 1804, a revival occurred. The first Methodist ministry had, it is said, some forty appointments in four weeks, extending 300 miles. The largest accession in any year, was 100, in 1843 or 4.

A Congregational church was formed in 1816, by the Rev. Jas. Johnson and A. Parmelee, in what is now Burke. Since the division of the town, there has been formed in Burke a separate church. The form was changed, April 4, 1842, to Presbyterian, and like the other churches of this order in the county, it belongs to the Champlain Presbytery. The church edifice at Chateaugay was begun in 1827, and dedicated July 4, 1842, sermon by Rev. Ashbel Parmelee. The clergymen have been Jacob Hart, Moses Parmelee, James Millar, Andrew M. Millar, —— Baxter and A. M. Millar, the present one, from whom most of the foregoing facts were received.

A Baptist church was formed Feb. 12, 1817, by Elder Isaac Sawyer. Israel Thayer was chosen deacon, and George W. P. Beman, clerk. The Baptist house of worship was commenced in 1820, and dedicated in 1838. The dedication sermon was preached by Elder Farr. The largest accession of their numbers occurred in 1830. The original number at the formation of the church, was about eleven. The Rev. Mr. Sawyer was succeeded by Rev. —— Johnson, who remained but a few months; Rev. David Byington, who remained a year, and Rev. Ephraim Smith, who has been, with some short intervals, the only minister employed since 1820. The Rev. Jeremiah Dwyer, during the above period, has been employed one year. On the formation of the town of Burke, about two-thirds of the members found themselves in the new town, and soon organized a new society, which, in the fall of 1852, are erecting a brick church in that town. The Baptist church of Chateaugay is at present quite small.

In 1835, there were classes of Protestant Methodists formed in town, and the numbers belonging to them were once somewhat numerous, but the church is now extinct.

CONSTABLE

Was formed from Harrison, March 13, 1807, embracing townships 1, 2, 3, and the Indian reservation. The first town meeting was held at the house of Jacob Settles, at which Albon Man was chosen *supervisor*; Ezekiel Payne, *clerk*; Joseph Wright, John Cadwell, Seth Blancher, *assessors*; Anthony Sprague, *collector*; Alric Man, Jonathan Hapgood, *overseers of poor*; Alric Man, Aseph Perry, Alexander McMillen, *com'rs of highways*; Anthony Sprague, Isaac Fairchild, A. McMillen, *constables*; John Smith, Seth Blancher, Amos Eldrige, *fence viewers*; Jno. Hapgood, David Danforth, Albon Man, *pound keepers*; John Livingston, Wm. Perry, Seth Blancher, David McMillen, Christopher Austin, *overseers of highways.*

Supervisors.—1807-10, Albon Man; 1811, Alric Man; 1812-13, Albon Man; 1814-23, Alric Man; 1824-5, Lewis Dubois; 1826, Guy Meigs;

1827, Ebenezer Man; 1828-31, Sylvester Langdon; 1832, J. G. Dickey; 1833, Sylvester Langdon; 1834-5, J. G. Dickey; 1836-7, Harry Horton; 1838, Sylvester Langdon; 1839, Augustus Martin; 1840-1, George W. Darling; 1842 3, Putnam W. Sumner; 1844-5, Sidney W. Gillett; 1846-7, J. G. Dickey; 1848, Washington Wooster; 1849, Lucian Wyman; 1850-1, Wm. Daggett; 1852, Joseph Hastings.

Notes from the Records.—Bounties on wolves, $5, in 1807; $10 in 1808 to '14, 1817-28; $15 in 1821; $20 in 1830. On foxes, $1 in 1819-20; $3 in 1821, with half this price for young foxes that had not left the burrow. On panthers, $20 in 1820. In 1812, voted in favor of making three towns of townships 1, 2 and 3. In 1814, $50 appropriated for burying the dead of the U. S. troops. 50 cts. penalty for geese running at large. In 1816, the question of diving the town again came up. In 1830, for abolishing the distinction between town and county poor. In 1846, on license election, 00, no license, 82. An act of April 21, 1846, required a tax of $250, for the erection or purchase of a town house, whenever the electors should direct.

William Constable, from whom this town is named, was a son of John Constable, a surgeon in the English army, during the French and English war, who in 1762, took a commission in the 1st regiment of the province of New York. He had but two sons, William and James. The former was born in Dublin, in 1761. A sister named Eweretta, married James Phyn, of Scotland, and another, Harriet, Thomas Pierce, of Bristol, England. James, was a bachelor, and died at New York, in 1807. Wm. Constable was married in Philadelphia, to Ann, daughter of Townsend White. Their children were Anna, Eweretta, William, John, Harriet, Emily and Matilda, all of which names occur among the names originally given the townships of the Great purchase. Of the daughters, the first married H. B. Pierrepont; the second, James Mc-Vickar; the the third, James Duane; the fourth, Dr. Samuel W. Moore, of New York; and the fifth, Edward McVickar. Wm. Constable became a leading director of the Bank of New York, and a merchant on an extensive scale, and sent one of the first ships from this country to China for trade, with Wm. Bell, as supercargo. During the fifteen years previous to his death, which occurred in May, 1803, Mr. Constable was actively and extensively engaged in land sales, and had great influence with the other persons concerned in these operations.

The first settlement in town was made on the south line of the town, by Jonathan Hapgood and Christopher Austin, from Milton, Vt., in 1800. These were related and formed but one family. They come as far as Chateaugay in March, and in June proceeded to the place they had selected for a settlement. William Cooper, of Salem, N. Y., Solomon Cook, and Ebenezer Titus, from Rutland county, Vt., Saul Clark, James Welch, Artemas and Thomas Smith, Peleg Austin, James Lyman, William Buell, and others had settled in town, in the year 1805, or previous. The first saw mill was erected by James Welch, in 1803. He settled a short distance south of the present village of Constable Corners. The first grist mill in town, was built soon after the war, by Joseph Colburn, of Vermont. The first school was taught in the summer of 1806, by Miss A. Mead, in a barn owned by J. Hapgood. At Constable Corners schools were not established earlier than 1811, when the first school was taught by one Blodget. The first physician who settled in town was Dr. Solomon Wyman. During the prevalence of the cholera, in

1832, a considerable number of cases occurred in town, some of which were fatal.

Religious Societies.—A Congregational society was formed May. 25, 1817, with Solomon Wyman, Samuel R. Nims, Alric Man, Oliver Bell, and John Child, trustees. A church was formed by Rev. J. Armstrong in 1822, who remained six years. His successors have been Jacob Hart, —— Butler, Tertius Reynolds, John L. Edgerton, Aaron Foster and Benjamin Marvin, none of whom have been installed the pastors. In 1847 its form was changed to Presbyterian. The society about 1844 erected a commodious church at an expense of $2500, of which Edward Ellice, the land owner, gave $400.

A Baptist church was formed May 4. 1833, of thirty one members. A Free Will Baptist church was formed in Malone and Constable, by Elder Samuel Hart, Moores Cole, a licentiate, in 1841. Pastors, Elder Samuel Hart, W. Warner, G. W. Town. Present number 20.

DICKINSON,

Was formed April 11, 1808, (to take effect April 1, 1809,) from Harrison, embracing Nos. 4, 5, 6, and all south. It has been reduced by the formation of Bangor and Moira, to its present limits. The first town meeting was held at the house of Appleton Foote. The name of the town is said to have been derived from a gentleman in New Jersey. At the time of formation, the entire settlement was in what is now Moira and Bangor. The first set of town officers were Samuel Pease, *supervisor;* Apollos Lathrop, *clerk;* Rufus Tilden, Chester Tuller, Elisha Drury, *assessors;* R. Tilden, *collector;* Appleton Foote, and Joseph Plumb, *poor masters;* Samuel Foster, John Potter, Robert Wilson, *com'rs highways;* R. Tilden, Edward Chapman, *constables.*

Supervisors.—1809, S. Pease; 1810-12, Joseph Plumb; 1813-22; Jonathan Lawrence; 1823, Jason Pierce; 1824, J. Lawrence; 1825-28, J. Pierce; 1829-32, Loderick Butterfield; 1833-34, Erastus Hutchins; 1845, Reuben Cady; 1836-41, E. Hutchins; 1842-43, Warren Ives; 1844-45, Peter Whitney; 1846-52, W. Ives. Bounties on animals have been voted as follows: For wolves, $10, 1809-10-12-17-18-19-20-28. $15 in 1811-12-13-21. $20 in 1815. For panthers, $10 in 1820. $15 in 1817. $20 in 1821. $25 in 1818. For foxes $2 in 1816 to 21. For bears, $3 in 1820; $5 in 1819-21. For catamounts, $20 in 1819. For crows, 37½ cents in 1816. For squirrels, 12½ cents in 1817. For chipmucks, 12½ cents in 1816. 1809, *resolved,* that all license money drawn from the town of Ezraville, and all that shall be due June 1, be appropriated for the use of the best kind of sheep. At a special meeting Nov. 10 1821, the bounties on animals withdrawn. In 1821 the poor moneys on hand amounted to $663.95 In 1830, opposed the poor house system. Dec. 10, 1830, voted to apply the poor moneys for schools. The town has usually voted for schools as much money as the law allows.

The earliest settlers in the present limits of Dickinson, is said to have been William Thomas, who located a short distance south of where the St. Lawrence turnpike was afterwards located. He had first settled in Hopkinton, and after a short residence here, returned to that town. Jonathan and Jesse D. Rice, from New Hampshire, settled at an early day. Reuben Cady and others had located in town previous to 1812. Most of the first settlement was limited to the St. Lawrence turnpike, which passes obliquely across the northern border of the town, and soon after its completion became a thoroughfare of great importance, especially in the military movements of the years 1813, '14. The Port Kent and Hopkinton road began to be settled soon after its construction, but the improvements along this route were scattered and limited. The present settlement of the town is limited to the central and western portions of Annastown, or township number seven. With the exception of three or four families on the Northwest Bay road, and a very small settlement at the head of Tupper's lake, near the southern extremity of the town, its whole extent is an unbroken wilderness. The facilities to market which the rail-road furnishes, has given new value to the timber of this region, in common with other portions of the northern counties, and has created several lumbering establishments in the depths of the forest, which will hereafter form the centres of settlements for farming purposes.

About midway between the Port Kent road on the south and the St. Lawrence turnpike on the north, and near the centre of number seven, is situated on Deer river a small village named *Thomasville.* It owes its origin and name to John Thomas, a former resident of Hopkinton, who in the latter part of the summer of 1839 commenced the erection of mills, and remained about a year. Deer river at this point affords a fine water power, which has been improved by the erection of two saw mills and a grist mill. The hamlet contains several mechanic shops, two stores, and a small cluster of dwellings.

A most melancholy accident occurred in Dickinson, on the 3d of Sept., 1852, in which the dwelling of Mr. Eseck Hawkins was burned, and his wife, and a son six years of age, perished in the flames. Most of the family lodged in the chamber, except the parents, who on discovering the house to be on fire, made vigorous efforts to rescue their children from the devouring element, and in this Mrs. H. perished. The father rushed into the room where his children were sleeping, and succeeded in rescuing all but one, which he found it beyond his power to save. The charred remains of the mother and son were collected, and interred in the same coffin. The funeral was attended by thousands of sympathizing friends and citizens, and the melancholy disaster spread a gloom over the surrounding community.

Religious Societies.—The Christian sect was organized in 1816, '17, by Eld. Spooner, and was for many years the only church in town. It prospered for some years, but has now become almost extinct. The whole number received was eighty. A Free Will Baptist church was formed in 1836. The clergy have been Chas. Bowles, John Kimble, and others; at present Eld. A. P. Walcott.

DUANE,

Was formed from Malone, Jan. 24, 1828, and in the erection of Harrietstown reduced to its present limits. It was named from James Duane, Esq., from Schenectady. who having acquired, by marriage with a daughter of W. Constable, the title of a considerable portion of the town, in 1821-2 caused the tract to be surveyed; in 1823-4 commenced improvements and erected a dwelling, and in 1825 removed with his family and made a permanent settlement. He was then nearly ten miles beyond neighbors, and the most remote settler in the forest. A considerable number located soon after, and the iron manufacture gave life and spirit to the settlements. A forge was erected in 1828, for the manufacture of iron from ore which had been discovered the year previous, but which from the disturbance of the needle in surveying, had been supposed since

1822 to exist. The ore wrought at this forge was the steel ore, so called, which occurred in its vicinity, the veins or beds running southeast and northwest in the direction of the strata of gneiss of the vicinity. The forge was carried off in a great freshet: afterwards rebuilt, burnt, and again rebuilt, to be a second time injured in a freshet. These misfortunes, together with the great expense of transportation, put an end to the enterprise after a few years. During the time that the forge was in operation, it made from a hundred to a hundred and twenty-five tons of iron annually. In 1838, a quarter furnace was erected by the Duane brothers, on Deer river, in the west part of No. 12, and was intended to be used for the reduction of primitive ores exclusively. The cold air blast was at first used, but afterwards the apparatus for heating the air was inserted. Immense difficulty was experienced in procuring iron, as the ores were very difficult to reduce, and many trials were found necessary to arrive at an economical method of fluxing and separating them. The business was continued seven or eight years, during which about six hundred tons of iron were made, a great part of which was made into castings on the premises. The difficulty of smelting, together with the great expense attending the manufacture in a situation several miles distant from the district that was to afford support to the laborers, and especially the prohibitory expenses of transportation to market, resulted in the loss of many thousand dollars to the enterprising projectors, and the works were discontinued in 1849. The stock of this furnace, and all the arrangements connected with it, were admirably constructed, and will compare favorably with any of the class in the state. This furnace is located on the Port Kent and Hopkinton road, fifty-seven miles from Lake Champlain. Deer river post office was established here for the accommodation of that section of the town, but discontinued in 1841.

For manufacturing steel directly from the mixed primitive and specular ores of Duane, a company was chartered by an act passed May 20, 1841, under the name of the Franklin Native Steel Manufacturing Company. James C. Dunne, Samuel W. Jones, Frederick A. Duane, Robert Duane, Benjamin M. Duane, and such as might join them, were to form the company. Capital $50,000; shares $100 each, with power to increase their capital to $150,000. This company was never formed.

The first saw mill in Duane was erected by the proprietor in 1823, on the west branch of Salmon river. In 1828, a grist mill was built on the same. The only religious society in Duane is the Methodist.

There was formerly a small Presbyterian society, but this has been broken up by death and removal of its members. The Episcopal service was performed statedly in town, by the Rev. Mr. Hart, from Malone, during several months in 1828. A building for religious meetings and public purposes, was erected by Mr. Duane in 1828. The greater part of township No. 12 was surveyed by John Frost, in 1821-2.

James Duane has been the supervisor of this town, except 1848, when Ezekiel Ladd was elected. The latter had been chosen in 1840, but at the election which followed the division of the town soon after, he was superseded.

FORT COVINGTON,

Was erected from Constable Feb. 28, 1817, and in the formation of Bombay, reduced to its present limits. Its name is derived from Brig. Gen. Leonard Covington, who was born in Maryland, Oct. 26, 1768, of respectable ancestry, and at an early age evinced a strong inclination to the profession of arms. He served under Wayne in the Indian wars at the west, and in 1809, was commissioned lieutenant colonel in the regiment of dragoons, was stationed in Louisiana, and became a resident of Natchez. In 1813, he joined the northern army, and in July was made brigadier general. At Chrysler's field he was wounded by a musket ball through his bowels, while at the head of his troops, of which he died on board a boat, on the way to French Mills, where he was buried with military honors. Several years after, his remains, with those of Col. Johnson and Lieut. Eaton, were taken to Sackett's Harbor.

It was at first proposed to name the town *Covington*, but this was anticipated by a new town in Genesee county. The first town officers were: Sebius Fairman, *supervisor;* Amos Welch, *clerk;* Isaac Fairchild, David Danforth, *assessors;* Isaac Fairchild, *collector;* Daniel W. Church, Wareham Hastings, Luther Danforth, *commissioners of highways;* Ambrose Cushman, Luther Danforth, *overseers of the poor;* Sebius Fairman, Seth Blanchard, Isaac Fairchild *commissioners of common schools;* Jonathan Wallace, John M. Rodgers, Ezekiel Payne, *inspectors of schools;* Isaac Fairchild, Wm. Whelpley, *constables;* Seth Blanchard, Luther Danforth, David McMillin, *fence viewers;* Ardus M. Hitchcock, David McMillin, B. D. Hitchcock, *pound masters.*

Supervisors.—1817–18, Sebius Fairman; 1819, Isaac Fairchild; 1820–2, S. Fairman; 1823, George B. R. Gove; 1824–5, Wm. Hogan; 1826–7, G. B. R. Gove; 1828–30, W. Hogan; 1830, James B. Spencer, to fill vacancy; 1831, no record; 1832, Wilson Randall; 1833, G. B. R. Gove; 1834, Uriah D. Meeker; 1835, Henry Longly; 1836-7, Tilness Briggs; 1838, James Campbell; 1839, G. B. R. Gove; 1840, Jonathan Wallace; 1841-2, Sidney Briggs; 1843, J. Campbell; 1844–5, S. Briggs; 1846–7, Warren L. Manning; 1848, Schuyler Button; 1849, W. L. Manning; 1850, Stephen V. R. Tuthill; 1851, J. Wallace; 1852, Preserved Ware.

Bounties have been offered for the destruction of noxious animals as follows: For wolves, $5 in 1829; $10 in 1817–18–19; $20 in 1821. For panthers, $10 in 1817–18–19; $20 in 1821. For foxes, $1 in 1820–1. For crows, 25 cents in 1817–18. For striped squirrels and black birds, 3 cents in 1817; for black birds, 6 cents in 1818. In 1817, voted $250, on condition that Constable will raise as much, to build a poor house. This was not done. In 1819, a town house was built by subscription, and finished in 1820. For one year it was used as an academy, and since as a district school house.

Much relating to French titles, &c., is excluded for want of space. In 1793, the chiefs of St. Regis leased to Wm. Gray, a tract on Salmon river for $200 annual rent, after the first four years. An inducement with the chiefs was, the promise of the erection of mills. Feb. 6, 1796, Gray and one Thomas Araquente, another chief, entered into terms of assignment, by which the latter gained the saw mill, then of no great value, but no regular papers were signed till Dec. 15, 1798, when the chiefs in full council, confirmed the conveyance. James Robertson, of Montreal, Dec. 29, 1798, bought this lease for $2,400 to T. A.. and the annuity of $200 to the St. Regis tribe, without a warranty on the part of Araquente, of the lands on both sides of Salmon river, from its source to a line to be drawn at a distance of half a mile from the mill. The mill and one mile square was, however, conveyed by warranty. Mr. Robertson and his brother Alexander, who had a joint and equal interest with him, continued to occupy until the death of J. R., when Neil and Patrick Robertson became entitled to equal moieties of his share. In 1804, (Sept. 11,) after spending $2,209 in the erection of a grist mill, it was swept off in a flood. $4,762 was soon after spent in rebuilding the mill, but before it was completed Alexander Robertson died, leaving Francis Desriviere, Esq., tutor and guardian of his minor children, by whom and the above Neil and Patrick Robertson, the mill was furnished and leased to Robert Buchanan, the person who built them. P. R. died in 1808 or '9, and N. R. in 1812, and a lengthy memorial in the archives of state, dated Jan. 30, 1818, from which the above facts are drawn, asserts that since the above deaths Mr. Buchanan, with others who had obtained leases within the mile square, had disclaimed the title of the Robertsons and refused to pay rent. This title was long a subject of litigation, and was not finally settled until after the treaty of 1818 and the award of the commissioners.

With the exception of a few French families who lived and worked around the saw mill, there was no settlement for agricultural purposes until about 1800. About this year or soon after, Samuel Fletcher, Aaron McLean, and Ambrose Cushman, located in No. 2, and John Hunsden, David Lynch, Robert,* Walter and Duncan Buchanan, (natives of Sterlingshire, Scotland,) settled near the mills. At the raising of the grist mill in 1804, help was invited from great distances in Canada, and the state, and when the frame was up it is said that the question arose which was the "smartest," to decide which the Glengarians and Yankees resolved to fight it out in a good natured way, and the result was that the former got severely whipped; and were obliged to own up beaten. The lands in the present village of Fort Covington (formerly French mills), on the east side of the river, within the mile square, were leased in such parcels and at such rates as he might be able to bargain for, by William Hawkins, who had acquired an irregular title, which was disclaimed by the state, and those who had paid for these lands were obliged to repurchase. In 1803, John Hunsden, an Irishman, having become a clerk to the Indians, induced them to cause a part of their tract near the mile square, to be surveyed out into farms, which were conveyed by durable leases, cleared up and improved. The terms were three years without rent, and $10 for every 100 acres annually afterwards. Upon the treaties of 1816 and '18, these settlers petitioned for their rights, and the surveyor general (Simeon De Witt), and two men appointed by the governor, (James S. Kip, of Utica, and Dr. Isaac Sargent, of Cambridge,) were directed to appraise the lands with and without the improvements. In their unpublished report which is before us, it is stated that the leases had been executed by virtue of powers supposed to be granted in the law of 1802, (see p. 154,) and the history of the titles is detailed at length. They reserved for a fort in case of war, 50 acres on the east side of Salmon river, and 14½ on the west side. They very strongly recommended an appropriation for roads in this section. To those who had made improvements on Indian leases, a preëmption was allowed, or if they declined purchasing the land they still might have a lien upon the improvements from those who bought the soil. Special provision was made for certain lots, and Hunsden was allowed $1,200 for services rendered. The legal heirs of the first Robertsons were entitled to the preëmption of a certain lot on condition of $120 being withheld for R. Buchanan. The appraisement and award of the commissioners will be found in the secretary's office at Albany. (*Field book, vol.* 35, *p.* 252.)

Most of the settlers availed themselves of the preëmption and purchased at the land office in Albany their farms. Those who chose to hold their improvements did so, notwithstanding the soil was sold to

Robert Buchanan died in town, October 31, 1828, aged 60.

others, until paid for. A portion of the lands were reappraised and have since been sold. The mile square was subsequently surveyed by the surveyor general into *house lots* and *out lots*, and sold by the state, excepting the two military reserves, which are rented for an indefinite period, and liable to revert whenever wanted for this purpose. Two or three proposals to fortify at this point have been made, and engineers have been on to examine the sites, but nothing has been done in this line and nothing is at present contemplated.

Upon surveying the tract granted in the treaty of 1818, there was found an excess of 307 acres, and a provision was inserted in the act of April 13, 1819, by which the governor was instructed to procure a release of the same and to stipulate an addition to their annuity at the same rates as for the purchase last made, or to pay them at once the present worth of the same.

On the declaration of war a block house was built in the village of French Mills, but never entirely finished, and during the first summer a drafted company of militia under Capt. Rufus Tilden, of Moria, posted as a protection to the frontier, and a guard to the provisions stored here for distribution among the St. Regis Indians. Moses Eggleston of Chateaugay, was lieutenant, and Aden Wood, ensign, and it consisted of about 40 men. During the summer two Troy volunteer companies under Capt. Higby and Lyon, and a drafted company of militia from Columbia county, under Capt. Miller, the whole under Major Young of Troy, were stationed here.

Shortly after the affair at St. Regis, the Troy and Columbia companies at French Mills, were withdrawn (Nov. 1812), and the Franklin county company again left alone. A British detachment of regulars, militia and Indians, made a descent from St. Regis through the woods, upon the post at French Mills. Capt. Tilden surrendered without resistance; the arms were broken and left, the ammunition thrown into the river, and men marched prisoners to St. Regis, and thence to Montreal. In Dec., they were exchanged for the same company which they had captured in Oct. Immediately after this two Columbia county companies under Major Tanner, Capt's Winslow and Gardner, were detached from Colonel Vosburg's regiment stationed at Chateaugay, which staid till March following. They were then withdrawn, and their place supplied by a volunteer company from Franklin county, raised and commanded by Captain David Irving, of Constable, who continued to hold the post until the arrival of Gen. Wilkinson, in November, 1813. Capt. Irving's company subsequently participated in the movements of Gen. Hampton, below Chateaugay. A further account of these operations will be given.

On the 13th of November, 1813, General Wilkinson, with his army, ascended the river in a flotilla of boats, and took up his quarters in the village, where he remained till February. The details of this event will be given in connection with our account of the war. While the American army were in winter quarters at French Mills, a citizen of New York was apprehended, suspected of having put up at the camp the following placard, addressed

"*To the American Army at Salmon River:*"

"NOTICE.—All American soldiers who are willing to quit the *unnatural* war in which they are at present engaged, will receive at the British outposts, the arrears due them by the American government, to the extent of five months pay. No man shall be required to serve against his own country." After numerous inquiries the author has been unable to ascertain from those who were in the service at the time, any particulars in relation to the above occurrence. The army had scarcely left the village than they were followed by the enemy, who remained a week, scouring the country to gather up whatever of public property they might be able to find, and pilfering such private property as the soldiers could conceal from their officers.

In not a single excursion it is said, did the enemy return with his full number, as great numbers deserted the ranks and left singly and in small parties, whenever opportunity offered. These mostly hastened into the interior of the country, going chiefly to Plattsburgh, Utica, &c. The frightful mortality of the troops here will be detailed in our future pages.

Soon after the war, an act was passed by congress, allowing magistrates to take affidavits of certificates of damages to private property during that period, which were to be audited and paid at Washington. A series of frauds was attempted, and to some degree successfully carried on, principally at French Mills, although instances occurred in St. Lawrence county, in which exhorbitant, fictitious and altered accounts were presented. In other instances, fair and honest accounts, were first certified by magistrates, and subsequently forged copies with the items changed, and greatly magnified, were sent to the department for audit and payment. The suspicions of a citizen of French Mills being excited, information was conveyed to government, and an agent was sent to detect and bring to punishment the offenders. This person acquired the confidence of the delinquents, and having become acquainted with the necessary details of their operations, promptly reported them to the civil authorities, who caused several of the party to be arrested. By a singular omission in the law there was no provision made for punishing these frauds, and several escaped from this cause. It is supposed that they were aware of this fact before engaging in them. The ring leader was sent to state's prison, and the others fled. Great numbers having just and honest claims, were cut off from their rights by these frauds.

The first and hitherto the only legal execution that has occurred in Franklin county, was that of Stephen Videto, in public at Malone, on the 26th of August, 1825, for the murder of Fanny Mosely, in this town, on the 2d of February previous. The circumstanc s were briefly as follows: The murderer was a young man a member of his father's family, who had formerly resided in Canada, and had there been slightly acquainted with his victim. He had lived in Fort Covington several years, on a small farm, and was previously remarkable for nothing but an excessively penurious disposition, which he possessed in common with his family. The victim was a person of superior enterprise, and having acquired a small sum of money by her industry, had been married in Canada to a reckless villain, who had abandoned her at Fort Covington, taking with him every thing valuable which she possessed. Being thus thrown desolate upon the charities of the world, she became a member of the Videto family, with whom she had been somewhat acquainted. For some time previous to the murder, some degree of criminal intimacy had been suspected, but the mortal dread of encountering the expense of a family, should they marry, and no alternative existing, is supposed to have led to the resolution of destroying her. To furnish a pretext for providing the means, and for carrying into execution this plan, he feigned to be in fear of his own life from the Indians, with some of whom he had quarrelled, and reported that he repeatedly saw them lurking around the premises, armed. He also became disturbed by the rats, and to destroy these purchased arsenic several days before the murder. He also borrowed a pistol and two muskets, for self defence, and one or two days before gave the alarm that Indians were lying in wait around the house, whom he affected to pursue. On the fatal night, notwithstanding his fears, he allowed a fellow lodger and a brother to go abroad, and neglected to fasten the doors and windows. He remained in the same room with the deceased, and was keeping watch in the night with his fire arms loaded, in readiness to repel any attack, while the woman was sleeping on her bed. Two discharges were heard in quick succession, accompanied by a crash of the window, and he rushed out of the house giving an alarm, and after running to some distance, returned with the statement that the Indians had broken in the window, shot the woman and fled. She was not instantly killed, and he produced some wine or other cordial for her to take. Upon subsequent examination it was noticed that there were no tracks in the snow to any distance; that the window had been broken *outwards*; that the position of the body had been such that it could not have been shot in the place it was, from without; that the scorched appearance of the clothing was such that the discharge must have been very near; and that the wine contained arsenic, a fact sworn to with the greatest directness by a medical witness. Unfortunately for his scheme he admitted that there had been no annoyance from rats; no one but himself had seen or been troubled about the Indians, and his own plans had not indicated in his own mind a belief of danger from that source. Moreover, he appeared indifferent about pursuit, and his manner and the facts were considered as warranting an arrest. He was tried at Malone, in July, 1825, before Judge Reuben H. Walworth, and the foregoing facts being adduced, he was judged guilty by the jury, after a consultation of fifteen minutes, and he was sentenced to be hung. Videto was hung in a field half a mile east of Malone, August 26, 1825. He continued till the last moment to assert his innocence, and on the gallows caused to be read a paper containing the following statement: "With regard to the crime for which I this day suffer, I have only to remark that I am perfectly innocent. By whose hand the unfortunate Fanny Mosely was deprived of life, I do not know; but I say it was not by mine, neither was I accessory to it; neither was I aware of the approach of that unhappy event; but at the time, was fearful of designs upon my own life." He declared his intention of holding the paper in his right hand when he died, if innocent. When the drop fell the paper was in his *left* hand, but the knot being improperly fixed, he was not strangled immediately, and after hanging some moments, he seized the paper in his right hand, and waved it to the crowd. This had its natural effect upon many of the spectators, but additional testimony which did not appear in the trial, renders the fact of his guilt certain in the minds of most of the citizens. The act of changing the paper can only be explained by supposing that consciousness remained after the drop fell, which he improved by consummating a resolution which had doubtless been for a long time uppermost in his mind. Many years afterwards, a vague report came back from the death bed of the criminal's mother, that she had confessed being privy to, or had assisted in the murder, but this report was so indefinite that it did not serve to change the belief of those who knew most of the circumstances, as to the guilt of the son. Indeed, it has much probability.

During the summer of 1832, some 8 or 10 died of cholera, and in 1847, the ship fever took off about 20. The commissioners of the land office, were, by an act passed April 1, 1841, directed to issue letters patent to Mary Gray, alias Lupin, and to her heirs and assigns, for a certain piece of land designated and known as the north middle subdivision of farm lot number six, of the St. Regis reservation, in the town of Fort Covington. This was in consideration of rights, supposed to be possessed by long residence in the place which she was said to have made her home from 1792, or about that period. She died a few years since.

This town, in July, 1849, suffered severely from running fires, which on the 20th, menaced the village, and nothing but a change of wind saved it from a general conflagration. The work of destruction in the adjoining towns of Bombay and Westville, was extensive and alarming, and in the former of these towns, not less than twenty dwellings and as many barns were said to have been burned. Such was the general feeling of insecurity, that applications for insurance multiplied beyond precedent, which led several insurance companies, including both of those located in St. Lawrence county, to insert a condition in their policies that they would not be responsible for damages done by running fires. This provision was subsequently abolished.

The village of Fort Covington is handsomely laid out east of Salmon river, half a mile from the boundary, and steamers from the St. Lawrence come up to within a short distance. The boundary of Jay's treaty of 1795, was designed to run upon the parallel of 45° north latitude. A glade through the forest was cut and cleared, and monuments erected. In 1818, upon the line being run after the treaty of Ghent, the true line was found to be north of the former, at Fort Covington, about 600 feet. By the Webster treaty of August 9, 1842, the former line was agreed upon, and permanent iron monuments erected by the side of each road or navigable stream at the place of crossing, and in the forest at intervals of a mile. These are of cedar cased with cast iron, about four feet high, square at the base, and gradually tapering upwards. On the four sides are cast the following inscriptions:

"ALBERT SMITH, U. S. COMMISSIONER." "TREATY OF WASHINGTON." "LT. COL. J. B. B. ESTCOURT, H. B. M. COMMISSIONER." "BOUNDARY, AUGUST 9TH, 1842."

The commissioners appointed to survey the boundary of 1818, were Gov. Van Ness and Gen. Peter B. Porter, who commenced at St. Regis.

A Library society was incorporated at French mills under a general act in February, 1815, under the title of the French Mills Miscellaneous Library, with James Campbell, David Jones, Ezekiel Payne, Wm. W. Herrick, Wareham Hastings, Luther Danforth, Joseph Spencer, trustees. The seal was to be the eagle, with the words *E Pluribus unum*, inscribed.

Religious Societies.—The First Presbyterian church arose from an Associate Reformed Scotch church, which belonged to the Synod of New York, and was organized mainly through the efforts of a Scotchman, who was usually known as Father Brunton. About 1821, Mr. B. left, and the organization in a measure went down, but two or three years after, the society was visited by the Rev. Alexander Proudfit, of Salem, N. Y., by whom it was revived, and under his influence, the Rev. Mr. Weller was engaged one year. The Rev. John A. Savage was employed during five years, as a stated supply, but was not installed. While Mr. Savage was here, the church left the Associate Presbytery of Washington Co., (Dec., 1828,) and joined the Champlain Presbytery, which is of the Constitutional Presbyterian, or New School order. After Mr. Brunton had left, a small Congregational society of about 15 members, mostly females, had been organized by Samuel Crosby, which were united by Mr. Savage, with the other church.

The Rev's Mr. Nickol, Jas. George, L. Tuller, Jas. E. Quaw, E. E. Wells, —— Williams, Joseph A. Rosseel, David C. Lyon, and Charles Gillette, have been successively employed at different times, but the latter is the only one who has been installed. The church edifice was built in 1828, at a cost of $4,000, and in 1845, a bell, weighing about 750lbs, was procured by the society. The pews are private property, and regularly deeded like a farm. Whole number since present organization 501. Present number on record, about 308. Present number residing near and belonging to church, 208.

A Baptist society was organized in 1824, at first by 9 members. The Rev. Nathaniel Culver, was its first minister. He has been succeeded by Hiram Sanford, —— Dodge, Wm. H. Rice, J. B. Drummond, L. H. Humphrey and J. M. Webb, the present clergyman. A church was built west of Big Salmon river, in 1829, as a cost of $1,000, which in 1851-2 was repaired and thoroughly finished at an additional expense of $1,700.

Fort Covington Wesleyan chapel was incorporated April 4, 1836, Humphrey Russell, Luther Danforth, Warren S. Manning, trustees.

St. Mary's church, (Catholic), was incorporated, March 8, 1840, Wm. Lahy, Patrick Holden and Michael Collins, trustees.

FRANKLIN,

Was formed from Bellmont, May 20, 1836, and made to embrace about half of township number 9, and the whole of number 10, of the Old Military tract. The first town meeting was directed to be held at the house of Henry B Hatch.

Supervisors.—1836-8, Harry B. Hatch; 1839-40, Norman Stickney; 1841, William Knowles; 1842, John R. Merrill; 1843-4, Harry B. Hatch; 1845, John R. Merrill; 1846, Norman Stickney; 1847-50, John R. Merrill; 1851, Hugh Martin; 1852, James B. Dickinson.

The earliest settlement within the limits of the town of Franklin, was begun by the erection of a forge and saw mill by McLenathan and Wells, from Jay, Essex Co., about the year 1827, at the settlement now known as Franklin Falls, but which then bore the name of *McLenathan Falls.* Difficulties attended these works which were finally suspended, and the place had mostly gone down, until the year 1846, when Fitz Geralds and McLean, from the village of New Sweden, town of Ausable, Essex Co., erected a saw mill for extensive lumbering purposes. One half of their right was sold to Keese & Tomlinson, of Keeseville, in 1847. In February 1848, Peter Comstock, of Port Kent, acquired an interest in the place. At about the time of the first settlement, at McLenathan Falls, a forge was erected by Uriah Sumner, on township number nine, of the old military tract. This enterprise was also abandoned. These two forges, were supplied by magnetic ore found in the town, which are said to be abundant. This town adjoins an extensive and valuable iron region in Essex county, which has employed a large amount of capital and given promise of future pre-eminence in this department of the useful arts. Besides magnetic ores, bog ore is said to occur in swamps, and may be found hereafter of much importance, when worked in connection with other ores, to improve the quality of the iron. The settled parts of Franklin are mostly along the Port Kent and Hopkinton road, and in the southern part of township number ten. The town is less broken than the country to the east and north, and will doubtless hereafter be found a good grazing district. The lumbering interests of the town give a market for domestic products, at present, but the natural outlet of the country to markets is down the valleys of the Saranac and Ausable rivers, to lake Champlain. A plank road with but four miles of interruption, connects Keeseville and Franklin Falls.

31

A most destructive conflagration occurred at the lumbering village of Franklin Falls, on the Saranac, on the 29th of May, 1852. For several days previous, a fire had been running in the neighboring woods, and on the day of the catastrophe, the wind was blowing almost a hurricane, and scattering the fire in every direction, so that all attempts to control it became unavailing. On approaching the village, which was situated in a ravine, it burst from the woods upon the settlement with such force, that every building in the place except two small ones was consumed. These were an extensive lumbering mill, together with twenty-three dwelling houses, a large store, a tavern, ane much lumber and valuable property, belonging to the owners of the mill. Nearly all the furniture in the houses was consumed, and some of the inhabitants escaped with their lives only with great difficulty. The principal sufferers were P. Comstock, J. B. Dickinson and Keese & Tomlinson, who were owners of most of the property destroyed. The extent and severity of this conflagration has never before been equalled in our counties, but the apparently hopeless ruin brought upon this place by its entire destruction, has not served to arrest, although it may have checked the enterprise of its spirited proprietors. A gang mill with a yankee * was commenced soon after, on a larger scale than before, and the village, phœnix-like, is rising from its ashes.

HARRIETSTOWN,

Was erected from Duane, March 19, 1841, and consists of townships Nos. 21, 24, 27, of Great tract No. 1, of Macomb's purchase. The first town meeting was directed to be held at the house of Micah E. Flanders. The circumstances which led to its formation are said to have been these: For several years the inhabitants of No. 21 had complained of the hardship of being under the necessity of taking a journey of thirty or forty miles around, to attend town meetings, and many had been accustomed to neglect them from the great labor and expense of time requisite. In 1840, however, by a concerted movement, they got a majority in town meeting, and had it adjourned to their own part of the town. The inhabitants in the north immediately originated a movement, which was forthwith consummated, by which the town of Duane was divided, and Harrietstown erected; and a provision inserted for a new town meeting in each town for the election of town officers.

Supervisors.—1841-4, Pliny Miller; 1845, Alanson B. Neal; 1846-50, P. Miller; 1851, A. B. Neal.

The town of Harrietstown began to be settled before the year 1812, by inhabitants of the adjoining counties, who located upon the northwest bay road. The town is named after the original or proprietary name of township No. 21. The latter received its name from a daughter of Wm. Constable, the wife of James Duane, Esq., of Duane.

The principal settlement is at present in the north part of township No. 21. Several lumbering establishments are erected and in contem-

---

* This term is applied to a number of saws placed in the same frame with a gang of saws, so that they will cut a log to the proper width while the gang of saws is making another into boards of marketable thickness. The two logs are placed side by side on the same carriage. A hotel on an extensive scale is in progress by Mr. Dickinson, and the place will probably before long regain its former size and prosperity. The Ausable river plank road, which terminates at this place, is destined to do much towards promoting its growth. The name of Franklin Falls was given to the village and settlement on the establishment of a post office, on the 31st of January, 1851.

plation in this town. The market for this section of the county is entirely down into Essex county and lake Champlain. There is at present no road leading directly from the settlement to Malone, without going through a corner of the town of St. Armand, in Essex county. There are at present three school districts in town.

Township No. 21 is very elevated, and its waters flow into the St. Lawrence, by way of the St. Regis, into lake Champlain, and into the Raquette.

MALONE,

Was erected, as Harrison, from Chateaugay, March 2, 1805, and at first included the whole of tract No. 1, and the Indian reservation. The first town meeting was directed to be held at the house of Jonathan Hapgood. In the formation of Constable, Dickinson and Duane, it was reduced to its present limits, that of townships Nos. 6 and 9, of tract No. 1. The former of these was owned by Richard Harrison, and surveyed by Joseph Beman, in 1801-2-3, assisted by Enos Wood. Its first agent was Judge Bailey. No. 9 was owned by Constable, Hammond and Mc Cormick. The south third owned by the latter, passed by way of Mr. Pitcairn, to A. O. Brodie, and is now mostly owned by James H. Titus, of N. Y. The middle third passed by deed to the estate of John Titus, N. Prime and Wm. Wallace, prior to 1830. April 11, 1808, the name of Harrison was changed to Ezraville (from Ezra L'Hommedieu), and on the 10th of June, 1812, the original name of Malone was restored.

The records commence in 1808, when N. Blanchard was *supervisor;* John H. Russell, *clerk;* Hiram Horton, Harry S. House and Thos. Spencer, *assessors;* H. Blanchard, *collector;* Cone Andrus, Oliver Brewster, *poor masters;* Samuel Pease, Jehiel Berry, Wm. Mason, *com'rs highways;* H. Blanchard, Joel Griffin and Apollos Lathrop, *constables;* Solomon Plumb, Stephen Holley, J. Barnum, D. Whipple and J. Lawrence, *fence viewers.*

Supervisors.—1808, Nathaniel Blanchard; 1809, Asa Wheeler; 1810-11, Hiram Horton; 1812, George F. Harrison; 1813-15, Harry S. House; 1816-17, Abel Willson; 1818-35, Asa Hascall; 1836, Martin L. Parlin; 1837, Asa Hascall; 1838-9, Jonathan Stearns; 1840-2, Asa Hascall; 1843-5, Hiram Horton, 2d; 1846-52, Wm. Andrus.

Bounties have been offered as follows: for wolves, $10, in 1808 to '13; $15, in 1816-17; $20, in 1818 to '21. For panthers, $10, in 1811-12-13; $20, in 1818 to '21. At a special meeting in 1821, called for the purpose of reducing the bounties; no action was taken; but in November of that year, they were rescinded. In 1845, voted against annexing a part of St. Lawrence to Franklin county, and in favor of petitioning for an appropriation for Clinton prison.

Settlements were begun in 1802, by Enos, Nathan and John Wood, from St. Albans, the town having been visited one or two years previous by the former. Nowell Conger, Luther Winslow, Jehiel Berry, Noah Moody, Roswell Wilcox, David and Lyman Sperry, and many others, came in 1803, or before. The emigrants of 1804 to '8, were quite numerous, and almost entirely from Vermont. The first child born in town, was a daughter of Luther Winslow, who was named *Malone,* after the township. N. and J. Wood, in 1804, built a saw mill, and J. Wood soon after began a grist mill, but the dam was carried off in a flood, and nothing was done towards rebuilding, till 1809, when Hiram Horton purchased the privilege, and erected a grist mill soon after. From the beginning, the citizens designed to establish an academy among them, and in 1806, they erected a building on a site given by Mr. Harrison, and still occupied, for the purpose. This building still stands, and has been used for a school house, meeting house, court house, jail and academy. An arsenal was built a little east of the village, in 1812. During the war, a volunteer company, consisting mostly of revolutionary soldiers, and styled Silver Greys, was formed under David Erwin. Their age exempted them from duty, but their inclinations led them to it. On the capture of Tilden's company, at French Mills, they started for that place, but did not arrive till after the surrender. A detachment of the army of Gen. Wilkinson occupied the village during the early part of the winter of 1813-14, but left in February. Very soon after, the enemy, hearing from spies, that a large amount of provisions was stored in the village, sent a detachment of about 1,200 regulars and 400 Canadian militia, under Col. Scott, who arrived towards evening on Saturday, February 19, 1814, posted sentinels on all the roads leading from the village, to intercept teams, and proceeded to search for stores. These were in a barn half a mile south of the village, and a considerable amount had been distributed among the inhabitants for concealment. On their first arrival, a considerable amount of firing occurred, principally to arrest teams which were attempting to escape. On Sunday morning, several of the Indians and militia commenced demolishing the arsenal, which had been left without arms, by the Americans, on leaving the place. The windows and gratings were torn out, and it was fired, but Colonel Scott, upon the earnest appeals of some of the more influential of the citizens, who represented the barbarity of this wanton destruction, issued orders for its preservation, and posted a guard around it for protection. He then convened some of the inhabitants, and gave them the building for educational purposes. For this act of lenity, he is said to have been censured by his government. A part of Sunday was spent in ransacking the town, and forwarding the stores they had seized, using the teams they had pressed for this purpose, and at noon they started on their return, by way of Chateaugay, losing great numbers by desertion. Private property, except arms, was generally respected. Col. Scott is said to have nearly lost his life from a drunken Indian, who reeled up to him, cursed him for not allowing them to plunder, and aimed his loaded gun for firing; but he was instantly seized. rudely bound on his back to a train, and taken off. An amusing case of smuggling occurred on this occasion. Jehiel Barnum, a revolutionary gun smith, living in Bangor, had been pressed with others, and sent off with a load of stores, and in charge of two soldiers, for French Mills. His team was young and restive, and gave him much trouble in keeping them from interfering with the sleighs before him, to avoid which, he got permission to turn off on a by-road, which he said would take them out right, and after going several miles, he drove up to *his own door*. His passengers here first discovered their dilemma, and he without difficulty persuaded them to remain, while the cargo was found very convenient in supporting the family.

In 1813, there were in town three saw mills, a grain mill, fulling and carding mills, and two bark mills.

The poor house of Franklin county was erected soon after the general law directing their establishment, on a farm of 110 acres, at a cost of $1.200. It has since been burnt and rebuilt. 1825, the large stone factory represented in our view of the rail road bridge, was built by John Stearns, and for a time gave employment to nearly a hundred operatives. It has been for some time discontinued. This extensive building stands in the deep ravine of Salmon river in the middle of the village, its upper story being on a level with the street. The Franklin Manufacturing company, was incorporated May 25, 1836, with a capital of $200,000, in shares af $250 each, for manufacturing cotton and woolen goods, but it was never organized.

A literary society was organized Oct. 2, 1840, for the purpose of procuring for the perusal of its members, periodical books, &c., and to establish lectures. It maintained an existence two or three years.

By an act of April 19, 1850, the commissary general was authorized to sell the several arsenals in certain counties, and Jan. 27, 1851, it was enacted, that when the arsenal and lot in the village of Malone should be sold, the proceeds, after deducting $200, should be applied to the improvement of a certain piece of ground, belonging to the state, situated in the village known as the Arsenal green and parade ground. The treasurer was directed to pay on the warrant of the comptroller, to Guy Meigs, Samuel C. Wead, and Hugh Magill, the above sum to be expended for these improvements. The grounds were to be graded, fenced, planted with trees, and laid out into walks, so far as might be without injuring the premises for purposes of military parades. These grounds were never to be sold for private purposes, without an act of the legislature. An appropriation was also made for inclosing and improving the grounds around the Academy in the western side of the village. Accordingly the Arsenal green, has been neatly and tastefully enclosed, and a row of shade trees planted around its border. This beautiful park, is crossed by the Northern rail road, which here required a deep cutting, but the two sides have been united by a foot bridge, and the premises are little marred by this work. There is scarcely a village in the state that can boast of two more elegant public parks than Malone, when this, and the grounds now in process of grading and enclosure around the Academy, shall have been completed, and the shade trees with which they are to planted, shall have attained a respectable growth. The public grounds in cities have been aptly compared to the lungs of the populace, and nothing can be more pleasant and healthful than an hour spent at the close of a sultry summer's day, in the refreshing coolness of a grove.

There is scarcely an inland town in the state, that will compare with Malone, in the thrift and improvement which it has exhibited since the completion of the rail road. Situated in the midst of a rich and rapidly improving agricultural district; enjoying ample facilities for manufacturing purposes; and the healthful moral influence of an excellent academy, in connection with the cheerful prospect which the southern and unsettled portions of the county exhibit for improvement, the business of which will very naturally centre here, all contribute to promote its growth and wealth. Prominent among the sources of its prosperity, is an extensive quarry of Potsdam sandstone, about a mile south of the village, which is being wrought on an extensive scale, and has already acquired a reputation and created a demand in many of our eastern cities, and in the western states. This stone occurs in a strata of very uniform thickness, and is raised with bars and wedges, marked with a chisel of any desirable size or shape, and broken with a remarkably even fracture. The great symmetry of size which can be obtained, the freedom from pyrites or other minerals that would stain or effloresce, by exposure; the extreme durability, as evinced by the sharp outlines of masses that have been exposed to the elements for thousands of years, and a delicate tinge of color which it presents, are combined in this material, and gives it a value which is seldom equalled. The quarries in Potsdam and other towns furnish stone equally valuable. The Malone quarry is owned by Mr. T. P. Chandler.

Malone has at present churches of the Presbyterian, Baptist, Episcopal, Universalist, Methodist, and Catholic denominations. Several of these are finely located, especially the Presbyterian church, which fronts upon the public square, and forms a prominent object in the village.

Two destructive fires, which occurred with a short interval, in the fall of 1852, led the citizens to see the necessity of an organization as a village, in order to raise by tax the means of providing against these calamities, and for the construction of internal improvements. Two fire engines were ordered, and the incorporation of the village is expected to be soon accomplished.

The valley of Salmon river presented an obstacle to the construction of the rail road, which was overcome by the erection of the elegant and substantial bridge, represented on the opposite page. It is built on the Burr plan with improvements; has a span of 150 feet and an elevation of 82 feet above the water. It has across it a double track, which here possesses a slight curve. The abutments contain 3000 cubic yards of masonry, and are 52 feet high, laid in good lime, mortar, and are very solid and permanent. To the passenger that crosses this viaduct in the cars, there is scarcely an opportunity of judging the merits of the work, or forming an adequate conception of its beauty, which can only be fully realized from the banks of the river below, where like the bow of promise, it is seen spanning the heavens far above the turmoil of the angry river. This highly creditable and successful work, was planned and executed under the direction of Charles L. Schlatter, the engineer of the road.

The settlement of township No. 9, was began in 1831, under the agency of the late Henry B. Titus, who then erected a grist and saw mill, and a scythe factory, at the great falls of Salmon river. It was the wish of the proprietor, James H. Titus, that this settlement should be called *Glenwood*, but it has lately received the name of *Titusboro*. After a few years, the investment proving ruinous from the want of an accessible market, these operations were discontinued, and have only been resumed since the completion of the rail road. The proprietor is now making a systematic effort to settle this tract, and an extensive gang mill has been erected by Meigs & Wead, of Malone, who have improved the Salmon river from near Wolf pond, to their mills for floating logs. Of the original immigration, a few remain, but the most had abandoned their locations. A large saw mill is about being erected at the outlet of Branch pond, a beautiful and romantic water. On lot No. 58, of the middle third, near Brandon, white limestone occurs, and is found to make excellent lime. This indispensable article is rather rare among the primary rocks of this county. The limestone from this town, has been examined chemically by Dr. Chilton, of New York, and found to contain but two per cent of impurities.

Religious Societies.—In 1806 or 7, the first Congregational church was formed by Ebenezer Hibbard and Amos Pettingill, missionaries, who were also instrumental in organizing several other churches, in this and St. Lawrence counties. In October 1809, the Rev. Ashbel Parmalee,[*]

---

[*] Few clergymen in this section of the state, have seen more of the rise and progress of our religious societies than Mr Parmelee. He was a native of Stockbridge, Mass., but at an early age removed with his parents to Rutland county, Vt., where he prepared for the

Bridge of Northern Railroad over Salmon River in the village of Malone, Franklin Co., N. Y.

A J HOFFMAN SC ALBANY

was employed; and on the 18th of February, 1810, he was installed the first pastor. This was the first ordination that occurred in the county, and took place in the upper room of the old Academy. The Rev. Messrs. Lemuel Haynes, of Rutland, Vt., Chauncey Cook, a missionary, Martin Powell, of Mooers, and Simeon Parmelee, of Westford, were present. About thirty members at first formed the church, but its present number is between four and five hundred, which is said to be greater than that of any other church of this sect in northern New York.

In 1826-8 a church was erected* and on the 7th of February 1828, it was dedicated. It cost about $1000. A new and elegant edifice was erected in 1851, and dedicated in February 1852. It is of brick and cost about $10,000. The Rev. Mr. Parmelee was succeeded, after a course of pastoral labors of thirty-six years, by the Rev. Elias Woodruff, the present clergyman. In the early part of the year 1816, a religious revival of unparalleled extent, occurred in Malone, in common with other places, which resulted in the addition of eighty or a hundred members to this church, among whom were thirty or forty parents of families. The years 1827 and 1831, were also noted as periods of unusual religious excitement. First Congregational church and society of Malone, was incorporated Jan. 8, 1828, with Jonathan Stearns, Asa Hascall and Harry S. House, trustees. St. Mark's church (Episcopal), was formed by Rev. Anson Hard, July 12, 1831. No clergyman employed till July 1833, when the Rev. A. Bloomer was engaged. His successors have been Rev. Amos Pardee, Alex' H. Call, Caleb Bingham, Henry Attwater, Wm. Long, Jubal Hodges, and A. C. Treadway. The present church edifice was erected in 1843. A Universalist society was formed not long after the war, but had for many years been lost, when Dec. 27, 1845, it was formed, which now numbers 78 members. It was formed through the efforts of Rev. E. A. Holbrook, who remained six years. A church was built at a cost of $2,300 in 1846. The present pastor is the Rev. G. Swan.

MOIRA,

Was formed with its present bounds from Dickinson, April 15, 1828. The whole of the poor moneys of Dickinson were given to Moira, as most of the settlement was in the new town.

Supervisors.—1828-30, Jason Pierce, 1831-2, Sidney Lawrence, 1833-6, J. Pierce; 1837, Orrin Lawrence; 1838, J. Pierce; 1839-40, S. Lawrence; 1841-3, O. Lawrence; 1844-8, Samuel Manning; 1849, Horace Dickinson; 1850-1, Darius W. Lawrence; 1852, Simon D. Stevens.

1830, at a special town meeting, voted to transfer to the school funds all the poor moneys in the hands of town officers. This was to be, and remain, a perpetual fund for the support of schools in town, agreeably to the provisions of an act passed April 27, 1829. $800 was directed to be loaned on security for the above purpose. All over the above sum was

duties of his station, and preached one year. He still continues his ministerial labors occasionally, and is said to have in preparation for the press, an account of his personal observations upon the progress of religious and other institutions, which have grown up under his notice.

* In April, 1851, there was found in taking down the walls of the Presbyterian church, first erected, a leaden plate bearing the following inscription. It was taken from the corner stone. " Laid by Northern Constellation Lodge, No. 148, Malone, May 30th, A. L., 5826. A. D 1826. Ind. U. S. A. 50th. Clark Williamson, M.; Stephen Van Rensselaer, G. M. S. N. Y.: De Witt Clinton, Gov. S. N. Y.; John Q. Adams, Pres. U. S. A.; Rev. Ashbel Parmelee, Pastor Con. So,; Orren Moses, Sculptor."

to be distributed among the several school districts, in the ratio of the other school moneys of the town were by law directed to be paid.

The town of Moira was apportioned to Gilchrist and Fowler, and the first settlement was made by Appleton Foote, from Middlebury, Vt., who in March, 1803, came into town as agent for the proprietors, to erect a mill and commence a settlement. He brought in Benjamin Seeley and family, to assist him, and the latter was the first family that settled here. They spent the first winter alone in the new settlement, and kept a rude accommodation for travelers, great numbers of whom were then passing through on their way to the new settlements in St. Lawrence county. Jonathan Lawrence and Joseph Plumb came into town on the 1st of March, 1804, having the previous year selected land and made arrangements for moving. Lawrence, Plumb, and one David Bates, were the only families that came in to reside in 1804. The first road to market was to French mills, from which a navigable communication exists to Montreal, and the first team that went through and back, a distance of about thirteen miles, is said to have occupied four days in the journey. In 1805, settlers came into town and settled in considerable numbers. The first Mills were built by Mr. Foote, who in 1803 erected a saw mill on the site of what is now Brush's Mills, and in the year following he added a single run of stones. The title subsequently passed to Luther Bradish, Robert Watts, and Peter Kean, who held the north middle and south thirds respectively. The present stone mill, near the rail road station of Brush's Mills, was erected by the proprietors about the year 1823. The north and middle thirds are at present owned, with the exception of parts sold to actual settlers, by Henry N. Brush. The first schools in town were opened in 1807.

The Northern rail road has two stations in town; one at Brush's Mills and the other near Moira Corners. At the former is an extensive wood station.

Wm. Pierce, a youth of 17, was tried at Malone, in July, 1839, for the murder of his father, and convicted. On the 10th of January previous, Willard Johnson and his son were working for the father of the prisoner. A dispute arose between the deceased and the prisoner, in relation to the use of a horse by the latter, to go to a spelling school. When they got to the field, where they were at work clearing land, Johnson directed the prisoner to cut a certain tree, to which he replied he would not, giving as his reason, that the old man would not let him have the horse, &c. About this time the father came up, and the dispute was renewed. The prisoner said his father promised him the horse, the father denied it, upon which the prisoner gave him the lie. On this the father threatened to flog him, and picked up a stick and struck him. The son stepped back, stood four or five seconds, raised his axe, and advancing rapidly four or five steps, struck his father with the axe in the right breast, driving the whole bit of the axe into the chest, of which wound the father died in about forty hours. The prisoner was sentenced to be hanged on the 2d day of September following. This sentence was commuted by Governor Seward to imprisonment for life.

Religious Societies.—The Christian sect originated in this town in 1816, under the labors of James Spooner, who came from New Hampshire, a young man of 20, and hired out as a laborer. In August, 1827, a church of 17 members was formed, and since continued, numbering 73 in all. Present number (October, 1852), 29. In connection with the Methodists, they have a church at Moira village.

A Congregational church and society exist in town, the latter having been incorporated April 26, 1823, with Horace Dickinson, Enos Day and John Cooper, trustees.

The Catholics are about forming a society at Brush's Mills.

WESTVILLE,

Was formed from Constable, with its present limits, April 25, 1829. Its name was suggested from its being the west part of Constable, and a post office named West Constable, had been established the year before. This has not since been changed. The first town meeting day having passed without election, Alric Man, Sylvester Langdon and Eseck Sprague, justices, filled the several offices by appointment, viz: Guy Meigs, *supervisor;* Ebenezer Leonard, *clerk;* Ebenezer Man, Goodrich Hazen, Stephen B. Clough, *assessors;* Samuel Fletcher, *collector;* Ira Briggs, Philemon Berry, *overseers of the poor;* Buel H. Man, Henry G. Button, P. Berry, *com'rs of highways;* S. Fletcher, Leonard Willson, *constables;* E. Man, John M. Rogers, S. B. Clough, *com'rs of schools;* Stephen Felton, E. Leonard, Samuel Coggin, *ins'r of com. schools;* P. Berry, *pound keeper.*

Supervisors.—1829, Guy Meigs; 1830, Philemon Berry; 1831-2, Goodrich Hazen; 1833-5, Alric Man; 1836-7, Henry G. Button; 1838-9, P. Berry; 1840-1, Buel H. Man; 1842-3, Alric Man; 1844-5, Samuel Coggin; 1846-7, James Walker; 1848-9, Samuel Man; 1850-1, Richard E. Morey; 1851, Ebenezer Man, to fill vacancy, occasioned by death of R. E. Morey; 1852, P. Berry.

The first settler in Westville, is said to have been Amos Welch, from Grand Isle, Vt., about 1800. —— Haskins, Elisha Sabins, Samuel Fletcher, John Reed, Alexander McMillen, Silas Cushman, John Livingston, Joseph and Thomas Wright and Alric and Dr. Albon Man, mostly from Vermont, settled in 1803, or before, principally on a road, that in 1800 had been made passable in winter from the settlements in Chateaugay to St. Regis. The two brothers Man were from Addison, Vt., and moved into town in March, 1803. The Wright families were from Salem, N. Y.

Amos Welch built the first saw mill in town, and before the lands had been opened for sale. Dr. Man built the second saw mill, in 1803. Wm. Bailey, for many years an inhabitant of Plattsburgh, and one of the first land agents in the county, and an early settler of Chateaugay, held with Albon Man, for many years, the agency of the town. The first sale of land was to Joseph Wright, Nov. 19, 1802. Alexander McMillen, Henry Briggs, Oliver Bell, Thomas Chamberlain, Barnabas Berry, Ezekiel Paine, Simeon Smith, settled at an early day; and for several years the settlements increased quite rapidly. The first school was taught in 1806, at the house of Dr. Man, by Samuel Russell. Townships 2 and 3 were surveyed into thousand acre lots in 1802, by Wright and Raymond, and subsequently subdivided into quarters.

Near the point where the principal road from Fort Covington to Malone, crosses Salmon river, in this town, is a forge for the manufacture of bar iron from bog ore, which occurs in the swamps of this town and Constable. This forge was erected by David Erwin, about 1810, and has been more or less used nearly every year since its first erection. It produced for many years the nails used in the country, which were made by the tedious and expensive methods in use before the invention of the machinery now used. Plates of iron of the width of a nail's length were first plated out under the forge hammer, and these were subsequently cut and headed by hand. The usual price for these nails, was thirty cents a pound, and the cost for this necessary article formed no small proportion of the expenses of building. There is another forge about three miles above.

In 1822, a part of No. 2, and the whole of No. 3, not previously sold, was conveyed to Edward Ellice, of London, as payment for money loaned by Alexander Ellice, to Constable, in the purchase of the tract. The most of this town, in common with that part of the county underlaid by standstone, is susceptible of high cultivation.

In the north part of Westville, about midway between the east and the west lines, and half a mile from the provincial boundary, is a medicinal spring, which enjoys a local celebrity for the cure of cutaneous diseases. The waters are strongly sulphurous, and slightly chalybeate. Several years since, limited accommodations were erected in the vicinity, for the convenience of those invalids who might resort thither, for medicinal aid.

Religious Societies.—Meetings were held at first by the Rev. Alex'r Proudfit, to whose congregation several of the first emigrants had belonged.

A Presbyterian church formerly existed in town, who employed the Rev. Mr. Reed as minister, but the society is now said to be scattered.

A Universalist society was formed in 1847.

The Westville Free church was erected in 1837, at a cost of $2,300, as a union church for the several orders in town. Mr. Ellice contributed $1,000 towards the expense.

CHAPTER VI.

SOCIETIES AND ASSOCIATIONS — THE PRESS — HISTORY
OF ACADEMIES.

MEDICAL society was formed in St. Lawrence county Oct. 14, 1807. The following statistics were politely furnished by Dr. Darius Clark, of Canton, the present secretary. At the first meeting, Joseph W. Smith was chosen president; I. W. Pier, vice-president; W. Noble, secretary; B. Holmes, treasurer; John Seeley, Powell Davis and B. Holmes, censors. Its presidents have been Joseph W. Smith, 1807 to '14, '18–19, '28–9, '33; Robert McChesney, 1815 to '17, '21, '41; Gideon Sprague, 1820, '35, '43; B. Holmes, '25; E. Baker, '26–7, '32, '45, '48; F. Parker, 1840; S. H. McChesney, 1830–1, '34, '44, '52; S. N. Sherman, 1836, '42, '47; J. A. Mott, 1837; S. Ford, 1838; Wm. S. Paddock, 1839.

A seal having for its device a lancet within the words "St. Lawrence Medical Society," was adopted July, 1811. The following have been elected honorary members: Henry S. Waterman, Levi S. Ives, —— Ambler, R. Bates. The following is an alphabetical list of members, with the dates of their admission, the first two figures of the year (18) being omitted:

Alvan Ames, '31; A. Ames, '44; B. F. Ames, '45; John Archibald, 15; Reuben Ashley, '27; Wm. Attwater, '21; Elijah Baker, '09; G. W. Barker, '28; Wm. Bass, '36; Daniel Brainerd, '11; Joseph Brayton, '28; Oliver Brewster, '29; M. L. Burnham, '43; R. Burns, '42; Wm. A. Canfield, '17; John S. Carpenter, '17; Wooster Carpenter, '29; Giles F. Catlin, '30; J. A. Chambers, '32; J. H. Chandler, '29; H. O. Chipman, '33; Darius Clark, '24; Jacob Clark, '31; R. L. Clark, '46; J. S. Cochran, '30; G. F. Cole, '38; D. L. Collamer, '30; J. S. Conkey, '44; Levi Crane, '22; I. B. Crawe, '36; R. Davidson, '52; Powell Davis, '07; J. H. Dunton, '42; Thomas Dunton, '43; J. W. Floyd, '23; Sylvester Ford, '28; Elkanah French, '24; W. F. Galloway, '47; Ira Gibson, '23; Geo. Green, '42; Woolcot Griffin, '28; Hiram Goodrich, '30; J. H. Grennell, '47; Thomas Harrington, '20; W. Hatch, '21; Henry Hewett, '42; B. Holmes, '07; J. H. Hyer, '52; C. F. Ide, '44; F. W. Judson, '16; H. D. Laughlin, '28; G. R. Lowe, '52; John McChesney, '21; Robert McChesney, '11; W. J. Manley, '44; John Marsh, '29; Samuel Marsh, '47; O. H. Mayhew, '43; H. Mazuzan, '36; Calvin S. Millington, '35; John S. Morgan, '28; James A. Mott, '12; James S. Munson, '29; Hiram Murdock, '28; Roswell Nash, '28; Rufus Newton, '22; D. S. Olin, '38; Nathaniel K. Olmsted, '21; Myron Orton, '11; Charles Orvis, '36; Wm. S. Paddock, '16; T. R. Pangburn, '43; Francis Parker, '21; O. F. Parker, '52; Ezra Parmelee, '41; Reuben Philips, '12; Ira W. Pier, '07; Caleb Pierce, '23; C. H. Pierce, '26; J. C. Preston, '52; Alanson Ray, '27; D. A. Raymond, '48; Jesse Reynolds, '52; Orra Rice, jr., '29; R. M. Rigdon, '32; J. H. Ripley, '34; J. W. Ripley, '28; L. Samburn, '28; Philip Scott, '14; John Seeley, '07; D. L. Shaw, '30; Lorenzo Sheldon, '28; Pierce Shepard, '08; A. B.

Sherman, '43; B. F. Sherman, '42; Mason G. Sherman, '40; Socrates N. Sherman, '27; Solomon Sherwood, '20; T. Van Sickler, '26; Royal Sikes, '16; C. Skidmore, '22; Benj. P. Smith, '32; Ira Smith, '14; J. W. Smith, '07; John Spencer, '09; Silas Spencer, '16; C. A. J. Sprague, '42; F. P. Sprague, '52; Gideon Sprague, '14; W. H. Sprague, '42; Alva Squire, '22; Lewis Stowers, '26; G. S. Sutherland, '52; Seymour Thatcher, '26; Albert Tyler, '28; S. C. Wait, '36; R. B. Webb, '27; E. Whiting, '34; Jason Winslow, '21; Wm. Witherell, '42; —— Wood, '33. Total, 121.

The Medical society of Franklin county was instituted in October, 1809, but the records are mostly lost, and a list of members from recollection is omitted on account of imperfections. Its seal has for its device a lancet within the name and date, and the words "ΑΕΣΚΥΛΑΠΙΟΥ," and "Triumphalia," the latter spelled backwards.

A series of benevolent societies were formed in St. Lawrence county more than twenty years since, which are at present the *Bible Society, Home Missionary Society, Tract Society, Foreign Missionary Society,* &c. Others have existed, but we have been unable to obtain their statistics, except that of the first named, to which we are indebted to the Hon. John Fine, who has been identified with it since the beginning. It was formed in January, 1820, and became auxiliary to the American Bible Society in April, 1820. It has paid $1,560 in donations to the parent society, and bought near $11,000 worth of Bibles and Testaments, of which it has distributed more than any other local society, except Monroe, Rensselaer and Brooklyn. It has twice supplied every family with a Bible, and once every Sabbath school scholar with a Testament. It has once supplied every reader with a Bible or Testament. It still continues in active operation and purchases yearly about $500 worth for sale and distribution. These societies are mostly auxiliary and hold anniversaries on the third Wednesdays of January in different parts of the county.

A similar series of societies exists in Franklin county, viz: *Bible Society,* organized Oct. 27, 1818, which has had 300 members. In 1850 it received $288·35, and in 1851, $239·36. Measures were taken in 1845, for supplying every family. The first officers were Hiram Horton, president; Asa Hascall, corresponding secretary; Francis L. Harrison, recording secretary; Cone Andrus, treasurer. A *Peace Society* formed at Constable, Feb. 23, 1848, with Henry Longley, president; G. C. Cotton, secretary. A *Tract Society* formed Jan. 20, 1842, which has distributed from 9,000 to 14,000 pages annually. The first officers were Gen. Prentice Sabin, president; G. C. Cotton, secretary. An *Anti-Slavery Society* formed in 1829. This met the other societies in their anniversaries, but did not transact business. A *Missionary Society,* Jan. 27, 1842, with Silvester Langdon, president; G. C. Cotton, secretary; Hiram Horton, treasurer. This in three years was dropped, as each denomination has one of its own.

The above hold anniversaries in January or February. We regret our inability to extend these notices from the full materials collected by Mr. Gideon C. Cotton, of Malone.

The first *Temperance society* of Northern New York, was formed in Constable, Feb. 1, 1829. The original pledge and subscription is before us, but our space forbids its insertion. The *Franklin county Temperance society,* was formed by the Rev. Mr. Axtel, agent of the State society, Oct. 15, 1829, it continued its meetings about six years, and its first officers were Col. Silvester Langdon, president, Dr. T. R. Powell, secretary. In 1837, it was reorganized. *The St. Lawrence Temperance society,* was formed in 1829, and like the former, was auxiliary to the State society. Local societies were formed as follows; with the numbers reported at the first annual meeting: *Oswegatchie*, March, 1828, 110; *Gouverneur*, March, 1829, 100. In 1828, 10,000 gallons of spirits sold. In 1829, 5,000; *Edwards*, Dec. 1829, 17. Two distilleries in town; *Russell*, Jan., 1829, 57. No distilleries, and no spirits sold in 1829: *Canton*, July, 1829, 112; *Potsdam*, Oct., 1828, 102. In 1828, 10,000 gallons of liquor sold; in 1829, none; *Parishville*, Jan., 1829, 40; *Hopkinton*, Nov., 1829, 35; *West Stockholm*, Jan., 1829, 20; *East Stockholm*, Jan. 4, 1830, 81; *Norfolk*, Jan. 4, 1830, 25; *Dekalb*, Feb. 1829, 66; *Waddington*, March, 1829, 38; *Richville*, Oct. 17, 1829, 47. Two or three buildings raised the year previous without the aid of ardent spirits. A County *Young Men's Temperance society*, was formed in Canton, March 21, 1834.

A *Teacher's association* was formed in Malone, Nov., 9, 1842, and continued but a short time.

A *County Lyceum*, auxiliary to a state Lyceum, and forming a part of a series embracing nation, state county, town, and school district lyceums, was formed at Canton, Feb. 27, 1833, and continued a few years. It had for its objects mental improvement, and the promotion of educational interests.

In the class of benevolent associations, we are proud to place those formed in 1847, for raising means to relieve the famine and distress which prevailed in Ireland and Scotland, from short crops, and the ravages of the potato rot, which brought the peasantry of these countries to the greatest want for food.

A public meeting was held at the Presbyterian house in the village of Ogdensburgh, on the evening of the 1st of March, 1847, of which the Hon. Henry Van Rensselaer, was chosen *president*. Joseph Rosseel, Elijah B. Allen, George M. Foster, and Sylvester Gilbert, *vice presidents*. H. G. Foote, and F. B. Hichcock, Dr. S. N. Sherman, and David C. Judson, were appointed a committee on resolutions. A series of resolutions expressing in the warmest language, commiseration for the *sufferings of the starving*, were passed, and an executive committee, consisting of D. C. Judson, H. Van Rensselaer, S. N. Sherman, G. N. Seymour, A. B. James, J. G. Hopkins, H. S. Humphrey, C. G. Myers, and John Fine, were appointed to collect and forward in the shortest time possible, such supplies as might be had for immediate shipment to Europe. In their appeal to the public, they said; "The wail of distress has come upon us, not in the single and casual cases of contagion and disease, or mingled with the shouts of victory from the battle field, but in the deep and dying groans of thousands perishing for want of food. Every new arrival from Europe, brings new and more extended accounts of the destitution of its inhabitants and of the miseries they are suffering. In the land of our forefathers, or from which those who are a part and parcel of us came, in England, in Scotland, and in Ireland, but mostly in the latter, does this destitution exist; and the miseries of starvation, of perishing of the want of sustenance occur to such an overwhelming extent, that the details are lost sight of in the magnitude of the general suffering and in the multitude of deaths—*for the want of food*. Shall we, who are blessed with abundance—who enjoy the bounties of Providence to almost an unlimited extent—shall we not be ready to part with some of that abundance to save the famishing in those countries with which our sympathies and feelings are most strongly united? * * The organization and arrangements in our principal cities and towns, (enlisting as they have the services of citizens of the highest character, for probity and intelligence) have already arranged channels of communication and distribution, through which our donations will be made sure of reaching their objects. We have here at the outset, the offer, (as will be seen by the proceedings of the meeting accompanying this) of the gratuitous conveyance of donations by the principal steam boat line from this place as far as their boats run, on the route towards the sea board, and we anticipate further evidence of liberality along the line, while at this place such arrangements have been made, that no charges will be made for storage, &c. Under such circumstances the committee offer their services and the facilities which they can command to their fellow citizens, not only of Ogdensburgh and its vicinity, but to the county of St. Lawrence generally, and they respectfully invite them to some early organized action in the different towns, by which the general sympathy existing in the community can be brought into action while the sleighing lasts, that their contributions may go forward with the opening of the navigation. The absolute destitution of millions of people, of means and of food, affords ample field for the exercise of charity, in any shape—in money, in wheat, in corn, in rye, in beans, in peas, in pork, in beef, in clothing, in short, every thing of food, or raiment, which will bear transportation. Let him who hath but little give but sparingly, and he who hath much give more, but let all give *something*, so that when we hereafter hear, as we fear we shall, of further suffering and perishing, we can each and every of us have the consolation of knowing and feeling that we have done our part to mitigate their calamities and relieve their distress."

This appeal had an effect throughout the county, generally, and on the 2d of June, the committee had forwarded 367 barrels, viz: 243 barrels of wheat flour, 43 of rye flour, 6 of oatmeal, 12 of beans, 4 of peas, 7 of pork, and one cask of sundries, for the Irish. Besides the foregoing, 52 barrels of provisions were forwarded to Scotland, by the same remittance, on further directions were given, than to bestow them upon the *needy and deserving*. The following is the communication of the committee to the central committee of New York, which accompanied the invoice.

"The Executive committee appointed by a meeting of the citizens of Ogdensburgh, to take into consideration, means for aiding the suffering in Ireland and Scotland, having sent forward the last of the supplies, which the benevolence and liberality of the inhabitants of St. Lawrence county have committed to their charge in pursuance of a resolution of the meeting appointing them, submit the following report.—That the appeal made by them to their fellow citizens of the county was more promptly and generally responded to than from the lateness of the season they had reason to expect, and has enabled them to send forward to the care and charge of the New York committee, 367 barrels of provisions, flour, &c. The corn meal came wholly from Waddington, where they have the means of kiln drying, which we not having here, induced the committee to exchange the contributions of corn, for an equal quantity of rye, which together with the wheat has been floured and packed in the best manner for exportation. Small quantities of oats, buck wheat, &c., have been exchanged for wheat. The whole business has been done without charge upon the cash fund, except some minor charges for repacking, cartage, &c. That the county of St. Lawrence, after the first of March, (in which to the opening of navigation our roads have been almost impassable), should by their spirited efforts have gathered together of their benevolent contributions, more than $3,000 worth of food, for a foreign suffering people, independent of cash contributions, is most creditable to their humanity and generosity." The efficiency of the aid received from Massena and Potsdam, is especially noticed by the committee.

Religious Associations.—The *St. Lawrence Baptist Association*, was organized in the fall of 1813, in Stockholm, in a log house on the St. Regis river, owned by Zephaniah French, by Elder Hascall, founder of Hamilton Seminary, Elder Starkwether, from Vermont, and a very few others. It embraces St. Lawrence and Franklin counties, and the following churches, with numbers in each in 1852; Brandon, 57; Burke, 66; Canton, 131; Chateugay, 34; Constable, 13; Edwards, 32; Fowler, 24; Fort Covington, 97; Gouverneur, 176; Hermon, 80; Madrid, 128; Malone, 203; Morristown, 50; Massena 49; Lawrence, 60; Nicholville, 82; Ogdensburgh, 184; Parishville, 172; Pitcairn, 24; Potsdam, 29; Russell, 2; Richville, 87; Stockholm, 53; total 1,961. During the previous year 32 had died, 55 added by baptism, and 66 by letter.

The Baptist Missionary Convention, was formed in 1827, auxilliary to a state society. It holds meetings annually on the first Wednesday of January, by rotation in the two counties. In connection with this, the *St. Lawrence Bible Society* of the Baptist denomination, meets and transacts its business. The latter was formed in September, 1836, and is auxiliary to a national society. During its first year it raised $198.63.

The St. Lawrence Quarterly Meeting (Free Will Baptist), was organized in 1837, and at the time embraced three churches in the two counties. The present number is nine. It extends into Jefferson county. The churches in De Kalb and Fowler, belong to the *Jefferson quarterly meeting*; and the other seven to the *St. Lawrence quarterly meeting*. The *St. Lawrence yearly meeting*, was formed at Fowler, in July, 1842, of the two quarterly meetings above named, to which a third (Clinton) has been added. It embraces 23 churches, 13 ordained ministers, 6 licentiates and 656 communicants.

Catholic Churches exist at St. Regis, Chateaugay, Malone, Fort Covington, Hogansburgh, Canton, Massena, Waddington, Potsdam, Ogdensburgh and Brasher. They belong to the Albany Diocese, and were built as follows: Brasher, in 1851, by Rev. James Keveny; Canton, built by Rev. James Mackey; Chateaugay (St. Patrick's), in 1845, by Rev. B. McCabe; Fort Covington (St. Mary's), in 1837-8, by Rev. John McNulty; Hogansburgh (St. Mary's), in 1833-4, by Rev. J. McNulty, who has been succeeded by Rev. James Keveny and Rev. Thomas Keveny; Malone (St. Joseph's), in 1836, by Rev. J. McNulty, who has been succeeded by Rev. J, Keveny, and it is now under the charge of Rev. Bernard McCabe. A larger place of worship is expected to be soon built here. Massena (St. Peter's), built by Rev. J. McNulty; Ogdensburgh (St. Mary's), now under the charge of Rev. James Mackey. A large stone church is being built here. Potsdam, built by Rev. P. Phellan; St. Regis, (see chapter 2 of this work); Waddington (St Mary's), built by Rev. James Mackey, now under the charge of Rev. P. Phellan.

The Northern Christian Conference, embracing Franklin, Jefferson and St. Lawrence counties, at present numbers about 250 communicants, and meets by adjournment on the Friday preceding the last Sabbath in June. In the foregoing pages, we have noticed the several churches of this sect.

The St. Lawrence Consociation (Congregational), was formed at Madrid, Feb. 9, 1825, and embraces the lay element of this church. The delegates that formed it were Rev. Oliver Eastman, Joseph Hulburt and Dea Caleb M. Foot, of Madrid; Rev. Moses Ordway and Dea. G. Stowe, of

Norfolk; Rev. R. Pettibone and Dea Aaron Warner, of Hopkinton; Dea E. Hulburd, of Stockholm; Dea N. Taylor and Jonas Matthews, of West Stockholm; and Nathaniel Crampton, of Parishville. This body at present meets by delegation on the last Tuesday of January, annually and semi-annually on the Tuesday preceding the third Wednesday in June, each church sending two delegates, one of whom must be its minister. It is strictly advisatory, and embraces the following churches, ministers and numbers (July, 1852); Brasher, 10; South Canton, 31; Brier Hill (Hammond), *S. Young;* De Peyster, *E. D. Taylor*, 55; Edwards, 18; Hopkinton, *E. Wood*, 94; Lawrenceville, *E. B. Catter*, 60; Lisbon, *M. L. Eastman*, 91; Madrid, *B. B. Parsons*, 128; Massena, 1st Ch., 40; 2d Ch., 46, *T. N. Benedict;* Norfolk, *G. B. Rowley*, 153; N. Lawrence; Parishville, B. Burnap, 99; Pierrepont, *P. Montague*, 25; West Potsdam, 30; Raymondville, *G. B. Rowley*, 31; Richville, *G. Cross*, 50; Russell, 27; Stockholm, P. C. Pettibone, 130; West Stockholm, —— *Dixon*, 58; Waddington, *C.F. Halsey*, 78.

The St. Lawrence Association, formed of the clergy of the above Congregational churches, was organized Sept. 14, 1844, at Madrid, and numbers 17 members. No churches of this order exist in Franklin county.

The Methodist Episcopal denomination, was among the first to organize. The *Black river circuit* was formed as a part of the Genessee district in 1803, and Barzillai Wiley, with John Husselkus, were appointed. In 1804 it had 90 members.

The St. Lawrence Circuit, with 84 members, was formed in 1811, and Isaac Puffer was appointed minister. In the same year, Malone Circuit, with 61 members, and John T. Adams, minister, was formed as a part of Champlain district.

In 1820, the Black river district was formed as a part of Oneida Conference, including both of our counties up to the period of the division. St. Lawrence circuit was supplied by the following preachers: 1812, Isaac Puffer, 144 members; 1813, Benj. G. Paddock, 160; 1814, Joseph Hickcox and Robert Menshall, 230; 1815, 262; 1816, Wyat Chamberlin and John Dempster, 251; 1817, Andrew Prindle and Thomas McGee, 231; 1818, Thomas Goodwin and Calvin N. Flint, 290; 1819, Timothy Goodwin and Thomas Demorest, 332; 1820, W. W. Rundall and Josiah Kies, 349; 1821, Ezra Healy and Orrin Foot, 398; 1822, Truman Dixon, Squire Chase and Roswell Parker, 343; 1823, Isaac Smith and R. Parker, 383; 1824, Gardner Baker, 315; 1825, do., 243; 1826. James Brown, 255; 1827, Andrew Prindle, 230; 1828, 152. In this year, this circuit was divided into several. Indian river circuit, embracing a part of St. Lawrence county, was formed in 1821. Potsdam circuit was formed in 1823, with Warren Bannister first preacher. The several circuits now existing were formed as follows: Ogdensburgh, 1826; Parishville, Waddington, Canton and Gouverneur, 1828; Heuvelton, 1829; Fort Covington, 1830; Hammond and Chateaugay, 1832; Hopkinton and De Kalb, 1833; Lisbon, Louisville, Massena and Bangor, 1835; Bombay and Stockholm, 1836; Westville, 1837; Russell mission, 1838; Rossie mission, Matildaville and Pierrepont mission, 1840; South Canton, Sprague's Corners, Norfolk, Buck's Bridge and Brasher mission. 1841; Macomb mission, 1842; Rackett river and West Stockholm, 1843: Edwards mission and Morristown, 1846; St. Regis mission, 1849; St. Lawrence, French mission, Duane mission and Moira circuit, 1850.

Black River Conference was formed in 1836, and two counties are now embraced in the Gouverneur, Potsdam and Ogdensburgh districts. The presiding elders of the Methodist Episcopal church, so far as the counties of St. Lawrence and Franklin have been concerned, since their organization, have been,

Albany Dist.—1804, Elijah Woolsey; 1807, Henry Stead.

Cayuga Dist.—1808, Peter Vannest; 1810, Wm. Case.

Oneida Dist.—1812, Wm. Case; 1814, Chas. Giles; 1818, Geo. Garey.

Black River Dist.—1820, Renaldo M. Everts; 1823, Dan Barnes; 1826, Goodwin Stoddard; 1827, Nathaniel Salisbury.

Potsdam Dist.—Formed in 1828, and embraced the two counties, and a portion of Jefferson. 1828, B. G. Paddock; 1831, Squire Chase; 1834, Silas Comfort; 1836, G. Loveys; 1837, W. S. Bowdish; 1839, Lewis Whitcomb. The district discontinued in 1840, and merged in Ogdensburgh district; renewed in 1842. 1842, A. Adams; 1845, Isaac L. Hunt; 1849, Geo. C. Woodruff.

Ogdensburg Dist.—Formed in 1851. 1851, Hiram Shepard.

Gouverneur Dist.—Formed in 1839; discontinued in 1844. 1839, W. S. Bowdish; 1841, Lewis Whitcomb; 1842, Nathaniel Salsbury.

Watertown Dist.—Lewis Whitcomb: 1849, Gardner Baker.

The St. Lawrence Conference of the Wesleyan Methodist Church was formed June 4, 1845, at Lisbon, and comprises Franklin, St. Lawrence, Jefferson, Lewis, Oneida and Herkimer counties, with a part of Oswego. Churches exist in Westville, Burke, Stockholm and Lawrence, Pierrepont and Parishville, Lisbon, Oswegatchie, Oak Point, Waddington, Louisville and Russell.

St. Lawrence Presbytery, is said to have been organized in De Kalb. According to the last official report, there were eight ministers, having under their care nine churches, and one candidate belonging to the Presbytery, which is of the new school order of the Presbyterian church, and constitutes a part of the *Utica Synod.* It embraces St. Lawrence county only, and there is much probability that it will be shortly united with the Ogdensburgh Presbytery (O. S.), from which it was separated by friendly agreement on the formation of the latter. The St. Lawrence Presbytery holds an annual meeting on the Tuesday preceding the third Wednesday in January, and a semi annual meeting on the second Tuesday of July. The present clergymen are Hiram S. Johnson, Roswell Pettibone, Elijah W. Plumb, Asa Brainerd, Bliss Burnap, Hiram Dyer, Branch B. Beckwith and Charles F. Halsey. Total number of members, 778.

The Ogdensburgh Presbytery (O. S.), was formed Jan. 21, 1839, soon after the division of the Presbyterian church, according to the provisions of the General Assembly of 1838, by the Rev. Messrs. James Rogers, John M. McGregor, John H. Savage, D. D., and elders from the Ogdensburgh, Oswegatchie and Hammond churches. This Presbytery at present embraces the following churches, clergymen and number of communicants! Hammond, 145; 1st, Oswegatchie, L. M. Miller, 247; 2d, do., 111; Morristown, R. T. Conant, 50; three churches in Jefferson county, viz: Le Ray, Wilna and Ox Bow, 140; total, 696. These churches in 1852 raised $4,100 for religious purposes. The churches of Franklin county belong to the Champlain Presbytery, which forms a part of the Albany Synod.

The St. Lawrence Association of Universalists was formed several years previous to 1840, but the records of the early proceedings could not be obtained. The present constitution was adopted in June, 1839. It is

32

embraced in the New York State Convention, and comprises the counties of St. Lawrence, Franklin and Clinton. Two delegates from each society, together with the clergyman of each, assemble annually by appointment, at different places, on the fourth Wednesday and Thursday of June, and constitute a council, for the discussion and regulation of the ecclesiastical business of the denomination. In June, 1851, a missionary society, for supplying destitute places in the three counties, was formed. There was formerly a Sabbath school society connected with the association, but this has been merged in the latter. The following is believed to be a complete list of the societies of this denomination, with the date of their admission, so far as could be ascertained:

Little York,* June, 1838. There is a church organization connected with this; Somerville,* June, 1843; Gouverneur and Hailesboro; Heuvelton;* Oswegatchie, June, 1842; Hammond, June, 1838; Canton,* formed before the association; has a church organization. Present number, 300; Madrid,* this, with the one that precedes and follows has a sabbath school connected; Potsdam,* organized before the association was formed; Massena; Hopkinton and Lawrence, June, 1843; Colton,* June, 1852; Nicolville; Morristown, June, 1843; Malone,* this has a church organization. The same with Madrid and Potsdam; Westville, June, 1844. Has an interest in the Union church in town; Plattsburgh,* June, 1845.

The standing clerks of the association since 1839, have been as follows: Z. N. Ellis, Wm. H. Waggoner, Jos. Baker, G. Swan and Martin Thatcher, who is the present incumbent.

ASSOCIATIONS FOR MUTUAL BENEFIT.

MASONS.—Being disappointed in procuring an official list, the following is offered as the best that could be obtained. It is defective in many points, and perhaps erroneous in some. *Aurora Lodge,* Fort Covington, very early. *Lodge of Benevolence,* formed at Hopkinton in 1811. *Columbia Lodge,* Madrid, August, 1825. Hiram Safford, M.; Oliver Spencer, S. W.; John Crawford, J. W. *Hamilton Lodge,* at that village, about 1810. *Harmony Lodge,* No. 187, Potsdam, 1808. The device of its seal was a square and compass. *Northern Constellation,* Malone, before the war; revived in the fall of 1852, with Clark Williamson, M.; F. P. Allen, 1st S. W.; Aaron Beeman, 1st J. W. *Northern Light,* Stockholm; removed to Lawrenceville, and is said to be the only one in the county that existed through the anti-masonic excitement. *Olive Branch,* Massena, 1806 or 7. *Racket River Lodge,* No. 213, Potsdam, fall of 1849. First officers, Joshua Blaisdell, M.; A. T. Hopkins, S. W.; J. H. Hyer, J. W. *Rainbow Lodge,* No. 12, Chateaugay, 1809. The regalia are said to have been stolen by the enemy in their incursion in 1814, which were bought up at Montreal by masons and returned. During the anti-masonic excitement, their charter, regalia and furniture disappeared. *St. Lawrence Lodge* No. 111, Canton, Dec. 1845. Lodges of masons existed before 1828 at De Kalb, Gouverneur, Rossie, Norfolk, Parishville, Ogdensburgh, and perhaps other places. They now exist at Ogdensburgh, Gouverneur, Canton, Potsdam, Lawrenceville and Malone.

Royal Arch Chapters existed at Malone, Potsdam and Ogdensburgh. At present they exist at Potsdam, Canton and Ogdensburgh. *St. Lawrence*

These churches have places of worship belonging to the several denominations of the different towns.

Chapter, No. 24, was formed at Massena, Feb. 9, 1809, with Elisha Dennison, H. P.; Daniel Robison, K.; John Polley, S. It was removed about 1816 to Potsdam. In 1828 it was suspended, and having funds at the time these were expended in the purchase of a library, which now numbers about 400 volumes. In 1851 it was revived. Device of its seal, a pot of incense.

ODD FELLOWS.—*Auriga Lodge*, No. 319, formed Aug. 6, 1847, at Madrid, with Joseph Baker, John A. Fuller, Cabot Pierce, Wm. J. Manley, Geo. Erwin, John Thomas, and Frederick Powell, charter members. Connected with this lodge are the Daughters of Rebecca, who are admitted to a part of each meeting. *Maslaqua Lodge*, No. 274, formed Feb. 5, 1847, at Potsdam, with Noble S. Elderkin, Chas. Boyington, Royal H. Munson, Josiah C. Gates, Shuball R. Gurley, and Norris Pierce, charter members. *Neshoba Lodge*, No. 78, formed March 15, 1848, at Malone, with S. P. Bates, H. S. Brewster, B. W. Clark, S. C. F. Thorndike, C. C. Whittlesey, and H. F. Heath, charter members. The device of their seal is an Indian in a canoe. *Norfolk Lodge*, No. 243, formed Aug. 22, 1849, with E. W. Sackrider, G. W. Floyd, H. G. Bradley, H. L. Sackrider, Q. D. Wicks, charter members. Seal, an eye with rays, a dove with an olive branch, and a scroll with the motto "In God we trust," encircled by the name, number, and date of the lodge. *Ogdensburgh Lodge*, No. 273, formed Feb. 24, 1847, with J. H. Haggett, J. M. Doty, D. Bingham, H. M. Smith, Geo. Boyd, F. B. Hitchcock, and A. M. Hepburne, charter members. *River De Grasse Lodge*, No. 425, formed at Canton, Jan. 29, 1852. Seal, an eye, three links, and the letters I. O. of O. F., within the name, number, and date. It is believed there is also a lodge at Waddington.

RECHABITES.—But one tent (Herculean Tent, No. 388), in the two counties. It was formed at Chateaugay in Sept., 1852, with the following as its first officers: A. M. Millar, Sh'd; E. A. Keeler, P. C. R.; A. S. Bryant, C. R.; D. C. Meigs, D. C. R.; G. Howe, L.; P. B. Fiske, R. S.; G. W. Goodspeed, F. S.; M. M. Roberts, T.; C. D. Silver, L G.; I. Spoon, O. G.

SONS OF TEMPERANCE.—*Oswegatchie Division*, No. 2, March 27, 1847. Charter members, Geo. Boyd, H. G. Foote, H. Rockwell, Geo. Guest, 2d, T. H. Hawley, G. W. Durgan, John Burke, Philip Hazen, Simeon Dillingham, A. M. Hepburn, Philo Abbott, R. G. James, A. M. Wooley, L. B. Stoor, R. S. Armstrong, and Joseph Bates. It meets on Fridays. *Stockholm*, No. 99, 1847; meets Wednesdays at East Stockholm. *Russell*, No. 100, 1850; meets Saturdays. *Chippewa St.*, No. 101, 1851, N. Hammond; meets Wednesdays. *Union*, No. 146, Somerville, Sept. 8, 1852. Charter members, Wm. R. Myers, Adam Myers, Hiram Hall, Wm. Harris, Chauncey Emmons, James McCarthy, E. Y. Kelsey, Harrison Emmons, F. White, C. G. Sharpstone, A. S. Sizeland. *St. Lawrence*, No. 258, Canton, June 26, 1847; meets Mondays. *Waddington*, No. 299, March 29, 1849. Charter members, James Redington, Richard Maguire, David Backus, James L. Buckley, Thos. Myers, Henry Stowers, Thos. Shea, Wm. Scott, S. E. Sanborn, G. R. Lowe, R. R. Hatch, A. L. Robinson, L. S. Wright, T. Short, 2d, John Proctor, L. J. Proctor, B. W. Daniels, J. B. Burdick, J. H. Bartholomew, and John Rand. It meets on Saturdays. *Centre*, No. 348, 1851, Parishville; meets Wednesdays. *Racket River*, No. 367, Potsdam, March 1848. Charter members, Ira Chandler, J. Blaisdell, B. Bachelor, H. Shead, T. Douglass, C. O. Hubbell, H. R.

Ames, B. C. Rich. It meets Monday. *Grass River*, No. 368, Madrid, May 6, 1848. Charter members, Noble Hosford, Hiram T. Fuller, Francis F. Pierce, Edgar P. Hill, Thos. Rea, Geo. A. Simons, Nathaniel L. Powell, Abraham Ross, and James A. Wright. Meets Thursdays. *Morley*, No. 369, 1850. *Minnesota*, No. 399, Raymondville, Jan. 1849. Charter members, Oliver Arnold, Jr., John Armstrong, H. B. Hall, Thomas Benedict, Joseph Clark, F. A. Clark, H. A. Bowland, and J. W. Denison. Meets Saturdays. *United Brothers*, No. 444, Ogdensburgh, Dec. 12, 1848. Charter members, S. F. Judd, David Burdett, James H. Russell, D. B. Bulsom, A. S. Sawtell, Wm. Lightfoot, Amos Wright, James Pendegrast, Thos. Child, H. Young, G. Boyd. Seva P. Taft, O. Fairbanks, J. B. Haggett, S. Low, P. W. Dunton, and S. L. Boyington. It meets Tuesdays. *Forest*, No. 463, Colton, 1851; meets Saturdays. *Massena*, No. 490, 1849. (gone down). *Gouverneur*, No. 544, Aug. 1849; meets Fridays. *Rickville*, No. 571, 1850. *De Peyster*, No. 586, 1849; meets Saturdays. *Ocean Rock*, No. 652, Millerville, April 9, 1850. Charter members, S. Sowls, C. Powers, M. Powers, B. P. Dowd, H. J. Clark, R. H. Miller, J. Miller, J. Gainer, J. Cole, H. Holland, G. W. Wright, W. Knight, and J. Barrell. Meets Saturdays. *Bounding Billows*, No. 653, Lawrenceville, 1850; meets Wednesdays. *St. Regis*, No. 659, Brasher Falls; meets Tuesdays. It is believed there are two or three other divisions in the county. In every instance application was made to some of the officers for facts, but many were disregarded, which renders it impossible to make our list perfect. This is stated that none may charge partiality or neglect upon us where it is not due.

In Franklin Co. *Franklin Division* No. 430, (Malone), Sept. 9, 1848, meets Tuesdays. *Northern Union*, No. 436, (Fort Covington), Sept. 1848. Charter members, J. C. Spencer, H. A. Paddock, C. M. Whitney, E. E. Whitney, S. Mears, R. H. Spencer, S. F. Lincoln, W. H. Payne, P. B. Wolff.

Cadets of Temperance, and *Daughters of Temperance*, have been in several instances, established, but it is believed none now exist.

Among associations for mutual benefit may be classed *Union Stores*, of which several exist in both counties. These form a part of a general system known as the *New England Protective Union*, which originated in Boston, in 1845. Each company is independent in pecuniary liabilities, and in organization. There exists a central agency at Boston, for the purchase of goods at a small commission, and delegates from divisions of 50 members or more, meet annually on the first Wednesday of October, at Boston, and though committees transact all business relating to the common interest. Business is done on the cash principle strictly, and traffic in ardent spirits is forbidden. Subdivisions are formed on application of 15 or more persons of good moral character, who do not use or vend intoxicating drinks. The first of these unions was formed at West Potsdam, in the fall of 1851. The following are their present number, location and capital of those existing at the close of 1852, as far as received. The facts were procured mostly through the kindness of Mr. Timothy Gibson, of Nicholville.

West Potsdam, No. 586, Oct. 14, 1851, capital $900, on an average. Trade since organization, $6000. Stephen Barnum, president; T. Bailey, secretary; *Morley*, W. Byington, president; Nicholville, 301, Nov. 1851, Rufus Alden, president; T. Gibson, secretary; capital $2000; Bicknellville, 307, Amos Bicknell, president; Silas Smith, secretary; capital, $2,500; Madrid, Norfolk 287, January 9, 1852, capital, $1,500; H. Attwater, president; Lloyd C. Yale, financial secretary; John Yale, recording

·cretary; Russell, 313, March 3, 1852; capital $500; W. P. Moore pre
·dent; Wm. E. Boyd, secretary; Stockholm depot, 312; B. Holmes, pre
·dent; Parishville, 315, March, 1852, capital $2000; L. Hatch, president;
·otsdam, 357, April 20, 1852, capital $200; sales $1000 monthly, Hexman
·'itten, president; T. Blaisdell, secretary; Lawrenceville, 399, J. Ferris,
·esident; P. Whitney, secretary; N. Lawrence, 400, Sept. 23, 1852; A.
·ownsend, president; L. R. Townsend, secretary; Dickinson, 392, C.
·aylor, president; Bombay, 405, Oct. 20, 1852, capital $2000; Jas. Mc
·oberts, president; S. B. Sowles, secretary; located at Bombay Corners

AGRICULTURAL SOCIETIES.—In the act of April 7, 1819, for encouraging
·ese, St. Lawrence received $100 for two years. A society entitled
*The St. Lawrence County Society for promoting agriculture and domestic
·inufactures"* having for its seal these words, encircling a sheaf of wheat,
·as formed in 1822. Membership 50 cents annually. A meeting was
be held on the last Wednesday of February, for the election of officers,
·d on the 3d Tuesday and Wednesday of October, for a fair, which was
be held at Canton, Potsdam and Madrid, alternately. This society was
·audoned in one or two years.
On the 4th of February, 1834, a second society was formed at Ogdens
·irgh, named the *"St. Lawrence County Agricultural Society."* Member
·ip $1 annually. Not less than two fairs were to be held annually at
·gdensburgh. Upon the last day of the first fair in each year, the offi
·rs were to be elected. Its first officers were George Parish, president;
·Van Rensselaer, Silas Wright, Jr., and J. C. Clarkson, vice presidents;
·nith Stilwell, secretary; Wm. Bacon, Smith Stilwell, Sylvester Gilbert,
·ivid C. Judson, U. H. Orvis, G. Ogden and Henry M. Fine, managers.
·is also subsisted about two years, and at its first fair distributed $247
·nong 37 competitors, principally on stock.
The general law of May 5, 1841, allowed this county $170 annually,
·r five years, and led to the formation of a third society, of which R.
·Harrison, was president, and a vice president was appointed to each
·wn, an executive committee of 7, and a treasurer and two secretaries.
·heir first fair (Oct. 7, 1841) distributed $361 in 66 premiums. Their
·cond (Sept. 14, 1842), $171 in 58 premiums. Nine years next ensued
·thout an agricultural society, when the board of supervisors, in 1851,
·ssed a resolution strongly in favor of another attempt, and designated
·e Thursday evening following for a preliminary meeting, to take mea
·res for an organization. Subsequent meetings were held, and on the
·of April, 1852, a convention was held at the court house, and a con
·tution adopted. Henry Van Rensselaer, was chosen president. Uriel
Orvis, Jonah Sanford and Hiram Johnson, vice presidents. Henry
Foote, secretary, and Ebenezer Miner, treasurer. A corresponding
·retary was appointed in each town. Elections are held on the 2d
·esday in June, at the court house, at 1 o'clock P. M., when the presi
·nt, vice presidents, secretary and treasurer, are chosen, and the execu
·e committee (who are the above officers), determine the time in Sept.,
·d place for holding the annual fair; decide upon the prizes, appoint
·iges or committees, and take such action as may promote the objects
·the society. Membership $1 annually, and none but members allowed
·compete for premiums. Citizens of adjoining counties entitled to a
·ance for premiums by paying $1. The fiscal year commences with
·tober. The constitution was signed by 50 delegates who attended the
·nvention.
The first fair of this society was held at Canton, Sept. 16–17, 1852, on
·mises finely adapted for the purpose, in the lower part of the village,

and near Grass river. The grounds had been leased for a term of five years, and enclosed in a close board fence. The side towards the road is descending and has numerous shade trees, while the rear part is level and affords a fine tour for the trial and exercise of horses offered for premiums. Both days were delightfully pleasant, and the crowds of intelligent farmers with their families who attended, bespoke the general interest that was felt, and augured well of the future. There were 396 articles offered for premiums, very many of which were highly creditable to the county.

Franklin county received $100 annually, by the law of 1819, and the board of supervisors raised a similar amount by tax for two years; a society was organized but was soon abandoned. By the act of 1841, this county was entitled to $50, but the effort that was then made for this purpose failed. On the 26th of August, 1851, a society was formed by a convention convened by the notice of the county clerk. Their constitution is as follows:

" We the undersigned, inhabitants of said county, have agreed, and do hereby agree, to be and are hereby associated together as a county society, for the promotion of agriculture in and for the said county of Franklin. And we severally agree to observe, perform, and abide by, the rules, resolutions and by-laws to be hereafter from time to time, adopted at any general meeting of this association, in conformity with the provisions of the legislature of this state, in relation to the formation, government and action of such societies. And we do further agree, that this society shall commence its operations from this 26th day of August, A. D., 1851."

The following officers were elected at the first meeting: President, Hon. Sidney Lawrence; secretary, Harry S. House; treasurer, Hiram H. Thompson; and a vice-president in each town.

The vice-presidents were appointed a committee to solicit subscriptions and obtain funds for the common benefit of the society. The first fair of the society was held October 6 and 7, 1852, on a plain half a mile east of the village, upon premises that had been leased for five years, and enclosed with a permanent fence, for the purpose of affording accommodations for succeeding fairs. The interest felt throughout the county in this fair, gives assurance that the association will be permanent and useful. There were eighty-one premiums awarded on domestic quadrupeds; eight upon fowls; sixteen upon dairy produce; thirty-two upon bread, fruit, and household goods; thirty-three upon miscellaneous manufactures; and eight upon farming implements. Three premiums were awarded upon the plowing match.

The St. Lawrence County Mutual Insurance Company was incorporated May 12, 1836. Silvester Gilbert, Zenas Clark, Tilden Hurlburd, John L. Russell, Edwin Dodge, Sylvester Butrick, Henry Van Rensselaer, George Redington, William Bacon, Smith Stillwell, Harvey Flagg, David C. Judson, and Baron S. Doty, were named in the act as first directors, their places to be supplied by an annual election by members of the company.

Persons insuring were to be members of the company while insured, and to have one vote for every hundred dollars of insurance. The existence of the company was limited to twenty years. The act has been amended May 12, 1836, March 26, 1849, and by several acts applicable to all insurance companies in the state. The company organized Oct. 13, 1836, and the first officers elected by the directors above named were,

Henry Van Rensselaer, president; Baron S. Doty, vice-president; Charles G. Myers, secretary.

The following statistics show the business which has been done by this company: Policies issued, 23,000; total insurance, $18,000,000; insurance in force, $15,000,000; premium notes, $420,000; paid losses from April 1, 1849, to April 1, 1852, $105,780·41.

The United States Mutual Insurance Company was incorporated under the general act of April 10, 1849, and its office is located at West Potsdam. The following is a list of the persons designated in the charter as first directors: Amos Blood, Martin Lester, Albert M. Skeels, William J. Barnum, Charles Dart, Orsemus L. Foote, Royal Barnum, Dennison G. Wilmarth, William A. Dart, Horace Allen, Truman Lillie, Jonah Sanford, Joseph Barnes, Martin Thatcher, Henry Barber, Amaziah B. James, Benjamin Lane, William E. Ellis, Alfred Goss, Lloyd C. Yale, C. B. Hawes, A. L. Lockwood, and James Lane. The directors are elected annually by the members, and choose from their number a president, vice-president, secretary and treasurer. The capital consisting of cash actually paid in, and of premium notes payable at such times as the directors shall determine, is fixed at not less than $100,000. Persons insured to have the option of giving premium notes liable to assessment in case of need, or of paying a sum of money for insurance in lieu of giving notes. The directors hold themselves indemnified and harmless from loss arising from default, neglect or misdeeds of the other directors. The duration of the company is fixed at twenty years. The funds of the company can not be used for traffic or banking, but may be loaned on good security payable on demand.

Cash premiums for one year, are taken in lieu of a note at 25 per cent on the amount which would have been demanded on the note, and the insurance may be renewed annually without a new survey. Steam mills, cotton factories, powder mills, distilleries, manufactories of printers' ink, and extra hazardous property not insured by the company. By the first annual report up to the 1st of January, 1852, the number of policies issued previously was 6,707, upon property valued at $4,918,679. Cash premiums less agent's commissions, $35,550·65. Losses and expenses paid, $13,085·23. Refunded on cancelled policies, $237·57. Balance of cash premiums, $22,237·84. A dividend of 30 per cent was declared on all risks of the first class, and 20 per cent on those of the second class which expired previous to Jan. 1, 1852. The company is responsible for the correctness of the surveys made by its agents, in this particular differing from some other mutual companies. Losses are allowed to the full amount insured.

The North American Mutual Insurance Company.—Was organized at Brasher Falls, July 1, 1851, up to Oct. 1, 1852, it had issued 1386 policies, and had at that time at risk $897,562·50.

The Franklin County Mutual Insurance Company.—Was incorporated, May 12, 1836, with Benjamin Clark, Hiram Horton, Jonathan Stearns, Jacob Wead, Aaron Beaman, Jonathan Thompson, William King, Sylvester Langdon, Jonathan Wallace, Henry N. Brush, Sidney Lawrence, Joseph Plumb, Timothy Beamar, directors. The business was to be carried on at Malone. The details of the provisions of this act were made to be like those of the Jefferson County Mutual Insurance Company, passed in March, previous. Policies were not to be issued until applications amounting to $50,000 had been received, and the duration of the act was limited to twenty years. An organization was, effected under this act, in June, 1836, by a meeting convened at the academy, and has continued in operation since. Benjamin Clark, Asa Hascall, Joseph H. Jackson, Samuel C. Wead, William King, and Abijah White, have been successively elected presidents. Uriah D. Meeker, A. B. Parmelee, and D. N. Huntington, have held the office of secretary, and Jonathan Wallace, Benjamin Clark, D. N. Huntington and Albert Andrus, that of treasurers. The last mentioned of each of the above are the present officers, up to Oct., 1852, it had issued about 4,200 policies, and has now about $1,000,000 worth of property covered by insurance, mostly in Franklin county. Within the last year, it has issued about 900 policies and paid $2,400 on losses.

Banks.—The wants of the county led the supervisors in 1825, to pass a resolution in which they asserted the unsound state of their currency which mostly consisted of Canada bills, from which loss constantly ensued and set forth the claims of Northern New York, to the benefits of the corporate privileges of banks. Passed by a vote of 11 to 7. On the 30th of April, 1829, the *Ogdensburgh Bank*, was incorporated for 30 years, capital $100,000, in 2,000 shares. Horace Allen, Amos Bacon, David C. Judson, Baron S. Doty, and Wm. Bacon, were appointed to open books for subscription of stock. This bank went into operation soon after, and has continued business without interruption. It is the only safety fund bank in the two counties.

On the 9th of Oct., 1838, articles of association were filed for a new bank, to commence operation Oct. 15, 1838, and continue 100 years, capital $100,000, in 1,000 shares, and to be managed by 21 directors, one third of whom to be chosen annually. It began to issue bills in Jan., 1839. The name assumed was *The St. Lawrence Bank.* After continuing business two or three years, it became insolvent, and its affairs were closed up.

On the 26th of Feb., 1841, *The Franklin Bank*, of Fort Covington, was to have begun operations, and continued till Nov. 2, 2301, on a capital of $100,000, in 2,000 shares, held by four citizens of Lewis county, but this never went into operation. *The Bank of Rossie*, projected by Samuel Linscott of Albany, was designed to commence business, April 15, 1844, with a capital of $100,000, but never organized. *The Citizen's Bank*, lately doing business in Ogdensburgh, was organized in Jefferson county, and in August, 1852, removed to Fulton, Oswego county. *The Drover's Bank*, now at Ogdensburgh, was originally established in Chautauque county. Circulation, Dec. 1, 1851, $98,887.

The Frontier Bank, of Potsdam, begun by Henry Keep, at Watertown, and removed to this place about May 1, 1851, owned by J. C. Dann, of Sackett's Harbor, H. P. Alexander, of Rockton, and Bloomfield Usher, of Potsdam, circulating, Dec. 1, 1851, $61,633. *The Bank of Malone*, was established in Sept. 1851, at Malone, and was owned by about 40 individuals, securities $35,110.80 in mortgages, and $65,000 in United States and New York stocks. The first directors were S. C. Wead, Hiram Horton, Wm. King and Wm. Andrus, of Malone, L. Fish, of Bangor, Henry B. Smith, of Chateaugay, G. A. Austin, of Orwell, Vt., O. A. Burton, of St. Albans, Vt., and D. P. Noyes, of Burlington, Vt.; S. C. Wead, president, Wm. A. Wheeler, cashier. A majority of the directors must reside in the county. This is the first bank for doing business in the county that has been established, and it is found eminently useful. *The Franklin County Bank*, principally owned abroad, and like the following, having no office of discount and deposit in the county, was founded several years since, but is mostly closed. In Dec., 1851, it reported a circulation of $2,811. *The Northern Bank of New York*, with a nominal existence at Madrid, but owned abroad, and with no office or circulation in the county, in Dec., 1851, reported $39,000 in circulation. *The Northern Exchange Bank* of Brasher Falls, of the same character as the preceding, reported $132,925 in circulation.

THE PRESS.

The first paper published in St. Lawrence county, was the *Palladium*, by John C. Kipp, and Timothy C. Strong, of Middlebury, Vt., who were furnished by David Parish and Daniel W. Church, with money to purchase a press and erect a building for the purpose of printing a paper in 1810. The enterprise was started in December of that year. The printers had a small quantity of type; Mr. Church built the office and sent for the press, while Mr. Parish furnished the money with which to begin business. Strong continued in the concern less than a year, when his partner took the office alone, and sold in the fall of 1812 to John P. Sheldon. The first paper was printed on a sheet 11 by 17½ inches, and had but two pages. Sheldon enlarged it to a folio, but difficulties being experienced in getting regular supplies of paper, many of the numbers were issued on a common foolscap sheet. It was printed on an old fashioned wooden press, published weekly, and distributed through the county by a foot post, an old Swiss about 60 years of age, acting as carrier. Sheldon discontinued his paper about 1814. From several numbers of this paper before us, it is learned that it was Federal in politics and denounced the war. For a time it had but three columns and two pages of 7 by 11 inches, exclusive of margin.

David R. Strachan and Platt B. Fairchild, purchased a Ramage press of James Bogart, of the Geneva Gazette, and commenced in Dec., 1815 a weekly paper under the title of the *St. Lawrence Gazette*, a small folio sheet, 20 by 25 inches, 5 columns to the page, at $2 per annum. Fairchild subsequently withdrew, and the paper was continued by the remaining publisher, until April 12, 1826, when Dan. Spafford and James C. Barter purchased the office and continued the paper without change of name or size, till Dec., 1829, when Spafford became publisher and continued it till about the 1st of January, 1830. He then sold it to Preston King, who had also purchased the *St. Lawrence Republican* previously issued at Potsdam. The Gazette thus ceased to exist, and the press on which it had been printed was laid away, and finally destroyed in the great fire of 1839. It espoused the cause of Mr. Adams, after his election in 1824, and advocated his reelection in 1828. Its politics were changed to republican on its union with the other paper.*

The Northern Light, an anti-masonic paper, was begun at Ogdensburgh, July 7, 1831, (20 by 26 inches), by W. B. Rogers, and in October, 1831, was assumed by A. Tyler and A. B. James, who published it about a year, when the latter became its editor. On the 10th of April, 1834, its name was changed to *The Times*, and at the end of the 4th volume it was enlarged to six columns, and its title changed to the *Ogdensburgh Times*. In July, 1837, Dr. Tyler again became associated with Mr. James,

* The author is indebted to a work entitled, The Typographical Miscellany, by J. Munsell, Albany, 1850, for numerous facts concerning the press of St. Lawrence county. They were prepared for that work by Mathew W. Tillotson, of Ogdensburgh, one of the present publishers of the St. Lawrence Republican. A very minute and extensive account was also furnished by Wm. H. Wallace, Esq. of Potsdam.

and the name was again changed to the *Times and Advertiser*. In July, 1838, Dr. Albert Tyler became its sole publisher, and continued until March, 1844, when it was transferred to Foote and Seely, and it became the *Frontier Sentinel*. Upon the change of parties about 1834, the politics of the paper became Whig, and it has continued till the present time, to be the organ of that party in the county, under the following names:

The *Frontier Sentinel* begun April 2, 1844, by Foote and Seeley, (six columns folio), at $1 per annum. Mr. Stephen B. Seeley, of the above firm, died August 17, 1844, and the paper was thenceforth continued by Henry G. Foote. On the 8th of June, 1847, the name was changed to the *Ogdensburgh Sentinel*, under which it has continued till the present time. It was at the same time enlarged to eight columns, and the price increased to $1·75. On the 27th of November, 1849, this paper was transferred to Stillman Foote, by whom it has been continued till the present time. In June, 1850, the price was reduced to $1. It has been printed since 1847, on an Adams power press.

The *Daily Sentinel* was the first attempt to establish a daily paper in St. Lawrence county. It was started April 14, 1848, by S. Foote, at one cent per number, and continued until Sept. 14, of the same year. Its pages were nearly square, and three columns in width. It was made up from the matter prepared for the weekly sheet, with a few advertisements. *The St. Lawrence Budget*, a very small advertising sheet, was issued from the press of the Sentinel, semi-monthly, for about two years, in 1850-1.

The Meteorological Register, was the title of a monthly quarto, commenced January 1, 1839, by J. H. Coffin, then principal of the Academy, and now of Fayette College, Easton, Pa. It was devoted to scientific inquiries, and continued but four numbers. It was issued by one of the printing offices in the village. This highly meritorious publication is believed not to have received the patronage which rendered its continuance practicable, although conducted with an ability very creditable to its editor. *The Ogdensburgh Forum*, was commenced April 24, 1848, by A. Tyler, to support the Whig party, and the interests of Gen. Taylor. It was of small sized folio, in small type, and at first issued tri-weekly and weekly, at $1·50, and 50 cts per annum. When first started it was issued in the quarto form, with four pages to the sheet, but at the end of six months the tri-weekly was discontinued, and after the first year the folio form was adopted. It was discontinued in February, 1851. The office from which this paper was issued had been supplied with new furniture complete, and was at first designed for a job office only, and it was the first attempt to establish an office of this kind in St. Lawrence county. After the paper was stopped it continued to do job work until 1852, when it was sold and removed to Gouverneur.

The first attempt to establish a daily paper in St. Lawrence county of a character comparable with the daily press of the cities, was made in March, 1852, by Wm. N. Oswell, a former editor of the St. Lawrence Republican, assisted by Mr. Fayette Robinson, in the editorial department. It was entitled the *Daily Morning News*; professed neutrality in politics, and was conducted with an ability and enterprise which entitled it to a liberal support. The presses, type and furniture of this office were new. In September, 1852, was commenced the issue from the press of the Daily News, a large sheet, neutral in politics, and devoted to literary and general intelligence, by the name of *The Weekly News*, by William N. Oswell. The latter paper soon after was temporarily suspended, but again issued in a smaller sheet, and continued as a daily paper. Both of these are believed to be now discontinued. *The Ogdensburgh Daily Times*, a second daily paper, was begun October 18, 1852, by William Yeaton and Warren Dow, and was printed at the Republican office. It proposed to act independent in politics, and the first number was a small folio, five columns to the page, and appeared to be edited with ability, but the publication was arrested by a disastrous fire after one or two issues.

The Potsdam Gazette was begun January 13, 1816, (neutral in politics), by Frederick C. Powell, 18 by 22 inches, from a screw press made by J. Ouram, in Philadelphia, and bought in New York for $150. It was discontinued in April, 1823. It was issued weekly, and contained four columns to the page. Zenas Clark was connected with it a few months. In January, 1824, Mr. Powell commenced issuing from the same press, a neutral paper, 20 by 24 inches, four columns folio, entitled *The Potsdam American*, which afterwards was published by Powell and Reddington, discontinued in April, 1829. In May, 1829, Elias Williams issued from this press and of the same size as the last, an anti-masonic weekly entitled *The Herald*, which continued but from May 29 till August. In April, 1830, Wm. Hughes printed on the same press an anti-masonic weekly called *The Patriot*. It was 20 by 26 inches, five columns to the page, and was stopped early in 1831, when the press was removed to Ogdensburgh, by W. B. Rogers, and used in publishing the *Northern Light*. This was afterwards sold to Judge Buell, of Brockville, for $25, and used for job work, and its place supplied in 1834, by an iron No. 3, Smith press.

The St. Lawrence Republican was commenced in Potsdam, in the fall of 1826, or early in the following year, by Wm. H. Wyman, on a Royal press. It was afterwards published in company with Jonathan Wallace, as a republican paper in opposition to the St. Lawrence Gazette, and was the first democratic paper in the county. It was 20 by 29 inches, weekly, and distributed by a post. In the summer of 1827, it went into the hands of Mr. Wallace, and in the winter of 1828, Wyman became the proprietor. In 1827 it was removed to Canton, and printed awhile as the *Canton Advertiser and St. Lawrence Republican*, and in 1830, to Ogdensburgh, where it was published by Preston King, until January, 1833. Samuel Hoard then purchased it. Up to this time, and until May following, this paper had been printed on a Ramage press, bought for $40 in New York, in 1826. It had a stone bed for its form, which being broken, it was replaced by a wooden plank. In May, 1833, Mr. Hoard brought from Fort Covington, an iron Smith press, and enlarged it to 21½ by 32 inches. In 1834, he took into partnership F. D. Flanders, the present editor of the Franklin Gazette. In December, 1834, it was taken by M. W. and J. M. Tillotson, and published two years, when the former withdrew, and it was continued by J. M. Tillotson until the fall of 1841. In April, 1839, the establishment was consumed by fire, but early in the summer resumed, and enlarged to 23½ by 36 inches, and with seven columns to the page. The new press was a Washington press, by Hoe & Co. In the fall of 1841, Franklin B. Hitchcock and Henry M. Smith, purchased the office, and issued it until July 16, 1848, when the former withdrew, and his place was taken by Wm. N. Oswell, who published the paper until December 3, 1851, when Hitchcock repurchased of Oswell, and it was continued by him and Smith till March 17, 1852. Mr. Smith's health then failing, he sold his share to M. W. Tillotson, a former proprietor, and it has since been continued by Hitchcock and Tillotson. While owned by Smith & Oswell, a steam power press by Hoe & Co., was procured. In the last and most destructive of the fires in Ogdensburgh in October, 1852, this office was again consumed, but the paper was continued on a small half sheet a short time, and is at the date of writing (January, 1853), published in folio, 22 by 25 inches, five columns to the page. Before its late disaster, this paper had attained a size, and was conducted with an ability that would compare favorably with any weekly paper in the country. It is proposed to enlarge it and provide new materials for an office during the coming season. This paper has long been the official organ of the democratic party of the county.

In 1827, while Mr. Wallace was publishing the St. Lawrence Republican, he issued a semi-monthly folio, 13 by 20 inches, called *The Day Star*. It was a Universalist paper, and continued six months, when it was united with the Gospel Advocate of Utica. While this paper was being published the press was removed to Canton.

In July 1832, C. C. Bill, started a whig paper in Canton, called the *Northern Telegraph*, and after printing it a time, sold his interest to Orlando Squires, who commenced publishing a democratic paper on the same press, which was called *The Canton Democrat*, who continued it a short time. A paper called *The Luminary of the North*, was published here in July 1834. *The St. Lawrence Democrat*, a whig paper owned by several individuals, and published by Edgar A. Barber, was commenced in September 1840, and its publication finally ceased in April 1842. It was printed on a No. 3 Washington press. *The Northern Cabinet, and Literary Repository*, a neutral and literary paper, was begun at Canton, Jan. 2, 1843, by Charles Boynton, in the quarto form, semi-monthly, at $1 per annum. The press and materials were the same as those which had been used in Mr. Barber's paper. On the 11th of April, 1844, Mr. Boynton commenced issuing *The Enquirer, and Tariff Advocate*, a campaign paper devoted to the whig party, and continued only till the November, following. It was a small folio, terms 50 cts., and issued from the same press as the preceding. In consequence of this the Cabinet became unpopular with the democratic party, and it was removed at the end of the second year to Potsdam, and continued weekly on the same plan as before, one year, when it was changed to folio. The literary matter of this folio was issued on a semi-monthly octavo in covers,—double columns— with title and index one year, under the name of *The Repository*, which was commenced July 20, 1846. At the end of the fourth volume, the Cabinet was sold to Wm. L. Knowles, and thenceforth issued under the name of *The St. Lawrence Mercury*. Mr. Knowles continued its publication two years, when he sold to William H. Wallace, who continued to publish it about two years longer under the same name, when he sold, in June, 1851, the establishment to H. C. Fay, who changed the name to *The St Lawrence Journal*, and continued its issue till July 1852, when it was united with the Potsdam Courier. It professed to be neutral in politics.

The Potsdam Courier was commenced by Vernon Harrington, in fall of 1851, and continued till July 1852, when it was combined with the Journal. It was issued from the same press which had been previously used at Gouverneur. It was neutral in politics. *The Potsdam Courier and Journal* formed in July 1852, by the union of the Courier and Journal, and published by Harrrington & Fay, is at present the only paper published in Potsdam. It professes to be neutral in politics, and is conducted with much ability. Terms $1 per year.

The Philomathean, a literary magazine, conducted by the Philomathean society of the St. Lawrence Academy, was started in the spring of 1849, and continued several numbers. It was made of selected productions of the members of the society.

It was proposed to be issued at the end of each academic term, or three numbers in a year, at a subscription price of 37½ cts.

The Northern New Yorker, a small folio weekly paper, neutral in politics, was commenced at Gouverneur, April 26, 1849, with the same press and materials which had been used in the Carthage papers several years previous. Published by W. M. Goodrich, and M. F. Wilson, and edited by Charles Anthony. Terms $1. At the end of the first volume it was undertaken by N. J. Bruett, who enlarged it one column, and continued it but twelve numbers. A very small sheet was continued five weeks longer, called the *St Lawrence Advertiser*. The office was then removed to Potsdam. Mr. Wilson commenced May 28, 1850, publishing at Columbia village (Madrid), with the press and type formerly used by the *Theresa Chronicle*.

The True Democrat. It was a small sized folio and professed to support the democratic party. At the end of ten months, it was purchased by O. L. Ray, and its politics changed from democratic to neutral. At the end of a year its name was changed to the *Columbian Independent*, and continued a year longer under the same title, when it was removed to Canton, and the name again changed to the *Canton Independent*, under which it is now published. Like the other county papers now published, is issued at $1 per annum. The *Canton Weekly Citizen* was the title of a very small folio, attempted to be published at Canton, commenced with the 1st of Jan. 1852, by J. S. Sargent. It continued four weeks.

The Labourer, is the title of a small but spirited weekly sheet, established at Gouverneur in July 1852, by Martin Mitchell, a gentleman well qualified to conduct a journal. It is issued from the same press as that which had been used in the Ogdensburgh Forum, and as a job press at Ogdensburgh. In 1852, it became the organ of the Free Soil movement, in Northern New York.

The Franklin Telegraph, the first paper ever published in Franklin county, was commenced at Malone, in 1824, on a Ramage press—had four columns to the page, and claimed to be *national republican* or whig, in politics. Its publisher was Francis Burnap. Upon the rise of the anti-masonic party, it supported that cause, and was published a short time by Elias Williams, as the organ of that party when Williams removed to Potsdam, and published an anti-masonic paper there a short time. *The Northern Spectator* was started at Malone, by John G. Clayton, who was sent from New York, with a new press and office complete, by William L. Stone, of the Commercial Advertiser, in the Spring of the year 1830. At the end of about two years, it passed into the hands of George P. Allen, and subsequently was issued by Frederick P. Allen. It was from the time of its first issue, devoted to the interest of the whig party and continued to be so after the change of name. It was discontinued in February 1835, and in the following month *The Palladium* was commenced with the same office by F. P. Allen, who continued to publish it ten years. March 1845, Mr. F. T. Heath, became the proprietor, and June, 1850, J. J. Seaver became a partner. It is now published by Heath and Seaver, and is the organ of the whig party in the county. This and the Franklin Gazette, were very lately the only papers published in the county, and for size, mechanical execution, and editorial management, they will compare favorably with any of the weekly issues from the country press.

The first newspaper published in Fort Covington was the *Franklin*

Republican, which was started in the spring of 1827, by J. K. Averill, upon a press from Plattsburgh. It had four columns to the page, and was published at $2.50 per annum. It was continued till June 1833. Six months after its commencement it was bought by Samuel Hoard, and James Long, but the latter continued but about a half year, and during the last year Mr. Hoard was reassociated with F. D. Flanders. Its politics were democratic.

The Franklin Gazette was begun in the fall of 1837, at Fort Covington, by F. D. Flanders, at $1.75 per annum; five columns to the page. It was democratic in politics. In the fall of 1847, it was removed to Malone, previous to which it had been printed on a Ramage press, but on its removal it was enlarged; a Smith press, previously used in the Sentinel office in Ogdensburgh, was procured, and it was published one year by Mr. Flanders, in company with Mr. Blaisdell. Since 1848, it has been published by Mr. Flanders alone. It has at present six columns to the page, and is published at $1 per annum. In state politics it has claimed to belong to the barnburner section of the democratic party, but in 1848, it advocated the election of General Cass to the presidency. A small paper called *The Messenger*, was published in 1850, at Fort Covington, at first by J. D. Fisk, and afterwards by J. S. Sergeant. It was continued a year, when it was discontinued and the press removed to Canton. It claimed to be independent in politics. At first it bore the title of *Salmon River Messenger*.

The Jeffersonian, is the title of a new democratic paper, recently established at Malone, in Jan. 1853. No particulars could be procured in time for our use in the work.

History of Academies.

The St. Lawrence Academy owes its origin to the spirited efforts of Benjamin Raymond, who in 1810 erected, at his own expense, a building for public purposes, and in the spring of 1812, employed Rev. James Johnson, of Lynn, Mass., a graduate of Harvard college, as a teacher and clergyman, entirely at his own cost. In December, 1812, a subscription was started to raise $5,000, in shares of $10 each, and Mr. Raymond headed the list by signing 100 shares, including the lot and building he had erected. Liberty Knowles, Azel Lyman, Samuel Pease, Robert McChesney, Benj. Burton, Anthony Y. Elderkin, Joseph P. Reynolds, Wm. Smith, James Johnson, Reuel Taylor, Pierce Shepard, Lemuel Pinney, John Burroughs, Sewall Raymond, David Parish, and Jacob Redington, each took ten shares. Eighteen others took shares of less number, making an aggregate of 312 shares.

In January, 1813, a petition for incorporation was presented, but this being lost or mislaid, on the 4th of April, 1816, a petition was again presented, and was successful. In this it is stated, that a lot near the centre of the village had been conditionally pledged to the trustees, on which was a building 36 feet by 24, having at one end a porch, with a belfry and cupola, and that there had been expended upon said building more than $700. A resolution of the town meeting was forwarded, praying that the lands in town reserved for literary purposes might be conveyed to the academy as a permanent fund. Benjamin Raymond, Liberty Knowles, Pierce Shepard, Azel Lyman, Joseph P. Reynolds, Sewall Raymond, Robert McChesney, David Parish, Nathan Ford, Louis Hasbrouck, Roswell Hopkins, Russell Attwater, and Ebenezer Hulburd, were recommended as trustees, and the name suggested for the institution was

Academy and public square in the village of Potsdam, St. Lawrence Co., N. Y.

the St. Lawrence Academy. This led to an act of incorporation with the above names as trustees, and a grant of the literature lot, which was never to be sold, but leased. It was found impossible to effect this, because land could be bought on reasonable terms, and none but loose and irresponsible characters could be found willing to become tenants, subject to an annual tribute. The trustees were accordingly, by an act of April 5, 1828, authorized to sell the lot, in whole or in part, and convey in fee simple, or otherwise, the lot of land previously granted, and invest the avails in a permanent fund, the annual income of which should be applied to the payment of the wages of tutors in the academy, and for no other purpose.

At the first meeting of the trustees, Sept. 17, 1816, it was resolved, " that the senior trustee and clerk, be directed to lease the land granted by the legislature, in lots not exceeding sixty acres each, for any term of time not exceeding fourteen years, for an annual rent of one peck of wheat per acre, after the first two years, payable at the village in this town on the first day of February, in each year. A preceptor was to be employed for one year, commencing on the first Monday in October next, on a salary of $420, and the prices of tuition were fixed at the following rates, viz: "Reading and writing, $2·50; English grammar, cyphering, mathematics, and book-keeping, $3; dead languages, $3·50; logic, rhetoric, composition, moral philosophy, natural philosophy, and French language, $4." On the 30th of Sept., 1816, a code of by-laws was adopted, which among other things provided, that none should be admitted as students who could not stand in a class and read in plain English readings; and that application for admission should be made in writing. Stated attendance at the church where the preceptor worshiped was required, unless a desire was expressed in writing by the parents or guardians of students, if minors, or by the students themselves, if 21 years of age, for the privilege of attending elsewhere. Strict observance of the Sabbath day and evening, and of Saturday evening, was enjoined, and strict morality was required.

On the 24th of April, 1818, a seal was adopted having for its device a pair of globes, and the inscription "St. Lawrence Academy, 1816," around them. Nahan Nixon, from Middlebury college, was employed by the trustees as the first preceptor in the fall term of 1816, and remained one year. At this period the trustees were unable to secure the services of any teacher whom they considered fitted for the station, and two years elapsed without a school being maintained. In the fall of 1819, the services of Levi S. Ives, now the Episcopal bishop of North Carolina, were secured, and he remained two years. On the 28th of January, 1822, the trustees petitioned the legislature, praying for the additional grant of the literature lots of Louisville and Stockholm, but failed.

In the fall of 1821, Charles Orvis, a graduate of Hamilton college, and at present a physician in Martinsburgh, Lewis county, was employed for one year, when the Rev. Daniel Banks succeeded and remained till his death in August, 1827. On the 25th of April, 1825, the first action was taken towards erecting a new building, and through the efforts of the Hon. Silas Wright in the senate, and the members from our two counties, procured a law April 9, 1825, requiring $2,500 to be raised by the sale of reserved literature lots, for the academy, on condition that a brick or stone edifice, worth at least $3,000 be first erected on ground owned by the trustees. The thanks of the board were tendered to Messrs. Wright, Vanden Heuvel, and Hascall, for their efforts in procuring this aid; and proposals were advertised for erecting a stone edifice to be 68 by 36 feet,

four stories high including the basement. The contract was taken by
Samuel Partridge, to be built under the direction and subject to the acceptance of L. Knowles, J. C. Smith and J. P. Reynolds. It is the one
on the north side of the Presbyterian church, and fronting on the public
square. The site of the St. Lawrence academy forms a part of a plat
given the town by the proprietors for that purpose, and held in trust by
the commissioners of highways. The latter were empowered by an act
of April 20, 1825, to convey such portion as they might deem necessary,
as a site for the erection of academic buildings. The corner stone of
the new edifice was laid with masonic ceremonies, by Harmony lodge,
on the 1st of June, 1825. Present, the trustees of the academy and several clergymen from the neighboring towns, and a large concourse of
spectators. Prayer by the Rev. Mr. Pettibone, of Hopkinton, now of
Canton. There was deposited under the stone a leaden box inclosing
a glass jar, corked and sealed, containing several manuscripts, pamphlets
and papers, among which was a copy of the Hartford Courant, containing
the "stamp act," and Washington's farewell address, and also a silver
plate, on which was neatly engraved the following inscription:

"Town of Potsdam, county of St. Lawrence, state of New York.
Settlement of this town commenced by Benjamin Raymond, Esq., from
Mass., A. D. 1803. St. Lawrence Academy chartered by the state
through his influence, A. D. 1816. Present trustees, Liberty Knowles,
Pierce Shepard, Azel Lyman, Joseph P. Reynolds, Sewall Raymond,
David Parish, Roswell Hopkins, Ebenezer Hulburd, Samuel Partridge,
Horace Allen, John C. Smith, John Fine, J. A. Vanden Heuvel. Rev.
Daniel Banks, principal; Mr. Noah Cushman, assistant. This edifice
erected A. D. 1825; expense, $4,000. Alanson Fisher, mason; Grey C.
Noble, joiner. This village contains 400 inhabitants; the whole town
2,700. De Witt Clinton, governor of the state. 'In prosperitate litera-
turarum, salutem reipublicæ consistere.' June 1, 1825. J. Davidson,
engraver."

An appropriate address was delivered by the Rev. James McAuley, of
Ogdensburgh. Last prayer by Rev. Roswell Pettibone, of Hopkinton.
Ceremony completed by sacred music, by a large choir of singers, ac-
companied by the Potsdam band.

Mr. Banks's place was filled till the close of 1827, by Joseph Hopkins,
who had been previously employed as an assistant. In the early part
of 1828, Mr. Asa Brainerd, from Danville, Vt., a graduate of the university
of Vermont, was employed, and continued to fill the post of preceptor
until 1847. He is now at the head of a female seminary in Norwalk,
Ohio. Wm. H. Parker, who for eight or ten years had been professor
of languages in the academy, was appointed principal, and held that
office two years, when he was succeeded by Wm. F. Bascom, the present principal. At an early period a teacher's class was formed for preparing instructors for common schools.

In 1835, this academy was selected by the Regents of the University
for the establishment of a teacher's department in the 4th senate district,
and the trustees took measures to provide facilities for it, by increasing
the number of teachers, and the erection of the stone building south of
the church. In their official report of 1837, the regents specially commended this academy for its success in forming a teacher's department,
and referred to it as an evidence of the utility of the plan. The town at
their annual meeting in 1835, adopted a petition for a law authorizing a
tax upon the town of $500, in each of the years 1836 and '7, for the pur-
pose of erecting an additional academic building, to accommodate the

prospective wants of this department. An act was accordingly passed, authorizing this tax, and in 1836, the academic building south of the church was erected. It is four stories high, 76 by 36 feet, having in the lower story, a lecture room 32 by 39 feet; a recitation room 23½ feet; an apparatus room 23 by 18½ feet; a fire-proof laboratory 16 by 9½ feet; and another room of the same size. The other stories were mostly devoted to rooms for students. The cost of this was reported $5,200, to pay which the tax of $1,000 and a subscription of $1,605, mostly among the trustees, was applied. The expenses thus incurred hung as a heavy burden upon the trustees until 1849, when an appropriation of $2,000 was received from the state treasury, by which it has been mostly relieved from debt. The teachers' department has been eminently useful, having furnished *during the last twenty-five years, on an average of* 100 *teachers annually* for common schools. A professorship of mathematics, and another of languages were instituted in 1835, with the view of increasing the facilities of this department.

The Gouverneur Wesleyan Seminary, resulted from a movement began March 31, 1826, on which date a subscription was drawn up for procuring funds to build a second story to the brick school house (then erecting) for academical purposes, and to be under the control of the subscribers. Every $10 entitled to one vote. By this means $540 or 54 shares were raised, and in November of that year, it was resolved that the new institution should bear the name of the *Gouverneur Union Academy,* to be controlled by three trustees elected on the first Tuesday of October, annually. This measure was not effected without considerable opposition from several inhabitants, who professed a strong attachment to the common schools, and attributed to *academies* an aristocratic tendency subversive of the general good. Some of these opposers have lived long enough to be ashamed of their conduct. The room was completed in 1827, and a school opened by a Mr. Ruger, a brother of the mathematician. He was succeeded by a Mr. Morgan. On the 25th of April, 1828, this academy was incorporated by the legislature under the name of the *Gouverneur High School.* John Spencer, Aaron Rowley, David Barrell, Harvey D. Smith, Josiah Waid, Alba Smith, Almond Z. Madison, Robert Conant and Joel Keyes, and their associates, were by this act incorporated as a body politic for the purposes of academical education, with a capital limited at $20,000 in shares of $10 each, which were to be deemed personal property. The institution was to be governed by nine trustees, chosen annually on the first Monday of September, and the persons named in the act were to be considered trustees until others were elected. In the autumn of the same year Isaac Green was employed as a teacher, with whatever salary might accrue from tuitions, and a free use of the school room in the brick school house was granted for the first term. On the 19th of February, 1829, the trustees made a formal application to the Regents of the University for a participation in the benefits of the literature fund, subject to their visitation. This request was accepted, and bears date from the time of application. The premises in the brick building being found inadequate to the wants of the school, efforts were made in the summer of 1830, to erect a new building on a scale commensurate with the prospective requirements of the institution. On the 6th of September in that year, 275½ shares, $2,755, had been subscribed for this purpose, and it was resolved to undertake a new building. The trustees at this period received proposals from Mr. Joseph Hopkins, a graduate of Hamilton College, who had previously been engaged as a teacher at Potsdam, in which this gentleman offered to subscribe $800 to

33

the stock of the institution, on condition that apartments for a family should be comprised in the plan, and that he should have the control of the school. His plan was to construct three long one story buildings, with a colonnade on each side, and so placed as to form three sides of an open court or square. A plan proposed by Mr. Philip Kearney, with modifications, was adopted. This consisted of a main building 30 by 40 feet, two stories high, the lower of 12 the upper of 10 feet. On each side was a wing 28 feet square, two stories high, with eight study rooms each. In consequence of the change of plan, $400 of Mr. Hopkin's subscription was relinquished. At this time the trustees possessed *but barely enough funds to erect the walls and roof*, but trusting in the sentiment in the motto of their seal,* that "brighter hours will come" they expended their money for these purposes, relying upon the generosity of the community for the means to finish their academy. In March, 1832, the trustees petitioned for $1000 from the literature fund of the state, but failed to receive it. In April, 1834, the building was completed, and the academy went into operation under the charge of Mr. Hopkins, who undertook it for the tuition money that might accrue, and the literature money that was received from the regents. In March, 1837, this gentleman resigned, and the trustees on the 29th of that month, entered into a compact with individuals representing the Methodist Episcopal denomination to the following effect:

John Loveys, Wm. C. Mason, J T. Peck, C. W. Leet and R. Reynolds, acting as a committee appointed by a convention of ministers of the Potsdam district, of the Methodist Episcopal Church, undertook the patronage and general care of the school, and engaged to provide the means to pay off a mortgage then existing upon the property, and employ one or more agents to solicit donations for its better endowment, and to engage as speedily as possible, three competent and faithful teachers; and that the institution should be open to students of any and all religious tenets, without preference. The school was to remain strictly a literary institution.

Lewis B. Parsons, Sylvanus Cone, Charles Goodrich, Harvey D. Smith and Ira A. Van Duzee, trustees, agreed that at least 100 shares of stock should be transferred conditionally to persons authorized to receive it in trust for the Methodist denomination, that Methodists might subscribe to any amount within the limits of their charter, and that the chapel might be used as a place of stated worship on the sabbath and for quarterly meetings, when not interfering with the regular exercises of the school. The trustees agreed that until a new election the present board would appoint such principal and assistant teachers as the committee should designate. It was stipulated that the bell should not be included in the property conveyed, as it had been procured by general subscription, and did not belong to the trustees. This compact was unanimously confirmed by the stockholders on the same day. The Black river conference, under whose care the academy thus came, has never formally sanctioned it, so as to become liable for its debts, although it has been customary to appoint preceptors and a board of visitors annually. They have claimed it in their list of seminaries.

The Rev. Jesse T. Peck (now president of Dickinson College, Carlisle, Pa.,) was appointed the first principal under the new regulations, and the institution had become quite prosperous when the building was accident

* Their seal adopted about this time, had for its device a lantern, with the above words around it.

MISS F. W. WRIGHT, DEL.

nlly burned on the night of the 1st day of January, 1839. By this accident most of their apparatus and a valuable cabinet of minerals was de-
stroyéd, but that which was regretted more than any other article, was
their silver-toned bell, which is still spoken of as having been one of the
clearest sounding and most excellent of its kind. At that time it was the
only one in the place. The institution was at this time heavily in debt,
and this catastrophe left their finances in a most deplorable condition. To
enhance this, an insurance of $1,800 in the Jefferson County Mutual
Company, was repudiated by some technical quibble, which led to fruitless litigation on the part of the trustees, and loss of reputation on that
of the company. Their remaining resources were $500 insurance in
New York; proceeds of subscription due in 1838-9, $1000; ditto, 1840,
$800; ditto, 1841, $800. Their debts amounted to $4000. In conse-
quence of the fire, the inhabitants at the ensuing town meeting, instructed
the trustees to petition the legislature for a loan of $2000, to be refunded
by a tax within four years. A very full attendance and only five or six
votes in the negative, bespeak the interest which the citizens felt in this
measure. This loan was accordingly procured at the following session:
new subscriptions of $1000 in each of the years 1840 and 1841, were
collected, and the trustees proceeded the same year to erect and finish
the present edifice, which is herewith represented. Edwin Dodge, Wm.
E. Sterling, Jesse T. Peck and Harvey D. Smith, were the building committee.

Meanwhile, the school was not allowed to be interrupted, but temporary
rooms were fitted up and occupied till the building was completely finished. The contemplated cost was $4000, but before finished it
amounted to $5,500. On the 25th of April, 1840, the name was changed
by the legislature to its present one. Mr. Peck resigned in December,
1840, and was succeeded by Loren B. Knox, who was principal till July,
1842, when the Rev. A. W. Cummings, was elected. He remained till
July, 1844, when the Rev. J. W. Armstrong, succeeded. This gentleman
continued to discharge the duties of principal with much success until
the summer of 1850, when he resigned, and Mr. W. W. Clark, was appointed to that office. The academy was long oppressed by debts, which
impaired its usefulness and embarrassed the trustees until 1851, when an
appropriation of $2000 was obtained from the state, with which they re-
moved all incumbrances, and it now enjoys exemption from this evil.
This debt arose in part from the fire and in part from the supposed misconduct of a fiscal agent. Its present facilities for imparting a thorough
classical and practical education, are superior, and the quiet, moral and
intelligent community in which it is located, render it peculiarly worthy
of patronage. It is enjoying a good degree of prosperity.

The Canton Academy, originated from a subscription circulated in the
spring of 1831, in which 25 citizens of that town, pledged themselves to
pay $1250, towards erecting a suitable building for an academic school.

These subscribers met on the 16th of May, 1831, and adopted articles
of association in the preamble of which are set forth the advantages of
education, and the necessity of a literary institution among them. They
provided that a building should be erected two stories high, with a
cupola and belfry, and not less than 30 by 50 feet. The subscribers
were to appoint a chairman and clerk, to hold their office during the
pleasure of the appointing power. Meetings to be legal must be held
by adjournment, or by written notice left at the residence (if in Canton),
of subscribers, indicating the time, place and objects of meeting. The
proposed building was to be owned in shares of $50 each, and every

share was to entitle to one vote. A building committee was to be appointed as soon as practicable, who were to solicit donations, and collect subscriptions, and to expend them on the proposed building, being required to render an exact account of their receipts and disbursements. To become a partner to the compact, a person was to subscribe his name and give his note to one of the building committee, in substance as follows, viz: "Five dollars payable in the month of August next, and the remainder in two annual installments payable in cattle, on or before the first day of October, or grain, on or before the first day of February following." These articles were to continue in force until the school should be incorporated, and for this, application was immediately to be made, by a committee of three, to be named at the next meeting of the subscribers. No subscription was binding until the sum of $1,200 was signed, and the site selected for the building.

Joseph Ames 2d, Isaac C. Paige and Wm. Noble, were appointed a building committee, and the present site opposite the county buildings was presented to the subscribers by David C. Judson, for that purpose. At the same meetings, Hiram S. Johnson, Silas Baldwin, Jun., and Minet Jenison, were appointed to solicit an incorporation from the board of regents, but the amount of property necessary for this was increased about this time, so as to put it beyond their present means to gain this object. On the 8th of May, 1835, an act was passed by the legislature, authorizing a tax of $500 upon the town of Canton, for a classical school, upon condition that an equal sum should be raised by subscription, which tax when collected should be paid over to the trustees of the gospel and school lot, to be safely invested, and the income to be paid annually for the support of the academy. A competent school must be maintained at least eight months in the year, to entitle it to the avails of this fund. The requisite sum was accordingly raised, and invested on bond and mortgage. On the 9th of April, 1837, another act was passed, authorizing a tax upon the town, of $500 annually, for three years, on similar conditions as the previous tax, and the requisite additional sum was subscribed.

An act of incorporation was passed, April 24, 1837, appointing Silas Wright, Jun., Minet Jenison, Thomas N. Conkey, Chauncey Foote, Thomas D. Olin, Richard N. Harrison, Daniel Mack, Joseph Ames 2d, Simeon D. Moody, Darius Clark, Henry Barber, and Amos G. Smith, trustees with the usual powers. Although a charter was not obtained until 1837, a good classical school had been sustained since 1831, under the charge of Messrs. Lockwood, Seymour and Barrett, successively, the latter having charge at the date of incorporation.

In 1839, the trustees purchased a lot of Mr. Judson, adjoining the one already in their possession, and erected a building upon it, to be occupied, a part of it by the female department of the academy, and a part, as a boarding house. After its completion, it was so occupied, until it was burned in Nov. 1844. During the summer of 1845, the building first erected was thoroughly repaired, and an addition made to it, for the accommodation of the female department, which is found to be a much more convenient arrangement than the previous one. This the trustees were enabled to do without incurring any liabilities, and they feel a satisfaction in still being able to say, that the academy is entirely free from debt. The cost of the buildings in their present condition is not far from $3,000. The presidents of the board of trustees, have been Silas Wright, Minet Jenison, and Thomas H. Conkey. The principals employed since the incorporation of the academy, have been George H.

Wood 1838 41; David Black, 1841-2; Sanford Halbert, 1842-3; Charles Williams, 1843-4; Franklin Wood, 1844-8; Edward W. Johnson, 1848-9; Abel Wood, 1849-50; Franklin Wood, from 1850 till the present time.

Ogdensburgh Academy.—An act of April 6, 1833, directed that the money then in the hands of the supervisor and poor masters of the town of Oswegatchie, should be delivered up to D. C. Judson, S. Gilbert, G. N. Seymour, M. S. Daniel and H. Thomas, who were appointed commissioners to receive these moneys, and enough more raised by tax upon the town, to make $2000, (on condition that a like sum were first subscribed in the village), and to purchase therewith a lot and buildings, for an academy, one room in the building being reserved for a town hall. The inhabitants of each school district in town, not in the village, were entitled to credit on the tuition of any scholar from their district, to the amount of the interest on the tax of the district. The supervisor and town clerk, and the president and clerk of the village, were made ex-officio trustees of the Academy, who were to audit the accounts of the commissioners and to fill vacancies. On the 24th of April 1834, the trustees were empowered to grant licenses for a ferry across the St. Lawrence, at the village, the rates and rules of which were to be established by the county court of Common Pleas. The income was to be paid over to the above commissioners, and when their term of office should expire, on the fulfilment of the duties for which they were appointed, to be paid to the treasurer of the academy. The rights thus granted were to continue ten years. On the 20th of April, 1835, the academy was incorporated with the following trustees.

"George Parish, John Fine, David Ford, David C. Judson, Henry Van Rensselaer, Royal Vilas, Bishop Perkins, Geo. N. Seymour, Baron S. Doty, Elijah B. Allen, William Bacon, Smith Stilwell, Sylvester Gillet, Amos Bacon, Thomas J. Davies, Joseph W. Smith, Ransom H. Gilbert, James Averill, 3d., Duncan Turner, George Ranney, Joseph Rosseel, Rodolphus D. Searle, Edmund A. Graham, James G. Hopkins, Silas Wright, Jr., William Hogan, Gouverneur Ogden, George Redington, and Augustus Chapman, together with the supervisor and town clerk, of the town of Oswegatchie, and the president and clerk of the trustees of the village of Ogdensburgh, for the time being. They were clothed with the usual powers of such officers. Those who held by virtue of town or village office, were to have the care of the town hall. Previous to the passage of these acts, an academic school had been established. On the 22d of May, 1834, the trustees at a meeting held at Canton, fixed the rent of the ferry at $300 per annum, for three years, commencing with the first of June. This rate has since been repeatedly changed, and at present amounts to $250 per annum.

On the 8th of October, 1834, Tayor Lewis, of Waterford, subsequently a professor of languages in New York University, and at present a professor of Greek and Latin in Union College, was appointed the first principal, with a salary of $600. On the following May, the trustees resolved to have four departments in their schools—two male and two female. This arrangement was never fully carried out. The first president of the board of trustees, was David C. Judson. He was succeeded by John Fine. In the fall of 1837, Mr. Lewis was succeeded by James H. Coffin, at present vice president and professor in Lafayette College, at Easton, Pa. In February 1838, Mr. Coffin was engaged for one year at $800, and on the 1st of April 1839, a new agreement was made by which he was to receive whatever income might be derived from tuition, ferry, and literature fund, reserving a sufficient sum for repairs. In the spring of 1840, the Rev. J. A. Brayton, was engaged, who continued in charge of the school until September 1843, when he resigned, and Mr. John Bradshaw was employed in November, of the same year. He continued the principal of the institution until the summer of 1841, when Messrs. Hart F. Lawrence, and Roswell G. Pettibone, entered jointly into an agreement with the trustees, in which they assumed the care and government of the institution, receiving whatever might accrue from tuition, literature fund and the ferry, excepting only sufficient to pay insurance and repairs. Under the direction of these gentlemen, the academy still remains, enjoying every facility which the ability and talents, of competent teachers can impart. Students from abroad are received as boarders at the academy, and are at all times under the care and government of the principal. This academy is free from debt. The Hon. John Fine president of the board of trustees, has filled this office for many years.

The Academic building, was erected by a company for a hotel in 1819, and opened in January 1820, as the Saint Lawrence House. Upon the organization of the academy it was purchased by the commissioners; the village of Ogdensburgh contributing $1000 to its purchase, with the privilege of the chapel for the use of elections and town meetings. This is the town hall of Oswegatchie. The academy is pleasantly located on the corner of State and Knox streets, directly opposite the old court house, and commands a beautiful prospect of the rivers and surrounding country. It embraces apartments for a family chapel, study and recitation rooms, a well selected library, and philosophical apparatus and every facility needed to impart a good thorough and practical education. The only assistance which this Academy has received from the regents for the purchase of apparatus, was $250, on the 28th of February, 1845. In the summer of 1851, a teachers' department was organized by the regents of the university.

Franklin Academy.—A building was erected for academic purposes in 1806, and at a special town meeting in 1810, the clerk was directed to solicit from Richard Harrison, a deed of the lot on which it stood, to be conveyed to the county judges until trustees were elected. A deed of four acres, exclusive of highways, was executed Oct. 12, 1810. A high school was maintained by private enterprise many years, under the name of the Harrison Academy. In May 1823, an unsuccessful subscription was attempted, and in September 1827, renewed and prosecuted until an incorporation was obtained from the regents April, 28, 1831. The first charter limited its duration to 20 years, and named Benj. Clark, Asa Hascall, Jacob Wead, Hiram Horton, Horatio Powell, John Stearns, Richard G. Foote, Samuel Peck, Samuel Hyde, Samuel Green, Oliver Westcott, Martin L. Parlin and Francis Burnap, of Malone, James Duane, of Duane, Joseph Plumb, of Bangor, first trustees. On the 25th of February 1833, an act was passed, granting $2000 from the state treasury for rebuilding the academy, which was to be charged as a debt against the town of Malone, and to be considered a part of the common school fund. To repay this, with 6 per cent interest, the supervisors were to levy a tax in 1837-8-9. The trustees had during the year 1835, erected the present stone edifice, which is three stories high, and 36 by 64 feet. It was finished in the following year. On the 15th of Dec. 1835, the old building had been injured by a fire.

The principals employed have been Simeon Bicknell, Nathan S. Boynton, Lorenzo Coburn, Worden Reynolds, Elos L. Winslow, George

Franklin Academy, Malone, Franklin Co., N. Y.

H. Wood, Daniel B. Gorham. The first charter having expired by limitation, application was made April 27, 1851, for its renewal, which was granted, on the condition that its endowment should never be diminished below $2500, that it should never be used for other than academical purposes, and that before the 27th of April, 1854 it should be reported free from debt. The first trustees under the new charter were Asa Hascall, Hiram Horton, R. G. Foote, M. L. Parlin, Wm. King, Wm. Plumb, Samuel Fisk, Samuel Field, Thomas R. Powell, S. C. Wead, and S. S. Clark. In 1851, $200 being the balance of the proceeds of the sale of a certain piece of land, formerly given by Cone Andrus for the use of the town of Malone, but recently sold by the commissary general, under the act of 1850, directing the sale of Arsenal lots was given, and in 1852, the premises were graded, and when enclosed and planted with trees will be highly ornamental.

Fort Covington Academy was incorporated April 21, 1831. William Hogan, John A. Savage, Samuel Hoard, and their associates, were to constitute a body politic for the promotion of literature, science, and the arts, and for improvement in education. Capital limited to $2,000, in shares of $25 each. The corporation was to be managed by nineteen trustees, and William Hogan, John A. Savage, Samuel Hoard, Hiram Safford, Jonathan Wallace, Allen Lincoln, George A. Cheeney, Roswell Bates, Jabez Parkhurst, George B. R. Gove, Luther Danforth, David L. Seymour, Aretus M. Hitchcock, Benjamin Raymond, James P. Wills, Ora F. Paddock, Daniel Noble, Daniel Phelps, and John More, were named the first. It was made subject to the visitation of the regents, and entitled to a share of the literature fund. The trustees met and organized in May, and to raise the required capital, proposed to take notes of those who wished to hold stock, leaving the principal in the hands of those who give them, and receiving the interest only. In default of payment the whole became due. By this means $2,965 was raised by 45 notes, and by a resolution of Sept. 2d of that year, the upper room in the town house was fitted up for academic purposes. In October, the Rev. John A. Savage was appointed principal. His successors have been Alex. W. Buel, Daniel Branch, Milton Bradley, H. Dodge, E. H. Squier, —— Miller, John Bradshaw, James C. Spencer, C. S. Sanford, Luther Humphrey, and Geo. A. Attwood. In 1831, a quantity of apparatus was purchased by the academy and village lyceum for their common use, and in the summer of 1832, the present stone edifice was built by permission granted by the legislature (April 13, 1832), on a public lot between the two rivers in the village. It is of stone, 33 by 44, two stories high, and if the common in front of the premises were enclosed and adorned with shade trees, would be an ornament to the place. This school has not been sustained in a liberal manner, and does not flourish.

Full returns are required to be made by the several academies to the regents, which are published annually, and show in a very satisfactory manner the comparative condition of the various institutions from year to year. From this source the following tables are derived, only a small portion of the returns being embraced.

STATISTICS OF THE SEVERAL ACADEMIES, FROM THEIR OFFICIAL REPORTS TO THE REGENTS OF THE UNIVERSITY.

Column No. 1 denotes the year; 2 the number of students; 3 the amount received from literature fund; 4 debts; 5 tuition; 6 total income.

ST. LAWRENCE.

1	2	3	4	5	6
1817	42	......	....	331	....
1818	....	90 80	....	....	....
1819	35	......	....	250	....
1820	114	......	....	416	....
1821	97	......	....	357	....
1822	89	......	....	....	....
1823	173	....	....	600	720 00
1824	172	170 37	210	500	661 00
1825	139	171 00		600	760 00
1826	227	255 32	....	800	1245 32
1827	89*	314 51	1006	763	1300 00
1828	110*	349 03	1275	900	1424 03
1829	117*	359 21	1100	1207	1715 65
1830	125*	336 53	1413	1735	2231 55
1831	110*	434 09	1400	1532	2126 49
1832	95*	231 45	1800	1476	1842 79
1833	90*	286 50	229	1302	1783 51
1834	98*	291 05	2248	1044	1452 05
1835	140*	433 07	1563	1279	1810 07
1836	82*	374 29	1490	1776	2294 29
1837	93*	347 75	3850	1747	2232 75
1838	144*	652 67	4300	1209	1685 00
1839	156*	815 50	4696	2120	2964 00
1840	150*	011 00	4547	2227	2975 00
1841	115*	433 93	4670	1461	2304 80
1842	115*	506 17	3564	1452	1956 00
1843	163*	410 31	4506	1733	2424 00
1844	282	464 32	4732	1944	2567 00
1845	255	422 98	5141	1795	2463 00
1846	228	431 49	5125	1647	2246 00
1847	190	369 13	4453	1305	1920 00
1848	193	284 52	3840	1250	1725 00
1849	175	290 66	2107	1183	1564 00
1850	220	279 14	1967	1455	1822 00
1851	237	253 68	1549	1513	1884 00
1852	258	......	670	1552	2150 00

GOUVERNEUR.

1	2	3	4	5	6
1830	39*	......	89	....	400 00
1831	35*	......	105	....	375 00
1832	37*	350 00	89	350	336 63
1833	66*	500 00	35	500	450 00
1834	57*	500 00	206	500	651 00
1835	46*	500 00	148	500	548 00
1836	30*	335 00	39	335	314 50
1837	115*	29 21	1495	576	....
1838	67*	194 73	2540	1536	1665 00
1839	91*	188 71	4801	889	1863 00
1840	77*	281 21	3350	1400	1736 00
1841	91*	294 68	2781	1714	2139 00
1842	65*	269 30	2497	1615	1666 00
1843	120*	448 41	3492	1500	1874 00
1844	209	322 66	3702	969	1488 00
1845	191	310 51	3961	1021	1379 00
1846	185	331 47	4238	930	1254 00
1847	185	371 33	4535	1249	1601 00
1848	285	364 29	4758	1486	1858 00
1849	299	452 95	5091	1666	2030 00
1850	277	276 98	6000	1487	1940 00
1851	226	180 03	5000	1211	1488 00
1852	217	......	500	1145	1332 10

OGDENSBURGH.

1	2	3	4	5	6
1839	34*	100 58	599	751	1202 00
1840	92*	114 57	511	669	1119 00
1841	83*	220 21	547	1451	2023 00
1842	54*	171 97	376	1008	1739 00
1843	115*	123 09	20	1050	1508 00
1844	....	236 10	84	1300	1848 00
1845	263	220 05	....	1300	2049 00
1846	234	251 46	....	1312	2095 00
1847	187	327 19	50	1200	1889 00
1848	149	268 56	...	800	1540 00
1849	173	109 00	....	937	1618 00
1850	211	243 42	....	1200	1559 00
1851	235	270 05	....	1504	1997 00

CANTON.

1	2	3	4	5	6		1	2	3	4	5	6
1839	99°	92 20	1038	753	921 00		1846	182	185 74	375	825	1091 00
1840	94*	142 35	1254	1006	1301 00		1847	164	226 51	328	725	1089 00
1841	59*	142 49	1354	820	1193 00		1848	116	135 61	....	617	1021 00
1842	51*	90 85	1091	758	1103 00		1849	109	133 23	....	358	899 00
1843	36*	108 44	864	610	915 00		1850	135	156 32	....	690	1001 00
1844	98	110 18	866	791	1124 00		1851	123	124 80	....	590	924 00
1845	126	88 02	600	625	913 00							

FRANKLIN.

1	2	3	4	5	6		1	2	3	4	5	6
1832	80*	109 65	249	818	......		1843	75*	187 57	1118	650	1148 00
1833	82*	145 16	260	840	......		1844	175	254 46	1078	837	1401 00
1834	45*	147 77	126	739	......		1845	235	383 86	1146	1070	1641 00
1835	58*	160 48	259	497	1097 48		1846	220	362 91	1276	933	1612 00
1836	37*	81 00	900	400	767 00		1847	160	327 19	847	768	1405 00
1837	45*	124 79	310	571	971 79		1848	153	239 31	1120	655	1242 00
1838	58*	241 75	874	647	1028 00		1849	169	297 93	908	732	1349 00
1839	37*	184 40	780	677	1169 00		1850	155	272 44	704	805	1414 00
1840	40*	145 82	816	762	1722 00		1851	221	192 30	765	1004	1265 00
1841	50*	113 35	931	680	833 00		1852	209	......	910	1078	2368 00
1842	81*	162 24	981	813	1245 00							

FORT COVINGTON.

1	2	3	4	5	6		1	2	3	4	5	6
1836	40*	69 83	50	....	......		1843	45*	102 58	225	800	1000 00
1837	50*	31 86	130	450	570 86		1844	243	398 74	....	....	.... ..
1838	25*	116 04	90	340	476 04		1846	60*	71 45	57	611	674 00
1839	68*	100 58	75	353	591 00		1847	102	47 54	100	241	375 00
1840	25*	45 33	150	500	720 00		1849	113	48 45	58	364	430 00
1841	73*	51 82	700	400	569 00		1850	104	35 73	25	289	388 00
1842	75*	100 58	607	800	956 00							

* Number at the date of the report. When this asterisk is omitted, it denotes the number during the year.

The comparative condition of the several Academies, as shown by late reports, is as follows.

	St. L. 1852	Gouv. 1852	Can. 1852	Og. 1852	Fr. 1852	F. C. 1851
Number of departments........	4	2	2	3	2	2
" teachers...........	5	5	2	3	2	1
" academic terms	2	3	3	3	3	3
" week's vacation.....	8	8	5	8	10	7
Value of lot and buildings......	$8,700	$6,600	$3,150	$8,000	$6000	$2,700
" library...........	530	400	260	393	241	200
" apparatus............	631	350	300	392	203	160
Other academic property.......	950	420	2,550	......	1,906	800
Total value of property........	10,801	7,770	6,260	8,785	8,350	3,860
Interest on academic property...	92	......	178	250	120	56
Total revenue................	1,884	1,488	924	1,997	1,265	388
Salaries for year previous......	1,603	1,193	500	1,668	896	307

CHAPTER VII.

INTERNAL IMPROVEMENTS, STATISTICS, &c.

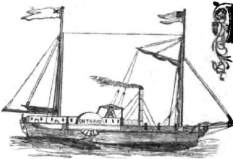

First steam boat on the great lakes, 1816.

ROM an early period attempts were made to improve the navigation of the St. Lawrence, and in an act of April 1, 1808, J. Wadington, D. A. and T. L. Ogden, were authorized to build a canal and locks at Hamilton, and to collect toll at the rate of 25 cents per ton, on all boats passing. Locks to be 50 feet long, 10 feet wide, and deep enough to receive boats having two feet draught. On page 343, is related what was done under this act. The north shore has always been chosen by *voyageurs*, and the difficulty of crossing over to these locks would have rendered their use limited. On the 5th of April, 1809, means were provided for carrying into effect a concurrent resolution of March 27th, directing the surveyor general to authorize some competent person to survey the St. Lawrence, and report. By an act of April 9, 1811, Russell Attwater and Roswell Hopkins, were appointed to expend $600, on the American shore from St. Regis to the Indian village in Lisbon. It is believed that a towing path was made along the shore in places, at an early day, and probably with this appropriation. In 1833, the subject of cutting a canal from the head of Long Saut to Grass river, was pressed upon the legislature, and a subscription raised to procure a survey. Grass river was considered navigable to within three miles of Massena village, and there intervened a ravine and low land, which it was found required a canal of six miles, one of which was through gravel and clay a depth of thirty-five feet. The fall from the head of the saut to Lake St. Francis, was found to be fifty feet. Estimated cost, $200,000. It was stated that in 1833, $48,000 was paid for cartage and towage past the Long saut, and the cost for towing one boat amounted to $500 per annum. This subject was also urged upon congress by a convention at Canton, Dec. 18, 1833. and D. C. Judson, Wm. Ogden, N. F. Hyer, H. Allen, and M. Whitcomb, were appointed to circulate petitions. Nothing was effected or afterwards attempted, as the Canadian government soon after undertook this labor.

The Oswegatchie Navigation Company, was incorporated April 28. 1831, for the purpose of improving, by means of locks, canals and dams, its navigation to Black lake, and to the town of Gouverneur; and from the Oswegatchie river, along the natural canal to Grass river, and up to Canton village. Capital to be $5,000, and Silvester Gilbert, Jacob A. Vanden Heuvel, Smith Stillwell, and Louis Hasbrouck, were appointed a board of commissioners to receive subscriptions. A certain portion of the work was to be accomplished within five years, and the duration of the corporation was limited to thirty years.

The previous act was renewed April 25, 1836, and continued in force thirty years. Baron S. Doty, Silvester Gilbert, Jacob A. Van Heuvel, Smith Stillwell, Henry Van Rensselaer, and E. N. Fairchild, were named commissioners to receive stock. Unless they met within three months, the act was to be void. In 1835, the capital stock was increased to $100,000. R. Harrison, D. C. Judson, S. Gilbert, H. Van Rensselaer, E. Dodge, A. Sprague, and S. D. Moody, were named commissioners to receive subscriptions. No actual improvements were ever undertaken under these acts. In the petition which procured the passage of the above act, it was stated, that at Heuvel locks had been commenced, and might be completed at small expense, that the expense of dams and locks to improve the natural channel of the Oswegatchie would not cost to exceed $12,000, and that a steam boat might be built for $5,000, sufficient to meet the business of the proposed company. The fall at Canton falls, is stated to be nine feet, and at Cooper's fall in De Kalb, as eight feet, which being overcome by locks would render the river navigable as far as the Ox Bow, in Jefferson county. A dam across Grass river, and a short canal near the eastern end of the natural canal, would bring Canton in navigable communication with the St. Lawrence at Ogdensburgh.

The plan of extending the Black river canal to Ogdensburgh, was brought forward in 1839, and a survey executed by Edward H. Brodhead, which is published in the legislative documents of 1840, embraced the several improvements above proposed.

Several acts have been passed for preventing the obstruction of the channels of our rivers by declaring them *public highways*. Raquette river from its mouth to Norfolk, and St. Regis from the province line to the east line of Stockholm, were so declared April 15, 1810. April 16, 1816, the Oswegatchie was made a highway to Streeter's Mills, in Rossie, and its obstruction forbidden under a penalty of $100. By a recent act this limit has been extened to Cranberry lake.

An act of 1849, for improving the sources of the Hudson for lumbering purposes, led in 1850, to petitions for grants to be expended on Raquette and Moose rivers. These were referred to a select committee, who through their chairman, Mr. Henry J. Raymond, made a very elaborate report, setting forth the advantages of the improvements, and describing the wonderful natural water communication of the primitive wilderness of Northern New York. This elevated plateau, averaging 1,500 to 1,870 feet above tide, gives origin to rivers, flowing in different directions. The Raquette, after a crooked and sluggish course through several large ponds, and receiving tributaries navigable for logs from many lakes in the interior, on arriving within 50 miles of the St. Lawrence, becomes rapid, and descends to near the level of that river before reaching Massena. In a multitude of places it affords fine cascades for hydraulic purposes, especially in the villages of Colton, East Pierrepont, Potsdam, Raquetteville, Norfolk and Raymondville, with many intervening places.

There is a peculiarity of this river that deserves special notice, which is its little liability to be affected by drouth and flood, in consequence of its being fed from lakes. The highest water commonly occurs several days later in this than the neighboring rivers, and a prudent policy should lead to the erection of sluices and flood gates at the outlet of the lakes to retain the excess of the spring flood against any want that might occur in the drouth of summer. Such a want has not hitherto been felt, but might if the interior country were cleared and cultivated. An act was passed April 10, 1850, declaring the Raquette a highway from its mouth to the foot of Racket lake, in Hamilton county, and on the 9th of April, an appropriation of $10,000 was made, to be expended by H. Hewitt, A. T. Hopkins and C. Russell, in removing obstructions, and improving the channel. These consisted in shutting up lost channels and straits around islands, in the erection of piers, dams, booms, &c.

The accession of capital and employment of labor from this improvement is remarkable. But one gang mill existed on the river at the time of the passage of the law, while at present there are either in operation or in course of erection, *eight*, and still more that are contemplated. The logs sawed at these are brought from the country adjoining Tupper's lake, Long lake in Hamilton county, many of the lakes and streams of Franklin county, and from the western borders of Essex county.

Much credit is due to Dr. H. Hewitt, of Potsdam, for exertions in procuring this improvement, and to Messrs. Wm. A. Dart, of the senate, and Noble S. Elderkin, of the assembly, for the zeal and ability with which they sustained the measure.

The first attempt to open a cheap and direct communication between the navigable waters of the St. Lawrence and the sea board, began in 1823, and arose from the wants which had been so severely felt during the war. A year or two after the peace, plans for uniting lake Champlain with the Connecticut, were discussed and attempted. Judge Raymond and Benjamin Wright, while surveying the country before its settlement, had formed projects for improving the natural channels of the rivers, and to them belongs the merit of the idea. The former was afterwards the ardent advocate of a canal. A meeting of the citizens of Clinton, Franklin and St. Lawrence counties, convened at Ogdensburgh, August 28, 1823, to concert measures for a canal, who appointed B. Raymond, of Norfolk, S. Partridge, of Potsdam, J. A. Vanden Heuvel, of Ogdensburgh, Wm. Hogan, of Fort Covington, Thomas Smith, of Chateaugay and Asa Hascall, of Malone, who prepared and published a lengthy report for distribution in the sections most to be benefited by the work. It was accompanied by a report from Judge Raymond, who had been employed to make a preliminary survey. This improvement proposed to use the Oswegatchie, Natural canal and Grass river, to Canton. The petitions and the friendly influences towards these works, led to an act for a survey under the direction of the canal commissioners, and Holmes Hutchinson, of Utica, was employed. The expense was limited to $1,500. The summit was found to be 811 feet above the St. Lawrence, at Ogdensburgh, and 966 above the lake. This work was commended to the legislature by Dewitt Clinton, in his annual message of 1825, but the work was found impracticable, and the idea abandoned.

A *Rail Road* began to be discussed in 1829, and a full meeting was held February 17, 1830, at Montpelier, for promoting a rail road from Ogdensburgh, and by way of lake Champlain and the valleys of Onion and Connecticut rivers, and through Concord and Lowell to Boston. A committee previously appointed, reported favorably on the plan and its advantages, and estimated that passengers and heavy freight could be taken over the whole route in 35 hours. They further predicted that 15 miles an hour would hereafter be performed by locomotives. On the 17th of March, 1830, a similar meeting was held at Ogdensburgh, and a committee of 12 appointed to collect information and report to a future meeting. Application was also made to congress for aid in constructing the work, but this failing, petitions were next forwarded to the state legislature, and a convention met at Malone, December 17, 1831, to promote this object. This failed, but was prosecuted until May 21, 1836. The lake Champlain and Ogdensburgh rail road was incorporated with a capital of $800,000. S, Gilbert and S. Stilwell, of St. Lawrence; B. Clark and J. Stearns, of Franklin, with two from each of the counties of Clinton and Essex, and James H. Titus, of New York, were empowered to open books for receiving stock. Some declining to act, a law of May 16, 1837, appointed Wm. H. Harrison, of New York, Wm. F. Haile, of Clinton, D. L. Seymour, of Franklin, and J. L. Russell, of St. Lawrence, in their place. About this time the plan of a rail road from Ogdensburgh directly through to Albany, was discussed. A convention met February 27, 1837, at Matildaville, for this object. The moneys subscribed for the road to lake Champlain, were first reloaned and afterwards refunded to subscribers. This company failing to organize, a convention met at Malone, August 8, 1838, and persons appointed to collect statistics. These show that there then existed in St. Lawrence county 8 iron furnaces, yielding 3,790 tons; 7 founderies, yielding 785 tons of castings; 8 trip hammers; 63 asheries, yielding 1,815 tons of pot and pearl ashes; 6 merchant mills; 42 grist mills; 3 lead mines, yielding 1,673 tons; 1 lead pipe factory; 1 copperas and alum works; 2 plaster mills and quarries, (the latter proving to be nothing but steatite, or soap stone); 4 marble mills; 137 saw mills, 11 of which make 717,700 pieces of lumber annually; 2 distilleries; 1 brewery and 2 sattinet and woolen mills. 571 tons of butter and cheese were made annually. and the whole amount of freight from the county was estimated at $117,294. In Franklin county were 6 iron works; 1 cotton factory; 17 grist mills; 49 saw mills; 2 woolen mills; 18 asheries; 12 tanneries; 3 trip hammers; 2 distilleries, and other works, yielding $23,181 worth of freight. These measures led to an act of April 18, 1838, authorizing a survey, which was executed by Edward F. Johnson, and the expense was limited to $4000. On the 14th of May, 1840, commissioners were appointed to survey and estimate the cost of a rail road by the several routes, and the public documents of 1841 contain the results. Both of the lines surveyed passed south east through the county and penetrated the wilderness. The *Port Kent route* passed up the valley of the Ausable, and down the St. Regis, and thence by way of Parishville and Potsdam, to Ogdensburgh. Length, 131 miles; summit, 1,733 feet above tide; cost, 2,714,003·89; maximum grade, 95 feet going east, and 90 feet going west; least radius of curve, 800 feet. The Plattsburgh route led to Malone and Moira, whence a route by Norfolk and Columbia, and one by Potsdam, was surveyed. Summit, 1,089 feet; distance by Norfolk, 120 and by Potsdam, 122 miles; cost of the Norfolk line, $1,778,459·24; of the Potsdam route, $1,923,-108·09; of both maximum grade, 40 feet; least radius, 1,300 feet. In connection with this report was given the probable cost of improving the rivers and Natural canal, the aggregate of which was $305,982. A convention met at Malone, December 22, 1840, who, through a committee, memorialized the legislature, and procured the opinions of several military men on the importance of the route as of national use in case of war.

This measure failed to become a law. Nothing discouraged, the friends of this improvement continued active, and finding it impossible to obtain assistance from the state began to importune for the privilege of helping *themselves;* and here they were met by the powerful opposition of the friends of the central routes, which was conciliated by their being themselves brought to the necessity of feeling the want of *votes* to carry one of their measures. In the session of 1845, Messrs. Hiram Horton, John L. Russell and Asa L. Hazelton, representing these two counties, a bill was introduced and early passed the assembly, but was delayed in the senate till near the close of the session. At this time not less than fourteen rail road bills were before the legislature, among which was one for increasing the capital of the Syracuse and Utica road. It was partly through the influence of the friends of this road who found themselves forced to *help* in order to *be helped*, that the bill finally passed, receiving the governor's signature but twenty minutes before adjournment. This act passed May 14, 1845, incorporating the NORTHERN RAIL ROAD, for fifty years, with a capital of $2,000,000, in shares of $50, and naming David C. Judson and Joseph Barnes, of St. Lawrence; S. C. Wead, of Franklin, and others from Clinton and Essex counties, and New York, commissioners to receive and distribute stock.

Measures were taken to raise the means for a survey, and in the fall of 1845, a delegation visited Boston, to induce capitalists to undertake the work. They were advised to return and raise along the road as much as possible first, which was done; but in their absence about $10,-000,000 of rail road stock had been taken, and their chances for success were much lessened. To set forth the advantages of the route, Mr. James G. Hopkins, of Ogdensburgh, in 1845, published a pamphlet, containing many documents and statistics relating to the matter. It is but justice to state that not only these estimates but those that preceded them, were so far as relates to the resources of the country, far below what time has developed. The Burlington people and those interested in the lines of New England roads connecting with Lake Champlain, early perceived the advantages that would ensue from a line which would turn a portion of the resources of the great west through their channels. In July, 1846, Mr. James Hayward, an experienced engineer, who, since 1828, had had his attention directed to this route, was employed to survey the route, who did so and reported.

In June, 1846, a company was organized at Ogdensburgh, having George Parish, president; J. Leslie Russell, of Canton, Hiram Horton, of Malone, Anthony C. Brown, of Ogdensburgh, Lawrence Myers, of Plattsburgh, Charles Paine, of Northfield, Vt., S. F. Belknap, of Windsor, Vt., Isaac Spalding, of Nashua, N. H., and Abbot Lawrence, J. Wiley Edmonds, Benjamin Reed, T. P. Chandler, and S. S. Lewis, of Boston, directors; S. S. Walley, treasurer; and James G. Hopkins, secretary. In the fall of 1847, a contract was taken by Sewall F. Belknap for the portion east of Malone, and by Chamberlain, Worral & Co., to be completed within two years. Work was begun in March, 1848, at the deep cutting in Ogdensburgh, and in the fall of that year was opened to Centreville from Champlain river. Late in 1849, it had reached Ellenburgh; in June, 1850, Chateaugay; October 1st, Malone; and in the same month through; the last work being done near Deer river bridge, in Lawrence.

The following are the *distances between intermediate stations*, in miles and hundredths: Ogdensburgh, 8·62 to Lisbon; 8·52 to Madrid; 7·48 to Potsdam; 3·00 to Knapp's Station; 7·60 to Brasher Falls and Stock-

Grain Elevator, Ogdensburgh R. R.

nolm; 5·74 to Lawrence; 5·79 to Moira; 2·35 to Brush's Mills; 5·70 to Bangor; 6·00 to Malone; 7·37 to Burke; 4·50 to Chateaugay; 7·50 to the Summit; 8·50 to Ellenburgh; 8·00 to Chazy, W. S.; 5·50 to Centreville; 3·31 to Moore's (junction of Montreal and Plattsburgh rail road); 7·29 to Champlain; 4·39 to Rouse's Point. Total 117·16 miles.

Length in the several towns, in miles and hundredths: Oswegatchie, 1·07; Lisbon, 11·61; Madrid, 5·48; Potsdam, 5·98; Norfolk, 0·97; Stockholm, 9·77; Lawrence, 7·70; Moira, 6·64; Bangor, 6·32; Malone, 8.66; Burke, 4·99; Chateaugay, 5·71; Clinton, 9·87; Ellenburgh, 3·92; Chazy, 9·49; Moore's, 9·71; Champlain, 8·23.

Height of stations above tide, in feet : Ogdensburgh, 239; Lisbon, 320; Madrid, 309; Potsdam, 320; Knapp's, 339; Stockholm and B. F., 311; Lawrence, 329; Moira, 363; Brush's Mills, 425; Bangor, 565; Malone, 703; Burke, 862; Chateaugay, 950; Summit, 1,146; Brandy Brook 935; Ellenburgh, 892; Chazy, 573; Centreville, 378; Moore's, 243; Champlain, 130; Rouse's Point, 84. Least radius 3,000 feet, except in the village of Malone, at which all trains stop, where it is 2,000 feet; highest grade per mile going east, 27 feet; going west, 40; west of Summit no grade either way more than 27 feet.

From their report of 1852, it is learned that this road has cost, including fixtures and equipment, $5,022,121·31, and possesses very ample facilities for the transaction of the immense amount of business in the freight department. Amount of land owned in July, 1851, 3077¼ acres, exclusive of road way. Its buildings at that date were as follows; Wharves, docks and piers, at Ogdensburgh 4,534 feet; at Rouse's Point, 165 feet wharf, and a pier of 1,650, which has since become a part of the bridge across Lake Champlain. Freight and passenger station at Ogdensburgh, 305 by 84 feet. One freight house at ditto, 402 by 82 feet; fire proof engine house for six locomotives, and numerous other buildings, the present dimensions and location of which may be seen by referring to the plan of the depot grounds on our map of St. Lawrence county. Among these, the grain warehouse and elevator, shown on the opposite page, deserves notice. It is built on piles in 14 feet water, and contains 42 bins, each 30 feet deep and capable of holding 4,000 bushels each, or 12 tons of wheat. All these delivered their grain on one tract by spouts, and each can load a car with 10 tons in eight or ten minutes, the load being weighed on a platform scale in the track. The elevators are driven by a steam engine of 15 horse power, and raise daily, 16,000 to 18,000 bushels, which is weighed as received in draughts of 30 bushels, and spouted into cars or raised into the bins if stored. The cars are sent in on one track and out on another, being changed by a traverse table. Vessels laden with grain on the upper lakes, are here unloaded with great facility, and the establishment is found to be eminently useful in promoting the business of the road. It was erected by N. Taggert, after plans by F. Pelletier the draftsman of the company, who has kindly furnished the above data. At Lisbon, Madrid, Potsdam, Stockholm, Lawrence, Moira, Bangor, Champlain and Hoyle's Landing, are depots, 50 by 100 feet: at Brush's Mills, 80 by 35 feet; at Chateaugay, 200 by 55, a passenger station 37 by 26, and a wood and water station, 330 by 35 feet; at Rouses Point a passenger and freight house, 500 by 104 feet, a station house and hotel, 78 by 50, repair shop, 175 by 80 feet; and numerous other buildings. Since the date of the last report before us, depots have been built at Knapp's, Burke, Malone, and other places.

Much opposition was met from the efforts made by the company to procure the right of bridging Lake Champalain, to enable it to connect with the eastern roads, and in the sessions of 1850, a special committee consisting of Wm. A. Dart, George Geddes and Robert Owens, Jun., was appointed, who in the recess of the legislature visited the locality and reported. An attempt was made to excite the jealousies of New York, against Boston, but an expression was obtained from the leading interests of that city disclaiming this, and concurring in the proposed improvement, and among the objections urged, were the obstruction to navigation, the division from the trade of the canals, and consequent loss of revenue to the state, and the obstruction it would be to the fortress of the United States government, north of the road and near the boundary. This matter has been since decided, and a floating draw bridge constructed so that trains pass freely over without hinderance.

It is less the amount of travel over this road than that of freight, that gives it importance. Being remote from the great lines of travel, it as yet, has not generally attracted that notice which it deserves, but when its advantages come to be known and appreciated, it can not fail of drawing a considerable amount of New England travel going westward. The officers of the Northern Rail road, can boast of one fact which few other roads would be able to do, viz: *that they have never caused the death or injury of a passenger who has entrusted himself to their charge.* This exemption from accident is not due to chance, but mainly to the admirable precision with which the trains are run, and it is doing injustice to no one to assert, that this is principally due to the talents and ability of the chief engineer Col. CHARLES L. SCHLATTER, who has from the beginning had the management of the road. Every employee is instructed in his duties, *and no excuses are received* for any violation or neglect of them. This inexorable rule has its advantages, which are felt and approved by all concerned, and it is said that men can be employed in running trains at less wages on this than on many other roads, from the feeling of security, resulting from these arrangements.

The officers of the company as given by the last, are T. P. Chandler, R. G. Shaw, Benj. Seaver, H. M. Holbrook, H. G. Kuhn, of Boston; Isaac Spaulding, of Nashua, N. H.; G. V. Hogle, of Champlain; Hiram Horton, of Malone; John Leslie Russell, of Canton; Geo. N. Seymour, and H. Van Rensselaer, of Ogdensburgh, James H. Titus, and Samuel J. Beals, of New York, *directors.* T. P. Chandler, *president.* James G. Hopkins, of Ogdensburgh, *secretary.* Wm. T. Eustis (office No. 14 Merchant's Exchange, Boston), *treasurer.* Chas. L. Schlatter, of Malone, *superintendent.*

The *Potsdam and Watertown Rail Road* originated from the dissatisfaction felt by Potsdam and Canton, in not having the Northern R. R. pass through their villages. Soon after the Rome and Cape Vincent rail road was opened, the want of a connecting link with the Northern road began to be felt, and it became an object of importance to decide whether this should connect at Ogdensburgh and run along the St. Lawrence or at a point east of this and through the interior of the county. In July 1851, a convention met at Watertown, and persons appointed to collect the means for a survey; Mr. E. H. Brodhead employed, and at a meeting held at Gouverneur, on the 8th of Jan. 1852, this report and survey were rendered, and a company formed the next day, under the general law of the state. In no place will the route vary three miles from a direct line; the grades will not exceed 36.96 feet to the mile, and with one exception, the shortest radius of curve does not

AND FRANKLIN COUNTIES.

exceed 2000 feet. Length 69 miles, estimated cost $293,721·50, for grading, bridging, and besides $6000 per mile for superstructure. A route was surveyed to Sackett's Harbor in connection with this.

From this time vigorous efforts were made to secure a sufficient amount of stock to commence the construction of the road, and by an act passed April 7, 1852, the company was authorized, whenever the subscription to the capital stock should amount to $5000 per mile, to exercise the powers, rights and privileges usually possessed by a company incorporated under the general act. This act was considered necessary in this case, in order to secure the rights of way, and made contracts for the same. In October 1852, the sum of $750,000 having been subscribed, the directors felt themselves warranted in entering into a contract for the making of the road, and accordingly contracted with Phelps, Matoon, and Barnes, of Springfield, Mass., by which the road was to be completed July 1, 1854. It will be one of the cheapest roads in the state, and must add immensely to the prosperity of the already rich and populous country through which it passes. Its present officers are O. V Brainard, Eli Farwell, Hiram Holcomb, Wm. McAllaster, Wm. E. Sterling, Edwin Dodge, Barzillai Hodskin, Orville Page, Zenas Clark, Samuel Partridge, Joseph H. Sandford, Wm. W. Goulding, A. M. Adsit, *directors*. Edwin Dodge, *president*. Zenas Clark, *vice president*. Daniel Lee, *treasurer*. H. L. Knowles, *secretary*.

Telegraphs.—Northern New York was first brought into direct communication with the great cities in 1849, by means of the Canadian line of telegraphs, operating on the Morse principle. A station was established at Brockville, and another at Prescott. The *New York State Line* extended a branch from Watertown to Ogdensburgh, by way of the Old Military road, in the summer of 1850. The only station in the county is at Ogdensburgh. In the summer of 1851, the *Vermont and Boston Line* originally intended to extend only as far as Burlington, was continued on to Rouse's Point and Ogdensburgh, partly along the line of the rail road, and partly along the highway. It has stations for receiving and transmitting intelligence at Ogdensburgh, Canton, Potsdam, North Potsdam, Malone, and Chateaugay. Both of these lines are operated on the principle of Bain's electro-chemical telegraph, and sufficient stock was taken up along the routes to defray the expense of erection.

Steam boat navigation was first attempted on the great lakes, by the building of the *Ontario*, in 1816, by Charles Smyth, David Boyd, Eri Lusher, Abram Van Santvoord, John I. De Graff, and their associates, who in February 1816, made an unsuccessful attempt to secure an incorporation as the Lake Ontario Steam Boat Company, with a capital of $200,000. In their memorial before us, they state that they had purchased of the heirs of Robert R. Livingston and Robert Fulton, the right to the exclusive navigation of the St. Lawrence. Their steamer, which is shown at the head of this chapter, is engraved from a drawing, by Capt. J. Van Cleve. The boat was 110 feet long, 24 wide, 8 deep, and measured 237 tons. She had one low pressure cross-head engine, of 24 inch cylinder and 4 feet stroke. The latter was made at the Allaire works, New York. She was designed to be after the model of the *Sea Horse*, then running on the Sound near New York, and was built mainly under the direction of Hunter Crane, one of the owners. The first trip was made in 1817, and her arrival was celebrated at all the ports on the lake and river with the most extravagant demonstrations of joy, and hailed as a *new era* to the commerce of our inland seas. In every vil-

34

lage that could muster a cannon, and from every steeple that had a bell, went forth a joyous welcome, and crowds of eager citizens from the adjoining country, thronged the shores to salute its arrival. Bonfires and illuminations, the congratulation of friends and the interchange of hospitalities, signalized the event. The trip from Lewistown to Ogdensburgh required ten days. Fare $16. Deck fare $8. Master, Capt. Mallaby, U. S. N. The Ontario continued till 1832, seldom exceeding five miles an hour, and was finally broken up at Oswego. The *Frontenac*, a British steamer, at Kingston, and the *Walk-in-the-Water*. on Lake Erie, followed soon after.

The *Martha Ogden*, was built at Sackett's Harbor, about 1819, with Albert Crane, managing, owner the first season. She was lost in a gale off Stoney point, and the passengers and crew saved by being landed in a *basket*, drawn back and forth on a rope from the wreck to the shore. No one was lost, and the engine was recovered and placed in the Ontario. The *Sophia*, originally a schooner, was fitted up as a steamer at S. Harbor, at an early day. The *Robins*, was another small schooner built over, but never did much business. The *Black Hawk*, built at French Creek, by G. S. Weeks, and owned by Smith, Merrick & Co., was used several seasons as a packet, and afterwards sold to Canadians, and the name changed to *The Dolphin*. The *Paul Pry* was built at Heuvelton, in 1830. by Paul Boynton, for parties in Ogdensburgh, and run some time on Black lake to Rossie. About 1834, she was passed into the St. Lawrence, at great delay and expense, and used as a ferry until from the affair at the Windmill, in 1838, she became obnoxious to the Canadians, and was run on Black river bay afterwards. The *Rossie*, a small steamer, was built near Pope's mills, about 1837, by White & Hooker, of Morristown, and ran two seasons on Black lake. This was a small affair and proved unprofitable.

An act of January 28, 1831, incorporated the *Lake Ontario Steam Boat Company*; capital, $100,000; duration till May, 1850. The affairs were to be managed by fifteen directors, and the office to be kept at Oswego. This company built the steamer *United States*, which was launched in November, 1831, and came out July 1st, 1832, under the command of Elias Trowbridge. Length, 142 feet; width, 26 feet beam, 55 feet over all; depth, 10 feet; engines, two low pressure ones of 40 inch cylinder and 8 feet stroke. Cost, $56,000. This steamer, so much in advance of anything that had preceded it on the American side, run on the through line till 1838, when, from having become obnoxious to the Canadians on account of the use made of her at the affair of the Windmill, she was run upon the lake only afterwards, and was finally broken up at Oswego, in 1843, and her engines transferred to the *Rochester*. This was the first and only boat owned by this company.

The *Oswego* was built at that place in 1833; of 286 tons; was used for several seasons on the through line, but after running six years, the engines were taken out and placed in the steamer St. Lawrence. She was changed to a sail vessel and lost. The *Brownville* was built on Black river, below the village of that name, in Jefferson county. In going down the St. Lawrence, she took fire and was burned to the water's edge, but was run on an island, and her crew saved. She was afterwards rebuilt, and run awhile with the former name, and subsequently lengthened at Sackett's Harbor, and her name changed to the *William Avery*. The engines, built by Wm. Avery, of Syracuse, which had previously been high pressure, were changed to condensing. With a few minor exceptions, there are at present no high pressure engines employed on the lake or river, except in propellers. In 1834, the Wm. Avery was run between Ogdensburgh and Niagara, with W. W. Sherman as master. She was dismantled in 1835. The *Charles Carroll* was built at S. Harbor, and run from Kingston to Rochester, in 1834. Afterwards she was rebuilt and lengthened at Sackett's Harbor, in the summer of 1834, and her name changed to the *America*. Her engine was high pressure. The America, with D. Howe master, was running from Ogdensburgh to Lewiston late in the season of 1834.

The *Jack Downing* was a very small steamer built by P. Boynton, at Carthage, Jefferson county, in 1834; drawn on wheels to S. Harbor, launched, fitted up, and intended as a ferry at Ogdensburgh; but used for this purpose a short time at Waddington, and afterwards run from Fort Covington to Cornwall. Her engine was in 1837, transferred to the *Henry Burden*, a boat on a novel principle, being supported on two hollow cylindrical floats and the wheel between them. It was afterwards taken by the Rideau canal to Ogdensburgh, and used a short time as a ferry.

The Oneida, of 227 tons, was built at Oswego, in 1836. A. Smith was her first master. Her owners were principally Henry Fitzhugh, of Oswego, E. B. Allen and G. N. Seymour, of Ogdensburgh. In 1838, and during some part of 1840, she was in the employ of government. With these exceptions, this vessel made regular trips from Ogdensburgh to Lewiston, until 1845, when her engine was taken out, and she was fitted up as a sail vessel. The engine of this boat is now in the steamer British Queen, one of the American line of boats from Ogdensburgh to Montreal. Lost as a sail vessel on Lake Erie. *The Telegraph*, a steamer having 196 tonnage, was built near Dexter, Jefferson county, and first came out in the fall of 1836. She was owned by parties in Utica, Watertown and Sackett's Harbor. Sprague was her first captain. She was in the employ of government in the fall of 1838, the whole of 1839, and some part of the spring of 1840. Changed to a sail vessel and burnt on Lake St. Clair. *The Express* was built at Pultneyville, Wayne county, H. N. Throop, master and one of the owners, about the year 1839. It was used on the through line for several years, and afterwards ran from Lewiston to Hamilton. It was finally laid up in 1850. The *Saint Lawrence*, 402 tons, was enrolled at Oswego in 1839, the engines being the same as those which had been used in the Oswego. In 1844, it was rebuilt, and the tonnage increased to 434 tons. Her first trip was performed in June, 1839. Cost about $50,000. It was run till 1851, most of the time as one of the through line, when it was dismantled at French Creek. This is said to have been the first steamer on this lake, that had state rooms on the main deck. Length, 180 feet; beam, 23 feet; hold, 11 feet. In 1839, she was commanded by John Evans; in 1840–6, by J. Van Cleve. Her place on the line was supplied by the Cataract.

The *George Clinton* and the *President*, were small boats built at Oswego, in 1842, and the former was wrecked on the south shore of the lake in 1850. About 1842, a stock company called the *Ontario Steam and Canal Boat Company*, was formed at Oswego, who in 1842, built the *Lady of the Lake*, of 423 tons, G. S. Weeks, builder; used on the through line until 1852, when she was chartered as a ferry in connection with the rail road from Cape Vincent to Kingston. This was the first American boat on this water that had state rooms on the upper deck. J. J. Taylor was her master for several years. The *Rochester*, built for this company by G. S. Weeks, at Oswego, in 1843, of 354 tons, and run on the lake and river until 1848, since which she has run from Lewiston to

Hamilton. In July, 1845, the *Niagara*, of 478 tons, came out, having been the first of a series of steamers built at French creek, by J. Oades. Her length was 182 feet; beam, 27½ feet; total breadth, 47 feet; hold, 7½ feet. Engine from the Archimedes works, with cylinder of 40 inches and 11 feet stroke. Wheels 30 feet in diameter. The *British Queen* was built on Long Island between Clayton and Kingston, in 1846, by Oades, the engines being those of the Oneida. Length, 180 feet; beam, 42 feet; engine double, each cylinder 26 inches in diameter. The *British Empire* was built at the same time and place with the last.

The Cataract, came out in July, 1837. She measures 577 tons, and was commanded the first season by James Van Cleve. Length of keel, 202 feet, breadth of beam 27½ feet, breadth across the guards, 48 feet, depth of hold 10 feet, diameter of wheels, 30 feet, engines built by H. R. Dunham & Co., at the Archimedes works in New York,' and the cylinder has a diameter of 44 inches, and a stroke of 11 feet, cost about $60,000. She was commanded in 1847-8, by J. Van Cleve; in 1849-51, by R. B. Chapman; in 1852, by A. D. Kilby.

Ontario, built in the summer of 1847, length of keel, 222 feet; a deck, 233 feet, and over all, 240 feet 6 inches; breadth of beam, 32 feet 2 inches, and over all 54 feet 8 inches; depth of hold, 12 feet; machinery made by T. F. Secor & Co., New York, cylinder 50 inches in diameter and 11 feet stroke; tonnage 900, cost about $80,000.

Bay State. This magnificent steamer came out for the first time in June, 1849, with J. Van Cleve, master, the first season. She has a tonnage of 935, and the following dimensions, viz: length 222 feet, breadth of beam 31½ feet, total breadth 58 feet; depth of hold 12 feet; engines from the Archimedes works, New York, with a cylinder 56 inches in diameter and 11 feet stroke; wheels 32 feet in diameter.

The Northerner, was built at Oswego, by G. S. Weeks, and came out in May, 1850, she has a tonnage of 905, length 232 feet, beam 30½ feet, total breadth 58 feet, depth of hold 12½ feet, wheels 32 feet in diameter, cost $95,000, engines by T. F. Secor & Co. of New York, with cylinder of 60 inches in diameter, and a stroke of 11 feet.

The New York, the largest American steamer on the lake, was built in 1851-2, and made her first trip in August last, with R. B. Chapman, master, cost about $100,000, tonnage 994, length 224 feet, beam 32½ feet, entire breadth 64 feet, engines built by H. R. Dunham & Co. New York, Cylinder 60 inches in diameter, with 12 feet stroke, wheels 34 feet in diameter.

Besides the above, there have been built or run upon the river and lake, the *John Marshall, Utica, Caroline, Prescott, Swan, Express, Gleaner*, and a few others, mostly small.

Shortly after the formation of the Steam and Canal Boat Company, a new one was organized, called the *St. Lawrence Steam Boat Company*. The two were, in 1848, united in one, which assumed the name of the *Ontario and St. Lawrence Steam Boat Company*, having a capital of $750,-000, and at present the following officers: E. B. Allen, president; E. B. Allen, G. N. Seymour, H. Van Rensselaer, A. Chapman, E. G. Merrick, S. Buckley, H. Fitzhugh, A. Munson, T. S. Faxton, H. White, L. Wright, directors; and James Van Cleve, secretary and treasurer.

This company is the owner of eleven steamers in daily service during the season of navigation. Their names, routes, and names of masters, as they existed in the summer and fall of 1852, are as follows:

Express Line.—From Ogdensburgh, by way of Toronto to Lewiston, and back, a daily line of two steamers, viz: *Bay State*, Capt. John Ledyard. *New York*, Capt. R. B. Chapman.

Mail Line.—From Ogdensburgh to Lewiston, touching at Kingston, and all the principal American ports, except Cape Vincent. A daily line of four steamers, viz: *Northerner*, Capt. R. F. Child. *Cataract*, Capt. A. D. Kilby. *Niagara*, Capt. J. B. Estes. *Ontario*, Capt. H. N. Throop.

The *American Line*, from Ogdensburgh to Montreal, a daily line of three steamers, viz: *British Queen*, Capt. T. Laflamme. *British Empire*, Capt. D. S. Allen. *Jenny Lind*, Capt. L. Moody.

Rail Road Ferry.—From Cape Vincent to Kingston: *Lady of the Lake*, Capt. S. L. Seymour.

Line from Lewiston to Hamilton, at the head of Lake Ontario; *Rochester*, Capt. John Mason.

It is a singular fact, that not a single accident has ever occurred upon any American steamer, on Lake Ontario, or the St. Lawrence, which has caused the death or injury of a passenger. This is not due to chance, so much as to skilful management.

It is believed that the steam packets on Lake Ontario, although they may be wanting in the gaudy ornaments, and dazzling array of gilding and carving, which is so ostentatiously displayed on the steamers of the North river, yet they will compare in real convenience, neatness and comfort, in the careful and attentive deportment of the officers and subordinates employed, in skilful management, punctuality and safety, with any class of boats in the world. This opinion will be readily endorsed by any one who has enjoyed the accommodation which they afford.

Of the above steamers, the Niagara, Cataract, Ontario, Bay State, and New York, were built at French Creek by John Oades, and the British Queen and British Empire, by the same builder at the foot of Long island, in the St. Lawrence. Of propellers, the pioneer on the lake was, the Oswego, built at that place in 1841, since which, about a dozen have been built on the lake. In 1851, a line now numbering ten propellers, was established by Crawford & Co., to run in connection with the Northern rail road for forwarding freight. In 1852, this line transported about 30,000 tons of flour and produce, eastward, and 20,000 of merchandise, westward. Most of these vessels have cabins for passengers. Most of them were built at Cleveland, Ohio.

Prominent among the enterprises which are destined to exert their influence for the promotion of the commercial interests of Ogdensburgh, may be placed the project which has been planned and is expected to be carried into effect during the coming season, which is the construction of a *submarine railway*, for taking vessels and steamers out of the river for repairs. The want of such a convenience has long been a desideratum, by the commercial interests of the St. Lawrence, but nothing was done towards effecting this object, till the 29th of September, 1852, when a meeting of parties interested was held, and a company formed, called the *Ogdensburgh Marine Railway Company*, with a capital of $15,000, and liberty to increase this amount at pleasure. This association was formed under the provision of a general act for the government of Marine Railway Companies, passed February 17, 1848. The following officers were chosen at the first meeting.

Henry Van Rensselaer, E. N. Fairchild, E. B. Allen, Edwin Clark, and Allen Chaney, *trustees.* Henry Van Rensselaer, *president.* Walter B. Allen, *secretary.* The duration of the company was limited to fifty years. Shares $50 each. It is proposed to construct this work on the west side of the Oswegatchie, above the village a short distance and near Pigeon point. The shore at the place can be made a good ship yard, and the business which this enterprise will create, must lead to the rapid settlement of the western part of the village. The cheapness of a marine railway, when compared with the cost of dry dock, for the repair of vessels, gives to the latter an incomparable advantage over the former, while the benefits arising from each are alike. This contemplated improvement, with a ship yard, will give to Ogdensburgh, when combined with other advantages which the place possesses, an importance in a commercial point of view, that will greatly promote its growth and prosperity.

State Roads.—Attention was early directed towards opening a southern route from St. Lawrence county, and a law of April 1, 1808, made provision for this by taxing the lands through which it passed for a road from *Canton* to *Chester*, in Essex county, and by several acts of 1810, to 1814, a further sum was appropriated for this purpose, and the road was opened under the direction of Russell Attwater, but was little traveled, and soon fell into disuse. On the 19th of June, 1812, a road was directed to be opened from near the foot of sloop navigation of the St. Lawrence, to Albany, and again in 1815, a further tax was laid with which a road was opened by Mr. Attwater, from Russell southwards, and made passable for teams, but like the other, soon fell into decay. Previous to 1810, the land proprietors had by subscription, built a bridge over the Saranac, which was swept away by a flood, and in opening a road towards Hopkinton, to aid which a law of April 5, 1810, imposed a tax on the adjacent lands, and appointed two commissioners to repair and construct a road from the North west bay to Hopkinton. In 1812, 1816 and 1824, a further tax was laid. The several towns were to be taxed four years for its support, and it was then to be assumed as a highway. A road was constructed and for some time travelled, but had so fallen into decay as to be scarcely passable. The several towns within two or three years have under taken to reopen it as a highway. In April, 1816, commissioners were appointed to lay out a road from Ogdensburgh, by way of Hamilton to Massena; from Massena through Potsdam to Russell, and from Russell through Columbia village to Hamilton, at the expense of the adjacent lands. On the 16th of April, 1827, John Richards, Ezra Thuber and Jonah Sanford, were directed to survey and level a route for a road from Lake Champlain to Hopkinton, and in 1829, $25,836 was applied for its construction. When done, the governor was to appoint three commissioners to erect toll gates and take charge of the road, which was soon after completed, and in 1833 a line of stages started between Port Kent and Hopkinton. This road is still used, the gates having for many years been taken down, and it has been and is of essential benefit to the country. An act of April 18, 1828, directed a road to be opened from Canton to Antwerp, at the expense of the adjacent lands.

Several other special provisions have been made for roads in the two counties. The first turnpike was made by the *St. Lawrence Turnpike Company*, incorporated April 5, 1810, and consisting of the principal land owners. It was designed to run from Carthage to Malone, and was opened by Russell Attwater, as agent for the company. In 1813, it was relieved from the obligation of finishing it beyond the line of Bangor east, or the Oswegatchie State road, west. After the war the road lost its importance, and in 1829 was divided into road districts. It still bears the name of the Russell turnpike. The *Ogdensburgh Turnpike Company*, was formed June 8, 1812, when D. Parish, L. Hasbrouck, N. Ford, J. Rosseel, Charles Hill, Ebenezer Legro, and their associates, were incorpornted with $50,000 capital, and soon after built what is since mostly a plank road from Wilna to Ogdensburgh, by way of Rossie. In April, 1826, the road was abandoned to the public. The *Parishville Turnpike Company*, was incorporated February 5, 1813, when D. Parish, N. Ford, L. Hasbrouck, J. Tibbets, Jr., B. Raymond and Daniel Hoard, were empowered to build with a capital of $50,000, the present direct road from Ogdensburgh through Canton, and Potsdam to Parishville. In March, 1827, this road was given up to the towns through which it passed, and in April, 1831, the part between Ogdensburgh and Canton, was directed to be improved by a tax upon the three towns of $500 for two years, to be expended by a commissioner named in each town. With this sum and tolls collected for its support, an excellent road was kept up. In 1850, the route was directed to be planked, and a sum not exceeding $10,000 was allowed to be borrowed on six years time, upon the credit of the tolls, and incidentally upon the credit of Ogdensburgh village, Lisbon and Canton. This has mostly been done.

Plank Roads.—A road from *Ogdensburgh* to *Heuvelton*, having been incorporated by a special act, was opened in September, 1849. Capital, $5000, with privilege of increasing to $20,000. Its earnings have been about $2000 annually. The *Gouverneur, Somerville and Antwerp Companies*, like the following, was formed under the general law. It was organized December 30, 1848, and finished September, 1850. Length, 12 miles, 124 rods; capital, $13,000. Six miles of this road are in Jefferson county. *First directors;* C. P. Egbert, S. B. Van Duzee, Gilbert Wait, Nathaniel L. Gill; *treasurer*, Martin Thatcher; *secretary*, Charles Anthony. The *Gouverneur, Richville and Canton Plank Road Company's* road extends from the village of Gouverneur to the line of Canton. Formed July 6, 1849; length 16 miles; capital, $16,000. Its first officers were Wm. E. Sterling, S. B. Van Duzee, John Smith, J. Burnett E. Miner, T. Cadwell, *directors;* E. Miner, *president;* Wm. E. Sterling, *treasurer;* C. A. Parker, *secretary.*

The Canton Plank Road, a continuation of the latter road, extending from the village of Canton to the town line of De Kalb, was built under a special act passed March 24, 1849, which authorized a tax in the town of Canton, of $6000 for the first year, and $1,500 annually, for three successive years afterwards, for constructing the road, which was to be owned by the town. Hiram S. Johnson, James P. Cummings and Benjamin Squire, were named as commissioners to locate the road. The nett earnings after keeping the road in repair and repaying money borrowed for its construction, were to be applied to the support of roads and bridges in town. Luman Moody, Theodore Caldwell and Joseph J. Herriman, were appointed commissioners to build the road, and superintend it after its completion. The latter were to be divided by lot into classes, and to hold their office for three years, vacancies to be supplied by election at town meetings.

The Canton, Morely and Madrid Plank Road Company, formed January, 1851; road finished August, 1851; length, 11¼ miles. Silas H. Clark, Alfred Goss, H. Hodskin, J. C. Harrison, E. Miner, R. Harrison, A. S. Robinson, first directors. *The Potsdam Plank Road Company,* was formed October 17, 1850; length 5 miles, 154 rods, from Potsdam village to the Northern Rail Road; cost $6 439·43; finished October 8, 1851; divided, 8 per cent; dividend, July 1, 1852; first directors, John McCall Robert

McGill, John Burroughs, Jun., Stephen Given, Jun., Benjamin G. Bald win.

The *Hammond, Rossie and Antwerp Plank Road Company*, formed January 23, 1850, completed in December following. Length 20 miles; capital, $35,000; 7 miles are in Jefferson county. There is an embankment 41 feet high at the Rossie hills, and the deepest rock cutting is 22 feet; directors, Ira Hinsdale, E. Brainerd, Z. Gates, A. P. Morse and D. W. Baldwin.

The *Morristown and Hammond Plank Road Company*, a continuation of the former, was laid along the route of the former road, and through a country which offered but few obstacles to its construction. President and treasurer, Moses Birdsall; secretary, Henry Hooker. Length, 10½ miles; capital, $10,000, in 200 shares of $50 each; organized in July, 1851; completed in May, 1852. This, with the preceding, forms a continuous plank road communication with routes leading to Utica, Rome, Watertown, &c., and terminating on the St. Lawrence river, in the village of Morristown.

The *Heuvelton and Canton Falls* (now Rensselaer Falls) P. R. Co., as originally organized, had a length of about ten miles. It has been continued to the road from Canton to Hermon, by the same company, and twelve chains on that road to meet a plank road in Hermon, since constructed, from the town line of Canton, through the village of Hermon. It is designed to continue this road through to Edwards. The first directors were Henry Van Rensselaer (president), Elijah B. Allen, E. N. Fairchild, D. Simpson and John Shull, jr.

The office of the company is in Ogdensburgh, at the land office of Mr. Van Rensselaer, who is the principal owner of the road. Through a part of the distance it was laid through unsettled lands, which have thus been brought directly into market and opened for settlement.

The *Hermon P. R. Co.* was formed on the first day of March, 1851. David W. Weeks, Seymour Thatcher, Edward Maddock, L. H. Sheldon, Noah C. Williams, were the first directors. Capital, $4,000, in shares of $50 each, and the length of the road is four and a half miles. It extends from the village of Marshville, to the town line of Canton, where it connects with the Canton Falls plank road to Ogdensburgh. The road was finished about the first of July, 1852. It has been proposed to extend this road on to Edwards, and thence through to Carthage, in Jefferson county.

The *Heuvelton and De Kalb P. R. Co.* was organized Feb. 6, 1849, and extended to intersect the Gouverneur and Canton plank road at a point three miles east of Richville. Its length is about 13 miles. The whole road is not yet finished, but it is expected that it will be opened through early in 1853. The first directors were Wm. H. Cleghorn, Wm. Thurston, John Pickens, R. W. Judson, Pelatiah Stacey, Andrew Rowlston, Lewis Sanford.

The *Norfolk, Raymondville and Massena P. R. Co.* was organized Feb. 14, 1851, to be completed in 1852. Length, 10 miles 44 chains; capital, $8,500, in 170 shares, of $50 each. A portion only of this road was completed at the close of the season of 1852. It is a continuation of the Potsdam road. It forms a direct communication between the rail road and several thriving villages. Uriah H. Orvis. G. J. Hall, N. F. Beals, C. Sackrider, B. G. Baldwin, E. D. Ransom, Hiram Attwater, Justus Webber and Marcus Robins were first directors. U. H. Orvis, president; G. J. Hall, secretary.

But about two miles of plank road exist in Franklin county, near the extreme southeast corner.

STATISTICS.

The following table exhibits the population of the several towns in the two counties, as shown by the censuses.

TOWNS.	1810	1820	1825	1830	1835	1840	1845	1850
Brasher,	.....	.....	401	828	939	2,118	2,218	2,548
Canton,	699	1,337	1,898	2,440	2,412	3,465	4,035	4,685
Colton,	.....	.....	.....	.....	.....	.....	466	506
De Kalb,	541	709	766	1,060	1,200	1,531	1,723	2,389
De Peyster,	.....	.....	787	814	788	1,074	1,138	906
Edwards,	.....	.....	.....	633	739	956	1,064	1,023
Fine,	.....	.....	.....	.....	.....	.....	243	293
Fowler,	.....	605	1,671	1,447	1,571	1,752	1,840	1,813
Gouverneur,	237	765	1,267	1,552	1,796	2,538	2,600	2,783
Hammond,	.....	.....	.....	767	1,327	1,845	1,911	1,819
Hermon,	.....	.....	.....	688	870	1,271	1,580	1,690
Hopkinton,	372	581	684	827	910	1,147	1,435	1,470
Lawrence,	.....	.....	.....	1,097	1,241	1,845	2,055	2,209
Lisbon,	820	930	1,474	1,891	2,411	3,508	4,376	5,209
Louisville,	.....	831	864	1,076	1,315	1,693	1,970	2,054
Macomb,	.....	.....	.....	.....	.....	.....	1,113	1,197
Madrid,	1,420	1,930	2,639	3,459	4,069	4,511	4,376	4,856
Massena,	955	944	1,701	2,070	2,288	2,726	2,798	2,915
Morristown,	.....	837	1,723	1,618	2,339	2,809	2,328	2,274
Norfolk,	.....	.....	665	1,039	1,373	1,728	1,544	1,753
Oswegatchie,	1,245	1,661	3,133	3,924	4,656	5,719	6,414	7,756
Parishville,	.....	594	959	1,479	1,657	2,250	2,090	2,131
Pierrepont,	.....	235	558	749	922	1,430	1,450	1,459
Pitcairn,	.....	.....	.....	.....	.....	396	553	503
Potsdam,	928	1,911	3,112	3,650	3,810	4,473	4,856	5,349
Rossie,	.....	869	1,074	650	655	1,553	1,386	1,471
Russell,	394	486	480	659	722	1,373	1,499	1,808
Stockholm,	307	822	1,449	1,944	2,047	2,995	3,293	3,661
Total,	7,885	16,037	27,506	36,351	42,047	56,706	62,354	68,617

TOWNS.	1810	1820	1825	1830	1835	1840	1845	1850
Bangor,	.....	370	910	1,076	1,035	1,289	1,606	2,160
Bellmont,	.....	.....	.....	.....	382	472	510	660
Bombay,	.....	.....	.....	.....	1,357	1,446	1,667	1,963
Brandon,	.....	.....	.....	316	417	531	578	590
Burke,	.....	.....	.....	.....	.....	.....	1,285	2,477
Chateaugay,	.....	828	1,364	2,016	2,039	2,824	1,952	3,728
Constable,	.....	637	1,016	693	724	1,122	1,177	1,447
Dickinson,	.....	495	899	446	597	1,005	1,074	1,119
Duane,	.....	.....	.....	247	237	324	178	222
Fort Covington,	.....	979	2,136	2,901	1,665	2,094	2,369	2,641
Franklin,	.....	.....	.....	.....	.....	192	361	734
Harrietstown,	.....	.....	.....	.....	.....	.....	129	181
Malone,	.....	1,130	1,633	2,207	2,589	3,229	3,637	4,549
Moira,	.....	.....	.....	791	798	962	1,013	1,340
Westville,	.....	.....	.....	619	661	1,028	1,159	1,301
Total,	.....	4,439	7,978	11,312	12,501	16,518	18,692	25,102

Names, ages and residences of Pensioners, from the census of 1840.

St. Lawrence County—Parishville.—Joseph Armsby, 76; Hepsebah Mitchell, 78; Simeon Howard, 79; Elijah Allen, 82.

Hopkinton.—Solomon Chittenden, 78.

Stockholm.—Ephraim Knapp, 83; Mercy Dunham, 78; Luke Fletcher, 81; Martin Brockway, 79; Rhoda Skinner, 83; Wm. Burrows, 81; Thomas Scott, 80; Elizabeth Whiston, 83.

Lawrence.—Elizabeth Sanders, 78; Sarah Barnes, 74.

Norfolk.—Daniel Bradish, 79; Tryphena Collamer, 79; Theodorus Woodard, 79; Elizabeth Lawrence, 81; Elijah Brown, 84; Jemima Sawyer, 75; Griffin Place, 78; Guy Carpenter, 56; Russel Attwater, 79.

Massena.—Daniel Kenney, 80; Elijah Flagg, 80; Daniel Kinney, 80; John Polley, 79; Eben Polley, 53; John Polley, 55.

Louisville.—Asa Day, 80; Oliver Barret, 79; Asher Blunt, 81; Elias Kingsley, 79.

Pierrepont.—Frederick Squire, 45; Reuben Butler, 45; Joseph Dirnick, 73; Nathan Crary, 78; David Bradley, 81.

Russell.—Miles Cook, 75; John Knox, 81; Samuel Barrows, 73; Abraham Wells, 83; Gilbert Ray, 76; John Gillmore, 87.

Fowler.—Ebenezer Parker, 84; Jacob Deland, 78.

Edwards.—Abel Pratt, 83; Comfort Johnson, 87.

De Peyster.—Joseph Shaw, 79; Jonathan Fellows, 78.

Oswegatchie.—Sarah June, 81; Benjamin Salts, 78; Esther Dollestun, 78; Richard Van Ornum, 82; Noah Spencer, 87; Daniel Chapman, 81.

Morristown.—Phinehas Maxon, 85; M. Demming, 80; Stephen Smith, 84; Sarah K. Thurber, 91; Wm. Lee, 74.

Hammond.—Emanuel Dake, 86.

Rossie.—Henry Apple, 86.

Gouverneur.—John Garrett, 85; Polly Hulbert, 72; Solomon Cross, 82; Eli Skinner, 81; Stephen Porter, 79.

Hermon.—David Page, 57; Asher Williams, 79.

De Kalb.—John C. Cook, 27.

Lisbon.—Isaac Mitchell, 80; Samuel Wallace, 80; Hughey Willson, 84; Amon Lawrence, 49; Jane Turner, 89.

Canton.—Asa Briggs, 88; Eber Goodnow, 75; Joshua Conkey, 80; Lucy Tuttle. 95; Isaac Robinson, 79; Lydia Low, 72; Olive Tuttle, 67; John Daniels, 80.

Potsdam.—Wm. Carpenter, 87; Eunice Perigo, 93; Elijah Ames, 79; Ebenezer Atwood, 74; Mary Aikins, 74; John Bowker, 85; Jane Dailey. 88; Stephen Chandler, 86; Lucy Chandler, 76; Daniel Shaw, 86; Nathan Estabrook, 80; Nathaniel Parmeter, 54; Nathan Parmeter, 81; Ruth Brush, 77; Dyer Williams, 81; Giles Parmelee, 76; John Fobes, 78; John Moore, 82; Ammi Courier, 75; Sylvanus Willes, 84; Thomas Palmer, 80.

Madrid.—John Erwin, 59; Samuel Daniels, 78; Abiram Hurlbut, 76; Peter Eaton, 58; Rebecca Packard, 66; Lucy Byington, 80; James Corey, 78; Isaac Buck, 77; Manasseh Sawyer, 81; Isaac Bartholomew, 78; Margaret Allen, 86; Jacob Redington, 81.—Total number, 118.

Franklin County—Malone.—Simeon Graves, 87; Enos Wood, 79; Aaron Parks, 75; Samuel Smith, 81; Jesse Chipman, 85; Samuel Forbs, 78; Nathan Beeman, 86; Chester Morris, 71.

Fort Covington.—Francis Clark, 86.

Dickinson.—Betsey Lathrop, 78.

Bombay.—Asa Jackson, 79.

Westville.—Barnabas Berry, 82.
Bangor.—Gabriel Cornish, 82.
Franklin.—Sally Merrill, 83.
Brandon.—Henry Stevens, 83.
Moira.—Jno. Lawrence, 78; Tho's Spencer, 84; John Kimball, 76; Elkanah Philips, 84; Uriah Kingsley, 80.
Bellmont.—Ebenezer Webb, 82.—Total number, 21.

In 1810, St. Lawrence county had five slaves. The state then contained 14,638 slaves. It had 247 looms making 19,047 yards woolen; 36,000 of linen, and 1,926 of mixed cloth; 5 fulling mills, dressing 14,000 yards; 2 carding machines, using 10,500 lbs. wool; 12 tanneries, using 1767 hides; 2 distilleries, making 25,000 gallons spirits, worth 80 cts. per gallon, and one trip hammer. Franklin county had 63 looms; 2 carding machines, and fulling mills; made 5138 yards of woolen cloth: 1913 of linen; 859 of cotton; 3 mixed, and 1076 hides, worth $425—and $175 during the previous year.

According to the census of 1850, the average number of deer killed in the county of St. Lawrence within the last year, was 3500, valued at $3 dollars each. By the same, the resources of the counties were shown as follows:

	St. Law.	Fanklin.		St. Law.	Fr'klin.
Acres impr'd,	337,086	103,203	No. of oxen,	6,555	1,945
" unimpr'd	262,627	64,156	" other cattle,	34,441	8,876
Val. of farms,	9,245,542	2,298,912	" sheep,	89,910	27,430
No. of horses,	13,811	3,650	" swine,	18,423	5,220
" of cows,	33,365	6,974	Val. of live stock,	2,144,176	502,589

The District of Onwegatchie was established March 2, 1811, and the following statistics, procured by the Hon. Preston King, at the treasury department, for this purpose, show the business of this district very satisfactorily. The collectors have been Alexander Richards, 1811-20; Aaron Hackley, 1821 to 1827; Nathan Myers, 1827-9; Baron S. Doty, 1829-36; Smith Stilwell, Oct. 1, 1836—Sept. 11, 1840; David C. Judson, Sept. 12, 1840, Feb. 16, 1849; James C, Barter, Aug. 7, 1849, till the present time. No duties were collected till 1815, since which the receipts have been as follows:

YEAR.	DOL. CTS.	YEAR.	DOL. CTS	YEAR.	DOL. CTS	YEAR.	DOL. CTS.
1815....	11.729·37	1825....	1,349·30	1835,....	2,954·75	1843 ...	743·35
1816....	4,409·80	1826....	1,207·87	1836....	10,551,00	1844...	2,032·09
1817....	6,176·02	1827....	768·02	1836....	2.228·97	1845...	2,884·26
1818....	5,155·98	1828....	2,103·33	1837....	4,316·79	1846...	1,852·26
1819....	2,716·01	1829....	2,044·91	1838....	2,847·52	1847...	4,550·09
1820....	1,677·01	1830....	2,329·76	1839....	2,497·68	1848...	5,106·75
1821....	1,339·45	1831....	3,314·60	1840....	1,111·25	1849*..	7,505·19
1822....	2,307·35	1832....	3,847·04	1840....	542·22	1849†..	1,325·19
1823....	2,462·07	1833....	3,295·99	1841....	1,420·08	1850‡	11,210·37
1824....	1,913·59	1834....	2,525·53	1842....	1,268·65	1851...	20,048·95

Subordinate offices exist at Oak Point, Morristown, Louisville, Massena and Waddington.

The District of Champlain, was established March 2, 1799, and includes Franklin county. From an official statement procured through the same channel as the above, it appears that Peter Sailly, F. S. C Sailly, David B. McNeil, Wm. F. Haile, Ezra Smith, and Oliver Pea-

* To Feb. 7. †From Feb. 7 to Aug. 6. ‡From Aug. 6, to Jan. 1.

body, have been collectors of the district. The deputies at Fort Covington have been, Seth Blanchard, John Hunsden, James Campbell, John McCrea, James B. Spencer, James Campbell, Samuel H. Payne, Ezra Stiles, George B. R. Gove. At Hogansburgh, B. Harrington, A. K. Williams, E. Bowker, and J. S. Eldridge. Belonging to the revenue department, are light houses at Ogdensburgh; Cross over island, Sunken rock, and Rock island, under the supervision of the collector of Oswegatchie district. They have stationary lights with parabolic reflectors.

Post Offices have been established in St. Lawrence county as follows with names of first postmasters and date of formation, as far as can be ascertained. A fire which destroyed the post office building in 1836, has made it difficult to settle some points. To such as are not known the star (*) has been prefixed, which denotes the time when the office commenced rendering. The author is indebted to the kindness of the Hon. Preston King for the following list:

Post Offices.	Date of establishment.	First Postmaster.
Black Lake (Oswegatchie),	Dec. 18, 1850,	Wm. H. Davis.
Blink Bonny (De Kalb),	Dec. 2, 1850,	Wm. Cleghorn, jr.
Brasher's Falls,	July 22, 1840,	Calvin T. Hulburd.
Brier Hill (Hammond),	March 6, 1851,	David Griffin.
Buck's Bridge (Potsdam),	March 30, 1836,	Owen Buck.
Brasher Iron Works,	July 14, 1849,	Isaac W. Skinner.
*Canton,	Dec. 27, 1808,	Daniel W. Sayre.
Colton,†	June 19, 1851,	Israel C. Draper.
Crary's Mills (Canton),	Dec. 10, 1849,	Truman Hunt.
De Kalb,	Dec. 9, 1806,	William Cleghorn.
De Peyster,	Sept. 10, 1827,	Smith Stillwell.
East Pierrepont,	Aug. 31, 1832,	Joseph Dimick.
East De Kalb,	July 14, 1851,	John H. Bartlett.
East Pitcairn,	Jan. 15, 1850,	Charles H. Bowles.
Edenton (De Peyster),	June 13, 1850,	Benjamin F. Partridge.
Edwards,	Jan. 4, 1828,	Orra Shead.
Edwardsville (Morristown),	March 22, 1837,	Jonathan S. Edwards.
Fowler,	Nov. 19, 1821,	Theodosius O. Fowler.
Flackville (Lisbon),	July 8, 1847,	Lauren Sage.
Fullersville Iron Works,‡	April 6, 1848,	Charles G. Edgerton.
Gouverneur,	Aug. 8, 1824,	Moses Rowley.
Hammond,	Oct. 16, 1824,	Arnold Smith.
Helena (Brasher),	Feb. 13, 1827,	David McMurphy.
Hermon,	Dec. 20, 1826,	Benjamin Healey.
Heuvelton (Oswegatchie),	Feb. 5, 1828,	George Seaman.
*Hopkinton,	Nov. 3, 1807,	Theophilus Laughlin.
Lawrenceville,	April 7, 1829,	Josiah Sanders.
*Lisbon,	July 1, 1810,	James Thompson.
*Louisville,	Sept. 11, 1811,	Benjamin Willard.
Louisville Landing,	April 9, 1850,	Ralph D. Marsh.
Lisbon Centre,	Dec. 19, 1850,	John McBride.
Madrid,	April 5, 1826,	John Horton.
Massena,	Sept. 19, 1811,	Calvin Hubbard.
Massena Centre,	July 13, 1851,	Augustus Wheeler.
Macomb,§	May 13, 1842,	David Day 2d.

† Formed as *Matildaville*, June 17, 1837, William R. Stark, postmaster.
‡ Formed as *Fullerville* about 1836.
§ Formed as *Washburnville*, July 27, 1837, David Day 3d, postmaster.

Morley (Canton),	April 3, 1839,	Lorenzo Fenton.
Morristown,	July 18, 1816,	David Ford.
Nicholville (Lawrence),	Jan. 7. 1831,	Clemens C. Palmer.
Norfolk,	May 22, 1823,	Phineas Attwater.
North Lawrence,	Dec. 12, 1850,	John H. Conant.
North Potsdam,	Dec. 30, 1850,	Rollin Ashley.
North Russel,	Feb. 17, 1848,	Linus A. Clark.
North Stockholm,	March 8, 1851,	Stephen House.
Oak Point (Hammond),	March 31, 1841,	James H. Consall.
*Ogdensburgh,	April 1, 1807,	Lewis Hasbrook.
Parishville,	Aug. 2, 1813,	Daniel Hoard.
Pierrepont,	June 5, 1820,	Peter Post.
Pitchirn,	June 5, 1840,	John Sloper.
Pope's Mills (Macomb),	July 14, 1849,	Russell Covell.
Potsdam,	April 21, 1807,	Pierce Shepherd.
Rackett River (Massena),	Feb. 28, 1842,	Peter Vilas.
Raymondville (Norfolk),	Sept. 2, 1840,	John Woodard.
Rensselaer Falls (Canton),	Dec. 19, 1851,	Archibald Shull.
Richville (De Kalb),	March 5, 1828,	John C. Rich.
Rossie,	May 16, 1816,	Roswell Ryon.
Russell,	June 27, 1812,	Pliny Goddard.
Shingle Creek (Rossie),	Feb. 6, 1828,	James Bailey.
Somerville (Rossie),	May 2, 1828,	Solomon Pratt.
South Edwards,	Sept. 16, 1828,	James C. Haile.
South Hammond,	Jan. 14, 1833,	Jonathan King.
Southville (Stockholm),	May 6, 1825,	Hosea Brooks.
*Stockholm,	Oct. 1, 1807,	William Gay.
Stockholm Depot,	April 23, 1851,	Jason W. Stearns.
Waddington,†	April 26, 1827,	Alexander Richards.
West Fowler,	Jan. 15, 1850,	Thomas Mitchell.
West Potsdam,	Sept. 22, 1847,	Wm. T. Galloway.
West Stockholm,	March 25, 1825,	Joseph H. Sanford.

FRANKLIN COUNTY.

*Bangor,	Feb. 17, 1812,	Henry Blanchard.
Bombay,	Jan. 3, 1838,	Wilson Randall.
Brush's Mills (Moira),	Aug. 11, 1849,	Henry N. Brush.
Burke (formerly	Nov. 4, 1844,	Hiram Miner.
West Chateaugay),	Feb. 25, 1829,	Ezra Stiles.
*Chateaugay,	April 1, 1807,	Amasa Fairman.
Dickinson,	June 10, 1828,	Benjamin Heath.
Duane,	March 25, 1833,	Franklin C. Hatch.
East Constable,	June 12, 1828,	Henry H. Hawkins.
Fort Covington,	May 7, 1818,	William Hogan.
Franklin Falls,	Jan. 21, 1851,	John Stearns.
Harriettstown,	Aug. 11, 1849,	Alanson B. Neal.
Flogansburgh (Bombay),	July 22, 1824,	William Hogan.
*Malone,	Oct. 1, 1810,	John H. Russell.
Merrillsville (Franklin),	July 29, 1837,	John R. Merrill.
*Moira,	Jan. 1, 1808,	Appleton Foot.
North Bangor,	Jan. 31, 1848,	George H. Stevens.
South Dickinson,	Feb. 3, 1842,	Eldred Baker.
Trout River (Burke),	Feb. 24, 1852,	Elisha Hollister.
West Constable,	Jan. 12, 1828,	Ebenezer Man.

† Formed as Madrid, December 14, 1807, A. Richards, postmaster.

List of those who have been admitted to practice in the court of Common Pleas, in St. Lawrence county, with the year when admitted. It embraces many lawyers living in adjoining counties:

Julius C. Abel, '32; Horace Allen, '16; Charles Anthony, '40; Frederick M. Attwater, '17; Jeremiah Bailey, '29; Benjamin G. Baldwin, '31; Cyrus W. Baldwin, '40; S. Baldwin, Jr., '28; Charles E. Beardsley, '28; Amos Benedict, '06; M. M. Berry, '21; Isaac W. Bostwick, '11; W. W. Bowes, '09; George Boyd, '10; A. C. Brown, '22; Wm. C. Brown, '40; D. W. Bucklin, '19 Justin Butterfield, '13; H. Wm. Channing, '16; David M. Chapin, '33; Samuel Chipman, '05; Palmer Cleveland, '10; Ela Collins, '15; George C. Conant, '10; John Cook, '17; Wm. C. Cooke, '43; Wm. A. Dart, '38; Charles Dayan, '25; Thomas Denny, '28; Edwin Dodge, '29; Stephen G. Dodge, '38; Joseph M. Doty, '41; James Edwards, '21; Edward Elderkin, '38; Charles A. Eldridge, '46; John Fine, '17; J. R. Flanders, '45; H. G. Foote, '43; Stillman Foote, '41; Jacob J. Ford, '22; Wm. D. Ford, '10; E. Fowler, '25; G. W. Gardner, '33; Ransom H. Gillet, '24; Edmund A. Graham, '25; John W. Grant, '27; Aaron Hackley, Jr., '21; Louis Hasbrouck, '11; Louis Hasbrouck, '38; A. Hayward, '32; Wm. B. Hickock, '45; Britton A. Hill, '38; J. G. Hopkins, '25; L. C. Hubbell, '21; C. T. Hulburd, '33; Richard S. Hunt, '44; N. F. Hyer, '32; A. B. James, '37; R. W. Judson, '38; Preston King, '30; Henry L. Knowles, '38; Liberty Knowles, '10; Wm. L. Knowles, '44; Alfred Lathrop) '17; Samuel Livermore, '10; Jno. Lynde, '12; A. McCollom, '03; James D. McLaren, '40; Henry C. Martindale, '11; Morris L. Miller, '03; Charles G. Myers, '32; Matthew Myers, '09; Gouv'r Ogden, '10; Lewis M. Ogden, '10; Wm. Ogden, '24; C. A. Parker, '45; Adriel Peabody, '05; Bishop Perkins, '15; Matthew Perkins, '02; Samuel H. Platt, '32; R. M. Popham, '10; Wm. S. Radcliff, '10; George Redington, '23; James Redington, '31; Amos Reed, '45; Alexander Richards, Jr., '17; Samuel Rockwell, '10; Cephas L. Rockwood, '30; J. L. Russell, '30; Tho's V. Russell, '38; Elam Rust, '33; John Scott, '10; S. B. Seeley, '37; Geo. C. Sherman, '32; Benjamin Skinner, Jr., '02; Levi Smith, '33; Simeon Smith, '40; Micah Sterling, '15; Egbert Ten Eyck, '03; Halsey Townsend, '21; J. A. Vanden Heuvel, '22; Wm. H. Vining, '17; James P. Warford, '07; Samuel Warford, '08; Samuel Whittlesey, '08; Charles B. Wright, '45; Silas Wright, Jr., '19;

Persons in St. Lawrence county admitted to the Supreme Court since 1847, in the order of their admission:

Bennett H. Vary, J. Addison Brown, Joseph Mac Naughton, Winslow T. Barker, Martin Thatcher, Ezekiel E. Cooley, Asahel Clark, Charles C. Montgomery, Theodore E. Parker, Orrin L. Ray, Benjamin H. Fuller, William H. Andrews, James H. Barter, Henry M. Eastman, John Powell, Jun., Sylvester T. Pierce, Charles Rich, William H. Sawyer, John H. Sigourney.

Members of the bar of Franklin county, derived from Mr. Joseph H. Jackson, of Malone, and by several lawyers in the county:

George S. Adams, William M. Berry,† Marshall Conant, Leander Douglass, George W. Field,† Putnam B. Fish, Edward Fitch, Richard G. Foote, Joseph R. Flanders, Azel Hayward,* Asa Hascall,* Albert Hobbs, William L. Horton, John Hutton, William Hogan,† Joseph H. Jackson,

* Dead.   † Removed.

David Jones,* Edgar A Keeler, Sidney Lawrence, William C. McVicker, Horace Meriam,† Joseph Moulton,† Henry A. Paddock, Ashbel B. Parmelee, Jabez Parkhurst, Walter H. Payne, ⸺ Purdy,* John H. Russell, Joel J. Seaver, Elisha B. Smith, James C. Spencer, Francis Storms,† Horace A. Taylor, Jonathan Wallace, Almon Wheeler,* C. H. Wheeler,* William A. Wheeler, George H. Wood,‡ Thomas Wright, Jun.†

ST. LAWRENCE COUNTY.

List of Public Officers.—The *Sheriffs* of St. Lawrence county, have been Thomas J. Davies, John Boyd, T. J. Davies, Joseph York, David C. Judson, Charles D. Raymond, Levi Lockwood, Minet Jenison, Lemuel Buck, Jonathan Hoit, Luman Moody, Benjamin Squire, Noble S. Elderkin, Josiah Waid, Henry Barber, and Reuben Nott. Mr. Lockwood first held the office by election, his predecessors having been appointed by the governor.

County Clerks.—Louis Hasbrouck, till March 1, 1817, with two years interval, in which Alexander Richards held the office. Myrtle B. Hitchcock, Joseph York, James G. Hopkins, Wm. H. Root, Alvin C. Low, John L. Russell, (appointed July 8, 1843, to fill for a short time the vacancy occasioned by the death of Mr. Low,) Martin Thatcher, George S. Winslow.

The following are fac similes of the signatures of clerks, with one exception, in which it could not be procured. It was inconvenient to arrange them in chronological order.

First Judges—Nathan Ford, 1802 till 1820. David A. Ogden, till 1824. John Fine, till 1825; D. A. Ogden, till 1829; John Fine, till 1838. Horace Allen, John Fine; from 1843 who held until the adoption of the new constitution. By this the office was made elective, and at a special election in June, 1847, Edwin Dodge was chosen, and in 1851, reelected.

Assistant Justices.—By appointment, Stillman Foote, John Tibbits, Jun., March 10, 1802; Luke McCracken, Robert Livingston, Daniel W. Church, March 5, 1806; Daniel W. Church, Stillman Foote, April 8, 1808; John Tibbits, Jun., Luke McCracken, Charles Cox, Daniel W. Church, Stillman Foote, David Ford, David Robinson, Reuben Ashman, March 6, 1811; Charles Cox, June 5, 1812; Daniel W. Church, John Tibbits, Jun., Stillman Foote, David Ford, Daniel Robinson, Reuben Ashman, April 5, 1814; Reuben Ashman, Jason Fenton, D. W. Church, Richard Townsend, Zephaniah French, Timothy Pope, John Polley, Charles Hill, Caleb Hough, Jun., April 15, 1815; Caleb Hough, Moses A. Bunnell, John Lyttle, Reuben Streeter, N. F. Winslow, March 16, 1818.

Judges.—Alexander J. Turner, Joseph Edsall, March 10, 1802; Russell Attwater, Benjamin Raymond, Alexander Richards and Joseph Edsall, April 8, 1808; Roswell Hopkins, March 27, 1810; R. Attwater, A. Richards, B. Raymond, R. Hopkins, Robert Livingston, David A. Ogden, March, 6, 1811; David A. Ogden, R. Livingston, June 5, 1812; R. Attwater, A. Richards, R. Hopkins, B. Raymond, D. Ogden, R. Livingston, April 5, 1814; R. Attwater, A. Richards, R. Livingston, Thomas J. Davies, N. F. Winslow, April 15, 1815; R. Attwater, R. Livingston, T. J. Davies, J. Fenton, A. Richards, March 16, 1818; Amasa Hackley, Jun., Jason Fenton, R. Livingston, Ansel Baily, Smith Stilwell, January, 24, 1823; R. Livingston, J. Fenton, S. Stillwell, A. Bailey, March 28, 1828; David C. Judson, Jabez Willes, Asa Sprague, Jun., Chauncey Pettibone, March 13, 1829; Minet Jenison, January 10, 1832; Minet Jenison, Jan. 13, 1837; Zenas Clark, March 27, 1835; Minet Jenison, Jan. 21, 1837; Edwin Dodge, George Redington, Phinneas Attwater, March 19, 1845. This list is necessarily imperfect from the defective manner in which the records of appointments were formerly kept. Among those who have held the office, not above mentioned, are James Averill, Anthony C. Brown, Isaac R. Hopkins.

Justices of Sessions.—(elected), Joseph Barnes, James C. Barter, 1847; Joseph Barnes, Chilleab Billing, 1849; Joseph Barnes, Silas Baldwin, 1850; Joseph H. Beard, Silas Baldwin, 1851; and reelected in 1852.

District Attorneys.—Amos Benedict, Samuel Whittlesey, A. Benedict, Jesse L. Billings, and Ela Collins, while Lewis and Jefferson were united with this county as a district. Since 1818, John Scott, was the first one who held the office in the county; he was succeeded by Bishop Perkins. This office is now elective, and Charles G. Myers, was chosen at the special judicial election of une, 1847, and reelected in 1851.

Surrogates.—Mathew Perkins, March 10, 1802. The earliest record of business done by the office bears date April 27, 1805. Andrew McCollom, Feb. 16, 1809. George Boyd, Gouverneur Ogden, March 3, 1813. Silas Wright, Jun., Feb. 24, 1821. Horace Allen, Jan. 21, 1824. James Redington, March 30, 1840. Charles G. Myers, March 30, 1844. Benjamin G. Baldwin, July 1, 1847.

All but the last named, held their office by appointment of the governor. Since the adoption of the present constitution it has become in St. Lawrence county a separate elective office.

Coroners.—Seth Ranney, William Shaw, Feb. 29, 1804. S. Ranney, Wm. Staples, Nicholas Reynolds, March 5, 1805. John Lyon, William Staples, Nicholas Reynolds, April 8, 1808. Benjamin Willard, Kelsey J. Thurber, John Boyd, Stephen Langworthy, March 6, 1811. Wm. S. Guest, Wm. Perry, Winslow Whitcomb, Clement Tuttle, June 15, 1812. Joshua Dewey, Stephen Slawson, Caleb Hough, Jr., March 3, 1813. John Herrick, Enoch Story, John Pierce, Levi Green, John Williams, Dyer Burnham, Kirtland Griffin, Jeremiah Matherson, March 2, 1814. J. Dewey, C. Hough, B. Willard, J. Boyd, K. J. Thurber, April 15, 1815. J. Dewey, C. Hough, B. Willard, J. Boyd, K. J. Thurber, March 16, 1816. Reuben Attwater, N. F. Winslow, C. Hough, Elijah Baker, John Lyttle, Ira Ransom, K. J. Thurber, March 16, 1818; R. Attwater, Elijah Baker, Ira Ransom, Joseph York, John Lyttle, Enos C. Eastman, April 8, 1819. R. Attwater, E. Baker, J. Lytle, J. York, E. C. Eastman, Wm. S. Guest, Charles Whalan, Hazen Rolf, and Jabez Willes, 1820. Wm. S. Guest, Peter Pollard, Ira Collins, Thomas Bingham, Hazen Rolf, Zoraster Culver. Caleb Hough, Henry C. Green, Thomas D. Olin, Nathaniel Ives, Feb. 28, 1821. In 1822, the same with the addition of Thomas Hill. We are not able to procure six years.

In 1828, John E. Perkins, Henry Foot, Samuel C. Barter, S. Pratt. In 1831, Darius Clark, Wm. S. Paddock, Justus Pickit, Michael S. Daniels. In 1834, Abijah Rowley, Allen McLeod, Jr., Gideon Sprague, Almond Z. Madison. In 1837, S. Pratt, D. Clark, John Stone, Rudolphus Searle. In 1840, D. Clark, Joseph H. Ripley, Royal Vilas, Smith Low. In 1843, D. Clark, Charles N. L. Sprague, Luther Lauphear, R. Vilas. In 1846, D. Clark, Henry D. Laughlin, Wm. S. Paddock, Heman W. Tucker. In 1847, Wm. S. Paddock, re-elected. In 1849, H. D. Laughlin, Cyrus Abernethy. In 1851, L. Lamphear, Wm. S. Paddock. In 1852, T. O. Benjamin, Alexander, R. Gregor, John C. Preston.

Loan Commissioners.—In 1808, $4,473 school moneys was received, to be loaned in the county, and the persons appointed to this trust up to 1840, have been Russell Attwater, Alex. Richard, Thomas J. Davies, Joseph W. Smith, Smith Stillwell, Jason Fenton, Geo. Ranney, Alvin C. Low, Joseph Ames, 2d. In 1837, $103,501, of the United States deposit fund was received for loaning in the county, and George Ranney and Joseph Ames, 2d, were the commissioners first appointed. In 1850, this and the loan of 1808, were consolidated, and but one set of officers are required.

Deputy Superintendents of Schools, appointed by the Supervisors.—Sylvester Ford, 1841, for the east section of Lisbon, Canton and Russell, and Jos. Hopkins for these and all the towns west. In 1843, George S. Winslow, for the whole county. Mr. Winslow resigned his office in 1844, and Charles Rich was appointed to the western, and Frederick P. Sprague, to the eastern sections. In 1845, Sprague resigned, and Mr. Rich was appointed for the whole county, for the ensuing year. In 1846, Luke Carton was appointed, and held the office till it was abolished.

Congressional Districts.—In March, 1802, St. Lawrence, with Herkimer and Oneida, were formed the 15th district. In 1812, with Lewis and Jefferson, the 18th. In 1822, with Oswego, Lewis and Jefferson, the 20th. In 1832, with Franklin, the 14th. In 1842, with Lewis, the 18th, and in 1851, with Herkimer, the 17th. The representations, so far as ascertained, have been as follows, the years given being those in which they came into office: 1811, Silas Stowe; 1813 and 1815, Moss Kent; 1817, David A. Ogden; 1821, Macah Sterling; 1823, Ela Collins; 1825, Nicol

Fosdick; 1827, Silas Wright; 1829, Jonah Sanford; 1831, Wm. Hogan; 1833 and 1835, R. H. Gillet; 1837, James B. Spencer; 1839, John Fine; 1841, Henry Van Rensselaer; 1843 and 1845, Preston King; 1847, Wm. Collins; 1849 and 1821, Preston King; 1853, Bishop Perkins.

Senators.—The journals of the senate contain the following names of members from St. Lawrence county. Russell Attwater, 1814; Silas Wright, 1824; Jabez Willis, 1835; James G. Hopkins, 1840. Under the old constitution this formed a part of the western district. Under that of 1822, a part of the 4th. Under that of 1846 with Franklin it formed the 12th, which has been represented by John Fine, Wm. A. Dart, and till 1854, by Henry B. Smith.

Assembly Districts.—This county was separated from Oneida and united with Jefferson and Lewis, about 1807, when Moss Kent, of Jefferson county, was the member. In 1808, Lewis Graves. In 1810 St. Lawrence was made a separate district, and has been represented as follows. In 1810-3, Roswell Hopkins; 1814; Louis Hasbrouck; 1815, David A. Ogden, 1816-18; Wm. W. Bowen; 1819-21, Joseph York; 1822, Wm. H. Vining; 1823-4, Nathaniel F. Winslow; 1825, Jacob A. Vanden Heuvel; 1826, Baron S. Doty.

From this period till 1847, the county elected two members on a general ticket, viz: 1827, Sylvester Gilbert, Baron S. Doty; 1828, Moses Rowley, Jabez Willes; 1829, Harvey D. Smith, Jonah Sanford; 1830, J. Sanford, Asa Sprague; 1831, A. Sprague, Joseph Freeman; 1832, Wm. Allen, Edwin Dodge; 1833, Wm. Allen, Sylvester Butrick; 1834, S. Butrick, J. Willes; 1835-7, Preston King, Wm. S. Paddock; 1838, P. King, Myron G. Peck; 1839, M. G. Peck, Asa Sprague; 1840, A. Sprague, Zenas Clark; 1841, Z. Clark, S. Pratt; 1842-4, George Reddington, Calvin T. Hulburd; 1845, John L. Russell, Asa L. Hazleton; 1846, A. L. Hazleton, Bishop Perkins.

The county is now divided into three assembly districts, as follows. In each of these one member is annually elected.

The first district comprises De Peyster, De Kalb, Fowler, Gouverneur, Hammond, Macomb, Morristown, Oswegatchie, Pitcairn, and Rossie.

The second district, Lisbon, Madrid, Norfolk, Canton, Russell, Hermon, Fine, Edwards, and Pierrepont.

The third district, Brasher, Massena, Potsdam, Stockholm, Lawrence Hopkinton, Colton, Parishville, and Louisville.

1847. Bishop Perkins, of Oswegatchie; 2d, Henry Barber, of Canton 3d, Phineas Attwater, of Norfolk. 1848. 1st, Charles G. Myers, of Oswegatchie; 2d, John S. Chipman, of Madrid; 3d, Benjamin Holmes, of Stockholm. 1849. 1st, Harlow Goddard, of De Kalb; 2d, J. B. Picket, of Edwards; 3d, Noble S. Eldrkin, of Potsdam. 1850, Harlow Goddard, of De Kalb; 2, John Horton, of Madrid; 3d, Noble S. Elderkin, of Potsdam. 1851. 1st, Smith Stillwell, of Oswegatchie; 2d, John Horton, of Madrid; 3d, Noble S. Elderkin, of Potsdam. 1852. 1st, Smith Stilwell, of Oswegatchie; 2d, Benjamin Smith, of Russell; 3d, Parker W. Rose, of Parishville. 1853. 1st, Barnabas Hall, of Gouverneur; 2d, Benjamin Smith, of Russell; 3d, Parker W. Rose, of Parishville.

PUBLIC OFFICERS, FRANKLIN COUNTY.

Sheriffs.—John Wood, Samuel Chapman, Zeruhabel Curtis, James Campbell, John Wood, by appointment; John Mitchell, elected in 1822; Reeve Peck, John Backus, Orrin Lawrence, Aaron Beeman, Guy Meigs

Wm. Andrews, Loyal C. Lathrop, Benj W. Clark, Rufus R. Stephens, and James C. Drake, elected in 1851.

County Clerks.—James S. Allen, Gates Hoit, Asa Wheeler, Gates Hoit, Asa Wheeler, and Ebenezer Brownson, successively by appointment. Asa Wheeler, elected 1822 8: Abel Wilson, 1828-31; Samuel S. Clark, 1831-4; Uriah D. Meeker, 1834-43; Lauriston Amsden, 1843-6; Henry S. Brewster, 1846-9; Samuel C. F. Thorndike, 1849-52.

County Treasurers.—Nathan Wood, Hiram Horton, appointed Dec. 5. 1810; Jacob Wead, June 12, 1821; Samuel C. Wead, April 24, 1843: S, S. Clark, Dec. 4, 1843. By election S. S. Wead, 1848; Wm. W. King, 1851.

First Judges.—Ebenezer Brownson, Feb. 21, 1809; Geo. F. Harrison, April 7, 1814; Joshua Nichols, Feb. 28, 1815; Albon Man, July 8, 1816; Hiram Horton, Nov. 10, 1820; E. Brownson, Jan. 31, 1823; Henry S. Waterman, April 18, 1823; B. Clark, March 19, 1825; W. Hogan, March 20, 1829; Roswell Bates, March 28, 1837; Henry B. Smith, February 24, 1843; Joseph R. Flanders, (elected) June 1847; John Hutton, (elected) November, 1851.

Assistant Justices.—Jesse Chipman, Solomon Wyman, February 21, 1809; Solomon Wyman, John Mazuzan, February 21, 1811; Amasa Fairman, February 26, 1812; Cone Andrus, Elisha Nichols, A. M. Hitchcock, Wareham Hastings, March 29, 1814; Seth Blanchard, James S. Allen, John H. Russell, March 13, 1817.

The following is a list of those who have been appointed judges, with the year of their appointment:

Cone Andrus, '17; Wm. Bailey, '08; Roswell Bates, '23; Seth Blanchard, '12; Ebenezer Brownson, '08; James Campbell, '17; Benjamin Clark, '23; Gideon Collins, '23; Silas Cushman, '09; Samuel Hard, '29; Geo. F. Harrison, '10; Wareham Hastings, '17; Wm. Hogan, '28; Hiram Horton, '14; Gates Hoit, '14; Moses Hoyt, '23; John B. Jackson, '22; Wm. King, '43; Sylvester Langdon, 34; Clark Lawrence, 31: Sidney Lawrence, 32; Albon Man, '10; Alric Man, '14; Joshua Nichols, '06; Jason Pierce, '24; Horatio Powell, '26; John H. Russell, '31; Elvin K. Smith, '43; Henry B. Smith, '33; Salmon Smith, '23; James B. Spencer, '14; Henry Stevens, '45: Henry B. Titus, 32; John Varnel, '29; Asa Wheeler, '08; Charles H. Wheeler, '22; Amherst K. Williams, '37.

Justices of Sessions.—(Elected) Elisha B. Smith, Frederick P. Allen, 1847; George W. Darling, Samuel Manning, 1849; Jonathan Wallace, Solon Parvin, 1850; Milton Heath, Elisha Hollister, 1851.

Surrogates.—Joshua Nichols, March 23, 1808; Albon Man, April 7, 1814; Ebenezer Brownson, July 8, 1816; James B. Spencer, July 8, 1828; Sydney Lawrence, May 16, 1837; Martin L. Parlin, March 31, 1843.

Since the adoption of the constitution of 1846, this office has been merged in that of the county judge. Joseph R. Flanders and John Hutton have accordingly acted in the capacity of surrogates since the adoption of the present constitution.

Coroners.—Ezekiel Payne, Oliver Brewster, 1808: Joseph Mason, Anthony Sprague, February, 1809; John Amsden, February 13, 1810; Noah Moody, Libius Fairman, February 26, 1812; John Wood, L. Fairman, March 30, 1813; L. Fairman, Abel Wilson, March 29, 1814; L.

Fairman, Leonard Conant, February 28, 1815; L. Fairman, L. Conant, March 16, 1816; N. Moody, March 27, 1816; John P. Andrus, July 8, 1816; N. Moody, John P. Andrus, March 13, 1817; N. Moody, Samuel Peck, June 16, 1818; N. Moody, S. Peck, L. Fairman, March 13, 1819; S. Peck, L. Fairman, February 12, 1820; S. Peck, S. Hyde, Warren Briggs, John Mitchell, C. M. Erwin, February 13, 1821; S. Peck, S. Hyde, W. Briggs, C. M. Erwin, Jeduthan Sherman, March 6, 1822.

Elected by the people under the late constitution:

Aretus M. Hitchcock, Samuel Hyde, Samuel B. Roberts, Luther Taylor, 1828; Asaph Watkins, Sidney Lawrence, Ezra Styles, Allen Lincoln, 1831; Leonard Conant, Lowell W. Gurnsey, George A. Cheeney, Timothy Beaman, 1834; Archibald Fisher, Leonard Conant, George A. Cheeney, Simeon Bellows, 1837; Luther Taylor, Timothy Beaman, Elisha Kellog, Milton Heath, Thomas S. Mears, 1840; Carlos C. Keeler, Lucius Plumb, Samuel H. Payne, Dorius Cox, 1843; Henry Mallon, Eli B. Smith, Reuben Cady, Samuel H. Payne, 1846; Samuel H. Payne (did not qualify in 1846), 1847; William Gillis, Thomas J. Looker, Jonathan Hoyt, Charles J. Rider, 1849; John R. Merrill, 1851.

Deputy Superintendents of Common Schools, for the county of Franklin, appointed by the board of supervisors:

Dana H. Stevens, of Moira (Mr. S. was a physician, and died in Moira about 1850), appointed November 12, 1841; Elos L. Winslow, appointed November, 1845; DeWitt C. Backus, appointed November, 1847, but the office was abolished before he entered upon its duties.

Congressional Districts.—In 1812, Franklin was, with Washington, Clinton and Essex, made the 12th district; in 1822, with Clinton, Essex and Warren, the 19th; in 1832, with St. Lawrence, the 14th; in 1842, with Warren, Clinton, and a part of Hamilton, the 15th; and in 1851, with Clinton and Essex, the 16th.

Superintendents of the Poor.—A. White, B. Roberts, S. Langdon, 1848.

Loan Commissioners.—Asa Wheeler, John Mazuzan, April 11, 1808; William Bailey, Amasa Fairman, February 13, 1810; John L. Fuller, March 30, 1813, in place of Fairman (declined); John H. Russell, 1814; Thomas Smith, Cone Andrus, February 5, 1820; John McCrea, February 25, 1822; James Campbell, Thomas Smith, February 7, 1824; Asa Wheeler, James Campbell, April 8, 1826; Oliver Westcott, James B. Spencer, February 20, 1829; Ebenezer R. Daggett, Orlando Furness, March 9, 1832; William King, in place of Furness (deceased), May 11, 1835; Aaron Beeman, in place of Daggett, February 13, 1840; Cephas Watson, in place of King, February 13, 1840; Hiram B. Miner, in place of Beeman, February 24, 1843; Ebenezer R. Daggett, in place of Watson, February 24, 1843; Ebenezer R. Daggett reappointed, March 19, 1845; Reuben Cady, in place of Miner, March 19, 1845; Thomas J. Looker, in place of Daggett, March 3, 1848; Samuel C. F. Thorndyke, in place of Cady, March 3, 1848.

At this period the old loan fund of 1808, was consolidated with the United States deposit fund.

Commissioners of U. S. Deposit Fund.—Orrin Lawrence, Goodrich Hazen, April 11, 1837; George B. R. Gove, in place of Lawrence, February 13, 1840; Joshua Dickinson, in place of Hazen, February 13, 1841; Hamlet B. Mears, in place of Gove, February 24, 1842; James Adams, in place of Dickinson, February 24, 1843; Martin R. Durkee, in place of Adams, March 9, 1845; John Roberts, 4th, in place of Durkee, March 3, 1848; Henry H. Hosford, March 3, 1848; Henry H. Hosford, March 19, 1850; John Roberts, 4th, March 19, 1850.

This county received $30,771·91 of the United States deposit fund.

Assemblymen from Franklin County.—By its act of incorporation, this county was attached to Clinton, forming one district, which was represented by the following persons: 1802, William Bailey; 1803-4, Peter Sailly; 1805, Benjamin Mooers; 1806, William Bailey; 1807, Nathaniel Platt; 1808, Elisha Arnold; 1809, Kinner Newcomb; 1810-11, Gates Hoit; 1812, no returns; 1813-14, Allen R. Moore; 1815, Robert Platt; 1816-17, Benjamin Mooers; 1818, Gates Hoit; 1819, Ebenezer Brownson; 1820-1, Platt Newcomb; 1822, Abijah North; 1823, William Hogan. In 1823, Franklin county was erected into a single assembly district, and has since so remained. 1824, George B. R. Gove; 1825-6, Asa Hascall; 1827, James Campbell; 1828-30, Luther Bradish; 1831-2, James B. Spencer; 1833-4, Jabez Parkhurst; 1835, Asa Hascall; 1836-8, Luther Bradish; 1839, Asa Hascall; 1840-1, John S. Eldridge; 1842, Thomas R. Powell; 1843, Joseph H. Jackson; 1844, Francis D. Flanders; 1845, Hiram Horton; 1846, Sidney Lawrence; 1847, Joseph R. Flanders; 1848, Elos L. Winslow; 1849, George B. R. Gove; 1850-1, Wm. A. Wheeler; 1852-3, Darius W. Lawrence.

CHAPTER VIII.

BIOGRAPHICAL NOTICES.

T is the most pleasing part of the historian's duties to record the names and services of those who have acted a leading part in the events which make up the annals of any period or of any country; and, in short, history may be considered but the record of the actions of leading men, as all popular movements and all the events of life are originated and guided by a few. In a work like the present, it is a delicate task to discriminate in the selection of subjects for notice, and numbers are necessarily omitted from the impossibility of obtaining data concerning them. We trust it will not be deemed invidious that a few living citizens are noticed in the following pages. We have been induced to this from a frequently expressed desire of numerous friends, and regret our inability to extend them to that of others, who through a long series of years, have been foremost in measures tending to the general welfare of the country, and the promotion of its internal improvement and prosperity.

RUSSELL ATTWATER was born June 20. 1762, at Cheshire, Ct., and was a son of Reuben Attwater, of English descent, and one of the committee of safety in New Haven county during the revolution. Mr. Attwater engaged in mercantile pursuits at Blanford, Mass., in early life, and while on business in New York in 1798, he was induced by McCormick, with whom he had dealings, to purchase parts of the present towns of Russell, Pierrepont, Hopkinton, &c., and to become an agent for McCormick, Harrison and others. An account of his labors has been given in our history of Russell, Norfolk and Brasher. In 1808 he was appointed an associate judge, and held the office many years. In the opening of the St. Lawrence turnpike, and the roads towards Lake George and Albany, he had the principal direction, and his energies were for many years devoted to the promotion of the various internal improvements of the country. In 1814 he was elected a senator, and in 1816 a presidential elector, and voted for Clinton. He died at the residence of his son, Phinneas Attwater, in Norfolk, in June, 1851.

THOMAS B. BENEDICT was a son of a clergyman, a native of Woodbury, Ct., where he was born October 23, 1783. When a young man, he came into De Kalb with judge Cooper, and engaged in mercantile pursuits. In 1812 he held a colonel's commission, and had principal charge of the military operations at Ogdensburgh in the summer of 1812. During the war he was promoted to a brigadier general. He was a man of much ability, and merited the confidence reposed in him, but military affairs impaired his relish for the quiet pursuits of peace, and presented temptations to which stronger men have yielded. He died at De Kalb, March 11, 1829.

JOHN BOYD was born in New York city, August 2, 1772, and settled in Hamilton in 1805. Being appointed sheriff, he removed to Ogdensburgh, and remained with an interval of two years, a citizen of that village till his death, July 17, 1833, after a long illness. He possessed much perseverance and energy, and was an active and useful member of society who deeply felt the loss occasioned by his death.

JAMES CAMPBELL. Few citizens of Franklin county have held more public offices or have seen more of the growth and progress of that country than Mr. Campbell. He was born in Rockingham, Vt., June 3, 1784, and in 1809 settled at French Mills, as a mechanic. In 1812 he was appointed inspector of customs, and during the summer of 1812, he acted as adjutant of the 66th regiment, then including the county, and assisttant U. S. store keeper, to receive the immense quantities of supplies ordered to the place during the sojourn of Wilkinson's army. From 1815 to 1818, he held the office of sheriff, and from 1818 to 1823, was one of the judges of the county. In 1820, as deputy marshall, he took the census of the county, and in 1827, was a member of assembly. In various military and civil capacities, as justice, presidential elector, and in numerous town and county offices, he has been equally useful.

DANIEL W. CHURCH, whom we have so often mentioned as a pioneer millwright, and to whom we are indebted for many facts relating to the  origin of the several towns, was born May 10, 1772, in Brattleboro, Vt., and moved into the county in 1801, and for many years was actively engaged in erecting the first mills in various parts of this county and Franklin. In the hardships and labors necessarily involved in these pursuits, there was constantly afforded an opportunity for the exercise of that presence of mind and self reliance which rendered him particularly useful to the country, and during the military operations at Ogdensburgh, which terminated with its capture in February, 1813, be was particularly active. He is living at an advanced age, with a son in Morristown.

THOMAS J. DAVIES, a native of Washington, Conn., came into the county in 1800, at the age of 33, selected a farm on Black lake, eight miles from Ogdensburgh, commenced improvements and in the following winter brought in his family by way of Vermont and Canada, and from an early period, took a leading part in political and public affairs, being the first acting sheriff of the county, which office he held for many years. He also for some time, held the office of county judge. He died on his farm at Black lake, April 18, 1845. Judge Davies, with only an ordinary education, possessed a business talent which joined with much energy of character, rendered him valuable as a public officer, and prosperous in his private affairs. He acted with the democratic party. His son, Charles Davies, has attained distinction as a mathematician, and for many years held a professorship in the military academy at West Point.

John Fine was born in New York, August 26, 1794, and was prepared for college by Andrew Smith, a Scotchman, a well known and severe teacher. He entered Columbia college in 1805, and graduated in 1809, at the age of 15, receiving the second honor, the English salutatory. Among his college classmates were bishops B. T. Onderdonk and J. Kemper, Rev. Dr. W. E. Wyatt, Rev. C. R. Duffee and J. Brady; Drs. J. W. Francis and E. N. Bibby, and the Hon. Murray Hoffman. Mr. Fine studied law four years with P. W. Radcliff, one year with G. W. Strong, and attended a course of law lectures of one year under judges Reeve and Gould, at Litchfield, Conn. He removed to St. Lawrence county in 1815, and formed a law partnership with Louis Hasbrouck, which continued until the death of the latter in 1834. In 1824 he was appointed first judge of the county, and was continued in this office by reappointment till March, 1839. In the fall of 1838, he was elected to congress, and in the latter of the two years was on the committee on foreign affairs. In 1844 he was reappointed first judge, and held that office until the adoption of the new constitution in 1847. During his service of over eighteen years on the bench, three only of his decisions were reversed. In 1848 he was elected to the state senate, and served one term, during which period he introduced and aided in carrying into a law, the bill to punish criminally the seduction of females, and also the bill to protect the property of married women. The latter has made a great change in the common law, and raises the female sex from a menial and dependant condition, as regards the control of their property, to an equality with man. The refinements of civilized society, and the spirit of the Christian religion, justify the law which has been incorporated into our code, and from the favor with which it has been received by the public, there is a probability it will never be repealed. Judge Fine received the degree of Master of Arts from Columbia college, in 1812, and that of Doctor of Laws, from Hamilton college, in 1850. In 1847 and 1849, he was nominated for judge of the supreme court, but on each occasion was unsuccessful, the venerable Daniel Cady, of Johnstown, being elected. From 1821 to 1833, he held the office of county treasurer, and upon resigning, the board of supervisors passed resolutions expressive of their confidence in his integrity and ability.* In 1852 he published a volume of lectures on law, for the use of his sons, of which Judge Cady has said: "I do not believe there is another work in the English language which contains so much legal information in so few words; all I read and hear of the lectures, strengthens my conviction that they should be in the hands of every student who wishes to acquire in the shortest time, a knowledge of the laws of his country." The high station and distinguished attainments of the one by whom this opinion was given, confer great value upon it. In the various benevolent movements of the day, and especially in the founding and support of the County Bible society, Judge Fine has been foremost, and he will long be regarded as the efficient supporter of this and other benevolent societies; as a distinguished lawyer, an able jurist, and as one who in every respect has adorned and elevated the society in which he has lived.

Stillman Foote, the first permanent settler of Canton, was born in

* "Resolved, That the board regrets that Mr. Fine finds the duties of the office incompatible with his other business, and that in accepting his resignation they have been governed by a desire to comply with his request.
Resolved, That this board have the fullest confidence in the able manner in which he has discharged his official duties, which have been highly satisfactory to the board of supervisor and to the public."

Yours Faithfully,
John Fine

Simsbury, Ct., Sept. 10, 1783, and was the son of Daniel Foote, who was one of the first settlers of Middlebury, Vt., where he erected the first mills. In 1840, at the age of 80, he divided his property among his children, and with that fondness for the life of a pioneer, characteristic with the family, he accompanied his son in 1801 to Canton, where he died. S. Foote was the first magistrate appointed in town, and for many years took a prominent part in public affairs. He died in 1834. George Foote, his brother, was born in 1749, and in the revolution was taken prisoner, but escaped. At an early day he settled in Canton, where he died May 12, 1830.

DAVID FORD, the pioneer of Morristown, was a native of New Jersey, and followed Judge Ford, his brother, to the county, in 1804. In early life he was a zealous politician, of the federal school, and in 1794, participated in the military expedition called out to suppress the whiskey riots of Western Pennsylvania. In this affair he held a major's commission in a troop of horse. He died at Ogdensburgh, Nov. 6, 1835, at the age of 75.

NATHAN FORD, was born at Morristown, N. J., Dec. 8, 1763, and having at an early age lost both parents, he spent his childhood with his paternal grand-father, Jacob Ford, and remained after the death of the latter in 1777, with the family, receiving but a common education. In 1779-80, he, though a youth of but 17, solicited a service in the continental armies, and obtained and faithfully discharged the duties of assistant deputy quarter master general during the memorable winter of suffering in which the American army lay encamped on the hills back of Morristown. While still a young man, he obtained the confidence of several of the parties, who had, many of them, been officers in the revolution, and who had become interested in the land speculations of Northern New York, and was sent by them in 1794 and 1795 to explore the northern part of the state where they had made their purchases, and also to examine and report upon several of the islands near Kingston, which they were proposing to purchase upon speculation.

We have given some of the details of his settlement at Oswegatchie, from which it will be learned that he was a man of indomitable energy and force of character, which proved adequate to the trying emergencies which surrounded him, and which would have discouraged common men from proceeding. The Oswegatchie Indians often proved annoying, especially when stimulated by ardent spirits, and on one occasion a number of them in the night time, entered the old stone garrison which he inhabited, seized Dick his negro slave, and was about to put him into the fire which was burning in the room, but the cries of the frightened negro aroused Mr. Ford, who seized his sword, and without waiting to dress, he rushed into the room, and succeeded with the help he assembled, in driving out the intruders. This affair probably occurred in a drunken row, for after the Indians had been driven from the house they began to quarrel among themselves, and one Battise, said to be a chief of the tribe, got stripped and beaten till he was nearly dead. During the night he knocked at the door of Mr. Lyon for admission, and was allowed to enter and spend the night on the floor. In the morning as he arose to depart, he stooped down to the hearth, blackened both hands with coal, and rubbing them over his face, he with a whoop and a bound, sallied forth to avenge the injuries he had received on the previous night. These Indians were peculiarly addicted to intemperance, having for many years resided near a post where liquors were easily procured, and in consequence frequent quarrels arose among them, and the night was often made hideous by their bacchanalian riots and yelling. Two or three of their number got killed at these revels in 1796 and 7.

Early in 1803, a dispute concerning timber on Ogden's island, alluded to on p. 343, had reached such a pitch that life was threatened, and the affair necessarily came under the notice of Judge Ford, who wrote to Governor Clinton as follows: "Upon my arrival here, I availed myself of the first safe opportunity to forward the letter (your excellency did me the honor to commit to my care), to the chiefs of the St. Regis village. Upon inquiry, I found they had carried a very high hand respecting the island business, and absolutely went so far as to threaten the taking of scalps. This threat was made by Gray, and was previous to Judge Edsall's sending the express forward. Upon my being informed of this outrageous conduct, I wrote Gray a letter upon the subject, and wished to know how he durst throw out such threats against the citizens of this state; and told him it was absolutely necessary for him to come forward and make such concessions as conduct like this required; that harmony and good understanding the citizens of this country were willing to cultivate, but threats like this they would be far from submitting to, and the sooner he gave satisfactory explanations upon the subject, the sooner harmony would be restored. Had he resided in the county or state, as a magistrate, I should have pursued a different method with him. Col. Lewis, who was on his way home from Oneida, (and who had not seen your excellensy's letter to the chiefs, or mine to Gray), called upon me. I explained to him the subject of your excellency's letter, and also mine to Gray. I told him it was a matter of astonishment, that he and Gray should have to act in such open defiance of the laws of the state as they had done respecting the sale of the timber upon the island; had it been by common Indians, some little apology might have been made for them, but for him and Grey, there certainly could be none, because they knew better, and they as certainly could have no doubt resting upon their minds as to the islands being comprehended in the sale of those lands to the state; and as an evidence that at the time of the treaty, he and Gray applied to your excellency, to know if the islands would not be taken possession of before the corn which was then upon them would be fit to gather. This was too strong a circumstance to admit of a quibble, and too well grounded in their recollection to be denied. He attempted a weak apology, and concluded by saying, he hoped good understanding would not be broken up, and that similar conduct would not take place. I then stated to him Gray's threats, and the necessity there was of his coming forward and making satisfactory acknowledgements which should be made as public as his threats had been. This he assured me he should do, and accordingly Gray came up, and after making the fullest recantation, declared he never meant or intended harm to any of the citzens of this state, and that he must have been in liquor when so unguarded an expression escaped him, and hoped the thing might be overlooked. I then talked with him upon the subject of the island. He did not pretend but that the islands were contained in the sales to the state, but attempted to apologize by impressing the idea of a grant made to the St. Regis people of that particular island, by the Oswegatchie Indians. I found no difficulty to confound him in this specious pretext, for it has been his and Lewis's uniform declaration to me, that the Oswegatchie Indians never had any claim whatever, to lands in this part of the state, consequently they could not grant an island in the river. In consequence of his excellency's letter, the business of the island I hope is happily concluded, and I hope a similar oc-

Engraved by [...]

believe me yours

A. Ford

casion will not present itself. I consider it proper to give your excellency the earliest information upon this subject, and it was but yesterday that Gray came forward."

Mr. Ford was appointed first Judge, which office he held for many years, and in this capacity he ever evinced that promptness and decision, joined with sound judgement, that rendered him peculiarly valuable to the public, and a terror to evil doers. In politics he was federal, and although he denounced the policy of the war, his course was such as to secure the confidence of the officers stationed at Ogdensburgh, and he was particularly useful in disuading from predatory incursions for plundering, which led only to retaliations. For several years previous to his death, which occurred in April, 1829, his constitution had been yielding to the insidious approaches of consumption, but the vigor of his mind remained unimpaired, and he continued to feel a deep interest in public affairs, after his strength had denied him the power of taking part in them. He had *seen* and *felt* the first feeble beginnings of a colony which had grown up to a populous and thriving town, and the howling wilderness traversed only by savages and wild beasts, transformed into cultivated fields and inhabited by an intelligent and prosperous people. With the progress of a third of a century before him, he looked forward into coming years, and with the prophetic faith natural to his employment, realized in his mental vision the change which a century would work in the condition of the country around him. Some time before his death, a friend conversing on this subject, asked him if, in his dreams, the future aspect of the town ever presented itself. The idea instantly struck him, and with an energy beyond his strength, and an eye kindling with enthusiasm he replied, *"Dream?* I *see* it! A rich and populous *city!* A wide extent of country covered with houses; a harbor crowded with the fleet of the lakes!" He then went on and in glowing language, portrayed the coming greatness and opulence which natural advantages were destined to confer upon the town. From the earliest period, Mr. Ford had taken the strongest interest in the welfare of the Presbyterian church in the village, and the day before his death, he had a conversation with some of the officers of the society, in which he said, " You know the deep interest I have always taken in the society, and how ardently I feel at the close of life for its welfare. I enjoin it upon you all to cultivate peace among each other, and let no jealousies or dissentions creep in among you. Let every one of you try to excell the rest in giving up their own individual wishes for the good of the whole. I am drawing near the close of life, I look forward to the salvation purchased by Christ, as abundantly sufficient to save all who will put their trust in him."

In person, Mr. Ford was thin and slender, and his features are well represented in the portrait given; his eye possessed unusual brilliancy, and when excited by any topic that engaged his whole soul, it sparkled with enthusiasm and feeling. In his manners he was courteous and graceful, and his hospitality was of that elegant kind which while it made its recipients at ease, gave them a sense of *welcome*, and a *home feeling*, so eminently pleasing to the guests. He was interred in the family vault, in the western part of the village, which is neatly enclosed in a wall, and the grounds within are suitably adorned with shrubbery.

ASA HASCALL, a native of Vermont, removed from Essex county where he had acquired the legal profession, and settled at Malone, in 1815. In 1818, he was elected supervisor of Malone which office he held till 1838. From 1840 to 1843, he held the same office. He was for many years a justice of the peace and district attorney for Franklin county. He also repeatedly represented his district in assembly. He died in Malone, January 5, 1852, at the age of 66, having for several years been disabled by a paralytic stroke. In his private and public life, he was a true specimen of the noblest work of God. In every station which he held he always acquitted himself like a man. The members of the bar in the county, were accustomed to look to him with a feeling bordering upon reverence, as a pattern of integrity and worth in their profession, whom they might safely imitate. As a citizen, as a lawyer, and above all, as a CHRISTIAN, his influence was great and unbounded, and employed to a good account."

LOUIS HASBROUCK, was the fifth in descent from a family of French Huguenots, who fled from France to Holland, and thence to New York, and settled on the Hudson, in the present town of New Paltz, Ulster county. He was born at New Paltz, on the banks of the Wallkill, April 22, 1777, and received his collegiate education at Nassau Hall, in Princeton, at which he graduated Sept. 25, 1797, and studied law in New York, under Josiah Ogden Hoffman and Cadwallader Colden. In August, 1801, he was admitted at Albany to practice in the supreme court, and in September following, to the Ulster court of common pleas. While at Albany, at the time of his admission to the supreme court, he met with Judge Ford, and was persuaded to come to Ogdensburgh to settle, and through the same influence he received an appointment as clerk of the county, March 10, 1802. In June he arrived at Ogdensburgh, and officiated at the first court held in the old garrison in that month. He came by horseback, with others, through the Mohawk and Black river countries. He returned in October, and continued for two years to spend his winters below, and his summers in Ogdensburgh. In May, 1804, he started with the view of making a permanent residence, accompanied by his wife, brother, a lady cousin, and a female slave, and proceeded up the Mohawk valley and the Black river settlements, in a wagon, as far as Coffin's tavern, in West Carthage. It being impossible to proceed further by wagon, he hired another horse of a Frenchman called Battise, and proceeded on from thence with three horses to the five travelers. One of the horses was used as a pack horse, and across it were laid two bags containing provision and clothing. Their outfit for a march of several days through a wilderness, with no guide but a line of marked trees, and only casual opportunities of procuring supplies from the huts of scattered settlers, consisted of some dried beef, a few lemons for making lemonade, hard crackers, and a little tea and sugar. For milk, bread, and other provisions, they trusted to the supplies they might procure along the road of inhabitants, or kill in the forest with their fire arms. Mr. Joseph Hasbrouck led the way, and the others followed in Indian file, adopting at times the practice of riding and tying, and at others mounting double. The route led through Wilna, Antwerp, and somewhere near the line of the Old State road, to the Oswegatchie, at the present village of Heuvelton, where they crossed the river in a scow. Their first night was spent at Lewis's, their second at Lee's (now Mordecai Cook's, in Antwerp), their third at Bristol's (De Peyster's), and their fourth at the old garrison in Ogdensburgh. The Hasbrouck mansion was erected the year previous, and finished in 1804. Mr. H. moved for a few weeks into Judge Ford's building, at the garrison. Mr. Hasbrouck arrived in the infancy of its settlement, and commenced the practice of law in that village, which he continued till his death. He held the office of county clerk until 1817. During a period of thirty-two years, in which he saw the progressive and rapid rise of the county, from a wilderness to a populous and prosperous district, he was intimately concerned with its business and its interests, and was extensively known to its citizens, by all classes of whom he was highly esteemed for the many excellent qualities he possessed. With the purest rectitude of principle in all his conduct, he united a kindness and benevolence of disposition, that made him alike respected and beloved by all. Modest and unpretending in his manners, he sought not public distinction, and preferred the walks of private life, from which he could not be prevailed to withdraw, until at the fall election of 1832, he reluctantly consented to allow his political friends to nominate him for the office of senator of this state. To this office he was elected, and continued until his decease, which resulted from the hydrothorax on the 20th of Aug., 1834. The members of the bar of the county of St. Lawrence, resident in Ogdensburgh, convened the day after, and testified their respect for the amiable character of the deceased by passing a series of resolutions highly expressive of their esteem for his merits, and sorrow at his death; and followed in a body to his last resting place, the remains of the citizen whose memory it was their privilege to honor. The trustees of the village also called a meeting of the inhabitants to consider the proper measures to be taken for paying suitable respect to his memory. The meeting thus assembled, adopted measures for testifying their sorrow and expressing their sympathy with the family of the deceased.

ROSWELL HOPKINS, was born in Amenia, Dutchess county, in May, 1757. At an early age he embarked in the arduous struggle of the revolution, and was engaged in the battle of Bennington, and also at the capture of Burgoyne, near Stillwater. He afterwards served two campaigns as a volunteer at West Point, and its vicinity. His campaign at this latter place, was terminated, however, by his being taken a prisoner, when he was put on board one of the British prison ships, and eventually landed at Newport, Rhode Island, where he was incarcerated with others for a considerable period, and for four days immediately subsequent to landing, without taking a morsel of food. He was released from this place on parole, about the close of the war. He settled in Arlington, in Vermont, where he resided till after he was appointed secretary of state, when he removed to Bennington, then the seat of the state government. Besides the office of secretary of state, (to which he was reëlected annually, by the general assembly, for ten years or more in succession, till he gave in his resignation), he held various other responsible state offices, and was once appointed elector of president and vice president of the United States. At the period of the early settlement of this region, Judge Hopkins purchased a large tract of land, including the township of Hopkinton, in this county, and removed his family from Vermont to his late residence. During all the hardships and privations incident to the settlement of a new country, a wide field is necessarily opened for the exercise of all those charities and acts of soothing kindness which have distinguished the conduct of some of the proprietors of this county. The course of Judge Hopkins with respect to the settlers of his land, to whom he stood in the relation of a father, was strongly marked by that unbounded generosity and munificence, which formed so prominent a feature in his character. Soon after the organisation of the county, he was appointed a judge of the court of common pleas, the duties of which station he discharged with his usual ability, for several years. He was elected to a seat in the legislature of this state, four years successively, from 1810 to 1813. For some years before his death he took no part in public affairs, but continued to enjoy the confidence and esteem of all who knew him. He died at the age of 73, Sept. 5, 1829, in Chazy, from injury sustained by being thrown from a wagon, and his remains were brought back and interred in Hopkinton.

HIRAM HORTON. Few persons held a more conspicuous place in public life among the pioneers of Franklin county than Judge Horton. He was a native of Springfield, Mass., and his ancestors were among the first settlers of that place. In his youth he failed to enjoy the advantages of an education, and was never able to attend a district school but six weeks in his life, but feeling the importance of this element, so necessary for the performance of the active duties of life, he set himself about the task of self-education, and at the age of twenty, had fitted himself to become the teacher of a district school, and was employed as an assistant by the secretary of state in Vermont. At about this time he removed to Brandon, Vt., where he purchased a commodious farm on Otter creek, and now in part occupied by the village of Brandon, and by a diligent and successful course of industry, acquired a considerable amount of property. In 1808, he removed to Malone, where he purchased the mill privileges on both sides of Salmon river, and erected the first mills worthy of the name. He subsequently filled the offices of supervisor, county treasurer, judge, and first judge, and was for many years an agent for Pierrepont and Ellice, in the sale and settlement of their lands. His death occurred Oct. 5, 1824, at Malone, at the age of 64. During the war he was a federalist, but sustained the measures of government in prosecuting that measure, and towards the close of his life his political preferences were in favor of Clinton.

DAVID C. JUDSON, came into the county of St. Lawrence in the spring of 1808, his father's family having settled on Black lake, in Oswegatchie, two years previously, from Washington, Ct. It being the period of the embargo, Mr. J. engaged in no permanent business, until 1811, when on the appointment of the late Thomas J. Davies, to the office of sheriff, he in connection with his friend Mr. York, undertook to do all the active duties of the office throughout the county, the former taking all east of the east line of Lisbon and Canton, and the latter the remainder.

He accordingly located at Hamilton, in Madrid, and this arrangement continued during the official term of Mr. Davies, and of Mr. York, his successor. In 1818, he was appointed sheriff, and assuming the active duties of the western half, and thus became thoroughly conversant with the entire county, and a witness of its early and feeble beginnings, which was of eminent service to him in subsequent life. In the division of the democratic party, during the era of good feeling in national politics, in relation to Mr. Clinton and his policy, Mr. J. adhering to Mr. C. was removed from the office of sheriff, on the triumph of the Bucktail party, in 1821.

He was immediately after nominated and elected to the senate from the eastern district. The constitution of 1821, coming into operation in 1822, by which all legislative and judicial offices were vacated, he declined renomination, and was principally instrumental in securing the nomination of Silas Wright, Jr., who was elected, and then first occupied the field in which he became so eminent. In the selection of a new suite for the public buildings, Mr. Judson from his intimate knowledge of the county, gave his influence for a change, believing that the public wants required it, and his identification with this measure contributed to his election to the assembly in 1818, the county having be-

Yours truly,
D. C. Hudson

fore been decidedly federal. The measure was brought forward this session, but defeated, principally through the influence of the late George Parish. In 1826 it was again brought forward, aided by Mr. Wright, in the senate, and Mr. Judson, notwithstanding his interests, and residence at Ogdensburgh, gave his influence for it. It was at last successful, having been made the issue of the election of 1827, and he was one of the building committee appointed to superintend the erection of the new buildings, which were completed in time for the fall term of 1829, at a cost of less than $7000.

From 1829 till 1840, he was one of the judges of the county court. In the fall of 1829, he was chosen cashier of the Ogdensburgh Bank, and remained till 1840, when he resigned, and in the fall of that year was appointed collector of the district of Oswegatchie, by Van Buren, and held this station under the different presidents, until 1849, since which he has enjoyed "the post of honor—a private station." It is seldom that an individual is found, who for nearly half a century, has been so extensively and so intimately concerned in public affairs, and it is but justice to add, that his worth is appreciated as extensively as his name is known, and in most of the public improvements of the county in general, and of Ogdensburgh and vicinity in particular, we witness some of the beneficial results of his influence.

Dr. ROBERT McCHESNEY, a native of Troy, studied his profession with Dr. Joseph White, of Cherry Valley, and David Little, of Springfield, N. Y., and in 1810, removed to Madrid, and in the year following to Potsdam. He there engaged in the practice of his profession with increasing reputation and success, until his death in May 1824, at the age of 36. He was a man of sound judgment and fine abilities, and enjoyed to a high degree the confidence of the public.

DAVID A. OGDEN, with his father Abraham Ogden, and his brother Thomas L. Ogden, all of whom then resided in Newark, New Jersey, purchased of William Constable in 1796, the town of Madrid. After the decease of their father the two brothers became the owners of this property, one third of which they sold in 1803, to Joshua Waddington, of New York. David A. Ogden, was the eldest of a family of twelve children. His father Abraham Ogden, was a native of New Jersey, where he spent the greater part of his life, and his ancestors were among the earliest settlers of that state. He resided in Morristown, during the time when the American army lay in winter quarters there, and his house was occupied by General Washington, as his quarters, during his sojourn there. Mr. Abraham Ogden, followed the profession of his father, that of a lawyer. Upon the organization of the general government, he received the unsolicited appointment of district attorney for the state of New Jersey, which office he held until his death, in 1798. Besides the purchase of Madrid as above stated, Mr. A. Ogden, in company with Mr. Hoffman, his brother-in-law, purchased a tract in Hague and Cambray, since called the Ogden and Hoffman tract. He was a brother of Samuel Ogden, the early owner of Oswegatchie, and the person from whom the present village of Ogdensburgh derived its name. D. A. Ogden, studied law in his father's office, and at about the period of the death of the latter, he removed to New York, and in company with his brother T. L. Ogden, commenced the practice of his profession, where they formed a business connection with Alexander Hamilton, which gave them a prominence in their profession, and terminated with the memorable duel between Hamilton and Aaron Burr, which cast a gloom of sorrow over the nation. Mr. Ogden continued the practice of his profession in New York until 1812, when he retired from that pursuit, to carry into execution a plan which he had for some years cherished, to remove to the St. Lawrence, and fix his permanent residence on its beautiful shores. In pursuance of this, he built a fine and substantial dwelling on the island opposite the village of Waddington and commenced its improvement as a farm, which comprises nearly eight hundred acres. He was at this time in the prime of life, and carried with him those tastes for rural employments, which he had imbibed in early life, which with his favorite literary pursuits, were well calculated to render his residence agreeable, not only to himself, but to those who might associate with him. He early turned his attention to improving the natural advantages of his location, not only as an agricultural but as a commercial and manufacturing district.

A feeling of brotherhood, and community of interest, was engendered by the difficulties encountered by the pioneer settlers, and many early emigrants speak with gratitude of the sympathy and assistance they received from him in time of need. He was once elected to congress, and for eight years held the office of first judge of the county court, when on account of declining health, he retired from the bench. At the announcement of his intention to do this, the grand jury then in session, passed a resolution expressive of their regard, and containing settlements highly complimentary to his character as a citizen and as a judge. With these exceptions he held no public offices. His death occured at Montreal, June 9, 1829, at the age of sixty. His remains were brought back to Waddington and interred. The St. Lawrence county bar, upon the news of his death being received, met and passed a series of resolutions highly expressive of their sense of the loss which they had to sustain in his death.

DAVID PARISH, was the second son of John Parish, an English gentleman, a resident of Hamburgh, who was the first to hold the office of United States Consul at that place. The subject of this notice was one of five brothers, whose names were John, David, Richard, Charles and George. The first is still living in Bohemia, and has attained much distinction as an astronomer, which science he has pursued as an amateur, and a number of important discoveries have been made by him at his private observatory. He is the proprietor of a large crown estate, and to which a great number of serfs belong; and he hears the title of Baron Seuftenberg. Charles Parish, and Richard Parish, the latter the father of George Parish, Esq., of Ogdensburgh, still reside at Hamburgh, in Germany. Mr. David Parish was educated as a banker, which pursuit was the business of his father; and the financial operations in which they were engaged, were on a most extensive scale. About the year 1808, there was an enterprise undertaken by some of the principal merchants and capitalists of Europe, in which they entered into an agreement with the French government, then in the hands of Bonaparte, to transfer a large amount of credits to Europe from the Spanish colonies in Mexico. The wars between France and England, and the restrictions upon commerce, which then existed, rendered the navigation of the Atlantic with valuable cargoes, extremely perilous, from their liability to capture by British cruisers, which swarmed in every sea where an opportunity existed for annoying the commerce of France. The only practicable way of transferring to Europe an equivalent for the specie which had been intercepted by blockade in the ports of the Spanish colonies, was to procure its shipment to maritime cities in the United States, where it could be invested in colonial produce, and shipped to

Gavit & Co. Albany

neutral ports in Europe, under the American flag, which in certain cases was allowed, by the arrogant British government, to pursue a commerce with Europe. The causes were then being developed which soon ripened into an open war between the United States and Great Britain, which principally grew out of the arbitrary assumptions of the latter government. The principal commercial house engaged in the enterprise above mentioned, was that of Hope &. Co., of Amsterdam, and Mr. David Parish was employed to visit the United States, to carry into effect the arrangements which had been made for the accomplishment of this object. Vessels built with express reference to speed, and manned by picked crews and experienced pilots, were employed to enter the blockaded ports whenever circumstances warranted, and convey the funds to such American ports as they might be able to enter. On several occasions very narrow escapes from capture occurred on these voyages, which were generally remarkably successful, and proved very lucrative to the projectors. While engaged in carrying these measures into effect, Mr. Parish resided in Philadelphia, and his business brought him in frequent contact with the financial men of that place, among whom were Robert Morris, Gouverneur Morris, the Ogden families and Le Ray de Chaumont. Among the more prominent of the subjects which engaged these gentlemen at that time, was the purchase and settlement of lands in the state of New York, and this subject being kept prominently before him, he was induced to listen to overtures from them on the subject of purchases. From the peculiar organization of European society, the ownership of large landed estates confers importance upon the possessor, and places him on a level far superior to that of the owner of a similar amount of capital invested in manufacturing or commercial pursuits; and this is coveted as the most desirable species of wealth, as well from its permanence and freedom from loss by accident or fraud, as from the certain revenues which it produces, and the importance in social life which it confers.

The gentlemen above mentioned were at that time engaged in settling their lands in the northern part of the state, and Mr. Parish, with the view of learning the value of the tracts offered him, sent Mr. Joseph Rosseel, then a young man, who had escaped from the military conscriptions of his native country, to explore the country, and make to him a report of its value. The result was the purchase of extensive tracts in Rossie, Antwerp, Hopkinton, Parishville, &c., and the village of Ogdensburgh, excepting parts previously sold. In September, 1814, the township of Hammond, and at various times, other tracts have been added to these purchases. Soon after acquiring an interest in these lands, Mr. Parish commenced the task of their improvement and settlement with much energy, and possessing resources which enabled him to undertake that which men of limited means would not have been able to accomplish. In 1810, he erected the large stone store on Water street, and his dwelling in Ogdensburgh, and in 1813, commenced the construction of a blast furnace at Rossie. The settlement of Parishville, and the opening of lines of communication between different sections of the county, and to the markets; the erection of mills, and opening of mines of iron ore, were among the enterprises in which he engaged, and which gave life and spirit to the settlements which he projected, and employment for the industry of those who had no other means to meet the payments due on their purchases, than the labor of their hands. The war checked the prosperity of Ogdensburgh, but scarcely affected the back settlements of Parishville and Rossie, which rather increased in proportion as

36

the front diminished in population, from the accessions which they received from the timid, and those thrown out of employment by the war.

While the war was pending, and in anticipation of the event, the government negotiated a loan of $16,000,000, and Stephen Girard and David Parish became parties to the loan of $7,000,000 of this sum. With occasional interruptions, Mr. Parish continued to be engaged in the improvement of his estates in St. Lawrence and Jefferson counties, until the year 1816, when he returned to Europe. Not long after this, he was induced, through the influence of Count Metternich, the celebrated Austrian minister, to engage in a partnership with the commercial house of Fries & Co., of Vienna, with the expectation that they should have a share of the patronage of the Austrian government in its financial operations. The parties with whom he became associated, sustained the style of living and equipage which can be afforded only by princes with imperial revenues, and although their dwellings contained galleries of paintings, and elaborate treasures of the fine arts, and they displayed all the dazzling parade of wealth, the real condition of the firm was most corrupt, and its affairs were fast tending to irretrievable bankruptcy. This fact Mr. Parish did not, unfortunately, discover, until it was too late to recede, and he found himself involved in the ruin which shortly overtook them.

A large portion of his European estates were sacrificed to satisfy the claims of the creditors of the house with which he was involved. The business in America, which had for some time previous been managed by David and George Parish, was soon after assumed by the latter. Mr. David Parish will long be gratefully remembered, by the citizen of St. Lawrence county, as their early benefactor, and is never mentioned by those who enjoyed an acquaintance with him, without a warm expression of esteem and respect. His wealth enabled him to extend those offices of kindness and support to those who needed, which with many would exist in intention only: the deserving poor found in him a benefactor; the man of enterprise and industry, a patron; the gentleman of cultivated mind, and enlightened views, a companion, who could appreciate and enjoy his society; and every member of the community in which he lived felt towards him a sentiment of respect and regard, which was as universal as it was deserved.

The portrait which we give, was engraved after a miniature, painted on ivory, by Spornberg, at Cheltenham, in England, in 1810, and is said by those who knew him, to be a correct resemblance. Mr. Parish was, by a special act of the legislature, passed in November, 1808, empowered to hold and convey real estate, but this act did not confer upon him the full right of citizenship.

GEORGE PARISH, was a younger brother of David Parish, who received a finished commercial education in Europe, and came to Ogdensburgh to reside, in 1816. He had previously held the office of collector in the East Indies, and was a gentleman of great intelligence, polished manners, and a capacity for the transaction of business which is seldom surpassed. He continued the improvements which his brother had commenced, and was among the first of our land proprietors who adopted towards settlers the equitable and accommodating system of receiving payments in kind, of whatever surplus grain, stock or labor he might have in exchange for land. The greater portion of the northern part of the state was purchased and held by capitalists, who bought upon speculation, and sold their lands through agents who received money only for their lands. The proprietors residing in the cities felt no personal interest in the affairs of their settlements, further than to realize as large a profit as possible, and expended money for roads and improvements only so far as it tended to enhance the value of their property and make it more saleable. The moneys received were usually remitted to the owners, and the country not benefited by its expenditure; and this system very naturally gave rise to a feeling of ill will towards the proprietor, which was evinced in various ways.

To this may be traced the causes of these abuses of power in voting for taxes, of which our past history affords many examples, and which, in some instances in Franklin county, grew into a studenduous system of fraud and crime, which required the action of the legislature to suppress, by withdrawing the power which had been exceeded.

The privations of a poineer settler, who has to contend against the rugged wildness of nature, in addition to poverty, want of access to markets, and the numerous casualties which befall those who advance beyond the precincts of civilization, and lay the foundation of what it is his ambition to make a *home*, and a *freehold*, are of such a nature that it requires persevering industry and rigid economy on the one side, and forbearance, liberal accommodation and easy terms on the other, in order that the purchaser and the landlord may each derive the greatest benefit, and the settlement prosper to their mutual advantage. During his residence in the county, he acquired the general respect of the inhabitants, by his courtesy and kindness. With the graces and urbanity derived from his early education and former associations, and a true sense of the requirements which genuine politeness, unattended with ostentation, or aristocratic airs, dictate, he assumed no position in the society of those around him which was calculated to convey a feeling of superiority. During his administration of the estates of the family in this country, he spent several years in traveling in the north and east of Europe. In the course of these journeys, he traversed Norway and Sweden, visited St. Petersburgh, Moscow, Astrachan and many other cities in the east of Europe, and was preparing to undertake an extensive tour over Asia, when he died suddenly at Paris, France, on the 22d of April, 1839, at the age of 58.

Dr. HORATIO POWELL, a native of Hartford, Vt., removed to Malone, and engaged in the practice of medicine, in 1811. From that period till within a few years before his death, he continued in the practice of that laborious profession, and acquired to a great degree the confidence and patronage of the citizens of Franklin county. For several of the latter years of his life, he was disabled by a paralytic affection. He died at Malone, November 12, 1849.

BENJAMIN RAYMOND, a son of Paul Raymond, was born at Richmond, Mass., October 19, 1774. In his youth he received such advantages as his native town afforded, and while a young man removed to Rome, and became acquainted with Mr. B. Wright, which led to a friendship that endured for life. In this way he became connected with the surveys of northern New York, of which we have given an account. While traversing the country, the several parties would occasionally meet, and spend the night together, exchanging the news which they might chance to pick up, compare notes, and speculate on the probable destiny which the future held in store for the country which they were exploring. On one occasion, Mr. Raymond, in a letter to Wright, distinctly expressed his belief, *that the navigable waters of the St. Lawrence would at a future day be united with those of lake Champlain, so as to afford a channel of communication between them;* and this germ of an idea of a canal be never lost sight of, but often and repeatedly urged it upon the public notice, and lived to see a concerted and general movement towards its realization, nor was the project wholly abandoned, until it gave place to a scheme for a rail road, which has but recently been completed.

Having traveled through St. Lawrence county in various directions as a surveyor, and observed the character of the soil and surface, he procured, on his return, from the proprietors of Potsdam, an agency for the sale and settlement of that town; and in this he was aided by the influence and recommendation of his friend Wright. In May, 1803, he started for his location from Rome, in a bateau, laden with iron for a mill, provisions for the season, and several men, and proceeded by the slow and difficult water route to Point Iroquois, above the present village of Waddington, where he hired teams, and opened a road sufficient to allow the passage of wagons to a point on Raquette river, about half a mile below the present site of Potsdam village. Here he built a raft, and floated up his effects to the falls, where he landed on the west side of the river, opened a land office in a bark shanty, and commenced the erection of mills. During the first year, he got in operation a saw mill, cleared a small tract and made arrangements for removing his family. In 1804, he returned and spent the summer, erecting a grist mill and a house, which was the first framed dwelling in town. The principal roads from the village to the neighboring towns are very direct, and were surveyed by Mr. Raymond, during the first season of his residence, with the view of making his settlement a central point with relation to the surrounding towns. During the second year of his residence, he opened a small store, for the accommodation of his settlers, and in 1810, he built a house, which he called an *academy*, and subsequently conveyed for that purpose. In the founding of this institution, and in securing its endowment by an appropriation from the state, he was peculiarly active and successful, and the St. Lawrence Academy may justly be considered as owing its origin to the zeal and energy of Mr. Raymond. He also took an active part in organizing the first religious society in town, and in securing the services of a clergyman.

About the year 1810, he became an agent for a tract of land in the town of Norfolk, and erected a warehouse at the head of navigation on Raquette river, and subsequently took much interest in the navigation of that stream, which was in early times regarded as a matter of much importance. The potash and other produce of the young settlements back of this place, was brought here for shipment, and the merchandise used in the country arrived by the same route.

In 1818, he removed to the settlement in Norfolk which bears his name, and which it received at the request of the inhabitants on the establishment of a post office. He remained at this place several years, as the agent of Mr. McVickar, having relinquished the agency of Potsdam, and engaged in the improvement of his new settlement, the erection of mills, and the formation of a line of boats to run between this place and Montreal. He was engaged in this business in partnership with Henry McVickar, and continued in this connexion until the death of the latter in Europe. Mr. Raymond was appointed one of the first justices of the peace on the organization of the town, and held that office as well as that of supervisor of the town of Potsdam, for many years. On the 8th of April, 1808, he was appointed a judge and justice of the county court. In 1823, he was employed by a committee chosen at a convention called

Benjamin Raymond

to concert measures for securing a canal from the St. Lawrence to Lake Champlain, to examine the route, and his report was instrumental with the petitions forwarded to the legislature in securing the passage of a law providing for the survey of the route by one of the engineers (Mr. Holmes Hutchinson), in the employment of the canal commissioners.

He continued actively engaged in his land agency, milling, farming, and merchandise, until 1824, when he went as an engineer and assistant of Benjamin Wright to the south, and engaged on the Delaware and Chesapeake canal, where he soon after sickened and died of a prevailing fever at St. Georges, Newcastle, Delaware, on the 26th of September, 1824. Mr. Raymond was tall and well built, and possessed a dignified and genteel deportment, which would lead one to select him in a crowd, as a man of superior ability and one who took a leading part in public affairs. His complexion and hair were light, and his features are admirably represented in the accompanying engraving. A single propensity in his character, impaired his usefulness and prevented him from being universally esteemed; which was a peculiar faculty for sarcasm that possessed a point and severity, and was expressed in language so *concise* and *pertinent*, that its sting often remained in the feelings of the unlucky subject long after the occasion had passed which induced it. This was not indulged from a cynical motive, nor from malicious feeling, for no man ever possessed a heart more open to the calls of humanity or a hand more ready to convey relief to the widow and the fatherless, the sick and the afflicted, than him; but rather to gratify a taste for the ludicrous, and to hold up in an absurd manner the arguments and motives of those from whose opinions he differed. Among those who had been politically and otherwise opposed to him on numerous occasions, and who had oftenest been the subject of his satire, the writer has not found one individual who did not concur in the assertion, that Mr. Raymond was a man of spotless integrity, great benevolence, and superior ability, in whatever station of public or private life he was called to fill.

ALEXANDER RICHARDS, was a native of New London, Conn., where he spent his early life. When a young man he removed to New Jersey, and becoming there acquainted with the Ogden family, he was sent by them as an agent to their lands in Madrid, where he located as the successor of Joseph Edsall in the land agency of that town in 1803. In 1811, he was appointed collector. During the war he was an active partisan, and being of the republican school of politics, he sustained that measure to the extent of his ability. He died at Waddington, Oct. 16, 1834, aged sixty-nine.

JOSEPH ROSSEEL, although never placed in a public station, yet from his early and prominent connection with the business of Ogdensburgh, has become in a measure identified with its history. He is a native of Ghent, Belgium, and came to America at the age of 25, with letters from the house of Hope & Co., of Amsterdam, introducing him to Mr. Parish, and to several commercial houses, *ostensibly* with a view of extending his commercial knowledge, but *in reality*, to avoid the military conscriptions of Napoleon. He reached Baltimore in August, 1807, and resided a year in Philadelphia, where he became acquainted with Robert H. Rose, late of Montrose, Pa., and with him took a tour into Pennsylvania. Late in 1807, he was sent by David Parish to explore the lands in Northern New York, which that gentleman proposed to buy, but from the lateness of the season was obliged to defer the exploration, which was accomplished in the summer of 1808, in which he traversed Antwerp

Rossie, and Kilkenny, then mostly a wilderness. In September, while on his way to "the garrison," he met D. Parish and G. Morris, and the latter offered strong inducements for him to locate at Morristown, and promised a gift of a mile square, where the village now is, if he would establish himself there; but Mr. Parish was convinced that Ogdensburgh would be *the* place, and his advice prevailed. With Mr. Parish's advice, and sustained by his capital, he commenced mercantile business with David M. Lewis,[*] under the firm of J. Rosseel & Co., and for several years did an extensive business, but an unfortunate speculation in western produce led to embarrassments, which Mr. Parish met. Having implicit confidence in Mr. R. he offered to again establish business, or to give him the general agency of his lands. He chose the latter, and has since continued in the employment of the family.

Dr. JOSEPH W. SMITH, was the first physician who settled in St. Lawrence county, at a period when the hardships of that laborious profession were unusually severe. The physician's avocation is always one of great responsibility, and requires for its successful prosecution the greatest amount of sagacity and skill, but especially amid the privations of a new settlement, where conveniences for the sick are sometimes not procurable, and the usual methods from necessity are supplanted by such as the exigencies of the moment may suggest, does it require in a special manner the exercise of sound judgment and a prompt and judicious action. Dr. Smith was born at Cheshire, Mass., Feb. 22, 1781. His father removed from Cheshire to Addison, Vt., and died in the year 1791. He studied with Dr. Ebenezer Huntington, of Vergennes, in 1799, and completed his professional studies with Dr. William Rose, at Middlebury, in 1802. In the following year, he removed to Lisbon, and commenced practice. During the time he resided here, his business extended to Madrid, Canton and Oswegatchie, and was one of great hardship from the want of passable roads, and the great distance which he was compelled to travel, often on foot from the impossibility of getting through otherwise, and exposed to the various vicissitudes incident to a new country. He has been known to travel on foot through the forest by torch light, at night, without a road, to Canton, a distance of 18 miles. In 1807, he removed to Ogdensburgh, and became the first physician at that place. He was the first president of the County Medical Society, and continued to fill that office during a great part of the time till his death. He also held the office of loan commissioner for some time. The following tribute to his memory, published soon after his decease, is believed to be but a just picture of his life and character:

"From the first settlement of the county till the close of his life, his whole time and energies were devoted to his profession. He underwent incredible fatigue in his extended practice in the country without roads, and never spared himself in his exertions to mitigate the pain of others; neither dangerous roads, or the darkness of night, or inclement weather, ever deterred him from attending to the calls of the sick, even though that call were made by the most poor and profligate of our race; all will bear him witness to his kindness, charity and compassion. It was no selfish principle that prompted his exertions. The love of gain seemed to have no influence with him, for he habitually did himself great injustice, as well in respect to the amount of his charges, as in his reluctance to collect those he had made. He was undoubtedly a man of great

[*] Mr. Lewis was private secretary of Mr. Parish, and died in New Orleans, June 1, 1834, aged fifty-eight.

science, skill and judgment in his profession. Perhaps no physician ever had the universal confidence both of his professional brethren and of his patients, than Dr. Smith; at the bedside of a patient he was rarely mistaken, either in the disease or its appropriate remedy. To the poor and distressed he was the good Samaritan, and in the various relations of professional and private life he was ever found exemplary."

He died at Ogdensburgh, July 4, 1835.

GURDON SMITH, was born in Windham, Ct., Feb. 12, 1775, where he resided till his 21st year, when he removed to Rome. Here he became acquainted with Mitchell and Wright, who had been extensively engaged in surveying, and becoming interested in this science, he commenced the study and subsequently assisted, as has been elsewhere stated, in the township surveys of St. Lawrence and Franklin counties. He was one of the first justices of the peace appointed on the organization of the town, which were Benjamin Raymond, John Delance and Gurdon Smith; the latter held his office about twenty successive years.

JAMES B. SPENCER, removed from New Haven, Vt., in 1810, to French mills; during the war he served his country with fidelity, in the capacity of captain in the 29th regiment of U. S. Infantry, and took part in several of the engagements of this frontier. He subsequently held many offices of trust, among which were those of magistrate, judge, deputy collector, member of assembly, presidential elector, and Indian agent, and in 1836 he was elected to congress. His tastes led him into the field of political strife, and he acquired much influence in the democratic party. A deep thinker and a man of an active temperament, he was well calculated to plan and execute whatever business of a political or a social nature he might undertake. Few citizens of the county have acquired more influence, or have been more highly esteemed than the subject of this notice. He died at Fort Covington, in March 1848, at the age of 64.

RICHARD TOWNSEND, was born at Hebron, New York, about 1768. In his youth he pursued the study of medicine but did not engage in its regular practice. He removed to Delhi, Delaware county, and engaged in the business of lumbering, when being in New York, in the course of his trade he became acquainted with Gouverneur Morris, by means of Gen. Lewis R. Morris, which resulted in his appointment as agent for the sale and settlement of wild lands in the townships of Cambray and Kilkenny, much of the former belonging to Morris, and the latter to Messrs. Fowler and Gilchrist. He was married about 1804, and in the year following made the first exploration with the view of settlement, of which a particular account is given in our history of Gouverneur. He settled in the village of Gouverneur, and spent the remainder of his life in that town, devoting his time to his agency, and to farming. During the epidemic of 1813, he practiced his profession, from necessity; but otherwise did not serve the public in that capacity except in cases of emergency. Towards the close of life he became a Quaker, and died in that faith, at his house two miles below the village, about 1826. He was interred at the Friend's settlement in Philadelphia, Jefferson county. He was active, intelligent and benevolent, and won the esteem of his settlers by his kindness and generosity.

WILLIAM HENRY VINING, was a young man of brilliant talents and endowed with a capacity which would have rendered him the ornament of his age, had his life been spared, but he was unfortunately for his country, stricken down early in life, but not until he had evinced on several occasions the splendor of his genius, and those traits of character which belong not to ordinary men. Mr. Vining's father was a member of congress from the state of Delaware, who died without wealth, and left his family dependent upon relatives. The mother also died while her sons were young, leaving the training of their children to a maiden aunt. Two of them were educated at West Point, but died young. Henry was received while a boy, into the family of Mrs. Gouverneur Ogden, his maternal aunt, and came to Waddington, where he afterwards lived. Adopting the legal profession he studied in the office of his uncle G. Ogden, and was admitted to practice in the supreme and county courts as an attorney in 1817, and as a counsellor in 1820. In 1821 he was elected to the assembly, but declining health prevented him from taking his seat. In the autumn of that year he sailed for the island of St. Croix, and arrived, as he expressed it in a letter to a friend, " A lonely invalid in the land of the stranger." In the spring he returned to New York without benefit from his voyage, and died in that city among his relatives in 1822. In the few cases at which he appeared at the bar, he evinced an eloquence and ability that elicited remark, and on an occasion of a slander suit, while pleading the cause of the plaintiff, it was said by several members of the profession that the plaintiff could well afford to be slandered, to be so eloquently defended. The management of his argument was masterly and its effect upon the jury and the audience was wonderful. On another occasion before the supreme court at Utica, he received the commendation of Chief Justice Savage, for the chasteness and purity of his language and careful preparation of authorities. He was a man of delicate sensibilities, a lively and poetic fancy, and of unsullied purity of character; he recognized in the beauties of nature the evidences of a God whom he loved and worshiped, and on every occasion which his brief career afforded, evinced that he possessed a heart that sympathizes with his fellow man, and a genius that needed but the opportunity to have rendered him eminent. The foregoing facts are derived from an article written twenty years after his death, by one who knew him well, and had been favored with his confidence.

Dr. HENRY S. WATERHOUSE, was a native of Salisbury, Vt., from which place he removed to Oneida, and thence to Malone, where he settled during the war, as a physician and surgeon. His tastes and studies led him to direct especial attention to anatomy, and he acquired much distinction as a surgical operator, and led to an appointment in the medical department of Vermont university, in 1826. He held this post about two years, and then removed to Key West, Florida, where he resided several years. He was drowned at Indian Key in Florida.

JOSEPH YORK, the second sheriff of St. Lawrence county, an active partisan in the war of 1812-15, and a citizen who enjoyed to a great degree the esteem of the public, was born in Clarendon, Mass., Jan. 8, 1781, and removed with his father's family at an early age to Randolph, Vt. From thence he emigrated in 1805, to Ogdensburgh, and for three years held the post of deputy sheriff under Thos. J. Davies, when he succeeded that gentleman, and held the office of sheriff four years. At the battle of Feb. 22, 1813, he was residing in the court house, and had care of the prisoners. Measures had been taken to raise a new company, and he was to have been one of its officers. He had charge of a cannon which was posted at the corner of Ford and Euphamia streets, and was the only person of his party who was not killed or wounded. He was captured and taken to Prescott, but soon after, at the intercession of his wife, he was paroled, and in a few weeks after exchanged. The prisoners in jail were set free on their own assertion that they were confined for political offences, but upon being assured of the contrary, they were mostly rearrested, and given up to Mr. York, who met the British authorities at the national boundary on the ice, in the middle of the St. Lawrence, and received them. Among these was one who had fled to Montreal upon his receiving his liberty, and was there captured. He had been confined on a charge of murder. During three successive years, Mr. York represented the county in the legislature. The town of York, in Livingston county, N. Y., derives its name from him. He died on the 6th of May, 1827, at the age of 46, after a lingering illness of several months.

Mr. York was a very public spirited man, and especially in times of danger or alarm, he was one of those who placed himself in front, and by his word and example encouraged others more timid or less qualified to think for themselves at moments of excitement. This was particularly the case in fires, on which occasion he never failed to take the lead in directing the means to be taken for suppressing the consuming element, and in rescuing property.

SILAS WRIGHT. This illustrous citizen was born in Amherst, Mass., May 24, 1795, and in infancy removed with his parents to Weybridge, Vt., where he formed his earliest associations. After an academic course, he entered Middlebury college, and graduated in 1815, and while still a student he entered warmly into the political discussions of the day, and became a republican in politics. Having studied law with Henry C. Martindale, at Sandy Hill, N. Y., he was in 1819, licensed to practice as an attorney in the supreme court, and in that year, being led to Canton on a visit to a friend, he was induced to settle in that new and thinly settled village. Here he commenced the practice of law, and soon acquired the esteem of his fellow citizens, and the confidence of the public generally, for his sound judgment and good sense. He was soon appointed surrogate, justice, commissioner of deeds, and post master; held several town offices, and passed through the several grades of military promotion to the office of brigadier general. As a magistrate he discouraged litigation, and as a lawyer he was especially eminent in the happy manner in which he drew from witnesses the statements bearing upon the case, without ever touching the feelings by rudeness or satire. His arguments were always lucid and logical, and carried with them a conviction not only of their truth and justice, but also of the genius and talents of their author.

In the various improvements of the town and county, he took an active part, and especially in the erection of county buildings, after the selection of the site, was he noted for his zeal and activity in collecting materials, and assisting the work.

The influence which the upright character and evident talents of Mr. Wright had acquired, led his friends to wish to try his abilities on a wider field; and his name was presented in the fall of 1823, without his previous knowledge, to the republican convention of the fourth senate district, then embracing the counties of Saratoga, Montgomery and Hamilton, Washington, Warren, Clinton, Essex, Franklin, and St. Lawrence. The opposition of De Witt Clinton and his friends to the convention of 1821, and other causes, had led to a new organization of parties, styled Clintonians and buck tails, anti-Clintonians or republicans. Mr. Wright was known to be friendly to the latter, but his known candor and liberality rendered him more acceptable to the Clintonians than any other candidate that could be offered, and he was unanimously nominated.

During the legislative session preceding the nomination of Mr. Wright to the office of senator, the republican members of both houses from the 4th district, met to decide by ballot which county in the senatorial district should be entitled to senator. The county designated was to be entitled to the privilege of selecting their candidate, thus dispensing with the formality of a convention of the whole district. After seven ballotings, and some feeling being created in the minds of some members, the choice fell upon St. Lawrence county. Mr. Wright was thus enabled to enter a field in which he was eminently qualified to excel, and his future career might have been quite different had the choice of a different county been the result of the balloting. The electors for president and vice president had, since 1789, been selected by the legislature in the same manner as senators of the United States are now chosen, which gave great additional importance to the members of the legislature, and from the relative prospects of the five prominent candidates for the presidential term to commence in 1825, (Crawford, Adams, Jackson, Clay, and Calhoun), the friends of Mr. Crawford believed that their interests would be promoted by retaining the existing law for the appointment of electors. Other parties proposed to restore the right of naming the electors, to the people, and most of the candidates of 1823 were questioned in relation to their views, and Mr. Wright among others. He freely declared himself in favor of giving directly to the people the choice of electors. No pledge was given or required beyond the faith reposed in the frank and unreserved declarations made by him in conversation. His vote in the county was 1,419, that of his opponent 20. In Canton it was 199 to 1. The one vote was doubtless given by Mr. Wright himself.

The session of 1824 was memorable for the spirit with which the passage of the electoral law, as the proposed change in the mode of electing presidential electors was called, and this became the engrossing subject of the session from the time of its opening till the final passage of the bill. Mr. Wright's course in this contest was such as to draw from his political opponents the admission that he was governed by upright and consistent principles, although at variance with their plans, and subversive of their cherished schemes. While in the senate, early in the session of 1825, a great number of applications for bank charters were presented in both houses, and such were the restrictions then in force, that banks that held charters virtually possessed great privileges for transacting pecuniary business, and hence charters were eagerly sought after. Mr. Wright opposed these applications to the extent of his ability, and was to a considerable degree successful. His influence constantly increased in the senate, and in 1826 he was elected to congress. The tariff question was then a subject that was agitated by the parties, and Mr. Wright became a member of a committee which had an important bearing upon this subject. At the next election for congress, Mr. Wright was defeated from the omission of the word *junior* in his name on some of the ballots, and from an irregularity in returns. Early in 1829, he was appointed comptroller, which office he filled with distinguished ability, until in 1833, he was chosen U. S. senator, and took his seat in this august body at the age of 38, and at the time when the nullification measures of South Carolina, the removal of the deposits from banks, the rechartering of the national bank, and other exciting topics distracted the national councils. Mr. Wright opposed the continuance of the bank in a speech of great ability. At the end of the short term to which he was chosen, he was, in 1837, reëlected, notwithstanding the powerful bank influences brought against him. At the national convention of

1844, the nomination of vice president was tendered to him, but declined. In 1842, his friends had solicited from him the privilege of nominating him for governor, but he declined, as he had also done that of the office of judge in the supreme court of the United States. In 1844, he was nominated for governor, and elected. During his official term, the constitution of the state was revised, and several subjects requiring in especial manner the exercise of promptness and discretion, arose.

In 1846 he was again nominated for governor, but Mr. John Young, his opponent, was elected. At the close of his official term, Mr. Wright returned to his residence in Canton, and engaged in that pursuit for which during a long period he had evinced a decided fondness,—that of practical agriculture. He was appointed in 1847, to deliver the address at the State Agricultural Fair, at Saratoga Springs, and accepted the appointment, but was suddenly attacked by a severe illness of which he died in two hours. He had for several months devoted his days to hard labor on his farm, and his nights to correspondence, which were believed to have been the proximate causes of his death. This sudden bereavement cast a gloom over the community, and the heavy tidings were received with sadness by his numerous friends, and the public generally. The democratic party were at this time looking about for a man upon whom they might unite at the next presidential canvass, and from every quarter there came expressions that indicated the preference they felt for Mr. Wright, and it is highly probable that had he lived he would have been selected as their candidate.

During his lifetime, his mercantile friends had procured a testimonial of their esteem which after his death was forwarded to Mrs. Wright. It consisted of 125 pieces of silver plate manufactured by Gerandus Boyce, of New York, each article bearing a suitable inscription, commemorating the occasion of the gift. The articles were two pitchers holding four quarts and one pint each; a silver tea kettle holding three quarts; a coffe pot, tea pot, sugar dish, cream pot, slop bowl, soup ladle, fish knife, crumb knife, ice cream slicer, pair of sugar tongs, four butter knives, and nine dozen table and dessert spoons and forks. The total value was about $1,900.

Soon after the death of Mr. Wright, his widow and family yielding to the solicitation of his *neighbors* and *friends*, accepted the offer which they tendered, of erecting a plain and simple monument over his grave, as a testimonial of personal esteem and private friendship. An ostentatious display of architecture was deemed inconsistent with the modest and unassuming character of the man whose name it bore, and unnecessary to perpetuate the memory of one who had become endeared in the hearts of the people. A subscription was drawn up in October, 1847, the amount of each contribution limited to $1, and its circulation to citizens of St. Lawrence county. With the avails of this, a simple shaft of pure white marble from the Dorset quarry, 15 feet in height, resting on a base of Canton granite 1¼ feet high, was erected and inclosed in a neat iron paling. This unassuming monument is shown at the end of the present chapter.

The shaft bears on one side his name and date of birth and death. On the other the inscription "erected by the citizens of the county of St. Lawrence."

The citizens of Weybridge and vicinity, in Vermont, (which town Mr. Wright always regarded with the feelings of a natal place), in the March following his decease, united in testifying their respect for his character, by erecting a monument to his memory. A series of resolutions highly expressive of regard, were drawn up, and a committee appointed to procure the means for erecting it and a steel plate engraving of it. Solomon W. Jewett and Samuel O. Wright, of Weybridge, and Samuel S. Phelps, of Middlebury, were appointed the committee, who, at a cost of about $4,400, erected in their village near the school house, and over the same ground where the Congregational church stood, at which Wright and his parents had worshipped, a shaft of white marble about thirty eight feet in height. The main shaft is twenty-eight feet high, three feet square at the base, and seventeen inches at the top. It stands upon a mound, and is supported by three bases; the first 8, the second 6½, and the third 5 feet square. Above this is a die four feet square, which is surmounted by the shaft. Inserted in the monument is a beautiful and accurate medalion bust, executed by E. D. Palmer, of Albany. The only inscription which it has upon it is, *Silas Wright.* It is surrounded by a circular iron railing six rods in diameter.

His biography has been ably written by the Hon. Jabez D. Hammond, and forms the third volume of the Political History of New York. The well known character and abilities of this talented writer, are a sufficient guaranty of its value.

We are indebted to Hammond's Life of Silas Wright, published at Syracuse, by Hall and Dickinson, for the portrait which faces our title. The reader will find in that work a very minute and correct account of the life and public services of this truly illustrious man. His memoirs have also been written by J. S. Jenkins.

Wright's Monument, Canton.

CHAPTER IX.

EVENTS OF THE WAR OF 1812—1815.

N the 5th of April, 1805, a regiment was formed in St. Lawrence county with Alex. J. Turner, *lt. col. commandant;* Joseph Edsall, *1st major,* and David Ford, *2d major;* and on the
11th a brigade, embracing Lewis, Jefferson, and St. Lawrence
counties was formed, having Walter Martin, its *brigadier general,*
He had previously been lieut. col., and his place was supplied by
Jonathan Collins, of Turin. On the 3d of April, 1806, the following appointments were made in Turner's regiment. Isaac Beach,
adjutant; John King, *paymaster;* D. W. Church, *quarter master;* Joseph
W. Smith, *surgeon;* Powell Davis, *surgeon's mate;* Louis Hasbrouck,
Timothy Pope, Timothy Crosset, Nathan Stone, Wm. Perry, Thomas B.
Benedict, Solomon Linsley, Jr., Isaac Bartholomew, Richard Flack,
Elisha Deniston, and Benjamin Stewart, *captains;* Jehiel Dimmock,
Kelsey Thurber, Samuel Armstrong, Martin Philips, Medad Moody, Pot-
ter Goff, Seth Gates, John Hawley, John W. Lyttle, Calvin Hubbard,
and Benjamin Bailey, *lieutenants;* and Jacob Arnold, Jr., Thomas Lee,
John A. Armstrong, Abner Wright, James Parkil, Jr., Joel Woodhouse,
Daniel Greene, Nicholas Reynolds, Robert Jackson, Seth Matthews and
David French, *ensigns.* An artillery company was formed April 6, 1807,
with Alex' Richard, *capt.;* Amos Wells, *1st lt;* Joseph Freeman, *2nd lt.* A
battallion of four companies, under Alric Man, *major commandant,* was
formed in Franklin co., June 4, 1808, and belonged to Gen. Benj. Moore's
brigade. Our space forbids the use of the details collected in relation to
subsequent organizations. The location of our counties upon the frontier, made them the theatre of events that will be briefly enumerated, and
checked their growth and settlement to a most lamentable degree; not
so much by the actual as the dreaded evils of war, and the entire cessation of trade, which had mainly found an outlet by the St. Lawrence.
With business stopped, the industry of the country palsied, and the
brightest prospects of the future blighted, it is not surprising that the
war was to a considerable degree unpopular, especially with those classes
whose business was interrupted by the measure, and whose property
was depreciated and in some instances rendered valueless by its occurrence. The measures which preceded and led to hostilities belong to
our national history. Grievances had existed for several years, and efforts had been made to settle the difficulties between the two nations by
diplomatic arrangements, but these failing, a resort to arms became the
only means effectual in attaining these ends which could not be accomplished peaceably.

On the 22d of Dec. 1807, congress laid an embargo upon all ships and
vessels in the ports of the United States, and directed that no clearance
should be furnished to any ship bound to any foreign port or place, except under the immediate direction of the president. In the event of

the suspension of hostilities between the belligerent powers of Europe, or of such changes in their measures, as would render the commerce of the country safe, the president was authorized, by an act passed on the 8th of April following, to suspend in whole or in part, the operations of the embargo. This applied to the lakes as well as the sea board. Early in 1809, Captains Samuel Cherry and Thomas Anderson, were stationed at Ogdensburgh, to enforce non intercourse and occupied temporary barracks erected for their use. These two companies of troops are represented as the worst set of men that ever lived, and were charged with being needlessly officious in searching persons crossing the river, which led to jealousies that almost ripened into hostility with the citizens. The latter, for their own protection, organized a nightly patroll to protect their gardens and hen roosts, and thus between the preservation of national and personal rights, the village bore the discipline of a camp, until, to the great joy of the citizens, the news arrived that the soldiers were to be withdrawn. This was too desirable an event to pass unnoticed, and preparations were made to celebrate it, which coming to the knowledge of the other party, an attempt was made in the night time, to seize an old French cannon, belonging in the village, which was to be fired on their departure, and to throw it from the bridge into the river. The plot was discovered, and the party sent was arrested by the citizen guard, and in the morning marched back to their quarters, and released-at the solicitation of their officers. As they were leaving, a citizen who went down to their boats to recover some stolen property, was seized and thrown overboard, which instantly raised an excitement, and as they left, they were followed by the hootings and cries of the irritated crowd. The old iron cannon, and the discordant music of a hundred tin horns with as many cowbells, assisted in expressing the general satisfaction. The books of a mercantile firm show an unsettled balance of $300 against one of these worthies. Congress, April 10, 1812, required 100,000 men to be raised in anticipation of the war, which were to be officered with present militia officers, paid at the same rates as the regular army, and were not compelled to serve longer than six months after arriving at the place of rendezvous. It was stipulated, that no non-commissioned officer musician or private, should be subject to corporal punishment by whipping, but stoppage of pay, confinement, and deprivation of rations, should be substituted. $1,000,000 was appropriated for this purpose. Gen. Jacob Brown, whose brigade included the county, wrote May 2, 1812, to Col. Benedict, to raise 43 men, including noncommissioned officers, to be held ready at a minutes warning, and two competent men as lieutenant and ensign. These he required to be embodied and stationed in the village of Williamstown, [De Kalb,] as soon as possible. Col. Stone, of Herkimer county, was also instructed to raise 37 men, and 1 lieutenant, to join the above. A company was accordingly raised of about 80 men, with Darius Hawkins, of Herkimer county, captain; John Polley, of Massena, and Elisha Griffin, of De Kalb, lieutenants. These were sent on to Ogdensburgh, and Col Benedict wrote, May 25, 1812, to D. W. Church, adjutant, in charge of the barracks, as follows :   They appear to have laid in for a stock of military supplies. "You will probably receive this letter by the hand of Lt. Polley, who has the command of a detachment of men from this encampment. I have ordered him to Ogdensburgh with the detachment. Lt. Griffin, as commanded, will follow in three or four days. They are to go to the public barracks. Lt. Polley is to be obeyed as commander, until the arrival of Lt. Griffin. You will receive by Whipple, four bbls. of pork, four axes, and one frying pan, which belong to the troops, together with one bbl. of whiskey, for their use. I expect to be at Ogdensburgh on or by Monday next, and until my arrival I have to request the favor of you to furnish flour, bread and other camp necessaries; in fine to be an assistant to the Lt., and lend him all the assistance in your power. On my arrival I shall make the necessary arrangements until the arrival of the proper officers."

These troops arrived on the last of May, and for a few days were quartered in the court house. The citizens, from their former experience, disliked the idea of having troops among them, and it is said that difficulty was experienced in getting their bread baked from this, cause. The declaration of war, in June 1812, was made known by the arrival of Major Darby Noon, to erect barracks, which were temporary and located a short distance below the village. No sooner was the news of the declaration of war received, than the greatest alarm was immediately created on both sides of the lines, from mutual fears of hostile incursion from the other side of the boundary.

In St. Lawrence county especially, this fear was greatly increased by rumors that parties of Indians were about to fall upon the settlements, then young and feeble, and lay waste the country with fire and tomahawk. On the slighest alarm, often from trivial or accidental causes, a rumor would originate and spread through an entire settlement; the timid would flee to the woods, and not unfrequently the most grotesque and ludicrous scenes were enacted. Families hastening off and leaving their houses open and the table spread with provisions, and fleeing on horseback and on foot, in carts, and in wagons, laden with such articles of value as they were able to snatch in their haste; some driving their flocks and herds before them, which others left behind, and each fugitive from the danger they apprehended, augmented the fears of the others, which they met by relating their own. Many of these did not return till peace and some never. By degrees it was remarked that no real danger from these sources existed, and confidence became reëstablished, so that before the close of the war, the former feeling of friendship had in some degree been renewed between the settlers along opposite the St. Lawrence. The first news of the war in June 1812, was the signal for general alarm, but before the close of the season, the minds of the settlers had become accustomed to these rumors and they were but little regarded. The sight of an Indian, however innocent and peaceable, his business, or of an Indian or squaw's track in the sand, was an especial subject of alarm, and this operated greatly to the distresses of the St. Regis tribe, who were thus cut off from their customary pursuits and compelled to remain at home, for fear of exciting alarms.

To say that this alarm was general, would be doing injustice to a large class of citizens who awaited whatever events the war might entail, with a constancy and steadiness which reflected great credit upon their character. In every town on the St. Lawrence, however most ludicrous scenes were enacted, originating in accidental alarms or the wanton reports set on foot by those who adopted this method of testing the personal courage of their neighbors. The settlers in De Peyster were on one occasion, driven to the woods by a report brought by a young man who rode through on horseback at great speed, and spread an alarm of Indians. This proved to be entirely groundless, and its author just a year afterwards, got severely flogged for this indulgence of his humor. A ludicrous incident occurred in Louisville, in June. An early settler who lived upon one of the points that project into the St. Lawrence, and who to a f' on ness for a practical joke, added much personal courage, became disgusted at the timid conduct of his neighbors, and feared that the Canadians would cross over for plunder, supposing the country deserted. He accordingly resolved one still beautiful evening, to try the effect of a stratagem which was to convince the people opposite within sight of his residence, that although some had fled, yet others were left, and that his government was not unmindful of the interests of its citizens on her northern frontier.

He accordingly, with the aid of two or three accomplices, built a great number of fires in a conspicuous point on the bank, and then passing up and down, he announced in a loud voice which resounded for miles across the placid waters of the St. Lawrence, the orders which it is customary to issue to the different companies and battallions of an army when taking their positions in a camp. These orders were duly responded to by his aids who were posted at suitable distances. The fires had attracted notice on the Canada shore, and the orders of the commander-in-chief were conclusive evidence that an army of Americans had arrived, and were about to precipitate themselves upon the British dominions. Immediately the cries of alarm, the barking of dogs, which their masters vainly tried to suppress, and the rattling of wagons announced that the settlers were on their way to the woods, where as it subsequently appeared, they spent the night in the greatest terror and confusion. One old Dutchman alone remained, declaring that the voice that came across the waters, was too much like that of an old fellow with whom he was acquainted.

As might have been supposed, the alarm spread in the vicinity of the fires, and a British army was reported to have landed and taken possession. Great numbers fled in terror to the thickets, snatching whatever was at hand capable of ministéring to the first necessities of nature, and remained several hours until two or three of their number who had been sent to reconnoitre and had crept cautiously up to the fires without encountering the picket guard or the line of sentinels, returned with a report of their observations. This little circumstance by showing the ridiculous consequences of false alarms, did much good by placing the citizens on their guard against them. The sayings and doings of diverse persons who headed this retreat, were not soon forgotten.

As soon as war was declared, Gen. Brown drafted six companies in the regiments of Colonels Benedict and Stone, which were under Captains Griffin, of De Kalb, Armstrong, of Lisbon, Cook and Hovey, of Lewis county, and Bell and Weaver of Herkimer county. Oliver Bush, of Turin, was 1st Major, and —— Whitman, 2d Major of Benedict's regiment. Col. Stone's regiment arrived soon after with several companies, among which was an independent rifle company under Capt. Noadiah Hulbard, of Champion. The militia captains on duty during a considerable part of the summer of 1812, were as follows in the order of their commissions: Nathan Adams, Nathan Cook, Imri Case, Jost Bell, Moses A. Bunnell, —— Howland, Jacob Hovey. When war was declared eight schooners were in Ogdensburgh harbor, which on the 29th of June, attempted to escape to the lake. Mr. D. Jones, an active partisan residing near the present village of Maitland, on the Canada shore, seeing the movement and appreciating the advantage that would result to the British interests if this fleet could be prevented from reaching Lake Ontario, raised a company of volunteers, pursued them in boats till he overtook them near the foot of the Thousand islands above Brockville. Two of the vessels, the Sophia and the Island Packet, were taken without resistance, as they were fitted for trade only, and had on board no armament. Several emigrant families on board, with the crew and a part or the whole of their effects were set on an island, and the vessels burned. The crews of the remainder immediately steered back to Ogdensburgh.

The following extract from the correspondence of Mr. Joseph Rosseel, conveys an account of the excitement produced by these measures:

" July 2, 1812. Since my last there has been much confusion throughout the town. This I intend sending by Mr. H., who is packing up to start with his family for Utica directly. This confusion commenced on Sunday morning with the setting out of a party from this place in a revenue cutter, in pursuit of 13 king's boats laden with cannon ball, swivels and ammunition; this pursuit proved unsuccessful, the wind failing the cutter. On Monday morning, Major Noon arrived here from Sacketts Harbor, in company with several merchants from Oswego, in a long boat, with men armed. His object was the arranging for barracks for 1000 troops and a hospital. The armed men came to accompany up eight vessels which lay here wind bound, when the news of the declaration of war reached us. These vessels with those of Ogdensburgh, holding out temptation to the enemy, sailed on that day at noon to the rejoicing of the inhabitants. We held a conference with Capt. Mayo, owner of the *Genesee Packet*, about sinking the Ogdensburgh vessels, but it was deemed improper. The remainder of that day was employed in keeping down the marauding spirit. The whole town met, and their proceedings were concluded with much propriety and harmony. All went on well till Tuesday, about noon, when five of the vessels which sailed the day before, returned to this port. That which excited a general alarm, was the circumstance of one of the returning vessels making signal of distress. The report was that two vessels had been burnt in the narrows by Indians and whites, who secreted themselves on the islands. This report which run through the country with the swiftness of lightning, together with the general orders which were at the same time issued to march to Ogdensburgh, all the men in town prepared for immediate action, created such confusion as is indescribable. In less than an hour all the settlements on Black lake and St. Lawrence, from hence upwards, were entirely deserted—people every where running through the woods in great dismay. At 2 P. M., we were all under arms, an immediate attack being expected from the enemy with a view, as was supposed, of burning our vessels;—our fears were not realized."

Very soon after, the *Prince Regent*, a new vessel of 10 guns, came down from Kingston, and fears were apprehended that an intention of attacking the town was entertained. On the 20th of July, Brigadier Gen. Stephen Van Rensselaer, arrived, and a rumor prevailed that two more vessels were coming down to destroy the fleet. As afterwards appeared, several plans were laid to take the vessels, but none were attempted; as a further security, they were taken above the bridge, and during an armistice that occurred in summer, were got up to the lake. Soon after the arrival of the Prince Regent; the *Earl of Moira* and *Duke of Gloucester*, the former of 18 and the latter of 10 guns, arrived at Prescott. A scheme was laid for destroying the Duke of Gloucester on the night of July 23, and from the original volunteer list before us, it appears that about 60 men offered themselves for the service who were to act under Colonels T. B. Benedict and Solomon Van Rensselaer. Three parties were to coöperate, but before night the vessel changed her position, and the at-

37

tempt was not made. In July, Gen. Brown despatched the schooner *Julia* of the navy, armed with one 18 and two iron 6 pounders, and laden with military stores, under the command of Lieut. H. W. Wells, of the government brig Oneida, and accompanied by Capt. Noadiah Hubbard with a rifle company in a Durham boat. She sailed July 29, and on arriving at Morristown, she was met at 3 o'clock on the 31st by the Earl of Moira, which soon as they came alongside, dropped their anchors, brailed up their canvass, and commenced a cannonade, which lasted, three and a quarter hours without intermission, but, singularly enough, without loss of life and with but little injury to the vessels. The Earl of Moira was hulled a few times, and the Julia received a slight injury from one shot. Near dark, the enemy's vessels were warped up to Elizabethtown (now Brockville), and the guns taken out and placed in battery on shore. The Julia weighed anchor and fell down the current, and by being towed by the Durham boat and the schooner's yawl, reached Ogdensburgh before morning. She lay off in the stream between Prescott and Ogdensburgh, until the fifth of September, under the command of Capt. Wm. Vaughan, sailing master in the navy. Samuel Dixon and Abram Shoemaker, volunteers, acting master's mates. Lieut. Wells returned the day after the affair to Sacketts Harbor.

A scout had been sent to notify the Julia of her danger from the two armed vessels, but did not arrive seasonably. The firing being heard at Ogdensburgh, and the occasion of it being surmised, Adjutant Church was sent, by Col. Benedict, to proceed with a party of volunteers to offer any assistance that might be possible. They hastily marched to the scene of the engagement but did not arrive until after the affair was over. From Mr. Church, the foregoing account was derived.

Samuel Dixon, who was on board the Julia and participated in this affair as a volunteer, had been in the employment of David Parish, as captain of the schooner, *Collector*. The principal merchant vessels on the lake, were bought up by government on their reaching the lake, and fitted up with an armament. Captain Mayo's schooner the *Genesee Packet*, had its name changed to the *Hamilton*. The *Experiment*, one of Mr. Parish's vessels became *The Growler*.

An incident occurred during the summer of 1812, while the militia were on duty at Ogdensburgh which created much talk at the time, and has since been a standing subject for a story; properly regarded it reflects high credit upon the military courage of the individual, and was at the time so regarded by his comrades. Had he been assigned a dangerous position in an assault, he would doubtless have acquitted himself in as conscientious and efficient a manner as he acted on the mistaken orders he received on the following occasion. An alarm had required a hasty draft of recruits from the militia of the adjacent towns, who arrived in the forenoon, and were from the necessity of the occasion put upon duty the same evening, before they had had time to learn the discipline of a camp, or the duties of the soldier. The articles of war were read in their hearing, in which the penalty of *death* was declared the doom of every offender, who should violate the rules of order, or be found wanting in deeds of omission, as well as commission, in the routine of the soldier's duty. To those who had just been called from the quiet labors of the field to participate in the events of war, and act a part in the rigid discipline of a camp, the soldier's life appeared to depend on more contingencies than casualties of battle, and the profession of arms to be a path beset with pitfalls and dangerous passes, so straight and narrow, that the utmost caution was required so to conduct one's deportment as not to incur the death penalty. Such doubtless was the sentiment of the subject of the following incident, when on the evening of his arrival, he was placed on duty as a sentinel, with the usual injunctions to allow no one to pass without the countersign.

This was not given him either through accident or design, and the omission was noticed by him at the time, and he enquired of one of the party who had previously known something of the usages of the camp, what he should do in this emergency, who replied that he must do as he had been ordered. He accordingly formed the resolution to obey orders to the letter; *to know no man in the dark, and to stop all persons passing by land or water.* There are those who believe that the sentinel was thus purposely left, in order to test his fidelity by endeavoring to deprive him of his arms, and thus make him a subject of ridicule. Indeed, one of the officers who was subsequently detained by him, is said to have boasted that he had got two or three guns away from sentinels on guard that night, and intended to get as many more.

The guard had all been posted and the serjeant and his party of some six or eight men, were returning to the guard house, when on approaching the spot where the man had been posted, without the countersign, they were ordered to stop and one by one were commanded to advance, lay down their arms and sit down upon the ground. Here they were kept in perfect silence and stillness by the resolute orders of the sentinel who noticed every motion, and with loaded musket threatened instant death to the first one who should offer to leave his place, or make the slightest move towards recovering his arms. The answer that the serjeant had returned, on being first hailed, which was the remark that Colonel B—— had given orders to allow a boat to pass up, had made the sentinel suspicious that something was wrong. About eleven o'clock at night, when preparing to go the grand rounds, the captain of the company on duty, made inquiries for the serjeant of the guard and his relief. No one knew what had become of them as they had not been seen since dark. The corporal of the guard was also found missing. Captain Hawkins, to whose command these belonged, Adjutant Church, and two privates, immediately started to go the rounds and ascertain the cause of the absence, and were proceeding along in single file, the two privates in advance, when they were stopped by the customary challenge, "Who comes there," to which it was replied, "Grand rounds." This was as unintelligible as Greek to the new recruit, who abruptly replied, "I'll grand rounds you," and he ordered the first one to advance and be seated. The captain was next disarmed and placed on a level with his privates, which altogether formed a group of a dozen or more, including all the missing ones, who were not only kept in their places, but kept still and silent by the resolute sentinel armed with a loaded musket. The other private was soon added to the captive party, and Adjutant Church was next ordered to advance, an order which with characteristic firmness, he promptly refused to obey. No sooner had he refused, when the sentinel instantly fired, but it being dark, the shot took no effect. Captain Hawkins, upon this sprang to his feet and endeavored to seize the musket, but he was collared and kept at arm's length by the iron grasp of the sentinel. A struggle ensued in which the bayonet was loosened from the musket, but retained by the owner, and the captain received a severe wound in the arm. The serjeant was also wounded in the leg, upon which the party retreated, leaving their arms on the field. In the excitement of the moment, the captain had ordered the stubborn guardsman to be shot, but a second thought dictated a more humane policy, and a line of sentries was posted around him to keep others from falling in his way till morning. The line beyond him was at length relieved, much wondering what strange event had kept them on duty so long. Meanwhile, our soldier, conscious of having committed some error, the nature and consequence of which he knew not, resolved still to act strictly upon his orders and to trust to common justice the event. He neatly stacked the weapons he had captured, hanging the swords and hats upon the bayonets, and upon the top of all he placed the military hat of his captain, and resumed his duties resolved to defend his position, at least as long as practicable. Two or three companies were ordered out to take him forcibly from his ground, but upon a little discussion it was thought expedient to let him remain. A young officer hearing of these occurrences offered to go alone and get him off, and he parted with that design, but nothing more was seen of him till after sunrise the next morning, when he was found sitting very quietly under guard, not far from the stack of trophies, of the last night's adventure.

The sentinel refused to let him off, notwithstanding some of his neighbors went to intercede in his behalf, until the man who had given him the orders on leaving him the night before should grant him the authority. But the latter had been wounded, and was unable to walk, and he was accordingly *carried* to within speaking distance of the sentinel, and succeeded in procuring his release. He still refused to leave his post, until assured by an officer with whom he was acquainted, that no harm should come from the last night's proceedings, and he appeared deeply affected at the mistake he had committed, and especially at the unhappy consequences that had resulted from it. The censure of public opinion, as soon as the first impulse was over, fell justly upon the officer who had placed a sentinel upon guard, with injunctions coupled with the death penalty, to stop all persons passing, and at the same time neglecting to give him the countersign. The man, who thus proved himself true to his orders, was Mr. Seth Alexander, still living in DeKalb.

About the middle of September, it was learned, that a number of bateaux were coming up the river laden with stores, and a party under Capt. Griffin, in a Durham boat, accompanied with a gun boat, having eighteen men and a brass six pounder, under D. W. Church, left Ogdensburgh in the evening, and late at night landed on Toussaint island, opposite the town of Lisbon, and near the place where the enemy lay. The only family on the island was secured, but the man managed to escape by swimming and gave the alarm, and the provincial militia were hastily rallied. The bateaux lay under the north shore behind the island. The party under Capt. Griffin, took a position near its head, while Church was directed to station his gun boat near its foot. A sharp firing soon began and was continued for some time, when the boat was abandoned with the loss of one man, (Macomb) and one wounded. It drifted down the channel, and was taken up by the enemy before it reached the foot of the island. The gun boat about sunrise came to anchor and was immediately fired upon; at the second discharge having five of the eighteen wounded, but before the third shot, the cannon was brought to bear, and very shortly after the regulars, who accompanied the enemy's boats, broke and run. Failing in its object, the party returned by land, and the gun boat was sent to Hamilton. Adjutant Fitz Gibbon, was said to have charge of the British party, two of which at the time were reported killed and several wounded. We had but one man killed.

Towards the close of the season, Capt. Benjamin Forsyth, with a company of riflemen, arrived at Ogdensburgh. Gen. Brown was frequently in the place. On the 2d of October, about forty British boats, escorted by two gun boats, were proceeding up the river towards Prescott, when a cannonade was commenced from the enemy's batteries upon the village, to cover the boats, which was returned a short time, until it was found that long shots had but very little effect. On the 3d, the firing was renewed, but not answered. On Sunday morning, the 4th, an attack was made by twenty-five boats and two gun boats, which had proceeded up the river nearly a mile, and were then seen to turn their course towards the village. The morning parade had just been dismissed, but the order to rally was instantly issued, and a wooden battery near the stone ware house was manned with the brass six pounder, under Adjutant Church, and an iron twelve pounder, under the orders of Joseph York, a volunteer citizen. There was but one embrasure which was occupied by the brass piece, the other being stationed at its end, and without protection. The regiment under the orders of Gen. Brown, and Forsyth's riflemen, which then lay encamped west of the Oswegatchie, was drawn up with the militia. The Americans numbered 1,200 men. Firing commenced from the enemy's batteries with the embarkation of the troops, and continued as they advanced, and was returned by our troops as soon as the boats arrived within musket range. The flotilla approached to within a quarter of a mile, when one of their gun boats having been disabled and two of their number killed, they returned to their own side. It was reported that one of their bateaux was sunk, but of this fact the author's informant was not certain. Not a drop of blood was lost on the side of the Americans, but some little injury was done to property and buildings by the shot of the enemy. About thirty rounds were fired from each of the two pieces at the wooden battery. The firing continued nearly two hours. The assailants in this attempt were commanded by Col. Lethbridge, and according to the accounts published by the British, they numbered 750 men. Christie, a British author, has thus described the affair: "They advanced without opposition to mid channel, when the enemy opened a tremendous discharge of artillery, which checked their progress. A confusion immediately ensued, and they were compelled to make a precipitate retreat, with the loss of three men killed and four wounded. The Americans were commanded by Brigadier General Brown, and are said to have behaved with much coolness and intrepidity. This enterprise, undertaken without the sanction of the commander of the forces, was censured by him, and the public opinion condemned it as rash and premature."

After this unsuccessful attempt of the enemy, nothing further of consequence occurred till the close of the year. The winter set in early, and was very severe. The drafted regiment returned home, and left the place under the protection of Captain Forsyth, with his rifle company, and a small detachment of Captain Kellog's artillery company of Albany volunteers. The remainder of that company had been detached to Sackett's Harbor. On the 6th of February, 1813, about a fortnight before the attack upon Ogdensburgh, Captain Forsyth, being told by spies and friends in Elizabethtown, (Brockville), that a large number of Americans were confined there in jail, and pressing news being repeatedly received that they were treated with severity, that some were claimed as British deserters, although they had become citizens of the United States, and that some of these would be executed by the authority of the British courts martial, it was resolved to attempt their rescue. A party consisting of Captain Forsyth's company, and citizen volunteers to the num-

ber of about two hundred, was organized, and ready to start about nine
o'clock in the evening, and leaving the town in the care of Captain Kellog, of the Albany volunteers, and a few citizens, they proceeded on foot
and in two or three sleighs (the latter in the rear), to Morristown. Having halted here a few moments, and procured a guide,* they crossed in
two divisions, marching in open order on account of the weakness of
the ice, Captain Forsyth leading one division, and Colonel Benedict the
other. Flank-guards were dispatched to each side of the town, to arrest such as might attempt to escape, while the main body marched into
the village, and stationed themselves in the square in front of the jail,
which then occupied the same site as at present. Adjutant Church was
ordered to detach platoons from the main body, and station them at
the corners of the streets, and those points best calculated to prevent resistance or a combination of forces. Lieut. Wells commanded the right
flank guard, and Lieut. Johnson the left. Sergeant Foster, of the main
guard, who had been stationed with a few men on one of the corners,
on hearing the approach of a company of men, hailed them with the
challenge, "who comes there?" He was answered by the reply, "not
friends of King George." Not hearing the first word in the reply, he
fired and wounded one man. The party proved to be the left flank of
the Americans, and an understanding was soon regained. Meanwhile
Captain Forsyth, with a few men, entered the jail, and demanded the
keys, which were surrendered without resistance, and every prisoner,
with the exception of one confined for murder, was removed. He naturally begged hard to share the fortune of the others, but was left. Some
of the more prominent citizens were taken prisoners, and (with the exception of one physician who was paroled at Morristown), taken to Ogdensburgh, at which place the party arrived before daylight. The rescued prisoners and citizens brought back, numbered about fifty-two, of
whom six or seven were officers. One man was wounded by a shot from
a window, with which exception no resistance was offered. The countersign of the party on this affair was *Americans.* Among the prisoners was Major Carley, three captains, and two lieutenants.

The following is a list of those taken, except officers: Stephen Chip-
man, David Wheeler, Charles French, Benjamin Gould, Wm. Graves,
Winthrop Tufts, Zea Castle, Ichabod Wing, George Allen, Henry Staats,
Timothy Buel, Abram McCue, Thomas Daehnbam, Alex. Campbell,
John Davis, Dan'l McMullen, Richard McBane, Joseph Trader, Isaac
C——, (name illegible), Uri Stone, Archibald Ladd, David Wheeler, John
W. Easton, Peter Whitman, Joseph Howard, Levi Stone, Thomas Thorn-
ton, Isaac Mather, Samuel Elliot, Joseph Woolley, James Smith, Horatio
Bradshaw, Gamaliel Tuttle, John Green, Joseph Ryon, Norris Loverin,
David Stevenson, Jehiel Smith, Thomas Rambley, Wm. Robinson, Rich-
ardson Cameron, Henry Smith, Cleveland Safford, John Joy, John
Whitlesy. Total 45, besides officers.

(From the original list.)

They also seized and brought away one hundred and twenty muskets,
twenty rifles, two casks of fixed ammunition, and some other public stores,
but no private property was either taken or destroyed. A writer from
Ogdensburgh, giving an account of this affair, says: "Captain Forsyth
was led to this enterprise by the repeated aggressions of the British
guards, who had been in the habit of crossing the river a few miles

* Arnold Smith, who kept a public house in the place.

above this place, and taking deserters, sixteen of whom they had in the jail at Elizabethtown, threatened with being shot. Capt. F. being informed of this, determined to effect their liberation, in which he succeeded. One prisoner confined in the jail for murder, he declined taking. Capt. F. speaks of the conduct of the officers and men in the highest terms of approbation. Two British officers, from Prescott, came over a few hours after the return of our troops with the prisoners, to effect their release. I understand they are all paroled, and are to return again to Canada this evening. The movement of the troops on the other side indicating an attack on this place, Col. Benedict was induced to call out his regiment of militia, so that we have now in Ogdensburgh about 800 men; and should an attack be made from Prescott, I have the fullest confidence in our success. .Indeed, from the high tone of our troops, it is difficult to restrain their ardor; and should they not be attacked from the other side within a few days, I should not be surprised were they to go over there."

This affair led the enemy to take measures for retaliation, and the governor arriving on his way to Upper Canada, Lt. Col. Pearson commanding at Prescott, proposed an attack upon Ogdensburgh, but the governor did not deem it expedient to order an attack; but as two men had deserted on the evening of his arrival and gone over to the Americans, who might, upon ascertaining the arrival of the governor, waylay him on his route, it was determined that Lieut. Col. Pearson should proceed on the ensuing morning with his excellency to Kingston, while Lt. Col. McDonnell, second in command at Prescott, should make a demonstration upon the ice in front of Ogdensburgh, as well with the view of engaging the attention of the troops, as by drawing out their forces to ascertain the strength of the garrison.

To afford the data from which to estimate the relative merit of the defence, the following account of the armament and force in garrison at Ogdensburgh is given, as derived from the memories of citizens then in town. It had been learned from spies that the British were preparing to attack the town, and Capt. Forsyth had written to General Dearborn, at Plattsburgh, soliciting assistance. To this Gen. D. sent word that he could afford him no help, and that he must do as well as he was able. If he could not defend the place he was at liberty to evacuate it, and it was left optional with him to do this before or after making an attempt to defend it. In his letter he said that the loss of the place might arouse the American spirit, intimating that the town was to be made a sacrifice for the good of the country.

Upon receiving this letter, Captain Forsyth assembled the officers around him, consisting of Captain Kellog, Lieutenant Smith of the rifle company, Lieutenant Baird, second lieutenant in the same, Lieutenants Lytle and Wells of the volunteers, then just raised, and Adjutant Church, who had at the request of General Brown joined Forsyth, to await the arrival of volunteers. A few others whose names are not remembered, were present. To these he read the letter of General Dearborn, and solicited their advice. The result of the deliberation that ensued was, that it was expedient to defend the place as long as practicable, and to abandon it only when compelled.

The defences of the place were as follows: Near the intersection of Ford and Eupharnia (now State) streets, stood an iron twelve pounder, under the command of Captain Kellog, of the Albany volunteers. It was mounted on a wheel carriage, and was one of the trophies won in the revolutionary war from Burgoyne at Saratoga. In front of the arse-sal* in Ford street, was a brass six pounder, on a wheel carriage belonging to the state of New York. It was under the command of Joseph York, with a few men mostly citizens and volunteers. A short distance north of the northeast corner of Mr. Parish's store, was a rude wooden breastwork, defended by an iron twelve pounder, which was mounted on a sled carriage. It was also one of the trophies won from Burgoyne, and was under the command of Captain Joshua Conkey, of Canton, but it is said was not fired, although it was so placed that it might have done the enemy much injury, and perhaps have checked them altogether. This piece had been on the armed vessel Niagara. On the point where the light house now stands, was a brass nine pounder, which had also been brought down on the Niagara, near the close of navigation. It is said to have been mounted on a sled carriage, and was under the command of a sergeant in the company of Captain Kellog. This piece was fired repeatedly with effect, and its commander was one of the last who retreated when the place was finally evacuated. Back of the old stone garrison were two old fashioned iron six pounders, which were mounted on sleds. They had formed a part of the armament of some gun boats that had dismantled the fall before. One of these pieces was under the orders of Daniel W. Church, and the other of Lieut. Baird, of Captain Forsyth's company. In front of the gateway between the two buildings which formed the stone garrison, was a six pound brass piece on a sled carriage. This piece had been in the village during the summer, and for some time previous had been used in their exercises by a company of flying artillery then being formed, but which was absent or scattered at the time when the place was taken. About twenty feet to the left of this, was a six pound iron cannon, on a sled carriage, which had been taken from a gun boat. Besides these, there were several cannon which had been thrown from gun boats upon the beach in front of the stone garrison, which were frozen into the ice, and which together with all of those above enumerated, were taken by the enemy, and were never recovered.

Below the town and not far from the present brewery, was an unfinished redoubt which had been commenced towards the close of the season previous, but which was at the time not occupied or defended. It had been commenced under the orders of General Brown, and was planned by M. Ramee, a French engineer, who had been in the service of Bonaparte, and was to have been quadrangular in form, and bore the name of Fort Oswegatchie.

" The troops stationed here have been employed since last Thursday, in building a fort—it progresses pretty fast, considering the number of men employed. It is believed, however, that it will not be finished before the winter sets in. The plan of the fort, we understand, was the production of Mr. Ramee, a French gentleman, who resides in this village." (*Ogdensburgh Palladium, vol. ii, No.* 46. *November* 10, 1812.)

The drafted militia had long since returned home, and Capt. Forsyth's company alone remained. Lieut. Lyttle had received orders for raising a company of volunteers, and Joshua Conkey, of Canton, had arrived a little before with thirteen men, towards a company. On the evening previous to the attack, an arrangement had been made, that in this case Adjutant Church was to have charge of the piece at the garrison, and Sheriff York the brass six pounder, near the arsenal. Early in the morning of Feb. 22, the governor departed, and at the same time Lt. Col.

* A store on the west side of Ford, between State and Isabella streets.

McDonnel marched out on the ice in two columns, with an intention, as stated by British authorities, of only making a demonstration, but which he turned into a real attack. One of these said to be five hundred strong, directed their march to a point where the breastwork had been thrown up below the village, but which at the time was without defense, and the other of about three hundred, approached from a point above the stone garrison. Besides the regulars, there were not more than fifty to show their faces to the enemy. Capt. Forsyth had drawn up his men in the rear of the garrison, and facing the column that was approaching from that quarter, and, when within half musket shot, he walked down in front of his men, and directed them to reserve their fire until the word of command was given. Near the right of the line, Lieutenant Baird was stationed with an iron six pounder, and Adjutant Church was about two-thirds the way down the line, with a brass six. No order was given to fire until the enemy had nearly reached the bank, where the snow had drifted about knee deep, and here they first fired, but without effect. Captain Forsyth then ordered his troops to fire, and a volley was at once discharged from the rifles and the two cannon. Upon hearing the order, the soldiers of the enemy fell prostrate, and immediately after the discharge, the company jumped up and ran off without ceremony, leaving eight of their number dead on the ice. This detachment consisted of provincial militia and volunteers, under British officers. The column of five hundred from below, under McDonnell, marched into the village without resistance. York and Kellog each fired upon them, but the gun of the latter was disabled, by the breaking of the elevating screw, at the first fire, which prevented it from being again used. York continued to fire till two of his men* were mortally wounded, and himself and party taken prisoners. Kellog and his men, after the accident which deprived them of further means of resistance, retired across the Oswegatchie, and joined Captain Forsyth. Meanwhile, the greatest confusion and alarm prevailed throughout the village, and numbers of citizens were hastening away, most of them in the direction of Heuvelton. The nine pounder, which was posted on the point under the charge of a sergeant, was fired with effect upon the first column, the moment they began to show disorder and commence retreat, but its position was such that it could not molest the other lower body. Captain Conkey surrendered himself without resistance. These three cannon being in their possession, together with the village, the enemy next directed his efforts towards the position of Forsyth.

There were planted in front of the stone garrison, occupied by him, one iron and a brass cannon, both sixes. These were loaded by Church and Baird, but when about to be fired, a white flag borne by two men was seen approaching. One of the bearers was Duncan Frazer, and the other Jonas Jones, who has since filled a high judicial station in Canada. The object of their visit was to present the compliments of Colonel Mc Donnel, and the conditional alternative, of " if you surrender, it shall be well; if not, every man shall be put to the bayonet." Captain Forsyth promptly replied, " Tell Colonel McDonnel there must be more fighting done first." The bearers of the communication immediately returned, and had no sooner entered the ranks, which were drawn up in Ford street, near the Hasbrouck place, when the two cannon before the gate way were immediately discharged. The brass piece was loaded with case shot, and disabled eight men; but being a little too elevated, it had

* Joseph Kneeland and —— Hyde, b)th citizens.

but little of the effect that would have been witnessed, had it been properly pointed.*

Immediately after this discharge, the enemy retreated behind the stone store of Mr. Parish, for shelter. Up to this time there had been none of Forsyth's company killed, and as there remained no enemy in sight, the latter ordered his men within the gates, as the British began to fire at his company from behind various objects, by which several were wounded, among whom were men by the names of Squires and Clark. They were not so badly wounded but that they were able to retreat. Lieutenant Baird lingered behind after the order for retreat was given, and only retired when a messenger was sent with a second command for him to leave. Soon after, some of the party, among whom were Church and Baird, went out to load the cannon in the rear which had been first used, hoping that some chance might occur for discharging them with effect, but on returning, both were wounded, the latter severely. Deeming further resistance useless, Captain Forsyth issued orders for his men to retreat, and to rendezvous at Thurber's tavern, on Black lake, and thence they proceeded to De Peyster Corners, where they arrived in the evening. The British took prisoners all the men in the hospital, eight in number, and Sergeant Carr, who had care of the arsenal. Lieutenant Baird was too badly wounded to retreat, and was conveyed to the house of Judge Ford, where he was taken prisoner. Adjutant Church, with the assistance of two of Forsyth's men, retreated. None of this company was killed, and with the above exceptions, none taken prisoners. There were on the side of the Americans five killed and eighteen wounded. As the enemy were marching down Ford street, some of the number on entering the store room used as an arsenal, were met by a lad at the door, by the name of Jones, from Canton who discharged a musket, and severely wounded one of their number, and was in the act of reloading his piece, when the soldiers, enraged at this resistance, fired a volley upon the courageous boy, and finished their work with him by a thrust of a bayonet, which pinned him to the counter. Further resistance not being offered, the enemy proceeded to ransack the town for public property and pillage, carrying off or wantonly destroying private property to a great amount. Fifty-two prisoners were taken over to Canada, where citizens were mostly paroled and allowed to return home, excepting those who had been found under arms. Conkey and his men, Sergeant Rogers, Lieutenant Baird, and a few others, believed to be about twenty, were sent as prisoners of war to Montreal, and thence by water to Halifax, until exchanged, except fourteen, of whom Rogers was one, who escaped from jail at Montreal, and returned home.

These prisoners were confined in an upper story of the prison; their window was grated with a double row of iron bars; a line of sentinels patrolled the premises surrounding, and the yard was enclosed with a stone wall. The manner in which they effected their escape, is said to have been as follows: Besides those taken at Ogdensburgh, there were several others confined in the same apartment, among whom was one who resided just south of the boundary on lake Champlain, who was known to be an active partizan, and had been seized on British soil, and

* The anecdote is related, that as Mr. Church was about to fire this cannon, Captain Forsyth stepped forward and ordered him to elevate it more. The former replied that it was high enough, but the commander, impatient of contradiction, peremptorily renewed his order, which was sullenly obeyed. It has been suggested that an additional turn of the screw was given to prove the soundness of his argument, and thus the lives of many of the enemy were saved.

confined, as a prudential measure. To him, however, on account of friends residing in the city, considerable indulgence was shown, and they were allowed to send him, from time to time, certain dainties from their tables. Being of ample corporeal dimensions, and enjoying an appetite adequate to its maintenance, the dishes were sometimes of proportionate size; and especially some of the puddings, which might have sufficed for a small party, but which were found to conceal numbers of sharp *files* and *saws*. With these the prisoners worked, whenever they could do so, unobserved, and at the end of two weeks, had so nearly severed the bars, that they could be removed with little labor. To conceal their operations, the notches worked with the files were filled with a sort of paste mingled with the filings in such a manner as not to be readily detected without close observation. At length a propitious night arrived for their flight. An inclement storm drove the sentinels to their boxes, and the tempest howled around the premises, deadening whatever sound they might accidentally make. Their bedding was torn up and twisted into ropes, the bars removed, and one by one, with the exception of the corpulent gentleman, from whose dinners the tools had been derived, they glided down the rope unobserved, and succeeded in scaling the wall and getting away. One of their number strained his ancle, and was unable to accompany them; but finding friends in the city, he remained two or three weeks, and finally in the garb of an agent of the commissary department, he was conveyed away, and Conkey and Baird remained prisoners till the close of the war.

To return to the subject: the enemy continued through the day to seek and carry away whatever commodities their caprice or their wants indicated, among which was a large quantity of provisions from the stone store, of which they were said to be much in need, and for which they paid the value. The prisoners in the jail, upon their own assertion that they were confined for political reasons, were set free, but upon a true representation being made afterwards, several were pursued, recaptured and given up to the sheriff.

The wanton destruction of private property, which is said to have extended to every house in the village except three, was perpetrated by swarms of the abandoned of both sexes from Canada, and by numbers of the dissolute class who belonged to the American side, and who seized this opportunity to gratify a morbid passion for gain, and for wanton ruin. The barracks were burned, and an attempt was made to fire the bridge, but without effect, as it was covered with ice and snow. The citizen prisoners captured at this incursion, were exchanged for those taken at Brockville. It is but just to observe that the wanton plunder of the enemy was disclaimed by those in command, and some efforts were made to procure the restoration of a few of the articles stolen.

The following are the British official accounts of this affair, dated Kingston, February 23, 1813:

GENERAL ORDERS.—His excellency the commander of the forces, has the satisfaction of announcing to the army in British North America, the complete success of an attack made by Lieut. Col. McDonnel, of the Glengary light infantry, and the detachment stationed at Prescott, yesterday morning, on the enemy's position at Ogdensburgh, which terminated in the capture of that place, and of eleven pieces of cannon, and all the ordnance and marine stores, provisions and camp equipage, and the destruction of two armed schooners and two gun boats. Such of the enemy's garrison as did not fly to the woods, were made prisoners. The conduct of every individual engaged, and which includes the whole of the troops, regular and militia, stationed at Prescott, appears to have been highly honorable to them. The following officers are particularly noticed by Col. McDonnel, as having distinguished themselves: Capt. Jenkins, of the Glengary light infantry, who, the commander of the forces laments to find, is severely wounded, as also Lieut. Empy, of the militia, who has lost a leg, and Lieut. Powell, of the King's regiment, slightly wounded, Staff Adjutant Ridge, of the King's regiment, who led the advance guard, and Lieut. McAuly, of the Glengary light infantry. Lieutenant McDonnel reports that he was well supported by Capt. Eustace, and the officers of the King's regiment; by Col. Fraser and Lieut. Col. Fraser, and all the officers of the militia, as well as by Capt. Le Lievre, of the Royal Newfoundland regiment, attached to the militia. The field artillery was well served by Ensigns McKay of the Glengary light infantry, and Kerr, of the militia, and the good conduct of the Royal engineers is likewise particularly noticed.

The commander of the forces was induced to authorize this attack, not by any means as an act of wanton aggression, the troops under his command having been ordered at all times to abstain from all acts of that nature; but as one of a just and necessary retaliation on that which was recently made on the British settlement of Brockville, by a party from Ogdensburgh, and in consequence of frequent depredations from that garrison committed on the persons and property of his majesty's subjects within its reach; and in announcing its results, his excellency feels much pleasure in publicly expressing his entire approbation of the gallantry and judgment with which it appears to have been conducted.

His excellency directs the officers and men taken prisoners on this occasion to be sent to Montreal, there to remain until further orders. A salute to be fired immediately.

JOHN HARVEY,
Lieut. Col. and Dep. Adj. Gen.

OFFICE OF THE ADJUTANT GENERAL'S DEPARTMENT, }
    Montreal, February 25, 1813. }

GENERAL ORDERS.—The major general commanding, has much satisfaction in announcing to the troops in the lower province, that he has received a report from Lieutenant Colonel McDonnel, of the Glengary light infantry, stating that in consequence of the wanton attack lately made by the enemy on the village of Brockville, it had been determined to retaliate by an assault on his position at Ogdensburgh. This took place, in a gallant and spirited manner, under the command of that officer, on the morning of the 22d inst., and was crowned with success after an action of an hour and a half, in which the enemy had about twenty killed, and a great number wounded.

Lieutenant Colonel McDonnel reports his having taken possession of all the enemy's artillery (with the exception of one piece), as well as naval, military, and commissariat stores; and of his having destroyed the barracks and shipping. A detailed return of the stores, has not yet been received, but eleven pieces of artillery and several hundred stand of arms had arrived at Prescott.

Lieut. Colonel McDonnel speaks in high terms of the conduct of the force under his command, particularly of the gallantry of Capt. Jenkins, of the Glengary light infantry, who was severely wounded. The lieut. colonel also mentions the assistance which he received from Colonel Frazer, Lieut. Col. Frazer, and all the officers of the militia, from Capt. Eustace and officers of the King's regiment, Capt. Le Lievre of the Newfoundland regiment, Lieutenant McAuley and the officers of the Glengary light infantry, and from Lieut. Gangrelen, of the Royal engineers; Ensigns M'Kay of the Glengary, and Kerr of the militia, who directed the service of the field pieces, as well as of the spirited manner in which the advance was led on by Staff Adjutant Ridge.

List of killed and wounded in the attack upon Ogdensburgh, 22d Feb., 1813.

Royal artillery—One rank and file killed. *King's regiment*—One sergeant killed; 12 rank and file wounded. *Newfoundland regiment*—One rank and file killed, and four rank and file wounded. *Glengary light infantry*—Two rank and file killed; one lieutenant colonel, one captain, one lieutenant, two sergeants, seven rank and file, wounded. *Militia*—Two rank and file killed; one captain, eight subalterns, one sergeant, fifteen rank and file, wounded. *Total*—One sergeant, six rank and file, killed; one lieutenant colonel, two captains, four subalterns, three sergeants, and thirty-eight rank and file, wounded. *Names of officers wounded*—Glengary light infantry, Lieut. Col. McDonnel, Capt. Jenkins, severely; Lieut. M'Kay. *Militia*—Capt. J. McDonnel, Lieut. Empy, severely; Lieut. M'Lean, and Lieut. M'Dermott.

J. ROWEN,
Deputy Assistant Adjutant General.

Capt. Forsyth announced to the secretary of war the event at Ogdensburgh, in the following letter, dated Feb. 22, 1813.

"SIR :—I have only time to inform you that the enemy, with a very superior force, succeeded in taking Ogdensburgh this morning, about 9 o'clock. They had about two men to our one, exclusive of Indians. Numbers of the enemy are dead on the field. Not more than twenty of our men killed and wounded; Lt. Beard is among the latter.

I have made a saving retreat of about eight or nine miles. I could not get all the wounded off.

We have killed two of the enemy to one of ours killed by them. We want ammunition and some provisions sent to us, also sleighs for the wounded. If you can send me *three hundred men, all shall be retaken,* and *Prescott* too, or I will lose my life in the attempt.

I shall write more particular to-day.

Yours, with due respect,
BENJAMIN FORSYTH, Cap. Rifle reg. com'g.

The following extracts convey additional facts in relation to this affair, and from having been written soon after the occurrence of the events, possess additional interest. The first is from Mr. Rosseel, and the second is understood to have been written by Mrs. York, to a brother in New York, and was published in Niles's Weekly Register.

"By the middle of the afternoon, having rigged out an apology for a one horse sleigh, I left Ogdensburgh with the land office papers, to rejoin my family, who left it the moment the place was being taken and came within an ace of receiving the contents of a 32 pounder, loaded with grape and canister, which stood at the four corners (near St. Lawrence tavern), in front of which the sleigh in which my family were, was driving furiously along, undistinguished from the enemy, and the dread effect of which discharge I witnessed from my window. Several of the British fell at the corner of Mr. Parish's premises [in the fence of which, what remains, may yet be seen to this day, the marks made by the grape shot.] I had received from General Arnold, of the militia, who was here prisoner on parole, a commission for Capt. Forsyth. that he prepare for an attack that night.   Forsyth and his rifle corps were at Kellog's [about a mile s. w. of Depeyster corners—on state road], and I found the militia at Remington's [Heuvelton].   They would not allow me to go further till I told them my errand.   The teamster who drove me was very drunk, and never minded the challenge from the pickets placed here and there along the road, which was narrow, I sometimes feeling their rifles touching our bodies.   At Kellog's I found almost all Ogdensburgh, soldier and civilian, all pell-mell.   But after I communicated to Capt. Forsyth my message from Gen. Arnold, the sound of the bugle cleared the room of riflemen, and the people breathed more freely.   After placing my family in safety, I returned to Ogdensburgh, between which place and Rossie Iron Works my attention was divided."

   Extract of a letter, February 26, 1813.   "I did not leave the house until the British were close to it, and not till they had shot a great number of balls into it.   I took nothing with me but some money, and my table spoons, and ran as fast as possible, with a number of other women; our retreat was to the distance of about 15 miles.   The next day I returned; our house was plundered of almost every thing, and my husband a prisoner on the other side.   You can easier imagine my feelings than I can describe them.   They did not leave any article of clothing, not even a handkerchief—they took all my bedding but left the beds; they broke my looking glasses and even my knives.   Thus situated I determined to go over to Canada, and accordingly went to a flag of truce, which was then in this village, for permission, which I obtained.   I went to one of my acquaintances on the other side, where I was favorably received. I applied to the commanding officer for the purpose of ascertaining whether I could procure any of my clothes; he assured me that I should have them if I could find them, but did not trouble himself to make any inquiry.   My journey was not lost; I procured the release of my husband, who was paroled and returned with me.   Most of the houses in the village were plundered. * * * You will be astonished when I tell you that they were not contented with what the Indians and soldiers could plunder during the battle, but after it was over, the women on the other side came across, and took what was left."   The partizan spirit of Mr. York, which was well known to the enemy, may have rendered his house an object on which to expend their antipathies. It was reported that a company of women, under the protection of a guard, was sent over to plunder, but this rumor is scarcely credible. The following anecdote, however, is doubtless reliable.   One of the provincial militia in crossing during the day, was met by a woman returning with a large mirror, which she said she had stolen from the Yankees.   She had scarcely spoken, when her feet slipped on the ice, which threw her prostrate, and her ill gotten booty was lost, while boasting of her success in obtaining it.

   Capt. Forsyth having retired with his company to Depeyster, the place was left defenceless, and the same day evacuated by the British.   Gen. Brown having received news of the affair arrived the next day, but did not enter the town, and soon returned home, and Forsyth proceeded to Sackett's Harbor, to join the forces at that place, which a few months after participated in the descent upon Little York.

   Most of the citizens who fled on the attack returned home, and the place was left entirely without military defence, or any semblance of resistance during the remainder of the war. This defenceless condition occasionally exposed them to insult, and in May 1813, some deserters having come over from the enemy, an officer was sent across with a flag, with a threat to commit the village to the flames, if they were not restored. To this requisition, Judge Ford, with his usual promptness replied, that they would do no such thing, for no sooner should he see them landing, *than with his own hands he would set fire to his own house, rally his neighbors, cross the river with torches, and burn every house from Prescott to Brockville.* The British officer seeing the consequences that might ensue, afterwards apologized for his conduct. In the fall of 1813, Col. Luckett, with a regiment of dragoons, forming a part of the regular service, was sent in advance of the army of Gen. Wilkinson, to examine the country and report.

He is believed to have been instructed to make no demonstration that would create alarm to the enemy, or lead to an attack. On the day of his arrival, Oct. 11, 1813, the town was filled with people, who had come to attend court, which was to commence its session on the following day. It was secretly reported the same evening, to persons still living, that there would be a flurry next day, the meaning of which in due time became apparent. The court met and had begun business, Benjamin Raymond presiding as judge, assisted by Daniel W. Church, and John Tibbits, assistant justices. The grand jury had received their charge and retired, and a case was being tried, when a cannonade was heard from the fort at Prescott, which led to much uneasiness, and after a little discussion, the session of the court was interrupted for the day, by the withdrawing of a juror, and the room was hastily evacuated. The grand jury also hearing the cannonade, adjourned for the day, and left the house. Their room was above the court room, in what is now a masonic hall. In passing out, the room was hardly cleared, and the last person of the number in the door, when a 24 pound shot entered the room, shattering an end beam in the house cut obliquely across the seats, but a moment before occupied by the jury, and lodged in the partition beyond. Fortunately no one was injured by the cannonade, but some damage was done to houses. As soon as the firing commenced Col. Luckett retired into the back country, and there are those who believe that a display of his force was designingly made to get up an excitement with the enemy.

In August 1813, a direct tax of $3,000,000 was apportioned throughout the United States, of which $770 was drawn from Franklin, $3,000 from St. Lawrence, $4,610 from Jefferson, and $1,960 from Lewis counties.

Before giving an account of Wilkinson's expedition, we will notice the operations in Franklin county, in the campaign of 1812. A company of militia from Lt. Col. Alric Man's regiment was drafted early in the summer, and commanded by Capt. Rufus Tilden, and about 18 mounted men, who were under the orders of the general officers of the regiment, to which Tilden was attached, viz: the 8th, commanded by Lt. Col. Thos. Miller, of Plattsburgh. Tilden's company were posted at French Mills, and commenced building a block house. Early in the fall, other companies of the 8th regiment, under Major Ransom Noble, of Essex, joined, and afterwards others under Major Young (p. 157). The mounted men were used as express men. This party acted in the descent upon St. Regis, which we have described (p. 156), but the merit of their boasted capture of *the colors*, loses its importance, if the following extract from Christie's history of the war (a British writer) be true.

" The Americans in plundering the village found an ensign or union jack, in the house of the resident interpreter, usually hoisted upon a flag staff at the door of the chief, on Sundays or Holy Days, which said the American Major in an order issued upon the occasion (not a little proud of the achievement,) *were the first colors taken during the war*."

The same author in giving an account of the affair at Toussaint island, states that the British force numbered 138 troops under Major Heathcoat. A detachment of militia commanded by Capt. Munroe had arrived near the close of the skirmish. Soon after the affair at St. Regis, Col. Young was withdrawn, and the enemy planned an attack upon Capt. Tilden, in retaliation for the first aggression. This took place on the 22d of November, according to Christie, by detachments of the Royal artillery, 49th regiment, and Glengary light infantry, amounting to seventy men, with detachments from the Cornwall and Glengary militia, of near the same number, the whole under the command of Lieut. Col. McMillan. The block house was not finished and had no roof, and the company was quartered in a house, on Water street, since owned and occupied as a dwelling by the late James B. Spencer. During the night an alarm had been brought in, and the company repaired to the block house. The British marched in on the old St. Regis road, west of Salmon river, crossed and paraded on Water street. The block house stood on a rising ground at some distance east of the river. Deeming it impossible to avoid it, Capt. Tilden surrendered his party prisoners to the number of 44, including himself and two subalterns. Many escaped, and the prisoners were sent to Montreal and imprisoned, one third being on parole each day until in three weeks they were exchanged for the very men they had taken at St. Regis, and released. At the affair at French Mills, Thomas Fletcher was shot in his door, having first discharged his rifle at a company of soldiers.

After Captain Tilden's company were taken prisoners, their place was supplied by militia and volunteers from Columbia county, under the command of Major Tanner, part of the 9th regiment New York State militia, who remained here until the first of March, 1813, when Captain David Erwin raised a company of volunteers who were stationed as a garrison for the block house, here, during the spring and summer of 1813. This company in the fall joined General Hampden's forces at Chateaugay, where he was intending to coöperate with General Wilkinson, after which this company was discharged.

Early in 1813, a plan of operations for the reduction of Canada was discussed in the cabinet, Gen. John Armstrong being the secretary of war, and Major General Henry Dearborn at the head of the northern armies. The following is a copy of the general outline proposed by Armstrong to Dearborn, February 10, 1813:

" 1st, 4000 troops will be assembled at Sacketts Harbor. 2d, 3000 will be brought together at Buffalo and its vicinity. 3d, the former of these corps will be embarked and transported under a convoy of the fleet to *Kingston*, where they will be landed. Kingston, its garrison, and the British ships wintering in the harbor of that place, will be its first object. Its second object will be York (the capital of Upper Canada), the stores collected and the two frigates building there. Its third object, Forts George and Erie, and their dependencies. In the attainment of this last, there will be a coöperation between the two corps. The composition of these will be as follows:

1st, Bloomfield brigade, 1,436; 2d, Chandler's brigade, 1,044; 3d,

Philadelphia detachment, 400; 4th, Baltimore detachment, 300; 5th Carlisle detachment, 200; 6th, Greenbush detachment, 400; 7th, Sacketts Harbor detachment, 250; 8th, several corps at Buffalo under the command of Col. Porter, and the recruits belonging there, 3000: total, 7000. The time for executing this enterprise will be governed by the opening of Lake Ontario, which usually takes place about the first of April.

The adjutant general has orders to put the most southern detachments in march as expeditiously as possible. The two brigades on Lake Champlain you will move so as to give them full time to reach their destination by the 25th of March. The route by Elizabeth will, I think, be the shortest and best. They will be replaced by some new raised regiments from the east. You will put into your movements as much privacy as may be compatable with their execution. They may be masked by reports that Sacketts Harbor is in danger, and that the principal efforts will be made on the Niagara, in coöperation with Gen. Harrison.

As the route to Sacketts Harbor and to Niagara is for a considerable distance the same, it may be well to intimate, even in orders, that the latter is the destination of the two brigades now at Lake Champlain."

The attack of Little York, and the operations on the Niagara frontier, were a part of the plan, and tended more or less to its accomplishment, but their details belong to our general history. On the 8th of July, 1813, Gen. Dearborn was withdrawn from the command of the northern army, and on the 5th of August, a communication was addressed to Gen. Jas. Wilkinson, proposing a plan of operations which he approved, and undertook to execute. This was to bring a combined force upon Canada, a part to descend the St. Lawrence, and another portion by way of Lake Champlain, which were to unite and coöperate as circumstances might dictate. The former of these was to be under the command of General Wilkinson, and the latter that of Gen. Wade Hampden. It remained to be discussed whether Kingston was first to be reduced, and in the advice of the secretary of war, this measure was strongly recommended. Gen. Wilkinson arrived at Sacketts Harbor, towards the last of August, and proceeded to the head of the lake to make preliminary arrangements for concentrating his forces. A series of unpardonable delays hindered him from effecting this object or of returning to Sacketts Harbor, before the 4th of October. The secretary of war was at that post, and on the day following a discussion was held between Generals Armstong, Wilkinson, Lewis and Brown, at which the reasons for and against making Kingston the first point of attack, were brought forward and examined in detail, but at length abandoned. The same delays and embarrassments continued and were increased by the storms incident to the lateness of the season. The forces assembled at Grenadier island. On the 28th of October, he wrote:

" The inexorable winds and rains continue to oppose and embarass our movements, but I am seizing every moment's interval to slip into the St. Lawrence, corps and detachments, as they can be got ready. Our rendezvous will be in Bush creek, about twenty miles below, and nearly opposite to Gananoqui, which position menaces a descent on the opposite shore. I shall sail from that position at 4 o'clock in the morning, and will pass Prescott about the same time the ensuing morning. We have had such a fluctuation of sick and well between this place and Sacketts Harbor, that it is impossible to say in what force we shall move; but I calculate on 6000 combatants, exclusive of Scott and Randolph, neither of whom will I fear be up in season, notwithstanding all my arrangements and exertions to accelerate their march."

38

On the first of November, 1813, the commander in chief wrote to Gen. Armstrong, as follows:

"You will perceive from the duplicate under cover (letter of the 28th of October), what were my calculations four days since; but the winds and waves, and rains and snow still prevail, and we have made several fruitless attempts to turn Stoney Point, one of them of great peril to three thousand men, whom I seasonably remanded to the harbor without the loss of a life. Our sick, one hundred and ninety six in number, have not fared as well; they were embarked in stout comfortable vessels, and sailed the day before yesterday morning for Sacketts Harbor, but they were driven on shore by a storm which continued with unremitting violence all night, and as no exertion could relieve them, I anticipated the loss of the whole; but the tempest having abated and the wind shifted from S. W. to N. E., boats were sent out yesterday morning, and Dr. Bull reports the loss of three men only. Other means of transport will be provided to-morrow, and these unfortunate men will be sent to the hospital at Sacketts Harbor. Brig. Gen. Brown, with his brigade, the light artillery, the riflemen, the gun boats, Bissel's regiment and a part of Macomb's are, I expect, safe at French creek, with the artillery and ordnance stores. These corps have made the traverse of the arm of the lake under circumstances of great danger, though fortunately without the loss of a life, but at the expense of some boats. I shall wait one day longer, and if the passage shall still continue impracticable to the troops, I will land them on the opposite shore, march them across the country to the St. Lawrence, and send the empty boats round to a given rendezvous. As Major General Hampton is under your orders, permit me to suggest to you what is worthy of reflection—whether he should take a position and wait the arrival of my command near the confluence of the St. Lawrence and Grand rivers, or whether he should move down the St. Lawrence and menace Chambly? If he is strong enough to meet Sir George, the latter will be the preferable plan, because it will have the effect to divide the enemy's force; otherwise, he should adopt the first idea, hazard nothing, and strengthen my hands. The enclosed copy of a memorandum from Colonel Swift, will show you what he is about, I flatter myself, to your satisfaction. The sole unpleasant circumstance before me, is our total ignorance of the *preparations* of Sir George, and what we may expect to meet on the island. I fear no consequences; but it must be painful to lead more than 6000 men to battle hoodwinked; and yet all my efforts to procure intelligence from Montreal, have proved fruitless."

The following account of the progress of the expedition down the St. Lawrence, is derived from the journal of Dr. Amasa Trowbridge, of Watertown, who attended in a professional capacity, and occasionally from the published diary of General Wilkinson.

On the 29th, Gen. Brown's brigade, with the light and heavy artillery, embarked and proceeded down the St. Lawrence, the entrance of which was about six miles from Bason harbor, and arrived safe at French creek the same evening. On the 31st, orders were issued directing the remainder of the army to follow, but a severe storm prevented the embarkation. The winds continued unfavorable till the 2d of November, when the whole embarked and arrived at Cape Vincent, nine miles, the same day, and encamped. General Brown, with the van of the expedition, had been attacked by the enemy's armed schooner and gun boats, but were repulsed with loss, and were compelled to move up the river and take a position eight miles below Cape Vincent. In the evening, about 10 o'clock, Commodore Chauncey came into the river from the lake, and anchored near the encampment. The army appeared much gratified at the appearance of the fleet.

On the 3d, the fleet weighed anchor and stood down the river. At seven the troops embarked and followed, with a favorable wind, and at nine passed our fleet at anchor, at the junction of the British channel with that on the south, in such a position as to oppose the enemy, should they attempt to annoy the army in descending. At 3 P. M., joined Gen. Brown at French creek. The 4th was spent in waiting, for boats with provisions and troops from Sackett's Harbor, and making necessary arrangements for the expedition. The 5th was a charming day, and in the morning orders were issued for sailing, and at six the whole army was under way, in about 300 small crafts and boats, and arrived the same evening at Morristown, a distance of forty miles; a favorable landing was selected, and the boats put in in good order. On the 6th the expedition proceeded on to within three miles of Ogdensburgh, and preparations were made for passing the fort at Prescott. At this place Gen. Wilkinson issued the following proclamation to the Canadians:

"The army of the United States, which I have the honor to command, invades these provinces to conquer, and not to destroy; to subdue the forces of his Britannic majesty, not to war against his unoffending subjects. Those, therefore, among you, who remain quiet at home, should victory incline to the American standard, shall be protected in their persons and property. But those who are found in arms, must necessarily be treated as avowed enemies. To menace is unjust, to seduce dishonorable; yet it is just and humane to place these alternatives before you.

Done at the head quarters of the United States army, this sixth day of November, 1813, near Ogdensburgh, on the river St. Lawrence.

    (Signed)   JAMES WILKINSON.

            By the general's command,

    (Signed)   N. PINKNEY,

                                  Major and Aid-de-camp."

"The powder and fixed ammunition were debarked and placed in carts, to be transported by land, under cover of the night, beyond the enemy's batteries. As soon as the general returned, orders were issued for the debarkation of every man (except so many as were necessary to navigate the boats), who were directed to march under cover of the night, to save useless exposure to the enemy's cannon, to a bay two miles below Prescott; and arrangements were made at the same time for the passage of the flotilla by that place, the superintendency of which devolved upon Brig. Gen. Brown, the general officer of the day. About 8 o'clock P. M., we had so heavy a fog, that it was believed we could pass the British fortress unobserved, and orders were accordingly given for the army to march, and the flotilla to get under way. The general, in his gig, proceeded ahead, followed by his passage boat and family; but a sudden change of the atmosphere exposed his passage boat to the garrison of the enemy, and near fifty-two twenty-four pound shot were fired at her without effect, while the column on land, discovered by the gleam of their arms, were assailed with shot and shells without injury. General Brown, on hearing the firing, judiciously halted the flotilla until the moon had set, when it got into motion, but was perceived by the enemy, who opened upon it, and continued their fire from front to rear, for the space of three hours; and yet out of more than three hundred boats, not one was touched; and only one man was killed, and two were wounded, Before ten next morning, the whole of the flotilla, except two vessels, reached the place of rendezvous."

[Another account states, that the general resorted to the expedient of sending some old boats forward, on which the British expended their long shot; and the army passed harmless, except from one shot, which killed two men and wounded three others.]

"About noon this day, Colonel King, adjutant general of the army of Gen. Wade Hampton, arrived, and waited on the commander-in-chief, whom he informed that he had been to Sackett's Harbor, with a despatch from Gen. Hampton to the secretary of war; that he had no communication, written or verbal, from Major General Hampton (the commander-in-chief), but that not finding the secretary of war at Sackett's Harbor, he had thought proper, on his return, to call for any communication which he (Gen. Wilkinson), might have to make to Gen. Hampton. The general had intended, in the course of the day, to send an express to Gen. Hampton, with an order to him to form a junction of his division with the corps descending the St. Lawrence, and availed himself of the opportunity presented by Col. King, to send the order. In passing Prescott, two of our largest vessels loaded with provisions, artillery and ordnance stores, either through cowardice or treachery, had been grounded in the river near Ogdensburgh, and opposite Prescott.

The enemy kept up so constant a cannonade on them, that we found it difficult, and lost half a day to get them out. We perceived the militia in arms at Johnstown, directly opposite us, and several pieces of field artillery in motion. Understanding that the coast below was lined with posts of musketry and artillery at every narrow pass of the river, Colonel Macomb was detached about one o'clock with the elite corps of about 1200 men, to remove these obstructions, and the general got under way about half past three o'clock.

Four or five miles below, we entered the first rapids of the river, and soon after passing them, two pieces of light artillery which Colonel Macomb had not observed, opened a sharp fire upon the general's passage boat, but without any further effect than cutting away some of the rigging.

Lieutenant Colonel Eustis, with a party of our light gun barges, came within shot of the pieces of the enemy, and a cannonade ensued without injury to either side. In the mean time, Major Forsyth, who was in the rear of the elite of Colonel Macomb, landed his riflemen, advanced upon the enemy's guns, and had his fire drawn by a couple of videts, posted in his route, on which their pieces were precipitately carried off.

The general came to at dusk, about six miles below the town of Hamilton, where he received a report from Colonel Macomb, who had routed a party at a block house about two miles below, and captured an officer."

On the morning of the 7th, information had been received that the enemy had taken a position on the river above Hamilton, at a narrow pass, and had fortified it to annoy the flotilla in passing. These were dislodged by Major Forsyth. A body of dragoons had assembled here for crossing, and the whole of the 8th and following night were devoted to transporting these. About noon, advice was received that two armed schooners, and a body of the enemy in bateaux, estimated at 1000 or 1500 men, had descended the river from Kingston, and landed at Prescott; that they had immediately sent a flag across the river to Ogdensburgh, and demanded the surrender of all public property there, under the penalty of burning the town. Not long after, we received information that the enemy had reëmbarked at Prescott, in their bateaux, and were following with seven gun boats.

While the expedition lay at the narrows near Hamilton, on the 8th, a council of war was held, Generals Wilkinson, Lewis, Boyd, Covington, Porter, and Swartwout, being present, in which the commander-in-chief stated that his force consisted of 7,000 men, and that he expected to meet 4,000 more under Gen. Hampden, at St. Regis; that his provisions amounted to ten day's bread and twenty day's meat; that from the best of his information the enemy's force was 600 under Colonel Murray, troops of the line at Coteau de Lac, strongly fortified with artillery; 200 on the island opposite, with two pieces of artillery, and about the same number on the south shore, with two pieces of artillery; 200 or 300 men of the British line of artillery, but without ammunition, at the Cedars; at Montreal 200 sailors and 400 mariners, with the militia, numbers unknown; no fortifications at that city or in advance of it; 2,500 regular troops expected daily from Quebec; the militia on the line reported at 20,000 men, Canadians chiefly. This information was procured by colonel Swift, who employed a secret agent for the purpose. Under these circumstances Major General Wilkinson submitted to the council the following proposition, viz: Shall the army proceed with all possible rapidity to the attack of Montreal? The above information was given by a confidential agent of reputed integrity, who left Montreal on the 3d instant; it was added, that two British armed vessels, with sixty bateaux with troops, had arrived at Prescott this morning, and that four hundred were the last evening at Cornwall, about thirty-three miles below this point. With these facts before them, the question was asked, "shall we proceed to attack Montreal?" to which Lewis, Boyd, Brown, and Swartwout, decided in the affirmative, and Covington and Porter expressed strong apprehensions from want of proper pilots, &c., but saw no other alternative.

A body of 300 provincial militia had, the evening before the arrival of the main army, been driven by Forsyth from a block house, with two 6 pound cannon, and this he had burned. On the evening of the 8th, the passage of the cavalry to the north shore was accomplished, and on the 9th at 6 A. M., the 2d brigade with two companies of the 2d artillery, the riflecorps and cavalry commenced their march by land to Williamsburgh, and in the afternoon the flotilla moved down the river. Very early in the morning, the enemy in the rear had a slight skirmish with the riflemen, in which we had one man killed, and the enemy retired. The object of Gen. Brown's being sent forward with a part of the army, was to clear the shore of any annoyances which the enemy might have erected, opposite the rapids and narrow defiles of the river. The flotilla passed down 11 miles, and came to for the night, and the army encamped on ground selected by Gen. Boyd, guards were posted, and all remained quiet for the night. The enemy continued to follow up the rear, and on arriving at Hamilton availed themselves of the opportunity to send to that village a peremptory demand for the restoration of some merchandise that had been captured under the following circumstances:

In October, 1813, some six or eight bateaux laden with merchandise, and owned in Kingston and Toronto, were passing along up the river, under the Canadian shore, and were moored for the night, not far from opposite the head of Ogden's island, when they were surprised, while most of the crews were sleeping, and captured without resistance. This expedition was planned and executed mostly under the direction of Benjamin Richards, of Hamilton, acting under a letter of marque, and assisted by a volunteer party of citizens. A part of the captured goods were stored in a warehouse in the village, and the cloths and lighter articles were taken to Madrid (Columbia village) and in other parts of the town for greater security. Soon after Gen. Wilkinson with his army had passed, Col. Morrison of the army which hung upon the rear of the Americans, stopped at the village, landed a part of his force, and demanded a surrender of the merchandise. No resistance could of course be offered or attempted, and he was proceeding to take what might be found of the property. While engaged in this, he heard a cannonade below, which made him impatient of delay, and he hastily spiked a 6 pound iron cannon which he found in the village, and ordered the goods and building in which they were to be set on fire. The day was beautifully dry and sunny, and the building, if burned, must have consumed a considerable part of the village. The principal citizens begged of the commanding officer of the enemy to consider this, and succeeded in getting the order countermanded under the stipulation that all the goods in the village which had been captured should be the next day landed on the Canada shore.

This agreement was fulfilled, but the portions which had been sent back to the Grass river were still in the hands of the captors. Some barracks belonging to the village of Hamilton, and which had been used by detachments of troops, were burned.

In January following, Capt. Reuben Sherwood, an active loyalist, of daring courage, who was well acquainted with the country, having acted as a surveyor, and who often appeared without disguise or concealment on the south shore of the St. Lawrence, crossed the river near Point Iroquois, with the design of recovering the remainder of the merchandise. He arrived late in the evening with a company of provincial militia, posted guards in the village to prevent resistance, pressed a number of teams with their drivers, and proceeded to Columbia village, where he succeeded in recovering, without difficulty, the greater part of what had been deposited in that place, which had not been purloined. The party engaged in this incursion returned about day light, decked out with ribbons and streamers of brilliant colors, which formed a part of their capture, and recrossed the St. Lawrence, without the loss of a man. Scandal relates that a party was hastily rallied to pursue and recover the goods, but that a quantity of *shrub*, a very agreeable mixed liquor, was left in a conspicuous place, which had its designed effect, and that the pursuing party were thus disarmed. This incursion, from the boldness with which it was conceived and executed, created a general feeling of insecurity among the inhabitants, and convinced them that the state of war was a reality; that they were at any moment liable to an unexpected and unwelcome visit from the enemy, and that their lives and property were alike at the mercy of the British. From this time forward, there was nothing attempted that might provoke retaliation, or invite an unceremonious visit from Canada.

To return from this digression: on the morning of Nov. 10, information was received that the enemy had collected at or near the foot of the Long saut, determined to oppose the passage of the flotilla. To dislodge these, Gen. Brown was sent forward, and about noon was engaged by a party of the enemy near a block house on the saut, erected to harrass the flotilla in its descent. At the same time the enemy were observed in the rear, who commenced a cannonade, which obliged the general to order two 18 pounders to be run on shore, and formed in battery, which soon compelled them to retire up the river.   These operations had so far wasted the day, that the pilots were afraid to enter the saut, and they came to anchor opposite the premises of John Chrysler, about nine miles above the head of the Long saut rapid.   At 4 P. M., a party of 50 men under Capt. Burbank, fell in with a party of the enemy in a grove about a mile in the rear of the camp, who were dispersed by a few volleys, losing one man and killing two.   A few minutes after this, a small body of mounted men appeared in the road near the river, who were fired upon by our rear guard of gun boats, and dispersed.   At 5 o'clock, a body of men appeared at the same place, with two 6 pounders, and opened a fire on our gun boats, which was returned, and kept up for some minutes.   Gen. Boyd advanced against these, who retired. As it was considered important to hear from Gen. Brown, whether the passage was clear before committing himself to the saut, from which there was no retreat, the American flotilla fell down a short distance, and came to under Cook's point,* about a mile below Chrysler's.

Before giving an account of the battle that ensued, it may be well to describe the topography of the country.   The Canada shore is here very level with the exception of three or four ravines, caused by rivulets, which would afford no obstacle to the crossing of troops, but would hinder the passage of artillery.   With the exception of a narrow strip of woods, between Chrysler's farm and Cook's point, the country was cleared.   Parallel with the river, and a mile distant, lays an ash swamp, which forbade the march of troops.   The current of the river at the point is very strong, the channel being but 1,300 yards over, and very deep, so that it would have been difficult for boats to retain a position, except near the shore.   During the whole voyage, and especially at the time of the battle, Gen. Wilkinson was very ill, and much of the time confined to his cabin.   Word having been received about 10 o'clock, that Brown had dislodged the enemy, and was proceeding down, orders were issued for the flotilla to sail, when eight of the enemy's gun boats appeared in the rear, and commenced a smart fire upon the rear guard of gun boats.   Several shots were directed at the flotilla, but none took effect.   A large row galley, carrying a 32 pound carronade, was the most formidable in the enemy's line.   The following is an extract from Gen. Wilkinson's official account of the events of the 11th of November:

"A variety of reports of their movements and counter movements were brought to me in succession, which convinced me of their determination to hazard an attack, when it could be done to the greatest advantage; and therefore I resolved to anticipate them.   Directions were accordingly sent by that distinguished officer, Col. Swift, of the engineers, to Brig. Gen. Boyd, to throw the detachments of his command assigned to him in the order of the preceding day, and composed of his own, Covington's and Swartwout's brigades, into three columns, to march upon the enemy, outflank them, if possible, and take their artillery.   The action soon after commenced with the advanced body of the enemy, and became extremely sharp and galling, and with occasional pauses, not sustained with great vivacity in open space and fair combat, for upwards of

---

* The river at this place is very narrow, and in the following summer, a small fort of earth and timber having the shape of the annexed plan was erected.   It enclosed a quarter of an acre, and was built under Lieut Ingles, from whom it received the name of Ingle's fort.   It has since been levelled.

two and a half hours, the adverse lines alternately yielding and advancing. It is impossible to say with accuracy what was our number on the field, because it consisted of indefinite detachments taken from the boats to render safe the passage of the saut. Gens. Covington and Swartwout voluntarily took part in the action, at the head of detachments from their respective brigades, and exhibited the same courage that was displayed by Brig. Gen. Boyd, who happened to be the senior officer on the ground. Our force engaged might have reached 1,600 or 1,700 men, but actually did not exceed 1,800; that of the enemy was estimated from 1,200 to 2,000, but did not probably amount to more than 1,500 or 1,600, consisting, as I am informed, of detachments from the 49th, 84th and 104th regiments of the line, with three companies of the Voltigeur and Glengary corps, and the militia of the country, who were not included in the estimate.

It would be presumptuous in me to attempt to give a detailed account of the affair, which certainly reflects high honor on the valor of the American soldier, as no examples can be produced of undisciplined men with inexperienced officers, braving a fire of two hours and a half, without quitting the field, or yielding to their antagonist. The information is derived from officers in my confidence, who took active parts in this conflict; for though I was enabled to order the attack, it was my hard fortune not to be able to lead the troops I commanded. The disease with which I was assailed on the 2d of September, on my journey to Fort George, having, with a few short intervals of convalescence, preyed on me ever since, and at the moment of this action, I was confined to my bed, and emaciated almost to a skeleton, unable to set on my horse, or move ten paces without assistance. I must, however, be pardoned for trespassing on your time a few remarks in relation to the affair.

The objects of the British and American commanders were precisely opposed; the last being bound by the instructions of his government, and the most solemn obligations of duty, to precipitate his designs on the St. Lawrence by every practicable means; because this being effected, one of the greatest difficulties opposed to the American arms, would be surmounted; and the first, by duties equally imperious, to retard and if possible, prevent such descent. He is to be counted victorious who effected his purpose! The British commander having failed to gain either of his objects, can lay no claim to the honors of the day. The battle fluctuated, and seemed at different times inclined to the contending corps. The front of the enemy were at first forced back more than a mile, and though they never regained the ground they lost, their stand was permanent and their courage resolute. Amidst these charges and near the close of the contest, we lost a field piece by the fall of an officer who was serving it, with the same coolness as if he had been at a parade or a review. This was Lieut. Smith, of the light artillery, who, in point of merit, stood at the head of his grade. The enemy having halted and our troops being again formed into battalion, front to front, we resumed our position on the bank of the river, and the infantry being much fatigued, the whole were reembarked and proceeded down the river without any further annoyance from the enemy or their gun boats, while the dragoons with five pieces of light artillery, marched down the Canada shore without molestation.

It is due to his rank, to his worth, and his services, that I should make particular mention of Brig. Gen. Covington, who received a mortal wound directly through the body, while animating his men and leading them to the charge. He fell where he fought, at the head of his men, and survived but two days. The next morning the flotilla passed through the saut, and joined that excellent officer, Brig. Gen. Brown, at Barnhart's, near Cornwall, where he had been instructed to take post and await my arrival. And where I confidently expected to hear of Major General Hampton's arrival on the opposite shore. But immediately after I halted, Col. Atkinson, the inspector general of the division under Major Gen. Hampton, waited on me with a letter from that officer, in which to my unspeakable regret and surprise, he declined the junction ordered, and informed me he was marching towards lake Champlain by way of cooperating in the proposed attack upon Montreal. This letter, together with a copy of that to which it is an answer, was immediately transmitted to a council of war, composed of my general officers and the colonel commanding the elite, the chief engineer and the adjutant general, who unanimously gave it as their opinion, that the attack upon Montreal should be abandoned for the present season, and the army near Cornwall should be immediately crossed to the American shore for taking up winter quarters, and that this place afforded an eligible position for such quarters.

I acquiesced in these opinions, not from the shortness of the stock of provisions, (which had been reduced by the acts of God), because that of our meat had been increased five days, and our bread had been reduced only two days, and because we could in case of extremity, have lived on the enemy; but, because the loss of the division under Major Gen. Hamilton, weakened my force too sensibly to justify the attempt. In all my measures and movements of moment, I have taken the opinion of my general officers, which have been in accord with my own.

I remained on the Canada shore until next day, without seeing or hearing from the "powerful force" of the enemy in our neighborhood, and the same day reached the position with the artillery and infantry. The dragoons have been ordered to Utica and its vicinity, and I expect are fifty or sixty miles on the march. You have under cover a summary abstract of the killed and wounded in the affair of the 11th inst. which shall soon be followed by a particular return; in which a just regard shall be paid to individual merits.

The dead rest in honor, and the wounded bled for their country and deserve its gratitude."

Killed.—Subalterns 3; serjeants 7; corporals 3; musicians 1; privates 88; total 102.

Wounded.—Brigadier general 1; assistant adjutant general 1; aid-decamp 1; colonel 1; major 1; captains 5; subalterns 6; serjeants 9; corporals 13; musicians 1; privates 198; total 237. Total killed and wounded, 339.

Names of the commissioned officers killed and wounded.—*Killed,* Lieut. Wm. W. Smith, of the light artillery; Lieutenant David Hunter, of the 12th regiment of infantry; Lieutenant Edward Olmstead, 15th do.; do.

Wounded.—Brig. Gen. Leonard Covington, mortally, (since dead); Major Talbot Chambers, assistant adjutant general, slightly; Maj. Darby Noon, aid-de-camp to Brigadier Gen. Swartwout, slightly; Colonel James P. Preston, of the 23d regiment infantry, severely, his right thigh fractured; Major W. Cummings, 8th regiment, severely; Captain Edward Foster, 9th do., slightly; Captain David S. Townsend, do. do., severely, (taken prisoner); Captain Mordecai Myers, 13th do., severely; Captain John Campbell, do., slightly; Captain John B. Murdoc, 25th do., slightly; Lieut. Wm. S. Heaton, 11th do., severely; Lieut. John

Williams, 23d, do., slightly; Lieut. John Lynch, do. severely, (taken prisoner); Lieutenant Peter Pelham, 21st do. severely, (taken prisoner); Lieutenant James D. Brown, 25th do., slightly; Lieut. Archibald C. Crary, do. do.. severely, in the skirmish the day before the action.

British Official Account of the Battle, dated LaChine, 15th Nov. 1813.

GENERAL ORDERS.—His Excellency the Governor General and Commander of the forces, has received from Lieut. Col. Morrison, 89th regiment, the official report of the action which took place on the 11th inst., at Chrystler's farm, 20 miles above Cornwall, between the corps of observation, consisting of the 49th and 89th regiments, and a detachment from the garrison at Prescott, under Lieut. Col. Pearson, the whole amounting to about 800 men, and the principal division of the enemy's army, commanded by Major General Boyd.   On the day preceding the action, an affair took place in consequence of the corps of observation pressing on the enemy, which after a short conflict, determined in his defeat, the British division occupying that night the ground on which the affair had taken place.   On the 11th, Lieut. Col. Morrison continued his pursuit, when the enemy concentrating his force, made a grand effort to relieve himself from so troublesome an opponent, and advanced with his heavy columns of infantry, supported by artillery, his front covered by ·a numerous body of cavalry and riflemen. Lieut. Col. Morrison fell back gradually, and took up a judicious position, (which he had previously made choice of), with his little band, his right on the river, consisting of the flank companies of the 49th regiment and a detachment of the Canada fencibles, under Lieut. Col. Pearsen, with a six pounder a little advanced, supported by the companies of the 89th regiment, under Captain Barnes; the 49th and 89th regiments formed the main body of reserve extending across the road to a pine wood, occupying a space of seven hundred yards. Major Heriot, with a detachment of the Canadian Voltigeurs, and a small band of Indian warriors under Lieut. Anderson, secured the left flank.   The action commenced about 2 o'clock, P.M., and in half an hour became general, the enemy attempting to turn the left of the British, but were repulsed by the 49th and 89th regiments, which advanced firing by wings and platoons.

The enemy having failed in this attempt, united their utmost efforts in an attack on the right, supported by four pieces of artillery and their cavalry, which was in like manner repulsed, the 49th and 89th regiments having moved up in echellon and formed in line; a charge commenced by the 49th regiment, was not persevered in, in consequence of the enemy's having charged upon the right, and threatened to gain the rear; but their cavalry were so gallantly received by the three companies of the 89th regiment under Captain Barns, and the well directed fire of the artillery under Capt. Jackson, that they were instantly repulsed, and by the rapid pursuit of Capt. Barn's party, a six pounder was captured from the enemy, whose attention was now solely directed to cover the retreat of his beaten forces. In this last effort he was foiled by a judicious movement of the corps under Lieut. Col. Pearson, who continued to pursue the enemy in his flight. [Here Col. Morrison speaks of the merits of Lieut. Cols. Pearson and Plenderleath; Majors Clifford and Heriot, of the militia, and Capt. Jackson; also of Lieut. Col. Harvey; Captains Skinner and Davis, of the staff ; Lieut. Anderson of the Indian department; and Lieut. Hagerman of the militia.]

It is with deep regret that Lieut. Col. Morrison transmits a list of casualties, containing the loss of several brave soldiers, but when the unequal contest, and the quadruple loss of the enemy, and the importance of this splendid victory are considered, the comparative British loss will appear less than might reasonably be expected.

[The particular returns of the several corps are omitted.]

Total.—1 captain, 2 drummers, and 19 rank and file, killed; 1 captain, 9 subalterns, 6 serjeants, and 131 rank and file wounded; twelve rank and file missing.

Names of Officers killed and wounded.—49th regiment, Capt. Nairne, killed; Lieut. Jones, wounded dangerously; Lieut. Clans, wounded, left leg amputated; Lieut. Morton, wounded severely, not dangerously; Lieut. Richmond, wounded slightly.

89th regiment—Capt. Brown, wounded severely, not dangerously; Ensign Leaden, wounded slightly.

49th flank company—Lieut. Holland, wounded severely.

Canadian Fencibles—Lieut. Delorimiere, wounded dangerously, since dead; Lieut. Armstrong, wounded dangerously.

By his Excellency's command,
EDWARD BAYNER, ADJ. GEN., N.A.

The preceding reports were made the subject of severe comments by the American press, generally.

The following account of the battle was prepared by Dr. A. Trowbridge, of Watertown, N. Y., who was present:

" Night came on and all schemes for meeting or attacking the enemy were changed for making suitable arrangements for the safety of the camp. The troops were marched back and posted on the same ground they occupied the night before. Strong guards were sent out in different directions, the troops were posted in line of battle, and directed to sleep on their arms. The night passed uninterrupted by alarms. It appeared evident from the movements of the enemy that a considerable force was advancing to attack us or pass our rear by land. The morning of the 11th was spent in making the usual preparations for marching. At 10 orders were issued for detachments of Generals Boyd's, Covington's and Swartwout's brigades, with 4 pieces of light artillery, and the remaining body of dragoons to march to join Gen. Brown, who it was understood had dispersed the enemy and taken a position at Cornwall. The movements had begun when the rear was attacked, the boats were brought to, and Gen. Swartwout sent back to meet the enemy. He dashed into the woods with the 2d regiment infantry, commanded by Col. Ripley, who, after a short skirmish, drove them back to a ravine, where they kept up a sharp fire upon our advancing columns, which charged upon the enemy, killed and wounded several, and took 20 prisoners. The enemy retreated in a scattered condition, in various directions. The main body of the enemy were now seen advancing in columns on the west extremity of Chrystler's field. They opened a fire of musketry, and from a six pounder which was heavy, and galling upon our troops composed of the 1st regiment and a detachment from the first brigade commanded by Col. Cole. This body was now ordered to flank the enemy's left. This was promptly done under a heavy fire from the enemy. Gen. Covington having been ordered up now took the position just left by Ripley and Coles, nearly in front of the enemy, and within rifle shot distance. The fight now become general and quite stationary.

Gen. Covington soon received a mortal wound by a rifle shot. Col. Preston next in command, was soon after wounded in the thigh by a ball, fracturing the bone. Major Cumins was next wounded, and was obliged to retire. Many platoon officers were wounded or killed, and within 30 minutes after, the whole brigade was in confusion and left the field. A few minutes previous, two six pounders were brought up by Lieut. Smith, and posted near some houses occupied by the enemy. Their position was favorable and their fire destructive to the enemy, but the lieutenant was soon killed, and most of his men wounded by musketry from the houses, and our piece taken. The enemy's fire was now turned upon Ripley and Coles flanking party retiring from their position. About this time a squadron of dragoons commanded by Maj. Woodferd, took a position in the rear, and suffered much from the enemy's fire. They were finally ordered to charge the enemy. This was made in the road upon the enemy in houses and behind board fences. The whole body soon returned with 30 horses without riders. The enemy's attention was so much diverted from Ripley and Coles retreating detachment, that by passing, partly covered by the forest, they made good their retreat. The guard left at the boats was ordered up commanded by Col. Upham. They occupied a position a few minutes in front of the enemy, who remained stationary in column, keeping up a steady fire from two six pounders upon every thing that appeared on the field to annoy them. Many of our wounded had been taken back to the boats; about 40 were left in a ravine and taken by the enemy. Gen. Boyd was the senior officer on the ground. Gen. Wilkinson was sick and confined to his boat and bed, and unable to muster forces without assistance. Gen. Lewis, next in command, was sick and unable to do duty.

The American troops were stationed on the margin of the river near the flotilla, and were reembarked with the wounded and sick, and proceeded down the river without further annoyance from the enemy or their gun boats, while the dragoons with 15 pieces of artillery, marched down the Canada shore, without molestation. The flotilla arrived at the head of the saut at 9 o'clock P. M., and encamped on the American side of the river. The badly wounded were placed in barns and log houses, and made as comfortable as circumstances would permit. The weather was cold, with snow and sleet, with storm and wind. The next morning the flotilla passed the saut, and joined Gen. Brown at Barnharts, near Cornwall. A council of officers was called which soon unanimously gave their opinion that the attack on Montreal should be abandoned, and that the army should be immediately crossed to the American shore for taking up winter quarters. The dragoons were recrossed and marched for Utica the same day, and the flotilla proceeded directly to French Mills, where they arrived the same night at 3 o'clock A. M. On the arrival of the army at French Mills the weather become intensely severe and remained so till the 23d of January. The soldiers have been subject to great fatigue; many had lost their blankets and extra clothing. The sick and wounded had no covering or shelter except tents in the severe latitude of 45 degrees. In the vicinity of French Mills, the country was a wildnerness. Provisions were scarce and of bad quality. Medicine and hospital stores were not to be found, and a supply could not be obtained short of Albany, a distance of 250 miles. It was ascertained that these stores were abundantly provided at Sacketts Harbor, but were, in stead of being placed on board of separate boats, distributed throughout the boats of the flotilla for which no officer could be made accountable. The want of these necessaries for the sick and wounded was severely felt.

Under these circumstances, sickness and mortality was very great, and excited general alarm."

On the 11th of November, Hampden wrote to Wilkinson that he would be unable to meet him at St. Regis, but would return to Lake Champlain, and coöperate by a descent from that place. "This reached Wilkinson at Barnhart's island. A council was convened and it was resolved to cross to the American shore, and take up winter quarters at French Mills, and accordingly the flotilla entered Salmon river and took possession. There a frightful mortality occurred, which is described by Dr. Lovell, a surgeon, as follows: The weather soon became intensely cold, and remained so all winter. In addition to the great fatigue to which the soldiers had been exposed, especially the division from Fort George, most of them had lost their blankets and extra-clothing on their march, or in the action of the 11th. Even the sick had no covering except tents, from the period they debarked at the Mills, until the 1st of January, in the severe latitute of 45°. Provisions were scarce and of a bad quality. Medicine and hospital stores were not to be found, having been lost or destroyed in the passage down the St. Lawrence. Under these circumstances sickness and mortality were very great. A morning report now before me, gives 75 sick, out of a small corps of 160. The several regiments of the army, in their returns, exhibited a proportionate number unfit for duty. Of the 75 referred to, 39 were reported of diarrhœa and dysentery; 18 of pneumonia; 6 of typhus; and 12 of paralysis of all the extremities. Many of the paralytics, on their arrival at the Mills, were attended with mortification of the the toes and feet. In a few of these the pain was severe, wherein opium not only relieved the pain but checked the progress of the mortification.

Stimulants, both externally and internally, were beneficial, and when these remedies were assisted by a nutritious diet, warm lodging and clothing, a cure was effected. The last complaint generally seized those who previously had been extremely reduced by disease, and under our unavoidably bad situation, frequently in a few days proved fatal."[*]

"In the vicinity of the French Mills, the country was a wilderness. Huts and hospitals were necessary to render the army comfortable. The erection of these was a work of great labor, and required several weeks to complete it. A supply of hospital stores could not be obtained nearer than Albany, a distance of 250 miles. The want of these necessaries for the support of the very wretched and enfeebled soldier, was most severely felt. The poor subsistence which the bread of the first quality afforded, was almost the only support that could be had for nearly seven weeks. These accumulated evils the army encountered with much patience and heroic fortitude. Now it was the chief surgeon, who was with the flotilla, found himself loaded with a weight of censure, of which he should be fairly exonerated, so far as he was blamed for the loss or waste of medicine and hospital stores on the St. Lawrence. It was abundantly demonstrated that no separate transportation for these stores, although expressly ordered by the commander-in-chief, had been provided; but that they had been improvidentally distributed throughout the boats of the flotilla, and for the security of which no officer had been, nor could have been made accountable.

The deaths, sickness and distress, at French Mills, excited general alarm. The great mortality had obvious causes for its existence. In all

*Mann's Medical ketches, p. 119.

such cases censure will fall on some department. And as each was disposed to exonerate itself, upon which was blame more probable to have alighted than the medical—than upon the surgeons of the army under whose immediate care the victims of disease were daily prostrated! There are to be found some, who ignorant of the effects of medicine on the human constitution, are too prone to believe its exhibition may be equally efficacious, under every circumstance and condition to which the patient may be subjected. Hence it was incorrectly inferred, when men were beheld expiring under the prescriptions of the surgeons, the mortality was a consequence of injudicious management or neglect of duty. Predispositions to diseases, the effects of obvious causes, the comfortless conditions of men exposed to cold, wanting the common necessaries of life, to support them in their exhausted states, are seldom taken into consideration. Dr. Lovell, one of the most able and indefatigable surgeons of the army, emphatically observed, " It was impossible for the sick to be restored, with nothing to subsist upon except damaged bread. '*   *   *   *   *   *   *

At MALONE HOSPITAL on the 1st of February, 1814, the number of sick had increased to 450. For an additional number of 200, sent from French Mills, rooms were wanted, which were promptly provided by Capt. Dwight, A. Q. M. G., who continued to give me his assistance."

For supplying the army of Gen. Wilkinson, an immense quantity of stores had been forwarded from Plattsburgh and Sackett's Harbor, at great expense. A portion of the latter was deposited at Hopkinton, and Malone, and these were constantly arriving when the order to evacuate the place was received. On the week before leaving, about 1400 barrels of pork and beef, a 100 casks of whiskey, and other parts of rations, were sent by James Campbell, assistant store keeper at the Mills. About 60 tons of hard biscuit, being considered not worth removing under the circumstances, was sank in Salmon river, in a hole cut in the ice, besides which about ten tons were distributed among the inhabitants, to keep from the enemy, but much of this was soon after seized by the British. The troops on evacuating, burned their boats (328 in number), down to the level of the ice, together with their barracks. The expenses to government during the time that the army tarried at French Mills, is said to have been $800,000.

" On the 9th of February, 1814, orders were issued to leave the cantonment. One division under Gen. Brown, moved up the St. Lawrence to Sackett's Harbor, the other under the immediate command of the commander-in-chief, directed its march to Plattsburgh. In consequence of the retrograde movement of the army from French Mills, the hospital at Malone, at this time under good regulations was broken up and the sick were ordered to proceed on routes destined for their respective regiments.   *   *   *   The few accommodations on the routes were wretched. The inhabitants although kind were not under circumstances to furnish means to render the situation of the sick men even comfortable. Nothing was omitted within their abilities to meliorate their miserable condition. Knowing that so large a detachment of sick and invalids could not be covered at night, if they moved in a body; the sleighs that transported them were successively put in motion in small divisions. Their line of movement, three days forming, extended the whole distance from Malone. The first division arrived at Plattsburgh, the place of their destination, about the time the last commenced its progress. About 20, very sick, who were left in the hospitals, under

*Mann,s Medical Sketches.

the care of a citizen physician, were made prisoners of war, by the British, who immediately followed the retrograde march of the army, as far as Malone. Those left in tho hospitals were not molested in their persons, but were only obliged to sign their paroles, the greater part of whom, after five or six weeks, joined the hospital at Burlington.* * *

The last of the American army had scarcely left French Mills, and a few teamsters were employed in removing what they might be able of the stores, when a detachment of British troops, marching in columns, and preceded by a hoard of savages, entered the village to plunder whatever of public property might be left.

An unlucky teamster, having lingered behind, and as the enemy approached, was attempting to escape, was shot by the officer who commanded the Indians. The ball lodged in the muscles of the neck, and still, it is said remains; the man, contrary, to all expectations, having survived. He still lives to relate the narrow and hazardous escape which he ran. An account of this incursion was published soon after, in the paper, from which we quote the following:

"On Saturday, the 19th, the enemy hearing that our troops had marched, ventured to cross the St. Lawrence, with a motley tribe of regulars, provincials, and a detachment of the devil's own,—sedentary militia, and their brethren, a band of savages. This martial body amused themselves at French Mills until one o'clock, P. M., and then marched, with eight pieces of artillery and two cart loads of congreve rockets. At the fork af the roads, eleven miles from the mills, a detachment was sent off to Malone, and the main body passed on to Chateaugay, where it arrived about 4 o'clock in the morning of the 20th. There, it is reported, a scene of plunder began, which greatly distressed several of the inhabitants, and every particle of beef, pork or flour, with every drop of whiskey which could be found, was seized on as public property, and carried away. By this gleaning, without discrimination between the individual and the public, it is believed the enemy carried off between 150 and 200 barrels of provisions of all sorts, good and bad—public and private."

During the winter some ten or fifteen teamsters had been hired in Lewis county, and many more from Jefferson, to convey flour from Sackett's Harbor to French Mills. They received each seven barrels, and were allowed nine days to perform the trip, at $4 per day and rations. They arrived at Hopkinton towards the last of January, where their loads were left (some 300 barrels, under the care of a few soldiers), and thence they proceeded to French Mills, to aid in removing the supplies from that place to Plattsburgh. They performed ohe trip, and were returning, when they were pressed at Chateaugny, and again compelled to return to Plattsburgh, with loads of provisions and stores. This they accomplished, and had got as far as Chatenugay, where 32 teams had stopped at a tavern, in the village for the night. There was a report in circulation, that the enemy were over, and their horses were left in their harnesses, ready for instant retreat if necessary. Meanwhile the party within, unmindful of danger, were singing and drinking to pass away the night, for sleep among such a crowd, was out of the question, when their gayety was suddenly arrested by the entrance of a British officer (Major Sherwood), who enquired of the landlord, who these gentlemen were, and on being told that they were American teamsters, he informed them that they were all prisoners of war. There were but 28 British soldiers, who were under the immediate command of Captain Conklin. The night was spent in searching for military stores and provisions, which were placed in the sleighs, and in the morning they commenced a retreat with whatever they could pick of public property.[*]

Gen. Hampden's movements have been alluded to. He had been ordered in September to proceed to Burlington, and raise recruits to join Gen. Wilkinson in his proposed operations. He advanced a short distance into Canada, and returned to Chazy, from whence he proceeded to Chateaugay.

His artillery consisted of 8 six pounders, 1 twelve and 1 howitzer, but was deficient in military supplies and provisions. On the first of October, an attack was made with 3 or 400 regulars and as many Indians, upon Col. Snelling, an outpost, but was repulsed. On the 21st of October, an incursion was made into Canada, but without accomplishing its object. An intervening forest of eleven or twelve miles existed before reaching the Canadian settlements on the Chateaugay, and the obscure road through this had been blocked up by fallen timber, and was defended by the Indians and light troops of the enemy. The following is an extract from the official account of Gen. Hampden;

"Brig. Gen. Izard, with the light troops and one regiment of the line, was detached early in the morning to turn these impediments in flank, and to seize the more open country below, while the army preceded by a strong working party, advanced on a more circuitous route for a road. The measure completely succeeded, and the main body of the army reached the advanced position on the evening of the 22d. The 23d and 24th were employed in completing the road, and getting up the artillery and stores. I had arranged at my departure under the direction of Maj. Parker, a line of communication as far up the St. Lawrence as Ogdensburgh, for the purpose of hastening to me the first notice of the progress of our army down. I had surmounted 24 miles of the more difficult part of the route, and had in advance of me seven miles of open country, but at the end of that distance commenced a wood of some miles in extent, which had been formed into an entire abatis, and filled by a succession of wooden breast-works, the rearmost of which was supplied with ordnance. In front of these defences were placed the Indian force and light corps of the enemy, and in the rear all his disposable force. As the extent of this force depended on his sense of danger on the St. Lawrence, it was a cause of regret that all communication from yourself or Major Parker, seemed to be at an end. As it was however believed that the enemy was hourly adding to his strength in this position if free from the apprehension of danger from above, an effort was judged necessary to dislodge him, and if we succeeded we should be in possession of a position which we could hold as long as any doubts remained of what was passing above, and of the real part to be assigned us. Our guides assured us of a shoal and practicable fording place opposite the lower flank of the enemy's defenses, and that the woods on the opposite side of the river, a distance of seven or eight miles, was practicable for the passage of the troops. Col. Purdy, with the light corps and a strong body of infantry of the line, was detached at an early hour of the night of the 25th, to gain this ford by the morning, and to commence his attack in the rear, and that was to be signal for the army to fall on in front, and it was believed the pass might be carried before the enemy's distant troops could be brought forward to its support. I had returned to my quarters from Purdy's column about 9

[*] Among other stores they took off a large cask, supposed to contain rum, but which when they reached French Mills, was found to hold nothing but water. The unfortunate cask was instantly knocked in the head, much to the amusement of the teamsters.

o'clock at night, when I found a Mr. Baldwin, of the quarter master general's dapartment, who put into my hands an open paper from the quarter master general, respecting the building of huts in the Chateaugay, below the line. This paper sunk my hopes, and raised serious doubts of receiving that efficient support which had been anticipated. I would have recalled the column but it was in motion, and the darkness of the night rendered it impracticable. I could only go forward. The army was put in motion on the morning of the 26th, leaving its baggage &c., on the ground of encampment. On advancing near the enemy it was found that the column on the opposite side was not as far advanced as had been anticipated. The guides had misled it, and finally failed in finding the ford. We could not communicate with it, but only waited the attack below. At 2 o'clock the firing commenced, and our troops advanced rapidly to the attack. The enemy's light troops commenced a sharp fire, but Brig. Gen. Izard, advanced with his brigade, drove him every where behind his defenses, and silenced the fire in the front. This brigade would have pushed forward as far as courage, skill and perseverance could have carried it; but on advancing it was found that the firing had commenced on the opposite side, and the ford had not been gained. The enemy retired behind his defenses, but a renewal of his attack was expected, and their troops remained some time in their position to meet it. The troops on the opposite side were excessively fatigued. The enterprise had failed in its main point, and Colonel Purdy was ordered to withdraw his column to a sheal four or five miles above, and cross over. The day was spent, and Gen. Izard was ordered to withdraw his brigade to a position three miles in the rear, to which place the baggage had been ordered forward. The slowness and order with which Gen. Izard retired with his brigade, could but have inspired the enemy with respect. They presumed not to venture a shot at him during his movement, but the unguardedness of some part of Purdy's command exposed him to a rear attack from the Indians, which was repeated after dark, and exposed him to some loss. These attacks were always repelled, and must have cost the enemy as many lives as we lost. Our entire loss of killed, wounded and missing, does not exceed fifty. In its new position within three miles of the enemy's post, the army encamped on the night of the 26th, and remained until 12 o'clock of the 28th. All the deserters, of whom there were four, having concurred in the information that Sir George Provost, with three other general officers, had arrived with the whole of his disposable force, and lay in the rear of these defences, and a letter from Major Parker (by express received in the evening of the 26th), having informed me that no movement down the St. Lawrence had been heard of at Ogdensburgh, and for some distance above. The following questions were submitted to the commanding officers of the brigades, regiments and corps, and the heads of the general staff, in a council convened for the purpose: "It is advisable under existing circumstances, to renew the attack on the enemy's position, and if not, what position is it advisable for the army to take, until it can receive advices of the advance of the grand army down the St. Lawrence?" The opinion of the council was expressed in the following words: "It is the unanimous opiniou of this council that it is necessary, for the preservation of this army and the fulfillment of the ostensible views of the government, that we immediately return by orderly marches to such a position (Chateaugay), as will serve our communications with the United States, eirher to retire into winter quarters, or to be ready to strike below." In pursuance of this opinion the army has returned by slow marches to this place, and now awaits the order of the government."

39

As soon as news reached Plattsburgh that the enemy had followed, a body of troops was sent back to meet them, but they were soon informed that the invading party had retreated. In our accounts of Hopkinton, Malone and Fort Covington, are given the details of this affair.

The unsuccessful issue of the military operations of the northern army in the campaign of 1813, created much dissatisfaction throughout the Union, and the conduct of the generals who had conducted the enterprises became the subject of severe censure, and both became the subject of investigation by courts martial. That of Gen. Wilkinson was by an order of the secretary of war, assembled at Utica, in January, 1815, and adjourned to Troy. He was charged, 1st, with neglect of duty and unofficer like conduct, stated in eight particulars; 2d, with drunkenness on duty, with two specifications; 3d, conduct unbecoming an officer and gentleman, with six instances; and 4th, in countenancing and encouraging disobedience of orders. To all of these he plead *not guilty*, and after a protracted trial, during which his actions and motives were severely canvassed, he was discharged. The official correspondence of the campaign was published by order of Congress.

On the 25th of March, 1814, the citizens of Franklin county held a public meeting at Malone, to unite in a petition to the legislature for protection against the insults and ravages of the enemy. With glowing and expressive language they represented their miseries, and invoked aid to protect their property from ravage and themselves from insult. The following is an extract from this document.

We, the subscribers, being chairman and secretary of a general meeting of the inhabitants of Franklin county, do respectfully represent:

That we are peculiarly and dangerously situated, and as freemen of this state, and citizens of our common country, ready to shed our blood in its defense, we ask for protection.

Like our brethren of the Niagara frontiers, many of our good citizens have experienced the spoliation of their goods, clothing and provisions, the locks of our desks and trunks have been broken, and books sacred and profane, valuable papers and money have been taken from them. We have escaped massacre and conflagration, but we have witnessed that whoever run was stopped by the force of powder and lead, and whoever submitted was under the humiliating and mortifying situation of being an eye witness to the spoliation of his goods. But this whole country is exposed to daily depradations. The barbarous savage may be prowling about our dwellings, and in our weak state of defense we must tamely submit to every insult and injury. The father experiences, with tenfold increase, the anxious solicitude of a parent and a husband. The mother hugs her infant closer to her breast, contemplating with fear and horror the dangers that await her.

The God of mercy only knows how soon the father may fall a victim to the brutal inhumanity of our enemy, in defending the land, the home of his affection; how soon the infant may be torn from the arms of its mother, and sacrificed to the sanguinary notions of a brutal foe; and how soon the house that shelters them from the stormy tempest, may be laid in ashes, and not a vestige of husbandry or cultivation be left to mark the residence of man.

Why have these calamities happened? Has it been the production of General Hampton's letters to the secretary at war, degrading the frontier settlements as almost improper subjects of protection, that the army should be ordered from their strong positions in this county, to the villages of Plattsburgh and Sacketts Harbor? These are strange movements, at a great sacrifice of public property, which we are unable to account for.

But our situation is too dangerous and degrading for us as American citizens, to have patience to sit peaceably under, and yet to flee our residences would but complete the ruin which is already begun.

We do further represent, that our enemies are continually drawing supplies of provisions from our frontiers, and the majesty of the civil law is trampled under foot, and the arm of the magistrate is put forth with little or no effect.

Our jail has been opened by our enemies, and prisoners set at liberty, and our military force is wholly insufficient to render us secure.

By an act of April 6, 1814, the sheriff of St. Lawrence county was directed to remove the prisoners in the county jail, to the Lewis county jail, for safe keeping.

In the summer of 1814, Capt. Thomas Frazer crossed the St. Lawrence at Hammond, with 60 men, and proceeded to Rossie to apprehend some horse thieves who were said to be lurking in the vicinity. Mr. James Howard was at the time holding a justice's court, which was hastily dissolved, and the parties sought were not secured. They made inquiries into the operations of the furnace then building, and are said to have exacted a pledge that munitions of war should not be cast there. In returning several persons volunteered to row them down the lake to the narrows, from whence they crossed to Canada. A plan was formed to attack them as they passed down the river, but this was discountenanced as only calculated to excite retaliation. This event occurring at about the time of the taking of Washington, gave rise to the presage, "that since the head and tail of the nation had both been captured, the remainder of the body would follow as a natural consequence."

CHAPTER X.

THE PATRIOT WAR OF 1837-40.

THERE had existed for several years in the Canadian provinces, a party which labored to obtain certain reforms in government, among which were the extension of the elective franchise and the procuring of a responsible elective council. This aroused a bitter feeling, and late in November, 1837, the press of the reformers was destroyed by a mob, which but increased the excitement, and at length the aid of the military force was called out to arrest certain prominent leaders of the reform party. The prisons became filled with persons charged with treason; martial law was proclaimed in the lower province, and numerous instances of wanton violence on the part of the soldiery occurred. Numbers fled to the states for an asylum, and the popular riots that ensued were only aggravated by the efforts made to suppress them. It is not our purpose to narrate the details of the causes or merits of the movement, but however much justice there may have been in the demands of the reformers, it will be the duty of the future historian to record the fact, that the pretext was seized by sundry American citizens, as a favorable opportunity to push forward their private schemes of personal aggrandizement and pecuniary speculation, and the planning of enterprises which they had neither the honor nor the courage to sustain when their support involved personal danger. The masses who acted in these movements, were doubtless actuated by sincere motives, and were blinded and misled by a few designing villians. The sympathies of our citizens have ever been on the side of political liberty, and our past history is filled with examples of its expression towards those seeking it, and this was the more sensibly felt from the vicinity of the arena of operations, and the belief that the sentiment of revolution, and aspirations for an independent republican existence were entertained by the masses of Canada. Refugees from the provinces were scattered through the northern states, who related with excited language, their version of the movements, and these causes, with many others concurring, led to efforts having for their avowed object the *independence of the Canadas.* The destruction of the American steamer CAROLINE,* Dec. 29,

---

* The *Caroline* was built as a small coasting sail vessel, in South Carolina, and her timber was the live oak of that section. At Troy she was changed into a small steamer, and under the name of *Carolina,* was run from Troy to Albany for some time. She was then taken through the Erie and Oswego canals to Lake Ontario, and plied as a ferry at Ogdensburgh. From this place she was taken through the Welland canal, and was used as a small ferry boat at Buffalo and vicinity, when she was employed in the patriot service, seized and destroyed by a party of Canadians.

1837, excited this feeling to an extraordinary degree, and public meetings were held throughout the country to express an honest indignation at the outrage and invoke the executive arm to protect our national rights. In this movement there was no political or sectional feeling. The subject became the absorbing topic of the press, and every mail was eagerly awaited to learn the news from the seat of the disturbances. On the 12th of Feb., 1838, Wm. L. McKenzie, a prominent leader of the movement, addressed the citizens of Ogdensburgh on the Canadian question, and in the evening and following morning a cannon was fired several times with the view of honoring the speaker, but with the effect of assembling crowds of excited citizens. In the evening several persons from Prescott crossed to ascertain the cause of the firing, who met a company of the Patriots, (as the friends of the movement were called,) who arrested and detained them till morning. This illegal proceeding irritated the Canadians, and increased the hostility. On the 18th of Feb. 1838, the state arsenal at Watertown was robbed, and a reward of $250 offered for the burglars. Active measures were taken to assemble arms and munitions of war along the frontier, and secret associations styled *Hunters' lodges*, were soon formed in the large villages, to organize a plan of resistance, and circulate early intelligence of the movements.

On the night between the 29th and 30th of May, 1838, the British steam boat *Sir Robert Peel*, on her passage from Prescott to the head of the lake, while taking fuel, at Well's Island, in Jefferson county, was boarded by a company of armed men, the crew and passengers driven on shore, and the steamer burned. The details of this infamous transaction, as collected soon after by several gentlemen from Ogdensburgh, are given below:

"On the 30th of May, the undersigned were informed that the steamer Sir Robert Peel, a British boat, had been boarded by a band of armed men, plundered and burnt, at a place known as Wells island, Jefferson county. We immediately started in the steam boat Oswego for the neighborhood of the outrage, and at Brockville took with us the purser and several of the hands of the steam boat Sir Robert Peel, with a view to obtain their testimony in aid of bringing the offenders to justice. On our arrival at French Creek, we learned that six men were then under arrest charged with the offence of burning and plundering the boat, and that three had been committed.

From the evidence taken, we think we can not err in saying the following is the substance of the facts relative to the destruction of the Sir Robert Peel: On the night of the 29th of May, the steamer on her passage up from Prescott to the head of the lake, touched at a wharf on Wells (a United States) island. The wharf was built entirely for selling wood to steam boats. There was no building, except one log shanty, belonging to the woodmen, within half a mile or more of the wharf, and there is not more than an acre of cleared land in sight of the wharf, on the island. When the boat first touched at the wharf, the man furnishing wood informed the captain of the boat that he had seen armed men on the island, and he was afraid they might be there with hostile intentions against the boat. The captain made light of the woodman's warning, let down the steam, and proceeded to take in wood. The captain, mate, and all the cabin passengers retired from the deck of the boat, and most of them were in bed. The boat touched at the wharf about 1 o'clock in the night, and had lain there about an hour, when a band of men armed with guns and bayonets, painted and dressed in Indian costume, suddenly rushed upon the boat, and by hideous yells and violent threats, drove all the officers, hands and passengers on shore. There were about ten passengers in the ladies' cabin who were driven on shore without their baggage, and in their night clothes; and the passengers lost a considerable portion of their baggage.

Immediately after the pirates got possession of the boat, they proceeded to sack and plunder it. Very soon after they had driven the officers, hands and passengers of the boat on shore, they cut her from the wharf. She floated out some thirty rods, and stopped at a small island or rock. About an hour after the armed band got possession of the boat, they set fire to her in several places, and then took to their boats, which they had in preparation. Most of the witnesses estimate the number of armed men from thirty to forty, who took possession of the boat.

On our arrival at French Creek, we found nine persons had been arrested on suspicion of being concerned in burning the boat. At French Creek we found one Thomas Scott, a surgeon, who had been a passenger on board the Sir Robert Peel, having come on board at Brockville. Doctor Scott is a citizen of Brockville, U. C., and his character as a most reputable man has been vouched for by several respectable inhabitants of Brockville. Upon the examination of the prisoners, Dr. Scott was sworn as a witness, and testified that he was a passenger on board the Sir Robert Peel; that after the band of armed men got possession of the boat, and he had been upon the wharf, he returned to the boat for his baggage, invited by one Robinson, another passenger, assuring him of safety, and was taken to the ladies' cabin to dress a wound of Hugh Scanlan, who said he had received a blow from a stick of wood. Scanlan was one of the prisoners, and identified by Dr. Scott. Dr. Scott states that while he was dressing the wound, the boat was cut from the wharf, and floated so that he could not get ashore, and after the boat was set fire to, to save his life, he went into the boat with the armed band, and they took him away to an island (we have since learned, called Abel's island). The band of men there had a kind of shanty or encampment. He remained with them until after sunrise the next morning. The pirates enjoined, and he promised, not to make any disclosures to injure them. They then allowed him to depart, and he got a farmer to take him ashore. He saw and counted all the persons who boarded the boat, and who went to the encampment, and he knows there were no more than twenty-two armed men who boarded the boat. He saw them all washed, and in their natural dresses, after sunrise, on the morning of the 30th of May.

It was talked and understood at the pirate's encampment, that all the persons, except two, who were engaged in the capture of the boat, were Canadian refugees, or Canadians who claimed to act in revenge for injuries. Dr. Scott states that if he could see, he could identify nearly every person engaged in the outrage. Nine of the persons concerned were fully committed for trial, and two or three, yet unarrested, are known, who were concerned in the outrage. Vigorous means have been taken to secure their arrest. The boat is wholly destroyed.

JOHN FINE, B. PERKINS, SMITH STILWELL."

At 5 o'clock in the morning, while the Robert Peel was still burning, the steamer Oneida, on her downward trip, arrived, and took off the passengers on the island to Kingston, the nearest British port, about 30 miles up the river. The cabin passengers, nineteen in number, acknowledged in the public papers their gratitude to Capt. Smith, of the Oneida, for thus generously relieving them from their unpleasant condition.

An outrage so flagrant as this, could not pass without the notice of government, and the most prompt and decisive measures were adopted by the authorities on both sides of the St. Lawrence, for the arrest of the authors of the act. The leader of the party that boarded and burned this steamer publicly acknowledged the act, with the motives which induced him to the attempt, in the following proclamation that was circulated through most of the newspapers:

To all whom it may concern: I, William Johnston, a natural born citizen of Upper Canada, certify that I hold a commission in the Patriot service of Upper Canada, as commander-in-chief of the naval forces and flotilla. I commanded the expedition that attacked and destroyed the steamer Sir Robert Peel. The men under my command in that expeditiou were nearly all natural born English subjects; the exceptions were volunteers for the expedition.

My head quarters were on an island in the St. Lawrence, without the jurisdiction of the United States, at a place named by me Fort Wallace. I am well acquainted with the boundary line, and know which of the islands do, and which do not, belong to the United States, and in the selection of the island I wished to be positive, and not locate within the jurisdiction of the United States, and had reference to the decision of the commissioners, under the 6th article of the treaty of Ghent, done at Utica, in the state of New York, 13th of June, 1822. I know the number of islands, and by that decision, it was British territory.

I yet hold possession of that station, and we also occupy a station some twenty or more miles from the boundary of the United States, in what was his majesty's dominions, until it was occupied by us. I act under orders. The object of my movements, is the *independence of the Canadas.* I am not at war with the commerce or property of citizens of the United States.

Signed this 10th day of June, in the year of our Lord, one thousand eight hundred and thirty-eight.

WILLIAM JOHNSTON.

On the 4th of June, 1838, Governor Marcy issued a proclamation, offering a reward for the arrest of certain persons, alleged to be concerned in the burning of the Robert Peel, viz: For William Johnston, $500; for Daniel McLeod, Samuel C. Frey and Robert Smith, each $250; and $100 each for the detection and delivery of other offenders. In a letter to the secretary of war, dated Watertown, June 3, 1838, he advised the coöperation of the governments of Canada with the United States, in endeavoring to clear the St. Lawrence of the Patriot forces, said to be lodged among the Thousand islands.

It was estimated that at least five hundred men well armed, and accommodated with boats adapted to the object to be accomplished, would be required to effect this purpose. The governor of Canada also offered a reward of £1,000, for the conviction of any person or persons concerned in the outrage.

On the morning of the 2d of June, 1838, the American steam boat *Telegraph,* while leaving Brockville, was hailed by two sentries, belonging to the volunteer militia, and fired upon with balls, six shot in all being fired, three of which struck the steamer. About the same time, several shots were fired from another wharf. Upon an examination which ensued, it appeared that the firing was not justified by orders, and it was asserted that no intention to hit the steamer existed. The sentries stated that they fired them as alarm guns. They were discharged, but no further action was taken in relation to the matter.

In a message from President Van Buren to congress, of June 20, 1838, it is stated that the outrages committed on the steam boat Sir Robert Peel and upon the Telegraph at Brockville, had not been made a subject of formal demand for redress by either government, as these acts were considered criminal offences committed within the jurisdiction of tribunals competent to enquire into the facts, and to punish those engaged in their perpetration.

Directly opposite the present depot at Ogdensburgh, stands a tall but massive stone tower, with a tin covered dome, whose enormous but dilapidated appendages indicate the purposes of its erection as a wind mill. This has been the theatre of a sanguinary conflict, the details of which were as follows:

Early in November, 1838, the Patriots, who had previously rallied in clubs and secret lodges, which had free and constant communication with each other, began to exhibit an intention of making fresh demonstrations upon Canada, at some point which was known only by those who were in their confidence. Unusual numbers of strangers were seen about Syracuse, Oswego, Sackett's Harbor, Watertown, &c., and large quantities of arms, many of which were of most beautiful workmanship, were collected and concealed.

About the 10th of November, two schooners named the *Charlotte of Oswego* and the *Charlotte of Toronto*, were noticed as being freighted at Oswego, from boats that had arrived from Syracuse, by the Oswego canal, under circumstances that were suspicious. After being laden they left the harbor, taking a northerly course. The steamer United States had been in port from Tuesday, the 6th instant, undergoing some repairs, which were not completed till Saturday the 10th. There had been a pretty heavy gale on the lake on Friday and previous days, which created a heavy swell, and made the navigation of that water unpleasant. The United States left Oswego about 9 o'clock on Sunday morning, the 11th instant, to continue her regular trip down the lake and river. On her leaving Oswego, she took about a hundred and fifty passengers, according to the testimony of Wm. Williams, the first mate. All of these, except one, were men passengers, without any baggage, except small budgets, and two or three trunks. There was a nail keg put on board, which fell in handling, and the head came out, when it was found filled with lead bullets, which rolled over the deck. There was also a number of boxes taken on board, marked for Cape Vincent. The steamer arrived at Sackett's Harbor between 1 or 2 o'clock, and lay there three-fourths of an hour, and here about twenty or thirty passengers came on board, all of whom were men.

The fire room was filled with men, the window of the fire room, in shore, was shut down, and in other respects the men were about the decks as usual. The United States passed the Telegraph (a steamer then in the service of the United States government), about eleven miles from Sackett's Harbor, opposite Point Peninsula. The passengers were on deck, and in open view of those on the government steamer. The mate of the United States testifies, that he heard some of the leaders of the men tell them to keep out of sight. The steamer stopped at Cape Vincent about half an hour, and here some ten or eleven passengers came on board. On arriving near the foot of Long island, below Millen's bay, the two schooners that had left Oswego, on the 10th, were discovered, and Capt. James Van Cleve, upon the request of a respectable looking passenger, who represented that they belonged to him, and were freighted with merchandise for Ogdensburgh, consented to take them in tow. Soon after the wind shifted, and blew more down the river, having previously been in such a quarter, that the vessels could not sail down to advantage. These schooners were lashed one on each side of the steamer, and her speed with them in tow was about eight miles an hour. The speed of the Telegraph was about nine miles an hour. The steamer touched at French Creek a few minutes, and seven or eight men came on to the schooners. Soon after leaving this port, the nature of the business of the passengers became evident, and swords and pistols were openly taken from boxes on board the steamer. The passengers being exclusively males, and unencumbered by baggage, and the suspicious character of the little freight which they did take on board with them, rendered it sufficiently evident that they formed a body of men designing some military enterprise against some point on the St. Lawrence. The boxes on board the steamers were here transferred to the schooners, which had not been long in tow before great numbers of men came from the latter on board the steamer, the greater part of them from the larger of the two, which was the Charlotte of Oswego. A consultation was now held between the captain and two of the owners of the stamboat present, and Hiram Denio, one of the bank commissioners, who was on board as a passenger, as to what was best to be done under the circumstances; and it was concluded to stop at the wharf at Morristown (the next American port), and cause information to be given to a magistrate of the character of the passengers on board of the steamer, and of their supposed objects, and of the steam boat having towed down the schooners, and also to send an express with like information to Ogdensburgh, with instructions to communicate the same to the marshal, if he should be there (as it was supposed he was), or if not, to a magistrate; and for the said steamer to remain at Morristown, until the express should have had time to arrive with the intelligence.

It was observed that one of the passengers on board the steamer, had a sword concealed under his cloak, and was looked upon by the others with that deference that indicated that they regarded him as their commander. Under his direction, about half of those on board entered the schooners, and the rest remained on board. Just before the steamer reached Morristown, (about eleven o'clock on Sunday night, Nov. 11), the schooners were unfastened, and dropped astern, and were seen no more by those on board the steamer, until their arrival in Ogdensburgh on the next morning. An express was sent on, as had been agreed upon. It is also believed that information was sent over to the village of Brockville, to the same effect. It had now become quite certain, that Prescott was the point against which the expedition was to be directed. The United States, after stopping two hours and a half, resumed her course to Ogdensburgh, where she arrived about three o'clock on Monday morning. The fires were put out immediately on entering the port, as usual, and the hands, with the exception of the customary watch, retired. The schooners, after parting company with the United States, proceeded on their way, and the wind being favorable, reached Prescott during the night. They contained, as has been above suggested, and as afterwards appeared, a military armament under the command of General John W. Birge, but which were under the more immediate command of one Von Schoultz, a Polish exile, who had seen much of military operations in his own country, and who doubtless had been induced to join this expedition from sincere motives, to promote a cause which he had been made to believe was just and honorable. Upon their approaching Prescott, one of the schooners was made fast to the upper wharf, and Von Schoultz urged his men to land, with bayonets fixed, and muskets unloaded; march into the village, and take possession of the fort at once.

A hesitation on the part of some of the leaders, and a difference of opinion as to the mode of attack, arose, which led to a delay, and the schooner was soon after cast off. Those who were conversant with the condition of the town, and the strength of·the garrison at Fort Wellington at that time, have expressed an opinion, that but little difficulty would have been experienced, at the first moment, in taking effectual possession. Soon after, the Charlotte of Oswego, grounded on the soft slimy delta of mud, which the Oswegatchie has deposited in the St. Lawrence, at its confluence with the Great river. About sunrise, on Monday morning, a crowd assembled on the dock, at which the United States was moored, and from the movements and conduct of those who took a leading part in the proceedings, it was evident they intended to seize that steamer, in order to assist in promoting their enterprise. Early in the morning, an iron six pounder cannon, belonging to the village of Ogdensburgh, and a brass four pounder, belonging to the state of New York, and in charge of an artillery company under Capt. A. B. James, were seized by the Patriots, and afterwards conveyed across the river in a scow, to the wind mill. Several of the owners of the steamer, upon perceiving that the demonstrations on shore, and the movements of the armed men, threatened the seizure of the boat, endeavored to obtain of the civil and military authorities assistance in preventing it. The marshal of the district was absent; the collector (Mr. Smith Stilwell), as was abundantly proven by evidence taken subsequently, upon a suit growing out of this affair, made strenuous and diligent efforts to prevent the proceedings which ensued, but without effect. Meanwhile the streets were filled with armed men, and it was perceived that the village of Prescott was alive with the bustle of preparation to resist the movements which were in progress against them. The leaders of the patriots in Ogdensburgh proceeded to muster a volunteer company to man the steamer, and openly derided the efforts of the civil authorities in preventing them. Having obtained a crew, partly it is said by volunteers and those whom they hired of the crew, and partly by those from on shore, the fires were kindled, and as soon as steam could be got up, they left the wharf, with loud cheers from the crowd, to go to the assistance of the schooner that had run aground. The schooner Charlotte of Toronto, after casting off from the upper wharf, fell down the stream, and took a position early in the morning, nearly opposite the wind mill, about a mile below. The walls of this were thick and massive, and the interior was divided into several stories. It had been formerly used as a grist mill, but for several years previous to this time, it had been deserted, and its machinery had fallen to ruins. Around it were several massive stone houses, at a short distance, the most or all of which were inhabited by families. The public road from Prescott down the river, passes immediately by it, and separates it from most of the stone houses. The point on which the wind mill stands, juts for some little distance into the St. Lawrence, and the margin of the river for a considerable distance above and below, as well as opposite, was overgrown by a thicket of cedar. Here from the schooner, and from a number of small boats that crossed the river, a lodgement was made, and a portion of the armament of the schooner was landed. The steamer United States did not succeed in getting off the grounded schooner, and presently returned to the American shore. The Experiment, a British steam boat, was lying at this time at the wharf at Prescott, and being armed with cannon, fired upon her without effect. Additional hands were now procured to navigate the steamer, which had herself grounded for a short time on her first trip, and she was again worked into the river, near where the schooner Charlotte of Oswego, lay aground, and soon after again returned. A demand was here made, from one on board to those on shore, for a longer hawser, which was promised from a neighboring store, and a quantity of bread and other provisions was conveyed aboard. On again leaving the dock, she went out into the channel, going between the grounded schooner and the British shore, and passed down the river nearly or quite to Wind Mill point, and was twice fired upon by the Experiment, but it is believed without effect. After arriving at Wind Mill point, she remained there some time, and about this time the Charlotte of Toronto, having remained opposite the wind mill till about the middle of the day, sailed up the river, and came to anchor near the American shore, not far from where the other schooner subsequently anchored, and remained till dark. The movements of the United States had consumed nearly half of the day, and she came up at about the same time with the Charlotte of Toronto, and apparently with a view to cover her from the fire of the British steam boat. She again went down to Wind Mill point, at each time of passing receiving a fire from the Experiment, which shot were cheered by those on board, who were assembled on the promenade deck; but as she was coming up on her last trip, with great speed. and apparently under a great press of steam, a cannon shot from the British steamer, entered the wheel house, and instantly beheaded a young man by the name of Solomon Foster, who stood as a pilot at the wheel. Upon arriving in port this time, the United States lay during the remainder of the day, near the wharf. During this time the boat was apparently under the orders of one Oliver B. Pierce, and had on board John W. Birge, of Cazenovia, Madison county, the reputed commander of the invading forces. Mr. Hiram Denio, who was personally acquainted with the former, was requested by the owners of the boat to go on board, and solicit the peaceable surrender of the property, which, after some consultation, was done, and the parties who had taken possession, withdrew from it.

During the last trip which the steamer made, it was particularly observed that but a small part of those who went over returned. The others were, it is said, landed at or near the wind mill.

Mr. Nathaniel Garrow, of Auburn, the U. S. marshal for the northern district of New York, arrived from Sackett's Harbor between seven and eight o'clock on Monday evening. and between eight and nine made a formal seizure of the steamer United States. In the afternoon of Monday, the *Paul Pry*, a small steam ferry boat, went over to the stranded schooner, in charge of a company of the Patriots, and succeeded in hauling her off. Not long after being relieved, she passed down and took a position near the other schooner, and in performing this service encountered a brisk fire from the steamer Experiment, which was returned with small arms. In the evening, she was also seized for a violation of the neutrality of the frontier. During the whole of Monday, there was frequent crossing of the river in small boats, and no attempt to prevent it was made or deemed practicable by the civil authorities. During the night, every thing remained quiet, and reports of cannon were heard at long intervals.

The unusual and very exciting state of things, however, which were evidently preparing for some crisis, kept the public mind awake, and every one anxious to learn what there might be known of the nature and progress of the expedition, its force, its chances of success, and the probabilities that they would be sustained by the Canadian population, or be reinforced by recruits from the states. Rumors of every kind floated through the town, and a meeting was held to concert measures for defense, but such was the novel and perilous crisis that had arrived, that nothing was effected. Some of the citizens warmly sympathized with the movement, and ardently wished it success, while another part, embracing most of those of influence and property, looked upon the proceedings as tending to nothing but ruin, and as calling upon the patriotism of every good citizen, to lend his aid in discouraging the prosecution of the enterprise, and in protecting the national honor and the interests of the village. Such, however, was the influence of the armed strangers in the streets, that this sentiment could scarcely be found to operate in efficient exertions. Monday night was spent by the patriots at the wind mill, and adjacent premises, in fortifying it as they might be able, under the direction of Von Schoultz, upon whom, in the absence of the superior officers, devolved the defence of a position, which it has been strongly insinuated and firmly believed, those who had incited and encouraged them to it, had not the courage to share with them.

It is difficult to estimate that moral baseness and utter depravity, that would, by the most solemn promises, engage to sustain the acts of others, and by means of these assurances, lead unsuspecting and inexperienced youths into a position in which utter ruin must inevitably await them, and having involved the destruction of their victims, meanly shrink from them.

This remark is not intended as a justification of the conduct of those who occupied the wind mill, but as an illustration of the character of those who originated the expedition, and were most loud and confident in their declarations and assurances of its ultimate success. On the following morning (November 13), the two schooners were seized at about ten o'clock, by the marshal. They at this time lay in the American waters, about thirty or forty rods from the pier or abutments of Creighton's brewery.

The Charlotte of Oswego, at the time of her seizure, had on her deck two or three cannon, one properly mounted on wheels, and the other two on small plank trucks. There were also on board, boxes and small casks, which contained guns and munitions of war. There were about half a dozen men, who were the captain (Sprague), and crew. The other vessel had on board some barrels of apples, but most of the munitions had been removed from her, and landed at the wind mill. Her captain (Quick), and three or four men, supposed to be her crew, were on board. These were put in charge of Colonel W. J. Worth, of the 8th U. S. infantry, who had arrived in the steamer Telegraph on Monday evening, and subsequently sent to Sackett's Harbor for safe keeping.

This steamer had visited the place on Saturday, to bring Colonels Totten and Thayer, of the engineer service, and was under the command of Capt. Hill, of the U. S. army. After the United States had been seized, her machinery was taken apart, so that she could not be used without the assent of the owners. The efforts of the military authorities, were directed to the prevention of all further communication with the Patriots and the American shore, and the arrival of the troops afforded the first means that the authorities had possessed of enforcing the laws. The testimony that was taken in a case growing out of this affair, concurs in proving, that on Monday, the arm of the civil law was powerless, and that there did not exist the means of preventing the proceeding which ensued. Colonel Worth had under his command two companies of government troops. On Tuesday, the British armed steamers Coburg and Victoria, having arrived at Prescott with a reinforcement of troops, at about seven o'clock, they, together with the Experiment, opened a discharge of cannon, and commenced throwing bombs at the Patriots in the wind mill, who fired with field pieces from their batteries on shore, in return. These exciting and novel proceedings, very naturally drew a large crowd of spectators from Ogdensburgh and the adjacent country, to Mile point, the present site of the rail road depot, and the most eligible point from which to observe the doings of the British, in their attempt to dislodge the Patriots. On Tuesday morning, a detachment of forty men of the 83d regiment, under Lieut. Johnson, and thirty marines under Lt. Parker, were landed and joined by detachments of militia. At a quarter before seven the British advanced in two columns. The left under Col. D. Fraser, consisting of the marines, Capt. G. McDonnel's company of L. G. Highlanders, Capts. Jones's and Fraser's companies of 2d regiment Grenville militia, and 100 men of Col. Martle's regiment of Stormont militia. The right column was led by Col. Gowan, of the Queen's borderers, and 100 of Capt. Martle's regiment. Soon after, a line of fire blazed along the summit of the hill, in the rear of the mill, for about eighty or a hundred rods, and the report of small arms made an incessant roar. The morning being dark and lowering, the gleam of the discharges became the more observable, and tended to heighten the horrors of the dramatic events that were transpiring. The Patriots were mostly protected by stone walls, and comparatively secure, while the British were fully exposed in the open field, and suffered greatly from the sharp shooters that were posted in the upper stories of the wind mill. The officers on horseback were seen distinctly to fall, here and there, on the field, and the ranks of the soldiers to waste away under the unequal contest. The British did not, at that time, have at Prescott guns of sufficient weight to make a sensible impression upon the massive walls of the tower, and their shot rebounded from the surface without producing effect.

After twenty or thirty minutes one party gave way, and retired out of sight over the hill, and at about nine o'clock the firing had ceased, apparently leaving the Patriots in possession of their strong hold, but without the ability to pursue, or to return to the American shore, or to maintain their present position for any great length of time, from want of provisions and munitions. At the time when the action commenced, the patriot forces are supposed to have numbered about one hundred and eighty, but during the engagement, a party consisting of fifty-two, who had pursued the retreating militia over the hill, were separated from their comrades, scattered, pursued and captured, in detail. The Patriot loss on this occasion, is said to have been five killed and thirteen wounded, while that of the British was said at the time, to have been about a hundred killed, and as many wounded. The official return of Colonel Young, gave two officers, and eleven rank and file killed, and sixty-seven wounded. It has been generally believed that their loss exceeded this number. Finding that the strong hold of the Patriots resisted any means of impression which they possessed, the British resolved to await the arrival of heavier cannon, and took precautions, meanwhile to prevent any reinforcement of the invaders. From nine till three there was but little excitement. An irregular firing was kept up on the windmill, and a body of regulars fired an occasional volley at a stone house, in which a portion of the Patriots were established. At three o'clock in the afternoon, a barn was burnt by the Patriots, as sheltering the British. During this time the Patriots occupied the wind mill, and several of the houses adjoining, and the brow of the hill. On the evening of the 13th, a requisition was sent to Sackett's Harbor, for more troops, to be ready, if necessary, to assist those already at Ogdensburgh, in restraining any attempt at reinforcement. Lt. W. S. Johnson, of the British army, belonging to the 83d regiment, was among the killed. The dead and badly wounded, lay on the field till the morning of the 14th (Wednesday), when the British sent a flag of truce, for permission to bury the dead, and both parties were for a short time, engaged in collecting and carrying off from the field the slain. The night between the 13th and the 14th, was quiet, and the wind blew so rough that all attempt at crosing the river, had nothing else prevented, would have been hazardous. At half past nine, troops were again marched to Fort Wellington, but no engagement ensued. In the forenoon of Thursday, Colonel Worth sent for several of the prominent citizens of Ogdensburgh, to come on board the steamer, who accepted the invitation. His object in doing this was to ask their opinions and advice, on the propriety of a course which he proposed, of applying to Colonel Plomer Young, the British commander, to ask of him the privilege of staying the further effusion of blood, by being allowed to remove the Patriots, and becoming responsible that they should attempt no further disturbance on this frontier. The humane intention of this measure, commended itself to the approbation of those to whom it was explained, and a citizen of high standing in the community, who was personally acquainted with Colonel Young, offered his services to procure an interview between Cols. Young and Worth, and accordingly visited Prescott, where he was politely received by the British officer, who accompanied him back to the steamer, and a private interview was held between the two colonels. The delicacy of the measure proposed, and the obvious charges that would be brought against the official character of an officer, who would consent to the escape of an enemy, who was entirely within his power, rendered a compliance with the request, a thing to be not for a moment entertained. He pointedly denied the favor asked, but from an intimation that was dropped, either from inadvertence, or design, that the machinery of the Experiment, 'the Colburg and Victoria having gone up the river the night previous), needed repairs, that would prevent her being used until two o'clock the next morning, it was very naturally inferred, that no means of annoyance would be in the possession of the British during the early part of the night. This opportunity Colonel Worth wished to have improved, and having consulted some of the citizens on the subject, it was understood that early in the evening, the steamer Paul Pry, should be at the service of a party of volunteers, who might safely approach the wind mill, and rescue the inmates, if they could be induced to improve the opportunity. This delicate and responsible service, was entrusted to Mr. Preston King, the post master of the village, who was selected as possessing the requisite qualifications for the duty.

A sufficient number of volunteers was raised for the occasion, and the steamer repaired to the vicinity of the wind mill. Among the volunteers was a man connected with the Patriots, who was said to be an officer of their organization, and to know their pass words; he was for these reasons, recommended as a suitable person to open the communication with them, and was sent on shore in a small row boat, to communicate the errand of the steamer, which as the shore was shoal, and there was no wharf, was compelled to lay off several rods from the shore to avoid grounding.

By subsequent information, it was ascertained, that some person who went ashore in the first boat, reported that a reinforcement of men and supplies might soon be expected by the Patriots, and they were advised to maintain their position.

After waiting a considerable time for a return from the row boat sen ashore, a small boat rowed by two men, brought to the steamer a wounded man from the wind mill, from whom and his companions, those remaining on board the steamer first heard of the report of reinforcements that had been made on shore. Mr. King then took a small boat, with one man, and repaired himself to the wind mill, made known the nature of his errand, stated the folly of looking for reinforcements which there was no reason to expect, and earnestly requested them to avail themselves of the only chance of escape that would be offered.

The delusive hope and divided councils arising from the report of reinforcements, produced delay and uncertainity in the movements of the Patriots to avail themselves of the opportunity to retire from their position. The men on board the steamer became impatient at the delay, and insisted upon the return of the steamer to Ogdensburgh. Mr. King was thus reluctantly compelled to return, without having accomplished his purpose, further than to bring off six or seven men from the mill, one of whom had been wounded in the thigh by a musket ball. He had scarce returned to port, when the British armed steamer was seen going down the river, and all chance of passing between the American shore, and the mill was cut off. The persons first sent on shore to communicate with the Patriots did not return to the steamer, but were left, and returned to the American shore in their row boat.

During the time the Paul Pry lay near the wind mill, firing along the line by the British piquet guards was kept up by musketry, which rendered the men on board the steamer impatient of inaction and delay. Had it not been for the false expectation of reinforcements, it is believed the patriots might at once have availed themselves of the opportunity offered for escape, and the sad events which subsequently followed, have been avoided.

On Thursday evening, the steamer United States (Captain Van Cleve), in charge of Captain Vaughan, sailing master of the navy, with a party of troops under Captain Wright, started for Sackett's Harbor, having along side in tow, the two patriot schooners, and manned by a company of United States troops. The schooners had on their decks, the cannon which had formed a part of their armament. Apprehending that they should meet a British force, expected from Kingston, to complete the capture of the wind mill, and believing it to be prudent to be provided against any emergency that might arise, Capt. Wright had caused the cannon to be loaded, and the military to be held in readiness. When they had arrived at a point just above Oak point, they met the British steamer Brockville, having two gun boats in tow. The United States was hailed, and ordered to " *lie to and send a boat aboard.*"

The peremptory and insulting tone in which this was expressed, forbade compliance on the part of the officer, who had the flotilla in charge, and the reply was made, that they might " *come aboard.*" The demand was again repeated, and answered with a coolness and pointedly laconic brevity, that did the highest credit to the courage and ability of Captain Wright. The parties having passed, the British steamer turned and followed for some distance, but no further notice being taken of her by the United States, the pursuer shortly resumed her original course.

On the morning of the 16th (Friday), the British having been reinforced with a regiment of four hundred regulars, and by gun boats armed with ordnance sufficient for the reduction of the place, set themselves at work systematically, for this purpose. An eighteen pounder was posted back of the mill, under Major McBane; a gun boat was posted below the mill, and a heavily armed steamer above it, so that the shot from these three points might not interfere with each other, and still have the mill in their focus. They were beyond the range of rifle shot, and sufficient to accomplish ere long the demolition of the tower. During the whole of Thursday, a white flag had been displayed from the mill, but no attention being paid to it, it was finally fastened on the outside. Three or four flags were sent out, and the bearers shot down, as soon as seen, as the British appeared to be inclined to receive no terms. At length on Friday, in the forenoon, the firing ceased, and an unconditional surrender being made, the prisoners, (for as such they were received, and regarded,) were marched out between files of regulars, and conducted to Fort Wellington, from whence they were sent to Fort William Henry, at Kingston, for trial. Had it not been for the interposition of the regulars, the prisoners would have been torn in pieces by the enraged militia, who exhibited a vindictiveness and animosity, that has scarcely found a parallel in the annals of French and Indian warfare. Every species of abuse and insult was heaped upon the unfortunate band. During the firing that ensued in celebrating the surrender, Captain Drummond, of the British army, was accidentally shot. The British burnt, at once, four dwellings and two barns, in the vicinity of the wind mill. Von Schoultz was said to be opposed to offering the enemy a flag of truce, and besought his men to rush upon the enemy, and die in the contest, but their ammunition and provisions were exhausted, and the fatigue of five days and nights incessant watching and labor, had made them indifferent to their fate.

British official return of killed and wounded in action with the Brigands, near Prescott, on the 13th November, 1838.

Killed.—83d regiment, 1 lieutenant. L. Glengary Highlanders, 4 rank and file. 2d regiment, Dundas militia, 4 rank and file. 1st regiment, Grenville militia, 2 rank and file. 2d regiment, Grenville militia, 1 lieutenant. Captain Edmondson's Brockville Independent company, 1 rank and file. Total, 2 lieutenants, 11 rank and file.

Wounded—83d regiment, 4 rank and file. Royal marines, 1 lieutenant, 14 rank and file. L. Glengary Highlanders, 1 ensign, 7 rank and file. 9th provincial battalion, 1 lieutenant colonel, 8 rank and file. 2d regiment, Dundas militia, 1 lieutenant, 12 rank and file. 1st regiment, Grenville militia, 4 rank and file. Capt. Edmondson's Brockville Independent company, 3 rank and file. Captain Jessup's Prescott Independent company, 1 sergeant, 4 rank and file. Gentlemen Volunteers, 2 rank and file. Total, 1 lieutenant colonel, 2 lieutenants, 1 ensign, 1 sergeant, 62 rank and file.

Names of Officers killed.—W. S. Johnson, lieutenant 83d regiment; —— Dulmage, lieutenant 1st regiment Grenville militia.

Wounded.—Ogle R. Gowan, lieutenant colonel 9th provincial battalion, slightly; —— Parker, Royal marines, slightly; —— Pardow, lieutenant 2d regiment Dundas militia, severely; Angus MacDonnell, ensign L. G. Highlanders, slightly.

P. YOUNG.

The board of supervisors were in sessions at Canton at the time, and the cannonade of the battle was distinctly heard at that place. Some of the board were warm sympathizers in the movement, and the following resolutions which were brought forward for action repeatedly, but failed to pass, shows the strong feeling that was entertained in relation to the patriot war, and may be regarded as a curiosity worthy of record.

The resolution of Isaac Ellwood is called up in the words following, to wit: · Whereas the members of the board of supervisors of St. Lawrence county, having received information and believing the same to be authentic, that the patriots have made a noble stand at Windmill point, near Prescott, in Upper Canada, and have had a severe engagement with the advocates and minions of British tyranny and oppression on the 13th inst. and having every reason to believe from said information, unless the said patriots are reinforced in the perilous situation in which they are placed, that they will meet with defeat, and sacrifice their lives in contending against a merciless and cruel foe: and whereas, this board feel a deep interest and intense anxiety in the success of that patriotic struggle which would spread the light of liberty over our oppressed brethren in Canada, and for the preservation of the lives of those patriots who are contending for the rights of men born free, and for the republican principles for which our venerable forefathers shed their blood.

Resolved, that this board adjourn, to meet again at the court house in the said county, on the last Monday of the present month, at 1 o'clock, P. M., in order to enable the members thereof to rescue that Spartan band of patriotic friends, and preserve their lives from the hands of their enemies, the tyrants and advocates of the British crown. On motion by Mr. Buck, seconded by Mr. Doty:—Resolved that the above resolution lie on the table until the same shall be again drawn up." The resolution was never called up from the table.

Bill Johnston, the avowed leader of the gang that boarded and burned the Robert Peel, had been seen publicly in the streets of Ogdensburgh for several days, and no one ventured to arrest him, until on the 17th, shortly after the surrender of the band in the windmill, he was seen to enter a boat with his son, and leave the harbor; the collector of the district, seeing him depart, called the attention of a deputy marshall to his movements, and advised that an attempt should be made to arrest him. Failing in this, he entered a boat belonging to the office, hoisted the revenue flag, and pursued him, in company with several others. Johnston and his son landed about three miles above the village, was pursued, headed, and finally induced to surrender, on condition that his arms might be received by his son. He was armed with a Cochran rifle, (with twelve discharges) and two large rifle pistols, with several smaller ones and a bowie knife. The merit of arresting Johnston has been claimed by different parties, and the bounty offered for his apprehension is said to have been paid to C. T. Buswell and A. B. James, who pursued on horseback as soon as he had landed, and were present when he surrendered his arms. The steamer Oneida, in the service of the United States government, and having on board a detachment of troops, was in the river when the boat in which Johnston and his son were escaping, was run on shore. The officers in charge of the steamer immediately steered towards the point where the boats landed, to afford any assistance that might be found necessary, and the captured party was conveyed on board the steamer, and taken to Sacketts Harbor.

On the Monday after the capture, the Hon. John Fine, in company with Charles G. Myers, consented at the solicitation of some of the friends of the prisoners to visit Kingston to carry a contribution of several hundred dollars to supply their wants, make inquiries into their condition, and offer legal council. The season of travel being passed and there being no direct communication with Kingston, they wrote to Colonel Worth at Sacketts Harbor, asking if he could be sent over from thence, and furnished with a letter to the commanding officer at Kings-

40

ton, both of these requests were declined. They then crossed the river to Prescott, to confer with Major Young, and on being escorted from the wharf to his quarters by a sentinel, they were kindly received, and furnished with a note of introduction to Colonel Dundas, at Kingston. A citizen of Prescott gave the use of a small steamer, without charge. At the hotels in Kingston, they found several Americans from Oswego, Salina, &c., on a similar errand, who stated that they had been there some time endeavoring to get access to the rooms of the prisoners but the sheriff had denied every application which had been made for this purpose. The next morning, they called upon Colonel Dundas, who stated that he had delivered the prisoners to the care of the sheriff, and that application must be made to him. He was told that the sheriff had positively refused, under any circumstances, any interview under orders from the governor, to several similar applications. They then added as a last resort, that being both lawyers they had some right to serve the prisoners in the capacity of legal counsellors, having been employed by their friends for that purpose. It was the boast of the English law which the Americans had inherited from the mother country, that every one was presumed innocent of a crime until proved to be guilty, and that the prisoners had a right to legal advice in this case, and the privilege of obtaining witnesses for their defense. Upon this the colonel arose and accompanied them to the fort, introduced them to the sheriff and requested that they might be permitted to see the prisoners. The sheriff said that the governor had sent orders that no one be permitted to visit them, but the colonel said that he would risk the responsibility, and requested the keys, which were given him. Several military officers were introduced and joined in the visit to the different rooms. These were above ground, large, cleanly, and contained about fifty prisoners each. Inquiry was made of those from St. Lawrence county, of their want of clothing, &c., which was afterwards procured and sent to them.* They said that they were furnished with good and sufficient food and were well treated. In one room was a company of about fifty boys under twenty-one years of age, and some as young as sixteen. Several of them alluded to the late events and the causes which had induced them to engage in the foolish enterprise, with sobbing and tears. Several of the officers present were much affected and proposed to leave. The Ogdensburgh citizens remarked to the boys, that there was hope in their case. The power of England was not so feeble as to fear the loss of Canada by the hands of boys, and the glory of England would not be enhanced by their sacrifice.

.They were advised to plead their infancy, and throw themselves upon the mercy of the government. The court martial was organized and one of the prisoners was on trial. Solicitor General Draper, conducted the examination of the prisoners with fairness. He allowed the accused the opportunity to state all the extenuating circumstances which he wrote down, and said he would send to the governor. In the evening an interview was had with Mr. Draper, at the rooms of the council, and at the suggestion of some of the citizens, an application was made to the governor general of Canada, through the medium of Judge Jones of the Queen's Bench, for the pardon of the boys. An answer was returned, that if the friends of the boys would exert their influence to prevent further aggressions, they should be released, and as an earnest of the performance of this promise, six were set free. From time to

---

* One of these boys on being questioned as to his wants, solicited some candy.

time others were liberated until most of those under age were allowed to return to their friends.

The issue of this expedition, did much to render the Patriot cause unpopular, and a healthy reaction was soon felt along the frontier, but a spirit of jealousy and hostility had been engendered that led to much difficulty. On the 21st of Dec., the village trustees resolved to organize a company, to be held ready at a minute's warning to act in preserving order, and repell if necessary any aggression. Arms were to be procured for them from Russell. On the last day of Dec., a crowded meeting was held to unite in a petition to Congress for protection of the frontier and intervention in favor of the prisoners. In support of the latter, they asserted for our government an equal merit in the capture, inasmuch as the Patriots had been cut off from their supplies by the official seizure of the schooners and armament. A becoming tribute was paid to the valor and courage of the misguided youths who had been seduced into the measure. On the 2d of Jan., 1839, another public meeting was held to discourage all further invasion of Canada. The call for this was signed by nearly seventy prominent citizens of all parties, and it was addressed by several of the inhabitants and by Major General Winfield Scott, in a very able manner. In his address, Gen. Scott, after conceding that a feeling favorable to Canadian independence pervaded the country, went on to enquire what act of that people had evinced their desire for a change, and pointed out in a masterly manner the folly of attempting to force upon them a measure which their acts proved that they did not desire. A series of resolutions was passed embodying the sentiment of the considerate of all parties, and appealing to all good citizens to aid in putting an end to these proceedings so destructive of the public peace and so perilous to our national welfare.

As the steam boat United States, Capt. Whitney, was leaving Ogdensburgh on the evening of April 14, 1839, with a large number of passengers, from 6 to 10 rounds of musket shot were fired from a wharf in Prescott, at which a crowd was assembled, but a subsequent inquiry failed to fix upon any one as the culprit, and the same evening she was fired upon from the wharf at Brockville. These insulting measures were greatly aggravated by a high handed outrage upon the schooner G. S. Weeks, —— Turner, master, on Friday, May 17, 1839, at Brockville, where she had stopped to discharge some merchandise. The usual papers were sent to the custom house, and a permit to unload was issued by the deputy collector. There was lying on deck a six pound iron cannon belonging to the state, consigned to Capt. A. B. James, to replace the one that had been seized by the Patriots, upon discovering which an attempt was made to seize it, but was resisted by the crew until the collector of the district came up and took possession of the vessel under some alleged irregularity of her papers. The gun was then taken by the mob, who paraded the streets with it and fired it repeatedly. Word was immediately sent to Col. Worth, at Sacketts Harbor, who repaired without delay to the place in the steamer Oneida, and sent a respectful inquiry to learn on what grounds the schooner was detained. To this the deputy could give no direct answer, and, but from what he could learn, Col. Worth inferred that the seizure was without justification, and resolved to vindicate our national honor in recovering the cannon that had been taken from it. On Saturday evening he repaired to Prescott, and peremptorily demanded of Col. Frasier, a release of the vessel and her cargo, to which at 10 o'clock the next day answer was given that the vessel and cargo should be released, but doubts were expressed whether the cannon could be got from the mob. To be prepared with an intelligent and prudent witness in case the necessity for extreme measures should arise, the Colonel invited Mr. Bishop Perkins, a legal gentleman of high standing in his profession to accompany him to Brockville. He had on board a company of about 100 regulars, who were well supplied with a double number of muskets and ammunition sufficient for the occasion. The steamers took up a position alongside the schooner, and a demand for the restoration of the gun was sent. The wharves and block house were densely crowded with an excited and furious mob, many of whom were armed, and all of them partaking of the excitement which the occasion called forth. The civil authorities endeavored to procure the restoration of the piece, but found themselves incapable of persuading or compelling the rabble to surrender it quietly. Had any of the crowd on shore in the exitement of the moment fired upon the steamer, there is little reason to doubt but that the fire would have been promptly returned by the regulars on board the Oneida, and the effect upon the crowded masses upon the wharves must have been signally fatal. Matters thus remained several hours, during which a collision was momentarily expected. At 4 P. M , a steamer from Kingston, with British regulars arrived, which had been sent for by the magistrates of the town, with the aid of which several of the ring leaders of the mob were arrested and lodged in the guard house. Having waited sufficiently long, Col. Worth notified the authorities for the last time that the cannon must be instantly returned, which was done with the utmost haste, and the prize was released. Col. Worth expressed the opinion that the civil magistrates evinced commendable zeal in their efforts to restore order and recover the cannon, but the utmost insolence was shown by the rabble towards the bearers of messages from Colonel Worth. The tidings of this event brought his excellency Governor Sir George Arthur, to Brockville, where he was presented an address signed by 266 persons, as an attempted justification for the recent outrage. They protested against the manner in which the gun had been given up at the demand enforced by the presence of an armed steamer in their harbor, and declared that they submitted only through the improper interference of some of his excellency's *prominent* and *courageous* officials in civil authority. In his reply the governor admitted that the seizure was illegal, and regretted that greater caution had not been exercised before that act. The step once taken he regretted that the seizure was abandoned without due authority, and more especially under the circumstances, although he admitted that some magistrates had acted with honest zeal and from a sense of public duty to advise the measure. He declared the seizure and firing of the cannon after it had been taken by the revenue officer, was a lawless proceeding, and regretted that personal abuse had been offered to the foreign officers who had entered the country on public duty. It is due to the Canadian press and the more considerate portion of the inhabitants, that they mostly denounced the seizure as wholly unjustified. The collector of Brockville was removed from office by Governor Arthur.

On Tuesday, June 25, 1839, a party from Prescott attempted to abduct a deserter from Ogdensburgh, but their plans being discovered, the gang was surrounded by a large concourse of people, covered with tar, and marched back to their boat under an armed guard. The leader of the gang was said to have committed suicide the next day. The British steamers commenced touching at Ogdensburgh in the latter part of June, and were well received. It was hoped that a renewal of friendly intercourse would do much to allay the animosity existing between the border inhabitants of the two nations.

As the American steam packet *St. Lawrence,* was passing down on her regular trip on the 4th of August, 1839, she was fired upon by an armed British schooner lying in the stream opposite Brockville. The particulars of this infamous outrage committed not by a lawless rabble, but by a government vessel, became the subject of a correspondence between the officers of the two governments in command of the naval and military forces along the frontier, a copy of which is before us. It appears that the steamer having numbers of passengers of both sexes was passing at about 5 P. M., when on approaching Her Majesty's armed schooner Montreal, she was hailed and ordered to show her colors, which being disregarded, several musket balls were fired by order of W. N. Fowell, commander. This being communicated to Col. Worth, an explanation was demanded, and the act was feebly attempted to be justified on the ground that they were afraid the steamer contained Patriots, that they wanted to know to what nation it belonged, &c. &c. These frivolous excuses, some of which would have been applicable on the high seas, when applied to the St. Lawrence, became extremely ridiculous.

On the 10th of August, 1840, Gen. Scott arrived at Ogdensburgh, in the Telegraph steamer, then in the service of government. He was on his way to Plattsburgh.

The continuance of secret lodges for the agitation of the Patriot question, led President Tyler to issue a proclamation September 5, 1841, calling upon all good citizens to discountenance them as tending to evil con sequences.

The following is a list, as nearly as could be procured, of the prisoners taken at the wind mill, and tried at Kingston.

The following notes and abbreviations are used: *g.,* plead guilty; *n. g.,* plead not guilty; *t.,* transported to Van Dieman's Land; *h.,* hung at Fort Henry; *a.,* acquitted; *w.,* wounded in the battle; *r.,* released without trial; *p.,* pardoned. Numerals denote the ages of prisoners. All, except those in italics, were sentenced to be hung.

Dorephus Abbey, 47 (Watertown), *n. g., h.* Dec. 12; Philip Alger, 23 (Bents, N. Y.), *w. r.;* Charles Allen, *p.;* David Allen, 24 (Volney), *t.;* Duncan Anderson, 48 (Livingston co.), *h.* Jan. 4; *Oliver Aubre* (L. C.), *w. r.;* Samuel Austin (Alexandria, N. Y.), *p.;* Thomas Baker (Winder, N. Y.), *t.;* Hiram W. Barlow, 19 (St. L. co.), *p.;* Rouse Bennett. 17 (Herk. co.), *p.;* Ernest Berentz (Poland, Europe), *p.;* John Berry, 40 (Columbia co.), *t.;* Orlin Blodget, 23 (Jeff. co.), *g. t.;* Geo. Bloudeau, 19 (Canada), *p.;* John Bradley, 30 (Ireland), *t.;* John A. Brewster (Henderson, N. Y.), *p.;* Chas. S. Brown (Oswego co.), *p.;* Geo. T. Brown, 23 (Le Ray, N. Y.), *n. g., t.; Bromley* (died of wounds in hospital); Christopher Buckley (Onondaga co.), *h.* Jan. 4; Chauncey Bugbee, 22 (Jeff. co.), *t.;* Hugh Calhoun (Ireland), *t.;* Paschal Cerventes (Vt.), *p.; Levi Chipman,* r. July 29; Truman Chipman, *p.; Culver S. Clark,* 19 (F. co.), *p.;* Eli Clark, (Oswego co.) *p.* on account of age and infirmities; Robt. G. Collins, 34 (Og'h), *t.;* Philip Coudrat (Germany), *p.; Hiram Coultman,* 19 (Jeff. co.), *w. r.;* Peter Cranker, 19 (Jeff. co.), *p.;* John Croukheit (Otsego co.), *t.;* Chas. Crossman (Jeff. co.), *p.; Jas. Cummings* (Canada), *r.* on account of insanity; Lysander Curtis, 33 (Og'h), *w., t.* (died in V. D.'s Land); Luther Darby, *t.;* Leonard Delino, 25 (Jeff. co.), *t.;* Wm. Denio, 18 (Le Ray), *g. p.;* Joseph Dodge (Mont. co.), *p.;* Aaron Dresser, Jr., 22 (Alexandria, N. Y.), *t.* (released in 1843); Joseph Drummond (Oswego co.), *p.;* David Dufekl, 22 (U. C.) *p.;* Moses A. Dutcher (Dexter, N.Y.), *t;* John Elmore (Jeff. co.), *p.; Shelah Evans,* 35 (Jeff. co.), *r.;* Ebon Fellows, *g., t.; David Field* (Granby, N. Y.); *Lorenzo F. Finney,* 21 (Watertown) *w.;* Michael Friar, 23, *t.;* Francis Gagnion, 18 (Canada), *p.;* Emanuel Garrison (Vt.) , *t.*; Wm. Gates (Lyme, N. Y.) *t.*; Daniel George (Lyme), *h.* Dec. 12 (paymaster); John Gilman, *t.*; Cornelius Goodrich, (Salina, N. Y.), *p.* 7 y'rs penitentiary; Gideon A. Goodrich (Mass.) *t.*; Price Gould, 21 (Jeff. co.), *p.*; *John Graves* (Plattsburgh), *r?* Jerry Griggs (Ct.), *t.*; Nelson J. Griggs (Onon. co.) *t.*; Hiram Hall, 15 (Jeff. co.), 7 y'rs pen'ry, *p.*; *Jacques Hered* (France), *w., r.*; Garret Hicks, 27 (Jeff. co.), *t.*; Edward Holmes (Syracuse), *p.*; Chas. Hovey (Lyme), *p.*; David Houth, 24, *t.*; Daniel D. Hustace, 27 (Watertown), *t.*; Jas. Ingles (Scotland), *t.*; Henry Jantzen, 29 (Ger.), *p.*; John M. Jones (Phil., N. Y.), *p.*; Geo. H. Kemble, 18 (Brownville), *w., p.*; John O. Koinski (Cracow, Poland), *p.*; Hiram Kinney, 20 (Onon.), *p.*; Oliver Lanton (Alb.), *p.*; Sylvester A. Lanton, 23 (Lyme), *h.* Jan. 4.; Andrew Leeper, 42 (Jeff. co.), *t.*; Joseph Lee, 21 (Oswego), *p.*; Joseph Lefort, 19 (Cape Vincent), *t.*; Lyman N. Lewis, *n. g.*; Daniel Liscomb (Lyme), *t.*; *Samuel Livingston* (Lisbon, N. Y.), *r.*; Hiram Loop, 26 (Oswego co.) *n. g., t.*; Foster Martin (Ox Bow), *t.*; J.; H. Martin, *t.*; Calvin Mathers (Salina), *t.*; Chauncey Mathers, 24 (Onon. co.), *t.*; *Fred'k Meals,* 21 (serv't of Von Schaltz, *w.,* died of wounds); *Alonzo Mignoteth, r?* Phares Miller (Watertown), *p.*; Justus Meriam, 17 (S. H.), *r.*; John Marriset, 26 (Canada), *w., t.*; Andrew Moore, 26 (Malta, N. Y.), *w., t.*; *Peter Meyer* (Syracuse), *r.*; Sebastian Meyer, 21 (Bavarian), *p.*; *Joseph Norris, a.*; *Wm. O'Neil,* 38 (Alex.), *n. g., a.*; Alson Owen, 24 (Oswego), *t.* (died in V. D.'s Land); *Jacob Paddo h.* 17 (Jeff. co.), *t.*; Joel Peeler, 50, *n. g., h.,* Dec. 22; Lawton S. Peck, 20 (J. ff. co.) *p.*; Ethel Penny, 18 (Jeff. co.), *p.*; Russell Phelps (Watertown), *h* Jan. 4; Jas. Pierce (Oneida co.), *t.*; Ira Polly (Jeff. co.), *t.*; *Lorenzo Phinney, w., r.*; *D. S. Powers,* (Brownville); *Gaius Powers, r.*; Asa Priest, 43 (Auburn), *w., t.* (died in V. D.'s Land); Jacob Putnam, 19 (M. co.), *p.*; Levi Putnam, 21 (do.), *p.*; Timothy P. Ransom, 21 (Alex.), *p.*; Solomon Reynolds (Salina), *t.*; William Reynolds (Orleans), *t.*; *J. B. Rozeau* (L. C.), *r.,* very young; Asa H. Richardson, 23 (Oswego), *t.*; Andrew Richardson (Rossie), *p.*; Lawrence Riley, 43 (Vt.), *t.*; *Edgar Rogers*; *Orson Rogers,* 23 (Jeff. co.), *r.*; Hiram Sharp (Onon. co.), *t.*; Henry Shaw, *t.*; *Truman Shipman* (Morristown); Andrew Smith, 21, *p.*; Chas. Smith (Lyme), *p.*; Owen W. Smith, 26 (Watertown), *t.*; Price Senter, 18 (Ohio), *n. g., p.*; Jas. L. Snow, 21 (Oa. co.), *r.*; Wm. Stebbins, 18 (Jeff. co.), *p.*; Joseph Stewart, 25 (Mifflin co., Pa.), *t.*; Tho's Stockton, 26 (Felt's Mills), *t.*; John G. Swanberg (Alex., N. Y.), *t.*; Dennis Suete (do.), *n. g., t.*; Sylvanus Sweet, 21, *g., h.* Dec. 22; *Giles Thomas,* 34 (Onon. co.), *w., r.*; John Thomas, 26 (Madrid, N. Y.), *t.*; John Thompson (Eng.), *p.*; Abner Townsend, 17 (Jeff. co.), *g. p.*; Nelson Trunx, 20 (Antwerp); Oliver Tucker, 17, *n. g., p.*; Geo. Van Ambler, 17 (Jeff. co,), *p.*; Cha's Van Warner, 21 (Ellisburgh), *p.*; *Martin Van Slyke* (Watertown), *a.*; Hunter C. Vaughan, 19 (S. Har.), *p* (from intercession of father); Nils Szoltereky Von Schoultz (general), *g., h.* Dec. 18; Joseph Wagner (Salina), *p.*; Saul Washburn (Warren co.), *t.*; Simeon H. Webster, *p.*; *James M. Wheelock,* 22 (Jeff. co.), *w.*; Patrick White, 22 (Irish), *t.*; Riley Whitney (Vt.), *t.*; Nathan Whitney (Ct.), *t.*; Hosea G. Wilkie (Orleans, N. Y.), *p.*; Cha's Wilson, *p.*; Edward A. Wilson, 23 (Pompey), *t.*; Sampson Wiley (Watertown), *p.*; Cha's Woodruff, 19 (Salina), *g., p.*; Martin Woodruff, 24 (Onon. co.), *h.* Dec. 19; Beman Woodbury, 24 (Cayuga co.), *w., t.*; Wm. Woolcot, 20 (M. co.), *w., p.*; Stephen S. Wright, 25 (Denmark), *t.,* released 1843.

All of those who were transported were after several years pardoned, and most have since returned. While detained in the penal colonies, they suffered incredible hardships, and numbers of them died. Those who survived, mostly came back with impaired constitutions from privations, and the hard labor to which they had been subjected.

CHAPTER XI.

GEOLOGY, MINERALOGY, METEOROLOGY, &c.

E have extended the foregoing chapters, so that the present must be necessarily concise From the map, opposite page 467, it will be seen that the southern part of these counties is underlaid by *primary* rock, as the oldest, formed of rocky masses, are designated by geologists. It is made up of a mixture of simple minerals, which often show in the structure and mode of arrangement, that they have been at some period subjected to the action of *heat*. The constituents of these primitive rocks, are generally quartz, hornblende, and feldspar, arranged in irregular and often very tortuous strata or layers, which are generally highly inclined. This peculiar mixture and arrangement of simple minerals is denominated *gneiss rock*. When stratification is wanting, it becomes *sienite*, and when mica takes the place of hornblende it is called *granite*. A great variety of minerals occur in gneiss rock in certain localities, and it is a valuable repository of lead and iron ores. In some places simple minerals occur in large quantities, to the exclusion of everything else, as serpentine, limestone, &c., which of themselves often become rock formations. The boundaries of the gneiss rock are very nearly as follows. They constitute the Thousand islands, the last of which lie before Morristown, although both shores of the St. Lawrence are here composed of newer rock. A narrow strip of this rock extends from Chippewa bay, up the valley of the creek of that name, two or three miles, being bounded on each side by a formation, which geologists have named Potsdam sandstone, of which a further account will be given hereafter. The gneiss rock next enters the county from Jefferson, near the line of the military road in Hammond, and its northern margin runs nearly in a direct line to Black lake, and forms all the islands in that water, although the north shore is sandstone. It leaves the lake in Depeyster, and runs across that town, De Kalb and Canton, leaving the most of these towns underlaid by gneiss, and passes across a small part of Potsdam into Parishville and the southern part of the settlements in Hopkinton, and thence through township No. 7, 8, and 9, of Franklin county, and the northern edge of Bellmont. With small exceptions to be mentioned, near Somerville, the whole of the country south of this line is primary, and to this region metalic ores, except bog ores, must be necessarily limited. At the village of Potsdam, the same rock comes up to the surface, like an island in the midst of sandstone, and at other places the same thing is observed. However irregular the strata of gneiss may be, they will generally be found to *dip*, or slope down towards the north, which explains a remark made by Mr. Wright in his early surveys, that the mountains [like all in the southern forest] afford very good land on the north side, and gradually descending, but on the south side have high perpendicular ledges."

The extensive forest of northern New York, is underlaid entirely by primary rock, which seems to have been thrust up through newer formations, that surround it. In some places, the latter are thrown into an inclined position by this intruded mass. Gneiss rock has but few useful applications. In early times (and still for coarse grinding), it was used for millstones, and in some places it occurs suitable for building, but is generally too hard to be wrought with profit. In the south part of Canton, a very fine grained and durable variety occurs, which has a uniform grey color and close texture, that recommends it where permanence is required. Towards the western part of St. Lawrence county, white limestone is of common occurrence with this formation, and it has given rise to much discussion, whether the limestone be primitive and coëval with the gneiss, or whether it be a later deposite, altered by heat. As this inquiry would be out of place in this work it will be omitted. One fact is well established, viz: that the white limestone *underlies* the sandstone, and many instances of this occur in Rossie, Antwerp, &c. In some cases there is a relative position between limestone and granite that strongly indicates the primitive character of the former, of which Prof. Emmons has figured, one near Hailesboro, which we give in figure 3, opposite page 684, in which *a* is limestone, and *b* granite. Another example is given below, in which *a* is a limestone, with a wavy structure, and *b* granite. This locality is in Lyndhurst, Canada.

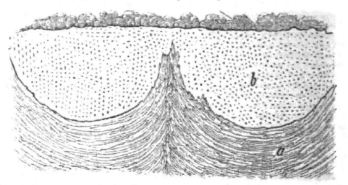

This limestone has been used to some extent as a marble, and mills for sawing it have existed in Rossie and Fowler, but its coarse crystaline texture impairs its value, except for the more massive kinds of architecture. For the manufacture of *lime*, however, there is probably nowhere in the world a material that will surpass this. It is generally in this rock, or along the line of junction with the gneiss, that the more splendid varieties of minerals occur, that are so eagerly sought by collectors. Limestone is rare in the primary rock of Franklin county; it, however occurs in township No. 9. In agricultural capabilities, the soil underlaid by primary rock varies in quality, and seems to be in a measure, dependent upon the prevalence of limestone, and the nature and amount of the loose drifted materials that overlie it. It has been generally conceded by geologists, that these transported materials, which in many instances constitute the soil, and modify to a great degree its agricultural capabilities, are derived from localities north of the place they now occupy. The northern border of the state, and for a great distance into Canada, is underlaid by rocks of a more recent period, in which lime is an important ingredient, and these give character to the soil for a considerable distance south, which can scarcely be said to differ from that immediately above them. The surface of the primary, is generally more or less broken by ridges of rock, often rising but little above the surface. These ridges have a prevailing direction of N. E. and S. W., which gives to the rivers, tributary to the St. Lawrence, their general course, and occasions the remarkable flexures, so strikingly noticed in the Oswegatchie and Indian rivers, which flow in natural valleys for a considerable distance be ween ridges of gneiss. Towards the southern borders of St. Lawrence county, the upheavals become of greater altitude, and as we go into the eastern part of this, and southern part of Franklin county, they attain the altitude of mountains, which in Essex, become the highest east of the Mississippi river. These bald and sterile peaks, support but a scanty vegetation, and overlook innumerable ponds and lakes, with fertile intervales; but thousands of acres will he found wholly unfit for tillage) and of no value beyond the timber on the surface, or the iron ores beneath it. These lands form an elevated plateau, liable to late spring and early autumnal frosts, but adapted to grazing, the uplands affording pasturage, and the intervales meadows. Of minerals interesting to the collector it has none, but it abounds in iron ores, which will hereafter employ the industry of great numbers, as it unites the three essentials of ore, water power, and fuel, to which, in a great degree, has been added in the Northern Rail road, an *access to market.* From an elevation of 1600 feet, the surface uniformly descends to the St. Lawrence, and in Franklin county, from the greater elevation, the descent is more perceptible, so that from almost any prominent point, the lower country north may be overlooked to a great extent, and the majestic St. Lawrence reduced to a silver line in the blue distance, with the Canadian villages dotted here and there, and the obscure outline of northern mountains, faintly appearing on the horizon, give a peculiar beauty to the landscape. Lying directly upon the gneiss, or in some instances upon the limestone, is a rock which presents a great variety of structure, called by geologists, *Potsdam sandstone,* from its great abundance above that village, and its remarkable adaptation for building purposes which it there exhibits.

Perhaps no material in the world will surpass in cheapness, elegance, and durability, the Potsdam sandstone, where it occurs in even-bedded strata, as in the towns of Potsdam, Canton, Stockholm, Malone, &c. The sharpness of outline which it preserves in localities where it has been exposed to the weather for centuries, indicate its durability, and being composed of nearly pure silex, occasionally tinged with iron, it affords none of the constituents which nourish parasitical mosses, Walls made of this stone never present the mouldy, decaying appearance, common to walls of limestone in damp situations. At the quarries of this stone in Potsdam and Malone, which at the latter place, has become a regular business for exportation, it cleaves into slabs, three or four inches thick, and several feet in length, and when first exposed to the air, it readily breaks when laid over a straight edge, with carefully

* On the flight of Sir John Johnson, mentioned on page 123, it is said. that as he passed down the Raquette, he noticed the *Potsdam sandstone* piled up in beautiful regularity by nature with all the symmetry of art, along its banks, and predicted *that a city would be built some day in the vicinity of that stone.* More than thirty years afterwards he enquired of one from that place at Montreal, if any use had been made of that stone ledge.

repeated blows of a stone hammer into pieces of any desirable length, or breadth with the greatest freedom. Exposure to the air hardens it in a little time, and it thenceforth is fitted for any purpose of paving, or the walls of buildings, for which uses it is unsurpassed. Walls laid with alternate courses of broad and narrow stone, present a very neat and substantial appearance.

The sandstone enters Rossie from Jefferson county, between the Oswegatchie and the iron mines, and runs across that town about two miles into Gouverneur. The first continuous mass of sandstone enters from Jefferson county in a bold escarpment, and forms a terrace overlaid by a soil of much fertility, and is generally quite level, except where accumulations of drifted materials occur, or valleys have been worn along the courses of existing streams. The south margin of this rock conforms to the course we have traced as the boundary of the gneiss, and it underlies some of the most valuable farming lands of Northern New York. A feature will be observed in the district underlaid by the sandstone, which is quite general, and is due to the little liability to disintegration which it exhibits, namely: the absence of gentle swells and sloping declivities. Wherever valleys occur, their margins are usually bounded by abrupt precipices of naked rock, and where deep ravines have been wrought by running streams, as at the falls on the Chateaugay river, the banks present bold projecting and overhanging cliffs, with intervening spaces, where from frost or running streams portions have been thrown down or swept away, leaving detached and almost isolated masses standing. In Hammond, instances occur in which outstanding masses of this rock, of the same height as the main body, but separated from it, often occurs. In texture, the sandstone differs greatly, being at times fine grained and uniformly stratified, as at all the quarries where it is wrought, and at times made up of angular or rounded masses of various sizes, cemented together, with little symmetry or appearance of stratification. It is among the last of these that several curious instances of structure exist, which indicate in themselves some of the causes that must have operated when the deposits were going on. *Ripple marks* are of common occurrence, proving that they formed the shores of ancient seas, by which the sands were thrown into slight undulating ridges, exactly as is seen on the borders of existing waters. In some places the rock is made up of balls, having a concentric structure like the coats of an onion, usually with a pebble as a nucleus, as if they had been formed by rolling over the surface, receiving an addition from the adhesion of sand, as we sometimes see snow balls rolled up by the wind on the surface of snow. In the vicinity of the iron mines of Rossie, this spheroidal structure is very common, and makes up the whole rock. They are of all sizes, from a pea to an orange. But perhaps there is no structure, either of this or of any rock, more worthy of study than the remarkable *cylindrical* stratification frequently observed in Rossie, Antwerp, Theresa, &c. These cylinders are vertical, and of all diameters, from two inches up to twenty feet or more, and their section where exposed to the surface, shows them to be made of concentric strata of sand of different colors and degrees of fineness, firmly consolidated and capable of being detached, when they present to the casual observer the appearance of huge logs of wood, and has led to their being called " petrified logs." As the kind of rock in which they occur does not possess cleavage, it is seldom quarried, and opportunities have not been found to learn the depth to which they descend. From what the author has seen, he infers that they are somewhat conical, and probably run out at no great depth. This sandstone contains but few evidences of organic existence, these being limited to obscure fucoids and one or two bivalve shells. At times the ripple marks have been seen much like sea weeds in their arrangement, and the fracture and cleavage of the stone near Potsdam, has at times shown a moss-like ramification, which may be due to manganese. The cylinders at times encroach upon each other, the last formed being perfect, while the older one has its stratification interrupted by the other. No rational theory has occurred to us by which this wonderful structure could be explained, *than that they were formed by vortices or whirlpools playing upon the surface of water, and imparting their gyratory motions to the mobile sands of the bottom, which gave the circular arrangement noticed, and which has since become consolidated and remains.*

The book of nature is ever open to give instruction, and may be read by all. In every department of the world around us, may be seen sufficient to call forth the admiration and fix the attention of the humble observer, who sees in the least and most casual occurrences, the operations of causes which may have operated at an exceedingly remote period, but which have written their history in characters more enduring than human monuments. The fancy would become weary in traveling back through the long period that has elapsed, since the surface of the ancient ocean that once evidently overspread this country, may have ebbed and flowed, obedient then as now, to physical laws which change not. The winds played upon the surface, and sent their waves to ripple along the shores, and the tinny vortex, formed by conflicting currents, spun then as now, and recorded its history in the sands beneath!

The Potsdam sandstone is bordered along the St. Lawrence, and extending back a few miles by the *calciferous sandstone,* which presents at many places near Ogdensburgh, definite fossil remains, which are however limited to a few species. Among these are many obscure masses, with a texture that indicates them to have been sponges, or the lower orders of zoöphytes, which have never been studied with the view of scientific interest. In an economical point of view this rock is of importance, both as a building stone and as material for lime, for which, however, it is far inferior to the white limestone of the primary region. At Massena and at Waddington, water lime has been manufactured from this rock, but this is not now done. The above enumerated form the principal of our rock formations, but over them all, is more or less extensively and very unequally spread a mass of soil, sand, clay, and boulders of rock, much of which bears evidence of having been drifted by agencies that have long since ceased from more northern localities, and deposited in its present form. This has received the name of *Drift,* and its study forms one of the most instructive departments of practical geology. Evidences of its northern origin, may be found in our ability to often trace loose masses of rock to the parent source, and especially to the polished and scratched surface of rocks when exposed, which bear testimony to the *fact* that they have been ground and furrowed by moving masses, which the direction of the scratches certify was from a northerly quarter. The evidence of the grinding of solid bodies moving in water, is often observed along streams at the present day. Near Cooper's falls, in De Kalb, is a cavity of several feet in depth which has been worn in this way, but it is at a level far above the present river; and in the gneiss rock, near the Ox Bow, in the edge of Jefferson county, is another example, which occurs on the face of a cliff some seventy feet in height, and is of so remarkable a nature as to have attracted general curiosity. The following cut is borrowed from Prof. Emmons's report on the geology of the 2d district, and correctly represents the shape of the cavity, but not the imposing height and grandeur of the cliff.

Pulpit rock, near Ox Bow, Jefferson county.

The pot shaped cavity is about 18 feet deep and 10 wide, at the largest part. It derives its name from its having been used as a pulpit on several occasions when the settlements were new. In one instance a Methodist quarterly meeting is said to have been held at the foot of this rock.

In De Kalb an instance is observed, in which the strata of sandstone have been pressed into waves, as is shown in fig. 3, facing page 704. This locality is mentioned by Prof. Emmons, from whose report these drawings are derived, as 80 rods north of De Kalb village. At another locality the strata are broken up, as shown in fig. 1, opposite page 684, which proves that these masses have been subjected to motion since formed and consolidated. Tortuous strata in the gneiss are extremely common, but nowhere can this be studied with better advantage than on the summit of the hill towards Hammond, in the village of Rossie.

Accumulations of drift are of common occurrence in Rossie, near Sprague's Corners, in Hermon, Pierrepont, Parishville and Hopkinton, &c.; and across Franklin county, near the village of Malone, they are very conspicuous. These hills may be readily known by their smooth, rounded outline. In the above instances, no prevailing direction can be noticed, but nearer the St. Lawrence, especially in the lower part of St. Lawrence county, continuous ridges crossing the river obliquely, may be traced considerable distances. In some cases, the surface is thickly studded with boulders, which have been noticed in continuous trains for half a mile or more, and groups of these, usually of similar materials, are of constant occurrence.

There is above the drift still another formation, consisting of sands and clays, and containing shells unchanged in texture, and of the species now living in the Arctic seas, which skirts the northern border of the two countries, from Ogdensburgh eastward, to which, from its extensive occurrence in the valley of the St. Lawrence, the term *Laurentian deposit* has been proposed. It exists in Canada over a great extent, and also in the valley of lake Champlain. The rail road cutting east of Ogdensburgh, was through this, and multitudes of the fossil shells of species named by naturalists, *Saxicava rugosa*, *Tellina grœnlandica*, and perhaps a few others occur, and may be gathered in quantities. The clay beds at Raymondville, which have a peculiar *columnar* structure, very much like starch, and no signs of stratification whatever, contain shells of the same species, proving that they belong to a marine formation of a *comparatively* very recent period. The clays at the latter place are overspread for miles by a light sandy loam, as is the case with the clay deposits near Albany and elsewhere. These recent fossils occur in ravines throughout a considerable part of the northern border of Franklin county. Of a still more recent period, are the bog ores still forming in swamps, the deposits of lime from a few springs, and the detritus brought down by rivers, and left at their mouths, of which the *rush bed*, at the mouth of the Oswegatchie, before the village of Ogdensburgh, is an instance.

Among the remarkable features of the primary, are trap dykes, of which many very interesting instances occur in Rossie, especially near Wegatchie, and metallic veins. As it is designed to render this notice of practical utility, many subjects of a theoretical nature will be passed. Of metallic veins, those of lead, copper and zinc are the principal, and of the first that at Rossie is preëminent. Indefinite reports of lead, silver, &c., based upon Indian traditions, were common among the early proprietors, and much effort was made to discover the localities, among which one, said to exist near the sources of Grass river, was sought after At Rossie, lead ore occurs in several veins, which descend nearly vertical, and the ores are associated with iron pyrites, calcite, celestine, anglesite and many other minerals, which will be enumerated. At the mines on Black lake, at Mineral point, zinc blende occurs in considerable quantities, as it also does, to some extent, with the galena of the St. Lawrence company's mines in Macomb. We consider the fact settled beyond a doubt, that lead ore exists in quantities that will render its mining very lucrative in St. Lawrence county, and from the discoveries that are being made, it is probable that many new and valuable localities will hereafter be opened. In all cases, so far as observed, this metal exists in true veins, with definite walls, and the geological features of the country are such as experience in other mining districts has shown favorable to the probabilities of ore in profitable quantities.

An association styling itself the St. Lawrence Copper Company, was formed under the exertions of H. H. Bigelow, of Boston, in 1846, for the purpose of working mines of copper in northern New York, and mining operations on a small scale were commenced in several places, but more extensively on the farm of Hubbard Clark, near the south line of Canton, where several thousand dollars were expended in the erection of machinery, and in sinking a shaft about sixty feet deep, with short levels. The ore occurs here in white lime stone, containing occasional crystals of brown tourmaline, and was the yellow sulphuret of copper. It formed a regular vein of one foot in width in some places, and was associated with calcite, iron pyrites and occasional stains of the green and blue carbonates of copper. The calcite of this place was at times found in crystals of huge proportions, coated with minute crystals of pearl spar. It is said that some eighty tons of ore had been procured, when the workings were suspended, and a small mass of native copper was reported to have been found near the locality. A reverberatory furnace was erected at Russell village, for working these ores, and others from Wilna, Jefferson county, but never got in operation. Mr. Bigelow subsequently went to California, was elected mayor of Sacramento, soon after wounded in endeavoring to suppress a riot, and afterwards died of cholera in San Francisco. Since the above period, no effort has been made to mine for copper, although in several places specimens of ore occur in such circumstances as to excite the belief that it exists in valuable quantities.

Next after the agricultural and manufacturing facilities of northern New York, her *iron mines* may be ranked among the elements of her wealth. These ores are of three distinct varieties, differing essentially in geological age, chemical characters, mineral associates, and the qualities of iron which they produce. These are the *primitive* or *magnetic*, the *specular* and the *bog* ores. The former, although of great abundance, mostly occur in sections yet unsettled, and difficult of access, in Pitcairn, Clifton, Chaumont, Sherwood, &c., and in the towns of Duane, Dickinson and Franklin in Franklin county. It is this variety of ore that is so largely wrought in Clinton and Essex counties, and that forms the wealth of Sweden. It is known to mineralogists as *Magnetite*, from its being magnetic, and is, so far as we have observed, interstratified with gneiss. Its mineral associates are few, being quartz, pyrites and pyroxene, from its being magnetic, it is readily separated from stone, by being crushed and passed under revolving magnets, which pick up the particles of ore. It is sparingly distributed through most of our gneiss rock, and the particles loosened by disintegration, form the black sand, so uniformly seen on the borders of lakes in the primary region. This sand often troubles the compass of the surveyor, and has led to the belief of mines of iron ore, in localities where nothing but iron sand existed. Specular and bog ores have no effect upon the magnetic needle. Primitive ore is difficult to melt, but makes good iron, and yields about 70 per cent. It may be worked in a forge or blast furnace, the former being most in use in Essex county. Some varieties make an iron that is exceedingly hard, as was the case with that wrought in Duane, which led to the belief that edge tools having the hardness and temper of *steel*, could be cast directly from the furnace. This, about the year 1840, led to much inquiry, and a resolution was passed by the assembly in the session of 1841, calling upon Professor Emmons, the geologist of the second district, embracing the northern part of the state, for information respecting this ore. In the report which this called forth, it was stated that the ore was a mixture of the *protoxide* and *deutoxide* of iron, two varieties, chemically differing in the amount of oxygen contained, but mechanically mixed in this instance, and that a part of the ore being first reduced, united with the carbon of the fuel, and became true steel, while the other part was melting. Although the edge tools stood the test of experiment, the opinion was expressed that they would not bear continued use, and this has been fully sustained by experience, which has shown that they will soon crumble and break. In his final report, the geologist expressed his belief, that the ores of Duane did not possess properties differing from those of Essex county. The iron from those ores is very hard, and well suited for those uses that require this property.

The *specular ores*, so called from the splendid lustre of the crystals of Elba and other localities, occurs under two varieties, distinct in situation, and accompanying minerals. The least important of these, is the *crystaline* variety, occurring in gneiss and white limestone, often beautifully crystalized in plates, and of variable and uncertain quantities, liable to thin out and again become wide, as is shown in figure 1, opposite page 685, which represents a locality in Gouverneur, where *a* is soil, *b* sandstone, *c* limestone, and *d* iron ore. It has not hitherto been wrought with profit. A mine in Edwards has yielded about eighty tons, which made excellent malleable iron. Quartz, apparently in twelve sided crystals, formed by joining the bases of two six sided pyramids, but really having a short prism between, is usually found with this ore, and cavities lined with crystaline groups of these minerals, form splendid cabinet specimens.

Between the gneiss and sandsone, and not elsewhere, occurs a red compact ore, chemically like the last, but so unlike to the eye as not to be classed with it, and this has hitherto been the ore most largely used in St. Lawrence, Jefferson and Lewis counties, for the manufacture of iron. The oldest of these mines is the Caledonia mine in Rossie, and has been more or less wrought since 1812. A few rods distant on the line of Gouverneur, is the Kearney iron mine, which was discovered by Lyman Adams, in 1825, and has produced about 50,000 tons of ore of excellent quality. It has been manufactured at the Carthage, Louisburgh, Fullerville, Freemansburgh, Alpina, Redwood, Wegatchie, Sterlingville, Antwerp and Rossie furnaces. It has been worked as an open pit to the depth of 50 feet, and an area of about a quarter of an acre. At first it appeared as a hillock not covered by other rock. The Caledonia mine is capped by sandstone, and has been wrought into caverns with huge masses of ore left to support the roof. In Fig. 2 opposite page 684, is shown the relative situation of the ore and rock, in which *a*, is ore; *b*, adit; *c*, a mineral supposed once to be serpentine, but now called a new species, *dysyntribite*, *d*, gneiss; *e*, sandstone. The relation of these two mines is shown in Fig. 1, opposite page 704, in which *a*, lis sandstone; *c*, Caledonia mine; *d*, ore. An apparent underlaying of the ore with respect to gneiss, is noticed by Prof. Emmons, in Fowler, as is shown in Fig. 8, opposite page 684, in which *a*, is sandstone; *b*, ore; *c*, gneiss. In Fig. 2, opposite page 704, is shown still another relation from the same authority, in which *a*, is serpentine; *b*, ore. Several very valuable mines of this ore occur along the junction of the primary and sandstone in Jefferson county, and it has been wrought to some extent near the village of Little York, in Fowler, since 1833. A part of this mine was purchased by the owners of Louisburgh furnace, several years since, and the remainder has been wrought at a tribute of from 2 to 4 shillings per ton to the owners. The ore here occurs in a hill of moderate elevation, and lies directly upon the gneiss, which has been uncovered to a considerable extent, although large quantities still exist. These red ores impart their color to whatever comes in contact with them, giving a characteristic tinge to every person and object about the premises. They are never crystalized, but occur in every variety of lamellar, slaty, botryoidal and pulverulent forms, and in some cases, cavities are found lined with beautiful and peculiar crystalizations of carbonate of lime, spathic iron, heavy spar, arragonite, quartz, iron pyrites, and more rarely cacoxene or chalcodite, and Millerite, the latter being the rarest and most beautiful of its associates. It occurs in- but one of our localities in brilliant needle shaped crystals, radiating from a centre like the fibres of a thistle down, and having the color and brilliancy of gold. Groups of crystaline specimens of these minerals, often form objects of great beauty. This variety of ore is constantly associated with a mineral much like serpentine, named by Prof. C. U. Shepard, dysyntribite, of which further notice will be given. In some form or other, this always makes its appearance in the mines, often in such large masses as to displace the ore, and render necessary an outlay to remove it. It is of every shade of green, yellow and red, often mixed in the same specimen, and its surfaces are many times grounded and polished as if it had slipped under great pressure, and before entirely solid. No profitable locality of red ore occurs east of the town of Gouverneur, although at the junction of the two formations in Pierrepont, a reddish pulverulent mass occurs, which has been ground and used as a paint. In some localities this ore bears unmistakable evidence of former igneous action, as shown by the contorted, folded and even *fused* appearance of the laminæ of which it is composed. Should this theory be correct, there must have been a peculiar susceptibility of the surface along the line of the two formations, where from its weakness, it yielded to the forces from below. In Gouverneur, near the Little Bow, is a locality of soft unctuous ore-like substance, occurring in white limestone, as shown in Fig. 2, opposite page 685, in which *a*, represents the soil, *b*, sulphate of barytes, and *c*, soft scaly ore. The red ores yield about 50 per cent in the large way as shown by our statistics of the Rossie furnace. It has been noticed that castings from this ore shrink a little upon cooling, which requires the patterns to be a little larger than the article to be made, while those from primitive ores lose nothing from this, the iron being probably more crystaline.

Bog ores are rather rare in the primary district, but more common in swamps in Madrid, Norfolk, Louisville, Bombay, Westville, &c., from which supplies for the furnaces at Waddington, Norfolk and Brasher Iron Works, have been derived, and they have supplied several forges. In favorable localities these superficial deposits are renewed after being dug over, and thus successive crops are obtained once in a dozen or twenty years. This ore makes very soft tenacious iron. A mixture of the primitive, red and bog ores in equal parts, was thought to make the best specimen of iron ever produced in Northern New York. Bog ores are generally lean, not yielding more than 20 or 25 per cent.

St. Lawrence has long enjoyed a deserved celebrity for the variety and beauty of its minerals, which indicates the propriety of giving a notice of the more important of these, as well for a guide to the mineralogist, as to convey to the inhabitants themselves, a just idea of the mineral wealth of their own neighborhoods, and perhaps serve to awaken a spirit of inquiry and observation, especially among the *youth* that will be productive of the best results. A neatly arranged mineral cabinet bespeaks the taste and intelligence of its possessor, and one need not travel beyond the precincts of St. Lawrence county, to collect one that shall possess both elegance and value, and be as remarkable for variety as beauty. It is conceded that this county is unrivaled for the variety of its mineral treasures, and this preëminence should be known and appreciated by its citizens.

Agate, of a coarse variety, occurs with chalcedony near Silver lake, in Fowler.

Albite, or white feldspar, is a common constituent of gneiss, in the towns underlaid by that rock, Gouverneur, Rossie, &c. Fowler affords examples, but there is nothing which possesses interest, either in crystal-

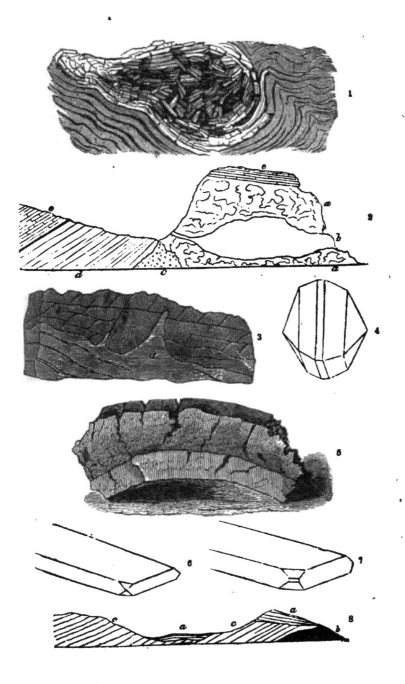

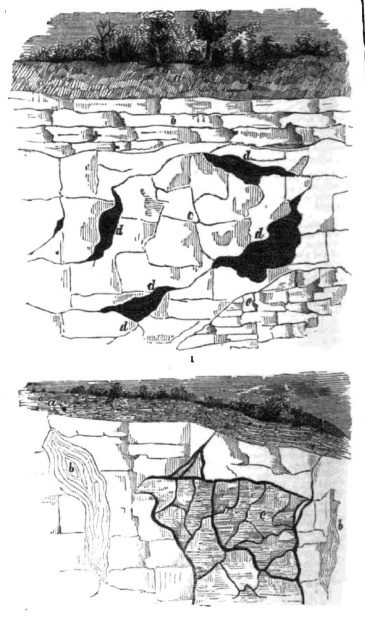

ine modification or quality, which renders the mineral an object of interest to the collector.

Amethyst (blueish violet, or purple quartz), to a limited extent, in Gouverneur. The banks of Yellow lake in Rossie, have also afforded inferior specimens.

Amphibole (basaltic hornblende), occurs frequently in bowlders, but not in rock formations. The crystals appear to be definitely formed and terminated, but so firmly imbedded in the rock, through which they are scattered that it would be impossible to detach them. Broken surfaces often present numerous-sections of crystals. In the town of Rossie it has hitherto been noticed most abundantly.

Anglesite (sulphate of lead), occurred sparingly in the lead mines of Rossie, with galena, but it was not of sufficient importance to be worthy of notice in an economical point of view, or of much interest to the mineralogist.

Ankerite (a variety of dolomite, containing iron), has been attributed to the iron mines of Rossie, but it scarcely differs from the spathic iron of that region, and can not be distinguished from it, if it exists, except by chemical tests.

Apatite (phosphate of lime), crystalized in six sided prisms, occurs at several localities in the white limestone formation, in St. Lawrence county. It was formerly found of a delicate green shade, a mile s. w. of Gouverneur village, but is not now met with there. At the Clark hill, in Rossie, small, but very pretty crystals have been found associated with sphene, crystalized feldspar, and pargasite. Near the head of Mile bay, on Black lake, this mineral has been found of a coarse quality, with its usual associates, but the finest locality hitherto observed in the county, is on the farm of Michael and Charles Harder, in the town of Rossie, in the vicinity of Grass lake. Crystals weighing 18 pounds, and 12 inches in length, have been obtained here, and those of less size, but finely terminated, are more common. The tender quality of the minerals renders it difficult to procure large specimens without fracturing. These, when perfect, are highly prized by mineral collectors, for their rarity and beauty. If procurable in quantities, it would be a valuable article for manures, being chemically the same as calcined bones. It is also used in the process of assaying gold and silver ores, and would command a high price for this purpose in the markets. The locality in Rossie was first noticed and wrought by Professor Emmons. In figure 5, opposite page 684, is a warped crystal of this mineral, which appears to have been bent after it had been formed, by some motion in the rock, in which it is bedded. This mineral also occurs in Gouverneur, two miles north of Somerville.

Asbestus, of a brown color, with fibres interlocking each other in a very intricate manner, occurs in the town of Fowler, associated with Rensselaerite, talc, and tremolite, between the villages of Little York and Fullerville. When broken, the fractured surface has some resemblance to rotten wood. It does not possess the quality of tenacity, or the property of being easily beaten up into a fibrous mass, which give value to this mineral in the arts, as a constituent of incombustible cloth, or a non conductor of heat, for the packing of iron safes.

41

Arragonite (needle spar), occurs in the iron mines, near Somerville, in beautiful white globular masses, in cavities of iron ore. When broken, these present a silken white radiated structure. Groups of these spherical masses, usually of about half an inch in diameter, often possess much beauty. The best that have been obtained came from a shaft sunk in the land of Mr. Parish, adjacent to the Kearney mine. From its occurrence with the ores of iron, this mineral is sometimes called *flos-ferri*, or the flowers of iron.

Automolite, has been attributed to the vicinity of Rossie village. Its existence is doubtful, and its locality is unknown. Recent examinations prove this mineral to be a variety of spinel, and identical with dysluite, one of the varieties of that mineral.

Babingtonite, has been said to occur in Gouverneur, coating crystals of feldspar. The locality, if it existed, has been lost.

Blende (sulphuret of zinc), was found associated with galena, at the lead mines at Rossie, sparingly, and at Mineral point, in the town of Macomb, more abundantly. It is more or less mixed with that mineral at the lead mines in Macomb, and in the towns of Fowler, Morristown, and De Kalb.

Calcareous tufa, formed by the deposit of carbonate of lime, from springs, is of common occurrence in Rossie, Gouverneur, and other towns. At some localities, it is found imitating in form, the fibres of moss, which it is popularly believed to be the petrification. This structure is found to occur where no vegetable matter could have existed, to give it the peculiar appearance.

Calcite (carbonate of lime), occurs in many localities, and is afforded at almost every mine that has been wrought, but at none with more brilliancy and beauty, than at the lead mines at Rossie and Mineral point. Limpid crystals, of great size, often with cavities containing water occurred here, and the modifications of form and combination of groups of crystals appeared to be infinite. Not unfrequently an instance would occur in which an original defect had been remedied, by a subsequent addition, and the form would be perfect, while the addition was evident from difference of color. On the right side of the Oswegatchie, two miles above the Kearney bridge, in the town of Gouverneur, in an oven shaped cavity in limestone rock, and imbedded in clay, are crystals of great size, rough externally but when broken quite transparent. A specimen more than a foot in length, nearly transparent, and weighing 75 pounds, was procured by Charles S. Bolton, of Wegatchie, from this locality. It is in the state cabinet.
Peculiar modifications represented in figures 1, 2, 3, 4, 7, 8, 9, 10, 11, opposite page 709, and a twin group shown in figure 4, opposite page 704, occur at the locality of Pearl spar, in Rossie. They are chiefly remarkable for form, rather than quality. The surface is often rough from calcareous depositions, and they are opake within. Just within the edge of Jefferson county, in the same range with the last locality, on the farm of Mr. Benton, a very interesting locality of calcite occurs, in which the same terminal planes as those represented in the figures occur. The spar at this place is sometimes tinged with a delicate rose tint, which is, however, liable to fade when exposed to the light.
On the left bank of the Oswegatchie, near the Natural dam, in Gouverneur, large crystals of calcite occur. The iron mines of Rossie,

afford crystals usually of the dog tooth form, in cavities of iron ore. Some of these with bright globular crystaline groups of nickeliferous iron pyrites, and spathic iron, form attractive cabinet specimens. The slender six sided pyramids are here, as in most other localities in the county, terminated by an obtuse pyramid, the planes of which are parallel with the plane of cleavage. The mines of the St. Lawrence Lead Mining Company, in Macomb, have furnished some interesting specimens of a smoky hue, and others tinged red. Cavities in white limestone, are often found to contain crystals of calcite, and it is noticed that all the crystals of a given locality possess some general resemblance or *family likeness*, which to one acquainted with the localities, would be sufficient to identify it among many others. This fact is interesting, as indicating that *similar conditions at the the time of formation, produce similar results,* and may perhaps lead to a knowledge of the causes which produce the varieties in crystaline form. In the town of Pitcairn, calcite, of a sky blue color, in coarse crystaline masses, occur on the south road, about two miles from Green's mill. At the copper mine, in Canton, crystals of calcite, nearly limpid, often a great size, and frequently coated with pearl spar, were found.

Celestine (sulphate of strontia), in crystals of a beautiful blue tint, was found in working Coal Hill mine in Rossie.

Chalcedony, occurs at a locality in Fowler, in interesting concretionary forms, but destitute of that polished surface, which is common with this mineral. It was found with calcareous spar, galena, blende, &c.

Chlorite, occasionally occurs in bowlders, but not in rock formation, in the northern part of the state. It is often associated with epidote.

Chondrodite, with its usual associates, *spinelle*, occurs in the town of Rossie abundantly about three fourths of a mile, west of the village of Somerville, in white limestone. It is of every shade of yellow, inclining to orange and brown, and is diffused in grains, and small crystaline particles, through the white limestone, appearing in relief, on the weathered surface. Detached bowlders on the shores of Yellow lake, contain the same mineral, and it is said to occur *in situ*, near the Clark hill, in Rossie.

Dolomite, or magnesian limestone, is of frequent occurrence, but not in sufficient quantities to give it geological importance. It is usually associated with white limestone, and is distinguished from it by its superior hardness, causing it often to appear in relief upon weathered surfaces. Rossie, Gouverneur, De Kalb, &c.

Dysyntribite, occurs at all localities of red iron ore.

Epidote, granular, and disseminated, in chlorite, is common in bowlders, but not in place.

Feldspar.—This important constituent of gneiss and granite, occurs abundantly throughout the the primitive region, but at only a few localities of sufficient interest to merit notice. At the locality of apatite, pargasite, &c., on the Clark hill in Rossie, crystals occur of considerable interest.

Fluor Spar.—One of the most celebrated American localities of this mineral was discovered many years since on Muscalunge lake, in Antwerp, near the borders of St. Lawrence county. Massive cubes variously grouped, and at times presenting single crystaline faces, a foot in extent, were here found. Externally they were usually rough, but within perfectly transparent, and of some shade of green, varying from the slightest to the deepest tinge. At the Rossie lead mines small quantities were found. Good specimens can not be now procured here. At a locality of sulphate of barytes in Gouverneur, two miles north from the Griffith bridge, a limited quantity was also found. Near the Rock island bridge, in the same town, it has recently been found in considerable quantity and of fine quality. This mineral possesses commercial value from its uses in the chemical arts. It is employed as a flux for separating metals from their ores, and in making fluoric acid, the most corrosive substance known, and which is used in etching upon glass. This acid is also used, with iodine and bromine, in the daguerreotype process.

Galena (sulphuret of lead).—This important ore the only ore hitherto employed in the country for the production of lead, occurs in Rossie and Macomb in quantities which will hereafter render these towns of great importance. This ore has also been found in Fowler, Pitcairn, &c., but not in such quantities as to repay the cost of working. It usually occurs in veins with calcareous spar, and of a highly crystaline structure, yielding the primitive form of the mineral (the cube), by cleavage with the greatest freedom. When crystalized, it has been in the form of the cube and octahedron, with the intermediate modifications. The Rossie lead mines have furnished groups of these crystals, which, for size and splendor, would compare with any in the world.

Garnet is found only in bowlders, and of coarse quality.

Graphite (carburet of iron), is a common mineral in the white limestone, although it has not hitherto been observed in quantities sufficient for any valuable purpose. Near the Big hill, in Rossie, it forms a vein in the old road, and a quarter of a mile further east, it also occurs. The apatite localities all afford scales of graphite. In Canton it occurs in gneiss. It has been found in considerable quantities in Duane in bowlders.

Greenstone is common in bowlders, and occurs in dykes in limestone in Rossie. The junction of the rock with the intruded mass, often exhibits evidences of the action of heat.

Hornblende, either in its proper color and crystaline form, or in its varieties as tremolite, asbestus, pargasite, &c., is one of our most abundant minerals. It is a constituent of gneiss, and coextensive with that rock. In Edwards is an interesting locality of glassy hornblende, which is very cleavable in one direction. It is two miles from the village, on the road to South Edwards, which runs on the right bank of the Oswegatchie. The color at this locality is greenish black, and it is very common to find the peculiar wedge shaped crystaline form of this mineral in the cavities. A similar but less interesting locality occurs in the town of Rossie, on the left bank of the Oswegatchie, a short distance above the village of Wegatchie. It occurs in De Kalb, Gouverneur, Potsdam, Pierrepont, &c.

Houghite.—This term has been applied by Prof. C. U. Shepard, of Amherst College, to a new mineral that occurs on the farm of Stephen Ayres, 1½ miles north of Somerville, associated with spinelle, serpentine, dolomite, phlogopite, &c. The quantity is abundant at the locality, and it has been found crystalized in octahedrons. The reader is referred to the American Journal of Science, since 1849, and the Transactions of the American Association, for 1851, for several articles by Profs. Shepard, Dana and Johnson, on this mineral. It has been suggested that it may be analagous to, or identical with, Völknerite, a Norwegian mineral, and it is at this time undergoing a rigid analysis in the laboratory of Yale College, that will probably settle the question.

Idocrase, in irregular fluted prisms, occurs in bowlders, and perhaps in rocks in *situ*, in several localities in Rossie, and probably other towns. It is usually clove brown, opake, brittle, and resembles some varieties of tourmaline in form. At Vrooman's lake, near the Ox Bow, it has been found in crystals, which possess terminal planes.

Iron pyrites (sulphuret of iron), is common, and will doubtless at a future time possess much economical importance for the manufacture of copperas, sulphuric acid, and soda ash. Of the former, several hundred tons were formerly made in the town of Canton, but the works have long since been discontinued. Some of the most brilliant specimens ever procured, were in the lead mines of Rossie, where it occurred in cavities of the veins, crystalized in cubes, with various modifications, and possessing a brilliant lustre which was not liable to tarnish. The iron mines of Rossie and those adjacent have furnished many interesting specimens. It here occurs massive and crystalized, the latter often associated with arsenic, constituting the mineral known as *arsenical iron pyrites*.[*] For variety of crystaline form, a locality on the farm of Mr. John Robertson, in the town of Gouverneur, is worthy of notice. The mineral here occurs in company with graphite and iron ore of a tarnished bronze color, and in small crystals, which possess the form of the cube, octahedron, dodecahedron, with every intermediate modification. Large octahedrons have been obtained in Gouverneur, at a working for iron ore on the farm of James Morse. The vicinity of the village of Hermon has furnished interesting specimens, and the mines which have been worked for iron, copper and lead, throughout the county contain more or less of this mineral. It is often imbedded in gneiss.

Labradorite (opalescent feldspar), occurs in bowlders, the best specimens having been found on the banks of the St. Lawrence, in the town of Oswegatchie, three or four miles above the village of Ogdensburgh. Several tons exist there, near the water's edge. It takes a beautiful polish, and would form an elegant gem. The play of colors is vivid, and the shades are mostly green and blue.

Isoxclase (feldspar with diagonal cleavage), occurs in Rossie at the celebrated locality of zircon and apatite, and this is the only hitherto reported locality. It occurs crystalized in the forms usual with feldspar, and when broken, presents a delicate bluish opalescence.

Magnetite, described above in our account of iron ores.

Mica.—See *Muscovite* and *Phlogopite.*

Muscovite.—This variety of mica does not occur in *situ* in northern New York, but is found in bowlders. One in Gouverneur, containing

---

[*] For an account of this mineral, see an article by Prof. Cha's U. Shepard, in the Transactions of the American Association, Albany session, 1851.

large plates of a black variety was examined in its optical properties, by Professor B. Silliman. Jr., of Yale College, and found to have an optical angle of 70° to 70° 30'.

Pargasite (green hornblende), occurs wherever apatite has been found in St. Lawrence county. It usually is crystalized in hexagonal prisms, of a delicate grass green, or bluish green color, sometimes in radiated crystaline fibres, in seams of rock, and at others in crystaline grains of ready cleavage. The finest locality of this mineral known in St. Lawrence county, is near the county line, in Rossie, and in a neighborhood called New Connecticut.

Pearl spar (crystalized dolomite), occurs in the town of Rossie, on the right bank of the Oswegatchie, about opposite the furnace at Wegatchie, where the river crosses the town the second time. It occurs in crevices of limestone, on a precipitous ledge thickly covered by small cedars, and is usually planted in clusters of crystals upon large dog tooth crystals of calcareous spar, and can be obtained in considerable quantities.

Phlogopite.—The mica of our white limestone formations occurs in numerous localities, and often in great beauty. At the serpentine locality of Gouverneur, near Somerville, at the hornblende locality of Edwards, and at other places in that town, in Fine, two miles from South Edwards, in Russell, De Kalb, Fowler, Hermon, Gouverneur and Rossie, it is of frequent occurrence, and at times of great beauty. The optical properties of these micas are given in vol. x, p. 374-8 (new series), of the American Journal of Science and Arts.

Pyroxene in prisms occurs in Rossie, Gouverneur, Hermon, De Kalb, &c. Near Grass lake, in the former town, a white variety occurs, in which the crystaline form is well exhibited. In Gouverneur it occurs in the vicinity of the apatite locality. It is here dark green, and greenish black.

Quartz, the most abundant of the simple minerals, and a constituent of gneiss and sandstone, occurs in many interesting varieties. The mines of crystalized specular iron in Gouverneur, Fowler, Edwards and Hermon all afford splendid crystals. The iron mine near Chub lake, in Fowler, afforded beautiful crystals, which were nearly transparent, and quite brilliant. On the farm of Joel Smith, in Gouverneur, at a locality opened for iron ore, similar crystals were found. At the apatite locality at Gouverneur, large smoky crystals have been obtained, and at that in Rossie similar ones, so rounded as to appear to have been partially dissolved, occur. The latter much resembles hyalite. At the iron mines in Rossie, delicate groups of needle shaped crystals occur in cavities in the ore.

Rensselaerite, of various shades, from white to black, through every intermediate color, and varying from a finely granular to a coarsely crystaline structure, occurs in limestone and gneiss in many places in the towns of Gouverneur, Rossie, Fowler, Russell, Fine, Pitcairn and Edwards. In Russell and Edwards, it has been wrought to some extent into inkstands and other small articles, and its softness, toughness, the beautiful gloss which it readily receives. and the diversity of color which it often presents, indicate it as a suitable material for any of the ornamental uses to which alabaster is applied. It can be turned in a lathe without difficulty. The manufacture from this material was never carried on as a regular business, and has been discontinued for many years. At Wegatchie, between 1836-9, about fifty tons were ground and sold for gypsum.

Rutile (titanic acid), has been attributed to Gouverneur, but its locality, if it ever existed, has been lost. This mineral is valuable, from the use made of it by the manufacturers of artificial teeth, to give a yellowish tinge to the enamel. It is worth about $6 per lb for this purpose.

Satin spar (fibrous calcite), is of frequent occurrence in seams of serpentine and Rensselaerite, in Fowler, Rossie and Edwards. At a locality near Silver lake, in Fowler, beautiful specimens occur. On the left bank of the Oswegatchie, between that river and Yellow lake, and opposite Wegatchie, in the town of Rossie, is a remarkable locality in a peculiar rock, supposed to be a new mineral. The satin spar is in vertical seams, while the fibres of the spar run across the vein. The width of the veins varies from a mere white line to an inch, and fine specimens are procurable in quantities. The same mineral occurs in narrow seams in serpentine, at the Dodge iron mine in Edwards. The quantity is small.

Scapolite, in pearly grey crystals, which are short and generally terminated, occurs at the locality of apatite, about a mile southwest of Gouverneur village. It is here abundantly diffused through limestone, and is readily obtained in separate crystals. Scapolite occurs in detached crystals very frequently in the white limestone formation.

Serpentine abounds throughout the primary section of the two counties, occurring generally with or near the white limestone formation, being usually disseminated in nodular masses through that rock. In the town of Rossie, on the island at Wegatchie furnace, in Gouverneur village, and at the Natural dam, two miles below: in Fowler, Edwards, De Kalb, Hermon, Russell, Pitcairn, Fine, Colton, Canton, &c., it occurs in greater or less quantity, but nowhere in sufficient abundance to form a rock of geological importance. At the locality of mica, &c., on the farm of Stephen Ayres, in Gouverneur, serpentine of a yellowish green color, and beautifully mottled, occurs. In Edwards, near the village, it occurs of various delicate shades of green and greenish white, which possess interest.

Spathic iron (carbonate of iron), occurs in the iron mines of Rossie, in beautiful crystaline groups, lining cavities in the ore, and associated with calcite, heavy spar and iron pyrites. The color is usually bronze, and various shades of brown, and the faces of the crystals often warped, and usually very brilliant. It also occurs massive diffused through the ore, and has been seen more rarely in botryoidal concretions, covering surfaces of red specular iron. Some of the specimens of this mineral from the Caledonia and Kearney mines, possess much beauty, and are highly esteemed by mineral collectors. The best specimens were obtained from the north end of the hill in which the Caledonia mine occurs.

Sphene, is of frequent occurrence in the western part of St. Lawrence county. At the apatite localities of Gouverneur and Rossie, it is found of a pale red color, and in imperfect crystals with its usual associates, pargasite, apatite, graphite, &c. Half a mile north of Gouverneur village, in a wall, black crystals with the angles rounded, as if by fusion, occur in quartz.

Spinelle occurs at the locality of chondrodite, in Rossie, and at the locality of serpentine and mica, on the farm of Stephen Ayres, in Gouverneur. At the former locality it has a pale reddish brown opake variety, generally well crystalized, and sometimes grouped into clusters. The small specimens are the best characterized, and some of them nearly transparent. Spinelle, when blue, is the *sapphire*, and when of a burning red, the *ruby*.

Sulphur, in a native state, occurs in concretions around the iron mines in Rossie, where it is formed by the decomposition of iron pyrites, and its deposition is said to be due to the action of vegetable matter. It may be expected to occur wherever iron pyrites is exposed to spontaneous decomposition in the weather. It is usually more or less mixed with sulphate of iron and other saline substances.

Sulphate of Barytes, is associated with limestone, in Gouverneur, about two miles from the Griffith bridge, where it occurs in an irregular vein with fluor spar. It presents externally a rusty brown color, and an irregular attempt at crystalization, the surface being covered by bundles of coarse crystaline fibres. Broken it presents a pure white color, and is fibrous and laminated. Several hundred pounds have been procured near the surface, and it is doubtless abundant in the vicinity. On the farm of James Morse, in the same town, this mineral occurs with a micaceous variety of iron ore, in crystaline plates, which by their intersection form irregular angular cavities. The forms represented in figs. 5 and 6, opposite page 709, were found here. In the town of Morristown, several tons were procured for manufacture into. white paint, a few years since. Its appearance was similar to that of Gouverneur. On yellow lake, in Rossie, and in the iron mines of that town, it has been found sparingly. At the latter, it is in small crystals, in cavities of calcite, and the forms shown in figs. 6 and 7, opposite page 684, have been observed. The lead mines of Rossie afforded it sparingly. On the farm of Robert Dean, in Antwerp, Jefferson county, near the county line, is an interesting locality in which this mineral, which naturally of great specific gravity, occurs light and spongy, from numerous vermicular cavities.

Sulphuret of copper, has been procured in quantities which justify the belief that it will be found in such abundance as will make it profitable as an ore of copper, in the towns of Macomb, Gouverneur, Canton, Fowler, Edwards, Russell, &c. Several explorations have been made for this mineral, but not to such extent as to decide the quantity that may be expected to occur.

Tourmaline, of a reddish brown color, and crystalized, is found imbedded in white limestone, in the towns of Rossie, Gouverneur, Hermon, Russell, &c. The quality of this is such that if it could be obtained of sufficient size, it would form the most excellent plates for examining the properties of polarized light. About two miles southeast of the village of Gouverneur, it has been found most abundantly. It also occurs one mile from that village, on the north side of the road leading to Somerville.

Tremolite, (white hornblende), occurs in the town of Fowler, between Little York and Fullerville, of a delicate rose color, in masses which have a broken crystaline structure. In De Kalb it is common in white crystaline blades and tufts, on white limestone, usually appearing in relief wherever the surface has been weathered. In Gouverneur, on the road from Richville to Little Bow, is a very interesting locality, on the farm of Stephen Smith; it here occurs in long crystaline masses, often interlocking each other, and forming specimens of great beauty. Near the Four corners, a mile from this locality, near the Rock Island bridge, and in an open field, beautifully radiated tufts are observed on the limestone rocks, which when broken present a silken gloss. No mineral can surpass in beauty of lustre or delicacy of fibre, specimens from these localities.

Zircon, much esteemed by mineralogists for its rarity and its containing zirconium, one of the rarest of the mineral elements, occurs at the apatite locality in Rossie, in square prisms, sometimes terminated by pyramids. It is of a brownish red color, and in small crystals is transparent. It occurs also on the farm of Lorenzo Heath, nearer the village than the former, and also on Grass creek, in the same town, associated with apatite. The peculiar modification represented in fig. 4, opposite page 684, occurs at the latter locality. When transparent, this mineral

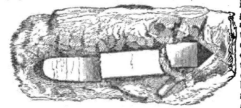 is cut and set as a gem, and its hardness and the beautiful lustre it is capable of receiving, render it peculiarly valuable for this purpose. None of this quality has ever been found in St. Lawrence county. The annexed cut is a crystal of zircon of the natural size, the parts of which have been displaced by some cause after it was formed. It is figured by Prof. Emmons in his final report.

METEOROLOGICAL NOTES.

Among the more striking of meteorological phenomena, are *tornadoes* of which several have occurred since our counties were settled. In traversing the forests, the tracks of these are often seen in lines of fallen timber, usually denominated windfalls. They generally travel eastward, and the whirl is in the opposite direction with that in which the hands of a watch move.

On the 21st of August, 1823, a tornado passed across the town of Constable, sweeping everything before it, but fortunately destroying no lives. It entered from Canada, and pursued a southeasterly direction until it passed the village of East Constable, when it turned eastward towards Chateaugay, and spent its force in the woods. The path was narrow, and for the first few miles it appeared to pass in two lines, which united. Its progress was slow, and the roar which accompanied it warned the inhabitants to seek safety in flight. The whirling of the vortex was excessive, carrying up and throwing out from its borders planks, rails, branches of trees, and whatever lay in its way, and it was said on respectable authority, that a *log chain* lying on the ground was carried ten or fifteen rods from its place. This report, so apparently incredible, is scarcely more so than others well authenticated by evidence, in which the turf has been torn up and carried off, and heavy metalic articles

swept away by the fury of the tornado. The day on which this occurred had been excessively hot and sultry, and the blackness, roaring and
violence of the phenomenon, were said to have been most sublime and
terrific. Towards the end of its course it ceased to progress, but moved
in spiral paths through a maple forest, many acres of which were prostrated.

Perhaps the most extraordinary tornado ever recorded without the
tropics, occurred in St. Lawrence county, Sept. 20, 1845. It was traced
from Upper Canada to Vermont. At 3 o'clock it was at Antwerp; at 5,
on the Saranac; at 6, at Burlington, Vt., and at Shoreham, Vt., in the
evening. Its length could not have been less than 200 miles, and its
course nearly east, till it reached Lake Champlain, which it appears to
have followed to its head.

On Saturday, at noon, (Sept. 20, 1845), some gentlemen standing on
the wharf at Coburg, C. W., happening to cast their eyes upon the water,
were struck with the appearance of a strong current setting directly out
from shore. It seemed as if the whole lake were going away bodily.
It presently returned to a height two feet higher than usual, and continued to ebb and flow at intervals of eight or ten minutes, till night. At
Port Hope, the steamer Princess Royal could not get into port at all. It
was at the time supposed to be the effect of an earthquake, and perhaps
was. The work of destruction began a mile east of Antwerp, and in its
course through the forest, it swept all before it, leaving a track of desolation from half a mile to a mile and a half wide, in which nothing was
left standing. Its appearance was described by those who observed it at
a little distance, as awfully sublime, it being a cloud of pitchy blackness
from which vivid lightnings and deafening thunder incessantly proceeded,
and the air was filled to a great height with materials carried up from
the earth, and branches torn from the trees. Torrents of rain and hail
fell along the borders of the track, and much damage was done by
lightning. It entered the county in Fowler, and crossed that town and
Edwards, when it entered the uninhabited forest, and was not further
witnessed. In its track on the Pitcairn road, and another passing through
Emmerson's and Streeter's settlements, some two miles apart, were sixteen buildings, barns, houses, and one school house, which were swept
away, yet wonderful to tell, no human lives were lost on the whole route.
In the house of a Mr. Leonard, were two women and five children, who
took refuge in the cellar, and escaped harm, except that one was
struck senseless by a piece of timber. In another house was a sick
woman, with a young child and a nurse attending them. Frightened by
the noise, the latter threw herself upon a bed, when the house was blown
down, and one of the logs, of which it was built, fell across her, and held
her fast. She was relieved by the superhuman exertions of the invalid.
Near this house, a man was driving a yoke of oxen attached to a wagon,
laden with coal. Two trees were brought by the wind and laid across
the wagon, which crushed it, without injury to the team or man. A
frame school house in Edwards, in which were several scholars and their
teacher, was unroofed without injury to its inmates. Immediately following the tornado was a storm of hail, some of the stones of which
were of great size, which severely lacerated such cattle as were exposed
to it. At Union falls, on the Saranac, in Clinton county, where it emerged
from the forest, it made a complete wreck of many of the buildings.
"Duncan's forge was considerably injured, and a brick school house near
the Travis forge, in Peru, was utterly demolished. A brick dwelling near
this, was partly destroyed. Two houses were blown down, over the

heads of the inmates, and it was miraculous that no lives were lost. Some 15 or 20 buildings were destroyed or injured in that vicinity, by the wind, which committed no further depredations until it reached Burlington, in Vt., where it unroofed a house, and blew down some barns. The steamer Burlington, near Fort Cassin, encountered the storm, but braved it handsomely, suffering no greater loss than some loose deck plank, which were picked up miles from shore." At Shoreham, in the evening, was a most majestic display of lightning [conceivable. The upper part of a dense cloud coming slowly from the north west, was almost constantly lighted up by flashes and spangled streaks, shooting in every direction. Occasionally it would strike the ground. As it approached, the thunder commenced its roar, and increased without intermission, until it passed.

At Clintonville, on the Ausable, the lightning struck a church edifice. Several other buildings were struck, some of which were destroyed by fire.

(See N. Y. Municipal Gazette, vol. 1, p. 524).

The extent and violence of this storm has seldom been paralleled, and had its track lain through a settled country, the loss of life must have been dreadful.

The data we possess in regard to our climate, is limited to the results of but a few years observations made under the direction of the Regents of the University at four academies subject to their visitation, and to a short period during which they have been reported to the Smithsonian Institution, by several voluntary observers. We possess reports of the Gouverneur Seminary, for 12 entire years, viz: 1831-2-3-4-5-8-9, 1841-2-3, (except rain gage in 1831 3, 1843); of the Ogdensburgh Academy, for 18 8; of the academy at Potsdam, for 21 entire years, viz: 1828 to 1846 inclusive; and of the Franklin Academy at Malone, for 1839-40-2. A similar series of observations have been made at 62 different stations in the state of New York, during an aggregate period of about 900 years, and the results embody a mass of facts bearing upon the climate of the state of great practical value. In 1850, the system first adopted, was discontinued, and another at fewer stations but with better instruments was substituted. To the farmer especially does the study of Meteorology commend itself, for to no pursuit has it so intimate a relation as this. It is a well established fact that changes of weather may often be predicted several hours before their occurrence, by the barometer, and thus especially in the haying and harvest seasons, a saving would often be effected sufficient to pay the cost of the instrument. That atmospheric changes are due to causes, none will deny. That these are within the scope of our investigation is probable, although from the necessity of the case, no amount of probabilities can ever establish an infallible prediction. If every season but one in a thousand had been remarkably cold, or wet, no certainty could be relied upon for the one. The accumulation of probabilities may, however approach such exactness, as to be of eminent practical service. The system observed in these records, enables us to form a comparative table of results, of variable value from the unequal time that they were maintained at each.

The first of the following tables is for *Potsdam*, the second for *Gouverneur*, and the third for *Malone*, and they show the results of the above observations, for the respective periods mentioned.

Months.	Thermometer						Resultant of winds.			Weather. Mean results.			
	Mean Temprature.			Highest degree.	Lowest degree.	Extreme range.	Mean direction.	Percentage.	Days.	Clear.	Cloudy.	Rain gage. Monthly mean.	Total fall of rain and snow.
	1st half.	2d half.	Whole month.										
January,.......	21.52	16.50	19.01	57	—34	91	s.78°30′w	32	9.78	11.55	19.45	1.40	28.15
February,......	16.00	21.61	18.80	67	—32	99	s.79 22 w.	26	95	11.88	16.40	1.08	21.24
March,.........	26.81	32.99	29.90	78	—28	104	s.67 45 w.	36	8.55	13.99	17.11	1.48	29.87
April,..........	41.39	46.18	43.73	84	—1	85	s.79 17 w.	22	6.60	14.50	15.50	1.76	34.13
May,...........	52.33	57.77	55.05	94	20	74	s.61 34 w.	31	9 45	15.78	15.22	3 03	60.52
June,..........	62.74	65.19	63.96	95	32	65	s.58 30 w.	35	15.37	16.62	13.36	3.31	66.25
July,...........	68.09	68.65	68.38	96	40	56	s.54 17 w.	34	16.27	18.00	12.05	4.03	60.70
August,........	67.71	65.76	66.73	95	34	61	s.63 45 w.	43	13.61	15.90	12.10	2.81	50.15
September,.....	60.36	54.96	57.66	88	23	65	s.62 59 w.	43	12 80	15.50	14.45	3.11	62.17
October,.......	47.83	42.18	45.00	86	12	74	s.58 48 w.	39	11.85	14.09	16.91	3.54	56.57
November,.....	37.14	30.14	33.64	71	—10	81	s.87 08 w.	31	9.40	9.02	20 98	1.93	38.52
December,......	25.35	18.94	22 09	59	—26	89	s.85 31 w.	26	7.94	10.43	20.52	1.44	28.85
Mean, ...	43.92	43.41	43.66	96	34	130	s.66 15 w.	34	10.29	14.18	15.96	2.38	47 79
January,.......	20.32	19.16	19.74	54	—25	90	s.83 45 w.	32	9.56	15.17	15.62	2.54	22.59
February,......	15 68	21.69	18.68	59	—32	91	s.71 32 w.	32	9.68	17.67	14.90	1.87	18.89
March,.........	28.49	23.54	31.01	72	—30	102	s.87 54 w.	34	10.30	15.35	12.25	1.68	15.12
April,..........	42.23	46.58	44.40	85	10	75	s.71 27 w.	32	6.96	15.69	14.78	1.94	17.46
May,...........	51.27	59.51	54.89	94	22	72	s.73 33 w.	36	10.83	16.17	14.80	2.44	22.09
June,..........	62.5	64.07	63.32	95	33	62	s.64 39 w.	32	9.71	17.89	12.12	2.89	23.97
July,...........	68 25	69.48	68.86	100	37	63	s.70 46 w.	59	17.67	18.99	12.08	2.34	21.60
August,........	67 50	67 51	67.50	99	32	67	s.79 46 w.	30	8.95	18.57	12.18	2.21	19.38
September,.....	60 79	55.59	58.11	93	22	71	s.81 29 w.	41	12.21	15.17	14.52	2.59	23.33
October,.......	49.09	44.52	47 10	80	10	70	s.82 48 w.	41	12.42	13.08	17.92	3 20	23.31
November,.....	36.56	30.19	33.37	73	—17	90	s.87 53 w.	32	9.80	10.60	20 00	2.16	19.49
December,......	21.84	18 14	20.49	55	—40	95	s.76 20 w.	29	8 80	11.68	19 92	1.67	15.06
Mean, ...	43 77	44 09	43.92	100	—40	140	s.81 29 w.	39	11.26	15.19	15.31	2.28	18.90
January,.......	18 18	18 25	15.21	54	—24	78	s 61 15 w.	56	16.70	11.50	19.50	1.73	5.19
February,......	23.80	28.49	26.14	68	—15	83	s.70 02 w.	52	15.58	7.53	20.50	2.22	6.68
March,.........	29.42	33.44	31.43	68	—12	80	s 83 12 w.	45	13.50	13.66	17.30	2.04	6.12
April,..........	41 82	48.33	45.07	90	11	77	s 86 36 w.	40	12.13	15.50	14.50	2.04	6.12
May,...........	47.85	58.16	53.00	88	25	63	s.51 07 w.	50	15.55	14.33	16 66	2.97	8.23
June,..........	57.54	49.57	53 55	89	31	57	s.77 32 w.	50	15 01	12.83	17.16	3.38	10.16
July,...........	65.69	68.12	66.90	94	39	56	s.84 03 w.	65	19.62	15.16	15.83	3.39	16.68
August,........	64 40	63.10	63.7	94	40	54	s.86 00 w.	33	9.80	16.16	14.84	1.57	4.71
September,.....	58 97	51.97	55.17	84	23	61	s.73 10 w.	58	17.54	12 33	17.66	2.75	8.26
October,.......	48 91	44 89	46.91	74	20	54	n.87 59 w.	36	10.54	14 66	16 33	2.92	5.72
November,.....	37 31	28.39	32.85	64	6	58	s.76 56 w.	42	12 58	6.50	23.50	1 44	4.22
December,......	26.02	16 42	21 22	45	—14	59	s.88 24 w.	43	12 80	6.86	24 14	1.09	6.2
Mean, ...	43 28	42.43	42 85	94	—24	118	s.88 57 w.	45	13 80	12.23	18.16	2 42	7.26

The first three columns after the months denote the mean temperature as derived from three daily observations, of which one was taken in the morning before sunrise, another in the warmest part of the afternoon, and the third an hour after sunset. The column headed " highest degree" denotes the greatest temperature observed, and the next column the least. The three columns headed "Resultant of Winds" is the product of much labor, and the first shows the angle or point from which all the winds have blown during the entire period. The column marked *percentage*, shows the prevalence of the winds in parts of a hundred, and that marked *days*, in that of the whole number of days in the month. To illustrate this, the month of January at Potsdam, may be taken as an example. The direction of the wind in the forenoon and afternoon was entered in the journal, and at the end of the month these entries were added up. The footings of 21 years showed that the average number of days of wind from each of the eight points were as follows in days and hundredths: N. 2.15: N. E. 5.46: E. 0.12: S. E. 0.59: S. 4.35: S. W. 9.69: W. 3.48: N. W. 5.16: total, 31.00. The columns showing these numbers we have been obliged to omit. From these numbers it remained to learn their value and mean direction (supposing the velocity of the wind to have been uniform), precisely as we would ascertain the direction and distance of a ship which should have sailed uniformly in the different courses for the above times, from the starting point. The eight directions were reduced to four by substracting opposite points; these reduced to two by a traverse table; and lastly these two were brought down to one by a trigonometrical calculation, and the aid of logarithms. In the instance cited, if the whole amount of winds or the whole time be called 100, then 32 of these, or 9.78 days of the 31.00, the wind came from a point S. 78° 30′ W., while during the remainder of the time (68 per cent or 21.22 days), the winds from opposite points balanced each other. The bearing which this inquiry has upon the questions of climate, and especially upon agricultural and commercial interests of the nation, renders it desirable, that these observations should be extended, and measures are now in progress to maintain on an extended scale a minute and judicious system of records. The colums headed *clear* and *cloudy* denote the relative periods during which the sky has been clear and overcast, the monthly mean of the rain gage indicates the average depth of rain in the several months, and the last column the total depth for the whole period, viz: 20 years at Potsdam, 9 at Gouverneur, and 3 at Malone.

The following table shows the results of a series of observations, made by Mr. E. A. Dayton, at Columbia village, with a set of standard instruments, placed as directed in the instructions, issued by the Smithsonian Institution, to which they have been reported. The time of observation have been 6 A. M., 2 P. M., and 10 P. M.

The instruments with which these observations have been made, were manufactured by James Green, of New York. The headings of the several columns render them sufficiently intelligible. In that marked Cloudiness, 10 represents a sky entirely overcast. In the column next to the last, the corrections for expansion of the mercury, and other modifying influences, are allowed for so that the number represent the actual mean height of the barometer, independent of modifying causes.

Months.	Thermometer.	Barometer.	Self Reg. Ther.		Prevailing winds.	Cloudiness.	Rain and m'l't snow.	Barom. cor. to freez. p'nt.	Range of Barom.
			High. est.	Low. est.					
July, 1851,.........	....	29.615	75.90	58.94	w.	3.9	...	29.608	560
Aug. "	....	28.410	76.97	57.06	s. w.	5.0	...	29.738	612
Sept. "	63.27	28.476	69.29	47.87	s. w.	6.0	2.46	29.829	1.153
Oct. "	45.92	29.644	....	....	s. w.	7.0	2.13	29.642	760
Nov. "	28.95	29.671	36.12	23.05	s. w.	8.5	4.54	29.668	1.462
Dec. "	16.52	29.779	25.34	8.11	w.	7.9	2.45	29.712	1.357
Jan. 1852,.........	11.62	29.639	19.00	2.04	w.	8.3	1.28	29.639	1.166
Feb. "	21.79	29.498	....	12.55	w.	6.9	2-96	29.495	1.651
Mar. "	26.39	29.694	34.63	17.04	w.	7.4	3.33	29.695	1.561
Apr. "	37.95	29.464	45.67	30.00	n. e.	6.9	0.77	29.484	989
Aug. "	66.41	29.725	76.37	54.26	s. w.	5.6	2.49	29.728	536
Dec. "	28.35	29.689	33.52	17.01	s. w.	8.8	4.94	29.689	1.302

We are under the necessity of omitting many observations which accompany the above.

The following is an abstract of observations made with similar instruments and for a similar object as the foregoing, at Ogdensburgh, by Mr. Wm. E. Guest, Esq., during 1851—1852. Parts of the two previous years are not included. Height above tide 279 feet.

Months.	Temperature.			Cloudiness	Rain and m'l't snow.	Barometer.	
	Mean.	High'st.	Lowest.			Mean.	Range.
January,........................	19.74	47	—22	6.8	1.85	49.653	1.365
February,........................	22.15	52	—17	6.3	2.81	59.702	1.032
March,........................	28.59	67	—12	6.5	3.15	29.688	0.660
April,........................	39.54	69	21	5.3	1.89	29.563	1.045
May,........................	53.56	83	34	3.9	3.25	29 671	0.947
June,........................	61.51	94	39	4.6	2.80	29.581	1.068
July,........................	67.75	95	50.3	8.3	3.19	29.615	703
August,........................	64.22	83	46	4.0	2.27	29.740	585
September,........................	57.51	88	32	4.8	2.43	29.798	1.113
October,........................	47.67	73	26	5.1	2.65	29.680	864
November,........................	31.64	52	13	4.9	4.06	29.654	1.305
December,........................	23.17	58	—14	7.0	4.68	29.684	1.355

A small part only of the record communicated, is embraced in the foregoing table.

A series of notes on our natural history, and a catalogue of plants growing without cultivation, which we had prepared, is necessarily omitted. It may not be amiss to remark, that the *beaver* still exists in scattered families between the sources of Oswegatchie and Grass rivers, although they do not build dams and villages as previously, from their fewness. The *moose* is said to be on the increase, and there is scarcely a year passes without one or more being taken. The *elk* is probably extinct, here although its horns are occasionally found, and it occurs in Canada. The panther, bear, lynx, fisher, otter, deer, and other animals that are pursued as game or for their furs, still continue to give employment to the pleasure seeking sportsman, and the professional hunter, nor are the waters that adorn the green woods and reflect the shadows of primeval forests, destitute of attraction to the followers of Izaak Walton. The lakes and rivers of the south part of Franklin county, are celebrated for their trout, while in the larger tributaries of the St. Lawrence, the sturgeon, pike, mullet, muscalange, pickerel, bass, perch, sunfish, and other species occur. Formerly the salmon abounded, but for many years none have been caught. To the naturalist, perhaps the most interesting fish in our waters, is the *bill-fish* (Lepidosteus oxyurus,) which occurs in Black lake, and the great rivers, and seldom fails to attract the curiosity of the most casual observer. F. Gabriel Sagard, Samuel Champlain, Father Charlevoix, and other French writers, described this fish, and its habits in the most absurd manner, probably guided by Indian traditions. The latter called it Chou-sa-ron, and the teeth were used as lancets for bleeding. This fish occurs sometimes five feet in length; its body is covered with hard bony scales, and it has a long narrow beak, armed with a double row of teeth. The interest to the scientific which it possesses, is derived from the fact that the structure of its teeth, under the microscope, prove it to be intermediate between fishes and reptiles, and with the exception of a somewhat similar fish of the Nile, the sole survivor of an early and deeply interesting geological period. In this we may study the structure and analogies of a race of animals, that at one period, were lords of the creation, but have long since given place to other forms of animal life.

Of birds there is probably nothing peculiar to this section, but a single fact relating to the chimney swallow may be noticed. It is well known that before the country was settled, this bird was accustomed to inhabit hollow trees, and countless myriads, would congregate in a single tree. Wilson in his ornithology, has given an animated and beautiful description of these colonies. A swallow tree of the description, formerly existed near Somerville, and attracted many curious visitors.

We inadvertently omitted in its proper place, to notice that an earthquake occurred in St. Lawrence county, on the evening of January 22, 1832, at about half past eleven o'clock, P. M. Houses were shaken at Ogdensburgh, so much as to awaken many from sleep, and the tremulous motion of stoves, crockery and windows, with a sound like distant thunder, beneath the surface of the earth, was distinctly perceived by those who had not yet retired to sleep. At Lowville, the sudden and violent agitation of the earth, was accompanied by a sound like that of several heavy carriages passing rapidly over frozen ground. It was also perceived very sensibly at Montreal, where the motion was compared to the shaking of a steamboat, whose machinery agitates her very much. It continued four seconds, and was accompanied with an indistinct noise.

APPENDIX.

NOTE A.

[Preferred from page 97.]

The surrender of Isle Royal was announced by the following proclamation of Governor Colden.

"By the Hon. Cadwallader Colden, Esquire, President of His [L. S.]   Majesty's Council, and Commander-in-chief of the Province of New York, and the territories depending thereon in America.

A PROCLAMATION.

Whereas, His Majesty's forces, under the immediate command of His Excellency General Amherst, have lately reduced the fortress and works erected by the enemy on an island in the St. Lawrence, called by the French Isle Royal, a few miles below Oswegatchie, an Indian settlement with a block house fort, which the enemy had before abandoned, from whence the inhabitants of this province, situated on the Mohawk river, have been so much annoyed by parties sent to harrass and disturb them, that they were kept in almost constant alarm, and many under strong apprehensions of their danger, abandoned their settlements. And whereas by this important acquisition, the people along the Mohawk river, will for the future remain quiet in their possessions, and as the improvement of the settlements there, and the cultivation of the adjacent uncleared country, can not but prove of the greatest advantage to the province. The general by his letter to me, dated below, the Isle Royale, the 26th ultimo, hath recommended that I would invite the inhabitants thereto and assure them of a peaceable abode in their habitation. I have heretofore thought fit with the advice of his majesty's council to issue this proclamation, hereby inviting the persons, who through fear of the incursions of the enemy on that side, have left their settlements, to return to their farms where they may now reap the fruit of their industry, in the utmost security, and as a further encouragement to others to become settlers in that part of the country, I do promise his majesty's grant of any of the vacant lands there to such persons as shall apply for the same, on the usual terms, and on condition of immediate settlements of the tracts that shall be so appropriated.

Given under my hand and seal at arms, in Fort George, in the city of New York, the fourth day of September. 1760, in the thirty fourth year of

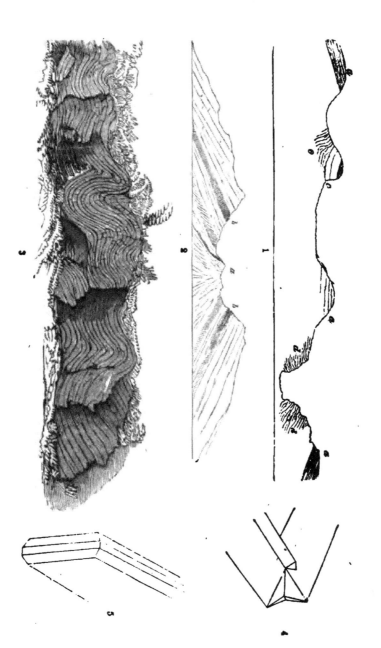

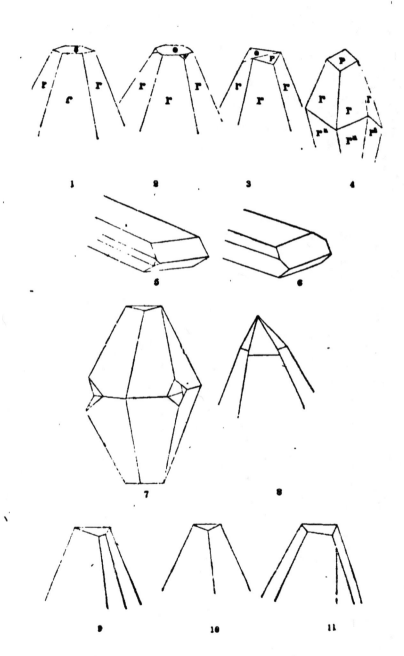

the reign of our sovereign, Lord George the second, by the grace of God of Great Britain, France and Ireland king, defender of the faith, and so forth.

By His Honors Command, G. W. BANYAR, *D. Sec'y.*
GOD SAVE THE KING.

We much regret our inability to refer to M. Pouchot, the commander of this post, at the time of its surrender.—(*Pouchot M. Memoires sur le Dernière Guerre des Amerique, Septentrionale, entre la France et l'Angleterre,* 3 *vols.* 12*mo, Yverdon,* 1781.

Two English historians (John Entick, in a work in 5 volumes 8vo, entitled *General History of the War in Europe, Asia, Africa and America,* London, 1763; and John Knox, in a work of 2 volumes, 4to., entitled *An Historical Journal of the Campaign in North America),* have detailed with minuteness the events of the campaign, and added other particulars. The latter accompanied the English army, and wrote from personal observation. We quote from his account:

"18th August. The weather is extremely unfavorable to our operations, yet the general, intent on the vigorous prosecution of his measures, resolves to lose no time. This morning was taken up with the repairs of the row galleys and prize vessel, and at 10 o'clock the engineers with the covering party returned, and made their report; but his excellency was predetermined, and the army are in readiness. The first division, consisting of the grenadiers, two battalions of light infantry, the right brigade of regulars, Schuyler's regiment, the greatest part of the Indians with Sir William Johnson, three row galleys and some field artillery, are to proceed down by the north shore, commanded by the general in person; pass the fort and take possession of the islands and coasts below it; at the same time the second division, composed of the left brigade of regulars, Lyman's regiment, two ranging companies, the remainder of the Indians, and two row galleys, under the command of Col. Haldiman, to row down to the south coast, and take post opposite to the fort, where they will not be exposed to the fire of the place, whilst the prize now deservedly called the Williamson brig, under Lieut. Sinclair, will sail down the centre of the river, between the two divisions, with direction to moor at random shot from the fort; Brig. Gen. Gage, with the rest of the army and heavy artillery, to remain at Oswegatchie. Such is the disposition his excellency made before the return of the engineers, and it was spiritedly executed accordingly, under a brisk and continued cannonade, directed against the brig and the general's column, whereby one galley was sunk, ten men were killed and wounded, one of whom lost a thigh, and many bateaux and oars were grazed with shot. As the north division rowed down in single files, it was 11 at night before the sternmost boat joined, and then the blockade of the fort was completely formed. Our Indians landed on the islands Gallop and Picquet, which the enemy abandoned with the greatest precipitation, having left a number of scalps, two swivel guns, some barrels of pitch, a quan-

42

tity of tools and utensils, with some iron behind them. Our Indians were so exasperated at finding the scalps, that they fired all their houses, not sparing even the chapel. Late in the night an attempt was made to weigh up the galley that was sunk, but we could not succeed.

19th. The general, with Col. Williamson and Lieut. Col. Eyre,* reconnoitered the fort and the islands nearest to it, on two of which ground is made choice of for batteries, about six hundred yards from the fort, as also for a third on an advantageous point of land on the south shore; and detachments are immediately ordered to break ground, cut and make fascines, with every other preparation for carrying on the siege. Orders were sent to Oswegatchie, for the heavy artillery, which are expected down this night. The Onondaga and Mohawk appeared to-day; they received orders, in like manner as the brig, to come to anchor at random shot from the fort, and if cannonaded, not to return it. The remainder of the army, except one Connecticut regiment, are ordered down from Oswegatchie, whence our heavy artillery arrived late at night, and the row galley with her gun was weighed up. The fort fired on the brig yesterday, which she spiritedly returned, until ordered to desist.

22d. The troops have worked with such diligence, that our batteries will be completed this night, and ready to play on Fort Levis to-morrow.

23d. The batteries were opened this morning, and had such effect, that the enemy drew in their guns, and endeavored to serve them à couvert. After some hours' firing, a disposition was made to storm the fort with the grenadiers of the army, in which the three vessels were to have assisted. For this purpose, a number of marksmen were judiciously placed on board each ship, with the view of compelling the enemy to abandon their guns; and they were ordered to fall down on the fort within the range of small arms; but whether the vessels were confused with the weight of the enemy's fire, or that the miscarriage may be imputed to the navigation or the wind, is difficult to determine; for the general, not approving of their manner of working down, sent orders to them to return to their former station, and desisted from his project for the present. The garrison expended a great deal of ammunition to little purpose; and our artillery were so well served, that the enemy were rather shy of standing to their guns.

25th. We have had warm cannonading on both sides, but their guns being at length dismounted by our superior fire, M. Pouchot, the governor, after displaying as much gallantry as could be expected in his situation, beat a chamade, and in the afternoon capitulated for his garrison, who are become prisoners of war; they consist of two captains, six subalterns and two hundred and ninety-one men, all ranks included; they had a lieutenant of artillery with twelve men killed, and thirty-five wounded. The ordnance mounted at Fort Levis, are twelve 12 pounders, two sixes, thirteen fours, four of one pound each, and four brass 6 pounders. Lieut. Col. Massey has taken possession of the fort, with three companies of his battalion. Fort Levis, on Isle Royale, is in a most advantageous situation. The island is small, and entirely comprehended within the works, which are carried on in the same irregular manner as nature has formed the insulary shore about it; but the area of

* This genteel fellow arrived at that rank solely by his merit, of which he had a large share. He was unfortunately drowned on his passage to Ireland, long after the conclusion of the war, and in the prime of his life. In his profession as an engineer, he was exceedingly eminent, and an honor to his country: the service, and the army, to whom he was a shining ornament, have sustained a very considerable loss by his death.

the fort is a regular square within four bastions only, which seems to have been the first intention in fortifying the island, so that the other defences, to all appearance, have been occasionally added, to render the place more respectable, and cut off communication to Montreal, to which it was an excellent barrier; at the head of a number of dreadful rapids, and commands, in a great measure, the navigation between lake Ontario and Canada. The country north and south is apparently even, rich and capable of great improvement inhabited principally by Indians, which, with the uncommon fertility of the circumjacent islands, producing Indian and other corn in great abundance, and the prospect of an immense fur trade induced the governor general to establish a strong settlement in this district. The batteries erected against Fort Levis consists of six guns each, besides mortars, though designed for a greater number, if necessary, and the two islands whereon they are constructed, are occupied chiefly by Col. Massey's grenadiers, with Brig. Gage's and Col. Amherst's corps of light infantry, who first took possession of them; and the remainder of the army, except Col. Haldiman's detachment, on the fourth point battery, are dispersed on other contiguous islands, in such a manner as to surround the fortress, and cut off the enemy's retreat, in case they had been inclined to abandon and retire."

NOTE B.

[Referred from page 109]

It had been our design to enumerate some of the evidence of superstition, as evinced in various enterprises of money seeking, by digging, draining the beds of streams, &c., &c., and searching for *vampires*, of which the annals of St. Lawrence county afford at least three instances. Our space forbids the details, revolting to humanity, and regard for the *living*, leads us to pass unnoticed these heathenish mutilations of the *dead.*

NOTE C.

[Referred from page 111.]

Instead of continuing our account of St. Louis, a short space will be devoted to the Mohawk dialect of the Iroquois. As it exists in Canada, it is said to have but 11 letters, viz: A, E, H, I, K, N, O, R, S, T, W, for the last of which a character like the figure 8, open at the top, is used. It is remarkable for the combinations of which it is susceptible, and which arises from the fewness of the roots or primitive words. The natives having but few ideas, and these of the most common and familiar objects, when it became necessary to speak of abstract ideas, as those of a religious character, the missionaries were obliged to use figurative terms, and comparisons couched in language suited to their capacity. From this cause, the speeches delivered at treaties abound in rhetorical figures, especially in metaphors. Hence arises a flexibility and range of modification in mood, tense and declension said to be much analagous, especially in the verb, to the Greek. The following is an instance of combination:

Ka-o-nwei-a, signifies a boat of any kind, (hence our word *canoe).*
Wa-ten-ti-a-ta, any thing "that goes by fire."
He-ti-io-kea, "on the ground."
Ot-si-re, "fire."
Watentiata-hetiiokea-otsiere, "a machine that runs on the ground by fire,"
i. e., a *rail road.*
Watentiata-kaonweia-otsire, "a boat that goes by fire," i. e., *steam boat.*

The Algonquin language has a relation with all those of the north and northwest. The dialect of this spoken at St. François, is the softest and most musical of all. For this reason the Iroquois call the latter *sken-so-wa-ne*, signifying a bird that soars and warbles. This arises from the prevalence of letter L, instead of R. The Iroquois called the Algonquins in derision, *Adirondacs*, or "wood eaters," which term has been applied to the lofty chain of mountains in Essex county. Mt. Marcy, the highest peak, is called *Ta-ha-was*, "that cleaves the sky."

The following are the numerals used in the Mohawk dialect, as given by Dwight, in the *Transactions of the American Antiquarian Society*, *vol. ii, p. 358.*

1, Oohskott; 2, tekkehnih; 3, ohson; 4, kubyayrelih; 5, wisak; 6, yah-yook; 7, chahtak; 8, sohtayhhko; 9, tihooton; 10, weeayhrlih; 11, oohskohyahwarrhleh; 12, tekkehninhyahwurrhlih; 20, toowahsun; 30, ohsonnihwahsun; 100, oohskohtowenyaoweh; 1000, towenyaowwehtse-realahsuhn.

We are indebted to Dr. E. B. O'Callaghan, editor of the Documentary History of New York, for the following:

THE LORD'S PRAYER IN MOHAWK.

(From Davis's Translation of Book of Common Prayer, New York. 1837, p. 80.)

Tagwaienha ne garon hiake tesiteron; Aiesaseennaien; A-onwe ne
Our Father who heaven   in   dwellest;   Glorified be thy name;   May come

Sawenniiosera; Tsinisarikonroten ethonaiawenne nonwentsiake, tsiniio
thy kingdom;   Thy   will   be   done   earth   on the,   as

ne garon hiake; Niatewenniserake tagwanataranontensek; nok sasani-
heaven in;   To day   our   bread give us;   and for.

konrhen tsinikon gwanikonraksaton; tainiiot ni-i tsiongwanikonrbens
give   us   our trespasses;   as   we   the trespasses forgive

nothenon ionk-hinikonraksaton; Nok tosa asgwatgawe nothenon aiong
those   against us who trespass;   And   lead   us not   into

gwanikonrotago; Noktennon heren tagwariwagwiten ne gariwaksen;
occasion of sin;   But   us   lead   away   from deeds evil;

Ise sawenniiosera, iah othenon tesanoronse, nok agwa saiataneragwat,
For tis   thy   kingdom,   power,   and the   glory,

iah tegagonte etho neniotonhake. Amen.
for   ever   and   ever.

NOTE D.

[Referred from page 245.]

As the name of Stephen Van Rensselaer is intimately associated with the early history of the purchases in Lisbon and Canton, and as the citizens of St. Lawrence county are indebted to him for the early and efficient interest which he manifested in promoting the construction of roads and internal improvements, we have deemed him fully entitled to a brief notice in the history of the county.

The first ancestor of the family was De Heer Kiliaen Van Rensselaer, who was originally a pearl and diamond merchant, and afterwards a commissioner appointed to take charge of the business of the Dutch West India Company, and one of its directors. He is said to have removed to New Netherlands, and acquired an extensive manorial title to lands on the Hudson, in the vicinity of Albany, having previously extinguished the Indian title to the lands by purchase. Stephen Van Rensselaer, the late patroon, was born in 1764, in the city of New York. At the age of nineteen he graduated at Cambridge University, and in 1786, was appointed a major of infantry, and two years after he received the command of a regiment. In 1790, he was elected to the state senate, and held this office five years. In 1795, he was elected by a large majority lieutenant governor, and was reëlected in 1798, and afterwards held several important and responsible offices connected with the state government. In 1810, and subsequently, he was entrusted with responsible duties in relation to the preliminary measures for the construction of the Erie canal, and in 1812, he was appointed by Governor Tompkins, major general of the New York militia, and was entrusted with the charge of the entire northern and western frontiers of the state, from St. Regis to the Pennsylvania line. His military career ended with this campaign. In 1801 and in 1813, he was nominated for governor, but was in the latter defeated by Mr. Tompkins. In 1816, he distinguished himself for his zeal in promoting the canals, and remained one of the canal commissioners till his death. He was several times elected member of assembly and congress, and in 1819 he was appointed a regent of the university, which office he held till his death. In 1821, he was a delegate to the convention for revising the constitution, and took a distinguished part in the deliberations of that body. But it is chiefly for the zeal and munificence with which Mr. Van Rensselaer engaged in promoting the causes of agriculture, science, and education. that his name will ever be venerated by the citizens of our state. In 1819, he had been successful in directing the attention of the legislature to the importance of fostering the agricultural interests in the state. Twenty-six county societies were organized in consequence of this movement, the presidents of which assembling in Albany in January, 1820, elected him president of the board of agriculture.

This movement had unfortunately but a brief existence; but his efforts did not cease with those of the public, and he caused to be made, at his own expense, an agricultural and geological survey of Albany and Rensselaer counties. He afterwards employed Prof. Eaton to execute a similar survey on a general scale, of the different rock formations along the line of the canal, which was executed in 1822-3, and this led the way to the state surveys since accomplished. The results of this exploration he caused, like the others, to be published with illustrations at his own expense. In 1826, there was incorporated an institution known as the

Rensselaer Institute, which he had established at Troy, and which was designed to impart a practical knowledge of chemistry, philosophy, natural history, and mathematics, and has since proved eminently useful in confering a thorough practical knowledge of the useful sciences. A peculiar feature in the mode of instruction adopted at this school, deserves mention. For several seasons it was the custom of Professor Eaton to take his classes with him in canal boats, fitted up for the purpose, through the canal to Lake Erie, that his pupils might have the opportunity of studying the different rocky strata in their localities, and of collecting the fossils and other objects of interest that might have relation to the subjects of their study. . Excursions for exercise in civil engineering, and the formation of collections in natural history, form a prominent feature of this school.

The Rensselaer Institute was founded and liberally endowed by him, and while he was bearing from his own purse not less than half of its current expenses, caused an invitation to be given to each county in the state, to furnish a student selected by the county clerk for gratuitous instruction, imposing as a condition that they should instruct in their own counties for one year on the experimental and demonstrative method.

Mr. Van Rensselaer took an active part in the formation and support of the Albany Institute, an institution devoted to the promotion of science, and till the close of his life continued usefully employed in fostering and encouragaing various measures for the public good. He was especially fond of giving encouragement to young men of genius and talent, but who, from the pressure of poverty, were unable to derive those advantages which they so eagerly desired, and who felt in all its force the reality of the sentiment expressed by the poet Beattie, in the following stanza:

> " Ah who can tell how hard it is to climb,
> The steep where fame's proud temple shines afar,
> Ah who can tell how many a soul sublime,
> Has felt the influence of malignant star,
> And waged with fortune on eternal war,
> Checked by the scoffs of pride, and envy's frown,
> And poverty's unconquerable bar,
> In life's low vale remote, have pined alone,
> Then dropped into the grave unnoticed and unknown."

Some of our most illustrious men of science owe their first impulse and encouragement, to the kindness and the munificence of Stephen Van Rensselaer. In his benefactions he was unostentatious, and it is only from indirect sources that it is learned that in the cause of agricultural and educational science alone, he expended not less than $30,000. He died Jan. 26, 1839, at Albany.

An author* who has written a sketch of his life and character, thus, with great justice, closes his eulogy upon him:

" What a mild splendor do the virtues of such a life shed around the horizon of the tomb. Far preferable to laurels won on battle fields or monuments of marble. We can not eulogize his military qualifications, although they were excellent, for such characters have abounded in all ages and among all nations. We much prefer his other qualities, of which the world does not afford so many shining examples; I mean h s

* See Ho gate's American Genealogy, p. 55.
A discourse on the life and character of Mr. Van Rensselaer, is also published in Munsell's Annals of Albany, vol. 3, pp. 251-327.

philanthropy and disinterested benevolence. He seems to have had great purity of character, a sound judgment, and well balenced mind. Entire confidence seems to have been reposed in his talents and patriotism. He died a Christian, having been admitted a member of the Reformed Dutch church at Albany in 1787, when 23 years of age."

NOTE E.

[Referred from page 436.]

We have stated that the town of Pierrepont derives its name from Mr. Hezekiah Beers Pierrepont, of Brooklyn, Long Island. This gentleman was so large a proprietor of lands in these counties, and so many of its inhabitants have derived their titles to land from him, that his name must always be connected with the annals of this district, and a short sketch of his life, therefore, will not be uninteresting.

He was born at New Haven, Connecticut, November 3, 1768, and was descended from the Rev. James Pierrepont, who was the first minister settled in that colony, at its establishment. It is worthy of note, that in 1684, the town plat apportioned to him has been ever since occupied by the family, and is still in their possession. It never has been sold since it was ceded by the Aborigines.

The immediate ancestor of the Rev. James Pierrepont, was John Pierrepont, of England, who belonged to the family of Holme Pierrepont, of Norman descent. John came to America with his younger brother Robert, about the year 1640, as tradition says, merely to visit the country, but married, and settled at Roxbury, near Boston. The name being French, became Anglicised, and has been spelt Pierpont, but the correct spelling is now resumed by this branch of the family.

The subject of this memoir being of a very active and enterprising spirit, was early dissatisfied with the prospect of a professional life, and left college without graduating, and entered into the office of his uncle, Mr. Isaac Beers, to obtain a knowledge of business. His uncle was an importer of books. He remained with him till 1790, when he went to New York, and at first took an engagement in the custom house, with the intention of obtaining a better knowledge of commercial business. The next year he associated himself with Messrs. Watson and Greenleaf, and acted as their agent in Philadelphia, where he realized a small fortune by the purchase of government debt. In 1793, he entered into partnership with Mr. William Leffingwell, and established in New York the firm of Leffingwell & Pierrepont.

France being then in revolution, neglected agriculture, and derived its supplies from abroad, principally from America. Mr. Pierrepont went to France, to attend to the shipment of provisions. The seizures that were made by England so embarrassed the trade, that he abandoned it, and made a voyage to India and China, acting as his own supercargo. On his return with a valuable cargo, his ship, named the Confederacy, was taken by a French privateer, and condemned and sold in France, contrary to our treaty stipulations and the laws of nations. He remained in France, making reclamations against the government, and had a fair prospect of recovering the value of his ship and cargo, when the United States made a treaty with France, by the terms of which it assumed the claims of its citizens against France. To the disgrace of this country, this claim, which is classed among many similar ones, under the title of "*claims for French spoliations prior to 1800*," has never yet been paid, though twenty-one reports in favor have been made in Congress, and many of the most distinguished and best men of the country have admitted their justice and advocated them. It has been admitted by one of the greatest opponents of the claims, that if they could be brought before the supreme court, they would beyond a doubt obtain a decision in their favor.

Mr. Pierrepont was in Paris during the most bloody days of the revolution, and saw Robespierre beheaded; he was also detained in England by the legal steps that were necessary to obtain his insurance, part of which he recovered. His neutral character as an American, enabled him to travel without difficulty on the continent, though war prevailed. Our country being represented abroad by able men, as well in, as out of, the diplomatic circles, he enjoyed their society and cemented friendships, some of which lasted during life. That with Robert Fulton was one of these, as a testimony of which Mr. Pierrepont named a son after him, who died an infant. After an absence of seven years. he returned to New York, and in the year 1802, married Anna Maria, daughter of William Constable. Wishing after his marriage to engage in some business of less hazard and uncertainty than foreign trade, he established a factory for the manufacture of gin, which was attended with great success, and the article which he manufactured attained a high reputation. He purchased a country seat on Brooklyn Heights in 1802, which he afterwards made his permanent residence. He was at that time one of only twenty-six freeholders, who owned a territory which has since become covered by a city, now the second in this state.

From his connection with Mr. Constable, who was a great land holder in this as well as other states, he had his attention drawn to lands in these northern counties, and purchased in 1806 the town of Pierrepont, and subsequently Louisville and Stockholm. He afterwards made large additions to his purchases from the estate of Mr. Constable and others, and became the owner of about half a million of acres. This extensive property engaged his whole attention ever afterwards, and his summers were devoted to visiting his lands. At his earlier visits he traveled on horseback, making thus the entire tour from Schenectady to Jefferson, St. Lawrence, and Franklin counties. His first visit having been in 1803, he saw the country, when as yet it was almost an unbroken forest, and had the gratification for a long series of years, of seeing its gradual settlement and improvement, much of which, in various sections, was the result of his own exertions. In his treatment of his settlers, for more than thirty years, he was uniformly kind and lenient, and he extended his indulgence in the collection of their dues for a long period, very much to his own pecuniary inconvenience. During the four years preceding his death, he surrendered the active care of his lands in these counties to his son Henry, who has since continued in charge of them. He died August 11, 1838, leaving a widow, who still survives him, two sons and eight daughters.

ADDITIONAL NOTES ON MADRID.

The following notes on *Madrid* were received from Mr. E. A. Dayton, too late for use in their proper place, and are here inserted as interesting addenda to the history of that town.

The Rutherford brothers, mentioned on page 341, were from Roxburgh-shire, Scotland, and emigrated in 1801. They were met in New York by Mr. Ogden, and induced to visit the town where they afterwards settled, in a neighborhood that has since been called Rutherford's Ridge. The land originally settled by them is still mostly occupied by their descendants. These families were two months in removing from Pittstown, N. Y., by the tedious water route of Oswego. Jesse Goss settled at Columbia village in 1801, and in 1823 built the first house east of the river at that place. It stood near the place of A. Goss's present store. He was the first to erect a cloth dressing and carding mill here. The present stone woolen factory was erected in 1835. Most of the east part of the village (known locally, as Brooklyn), has been built since that time.

Joseph Freeman and his brothers Asa, Elisha and Rufus were natives of Dalton, Mass., and removed to Madrid in 1850. The former was born May 7, 1773, and in 1798 removed to Johnstown, in Canada, and thence to Madrid, crossing on the ice, and losing by an accident his stock of provisions. In 1801, Cyrus Abernethy, from Vermont, settled on the place now owned by Roswell Abernethy. The first marriage in the south part of the town, was Eezkiel Abernethy to —— Linsley. The first mill at Columbia village, built by Seth Roberts, was afterwards burned and the land and water privilege were bought by Timothy Reed, who built a new dam, and a saw and grist mill. The first store at this place was built by Buck & Meach, on the present site of the burying ground. In the summer of 1800 an attempt to navigate Grass river was made with a flat bottomed boat, but without much success, as in ascending, the loading had often to be taken out, and the empty boat dragged up with great labor.

In 1808 or 9, Eli and Nathaniel Hamblin, and Wm. Castle built a small distillery on the river below the mill, and it was used till about 1830.

Samuel Allen, originally from Vermont, settled in town among the very first. In 1797, having previously made a short sojourn in Chateaugay, and been engaged with his father, brother and a man by the name of Whelpley, in cutting the first road from that place to the French Mills. He states that on the 11th of March, 1797, there was but one family in town, which were Dutch. They lived in a hut in the present village of Waddington, and every member of it were clad in garments of deerskin. The first death of a white known to have occurred in town, is said to have been that of Daniel Tuttle, who lived a short distance above Point Iroquois on the river. The first birth among the white settlers, was that of Wm. L., son of Samuel Allen, Oct. 19, 1797. He was one of the unfortunate party at the windmill, at Prescott, in Nov. 1828, and is supposed to have been killed there, as he was never heard of after that event.

On the 4th of July, 1798, the first celebration of our national independence was held in town, on the extreme end of Point Iroquois, at which about 12 or 15 were present. The declaration was read by Jacob Redd·ngton, Esq., who delivered a short oration, which was followed by the firing of guns, and cheering. This uproar attracted the notice of the Canadians, who did not know what could be the cause of the disturbance among the Yankees, and they sent over a "flag of truce" to learn what might be the matter. They were told that they would not be hurt, and upon this assurance returned. The exercises of the day were concluded by a *ball*, for which they lacked none of the requisites but music of some kind, and this was supplied by the voice of Mrs. A——, who sang while the others danced, and the sport went on with as much spirit as if there had been a hundred fiddlers.

Tradition relates that the first town meeting in Madrid, was held in the fields, the presiding officer, seated on a pine stump.

The first Associate Reformed Society, of Madrid, erected a church edifice in 1819, at a cost of $800. Wm. Taylor, the first pastor, remained from September, 1819, till 1837. In 1840, the Rev. John Morrison, the present pastor, succeeded. A parsonage was built soon after the church was burned in 1841, and the society have since built one of stone. A second church was built in 1842, since which meetings have been held alternately in each. In December 1852, thirty-six members residing in north Potsdam, formed a separate organization, and are now erecting a church. Present number in Madrid 350.

INDEX.

ERRATA.

The reader is requested to make the following corrections.

15, 3d line from bottom, for 1849 read 1749.
66, last line, for *debilitated* read *invigorated.*
88, 13th line from bottom, for 1957 read 1757.
100, 4th line from bottom, for *solitude* read *solicitude.*
136, top line, for *table* read *talk.*
156 last line, for 18 read 1802.
195, 4th line from bottom, for *Parial* read *Parish.*
198, 2nd line from top, for *reserved* read *preserved.*
236, 7th line from top, for *ragged* read *rugged.*
243, 11th and 12th lines from the top, erase the words "who married a daughter of Wm. Constable."
244, 23d line from top, for *LeRay* read *LeRoy.*
267, Canton was organized in 1805 instead of 1808
" Pierrepont was taken from *Russell and Potsdam.*
274 6th line from top for *Merriman* read *Herriman.*
280. 16th line from top, read *C* instead of *G* in Mr. Page's name.
311. First word should end with *n* instead of *u.*
311. 3d line from bottom, for *Mr.*, read *M.*
312. 17th line from top, for *Arnod* read *Arnot.*
316. 1st word begins with *K* instead of *R.*
321. 5th line from top, for *house* read *horse.*
324. Top line, for *effectual* read *effected.*
366. 26th line from top, for *Jordan* read *Judson.*
415. 21st line from bottom, for *R.* read *C. Slade.*
417. 11th line from top, for *Judge* read *Jude.*
434. 20th line from top, for *the* read *Mr.*
452. 22d line from bottom, for *McLarer* read *McLaren.*
456. 20th line from bottom, for *Narsh* read *Nash.*
540. 27th line from top, for *Grey* read *Guy.*
547. 25th and 26th lines; first words of these lines transposed.
555. 6th line from top, for $5,000 read $50,000.
557. 2d line from top, for *John* read *John H.*
" 9th line from top, for *T.* read *J.*
" 12th line from top, for *S. L.* read *I. L.*
569, 23d line from top, for *Companies* read *Company.*
" 26th line from top, for *Egbert* read *Egert.*
589. Top line, for 1783 read 1763.
" 3d line from top, for 1840 read 1800.
593. 21st line from top, for *employment* read *temperment.*
596. 18th line from bottom, after the word *sheriff* erase the word *and.*
" 9th line from bottom, for *suite* read *site.*
600. 18th line from bottom, for *Seuftenberg* read *Senftenberg.*
620. 12th line from bottom, for *Hulbard* read *Hubbard.*
693. 10th line from bottom, for *Ioxoclase* read *Loxoclase.*
704. 1st line, for *Preferred* read *Referred.*

2